The Complete Works of
WASHINGTON
IRVING

Richard Dilworth Rust
General Editor

LETTERS

Volume III

Scudding Clouds after a Shower
watercolor of Sunnyside by George Harvey
c. 1836–1840

WASHINGTON IRVING

LETTERS

Volume III, 1839-1845

Edited by

**Ralph M. Aderman, Herbert L. Kleinfield
and Jenifer S. Banks**

Twayne Publishers

Boston

1982

Published by Twayne Publishers
A Division of G. K. Hall & Co.

Copyright © 1982 by

G. K. Hall & Co.

The Complete Works of Washington Irving
Volume XXV

The preparation and publication of this volume
were made possible (in part) by grants from the
National Endowment for the Humanities,
an independent federal agency.

CENTER FOR EDITIONS OF
AMERICAN AUTHORS

AN APPROVED TEXT

MODERN LANGUAGE
ASSOCIATION OF AMERICA

®

Library of Congress Cataloging in Publication Data

Irving, Washington, 1783–1859.
Letters.

(His The complete works of Washington Irving ;
v. 23–26)
Includes indexes.
CONTENTS: v. 1. 1802–1823.–[etc.]–v. 3. 1839–1845.–
v. 4. 1846–1859.
1. Irving, Washington, 1783–1859–Correspondence.
2. Authors, American–19th century–Correspondence.
I. Aderman, Ralph M. II. Kleinfield, H. L.
III. Banks, Jenifer S.
PS2081.A4   1978   818.209 [B]   82–10907
ISBN 0–8057–8524–8 (v. 3)

Manufactured in the United States of America

ACKNOWLEDGMENTS

In addition to the acknowledgments in volume 1, the editors wish to mention the help and encouragement of other individuals in the preparation of volumes 3 and 4. Many of the persons named earlier have continued their invaluable support, and others have joined them. Lewis Leary and Walter A. Reichart have checked the transcriptions and annotations of the last two volumes and have offered useful suggestions. Richard D. Rust and his assistants, Page Davis and Marjorie Harris, have read typescripts and proofs carefully and cheerfully under the pressures of deadlines. Pierre Ullman has continued to assist with the transcription and annotation of Irving's Spanish letters. For the preparation of the genealogy in volume 4 the editors are grateful to Alice Aderman, the major investigator, to the Irving descendants who graciously supplied details about the family, and to the staff of Sleepy Hollow Restorations for access to their collection of documents and memorabilia relating to the Irvings. Miss Banks wishes to thank Cindy Hoffman, Donna Kern, and Kathy Laube for their help in proofreading, and Mr. Aderman is indebted to Alice Aderman, Dusky Loebel, Janet Montross, and Jeffrey Aderman for proofreading and editorial chores. Although it is not possible to mention everyone who contributed to this project over the past eighteen years, the editors do wish to thank all of the unnamed scholars, librarians, associates, and friends who have helped in one way or another. Although Herbert J. Kleinfield did not live to see the completion of the project, his influence will be found throughout these volumes. His industry and perseverance have remained a constant source of inspiration and admiration.

R. M. A.

J. S. B.

CONTENTS

LETTERS, 1839–1845

ILLUSTRATION

FRONTISPIECE

From *Scudding Clouds after a Shower*, c. 1836–1840.

A watercolor of Sunnyside
by George Harvey (c. 1800/01–1878).
This view of the riverside shows the striped awnings
which were used on the house during the summer.

Reproduction courtesy of Sleepy Hollow Restorations.

EDITORIAL PLAN
TO LETTERS

Although Irving's letters are scattered over the eastern United States and western Europe, several institutions have brought together a large number of them. The New York Public Library, with its Seligman, Hellman, and Berg collections, is especially rich; and these, together with other holdings, form the largest body of Irving correspondence held by a single repository. Another valuable group is to be found in the Clifton Waller Barrett Collection of the Alderman Library of the University of Virginia. At Tarrytown, Sleepy Hollow Restorations has assembled an important collection of letters along with photocopies of items held elsewhere. Other noteworthy concentrations of Irving's letters repose in the libraries at Yale, Harvard, and Columbia Universities, in the Historical Society of Pennsylvania, and in the archives of John Murray, Irving's chief British publisher. The National Archives in Washington contain Irving's official diplomatic communications, as well as letterbook copies of his dispatches and letters written as minister to Spain. A few letters remain in the hands of private collectors but the bulk of those extant are preserved in institutional libraries. Others are widely scattered, as may be observed by consulting the notes that identify the location or source of each letter printed, or, if the information is sought in summary form, by referring to the cumulative calendars appended to the final volume of this collection of Irving's letters.

This edition, arranged in chronological order, is the first comprehensive collection in print of all letters of Washington Irving presently known and available, both published and hitherto unpublished. But a considerable number of letters have escaped detection, although they have been identified through a systematic search of dealers' and auctioneers' catalogs, as well as by evidence found in journals and other letters, or from other sources. They are enumerated, along with the ones printed in these volumes, in an appendix to the final volume in order to supply the broadest possible record of Irving's letter-writing available at the time of this publication. It is hoped that this checklist will eventually lead to the discovery of additional holograph material. Letters that came to the editor's attention too late to be presented in their proper place in these volumes are printed in an appendix at the end of the final volume, in a chronological ordering of their own.

Since the present edition is not designed to include surviving letters written to Irving, no exhaustive effort was made to locate or list all of them. Many of them are not directly related to Irving's letters, and the contents of many may be inferred from what Irving wrote. Those having a special bearing on Irving's letters to these correspondents are quoted or summarized in appropriate notes, and all of them are listed, with location when known, in a separate calendar at the end of the final volume in the hope that the utility of the collection may be enhanced.

The great bulk, at least eighty-five percent, of the letters here presented has been taken from the original manuscripts. Although transcriptions of holographs are derived from photocopies, they are checked for accuracy by four or more readers, and all transcriptions were read (often twice) against the holographs. In the absence of holographs, letters derived from a printed source were collated against any other existing printed versions and explanatory notes added wherever warranted.[1] This is not to claim absolute authenticity for resulting text, but represents the best that can be done with the evidence at hand. Equally difficult are the cases where the only available text is a copy made by someone other than Irving (known or unknown), presumably from a holograph no longer extant.[2] Here again the editors can only reproduce what is before them, while noting whatever facts they have regarding the transmission of the text, and hoping that the original letter may yet come to light.

Fragments of letters, whether derived from manuscript or printed sources, are incorporated in sequence, unless they are mere scraps of little meaning or significance, in which case they are relegated to an

---

1. A comparison of Pierre M. Irving's four-volume *Life and Letters of Washington Irving* (1862–1864) with the three-volume edition (copyrighted 1869) reveals numerous instances of the biographer's effort to refine his earlier work. The second edition omits many letters of the first edition (or extracts them), and further bowdlerizes those remaining. The two editions of George S. Hellman's *Letters of Washington Irving to Henry Brevoort* (1915 and 1918), on the other hand, reveal few alterations. In both cases, first and later printings were collated for variants, editorial decisions were made in accord with Irving's known practice or other available evidence, and explanatory notes were added wherever indicated. These are the only two bodies of Irving letters in book form that went into second editions or settings. Other letters lacking holographs that are not in these two collections but that exist in printed forms differing from each other (some of them appearing in periodicals) are similarly treated.

2. For example, the letterbook copies of Irving's diplomatic correspondence for which holographs are not available.

appendix at the end of the last volume, where they appear in sequence with notations on whatever information may be available and desirable regarding their authenticity, for many of these scraplike fragments are derived from biographical and other secondary works, some from catalogs of book dealers or autograph dealers, as well as from auction catalogs.

The circumstances under which Irving wrote determine the varying conditions of the existing holograph letters, as much as the writing materials at his disposal or the conditions under which they were stored during the long lapse of years since they were written. During his first trip to Europe in 1804 to 1806, Irving drew ˙upon entries in his journals and frequently copied them precisely into letters to his friends and relatives in New York.[3] During periods of protracted residence in one place—whether in New York, London, Paris, Madrid, at Sunnyside, or elsewhere—he often wrote leisurely and carefully, but there is sometimes a marked falling-off in precision as a letter stretched out under his hand. Generally his business letters and official diplomatic or consular dispatches were written with greater care than personal letters. At other times, especially between stints of travel, or when pressed for time, he wrote in a careless, almost illegible scrawl, with whatever pen, ink, or grade of paper came to hand. Often he used a thin or low grade of paper and a blunt pen which caused the ink to bleed through the paper. On a few occasions when he resorted to writing with pencil, the result made the work of the twentieth-century editor doubly difficult. Letters may be presumed to have been written in ink except where there is a note to the contrary. Variations in the inks used are often no longer precisely distinguishable and are not recorded unless an unusual circumstance makes a description desirable, in which case a notation is made in the notes. Similarly, the paper used covers a great variety of grades, from good to bad, laid and wove, white and tinted, lined and unlined, with and without watermarks, and of various shapes and sizes; in short, he appears to have used whatever was available. Description of kinds of paper is not attempted except in a few exceptional cases where it has textual significance.

While the editors have made every effort to record what Irving wrote, the conditions of some manuscript pages and the anomalous readings occasioned by Irving's erratic handwriting produced so many prob-

---

3. This parallelism between the journals and letters has been indicated in Nathalia Wright's edition of *Journals and Notebooks*, Volume I, of the present edition. Parallel passages of this kind will be noted in successive volumes of the journals and letters as they appear.

lems which the eye cannot resolve that recourse was had to a set of ground rules, the chief of which is that when a word, character, spacing, construction, or mark of punctuation is in doubt, presenting equally defensible alternatives, the reading is rendered in conformity with the contextual requirement (if ascertainable), insofar as it accords with Irving's practice (if known) or with accepted usage in his day. In short, the aim has been to produce a reliable text, short of an absolutely literal transcription, which is manifestly impossible, as the sequel will demonstrate.

It does not follow that Irving's errors and inconsistencies are eliminated. Indeed, the aim of the editors, which is to present Irving as faithfully as possible, precludes this possibility. To correct his miscues and normalize his idiosyncrasies would destroy the distinctive texture of his writing. So it is that the two primary objectives of the editors—fidelity to Irving's text and utility for the reader—are constant but not always compatible aims, causing the editors to tread a very narrow line between what is ideally desirable and what is practically possible or permissible.

Despite the variety of difficulties, the editors have made a conscientious and considered effort to render faithfully the text as Irving wrote it—his oversights, inconsistencies, and often his errors included. No effort was made to correct or "improve" the holograph version, unless the error or flaw is clearly unintentional, and failure to amend would lead to misreading or misconstruction of Irving's meaning. In all such cases, editorial alterations made are signaled by square brackets or explained in the notes. No alteration is made silently. Hence any odd or erroneous idiom or phraseology, error in punctuation or spelling, or omission or transposition of letters or words in the text are to be presumed to be Irving's.

This policy of reproducing the holograph as accurately as possible perpetuates various inconsistencies, sometimes on the same page, even in the same paragraph, occasionally in the same sentence. Thus the same sentence may spell out a numeral and subsequently use the arabic form, or it may use "and" as well as the ampersand for both "and" and "et cetera," in the latter case usually "&c" without a period. Words normally written as one are often separated ("every thing"), and others commonly separated or hyphenated are joined ("forgetmenots"). Irving's contractions follow no recognizable pattern, but do not often lead to obscurity or misinterpretation; when they do, missing elements are added in brackets or clarified in the notes. Similarly, his misuse or neglect of the apostrophe is not corrected unless it leads to misconstruction, in which case editorial emendations are bracketed and noted. His superscripts are uniformly brought down to the line. Often he omitted the period following a superscript but signalized the contraction or abbreviation by adding one or more dots under the superscript, by underscoring it, or by adding a dash after it. These signals are all rendered as a period, thus honoring his intention while ridding the page of eccentric mannerisms very difficult to reproduce on the printed page.

Irving's erratic terminal punctuation presents special problems. Often he used a dash, rather than a period, at the end of the sentence. This sometimes seems to have happened inadvertently because he failed to lift his pen cleanly from the paper and so elongated an intended period to look like a dash; at other times he clearly meant to write a dash. In all cases his dashes at the ends of sentences are respected as deliberate terminal punctuation. His sentence beginnings and endings are rendered as he wrote them, with or without period (or dash) if the succeeding sentence in the same paragraph begins with a capital letter, except in cases where the next sentence begins with "I" or a proper noun, in which case a bracketed period is added as a necessary signal for the reader. When the following sentence begins with a small letter, preceded by a period (or dash), it is so rendered. Only when it begins with a small letter and Irving failed to supply a period (or dash) is a bracketed period (sometimes a semicolon) added. No missing period is added at the end of the paragraph.

Similarly, his internal punctuation is respected; any necessary marks of punctuation added or changed for clarity are bracketed or footnoted (usually the former). When doubt exists among his uses internally of commas, colons, semicolons, or dashes, the questionable marks are rendered in accord with the demands of the context, compatible with Irving's general practice or the usage common in his time. His occasional use of the colon instead of a period to denote an abbreviation (usually in connection with titles of books) is respected. If, as is true in a few instances, he used what seems to be a period for a comma, or what seems to be a comma for a period, and the error is corrected, it is so noted. Commas, parentheses, dashes, and quotation marks missing from intended pairs are added in square brackets. Missing sets of quotation marks are added (in brackets) when their omission would result in misreading. Quotation marks when used by Irving at the beginning of successive lines of a quoted passage (verse or prose) are omitted.

Carets, which Irving sometimes used to indicate inserted matter, are transcribed as arrows in accordance with the system of editorial symbols explained in the table below. His abbreviations stand as he left them unless clarity demands amplifications or corrections, which are then bracketed or noted, normally the former. His occasional use of the long form of "s", "ſ" usually when the letter is doubled, is not reproduced.

Irving often wrote participial forms normally ending in "ed" without the penultimate *e*, and without an apostrophe indicating an elision or a period designating an abbreviation. These are rendered as he wrote them: i.e., "servd" rather than "serv'd" or "serv^d" or "serv[e]d." In a very few cases where the elision involves more than the *e* or some other single letter, and misreading is likely to result, missing elements in brackets are added.

Certain misspellings occur so frequently as to become routine and not worth noting or correcting, unless they convey false information, in which case a note is added. Names of passing acquaintances, even of friends and long-term associates, may vary from page to page. In the interest of unencumbered text these are allowed to stand, but where the proper form is ascertainable, the correct form is given in a note keyed to the first occurrence, and also in the index.

Loosely associated with the problem of handling proper names is the problem of distinguishing between capital and lowercase forms of initial letters of his words—not only of nouns but of all parts of speech. Often the formation of a letter is not sufficiently distinctive nor its size in relation to adjacent letters sufficiently marked to indicate clearly which Irving intended. He commonly wrote the initial letter of a word beginning with a consonant with an upward sweep which often raises it higher than the letters which follow it. This upward flourish is especially noticeable when the initial letter *y* appears at the beginning of a new line. When conformation of the letter in question is not sufficiently distinctive and the context indicates a lowercase form, the letter is rendered lowercase. Conversely, if the content calls for a capital, and the letter rises only slightly above adjacent high-rise lowercase letters, it is capitalized; it need not reach the height of high-rise letters which follow it. A more objective procedure, based on a mechanical measurement of differences in height, introduces a new body of inconsistencies and a maze of contradictions and indefensible readings or renditions, and invariably increases the incidence of error. Throughout, the editors have followed the principle that where Irving seems to use capital letters for lowercase words, the transcriptions of those letters have been rendered to accord with knowledge of his customary practice and the customary orthographical practice of his time, by transcribing as capitals only those letters which are clearly so—all intermediate forms being rendered in lowercase.

The height of initial letters in Irving's complimentary closings is also often troublesome. They can vary from an apparent "yrs Truly," "yours Very truly," "Very truly Yrs," or almost any other combination of initial lowercase or capital letters. These and other such doubtful cases are rendered as "Yrs truly," "Yours very truly," or "Very truly yrs," only the initial letter in the first word in the closing capitalized in accord with Irving's usual practice and the common usage of his time. Less formal closings such as "ever your devoted friend," are transcribed in conformity to the demands of the text, as ascertained. When doubt rises between what the eye measures and what knowledge of Irving, his handwriting and habits of expression suggest, then Irving is given the benefit of that doubt.

Another problem which occasionally presents itself is that of Irving's ending a paragraph at the bottom of a page with a short line containing very few words. He would then on the following page begin a new paragraph on a new subject with little or no ascertainable indentation of the first line of that paragraph. Rather than submit to a policy of strict measurement, the editors in such instances have honored Irving's intention by indenting the first line of the new paragraph.

Occasionally Irving would so crowd what he had to say on the last page of a letter that he left little space for a complimentary close and signature, writing, for example, "Truly your friend Washington Irving" on, or so nearly on, the last line of the text that it is often impossible to determine whether he intended a new line or new lines. In such instances the complimentary close and the signature have been given each a line to itself in accordance with his customary practice.

In short, though mindful of Irving's request to his brother Peter, in a long letter of July 7–25, 1804, that "If you find anything . . . in the letters I may write that you thing[k] proper to publish, I beg that you will arrange and finish it *handsomely*," the editors have avoided complete compliance with that request, thinking it useful and instructive to present as exactly as possible what Irving wrote, sometimes in informal haste without care for niceties of spelling or punctuation, or even consistent capitalization of proper nouns, and sometimes in handwriting filled with orthographic peculiarities which are rendered in his favor when consistent with the guidelines already mentioned. The editors will try to present him as handsomely as modern textual principles allow.

In those letters where a covering sheet has been preserved, postal markings and other information which it contains have been recorded. Lines or elements of postal markings are separated one from the other with a horizontal line; when two or more discrete postal markings appear, each is separated from the other by a double horizontal line.

Lacunae in the manuscript and torn places in a page that remove a word or passage are explained in the notes. If the missing element can be conjectured, it is supplied in brackets and noted if necessary. Doubtful or alternate readings are indicated by the appropriate editorial symbol and needed explanation is supplied in the notes. Erasures and cancellations in the holographs, when recoverable, are inclosed in angle brackets. Unrecovered cancellations are marked "⟨[*unrecovered*]⟩." Some

cancellations have obviously been made by persons other than Irving—
some of them almost certainly by Pierre M. Irving, in the interest of
what the nephew-biographer considered propriety. When one or more
letters are canceled or written over (i.e., traced over), the substitution
appears immediately after the canceled matter, without intervening
space; for example "the⟨ir⟩re" and "3⟨7⟩8." Cancellations which are
identical with the substitution, canceled fragments of characters which
are illegible, obvious slips of the pen, and meaningless false starts (which
often occur at the ends of lines and indicate merely that Irving ran
out of space and elected to begin the word anew on the next line but
neglected to strike the false start made at the end of the preceding
line) are not reproduced. There are many instances of this kind, even
in the letters which he seems to have written with more than usual
leisure or care.

Most of the marks in the margins and at the beginning and end of
passages (usually in pencil)—crosses, x's, checks, arrows, vertical and
horizontal lines, encirclings, parentheses, and slashes—are the work of
earlier owners or editors of the manuscripts including Pierre M. Irving,
while preparing his uncle's biography. Only those demonstrably Irving's
are reproduced. Irving's catchwords, placed at the bottom of a page
and repeated as the first word of the next page, are not reproduced.
On rare occasions Irving numbered the pages of his letters; but since
the significance of these numbers is slight, having no relevance to the
present edition, they are not reproduced.

No effort is made to reproduce Irving's irregular spacings between
characters, words, sentences, or paragraphs—unless the space has a
special significance, e.g., to indicate a change of subject matter or to
begin a new sequence.

Quotations, allusions, and literary, historical, or biographical references are identified wherever possible. Such identifications are made
at their first occurrence only. Quotations of poetry in the text are
printed in reduced type size when they are known to be from other
authors. Quotations are to be presumed Irving's unless otherwise indicated, and accordingly are printed in the same type as the text.

Irving's infrequent notes, usually at the bottom of the manuscript
page or along the side, are reproduced in the notes and labeled as his.

Many of the foregoing forms and procedures in preparing the text
of Irving's letters stem from peculiarities of his handwriting, and consequently do not differ materially from those adopted for the editing
of his journals and notebooks and therefore are not dealt with in the
same detail with which they are explained by Nathalia Wright in
Volume I of the present edition, where they can be consulted on

pp. xix–xxvi. But the inherent differences in genre between journals and letters accentuate certain aspects of form and procedure sufficiently unique or peculiar to the letters as to require special treatment by the editors, and consequently need particularization and explanation.

Basic to these procedures is the numbering of the letters in simple chronological order throughout the four volumes, which correspond roughly to periods in Irving's life. A single introductory essay discussing the relation of the letters to his literary career has been adopted as the most suitable way for the reader to see them in context; there is no introductory note for successive volumes after the first, but a chronological table of Irving's activities corresponding to the period covered in each volume is provided for the reader's orientation. Each volume also has a table of editorial symbols, abbreviations, and short-title forms used, as well as a self-contained index, the last volume having the cumulative index instead.

Each letter is assigned an arabic number in accord with its position in the entire sequence. This numeral printed flush to the left margin, is followed by the name of the addressee, printed in its accepted spelling, unless the notation "To ——–" appears in its place. This entire line is set in italics to serve as a caption and provide ready identification.

The transcription itself begins, in accord with Irving's normal practice, with the local or street address (if given), name of the city or place, and date on the first line. The year (or other element of the date), if not given, is added in brackets, whenever ascertainable. These elements, in whatever order, are reproduced as Irving wrote them, punctuation included, except that their location on the page (which in the holograph may appear anywhere, left to right) ends flush with the right margin, with slashes added if they occupy more than one line in the original. If Irving wrote the date at the end of the letter, it is so printed, but it is also added in brackets in the usual place at the head of the letter, so that this necessary index for cross-referencing can be found readily.

In cases of misdating, the correction is made in brackets immediately following the erroneous date, and the letter is placed in its proper chronological order. Incomplete or missing dates are supplied in brackets if they can be ascertained from postmarks, internal evidence, biographical information, perpetual calendar, or other sources. The evidence for dates supplied by the editors is explained in the notes. A letter that is dated ["Fall, 1823,"] and for which no closer dating can be made, appears at the end of November, 1823; one simply dated "1812" appears at the close of that year. Letters that cannot be dated conjecturally appear in alphabetical order according to the recipient's name at the end of the final volume immediately following the appendix which contains letters received too late to be incorporated in the regular chronological sequence. Following the undated letters are printed those for which both date and addressee are unknown.

The inside address, in whatever manner Irving wrote it, follows his text except that it is printed flush left, with slashes if separate lines need to be indicated. Immediately following is the salutation, again flush left. Following the body of the letter, the complimentary close, usually occupying several lines in the holograph, is printed in one line, flush right, with slashes if lineation needs to be indicated. The signature follows, also flush right. If, instead of placing the inside address at the beginning of the letter, Irving wrote it at the bottom of the first page or at the end of the letter, it is positioned at the end, on one line, flush left, with slashes, if needed; and if the date appears at the end, instead of the beginning, it is so placed, again flush left. The recording of postmarkings has been explained in vol. I, p. lxvi. above.

The introductory and concluding elements appear in the originals in so confusing a variety of forms and locations that they defy exact reproduction on the printed page. Hence a degree of regularization is adopted as a simple, sensible means to bring order and uniformity into Irving's calligraphic vagaries, without doing violence to his general ordering of these parts or to his intended meaning. Included in this category is the regularization of salutations for letters derived from secondary sources, such as George S. Hellman's edition of the Irving-Brevoort correspondence and Pierre M. Irving's biography of Irving, where capital letters throughout or a combination of large and small capitals are used. These are all rendered uniformly in capital and lowercase letters in accord with Irving's own practice, thus: "My dear Brother," not "MY DEAR BROTHER" or "My Dear Brother."

The first unnumbered note presents significant information on the address leaf or envelope, if available, in the following order: name of addressee, address, postmark or docketing, followed by any other details, such as the name of the ship or carrier, regular mail, ambassador's pouch, or whatever the means of conveyance, as well as endorsements and postmarkings including date on which letters were received or answered, etc. These details vary widely from letter to letter, and any omissions are to be understood as indicating that they are missing from the original. However, the numbers indicating the cost of postage or carriage are not reproduced, nor are extraneous words or symbols added by owners or readers of the letter.

The second unnumbered paragraph gives the ownership and location of the manuscript or text from which the transcription was made, and details about previous publication, transmission and provenance of the text, and other pertinent data. For letters transcribed from a printed version, only the copy-text (usually the first printed) version is cited, unless unusual circumstances obtain (e.g., variations in two or more printed forms), in which case a description or explanatory note is added.

A third unnumbered note gives biographical details about the recipient. This biographical note, usually more detailed than notes identifying persons merely mentioned in the letters, is attached to the first letter addressed to him by Irving. Earlier or later casual mentions of the addressee are cross-referenced to this main biographical notation. Biographical notes of this kind can be located through the index, where they are starred.

Numbered notes following each letter identify persons, places, events, allusions, quotations, or circumstances necessary for an understanding of the letter.

A list of abbreviations and of short titles for books cited three or more times as sources of information in the notes is supplied at the end of each volume, and a list of Editorial Symbols appears at the beginning of each volume.

Cross-references are made by date, and should be understood to include both text and relevant notes. In the case of two or more letters for a given date, the name of the addressee is added.

The first three volumes are separately indexed; the last volume provides a cumulative index, as well as an Index of Recipients and a Catalog of Sources.

CHRONOLOGICAL TABLE
1839–1845

1839 January 18, relinquished writing of the history of the conquest of Mexico to W. H. Prescott; March–February 1841, monthly contributor to *Knickerbocker Magazine*.

1840 November, issued revised *Biography of Oliver Goldsmith*.

1841 June, brought out *Biography and Poetical Remains of Margaret Davidson*; July, visited Gouverneur Kemble at Cold Spring; fall and winter, worked on the *Life of Washington*.

1842 February 10, nominated as U.S. minister to Spain; April 10, sailed for Europe; May, visited his sister, Mrs. Henry Van Wart in Birmingham; June, visited Sarah Paris Storrow, his niece, in Paris; July 25, reached Madrid to assume diplomatic post; August 1, presented credentials to General Espartero, the regent of Spain, and met Isabella II, the twelve-year-old queen; November–December, insurrection in Barcelona.

1843 Winter and spring, bothered with an inflammation of the skin; July, besieged in Madrid; September 8–November 30, on leave in Paris for treatment of skin ailment.

1844 March 21, witnessed the return of the queen mother, Maria Christina, from exile; June 26, went to Barcelona, the summer residence of the queen, to present letters from President Tyler; July 29–November 17, on leave; visited Sarah Storrow in Paris and the Van Warts in Birmingham.

1845 September, gave up his official residence in Madrid, left for a visit in Paris; December, met Louis McLane to assist in negotiations on the Oregon question; December 12, submitted resignation as minister.

EDITORIAL SYMBOLS AND ABBREVIATIONS

EDITORIAL SYMBOLS

[roman]   Editorial additions.
[*italic*]   Editorial explanations.
⟨   ⟩   Restorations of canceled matter.
? ? or [?]   Doubtful or alternate readings. The former are used
                   within angle brackets. The latter is used for a single
                   doubtful word, and appears immediately after the word
                   or character in question, with no intervening space.
[*unrecovered*]   Unrecovered word. When more than one word is in-
                   volved, the fact is indicated (*"three unrecovered words"*
                   or *"two unrecovered lines"*).
↑ ↓   Interlinear insertions, above or below the line.
Editorial situations not covered by these symbols are explained in the
notes.

ABBREVIATIONS AND SHORT TITLES

Aronson, *Royal Vendetta*: Theo Aronson, *Royal Vendetta, The Crown of
    Spain, 1829–1965.* Indianapolis, 1966.
A Bibliography of WI: Stanley T. Williams and Mary Allen Edge, *A
    Bibliography of the Writings of Washington Irving.* New York, 1936.
Bowers, *Spanish Adventures of WI*: Claude G. Bowers, *The Spanish Ad-
    ventures of Washington Irving.* Boston, 1940.
Bulletin NYPL: Bulletin of the New York Public Library.
Butler, *WI's Sunnyside*: Joseph T. Butler, *Washington Irving's Sunny-
    side.* Tarrytown, 1968.
Christiansen, *Military Power*: E. Christiansen, *The Origins of Military
    Power in Spain, 1800–1854.* Oxford, 1967.
Columbia: Columbia University Library.
*Correspondence of Prescott: Correspondence of William Hickling Pres-
    cott, 1833–1847.* Edited by Roger Walcott. Boston & New York, 1925.
Diary 1828–1829: Washington Irving Diary Spain 1828–1829. Edited by
    Clara L. Penney. New York, 1926.

Ford, *A Hand-Book for Travellers*: Richard Ford, *A Hand-Book for Travellers in Spain and Readers at Home*. 3 vols. Carbondale, 1966.

Harvard: Harvard University Library.

Hasse, *Index to U. S. Documents*: Adelaide R. Hasse, *Index to United States Documents Relating to Foreign Affairs, 1828–1861*. 3 vols. Washington, 1914–1921.

Hellman, *WI Esquire*: George S. Hellman, *Washington Irving Esquire, Ambassador at Large from the New World to the Old*. New York, 1925.

HSA: Hispanic Society of America.

HSP: Historical Society of Pennsylvania.

Huntington: Henry E. Huntington Library and Art Gallery.

Ireland, *NY Stage*: J. W. Ireland, *Records of the New York Stage*. 3 vols. New York, 1966.

J&N, I: Washington Irving, *Journals and Notebooks*, Volume I, 1803–1806. Edited by Nathalia Wright. Madison, Wisc., 1969.

J&N, III: Washington Irving, *Journals and Notebooks*, Volume III, 1819–1827. Edited by Walter A. Reichart. Madison, Wisc., 1970.

Journal 1828: Washington Irving, *Journal of 1828, and Miscellaneous Notes on Moorish Legend and History*. Edited by Stanley T. Williams. New York, 1937.

Journals of WI: *The Journals of Washington Irving*. Edited by William P. Trent and George S. Hellman. 3 vols. New York, 1919.

July, *Verplanck*: Robert W. July, *The Essential New Yorker: Gulian Crommelin Verplanck*. Durham, N. C., 1951.

Langfeld & Blackburn, *WI Bibliography*: William R. Langfeld and Philip C. Blackburn, *Washington Irving, A Bibliography*. New York, 1933.

LBI: *The Letters of Henry Brevoort to Washington Irving*. Edited by George S. Hellman. 2 vols. New York, 1916.

LC: Library of Congress.

Leslie, *Autobiographical Recollections*: *Autobiographical Recollections by the Late Charles Robert Leslie, R. A.* Edited by Tom Taylor. Boston, 1860.

Letters of J. K. Paulding: *The Letters of James Kirke Paulding*. Edited by Ralph M. Aderman. Madison, Wisc., 1962.

LSS: Washington Irving, *Letters from Sunnyside and Spain*. Edited by Stanley T. Williams. New Haven, 1928.

Manning, *Diplomatic Correspondence*: *Diplomatic Correspondence of the United States: International Affairs: 1831–1860*. Edited by William P. Manning. Vol. IX Spain (Washington, 1939).

MHS: Massachusetts Historical Society.

Moore, *International Arbitrations*: J. B. Moore, ed., *History and Digest of the International Arbitrations to Which the United States Has Been a Party.* 6 vols. Washington, 1898.

Moore, *Digest of International Law*: J. B. Moore, *Digest of International Law, as Embodied in Diplomatic Discussions, Treaties, and Other International Agreements, International Awards, the Decisions of Municipal Courts, and the Writings of Jurists, and Especially in Documents, Published and Unpublished, Issued by Presidents and Secretaries of State of the United States, the Opinions of the Attorneys General, and the Decisions of Courts, Federal and State.* 8 vols. Washington, 1906.

Munroe, *Louis McLane*: John A. Munroe, *Louis McLane: Federalist and Jacksonian.* New Brunswick, N. J., 1973.

NA, RG: National Archives, Record Group.

NYEP: New York *Evening Post.*

NYHS: New-York Historical Society.

NYPL: New York Public Library.

NYSL: New York State Library.

Odell, *NY Stage*: G. C. D. Odell, *Annals of the New York Stage.* 15 vols. New York, 1927–1949.

Penney, *Bulletin NYPL*: Clara L. Penney, "Washington Irving in Spain: Unpublished Letters Chiefly to Mrs. Henry O'Shea, 1844–1854," *Bulletin NYPL*, 62 (December, 1958), 615–31; 63 (January, 1959), 23–29.

PMI: Pierre M. Irving; and Pierre M. Irving, *Life and Letters of Washington Irving.* 4 vols. New York, 1862–1864.

Porter, *Astor*: Kenneth W. Porter, *John Jacob Astor, Business Man.* 2 vols. New York, 1966.

Scoville, *Old Merchants of NYC*: J. A. Scoville (used pseudonym of Walter Barrett), *The Old Merchants of New York City.* 5 vols. New York, 1885.

SHR: Sleepy Hollow Restorations.

Simison, *Keogh Papers*: "Letters to Sarah Storrow from Spain by Washington Irving," edited by Barbara D. Simison in *Papers in Honor of Andrew Keogh, Librarian of Yale University By the Staff of the Library 30 June 1938.* New Haven, 1938.

STW: Stanley T. Williams, *The Life of Washington Irving.* 2 vols. New York, 1935.

Va.—Barrett: Clifton Waller Barrett Collection of American Literature, University of Virginia.

WI: Washington Irving.

WIHM: Ben Harris McClary, *Washington Irving and the House of Murray.* Knoxville, 1969.

Yale: Yale University Library.

Young, *WI-Bordeaux*: John-Perry Young, *Washington Irving à Bordeaux*.
Niagara Falls, Ontario, 1946.

LETTERS, 1839–1845

Volume III

1251. To Samuel Ward

Greenburgh Jany 12d. 1839

My dear Sir,

If you can give your good word in favor of my nephew Pierre Munro Irving as Notary to Your New bank, you will be promoting the interest of a very worthy young man and conferring an obligation on Yours, my dear Sir—

Very truly
Washington Irving

Samuel Ward Esqr

ADDRESSED: Samuel Ward Esqr / New York DOCKETED: Washn Irving / recommending / Pierre M Irving / as Notary to Bk of Commerce / 12 Jany 1839
MANUSCRIPT: Brown University Library.

Samuel Ward (1786–1839), who was a partner in the mercantile firm of Prime, Ward and King, established the Bank of Commerce and served as its first president.

1252. To Stephen Whitney

Greenburgh. Jany 12th. 1839

Dear Sir,

May I ask the favor of your influence in behalf of my nephew, Pierre Munro Irving:[1] son of my deceased brother William Irving,[2] for the office of Notary to your new bank.[3] He is brother in law to Mr Moses Grinnell;[4] who I am sure will likewise feel greatly obliged by your interest in his favor.

Very respectfully/Yours &c
Washington Irving

Stephen Whitney Esqr.

MANUSCRIPT: NYPL—Seligman Collection.

Stephen Whitney (d. 1860), a director of the Bank of Commerce and a businessman in New York since 1805, lived at No. 7 Bowling Green.

1. Pierre Munro Irving (1802–1876), a lawyer who had speculated in land in Illinois and in Toledo and editor of the Toledo *Blade*, had assisted WI with the research for *Astoria*.

2. William Irving (1776–1821), a merchant and prominent citizen of New York, was WI's oldest brother.

3. The Bank of Commerce at 28 Merchants Exchange had announced that it was selling shares at ten dollars each for a total capitalization of $3,495,000. See NYEP, January 12, 1839, and February 13, 1839.

4. Moses Hicks Grinnell (1803–1877), who had married WI's niece Julia (1803–1872) in 1836, was president of the Phoenix Bank in New York and a partner in the shipping firm of Grinnell, Minturn and Company. He served in Congress from 1839 to 1841.

1253.   To William H. Prescott

New York, Jany 18—1839

My dear Sir,

Your letter[1] met with some delay in reaching me, and since the receipt of it, I have been hovering between town & country, so as to have no quiet liesure for an earlier reply.

I had always intended to write an account of the Conquest of Mexico, as a suite to my Columbus, but left Spain without making the requisite researches. The unsettled life I ⟨have⟩ subsequently led for some years, and the interruptions to my literary plans by other ⟨p⟩ occupations, made me defer the undertaking from year to year. Indeed the more I considered the subject, the more ⟨it⟩ I became aware of the necessity of devoting to it great labour, patient research and watchful discrimination, to get at the truth and to dispel the magnificent *mirage* with which it is envelloped; for unless this were done, a work, however well executed in point of literary merit, would be liable to be subverted and superseded by subsequent works founded on those documentary evidences that ⟨may⟩ ↑might↓ [be][2] dug out of the chaotic archives of Spain. These considerations loomed into great obstacles in my mind and, amid the hurry of other matters, ⟨kept me from⟩ ↑delayed me in↓ putting my hand to the enterprize. About three years since I made an attempt at it, and set one of my nephews[3] to act as pioneer and get together materials ⟨for⟩ under my direction, but his own concerns called him elsewhere, and the matter was again postponed. Last autumn, after a fit of deep depression, feeling the want of something to arouse and exercise my mind; I again recurred to this subject. Fearing that, if I waited to collect materials I should never take hold of the theme, ⟨I determined⟩ and knowing my own temperament and habits of mind, I determined to dash into it at once; sketch out a narrative of the whole enterprize, ⟨digested from the⟩ using Solis, Herrera & Bernal Diaz[4] as my guide books; and having thus acquainted myself with the whole

ground, and kindled myself into a heat by exercise of drafting the
story; to endeavour to strengthen, correct, ⟨and⟩ enrich and authenticate my work, by materials ⟨g⟩ from every source within my reach. I
accordingly set to work, and had made it my daily occupation for about
three months, and sketched out the groundwork for the first volume
when I learnt from Mr Cogswell[5] that you had undertaken the same
enterprize. I at once felt how much more justice the Subject would
receive at your hands. Ever since I had been meddling with the theme
its grandeur and magnificence had been growing upon me; and ⟨my⟩
I had felt more and more doubtful whether I should be able to treat it
conscientiously—that is to say, with the extensive research and thorough
investigation which it merited. The ⟨early⟩ history of Mexico prior to
the discovery & conquest, & the actual state of its civilization at the
time of the Spanish invasion; are questions in the highest degree
curious and interesting, yet difficult to be ascertained clearly from the
false lights thrown upon them. Even the writings of Padre Sahagun[6]
perplex one as to the degree of faith to be placed in them. These themes
are connected with the grand enigma that rests upon the ⟨mo?⟩ primitive population and civilization of the American continents, and of which
the singular monuments and remains scattered throughout the wilderness serve but as tantalizing indications—The manner in which
you had executed your noble ⟨work⟩ history of Ferdinand and Iza-
bella gave me at once an assurance that you were the man to undertake
this subject; your letter shews that I was not wrong in the conviction, and that you have already set to work ⟨to⟩ on the requisite preparations. In at once yielding up the theme to you I feel that I am but
doing my duty ⟨towards the literature of my country⟩ in leaving one
of the most magnificent themes in American history to be treated by
one who will build up from it an enduring monument in the literature
of our country. I only hope that I may live to see your work executed
and to read in it ⟨[*unrecovered*]⟩ an authentic account of that conquest,
⟨and an adventure of⟩ ⟨and of the⟩ and a satisfactory discussion of the
various questions connected with Mexico and the mexicans, which,
since my boy hood have been full of romantic charm to me, but which,
while they excited my imagination have ever perplexed my judgement.

   I am sorry that I have no works to offer you that you have not in the
Boston Libraries—I have mentioned the authors I was making use of;
they are to be found in the Boston Athenaeum; though I doubt not
you have them in your own possession—While in Madrid I had a few
chapters of Padre Sahagun copied out for me,[7] relating merely to some
points of the Spanish invasion. His work you will find in Lord Kings-
boroughs collection;[8] it professes to give a complete account of ⟨the
Mexican⟩ Mexico, ↑prior to the Conquest↓ its public institutions; trades,

callings, customs &c &c Should I find among my books any that may be likely to be of service ⟨to you⟩ I will send them to you. In the mean time do not hesitate to command my services in any way you may think proper.

I am scrawling this letter in great haste, as you will doubtless perceive—but beg you will take it as a proof of the Sincere and very high respect and esteem with which I am—Your friend & sevt

Washington Irving

Wm H Prescott Esqr

MANUSCRIPT: MHS. PUBLISHED: PMI, III, 137–40; George Ticknor, *Life of William Hickling Prescott* (Boston, 1864), pp. 158–60.

William Hickling Prescott (1796–1859), who had completed *The History of the Reign of Ferdinand and Isabella the Catholic* late in 1837, was gathering materials for his contemplated study of the Spanish conquest of Mexico and Peru, a topic on which WI had been working during the last three months of 1838.

1. In his letter of December 31, 1838, Prescott stated that Joseph Cogswell had told him of WI's "liberal conduct" in offering to relinquish the subject of the conquest of Mexico to him. For the complete letter, see PMI, III, 134–37.

2. WI omitted this word.

3. Pierre Munro Irving does not mention these researches in his life of WI. See also STW, II, 104.

4. WI's library at Sunnyside contains Antonio de Solis, *Historia de la Conquista de Mexico* (Madrid, 1732); Antonio de Herrera y Tordesillas, *Historia General de los Hechos de los Castellanos en las Islas y Tierra Firme de Mar Oceano*, vols. 2–4 (Madrid, 1726–1730); and Bernal Diaz del Castillo, *Historia Verdadera de la Conquista de Nueva-Espana* (Madrid, 1632). A copy of *Conquista de la Neuva Espana*, without a title page and possibly by Diaz, is also in the library at Sunnyside.

5. Joseph G. Cogswell (1786–1871), who had studied at Göttingen with Edward Everett and George Ticknor and had traveled widely in Europe, had started the Round Hill School at Northampton, Massachusetts, with George Bancroft in 1823. Later Cogswell, after advising John Jacob Astor in the creation and development of the Astor Public Library, served as its superintendent from 1848 to 1861.

6. Bernardino de Sahagún (1499?–1590) prepared *Historia de la Conquista de Mexico*, which was not published until 1829.

7. This transcript is now at NYPL.

8. Edward King, Viscount Kingsborough (1795–1837) had prepared *Antiquities of Mexico: Comprising Fac-similes of Ancient Mexican Paintings and Hieroglyphics, Preserved in the Royal Libraries of Paris, Berlin and Dresden, in the Imperial Library of Vienna, in the Vatican Library . . . Together with the Monuments of New Spain, by M. Dupaix* (London, 1830–1848).

1254. To Messrs. Lea & Blanchard

New York, Jany 25th. 1839

Messrs. Lea & Blanchard
Gentlemen,

A friend of mine, Mr George Washington Montgomery,[1] at present employed in the state department at Washington, was sent last spring on a Mission to Guatemala, in the course of which he traversed the Mountains of Central America. He has written a very lively account of his expedition[2] containing sprightly travelling incidents, picturesque discriptions, touches of character and considerable information of a very interesting kind about the actual state, resources &c &c of that country. It would make one light octavo volume—I have read it with much pleasure and interest, and think it would be very acceptable to the public. The Manuscript is in my possesion, to dispose of for the author. Are you disposed to undertake the publishing of it, and on what terms. Mr Montgomery is an old friend of mine, a brother in law of Mr O Rich, the American Bibliopole.[3] He is an accomplished scholar, acquainted with the learnd languages and elegantly versed in the modern. He has published two or three works on Spain and in Spanish, and one of them has been translated into English and published in this Country (Bernardo del Carpio)[4] His present work is dedicated to Mr Forsyth,[5] Secretary of State.

I will thank you to let me hear from you soon in reply.

Very truly yours
Washington Irving

ADDRESSED: Messrs. Lea & Blanchard / Philadelphia POSTMARKED: NEW-YORK /
    JAN / 25   DOCKETED: Rec Jan 26 / Ans [Jan] 28
MANUSCRIPT: NYPL—WI Papers.

Isaac Lea and William A. Blanchard were operating the publishing business formerly known as Carey, Lea & Blanchard. See David Kaser, *Messrs. Carey & Lea of Philadelphia* (Philadelphia, 1957), pp. 62–63.

1. George Washington Montgomery (1804–1841), whom WI knew in Madrid during his Spanish residence, was attached to the United States legation there. Montgomery's Spanish translation of WI's *The Conquest of Granada* was published in 1831. See Stanley T. Williams, "The First Version of the Writings of WI in Spanish," *Modern Philology*, 28 (1930), 191–92.

2. Subsequently published by Wiley and Putnam of New York as *Narrative of a Journey to Guatemala in Central America, in 1838.*

3. Obadiah Rich (1783–1850) was American consul in Spain and secretary of the American legation when WI went to Madrid in 1826. WI lived for a time

with Rich and used his library of early Spanish books in his researches on Columbus and Spanish exploration.

4. Montgomery wrote a novel, *El Bastardo de Castilla*, adapted from a story by Bernardo del Carpio. See Williams, "The First Version of the Writings of WI in Spanish," p. 192.

5. John Forsyth (1780–1841), a Congressman and Senator from Georgia, served as secretary of state under Presidents Jackson and Van Buren from 1834 to 1841.

1255. To Jonathan Goodhue

New York, Feb 13th. 1839

My dear Sir,

Will you have the kindness to interest yourself with your partner Mr Perit[1] in behalf of my nephew Pierre Munro Irving, son of my deceased brother William Irving, for the situation of notary to the Bank of Commerce. I take very deep interest in procuring this appointment from a wish to fix my nephew near me, in this his native city. I can respond in the fullest manner for his fitness for the office, from his high moral character, his talents and his scrupulous good faith. I cannot take the liberty of making the application to Mr Perit personally, but shall take it as a very great obligation if he will ⟨promote⟩ gratify my wishes in this matter

Very truly my dear Sir / Your friend
Washington Irving

Jno. Goodhue **Esqr**

ADDRESSED: Jonathan Goodhue Esqr.   DOCKETED: Washington Irving / Feby. 13, 1839.
MANUSCRIPT: New York Society Library.

Jonathan Goodhue (1783–1848), a prosperous New York merchant, was a trustee of the Bank for Savings in the City of New York from 1823 until his death. See Charles E. Knowles, *History of the Bank for Savings in the City of New York, 1819–1929* (New York, 1929), p. 180.

1. Pelatiah Perit (1785–1864), a director of the newly established Bank of Commerce, had been with Goodhue's firm since 1819. He later served as president of the Chamber of Commerce from 1853 to 1863. See Scoville, *Old Merchants of NYC*, V, 265; and NYEP, January 12, 1839.

1256. To Messrs. Lea & Blanchard

New York, Feb. 13. 1839

Messrs Lea & Blanchard,
Gentlemen,

I received your letter[1] declining to undertake the publication of the
Journey to Guatemala,[2] as not wishing to risk ⟨the⟩ any loss. Would you
be willing to publish an edition at the risk of the author. He is informed
that the cost of publishing such a book as his Mss. would make would
be from 25 to 50 cents per Copy on 500 Copies; that is to say about
$150 for that number of Copies. and is willing to incur that expence.
I will guarantee his fulfilling such an engagement and would really
take it as a favor if you would facilitate his wishes and get the work
speedily into circulation. If you are disposed to do so I will forward
the Mss. on receiving your reply.

Very truly yours
Washington Irving

P. S. Direct to me *"Tarrytown Westchester Cy* N. Y.["]³

DOCKETED: Red & Ans Feb 14
MANUSCRIPT: Yale.

On the lower half of page 2 is the draft of a reply, written very faintly: "Send
on the Mss & we will find a [*unrecovered*] for it somehow, but in doing it it will
be more to ⟨assist [*word unrecovered*]⟩ oblige You than expectation of profit If any
arise we will take care of the author. The risk we will undertake."

1. This letter has not been located, but probably it was written on January 28,
1839, as indicated in the docket of WI's letter of January 25, 1839.
2. The work by George Washington Montgomery. See WI to Lea & Blanchard,
January 25, 1839.
3. WI omitted the final quotation marks.

1257. To Russell H. Nevins

New York Feb. 13. 1839

My dear Sir,

I have called at your office without having the pleasure of seeing
you. The object of my visit was to interest you in favor of my Nephew
Pierre Munro Irving, for the situation of Notary to the Bank of com-

merce. I believe you are a friend of his father my deceased brother
William. This young man inherits his fathers worth and talents; ⟨he
is⟩ and is every way fitted for the appointment. I should have addressed you before by letter but I had intended to See you personally.
Excuse the liberty I take, but I cannot tell you how much interest I
take in this application.

With great respect / Your friend & servt.
Washington Irving

Russell H Nevins Esqr

MANUSCRIPT: Yale.

Russell H. Nevins, a broker at 42 Wall Street, was a director of the Bank of
Commerce. See *New York City Directory for 1837-38*, p. 460.

1258.   *To Charles Elliott and J. W. Royer*

Greenburgh, Feb. 24th. 1839.

Messrs. Charles Elliott / & J W. Royer / Corresponding Committee &c

Gentlemen,

I have to acknowledge the receipt of your letter informing me of my
having been elected by the Washington Literary Society of La Fayette
College,[1] to deliver an address before the faculty and students at the
next commencement.

I cannot but feel deeply sensible of this mark of consideration on the
part of your association; but regret to say that an insuperable diffidence
in regard to public speaking has compelled me to decline all invitations
of the kind. I beg you to make this known to your society and to present
them my most grateful thanks for the honor they have done me by
the election.

Very respectfully yours
Washington Irving

MANUSCRIPT: Lafayette College Library.   PUBLISHED: *American Literature*, 43
(March, 1971), 115.

Charles Elliott (1815-1892) was valedictorian of the class of 1840 at Lafayette
College and a member of Phi Beta Kappa. He attended Princeton Theological

Seminary and later taught at several theological seminaries and colleges in Pennsylvania, Ohio, and Illinois before returning to his alma mater. Joseph Warren Royer (d. 1910) graduated in the class 1841 and after taking a medical degree was a physician at Trappe, Pennsylvania, for the rest of his life. (Information from Robert G. Gennett of the Lafayette College Library, letter of January 30, 1975.)

1. This group was founded in 1830 as the Manual Labor Academy Philamathean Society but changed its name to the Washington Literary Society in 1832. Its records and library were destroyed in a fire in 1897. (Information from the letter of Robert G. Gennett, January 30, 1975.)

1259. To Henry R. Schoolcraft

Greenburgh, Feb. 24th. 1839.

Dear Sir,

I enclose you a letter to my friend Colonel Aspinwall,[1] but regret to say that the last time he wrote to me he was in great uneasiness apprehending the loss of one of his daughters[2] who appeared to be in a rapid decline. In a previous letter, also, he expressed an unwillingness to undertake any further literary agencies (excepting for myself on the score of old friendship) as he found them extremely troublesome, unprofitable and very apt to be unsatisfactory to all parties. From the foregoing circumstances combined he may decline acting in your case; though I should think your name would carry with it peculiar claims to his attention.

Perhaps you may be able to make an advantageous arrangement with Messrs Wiley & Putnam Booksellers in Broadway; who have a house established in London for the publication of American works.

Wishing you the highest success in your enterprize I am Dear Sir,

with great respect and esteem / Very truly yours
Washington Irving

Henry R Schoolcraft Esqr

MANUSCRIPT: LC.

Henry Rowe Schoolcraft (1793–1864), who, while serving as Indian Agent for the Lake Superior tribes, discovered the source of the Mississippi River in 1832, was superintendent of Indian Affairs for Michigan from 1836 to 1841. He had published books on the Missouri lead mines in 1819 and descriptive accounts of the Mississippi valley in 1825 and 1834 and was presently trying to find a publisher for *Algic Researches, Comprising Inquiries Respecting the Mental Characteristics of the North American Indians,* a work which appeared later in 1839 in two volumes under the imprint of Harper & Brothers.

1. Colonel Thomas Aspinwall (1786–1876), a soldier in the War of 1812 who was U.S. consul in London from 1815 to 1853, acted as WI's literary agent with English publishers. See *Proceedings of the Massachusetts Historical Society,* 2d ser. 8 (November, 1891), 36. WI's letter to Aspinwall has not been located.
2. Aspinwall's daughter, Juliana (b. March 13, 1822), had died on January 26, 1839. See *The Aspinwall Genealogy,* comp. Algernon Aiken Aspinwall (Rutland, Vermont, [1901]), p. 81.

1260.   To [*Lewis G. Clark*]

[February?, 1839?]

Sir: I send you a few more extracts from my travelling note-books. They are the first sketchings of a series of essays, narration, description, and character, which I intended to improve and extend at my leisure, but which I have suffered for years to be neglected among my papers, until the subjects of which they treat are almost out of date. Such as they are, I trust them to the indulgence of your readers.

Your obt Servt.
Geoffrey Crayon

MANUSCRIPT: Va.–Barrett.

1261.   To Sarah Van Wart

New York, March 26t. 1839.

My dear Sister,

I have just returned from being present at the wedding of Irving and Miss Ames.[1] None of our family were present but Pierre Munroe Irving and myself, nor of Mr Ames family[2] excepting his immediate household—Two of Miss Ames's schoolmates were the only persons present, not related to the parties. The bride looked very interesting; she is a most amiable little being, and her situation was a trying one, on the point of being severed from her family and home, and to launch at once into a new kind of life, in a new place, without any connexions round her. She acquitted herself charmingly, and I felt my heart completely linked to her. I shall make a point of visiting the young couple early in the Summer, by which time I trust they will be completely settled in their rural habitation near Philadelphia. In Mr Ames I found an old and very worthy acquaintance, made at Liverpool some twenty four years since. We have renewed our acquaintanceship, and I shall make a point of cultivating it. This match promises to be a very happy one for Irving and I trust he will make it a happy one to the dear little girl who has embarked all her prospects in life so completely with him. God bless them both!

I shall ⟨t⟩ now hasten back to my little Cottage where the opening of Spring calls for my constant presence and attention. Three of the girls are in town on a visit, to see their friends and get the Spring fashions. The rest, with Sister Catharine, are snug at home. Our home has been a very sweet and happy one this winter, and the return of Spring makes it doubly delightful. I never saw Sister Catharine so delighted by the first symptoms of Spring: the singing of the little birds round the cottage, who have begun the year earlier [*end of MS*]

ADDRESSED: Mrs. Henry Van Wart. / Care of Henry Van Wart Esq / Birmingham /
   per Great Western   POSTMARKED: BRISTOL / SHIP LETTER
MANUSCRIPT: Va.—Barrett.

Sarah Irving Van Wart (1780–1849), WI's youngest sister, was married to Henry Van Wart (1783–1873), an American engaged in the hardware and cutlery business in Birmingham, England. During his early years in England WI was a frequent visitor at the Van Wart home.

1. Irving Van Wart (b. 1807) and Sarah C. Ames were married in New York on March 26, 1839, by the Reverend Mr. Dewey. See NYEP, March 27, 1839.

2. Barrett Ames, the father of the bride, was a New York businessman who lived at 2 Lafayette Place. See *New York City Directory for 1838–39*. WI was to take his son Hector with him in 1842 as a clerk in the U.S. legation in Madrid.

1262.   *To Messrs. Marsh, Capen, Lyon & Webb*

                                              Greenburgh. April 15th. 1839.

Messrs. Marsh, Capen Lyon & Webb

Gentlemen,

Various occupations and engagements have so crowded upon me of late as to make me more than usually remiss in my correspondence which is the reason of my not having earlier replied to your letter of the 15th. ult.[1]

I wish to have my Ms: of Mahomet[2] back again, at all events, before publication, as I am sensible some revision is necessary. I do not think any thing would tempt me again to submit a manuscript of mine to such an ordeal as I find it would have to undergo at your board; though I am sensible such a process is necessary to ensure perfect success and a high standing to your enterprize[.] I shall leave to my brother[3] to arrange with you as to the terms of publication. There is one thing to be considered. In publishing in your series[4] I lose my chance of making a sale of the work in England, and for this very work, which was written for Murrays Family Library, he offered me Five hundred guineas, and I accepted his offer; though his subsequent embarrassments prevented the publication from taking place[5]

It is not in my power to contribute the Sketch Book and the Companions of Columbus to your series, these being comprised in a number of my works leased to Carey Lea & Blanchard for a term of years.

I have not been able to attend to the plan suggested for a Work concerning the early voyages of discovery; nor have I been able to write the preface you require; nothing presenting itself to my mind that would not appear to be merely foisted in. If any thing should suggest I will strike it off—though I think the work might be very well published as it stands.

Very respectfully Gentlemen / Your obt Servt
Washington Irving

Manuscript: NYPL—Berg Collection (draft).

Marsh, Capen, Lyon & Webb was one of the twenty bookselling and publishing firms located in Boston on Washington Street between State and Milk Streets. Details about these firms have not been preserved. See W. S. Tryon, *Parnassus Corner: A Life of James T. Fields* (Boston, 1963), pp. 50–51.

Appearing in WI's hand along the left margin of the first page is "Draught of a reply—afterwards somewhat modified."

1. This letter has not been located.

2. WI had apparently sent the publisher an earlier version of *Mahomet*, perhaps the same one submitted to Murray in 1831.

3. Ebenezer Irving often acted as WI's agent with American publishers.

4. WI is probably referring to "The School Library," a series of volumes published "under the sanction of the Board of Education of the State of Massachusetts." His abridgment of *Columbus* was the first volume in this series. See Jacob Blanck, *Bibliography of American Literature* (New Haven, 1969), V, 45.

5. Through the agency of Colonel Aspinwall WI had delivered the manuscript of *Mahomet* to John Murray in the fall of 1831; but, owing to differences between them, WI requested the return of the manuscript. See WI to John Murray, October 29, 1831; WIHM, pp. 126, 157–63.

1263. To Gulian C. Verplanck

Greenburgh, May 11. 1839.

My dear Sir,

Permit me to speak as warmly as I can in favor of Dr Dudley Atkinson, for the post either of Resident Physician or Health Commissioner. I owe him a strong debt of gratitude for his skilful treatment and devoted care of a young friend ⟨and⟩ of mine (Mr Coolidge[1] of Boston) many years since at Paris, at the time that Dr. Atkinson was attending lectures there. He had to contend not merely with the malady, but with the obstina⟨t⟩cy and Contumely of the ⟨Br⟩ Physician to the British Embassy, who treated him with great superciliousness and slight, ⟨as a⟩ but who eventually, after having brought the patient to deaths door, had to abandon the case to him. The rapid recovery of my friend, under the opposite treatment of Dr Atkinson was a triumph to him and an indiscribable relief to me—All that I have since known of Dr Atkinson has confirmed the good opinion I then ⟨enterta⟩ concieved for him, and it will give me the sincerest pleasure to be in any degree instrumental in procuring for him either of the before mentioned appointments

Very truly your friend
Washington Irving

Hon Guilian C Verplanck &c &c &c

MANUSCRIPT: Andrew B. Myers.

Gulian C. Verplanck (1786–1870), a longtime friend associated with WI on the *Analectic Magazine* in 1814, was now a member of the Finance Committee of the New York Senate. See July, *Verplanck*, p. 225.

1. Joseph Coolidge (1798–1879) of Boston traveled in Europe in the early 1820's after taking his M.A. at Harvard. WI met him in Paris. See WI to T. W. Storrow, August 20 and November 10, 1822.

1264. To the Reverend Robert Bolton

Greenburg, May 27th. 1839

My dear Sir,

The Sun blinds to which you allude are made of what is called Tent cloth. I had to ⟨[unrecovered]⟩ order it from France as none was to be procured in New York. The maker of the blinds was a Mr Farrand,[1] No 219. Hudson Street, where the same business is followed by his successor George Gatty.² If you have any friend in France you could, by the present rapid means of communication, soon get a supply. Or if you would write to Mr Thomas ↑W↓ Storrow ⟨Junr⟩ at Paris (who procured it for me) and use my name, he would readily procure and send it to any house in New York that you might direct. It comes in pieces of, I should think, about 25. or 30 yards long—and a yd & half wide. I received a letter from you some time since,³ requesting Autographs—I have neglected to reply to it, not having any autographs on hand and intending to forward you some, as soon as I could procure any. I shall rummage my papers soon, and endeavor to furnish You with some, but I fear ⟨it⟩ my chance stock has been completely gleaned.

I have had a busy Spring, pruning, grafting, ploughing, harrowing, tilling, making fences &c &c—but hope to get a little liesure [in] [MS blotted] the course of a fortnight. I am anxious to see your new mansion and shall endeavor to ride over some morning, in the early part of Summer.

with kindest remembrances to Mrs Bolton⁴ and the young people.⁵ I am, my dear Sir,

> Yours very truly
> Washington Irving

The Rev. Robt **Bolton**

ADDRESSED: The Rev. Robert Bolton / New Rochelle / N. Y. POSTMARKED: NEW-YORK / MAY / 27 // GREENWICH / Mauy / 28 / CT DOCKETED: [unrecovered]
MANUSCRIPT: SHR.

The Reverend Robert Bolton (1788–1857) was a merchant whom WI had known in Liverpool during his early years in England. He later took the orders in the Protestant Episcopal Church and became rector of Christ Church, Pelham, Westchester County. See J. T. Scharf, *History of Westchester County*, 2 vols. (Philadelphia, 1886), I, 607; and Henry Carrington Bolton and Reginald Pelham Bolton, *The Family of Bolton in England and America, 1100–1894* (New York, 1895), chart 22, and pp. 330–37.

1. James H. Farrand, blindmaker, is listed in the *New York City Directory* through the 1837–1838 issue. See p. 235.
2. George Gatty is listed in the 1838–1839 *New York City Directory* at the address previously occupied by Farrand. See p. 266.
3. This letter has not been located.
4. The former Anne Jay (1793–1859) of Bath, England, and mother of his fourteen children.
5. Among Bolton's children were five daughters born between 1825 and 1831. For other details, see WI to Bolton, December 24, 1846.

1265. To Joseph L. Chester

Greenburg [June] 26th. 1839

Dear Sir,

I have just received your letter of the 21st. instant,[1] and regret to say that my literary arrangements are such as to prevent my being a contributor to Your magazine.[2] I feel, also, a repugnance to furnish the commendatory letter you request, such letters always savouring too much of bookselling management, and arguing some degree of self confidence in the person furnishing them, as if his opinion was to stamp a current value on the work. As there is now an abundance of young and vigorous native talent pressing into the carreer of letters, I make no doubt you will soon recruit your ranks with names destined to rise into celebrity.

With best wishes for your success / I am very respectfully, /
Your obt Servt.
Washington Irving

Joseph L Chester Esqr

ADDRESSED: Joseph L Chester Esqr / 71 Cedar Street / New York   POSTMARKED: TARRYTOWN N. Y. / JUN 26 DOCKETED: Washington Irving Esqr / *June 28, 1839* / Washn. Irving / *June 28. 1839.*
MANUSCRIPT: Haverford College Library.

Joseph L. Chester (1821–1882), a writer who contributed frequently to the weekly and monthly periodical press, was a merchant in New York and Philadelphia until 1858, when he removed to England.

Although WI wrote "July" as the month, the postmark and the dockets clearly establish that it was "June."

1. This letter has not been located.
2. Since Chester's enterprise did not succeed, the name of his prospective magazine is not known.

1266. To Martin Van Buren

Greenburgh July 2d. 1839.

My dear Sir,

I had intended to come to town to ⟨search⟩ meet you, but fear I shall be prevented, as I am suffering under the effects of a severe cold, attended with acute pain in the head. I wish you would drop me a line to let me know when I may expect you at my cottage, where I shall be most happy to receive you.[1] I can only promise you plain country fare, but you shall have chicken dressed in the true Dutch Style as we used to have them during our tour through the Dutch neighborhoods of the Hudson[.] above all, you shall have a hearty welcome from one who has as honest a regard for you as if you were not in place and power

Yours ever
Washington Irving

ADDRESSED: Martin Van Buren / President of the U S. / New York.
MANUSCRIPT: LC.   PUBLISHED: George S. Hellman, *WI, Esquire*, p. 256.

Martin Van Buren (1782–1862), the president of the United States at this time, had worked closely with WI in London at the U.S. legation in 1831 and 1832.

1. Van Buren left New York City about noon on July 10 and was to depart from Sing Sing on the morning of July 12. Unless the visit could not be worked into his schedule, Van Buren probably dined with WI on July 11. See NYEP, July 10 and 11, 1839.

1267.   To Israel K. Tefft

Greenburgh July 21st. 1839.

Dear Sir,
I have to acknowledge the receipt of your letter of the 9th. instant,[1] informing me of my being elected an honorary member of the Georgia Historical Society.

I beg you to express to the Society the grateful sense I entertain of this very flattering mark of their esteem.

With best wishes for the prosperity of Your institution I remain, dear Sir

Very respectfully / Your obt Servt.
Washington Irving
I. K. Tefft Esqr / Corresponding Secretary &c.

MANUSCRIPT: Georgia Historical Society.

Israel Keech Tefft (1794–1862), an autograph collector and a banker associated with the Georgia State Bank from 1822 to 1862, helped to found the Georgia Historical Society and served as its corresponding secretary until his death.

1. This letter has not been located.

1268. To David Hoffman

New York, Aug. 22d. 1839

My dear Sir,

I have no apology to offer you for Suffering your letter[1] to remain so long unanswered. but that of habitual procrastination in letter writing, encreased by a multiplicity and variety of casual cares and occupations. I am, in fact, a man of but little method and less leisure; and am continually behind hand in my correspondence, which unluckily is daily augmenting and crowding upon me.

In respect to your literary plans, I scarce know what council to give you. Literature seems to me to be in a great measure a lottery to those who engage in it, and it is difficult to account for the success of some and the failure of others. Your writings appear to me to possess sterling merit, and I should think contained the elements of popularity in a superior degree to many that have attained wide currency. Your essays of the Grumbler[2] especially I should have thought calculated to obtain a ready and extensive circulation in this country. I would barely point out one thing which I have heard objected to; ⟨th su⟩ the use of a kind of Classic nomenclature for your persons, Such as Honestus, Candidus &c instead of familiar every day names. This has the high authority and example of Johnson[3] and other of the Standard Essayists; but it is thought to ⟨p⟩ give the narratives a cold and artificial look, and to raise them above the sympathies of every day life—

I really do not know what course to reccommend to you in dealing with the Booksellers. Do what you may they always continue to have the Lions share. I have tried every way; have had books published on my own account, and disposed of them to various Booksellers—Have published on shares, and have sold editions. I have generally found ⟨tha⟩ ↑it↓ best ⟨way is⟩ to make the terms such as that the Bookseller would find it his interest to push the work into wide circulation. As you propose to publish a number of works, I think you had better sacrafice all thought of profit on one, and even make up your mind to Sustain a loss upon it, so that you could get the booksellers to foster and circulate it, and thus diffuse your name throughout the country. One work, thus circulated, if it should meet with approbation, would command attention for its successors; and out of the sale of the latter you might indemnify yourself for any preceding loss you might have sustained.

The vast influx of British literature, aided by the state of our Copy right law, renders it hard for Native writers to get their heads above the surface. I found it impossible some months since, to get any bookseller to make an offer for an American work of merit,[4] entrusted to my care,

or even to take the trouble of printing & publishing it at the authors risk; until Wiley & Putnam of New York, undertook it, as a matter of friendship toward myself—I believe the author will lose money by it.
   With best wishes for your success

I am my dear Sir / Yours very truly
Washington Irving

David Hoffman Esqr.

ADDRESSED: David Hoffman Esqr / Baltimore   POSTMARKED: NEW-YORK / AUG / 23   DOCKETED: Washington Irving / 28 Sept 1839. MANUSCRIPT: Va.—Barrett.

   David Hoffman (1784–1854), who was a professor of law at the University of Maryland from 1817 to 1836, published legal treatises and familiar essays and later practiced law in Philadelphia.

   1. This letter has not been located.
   2. Hoffman's *Miscellaneous Thoughts on Men, Manners, and Things, by Anthony Grumbler, of Grumbleton Hall, Esq.* had appeared in 1837.
   3. Samuel Johnson's *The Rambler* (1750–1752) and *The Idler* (1758–1760) probably served as models for Hoffman.
   4. Probably George W. Montgomery's *Narrative of a Journey to Guatemala*, which WI had offered to Lea & Blanchard but which was published by Wiley & Putnam. See WI to Lea & Blanchard, January 25, 1839, and February 13, 1839.

1269.   *To James Nack*

New York, Aug. 22d. 1839

My dear Sir,
   I cannot but feel deeply sensible of the proof of esteem and regard you have given me in dedicating to me your charming volume of poems,[1] but I feel still more sensible of the assurances you give in your work that my writings have been so fortunate as to administer solace, and even pleasure, to you under your great bereavements. Believe me Sir when I assure you that this has given me a truer and honester glow of Self Satisfaction than has ever been excited by the most flattering eulogies of the press.

I am, my dear Sir / Very truly & respectfully / Your obliged
Washington Irving

James Nack Esqr

ADDRESSED: James Nack Esqr / No 20. City Hall / N York   POSTMARKED: NEW-
    YORK / AUG / 23
MANUSCRIPT: Harvard.

James Nack (1809–1879), who lost his sight and speech in a childhood mishap,
attracted attention with *The Legend of the Rocks, and Other Poems* (1827) and
An Ode on the Proclamation of President Jackson (1833). As a result, he was made
an assistant to the clerk of the city and county.

1. *Earl Rupert, and Other Tales and Poems* (New York, 1839).

1270. To ————

New York, Sept. 2, 1839.

I understand[1] that my friend, the Rev. Mr. Warner, proposes to
receive into his family at Paris, a limited number of young gentlemen,
for the purpose of superintending their education and moral improvement. I know of no person better fitted for such a task. Indeed, from
the knowledge I have of his private character and personal qualities,
and of the excellent tone, both as to morals and manners, prevalent in
his domestic circle, I think those parents singularly fortunate, who, in
seeking to give their sons the advantages, without exposing them to
the risks, of Paris, can obtain for them his guardian eye, and admission
into the bosom of his family.

Washington Irving

PUBLISHED: *The American Lyceum in Paris* (Paris, 1840), pp. 20–21; *Emerson
    Society Quarterly*, no. 52 (Third Quarter, 1968), 82.

The Reverend Thomas T. Warner (d. 1849) was chaplain and professor of
moral philosophy at the U.S. Military Academy from 1828 to 1838. He moved to
Paris in 1839 to promote the lyceum there, carrying letters of introduction from
James Fenimore Cooper and WI.

1. The version of the letter printed in *The American Lyceum in Paris* omits
the *s*, probably because of careless proofreading.

1271. To John S. Littell

Greenburgh Octr. 13th. 1839

Dear Sir,
    I have to acknowledge the receipt of your letter of the 7th. inst.[1]
proposing that I should write a History of the American Revolution.

It is certainly a noble subject and one that I should be proud to grapple with; but my occupations and engagements are such at present as to put it out of my power to undertake the subject; and I have already had to decline propositions similar to your own, from various quarters.

Very respectfully / Your obliged & humble Servt.
Washington Irving

John S. Littell Esqr.

MANUSCRIPT: Va.—Barrett.

John S. Littell (1806–1875) edited Alexander Graydon's *Memoirs of His Own Time* (Philadelphia, 1846) and the *Life, Character, and Services of Henry Clay* (n.p., n.d.).

1. This letter has not been located.

1272. *To Maria Hale Irving*

Greenburgh Octr. 26th. 1839

My dear Maria,
I return you your two fine boys,[1] with many thanks for the *loan*. They have behaved themselves like fine little fellows, and I shall always be happy to see them at the cottage; which I hope they will henceforth consider one of their holyday resorts.

Affectionately your uncle
Washington Irving

ADDRESSED: Mrs Lewis G. Irving / Sing Sing
MANUSCRIPT: Helen Irving Horton.

Maria Carleton Hale (1797–1869) married Lewis Graham Irving (1795–1879), son of William and Julia Paulding Irving, on June 16, 1823.

1. Lewis (1825–1861) and Charles (1826–1895).

1273.   To William H. Seward

Greenburgh. Oct. 27th. 1839

My dear Sir,

Permit me to present to you my nephew Mr Irving Paris,[1] who goes to Albany to stand his examination for admission to the bar. He is a young gentleman of whom I can speak confidently as to his qualities both of head and heart.

He is desirous of obtaining the appointment of commissioner of Deeds, to assist him in his first launch into business. If it would be convenient to you to give him your countenance in this matter you would greatly oblige me.

I may as well add that he is the brother of my niece Miss Sarah Paris,[2] the young lady who accompanied me in my evening visit to your house at Auburn;[3] of which most agreeable visit she, as well as myself, ever retains the liveliest reccollection.

With kind remembrances to Mrs Seward.[4]

I am my dear Sir, / ever very faithfully yours,
Washington Irving

His Excellency / Wm H. Seward / &c &c &c

ADDRESSED: His Excellency / William H. Seward / &c &c &c / Albany / *Mr Irving Paris.*   DOCKETED: Irving Paris N. Y. / Commissioner of Deeds.
MANUSCRIPT: University of Rochester Library.

William H. Seward (1801–1872), governor of New York at this time, served in the U.S. Senate from 1855 to 1860 and as secretary of state under Presidents Lincoln and Johnson.

1. Irving Paris (1816–1879) was the son of Daniel and Catharine Irving Paris.
2. Sarah Paris (1813–1885), who married Thomas Wentworth Storrow, Jr. on March 31, 1841, was probably WI's favorite niece.
3. WI had visited Seward's home in August, 1838. See WI to Seward; September 22, 1838.
4. The former Frances Miller (1805–1865), daughter of Seward's law partner, Elijah Miller. See Glyndon Van Deusen, *William Henry Seward* (New York, 1967), pp. 10, 416.

1274.   To Martin Van Buren

Greenburgh, Nov. 2, 1839

My dear Sir

The recommendation of Mr Anthony J Bleecker[1] for the office of U. S. Marshall for this district is I believe already before you backed by many of the weightiest ⟨names⟩ friends of the administration. To this let me add my good word in his behalf as a gentleman of high integrity and much ability and well qualified to discharge the duties of the office; let me moreover speak of him in a point of view that I confess has great interest with me as one of the *original, well-tried stock* of "Old Yorkers" who ought to be cherished and taken care of as the real *seed* corn of our population

Ever with truest regard / Yours
(signed) Washington Irving

Martin Van Buren, President of U. S.

MANUSCRIPT: Paul Fenimore Cooper. A copy, not in Irving's hand.
PUBLISHED: *Correspondence of James Fenimore-Cooper*, ed. James Fenimore Cooper, 2 vols. (New Haven, 1922), II, 406–7.

1. Anthony J. Bleecker (1799–1884), who also secured the support of James Fenimore Cooper in his application for the post, was appointed U.S. marshall for the New York District in December, 1839. See *The Letters and Journals of James Fenimore Cooper*, ed. James F. Beard, 6 vols. (Cambridge, Mass., 1960–1968), III, 446–47; NYEP, December 18, 1839.

1275.   To Edgar Allan Poe

Greenburgh, Nov 6. 1839.

Dear Sir,

The magazine[1] you were so kind as to send me, being directed to New York, instead of Tarry Town, did not reach me for some time— This—together with an unfortunate habit of procrastination, must plead my apology for the tardiness of my reply.

I have read your little tale of William Wilson[2] with much pleasure. It is managed in a highly picturesque Style and the Singular and Mysterious interest is well sustained throughout—I repeat what I have said in regard to a previous production,[3] which you did me the favor to send me, that I cannot but think a Series of articles of like Style and merit would be extremely well received by the public.

I would add, for your private ear, that I ⟨like⟩ ↑think↓ the last tale much the best, in regard to style. It is simpler. In your first you have been too too anxious to present your pictures vividly to the eye, or too distrustful of your effect, and have laid on too much colouring. It is erring on the best side—the side of luxuriance. That tale might be improved by relieving the Style from some of the epithets. There is no danger of destroying its graphic effect, which is powerful—[4]

> with best wishes for your success / I am my dear Sir/
> Yours respectfully
> Washington Irving

Edgar A Poe Esqr

ADDRESSED: Edgar A. Poe Esq / Philadelphia   POSTMARKED: 7 November / Dobbs Ferry / N. Y.   DOCKETED: W. *Irving*
MANUSCRIPT: NYPL—Berg Collection.   PUBLISHED: George E. Woodberry, *The Life of Edgar Allan Poe*, 2 vols. (Boston, 1909), I, 216–17.

1. *Burton's Gentleman's Magazine* for October, 1839. Poe had joined the magazine in July, 1839, and remained with it for about a year.
2. This story also appeared in Eliza Leslie's annual, *The Gift*, for 1840. See Poe to Philip P. Cooke, September 21, 1839, in *The Letters of Edgar Allan Poe*, ed. John Ward Ostrom, 2 vols. (Cambridge, Mass., 1948), I, 119.
3. Probably "The Fall of the House of Usher," which was published in *Burton's Gentleman's Magazine* for September, 1839.
4. On November 11, 1839, Poe wrote to Joseph Evans Snodgrass that "I am sure you will be pleased to hear that Washington Irving has addressed me 2 letters, abounding in high passages of compliment in regard to my Tales—passages which he desires me to make public—if I think benefit may be derived. It is needless to say that I shall do so—it is a duty I owe myself—and which it would be wilful folly to neglect, through a false sense of modesty. . . . Irving's name will afford me a complete triumph over those little critics who would endeavor to put me down by raising the hue & cry of *exaggeration* in style, of *Germanism* & such twaddle. You know Irving heads the school of the *quietists*" (*The Letters of Edgar Allan Poe*, I, 121).

1276.   To William Jerdan

Greenburgh, Novr. 16th. 1839.

My dear Sir,

This will be handed you by my friend Mr George Catlin,[1] who has resided for several years *as an artist*, among our wild tribes of the Prairies diligently studying their characteristics, and making sketches on the spot, of their persons, dresses, ceremonies, hunting scenes, &c.

He has made also a complete collection of curious and splendid Indian dresses; of their weapons, tents &c &c. All these he has formed into a gallery, which ⟨presents⟩ ↑gives↓ a most vivid and faithful idea of the natural scenery of the Far West and the picturesque life of its savage tribes. Mr Catlin, moreover, is full of anecdote of Indian scenes and adventures, and I ⟨am of a⟩ know of no one who gives so graphic and dramatic an account of the wild scenes of the Far West. I would reccommend him most confidently to your acquaintance and civilities being convinced you will be interested in his acquaintance

> Very truly my dear Sir / Yours
> Washington Irving

William Jerdan Esq / &c &c &c

ADDRESSED: William Jerdan Esq / Editor of the Literary Gazette / London / [*above the address*:] 7 Wellington St. [*unrecovered*] / [*below the address*:] 13 Portsmouth St.   DOCKETED: Washington Irving / Intr. Mr Catlin / Jany 9th.   MANUSCRIPT: Iowa State Education Association.

William Jerdan (1782–1869) was a journalist, editor of the *Literary Gazette* from 1817 to 1850, and one of the founders of the Royal Society of Literature, which conferred its 50 guinea medal on WI in 1830. See WI to Peter Irving, April, 1830.

1. George Catlin (1796–1872) was an artist who lived among the Western American Indians between 1829 and 1838. He painted portraits of 600 distinguished Indians, plus many scenes of Indian life and culture. He exhibited his materials in the United States and abroad from 1837 to 1852.

1277. To Irving Van Wart

> Greenburgh, Nov. 27th. 1839

My dear Irving,

I had intended before this time to have made you a visit, but your aunt Paris has had a return of her dismal nervous complaint, and I find my presence at the cottage so important to her comfort and her quiet of mind, especially at this season of the year, when there are not so many agreeable things occurring to engage her attention and amuse her thoughts, that I have given up several excursions which I had in mind, and have resolved to remain at home, until she recovers her usual state of health and Spirits.

I had anticipated much pleasure in meeting with Mrs Butler;[1] indeed I know of no one I should be happier to see, or ⟨who⟩ meeting with whom would awaken more interesting and heartfelt reccollections. I hope, however, to have this satisfaction before very long; in the mean time, when you see her, give her my kindest remembrances.

With my best love to your precious little wife whom I hold "in my hearts core."[2]

I am my dear Irving / your affectionate Uncle
Washington Irving

Irving Vanwart Esqr.

ADDRESSED: Irving Van Wart Esqr / Philadelphia POSTMARKED: NEW-YORK / NOV / 29
MANUSCRIPT: HSP.

1. Possibly Frances Anne Kemble (1809–1893), the English actress who married Pierce Butler of Germantown, Pennsylvania.
2. *Hamlet*, II, ii, 78.

1278.   To William H. Seward

Greenburgh Decr 19th. 1839

My dear Sir,

Understanding that my neighbor Mr Stephen B Tompkins[1] is candidate for the office of Surrogate[2] of this county, I beg leave to reccommend him most heartily for the appointment. He is active, intelligent, liberal and public spirited, and by the constant exercise of those qualities has contributed greatly towards promoting the prosperity of this neighborhood.

Excuse the liberty I take in meddling in these matters, but, at a time when you have so many reccommendations pressing upon you for mere party purposes, it may be worth while to have one, now and then, dictated by a simple wish for the public good.

Very sincerely your friend
Washington Irving

His Excellency / William H Seward / c& &c &c / Albany

ADDRESSED: Hi[s] excellency / William H Seward / &c &c &c / Albany DOCKETED: Stephen B. Tompkins / Surrogate / Westchester County
MANUSCRIPT: University of Rochester Library.

1. Stephen B. Tompkins, a resident of the Tarrytown area, was buried in the Old Dutch Churchyard there. He is not listed among the surrogates of Westchester County in J. T. Scharf, *The History of Westchester County*, I, 232, 297.

2. The surrogate was a judicial official dealing with settlement of wills and estates. Until 1894 such officers in New York were appointed by the governor. See Lynton K. Caldwell, *The Government and Administration of New York* (New York, 1954), pp. 114–15.

1279.   To Eliza Leslie

Greenburgh, Decr 20th. 1839.

My dear Miss Leslie,

I have a regular engagement with the Knickerbocker,[1] which, while it occupies all the time I can devote to literary occupations, renders it as I concieve, improper for me to furnish articles to any other Miscellany. I have, therefore, felt obliged to decline numerous applications of the kind contained in your letter.

I have heard the most gratifying accounts of your brothers coronation picture.[2] I hope he will make a copy and send it to this country for exhibition. I think it would pay well. His success in this picture will no doubt be a most fortunate hit for him in England.

Very truly & respectfully / Your friend & Servt
Washington Irving

Miss Eliza Leslie.

ADDRESSED: Miss Eliza Leslie / care of Messrs. Carey & Hart / Philadelphia
MANUSCRIPT: Va.—Barrett.

Eliza Leslie (1787–1858), a prolific writer of juvenile stories and domestic works, was editor of *The Gift*, a literary annual published in Philadelphia.

1. WI had signed a contract with Lewis Gaylord Clark and Clement M. Edson, editors of the *Knickerbocker Magazine*, on February 7, 1839, to contribute regularly to it. Between March, 1839, and October, 1841, WI prepared thirty essays, tales, and sketches for the magazine. See STW, II, 360, n. 99.

2. Charles Robert Leslie (1794–1859), whom WI knew intimately during his residence in England, had painted "The Queen Receiving the Sacrament after the Coronation, June 28, 1838," a work which greatly pleased Queen Victoria. See Leslie, *Autobiographical Recollections*, pp. 110–11.

1280. To Lewis G. Clark

Greenburgh, Dec. 21st, 1839.

My dear Sir:

Your letter dated Monday 15th,[1] with the accompanying MS., did not reach me until last evening, (Saturday.) I have supplied the hiatus in "Pelayo," and will send it to town by a gentleman who goes to-morrow (Monday) afternoon, and who will put it in the post-office.

The other article for the January number, entitled "The Bermudas: a Shaksperian research," must be at the lodgings of my nephew Pierre, as I left it with his wife just as I was departing from town. It was wrapped up in a parcel with a shirt that was to be sent to the laundress. I hope the MS. may not have gone there too, or I shall be literally "in the suds."

As to Mr. ———— ————, I have heard from one or two other quarters of his surprise and chagrin at my not having noticed a letter of introduction which he says he brought to me from Mr. ————. The simple fact is, I have never received such a letter. It may be sleeping in some out-of-the-way post-office in Westchester county, as is frequently the case of letters addressed to me. The only post-office at which I inquire is that at Tarrytown, and God knows I receive five times as many through that as I care for, or can attend to.

I have never known any thing of the plan of Mr. ———— until I received the copy you sent me. If you should be in communication with him, let him know these facts; as I would not be on ill terms with a person of his universal acquaintance, wonderful ubiquity, and windy vocation.

Yours, very truly,
Washington Irving

PUBLISHED: *Knickerbocker Magazine*, 55 (February, 1860), 231–32.

1. This letter has not been located.

1281. To James K. Paulding

Greenburgh, Decr 26th. 1839.

My dear Paulding

Let me reccommend to your favorable attention, the application of Mr Edwin Doty, for an ⟨situation⟩ appointment in the Marine Corps.

He is the son of Isaac Doty, well known ↑in this County↓ as a pure and uncompromising patriot in the time of the revolution, and who suffered both in person and fortune in the service of his country.

Mr Edwin Doty has for some time been a resident of Whiteplains, where he is universally esteemed for his correct moral deportment, and gentlemanly bearing. Should he make his application in person, you will be able to judge for yourself, how decidedly his appearance and deportment are in his favor, and corroborate those representations. I sincerely hope you may be able to promote his views, and though I know you have a rigid determination to act in all your appointments with strict impartiality, yet I cannot help endeavoring to awaken a kind feeling towards *old Westchester County*

Wishing you and yours a Merry christmas

I am my dear Paulding / Yours ever
Washington Irving

Hon Jas K Paulding / &c &c &c

MANUSCRIPT: LC.

James Kirke Paulding (1778–1860), who had collaborated with WI on *Salmagundi* and associated with him in the Lads of Kilkenny thirty years earlier, was now serving as Van Buren's secretary of the navy, a post which had first been offered to WI.

1282. *To Gouverneur Kemble*

Greenburgh, Decr 28th. 1839

My dear Kemble,

I return you Godfreys letter.[1] I approve of your idea of having the security reduced a thousand dollars before we accept of Mr Maynard[2] in lieu of Godfrey. I approve likewise of your other precautions. Mr Maynard may be one of the richest men in Michigan, but we know the airy nature of those great fortunes of the West; I feel confidence in Godfreys honesty and in his good intentions, and do not like to let go my hold upon them without an equivalent. I am disposed to give him every reasonable indulgence; but the times are hard with us as well as with him, and, as we have treated him as a friend rather than a debtor, he must do the best he can for us.

I do not wonder the President has grown so lusty—having remained so long undelivered of so thumping a Message. I trust his safe accouchement will bring him down to his usual proportions. I have read his speech with great satisfaction.[3] It is very lucid and puts the financial question in a clear light that I think will ⟨be⟩ have an effect upon all plain thinking unprejudiced people throughout the union.

I write in haste, by one of my nephews just starting for the Tarry-town Post office.

Yours ever my dear Kemble
Washington Irving

Hon Gouvr Kemble.

ADDRESSED: Hon. Gouverneur Kemble / Washington City POSTMARKED: NEW-
    YORK / DEC / 29 DOCKETED: W Irving / 28 Dec 1839
MANUSCRIPT: Lehigh University Library. PUBLISHED: ˙American Literature, 35
    (May, 1963), 165–66.
Gouverneur Kemble (1786–1875), one of WI's friends of his youth and pro-
prietor of the West Point Foundry, was serving in Congress at this time.˙

1. David Godfrey (1800–1885) was a Michigan resident who acted as agent for WI and Kemble in their Western land speculations.

2. It is not clear whether WI was referring to Ezra, J. W., or William S. May-nard, all of whom were early settlers in the Ann Arbor area. See Reports of the Pioneer Society of the State of Michigan Together with Reports of County, Town, and District Pioneer Societies (Lansing, 1900), I, 329, 334, 335.

3. Van Buren sent his address to Congress on December 24, 1839. In it he advocated enactment of the Independent Treasury bill and the enforcement of the legal-tender clauses requiring that all financial transactions of the government be made in hard money. See Senate, Congressional Globe, 26th Cong., 1st sess., pt. 8, app., pp. 1–8.

1283. To William H. Seward

Greenburgh Decr 30th. 1839.

My dear Sir,

When I wrote to you lately[1] in favor of my worthy neighbor Mr Tompkins for the office of Surrogate of this county I was not aware that my nephew Lewis G Irving was a candidate for the Same office. With-out wishing in the least to impair my reccommendation of Mr Tompkins I write this explanation merely lest Silence on my part should be construed ⟨into⟩ unfavorably to my Nephew, as if I know some reason why he ought not to succeed: which certainly is not the case.

Very respectfully my dear Sir / Your friend
Washington Irving

His Excellency / Govr. Seward.

ADDRESSED: His Excellency / Governor Seward / Albany POSTMARKED: NEW-
   YORK / JAN / 1 DOCKETED: Lewis G Irving / West. Co / Surrogate
MANUSCRIPT: University of Rochester Library.

The address leaf includes the frank "Frm M H Grinnell / *M C*" in the upper
right corner.

1. See WI to Seward, December 19, 1839.

1284. To Lewis G. Clark

[Before January 10, 1840]

To the Editor of the Knickerbocker.

Sir:
   Having seen it stated, more than once, in the public papers, that I
declined subscribing my name to the petition, presented to Congress
during a former session, for an act of international Copy-right, I beg
leave, through your pages, to say in explanation, that I declined, not
from any hostility or indifference to the object of the petition, ⟨about⟩
↑in favor of↓ which my sentiments have always been openly expressed,
but merely because I did not relish the phraseology of the petition,
and because I expected to see the measure pressed from another quarter.
I wrote about the same time, however, to members of Congress, in
support of the application.
   As no other petition has been sent to me for signature, and as
silence on my part may be misconstrued, I now, as far as my name
may be thought of any value, enroll it among those who pray most
earnestly to Congress for this act of international equity. I consider
it due, not merely to foreign authors, to whose lucubrations we are
so deeply indebted for constant instruction and delight, but to our
own native authors, who are implicated in the effects of the wrong done
by our present laws.
   For myself, ⟨whose⟩ my literary career, ↑as an author,[1]↓ is drawing
to a close, and cannot be much affected by any disposition of this question; but we have a young literature springing up, and daily unfolding
itself with wonderful energy and luxuriance, which, as it promises to
shed a grace and lustre upon the Nation, deserves all its fostering care.
How much this growing literature may be retarded by the present state
of our Copy-right law, I had recently an instance, in the cavalier treatment of a work of merit, ↑written↓ by an American, who had not yet
established a commanding name in the literary market. I undertook,

↑as a friend,↓ to dispose of it for him, but found it impossible to get an offer from any of our principal publishers.[2] They even declined to publish it at the Authors cost, alledging that it was not worth their while to trouble themselves about native works, of doubtful success, while they ⟨had the⟩ could pick and choose among the successful works daily poured out by the British press, *for which they had nothing to pay for Copy-right.*

This Simple fact spoke volumes to me, as I trust it will do to all who may peruse these lines. I do not mean to enter into the discussion of a subject ⟨which⟩ ↑that↓ has already been treated so voluminously. ⟨nor to urge the various arguments that might be advanced⟩ I will barely observe, that I have seen few arguments advanced against the proposed act, that ought to weigh with intelligent and high-minded men; while I have noticed some that have been urged, so sordid and selfish ↑in their nature, and so narrow in the scope of their policy,↓ as almost to be insulting to those to whom they were addressed.

I trust that, whenever this question comes before Congress, ↑it will at once receive an action prompt and decided,↓ ⟨the action upon it to will be so prompt and the favorable⟩ ↑and be carried by an overwhelming, if not unanimous,↓ ⟨vote so overwhelming, as at once to wipe off a Stigma which remains⟩ vote, worthy of an enlightened, a just, and a generous nation.

Your ob. Servt.
Washington Irving

ADDRESSED: Editor of the Knickerbocker / New York   POSTMARKED: TARRYTOWN N. Y. / JAN 10[?]

MANUSCRIPT: Va.—Barrett. PUBLISHED: *Knickerbocker Magazine,* 15 (January, 1840), 78–79; PMI, III, 149–51; and Homer S. Barnes, *Charles Fenno Hoffman* (New York, 1966), pp. 110–11 (in part).

Since this letter was printed in the *Knickerbocker Magazine* for January, 1840, and since the unrecovered numeral in the postmark is a single digit, the letter was written before January 10, 1840.

Numerous editorial marking and instructions for the printer suggest that WI's original letter was used as copy text for publication in the *Knickerbocker.*

1. The phrase "as an author" and the commas before and after it have been added in another hand, probably Clark's.

2. Probably WI is alluding to his attempt to persuade Lea & Blanchard to publish George W. Montgomery's *Narrative of a Journey to Guatemala.* See WI to Lea & Blanchard, January 25, 1839; and to David Hoffman, August 22, 1839.

1285.   To Martin Van Buren
(Confidential)

Tarrytown Jany 13th. 1840

My dear Sir,

I am about to appeal to your friendship in a way I once little dreamt of doing; by asking a favor in which my own personal interests are involved. The explanation I shall make *in confidence* will I hope plead my Apology. I wish to obtain a respectable and reasonably profitable appointment for my brother Ebenezer Irving; and I presume the Sub treasury scheme, when it goes into operation, will put something of the kind at your disposal.[1] I believe you are acquainted with the character of my brother, if not, Paulding and Kemble, who know him well, can vouch for his spotless integrity and thorough worth, and his capability, industry and punctuality as a man of business.[2] In politics, like all my brothers he has never been of the same School with yourself, and has been sincere and disinterested in his politics, having never asked a favor.

The vicissitudes of the times have of late years born hard upon him, and his means have been gradually diminishing. I have done all I could to buoy him up; and his charming family of daughters have long, been the inmates of my cottage and made it a delightful home to me. My own means, however, are hampered and locked up so as to produce me no income,[3] and I have had to depend upon the exercise of my pen, daily growing more and more precarious, to keep the wolf from the door. The least interruption of health and good spirits would reduce me to painful embarrassments. In the mean time I find my brothers usual source of income is likely soon entirely to cease, and this fills me with solicitude both on his account and my own. I have now, I trust, said enough to shew you how materially you would lighten a load of care that presses upon me, by giving my [brother] [*MS torn*] a situation that would help to provide for h[is own?] [*MS torn*] little flock. As I said before—I make the [disclosure?] [*MS torn*] to you *in confidence as a friend,* for if I did [not think?] [*MS torn*] of you from my own heart, and believe you to be [my] [*MS torn*] friend you would never have heard from me in [this?] [*MS torn*] manner.

Before I conclude let me tell you how much I have been gratified by your Message. It is a glorious paper, and sheds a light upon the whole labarynth of financial subtelties and corruptions that must lay it open to the simplest mind.

Ever very truly yours
Washington Irving

His Excellency, Martin Van Buren

MANUSCRIPT: LC.   PUBLISHED: STW, II, 95 (in part).

1. Apparently nothing came of this request. "Ebenezer did not benefit by the Sub-Treasury plan." See STW, II, 70.

2. Paulding spoke to Van Buren in Ebenezer's behalf. See Paulding to WI, March 3, 1840, in *Letters of J. K. Paulding*, p. 275. It is possible that Gouverneur Kemble, in Washington at this time as Congressman, also spoke to Van Buren, but no record of it has been found.

3. On December 1, 1838, WI had observed to Sarah Van Wart, his sister, that most of his "actual capital" was tied up in "unproductive property." WI lost money in land speculations in Mississippi and Toledo. See PMI, III, 87, 119.

1286.   To Gouverneur Kemble

Tarrytown, Jany 21. 1840

My dear Kemble,

I find some of the heirs of Joseph Youngs[1] are disposed to urge their claim for remuneration for the destruction of his house, in the Sawmill River valley,[2] by the British during the revolutionary war. The late Samuel Youngs[3] of this neighborhood was for many years an applicant to congress in the matter. He is dead, but the claim survives to other heirs. I have not the least doubt that the claim is a just one, and more entitled to consideration than four out of five of those listened to. Joseph Youngs house was made head quarters by our troops, which drew upon it the wrath of the enemy. The Youngs family was active in the service of the country and suffered much. Give the claim a good lift whenever it comes up.

Yours ever,
Washington Irving

Hon Gouvr Kemble.

ADDRESSED: Hon. Gouverneur Kemble / Washington City   POSTMARKED: TARRY-
      TOWN N. Y. / JAN / 22   DOCKETED: W. Irving / 21 Jany 1840
MANUSCRIPT: Lehigh University Library. PUBLISHED: *American Literature*, 35
      (May, 1963), 166.

1. Joseph Youngs, who lived four miles east of Tarrytown at "Four Corners," the intersection of County House and Unionville Roads, was involved in several skirmishes with the British. His house, used to quarter the militia, was set afire by the British, Hessians, and Tories on February 3, 1780. See Otto Hufeland, *Westchester County during the American Revolution, 1775–1783* (White Plains, 1926), pp. 254, 324; and J. T. Scharf, *History of Westchester County*, II, 312–15.

2. The Sawmill River, running parallel to the Hudson River, intersects County House Road about halfway between Tarrytown and the Youngs house.

3. Samuel Youngs (d. 1838), the son of Joseph Youngs, had a thriving law business and served several years as surrogate of Westchester County. See Scharf, *History of Westchester County*, I, 534, 541.

1287.   To William H. Prescott

Greenburgh Jany 21. 1840

My dear Sir,

Your letter of the 24th. ult.[1] reached me just after I had sent a letter to the Knickerbocker, signed with my name, and expressive of my opinions and wishes in respect to the ↑proposed↓ Act of international Copy right.[2]

You have applied to the very worst person to draft and set on foot ⟨another⟩ ↑a↓ petition on the subject. I have already kept shoving the matter off of my mind ever since I received your letter, and I now write to inform you that if the business is left to me it will be put off until too late, if it is done at all. I have no turn for such matters, and have a fatal habit of procrastination in all things of the kind: and my residence in the country removes me from the sphere of personal influence and activity in circulating a petition. If you will have a petition set on foot I will sign it and do my best to promote its success.

I understand the committee in the Senate to which was referred a petition on the subject have reported unfavorably.[3] This is extremely discouraging; yet I can hardly think our legislators are so insensible to all arguments of justice, true policy and enlightened liberality to persist in refusing such a law. If the copy right law remains in its present state our native literature will have ⟨as⟩ to ⟨hard⟩ struggle with encreasing difficulties. No copy right to protect it in England and an influx of foreign and cheap literature to drown it at home.

I am glad to hear you are accumulating such rich and copious stores for your new histories and should delight in rummaging the antique works and rare documents of which you speak[4]—I have a great relish for "Auld world" reliques of the Kind.

Ever my dear Sir / with great respect and regar[d] [*MS torn*] /
Yours faithfully
Washington Irving

Wm H Prescott Esqr

ADDRESSED: William H Prescott Esq / Boston   POSTMARKED: TARRYTOWN N. Y. / JAN / 22
MANUSCRIPT: Va.—Barrett.

1. Prescott's letter to WI, December 24, 1839, printed in PMI, III, 151 (in part); in George Ticknor, *Life of William Hickling Prescott* (Boston, 1864), pp. 164–66; and in *The Papers of William Hickling Prescott*, ed. C. Harvey Gardiner (Urbana, 1964), pp. 152–53.

2. WI's letter appeared in *Knickerbocker Magazine*, 15 (January, 1840), 78–79. For details about the copyright ferment, see Andrew J. Eaton, "The American Movement for International Copyright, 1837–60," *Library Journal*, 15 (April, 1945), 95–122.

3. See Senate, *Congressional Globe*, 26th Cong., 1st sess., pt. 8, p. 107.

4. Prescott reported in his letter of December 24, 1839, that he had received copies of Navarrete's materials relating to Mexico and Peru, plus those of Muñoz and Vargas Ponce. In addition, he reported that he had located a set of Lord Kingsborough's *Antiquities of Mexico*.

1288. To Mary Irving

[February 3, 1840]

My dear Mary.

I enclose a precious little billet[1] which I received a day or two since and which I beg you to lorck[2] up ⟨company?⟩ with my fifty guinea medal.[3] I had some thoughts of having it treasured up among my papers in your fathers iron chest, but conflagrations are so frequent down here that I feared it might be burnt up.

Your afft uncle
W. I.

ADDRESSED: Miss Mary Irving / (*confidential*)   DOCKETED: [*across top of MS page 1*] received on February 4th. *1840*.
MANUSCRIPT: SHR.

Mary Elizabeth Irving (1820–1868) was a daughter of Ebenezer Irving.

The letter is dated as February 3, 1840, on the assumption that WI wrote it the day before his niece received and docketed it in New York City.

1. The nature of this "billet" has not been determined.

2. WI probably intended to write "lock."

3. WI received a fifty guinea gold medal from the Royal Society of Literature on April 29, 1830. It is now at Sunnyside. See PMI, II, 429; and STW, II, 331, n. 105.

1289. To Gouverneur Kemble

New York, Feby. 4th. 1840

My dear Kemble,

In compliance with your suggestions I have endeavored to make some interest among the leaders of the party in behalf of my brother, E. I, but you [know][1] how little I am acquainted with the politicians of New York, and how excessively irksome to me is such solicitation. Nothing but my deep solicitude for the welfare of my brother and his family of daughters, (which has in fact formed the constant care upon my mind for years past) could induce me to take this step. I am not much acquainted among the leaders of the party, but have spoken to such as I know. Walter Bowne,[2] who knows my brother E. I. promised his influence and good word. He said he would have occasion to write Mr. V. B. in the course of a day or two, and would speak in favor of E. I. in the letter. John Targee,[3] an old friend of the family, entered into the matter heartily and promised to do all he could to favor the appointment. He did not think it adviseable to write to the President until the act should have passed, and the appointments should be about to be made, when he assured me he certainly would. You may consider him therefore as reccommending the appointment. I have written to one or two of our N. Y. representatives at Albany,[4] and shall see what I can do more in N. Y. but I am a wretched canvasser for favors. I have not heard of any rival candidates for the office but one, who however has been already so gorged with fat offices that I should not think him likely to be formidable. Other candidates, however, there no doubt are, but I doubt whether any can be found who, in these times of knavery and defalcation, would present a more satisfactory and unquestionable name to the public than my worthy brother.

I take the application of my brother deeply to heart on more accounts than one. You know the solicitude I have felt about him for a long time past, from his diminishing means and numerous family. His means are now almost dying away, and my own are incessantly tasked to keep all afloat. My own little capital is all invested in such a manner as to produce me nothing; the sum recently received from you on a/c of the Godfrey purchase, is all that I have received from my property for some time past. It is the current exercise of my pen that keeps the wolf from the door—and that is, at my time of life, rather a precarious resource to depend upon. This office for my brother has suddenly suggested itself as a means of creditably providing for him, and of lightening my own burdens—

⟨I would be⟩ I wrote sometime since to Mr Van Buren on this subject and did not intend to make interest in any other quarter, but from the tenor of your letter I am induced to believe that he has conferred with you in the matter, and that the suggestion that ⟨I⟩ my brothers application should be backed by some of the party leaders, takes its rise with him. I shall go on to act upon it as far as I am able, but I confess, after having taken these steps, should I prove unsuccessful, it will be a humiliation that will grind my spirit for the rest of my days. While this thing is pending I cannot accept your kind invitation to come to Washington. I might appear to be seeking for favors. Should it succeed, I shall probably be with you towards spring, and perhaps bring Sarah Paris with me. I wish you would drop me a line to let me know ⟨how the⟩ when the subtreasury question is likely to come up in the lower house—and tell me something of affairs in general. There is some talk here that Genl Harrisons prospects[5] are brightening—I cannot think it possible he should succeed, though the distresses of the country when they press upon the agricultural classes, may be wrested to the disadvantage of the administration.

I thank you for the documents. I am pleased with the direct unostentatious report of Paulding[6] and amused with his ⟨sturdy⟩ contest with the sturdy beggars of the pension list

Yours ever
W Irving.

P S. Write to me at N York, as I shall be here for some few days.

I have just seen Jeronimous Johnson who has promised to interest himself in behalf of my brother—and will write to Mr Van Buren on the subject when the bill shall have passed. Let me know of any other names you may think desiriable

DOCKETED: [top of MS page 4] W. Irving / 4 feby 1840
MANUSCRIPT: Lehigh University Library.   PUBLISHED: *American Literature*, 35 (May, 1963), 166–68.

1. WI omitted "know."
2. Walter Bowne (1771–1846), a hardware merchant who served as mayor of New York from 1827 to 1831, was an influential member of the Tammany Society. See Martha J. Lamb, *History of the City of New York*, p. 724.
3. John Targee (ca. 1772–1850), a silversmith, bank director, and almshouse commissioner, was active in the Tammany Society. See New York *Sunday Times*, February 17, 1850.
4. Among the city representatives elected to the state legislature in November, 1839, were William B. Maclay, James J. Roosevelt, Cornelius H. Bryson, Ulysses D. French, Paul Grout, Norman Hickok, Thomas Heritell, Francis W. Lasak, Edmund J. Porter, Thomas Spofford, Solomon Townsend, George Wier, and John

J. Morgan. See NYEP, November 13, 1839. It has not been possible to determine which men WI wrote to.

5. William Henry Harrison (1773–1841), a soldier in the War of 1812, was chosen as the presidential candidate of the Whig party on December 7, 1839. See James A. Green, *William Henry Harrison, His Life and Times* (Richmond, Va., 1941), pp. 333–34.

6. James Kirke Paulding's report as secretary of the navy was dated November 30, 1839. He called for stricter regulations in the granting of Navy pensions. See Senate, *Congressional Globe*, 26th Cong., 1st sess., pt. 8, pp. 26–28; and NYEP, January 4, 1840.

1290. To My Six Nieces

New York, Feb. 4th. 1840

My dear Girls,

I write to let you know that it is quite uncertain when I shall return home. I am leading a very busy and dissipated life and am now writing in bed at four O clock in the morning, having no leisure in the day time. And now for gossip, which I know is what you all love dearly. Pierre and Helen[1] like the birds, are looking out for a new nest at the approach of Spring time. They seem bothered ↑to dicide↓ between two excellent places, Miss Setons in the upper part of the City, and Mrs Laidlaws in Warren Street, and having thus got into a state of indecision are likely to remain there for some time to come. Helen showed me a letter from Julia,[2] who appears to be enjoying herself very rationally at Washington. She had not been out much, as gaieties had not commenced, but had been with Mrs Paulding[3] leaving cards and paying visits. She was to dine in the course of a day or two at the Presidents. She found Mrs Paulding an invaluable guide and companion to pilot her through the perplexities of a first launch in Washington. I have not been able to get to Auntabbys until yesterday. All are well there. Carry Blackwell[4] is on a visit ⟨there⟩ to your cousin Abby,[5] and the young folks appear to be enjoying themselves mightily. ⟨I am sorry⟩ your Auntabby[6] is ⟨but⟩ on the point of losing all her good servants, for which I am very sorry.

I saw Mrs Constant[7] several days since looking like herself again—which you know is every thing that is lovely and lovable. She is passing her time very pleasantly in New York, and so is the Judge and so is Willie.[8] I met the judge at ⟨a⟩ dinner at Mr Carys, where I also met Mr Ludlow,[9] so that Westchester was ably represented there. The Judge complains of the severe duties of the knife and fork which he has to perform, yet he appears to thrive in spite of hard work. One gentleman at table (Mr March) asked me about my *handsome* niece—I asked him which of the six he meant, as they ⟨were⟩ all came under that description

On Sunday I took a family dinner at Mr Schermerhorns,[10] and in the evening there was a gathering there from Treats[11] and the Generals. It was very pleasant. The three establishments being so near together enables them to meet often and promptly at each others houses and renders them quite independent of Society at large. Mr Schermerhorns new house is extremely commodious. He has fitted it up with much taste. Annies[12] room, which during the occupancy of Mr Ruggles[13] was painted in fresco by Brigaldi, is elegantly furnished, and is altogether, I should think, the most beautiful bed chamber in New York.

On Monday evening I was at Mr Saml Wards (who married Miss Astor)[14] He has commenced housekeeping in Bond Street, in very pretty style. There was no company there excepting Mr William Astors[15] family and three or four foreign artists and literati, beside Mr Longfellow.[16] We had some exquisite music from a young German performer,[17] a successor to Schlessinger,[18] and, to my taste, superior to him. Mrs Ward sang two or three things very well. She has taken great pains with herself and is constantly improving in her singing.

To day I take a ghostly dinner with my ⟨[unrecovered]⟩ ↑pious↓ and reverend friend Dr Wainwright;[19] and tomorrow I t[ake] [MS torn] a sympathizing dinner with the "Vidder and the fatherless["]—so you see what an edifying life I am leading.

I enclose you cards of invitation for the Great Brevoort Fancy ball,[20] which is convulsing the whole fashionable world. If any of you are inclined to go, I will take you there. No extra expense of any consequence need be incurred, ↑(and I will bear it)↓ as a few ribbands fancifully disposed can constitute a passable fancy dress. I think Kate might arrange a primitive dutch dress and go as Katrina Van Tassel just from the Van Tassel cottage—

As Kate says "the Carriage is at the door" so I must conclude—with love to the Lady Abbess.[21]

Your affectionate uncle
W.I.

MANUSCRIPT: Yale. PUBLISHED: Yale Review, 16 (April, 1927), 461–62; LSS, pp. 5–7.

The six nieces were five unmarried daughters of Ebenezer Irving: Catharine Ann (1816–1911), Sarah (1817–1900), Julia (1818–1861), Mary Elizabeth (1820–1868), and Charlotte (1824–1911), plus Sarah Paris (1813–1885).

1. In 1836 Pierre Munro Irving had married Helen Dodge (1802–1885), his cousin, after the death of his first wife, Margaret Berdan (1809–1832).

2. Julia (1803–1872), daughter of William Irving, was married to Moses Hicks Grinnell.

3. Gertrude Kemble Paulding (1791–1841), wife of James Kirke Paulding, Van Buren's secretary of the navy.

4. Possibly the daughter of Robert Blackwell, a New York merchant who sold the island bearing his name to New York City in 1828. See Charles H. Haswell, *Reminiscences of an Octogenarian of the City of New York* (New York, 1896), p. 30.

5. Abigail (1822–1906?), the daughter of John Treat Irving.

6. Abigail Spicer Furman Irving (1779–1864), the widow of John Treat Irving.

7. The wife of Joseph Anthony Constant (1805–1860), one of WI's neighbors in the Tarrytown area. See J. T. Scharf, *History of Westchester County*, II, 183; Ernest F. Griffin, *Westchester and Its People* (New York, 1946), I, 346; II, 488; and Robert Bolton, *The History of the Several Towns, Manors, and Patents of the County of Westchester* (New York, 1881), I, xv.

8. Mrs. Constant's husband and son.

9. Probably Thomas W. Ludlow (1795–1878), a New York lawyer and financier who as Van Buren's envoy had tried to place U.S. Treasury notes in Europe from 1837 to 1839, had a country home in Westchester County.

10. Abraham S. Schermerhorn (1783–1850) was a wealthy New York mechant and social leader. His daughter Helen (1820–1893) had married John Treat Irving, Jr., in 1838. See Richard Schermerhorn, Jr., *Schermerhorn Genealogy and Family Chronicle* (New York, 1914), pp. 166–68.

11. John Treat Irving, Jr. (1812–1906), son-in-law of Abraham Schermerhorn.

12. Anna Schermerhorn (1818–1886), daughter of Abraham Schermerhorn. See *Schermerhorn Genealogy*, p. 166.

13. Probably Samuel B. Ruggles (1800–1881), an attorney and a director of the Bank of Commerce who was well known in New York financial circles.

14. Samuel Ward (1814–1884), son of the founder and first president of the Bank of Commerce, was married to Emily Astor (1819–1841), daughter of William B. Astor (1792–1875).

15. Astor was married to Margaret Armstrong (1798?–1872).

16. Henry W. Longfellow (1807–1882), a professor of modern languages at Harvard, had first met WI in Madrid in 1827.

17. Possibly William Scharfenberg (1819–1895), a German pianist who first appeared in New York in concert on November 15, 1838. See Odell, *N Y Stage*, IV, 325.

18. Daniel Schlesinger (1799–1839) was a German pianist and composer who first performed in New York on June 6, 1837. See *The Macmillan Encyclopedia of Music and Musicians*, ed. Albert E. Weir (New York, 1938), p. 1668; and Odell, *N Y Stage*, IV, 180.

19. Jonathan M. Wainwright (1793–1854), who had been rector of Grace Episcopal Church from 1821 to 1834, was in charge of St. John's Chapel of Trinity Church.

20. On February 27, 1840, a fancy dress ball was held at the Brevoort mansion on Fifth Avenue, with 500 guests present. See *The Diary of Philip Hone, 1828–1851*, ed. Allan Nevins (New York, 1927), I, 462–65; and Charles H. Haswell, *Reminiscences of an Octogenarian*, p. 348.

21. Probably WI's facetious reference to his sister, Mrs. Catharine Paris, who was staying at Sunnyside with his nieces.

1291.   To Gouverneur Kemble

New York, Feb. 5th. 1840

My dear Kemble,

Godfreys letter[1] is rather confused and I cannot say that I fully understand it. It would seem he wishes to release the property he holds from
the mortgage to us, and offers two notes of Mr Maynards, one for
$2,244.95 due 17 Aug. 1839 less $250, said to be paid, and the other for
$2310.33 due 17 Feb. 1840—the difference between the notes and the
amount owing to us to be immediately paid, as I presume, though he does
not say so. These notes he states are secured by mortgage "on two
good improved farms" in that county, which Kingsley, Ramsdell & Morgan,[2] in their memorandum at the close of his letter, state to be amply
sufficient and that there will be little or no delay in collecting the amount
of the note. If these mortgages are assigned to us and the notes transferred to us with Mr Godfreys endorsement, he will be still held, unless
they are indorsed *without recourse to him.* And if the farms are *in these
times* worth one half more than the amount of the notes it may be safest
to take them, for, one being past due and the other due in a fortnight,
the mortgages can be foreclosed at once, should it be thought adviseable
to coerce payment. I do not understand Mr Gs. meaning when he says that
"if they fore close he will draw ten per cent." It may be that, on fore-
closing a mortgage the mortgager has a right of redemption for a certain term during which interest accrues at ten per cent per ann.

Another offer is, that Mr Maynard will pay all over $4000 immediately,
and give his notes (a *bond* is better than a note) for the $4000 payable in
1, 2, 3 & 4 years $1000 each year with interest annually at 7 per cent
per annum "Secured by real estate for twice the amount, appraised by
men under oath"—If the amounts are made payable at the exchange
current in this city, or equal to specie with interest at 7 per cent—this
offer may be acceptable. We ought to be well satisfied that the real
estate mortgaged is unencumbered, and fully worth double the amount
of debt as proposed—the danger may be that it may be appraised by
holders of lands at high prices, who though under oath, may be apt to
overrate it, and yet intend to act conscientiously. It would perhaps be
better to have from him a tolerably minute description of the lands proposed to be mortgaged; location, quantity, quality, estimated value &c
and the same of the two farms—you may then be able to learn from some
of the members from that quarter how correct the statements are with
the real worth of the property.

—I write the foregoing under the dictation of my brother, who has
looked into the matter with the eye of a man of business; which I can-

not pretend to. You may avail yourself as far as you think proper of his cautious suggestions. As you are more conversant with the whole affair you are better qualified to judge than I, which is the best of the two propositions or whether it may be adviseable to hold on to the securities we have—I leave the matter to your judgement, and will conform to any decision you may make.

Yours ever my dear Kemble
Washington Irving

Hon. Gouverneur Kemble.

ADDRESSED: Hon. Gouverneur Kemble / City of Washington POSTMARKED: NEW-YORK / FEB / 5 DOCKETED: W Irving / feby 1840
MANUSCRIPT: Lehigh University Library. PUBLISHED: *American Literature*, 35 (May, 1963), 168–70.

1. This letter has not been located.
2. James Kingsley, Norton R. Ramsdell, and Elijah W. Morgan were attorneys practicing in Ann Arbor, Michigan at this time. See *Pioneer Collections, Report of the Pioneer Society of the State of Michigan*, 1 (1877), 337; 21 (1892), 231; 35 (1907), 110–15; and 37 (1909–1910), 417–18.

1292. *To Gouverneur Kemble*

New York, Feb 6th. 1840

My dear Kemble,

I mentioned in my letter a day or two since that Mr Jeronimus Johnson had promised to write, and to exert himself in favor of my brother. I now find he is anxious to make a bargain for himself. He mentioned to me yesterday several names that he thought he could procure to back my brothers application; but stated that, in case his exertions were successful, he wished my brother to give his son a clerkship under him. I told him I had no doubt my brother would do so, provided his son were fitted for the situation. To day he tells a different story. He says Mr Wright,[1] who brought in the bill, promised to use his influence, which he presumed would be effectual, to get *him* the appointment. He still offers to speak to the persons he had previously named in favor of my brother, but wishes to go on to Washington and confer with Mr Wright—either to ⟨wish⟩ give up all pretensions to the appointment, and content himself with my brother giving a clerkship to his son; or, should Mr Wright think his chance best with Mr Van Buren, and wish him to take the office, then to have my brother appointed to his vacated office of appraiser—

I confess I do not relish this finessing—it is out of my line. The office I have asked for my brother is a gentlemanlike, respectable one, involving responsibility and of course betokening confidence. I wish him to have it and not to be served at second hand, with an inferior station. I fear we cannot depend much upon the services of Mr Johnson, and doubt whether we have not roused a rival candidate. ⟨though he says either of the before mention⟩ I shall try, therefore, to get a few more names myself, but I feel a loathing to the task.

You may communicate the foregoing to Mr Van Buren if you think proper—Let me know if in fact any interest has been made for Mr Johnson—I rather think he is trying to have two strings to his bow.

Ever my dear Kemble yours
W I.

DOCKETED: W. Irving / 6 feby 1840
MANUSCRIPT: Lehigh University Library. PUBLISHED: *American Literature*, 35 (May, 1963), 170–71.

1. Silas Wright (1795–1847), a close friend of Martin Van Buren and Democratic senator from New York from 1833 to 1844, was governor of New York from 1845 to 1847.

1293. *To Gouverneur Kemble*

New York, Feb–8–1840

My dear Kemble,

I wrote to you a day or two since in a moment of vexation on account of some double dealing on the part of Mr Jeronimus Johnson, who instead of aiding my brothers application, as he promised, had set out to get the office for himself. I understand he has written to Wright on the subject, but I do not fear his rivalry; and think he will have to remain content with the snug office he has already held for years. It is vexatious and disgusting, however to meet with such trickery

I enclose a letter ↑to the president↓ from a very different kind of man Benjamin F. Butler:[1] you can either hand it to Mr Van Buren yourself or put it in the post office. I am in hopes of getting a few more names, but I am a bad canvasser, and not much acquainted among the city politicians; beside there appears to be two or three other candidates in the field, and some to whom I have applied, such as the Mayor,[2] & postmaster,[3] have already committed themselves. Not one, however, but has expressed the highest opinion of my brothers ⟨[*unrecovered*]⟩ fitness for the office, and their disposition to aid him, should their own candidate withdraw—so that I feel confident his appointment, should it take place, would meet with no cavilling

Excuse my dear Kemble, the ⟨[*unrecovered*]⟩ my troubling you so repeatedly on this subject, but I am committed in the matter; and my domestic comfort and the welfare of my family circle are so much involved in it, that cannot help urging it forward.

Yours ever,
W. I.

Hon. Gouverneur Kemble.

MANUSCRIPT: Lehigh University Library.

1. Benjamin F. Butler (1795–1858), a New York attorney and Democratic stalwart, served in Jackson's cabinet as attorney general from 1833 to 1837 and as acting secretary of war from October, 1836, to March, 1837. From 1838 to 1841 and from 1845 to 1848 he was U.S. attorney for the Southern District of New York.

2. Isaac L. Varian, a Democrat, was mayor of New York City from 1839 to 1841.

3. Jonathan I. Coddington (1783–1856) was appointed to the postmastership of New York by Andrew Jackson in 1836.

1294. To Sarah Irving and Other Nieces

[Brooklyn, February 12, 1840]

My dear Girls,

I should like some of you to be at Mrs Brevoorts ball[1]—As I said before, I will gladly defray any expense it may require, either for dresses for the ball, or dresses for town. If you do not choose to accept Mrs Jones[2] kind invitation you can ⟨come⟩ make your visit to ⟨[*unrecovered*]⟩ Chamber Street a little earlier; though I should think, the former would be pleasant. A young lady owes something to her position in society, and an appearance once in a while on an occasion of the kind Serves *to keep her in her place.*

In casting my eye accidentally and unintentionally on the other page I observe your uncle[3] has related something about the affair of Mrs March[4]—I have not a doubt that the poor woman has been for a considerable time, afflicted with a species of monomania—Her intellects are in no respect strong, and every thing I have seen or heard concerning her persuades me that she has had a singular streak of insanity through

her mind. I have heard in my time of other cases of the kind.
With love to Aunt Paris

Your affectionate Uncle

W I.

ADDRESSED: Miss. Sarah Irving / Care of Washington Irving Esqr / Tarrytown /
Westchester County / N. Y. / In fav of / L. G. Irving *Esq*   DOCKETED: 1840
MANUSCRIPT: SHR.   PUBLISHED: STW, II, 93.

WI's letter is written on the third page of a double sheet, the first two pages of
which contain a gossipy letter by Ebenezer Irving, dated February 12, 1840. The
address is in Ebenezer's handwriting.

1. This costume ball, held at the Brevoort mansion on Fifth Avenue, was the
most important social event of the season. For other details, see WI to his six nieces,
February 4, 1840.
2. Mrs. Colford Jones, one of WI's Tarrytown neighbors.
3. WI probably intended to write "father."
4. In his section of the letter Ebenezer tells of an unnamed woman who took
a vase and sold it to a manufacturer who, after melting it down, read about its
theft and notified the owner. Ebenezer observes, "I should hardly think that the
woman could be in her right senses; and yet hear that her husband will not allow
that she is demented" (letter at SHR).

1295.   To John K. Mitchell

[February 28, 1840]

Mr Washington Irving presents his compliments to Dr J. K Mitchell and
regrets that he cannot have the pleasure of accepting his very obliging
invitation for tomorrow Evening—

P. S. Mr Irving, being in town, has but just received the card of invitation which had been addressed to him at his residence in the country.

New York. Friday. Feb. 28th. [1840]

ADDRESSED: Dr J K Mitchell / Philadelphia   POSTMARKED: NEW-YORK / FEB /
29
MANUSCRIPT: Va.–Barrett.

The year has been determined by the perpetual calendar.
Dr. John Kearsley Mitchell (1793–1858) was a Philadelphia physician, chemist,
and physiologist. He entered practice in 1822, and from 1841 until his death he
held the chair of theory and practice of medicine at the Jefferson Medical College
in Philadelphia.

1296.　To Lewis G. Clark

Greenburgh, March 17th. 1840

My dear Sir,

In consequence of not sending to the post office for several days I did not receive Your letter[1] calling so lustily for help until yesterday (Monday) after post hours. I have nothing at hand to send to You, and fear, if I had, it would come too late. We have nothing new in these parts, excepting that there has been the deuce to pay ⟨in S⟩ of late, in Sleepy Hollow; a circumstance, by the bye, with which You of New-York have some concern, as it is connected with Your Croton Aqueduct.[2] This work traverses a thick wood, about the lower part of the hollow, not far from the old Dutch haunted church;[3] and in the heart of the wood, an immense culvert, or stone arch, is thrown across the wizard stream of the Pocantico, to support the Aqueduct. ⟨At this About this⟩ As the work is unfinished a Colony of Patlanders[4] ↑have been↓ ⟨are⟩ encamped about this place all winter, ⟨shut?⟩ formerly a kind of Patsylvania, in the midst of a "wiltherness." Now whether it is that they have heard the old traditionary stories about the Hollow, which, all ⟨fabling⟩ fanciful fabling and idle scribbling apart, is really one of the most haunted places in this part of the country; or whether the Goblins of the Hollow, accustomed only to tolerate the neighborhood of the old Dutch families, have resented this ⟨incur⟩ intrusion into their solitudes by strangers of an unknown tongue, certain it is, that the poor paddy's have been most grieviously harried, for some time past, by all kinds of apparitions. A ⟨roa⟩ waggon-road cut through the woods and leading from their encampment past the haunted church, and so on to certain whisky establishments, has been especially beset by five fiends; and the worthy patlanders, on their way home at night, ⟨have⟩ beheld misshapen monsters whisking about their paths sometimes resembling men, sometimes hogs, sometimes horses, but invariably *without heads;* which shews that they must be lineal descendants from the old goblin of the Hollow. These imps of darkness have grown more and more vexatious in their pranks; ⟨Some⟩ occasionally tripping up, or knocking down, the unlucky object of their hostility. In a word, the whole wood has become such a scene of *spuking* and *diablerie*, that the paddys will not any longer venture out of their shantys at night, ⟨but⟩ and a Whisky-shop, in a neighboring village, where they used to hold their evening gatherings, has been obliged to shut up, for want of custom—This is a true story, and you may account for it as you please. The corporation of your City should look to it, for if this harrying continues, I should not be surprized if the Paddies,

↑tired of being cut off from their whisky,↓ should entirely abandon the ↑Goblin↓ regions of Sleepy Hollow, and the ↑completion of the↓ Croton Waterworks be seriously retarded

————————

You may make what use of the foregoing you please. I have scribbled it in all haste as breakfast is waiting, and ⟨my⟩ ↑one of my↓ Nephews who takes this with him to town is impatient to be off—

Yours truly
W I.

P. S. The above story was told me last evening by one of the young Engineers[5] who was on a visit to the cottage

ADDRESSED: L—G. Clark Esqr / office of the Knickerbocker / Fulton Street / New York

MANUSCRIPT: SHR. PUBLISHED: *Knickerbocker Magazine*, 15 (April, 1840), 349–50 (in part); 55 (April, 1860), 442–43.

1. This letter has not been located.

2. In the spring of 1835 the voters of New York City approved the construction of an aqueduct bringing water from the Croton River, which was dammed to create a lake. Opened on October 14, 1842, the aqueduct conveyed water about forty miles to a reservoir at 86th Street and Sixth Avenue, from whence it was distributed throughout the city. See Mary L. Booth, *History of the City of New York* (New York, 1880), pp. 745–47; and William Thompson Bonner, *New York, the World's Greatest Metropolis* (New York, 1924), p. xii.

3. The Sleepy Hollow Church, built in 1699 by Frederick Philipse, was the oldest religious edifice in the state. See Roland Van Zandt, *Chronicles of the Hudson* (New Brunswick, N.J., 1971), p. 312.

4. Irish laborers.

5. This may be James Renwick, Jr. (1818–1895), son of one of WI's old friends, who was an assistant engineer on the Croton project. See Bonner, *New York, the World's Greatest Metropolis*, p. 274.

1297. *To Gulian C. Verplanck*

Greenburgh April ⟨8⟩ 7th. 1840

My dear Verplanck

Supposing there was a disposition at Albany to supply my place at the board of Regents[1] by a more attentive and efficient member, and that there might be some scruple of friendship or delicacy about superseding me, I had intended to send up my resignation It is an office of which my negligent habits render me unworthy, and which might be infinitely better conferred. Your kind letter,[2] however, and the wishes you convey of the other Regents, have determined me, if permitted, to continue in the office, and I will come up to Albany at the time you mention, though I would rather come before that time, should there be a previous meeting of the board, having engagements which call me elsewhere early in the month of May.

Believe me ever with the truest esteem and regard

Yours faithfully
Washington Irving

To Gulian C. Verplanck

MANUSCRIPT: SHR (copy).

1. The Board of Regents of the University of the State of New York was a twenty-three member group which included the governor, lieutenant governor, and the secretary of state. It inspected colleges and academies and their curricula and reported annually to the state legislature. It had the power to issue charters to schools and to grant degrees beyond the master's level. See July, *Verplanck*, p. 260.

2. This letter has not been located.

1298.   *To* ———

Greenburgh, April 11th. 1840

Sir,

Your letter of the 28th. March,[1] having been directed to me at *Westchester* instead of Tarrytown, has but just reached me. I beg you to present my grateful acknowledgements to the Institute for the mark of good will conferred upon me in electing me an Honorary member. No motto occurs to me at this moment for your association, and it is very probable, as nearly a fortnight has elapsed since the date of your letter and you wished a reply by return of mail, you have already devised one to suit you.

Very respectfully / Your obliged & hble servt
Washington Irving

MANUSCRIPT: Haverford College Library.

1. This letter has not been located.

1299.   To Lewis G. Clark

[April, 1840]

My dear Clark:

I hope you have performed your promise, and that we shall see an extended critique on Cooper's new work in your next number,[1] in which the author will receive ample justice. I have just read the "Pathfinder," and it has given me a still higher opinion than ever both of Cooper's head and heart. It is an admirable production; full of noble pictures of exalted virtue in the humbler paths of life. The characters of the "Pathfinder" and "Mabel Dunham" are noble conceptions, and capitally sustained. The old salt-water tar captain, also, is a master-piece, with his nautical wisdom, his contempt for fresh water, and his "point no point" logic. Let no one say, after reading "Mabel Dunham," that Cooper cannot draw a female character. It is a beautiful illustration of the female virtues under curious trials, some of the most terrific, others of the most delicate and touching nature. The death-bed scene, where she prays beside her father, is one of the most affecting things I have ever read; and yet how completely free from any overwrought sentiment or pathos!

The proof to me of the great genius displayed in this work, is the few and simple elements with which the author has wrought out his effects. The story has nothing complicated; it is a mere straightforward narrative; the characters are few.

I am interrupted by a call to breakfast; my brother is about to set off, so I must break off.

Very truly yours,
Washington Irving

PUBLISHED: *Knickerbocker Magazine*, 55 (January, 1860), 94; 15 (May, 1840), 449 (in part).

WI's letter appraising *The Pathfinder* was published in two versions in the *Knickerbocker Magazine,* as indicated above. The earlier version is abridged, with some changes in wording. The later printing is used as copy-text, except that the initial letter of the first word of the fifth sentence has been capitalized as it was in the first printing.

The date has been ascertained by WI's allusion to the review of *The Pathfinder*.

1. In the *Knickerbocker Magazine*, 15 (April, 1840), 344–45, Clark indicated that he had not finished the reading of the novel before the publication deadline. He promised a more extended notice in a later number, but because of long articles and the pressure of time he concluded the *Knickerbocker's* discussion in the May issue (p. 449) by quoting from WI's letter.

1300.   To Pierre M. Irving

April, 1840

I am convinced that, by exercising my pen in my former independent way, and taking my time to collect my writings into volumes,
I should make much more money eventually, and escape a monthly
recurring task.[1]

PUBLISHED: PMI, III, 152.

1. WI is probably referring to his arrangement to contribute a monthly piece
to the *Knickerbocker Magazine*.

1301.   To Sarah Van Wart

Greenburgh May 4th. 1840

My dear Sister,
I have just received your letter of April 11th[1] repeating the information given in a former letter of the matrimonial engagement of
Matilda.[2] I am glad to find the choice she has made is so satisfactory to
you, and hope and trust you may both derive all the happiness from the
connexion which you anticipate. I often wish my dear Sister, that I
could transport myself at once to the Shrubbery[3] and mingle once more
in your happy little domestic circle, and I please myself with the idea
that some time or other I may make another visit to England. But time
rolls on, ties and obligations accumulate to bind me at home, and
render my presence here important, if not indispensible, to the happiness and welfare of the family connexion, and the prospect of the visit
becomes more and more vague. Still I do not give up the hope that
some time or other I may be able to give home the slip and make a
brief excursion across the Atlantic.
I am sorry to find, by your letter, that Irvings[4] affairs are in such a
situation as to oblige him to look round for some new means of support.
I have ⟨not⟩ never enquired much into his concerns, as he seemed sensitive in the matter, but had hoped his Sheffield connexion[5] might have
proved a source of abundant profit. I am grieved that he should have
made any application about the Agency held by his uncle, but I
believe he was led to do so from learning that I was endeavouring to
get an official appointment for brother Ebenezer;[6] and ⟨I have⟩ from
expecting confidently that I would be successful. I have been making
such an effort; for I found Ebenezers means continually diminishing

during these hard times, while my own were so limited and shackled, that I had to depend upon the current exercise of my pen (which any mental or bodily affliction might instantly interrupt) to aid him in keeping the family afloat. Various circumstances concur, however, to render the chance of my getting the situation for him almost hopeless; and even if I should succeed, the office will be precarious, and liable to be abolished should there be a change in the administration. It is consoling to me to find by your letter that both you and Mr Van Wart entertain proper feelings on the subject of Irvings application,[7] and that "you can never bear the idea of the agency being taken from Ebenezer" Poor fellow—It would be sad indeed in these times of difficulty to take from him the feeble staff on which he has to lean. Heavens! how I wish my means were competent to put an end to all these miserable questions and concerns that poison the intercourse of families,—but some how or other, every attempt I make to enlarge my means for the purpose, only results in impairing them. However, God grant me a little longer health and spirit to work, and good will on the part of the public to recieve my poor productions, and I will try hard to get once more ahead. I think, as poor Scott said, I have yet a good deal of work in me, though as years gather on, it seems harder than formerly to bring it out. I have to bring this letter to an abrupt conclusion, as the opportunity to take it to town is about departing. I will write to you soon again and endeavor to Give you a more entertaining letter.

With love to all the family I am my dear Sister

Yours most affectionately

W. I.

ADDRESSED: Mrs. Henry Van Wart. / care of Henry Van Wart Esq / Birmingham/ *per Great Western*
MANUSCRIPT: Va.—Barrett.

1. This letter has not been located.

2. The fourth child of Sarah and Henry Van Wart who married Charles Aylett Kell.

3. The name of the Van Wart residence in Edgbaston, a suburb of Birmingham.

4. Irving Van Wart, who had married Sarah Craig Ames in New York on March 26, 1839, and had established himself in business in Philadelphia. See WI to Sarah Van Wart, March 26, 1839.

5. Probably WI is referring to an arrangement for young Van Wart's importing merchandise from Sheffield.

6. WI had written to President Van Buren on January 13, 1849, and to Gouverneur Kemble on February 4, 1840, seeking an appointment in the New York subtreasury office for Ebenezer.

7. Apparently unaware of the efforts being made on Ebenezer's behalf for the subtreasury post, Irving Van Wart applied for the same position.

1302.   To Alexander Valteman

Albany, May 7th. 1840

Dear Sir,

I regret extremely that engagements, which require my departure for New York will prevent my having the pleasure of attending at the meeting to be held this evening for the consideration of your plan for a system of exchange between Governments and learned institutions throughout the civilized world, of duplicate Specimens in natural history and productions in Literature. It is a noble and magnanimous scheme, worthy of the civilization of the age, and the advantages of which are so obvious and striking that ⟨I cannot⟩ they must strike every intelligent mind at a single glance. These advantages, too, would be peculiarly felt in this country, in which our learned institutions and collections are yet almost in their infancy; for it is the singular operation of your plan to germinate libraries and collections promptly and almost without cost.

Wishing you the utmost success in Your generous and philanthropic undertaking I remain

very respectfully / Your friend & Servt
Washington Irving

Alexander Valteman, Esq

MANUSCRIPT: SHR.

1303.   To ———

[May 20, 1840]

My dear Sir,

I understand that Henry Landman wishes to rent a house of you for a year. I ⟨felt⟩ consider him a very trust worthy person and think you will be perfectly secure in accepting of him as a tenant

Very respectfully / Your friend & Servt
Washington Irving

Greenburgh. May 20th. 1840

MANUSCRIPT: Va.—Barrett.

1304. To Conêgo Januário da Cunha Barbosa

New York, June 29th. 1840

Sir,

I have the honor to acknowledge the receipt of your letter[1] informing me of my. having been elected an honorary member of the Historical and Geographical Institute of Brasil, and enclosing a Diploma.

I beg you to communicate to the Institute the high sense I entertain of this distinguished mark of their esteem, and to assure them that it will give me at all times the greatest pleasure to promote as far as lies in my power, the objects of their association

Very respectfully / Your obliged & humble Servt
Washington Irving

Congo J dal Barboza Esqr. / Perpetual Secretary / &c &c &c

DOCKETED: Lida em sessao de / 14 de Novembro de / 1840 — /Lagos. / 2o So
    [Second Secretary]
MANUSCRIPT: Instituto Historico e Geographico Brasileiro.

Canon Januário da Cunha Barbosa (d. February 22, 1846) was first secretary of the Historical and Geographical Institute of Brazil from its founding in August, 1838, until he assumed its presidency, a post he held until his death. See *Revista do Instituto Histórico e Geográphico Brasileiro*, 5 (1843), 538; 8 (1846), 144–45.

1. This letter has not been located. WI was proposed for honorary membership by Henrique Julio de Wallenstein, consul general of the Russian Empire to Brazil, at the meeting of the Institute on November 30, 1839. See *Revista do Instituto*, 1 (1839), 291, 296.

1305. To Jared Sparks

Tarrytown June 29th. 1840

Dear Sir,

I must crave your indulgence to pardon my delay in answering your very kind letter of February last:[1] but I am at best but a very irregular and dilatory correspondent, and letters multiply upon me with an encreasing frequency and abundance that baffle every exertion ⟨at⟩ to attain tolerable punctuality.

I have under this same date, written a letter to the Secretary of the Historical and Geographical Institute of Brasil at Rio de Janeiro,[2] expressive of my grateful sense of the honor conferred upon me,[3] and

I have also written to Mr de Wallenstein,[4] acknowledging his very flattering and unlooked for mark of consideration in nominating me to the Institute.

Believe me, dear Sir

With great respect and regard / Your obliged
Washington Irving

Jared Sparks Esqr

ADDRESSED: Jared Sparks Esqr / Care of Thos W. Storrow Esq /New York. POST-MARKED: TARRYTOWN N. Y. / JUN / 30   DOCKETED: From / W. Irving. / June 30. 1840
MANUSCRIPT: Harvard.

Jared Sparks (1789–1866) had devoted himself to collecting and editing *The Diplomatic Correspondence of the American Revolution*, 12 vols. (1829–1830), *The Writings of George Washington*, 12 vols. (1834–1838), and *The Works of Benjamin Franklin*, 10 vols. (1836–1840). He also edited the *Library of American Biography*, 10 vols. (1834–1838). In 1839 he became professor of history at Harvard and served as president of Harvard from 1849 to 1853.

1. This letter has not been located.
2. The secretary was Dr. Emilio Joaquim da Silva Maia, a professor at the College of Medicine of Pedro II in Rio de Janeiro. The receipt of WI's letter was noted in the minutes of the meeting of the Institute for November 14, 1840. See *Revista do Instituto Histórico e Geográphico Brasileiro*, 1 (1839), 7; 2 (1840), 529.
3. WI was proposed for honorary membership in the Institute on November 30, 1839, along with Sparks, Sir Gore Ousley, Sir William Ousley, and several other persons. See *Revista do Instituto*, 1 (1839), 291.
4. Jules de Wallenstein.

1306. To Charles A. Bristed

Greenburgh Septr 28th. 1840
My dear Charles,

The length of time that has elapsed since my leaving England; and the absence of all correspondence with those I knew there render it an embarrassing matter for me to furnish ⟨f⟩ letters of introduction. I enclose you a couple[1] which I think will be of service; I shall see you before your departure and, in the mean time, will think if there are any others to whom I can introduce you with advantage.

With great regard / Your friend
Washington Irving

Charles Bristed Esqr

ADDRESSED: Charles Bristed Esqr / care of John Jacob Astor Esq / New York.
    POSTMARKED: NEW-YORK / SEP /28
MANUSCRIPT: Va.—Barrett.

Charles Astor Bristed (1820–1874), grandson of John Jacob Astor, had graduated
from Yale in 1839 and was about to set out for England to attend Trinity College,
Cambridge, from which he graduated in 1845 as a foundation scholar. Upon returning to New York, he married Laura Brevoort (d. 1860) in 1847 and served as trustee of the Astor Library from its establishment until his death.

    1. These letters have not been located.

1307.   To Charles A. Bristed

[October 1, 1840]

My dear Charles,
    I enclose two more letters—One to William Jerdan,[1] Editor of the
Literary Gazette, and center of a clique of popular writers—The other
to Mr Frank Mills,[2] a man of talents and excentricity, who, should he be
in London, or Paris, could put you in the way of seeing something of
life. He is or was a bachelor, and may be heard of at the Garrick club.[3]
    I also enclose you a letter to John Murray the renowned bookseller[4]

Yours[?] ever very truly / Washington Irving
Octr 1. 1840

MANUSCRIPT: New York University Library.

    1. WI's letter to Jerdan has not been located.
    2. Frank Mills was an Oxford scholar whom WI met in Paris in 1824. He is
mentioned frequently in WI's journals. See WI to Peter Irving, June 10, 1824.
    3. The Garrick Club, established in 1831, promoted the patronage of the drama.
For other details, see WI to Frank Mills, September 4, 1832.
    4. This letter is preserved in the John Murray Archives, London.

1308.   To John Murray II

New York, Oct 1. 1840

My dear Sir,
    Permit me to present to you my young friend and countryman Mr
Charles Bristed, a young gentleman of fortune; grandson of the celebrated Mr John Jacob Astor, founder of Astoria[.] Mr Bristed visits

Europe for the purposes of instruction and the gratification of a liberal curiosity. He has already given evidences of literary talent from which we indulge strong hopes. Any attentions you may find it convenient to bestow on him will add to the many obligations of

Yours ever very faithfully
Washington Irving

John Murray Esqr / &c &c &c

ADDRESSED: John Murray Esqr / &c &c &c / Albemarle Street / London
MANUSCRIPT: John Murray.   PUBLISHED: WIHM, p. 176.

John Murray II (1778–1843) was WI's English publisher during the 1820's until a misunderstanding cooled their business relationship. For a full account of their association, see WIHM.

1309. *To Gouverneur Kemble*

Greenburgh, Oct. 31t 1840

My dear Kemble,

I have just received yours of the 30th. inst,[1] and thank you for the kind solicitude you manifest lest by any "unsatisfactory display of my present feelings," I should draw upon myself the attacks of the administration party. I am not aware of my having made any such display. I have expressed to some of my friends my opinion of Mr Van Burens conduct in the matter of my brothers *candidateship*,[2] which I thought betrayed heartlessness in friendship and low mindedness in politics; and my opinion of his Conduct was not elevated by the excuse you gave for him, that he was under the Control of a clique at Washington, and obliged to yield to the dictation of low demagogues in New York. Concluding him, therefore, unfit for his high station, I determined to abstain from voting for him.[3] The recent affair in New York in which the character of Grinnell and others was assailed,[4] ⟨and⟩ the most unfair means taken to poison the public mind on the eve of an election and the forms and institutions of Justice and the rights of individuals violated for party ends, determined me to go further and to give my vote for the opposition ticket. I shall do so. But it is not nor has it been my ⟨dep⟩ intention to take any more active part in politics than I have hitherto done. I am not and will not be a political partizan—If I am to be assailed for the quiet exercise of my right of voting according to my conscience and inclination, it will but be another proof how little the sacred rights of individuals are regarded in the struggle for political ascendency—

God bless you my dear Kemble and extract you as soon as possible from this mire of politics which is far from being your true element

Yours ever
Washington Irving

Hon Gouv Kemble

MANUSCRIPT: Richard Kemble.

1. This letter has not been located.
2. WI had written to Van Buren on January 13, 1840, urging Ebenezer's appointment to a post in the subtreasury office in New York.
3. WI's decision to support the Whigs was reported to Van Buren on October 3, 1840, by WI's longtime friend, Commodore John B. Nicholson: "I regret to say, that I have understood our old friend Irving has got off the Fence and shewn himself in his true colors—by being a whig and a resident one. He is said an abusive one[.] I the more deeply regret it, as we have at all times looked upon him as a pure and highly honorable man, it is like throwing himself away. . . . It was no doubt because his infirm[?] Brother was not placed in the office now filled by Mr. Allen.—I understand he complains of your *not* answering some late letter he addressed to you. This he considers a great grievance and has some idea of demanding back the letter he wrote you. . . . I have not seen Irving, and hope I shall not although I would like to ask his motives for becoming an opponent to one who has been kind and friendly to him for years past" (Van Buren Papers, LC).
4. Moses Grinnell (who was married to WI's niece Julia) and other Whig politicians were charged with importing "hordes of hired vagabonds" from Philadelphia to stuff the ballot boxes in the autumn election in 1838. See NYEP, October 22–28, 1840.

1310. *To William L. Stone*

Tarrytown Nov 8th 1840

My dear Sir,

I am sorry you should think it necessary to make an apology for writing to me. I shall be happy at all times to reciprocate all offices of friendship with you

The biographical sketch of Campbell[1] was written by me, but rather against the grain, and wrought up from very slight materials. I should like, if I could, to knock it in the head, but since I cannot do that, I must endeavor to prune it a little. I shall be in town in the course of a few days and will see Messrs. Wiley & Putnam on the subject.

I am, dear Sir, / with great respect & regard. / Yours truly
Washington Irving

William L. Stone Esqr

MANUSCRIPT: Stanford University Library.

William Leete Stone (1792–1844) was a journalist who edited the New York *Commercial Advertiser*. His *Tales and Sketches* (1834) contains popularized historical fiction; and *Life of Joseph Brant* (1838) and *The Life and Times of Red Jacket* (1841) reflect his deep interest in the Indian.

1. WI's life accompanied a selection of Campbell's poems which appeared in 1810. (See Langfeld & Blackburn, *WI Bibliography*, p. 3.) Stone had apparently approached WI about including the biography in a volume which he was preparing. It appeared as *The Poetry and History of Wyoming: Containing Campbell's Gertrude, With a Biographical Sketch of the Author, by Washington Irving* (New York, 1841).

1311. *To Charles Storrow*

Greenburgh Nov 8t. 1840

My dear Charles,

I have been slow in answering your letter[1] partly because I am a dilatory correspondent and chiefly because I am always overwhelmed with correspondence.

As to Thomas's inroad into my domestic circle I scarce know how to speak of it, it is so gratifying in some respects and so painful in others. He takes from my side a most affectionate girl,[2] who, more than any other member of the family, has been my companion, the sharer of my thoughts and feelings, and the kind and zealous promoter of all my domestic plans and comforts since my return home. I cannot but feel the loss of her constant companionship as a great bereavement, and hardly know how I shall get reconciled to it. Still I know no one to whom I would more gladly see her united than to your brother, and I feel a consolation in the certainty that they are suited to each other and will be most happy together

It will give me and give us all the greatest pleasure to see you at the cottage—and ↑I↓ hope you will not fail to make the visit you promise

Ever my dear Charles / affectionately yours
Washington Irving

Charles S. Storrow Esqr

ADDRESSED: Charles S. Storrow Esqr / Boston POSTMARKED: New York / NOV. 9.
MANUSCRIPT: MHS.

Charles Storrow (b. 1809) was the son of Thomas Wentworth Storrow (1779–
1862), an English businessman living in Paris with whom WI was intimate during
his residence in Paris.

1. This letter has not been located.
2. Thomas Storrow (1805–1861), the eldest child of Thomas Wentworth Storrow, married Sarah Sanders Paris on March 31, 1841. As WI indicates later in the
letter, Sarah was his special favorite among his nieces.

1312. To Sarah Van Wart

Greenburgh Nov 25th. 1840

My dear Sister,

I find by your recent letters to sister Catharine[1] that you had seen
Thomas Storrow and learnt from him all about his eventful visit to the
Cottage.[2] It is a visit which I hardly know whether to rejoice or mourn
over; for though it adds another link to a family connexion which has
already proved so very satisfactory, and gives to Sarah a partner and
protector for life, acceptable to us all, and with whom she cannot but
be happy; yet it gives a sad blow to the little domestic circle of our
rural retreat, which has been such a delightful one, and produces changes
in the whole plan of life of some of us, the consequences of which I
cannot foresee. For my own part, it will be a bereavement to me. Ever
since my return to the United States Sarah has been peculiarly my companion; taking the strongest and most affectionate interest in all my
concerns, and delighting me by her frank, natural, intelligent, and social
qualities. She is especially identified with the cottage and all its concerns, having been in all my councils, when building and furnishing it,
and having been the life of the establishment ever since I set it up.
How I shall do without her I cannot imagine, or how I shall reconcile
myself to her entire absence from a place where every path, tree shrub
and flower, is more or less connected with her idea. Thus you see,
though a bachelor, I am doomed to experience what parents feel, when
their children are widely separated from them by marriage. But this is
a world of changes; and we were all too happy in our delightful little
nest, for our domestic quiet to remain uninterrupted.

The effect of the contemplated marriage on Sister Catharines plans
and prospects, however, is what most perplexes me. I really know not
what to think or what to advise in the matter. She is of such a sensitive,
nervous temperament; So easily acted upon by mental and external

circumstances; so fragile in constitution, yet so exciteable, and when excited, so prone to exceed her physical forces and to throw herself into a state of complete bodily derangement, that we have had to treat her like a hot house plant. Sarah has for years been with her constantly day and night ⟨and⟩ until their very existences are woven together. How she would bear a Separation from this only daughter, and a separation, which would appear to her for life, I cannot ⟨[*unrecovered*]⟩ concieve, ⟨and⟩ ⟨yet⟩ it would be perfectly desolating,—and yet, at her time of life, with her frail constitution and susceptible feelings to leave home, friends, connexions, ⟨and⟩ domestic quiet, and all the domestic arrangements ⟨to⟩ which have grown up around her and been adapted to her tastes and habits, to cross the ocean, ⟨and⟩ brave all the fatigues ⟨and⟩ changes and excitements of travel, and to pass the rest of her days in strange countries, and in a great measure among strangers; these are trials for which it is questionable whether she is competent—Sometimes her spirits rise to the task, and she talks of crossing to England and making Birmingham a resting place, at least, at other times, when her physical energies give way, she shrinks from the idea, and endeavors to persuade herself, that she can remain contentedly at home, ⟨so⟩ comforted with the assurance of her daughters prosperity and happiness. I confess, as I said before, it is a subject on which I cannot pretend to advise her; for view it in either light, it is full of difficulty. ⟨ I but?⟩ Which ever way she .may make up her mind, I look forward with anxiety to the trial her feelings must undergo.

For my own part, this affair will probably quicken my movements with respect to a visit to Europe which I have for some time had in contemplation, but which various circumstances have conspired to prevent me from making. I do not yet know when my presence can be spared from my little rural establishment, and from the family connexion to which during the late years of "hard times" my aid and management have been very essential; neither do I know whether in addition to the expenses of keeping up the cottage, I can afford what will be necessary for the "travelling purse"; ⟨If as?⟩ as soon as I can, however, I will make the effort; though my visit must necessarily be a short one. If times ever again come smooth and flush with me, so that I can command a decent income independent of the irksome fagging of my pen, I ⟨should⟩ ↑shall↓ think nothing of an occasional trip across the atlantic, now that Steam has made the voyage so short and commodious; but cares and claims multiply upon me as I advance in years, and I begin to think I shall continue to have a "hand to mouth" existence until the last gasp.

I have not seen Irving[3] for some time; when last I was in town he was on the point of setting off with his little wife[4] on a visit to Philadelphia.

I believe they intend to spend the winter with Mr Ames.[5] What will be Irvings ultimate plans I am at a loss to conjecture. He is not fitted for business; being too restless and indiscreet. I hope years will calm down this vivacity of temperament that requires constant change and variety. Mr Ames has been talking of making a purchase of a farm; in such case he might find occupation ⟨of⟩ for Irving of a kind that he would relish; his little wife would be delighted with country life, and is well calculated to make a rural fire side a happy one. She is a most excellent and loveable little being.[6]

MANUSCRIPT: Va.—Barrett.   PUBLISHED: PMI, III, 153–55 (in part).

1. This letter has not been located.
2. WI refers to Thomas Wentworth Storrow, Jr.'s proposal to Sarah Paris. For other details, see WI to Charles Storrow, November 8, 1840.
3. The son of Mrs. Van Wart and WI's nephew.
4. Irving Van Wart had married Sarah Craig Ames in New York on March 26, 1839.
5. Barrett Ames, who was Irving Van Wart's father-in-law.
6. The manuscript ends at this point.

1313.   To William L. Stone

Tarrytown, December 2, 1840

. . . he is mistaken in the idea that I have any work in hand connected with the landing of Columbus. The report . . . must have originated in Mr. Cooper's being occupied in a novel on that subject. . . .[1]

PUBLISHED: Catalogue of Chicago Book and Art Auctions, Inc., February 18–19, 1937, item 272.

1. *Mercedes of Castile*, which was published by Lea and Blanchard of Philadelphia on November 24, 1840. See Robert E. Spiller and Philip C. Blackburn, *A Descriptive Bibliography of the Writings of James Fenimore Cooper* (New York, 1934), p. 110.

1314.   To Sarah Van Wart

[Early December, 1840]

I find by your correspondence with Sister Catharine[1] that she gives you many details of our country neighborhood and circle, and that you take great interest in every thing relating to "old Tarry-town." You would scarcely recognize the place, however, it has undergone such changes. These have in a great degree taken place since I have pitched my tent in the neighborhood. My residence here has attracted others; cottages and country seats have sprung up along the banks of the Tappan Sea, and Tarrytown has become the metropolis ⟨of quite⟩ a fashionable vicinity.[2] When you knew the village it was little better than a mere hamlet, crouched down at the foot of a hill, with its dock for the accommodation of the weekly market Sloop. Now it has mounted the hill; boasts of its hotels and churches of various denominations;[3] has its little gothic Episcopalian church with an organ;[4] the gates of which on Sundays are thronged with equipages, ⟨from⟩ belonging to families resident within ten ⟨mil⟩ or a dozen miles along the river banks. We have, in fact, one of the most agreeable neighborhoods I ever resided in. Some of our neighbors are here only for the Summer, having their winter establishments in town; others remain in the country all the year. They are generally in opulent, or at least easy, circumstances; well bred and well informed; most of them having been abroad and passed some time in Europe. We have frequent gatherings at each others houses, without parade or expense, and I do not know when I have Seen more delightful little parties; or more elegant little groups of females. We have occasionally excellent music, for several of the neighborhood have been well taught, have good voices, and acquit themselves well both with harp and piano; and our parties always end with a dance. We have pic nic parties, also, Sometimes in ⟨the⟩ some inland valley, or piece of wood, Sometimes on the banks of the Hudson, where some repair by land and others by water. You would be delighted with these picturesque assemblages, on some wild woodland point jutting into the Tappan Sea. With gay groups ⟨Under th⟩ on the grass under the trees; carriages glistening through the woods; a yacht with flapping sails and fluttering Streamers anchored about half a mile from shore; and row boats plying to and from it filled with lady passengers. Country life with us at present is very different from what it was in your youthful days. It has a politer tone; there is more of morning visiting, like in country life in England; still it differs essentially from English rural life. The nature of our climate influences our habits. We have so much sunshine and fine warm weather during the genial months of the year, that we live more out of doors, and in a more free and unceremonious style—Our very winters, though sometimes intensely cold, are brilliant and beautiful from the purity of the atmosphere and the prevalence of Sunshine. For my part, I am almost a worshipper of the Sun. I have lived so much of my life in climates where he was all powerful; that I delight in his vivifying effect on the whole face of nature and his gladdening influence on all animate creation. In no climate within the range of my experience is Sunshine more beautiful in its effects on landscape than in this; owing to the transparency of the atmosphere, and at the same time, the variety of clouds with which our skies are diversified. To my mind neither Spanish nor Italian skies, so bright and cloudless, can compare with ours, forever shifting in their tints, and at times so gorgeous with their floating regions of "cloud land"

Your letters give happy accounts of your domestic arrangements. You are fortunate in having two little Colonies, (Williams and Matildas)[5] within such an easy distance of the *Mother Country*. Your visits from one to the other serve to diversify life and to give you variety enough within your fami[ly] [*MS torn*] circle—It is a most happy circumstance that the connexions formed by your children are so perfectly in unison with your own tastes and inclinations and that you all harmonize so ⟨perfectly⟩ ↑thoroughly↓. A well united family connexion is a world within itself and renders its members independent of all the world beside.

Give my love to all your household and to those of the colonies who care for it. I am a remiss correspondent and may therefore drop out of the thoughts and affections of some of you, but I cannot help it. It is not for want of thinking of you all; but it is that I have to spin my poor brain to provide the ways and means for others as well as for myself; and he who has to fag his pen for a livelihood, has very little inclination to take it up when he ⟨can⟩ is not driven thereto by sheer necessity.

Ever my dear Sister most affectionately yours,
W. I.

ADDRESSED: Mrs Sarah Van Wart / Care of Henry Van Wart Esqr / Birmingham / per British Queen / St Ship STAMPED: SHIP LETTER POSTMARKED: G / [*unrecovered*] / 1840 // BIRMINGHAM / DE 23 / 1840

MANUSCRIPT: NYPL—Berg Collection. PUBLISHED: PMI, III, 153–55 (in part); and Butler, *WI's Sunnyside*, p. 9 (in part); (1974 ed.), pp. 30–31 (in part).

PMI (III, 153) implies that this letter is part of WI's letter of November 25, 1840. The date of receipt in Birmingham was December 23, 1840, a fact which suggests that WI wrote a week or two after November 25. Also the size of the paper and the handwriting differ from that letter.

1. This letter has not been located.

2. WI recounted the changes in the Sleepy Hollow area in an article in the *Knickerbocker Magazine*, 13 (May, 1839), 404–11. Among WI's neighbors were Anthony Constant, William Creighton, Moses Grinnell, George D. Morgan, F. Cottinet, and the Danforths. See J. T. Scharf, *History of Westchester County*, II, 281.

3. Among the churches were the Asbury Methodist Episcopal Church, established

in 1807, with a new building on Washington Street, and the Second Dutch Reformed Church, which used two buildings for worship. See Scharf, II, 251.

4. Christ Church (Protestant Episcopal) was housed in a building erected in 1837. The Reverend William Creighton was rector. See Scharf, II, 251.

5. Married children of the Henry Van Warts. For details about Matilda's marriage, see WI to Sarah Van Wart, May 4, 1840.

1315. To William H. Seward

New York Decr 11. 1840

My dear Sir,

I have lately been induced to contribute a small work[1] to Harper & Brothers School and District Libraries. This has called my attention to the undertaking of these enterprizing publishers, and the more I have considered their plan the more I have been struck with its utility. The works comprised in their series[2] have generally been very well selected, and those, either original or digested from other publications, to be ⟨very⟩ well executed; they are improving likewise in their contributors. The whole of th⟨is⟩eir series, when completed will form a body of literature and science portable in form and cheap in price, so as to be easily transported to the most ↑remote and↓ retired parts of the country and to come within the means of individuals of moderate circumstances or of the poorest communities and neighborhoods. They will form a variety and selection, as to subjects and authors, that persons often find it difficult to make from their own knowledge or judgment. I cannot but think, therefore, that an enterprize of the kind, ⟨which presumes⟩ calculated to throw knowledge in cheap masses, into every part of ⟨the⟩ our vast country, deserves every countenance and encouragement. The publishers inform me that they have staked a great amount on their undertaking, and have put their works at so cheap a rate that nothing but an immense circulation will remunerate them.

Under all these circumstances I have thought it might not be deemed an intrusion in me to call your favorable attention to this enterprize and to commend it to any favorable notice you may think proper to bestow upon it.

Let me congratulate you on your re election to the honorable post which you have filled so ably and receive my best wishes for your prosperity both in public and private life. With kind remembrances to Mrs Seward I remain my dear Sir,

Yours very faithfully
Washington Irving

His Excellency / Governor Seward

ADDRESSED: His Excellency / William H Seward / &c &c / Albany.   POSTMARKED:
   NEW-YORK / DEC / 12   DOCKETED: Washington Irving / Dec 11. 1840
MANUSCRIPT: University of Rochester Library.

1. WI's *Life of Goldsmith* was published as part of the School District Library
at this time. It was reviewed in the *New York Review* for January, 1841. See Jacob
Blanck, *Bibliography of American Literature*, V, 46.
2. In 1838 the Harpers assembled a boxed set of fifty volumes for circulation
among schools and sold it for twenty dollars. After the New York legislature passed
a law in 1839 that all school districts with a population of over 10,000 should have
libraries, the Harpers won the contract to provide books to the school systems.
The School District Library was continued through 1845–1846. In all, 212 titles
and 295 volumes were issued, mostly in cloth, and sold to the schools for thirty
to thirty-three cents per volume. See Eugene Exman, *The House of Harper* (New
York, 1967), pp. 22–23.

1316.   *To Sarah Van Wart*

Greenburgh—Decr 26th. 1840

My dear Sister,
   I hope you have had a right Merry Christmas with your family
gathered around you. Your letters give a delightful idea of your domestic arrangements; the "Mother Country" of the Shrubbery and the two
colonies at no great distance. The constant intercourse between you all
must give rise to daily expeditions and give sufficient variety and excitement within your domestic circle to make life animated and cheerful.
We have had a pleasant Christmas gathering at the Cottage, though
we missed brother Ebenezer and Mr Storrow, who ought to have been
of our party, but were detained in town by business. Christmas day
was bright and sunny, but the weather changed in the night and now
a snow storm is prevailing which promises to be a severe one. This,
however, is rather a welcome event in the country as it produces fine
Sleighing and sets all the country in movement. I know nothing more
exhilarating than the first sleigh rides; skimming over the sparkling
snow, the air so pure and bracing; the Sunshine so splendid; the very
horses seem to ⟨delight in the⟩ share your animation and delight, and
dash forward merrily to the jingling of the sleigh bells
   Sister Catharine is passing the holydays with us; for some weeks
past she has taken up her residence with our niece Mrs Romeyn,[1] at
Tarry town. I presume she has informed you that she has finally given up
all idea of accompanying Sarah across the Atlantic, fearing the under-

taking would be too much for her strength and constitution. She is now endeavoring to prepare herself for the approaching separation[2] by absenting herself from Sarah, and sojourning with Eliza. I confess there is something in the very expedient so painful and forlorn that I cannot bear to dwell upon it. She has much fortitude and has been accustomed to trials, but I confess I look forward with solicitude to the one she is destined to undergo. Her great consolation is the certainty that her daughter will be united to one so calculated to make her happy.

⟨I am⟩ I had at one time entertained some vague ideas myself of accompanying the newly married couple across the Atlantic and paying you a brief visit, but I have to relinquish the idea. ⟨In⟩ I cannot afford the expense, having to task myself to the utmost to keep my little domestic establishment afloat and meet the current expenses of the year. I hope times may become better by and bye, and I may find myself more flush than at present, but expenses seem to encrease with me as means diminish. It is a pretty hard thing to bring up the rear of a family and have the care of all that fall behind hand. However, so long as I have any work left in me, and can task my poor weary brain, I shall not despond.

Irving and Mr Ames paid us a visit not long since. They were look-ing at Mill seats in the neighborhood for the purpose, Irving said, of setting up a manufactory with the assistance of his father. I have since heard they think of hiring a Mill Seat in Orange County belonging to Mr Ames father in law. I did not learn from Irving the particulars of his plan, but I hope, if Mr Van Wart is really going to enter into such an enterprize he will not trust the management entirely into the hands of Irving. I speak this for *Irvings* good. He has amiable and excellent qualities, but he has not the qualities requisite for the safe management of a manufacturing establishment. In a little while he would involve himself in perplexities and losses. He has no idea of the ⟨value of⟩ importance of economy either in the conduct of business or in his pri-vate expenses. I should feel easy in this matter if I thought Mr Ames was to take a part in the undertaking and to have a supervision and controul. He is a prudent and experienced man of business. [I] [*MS torn*] am happy to see that he and Irving appear to be on excellent terms. His mode of conducting towards Irving is full of kindness and respect. Irvings wife is a precious little being whom it is impossible to know and not to love. I wish Irving could have enough interest in a concern to keep him busy and pay his expenses, but not to give him an unlimited com-mand of capital and credit. As I said before, I speak all this for *his own* good, and from close observation of his character.

You have made enquiries recently whether I do not write for some other work beside the Knickerbocker—I do *not*—and after the month of February my regular engagement with the Knickerbocker will cease,[3] and I must make some other literary arrangement to help out my income. I have recently written a biography of Goldsmith for Harpers family library, and will send it to you ————

Give my love to all at the homestead and at the two Colonies—I will write to you again as soon as I can command a little liesure and an *unfagged* pen. God bless you and yours my dear Sister

Your affectionate brother
W. I.

ADDRESSED: Mrs Henry Van Wart. / Birmingham / *per Cambridge* / LIVERPOOL / SHIP LETTER POSTMARKED: [*unrecovered*]
MANUSCRIPT: Va.–Barrett. PUBLISHED: PMI, III, 155–56 (in part).

1. Eliza Romeyn (1801–1887) was the daughter of Ann Sarah Irving (1770–1808) and Richard Dodge (1762–1832). Details about her first marriage are lacking. On April 3, 1845, she married Oscar Irving (1800–1865), son of William Irving and her first cousin.

2. The approaching marriage of Sarah Paris to Thomas Wentworth Storrow, Jr., who planned to go into business in Paris. See PMI, III, 160.

3. WI had made a two-year commitment to contribute monthly pieces to the *Knickerbocker Magazine*. For a listing of his contributions see *A Bibliography of WI*, pp. 166–67.

1317. To D. Henderson

Greenburgh Jany 13th. 1841

Dear Sir,

I am not aware ⟨of⟩ that I can claim any direct relationship to the William Irving ⟨You sp⟩ ↑of Lochmaben↓ of whom you make mention, though we may both be of the same stock. My father, whose name was William Irving emigrated to this country about the Year 1760, but he was from a different part of Scotland. We consider ourselves descended from the ⟨Irving's or rather Irvine's of Drum,⟩ ↑House of Irvine of Drum↓ (originally ⟨B⟩ of Bonshaw)—from a branch of the family that ↑was either exiled or↓ took refuge in the north of Scotland, during the civil wars.[1] Perhaps a description of the armorial bearings preserved among us, may enable Dr Irving to know whether we are of the same stock ⟨The following is the technical description.⟩ ↑I give it to you in the technical terms in which it stands record↓ Three small sheafs or bundles

of ↑each of the↓ Holley, ⟨each ↑of↓ three⟩ leaves, vert, banded ↑to-
gether↓ gules, on a shield argent The crest an armed hand ⟨grasping⟩
↑holding↓ three holley leaves. The motto *Sub Sole Sub umbra Virens*[2]

I remain dear &c &c

MANUSCRIPT: NYPL—Seligman Collection (draft).

This letter is apparently a draft of WI's response to a query from D. Henderson of Jersey City written on January 4, 1841. On the manuscript WI had written
"1840," and "1?" is written above the "0," presumably by someone aware of Henderson's letter (also preserved in NYPL—Seligman Collection). WI probably forgot and inadvertently wrote the old date.

1. For details about the background of WI's family line, see STW, II, 241–54.
2. The crest of Alexander Irving of Drum, Aberdeenshire, Scotland, is described
as "a sheaf of nine holly-leaves vert. *Sub sole, sub umbra virens.*" See James Fair-
bairn, *Fairbanks Book of Crests of Families of Great Britain and Ireland* (reprint
ed., Baltimore, 1968), p. 299. For an illustration of the crest, see *Armorial Families,
A Directory of Gentlemen of Coat-Armour*, ed. Arthur Charles Fox-Davies, 2 vols.
(Rutland, Vt., 1970), II, 1029. The motto might be translated as "under the sun,
under the verdant shadow." The Irving coat of arms was placed on one of WI's
watch fobs, a picture of which is reproduced on the title page of Butler, *WI's
Sunnyside* (1974 ed.).

1318.   To George Roberts

Greenburgh Jany 14th. 1841

Dear Sir,

Your letter of the 26th Decr.[1] having been detained in New York,
has but just come to hand. I regret that I cannot comply with your wishes
in respect to your next Double Number. The nature of my literary
engagements preclude my contributing, for the present, to any but one
periodical work,[2] and I have had to decline applications, Similar to
your own, from various quarters, some of them accompanied by the
most lucrative offers.

Wishing you every success in your spirited undertaking I am

Very respectfully / Your obt Servt.
Washington Irving

George Roberts Esqr

MANUSCRIPT: HSA.

George Roberts, who was one of the founders of the Boston *Times*, also published the Boston *Notion*, a weekly which reprinted articles from the *Times*, plus other material, including original contributions.

1. This letter has not been located.
2. WI had agreed to contribute exclusively at this time to the *Knickerbocker Magazine*.

1319. To Sarah Van Wart

Greenburgh, Jany 1⟨8⟩9th 1841

My dear Sister,

I received yesterday yours of Decr. 23d.[1] and, as I have a morning of liesure, will answer it on the spot; for in my life of multifarious occupations and engagements a letter once deferred is apt to be entirely neglected. Our winter at the Cottage has been quiet and comfortable, but not so joyous as usual. The approaching change in our domestic circle though rarely spoken of, throws a cloud over all. Sister Catherine has been at home ever since christmas. She is schooling her mind to bear up against the parting; but I can see it wears ⟨to⟩ both mind and body. It is now nearly a month since brother Ebenr. has been at the Cottage. I never have known him to be so long absent before, unless when on a journey. Business has detained him in town. His prolonged absence is quite an affliction to his good little daughters. I never knew children more tenderly attached to a parent; ⟨and indeed his⟩ their affection encreases in tenderness as age creeps on him, and indeed his most amiable and exemplary conduct towards them on all occasions and through all trials and vicissitudes deserves their love. I think him one of the most perfect exemplifications of the christian character that I have ever known. He has all fathers devotion and zeal without his strictness ⟨in mind & [*unrecovered*]⟩ Indeed his piety is of the most genial and cheerful kind; interfering with no rational pleasure or elegant taste, and obtruding itself upon no ones habits, opinions or pursuits. I wish to god I could feel like him. I envy him ↑that↓ indwelling source of consolation and enjoyment which appears to have a happier effect than all the maxims of philosophy or the lessons of worldly wisdom.

I promised in a late letter to send you a copy of my biography of Goldsmith ⟨that I⟩ recently published.[2] I have not been to town since, but when I do go I will procure a copy and forward it. In the Spring I shall publish a biography of Miss Margaret Davidson, with her posthumous writings.[3] She was a sister of Lucretia Davidson,[4] whose biography you may have read, a lovely American girl, of surprizing precocity of poetical talent who died at the age of 17 or 18. The one whose biography I have just written died a year or two since, between 16 and 17 years old. I saw her when she was about 11 years old and again when about 14. She was a beautiful little being; as bright and as fragile as a flower, and like a flower she has passed away. Her poetical effusions are surprising—and the spirit they breathe is heavenly—I think you will find her biography one of the most affecting things you have ever read. It is made up in a great degree from memorandums furnished by her Mother; who is of almost as poetical a temperament as her children. The most affecting passages of the biography are quoted literally from her manuscript. You may reccollect the family of Mrs Davidson;[5] she is one of a number of sisters very beautiful girls, ↑[*unrecovered*] name of Miller,↓ who ⟨now?⟩ in your younger days lived in Maiden lane. One of them married Mr Coe a clergyman. Another married a Mr Schuyler—the third married Dr Davidson. They had a brother named Morris Miller,[6] a cheery handsome, fine tempered fellow, who used to know some of our family.

The coming month of February finishes my regular engagement with the Knickerbocker; though I may contribute to it occasionally. I find these monthly obligations to write extremely irksome. The proprietors of the Magazine also are not punctual in their pay. So I must cast about for some other mode of exercising my pen and making out the expenses of the year. Would that I could throw it by altogether, or at least only exercise it for my amusement. Had I only myself to take care of I *would* ⟨some⟩ renounce this drudgery of the pen, for I could content myself on a pittance; but I have those to help on who cannot live out of the eye of the world, as a bachelor can; So I must work on to keep all in proper trim.

I am surprised to learn that you are about to sell the shrubbery. I can readily imagine that you can find a cottage in the neighborhood where you will be fully as well situated in point of scenery &c but I had supposed long occupancy had rivetted you to the spot. I hope economical considerations may not press too rigidly upon you—but they press upon every body in these hard times.

Before this letter will reach you you will have been astonished by a sudden invasion of a whole detachment of the family: Gabriel Irving and his party.[7] ⟨Their dep⟩ The news of their intended departure reached me but a few days since; they were then to sail the next morning. I never was more surprised by any movement of the kind in my life, for I had seen them all but a short time previous when nothing of the kind was in contemplation. After this I suppose you will not be astonished if any of our family household suddenly uproots itself and scuds across the Atlantic. I hope you have had time to see something of the party. Gabriels wife is a most excellent little being; strong minded, sweet tempered and with a heart full of generosity and kindness. Little Abby is a little jewel, but you must know her well to know her fine qualities of head and heart. She passed some weeks with us last spring and was the life of the Cottage. Gabriel is a plain, sensible, manly fellow with some spice of humor; but who, through a contempt for the follies and false refinements of fashionable life, sometimes errs in the opposite extreme. He is however, a man of integrity and worth.

I have not seen Irving since last I wrote to you. I hope what I then said on the subject of his manufacturing schemes may not have been misunderstood. I feel truly anxious for his welfare—but I am anxious that whatever he undertakes should be under the eye and check of some-one of superior discretion. I dread lest in ⟨seeking⟩ striking out in some new and unknown path he should involve himself or his father or both, in perplexities and losses. I shall make a point of seeing him when I go to town.

—I have just made up my mind to go to town this afternoon, provided the Steam boat runs. The weather has been uncommonly mild for a fortnight past and the River has been open, but last night was severely cold and there is much ice, so that navigation may be interrupted—I shall leave my letter open, to finish it in town should I go there [end of MS]

Manuscript: Va.–Barrett.   Published: PMI, III, 156–57 (in part).

1. This letter has not been located.

2. WI had mentioned this work in his letter to William H. Seward, December 11, 1840.

3. *Biography and Poetical Remains of the Late Margaret Davidson* was published by Lea and Blanchard in June of 1841. (See Langfeld & Blackburn, *WI Bibliography*, p. 39; and Jacob Blanck, *Bibliography of American Literature*, V, 46.) Margaret Miller Davidson (1823–1838), who was reading the English poets and writing verses at the age of six, contracted tuberculosis and died of it in her sixteenth year.

4. Lucretia Davidson (1808–1825), a precocious student and poetess and sister of Margaret, died of tuberculosis a month before her seventeenth birthday.

5. Mrs. Margaret Miller Davidson (1787–1844) brought out *Selections From the Writings of Mrs. Margaret M. Davidson, the Mother of Lucretia Maria and Margaret M. Davidson* (Philadelphia, 1843).

6. Morris Smith Miller (1779–1824), a lawyer from Utica who was in Congress from 1813 to 1815, was a friend of WI and James Kirke Paulding during the period when they contributed to the *Analectic Magazine*.

7. Gabriel (1807–1845), son of John Treat Irving, was married to Eliza Eckford. In addition to Abby, mentioned later in the letter, they had two daughters, Henrietta and Elizabeth.

1320.   To Sarah Paris

New York Jany 25th. 1841

My dear Sarah,

I received by the last packet a letter from Thomas Storrow[1] the purport of which he wished me to communicate to you, being probably prevented by diffidence from being as explicit in his letters to you, concerning his plans and wishes. He intends to sail for Boston on the 4th. February, so that we may expect him with us ⟨lat⟩ in the latter part of that month. It is his wish that the wedding should take place early enough to allow time to visit ⟨his⟩ some of his family in Boston and to make suitable arrangements to Embark for Europe by the 15th April, or at the latest by the 1st. May: As his affairs in Paris will require his return by that time.

I hope your mother may be able to reconcile her mind to this early separation; indeed I doubt whether any thing would be gained on the score of the feelings by further procrastination; while a prolonged detention in this country during the early part of the present year, when business will be reviving from its long torpor, might be of serious detriment to the interests of Mr Storrow. I am speaking in this matter sorely against the current of my own inclinations, for I look forward to the parting with you as one of the greatest bereavements I have ever experienced—but I forbear to say another word on this subject.

I shall not return home as soon as I had intended. Julia goes to Mr Schermerhorns ball, and to the city assembly and as Mr Grinnell will not be here, I have offered to attend her; so that I am launched into gaieties which I feel little disposition to enjoy. I dined yesterday (Sunday) with Mrs Colford Jones: there was no one there but the two families. The dinner was extremely agreeable. Many kind inquiries were made after you all.

Charlotte[2] will have told you all the family news, and I am, ⟨in the⟩ even in the best of moods, but a poor gossip and today feel quite flat— So with love to all I will subscribe myself

Your affectionate uncle
Washington Irving

P. S. You talked of coming to town for a day or two. I[f] [*MS torn*] you are disposed to come down, with your Uncle[3] the begi[nning] [*MS torn*] of next week, and will write me word by mail, to that e[ffect,] [*MS torn*] I will remain in town and take you back: otherwise I [will?] [*MS torn*] return on Saturday next. Drop me a line to say whether you will or not.

MANUSCRIPT: Yale.

1. This letter has not been located.
2. Charlotte Van Wart Irving (1824–1911), daughter of Ebenezer.
3. Probably Ebenezer.

1321.   To D. H. Williams

New York, Feb—17th. 1841

Dear Sir,

When I talked with you of the probability of my contributing to your annual for the present year I was not aware that the manuscript would be wanted soon. My occupations and engagements are such at present as to make it very doubtful whether I would be able to get any thing ready in time.[1]

I stated to you, when I had the pleasure of conversing with you, the terms on which I contributed to the Magnolia, and which were those proposed by the publisher. Those terms were three hundred dollars for fifty pages of the letter press of that work, payable on the delivery of the manuscript, with the right to publish the contributions among my other works after the lapse of two years.

⟨Such⟩ Should those terms suit you I will endeavor to get something ready for your work, though, as I before observed, I very much doubt whether I shall be able to do so at a sufficiently early period.

Very respectfully / Your obt Servt.
Washington Irving

D. H. Williams Esqr

MANUSCRIPT: Captain Hobbs, Essex, England (on deposit at Corpus Christi College Library, Cambridge University).

David H. Williams of Boston became the publisher of *The Token* in 1841 and brought out the 1842 volume in the fall of 1841. See Ralph Thompson, *American Literary Annuals and Gift Books: 1825–1865* (New York, 1936), p. 66.

1. *The Token* for 1842, the last annual volume issued, did not include a contribution by WI.

1322.   To William and John Lyon

Greenburgh Feb. 24th. 1841

Messrs. Lyon / Irving Institute
Gentlemen,

This will be handed to you by Capt Fazio[1] late of the United States Navy, who is desirous of delivering one or more of his course of Oriental lectures before the young gentlemen of your institution. I have not had the pleasure of hearing one of his lectures, but understand they are both entertaining and instructive having in the course, of an active and enterprizing life, visited and observed the various countries concerning which he lectures. I have no doubt you would find his lectures very satisfactory

Very respectfully gentlemen / Your friend & Servt.
Washington Irving

ADDRESSED: Messrs Lyon / Irving Institute.   DOCKETED: W. Irving / Greenburgh / Feb. 24 1841
MANUSCRIPT: Washington's Headquarters, Newburgh, New York.

William P. and John Lyon established a private boarding school for boys on Beekman Avenue in Tarrytown in 1838 and named it the Irving Institute with the approval of WI. William Lyon served as principal until 1853. In the late 1840's and early 1850's the school discontinued operation for a time but was subsequently revived. See WI's letter to an unidentified correspondent, April 26, 1851; and J. T. Scharf, *History of Westchester County*, II, 258, 302, 584.

1. No person named Fazio is listed in the roster of officers of the U.S. Navy. WI may have been referring to L. C. Fatio, about whom he speaks at length in a letter to Sarah Storrow on September 1, 1841.

1323.   To Messrs. Lea & Blanchard

New York, Feb–25th 1841

Messrs. Lea & Blanchard,
Gentlemen

I have a volume ready for the press containing a Memoir of the late Margaret M Davidson with her poetical remains. This was a younger sister of the celebrated Lucretia Davidson, equally lovely in ⟨[*unrecovered*]⟩ person & character and equally remarkable for precocity of talent.[1] She died in her sixteenth year, leaving behind her writings really surprising for one of her age. I knew her personally. I have digested the memoirs from facts and memoranda furnished by her family and if I may judge from the effects upon my feelings of the crude materials, the narrative of her life will be deeply interesting and affecting. Her ⟨writing⟩ poetical writings are full of beauty: and there runs a vein of the purest and most elevated piety throughout her conduct, character and writings that will cause ⟨them⟩ ↑the work↓ to ⟨p⟩ be put in the hands of the young, and will contribute to its circulation—I cannot but think it will attract much attention. I am treating in behalf of her family, who will chiefly benefit by the profits of the work. What terms are you disposed to offer. The ⟨mem⟩ volume will be about the size of a volume of Bracebridge Hall[2] and the memoir ⟨to oc⟩ will occupy about one half. I presume the terms on which we arranged for the Crayon Miscellany[3] will be a good guage to go by.

Very respectfully / Your friend & Servt
Washington Irving

P S—I do not propose to Stereotype the work

MANUSCRIPT: HSP.

1. For other details about the Davidson girls, see WI to Sarah Van Wart, January 19, 1841.

2. *Bracebridge Hall* was published by Carey & Lea in various printings in octavo format.

3. WI received thirty cents per volume printed for each of the numbers of the *Crayon Miscellany*. See *The Cost Book of Carey & Lea, 1825–1838,* ed. David Kaser (Philadelphia, 1963), pp. 141, 169, 173, 183.

1324.   To Sarah Van Wart

Greenburgh, Feb 26th 1841.

My dear Sister,

The cottage has been enlivened by the arrival yesterday of Thomas Storrow, who for three or four days previously had been constantly looked for; the customary time for the voyage having expired. He had a somewhat longer voyage than usual and a rough one, but arrived in fine health and spirits. I presume the wedding will take place early in April,[1] so as to allow time to pay a visit to Mr Storrows friends in Boston and return here previous to Embarking for England about the first of May. Sister Catharine is at home, and keeps up a cheerful countenance; she cannot but be gratified by the worthy choice her daughter has made, but the prospect of the separation wears hard upon her mind. For my part I now wish it was all over, ⟨and⟩ that there was an end of these anticipations and that our little rural household had come to the footing upon which it must eventually go on. I feel that it is to be sadly crippled, and, since it must be so, the sooner the better that we may become accustomed to it.

In your last letter[2] you talk of my coming out to Europe in the Autumn. I most sincerely wish I could but I most seriously fear I cannot. I am trammelled and fettered in a way of which you do not seem to have an idea. Poor hand as I am to conduct a household and country establishment there is no one but myself to do it, and I do not know what would become of the cottage and its inmates if I were to absent myself. Then I have to find the ways and means to make both ends meet, and hard it is in these precarious times and with my precarious resources. If I can get through this year without going behind hand I shall esteem myself fortunate, but where I am to find a bag of money for travelling expenses I cannot divine.

I dined at Mr Ames's last week. Poor little Sarah has had a trying time, but I trust now will soon be regaining strength. The twins are two fine little fellows.[3] Mr Ames appeared to be quite relieved in mind, for he had been extremely anxious. I was pleased to find, in conversation with Irving, that the manufacturing project was laid aside for the present; my doubts and fears concerning it had been considerably augmented on learning that it originated with Dr Church (Dousterswivel, as your son William used to call him) of Steam Carriage memory. I think there ought to be a new clause inserted in the Litany "From all inventors, projectors and other devisers of sudden wealth Good Lord deliver us!" I have written to Mr Grinnell (Julias husband) to make interest with the new Collector, whoever he may be, to get Irving a situation in the Custom House; but I do not feel sanguine of success: Irving ⟨however[?]⟩ being almost a stranger in the city, and there being swarms of applicants who have rendered and are rendering political service. I have at the same time written to prevent Mr Davids (Mr Van Warts brother in law) from being displaced in the approaching ⟨[unrecovered]⟩ overturn of the establishment, and shall attend personally to keep him in his place. I was amused by your question in one of your late letters to Sister Catharine, "whether I was to be appointed Collector of N York?["] This originated I presume in a paragraph in an Excentric paper called The Herald, the editor[4] of which, after a great flourish, reccommended me for the office. This is one of the fat offices that is only given to most efficient political partizans—I have no claims of the kind. Indeed I have taken no active part in politics, and was ⟨rash[?]⟩ always considered of the Van Buren party from my personal friendship for him. Unworthy conduct on his part toward me, however, forfeited that friendship, and a conviction of the ruinous policy of his party induced me, at the last election, to take a decided stand with the Whigs; at least as far as a public vote would go. However, I am too quiet a man to be of much value in the eyes of political leaders.

I am anxious to hear how Gabriel and his flock make out on their travels. Since the days that the renowned Captain Greatheart set out with Christiana and Mercy and all the children of honest Christian,[5] I ⟨have⟩ do not think there has been a more resolute pilgrimage we shall look anxiously to your letters for particulars of their wayfaring as far as the Shrubbery.

I have made two visits (one of three weeks) to Julia Grinnells this winter. She is living very happily; with a beautiful establishment, a noblehearted fellow for a husband and two fine children, and acquits herself most admirably in the married state. When I was last in town she told me that she had recently written to you, so I presume she gave you a budget of ⟨her⟩ domestic matters. In a few days more her husbands term of service as member of Congress expires,[6] when he will gladly return into the bosom of domestic life. He is one of the most popular men in our community. Give my affectionate regards to ⟨the⟩ all at the mother establishment and the two Colonies.

Your affectionate brother
Washington Irving

ADDRESSED: Mrs. Sarah Van Wart / Care of Henry Van Wart Esq / Birmingham / *per Columbia* POSTMARKED: BIRMINGHAM / [MA]R 16 / [18]41 // AMERICA / L
MANUSCRIPT: NYPL—Seligman Collection.

1. Actually the marriage occurred on March 31, 1841.
2. This letter has not been located.
3. Irving and Ames, the twin sons of Irving and Sarah Ames Van Wart, were born on January 20, 1841. Barrett Ames was the maternal grandparent.
4. James Gordon Bennett (1795–1872) founded the New York *Herald* on May 6, 1835 and edited it until he retired in 1867. His sensational crusades against fraud and hypocrisy attracted a large readership.
5. WI alludes to characters in John Bunyan's *The Pilgrim's Progress.*
6. Moses Grinnell (1803–1877) served as a Whig representative in the 26th Congress from December 2, 1839, to March 3, 1841.

1325. To John S. Popkin

Greenburgh March 6th. 1841

Sir,

In reply to your inquiry whether I have known or heard of any persons of your name in Europe I would observe that in 1824 I was slightly acquainted with a widow lady of that name[1] but whether she spelt it Popkin or Popkins I do not reccollect. I understood her husband had been a person of highly respectable standing, but do not know ↑from↓ what part of Great Britain he claimed his origin. The lady in question appeared to be opulent, and circulated in the best society. Her parties were attended by the English fashionables resident at Paris. I have been at a very brilliant private concert given by her She was Sister of the late Miss Lydia White,[2] celebrated in the aristocratical & literary circles of London, whose house was a rendezvous of the fashionable literati and titled blue stockings of the English metropolis. I am sorry, Sir, that I cannot give any more minute information on the subject of your inquiry

Very respectfully / Your obt Servt
Washington Irving

Rev. John. Snelling Popkin D. D.

ADDRESSED: Rev. John Snelling Popkin D. D / Cambridge / Mass. POSTMARKED: NEW YORK / MAR 8
MANUSCRIPT: MHS.

John Snelling Popkin (1771–1852), who graduated from Harvard in 1792 and served as pastor of the Federal Street Church in Boston from 1799–1802, was an erudite Greek scholar who wrote *A Grammar of the Greek Language* in 1828.

1. In his journal for January 26, 1824, WI indicates that he went with Captain Medwin in the evening and called on "Mrs. Popkins." He also saw her on November 24, 1824, and her husband on March 26, 1825. See *J&N*, III, 279, 429, 469.

2. Lydia White (d. 1827), whose home in London WI visited on June 4 and July 16, 1824, was a wealthy Irishwoman known for her lavish entertainments. Byron caricatured her as "Miss Diddle" in "The Blues." See *J&N*, III, 340, 365; and *The Journals of Thomas Moore,* ed. Peter Quennell (New York, 1964), p. 35.

1326. To Messrs. Lea & Blanchard

New York, March 14th. 1841

Messrs Lea & Blanchard
Gentlemen,

I put the Memoirs and poems of Margaret Davidson[1] in the hands of Messrs Wiley & Putnam yesterday, to be forwarded to you. You will be able after looking over the memoir, to judge what chance it has to make an impression, and what number of copies it will be adviseable to publish. You may stereotype it or not as you think proper, and make an allowance at the rate you proposed in your letter. I wish ultimately, when it has had its run in a handsome edition, to put it in Harpers Family library,[2] that it may yield as much profit as possible to the family of the deceased. I will thank you to put it to press as soon as possible and forward me proofs struck off while the type is in galleys, so that in case of any material corrections there will be no need of breaking forms. I should like very much to have the proofs, ↑of the memoir,↓ within a fortnight, or three weeks at farthest. When ⟨I am informed⟩ you have determined upon the mode of bringing out the work, and we have settled definitively as to the terms, we can draw out a memorandum[3]— I wish the work to be handsomely printed so as to make a very presentable volume.

Very respectfully gentlemen / Your friend & Servt
Washington Irving

ADDRESSED: Messrs. Lea & Blanchard / Philadelphia POSTMARKED: NEW-YORK / MAR / 14 DOCKETED: [on MS page 1] Recd March 15 / on 29th
MANUSCRIPT: HSP.

1. WI had proposed the publication of the book to Lea & Blanchard on February 25, 1841.

2. This series of books, which emphasized biography, travel, and history, included J. K. Paulding's *Life of Washington*, W. C. Bryant's *Selections from American Poets*, and WI's *Life of Oliver Goldsmith*. The Family Library, started in 1830 and continued until 1845, contained 187 volumes which sold for forty-five cents each. See Eugene Exman, *The House of Harper*, pp. 10–11.

3. WI had proposed earlier that royalties similar to those which he had received for the *Crayon Miscellany* be turned over to the Davidson family. See WI to Lea & Blanchard, February 25, 1841.

1327.   To Messrs. Lea & Blanchard

[April 2, 1841]

Messrs Lea & Blanchard
Gentlemen
  Please to furnish to the Marshall Institute[1] of Philadelphia a copy of the History of Columbus, of the "Companions" to the same, and of Astoria and charge the same to my account

very respectfully / Your obt Sert
Washington Irving

Tarrytown April 2d, 1841

MANUSCRIPT: Andrew B. Myers.

1. The Marshall Institute was a Philadelphia literary association which promoted culture through library services and lectures. See "The Diaries of Sidney George

Fisher," *Pennsylvania Magazine of History and Biography*, 77 (January, 1953), 99–100.

1328.   To Daniel Webster

Tarrytown, April 2d. 1841

My dear Sir,

I trust you will excuse the liberty I take in Speaking a word in favor of a gentleman at present employed in your department, Mr George Washington Montgomery. His father was once American consul at Barcelona and he himself passed much of his youth in Spain—I became acquainted with him in Madrid when he rendered me essential services when I was preparing the life of Columbus. I found him a person of most upright, honorable and reliable character; a good scholar, and well acquainted with the Modern languages. He writes Spanish correctly and elegantly and has published works in that language which have gained him a reputation in Spain. Mr Forsyth[1] who knew his merits and was acquainted with his family, gave him various employs; and at one time sent him on a confidential mission to Guatemala; of which expedition, on his return he published a very interesting account.[2]

As there will probably be some changes in your department I have thought proper to submit these particulars to your consideration, and shall feel highly gratified if they may have sufficient weight to secure for Mr Montgomery a continuance of official employ.

Ever my dear Sir / Very respectfully & faithfully yours
Washington Irving

Hon Danl Webster.

MANUSCRIPT: New Hampshire Historical Society.

1. John Forsyth (1780–1841) had been Van Buren's secretary of state.

2. For details about Montgomery's *Narrative of a Journey to Guatemala in Central America, in 1838,* see WI to Lea & Blanchard, January 25, 1839.

1329.   To Catharine Irving

[April 12, 1841?]

My dear Kate,

I hasten to inform you that the bride[1] was dressed in rich white satin with three broad flounces of point lace which covered the whole skirt. Her veil, of the costliest lace, came from Paris. She wore diamonds enough to content a dowager and had an exquisite bouquet of white japonicas All this I have from the best authority for I dare not trust my own judgement in such matters. She was the prettiest girl in the whole room except six; who the six were I will not venture to particularise.

Indeed the whole company looked inexpressibly beautiful. Several very interesting young gentlemen asked me if you were coming. I told them no—that you were indisposed; where upon they all fainted away and were carried out.

I send you a chest of wedding cake to dream on. It has all been passed through the ring—I saw it myself.

Yours devotedly
W. I.

April 12th. [1841?]

Manuscript: SHR.

1. Probably WI is referring to Sarah Paris, his favorite niece, who married Thomas Wentworth Storrow, Jr., on March 31, 1841.

1330.   To ———

New York April 15th. 1841

Understanding that John McCabe is about to open an Intelligence Office for Servants[1] &c I reccommend him as a person particularly well qualified for such an undertaking; as intelligent, upright, obliging and as one whose word is thoroughly to be relied on

Washington Irving

Manuscript: Andrew B. Myers.

1. An intelligence office was an employment agency for household servants and domestic help.

1331.   To Francis Granger

New York, April 16th 1841

My dear Sir,
Permit me to introduce to you my nephew Mr James R Dodge[1] of North Carolina, who visits Washington on business. Any facilities you may find it convenient to afford him ·will be considered as personal favors conferred on

Yours ever my dear sir
very faithfully
Washington Irving

Hon Francis Granger
&c &c &c

ADDRESSED: Hon Francis Granger / Post Master General / Washington / James R
    Dodge Esq
MANUSCRIPT: Harvard.

Francis Granger (1792–1868) was a Whig congressman from New York from 1835 to 1843, except for the interval when he was Postmaster General.

1. James Richard Dodge (1795–1880) was the son of Ann Sarah Irving and Richard Dodge.

1332.   To Messrs. Lea & Blanchard

New York, April 16th. 1841

Messrs Lea & Blanchard
Gentlemen,
I have been for several days without receiving a proof sheet.[1] As I have remained in town for the purpose of correcting & expediting them your tardiness puts me to singular inconvenience. I beg you to make an exertion and have the whole of the memoir set up at once, I am sure you could do it with very little trouble otherwise, as the weather improves and my country avocations call for my attention the work may experience delay on my part.
I wish the following verse to be inserted as an epigraph on the title page

Thou wert unfit to dwell with clay,
For sin too pure, for earth too bright!

And death who called thee hence away
Placed on his brow a gem of light![2]

From lines of Margaret to her Sister.

I am gentlemen very respectfully yours

Washington Irving

ADDRESSED: Messrs Lea & Blanchard / Publishers / Philadelphia POSTMARKED:
NEW-YORK / APL / 17 DOCKETED: Memoir—notice 150 pages— / [ditto] 58
pages / [on MS page 1] Recd Apl 18
MANUSCRIPT: HSP.

1. Of *The Biography and Poetical Remains of the Late Margaret Miller Davidson.*
2. From "To My Sister Lucretia," in *The Biography and Poetical Remains of the
Late Margaret Miller Davidson* (Philadelphia, 1841), p. 73. This epigraph appeared on the title pages of both the American and English editions. See Langfeld &
Blackburn, *WI Bibliography*, p. 39.

1333. To Sarah Van Wart

New York, April 30th. 1841

My dear Sister,

This will be handed you by our niece Sarah,[1] who will be able to
tell you every thing concerning family affairs, so that I shall be brief—
I cannot let her go however without scrawling a line. I feel greatly relieved that the parting scenes at the Cottage are over, for I had looked
forward to them with dread. Sister Catharine had borne up with great,
though forced, cheerfulness ⟨during⟩ ↑after↓ Sarahs return from Boston,[2] but as the time approached for seperation she grew nervous and
agitated, and went to Eliza Romaynes,[3] to be out of sight of the packing
up, and other preparations for departure. Sarah visited her every day,
and Mr Storrow and myself agreed to manage matters so as to prevent
any parting scene. Their last interview was on Tuesday, and was a long
and cheerful one, for both supposed ⟨they⟩ the day of departure was to
be Thursday and that they should see each other in the intervening day.
On Wednesday they were both apprised that we had fixed on that
afternoon for the departure from the Cottage and had determined that it
would be best for both of them not to see each other again—so that
they might be spared the agony of a parting scene. As you may suppose
they were both excessively shocked and affected by the arrangement,
but after a time, saw and felt that it was for the best. Indeed they could
neither of them have stood it. The parting from the cottage alone was a
heart rending trial for poor Sarah. I accompanied her and Mr Storrow

to town where they are staying at Julia Grinnells. Sarah has resumed her tranquility and at times her cheerfulness; but she is thin and pale and shows signs of mental suffering. Tomorrow is the day of embarcation,[4] but I do not mean to have any leave taking with her. I feel that I could not stand it. Storrow has shown himself throughout a most amiable, affectionate considerate fellow, and it is a great consolation to us that in ⟨parti losing Sarah she⟩ in[5] being seperated from us Sarah is with a protector that will be every thing that is kind and devoted to her We have had wretched *wretched* weather for weeks past—almost continual storms, and this has added to the gloom of this separation. I trust however we shall have fine weather in the course of a day or two, when Spring, which has been sadly kept back, will break forth with all its beauty, and sunshine will give cheerfulness to the cottage.

    With love to all I am my dear Sister

                                        Your affectionate brother
                                            Washington Irving

Mrs S. Van Wart.

MANUSCRIPT: NYPL—WI Papers.

    1. Sarah Paris Storrow, who visited her Birmingham relatives en route to Paris, where her husband was in business.
    2. The newlyweds had gone to Boston to visit Storrow's family and relatives.
    3. The niece with whom Mrs. Paris had also stayed before Sarah's wedding. See WI to Sarah Van Wart, December 26, 1840.
    4. The young couple apparently took the *Great Western*, a steamship which sailed for Bristol on May 1. It is the only ship departing for England on this date. See NYEP, May 1, 1841.
    5. WI apparently forgot that he had not canceled "in."

1334.   To John Murray II

                                        New York, May 1. 1841

My dear Sir,

    Permit me to make you acquainted with Mr Thomas W Storrow, who has recently married a favorite niece of mine, and with his bride is on the way to Paris, where they are to take up their residence. Any civilities you may find it convenient to bestow on them during their brief sojourn in London will add to the many favors conferred on

                            Yours ever my dear Sir: / Very faithfully
                                            Washington Irving

John Murray Esq

MANUSCRIPT: Pforzheimer Library.

1335. To Sarah Storrow

[May 3, 1841]

My dear Sarah,

Though I have nothing of moment to say, I will not suffer the Packet[1]
to sail without a line from me. I know the value of the first letters from
home, and how eagerly you will look for them on your arrival at Paris;
and though they may bring but the events of a day or two after your
departure, yet the long interval that will have elapsed before their reception will make them appear to contain the budget of a month.

I returned to the Cottage the afternoon of your departure It was a
gloomy evening there, as you may suppose; for every one there seemed
to realize the loss that had been sustained by our happy fireside. I shall
not dwell, however, on painful scenes but will hasten to inform you that
they have been transient; that your mother, about whom we felt most
solicitude, has borne the trial with more fortitude than we had hoped,
and ⟨after⟩ though her first night was sleepless, has since that had her
usual share of sleep and has resumed her serenity. As the season will
be favorable for ⟨out⟩ driving out in the carriage, ⟨she⟩ and for sunning
herself about the walks and green banks, I think you will have nothing
but cheerful accounts of her.

On Sunday we had the carriage and gig in readiness and meant to
turn out "en masse" for church, but the weather again became stormy
and only a few of us went in the carriage. I saw Phil Paulding[2] in the
course of the morning. He told me that he called at the Cottage on Wednesday evening, ⟨the day⟩ to pay you a farewell visit, supposing you
were to go to town the next morning: and was disappointed at finding you
had already gone. He begged me, when I wrote to you, to mention this.
I was touched by this proof of attention and kind feeling on the part
of the worthy fellow. He passed Sunday evening at the Cottage; Your
brother[3] was there also, and the evening passed cheerfully among the
young folks. It is in these evening gatherings, however, that I miss you;
I find myself unconsciously looking round for your countenance, or expecting to see you enter the door; and as they are all chatting around me
the words of the song come to my mind—"Oh for thy voice—thy happy
voice!"—but we must not talk of this.

Monday was a sunshiny day—a rarity in this most dismal season. As I
saw Kate[4] was not in a very bright mood I proposed to her to accompany
me in a round of errands and calls to which she gladly assented. We ac-

cordingly started off in the little gig waggon, with Charlotte[5] on the
back seat, whom we safely deposited at school, and then Kate and I set
off on one of those rambling cruizes that you and I have so often taken
together. We had a beautiful drive through Beekmans woods; the trees
in many sheltered places were beginning to put forth buds and young
leaves, and to give those first indications of reviving verdure that are so
cheering. We talked of you my dear Sarah, the whole day, for in this
neighborhood every object brings you to mind. Our first stopping place
was the McKenzies.[6] It was too early an hour for a regular visit and I intended only to ask for McKenzie with whom I had some business. He
was from home, however and his excellent little wife[7] received us with
her accustomed warmth and frankness We paid her a long visit and to
me it was a most interesting one, for I feel a strong and growing regard
for this noble hearted little creature and a deep sympathy in the fortunes of her worthy husband. He has anxious moments I fear, poor
fellow, and looks forward with a dubious eye, but then he has a treasure
at home, better than all the worlds wealth and of which the world cannot
deprive him. Mrs McKenzie told me she expected in the course of the
Spring to have her Sister Fanny and her husband,[8] and several of her
own family to pay her a visit of several days. Where the blessed little
being is to put them all and how to accommodate them heaven only
knows. One would think her mansion was as large as her heart. While
we were yet talking with her McKenzie arrived from the landing; with
his waggon filled with young trees, flowers &c[.] I think he begins to
look care worn; though he only wants a little money to make him one
of the happiest of mortals. Indeed when I saw him seated by his fireside, with his wife beside him and his bright looking child[9] on his knee,
I would not have exchanged his lot for that of the richest man of my
acquaintance.

From McKenzies we drove through the fields and by a new carriage
track winding along the skirts of beautiful pieces of wood down to
the new mansion of the Perrys.[10] Oh! how I wished for you there, to see
one of the most picturesque objects in the neighborhood When the
trees are all in leaf it will be positively lovely. We found the house and
all about it in complete confusion. The family being dislodged from
their quarters at Sing Sing, had to move into the new house before it was
finished, so that ⟨it was⟩ carpenters and painters where[11] still at work,
while household furniture stood higgledy piggledy about all the rooms
and passages. Mrs Perry managed to ⟨save⟩ find one room in which we
could sit down, and we ↑passed↓ half an hour with her very pleasantly—
I think we shall find our ⟨neighbor⟩ new neighbors in Beekmans woods
among the very pleasantest of our intimates. The rest of our mornings
drive was taken up with calls at farm houses &c where I had errands

to execute, which furnish nothing worth mentioning. My afternoon was taken up with superintending the improvements about the place; and with trimming ⟨and set⟩ trees and clearing out paths. This, however, is a kind of work I shall have to postpone for the present. It is too apt to bring you before me. I attempted to clear up about the "Haunted Oak" where it has all grown wild and where I intend to put a Seat for your sake, but I found I must leave that for a future day, and turn my hand to the new walks which are not so full of reccollections.

On Tuesday I came to town, and here I have remained until today (Thursday) intending to return to the Cottage this afternoon The weather continues unsettled and comfortless—never have I known so dreary a season: but we must soon get into more genial weather. You, I trust, have by this time got far beyond the reach of these clouds and storms that have overshadowed us for so long a time Before this letter reaches you you will have accomplished your tour in England and will be surrounded by the wonders and splendors of Paris and I almost smile to think how all the scenes and concerns of our little neighborhood will have dwindled in your eyes after the striking and constantly varying scenes through which you will have passed—However, the scenes I treat of are *home* scenes—and these I trust will long continue to speak to your heart, however simple and homely they may be.

And now God bless you my dear girl for I must conclude this scrawl which I am ⟨be⟩ writing between moments of hurry; ⟨as always I have tried to⟩ At another time I shall write more copiously, and I trust in a more entertaining vein. I was determined not to let the first opportunity depart without a line from me, but ⟨as yet⟩ it is rather up hill work. Remember me most kindly to Mr Storrow. I hope he will not look back upon our Cottage as a dismal little abode. Tell him when he Revisits it he will find nothing but Smiles and Sunshine.

> God bless you my—dear—dear Sarah / Your affectionate uncle
> W I.

ADDRESSED: A Madame / ⟨Monsieur⟩ Madame Storrow / aux Soins de Monr T. W. Storrow / No 17 Rue du Faubourg Poissonniere / à Paris /per Albany / for Havre   POSTMARKED: OUTRE MER [*unrecovered*] / 1 / Jun / 41 // [*unrecovered*] / PARIS / [*unrecovered*]   DOCKETED: May No 1 1841 / No 2
MANUSCRIPT: Yale.

1. As the address leaf indicates, WI sent this letter by the *Albany*, under the command of Captain Watson. The ship left New York on May 7, 1841. See NYEP, May 7, 1841.

2. Philip R. Paulding (1816–1864) was the son of William Paulding, mayor of New York from 1823 to 1827, and the nephew of James Kirke Paulding. He became engaged to Catharine Irving but broke the engagement a few months later. See WI to Sarah Storrow, December 1, 1841, and April 13, 1843.

3. Irving Paris (1816–1879).

4. Catharine Ann, the daughter of Ebenezer. See note 2 above.

5. Charlotte, the sister of Catharine Ann.

6. Alexander Slidell Mackenzie (1803–1848), whom WI had known in Spain as Slidell, had officially changed his name in 1837 at the request of a maternal uncle. After completing a tour of duty in the navy, he settled on a farm north of Tarry-town and wrote a biography of John Paul Jones for Jared Sparks's series on American biography.

7. Catherine Alexander Robinson, whom Mackenzie had married in 1835.

8. Nothing has been discovered of Mrs. Mackenzie's sister, Fanny.

9. Ranald Slidell Mackenzie (1840–1889), who was born in Westchester County, graduated from West Point in 1862 and distinguished himself in the Civil War and in the Indian campaigns in the West afterward.

10. Matthew Calbraith Perry (1794–1858) had married Jane Slidell, the sister of Alexander Slidell Mackenzie, on December 24, 1814.

11. WI probably intended to write "were."

1336. To Joseph C. Cabell

Sunnyside Cottage, near Tarry town / May 8th. 1841

My dear Sir,

Though many a year has passed and gone since we have seen, or heard from, each other, yet I make bold to call to your remembrance a brother pilgrim who in days of yore visited with you the shrine of our Lady of Loretto, and scaled the heights of St Gothard.[1] Since those days of rambling juvenility you have led a quiet, regular, useful life, in the bosom of your native land, and devoted to objects of public utility; while I have kept on wandering, and living about the world in the most miscellaneous and often I fear the most unprofitable manner. For a few years past, however, I have been ⟨anchored⟩ ↑nestled↓ on the banks of the Hudson, in a little mansion of my own rearing where I should be most happy at any time to have you for a visitor that we might talk over the scenes of our ancient travel.

The object of my present letter is to speak a word in behalf of a nephew (Theodore Irving) who is a candidate for a professorship in the University of Virginia of which I understand you are one of the Visiting Committee. When he was just grown up he came out to me in Spain, and remained some few years under my care, ⟨in⟩ part of which were spent in the office of the Legation at London. I directed his attention to the modern languages and he made himself quite a proficient in French, Spanish and Italian. For five years past he has been a professor at Geneva College in this state,[2] and has acquitted himself with great zeal and fidelity. I understand he has shewn quite a tact for teaching and has excelled in commanding the respect and winning the regard of his pupils. In fact he has one of the finest tempers I have ever known, and his manners are most urbane and gentleman like.

I do not wish, however, to ask any favor in his behalf; I only wish to secure an attentive consideration to his application: let his merits be carefully scrutinized and let his success depend entirely upon their sufficiency.

Give my kindest remembrances to Mrs Cabell,[3] if she still bears me in her reccollection, and believe me ever my dear Sir, with faithfully cherished regard

Yours most truly
Washington Irving

Joseph C. Cabell Esq

ADDRESSED: Joseph C. Cabell Esq / Richmond / Virga— FRANKED: Free / W C Rives   DOCKETED: G. W. Irving. / May 8th — 1841. / ansd. June 24. 1841. MANUSCRIPT: University of Virginia.

Joseph C. Cabell (1778–1856), with whom WI had traveled in Europe from March to June, 1805, was a Virginia lawyer interested in agricultural improvements. He worked closely with Thomas Jefferson in the establishment of the University of Virginia. For details about the earlier association of WI and Cabell, see Richard Beale Davis, "Washington Irving and Joseph C. Cabell," *University of Virginia Studies*, 5 (1941), 7–22.

1. WI alludes to their visit to the shrine of Loretto on April 19, 1805, and to St. Gotthard's pass on May 7 and 8, 1805. See *J&N*, I, 310–13, 369–74.

2. Theodore Irving taught at Geneva College from 1836 to 1848, his application at Virginia being unsuccessful.

3. Mary Walker Carter of Lancaster, Virginia, whom Cabell had married on January 1, 1807. See Davis, "Washington Irving and Joseph C. Cabell," p. 20.

1337. To William C. Rives

Sunnyside Cottage, near Tarry town / May 8th 1841

My dear Sir,

Understanding that you are one of the Visiting Committee of the University of Virginia I would ask your attention to the application of my nephew Theodore Irving for the professorship of Modern languages, &c. I do not know whether you reccollect him in Europe, where he passed some few years under my care in Spain France and England; part of which time was spent in the office of the legation at London. While with me he made himself a proficient in French, Spanish and

Italian; beside pursuring other Studies. He has since his return to the United States produced an Historical work, The Conquest of Florida, which you may have seen. For five years past he has been professor of Modern languages, Belles lettres &c &c at Geneva College in this state, and has acquitted himself so as to give great satisfaction.

He is admirably calculated for the instruction of youth, from the excellence of his disposition the suavity and at the same time the gentleman like correctness of his manners, and has been a favorite both with the faculty and the students of the College in which he has officiated

In calling your attention to his application, however, I wish you distinctly to understand that I ask nothing for him as a matter of favor either to him or to myself. Let his abilities for the situation, and ⟨the⟩ his character and conduct be rigorously enquired into and let his merits alone entitle him to success.

Ever my dear Sir

Very respectfully & truly yours
Washington Irving

Hon William C. Rives

ADDRESSED: Hon. William C. Rives / Castle Hill / Albemarle Co / Va.   FRANKED: ⟨Paid⟩   DOCKETED: Washington Irving Esq. / on behalf / of Theodore Irving / *for Mod. languages.*
MANUSCRIPT: University of Virginia.

William C. Rives (1793–1868), a Virginian who served in both houses of Congress at various times between 1823 and 1845, was U.S. minister to France in August, 1830, when WI joined him to attend the inauguration of Louis Philippe. See WI to Rives, August 10, 1830.

1338.   To Sarah Storrow

Sunnyside Cottage Saturday May 8th. 1841

I wrote to you a few days since, my dear Sarah, while I was in town, and my letter was to go by the Havre packet.[1] ⟨The soiree⟩ I forgot to mention among my town gossip that I was at a musical soireé at Mrs Brevoorts, which was conducted in very elegant style, and where we had an agreeable assemblage and very good music both vocal and instrumental. Julia Grinnell and her husband were there and were much pleased. Among the guests was Mrs Hammersley.[2] It was the first time I had met her in public since her fathers death.[3] She greeted me most cordially and we had much conversation together. I was delighted with her appearance and manners, so lovely in person, and then so amiable, quiet and lady like. I was more than usually pleased and interested with her because she talked of you so sweetly and kindly and seemed to appreciate your character so justly. I was grieved, however, to see that there was no intercourse between her and her sisters, though in the same room and not far from each other. I presume they had spoken to each other when they met, but I observed no communication between them throughout the evening. And yet you remember how closely and tenderly they were but recently entwined together in sisterly affection. I cannot concieve any excuse ↑sufficient↓ for such alienation—at least none that I hear suggested. What are the sordid considerations of pounds shillings and pence to these dearer concerns of the heart: and what have the jars and janglings of husbands to do with the affections of sisters that have sprung up from the cradle and should continue to the grave. Good heavens what contradictory mortals we are!—We grieve and repine at the separation that death and distance effect between kindred hearts—and here are sisters, but five paces asunder, yet apparently as severed in all the sweetest sympathies of our nature as if half the world were thrust between them!

—The evening before last I returned to the dear little family circle at Sunnyside, and found all well, and as cheerful as the continued bad weather would permit. Your mother had taken ⟨[*unrecovered*]⟩ ↑advantage of↓ two transient intervals of sunshine to drive to Elizas, and had enjoyed her drives and her visits. She sleeps very well, and keeps up her usual tone of spirits. I long for genial settled weather that she may drive out daily and enjoy the opening season.

This is a bright Sunday morning—one of the very–very few real Spring mornings we have had this season. For the first time this year the girls have sallied out after breakfast without hat and shawl, and loitered around the porch; and admired the honeysuckles; and played with the dogs and pigeons and strolled arm in arm about the grass plots. As I ⟨watched⟩ gazed on the well known scene I felt my heart and my eyes filling, and ⟨the⟩ found myself humming the burden of the song— "But where art thou!—oh where art thou!" But I checked the feeling, and reproached myself, when so many were left for me to love, and, I trust, to love me, at repining so severely that one should be seperated from the domestic groupe. Still it takes time, when one ↑like myself↓ is "in the sere, the yellow leaf"[4] to get over these sudden loppings off. With you, my dear girl, the case is different, your heart is yet green, and can furnish growth to many a new and sweet affection, and I console myself with picturing you in my imagination, mingling among your relatives in England, forming new ties and attachments, which you will be near enough to each other to cherish and enjoy—or settled in a pleasant house in Paris, ⟨with⟩ entering upon a new character; with domestic interests, occupations, pleasures and affections springing up around you and forming a new era in your existence.

—As we were not go to church until afternoon, and as this lovely sabbath morning was too precious to be wasted, I have taken the girls out to enjoy it, as profitably I trust as between church walls, in strolling about the walks and glens and green banks, and inhaling the blessed breath of Spring, which ⟨after the late⟩ is sufficient to thaw the inmost fountains of the heart and set all the affections in a flow. I do not know when I have been more sensible of this tender influence of the weather: but in fact all nature, which during this cold tardy, hardhearted season, has remained spell bound; seemed to start into life this morning. The birds, which hitherto have only now and then ventured a few dubious half melancholy notes, ⟨war⟩ now warbled out boldly in the sunshine; the bees hummed about the scantily opened blossoms, and the pigeons in their frolick morning flights, swept down to the river banks and then circled among the tree tops. The Tappan Sea too had put on all its atmospherical charms. There was scarce a ripple on its surface, and its sunday fleet of sloops gleamed here and there about its wide sunny reaches, or faded away into the blue distance. How often have you and I watched those opening indications of Spring ⟨[*unrecovered*]⟩ together. I only wish they could have occurred this season more early; that your last reccollections of the Cottage might have been full of beauty.

Thursday 13th. This letter has been lying in my drawer for several days. I have been to town for a day, and when at home have kept as much out of doors and as busy as the uncertain weather would permit. The bright Sunday morning on which I have dwelt so much in the forepart of this letter, was a mere mouthful of sunshine in this rainy season, and the weather soon relapsed into its vapouring and whimpering fits. Yesterday, however, gave better signs, and this morning dawns most auspiciously, so I begin to hope we are about to get once more into our usual climate. Your mother caught a slight cold in one of her visits to Eliza and for part of the week has been somewhat feverish: we feared an attack of her ⟨usu⟩ customary Spring indisposition; but good housing and good nursing have parried the attack and driven off the fever. Nothing could be more amiable and affectionate than the attention of the dear girls to her; they watch over her with the tenderness of daughters; endeavor to anticipate all her wishes, and by their constant, but quiet companionship, prevent her feeling lonely.

As Kate is writing to you I trust to her to give you whatever ⟨there may⟩ I m[ay] [*MS torn*] omit of domestic news. Yet what news have we to furnish from our quiet little home, where one day passes so much

like another, ⟨in⟩ especially at this season, where we are almost entirely
shut up within ourselves and have no visitors. For my part, as I before
observed, I keep out doors, and busy myself about the garden and the
fields all day, whenever not absolutely driven in by the rain—So that
when evening comes I am completely fagged, and am apt to doze
over my book in the drawing room; but then I gain a good nights
sleep, and that is always worth working for. In the mean time, in spite
of wind and weather, the Spring is advancing; the trees are every day
putting out their leaves more and more, and the blossoms beginning to
open. We have occasional gleams of sunshine and intervals of warmth,
and I think we feel them more sensibly this season on account of their
rarity. Within these three days the little Boblinks have begun their
tinkling songs among the apple trees and the Cat birds are whisking
and pecking and carolling about the Cottage, and as these are warm
weather birds, we hail them as harbingers of sunshine. The nest of the
little Phoebe bird under the porch, however, remains unoccupied. This
is the second season it has been deserted, but I wont allow it to be
disturbed—It shall always remain ready for her.—*The Phoebe bird will
come back again*!

The most pleasing tidings I have heard for some time is that Mrs
Constant is likely to return home in the course of a few days. She is in
New York, and only waiting I believe until the weather shall be settled
and genial. How delighted I shall be to see her once more restored to
health and to that home which she so much adorned and rendered so
happy. I believe she is yet far from being completely recovered; but
there is every prospect of her thorough convalescence. Her restoration
to home and health will really be an event in ⟨the⟩ this neighborhood.

I am writing before breakfast and I hear the ringing of the breakfast
bell and the pattering of footsteps. The sun is shining in at my window and promising a fine day. If it keeps its promise I will turn out
horse and vehicle and make ⟨an⟩ the first irruption this spring into
Sleepy Hollow. The little valley must be by this time in blossom, and
it is a long while since the girls have had a real excursion for pleasure.
By the time this reaches you the garden of the Tuilleries will be in all its
beauty, and I can fancy your delight in strolling through its noble alleys,
and about its terraces and fountains. How many a delightful morning I
have passed there with your poor uncle Peter. Versailles, St Cloud St
Germain, also, thanks to the rapidity of rail roads, will now be close
at hand; ⟨their⟩ with their glorious parks and gardens. With such resorts
at command what a residence is Paris!

Before closing this letter I must furnish you with a bulletin of your
mothers health. She has passed a comfortable night—is entirely free

from fever and enlivened by the prospect of fine weather. If the latter continues fair I presume she will commence her daily drives tomorrow.

With kindest remembrances to Mr Storrow, I remain my dear Sarah

Ever most affectionately your uncle

W I.

Addressed: Packet Letter / à Madame / Madame Storrow / aux Soins de M. T. W. Storrow Jr. / Rue du Faubg Poissoniere / a Paris / *per Brittania from Boston* Postmarked: NEW-YORK / MAY / 15 // [*unrecovered*] / JUIN / [*unrecovered*] // EX / 10 JU 10 / 1841 // PACKET LETTER
Manuscript: Yale. Published: *Yale Review*, 16 (April, 1927), 463–65; LSS, pp. 8–12.

1. See WI's letter of May 3, 1841.
2. Sarah Mason, who was married to Andrew Gordon Hamersley (ca. 1806–1833).
3. John Mason (b. 1773), a prominent New York merchant and banker, had died on September 26, 1839.
4. *Macbeth*, V, iii, 23.

1339. To ——

Greenburgh, May 9th. 1841

During my residence in Europe my nephew Theodore Irving passed some few years with me and under my guidance, in Spain, France and England. During this time he was principally occupied in acquiring a knowledge of the French, Spanish and Italian languages, with his proficiency in which I was very well satisfied. He has of late years held a professorship in Geneva College in this state, where he has taught the Modern languages, History, Moral Philosophy, Belles lettres &c and as far as I can learn, has given much satisfaction. I can confidently vouch for his extreme assiduity, his correct principles, the amiableness of his disposition and the perfect urbanity of his manners.

Washington Irving

Manuscript: University of Virginia Library.

1340. To Aaron Vail

New York May 11th. 1841

My dear Sir,

This will be handed you by my excellent and highly esteemed friend Mr T. W. C. Moore[1] for whom I would solicit your kind civilities. He visits Madrid on some business which he will explain to you, on behalf of the Messrs. G. G. & S Howland[2] of this city. These gentlemen are among the most eminent and estimable of our New York Merchants, and persons for whom I entertain the highest regard. Any facilities you may be enabled to furnish Mr Moore in the prosecution of his business will be services most worthly[3] rendered and which will be duly appreciated by all the parties concerned, as well as considered personal favors to

Yours ever, my dear Sir / Most faithfully
Washington Irving

Aaron Vail Esqr / &c &c &c

ADDRESSED: Aaron Vail Esq / Charge d'affaires / of the United States / Madrid
    DOCKETED: Washington Irving / 11th. May 1841 / recd. 26 June — / Mr
    Moore
MANUSCRIPT: Va.—Barrett.

Aaron Vail (1796–1878), whom WI had known in London, had served as chargé d'affaires at the legation there from 1832 to 1836. Currently Vail was American chargé at Madrid, where WI would follow him as minister in 1842.

1. Thomas W. C. Moore, son of the Royalist John Moore, who was customs collector for the British during their occupation of New York City during the Revolutionary War, was a patron of the arts, a writer of light verse, and an intimate friend of Fitz-Greene Halleck. He is credited with having John Searle's 1822 watercolor of the Park Theater audience copied and preserved at NYHS. He also lent paintings by Rembrandt and Velasquez in 1839 for the May Exhibition of the Apollo Association. See Martha J. Lamb, *History of the City of New York: Its Origin, Rise and Progress*, II, 685; *Memorial History of the City of New-York* (New York, 1893), ed. James Grant Wilson, IV, 517n.; and Mary Bartlett Cowdrey, "American Academy of Fine Arts and American Art Union, Exhibition Record, 1816–1852," *New-York Historical Society Collections*, 77 (1944), 297, 369.
2. Gardiner Greene Howland (1787–1851) and his brother Samuel Shaw Howland (1790–1853) began in 1816 a shipping firm specializing in the South American and Pacific trade. In 1834 the brothers retired from active management of the firm, leaving the business to Gardiner's son William and to their nephew, William H. Aspinwall (1807–1875).
3. WI probably intended to write "worthily."

1341.   To Sarah Storrow

Sunnyside, May 25th. 1841.

My dear Sarah,

I have been picturing you to myself, for some time past, as travelling about, in England, in the loveliest season of the year, ⟨and⟩ gazing about you with almost an intoxication of feeling on the delicious rural scenery, and visiting old castles, ⟨als⟩ cathedrals and ruined abbeys with insatiable curiosity and intense, but reverential, delight. Such at least were my own feelings on first ⟨landing⟩ visiting English Scenes, and I am apt to think that, in these matters, we feel very much alike. I am glad too, to fancy you on firm land and ⟨in a manner⟩ at the end of your voyage, for it was painful to me to think of you every day and hour and minute as urging your way across the broad atlantic, and adding to the space that separated us from each other. We shall now be looking forward to the receipt of letters from you, and the first that arrives will break the spell of silence and uncertainty and once more link us, by inter communion of thought and word, together.

In my last I mentioned that your mother had caught a slight cold and had some degree of feverishness. It wore off, but returned for a day or two. She is now quite free from it; walks out about the grounds before the cottage and intends to pay a visit of a few days to town, at the end of the week. Her spirits are good, she has comfortable nights sleep, and is altogether in a healthier frame of mind than she was at any time during the winter. The season too has its effect for within a few days the Spring has broke upon us; hand in hand with Summer, leaves and blossoms and singing birds have all come together and the whole Scene round the Cottage has been a perfect paradise. The girls have all exerted themselves, in every way, to contribute to your mothers enjoyment; ⟨they are⟩ indeed they seem to me to exert themselves in all respects, to make up for your absence, and what with the amiableness and affection within doors, and the bright and lovely weather and sweet scenery without, the little Cottage is once more regaining its charms and becoming a happy home. Julia and Mr Grinnell came up by land on Saturday last and stayed until monday morning. The weather was delightful and they appeared to be greatly pleased with their visit and with every thing about them. From various circumstances I am led to believe that Grinnell would like to have a little Summer retreat in this neighborhood, and I am sure Julia would. However, the most convenient places in our immediate neighborhood are now taken up. He enquired repeatedly about the cost of the different cottages erected in the neighborhood; the arrival & departure of the Steamboats &c and observed that one could get to and from town to this neighborhood as quickly as one could to the part of Staten Island at which .they boarded last year—I wish he could be persuaded to put up a nestling place in the vicinity, but I fear the idea will pass out of his mind without being carried into effect.

I have been working about the grounds and especially about the ⟨fallen⟩ old ↑fallen↓ chestnut tree, where you took your seat ⟨on⟩ in the course of one of our last rambles. I have new paths leading to and from it along the brook, and it is really one of the prettiest places in my whole grounds. The trees and shrubs this Spring have come out in great luxuriance, improved in size and shape, indeed I think I have never seen the place so beautiful.

I have received two or three letters recently which I know would please you, and as I have not you ⟨at hand to⟩ at my elbow to hand them to, as I always did all my correspondence of an interesting nature, I will transcribe them. The first is from that excentric but excellent fellow Van Bibber,[1] of this I will merely give a scrap, as the greater part relates to his private concerns and to a drama in two acts which he has just finished and is disposed to risk on the stage. His whole letter is charmingly written, and ⟨show⟩ evidences a mind imbued with classical literature and with the golden old literature of England. I give you ⟨h⟩ merely his conclusion which is quaint but picturesque, ⟨and⟩ full of kindness and not deficient in beauty—

"Avon Dale, Sweet lady, has just donned her annual garniture of buds and flowers; her head is crowned with a garland of lilac, peach and apple blossoms, her feet covered with Slippers of woven cowslips and Polyanthus. Every morning I catch her twining some new bud or wreathing some new flowret into her Coronet. Come, Sir, I must renew my invitation for a visit; our means will not allow us to offer you those costly juices ripened beside the Rhine or Marne, to which you have doubtless been ever accustomed; but if you are fond of rich cream, fresh milk and clear water (with ever and anon a sparking glass of aromatic mint julep,) if you love deep woodland solitude and the voice of plaintive turtle doves (I never in any other place knew half so many or half such musical ones)—then come, dear Sir, to Avon Dale, and I will ensure you a hearty welcome, a room (when you wish it) to yourself, a horse to ride on when you list, abundance of pure-fresh air and a glorious view of the distant mountains of Catockton. But if you still turn a deaf ear to my invitations, and prefer to all this ↑the↓ company of your fair nieces, the manifold pleasures of Sunnyside Cottage and the delicious reveries inspired by Sleepy Hollow, then—my only wish is that your own orchard may shower down its choicest blossoms on your head, and that, during all this merry Spring time, you may have sweet thoughts, pleasant dreams and frequent visits from the muses"—

Is not that delightfully said? and does it not give a delightful idea of the man and his wild wood retreat? I declare to you, that, if I could possibly tear myself from the Cottage at this moment when it is all in bloom and beauty and fragrant with lilacs, I should be delighted to ⟨t⟩ pay a visit to the poetic retreat of the Van Bibbers.

The next letter is from my friend James[2] the novelist, dated from Bruxelles. 17 Jany last.

"My dear Irving,

I cannot let slip the opportunity of the return of my young acquaintance Mr Meline[3] to the United States to write you a few lines, though it is now alas many a year since we met and the broad Atlantic rolls between us perhaps forever. The memory of our intercourse while you were resident in the old world still remains fresh and pleasurable with me, and I trust that I am not forgotten either; but that when you see the name of one of my paper things you think of him who wrote it. My productions in that way have been many, yours all too few, but those that you have written have given me intense delight, especially Astoria every word of which I dwell upon with feelings of excitement and interest and longings for adventure which I thought were gone with my boyhood. I am even now writing something for the Knickerbocker which I hear, you take an interest in; as indeed you should in your God-child; and what I shall require as payment shall be a few lines from your hand to tell me how you are and that you have not forgotten your English friends. ⟨I am⟩ My address for the present must be at Messrs Longmans Paternoster Row for I am now wandering having lately met with a ↑severe↓ family affliction which made changes of Scene and air advisable for me. I shall soon, however, settle again, and if ever you should be tempted once more to cross the broad stream I trust that one of the first fire sides at which you set down will be that of yours ever truly &c"

Is not this a most kind and friendly letter? and how little have I deserved it! I who have let his former letter remain unanswered and a book which he sent me unacknowledged, and unthanked for—but I will reform! And now comes the third letter—from that glorious fellow Dickens (Boz)[4] in reply to the one I wrote,[5] expressing my heartfelt delight with his writings and my yearnings towards himself—See how completely we sympathize in feelings.

"My dear Sir,

There is no man in the world who could have given me the heart felt pleasure you have by your kind note of the thirteenth of last month. There is no living writer, and there are very few among the dead, whose approbation I should feel so proud to earn. And with every thing you

have written upon my shelves, and in my thoughts, and in my heart of
hearts, I may honestly and truly say so. If you could know how earnestly
I write this, you would be glad to read it—as I hope you will be, faintly
guessing at the warmth of the hand ⟨which⟩ I autobiographically hold out
to you over the broad Atlantic.

I wish I could find in your welcome letter some hint of an intention
to visit England. I can't. I have held it at arms length, and taken a birds
eye view of it after reading it a great many times, but there is no greater
encouragement in it this way than in a microscopic inspection. I should
love to go with you—as I have gone God knows how often—into Little
Britain, and East Cheap, and Green Arbour Court, and West minster
abbey.[6] I should like to travel with you, outside the last of the coaches,
down to Bracebridge Hall.[7] It would make my heart glad to compare
notes with you about that shabby gentleman in the oil cloth hat and
red-nose who sat in the nine-cornered back parlour at the Masons arms[8]
—and about Robert Preston[9]—and the Tallow Chandlers widow[10] whose
sitting room is second nature to me—and about all those delightful places
and people that I used to walk about and dream of in the day time
when a very small and not over-particularly-taken-care of-boy. I have a
good deal to say too about that dashing Alonzo de Ojeda[11] that you can't
help being fonder of than you ought to be—and much to hear concerning
Moorish legend and poor unhappy Boabdil.[12] Diedrich Knickerbocker
I have worn to death in my pocket—and yet I should shew you his
mutilated carcase—with a joy past all expression. I have been so accustomed to associate you with my pleasantest and happiest thoughts, and
with my leisure hours, that I rush at once into full confidence with you,
and fall—as it were naturally, and by the very laws of gravity—into your
open arms. Questions come thronging to my pen as to the lips of people
who meet after long hoping to do so. I dont know what to say first,
or what to leave unsaid, and am constantly disposed to break off, and
tell you again how glad I am this moment has arrived.

My dear Washington Irving I cannot thank you enough for your
cordial and generous praise or tell you what deep and lasting gratification
it has given me. I hope to have many letters from you and to exchange
a frequent correspondence. I send this to say so. After the first two or
three I shall settle down into a connected style and become gradually
rational

You know what the feeling is after having written a letter, sealed it
and sent it off. I shall picture you reading this and answering it, before
it has lain one night in the Post office. Ten to one that before the fastest
packet could reach New York I shall be writing again.

Do you suppose the Post Office clerks care to receive letters? I have
my doubts. They get into a dreadful habit of indifference. A Postman I

imagine is quite callous—Conceive his delivering one to himself, without being startled by a preliminary double Knock—!

Always your faithful friend
Charles Dickens—[13]

May 26th. Since copying the foregoing letters I have answered them all[14] so you see I am becoming quite a prompt correspondent. When you next visit England I will procure you the ⟨q⟩ acquaintance of Mr Dickens, who I have no doubt must be a delightful character,—I shall be anxious to know whether you have seen any of my literary friends in England to whom I gave Mr Storrow letters. Among the artists I learn ⟨an?⟩ that Sir David Wilkie[15] was absent on a visit to the Holy land! I regret that you have missed him; the letter however will serve for another time.

Within these few days past Mrs Constant has returned home. I have not yet seen her, but shall do so this afternoon. She is yet weak; insomuch that the drawing room is turned into a bedroom to spare her the fatigue of going up & down stairs. It is the intention of Mr Constant to take her soon to Rockaway, where they will remain for the greater part of the Summer.

I have commenced the barricade at the foot of the ban[k and] [MS torn] trust before long to be protected against all the Surf an[d] ⟨?↑warmth↓?⟩ [MS torn] of [the] [MS torn] Tappan Sea and the evil influence of the Erie Rail Roa[d.] [MS torn] Our Neighborhood is filling up for the Summer. The Hamiltons[16] are at home; Mrs Colford Jones and her family came up yesterday, and Mrs Sheldon is to come up about the beginning of the month. Poor Mrs Sheldon still remains as lame as ever; while Mr Henry Sheldon is looking uncommonly well, and can limp faster than any duck on the place—What a striking reverse of situation—how mysterious are the visitations of providence! By the way there is a report that Mr Henry Sheldon[17] is engaged to Miss Hetty King—but you know how apt the public is to ⟨marry off⟩ engage old Bachelors in this neighborhood without their knowledge. If it should be the case he will get a capital wife, and one that ⟨he⟩ will grace his cottage—but I doubt the fact.

Evening. I have been with Kate to see Mrs Constant. She looks thin and pale, and is quite weak, for though she has been home several days she has been able ⟨to⟩ but once to get down as far as the garden—Yet she is evidently better in health and spirits and talked very cheerfully. As you may suppose she enquired most kindly after you and spoke of you in the most affectionate manner. She goes to Rockaway in July to pass a month there, So that she will not be as long absent from the neighborhood as I had apprehended. It was delightful to see her once more under her own roof among those scenes which she has so graced and gladdened.

And now my dear Sarah I must conclude this letter, which has been so much taken up with myself. I only ask in return that you will in your letters be equally egotistical. Tell me all about yourself; your movements, your occupations, your amusements; all that you see think and feel. let me have as much of yourself as possible that I may not feel as if we are severed in Spirit by the distance between us. I shall be eager to hear of your final establishment in your own habitation at Paris, and in what quarter of the great city you are fixed, and how you acquit yourself in housekeeping. Mr Storrow, however, is an able and experienced hand who will arrange every thing, I make no doubt, to your hearts content. Remember me to him most kindly and heartily and believe me my dear— dear Sarah

ever your affectionate Uncle
Washington Irving

Mrs. Sarah Storrow

ADDRESSED: A Madame / Madame Storrow / Aux Soins de M T. W. Storrow / Rue du faubg Poissonniere / à Paris / per Charles Carroll POSTMARKED: [unrecovered] DOCKETED: May 21st 1841 / No 4x
MANUSCRIPT: Yale. PUBLISHED: PMI, III, 163–67 (in part); The Letters of Charles Dickens, ed. Madeline House and Graham Storey (Oxford, 1969), II, 395.

1. Probably Thomas Emory Van Bibber (1812–1881), who wrote a narrative poem, The Flight into Egypt (1880) and was joint author, with W. C. Van Bibber (1824–1892), of The Spendthrift (1884). See Dramatic Compositions Copyrighted in the United States, 1870 to 1916, 2 vols. (Washington, 1918), II, 3487.

2. George Payne Rainsford James (1801–1860) was a prolific popular English novelist whom WI had met in Bordeaux on October 1, 1825, and had encouraged in his writing career. WI was to see him in England in 1842, and James dedicated his novel Thirty Years Since (1848) to WI and described him in it. See STW, I, 464; II, 365, 388; and J&N, III, 527.

3. James Florant Meline (1811–1873), a journalist, biographer, and consular official, studied for three years in Europe.

4. Charles Dickens (1812–1870), who had attracted attention with his Sketches By Boz (1836–1837), Pickwick Papers (1836–1837), Oliver Twist (1837–1838), Nicholas Nickleby (1838–1839), The Old Curiosity Shop (1840–1841), and Barnaby Rudge (1841), had written to WI on April 21, 1841. See The Letters of Charles Dickens, II, 267–69.

5. As Dickens points out in his letter, WI had written on March 13. Although WI's letter has not been located, it has been described by Dickens's biographer as "a very hearty letter ... about little Nell and The Curiosity Shop, expressing ... delight with his writings." See John Forster, The Life of Charles Dickens, 2 vols. (London, 1872), I, 259.

6. These allusions are to places described in The Sketch Book.

7. This trip by coach to Bracebridge Hall is presented in *The Sketch Book*...

8. See "The Boar's Head Tavern, Eastcheap" in *The Sketch Book*.

9. The drawer at the Boar's Head Tavern.

10. The historian of the tavern, to be found in the same sketch.

11. A Spanish cavalier who accompanied Columbus on his second voyage. See *The Voyages and Discoveries of the Companions of Columbus*, Author's Revised Edition (New York, 1850), pp. 17–33, 51–101.

12. Boabdil el Chico, the unfortunate king of Granada at the time the city was taken by the Spaniards. WI relates his story in *A Chronicle of the Conquest of Granada*.

13. WI's transcription differs slightly from the one taken from the manuscript in the Huntington Library and included in *The Letters of Charles Dickens*, II, 267–69.

14. WI's replies to James and Dickens have been preserved.

15. Sir David Wilkie (1785–1841), whom WI knew intimately in Madrid and Seville in 1827 and 1828, died on June 1, 1841, on the return voyage from the Holy Land.

16. The James Hamiltons, whose estate, Nevis, was a short distance south of Sunnyside.

17. Henry Sheldon was a silk merchant who lived at Tarrytown. See J. T. Scharf, *History of Westchester County*, II, 245, 297.

1342. To Charles Dickens

Sunnyside Cottage May 26th. 1841

My dear Sir,

I cannot tell you how happy the receipt of your letter[1] has made me, for it has convinced me that I was not mistaken in you; that you were just what your writings made me imagine you, and that it only wanted a word to bring us together in heart and soul. Do not suppose me, however, a man prompt at these ⟨[*unrecovered*]⟩ spontaneous overtures of friendship. You are the only man I have ever made such an advance to. In general I seek no acquaintances and keep up no correspondences out of my family connexion; but towards you there was a strong impulse, which for some time I resisted, but which at length overpowered me; and I now am glad it did so.

You flatter my languid and declining pride of authorship by quoting many of my sketchings of London life,[2] written long since, and too slight as I supposed, to make any lasting impression; but what are my slight and isolated sketches to your ample and complete pictures which lay all the recesses of London life before us? And then the practical utility, the operative benevolence which prevade all your p⟨ain⟩ortraitures of the lowest life, ⟨which⟩ ↑and↓ give a value and dignity to your broadest humor; that exquisite tact which enables you to carry your readers through the veriest dens of vice and villainy without a breath

to shock the ear or a stain to sully the robe of the most shrinking delicacy. It is a rare gift to be able to paint low life without being low, and
to be comic without the least taint of vulgarity. I have a peculiar relish
for ↑your↓ pictures of low English life, and especially those about the
metropolis, and connected with public fairs &c, from having studied
them much during my residence in England. I had a perfect passion for
exploring London, and visiting every place celebrated in Story or song;
or mentioned in novels and essays, or connected with the biographies
of distinguished characters; or rhymed in old ballads, ⟨noted in th⟩ ↑or↓
rendered notorious ⟨in⟩ by the confessions of robbers and highwaymen.
I used to prowl by myself through all the intricate regions of the City;
East Cheap, Tower Hill, Wapping &c &c, and skirt all the environs, visit
the neighboring villages; eat my solitary beef steak at Jack Straws
Castle,[3] or at the country Inns renowned by the equestrian expedition
of Johnny Gilpin.[4] I attended all the fairs held in the vicinity of London,
many of which have now declined or have been abolished—West end,
Brook Green, Fairlap &c &c.[5] I wanted to write about all these scenes,
and to write copiously; but some how or other my pen seemed spell
bound; ⟨I could⟩ it could only throw off a few disconnected sketches,
which were so slight and unsatisfactory as only to worry me. I felt too
much like a stranger in the land and feared to give full scope to the bent
of my humor and inclination All this makes me the more sensible to the
fullness as well as the fidelity of your picturings. They place before me
the very scenes and people I have so often studied, and been eager to
describe—but they depict them with an accuracy, minuteness yet breadth
of painting that I could never have ⟨maintained.⟩ ↑attained.↓

I have just been reading again your Pickwick papers[6] which grow on
me more and more with every perusal. Old Pickwick is the Quixote of
commonplace life and ⟨like⟩ ↑as with↓ the Don, we begin by laughing at
him and end by loving him. ⟨Of?⟩ Sam Weller and his father I could
swear I had seen fifty times in my loiterings about coach offices and Inn
yards—all the world knows the truth and force of their portraits. I have
a great fancy ⟨for⟩ however, for the less obtrusive merits of those
worthies Bob Sawyer and Ben Allen; how much have I seen of the
make shift life, of the scrub junketting, ⟨and⟩ pot boy dissipation ⟨of
those?⟩ ↑practical joking, and pushing familiarity,↓ such half scamps, half
gentlemen in England! Dick Swiveller[7] too, the exquisite Dick Swiveller who is so continually within a hairs breadth of becoming a scamp
but is carried safely through every temptation by the native goodness
of his heart. And then the measured degree of good fortune meted out
to him in the end; his hundred and fifty pounds a year his little cottage
at Hampstead, ⟨&⟩ with a smoking box in the garden and the small
servant for a wife to play cribbage with him for the rest of his days!

Let me ask you one question. Mantalini,[8] the inimitable Mantalini! is
he a mere creation of the brain or did any mortal ⟨stan⟩ sit for the portrait. Judging as an artist, I should think you had the "living subject"
for ⟨the ground work⟩ a model, but that you clothed and heightened it
by the copious additions of your fancy.

I have been dwelling on your comic picturings but you have proved
yourself equally the master of the dark and terrible of real life: not the
robbers, and tyrants and villains of high strained romance and feudal
times and castellated scenes: but the dangerous and desperate villainy
that lurks in the midst of the busy world and besets the every day haunts
of society; and starts up in the ⟨humble⟩ path of the plodding citizen, and
among the brick walls of the metropolis. And then the exquisite and sustained pathos, so deep, but so pure and healthy, as carried throughout
the wanderings of little Barbara and her poor old Grandfather.[9] I declare
to you there is a moral sublimity and beauty wrought out with a match-
less simplicity of pencil in the whole of this story, that leaves me at a
loss how sufficiently to express my admiration—and then there are
passages (like that of the schoolmasters ⟨med⟩ remarks on neglected
graves) which come upon us suddenly and gleam forth apparently
undesignedly, but which are perfect gems of language.

But I must restrain my pen or it would run riot on this theme and yet
would mere hint forth the images and reccollections with which you
have crowded my mind.—Do you know Leslie the painter, the one
who has recently painted a picture of the Coronation of Queen Victoria.[10] If you do not I wish you would get acquainted with him.
You would like one another. He is ⟨a⟩ full of talent and right feeling.
He was one of my choice and intimate companions during my literary
sojourn in London. While I was ⟨in?⟩ making my early studies with
my pen he was working with his pencil. We sympathized in tastes and
feelings and used to explore London together; and visit the neighboring
villages, and occasionally extend our researches into different parts
of the country. He is one of the purest and best of men; with a fine
eye for nature and character, and a truly Addisonian humor. ⟨Rodgers⟩
↑Rogers↓[11] knows and values him, and would make you acquainted;
though you need nothing to usher you to his acquaintance but your own
card. By the way I see by the dedication of your last work[12] that you
properly appreciate the character of Rogers; intrinsically a most benevo-
lent man, full of sympathy for the poor mans joys and sorrows; and, as
a lady of my acquaintance ↑once↓ so beautifully said of him "So kind
to those in affliction!" He was one of the last persons I saw in London.[13]
I breakfasted with him. On taking leave he followed me to the street
door; pressed my hands, and bade me farewell with a warmth and kindness that I shall never forget.

You speak to me about my revisiting England. I should delight to do so, but I know not when I shall. I have built me a little cottage on the banks of the Hudson in a lovely spot endeared to me by the reccollections of my boyhood. I have a pleasant and friendly neighborhood, and a happy household of young nieces who are like daughters to me, and who would be in despair if I should leave them. Judge then how fast I have taken root.

ever my dear Sir Yours most faithfully
Washington Irving

Charles Dickens Esqr

ADDRESSED: Charles Dickens Esqr / Devonshire Terrace / York Gate / Regents Park / London / per *Caledonia* POSTMARKED: PAID / NEW-YORK / MAY / 31 // AMERICA / L // [*unrecovered*] / JUL • 5 / 1841
MANUSCRIPT: Huntington. PUBLISHED: *The Letters of Charles Dickens*, II, 269–70, 395 (in part).

1. Dickens's letter of April 21, 1841. See *The Letters of Charles Dickens*, II, 267–69.
2. See WI to Sarah Storrow, May 25, 1841, for specific details.
3. An inn in Hampstead, named after Jack Straw, one of the leaders of the Peasants' Revolt (1381). "This noted hostelry has long been a famous place for public and private dinner parties and suppers, and its gardens and grounds for alfresco entertainments." See Edward Walford, *Old and New London: A Narrative of Its History, Its People, and Its Places*, 6 vols. (London, n.d.), V, 454–55.
4. The main character in William Cowper's poems, "The Diverting History of John Gilpin, Showing How He Went Farther Than He Intended, and Came Safe Home Again" (1782). Gilpin and his wife had planned to dine at the Bell Inn in Edmonton until his runaway horse carried him to Ware, ten miles away. For details, see Walford, *Old and New London*, V, 564–67.
5. These fairs were held in villages on the perimeter of London. West End Fair occurred in July in the western part of Hampstead, northwest of London; Brook Green Fair took place in May in Hammersmith, west of the Kensington section of London; and Fairlap Fair was held in Hainault Forest near Epping, northeast of London. See Walford, *Old and New London*, II, 137; V, 503; VI, 533.
6. *The Posthumous Papers of the Pickwick Club*, which appeared serially from April, 1836, to November, 1837, was published in two volumes in 1837. Pickwick, Sam Weller, Bob Sawyer, and Ben Allen are characters in the *Pickwick Papers*.
7. A character from *The Old Curiosity Shop*.
8. A character from *Nicholas Nickleby*.
9. Characters from *The Old Curiosity Shop*.
10. In the fall of 1838 Charles Robert Leslie began painting "The Queen Receiving the Sacrament at Her Coronation" and continued on it into the summer of 1839. See Leslie, *Autobiographical Recollections*, pp. 310–15.
11. Samuel Rogers (1763–1855) was the author of *The Pleasures of Memory* (1792) and a social figure known for his literary breakfasts. WI met him in his early years in London and remained on friendly terms with him.
12. In his dedication, published in installment 26 of *Master Humphrey's Clock*

and later given to *The Old Curiosity Shop* when it and *Barnaby Rudge* were detached and published separately, Dickens wrote: "Let me have *my* Pleasures of Memory in connection with this book by dedicating it to a Poet whose writings (as all the World knows) are replete with generous and earnest feeling; and to a man whose daily life (as all the world does not know) is one of active sympathy with the poorest and humblest of his kind." See *The Letters of Charles Dickens*, II, 125.

13. In his journal for March 30, 1832, Thomas Moore wrote: "Breakfasted with Rogers, to meet Washington Irving, who is about to start for America." See *Memoirs, Journal, and Correspondence of Thomas Moore*, ed. Lord John Russell, 8 vols. (London, 1854), VI, 252.

1343. To G. P. R. James

Sunnyside Cottage, May 26th. 1841

My dear James,

I have just received your letter dated at Brussels the 7th. of last January,[1] but have not seen the bearer Mr Meline,[2] as I am residing in the country and he left it at the house of one of my relatives in New York, without putting his address on his card.

I do assure you I have ever entertained the most pleasureable reccollection of our first meeting at Bordeaux and our subsequent intercourse in London,[3] and have watched your literary career with the warm exultation of a friend. I have been delighted also to notice the kindliness of feeling, the purity of taste and the soundness of principle maintained throughout your various writings; this too at a time when there is such a meretricious taste and such a specious profligacy prevalent in literature throughout the world. I understand you have recently been visiting some of the scenes on the continent connected with the story of Richard Coeur de Leon, preparatory to a work on that subject.[4] I reccollect making an excursion from Vienna to the Ruins of a castle on the Danube, where he ⟨had⟩ was once confined.[5] It was a picturesque scene, and I saw it under magical effects of weather. I hope you have visited it, and if so, that you have visited a magnificent and hospitable monastery[6] on a mountain on the opposite side of the Danube and partaken of the ⟨good⟩ ↑worthy↓ abbots good cheer and good wine. If so, I beg you to commemorate all these things in your book if they will work in tractably with the story.

I thank you for your kind invitation to your firesi[de] [*MS torn*] It would indeed give me heartfelt pleasure to revisit my friends in the old world; and I constantly promise myself to do so sometime or other: but here I am, fast rooted on the banks of the Hudson, in a cottage which I have built, myself, amidst grounds which I have laid out and trees which I have planted, amongst ↑the↓ scenes of my boyhood, ↑and↓ about which I have scribbled in after years, with a most friendly, polite and agreeable neighborhood, and a house full of young nieces who make my home the happiest one that ever old bachelor inhabited. You may imagine then how difficult it is for me to uproot myself and how likely I am to keep putting off my proposed visit to Europe from year to year, as I have for some years past. Still I ⟨am⟩ may be carried across the Atlantic by some sudden impulse, as I came very near being not long since, on a favorite niece ⟨my⟩ being taken from my side by matrimony and setting off with her husband to reside at Paris.

I notice your kind intentions with respect to the Knickerbocker. It is a periodical work which I wish well to; but I have no property in it. I wrote for it for a couple of years, but have ceased to do so, wishing, if I can to devote my attention to some regular work though I grieve to say I begin to grow very reluctant to handle my pen, and would much rather ramble about my grounds; prune trees, lay out paths, and super-intend the police of my poultry yard.

If ever you should cross the Atlantic, (and now that steam navigation has narrowed the ocean it is nothing to do so) I would rejoice to see you at my cottage and display to you my skill in husbandry, by which I am enabled to raise all kinds of produce at not much more than twice as much as it would cost in the market.

> ever yours most faithfully
> Washington Irving

G. P. R James Esqr

ADDRESSED: G. P. R James Esq / &c &c &c / care of Mess Longman & Co / Pater-noster Row / London / *per Caledonia* POSTMARKED: NEW-YORK / MAY 31 MANUSCRIPT: NYPL–WI Papers.

1. WI quoted James's letter in his letter to Sarah Storrow, May 25, 1841.

2. Probably James Florant Meline. See WI to Sarah Storrow, May 25, 1841.

3. The dates of the meetings of WI and James in London have not been deter-mined.

4. James's *History of the Life of Richard Coeur de Leon, King of England* was noted in NYEP, December 30, 1841.

5. On his return to England from Jerusalem while traveling in disguise, Rich-ard I (1157–1199) was arrested near Vienna on December 21, 1192, and imprisoned in the castle of Dürnstein for fifteen months before he was ransomed. WI had visited the ruins of Dürnstein on November 9, 1822. See J&N, III, 67.

6. The Benedictine abbey and monastery of Göttweig is located south of the Danube about five miles from Dürnstein. For details, see J&N, III, 66–67; WI to Sarah Van Wart, October 27–November 10, 1822; and to Susan Storrow, November 10, 1822.

1344.   To Sarah Van Wart

[ca. May 1841]

Thus you see, though a bachelor, I am doomed to experience what parents feel, when their children are widely separated from them by marriage.[1] But this is a world of changes; and we were all too happy in our delightful little nest, for our domestic quiet to remain uninterrupted.

PUBLISHED: PMI, III, 160.

1. WI is alluding to the departure of his niece Sarah Paris after her marriage to Thomas Wentworth Storrow, Jr.

1345.   To Sarah Storrow

Sunnyside June 13th. 1841

My dear Sarah,
    We have all been made most happy by your letters[1] by the Great Western[2] giving account of your first few days in England. If you could have seen with what eagerness they were read, and how they were handed from one to the other round the centre table in our little drawing room and the expressions of affection and delight that were continually breaking forth, you would have felt well repaid for the task of writing them. It is fortunate for you, my dear Sarah, that you do not value yourself on a talent for letter writing; you do not attempt to write *fine* letters and therefore you write *good* ones. Your letters have all the freshness and truth of your own feelings; I find in them continually those qualities which I prized in you, and which made you one of the most delightful companions to me that I was ever blessed with—It is not fine periods and fine thoughts that make the real letters of friendship and affection; these come from the head and speak to the fancy; but we want the simple unstudied language of the heart, that speaks to the heart. Your letters present me a perfect picture of your feelings, as I was sure they would be affected on your arrival in England; that tumult of excitement and delight; that crowd of Sensations and impressions which distract and almost overpower the mind and for a time set analysis and sober narrative at defiance. When you express your despair at the limited power of letter writing ⟨to give utterance to⟩ (and, especially of your own powers of letter writing,) to give utterance to all you see and think and feel, you give the most vivid picture of

your ⟨own⟩ self and your actual state of mind; and make us understand how exquisitely alive you are to the novelties and wonders that are continually breaking upon you. It is this fresh susceptibility to every thing new and striking and beautiful, this joyous faculty of imbibing delight from all right sources, that made me always covet you for a travelling companion, and I do not know what I would not have given to have been with you on your first landing in England, and first mingling among the historic monuments of the old world. Oh! if I could only have visited old Chapstow Castle and Tintern Abbey and traversed the sweet valley of the Wye[3] with you. You have called it all up to my reccollection and made my tour through that lovely region pass like a dream before me. Your feelings on first visiting the ruins of old castles, and abbeys; and treading the vaulted aisles of cathedrals recall all my first impressions and shew me how much we feel alike in these matters. I shall look with eagerness for your account of the rest of your English tour. You were about to set off for a succession of ⟨[unrecovered]⟩ remarkable places, Warwick Castle,[4] Stratford on Avon,[5] Blenheim,[6] Oxford and old Babylonian London—I think when you get to the end of such a tour you will find your head more crowded and confused than ever. When I ⟨first⟩ made my first tour in Europe I used to keep a journal, and set down the events and sights each day; but Rome, Paris and London completely overpowered me, and for a time after my arrival in each of these cities my journal was suspended.

By the way, to return to Chapstow Castle. Your mention of it recalls it strongly to my mind. At the time I visited it with Renwick[7] it was shewn by an old woman who ⟨had⟩ with six grand children inhabited ⟨two⟩ ↑one↓ of the towers ↑above the dungeon.↓ She had lived there 20 years, and an aunt had been born in one of the towers and lived there ninety years; so fixed and old are things in the old country. She had gardens and wall fruit in the courts of the castle which were apt to be plundered by the boys of the village. I reccollect the great Walnut tree in the center of the court; I reccollect, also, that Renwick and myself sat on the grass in the court yard, on a Sunday morning, listening to the distant tolling of the bell of the village church and watching the sea gulls soaring round the castle tower, when we were startled by a thundering knocking at the great gate ⟨and⟩ ↑The old woman hastened to throw it open & we↓ expected to see some armed knight entering on his charger through the echoing barbican—when ⟨thr⟩ lo & behold—enter a ragged urchin driving a couple of donkies—So much for the modern chivalry of Chapstow—I reccollect our route on the same day to Tintern; ⟨the thougt⟩ and a romantic one it was, across a high hill and through scenery similar to the glens in the highlands of the Hudson—and then the ⟨sweet⟩ ↑lovely↓ Valley in which Tintern

Abbey is situated—the villagers were wending along ⟨there⟩ the banks
of the Wye to church, and the village bell was sounding sweetly down
the valley.—But all this is like reading old allmanacks to you—Let me
talk a little about home—

Our Spring, though late and brief has been beautiful. Indeed I can
scarcely say we have had any spring but a little mingling of the fag
end of winter and the beginning of Summer. In consequence, however,
of vegetation being so much retarded, it burst forth all at once, and
the country was suddenly in all its freshness and bloom and fragrance.
I never have seen it look more beautiful—and I think ⟨about⟩ the little
domains about the cottage have been more beautiful than ever—The
trees and shrubs and clambering vines that have been transplanted
within the last year or two, have now taken ↑good↓ root and begin to
grow luxuriantly. If vegetation goes on at this rate we shall before long
be buried among roses and honeysuckles and ivy and sweet briar. All the
groves too about the place are magnificent this year. Most of the
↑forest↓ trees you know, ⟨th⟩ are ⟨still within⟩ young, and scarce any
past their prime; so that every year ⟨they⟩ the groves grow more dense
and stately. The new walks are very popular ⟨and⟩ especially that to
the fallen Chest-nut tree, which is one of the most shady cool and delightful resorts ⟨for⟩ ↑of↓ a warm sunny day that you can imagine. I
never was more conscious of the sweetness of the country than this
season.

I have nearly completed my bulwark along the foot of the bank. It
will not merely be a complete protection against the encroachments
of the river, but ⟨it will be⟩ ↑also↓ a great improvement to the place—
I shall have the whole bank finished off and in some places sloped
down to the wall, with footpaths leading down to it, and seats under
the trees. The shore of the river too is cleared of all the rocks and
stones that encumbered it and the whole aspect of the place along the
river is changed.

⟨[unrecovered]⟩ You will no doubt hear from others of the family,
of the gay times that "Kate and I" have been leading; dining out two
days successively in the neighborhood, to meet Mr Edward Jones and
his bride; who were passing a few days with Mr George Jones. Our
first dinner was at the widows, our second at the widowers, and both
very pleasant. Mrs Mary Jones and her family were present on the first
occasion, and ⟨Mr McKen⟩ Mr. & Mrs McKenzie[8] on the last. Miss
Elizabeth Jones ⟨was also present⟩ ↑at both↓. I am much pleased with
Mrs Edward Jones—both with her appearance and manners. She looks
very much like her sister Mrs McKenzie; I wish the latter resembled
her in fortune—Still if Mrs McKenzie were rich I should not feel half
the interest in her that I do. I love her for the heart and soul with

which she devotes herself to her husband and his scanty lot. I was contrasting the fortunes of the two sisters the other morning to Mary
Hamilton,[9] ⟨and expressing⟩ as if rather pitying the hardness of that
of Mrs McKenzie, "Pity her!" cried little Mary with sudden warmth—
"I'd rather a hundred times have her choice than _____" here she
reccollected and checked herself, but I have felt still more kindly
toward little Mary since that sudden and generous outbreak.

Mrs. Constant was at the cottage a few days since looking most
sweetly. She is in better spirits and evidently in better health, and I
trust will be greatly benefited by her intended visit to Rockaway.
I am thinking of taking little Mary to ⟨the⟩ Rockaway during Mrs
Constants visit there, and giving her the benefit of the sea air and sea
bathing. Her health continues precarious and her constitution needs
building up.

Irving Van Wart with his little wife and brace of chaffing boys are
at Eliza Romeyns, to pass some time there. Oscars wife[10] is at Mrs.
Fields where Ogden[11] likewise boards, so that there is quite a family
colony at Tarrytown. The Berrians are also boarding at Mrs Fields and
I believe will pass the summer there. Catharine (Oscars wife) has been
to Washington for her health and has returned much benefited by
her excursion; still there is solicitude felt concerning her.

Your Mother ⟨passed⟩ made a long visit to town lately and enjoyed
her visit greatly. The receipt of the first letter from you, written while
on board ship, contributed to make her visit pleasant as it lightened
her heart of much lurking uneasiness; for, though she had great confidence in the excellence of your ship and captain, yet the fearful mystery
that hung over the fate of the Steam Ship President,[12] had an irresistable
effect to inspire vague apprehension. Julia & Mary remained with her
until her return, and ⟨wh⟩ were extremely attentive to her. They all
returned with great delight to the cottage; ⟨which⟩ indeed I do not
know when I have known your mother to express more vividly her
feeling of enjoyment in finding herself once more surrounded by the
freshness and sweetness of the country. Every thing had come out
into full beauty & luxuriance during her absence. The locust trees were
in blossom, the Honeysuckles loaded with flowers; the sweet briar and
roses just beginning to bloom, and the boblinks were singing among
the appletrees and clover blossoms. Your Mother has been in cheerful
spirits ever since her return and your late delightful letters have made
her quite happy. My dear Sarah, if you could have heard all that was
said about your charming, natural, kind hearted letters you would no
longer doubt your talent at letter writing. Your letters breathe your
own spirit—and that is just what those who love you want. When you
write to me scribble away whatever comes into your head without

caring how you express it, or how your letter may be scrawled and blotted: only write copiously and tell me about all your amusements, occupations acquaintances &c &c.

Your brother Irving came up to the cottage with your Mother and the girls, and has been passing three or four days here. The day before yesterday he & Washy[13] set off for Yonkers in the boat, to take the Miss Blackwells[14] across to the Pallisades. They had a small pic nic on the top of the Pallisades and after enjoying themselves greatly, set off on their return. They were overtaken by a tremendous squall—drenched to the skin and reached Yonkers ⟨looking like drowned rats They⟩ with some difficulty. They [r]eturned [*MS blotted*] to Mr Wells's[15] old mansion looking like drowned rats but were soon rigged off in suits of the old gentlemans clothes; ↑and old fashioned ruffled shirts.↓ ⟨When they⟩ They reached home late in the evening, in more uncouth equipment than Mr Dakin on our famous ⟨ruin in the⟩ ride in the thunder storm. Washy especially ⟨was⟩ nearly suffered a total eclipse by his nether garment, his chin just peering above the waistband.

You ask in one of your letters after little Vaney.[16] I am almost affraid to tell you that the poor little fellow has come within an ace of suffering an untimely death. For some days he was strangely out of order and I feared [he] [*MS torn*] was going mad. I had him shut up repeatedly; but he would get out & [go] [*MS torn*] about howling in the most doleful manner. At length I felt compelled to order that he should be drowned, when just as the sentence was about to be executed old Mr Mann[17] who happened to come by informed us that the poor animal had been wantonly shot by a vagabond of the neighborhood. It was a most fortunate reprieve; for had I learnt the fact too late I should never have forgiven myself. I have taken the poor little animal into ten times more favor than ever—I always reccollect that he was your favorite—and I think of you whenever he comes bounding towards me, and reproach myself for having thought of sacraficing him. He is now perfectly recovered, and full of life and spirits.

I must bring this letter abruptly to a conclusion though I have ⟨[*unrecovered*]⟩ still much to say, but breakfast time approaches, after which the letter must be dispatched to town—Give my kindest remembrances to Mr Storrow and believe me my dear Sarah ever most affectionately your uncle

Washington Irving

MANUSCRIPT: Yale.

1. Sarah Storrow's letters to WI and other members of her family have not been located.

2. The *Great Western* arrived from Bristol on June 10. See NYEP, June 11, 1841.

3. Chapstow Castle, a ruin on the west bank of the Wye River in Monmouthshire, dates from the thirteenth and fourteenth centuries. Tintern Abbey, also a ruin farther up the Wye valley, was founded in 1131 by the Cistercian monks.

4. Warwick Castle, built on the site of fortifications of the tenth century against the Danes, was started by Thomas Beauchamp, earl of Warwick, in 1330, with additions to the walls and interior made in the fifteenth and seventeenth centuries. It is located on the River Avon about 21 miles southeast of Birmingham.

5. Stratford-on-Avon was the site of Shakespeare's birth in 1564.

6. Blenheim Palace, near Woodstock, northwest of Oxford, was built by the English Parliament for the first duke of Marlborough to express the nation's gratitude for his victory over the French and Bavarians at Blenheim on the left bank of the Danube in Bavaria on August 13, 1704.

7. WI and James Renwick (1792–1863) toured Wales from July 31 to August 14, 1815, shortly after WI arrived in England. They visited the ruins of Chapstow Castle on August 5 at sunset and went on to Tintern Abbey the next day. See *Journals of WI*, I, 7–8.

8. Mr. and Mrs. Alexander Slidell Mackenzie. See WI to Sarah Storrow, May 3, 1841.

9. Probably the daughter of James A. Hamilton, one of WI's neighbors. See WI to James A. Hamilton, June 8, 1838.

10. Catharine E. C. Dayton (1800–1842), wife of Oscar Irving, WI's nephew.

11. Henry Ogden Irving (1807–1869), son of William and Julia Paulding Irving.

12. The steamboat *President* sailed for England on March 21, 1841, and was never heard of afterward. See Charles H. Haswell, *Reminiscences of an Octogenarian of the City of New York* (New York, 1896), p. 274.

13. Probably Washington Irving (1835–1910), a son of Edgar and Amanda Tenant Irving.

14. Probably girls of the same Blackwell family mentioned in WI's letter of February 4, 1840.

15. Probably Lemuel Wells (1760–1842), a New York merchant who lived in Yonkers on an estate along the Hudson across from the Palisades. See J. T. Scharf, *History of Westchester County*, II, 18.

16. One of the dogs at Sunnyside. See Harold Dean Cater, "Washington Irving and Sunnyside," *New York History*, 38 (April, 1957), 154.

17. Possibly John Mann, a resident in the Sunnyside area. See J. T. Scharf, *History of Westchester County*, II, 240.

1346.   To William W. Waldron

Sunnyside, June 14th, 1841

My Dear Sir:

You have my cheerful permission to put my name on your list of subscribers for a copy of your forthcoming work,[1] but I fear the retired life I lead in the country will afford me little opportunity of making interest in its favor. Are you aware that Mrs. Sigourney,[2] an American lady of poetic celebrity, is about to publish a poem of the same subject that you have chosen?

Very respectfully, your obedient servant,

Washington Irving

William W. Waldron, Esq.

PUBLISHED: William H. Waldron, *Washington Irving and His Cotemporaries* (New York, 1867), p. 246.

1. *Pocahontas, Princess of Virginia; and Other Poems,* published in New York by Dean and Trevett in 1841.
2. Lydia Huntley Sigourney (1791–1865), the "Sweet Singer of Hartford," was a widely read writer of sentimental verses. WI refers to her *Pocahontas, and Other Poems,* published by Harper and Brothers later in 1841.

1347.   To Sarah Storrow

Sunnyside, June 21. 1841

My dear Sarah,

We have again been rejoiced by the arrival of letters from you to your father, and Irving,[1] which, of course, were transmitted forthwith to the Cottage and read by us all with the greatest avidity. If you only could witness the delight given by these letters you would no longer hesitate to scrawl down any thing in any way; and would not think it necessary to make apologies. All I regret is that you have had to hurry through such a succession of the most interesting scenes and places without having time to see and enjoy them properly or to receive suitable impressions However, this was not to be helped; and it was well to secure a sight of them at any rate. I do not wonder that your mind became fatigued and that you longed for a little repose. You revert to your impressions of Gloucester Cathedral.[2] Did you visit the Crypt of that Cathedral. Almost all these cathedrals have Crypts, or ⟨imp⟩ immense vaults under them, almost equal in extent to the super incumbent edifice. They were often used as places of Sepulture. That of Glocester Cathedral was uncommonly fine; consisting of low vaults supported by massive Saxon columns and arches. In one of its gloomy recesses a place is pointed out ↑in the wall↓ where, during a time of persecution, two bishops were chained, immured and starved to death.[3]

Your letters set me to rummaging my old travelling notes and memorandums and I am enabled occasionally to edify the household at the

Cottage by illustrations of your brief sketches. Thus I have illustrated to them the Spectral tomb in the vaulted passages of Westminster Abbey,[4] which startled and discomfited you on your moonlight visit. It is a mural monument of one of the Pultneys:[5] a figure in white marble reclining at full length on a sarcophagus. It is ⟨against⟩ ↑erected against the wall at↓ the end of the Cloisters immediately facing the vaulted ⟨court⟩ passages opening from what is called the Deans Yard. A strong gas light suspended from the vault of the Cloisters falls immediately on the figure and gives it a striking effect, as seen from the vaulted passages.[6] I have passed that figure many a time at night on my way to and from the residence of a bachelor friend, Mr Bandinel[7] of the foreign office, who had a most quaint residence deep in the old conventual part of the Edifice; which he had fitted up with all kinds of antique and outlandish furniture, reliques &c and used to give most hospitable and intellectual entertainments. Before I knew him, however, the cloisters of Westminster abbey used to be one of my favorite haunts at all times of day and night. The view of the abbey by moonlight, looking up at it from under the arcades of the cloisters is wonderfully fine. On the pavement of the cloisters close by the tomb which startled you, are the monumental stones of three of the old abbots—Vitelis, 1082 and Gislebertus 1114 and Laurentius 1176.[8] Their ⟨figures⟩ ↑effigies↓ and the inscriptions are ⟨now⟩ nearly trodden out by the footsteps of centuries. I subjoin a copy of a slight sketch[9] which I once made of the Spectre tomb from the vaulted passages—by which you will see that it struck me as forcibly as it did you; though from being ↑more↓ accustomed to tombs and vaulted passages and all kinds of Spectral apparitions I was not as much frightened. I shall look forward to some further accounts of your impressions concerning the abbey in your future letters; as you have merely given us your first visit by moonlight, when you penetrated no further than the Cloisters.

Your letters have had a most cheering and animating effect upon your mother. You have no doubt heard from other correspondents how gay she has become lately; paying visits about the neighborhood to Mrs Sheldon, Mrs Constant & Mrs Colford Jones. She was very much delighted with Mr Sheldons cottage and the superb view which it commands: the new piazza has been a beautiful addition to the building and will make it a delightful summer residence. The same ⟨day⟩ ↑morning↓ that she visited Mrs Sheldon we drove down, on our way home, to Philip Pauldings new mansion with which your mother was also greatly pleased. They are now busy putting up the piazza, which will be a noble one. The building when complete will be both picturesque and convenient.

I am projecting an expedition, in the course of the season, to the

Priory[10] with your mother. We will take two days for it: putting up for the night at the Hotel at New Rochelle. I think it is an expedition which she will enjoy greatly.

June 22. Yesterday ⟨I⟩ afternoon I drove with Kate and Sarah & William to Stephen Archers[11] to visit two Mrs Ogdens who are quartered there for the summer. They are sisters, ⟨one of them⟩ once Miss Hunters. You must reccollect one of them the beautiful Ruth Hunter. She is still handsome, and has a fine style of countenance, marked and expressive, with superb dark eyes. Kate says she put her in mind of Fanny Kemble when on the stage and there is some resemblance in the character of her countenance. We mad[e][12] a most agreeable visit, and I hope to see a good deal of them this summer. Ruths husband has been unfortunate in business since their marriage. Her father too, Mr Schuyler, formerly of Saratoga, has fallen into embarrassments of late years. I reccollect dining with him at Saratoga the year after my return from Europe, when he lived elegantly and hospitably, surrounded by a young and lovely family. The misfortunes of her family have doubtless had an effect upon the spirits and the character of the beautiful Ruth, but the effect has been beneficial. I thought her a bright beautiful young creature several years since when I sat beside her at her fathers table; but I was infinitely more interested with her when I saw her at Stephen Archers with a shade of thoughtfulness and melancholy thrown across her fine countenance. All fine natures are improved by affliction. What corrodes base metal purifies true gold; ⟨I do not think⟩ and the choicest fruits of the finest flavor ⟨are not refined that⟩ ↑are those that have experienced↓ the occasional shade and shower.— And so much for that visit. From the "Pilgrims Rest"[13] we drove to the Howlands[14] where however we found none of the family home but Miss Howland. Mr H has been sadly afflicted of late with the inflammatory rheumatism which for a time rendered him perfectly helpless, so that he had even to be fed by others, like a child. He is now nearly well, but still has not recovered the free use of his arms. We concluded our afternoon by a lovely drive along the Valley of the Neperan,[15] which was in its perfection: the foliage of the trees being fully developed, and every leaf in its tender freshness. Indeed I have never seen the country in general more beautiful than it has been this season, since it has struggled through the protracted chills and storms of winter. Still, the season is very precarious, and we have but fitful gleams of summer and summer heat, and as yet have ⟨only⟩ had a very few evenings in which we could enjoy the piazza. By the way, I am glad to see that after leaving Birmingham you had again fine weather, and was enabled to see Warwick Castle, Kenilworth, Stratford on Avon, Oxford, &c &c to advantage. I want to know whether you saw the

interior of Windsor Castle.[16] I am affraid you left London without getting
a sight of Queen Victoria.[17] I have a thousand questions to ask you,
but fear to task your pen and your patience. I would give you one
general rule for your correspondence with the family. Do not attempt
to write to several persons by the same opportunity. Write at one time
to your father at another time to your mother, so to your brother, to
Kate & to myself. One letter at a time will serve for us all, and will
be considered as intended for us all; you can then make it full and
minute without fatigue to yourself. I ⟨speak⟩ mean this for your direction when you are pressed for time, in travelling, or in the hurry of
occupations and engagements. When you have perfect liesure and are in
the mood, we shall all be glad to hear from you severally; only let
me beg you most earnestly not to distrust your talent at letter writing,
and not to neglect it through diffidence or distaste. Reccollect, my
dear Sarah, it is all the communion and intercourse we can now have
with each other; and these few and fitful scrawlings of the pen, which
at most afford but a few moments perusal, are to stand in the place of
the daily and hourly interchange of kind words kind looks, kind actions,
and the thousand endearments that bind heart and heart together in
the happy communion of domestic life. Sum up all that the most active
correspondence amounts to, and what a small portion of existence does
it occupy, and what a still more scanty amount of ⟨our substance⟩ our
being and doing, our thinking and feeling does it communicate. Yet
this feeble tie is all that keeps kindred hearts from falling asunder and
growing strange to each other. Let us all cherish and cultivate it therefore, while it is our lot to live apart.

June 24. A glorious bright morning. Your mother has made a sudden
move and has gone off in the carriage with three of her maids of honor,
on a visit to Eliza.[18] It is her intention ⟨of⟩ to pass a few days there;
not that she needs the change on account of low spirits, for she is perfectly cheerful; but she had promised Eliza a visit and she wishes
to make it and be back to the Cottage before the 4th of July; as Jock
is to come up here and help celebrate it. Sarah Van Wart and her
fine brace of little urchins are still at Elizas and likely to remain some
time there for they all appear very happy together. Catharine (Oscars
wife) is at Mrs Fields under the hill, so your mother will have plenty
of company, and I have no doubt will enjoy her visit. I have nothing to
tell you of domestic news, excepting that my bulwark is nearly completed, and my bank secured—that we take delightful drives in the
afternoons; and long strolls about our walks, which are now quite
extensive; and that in these drives and ⟨walks⟩ strolls you my dear,
dear Sarah are ever present to our thoughts and the theme of our
conversation

June 26. Yesterday Kate, Sarah and myself dined with the Constants. Your mother likewise was invited, but being at Elizas we did not think proper to send her the invitation. Mrs Colford Jones and her two daughters & Mr George Jones were there. We had a most pleasant dinner and a delightful evening. Mrs Constant is still ⟨so?⟩ rather thin and pale, but looked like herself again and was in excellent spirits. She is still weak, but has recovered her cheerfulness Mr Constant says she ⟨has⟩ is better than she has been at any time for two years past. She sang for us repeatedly, as did also Mrs C Jones: who, I apprehend has been under the tuition of Mr Bagioli[19] of late, for she is exceedingly improved in the style of her singing—however, I may be prejudiced you know.

I presume by the time this reaches you, you will have seen a good deal of Paris. Some of the finest points of view are from the bridges. When I was first in Paris the Pont des arts[20] was a favorite promenade; being shut up at each end by toll gates. Since it has been thrown open to the public it has ceased to be frequented for mere recreation: but it commands fine views up and down the Seine. The Garden of the Tuilleries will of course be a frequent resort for a promenade. I used to like the retired parts, not much frequented by the company: where I could stroll or lounge with a book in my hand. There is one place, just under a high terrace, much frequented by nursery maids with their young folks and by old Frenchmen who seek sunshine in cool weather. I used often to amuse myself with the pretty and the quaint groupes that used to assemble there, in the mornings in Spring and Autumn—and in fine days in winter

28. I have written my letter by scraps. ⟨and⟩ It is now Monday morning. Your brother came up on Saturday and we have had a happy housefull. Yesterday all were at church at Tarrytown. In the evening Phil Paulding & Ogden were here and there was great strolling about the paths, by a kind of dubious mixed twilight and moonlight—My new paths are quite popular and beguile the girls into extensive promenades. With kind remembrances to Mr Storrow

Your afft. uncle W.I.

Addressed: A Madame / Madame Storrow / aux soins de M. T. W Storrow / Rue du Faubg Poissonniere / à Paris / per Columbia   Postmarked: NEW-YORK / JUN / 29 // J / 15 JL 15 / 1841 // ANGE CALAIS / 17 / JUIL / 41 // Packet Letter // AMERICA / L   Docketed: June 21st 1841 / No 6 Manuscript: Yale.

1. These letters have not been located.
2. The earliest building on the site was a nunnery established in 681 and destroyed in 727. It was used by the Benedictine monks in 1022, and a church was built in 1058. Following the Norman Conquest a new church was erected and con-

secrated in 1100. See Marianne Schuyler Van Rensellaer, *English Cathedrals* (New York, 1910), p. 300. WI and Renwick visited it on August 2, 1815. See *Journals of WI*, I, 5.

3. WI drew the details of this sentence from his journal entry of August 2, 1815. See *Journals of WI*, I, 5.

4. See "Westminster Abbey" in *The Sketch Book* for many of the same details.

5. This is Daniel Pultney (d. 1731), M.P. for Preston and lord of the admiralty. It is called by Arthur Penrhyn Stanley "the most conspicuous monument in the Cloisters." See *Memorials of Westminster Abbey*, 3 vols. (New York, 1889), II, 84.

6. A passage added in an "Appendix. Notes Concerning Westminster Abbey" to posthumous editions of *The Sketch Book* echoes some of the phrases of the two preceding sentences: "On entering the cloisters at night from what is called the Dean's Yard, the eye ranging through a dark vaulted passage catches a distant view of a white marble figure reclining on a tomb, on which a strong glare thrown by a gas light has quite a spectral effect. It is a mural monument of one of the Pultneys."

7. James Bandinel (1783–1849), a clerk in the British Foreign Office whom WI knew when he was secretary of the U.S. legation. See WI to James Bandinel, May 28, 1830.

8. WI had described the inscriptions for these three early abbots in the fourth paragraph of "Westminster Abbey" in *The Sketch Book*.

9. WI's sketch, about one fourth the length and one third the width of the sheet, is on the left side of the page starting after the sixth full line and causing the next sixteen lines to be indented around the sketch.

10. Probably Bolton Priory in Pelham Manor, New York.

11. Steven Archer (1803–1877) was a physician of Tarrytown. See J. T. Scharf, *History of Westchester County*, I, 576.

12. WI omitted the *e*.

13. Apparently the name of Steven Archer's residence.

14. Probably Gardiner Greene or Samuel Shaw Howland, New York merchants mentioned by WI in his letter to Aaron Vail, May 11, 1841. Apparently one of them had a residence in the vicinity of Tarrytown.

15. Another name for the Saw-Mill River, which flows through Greenburgh and Yonkers. See J. T. Scharf, *History of Westchester County*, I, 6.

16. Located west of London, Windsor Castle was the main residence of British monarchs since William the Conqueror.

17. Victoria (1819–1901) was the queen of England from 1837 to 1901.

18. Eliza Dodge Romeyn, WI's niece.

19. Antonio Bagioli directed the performance of the opera *Cenerentola* at the Richmond Hill Theater on October 6, 1832, and gave private singing lessons in New York City. See Ireland, *NY Stage*, II, 61.

20. An iron footbridge built in 1802 to 1804 between the Louvre and the Institute. See Karl Baedeker, *Paris and Its Environs* (Leipzig, 1900), p. 245.

1348. (*deleted*)

1349.   To Daniel Webster

Sunnyside Cottage (Tarry town) July 3d./41

My dear Sir,

I am informed that Mr James Baker, at present resident in Norfolk, Virginia, is an applicant for some situation in the gift of any one of the departments. Should his name come as an applicant before you, I would reccommend him as a person I believe to be highly trustworthy. He is a native of the city of New York, a son of Gardiner Baker[1] of yore, who first established a museum in the city. When he was quite young, in 1812, I was instrumental in procuring him a Commission of 2d Lieutenant of Artillery in the United States Army. He served throughout the war with ability, and was the Commandants adjutant of all the artillery at the Norfolk station during the most critical period. He has since been resident at Norfolk, and has uniformly ⟨born⟩ sustained the most excellent and popular character; as I learn from numerous vouchers from the most respectable persons: the originals of which have been forwarded to Washington, and are to be seen in the office of the Secretary of War.

Feeling thus authorised to speak in his favor, and having a strong inclination to do so, from reccollections and associations of former times, I take the liberty, my dear Sir, of begging your kind consideration of any claim he may lay before you.

With the highest respect and regard / Yours ever very faithfully
Washington Irving

Hon. Daniel Webster / &c &c &c

ADDRESSED: The Hon Daniel Webster / Secretary of State / Washington POST-
    MARKED: TARRYTOWN N. Y. / JUL / 6   DOCKETED: Office Indefinite /
    Baker J. / recommended / by Washington / Irving. / 1841
MANUSCRIPT: Brandeis University.

1. Gardiner Baker was keeper of the American Museum, started in 1791 to collect material relating to the history of the United States and housed in the rooms of the Tammany Society. Subsequently Baker took over the ownership of the museum, sold it to John Scudder, who later offered it to P. T. Barnum. Details about Baker's military service have not been located. See J. G. Wilson, *Memorial History of the City of New-York*, III, 76–78; and William T. Bonner, *New York, The World's Metropolis*, p. 201.

1350.   To Lewis G. Clark

Sunnyside Cottage, July 8, 1841.

My dear Sir:

I have not sooner replied to your letter of the eighteenth of June,[1] communicating the intelligence of the untimely death of your twin-brother,[2] because, in fact, I was at a loss how to reply. It is one of those cases in which all ordinary attempts at consolation are apt to appear trite and cold, and can never reach the deep-seated affliction. In such cases, it always appears to me better to leave the heart to struggle with its own sorrows and medicine its own ills: and indeed, in healthful minds, as in healthful bodies, Providence has beneficently implanted self-healing qualities, that in time close up, and almost obliterate, the deepest wounds.

I do not recollect to have met your departed twin-brother more than once; but our interview left a most favorable impression upon me, which was confirmed and strengthened by all that I afterward knew of him. His career, although brief, has been useful, honorable, popular, and happy; and he has left behind him writings which will make men love his memory, and lament his loss. Under such circumstances a man has not lived in vain: and although his death be premature, there is consolation to his survivors, springing from his very grave.

Believe me, my dear Sir, yours very truly,
Washington Irving

PUBLISHED: *Knickerbocker Magazine*, 55 (January, 1860), 114.

1. This letter has not been located.
2. Willis Gaylord Clark (b. October 5, 1808), who had died of tuberculosis on June 12, 1841, had assisted his brother in editing the *Knickerbocker Magazine*. He had published a book of verses, *The Spirit of Life*, in 1833.

1351.   To Sarah Storrow

Hellgate, July 11th. 1841

My dear Sarah,

Your letters to your Mother and to Kate,[1] dated from Meurices Hotel, Paris, were received a few days since. I am looking now for the intermediate letters which must be coming by ↑a sailing↓ Packet, one of which, you say, is to me; and which must give us some account of your travels from London to Paris, and your arrival at the latter city.

I want to know every step of your progress and of your "whereabout."
Some casual expressions in your last letters have pained me to the quick.
You speak of yourself as being pale and thin—of shedding tears—of
feeling at times lonely and homesick. These expressions haunt my mind;
they have formed themselves into pictures, and are continually presenting themselves before me. I have always been accustomed to see you
so bright and joyous; always receiving and communicating happiness—
that it distresses me to think of you otherwise—But you will soon be so
again. I am sure you will. I know your buoyant nature; your quick
susceptibility to every thing that is good and beautiful and pleasant.
You are surrounded by all kinds of objects to delight a cheerful spirit
and exercise an intelligent mind. You will soon get over the strange-
ness of your situation and of the scenes and persons about you. You will
gradually form new habitudes, and with them new sources of intellectual gratifaction; and will cease to think with painful longing of
your former home, as you take more and more interest in the home that
will be ⟨springing⟩ forming itself around you.

Kate wrote to you by the last packet,[2] and gave you a chronicle of the
events at the cottage, which, as usual, have nothing in them very
striking. The fourth or rather 5th. of July was celebrated at Mrs Colford
Jones by fire works, a supper &c at which most of the neighborhood
were present, with some few guests from town. The fireworks went off
better than last year, but the fête generally, not as well. We missed you
and Mrs Constant, and I think your absence had a dampening effect
with many. It certainly had with me. I never feel your absence more
my dear Sarah, than when I mingle in these little gatherings of the
neighborhood, to which you always accompanied me. I feel now how
much of my pleasure was reflected from your own happy looks, and from
the animated part you took in the Social Scene. Mrs Sheldon was among
the guests at Mrs Jones; She is gradually getting better of her lameness—but very slowly. I had not much to say to her, nor indeed to any
one else on that occasion, for I was not in a talkative mood. I do not
find any disposition in the neighborhood to get up musical meetings
this season; nor is there any talk of pic nics. I have not stirred in the
matter myself; for I have not felt much inclination. I have satisfied
myself with rural occupations about my place; and with occasional
long drives about the country; for which the occasional cool delightful
days which we have had this summer have been very favorable. All
I want in these drives is a bright communicative companion, that will
respond to my feelings and remarks— and this unluckily is ⟨[unrecovered]⟩
a perpetually recurring want that makes me feel your loss.

I suppose Kate has informed you that we are to lose the Perrys from
our neighborhood. Capt Perry has been ordered to take command at the

⟨[*unrecovered*]⟩ Navy yard at Brooklyn;[3] where a house is provided for him. This will fix him for three or four years, after which he will probably be ordered to sea. Finding there was no likelihood of his being able for several years, to reside at the rural establishment he had just set up; he has offered it either for sale or to rent for a term of years. We all regret this circumstance extremely for we were highly pleased with the Perrys and hoped to be very intimate with them.

Among the 4th of July guests at Mrs Colford Jones was my friend West the painter.[4] He passed three or four days there, and was frequently at the Cottage. He intends making Mrs Jones another visit soon after which I expect to make an excursion with him to the Highlands. I received a letter not long since from Gouverneur Kemble urging me to make him a visit. He has resumed his station as president of the company,[5] and keeps up his old establishment. His sister Mary[6] has been rather out of health ever since the death of poor Mrs Paulding.[7] I fear I shall find a visit there very melancholy. There are too many associations with that place, that will now be extremely painful to me. I rather think I shall stay there but for a day or so, and make the most of my Highland visit at Brevoorts; who has taken the old Beverly House;[8] (a mile or two below Mr S. Governeurs)[9] which formerly belonged to the family of the Robinsons,[10] and is associated with the history of the Arnold treason. It is a fine old country seat, with venerable trees, and commands a noble prospect. Mr Brevoort has urged West and myself to pass some days with him.

I am just now on a brief visit to Mr Astor; I came here yesterday (Saturday[)] and think I shall return home tomorrow. I presume you have heard of the trouble in Mr A's family: arising from a clandestine marriage of his grand daughter, Miss Louisa Langdon, with young Kane.[11] Mrs Langdon had set her face against this match and had thought she had prevented it, she was therefore excessively indignant at being deceived, and departed for Europe without seeing her daughter, or becoming in any degree reconciled to her. She even went so far as to prevail upon Mr Astor to disinherit her. I presume, however, that this affair will end in the ⟨so⟩ usual way—by a forgiveness of the parties, after many unkind things have been said and done that will be hard to be forgotten. What constant troubles and heartburnings, and dissentions are occurring in these rich families—let us congratulate ourselves, my dear girl, that the curse of wealth has never fallen, nor is likely to fall, on our numerous connexion.

I presume before this you have received the volume containing Miss Davidsons memoir and poetical remains, as I directed one to be forwarded to you. It has met with great success; which I do not attribute to any merit of mine; but to the extreme interest and pathos of the materials placed in my hands. I remitted to the mother the note of hand given by the booksellers for the edition, and transferred to her the copy right, reserving merely [the] [*MS torn*] right to publish at any time, the memoir, in connexion with my [own] [*MS torn*] writings. I am occasionally exercising my pen in rearranging & modifying old articles, some of which have ↑already↓ appeared in periodical publications. I do this more to get myself into a literary vein, and in hopes that I may, after a time, strike into something new. Oh! if I could only have a "run of luck" as gamblers say— it would quite set me up again; but I am so pestered with petty cares and concerns, ⟨and⟩ most of them about the affairs of others, and am so taken up and interrupted by all kinds of interruptions and engagements, that I am like a poor fly in a cobweb that can neither move leg nor wing and can do nothing but buz.

July 13. I did not return home yesterday; but accompanied Mr Astor in an excursion on the water. We embarked at Hellgate Ferry on board of a Sloop hired for the purpose and intended to make a cruise to the Hook; but light baffling winds and calms prevented our getting farther than Corlears Hook and the navy yard. Still it was a pleasant and an interesting excursion to me. The day was splendid, and quite cool and temperate. We coasted along those beautiful shores which you have occasionally coasted with me in sail boats and as I saw the old Jones country seat peering through the trees, with its half ruined out houses and weedy garden, I recalled our stroll about its haunted grounds. So you see, my dear Sarah; go where I may, you are associated in my mind with every scene.

I am glad to find you were about to undertake the study of the French language in good earnest. It will be an occupation for your lonely hours, and will enable you to enjoy every thing around you. Indeed, you have abundant occupation for every spare moment, if you prepare yourself properly for mingling to advantage in European society and ⟨for⟩ enjoying and profiting by European scenes. not the mere study of languages, but a great range and variety of reading is necessary to prepare the mind for the objects ⟨continually⟩ and themes continually ⟨[*unrecovered*]⟩ presenting themselves: and the studies thus prompted and stimulated by the necessity ⟨of⟩ or impulse of the moment, are always delightful. You have now to revive all your historical and literary associations, and to acquire new ones. You are to read treatises in the arts, that you may be able to appreciate the master pieces in every department which will now be before you. Paris is a vast wilderness of Knowledge and of Elegant enjoyment; but intellectual guides are necessary to ↑to enable one to↓ thread its mazes. My dear Sarah your present position ⟨properly⟩ abounds with opportunities for self cultivation and improvement which, ⟨if⟩ even though you avail yourself of them in but a moderate degree, cannot fail to have the most advantageous effect upon you. Do not be careless about your intellectual powers as if not worth cultivating. *Believe in yourself*, you have mental qualities that have never had their due exercise and development; and now that you are thrown more upon your own resources I make no doubt they will be more and more unfolded to you and you will become sensible how much they may be heightened and extended by proper cultivation, and how independent they may make you of others for your enjoyments. You have hitherto been constantly surrounded by young companions, whose mere chat whiled away the time and prevented the exercise of much thought or reflection. You will now be for a time at least, a good deal alone. This at first will be irksome, but *it is good to be alone*   It is necessary for the full development of mind, and the acquisition of habits of meditation and reflection, and, after a while, we come to understand and feel the delights of occasional solitude

And now I must bring this somewhat prosy letter to a close as I am about to descend to breakfast, after which I shall set off for town and shall have no liesure to add any thing further. Give my kindest remembrances to Mr Storrow and tell him I will answer his letter by the next opportunity. It gives us all great consolation, in being separated from you my dear Sarah, to think you have so tender attentive and excellent a protector.

Your afft uncle
Washington Irving

ADDRESSED: a Madame / Madame Storrow / Aux Soins de Mr T. W Storrow / Rue du Faubg. Poissonniere / à Paris. / per Francois Ier   POSTMARKED: OUTRE-MER DE HAVRE / 12 / Aout / 41 // PARIS [*unrecovered*] / 13 / AOUT / 41   DOCKETED: July 11th 1841 / No 7
MANUSCRIPT: Yale.

1. These letters have not been located.
2. This letter has not been located.
3. Matthew C. Perry served as commander of the Brooklyn Navy Yard from the summer of 1841 to mid-April of 1843. See Samuel Eliot Morison, *"Old Bruin": Commodore Matthew C. Perry, 1794–1858* (Boston, 1967), pp. 124, 163.
4. William Edward West (1788–1857), whom WI had known in Paris in 1824 and in London in 1829, painted portraits of Byron and other well-known Englishmen. He lived in New York from 1840 to 1850. See *J&N*, III, 436.
5. Kemble returned to the West Point Foundry after serving in Congress from 1839 to 1841.
6. Mary Kemble (b. 1799) had married Robert Parker Parrott, an engineer at the West Point Foundry, in 1839.

7. Gertrude Kemble (b. 1791), wife of James Kirke Paulding, had died on May 25, 1841, after a lingering illness. See *Letters of J. K. Paulding*, p. 307.

8. The Beverley house, which was occupied by WI's old friend Henry Brevoort in 1841, was located in the Highlands of the Hudson about five miles from Gouverneur Kemble's residence at Cold Spring and about one and one-half miles south of West Point on the east bank of the Hudson. It was built in 1758 on land which Mrs. Robinson inherited from the Philipse estate in the Philipstown area at the foot of Sugar Loaf Mountain. WI described it in a letter to Sarah Storrow on July 31, 1841, as "the house at which Arnold received the letter from André, apprising him that his treason was discovered, and from which he made his hair breadth escape." See PMI, III, 168; Wallace Bruce, *The Hudson, Three Centuries of History, Romance, and Invention* (New York, 1907), p. 87, and map between pp. 120 and 121; and H. D. Eberlein and C. V. D. Hubbard, *Historic Houses of the Hudson Valley* (New York, 1942), p. 34.

9. Samuel Gouverneur (1799–1867), who in 1820 had married Maria Monroe, the daughter of President James Monroe, was postmaster of New York City for nine years. See Martha J. Lamb, *History of the City of New-York*, II, 687.

10. Beverley Robinson (1722–1816), a Loyalist who refused to take the oath of allegiance to the state of New York in 1777, had his property confiscated. Beverley, his former home, was then used by Benedict Arnold, the commandant of West Point, who fled from it when he learned of Major André's capture. See Eberlein and Hubbard, *Historic Houses of the Hudson Valley*, pp. 34, 36.

11. Louisa Dorothea Langdon (b. 1820) had eloped with Oliver DeLancey Kane, much to the distress of her parents. Ironically, Dorothea Astor (1795–1853) and Walter Langdon (d. 1847), the parents, had also been married during an elopement in 1812. See Porter, *Astor*, II, 1040; Lucy Kavaler, *The Astors, A Family Chronicle of Pomp and Power* (New York, 1966), p. 56; and Harvey O'Connor, *The Astors* (New York, 1941), pp. 76–77; genealogical table on pp. 463–65.

1352. To Sarah Storrow

Sunnyside Cottage Sunday July 18th. 1841

My dear Sarah,

We have this day recieved your letters by the Havre Packet,[1] giving an account of your arrival at Havre & your journey to Paris. We had been looking for them for some days quite impatiently, having already received those written several days after. I thank you, my dear girl, for your most affectionate letter from Havre, and for the account you give of my worthy, my excellent friend Beasley.[2] I feel towards him like a brother; and it does my heart good to find that you met him with such cordial warmth. But I was sure you would. It seems to me as if I can always *feel* how you would act on any particular occasion; I know you so well, and we feel so much alike in most matters.—though I am flattering myself grossly in saying so. My dear Sarah I must again repeat how much I am delighted with your letters. They are so natural, so fresh, so direct from the heart. Your little pictures of French street scenes; of the norman peasants with their high caps; their bright dresses; their donkeys and market baskets; of the old streets; the cathedrals &c &c are all perfectly graphic and bring up a thousand pleasant reccollections. Did you notice what a perfect city of Parrots Havre is? Scarcely a house but has one or more of these birds of abomination ⟨chai⟩ perched on its window sills, or swinging in a ring, or clambering with beak and claw up and down its wire cage and chattering and squalling like a very imp of Satan. These horrid birds were first brought to Havre in its colonial ships, and now the place ⟨has⟩ seems to have become a mart for them from whence all France is supplied. I ought to have given you a little itinerary of the Seine; up which your Uncle Peter and I have so often voyaged and the ⟨river⟩ banks of which we have so often explored. I should have pointed out Tankerville Castle, where we had once a delightful pic nic, and ⟨La Mal⟩ the fine old Chateau of ⟨La Mollairie, Mollerie; Mallerie⟩↑La Maillerie↓ (or some such name) about the vicinity of which we loitered for a day or two. And Quilleboeuf where we once put in in a storm with a large and merry party on the way to Paris.[3] And the ruins of the ancient abbey of Jumeage,[4] ⟨where I⟩ among which I spent a solemn but delightful summer day alone. And the Convent of the *Corset Rouge* about which your uncle used to tell a romantic little story; and the ruins of the castle of Robert the Devil,[5] father of William the Conqueror; which I visited in company with Mr Ritchie of Boston. But all these regions are full of romantic reccollections to me. When at Rouen did you visit the church of St Ouen;[6] which is a wonderfully fine piece of gothic architecture? The interior is superb, with lofty columns that spring up from the pavement to the roof. And did you visit the place where the Maid of Orleans was executed;[7] and the town house adjacent,[8] in the court yard of which, the walls have fine old sculpture in relief, representing the famous meeting of Henry VIII and Francis I on the field of the cloth of gold? And did you see the great gothic town Hall;[9] one of the largest halls or chambers in Europe unsupported by columns? If you have not seen all these, they will serve to occupy you on your next visit. You must, if possible, make Beasley a visit and accept of his proferred hospitality. You will give him heart felt pleasure, and he will make your sojourn truly pleasant. What I would give to be able to be there with you and to pass a little time upon the charming *Cote*! What delightful times I have passed there, when Mrs Beasley[10] was alive and your uncle Peter was with me! My dear girl your letters make me live over past scenes, and ⟨[*unrecovered*]⟩ make me repine that I cannot be with you and share your enjoyment of the novelties continually presenting themselves to you.

To come to home affairs—.I wrote to you a few days since from Mr

Astors where I was paying a visit.[11] I returned home on Tuesday last and found all well at the Cottage. Your mother really has been quite animated and active of late; paying visits and taking long drives, which she relishes greatly. On Wednesday evening "Kate & I" accompanied the Mrs Jones's[12] on a visit to the Howlands. We all went in Mrs Colford Jones ⟨[unrecovered]⟩ omnibus; Mrs Mary Jones & I on the back seat; ⟨[unrecovered]⟩ Mrs Colford & Kate on the middle seat; Mary and Helen Jones on the front seat; and William the coachman, and Peter the African imp on the Dickey. We had a delightful drive, and made a charming visit. Mrs Howland kept us to tea, which was served up at table in the good old rural style. We loitered about the place until flying clouds and a muttering of thunder behind the hills warned us that a shower might be gathering. The carriage was therefore summoned, we all embarked, and drove off merrily—chatting and laughing, and felicitating each other on our happy excursion. as we ascended the heights on the cross road, however, just past the old hermit basket makers; the looks of the weather began to grow wild. The clouds ⟨had⟩ seemed to gather up from all quarters; lightening played in every direction, but ⟨still⟩ there was as yet no thunder, and not a ⟨lea⟩ drop of rain. William pushed his horses; we hoped to get home before the storm began; but the air had the chill feeling of approaching rain; it was growing dusk, and the lightening became more and more vivid. By the time we passed the Presbyterian church[13] it began to patter, and before we reached Stevens Inn (The Dobbs Ferry post office) we had a rattling shower. The ladies proposed to stop until the shower should be over. We accordingly alighted at the Inn and sent the carriage to take shelter in the barn or under the shed. And now came on, not a shower, but a deluge—torrents of rain, sheets of lightning, peals of thunder—now and then it would pause a few moments to take breath and then begin again with redoubled fury. There we sat, in the back parlour of the little tavern, illumined by a small lamp and a tallow candle and decorated with rueful engravings of all the presidents, beside a forlorn likeness of myself. What was to be done. The storm seemed likely to last all night; it was either a glare of lightning or pitchy darkness—The Mrs Jones' were inclined to pass the night at the Inn, though poor Mrs Mary dreaded the horrors of a country feather bed. At length, about ten O clock, there was a kind of intermission—It did not rain "cats and dogs," but only small Kittens. Councils were held; a thousand minds were made up and as soon changed—The Coachman was consulted. He changed his mind a dozen times to suit his mistress. I was appealed to, but could only answer that, for myself, I should not have the least hesitation to set out, but then I was not a proper person to consult as "I never knew when there was any danger"—At last it was determined to tempt the elements—This consultation exhausted a great part of the interval of the storm. The difficulty now was to get the carriage from the stable. ⟨The⟩ Peter had disappeared—he was a "perfect pest"—"never at hand when wanted" &c &c. At length he was found—the carriage was summoned and drawn up to the door; but it had been too long to go under the shed the rain had beat in it and the bottom was full of water— ⟨[?Here it was?]⟩ Mrs Mary had got in but scrambled out again, dripping from every feather Then there was mopping, and rubbing and scrubbing until it was tolerably dry—then dry shoes were borrowed of the land lady; and lanterns provided to be held up by Peter & the Coachman—At length, having nearly exhausted the interval of calm we set out. "Now William! take care William! Drive slow William—Hold up the lantern Peter! Are you sure you see the road William? Oh yes Maam—Oh William! William! a little more to the left William!—Now William—William a little more to the right—are you sure you are in the road? &c &c &c—Kate laughed. How can you laugh exclaimed Mrs Mary—"its really tempting providence." For my own part I sat mute. I dared not say I was not afraid, lest it should be taken unkindly. On we went, at a snails pace; claps of thunder, sheets of lightning; ⟨b⟩ deluges of rain; Every now and then there was a scream, and at the least jolt Mrs Mary was in an agony. When we reached [?Jawals?] hill the little African imp was made to alight and go ahead like a Jack o lantern, to ⟨guide the hor⟩ show the way. Turn the light this way Peter—Do you see the road William—Yes Maam." Better than before—Yes Maam—Ah thats right. Keep ahead—Peter—Never mind the rain Peter—⟨Nev⟩ Oh after all Peter is a good boy—Never mind your shoes Peter—you shall have a new pair tomorrow—hold up the light Peter—Ah well—Peter is a good boy after all &c &c—At length we reached Mrs Colfords about eleven at night; where I deposited Kate, and, borrowing a pair of India rubber overshoes and an umbrella made the best of my way home.—The Jones' now give a history of the evenings adventures to all their friends, and consider that they escaped miraculously from all kinds of deaths and dislocations. I am sorry to say that their gratitude to the redoubtable Peter, like the vows of ⟨shipm⟩ tempest tost mariners to the saints, was forgotten as soon as the danger was over—he is doomed to be turned off forthwith, having by dint of indulgent treatment, become a perfect little scamp. ↑I had nearly forgot to mention that a good natured bare legged servant girl at the Inn was very kind & attentive to the ladies; ⟨when⟩ and that on parting Miss Mary Jones rewarded her magnificently by giving her her French silk ridicule!↓

This morning we were at church at the Dobbs Ferry church.[14] Quite a full congregation all the neighbors, and several persons from town. ⟨Mrs⟩ Mr Constant was there. ⟨He has⟩ Mrs Constant who is still at

Rockaway begins to find benefit ⟨to⟩ from the sea air and ventures to bathe a little, though she will not venture to take the surf. She was terrified by her first trial of it, when the water was very rough. ⟨and⟩ the Irishman who officiates to take care of the ladies in the surf was quite indignant—"By the powers" said he "I have bathed ladies without number. I have bathed *queens* among the rest—but I never bathed any one that behaved so bad."

July 20th   I have just received your long and delightful letter of June 26[15] (by the Caledonia Steamer) and have again to express to you how much, how very much I enjoy the fresh and natural expression of your feelings, and the graphic little sketches you give of every thing that strikes you. I know the very balcony of your appartment and the splendid view which it commands; and have many a time looked down upon just such scenes as you describe, from a similarly situated apartment in an old Hotel that used to stand next to Meurices:[16] It is one of the most splendid and at the same time amusing city views in Europe. Many and many a time have I hurried to my window (like yourself) ⟨to⟩ at the sound of the Military Music to see the Guards pass by; and many a time have I been amused with the pomposity and ⟨pa⟩ ludicrous parade of that lofty personage the Drum major. This functionary, all over the world, is made to cut these solemn capers and make thes[e] whimsical gesticulations; which in fact, mark the time of the music &c. Every thing is regulated by his huge silver headed cane. Your Sunday visit to St Cloud also is perfectly delicious. I enjoy your descriptions the more from being so perfectly familiar with the scenes and places, and from their bringing up so many reccollections of past pleasures; but there is a joyousness in your own manner of mentioning things, my dear girl, that ↑gives↓ effect to every expression. Continue to write on, in the same rapi[d] unstudied way; never trouble yourself about turning a period, or, what is still less important, writing a neat hand, but scribble and scrawl as fast and *as much* as you can, and never ⟨fear⟩ ↑doubt your↓ giving delight to those with whom you correspond above all, never fear criticism from me; I love you too well to criticise. I can do nothi[ng] but enjoy your letters; and I read them over and over again, as pictures of yourself. But oh, my dear Sarah, how much these letters make me deplore our separation. I continually find in them instances of that quick and every varying susceptibility to to[17] every thing calculated to touch the heart, arouse and elevate the feelings; delight the imagination and amuse the fancy, which made you so precious to me as a companion; and I repine that I cannot be by your side, to see every thing with you, and to catch, as I so often have done, pleasure from your ⟨own⟩ exclamations and remarks; and from your ⟨own⟩ kindling animation. These last two letters, to your mother and myself, are gratifying also from the buoyant tone in which they are written. They breathe nothing but innocent enjoyment of the bright and beautiful scenes around you. There are no sad passages to sadden us. We picture you to ourselves happy, and that *half* consoles us for our separation. But I know the constitution of your mind, and I know your heart to its very core, and I know that morbid melancholy has no abiding place in your nature. There are tears, quick delightful tears, like summer showers, that soon pass away and serve to soften and freshen the feelings—but there are no mists and fogs, and lowering clouds and long rainy days in your composition—God bless you, my dear girl, and keep your warm, generous, affectionate heart always light and sunshiny!

Evening—You make mention in your letter of an uncommonly fine old gentleman a quaker, with whom and his family you became acquainted, but you do not mention his name—Never omit to do so, as I may often be acquainted with the individual, by reputation, if not personally. Nine years, however, is an interval that wipes out many a reccollection, and I daily find persons and scenes in Europe fading away like the lingerings of a dream.—You ask me if I ever was at Richmond[18]—Many a time and oft—and ⟨many a⟩ ↑several↓ pleasant rural rambles ⟨have⟩ and rural repasts have I had there with Leslie, Newton and others of my London cronies. The view from the terrace is one of the most magnificent landscapes in England. It is a perfect summing up of all the beauties of English scenery.

The sweet briars which you and David[19] planted, and which you inquire about, are flourishing finely—You need not fear that they will not be taken care of. We value too highly every thing that reminds us of you. All our clambering vines have been very luxuriant this season, and are gradually clothing the cottage with verdure. Some of the trumpet creeper too begins to flower; and by another year we shall have the east wall quite gorgeous

July 21. *On board of the Steamboat bound to New York.* I am making preparations for an excursion to the Highlands in company with Mr West—to pass a few days with Gouvr. Kemble & Mr Brevoort. I believe I informed you in a former letter[10] that Mr Brevoort has hired the Beverley House, in the Highlands, ready furnished, for the Summer. How much I shall miss you in this annual visit, in which of late years you have always accompanied me—and how much I shall feel the loss of poor Mrs Paulding, whom we used to meet on these occasions, and whose presence diffused such happiness around her. Poor Mary[21] has been sadly afflicted by the death of her sister, and has suffered much in health. She has taken charge of little Jimmy[22] who is to remain for two or three years with her. Mr Paulding continues to keep house in St Johns Square; and has an excellent woman as a housekeeper, who formerly lived with your uncle Ebenezer. I forget her name. I have not seen Mr Paulding for some time, but think it probable I shall meet him in the Highlands where he makes a visit every fortnight. I shall not set out for two or three days yet—and shall return to the Cottage this evening.—Mrs Colford Jones and her young flock set off for Niagara next week. The good lady is full of anticipations of all kinds of difficulties and bothers on the road; having no one to take the lead; Mrs Mary Jones, who has usually been her protector & dictator, intending to open a campaign with Miss Mary, at Saratoga Springs. I make no doubt ⟨[unrecovered]⟩ I shall have a whole chronicle to relate to you hereafter of the Summer adventures of this most eventful family. Miss Mary has at present a devoted admirer in young Harmony, Nephew of the rich old bachelor merchant, Peter Harmony (alias Ximenes) of Cadiz.[23] The young gentleman appears to be well received by the family; makes frequent visits to "Silver Spring" and ruralizes and sylvanizes with Miss Mary about the glades and groves. He is a pleasant, good looking, good natured fellow, and, should he gain her hand I hope he may become a good protestant, a rich heir and an excellent husband; and that the Jones family in general, may be all the happier for having *Harmony* among them, excuse the pleasantry.

Tomorrow I dine with Mr Henry Sheldon, who has a gentlemans party to meet old Mr Gallatin at present on a visit to him. Mrs Sheldon is still suffering under the visitation of providence, for having joked about her worthy brother in law, and his limping after the little ducks to make them keep in the pond. She Still continues to limp about the house, and cannot walk any distance. I am affraid, however, this awful lesson has had no effect upon her; she is as full of mirth and mischief as ever. The report I cited in a former letter about ⟨the⟩ ↑her↓ worthy old bachelor brother in law being engaged to Miss Hetty King is, I apprehend, as groundless as other reports about old bachelors in the neighborhood. The worthy man is suffering great anxiety this Summer. In consequence of the drought, the forest of trees which he has transplanted is in a very languishing condition, and the waterfall, which [MS torn] to be the ⟨comfor⟩ "pride["] and comfort of his old age has dwindled [MS torn] [u]ntil it has scarce strength enough left to run down hill. [MS torn] evenings since I set out alone on foot to pay a visit to the Ha[milton]s. [MS torn] [I do n]ot [MS torn] know what possessed me after all the experiences I have had, to try a short cut across the fields, instead of going by the road or the aqueduct. Such a time as I had—our memorable expeditions though brake and bramble were nothing to it. I lost my way in ploughed grounds and cornfields; tumbled down a ravine; pulled down a stone wall on my heels and finished by jumping into the midst of a quickset hedge, set up by the illstarred Captain

Rocket. I arrived at the Hamiltons utterly Kilt as an Irishman would say; but recovered sufficiently to pass a very pleasant evening. Mary played for me most charmingly, Bo sang his best and all the rest were as affable and agreeable as usual. In the course of the evening Schuyler and Alexander Hamilton came straggling in from one of those fortuitous voyages incident to this family. They had come up in a steam ferry boat, just built by Schuyler and on a voyage of experiment; ⟨and⟩ had been put ashore at some miles distance from the house, and reached there dusty, hungry but as usual in high spirits. The Dream has been fitted up anew this year and carrys an immense press of canvas; but from some defect in her trim, disappoints them all in her sailing. I have not been on board of her. She bore down to the cottage in gallant style on the fourth of July; displayed all her colours and fired us a salute. There is quite a mania for yachts this season, and they are beautiful objects on the river. The Hamiltons made many kind enquiries about you and the young ladies expressed great envy of your position in the center of the gay metropolis; the heart of the civilized world. Mrs Hamilton expressed a wish that your mother would ⟨come⟩ pay them a sociable visit and take tea as she heard that she had taken to visiting about lately and seeing the world. I told her, what was the fact, that your mother intended to pay them a visit soon, but that her remaining to tea was out of the question—In fact your mother is quite "coming out" this Summer and I should not be surprized if she becomes quite a belle.—The steamboat has arrived at N York and I must conclude—

1 Oclock. I have barely time to scrawl a line in conclusion[.] I have just made Jock perfectly happy by handing him ⟨the⟩ ↑your↓ letters to your mother and myself: and he has posted off to shew them to your father.

I had intended to write by this opportunity to Mr Storrow, but shall not ⟨[unrecovered]⟩ have time. Remember me to him most kindly, I can see from the tenor of all your letters, the kind considerate attention paid by him ↑on all occasions↓ to render every thing pleasant and gratifying around you; and it is an unspeakable source of satisfaction, in being severed from you, to feel persuaded you have a most amiable generous spirited and delicately minded protector—one who knows how a lady ought to be taken care of.

Ever affectionately your uncle
Washington Irving

ADDRESSED: a Madame / Madame Storrow / Aux Soins de Mr Thomas W Storrow / No 17. Rue du Faubourg Poissonniere / à Paris / per Packet Ship Burguntly /

for Havre   POSTMARKED: OUTRE MER LE HAVRE / 12 / Aout / 41 //
PARIS [unrecovered] / 13 / AOUT / 41   DOCKETED: July 18th 1841 / No 8
MANUSCRIPT: Yale.   PUBLISHED: PMI, III, 167, 168 (in part); Yale Review, 16
(April, 1927), 468–73; LFSS, pp. 17–24.

1. These letters have not been located.

2. Reuben Beasley (d. 1847), who was appointed U.S. consul at Le Havre in
1817, was involved in a Seine River steamboat venture in which he persuaded WI
to invest money. Peter Irving was a frequent visitor at the Beasleys during his
residence in Europe.

3. WI frequently saw Tancarville and its castle when he traveled on the Seine
between Le Havre and Paris. La Mailleraye was "a magnificent chateau on a point
of the river" about sixty kilometers up the Seine from Le Havre. Quilleboeuf was
another village near the mouth of the Seine with an imposing chateau. For WI's
initial reactions to these places, see J&N, III, 222–24, 496–98; and WI to Mrs.
Thomas W. Storrow, June 29, 1825.

4. The abbey of Jumièges, founded in the seventh century by St. Philibert, was
destroyed by the Northmen but rebuilt by William of the Long Sword. Although in
decline after the fifteenth century, it was wrecked during the French Revolution.
It is about thirty kilometers downriver in a direct route from Rouen. See Sisley
Huddleston, Normandy (Garden City, 1929), pp. 65–66.

5. This castle, which was largely destroyed in the fifteenth century by the English, had six towers. As WI suggests, it took its name, Chateau Robert le Diable,
from Robert le Magnifique. See Huddleston, Normandy, pp. 61–62; and Normandie
(Les Guides Bleus) (Paris, 1972), pp. 411–12.

6. This church was started in 1318 on the site of an earlier Romanesque church
and completed two years later. See Huddleston, Normandy, pp. 52–53; and Normandie (Les Guides Bleus), pp. 151–53.

7. Joan of Arc was burned at the stake on May 30, 1431, in the Place du Vieux-
Marché, a few hundred meters from the cathedral of Rouen. See Huddleston, Normandy, p. 37; Normandie (Les Guides Bleus), pp. 144–45.

8. The Hôtel de Bourgtheroulde, built in Flamboyant Gothic style between 1518
and 1532 by William the Red, is known for the bas-relief depicting the meeting
of Francis I and Henry VIII in 1520. See Normandie (Les Guides Bleus),
pp. 145–46.

9. The Hotel de Ville, adjacent to the Church of St. Ouen, occupies a wing of the
ancient abbey which antedated the church. See Normandie (Les Guides Bleus).
p. 153.

10. Mrs. Beasley was the former Jenny-Adelaide Guestier, daughter of Daniel
Guestier and sister of Pierre François Guestier of Bordeaux. WI visited the latter
in October, 1825. See J&N, III, 212, 527–28, 531–37.

11. See WI's letter of July 11, 1841.

12. The Joneses were WI's neighbors who are frequently mentioned in his
letters. Helen Jones is probably the Helen Colford Jones who married Woodbury
Langdon on November 9, 1847. See The Diary of George Templeton Strong, ed.
Allen Nevins and M. H. Thomas, 4 vols. (New York, 1952), I, 317.

13. The congregation of this church, organized in 1825, erected a wooden-shingled
building in 1827 on Ashford Avenue near Broadway. It was torn down in 1880.
See J. T. Scharf, History of Westchester County, II, 187.

14. Zion Episcopal Church, with a stone building on Cedar Street, was or-

ganized in 1833. WI was later one of its vestrymen. See Scharf, *History of West-chester County*, II, 187.

15. This letter has not been located.

16. The Hôtel de Meurice was located at the corner of Rue de Rivoli and Rue de St. Honoré near the Jardin du Carrousel and the Palais Royal. See *Guide de Paris 1828* (facsimile ed., Paris, 1970), p. 105.

17. WI repeated "to."

18. Richmond, a village sixteen miles up the Thames from London Bridge, was the site of a large park enclosed by Charles I. WI probably visited the area in 1819 and 1820 when he was intimate with Charles Robert Leslie, Gilbert Stuart Newton, Peter Powell, William Willes, and the Bollman family. See *The Victoria History of the County of Surrey*, ed. H. E. Malden, 4 vols. (London, 1902–1912), III, 533–41; and WI to Leslie, September 13, 1819, and October 31, 1820.

10. David Davidson (d. 1803), WI's hired man for whom he later secured a position at Wiley and Putnam's publishing firm. See WI to Sarah Storrow, September 1, 1841.

20. See WI to Sarah Storrow, July 11, 1841.

21. Mary Kemble Parrott, sister of Gertrude Kemble Paulding.

22. James Nathaniel Paulding (1833–1898), youngest son of James Kirke Paulding.

23. Peter Harmony was a shipping merchant and foreign importer known for his trade in fine wines. He had an imposing residence on Broadway near Rector, near old Grace Church. His wealth was such that he was taxed on $30,000 of personal property in 1815 and on $55,000 in 1820. See W. T. Bonner, *New York, The World's Metropolis*, p. 73; and Scoville, *Old Merchants of NYC*, I, 194, 226–27; II, 128.

1353. To Messrs. Lea & Blanchard

New York July 21. 1841

Gentlemen

I have to acknowledge the receipt of the letter of your Mr Lea of July 17th.[1] Relative to a second edition of Miss Davidsons Memoir &c. You will use your discretion as to the number of copies &c of the edition, on the same terms as the first edition—The note for the amount in payt., as before, You will make out in favor of Mrs Davidson. I am not aware of any alterations ⟨to be made⟩ necessary or advisable in the second editions; if there are any corrections they will be very trifling and may be specified in a letter, but I do not think there will be any. You may proceed with the edition therefore at your convenience

Very respectfully / Your obt Servt.
Washington Irving

ADDRESSED: Messrs Lea & Blanchard / Booksellers / Philadelphia   POSTMARKED:
NEW-YORK / JUL / 22   DOCKETED: [upper left corner of p. 1] Recd. July
23d —
MANUSCRIPT: Pforzheimer Library.

1. This letter has not been located.

1354. To Sarah Storrow

Cold Spring, July 26th 1841

My dear Sarah,

I am here at my friend Kembles little nest among the Highlands,
where you have so often been with me. How sadly do I miss you! I do not
know when you have been brought more tenderly and painfully to my
mind. I reccollect the buoyancy of spirit and the romance of feeling
with which you used to enjoy these glorious mountain scenes, and the
refreshment of heart which I used to experience in exploring them with
you. I arrived here the evening before last (saturday evening) in company with Mr West We had a splendid evenings voyage through the
Highlands, which looked, to me, more magnificent than ever. I found Mr
Kembles house a real "bachelors hall" having no longer a lady to preside
there. Mary has her Cottage in the bosom of the hill, and the glorious
being who used to grace and gladden this little mansion with her presence
is gone forever! I cannot express to you how dreary I have occasionally
have[1] felt since I have been here. Yesterday morning I went up to
Marys residence. The Cottage originally built by Mr Parrot[2] has been
enlarged and is very pretty and picturesque, though perfectly simple.
The view it commands is really splendid: and quite took me by surprize,
—though I had expected something striking. It commands a view ⟨above
the⟩ of an immense ampitheatre of mountains, with the Hudson making
its singular bend through it—; gleaming here and there from among
rocks and precipices and eternal forests. ⟨All⟩ The foreground is like a
morsel of park scenery; with noble forest trees, and grassy glades. Altogether I think it one of the noblest prospects on the river. Mary
received me with her usual warmth and kindness; but there was a
sadness in her look and manner that shewed how much she felt the
loss of her glorious sister. Mr Paulding is on a visit to her; and little
Jimmy is under her charge. The latter has grown considerably, and is
odder than ever. In fact there is great danger of his becoming a ⟨perfect⟩
complete oddity. He has been so much petted for his whims and excen-
tricities that the little creature seems to be continually making grimaces
and, playing a part, for the purpose of attracting notice. He cannot

say or do anything naturally, like other children. Little Gouvr[3] has improved greatly and is a very fine boy. Willy[4] is tall and slender; a perfect lance in shape; his face as fine as ever, and in his nature inheriting all his mothers nobleness of spirit. Kem[5] is the same ⟨balderdashed⟩ being that you knew him: naturally apt and intelligent, with honorable principles, ⟨but⟩ and gentlemanlike notions, but sadly balderdashed by "good society," and by having figured as a little man before he had ceased to be a boy. Still I have hopes that when his nonsense years are completely passed he will make something good; though his gentlemanly habits of indolence and amusement are sadly against him. Mr Brevoort came here yesterday morning from his residence at the old Beverley Countryseat, about five miles off. He passed the day and night here, and is here still. This evening Mr West and myself accompany him home, and tomorrow morning I shall set off with him for Kingston (old Esopus) to meet the Directors of the Delaware & Hudson Canal Company,[6] who are about to make a visit of several days, to various points of their canal. This will take us through a variety of fine mountain scenery; and, as the directors take care to have their way made smooth before them, and all kind of conveniences provided, I expect to make a very pleasant excursion.

I presume other letters from home will tell you of the trouble and vexation we have had at the Cottage from the misconduct of that most unlucky fellow William I.[7] It seems that he took it into his wise head to pay clandestine attentions to a daughter of Genl Benedicts;[8] the one who was a day scholar at Eliza Romeyns. A correspondence was carried on between them in which he most culpably made his little sister Charlotte[9] an agent; they met and strolled together in the environs of the village, Their meetings were noticed, ⟨by⟩ and the brothers of the young lady[10] received annonymous letters on the subject. They supposed the intentions of William to be dishonorable and in a moment of exasperation, way laid him, and without regarding his protestations of the innocence of his views and conduct, inflicted on him a severe personal chastisement, publicly, in the village. William subsequently addressed a letter to Milton Benedict, ⟨the⟩ his principal assailant, avowing himself engaged to his sister and that nothing had ever passed between them that was not customary and innocent in such a relative position; demanding that he should publicly retract the imputation which he had cast on his sisters character and apologize to himself for the outrage he had committed on him. This ⟨wa⟩ note was unattended to. He then wrote a second demanding personal satisfaction, (in a word a challenge to a duel) Both notes were returned to him under a blank cover. He then caused Milton Benedict to be posted in various parts of Tarrytown as a defamer of the reputation of his sister; as a coward &c—I have taken

no part in this disgraceful matter, nor had anything to say to William
since the affair transpired. He left the Cottage and took up his residence
at a farm house on the opposite side of the river when he sent the challenge; and I shall take care that he shall no longer incommode the
household by his presence. He was grossly reprehensible in the first
part of this affair, in the clandestine manner in which he paid his
addresses to this inexperienced school girl. The brothers were rash in ⟨the
mode they took to⟩ attacking him, without ⟨being⟩ carefully investigating
the matter. Still, they were excusable, acting as they did under a strong
belief of his criminality. They have put themselves in the wrong by
refusing to apologize after ⟨he avowed⟩ being satisfied, as they admitted
they were, ⟨of⟩ that their sister had not been dishonored, and after he
avowed himself engaged to her. In thus refusing an apology they
↑virtually↓ persisted in a gross outrage upon him, and in their original
stigma on the ↑character↓ of their sister. The subsequent challenge
and posting were in the usual course by which a gentleman seeks to
extricate himself from a gross indignity.–The one I most feel for in the
matter is the poor little girl, whose name ⟨is⟩ has been most sadly bandied
about in the brawl between rash and inconsiderate men, and who I
believe to be a very amiable innocent hearted little being. As fate
would have it, old General Benedict, who has been lingering for two
years on the verge of the grave, died the very evening of the day on
which the posting took place—He was perfectly ignorant however of the
whole transaction. I left home the ⟨morn⟩ next morning, on my present
visit to the Highlands, which had been for some time in contemplation;
but I was not unwilling to be absent from the neighborhood for a time
until this paltry business ⟨had [*?turned?*]⟩ had ceased to be a theme of
country gossip. Is it not hard that one cannot set up a little quiet modest
retreat, without having it harrassed and disgraced by such mischievous
inmates But enough of this most offensive subject.—

—You mention in two of your letters having sent me parcels of Galig-
manis papers. I should be glad to receive them, but they have never
come to hand.

I sent you some time since a copy of Miss Davidsons works & memoir,
which I trust you have received before this. It has been well received and
meets with so good a sale that a new edition is about to be put to press.
I hand all the profits of the work to Mrs Davidson

I had intended to keep this letter open and finish it this evening
or tomorrow morning at Beverley; but Mr William Kemble[11] goes down
to town this afternoon, so I will send it by him that it may be in time
for the Steam Packet. I have been up this morning on a second visit
to Mary's cottage, and am still more delighted with it. It is positively
one of the most charmingly situated residences I have ever seen. The little

mansion itself, ⟨and⟩ the ⟨gr⟩ furniture; the grounds around it &c &c all ⟨bear⟩ give evidence of taste and elegance of feeling; but the prospect of these grand mountains clothed with forest, with the glorious Hudson rolling at their feet, is perfectly magnificent. Marys husband is I believe a very worthy amiable man, but he is silent and quiet, and looks as if he was a *cast iron man* from his own foundry.

The day before I left the cottage I dined at the Sheldons to Mr & Mrs Gallatin[12] (the old people) who were on a visit there. Mr George Jones was the only guest beside myself from the neighborhood. We had a very elegant dinner and a very cheerful one. Mr Gallatin was in fine spirits and full of conversation. He is upwards of eighty, yet has all the activity ⟨of a⟩ and clearness of mind and gaiety of spirits of a young man. How delightful it is to see such intellectual ⟨age and⟩ and joyous old age; to see life running out clear and sparkling to the last drop. With such a blessed temperament one would ⟨content⟩ be content to linger and spin out the last thread of existence.

Give my kindest remembrances to Mr Storrow.

Your affectionate uncle—

WI.

ADDRESSED: à Madame / Madame Storrow / aux Soins de Mr Thomas W Storrow / 317. Rue du Faubourg Poissonniere / a Paris / *per Caledonia* / from Boston
    POSTMARKED: NEW-YORK / JUL / 1 // Packet Letter // AMERICA / L //
    2 [FR]ANCE 2 CALAIS   DOCKETED: July 26th 1841 /No 9
MANUSCRIPT: Yale.   PUBLISHED: PMI, III, 167–68 (in part).

1. WI repeated "have."

2. Robert Parker Parrott, the husband of Mary Kemble and the brother-in-law of Gouverneur Kemble.

3. Gouverneur Paulding (1829–1913), the third child of James K. and Gertrude Kemble Paulding.

4. William Irving Paulding (1825–1890), the second child of the Pauldings.

5. Peter Kemble Paulding (1819–1900), the eldest Paulding child, named after his maternal grandfather.

6. WI has more to say about the canal in his letter to Mrs. Van Wart on August 1, 1841. The 108-mile canal, opened in 1828 and continued until 1899, extended from Honesdale, Pennsylvania to Kingston, New York on the Hudson and carried anthracite coal eastward. The directors included Philip Hone (1781–1851), Maurice (d. 1854) and John Wurts; engineers on the project were Horatio Allen (1802–1890), John A. Roebling (1806–1869), Benjamin Wright (1770–1842), John L. Sullivan (1777–1865), and John B. Jarvis (1795–1885). See Carter Goodrich, Julius Rubin, H. Jerome Cranmer, and Harry H. Segal, *Canals and Economic Development* (New York, 1961), p. 185; and Harry Sinclair Drago, *Canal Days in America, The History and Romance of Old Towpaths and Waterways* (New York, 1972), pp. 87–98.

7. William Irving, who was thirty years old.

8. James Benedict (1784–1841), who married Deborah Coles in 1812 and fought

in the War of 1812, continued in the state militia and was promoted to major general in 1826. His home was located west of Broadway near the center of Tarrytown. See Martha J. Lamb, *History of the City of New-York*, II, 690; and J. T. Scharf, *History of Westchester County*, II, 251.

9. Charlotte Van Wart Irving, who was seventeen at this time.

10. Probably Milton and Theodore Benedict.

11. William Kemble, the brother of Mrs. Parrott and Mrs. Paulding.

12. Albert Gallatin (1761–1849), the Swiss-born financier who served as secretary of the treasury under Jefferson and Madison from 1803 to 1814, was on diplomatic missions abroad for the next ten years. From 1831 to 1839 he was president of the National Bank of New York and used his influence to restore financial stability after the Panic of 1837. On November 11, 1793, Gallatin married the former Hannah Nicholson (1766–1849), the daughter of Commodore James Nicholson of the U.S. Navy. See Raymond Walters, *Albert Gallatin, Jeffersonian Financier and Diplomat* (Pittsburgh, 1966), pp. 52–56, 380.

1355. To Sarah Storrow

Honesdale, ↑Saturday↓ July 31. 1841

My dear Sarah,

I wrote to you a few days since from Mr Kembles at Cold Spring[1] giving you some account of our friends in the Highlands. I left Cold Spring on Monday afternoon, in company with Mr Brevoort and Mr West; for Mr Brevoorts residence at the old Beverley House, about a couple of miles below Mr Gouverneurs. It was a fine evening and we had a delightful drive through Scenes which you will well reccollect, ⟨We passed⟩ and which, on our first visit to the Highlands, made such a vivid impression on you. I thought of you (but when do I not think of you!) as we crossed the Indian Brook;[2] one of your favorite resorts; and I really had a sad twinge at the heart as we drove by the Spot where, on our memorable expedition by land, I left you ⟨seated⟩ by the road side, seated by the wreck of our waggon, when I went in quest of aid. I cannot tell you, my dear Sarah, how sweet yet sad these scenes and memorials of our past companionship are to me. They constantly make me feel how precious you were to me, and what I have lost in losing you.

After passing by the road leading down to Mr Gouverneurs we continued parrallel to the river, though nearly a mile from it; with a range of woody mountains on our left. The road ran through the property of Mr Arden,[3] and became grass grown, crossed occasionally by gates and bars, and shaded by magnificent trees; oaks and elms of immense size; with here and there a neglected avenue; speaking of former style but latter decay. It was about dusk when we arrived at Beverley. It is an irregular old mansion; part of it intended as a polite

residence, ⟨of⟩ the rest a mere farm house. It has never had any pretension, to architectural merit; though the panneld ⟨room⟩ wainscots, tiled
chimney pieces, in some of the rooms have an air of respectability and
quaintness. The chief interest about it is, its having been the house
at which arnold received the letter from Andrè, ⟨w⟩ apprising him that
his treason was discovered, and from which he made his ⟨[unrecovered]⟩
hair breadth escape. We drank tea in ⟨the⟩ ↑an↓ old room, with low
cieling and beams over head, in which Arnold was at breakfast when
the letter was delivered him; and the foot path is still shewn, by which
he escaped through the woods to the river side. The old mansion is in
a very lonely situation, just at the foot of the mountains, ⟨and⟩ out of
sight of the river; and out of the way of travel. The Brevoorts have
half furnished it, in a very simple style; they have their harp and piano
and plenty of books; their swing under ⟨the⟩ lofty trees &c and are
perfectly enchanted with their rural retreat. They really are quite the
kind of people to enjoy the country; living very much out of doors;
rambling about the woods and fields, and casting off all the common
place of city life—I was quite sorry that I could not pass a few days
with them in this old haunt of treason; but Brevoort and myself had
arranged to set off the following morning, on our expedition up the river
to meet the Directors of the Delaware & Hudson Canal Company.
Our evening was very pleasant. Mrs Brevoort and Laura gave us some
excellent music and we had some very agreeable conversation. The next
morning, leaving Mr West in charge of the family, Mr Brevoort and
myself crossed the river to West point and there got on board of an
Albany steam boat, which after a very fine sail up the river landed us at
Kingston. By some mistake we arrived at the place of rendezvous
↑three or four hours↓ after the Directors had set off in the canal boat so
we had to get a carriage and endeavour to overtake them. The object
of their expedition was an annual visit along the line of the canal and
to the coal mines among the mountains. We had a splendid drive of
twenty five miles through glorious mountain scenery; the CatsKill
mountains on the north, the Shawnagunk Mountains on the south, and
the beautiful wild river the Rondout, winding through a romantic
valley, equal to the Ramapough. It was after dark before we overtook
the canal boat, where we were most cordially welcomed by the directors,
among whom was Mr Philip Hone.[4] The canal boat was fitted up with
every convenience & well supplied with PROVANT for the expedition;
we accordingly had a very soccial and merry time of it; one night we
slept on board, and twice on shore; but the scenery through which we
passed was beyond my most sanguine anticipations. You remember
the glorious variety of mountain, and forest, and deep rich valley and
shining rivers, ⟨th⟩ which we traversed on our memorable ⟨ex⟩ return

from the Western part of the state—Fancy a succession of such scenery
for upwards of a hundred miles. For a great part of the way we tracked
the course of the Rondout; then the Delaware; then the Lackawaxen &c.
The canal itself was like a beautiful winding river; but at times it was, for
many miles, built along the face of perpendicular rocky cliffs; with
great precipices butting over head, with immense trees growing out of
every fissure, while far below, at the foot of an artificial wall, roared
along the Delaware. I think I never in my life have been more impressed
with natural scenery; probably from its being so unexpected;—and then
the stupendous works of art I was contemplating—this daring enterprize
of building such an immense watry high way along perpendicular mountains and through the heart of an almost impracticable wilderness. We
reached this place yesterday morning. ⟨[It]⟩ is the great coal deposit;
whither the coal is brought from the mines (16 miles distant) in cars
along a rail road and whence it is transported in the canal boats. The
place is new but very bustling and promises to rise to importance. It
is ⟨[prettily]⟩ well laid out and prettily built, and is named after Philip
Hone who has been one of the most efficient persons ⟨to promote⟩ ↑in
promoting↓ this great enterprize. What I have continually felt throughout
this journey was the want of some companion to whom I could
express my delight, and who could sympathize in my impressions My
fellow travellers were all men of business; with the exception of Brevoort, who was unusually obtuse, and Hone, who was in general too
much taken up with himself. But I have been spoiled of late years
by having you so much with me in my excursions after the picturesque,
and accustoming myself to turn to you on all occasions when I wanted
some one to help me enjoy a landscape.

Saturday August 1. We have been overtaken by an easterly storm
and have to postpone our expedition by rail road to the Coal mines
until tomorrow. What a contrast between the Sunday I am passing at
this place and that which you are contemplating at Paris. Here it is
literally a day of rest. A mere repose from labor; a universal stillness,
⟨and⟩ but an absence of all enjoyment. Nothing can be more dull and
monotonous than a Sunday in one of these little, commonplace, orderly
country towns. I have been to a common place little church of white
boards, and seen a congregation of common place people and heard a
common place Sermon, and now cannot muster up any thing but
common place ideas; so that I will forbear writing any more for the
present. Good lord deliver me from the all pervading common place
which is the curse of our country. It is like the sands of the desart, which
are continually stealing over the land of Egypt and gradually effacing
every trace of grandeur and beauty and swallowing up every green

thing. I must confess I envied you your half wicked Parisian Sunday; at church in the morning and at St Cloud in the afternoon.

Aug. 3. Carbondale.[5] If I have wished for you repeatedly on former parts of my route I have been well satisfied you were not with me on the journey from Honesdale to this place, and yet it has been one of the most striking and interesting parts of the whole expedition. We have come entirely by rail road, in rough cars or boxes, made for the transportation of coal, fitted up with rude benches, with buffalo skins thrown over them. We were drawn by horses, but came at the rate of little more than two miles an hour. In fact our route for the most part of the way was up and down steep hills, across deep valleys and rapid Streams and over the back of a mountain. There were eight places where we had to be drawn up or let down inclined planes by the aid of machinery, some of them about a mile in extent; where the breaking of a cable or starting of a bolt would have sent us whirling down hill and dashed us to pieces; we were often elevated thirty and forty feet in the air, on a narrow rail road just wide enough for one train of cars, without foot walk; in this way we traversed valleys and saw wild streams dashing along below us. Several of these ascents took us to the top of the Moosick Mountains,[6] from whence we had a vast view over a boundless wilderness of forests; with the Cats Kill mountains raising their blue aerial peaks upwards of fifty miles distant. ⟨From⟩ This mountain divides the waters which flow into the Delaware and the Susquehanna. After crossing this mountain we descended into the beautiful woody valley of the Lackawanna in which this village is situated. The weather, as in the previous part of our journey was splendid, and we passed through some enchanting forest scenery; but my dear Sarah, had you been with me you would have been in continual dread. This place is in the region of coal mines and yesterday afternoon we penetrated one for the distance of a mile, beheld the miners at their work, and were present at a blasting with gunpowder, which ⟨?men?⟩ reverberated through the mine like thunder. In the evening half the population were about the hotel to welcome the Directors; ⟨and⟩ with a band of music, firing of canon &c. Mr Hone and myself were quartered for the night at the house of Mr Archibold, the Superintendent and director of the mines, a man most highly prized by the company, and who has risen into esteem and prosperity by his merits. I ⟨found⟩ had become acquainted with him in the latter part of the route when he joined our party, and had been delighted by his simple, quiet manners, his varied and extensive information and his original vein of thinking. I was much pleased also with his little establishment, where every thing was well regulated and in good taste, though extremely simple. His wife too, was an intelligent and agreeable woman, and ⟨took⟩ acquitted herself well in conversation. I was quite surprised when she enquired after your mother, and appeared to be well acquainted with you all, and with every on[e][7] at Johnstown. A moments enquiry, however, accounted for it. I found she was a sister of Mr Frothingham (Jane Anns husband)[8] and that her husband had been brought up in Johnstown and its vicinity. She does not appear, however, to have any of the defects of her brother; her little household seems to be a most happy one.

We have now got through with our examination of the various parts of this great mining enterprize, and this afternoon we turn our faces homeward. This evening we shall reach Honesdale; thence we take an extra stage to Goshen, and thence I shall shape my course either by New burgh to the Highlands; or ⟨perhaps b⟩ by the rail road to Tappan, and so to the Cottage. I long to get back to little Sunnyside, from whence my absence has been most unexpectedly prolonged by this wild expedition, and from whence I have heard nothing since my departure and shall hear nothing until my return. I find the great western has arrived, there are therefore letters from you, to some of the family if not to myself. Gabriel and his flock must also have arrived; from whom I shall learn so much about you. These considerations make me long to be at home, much as I am delighted by the grand and beautiful scenes I am continually beholding. I hope you apply yourself diligently and perseveringly to the study of the French. Make yourself well acquainted with the conversational exercises, and practice unremittingly on the verbs; you will then get ⟨con⟩ a colloquial ⟨convers⟩ fluency that will be an ⟨import source of⟩ immense advantage to you, in your intercourse with French society. I again entreat you to avail yourself as much as possible of the many hours you will now have to yourself, ⟨alone⟩ to cultivate your mind in the various branches of knowledge that fit one for polite and intelligent society. My dear Sarah you have admirable elements in your nature that have never been sufficiently brought out; I wish you could ⟨only⟩ be brought to think of yourself only half as well as I think of you, and you would then ⟨become⟩ be stimulated to cultivate and work up those powers which I know lay latent in your mind, but for which you do not ⟨think you⟩ give yourself credit. Set your mind as much as possible on intellectual objects and pursuits. As to mere fashion and finery, in dress or in any thing else, consider them as ⟨inferior⟩ objects, to be attended to of course, but quite of secondary importance in the estimation of a noble minded woman. With proper tastes and proper emulation, what a glorious opportunity of self cultivation has an intellectual woman in the center of Paris!

New York, Aug 6th. We left Carbondale on the afternoon of the

3d. and had a fine drive through the mountains to Honesdale, where
we were warmly welcomed. Indeed I was quite surprised by the cordial attentions I experienced in these villages in the wilderness, and by
a compliment that had been paid me during my absence. ⟨The Last⟩
↑On↓ Sunday afternoon I had rambled with some of my fellow travellers
to the summit of a peculiar and very picturesque cliff on the crest of a
woody height; that ⟨almost⟩ overlooks the pretty village of Honesdale
and its romantic valley; and had returned home by a beautiful walk
along the foot of the mountain, overhung with rocks and trees, with
thickets of Kalmias, Rododendrons &c and a wild little river babbling
along, and dividing it from the village—It was a perfect green alley
carpeted with verdure, one of the most delightful walks I had ever
seen in the vicinity of a village. Several of the young people of the
village were taking their Sunday stroll in it. I expressed my ⟨[unre-
covered]⟩ hope that so charming a prominade might never be laid
desolate by the hand of improvement ⟨and suggested that it⟩· ↑but↓
might be kept up as a public resort—and suggested that it might be
called [Lady]wood [MS torn] Lane; to secure for it the all potent protection of the ladies. On [my re]turn [MS torn] from Carbondale, the two
rival newspapers of Honesdale were [put in] [MS torn] my hands, in
which I found my sojourn in the village mentioned at large, my visit to
the ⟨cut⟩ cliff &c—and that the latter had been named Irvings cliff in
memorial of my visit, and the beautiful green alley had received the
name of Lady Wood Lane—I furthermore heard before my departure
that in the course of the week the ladies were to have a rural fete in the
lane by way of conferring on it its name in style—We left Honesdale
early on the morning of the 4th. in an extra stage; and had a rough but
interesting journey through forests and across mountains—something
like that we made on our return from Theodores wedding.[9] We reached
Goshen late in the evening. And yesterday morning drove from thence
to Newburgh, about twenty miles, through some of the most enchanting scenery I have ever seen in this country. At Newburgh we embarked
in an Albany Steamboat, and reached New York ⟨in the⟩ about five
oclock. My heart yearned as I passed the cottage and saw it peeping
from among the trees and thought of the dear little folks nestled there,
and regretted that I could not be landed any where in its vicinity.
I learn however that they are all well—and that there is a letter from
you, waiting for me; which I am glad to hear your mother has opened
and read. I shall return to the cottage this afternoon Your mother, I
understand has been at Eliza Romeyns for a week past; and is in good
health and Spirits. I am disappointed at not finding Gabriel Irving
and his party at home. They were to sail about the beginning of July,
in a sailing packet and will have a long voyage. Your favorite Steam

ship the Great Western, which sailed ⟨several⟩ a week or two after them has been in port for some days.

I have just heard that two of the parcels of Galegnanis Messengers which you had the provident kindness to send me, have arrived and been sent up to the cottage.

I am at Mr Grinnells. Julia and her children are at New Bedford, where Mr Grinnell generally goes on Fridays and returns on Tuesday or Wednesday. I have partly promised to accompany him next Friday, if I find I can be spared from home.

And now my dear Girl I must conclude this rambling letter which, for the most part is about scenes in the Wilderness, which will not interest you so much as home scenes; but I could not help still taking you with me on my travels. Farewell, may every blessing attend you and keep your heart as light and happy as it is good and kind. With kindest remembrances to Mr Storrow

Your affectionate uncle
Washington Irving

ADDRESSED: A Madame / Madame Storrow / aux Soins de Mr Thomas W Storrow / Rue du faubg Poissoniere / à Paris   DOCKETED: July 31st 1841 / No 10 MANUSCRIPT: Yale.   PUBLISHED: *Yale Review*, XVI (April 1927), 473–78; LSS, pp. 24–31.

1. See WI's letter of July 26, 1841.

2. Indian Brook is a stream flowing into the Hudson just south of Constitution Island, about one-eighth mile north of the Gouverneur estate and about three miles south of Gouverneur Kemble's residence. See Roland Van Zandt, *Chronicles of the Hudson, Three Centuries of Travelers' Accounts* (New Brunswick, 1971), pp. 202–3, 212, 332, 334; and Wallace Bruce, *The Hudson, Three Centuries of History, Romance and Invention* (New York, 1907), map opposite p. 120.

3. Colonel Thomas Arden, who owned land along the Hudson south of the Gouverneur estate and about three fourths of a mile north of the Beverley House occupied by Henry Brevoort. See Bruce, *The Hudson*, map opposite p. 120.

4. Philip Hone (1781–1851), a successful merchant and businessman and mayor of New York in 1825 and 1826, was part owner of the coal mine near Honesdale. He is remembered today for his diary (1828–1851), which preserves details about social life in New York City.

5. This town, about thirteen miles northeast of Scranton and about fifteen miles west of Honesdale, was the site of the first underground anthracite mine, which opened in 1831.

6. These mountains made a barrier 1000 feet high between the Delaware River and the coal fields. See Harry S. Drago, *Canal Days in America*, p. 91.

7. WI omitted the *e*.

8. Jane Ann Dodge (1799–1875) married John Frothingham (1789–1869) in December, 1816.

9. In a letter of September 22, 1838, WI spoke of the wedding of Theodore Irving to Jane W. Sutherland on August 28, 1838.

1356. To Sarah Van Wart

Honesdale, Aug 1st. 1841

My dear Sister,
  I write from among the Mountains in the upper part of Pennsylvania,
from a pretty village which has recently sprung into existence, as the
Philip Hone, who was extremely efficient in directing enterprize
into this quarter. I came here along the Delaware and Hudson canal,
which extends from the Hudson River near the Cats Kill mountains,
upwards of a hundred miles into the interior; traversing some of the
most beautiful parts (as to Scenery) of the State of New York, and
penetrating the State of Pennsylvania. I accompanied the Directors of
the Delaware & Hudson Canal on their annual visit of examination;
among the directors are Philip Hone and my friend Brevoort. I do not
know when I have made a more gratifying excursion with respect to
natural scenery, or more interesting from the stupendous works of art.
The canal is laid ⟨for⟩ a great part of the way along romantic valleys,
watered by the Rondout,[1] the Lackawaxin[2] &c for many miles it is built
up along the face of perpendicular precipices, rising into stupendous
cliffs with overhanging forests; or strutting out into vast promontories;
while on the other side you look down upon the Delaware, foaming
and roaring below you at the foot of an immense wall or embankment
which supports the canal. Altogether it is one of the most daring undertakings I have ever witnessed, to carry an artificial river over ⟨moun⟩
rocky mountains and up the most Savage and almost impracticable
defiles: and all this too, has been achieved by the funds of an association composed of a handful of individuals. For upwards of ninety miles
I went through a constant succession of scenery that would have been
famous had it existed in any part of Europe; The Cats Kill mountains
to the north, the Shawangunk mountains to the south, and between them
lovely valleys, with the most luxuriant wood lands and picturesque
Streams. All this is a region about which I had heard nothing: a region
entirely unknown to fame—but so it is in our country. We ha[ve] [*word
ran off edge of paper*] some main routes for the fashionable traveller,
along which he is hurried in Steam boats and rail road cars: while on
every side extend regions of beauty about which he hears and knows
nothing. Some of the most enchanting scenes I have beheld since my
return to the United States, have been in out of the way places, into
which I have been accidentally led.
  I received a letter from you shortly before I left home; by which
I find you are likely to remain some time longer at the Shrubbery. I

hope times may improve and business revive, so that you may not find it necessary to change your residence; or, if it should still be advisable to do so, that you may find a good purchaser. We are gradually getting through this "valley of the shadow of death"[3] which the whole busy world has had ⟨of⟩ for some few years past to traverse, and I am in hopes that the severe lessons received this time will ⟨ha⟩ be held in remembrance and have a wholesome effect for the residue of our existence. The world at large is suffering the penalty of its own avarice; for avarice for a time was as extensive and deleterious in its sway as the cholera Every one was siezed with the mania of becoming suddenly rich; and in yeilding to the frantic impulse has impoverished himself. The only consolation to each individual sufferer is that he is not worse off than most of his neighbors. It has been a mania too that has infected the most knowing as well as the most simple minded; ⟨and that⟩ indeed some of the shrewdest calculators have been the most taken in. [*end of MS*]

MANUSCRIPT: NYPL—Seligman Collection.   PUBLISHED: PMI, III, 152–53, 168–70 (in part).

1. Rondout Creek rises in the Catskills in western Ulster County and flows into the Hudson River at Kingston, about fifty miles away.
2. The Lackawaxen River flows from Honesdale a distance of twenty-five miles and enters the Delaware River at the village of Lackawaxen.
3. Psalms 23:4.

1357.   To Messrs. Lea & Blanchard

Tarrytown Aug 9th. 1841

Messrs Lea & Blanchard

Gentlemen,
    In the 2d edition of Margaret Davidsons Memoirs, at the last line of Page 13. for "letters in writing" read "lessons in writing"
    After line 17. P 136 insert the following
We here interrupt the narrative of Mrs Davidson to insert a copy of verses addressed by Margaret to her brother, a young officer in the army and stationed at a frontier post in the Far West. They were written in September about two months before her death, and are characterized throughout by her usual beauty of thought and tenderness of feeling; but the last verse, which alludes to the fading verdure, and falling leaf, and gathering ⟨sadness⟩ ↑melancholy↓ and lifeless quiet of the

season as typical of her own blighted youth and approaching dissolution, has something in it peculiarly solemn and affecting

To My Soldier brother—in the Far West.[1]

'Tis an Autumn eve, and the tints of day
   From the West are slowly stealing,
And the clouds round the couch of the setting sun
   Are gently and silently wheeling.
—'Tis the scene and the hour for the soul to bathe
   In its own deep springs of feeling—
And my thoughts from their galling bonds set free,
Have fled to the "far-far West" to thee!

And perchance 'mid the toils of thy varied life
   Thou also art pausing a while,
To behold how beautiful all things look
   In the Sun lights passing smile;
And perchance reccollections of kindred and home
   Thy cares for a moment beguile
Thy thoughts have met *mine* in their passage to thee,
And though distant far distant, our spirits are free!

I know thou art dreaming of home
   And the dear ones sheltered there,
Of thy mother, pale with the pain of years,
   And thy sire with his silvered hair;
And with *them* blind thoughts of thy boyish years
   When the world looked all so fair,
When thy cheek flushed high at the voice of praise
   And thy breast was unknown to care,
And while memory burns her torch for thee
I know that these thoughts and these dreams will be!

But when, in the shade of the Autumn wood,
   Thy wandering footsteps stray;
When yellow leaves and perishing buds
   Are scattered in thy way;
When all around thee breathes of rest
   And sadness and decay—

With the drooping flower, and the falling tree,
Oh! brother blend thy thoughts of me!

The following fragments, continues Mrs Davidson, appear to be &c (here
resume the narrative at line 18 of Page 136)

I am gentlemen,

Very respectfully / Your friend & Servt.
Washington Irving

DOCKETED: Recd Aug 12 / And [Aug] 12 [The second line is under the first line,
and in place of "Aug" the writer has used ditto marks]
MANUSCRIPT: University of North Carolina Library.

1. At this point WI has an asterisk, with the following note at the bottom of the
page: "This copy of verses has come to hand since the publication of the first
edition of this memoir."

1358.   To Sarah Storrow

Sunnyside Cottage Sept. 1. 1841

My dear Sarah,

Your mother I believe has given you in her letter a daily bulletin of
my health during my recent malady; finding myself, however, fairly
emerged out of the "Dark Valley" I hasten to give you, under my own
hand, assurance of my returning health. I have indeed received a lesson
which will cure me hereafter of that heedless confidence in my constitution which made me think myself proof against heat or cold, wind or
rain, and ↑rendered me↓ regardless of every exposure. I believe the
last day of my tour to the coal region, when, for the sake of ⟨b⟩ seeing the
mountain scenery I ⟨rode⟩ sat from morning till night beside the driver,
exposed to the intense heat of the sun, after my system had been deranged
by previous fatigues and exposures, gave the effectual blow to my health.
I returned home completely out of order and in the course of three or
four days my indisposition terminated in a violent fever. I have never
known before what a real fever was—indeed my health has been so uniformly good that I have scarcely ever had a serious malady of any kind.
Perhaps this may have made my actual illness appear the more severe
to me. ⟨In the⟩ at times when I lay panting with fever, my whole frame
in a state of indiscribable irritability; my mind at intervals wild with
delirium; it seemed to me as if I could not exist under it; as if the fever
must sieze upon my brain, deprive me of my senses and hurry me out
of existence. But how can I express myself in sufficient terms of affection-

ate gratitude for the tenderness, the watchful, the devoted, the unwearied tenderness with which I have been treated! Your dear mother
has been constantly by my bed side; forgetting her own weakness and
infirmities; watching every varying symptom; and attending upon me
almost with the alertness and activity of youth. And then the dear girls
have been hovering about me like ministering angels. The dear good
little Sarah, with her ⟨effective⟩ provident and effective care, and with
the mature judgement and experience of a matron, was my thorough
nurse; attending to all the directions of the doctor, punctually administer-
ing his prescriptions; preparing my cooling drinks and studying every
thing that might relieve and comfort me. Poor little Mary, too, would sit
by me and fan me during the wild paroxysms of my fever; endeavoring
with quiet assiduity to arrange and smooth the pillows for my throbbing
and restless head; and turning aside continually to wipe away the tears
that kept trickling down her cheeks.

[*Along the left-hand margin of the page appear the following sentences.*]
    I wish Mr Storrow to procure and send out to me as soon as possible
the following works on the subject of American discovery—Gumilla[1] in
Spanish, or in French—the former preferable. *Pedro Simon*[2] I presume in
Spanish—and *Pedrahata* [?][3]—Mr Warden[4] probably has them or can
tell where they may be procured

    It is almost worth being ill to experience such tenderness. I used to
look forward with doubt and distrust to the time when through age and
infirmity I might be unable to take care of myself, and, having no child
of my own to cherish and bear with me, I might become an irksome
burthen upon others. I have no longer such apprehension. I feel that I
have affectionate tender hearted beings about me, that would be to me
like children, and love and cherish me the more for my very infirmities.
Thank god, my malady has passed away and I begin to be myself again.
Yesterday, for the first time, I drove out in the carriage with your mother
and Julia (Sanders wife) We had a lovely drive past Mr Constants,
through the new road to the Saw mill River, and up that delightful valley
and by the Dobbs Ferry road house. Oh how beautiful every thing
looked; my heart was full of love and gratitude and enjoyment. This
morning opens bright and exhilirating; a pure bracing north west wind
has made the air light and elastic and seems to give new vigor to my
frame. I feel in the happiest of moods, and my happy feelings are reflected from every affectionate countenance around me. It is the fifth
anniversary of our taking up our residence at the dear little cottage which
has proved such a happy home to us all.
    During an early stage of my illness I received your long delightful

letter written at different dates; the last the 31st July.[5] Your animated descriptions of the fêtes of Paris, and of your excursions to places in the vicinity bring up the most pleasing reccollections. I am continually gratified to find how much we coincide in our impressions of scenes and places: and how much we are struck ⟨with the same⟩ and pleased with the same circumstances. I agree with you as to the view from the terrace at St Germains; it is vast ↑diversifed↓ and noble, but by no means so beautiful as that from Richmond. Meudon was a favorite resort of mine when I sojourned part of one Summer at the village of Auteuil. I used to stroll there on foot and from thence to St Cloud. The prospect from the terrace at Meudon[6] is indeed superb. The village of Meudon was classic ground to me, having been the residence of Rabelais an old French writer of admirable wit and humor, though too gross and obscene for female perusal. Have you ever in your excursions stopped at dear little Auteuil. It lies on the border of the Bois de Bologne, between that and the Seine. The Storrow family had a country retreat there for two or three Summers at which Peter and myself passed many a happy day and I once took lodgings nearly opposite their mansion for several weeks, to escape the turmoil of Paris and finish a work I was writing. Many a morning have we passed with the Storrows, strolling in the Bois de Bologne or seated under the trees.

I presume you often walk on the Boulevards of Paris They used to be a most amusing study to me. Every quarter of the Boulevard has a class of frequenters peculiar to itself and differing in style, dress &c from the others. The fashionable throng in one part; the bourgeoisie in another; and the motley population beyond Port St Martin. It is on the boulevards that one sees the population of Paris in all its varieties; it is a constantly moving puppet show. The alleys of the Tuilleries only give you Paris in its gala dress.

Sept 2d. Has your mother given you an account of the Maratime invasion of the Cottage by that crack brained navigator Capt Fatio?[7] You no doubt reccollect this odd genius; and his tour through the country as a strolling lecturer. It seems government has given him the command of a revenue cutter, and he is a complete beggar on horseback. His first move was to take himself a wife; whom he married at Washington. rather a pleasing genteel looking person, whom he presents as Mrs America Fatio. She for the present presides over the cabin of the cutter, ⟨and⟩ the Captain treating her to a cruise during the Honey Moon. In the course of this matrimonial cruise he came up into the waters of the Tappan Sea; intending to proceed up to West Point, make a grand flourish and fire a salute for the military academy. His swaggering cruise was suddenly checked by orders which overtook him to return to New York. He anchored off Tarrytown; visited Eliza, invited her and several others

to a breakfast on board of the cutter and sent me an invitation to me
to the same effect. A freak of bad weather prevented his fête and I
hoped we were rid of him: but lo, in the afternoon he appeared off the
cottage; dropped anchor, displayed his colours and fired a salute. a
couple of boats were then manned for shore, in one of which came the
captain, inviting us all to tea with Mrs America Fatio. Fred[8] and Philip
Paulding and Irving Van Wart were on board. There was no such thing
as parrying the Captains importunities; and as I thought a visit on board
the cutter might be curious and amusing to the girls I took Kate and
Julia with me. Such a time as we had with the overpowering civilities
and the perpetual fuss of the Captain. His wife was well bred and pleasing enough; but the Captain hardly gave her an opportunity to say a word.
He was interfering in every thing and bothering every body with his
commands from the sailors on the rigging to the poor devil who waited
on table. And then such an arrant drawer of the long bow; ⟨He had a⟩
such stories about his exploits; and such a gross hyperbolical flatterer. The
malady which was to pull me down was lurking in my veins; I was
nervous and impatient; and in this state had for three mortal hours to
endure the incessant palaver and overpowering blarney of this poetical
vagabond. I was several times tempted to jump overboard and swim
ashore or be drowned. To finish our entertainment in style, just as we
made a move to depart, the music of the Cutter, a cursed drum and fife,
struck up and for half an hour played a variety of tunes enough to drive
one mad. The captain was vain of his drummer; he was a chimney sweep
he had picked up in the streets and meant to make a first rate musician
of him. I wished the captain were up the chimney and the drummer
sweep at the bottom; to drum there to all eternity. We got ashore between nine and ten Oclock: the ⟨drum was⟩ captain and his drum haunted
my dreams all night and I believe this nautical regale contributed to
hurry me into a fever. The captain weighed anchor the next morning—
he is destined to cruise on the Florida coast. I hope government will
keep him there and that we may never see his flag again in the Tappan
Sea.

Sept. 3. The weather continues bright and beautiful. I presume your
mother gives you an account of the visitors at the cottage. They have
been numerous during my illness; and have been very kind in their enquiries. The evening before last there was a Soiree at Mr George Jones;
quite a gathering of the neighborhood. I was not well enough to attend.
Yesterday afternoon I took a delightful drive with your mother and
Sarah Irving, and on our way home we called at the Hamiltons. The
girls were all out, but Mr & Mrs Hamilton and old Mrs Hamilton[9] were
at home—and two visitors. Your mother was received in the most cordial
manner. Mrs Hamilton said she considered ⟨it qu⟩ her visit quite a favor.

We sat there some time, and your mother came away delighted with every body and every thing. She enjoys these little visits extremely. Indeed, I have not seen her so alert in body and mind for a long time. Our next visit is to be to Mrs Howlands.

I presume you know that David[10] has left us. I received a letter ⟨which⟩ while I was ill, which lay by me three days unopened. It proved to be from Messrs. Wiley & Putnam, informing me that they had a vacancy in their retail department, with a salary of $200 a year to begin with, and that they wished me to send the candidate at once. We dispatched David the same afternoon, to secure the place. He returned the next day to make his final arrangements, and two days after there was a sad leave taking on all sides. He expressed great regret at leaving me while on a sick bed; but I would not have him risk so good a place.

I have no doubt of his doing well. He is a thoroughly excellent lad. We have a little fellow in his place; one John Mitchell, (Scotch) who really promises to be very regular, intelligent and handy; so that I ⟨hope⟩ ↑begin to think↓ we have again drawn a prize.

We have seen nothing of Gabriel or his party since their return. I hope we shall have little Abby on a visit to the Cottage before long; but you know nothing is more uncertain than her movements while under the maternal wing. Today or tomorrow we expect letters from you by the Boston Steamer which must arrive about this time. Your mother, as usual, is in eager expectation. Farewell my dear Sarah; give my kind remembrances to Mr Storrow. ever your affectionate uncle

Washington Irving

ADDRESSED: à Madame / Madame Storrow / aux Soins de M. T W Storrow / Rue du faubg. Poissonniere / à Paris / *per Albany*   POSTMARKED: OUTRE-MER / 16 / OCT / 41 / LE HAVRE   DOCKETED: *September 1st 1844* / No 11
MANUSCRIPT: Yale.   PUBLISHED: *Yale Review*, 16 (April, 1927), 478–80; LFSS, pp. 32–35 (in part); PMI, III, 170–72 (in part).

1. WI's library included Padre Joseph Gumilla, *Historia Natural . . . de las Naciones en la Riveras del Rio Orinoco*, 2 vols. (Barcelona, 1791).

2. Among the books in WI's library is Pedro Simon, *Noticias Historiales de la Conquistas de Tierra Ferme en las Indias Orientales* (Cuenca, 1629).

3. This title has not been identified.

4. David Baillie Warden (1778–1845), an Irishman by birth, came to the United States for political reasons and taught in several colleges. Later he was appointed secretary of the American legation in Paris and subsequently served as U.S. consul in Paris for forty years. He was a bibliophile interested in books on the explorations and history of the Western hemisphere.

5. This letter has not been located.

6. Meudon, a suburb of Paris about seven miles southwest of Notre Dame Cathedral, was dominated by a chateau with a wide terrace laid out in the seventeenth century. See Karl Baedeker, *Paris and Its Environs*, pp. 298–99.

7. L. C. Fatio, who was appointed a midshipman in the U.S. Navy on March 8, 1822, is probably the person referred to as Fazio in WI's letter to William and John Lyon, February 24, 1841. See Edward W. Callahan, *List of Officers of the Navy of the United States and of the Marine Corps from 1775 to 1900* (New York, 1901), p. 190.

8. Frederick W. Paulding (1811–1859), son of William Paulding and older brother of Philip Paulding. See also WI to Sarah Storrow, May 3, 1841.

9. Probably Elizabeth Schuyler Hamilton (1757–1854), mother of James Alexander Hamilton and widow of Alexander Hamilton.

10. David Davidson. See WI to Sarah Storrow, July 18, 1841, note 19.

1359. To Francis Granger

Sunnyside Sept 15th. 1841

My dear Sir,

I had written the enclosed letter[1] and was about to send it, when I learnt, to my great regret, that you ⟨had⟩ were about to leave the cabinet. This quite disconcerted me for the moment. On after thoughts I have determined to send the letter notwithstanding. It may not come too late for you to act upon it; if it should, however, you may hand it over to your successor.[2] He may be some person with whom I have no acquaintance, or none of sufficient degree to warrant a direct application of the kind; and yet he may be influenced in favor of the application, by the facts stated in my letter.

It is indeed with great regret that I find the course of political events is about to deprive the public of your valuable official services; hoping and believing however, that whatever your future career may be it will be one of honor and prosperity, I remain my dear Sir

Yours very faithfully
Washington Irving

Hon Francis Granger / &c &c &c

ADDRESSED: The Hon. Francis Granger / Postmaster General. / Washington City POSTMARKED: NEW-YORK / SEP / 16 DOCKETED: W. Irving / Sep: 15. 1841. / The enclosed letter related solely to the / establishment of a New post office & / therefore I handed it to Mr Fuller / J. M.

MANUSCRIPT: Ontario County Historical Society, Canandaigua, New York.

Francis Granger served as postmaster general from March 6 to September 18, 1841, when he resigned to run for Congress.

1. This letter has not been located. According to the docket, it dealt with the establishment of a new post office.

2. Charles A. Wickliffe (1788–1869), who had served in Congress from 1823 to 1833 and as governor of Kentucky from October, 1839, to September, 1840, succeeded Granger as Tyler's postmaster general.

1360. *To Sarah Storrow*

New York, Sept 23d. 1841

My dear Sarah,

Since last I wrote to you we have received your delightful letters from Versailles,[1] written in a true spirit of enjoyment, and giving a lively and graphic picture of your sojourn at that place of artificial enchantment and your ⟨ex⟩ visit to the Fair at St Germains.[2] These letters as usual call up a thousand delightful reccollections in my mind, for Versailles has been a frequent resort, ⟨of mine⟩ and at one time a transient residence, ↑of your Uncle Peter & myself[.]↓ I have been too at the Fair of St Germains and the picturesque and merry groupes, about its terraces and its groves and woodland alleys are fresh before me.

Since I wrote to you last I have quite recovered my health, and almost entirely my strength, and have again been able to make excursions and attend the Social gatherings of our neighborhood. I made a very pleasant expedition with the Mrs Jones's and some ↑members↓ of their famil⟨y⟩ies to·lake Mayopec;[3] and took Mary with me, whose health, though much restored, is not altogether so firm as I could wish. We went by steam boat to Peeks Kill, and thence in Mrs C Jones's large waggon and Lewis's little pony waggon, to the lake. On our way we passed by the grove on the border of the lake, the scene of ⟨the⟩ ↑our↓ little Pic Nic, on that memorable highland excursion which you and I made in company with Mr G Kemble & Mr [?Doftham?]. The sight of it gave me a sad twinge of reccollection; but where can I go my dear Girl that there is not something or other to call you to my mind, So completely have our lives be⟨come⟩en woven together for several years past.

We passed a part of three days at the lake very agreeably, though my strength was not sufficiently restored to cope with the exhuberant spirits and constant activity of my travelling companions. You would have been charmed with the lake. We made excursions about it in rowboats, and visited its beautiful islands; on one of which we passed a great part of a morning listening to a young French Gentlemen ⟨Mr⟩ ↑the Baron↓ Too brilliant (who was one of our travelling party,) reading an amusing little French comedy. We returned from the lake by land, through wild and beautiful scenery; part of it along the Croton, where the roads were exceeding rough and the Jones's of course in frequent panics.

Since my return home there ha⟨s⟩vc been ⟨an⟩ several very pleasant little gatherings, or visitations in the neighborhood, which have brought our rural circle together; but we have had no pic nics nor musical soirees as we had last year. I ⟨pre⟩ refer you to the letters from the girls and from your mother for the gossip of the Cottage and the neighborhood not having time to enter into particulars. You will be delighted to hear that Mrs Constant ⟨has⟩ is really to sail for France in the latter part of October. ⟨Th⟩ Mr Constant talks of being absent eighteen months or two years; Miss Johnson accompanies them and they take Willy with them. What a joyful meeting you will have with her at Paris. She is looking most lovely, yet I understand is extremely nervous. Much as I regret to lose her ⟨to⟩ from the neighborhood, I am rejoiced that this measure is finally determined on; for I trust it [will] restore her to us in perfect health and spirits, to be once more the pride and delight of our rural neighborhood.

Rebecca McLane[4] is on a visit to the Hamiltons, where she arrived a few days since, looking very thin and rather out of Spirits from some domestic trials; the recent death of a favorite uncle,[5] and the sickness and death of an overseer of the estate at Bohemia,[6] who was much prized by the family, and who Rebecca attended with the most generous and kindhearted Solicitude in his last illness. Rebecca enquired after you in the warmest and most affectionate manner, and asked whether I thought you would like to receive a letter from her. I told her that I knew of no one whose letters would be more acceptable to you—I hope she will write to you; but you know her impulses though ardent and sincere, are not always apt to be acted upon.

I am scrawling this hasty line at your uncles counti[ng house?] [MS torn] and in a great hurry—It is a mere apology for a letter. I will write a longer one at a quieter moment. Yesterday there was a grand opening of the Hudson and Erie Rail road,[7] from the great Pier opposite the Cottage to Goshen—a distance of about 45 miles. I was invited to attend, and crossed in my boat from the Cottage to the Pier head. About ½ past ten in the morning a Steam boat arrived from New York, laden with invited guests—about 500—It seemed as if every gentleman that I knew in New York was there. We started forth with in the cars; which are spacious and convenient, and had a splendid drive through the valley of the Ramapo, and a succession of that Romantic scenery through which you and I passed on our delightful tour from the Highlands to Hoboken— at Goshen there was all the country assembled; and one of the most enormous dinners I ever was present at—tables being spread in temporary buildings, and in the ⟨Hot Slee⟩ Rail road Hotel—We returned in the cars in the evening and I continued down to New York in the Steam boat and am scribbling this letter with all the ⟨nervous⟩ irritation of

nerve consequent to such an expedition and such a tumultuous festival—
Which I give as an excuse for this letter, not being much longer and
much better—

Remember me affectionately to Mr Storrow

                              Ever my dear Sarah your affectionate Uncle
                                                                    W I.

ADDRESSED: À Madame / Madame Storrow / aux Soins du Monsr. T W Storrow /
    Rue du faubg Poissoniere / à Paris. / par Gt. Western   POSTMARKED: [*unre-
    covered*] // BRISTOL / SHIP LETTER   DOCKETED: September 23d. 1841 /
    No 12
MANUSCRIPT: Yale.

    1. These letters have not been located.
    2. This annual festival was held on the Sunday nearest August 30 and the nine
following days at Saint-Germain-en-Laye, a suburb about eleven miles northwest of
Paris. See Karl Baedeker, *Paris and Its Environs*, pp. 332–33.
    3. Lake Mahopac, named after a local Indian tribe, was in Putnam County about
ten miles east of West Point and twenty miles northeast of Tarrytown.
    4. Rebecca McLane, the eldest daughter of Louis McLane, later married Philip
Hamilton (1802–1884), the youngest son of Alexander Hamilton and the brother
of James Alexander Hamilton, who was WI's neighbor.
    5. George Baldwin Milligan, the brother of Catherine McLane. See Munroe, *Louis
McLane*, p. 488.
    6. The family home of Mrs. McLane, a plantation of which she inherited a part
upon the death of her father in 1806. See Munroe, *Louis McLane*, p. 41.
    7. For details of the festivities attending the opening, see NYEP, September 24,
1841; and *The Diary of Philip Hone*, II, 564–65.

1361.   To Sarah Storrow

                                              New York, Oct. 3d. 1841

My dear Sarah,
    I have been passing a few days partly in town, on business, and partly
at Mr Astors, and am writing this, on a rainy Sunday morning, at Mr
Grinnells. The evening before last I was at Mrs Frederick Rhinelanders:[1]
it was a delightful visit, though it brought up many half melancholy reccollections of former times, and of visits that we have made there together. You were spoken of repeatedly, ⟨with⟩ ↑in↓ the kindest and most
affectionate terms; but it is needless for me to dwell on this visit as it is
probable this letter will be delivered to you by Mary Rhinelander (Mrs
King)[2] herself, who sails ⟨in the⟩ for Havre in the packet of the 8th inst.

What a joyful meeting you will have with this warm hearted generous spirited little being. I think you will like her husband also, who appears to be frank, manly and amiable. Our little friend Posey, whom you may reccollect, with her blooming cheeks and pink ribbons, has grown up into a lovely girl; as fresh, as sweet and artless as ever; with a stock of natural, unassisted beauty, that would furnish a capital for half a dozen Parisian belles.

I was at a little evening party at Mrs Constants, a few days before I left the country. She is looking very lovely, and her general health is much improved. I trust her tour in Europe will effectually restore it. When last I saw him Mr Constant was in doubt whether to sail in the Havre packet of the 25th of this month, or to wait and sail with Capt Funk[3] on the 1st. of November. The worthy little captain is a great favorite with both Mr & Mrs Constant

You will soon have a little home circle of friends forming around you, and will cease to feel lonely and a stranger in Paris. I long to hear of your being comfortably settled in appartments furnished by yourselves; which will contribute greatly to give you a home feeling. You have passed the hardest part of the ordeal in a separation from home, and will daily be forming ties, and occupations and habitudes, incident to your change of position, and productive of future ⟨enjoyment⟩ ↑happiness↓ and advantage. You have the highest sources of elegant and intellectual enjoyment and improvement around you, and you must ⟨seek⟩ task yourself diligently to improve them. I think, my dear Sarah, you are apt to undervalue yourself, and to be careless about the cultivation of your tastes and of your intellectual powers. I do not know but this has been the result of an error on the part of your mother, who always appeared to me to be more prone to twit you about your defects, than to arouse your ambition and energies on the points on which you were calculated to excel. I do not think any one appreciates ⟨you as j⟩ your mental powers as justly as I do; though I have only seen them exercised in a desultory manner. I know too the difficulties you have to contend with in any mental application, from the want of early and ⟨com⟩ regular dicipline of the mind, and from a long cessation of all direct study, ⟨and⟩ or continued course of reading; but I know the quickness of your perceptions; the excellence of your judgement, the intuitive correctness of your taste, and that quick convertability of your mind, which turns all that you read, not into a stock of facts for the memory, but of ideas for the understanding therefore, do not be discouraged when you find yourself somewhat incapable of mental drudgery, and somewhat impatient of tasks on the memory; keep on as well as you can, and trust me in the end you will find yourself an immense gainer. ⟨I do not try⟩ Were I to talk in this way to any one else it might seem like flattery; but you, my dearest girl, know my object which is to stimulate you to exertion and to counteract an unfortunate Self distrust ⟨of your capability⟩

I saw yesterday little Abby[4] for the first time since her return, looking fresh as a rose and plump as a little partridge. She gave me many very interesting particulars about you, and spoke with delight of her sojourn at Paris, which she would be rejoiced to revisit. She and her mother are in town taking care of old Mr Furman[5] who is ill of an intermittent fever, but on the recovery. She tells me that you confidently expect me at Paris this autumn, and some of your letters intimate the same expectation. My dear girl *it is out of the question.* ⟨Nothing⟩ I cannot consult my own wishes in this matter—I must stay at home and endeavor to take care of those about me. Mr Van Wart has signified to your Uncle E.I. that his agency must come to a close. This leaves him for the present without any means of support; and what new mode he is to devise at this time of life and with his infirmities, it is difficult to imagine—How I shall be able to keep all afloat with my cramped and diminished means, and with debts incurred on behalf of others hanging over and threatening me is an equally harrassing question. ⟨Thes Wh⟩ These thing[s] [*MS blotted*] break my rest and disturb my waking thoughts; they haunted me sadly during my illness. However, as poor Scott said, "I have a good deal of work in me yet" If I can but fairly get my pen under way I may make affairs wear a different aspect: but these cares and troubles bear hard upon the capability of a literary man "who has but his good spirits to feed and clothe him." The Doctor who attended upon me in my illness and who was curious in studying my Constitution, said "I had a large heart that acted powerfully on my system." God knows I have need of a stout heart at times, but I certainly have always found it rally up to the charge in times of danger or difficulty. On that I will still rely.

I am writing a brief and uncomfortable letter; but my mind is so much occupied just now by a variety of matters that I have no mood nor time for cheerful gossip. I will soon write to you again and I trust in a brighter vein—

Remember me kindly to Mr Storrow

Your affectionate uncle
W.I.

MANUSCRIPT: Yale. PUBLISHED: *Yale Review*, 16 (April, 1927), 481–82 (in part); LFSS, pp. 36–38 (in part).

1. Probably the former Mary Lucretia Lucy Ann Stevens (1798-1877), whose husband, Frederick William Rhinelander (b. 1796), had died in 1836. See the manuscript genealogy by William Kelby in NYHS vertical file of the Rhinelander Family.

2. Mary Rhinelander (1818–1894) married John A. King, Jr. (1817–1900) at

Hell Gate on February 21, 1839. See *American Families of Historic Lineage* (New York, n.d.), p. 76; and Kelby, Rhinelander Family genealogy at NYHS.

3. According to an ad in the NYEP on November 1, 1841, Captain James Funck was leaving for Le Havre on the *Oneida* on that day. Funck was a friend of Peter Irving. See WI's letters of June 10, July 8, and December 25, 1835, and January 10, 1836.

4. The daughter of Gabriel Irving.

5. Probably Gabriel Furman (1756–1844), the great-grandfather of little Abby.

1362.   To Daniel Webster

Sunnyside Cottage, Oct 25th. 1841

My dear Sir,

Understanding that Mr Thomas B Adair. of Baltimore is an applicant for the office of Consul at his native place, Belfast Ireland, I take the liberty of Speaking a word in his favor. He has been for about fifteen years a citizen of the United States, and resident of Baltimore, where he married a daughter of the late Col. Tennant. He is a worthy man, well acquainted with commercial affairs, and well calculated for the office he solicits; but on these points I apprehend you will receive ample testimonials from the wide circle of his friends and connexions at Baltimore Being in some degree connected with him through family inter-marriages I feel some personal interest in the Success of his application

Ever my dear Sir, with the highest respect / and regard, yours faithfully

Washington Irving

The Hon Daniel Webster &c &c &c

ADDRESSED: The Hon Daniel Webster / Secretary of State / Washington   DOCK-
     ETED: Washington Irving
MANUSCRIPT: Brandeis University.

1363.   To Sarah Storrow

Sunnyside Oct 29th 1841

My dear Sarah,

Though but little in the mood for letter writing I will not suffer the Steampacket to depart without scrawling you a line. Some of your recent letters have given us very animated and graphic accounts of your sojourn at Versailles, and I have been delighted with the Spirit of true and happy hearted enjoyment which breathed through them; shewing that you were really beginning to feel yourself at home, to identify yourself with your new situation, and to enter with entire zest in the scenes around you. You are indeed most happily situated; and when you are completely settled in your own little snug *Menage* at Paris, you will find a delightful home of your own forming itself under your hand. You mention that you have a room which you call mine. My dear dear girl how happy should I be to occupy that room. I never longed to be with you so much as now, when at times I feel a little weary ⟨in⟩ at head and heart; but things must have their course; and I look forward with hope at some future time to occupy that room, and to enjoy with you some of the intellectual delights of Paris.

I had a letter a few days since from Dickens.[1] (Boz) He says in the course of it "Rogers[2] has been in great distress and desolation at having missed your niece. He was with me last night and bewailed his affliction in very moving terms He begged me to say as much to you, and to remember him heartily"—What do you think. Dickens is actually *coming to America*. He has ⟨taken⟩ ↑engaged↓ a passage for himself and his wife in the Steam Packet for Boston for the fourth of January next[3]—He says "I look forward to shaking hands with you with an interest I cannot (and I would not if I could) describe. You *can* imagine, I dare say, something of the feelings with which I look forward to being in America. I can hardly believe I am coming" In a few days after the receipt of this letter you will have Mrs Constant with you! What a meeting it will be for you both; for she, newly ⟨landed⟩ arrived in a Strange land, will equally with yourself, [enjoy][4] the value of a "home" friend. She will give you all the news of our neighborhood. Our summer has not been a gay one: at least we have not had pic nics nor musical gatherings. Mr & Mrs Constant were absent part of the time. I have been absent and ill; At the Cottage we have given no parties, and have never put up the tent Saloon which was erected so ⟨promp⟩ suddenly last year. Your absence from the Cottage has in fact given a check to our domestic gaiety and sociability which it will [take][5] some time to get over. I continually feel the want of some one to second me, or to sympathize with me in all my social connexions. I am made more and more sensible of the sad void in my household, which nothing seems to supply. We are not, however, in want of numbers. The little Cottage has been completely crammed. Anna[6] has been ⟨st⟩ here with four of her children, beside a visitor or two at the same time. I was delighted with your little favorite Hatty;[7] who is one of the oddest, merriest, cleverest little beings that I have seen for a long time: and is growing very pretty. Anna, though merely eleven years of age is as tall as a girl of fifteen, and will make a very fine girl—Eliza Romeyn is likewise quartered at the cottage having broken up her establishment at Tarry town; finding it was going behind hand. I am glad to get her away from that losing, yet toilsome concern, which was calculated to wear out her fine cheerful temper and break down her spirit.

Your mother has taken the idea of going to town for the winter provided your father can find lodgings to Suit her. She feels your absence, as winter approaches, and wishes to be with your father and Irving. I do not know that she will carry this plan into execution and hope she will not; yet I would not interfere with any arrangement she may think conducive to her comfort. Her room at the cottage will always be kept ready for her at all events; and, if she does go, ⟨it⟩ a few weeks residence in town may suffice her—I feel at times too much deadened in spirit to do much towards striking out plans for others; ⟨and⟩ or to interfere with plans they may strike out for ⟨myse⟩ themselves; my only regret is that my straitened means and accumulating cares diminish my power of contributing to the cheerfulness of those around me. However I trust we shall all get into brighter times before long, and that the little Cottage will continue to merit the name of Sunnyside—I am ⟨scrawling⟩ ↑finishing↓ this on board of the steamboat & must conclude. Give my kindest regards to ⟨St⟩ Mr Storrow and tell him I daily feel more and more drawn towards him in heart for the delicate ⟨a⟩, tender and unremitting attention ⟨which he pays⟩ with which he studies to promote your happiness —God bless him for it!

Your affectionate uncle
W I.

ADDRESSED: À Madame / Madame Storrow / Aux Soins du Mr. T. W. Storrow / Rue du Faubg Poissonniere / à Paris / *per Columbia*   POSTMARKED: NEW-YORK / OCT / 30 ANGL / 18 / NOV / 41 / [*unrecovered*] / AMERICA / 16 NO 16 / 1841   DOCKETED: October 29th. 1841 / No 14
MANUSCRIPT: Yale.   PUBLISHED: PMI, III, 173 (in part).

1. See Dickens to WI, September 28, 1841, in *The Letters of Charles Dickens*, II, 394–97.

2. Samuel Rogers was mentioned by WI in his letter to Dickens on May 26, 1841.

3. Dickens and his wife arrived in Boston on January 22, 1842, and traveled in the United States, going as far south as Richmond and as far west as St. Louis before sailing from New York on June 7. During the visit WI entertained Dickens at Sunnyside, presided over a dinner for him in New York on February 18, and met him in Washington and Baltimore. See Edgar Johnson, *Charles Dickens, His Tragedy and Triumph*, 2 vols. (New York, 1952), II, 362, 364, 385, 387, 391, 402, 406.

4. WI omitted the bracketed word.

5. WI omitted the bracketed word.

6. Anna Henrietta Duer Irving (1807–1874) was the wife of Pierre Paris Irving. She had five living children in 1841: Pierre Leslie (1828–1891), Anna Duer (1830–

1884), Elizabeth (1834–1906), Harriet Robinson (b. 1835), and Ellen (1840–1895).

7. Harriet Robinson Irving.

1364.   To J. Mills Brown

Sunnyside Octr. 30th. 1841

Dear Sir,

Indisposition, and subsequently the hurry of various engagements and occupations have prevented me from replying to various correspondents and among others from acknowledging the receipt of the copy of verses which you had the kindness to send me through the hands of my friend Mr Brevoort, and which I have read with much satisfaction. Accept my sincere thanks for this delicate testimonial of regard and believe me very respectfully

Your obliged friend & servt
Washington Irving

Mills Brown Esqr

ADDRESSED: J Mills Brown Esq / Birds Nest / near Cold Spring / Putnam County
   POSTMARKED: NEW-YORK / NOV / 1
MANUSCRIPT: NYPL—WI Papers.

1365.   To Sarah Storrow

Sunnyside, Nov 19th 1841

My dear Sarah,

Your late letters[1] giving us an account of your preparations for housekeeping have given us great delight, for they are written in a happy vein, shewing that you are beginning to feel yourself really at home and to enjoy every thing around you without alloy. You are indeed, my dear girl, surrounded with advantages calculated to delight and to improve you and you have a most kind and affectionate guardian beside you, who seems to Study, with discriminating eye, every thing that can administer to your happiness. Your last letter to me, giving an account of your first visit to the Italian Opera; your presence at a royal review, your meeting Mr Thiess[2] in the street &c had all that freshness and vivacity of spirit that used to be the charm of your conversations at home, when you would relate and depict what you had seen abroad. I have enjoyed, also, your accounts to your mother and the girls of your furniture, servants; your dresses &c Do not fear to be too minute in these details. You cannot imagine how they put you before us in your every day life and occupations, and in your personal appearance.

I have written you rather a gloomy letter[3] lately and am sorry for it; but for a time I was depressed in spirit by a concurrence of uncomfortable circumstances. I have always had a principle of reaction in my nature, however, which I am happy to find is not extinguished. I have taken pen in hand, and have been writing steadily for some weeks past.[4] I do not know that what I have written will be of a nature to command much popularity or circulation, nor do I think I shall offer it soon to the press; but the manner in which I have executed it satisfies me that I have "good work in me yet," and I am determined to keep on until I have fairly worked it out. The effect too has been immediate on my spirits. ⟨I feel⟩ My mind is steadily and cheerfully occupied; I feel that I am going ahead, and that if I can keep on in this manner I can make every thing smooth for those around me. The moment I finish the work I am busied upon I shall throw it aside and commence something else; If I continue in health and good spirits I shall soon have a little capital lying by me in Manuscript.

Your uncle E.I. is without employment and is with me at the cottage. He is in good spirits, however, and I trust we shall be able to devise something before long to give him occupation. I hope at any rate, by my own exertions, to be able to keep all afloat. Eliza Romeyn has sold her house to a Mr Tredwell[5] a worthy biscuit baker who has amassed a fortune by honest industry She gets $9000 Dollars for it; and will now stand free of all debts. She is at present on a visit ⟨G⟩ at Gabriel Irvings but will soon return to the Cottage.

Pierre M Irving has ⟨had⟩ been appointed by the Bank of Commerce[6] agent for the payment of Govt. Pensions; this will make an addition to his means of about twelve hundred dollars a year besides office rent, fuel, lights Stationary &c so that he is getting up in the world.

Your mother left us the day before yesterday on an experimental visit to town, where your father has taken lodgings for her in a very respectable house. She however will give you all the particulars. I cannot tell you how much I felt this ⟨circumstance⟩ ↑move↓ when first it was suggested. It seemed like breaking up our home, but I am reconciled to it, as it will be but for a visit, with the difference that she will be in lodgings of her own, without being obliged to others. I wanted her, however, to have one of the girls with her by turns, and hope yet she will make such an arrangement. If she finds the residence in ⟨th⟩ town not to prove agreeable she has promised to return instantly. At any rate she will return in the Spring, for after all, *this is her home.*

I must conclude for this letter is to go down on the morning boat, that

it may be in time for the Great Western and I am summoned to breakfast. Give my kind remembrances to Mr Storrow. ever my dear Sarah

Most affectionately your uncle
W. I.

P.S. I am looking for the books Mr Storrow is to send me[7] ⟨from wh⟩ on
which I mean to go to work almost immediately; having a literary use to
make of them.

ADDRESSED: a Madame / Madame Storrow / Aux Soins du M T. W. Storrow / No
17 Rue du Faubg Poissoniere / à Paris / P. *Great Western*   POSTMARKED:
NEW-YORK / NOV / 25 // SHIP LETTER
MANUSCRIPT: Yale.   PUBLISHED: PMI, III, 173–74 (in part).

1. These letters have not been located.
2. Probably Léon Thiessé (1793–1854), a French writer, translator, and editor
who served as head of the department of Basses-Alpes after the Revolution of 1830
until his retirement in 1841.
3. See WI's letter of October 29, 1841.
4. WI may have been working on a section of his biography of George Washington. See STW, II, 360.
5. Ephraim Treadwell of 725 Washington Street and Francis C. Treadwell of 110
Beekman Street are listed as bakers in Longworth's *New York City Directory* of
1841–1842 (p. 707). One of them may have purchased Mrs. Romeyn's house in
Tarrytown.
6. PMI had been appointed notary at the Bank of Commerce, 28 Merchants Exchange, in 1839 after WI had written letters of solicitation to Stephen Whitney,
January 12, 1839; to Samuel Ward, January 22, 1839; and to Russell H. Nevins,
February 13, 1839. As WI indicates, the new post represented an advancement for
PMI.
7. In his letter of September 1, 1841, WI had asked Storrow to send him several
books relating to American discovery.

1366.   To Sarah Storrow

New York, Decr. 1. 1841

My dear Sarah
I have read lately with great delight your letter to Irving[1] in which
you give an account of your excursion to Pallaisseau.[2] I have never been
there, and knew nothing of the existence of such a scene, not that the
story of the Maid & magpie[3] had a real foundation and locality. It is these
Storied and picturesque localities that give a charm to Europe that we
want in our own magnificent country.
I am passing a few days in town at Mr Astors, having brought Julia

& Mary on a visit to Julia Grinnells. You will hear by this opportunity no doubt, from other quarters, of the engagement of Kate to Philip Paulding. It has taken place since I came to town. I am glad the affair has come to this conclusion, for ⟨P⟩ our dear Kate has been sadly out of Spirits of late from some doubts and cross purposes in their love affairs of which I knew nothing. I hope and trust they may be happy together; they know each other well, from an intimacy of years and have nothing to find out as to each others faults or peculiarities. I am told your uncle E.I. is well pleased with the circumstance, and I can readily suppose it must contribute to take much care off of his mind in respect to the future fortunes of his girls; though he must feel satisfied that as long as I have a morsel to share with them they shall not want. It is a great ⟨gratification that⟩ satisfaction to think that Kate, though she may leave the Cottage, will yet to be in the immediate neighborhood; and I shall now look to the White house on the hill with tenfold interest. Mr George Jones is advertising his place for sale. He finds it impossible to attend to it properly, and that his life is rendered unsettled and comfortless by shifting incessantly from town to country. I shall look with anxiety to the neighbor who is to succeed him; and fear I shall never have one so ⟨t⟩ acceptable as himself.

The town has been running mad (or foolish) about two or three distinguished visitors: The Prince de Joinville,[4] Lord Morpeth[5] &c &c and there has been nothing but public dinners, balls, routs &c &c as yet I have steered clear of them all but today I am to meet Lord Morpeth at dinner at Mrs Hones, and in the evening at a ball at Mrs Mary Jones. By the way, there has arisen a terrible feud in the crambo fashionable world of New York, between Mrs Mary ↑Jones↓ and Mrs Doctor Mott,[6] in consequence of Mrs Doctor Mott omitting to invite Mrs Mary Jones and Miss Mary Jones to a ball which Mrs Doctor Mott gave to the Prince de Joinville and at which all the fashionable world was present. Mrs Doctor Mott did it avowedly in revenge of some "airs" which she said Mrs Mary Jones and Miss Mary Jones gave themselves towards herself and her daughter on divers occasions. Mrs Mary Jones and Miss Mary Jones have been eloquent in assuring the whole world how little they cared for Mrs and Miss Doctor Mott and their party, and to prove it, are this evening to give a ball to the whole world, to which Mrs and Miss Doctor Mott will be most particularly uninvited. I cannot but observe, however, that in this momentous affair Mrs Doctor Mott has shewn herself a great general. She has ⟨looked⟩ for some time past been endeavoring to get a stand in the fashionable world, with but limited success but this double achievement of ⟨giving⟩ having the Prince de Joinville at her ball, and cutting Mrs Mary Jones and Miss Mary Jones has established her house for ever. I am told now wherever she goes she is pointed out as the lady who cut Mrs Mary and Miss Mary Jones, whereupon every body begs to have the honor of being introduced to her.

You ask me in one of your letters whether I received the one containing a copy of a note from my excellent friend Rogers.[7] I did so and read it with a heart full of affection towards him for his delicate attention to you. I can assure you of a most kind reception from him when you revisit England.

I have been about a week in town and begin to long most heartily after the Cottage; where if nothing occurs ⟨to⟩ imperatively to call me away I shall remain through the winter, hard at work, that I may once more get a little ahead of the world, and cast dull care behind me. I expect to have ⟨my⟩ now and then a bright ray from the Parisian world, reflected into our little fireside world by your letters;

Decr 7th. In the hurry of town occupations and engagements this letter has lain neglected and I now take it up merely to scrawl a conclusion. I have been dreaming about you continually for a few days past. In one of my letters[8] I was walking with you among the most delightful gardens, amidst groves and statues and fountains and rejoicing that we were once more together; and in another dream I was ill and you were taking care of me. I presume the dreams were in consequence of reading some of your late letters some of which were taken up with the gardens of Versailles and the other with my late indisposition. I cannot express to you how these dreams waken up old feelings.

I am now about to pack up my things as we set off at half past two oclock on our return to the Cottage, where I heartily long to be. I want to see my dear dear honest hearted little Kate, now that all her troubles and perplexities are over; and I want to be quiet and at work in my little study. I have staid until today to be present at the Anniversary of the St Nicholas Society[9] which went off yesterday in great style. The dinner was more numerously attended than on any former occasion. We had Lord Morpeth there, who of late has been the universal guest. He made a very neat speech on the occasion—My health was drunk in the course of the evening and I was absolutely hurra'd up on my legs to make a speech but, agitated and abashed as usual and overcome by the prolonged and deafening testimonials of good will, I blundered through two or three indistinct sentences and sat down amidst thundering applause—I never shall figure as an ⟨[unrecovered]⟩ orator.

Your mother is looking extremely well and appears to enjoy her residence in town. She is in the midst of her connexions, and has visits in the course of the day which serve to enliven and amuse her. Upon the whole I now think her coming to town a good move. She will pass her time more cheerfully than in the confinement of a winter residence in the Country, and will ⟨enj⟩ doubly enjoy the cottage, returning to it in the time of the birds and-flowers.

Give my kindest remembrances to Mr Storrow—as well as to Mrs Constant and Mrs King, who I trust are with you at present

Your affectionate uncle
WI.

P S I ought to have told you that the ball at Mrs Mary Jones was very choice and brilliant. Lord Morpeth and several distinguished strangers were there, but not the Prince de Joinville, who had sailed. Julia & Mary made their appearance there, and looked very well and enjoyed themselves. Mrs Doctor Mott and Miss Doctor Mott were not invited

ADDRESSED: À Madame / Madame Storrow / Aux Soins du M T. W Storrow / Rue du Faubg Poissonnicre / à Paris   POSTMARKED: OUTRE-MER / 29 / Dcc. / 41 // LE HAVRE / PARIS / 30 / DEC / 41   DOCKETED: *December 1st 1841* / No 16
MANUSCRIPT: Yale.   PUBLISHED: *Yale Review*, 16 (April, 1927), 483–84 (in part);

LFSS, pp. 39–41 (in part); PMI, III, 174–75 (in part).

1. This letter to Irving Paris has not been located.
2. Palaisseau is a town southwest of Paris, about eleven miles from Notre Dame Cathedral.
3. WI was familiar with this story in its dramatic and musical transmutations. Genest sums up the plot of the dramatic piece: "about a fortnight before it begins, Dame Gervas [a farmer's wife] has lost a silver fork—in the 2d act, she discovers she has lost a silver spoon—Annette [servant of Mme. Gervas] is suspected of having stolen it, as she had sold a silver spoon to the Jew [Isaac, who is passing through the vicinity of Palaiseau]—she has a particular reason for not saying that the spoon, which she had sold to the Jew, was given to her by her father—Annette is con-demned—the Magpie steals a shilling from Blaisot [the servant of Gervas], and carries it into the belfry of a church—Blaisot gets into the belfry, and finds not only his shilling, but the silver fork and spoon which the Magpie had stolen—Annette is of course freed from all suspicion." Originally the story had appeared as *La Pie Voleuse* (1815), a melodrama by Louis-Charles Caignez and Jean-Marie-Théodore Baudouin d'Aubigny which caught the eye of English producers. *The Maid and the Magpie, or Which Is the Thief*, in a translation made by Samuel James Arnold, was acted at the Lyceum Theatre in London on August 21, 1815. This was followed by Thomas Dibdin's version, *Magpie, or the Maid of Palaiseau*, which was first produced at Drury Lane on September 12, 1815, and followed by thirty-eight other performances in the 1815–1816 season. On September 15, 1815, a third version, which was translated by John Howard Payne and adapted by Isaac Pocock, was performed at Covent Garden and repeated twenty-six times during the season. Although Payne did not receive formal credit for this version, he probably told WI about his work on it during their intimacy in the 1820's, when they were adapting other foreign plays for the English stage. WI was familiar with *La Gazza Ladra*, Rossini's opera of 1817, which used the French play as the basis for its libretto

and which was first performed at the Haymarket on March 10, 1821. WI probably was also acquainted with Henry Bishop's musical adaptation in English, *Ninetta, or the Maid of Palaiseau,* which was performed at Covent Garden on February 4, 1830, when WI was working at the U.S. legation in London. See Genest, *Some Account of the English Stage,* VIII, 515–16, 539; *J&N,* III, 448, 474, 540; Arthur Hobson Quinn, *A History of American Drama . . . to the Civil War* (New York, 1923), 168–69; Herbert Weinstock, *Rossini: A Biography* (New York, 1968), p. 75; and *Grove's Dictionary of Music and Musicians,* 5th ed., ed. Eric Blom, 10 vols. (New York, 1968), III, 584.

4. François Ferdinand Philippe d'Orléans (1818–1900), prince de Joinville, the third son of Louis Philippe, was a captain at this time in command of *La Belle Poule,* which arrived in New York on September 20, 1841. He visited Washington, St. Louis, and Boston before returning to New York for a lavish dinner at the Astor House on November 27. See NYEP, September 21, October 1, November 17, 26, 29, 1841.

5. George William Frederick Howard (1802–1864), 7th earl of Carlisle, was also called Lord Morpeth. He was a member of Parliament from 1826 to 1841, when he resigned and spent a year in the United States and Canada. He resumed his parliamentary career in 1846. He had arrived in New York on November 13, 1841. See NYEP, November 16, 1841.

6. Louisa Dunmore Mums, the wife of Valentine Mott (1785–1865), a prominent New York surgeon and social figure.

7. This note has not been located.

8. WI probably intended to write "dreams" instead of "letters."

9. The meeting of the St. Nicholas Society was held in the American Hotel at 4:30 on December 6, 1841. See advertisement in NYEP, November 29, 1841.

1367. To William C. Rives

Sunnyside Cottage Dec 8h. 1841

My dear Sir,

I have to acknowledge the receipt of your kind favor of Nov 4,[1] inclosing a note from Mrs Rives, as also the receipt subsequently, of the charming little volume which she has had the kindness to send me. I enclose a letter of thanks to her which you will have the goodness to convey to her. I trust this first literary essay will be crowned with such success as to encourage her to favor her friends and the public with further productions from her pen. She sees things with a happy eye and a kind heart and has a felicitious mode of conveying her impressions: these are the essentials for a popular writer.

With kindest wishes, my dear Sir, for your prosperity both in your public and private walks of life, which with you are paths of rectitude and honor, I remain very faithfully

Your obliged friend
Washington Irving

The Hon Wm C. Rives / &c &c &c

ADDRESSED: The Hon. William C. Rives / &c &c &c / Washington City   POST-
    MARKED: TARRYTOWN N. Y. / DEC 11
MANUSCRIPT: LC.

1. This letter has not been located.

1368.   To Mrs. William C. Rives

Sunnyside Cottage, Decr 8. 1841

My dear Madam.

Accept my kindest thanks for the Copy of your very elegant little
work;[1] which is going the rounds of my rural household and giving great
delight. I hail this first adventure[2] in to the perilous fairy land of literature, and hope your path through it may always be strewn with flowers.
I am sure the sternest critic must be disarmed of all rancour at the appearance of a Lady Errant, who comes with ⟨such⟩ so gentle and amiable
and winning a grace.

Your residence in Europe, so diversified and under such peculiar and
favorable auspices, must have given you a vast fund for the memory and
the imagination to draw upon, and I trust the little volume you have
now put forth is but the harbinger of more extended lucubrations with
which you are to favor the public.

With best wishes for your success I am, my dear Madam,

very truly and respectfully / Your obliged
Washington Irving

Mrs William C Rives

ADDRESSED: Mrs. William C. Rives / Carth Hill
MANUSCRIPT: LC.

Judith Page Walker (1802–1882) had married William C. Rives in 1819 and
accompanied him on his diplomatic mission to France a decade earlier.

1. *Tales and Souvenirs of a Residence in Europe*, published by Lea & Blanchard
of Philadelphia. It was advertised as "just published" in NYEP, November 16, 1841.
2. WI was apparently not aware that she had brought out *The Canary Bird*
in 1835.

1369.   To Messrs. J. and H. G. Langley

Sunnyside (Tarrytown) Dec 13. [1841]

Gentlemen,

I am looking over the ground in order to make up my mind about the proposed work—To aid me in this I should like to have two or three works that have been published on the subject—such as Pauldings life of Washington.[1] Weems Do.[2] Custis Memoirs of Mrs Washington, published in the 1st vol of American Portrait Gallery[3]—These and any other works relative to the matter ⟨I⟩ (excepting Sparks[4] & Marshall[5] which I have) I would thank you to procure for me and send them to No 37 Murray St. directed to E Irving Esqr. When I have done with them, I will return them to you

Very respectfully / Your obt Servt
Washington Irving

ADDRESSED: Messrs. Langleys. / Booksellers / Chatham St.   DOCKETED: Washington Irving / *Decr. 13 1841*
MANUSCRIPT: Long Island Historical Society.   PUBLISHED: STW, II, 227 (in part); *Historical Magazine*, 2d ser. 3 (January, 1868), 20.

1. James Kirke Paulding, *A Life of Washington* (New York, 1835).
2. Mason Locke Weems, *A History of the Life and Death, Virtues and Exploits of General George Washington. Faithfully Taken from Authentic Documents* (Philadelphia, [1800]).
3. WI is referring to *The National Portrait Gallery of Distinguished Americans*, ed. James B. Longacre and James Herring (Philadelphia, 1834), pp. 29–38. The sketch of Martha Washington was prepared by George Washington Parke Custis.
4. Jared Sparks, *The Life of George Washington* (Boston, 1839).
5. John Marshall, *The Life of George Washington*, 5 vols. (Philadelphia, 1804–1807).

1370.   To Cornelius Mathews

Sunnyside, Decr. 18th. 1841

My dear Sir;

I thank you most heartily·for the acceptable little parcel of ⟨y⟩ works which you have had the kindness to send me. Your poem I have read with both pleasure and pride; being proud that a chance spark of mine should have been able to light up such a blaze.[1] I shall be happy to receive the continuation of Puffer Hopkins, and will immediately set about reading the commencement, which I have hitherto abstained from doing, as I generally avoid reading any of these works published by instalment until I have the whole series before me.[2] Your Arcturus[3] has had my hearty good wishes from its very commencement; for it struck out in a style that hit my humor, and smacked to me of the good old school, sufficiently modernized to suit and benefit the times. I am glad to find it maintains its course cheerily and healthfully, and wish it all possible success. As to the question of International Copyright[4] I am too much out of the way of feeling the public pulse to know as to the time most favorable for agitating the subject. The present session of Congress is perhaps a propitious one, as, in the ⟨present⟩ singular position of parties, there is a temporary pause in the all absorbing business of president making, and the humble interests of literature may stand some little chance of being attended to. It will be necessary, however, that the movement be combined and urgent, for the friends of Copy right are scattered and individually of feeble means; whereas the opponents are wealthy publishers, who can afford to keep hired agents about the avenues of Congress. It is really humiliating as well as irritating that the feelings and opinions of the nation on a subject that so deeply affects its character for intelligence and high civilization should be slyly managed by the tamperings of vulgar minded and mercenary monopolists; but I fear the time for the full establishment of authors rights is not yet arrived. The sordid sons of this world have yet too much advantage over the children of light. One thing however may be done, even if in the coming attempt we should fail—Ascertain who are the real and efficient opponents of the measure—and, if they prove to be influenced by Sordid motives, turn the whole indignation of ⟨insulted⟩ wronged and insulted literature upon them.

I have no idea of "employing my pen publicly in advocacy of this interest." if I had, I know of no work in which I would be more pleased to appear than in the Arcturus. I will be most happy, however, to aid the good cause as far as in me lies by writing to Such persons ↑of my acquaintance↓ at Washington, both in and out of Congress, as I may think likely to be of Service.

Very respectfully my dear Sir / Your obliged friend & Servt

[Signature clipped]

Cornelius Mathews Esqr

ADDRESSED: Cornelius Mathews Esqr / office of Arcturus / 14 Pine St / New York
    POSTMARKED: TARRYTOWN N Y / DEC / 20
MANUSCRIPT: Harvard.

Cornelius Mathews (1817–1889), a graduate of Columbia and a lawyer who never practiced, made his reputation as a writer of fiction and drama and as an editor.

He worked tirelessly for an international copyright and spoke on that subject at the Dickens dinner in 1842.

1. Mathews's poem, "Wakondah, The Master of Life," is preceded by a quotation from WI's *Astoria* (I, 265): "We have already noticed the superstitious feelings with which the Indians regarded the Black Hills; but this immense range of mountains (the Chippewyan or Rocky Mountains) which divided all that they know of the world and gives birth to such mighty rivers, is still more an object of awe and veneration. They call it, 'The Crest of the World,' and think that Wakondah or the Master of Life, as they designate the Supreme Being, has his residence among these aerial heights." See *The Writings of Cornelius Mathews* (New York, 1843), p. 162.

2. *The Career of Puffer Hopkins* was published serially in *Arcturus* from June, 1841, to May, 1842.

3. Founded by Mathews and Evert A. Duyckinck, *Arcturus* was published from December, 1840, to May, 1842. Its purpose, as stated in the first issue, was "the cultivation of good literature, honest mirth, and truth." See Frank Luther Mott, *A History of American Magazines, 1741–1850* (Cambridge, Mass., 1930), p. 711.

4. WI had written to Lewis Gaylord Clark about the international copyright on December 21, 1839, expressing his desire for Congressional action to protect American literary property. See *Knickerbocker Magazine*, 15 (January, 1840), 78–79; and PMI, III, 149–51.

1371. To Sarah Storrow

Sunnyside Decr 26t. 1841

Here we are my dear Sarah, in the Christmas holydays; the Cottage dressed in evergreens and enlivened by cheerful voices, but oh how sadly, sadly do I feel your absence. It is the first christmas celebrated at the Cottage ⟨that⟩ at which you have not been present, and I have continually missed your bright and happy countenance that ⟨g⟩ used to be like sunshine to us all. Still we have passed a pleasant christmas day. It does not take much to make a fête in our simple little establishment. We had Pierre and Helen from town and Philip Paulding, ⟨Mr⟩ Ogden Irving & Mr Anthony to dine and pass the evening with us; there was music and dancing and all seemed to enjoy themselves.

The winter is an open one; we have had a little snow and a little sleighing; but the river keeps open, ⟨and⟩ the Steam boats continue to run and communication with town is kept up. The Cottage is well filled. Eliza Romeyn is one of the inmates as also your Uncle E.I. who, since his affairs have passed through a crisis, appears to be more comfortable in mind than he has been for a long time.

The girls are all busy fitting Kate out for that "Awful change"[1] which I presume will take place some time in the early part of the Spring. The young couple carry on their courtship in their own shy, quiet way and appear to be both very much relieved in mind now that the matter is settled. The white house is nearly finished, and will be very elegant as well as convenient in all its internal arrangements. Its vicinity to the cottage promises to be a source of great enjoyment to the inmates of both establishments, as there doubtless will be a daily intercourse kept up. The occupation of Mr Constants house by the Grinnells will likewise tend to animate and enliven our domestic circle—

I have written you two or three very uncomfortable letters lately and am sorry for it; but I was discouraged by evils that seemed thickening around me, and felt doubtful whether I still retained mental force and buoyancy sufficient to cope with them. Thank God, the very pressure of affairs has produced reaction; a stout heart, not yet worn out, has rallied up to the emergency, and I am now in a complete state of literary activity. I shall keep on without flagging or flinching, as long as health and good spirits are continued to me, and I trust I shall be able to take care of all around me. Never did I feel the value of life and health more than at this moment, and never did I take a deeper interest in existence. I believe it is good for man to be thus roused to new exertion (even though by the stimulus of adverse circumstances) when the game of life ⟨is⟩ ↑would otherwise be↓ growing tedious and uninteresting.

Tell Mr Storrow I have received the books which he was so kind as to procure for me, and will account to him for the cost, which was not beyond what I had expected ⟨as⟩ They are very rare works, not to be met with in this country, but indispensible to a work which I have in contemplation[.] I feel very much obliged to him for the prompt manner in wh[ich] [MS torn] he has attended to my wishes

I have just read your letter to your mother dated the 1st December, and also a previous one dated in November, to your father.[2] They concur in shewing us that you are nestling yourself delightfully in your new quarters and making a happy little home for yourself in Paris. I know my dear Girl that you have a fund of happiness within yourself, from your own buoyant disposition, and, generous affectionate heart, and I am constantly gratified by the proofs your letters furnish of the kind, delicate and considerate attention incessantly payed by Mr Storrow, to promote your comfort and enjoyment God bless him—he has the true spirit of a gentleman.

I must hasten to conclude this hurried scrawl, which is all that circumstances will permit me at present to furnish; but I am determined not to let another packet depart without sending you a line. I am now so much engrossed by my literary avocations that I shall not be able to write to you as often or as circumstantially as before—but you know the reason and I am sure will not complain. Give my kindest remembrances to Mr Storrow.

Ever my dear Sarah / Most affectionately your Uncle
W I.

MANUSCRIPT: Yale.   PUBLISHED: PMI, II, 175 (in part).

1. A reference to Kate Irving's impending marriage to Philip Paulding.
2. These letters have not been located.

1372.   To A. P. Upshur

Sunnyside Cottage (Tarrytown) Jany 24th. 1842

Dear Sir,

Permit me to offer as a candidate for a Second Lieutenancy of Marines my nephew Washington Irving Jun[1] He is now in his twentieth year, and recently from Geneva College in this state, where he has been educated. He is a youth of good parts, a generous temper, great personal activity and aptness, and an intrepid spirit. He has a strong inclination for the sea, and I think would make an excellent officer in the service for which I take the liberty to reccommend him.

I do not feel that I have any right to ask favors of you, Sir, and should therefore esteem it the greater kindness on your part if my application should prove successful.

Very respectfully / Your most obt Servt.
Washington Irving

The Hon. A. P. Upshur / &c &c &c

MANUSCRIPT: Boston Public Library.

Abel P. Upshur (1791–1844), a member of the Virginia Supreme Court from 1826 to 1841, was appointed secretary of the navy by President Tyler. He died in a gun explosion on the battleship *Princeton.*

1. Washington Ebenezer (1822–1894), the twelfth child of Ebenezer and Elizabeth Kip Irving. He is not listed in the rosters of officers of the Marine Corps or Navy.

1373. To S. B. Grant et al.

Sunnyside (Tarrytown) ⟨Jan⟩ Feb 1st. 1842

Messrs. S. B. Grant. James Dixon
⟨Jas. Holbrook⟩ Chạs G. Gilbert
A Brigham   E. B. Green
E. E. Marcey   Geo Brinley Jr
I W Stuart & W J Hamersley
Committee of Arrangt

Gentlemen,

I feel greatly flattered and obliged by the honor you have done me in inviting me to the dinner to be given to Charles Dickens Esqr.[1] It would give me the highest pleasure to join with you in this tribute of gratitude for the delight we have all experienced from the inimitable productions of that great genius but I regret to say that circumstances will not permit me to be present on the occasion

With high respect I am Gentlemen

Your obliged & hbl Servt.
Washington Irving

ADDRESSED: Messrs. S. B. Grant / James Dixon / & others. / Committee of Arrangement / Hartford Con.   POSTMARKED: TARRYTOWN N. Y. / FEB / 3 MANUSCRIPT: Litchfield Historical Society, Litchfield, Connecticut.

James Dixon (1814–1873), a poet and writer for the *New England Magazine*, served on various occasions in the Connecticut legislature and in the U.S. House of Representatives and Senate; Dr. Amariah Brigham (1798–1849) was superintendent of the Hartford Insane Asylum, which Dickens visited while in Hartford; George Brinley, Jr. (1817–1875) was later known as a collector of Americana who bequeathed his books to Yale; I. W. Stuart (1809–1861) was a local historian; William J. Hamersley, the mayor of Hartford, presided at the Dickens dinner. The other addressees have not been identified.

1. The dinner for Dickens in Hartford was held at the City Hotel on Tuesday, February 8. Dickens, who had arrived from Worcester on the preceding evening, remained in Hartford until February 11, when he left for New Haven. See NYEP, February 11, 1842; and John Forster, *The Life of Charles Dickens*, I, 293–94.

1374. To Lewis G. Clark

[February 9, 1842]

My dear **Sir,**

Your note did not come to hand until since my arrival in town. It will give me great pleasure to meet Mr Dickens at your house any day you may appoint.[1] I am at present at Mr Astors

Very truly yours,
Washington Irving

L Gaylord Clark Esqr.

ADDRESSED: L Gaylord Clark Esqr / Henry Street. / or Office of the Knickerbocker. MANUSCRIPT: NYPL—Hellman Collection.

1. The meeting with Dickens at Clark's home took place on Wednesday, February 23, 1842, with WI, Bryant, Halleck, Henry Brevoort, Henry Inman, C. C. Felton, Bishop Wainwright, and others in attendance. On February 15, Dickens, suffering from a sore throat, had asked Clark to postpone a breakfast for a day or two. The dinner mentioned above was probably a substitute worked into Dickens's busy schedule. WI had called upon Dickens on the day of his arrival in New York and stayed with him at his hotel until 10:00 P.M. See Lewis Gaylord Clark, "Charles Dickens," *Harper's Monthly Magazine*, 25 (August, 1862), 376–77; Dickens to Clark, February 15, 1842, and March 2, 1843; and Dickens to John Forster, February 17, 1842, in *Letters of Charles Dickens*, ed. Madeline House and Graham Storey (Oxford, 1969), III, 62, 70, 453.

1375. To Ebenezer Irving

New York, Feb. 10, 1842.

My dear **Brother:**

I have been astounded, this morning, by the intelligence of my having been nominated to the Senate as Minister to Spain. The nomination, I presume, will be confirmed.[1] Nothing was ever more unexpected. It was perfectly unsolicited.

I have determined to accept. Indeed, under all the circumstances of the case, I could not do otherwise. It will be a severe trial to absent myself for a time from dear little Sunnyside; but I shall return to it better enabled to carry it on comfortably.

PUBLISHED: PMI, III, 177.

1. WI was nominated U.S. envoy extraordinary and minister plenipotentiary to Spain on February 8, 1842, and confirmed by the Senate two days later. See Senate, *Journal*, 27th Cong., 1st sess., pt. 6, p. 25.

1376. (deleted)

1377. To Ebenezer Irving

February 16, 1842.

Nothing could be more gratifying than the manner in which this appointment has been made. It was suggested by Mr. Webster to the President,[1] immediately adopted by him, heartily concurred in by all the Cabinet,[2] and confirmed in the Senate almost by acclamation. When it was mentioned, Mr. Clay,[3] who has opposed almost all the other nominations, exclaimed: "Ah, this is a nomination everybody will concur in! If the President would send us such names as this, we should never have any difficulty." What has still more enhanced the gratification of this signal honor, is the unanimous applause with which it is greeted by the public. The only drawback upon all this is the hard trial of tearing myself away from dear little Sunnyside. This has harassed me more than I can express; but I begin to reconcile myself to it, as it will be but a temporary absence.

PUBLISHED: PMI, III, 179.

1. John Tyler (1790–1862), a Virginian who had served in the state legislature and in the U.S. Congress, succeeded to the presidency upon the death of William Henry Harrison on April 4, 1841.
2. WI is echoing the news story reprinted from the *Express* in NYEP, February 11, 1842.
3. Henry Clay (1777–1852), a Kentucky statesman who was a perennial candidate for the presidency, was a U.S. senator at this time.

1378. To George Ticknor

New York, Feb. 16th. 1842

My dear Sir,

I have this moment received your letter of the 13th. inst.[1] Several days since I sent an earnest request to Washington that Mr Cogswell[2] might be appointed Secretary to the Legation, and have repeated the request. I know and feel the truth of all that you say concerning him and shall be excessively disappointed if my wishes are not attended to. I trust however that he will receive the appointment.

For the kind expressions ⟨con⟩ of your letter concerning myself accept my sincere thanks and believe me with great esteem and regard

Yours faithfully
Washington Irving

Geo Ticknor Esqr.

MANUSCRIPT: Dartmouth College Library.

George Ticknor (1791–1871), who had studied in Europe from 1815 to 1819, served as professor of modern languages at Harvard from 1819 to 1835 and then resigned to work on a history of Spanish literature.

1. This letter has not been located.
2. WI's recommendation of Joseph G. Cogswell as secretary of the Madrid legation was vigorously supported by letters to Daniel Webster from Moses H. Grinnell (February 12, 1842 [Brandeis University]) and W. H. Prescott (February 14, 1842 [Dartmouth College]).

1379. To Daniel Webster

Private[1]   Private

New York Feb 16th. 1842

My dear Sir,

I have hitherto forborne writing to you on the subject of my appointment as Minister to Spain, not daring to give vent to my feelings in their excited and agitated state. I never have been so completely taken by surprise, or so overwhelmed. Such a signal honor on the part of my government, so warmly applauded by my countrymen, seems to me something too great for one of my pretensions, and I am at times almost inclined to doubt whether it is not all a dream. But what still heightens the effect of this crowning honor of my life is ↑the conviction of↓ *the hand* by which it is conferred; for, though deeply sensible of the readiness with which the President adopted the suggestion, I am fully aware my dear Sir, that this measure originated with yourself, and I regard it with heart felt pride, as a magnificent testimonial of your friendship.

Having received no official communication from Government[2] I am at a loss how to regulate my departure. I observe ⟨b⟩ a paragraph in the papers stating that a Frigate is ordered to be in readiness to take me out, but this I presume to be a mere rumor. I should be well disposed to make the voyage in a quieter manner—I do not wish to ask any unreasonable indulgence but a little delay is necessary for me to ⟨reg?⟩ arrange my affairs, which otherwise would be left in confusion. If it would not be incompatible with the objects and exegancies of my mission, also, I should like to be permitted to go by the way of England and France, that I might see my relatives in these countries; especially a sister from whom I have been separated for ten years, and whom I otherwise may never see again. I should make no delay for mere purposes of pleasure; my whole stay in England would but be a few days as I should not make any sojourn in London: the whole difference in time between this route and one direct to Spain would be but a very few weeks. I have already intimated through another channel my desire to have Mr Joseph G. Cogswell appointed as Secretary of the Legation. He is a gentleman with whom I am on terms of confidential intimacy and I know no one who, by his various acquirements, his prompt sagacity, his knowledge of the world, his habits of business and his obliging disposition is so calculated to give me that council, aid and companionship so important in Madrid, where a stranger is more isolated than in any other Capitol of Europe.

If you could find liesure to drop me an unofficial line, however brief (directed to me at New York) in reply to these matters, and signifying when it will be expedient *for* me to come on to Washington you will relieve me from some anxiety and suspense.

Ever my dear Sir / very faithfully and fervently yours
Washington Irving

Hon. Daniel Webster / &c &c &c

DOCKETED: *Private.* / Washington Irving. / 16th Febry. 1842.
MANUSCRIPT: NYPL—Berg Collection. PUBLISHED: PMI, III, 180–81 (in part).

1. This word is not in WI's handwriting.
2. WI received an unofficial letter from Webster on February 14, 1842. See PMI, III, 177–78.

1380. To Ebenezer Irving

February 17, 1842.

I now abandon the care of the place entirely to you. You will find, in my little library, books about gardening, farming, poultry, &c., by which to direct yourself. The management of the place will give you healthful

and cheerful occupation, and will be as much occupation as you want.
* * * So content yourself at Sunnyside, and never think of seeking any
other "berth" for the rest of your days. Try if you cannot beat me at
farming and gardening. I shall be able to bestow a little more money
on the place now, to put it in good heart and good order.

Tell the girls they must not repine at my going away for a time, but
must cheer me off with pleasant faces. The parting from Sunnyside will
be hard for me, and must be rendered as cheerful as possible. * * * I
shall apply myself steadily and vigorously to my pen, which I shall be
able to do at Madrid, where there are few things to distract one's attention, and in a little while I shall amass a new literary capital. I shall
therefore return to Sunnyside with money in both pockets, be able to
"burn the candle at both ends,"[1] and to put up as many weathercocks as
I please.

PUBLISHED: PMI, III, 179–80.

1. Alain René LeSage, *Gil Blas*, VII, xv.

1381. To Daniel Webster

New York, Feb. 18th. 1842

The Hon. Daniel Webster / Secretary of State / Washington.
Sir,
I accept with no common feelings of pride and gratitude the honorable
post offered me by the Government, of Envoy Extraordinary and Minister
Plenipotentiary to Spain. It will take some little time for me to arrange
my affairs preparatory to so sudden and unexpected a change of position
and pursuits; but I trust to be ready to depart early in April; previous
to which time I will visit Washington to receive my instructions
                            I am Sir, very respectfully / Your obedient Servant
                                                    Washington Irving

DOCKETED: Recd Feby 25 / [*unrecovered*] Hill
MANUSCRIPT: NA, RG 59.   PUBLISHED: PMI, III, 180.

1382. To Daniel Webster

(Private)

New York, Feb. 18. 1842

My dear Sir,

In my letter of yesterday[1] I expressed my wishes respecting the person to be appointed secretary to the Legation. Since then I have heard a report of two or three persons being candidates for the office. I beg leave, most respectfully, once more to urge my wishes that Mr Cogswell may receive the appointment. There are various circumstances that make him peculiarly fitted for the place. From some little experience in these matters I know the importance to the comfort and the successful conduct of a legation that there should be harmony between the Minister and the Secretary; and I know of no one more likely to ensure it in the present instance than Mr. Cogswell. ⟨Spain⟩ The minister at Madrid, moreover, is so much more isolated than in any other court, that his comfort, and well being depend in a great measure upon the domestic arrangements of the mission. I hope you will excuse my urgency in this matter; but I feel I have much at stake upon it as to my residence in Madrid.

Ever my dear Sir / Very faithfully yours

Washington Irving

The Hon Daniel Webster

MANUSCRIPT: MIIS; NA, RG 59 (copy).

1. Probably WI is referring to his letter of February 16, 1842, to Webster.

1383. To T. L. Ogden

New York, Feby. 20th, 1842

My dear Sir

At the request of Mr Samuel Ward[1] I address you a few lines respecting Professor Mersch,[2] a friend of his, whom I have the pleasure of meeting frequently at Mr Astors, and who, I understand, is a candidate for the professorship of German about to be established in Columbia College. From my knowledge of Mr Mersch I judge him to be well qualified for this place, and in general attainments and intelligence he is evidently entitled to a high rank—Having received his education in Germany there can be no doubt of his being well prepared for the duties of an instructor. Mr William B. Astor and other mutual friends who know him more intimately than I do speak of him in very high terms both as a gentleman and a Man of Science.

I am my dear Sir

with great regard / Yours truly
Washington Irving

T. L. Ogden, Esqr.

MANUSCRIPT: Columbia.

Thomas Ludlow Ogden (1773–1844), a prominent New York lawyer, was a first cousin of WI's legal mentor, Josiah Ogden Hoffman. WI had accompanied them on a trip to upstate New York and Montreal in the summer of 1803. See STW, II, 28–34; and J&N, I, xxvii, 3–4.

1. Samuel Ward, Jr., a banker, was married to Emily Astor, the granddaughter of John Jacob Astor.
2. Mersch, who served as Astor's German agent in the settling of German immigrants in Green Bay, Wisconsin, did not receive the appointment. See Porter, *Astor*, II, 1127; and Horace Coon, *Columbia, Colossus on the Hudson* (New York, 1847), p. 72.

1384. To Lucius D. Baldwin

New York, February 22d. 1842

Sir,

A gentleman is already nominated for the place of Secretary of ⟨the⟩ Legation to Spain and I have no doubt the nomination will be confirmed There are no other official situations in connexion with the mission

Very respectfully / Your obt Servt.
Washington Irving

Lucius D. Baldwin Esqr.

MANUSCRIPT: Va.—Barrett.

1385. To Messrs. Lea & Blanchard

Sunnyside, (Tarrytown) Feb 26h. 1842

Messr Lea & Blanchard
Gentlemen,

Previous to my departure for Europe I should like to form a new arrangement with you respecting my works which you have in your hands.[1] I propose to give you the exclusive privilege of publishing the whole of them for a specific term of years, in any creditable form you may choose. I to furnish new and revised editions, with corrections additions, notes &c so as to give them novelty and effect. I also to prepare from time to time, detached volumes, forming collections of tales, of essays, of historical passages and pictures, selected from the general mass of my works These volumes may be sold separately and may form handy books for travellers; presents for young people &c. This agreement will also comprise two volumes of tales essays &c never yet published in a collective form; also a volume containing the biography of Goldsmith and the Memoir of Margaret M Davidson, both of which I have the privilege of publishing in connexion with my other works. As this will throw all my works into a new form, and be the last and improved edition, beside embracing works never hitherto published collectively the terms I ask are three thousand dollars a year for a certain number of years hereafter to be agreed upon.

I shall be happy to hear from you as soon as your convenience will permit, as my ⟨stay in this country must⟩ ↑departure cannot↓ long be deferred.

I am gentlemen, with great respect / Yours very truly
Washington Irving

ADDRESSED: Messrs Lea & Blanchard / Booksellers / Philadelphia   POSTMARKED: [TARR]YTOWN N. Y. / FEB / 8   DOCKETED: Recd March 1st [*upper left corner of MS page 1*]
MANUSCRIPT: Harvard.

1. In 1835 WI had entered into a seven-year contract with Carey & Lea, the predecessor of Lea & Blanchard. It provided for the publication of all his writings except the abridgment of *Columbus* at an annual fee of $1,150. See David Kaser, *Messrs. Carey & Lea of Philadelphia*, p. 86.

1836. *To the Senate and House of Representatives*

[February, 1842]

To the Honourable The Senate and The House of Representatives in Congress Assembled.

Your memorialists respectfully request that the attention of Congress may be directed to the subject of an international copy-right law. By the recent legislation of the English parliament, the privilege of copy-right is extended only to the citizens of those nations by which the benefit is reciprocated; so that it is by courtesy alone, and by no legal surety, that American writers can at present derive any advantage from the sale of their works in Great Britain. Your petitioners regard the license of the existing system in this country as fatally subversive of the interests of our youthful literature, and as unjust and ungenerous towards foreign authors. Can it be reasonably expected that our publishers will pay an adequate price for native works, when they can obtain their supply of new books (a supply often far beyond the demand) for English authors for *nothing*? Your petitioners are at a loss to perceive why literary property is not as much entitled to protection as the production of manual handicraft or labour. The toil of the author is as exhausting to the physical energies as the toil of the mechanic, and yet the foreign mechanic can transfer the products of his industry to his agent in this country and reap the benefit of their sale, while the foreign author may see his works pirated and mutilated, and sold for the advantage of another, and be unable to obtain redress. Your petitioners sincerely believe that the proposed change in the copy-right system would not be prejudicial to the interests of any craft or profession in the United States; and even if it were so, they think that the dignity and paramount interests of the country would still imperiously demand that an international copy-right law should be adopted. Your memorialists will ever pray, &c.

February, 1842

Washington Irving	Tarry Town, N York
W. A. Duer	Cos-Cob—N.Y.
Jas Renwick	Cos-Cob N.Y.
Gov. P. Morris	New York
Rufus Dawes	New York
James Fred: Otis.	New York
Wm. T. Porter	New York
William [L.?] Stone	New York
John O. Sargent	New York
David Hale	New York
[C?] Fenno Hoffman	New York
W. C. Bryant	New York
[I?] [J?] M Mathews	New York
Taylor Lewis	New York University N. Y.
C. S. Henry	New York University N. Y.
Charles A Lee	New York NY.
Rufus W. Griswold	New York
Auguste [Daryae?]	New York.
J. L. O'Sullivan	New York
H.Hastings Weld	New York
L. Gaylord Clarke	New York

Epes Sargent   New York
N. P. Willis   New York
J H ?   Mississippi
Fitz-Green Halleck   New York

DOCKETED: 27th Cong / 2. Sess Memorial / of Washington Irving / & others, praying the / enactment of an inter- / national copy-right law. / 1842 March 30th Referred to the / Com: on the Judiciary / Mr Clay.
MANUSCRIPT: LC.

1387. *To George Ticknor*

New York, March 7th. 1842

My dear Sir,

Uncertainty as to my movements, and the pressure of various engagements have prevented my replying at an earlier date to your kind letter of the 22d ult.[1] I have now the satisfaction of learning that Mr Cogswells nomination is confirmed;[2] but I am still uncertain as to the mode and time of my embarkation for Europe. I rather think I shall sail in a packet Ship from this port. Should I embark at Boston, however, which is very improbable, I shall not fail to avail myself of your very hospitable invitation, for which I return you my most cordial thanks.

With great respect and regard / Yours very faithfully
Washington Irving

Geo. Ticknor Esqr

MANUSCRIPT: Dartmouth College.

1. This letter has not been located.
2. Cogswell was commissioned secretary of the legation on March 4, 1842. See Senate, *Journal*, 27th Cong., 2d sess., pt. 6, pp. 31, 35.

1388. *To Messrs. Lea & Blanchard*

New York, March 10th. 1842.

Messrs Lea & Blanchard
Gentlemen

I am sorry to say your answer[1] to my proposition does not by any means meet my views. I will now make another proposition.

Our present arrangement, which expires I believe in the month of May next, to be continued for two years longer on the present terms, at the end of which time the terms to be increased to $2500 per annum, and so continue for Seven years; the whole contract embracing a period of nine years. From the Commencement of the second term (viz in May 1844) you to have the exclusive privilege of publishing all my works *now in print*, in any creditable form you may please, excepting one or two minor works. Such as the life of Goldsmith &c to which I cannot extend an *exclusive* privilege.

During this second term (I E. from the month of May 1844) I to furnish you with new and revised editions, with such additions alterations notes &c as shall give them an air of novelty and a decided preference over all preceding editions: this edition may be served up volume by volume with pictorial illustrations &c

I to furnish you, after May 1844 with detached volumes containing collections of tales of essays, of historical passages and Scenes, selected from the Mass of my works; and which volumes may be sold separately and individually

I to furnish you also, after May 1844 with two volumes to be published in connexion with my other works, as forming part of the series, one made up of essays from Salmagundi; of Naval biographies and other early writings; and the other to contain the biographies of Goldsmith and Miss Dàvidson.

This arrangement will *not* comprise the "two volumes of Tales and Sketches never before published Collectively" alluded to in my former proposition. They, as well as all other new works, will be the subjects of Separate bargains.

As I am desirous of arranging these matters before my departure I will thank you for a definite answer as soon as convenient; and, being rather pressed for time, I trust you will not take it amiss, should your answer be still wide of the mark, if I endeavor to make a satisfactory arrangement elsewhere. I trust, however, we may both find it to our interest to continue a connexion which has Subsisted for so many years with perfect harmony

Very respectfully gentlemen / Your obt Servt.
Washington Irving

ADDRESSED: Messrs Lea & Blanchard / Booksellers / Philadelphia   POSTMARKED: [NEW-YORK N. Y.?] / MAR / 11   DOCKETED: Recd. *March 11th* / ansd [ditto] 12th. [*upper left corner of MS page 1*]
MANUSCRIPT: Harvard.

1. On March 3, 1842, the publishers responded to WI's letter of February 26

by rejecting his suggestion of a new edition of his works, giving as their reason "the present distressed state of almost every portion of the country." They countered with the following offer: "For the present we should prefer to continue our arrangement for two years at one thousand dollars per annum & include the right to publish Astoria, Miscellany, etc in it, Or if you wish to publish 'Mahomet' this spring & the two volumes of Tales, mentioned in your letter, to follow by June or July—these might be included in the two years right with the others, say the whole for five thousand dollars for the two years commencing at the time of publication of the last—we to reserve the right at the end of that period to publish a new edition of your works as you propose with the other vols selected, say for five or more years at the price of $2500 per annum." See Earl L. Bradsher, *Mathew Carey, Editor, Author and Publisher* (New York, 1912), p. 91.

1389. To Joseph G. Cogswell

Washington March 15th. 1842

My dear Cogswell.

I find government perfectly accommodating as to my mode and time of departure; which I think will be in the Liverpool Packet of the 7th April[1] It will take me about a week ↑here↓ to put myself *au courant* of the affairs of the Legation, there being much correspondence and many documents to read and take notes of. It will be well for you to come on soon and do the same thing, as I am told the mission has more important concerns on hand that the public are aware of.

If no other way presents of forwarding books and the heavy luggage they can be sent to Liverpool and shipped thence to Cadiz.

As you may want to know something on the Subject of pay. I understand the Ministers pay commences about a month prior to Sailing;[2] he having that time to make preparations. I presume the Secretaries commences at the same time

Let me hear from you if there is any thing of moment, and let me know when you will be likely to come on[.] I put up at Browns Hotel[3]

Very truly yours
Washington Irving

Manuscript: NYPL.

1. WI apparently boarded the *Independence* for Liverpool on April 7, 1842, but did not sail until April 10. See NYEP, April 7 and 12, 1842; and WI to Catharine Paris, April 10, 1842. For a discussion of the discrepancies in WI's sailing date from New York, see "Letters to Sarah Storrow from Spain by Washington Irving," ed. Barbara D. Simison, in *Papers in Honor of Andrew Keogh, Librarian of Yale University By the Staff of the Library 30 June 1938* (New Haven, 1938), p. 230.

2. The minister's salary was $9,000 a year, and the secretary's, $2,000. See Senate, *Congressional Globe*, 27th Cong., 2d sess., pt. 2, p. 982; STW, II, 115, 143; and Porter, *Astor*, II, 1094–96. As WI reported to Cogswell on March 22, 1842, the salary started from the date of the commission.

3. Probably the Indian Queen Hotel, the proprietor of which was Jesse Brown. Later it was known as the Metropolitan. See Rufus R. Wilson, *Washington, The Capital City*, 2 vols. (Philadelphia, 1902), I, 203–5; and Ben Perley Poore, *Perley's Reminiscences of Sixty Years in the National Metropolis*, 2 vols. (Philadelphia, 1886), I, 42, 481.

1390. To Ebenezer Irving

Washington, March 16, 1842.

My dear Brother:

My reception in Washington, by all persons and parties, has been of the most gratifying kind. The Government seems disposed to grant me every indulgence as to the time and mode of my embarcation, my route, &c. I shall remain here until some time in the early part of next week, to read the correspondence and documents connected with my mission, and to make myself acquainted with the affairs of the legation, after which I shall return home to make my final preparations for departure.

I dined with Mr. Granger[1] yesterday; Mr. Webster to-day; I dine to-morrow with Mr. Preston,[2] of the Senate, the next day with the President, and on Saturday with Mr. Tayloe;[3] so you see I am launched in a complete round of dissipation. Last evening I was at the President's *levee*—a prodigious crowd. I set out to walk, with Julia Sanders[4] on my arm, but was penned up against the wall, and for an hour had to stand shaking hands with man, woman, and child from all parts of the Union, who took a notion to *lionize* me. I thought I had become so old a story as to be past all such bozzing, but they seem to think me brought out in a new edition at Washington. * * *

March 17th—I have nearly finished my business here. I have read all the correspondence and documents of importance connected with my mission, and had private conversations with the Secretary of State. I have received my letter of credit on the Rothschilds,[5] London, for my salary, which, I find, commences from the date of my commission—10th of February last. I shall receive a draft for my outfit on Tuesday next. I intend paying a visit to Mount Vernon[6] on Monday, and hope to leave this for Baltimore on Tuesday afternoon. As I shall stop in Philadelphia to see my booksellers,[7] I shall not reach New York until toward the end of the week. I still shall endeavor to make all my arrangements so as to sail in the Liverpool packet on the 7th April, as I am anxious to get out to Europe early enough to have a portion of the fine season for travelling.

Yesterday I dined at the President's, and had a very pleasant dinner. Mr. Tyler has all the air of a very good-hearted, fine-tempered man, and I have experienced the most cordial reception from him. I sat next to his daughter-in-law,[8] a daughter of my early friend, Mary Fairlie,[9] and we had much interesting conversation about her mother, among whose papers she had found many of my letters during the time that, in our young[10] days, we kept up an amusing correspondence.

PUBLISHED: PMI, III, 185–87.

1. Francis Granger, a New York Whig who had been Harrison's postmaster general, was now serving in Congress.

2. William C. Preston (1794–1860), a South Carolinian with whom WI had traveled in Europe in 1817, was in the U.S. Senate from December, 1833, to December, 1844.

3. Benjamin Ogle Tayloe (1796–1868), who had studied law with Benjamin Rush and served as his private secretary while he was U.S. minister to England in 1817, lived and entertained lavishly in a spacious home in Lafayette Square near the White House. See Rufus R. Wilson, *Washington, The Capital City*, I, 232–33; and Harold Donaldson, *Historic Homes of Georgetown and Washington City* (Richmond, 1958), pp. 285–90.

4. WI is referring to Julia Granger (1822–1897), the wife of Sanders Irving, in this way to distinguish her from Julia Irving, the wife of Moses Grinnell. WI used the same method and spoke of Helen Pierre and Helen Treat to refer to the wives of Pierre M. and John Treat Irving, Jr.

5. N. M. Rothschild and Sons was the London branch of the banking family which dominated European financial circles. See Frederic Morton, *The Rothschilds* (New York, 1962), pp. 144–46.

6. WI was probably gathering material and impressions for his biography of George Washington.

7. Lea & Blanchard.

8. Elizabeth Priscilla Cooper (1819–1896), who married Robert Tyler (1816–1877) on September 19, 1839, acted as official hostess at the White House during her mother-in-law's invalidism and after her death. See Oliver P. Chitwood, *John Tyler, Champion of the Old South* (New York, 1964), app. D, p. 478; and Elizabeth Tyler Coleman, *Priscilla Cooper Tyler and the American Scene* (University, Ala., 1955), p. 87.

9. Mary Fairlie (1790–1833), who served as the model for Sophy Sparkle in *Salmagundi*, had married the actor, Thomas A. Cooper, in 1812.

10. The printed text has "voung" an obvious misprint.

1391. To Aaron Vail

Washington, March 17th. 1842

My dear Sir,

You will have heard long before the receipt of this of my appointment
⟨to⟩ as Minister to Spain. Whatever Satisfaction I may receive from this
mark of confidence and esteem on the part of my government is diminished by the idea that I have to take the place of yourself, for whom I
have ever entertained so sincere a regard. However, the change in the
mission had been determined upon, and had the post not been given to
me, I am told it would have been given to a third party.

I expect to embark on the Seventh of April in a packet Ship for Liverpool, my sojourn in England will be brief; I shall pass some little time
in Paris and shall reach Madrid as early as possible in July. I hope it
may suit your convenience to wait there until my arrival and induct me
into the duties of my new office. As I shall have to form an establishment
on my arrival, and as you may be laying down one, we may perhaps
make some arrangements mutually accommodating. I shall also be in want
of Servants—in fact I shall be in want of every thing. I wish you would
drop me a line to Paris[1] letting me know of your proposed movements,
and of your wishes as to the time of departure. Also as to the state of
the.roads as to robbers; and whether it will be necessary to provide an
escort. In fact any information you can give me on all the above points,
and any other that may suggest themselves to you, will be very acceptable. Address your letter to the Care of Thomas. W Storrow Jr. Rue du
Faubourg Poissonniere, Paris. If I can be of any service to you in that
city I beg you will command me.

Ever my dear Sir with high esteem and regard

Yours faithfully
Washington Irving

Aaron Vail Esqr. / &c &c &c

MANUSCRIPT: NYSL.

1. Vail's letter of May 22, 1842, to WI is preserved at Va.—Barrett. In it he
offers to provide an escort for WI, to make reservations for a diligence, to see that
his luggage is forwarded, to vacate his apartment just before WI's arrival, to leave
household items for WI's use, and to arrange for servants for WI.

1392. To Joseph G. Cogswell

Washington March 22d. 1842

My dear Cogswell,

Your commission has been made out and lying on the table of the head clerk of the Department of State[1] for many days. It would have been forwarded to you, but I gave him reason to suppose you would be on here shortly. You can come on at your convenience; there is no absolute necessity for it; but I think it will be advisable, as you will be able by perusing the correspondence of the legation to put yourself up to the business we may have to conduct, and you will be able likewise to inform yourself of the routine of official affairs, and to make some valuable acquaintances.

There is no advance made to the Secretary, he is empowered to draw quarterly for his pay on the Rothschilds in London; but his first quarter must expire before he can draw. I have requested the head clerk to send on your commission with a printed letter of instructions &c Your pay commences from the date of your commission, which is the 4th – of March.

I hope Mr Astor will not be able to seduce you from the diplomatic career now opened to you,[2] even though he should grant you the *sine qua non*[.] I leave this place either this afternoon or tomorrow but, having to stop at Baltimore & Philadelphia on my way back, will not be in New York until towards the end of the week; when I will join you at Mr Astors; to whom I beg you to present my kind remembrances. I still hold it in mind to embark on the 7th April for Liverpool

Yours with cordial regard
Washington Irving

Manuscript: NYPL.

1. Daniel Fletcher Webster (1813–1862), son of the secretary of state, served from March 6, 1841, to April 24, 1843. See Ben Perley Poore, *Political Register and Congressional Directory* (Boston, 1878), p. 223; and Claude M. Fuess, *Daniel Webster*, 2 vols. (Boston, 1930), I, 121; II, 92, 360.

2. Cogswell's feelings toward WI's offer can be traced in his letters of this period. On February 14, 1842, to George Ticknor, Cogswell commented: "I am inclined to go, . . . but I have by no means decided upon it." Ten days later to C. S. Daveis he observed: "Mr. Irving has said so much to me of the satisfaction it would give him to have me of the legation, and other friends have urged me so strongly to go that I have fully made up my mind to become a diplomatist if the opportunity is offered. Mr. Astor is very much against it, being very reluctant to have me leave him. . . ." To Ticknor on March 10 Cogswell reports: "Mr. Astor is greatly distressed

at my leaving him, thinking that for a public object as important as is that of the immediate execution of his library plan I should have been justified in declining the appointment, as I gave no previous pledge to accept. I told him I would give up the Secretaryship if he would engage to begin at once upon the library, and that unless he did so I should certainly accept it. . . . Nothing short of a miracle will induce him to undertake it during his life." However Astor's persistence and persuasion changed Cogswell's mind, as he tells Ticknor on March 28: "Do not cry out upon me for fickleness, when you read that I am not going to Spain. I have made the sacrifice of honors to honor. . . . At the last moment Mr. Astor agreed to all that I asked of him: to go on immediately with the library, to guarantee me the librarianship with a salary of $2,500 a year, as soon as the building is finished, and in the mean while $2,000, while engaged upon the catalogue, or otherwise employed. . . . Irving not only consents, but fully approves what I have done, but he is desirous not to have it known, until he has made all arrangements for my substitute. . . ." See *Joseph Green Cogswell, As Sketched in His Letters*, ed. Anna E. Ticknor (Cambridge, Mass., 1874), pp. 228–32. Cogswell's decision also prompted a comment from Philip Hone on April 6: "Mr. Coggeswell of this city, who was appointed secretary of legation to accompany Mr. Irving, does not go. Mr. Astor, who enjoys his society, has bribed him to remain. He is willing to pay as much for the velvet cushion on which it is his pleasure to rest his head as the secretaryship would have produced, and it comes in the shape of a permanent salary to Mr. Coggeswell as librarian of a great public library which Mr. Astor has signified his intention to establish and endow in this city, which he proposes now to anticipate. That gentleman wisely determines to receive his equivalent and stay at home, write articles for the New York *Review*, and accompany his patron in his daily drives from Broadway to Hell Gate. Maecenas keeps Horace near him, and Horace knows when he has a good thing" (*The Diary of Philip Hone*, ed. Allan Nevins, II, 595).

1393. *To Joseph G. Cogswell*

[March 22?, 1842]

My dear Cogswell,
   Your letter of credit is not enclosed in this despatch, but will be delivered to you when you come to Washington.

                                                                    yours truly
                                                                    Washington Irving

MANUSCRIPT: Va.—Barrett.
ADDRESSED: Joseph G. Cogswell

   This letter is tentatively dated March 22?, 1842. The tenor of the note and the absence of a specific address suggest that it may have been an addendum to WI's letter of March 22, 1842, to Cogswell.

1894. To Daniel Webster

Washington, March 22d, 1842

My dear Sir,

In taking my departure for Spain I have to leave behind me a nephew, Washington Irving Junr about nineteen years of age, in whose welfare I take great interest. I have asked for him of Mr Upshur the commission of Second lieutenant of Marines.[1] He would make an excellent officer. He is active, intelligent, apt and fearless, and has a predilection for the seas. I will take it as a great kindness if you would, at any convenient time, bring his name to the reccollection of Mr Upshur, and add any word in his favor you may think proper. Excuse this additional claim on that friendship which you have manifested for me in so signal a manner; but really I feel toward this youth as a parent who leaves a son behind him unprovided for, and (left) ↑exposed↓ to the hazards of idleness.

Ever very truly and gratefully / Yours
Washington Irving

Hon Daniel Webster / &c &c &c

ADDRESSED: Hon. Daniel Webster / Secretary of State / Washington   DOCKETED: Referred to / the Secy of / the Navy. [*in pencil*] / D. S. — Recd. 25 March. / *Sec. Navy* [*top of MS page 1*]
MANUSCRIPT: Dr. Noel Cortes, Philadelphia.

1. See WI to A. P. Upshur, January 24, 1842. Apparently nothing came of WI's solicitation.

1395. To Gardner G. Howland

[March 25, 1842]

My dear Howland,

You need not write to Mr Moore[1] by tomorrows packet, on the subject of his return. Should I find it expedient to proceed in the matter about which we conversed this afternoon it will be time enough to write to him by the Steam Ship of the 1st. April. In the mean time I beg of you not to say any thing to any body on the subject

Yours very truly
Washington Irving

Friday Evg. March 25th [1842]

ADDRESSED: Gardner G. Howland Esqr / Washington Square
MANUSCRIPT: Minnesota Historical Society.

1. T. W. C. Moore was a foreign agent for G. G. & S. Howland, a New York shipping firm. See WI to Aaron Vail, May 11, 1841.

1396. To Benjamin Rush

New York, March 26th. 1842

Dear Sir,

My connexion with the Knickerbocker has long since ceased, and I am ignorant of the terms it offers,[1] to occasional contributors, and whether there is any room in its pages for their contributions. Under its former arrangement the proprietors of the work were extremely unpunctual in their pay: and I now hold their dishonored notes for money due two years since. Within a few months they have sold one half of their establishment, to a business house in Boston,[2] and its affairs may now be conducted with more punctuality; and I think it probable they are so. I have had no dealings with any other periodical, and am unable to give you the information you require: a direct correspondence with the Editors would perhaps get you a satisfactory answer; but I would generally advise you, in all your dealings, to bargain for *cash*. Never were the ⟨liter⟩ wages of literary labor more unfaithfully paid than at the present day.

I feel very much obliged to you for the kind expressions contained in your letter and for the very kind and flattering notice you have taken of my appointment;[3] and can only in return offer you my best wishes for your success in your literary career; and my regrets that I cannot be of more effective service to you

Very respectfully / Your obt Servt
Washington Irving

Benj Rush Esqr

MANUSCRIPT: Princeton University.

Benjamin Rush (1811–1877), son of Richard Rush, the diplomat and statesman, had served as secretary of the U.S. legation in London from 1837 to 1841. WI's letter is in reply to one written by Rush on March 21, 1842.

1. From March, 1839, to October, 1841, WI had contributed articles, tales, and sketches to the *Knickerbocker Magazine* on a monthly basis for a sum of $2000. See STW, II, 106–7.

2. Probably John Allen, who was publisher of the *Knickerbocker* from 1842 to

1847. He had been William D. Ticknor's partner in Boston from 1832 to 1834 and then operated his own publishing business until 1837, when he moved to New York. Apparently WI still associated Allen with Boston. See F. L. Mott, *History of American Magazines, 1741–1850*, p. 606; Charles A. Madison, *Book Publishing in America* (New York, 1966), p. 40; and *The Cost Books of Ticknor and Fields and Their Predecessors, 1832–1858*, ed. W. S. Tryon and William Charvat (New York, 1949), p. xv.

3. In his letter of March 21, Rush had written: "I beg leave most respectfully to offer my congratulations on your recent appointment to Spain, and I venture in this connexion to put under cover to you the Philadelphia Inquirer of the 5th. inst. in which you will see a short article signed 'One Citizen,' which I had great pleasure in writing, though well aware how much more might have been said" (draft copy, Princeton).

1397. To Hugh S. Legaré

New York, March 28th. 1842

My dear Sir

In consequence of Mr Astors having determined with the aid of Mr Cogswell to carry out his project of founding a public library, the latter has been induced to decline the appointment of Secretary of Legation to Madrid[.] I have reccommended, therefore, in his place Mr Alexander Hamilton Junr.[1] As you are well acquainted with this young gentleman you must be aware how well fitted he is for the office; and you must be sensible, from my intimacy with him and his family, how very acceptable the appointment would be to me[.] I am sure therefore you will do your best to carry it into effect.

Very truly and cordially yours
Washington Irving

Hon Hugh S. Legare / &c &c &c

MANUSCRIPT: Maine Historical Society.

Hugh Swinton Legaré (1797–1843), a South Carolina legislator in the 1820's and U.S. chargé d'affaires at Brussels from 1832 to 1836, served as Tyler's attorney general until his death on June 30, 1843.

1. Alexander Hamilton, Jr. (1816–1889), who was the grandson of Washington's secretary of the treasury, lived near Sunnyside with his parents, the James Alexander Hamiltons.

1398. To William C. Preston

New York, March 28th. 1842

My dear Preston,

Mr Cogswell having declined the appointment of Secretary of Legation to Spain to my great regret and embarrassment, I am extremely
anxious to have Mr Alexander Hamilton Jr of this city appointed in his
place. He is a young gentleman every way qualified to do credit to the
office, and he would be a most acceptable companion and coadjutor to
myself, having long been in habits of cordial intimacy with him as well
as with his family who are my near neighbors in the country[.] I beg
you therefore to give him your support.

With kind regards to Mrs Preston

Yours ever very truly
Washington Irving

Hon Wm C. Preston / &c &c &c

Manuscript: Va.–Barrett.

1399. To William C. Rives

New York, March 28th. 1842.

My dear Sir,

Mr Cogswell having been induced by important considerations, to
decline the appointment of Secretary of Legation to Spain, I am desirous
of having Mr Alexander Hamilton Junr, son of James Hamilton Esqr
appointed in his place. He is a young gentleman of great promise and
would do honor to the appointment. You are no doubt acquainted with
his numerous and influential connexions in this State, who would be well
pleased at his receiving this mark of confidence from the government

To me it would be extremely gratifying, having long been in habits
of cordial intimacy with him; and you know from experience how
important to the comfort of a Minister is a good understanding with the
Secretary

With kindest regards to Mrs Rives

Yours very faithfully
Washington Irving

P S. Receive my congratulations on your recent able and effective Speech.

MANUSCRIPT: LC.

1400. To John Tyler

New York, March 28t. 1842

My dear Sir,

Mr Cogswell having been induced by considerations of a substantial and satisfactory nature to decline the appointment of Secretary of the Legation to Spain, I take the liberty of reccommending in his place Mr Alexander Hamilton Junr. of New York, son of James Hamilton Esqr once District Attorney. ⟨This⟩ ↑He is a↓ young gentleman of high moral worth, sterling talents and varied acquirements and promises fair, at no distant period, to take an honorable and popular stand in public life. He is the author of a Series of articles that have recently appeared in the Courier and Enquirer in defence of Mr Websters position in the case of the Creole.[1] His appointment would give great satisfaction to an extensive and influential connexion in this state, who were very efficient in the Support of General Harrison and yourself in the last election, and who regard this young man with hope and pride

Lastly I would ask his ⟨as⟩ nomination as a *great personal favor to myself*. On my relations with the Secretary of Legation will depend in a great degree my comfort, and the prosperous conduct of my mission in a place like Madrid; so isolated, so apt to be distracted by factions and tumults, and where an American Minister has none of his countrymen to rally round him and render him counsel and support in cases of emergency. Mr Hamilton I know intimately; his family reside in my immediate neighborhood in the Country. We have been in habits of cordial intercourse for years and in having him by my side I shall feel as if I were taking a portion of my home with me

With kindest regards to your family I remain

Dear Sir very respectfully & truly / Your obliged friend & Servt
Washington Irving

John Tyler / President of the United States.

MANUSCRIPT: LC. PUBLISHED: Hellman, *WI, Esquire*, pp. 257–58.

1. The American brig *Creole* carrying tobacco and slaves from Hampton Roads to New Orleans was seized by some of the slaves who had overpowered the crew and killed the captain. They sailed the vessel to Nassau, where the British held

nineteen blacks accused of murder and freed the rest. Webster demanded the extradition and return of all slaves, plus damages, but Lord Ashburton rejected his claim. See Claude M. Fuess, *Daniel Webster*, II, 112–13.

1401. To Daniel Webster

New York, March 28. 1842

My dear Sir,

Mr Cogswell having, for cogent reasons, declined the appointment of Secretary of Legation to Spain permit me to reccommend in his place Mr Alexander Hamilton Jr Son of James Hamilton Esqr of New York. He is a young gentleman of high and honorable nature, and well qualified by talents, attainments and manners for the office. His appointment would be very gratifying to his connexions, who, you must be aware are numerous and influential: it would be peculiarly satisfactory to me, having long been in habits of cordial intimacy with him, and with his family who are my near neighbors in the country

I may add that he is of much promise in political life; having taken an active and efficient part in support of the whig ticket during the last presidential election; and having recently, as I understand, ably defended with his pen in the public papers, your positions with respect to the case of the Creole.

I am extremely anxious to have this matter settled soon, that I may embark with my mind at rest on a subject so important to the comfort of my residence in Madri[d]

Ever my dear Sir / with devoted regard / Yours
Washington Irving

Hon Daniel Webster

DOCKETED: Answered 30 March 1842
MANUSCRIPT: NA, RG 59.

1402. To Daniel Webster

New York, April 2d. 1842.

My dear Sir,

On arriving in town this evening from my place in the country I found your letter of 30th March.[1] I do assure you that no one has been more embarrassed and annoyed by the resolution of Mr Cogswell to decline

the appointment to Spain than myself. It took me by surprise on my
return from Washington; at which time he had just received his commission and its accompanying letter. It was made at such a late day in
consequence of a tardy agreement made by Mr Astor at the eleventh
hour, to carry into immediate effect the building and establishing of his
great public library, on condition that Mr Cogswell would remain to
superintend it as librarian[2] As this was an enterprise to which Mr Cogswell had long considered himself pledged; as it secured to him an
honorable provision for life; and to the public an important institution
which has long been a desideratum in our community, I felt compelled
to acquiesce in his decision   As to the appointment of his successor I
still flatter myself with the hope that the earnest application I have made
in behalf of Mr Hamilton will have its effect. He is the person I had
originally in view; when I was induced to give the preference to Mr
Cogswell in compliance with the wishes of Mr Legare. My choice of Mr
Hamilton has been made carefully and deliberately in consequence of
an intimate acquaintance with him and the knowledge of ⟨the⟩ ↑his↓
fitness for the office. I believe in appointments of this kind it is customary,
in a great degree, to consult the wishes of the Minister, when they are
not at variance with the good of his mission; and I cannot but hope the
President will especially exercise this courtesy and indulgence, where
the mission places the Minister in so isolated a position as that of
Madrid.

Excuse my earnestness in this matter my dear Sir but it is of vital
interest to me. I shall not be here to press it any further; but leave it
with confidence in your friendly hands

> Very respectfully and truly / Your friend & Servt
> Washington Irving

Hon Daniel Webster / &c &c &c

DOCKETED: *Private.* / Washington Irving. / 2d. April 1842
MANUSCRIPT: Va.–Barrett.

1. This letter has not been located.
2. For other details about this arrangement and WI's recommendation of Alexander Hamilton, Jr., see his letters to Hugh S. Legaré, William C. Preston, Daniel
Webster, and John Tyler, all dated March 28, 1842.

1403.   To Richard Bentley

New York April 4th 1842

My dear Sir,

This will be handed to you by Mr Henry R Schoolcraft;[1] a gentleman of literary celebrity in this country, and of great private worth and respectability He has been for twenty years a resident of the "West," as government agent among the Indian tribes and has made great researches as to their manners, customs, oral tales, traditions, &c &c. These he proposes to publish in a collective form under the title of *Cyclopedia Indianensis*.[2] Any services you may find it convenient to render him in the prosecution of his plan, and any personal civilities you may shew him will be gratefully considered by myself

Very truly your friend & Servt
Washington Irving

Richard S Bentley Esq

ADDRESSED: Richard S Bentley Esq / Bookseller / London / *Mr Henry R. School-craft*
MANUSCRIPT: Va.–Barrett.

Richard Bentley (1794–1871) was a successful London publisher and proprietor of *Bentley's Miscellany* (1837–1868).

1. Schoolcraft and WI, who had a mutual interest in the American Indian, had corresponded since 1835.
2. Schoolcraft eventually brought out his studies in six parts under the title of *Historical and Statistical Information Respecting the History, Condition, and Prospects of the Indian Tribes of the United States* (Philadelphia, 1851–1857).

1404.   To John G. Chapman

New York, April 4th 1842

My dear Sir,

I had intended to call on you on the last day of my sojourn at Washington,[1] but was so completely occupied at the State department and else where to the last moment that I had barely time to reach the cars before they started. I shall be very glad to receive the MS. relative to the Fairfax family,[2] but fear it will not reach New York before I sail, which will be on Thursday next. (the 7th) It will however, be sent after me. Any other MSS. ↑or letters↓ you may have occasion to send me from time to time you can leave with Mr Markoe[3] at the State department, who will forward them with my despatches. I have never seen the "Travels of the Rev Andrew Barnaby"[4] and should like to have any minutes of its contents that may relate to my subject.

I have not seen the Langleys[5] since my return but shall see them before my departure. I trust you will have sufficient encouragement from them to go on with your Washington sketches.[6] It will give me great pleasure to hear from you from time to time on this or any other topic, and I assure you one of the greatest sources of satisfaction I have derived from my late visit to Washington is the friendly intercourse which I trust it has established between us

Very truly my dear Sir / Your obliged
Washington Irving

John G Chapman Esqr

MANUSCRIPT: Wellesley College Library.

John Gadsby Chapman (1808–1889) was a painter with a studio in Washington. He was commissioned to paint *The Baptism of Pocahontas* for the Capitol Rotunda, and he may have been working on it at this time.

1. WI was receiving instructions and briefings concerning his duties as minister to Spain.

2. WI was gathering material for a biography of George Washington, and he was eventually to deal with the Fairfaxes early in the first volume of this work. In 1748 Washington accompanied George Williams Fairfax on a surveying expedition into the area west of the Blue Ridge Mountains. See *The Life of George Washington* (New York, 1855), I, 35–40.

3. Francis Markoe was a clerk in the State Department at this time. See *The Memoirs of John Quincy Adams* (Philadelphia, 1876), X, 469. For other details, see WI to Markoe, April 4, 1842.

4. Andrew Burnaby, *Travels Through the Middle Settlements in North America, in the Years 1759 and 1760, With Observations upon the State of the Colonies* (London, 1775). Probably Chapman had suggested the book for background details for WI's life of Washington.

5. J. and H. G. Langley were booksellers on Chatham Street in New York City from whom WI ordered several books containing biographical materials on Washington. See WI to J. and H. G. Langley, December 13, [1841].

6. The nature of the Langleys' encouragement to Chapman has not been ascertained.

1405.   To Philip Hone

New York, April 4t. 1842.

My dear Hone

I have just received your kind note of the 1st Inst[1] enclosing an invitation signed by a number of my towns-men to partake of a public dinner,[2] as a farewell expression of their regard, prior to my departure for Spain.

I cannot but remember with deep sensibility, a similar testimonial of their good will,[3] with which I was surprized and overpowered on my return home after so long an absence that I had almost feared it had alienated me from their affections; and it is a proud gratification to me to find that, after ten years of familiar intercourse the same good will appears still to be exhibited. Indeed the manifestations of public regard have thickened upon me, rather than declined with the lapse of years and when I have made up my mind to find myself naturally waning in popular favor, and rightfully giving place to younger and fresher candidates, I am surprized by new marks of popular esteem and a national confidence, surpassing all that have gone before. Thus have I continually been paid, and overpaid, and paid again, for all the little good I may have effected in my somewhat negligent and fortuitous career, until at times, I feel as if in receiving such unmeasured rewards, I am tacitly pocketing what is not due to me.

In the present instance this shall not be the case, indeed the nature of my preparations, on the eve of departure for a post of important and untried responsibilities, leaves me neither the leisure nor the frame of mind necessary to participate in such a festivity as is proposed; but I beg you to assure my towns men, that, while I excuse myself from accepting their proffered dinner, I will treasure ⟨it⟩ up in my "heart of hearts" the cordial "Farewell" intended by it, as one of the dearest of the many testimonials of regard received by me from my native place.

For you, my good friend, who have known me "from my childhood on," accept my thanks for the kind expressions with which you have accompanied this invitation, and my sincere wish that, should I live once more to return to my native land, I may find you in the full enjoyment of health and prosperity

Yours very faithfully
Washington Irving

Philip Hone **Esq**

MANUSCRIPT: NYHS.   PUBLISHED: NYEP, April 7, 1842; *New-York Mirror*, 20

(April 16, 1842), 123; PMI, III, 190–91; *The Diary of Philip Hone*, ed. Allan Nevins, II, 595–96 (in part).

1. Hone had written: "The agreeable duty is deputed to me to transmit the enclosed invitation, and to request that your answer (which it is confidently hoped will be favorable) may be communicated to, dear sir, your faithful friend and servant, (Signed) Philip Hone." See *New-York Mirror*, 20 (April 16, 1842), 123.

2. The text of this invitation, dated March 29, 1842 and signed Robert H. Morris, Hone, G. C. Verplanck, and forty-six others, is printed in NYEP, April 7, 1842; and *New-York Mirror*, 20 (April 16, 1842), 123; and PMI, III, 189–90.

3. On May 30, 1832, WI was given a public dinner at the City Hotel which was attended by many prominent citizens of New York. For details see New York *American*, June 2, 1832; *New-York Mirror*, 20 (June 9, 1832), 386; and PMI, II, 486–91.

1406. To Francis Markoe, Jr.

New York April 4th. 1842.

My dear Sir,

I have received your letter[1] informing me of my being elected a corresponding member of the National Institution for the Promotion of Science.[2] It will give me great pleasure to do all in my power to promote the objects of the Institution.

Mr Chapman[3] the artist is collecting facts for me relative to the Life of Washington. I have directed him to leave with you, any letters he might write to me on the Subject, and will be much obliged to you if you will forward them with my dispatches

I shall sail in the Packet Independence for Liverpool on Thursday the 7th inst

With kind remembrances to Mrs Markoe I am my dear Sir

Your obliged friend & servt
Washington Irving

Francis Markoe Jr.

ADDRESSED: Francis Markoe Jr Esqr / Corresponding Secretary / of the National Institute / Washington   POSTMARKED: NEW-YORK / APL / 4
MANUSCRIPT: Pierpont Morgan Library.

Francis Markoe, who eventually became chief clerk in the Department of State, was one of the founders and for a number of years the corresponding secretary of the National Institution for the Promotion of Science. See letter from S. Dillon Ripley, secretary, Smithsonian Institution, Washington, D.C., April 8, 1975.

1. This letter has not been located.
2. The National Institution had been established by an act of Congress in Febru-

ary 1841, with Joel R. Poinsett, James K. Paulding, John Quincy Adams, John J. Abert, Joseph G. Totten, A. O. Dayton, Francis Markoe, Levi Woodbury, William Cranch, Henry D. Gilpin, and William J. Stone as members of the corporate body. The National Institution, which was the custodian of the collections of the U.S. Exploring Expedition and materials from the bequest of James Smithson, was incorporated into the Smithsonian Institution when it was chartered by Congress in 1846. See William Jones Rhees, *The Smithsonian Institution*, 2 vols. (Washington, 1901), I, 217, 1011–12.

3. See WI to Chapman, April 4, 1842.

1407. To John Murray II

New York, April 4th 1842

My dear Sir

Permit me to introduce to your acquaintance and reccommend to your civilities Mr Henry R. Schoolcraft; a gentleman of celebrity in this country, and who, during his residence of many years as Indian Agent, among our aboriginal tribes, has made great researches into their manners, customs traditions, oral tales &c &c These he intends to throw into a collective form and publish under the title of *Cyclopedia Indianensis*. ⟨He is⟩ Any good offices you may find it convenient to render him in the prosecution of his plan and any personal attentions, which from his private[1] worth and general intelligence he well merits, will be considered favors done to myself

Ever my dear Sir with great regard / Yours faithfully
Washington Irving

John Murray Esqr

ADDRESSED: John Murray Esqr / Albemarle Street / London / *Mr Henry R Schoolcraft*   POSTMARKED: [*unrecovered*]
MANUSCRIPT: John Murray.   PUBLISHED: WIHM, pp. 176–77.

Schoolcraft apparently mailed the letter after he reached London, for the address leaf bears a one-penny British stamp.

1. WI wrote "pivate."

1408. To Gouverneur Kemble

New York, April 5th. 1842.

My dear Kemble,

I begin to fear I shall depart without seeing you; which will be a great disappointment. I received your letter[1] some time since, but have ever since been in such a turmoil in making preparations for this sudden and unexpected change in my life and pursuits, that I have been unable to keep up the course of correspondence. I leave my sweet quiet little home with great regret; but really I do not know how I should have been able to carry it on much longer in these hard times; when every resource seemed withering and drying up. I leave a full power of attorney with my nephew Pierre M Irving, to transact all my affairs;[2] and to him you will pay any interest that may accrue from the Godfrey purchase,[3] and he will be empowered to do all that is necessary in the matter.

I leave my usual household at the Cottage, under charge of my brother Ebenezer, who is Laird of Sunnyside pro tem. I shall hail with joy the day that I return to nestle myself down there for the remainder of my life.

If I should not indeed see you before I sail I leave you my heartfelt wishes for your prosperity and happiness, and so God bless you my dear Kemble.

Yours ever
Washington Irving

Gouverneur Kemble Esqr.

ADDRESSED: Gouverneur Kemble Esqr / West point Foundry / Putnam Cy   POST-
    MARKED: NEW-YORK / APR / 6
MANUSCRIPT: Lehigh University Library. PUBLISHED: *American Literature*, 35
    (May, 1963), 171.

1. This letter has not been located.
2. This document, dated April 6, 1842, is preserved in Va.–Barrett.
3. WI refers to land speculation in Michigan in which he had invested money a few years earlier. See WI to Kemble, September 28, 1836; September 13, 1837; June 2, 1838; December 28, 1839; and February 5, 1840.

1409. To George Ticknor

New York. April 6th. 1842

My dear Ticknor,

It will give me great pleasure to execute your wishes not only in the matters you suggest[1] but in any other you may point out during my residence abroad.

With many thanks for your kind expressions and good wishes believe me ever

Yours very truly
Washington Irving

Geo Ticknor Esqr

MANUSCRIPT: Va.–Barrett.

1. On March 31, 1842, Ticknor had written to WI, asking him to meet his assistant, Pascual de Gayangos, in London and to receive "a written memorandum of what he has ordered for me in Madrid, the person of who, he has ordered it, and the best mode of accomplishing there all I desire. . . ." Ticknor planned to use the copies of these materials from Madrid and the Escorial in his *History of Spanish Literature*, which appeared in 1849. See *Life, Letters, and Journals of George Ticknor*, ed. Anna Ticknor, 2 vols. (Boston, 1876), II, 245–46.

1410. To Sarah Irving

[New York, April 7, 1842]

My dear Sarah,

I have given Pierre M Irving a full power of attorney to act in my name, and have made arrangements with him for the conduct of my pecuniary affairs. You will draw on him therefore, from time to time, for such funds as may be requisite to keep every thing at the Cottage on the usual footing. Out of these funds you and your sisters ⟨wh⟩ will help yourselves, as circumstances may require, for your personal expenses, regulating yourselves by an allowance of one hundred dollars a year each, commencing on the 1st. of the present month of April. This allowance is to be in addition to the dividends &c which you may receive from the Stocks which I hold ⟨for⟩ as trustee for you and your Sisters.

Let Pierre know some little time before hand, when you are about to draw on him, that he may provide the funds without inconvenience.

And now my dear, good little girl, God bless you! You have been like a daughter and an affectionate one to me, and so have all your Sisters; and have by your ⟨affec⟩ kind attentions made the years I have lived among you one of the happiest portions of my life. In a little while we shall come together again, better supplied I trust, with the ways and means of carrying on our simple little scheme of household comfort and then we will have merry times at sweet little Sunnyside

With my love to all the flock

Your affectionate Uncle
Washington Irving

New York, April 7th. 1842

MANUSCRIPT: SHR.   PUBLISHED: PMI, III, 192 (in part).

1411. To Morgan Lewis

New York April 10th. 1842

My dear Sir,

I had intended to call on you previous to my departure, but have been so much hurried as not to find a moment of liesure. I am occupied upon a life of Washington, which I shall finish while in Spain. You must be rich in personal reccollections ⟨abo⟩ of him, and may have interesting documents concerning him and concerning the American revolution.[1] Any thing of the kind that you can furnish me will be considered a most valuable favor. Should you find it convenient to attend to this application ⟨and⟩ any letter you may wish to forward to me can be sent to the counting house of Messrs. Grinnell Minturn & Co.[2]

With best wishes for your health & happiness

I remain my dear Sir / Yours very faithfully
Washington Irving

Genl Morgan Lewis / &c &c &c

ADDRESSED: Genl Morgan Lewis / &c &c &c / New York.   POSTMARKED: NEW-YORK / APR / 10   DOCKETED: W Irving
MANUSCRIPT: SHR.

Morgan Lewis (1754–1844) had served with General Horatio Gates in the Ticonderoga and Saratoga campaigns in 1777 and 1778. Following the war he was admitted to the bar and served as attorney general, justice of the New York Supreme Court, and governor of the state. During the War of 1812 he was quartermaster general of the American forces.

1. Apparently Lewis could not provide materials, for WI did not acknowledge his assistance when the biography of Washington appeared.
2. The business offices of the firm were located at 134 Front Street at the corner of Pine.

1412. To Catharine Paris

Ship Independence April 10th 1842

My dear Sister,

I was on the point of coming in to see you this morning, for I was at the Street door but I reflected that a parting scene would only be agitating to us both, and harrassing to your nerves, so I refrained. I now go off with a stout heart, cheered by a confident hope that this temporary absence will have ↑a↓ prosperous effect upon my home and all my family and that I will return after a little while the better enabled to pass the residue of my days happily among you all. I shall write to you from England, and when I get to Paris will give you a full account of Sarah and all her concerns.

God bless you my dear Sister/ Your affectionate brother
Washington Irving.

MANUSCRIPT: Yale.

Although WI's departure was scheduled for April 7, it was delayed until April 10, possibly because of the weather. See NYEP, April 7, 12, 1842.

1413. To Edward Everett

[May 3, 1842]

My dear Sir,
    It will give me great pleasure to call with you on Lord Aberdeen.[1] I will be at home at the time you mention

Yours very truly
Washington Irving

Thomas's Hotel[2] / Tuesday May 3d [1842][3]

MANUSCRIPT: MHS.

At the top of the sheet in another hand is written "Edward Everett."

Edward Everett (1794–1865), who had taught Greek at Harvard, edited the *North American Review*, served in the U.S. Congress from 1825 to 1835 and as governor of Massachusetts from 1836 to 1839, was U.S. minister to Great Britain, a post which he held until August, 1845.

1. George Hamilton Gordon, 4th earl of Aberdeen (1784–1860), who had served as foreign minister in Wellington's ministry from 1828 to 1830, had assumed that post again in September, 1841, and was to hold it until July, 1846. Taking a conciliatory approach toward relations with the United States, Aberdeen actively supported the Webster-Ashburton Treaty (1842) and the Oregon Treaty (1846) setting the boundary at the 49th parallel.

2. Probably St. Thomas's Hotel, Berkeley Square.

3. In another hand "1843?" has been written. The perpetual calendar establishes the date as 1842.

1414. To Catharine Paris

London May 3d. 1842

My dear Sister,

I have arrived in England *before my ship*, and in London before visiting Birmingham; and these are the circumstances of the case. We had
a fair wind and fine voyage until we made the Irish coast, when the wind
came a head. After beating for a day or two in the channel with the
prospect of passing several more days on shipboard a Steam packet hove
in sight. A Signal brought it within hail. It was bound from Cork for
Bristol, where it would arrive on the following day. Several of ⟨the f⟩
my fellow passengers and myself, therefore, got on board, and were
landed on the following day, (30 April) at Bristol: where our dear Sarah
landed about a year previously. As ⟨I⟩ we entered the mouth of the
Severn and sailed up to the city I recalled Sarahs account of the delight
she received from the beautiful scenery; and I found it well worthy of
her enthusiasm. We ⟨I⟩ landed after dark, and the next morning I set
off in the rail road cars for London. These rail roads have altered the
whole style and course of travelling in England. You fly through the
country rather than ride: ⟨and yet⟩ We were about four hours travelling
a distance of one hundred miles: and such admirable vehicles. I sat as
comfortably cushioned and accommodated as in my old voltaire chair
at the Cottage. The rail roads too are so well finished that you experience
none of the jarring and vibration that are felt in ours. In this way we
were whirled through a succession of enchanting scenery, in all the
freshness of spring; the weather was lovely, and the sunshine worthy of
our own country.

I had intended merely to touch in London and proceed by rail road
to Birmingham; which is now but a five hours journey from the Metropolis; I found, however, once here, it was impossible to get away as
readily as I had supposed. I waited on our Minister Mr Everett, and
had some matters to arrange with him, and understood that it would
be proper for me to appear at the ⟨drawing room⟩ Levee and be presented to the Queen on Wednesday morning (tomorrow)[1] Then I had
to order some addition to my Diplomatic uniform for the occasion to
get clothes &c. &c It worries me extremely to be thus detained from
seeing sister Sarah, and I fear she will be grieved at my delay. I shall
endeavor to break away from town the day after tomorrow, and put off
all further business and arrangements until my return. In fact I am not in
mood and trim to enter upon the bustle and agitation of ⟨[*unrecovered*]⟩
public life. ⟨and⟩ The hurried transitions of the latter part of my voyage,
and of my arrival have excited me too much; I arrived here, flushed

and heated and agitated, and since that have experienced something of depression. I have avoided making any calls that might involve me in engagements, or hurry me into society, and have felt a singular reluctance to commit myself once more to the current of society and the turmoil of the world. I have caught myself repeatedly experiencing something of the homesickness that poor Sarah complained of: and looking back with ⟨obliging⟩ an eye of regret to the unpretending quiet of dear little Sunnyside. However all this will pass away. When I have made my visit to Birmingham I will come back and plunge into the stream, and trust to the buoyancy and activity of my spirit to enable me once more to ⟨[unrecovered]⟩] buffet with the waves. I find that, by getting on board the Steamer and landing at Bristol I escaped the bother of a public dinner which they were prepared to offer me at Liverpool[2]—this is a great comfort—

I called on Mrs Bates[3] yesterday who gave me news from Birmingham Mr Van Wart was in London a few days since and brought her a letter from Marianne. I learn that all are well there, and looking out f[or] [MS torn] me. What a visit it will be for me. My heart beats at the thoughts of it.

⟨Befor⟩ Long before this letter reaches you you will have heard of our dear Sarahs confinement; the first news of which I received yesterday. By this time I presume she sees company again as I hear she had a very favorable time. What a happy addition this will be to her stock of domestic enjoyments! What new ties and delightful duties it creates! It will be a strange sight for me to see Sarah, with her infant in her arms! Dear, dear girl, how my heart yearns toward her! I question whether I shall get away from England until ↑toward↓ the end of the month; and then I shall hurry on to Paris: where I expect to be joined by Mr Hamilton; who I trust will bring me letters and accounts from you all, and from dear little Sunnyside. This letter must answer for the family. It is written in a scanty moment, snatched from amidst the hurry of various occupations. All letters for me had best be sent to Mr Daniel Le Roy New York,[4] ⟨to be⟩ the agent for forwarding letters for the legations. They will then come one[5] with the despatches to the distributing agents at London; who will forward them to me wherever I may be.

With love to all.

Your affectionate brother
W. I.

ADDRESSED: Mrs. Daniel Paris. / ⟨Care of E. Irving / New York.⟩ / Tarrytown N Y
    POSTMARKED: BOSTON / SHIP / [unrecovered] // NEW-YORK / MAY 23
    DOCKETED: Washn. Irving to Mrs. Cath. R. Paris. London / May 3d 1842
    FRANKED: Washington Irving

MANUSCRIPT: SHR.   PUBLISHED: PMI, III, 193–95 (in part).

1. WI was officially presented to Queen Victoria (1819–1901) by U.S. Minister Edward Everett at her levee in St. James Palace on the afternoon of Wednesday, May 4, 1842. See London *Times*, May 5, 1842.

2. See WI to Thomas Todd, May 5, 1842, for the invitation from Liverpool and WI's reply.

3. The wife of Joshua Bates, an American businessman in London.

4. Daniel LeRoy is listed as a broker at 44 Wall Street in *Longworth's New York Directory for 1842–43* (p. 378).

5. WI probably intended to write "on."

1415. To Thomas Todd

London, May 5, 1842

Dear Sir,

I have to acknowledge the receipt of your letter of 2d inst.,[1] informing me of the very kind intention which had been entertained, by some of the inhabitants of Liverpool, of offering me a public dinner on my expected arrival at that port, and of their regret and disappointment at the accidental change in my route. I beg you to assure those gentlemen of the very deep and grateful sense I entertain of this signal evidence of their good opinion and good-will, and of the very flattering expression of respect, and the cordial wishes for my prosperity, which they have deputed you to convey to me. Permit me to add, that, from certain passages of your letter, I am led to view this public honour intended me in a higher light than as a mere compliment confined to myself. I perceive in it a desire to manifest, through me, a conciliatory disposition toward my country at a moment when untoward circumstances prevail, and when, as you intimate, inconsiderate and designing men may seek to sow discord between the two nations. Such a conciliatory disposition, I am confident, prevails among the right-minded and right-hearted of both countries, and, I trust, will be sufficient to neutralize any such mischievous efforts as those to which you allude. There is no question at present existing between the two countries,[2] however difficult at first it may appear, which is not, in my mind, susceptible of an amicable adjustment, if negotiated in that mutual spirit of forbearance, with that delicate consideration for the peculiar position and circumstances of each other, and with that magnanimous regard for each other's honour and interests, which ought to govern the opinions and dealings, public and private, of two great and kindred nations, whose honour and interests

are in so many respects identical. I have the honour to be, very respectfully, your obedient servant,

Washington Irving

Mr Thomas Todd, &c.

PUBLISHED: London *Times*, May 12, 1842, quoted from Liverpool *Albion*, May 9,
1842.

1. This letter has not been located.
2. WI was probably referring to the controversy over the northeastern boundary
between Maine and New Brunswick which was resolved by the Webster-Ashburton
Treaty of August 9, 1842.

1416. To Catharine Paris

The Shrubbery, May 7. 1842

My dear Sister,
  I wrote you a hasty scrawl a few days since from London. I was detained in town three or four days by business, and then[1] set off for
Birmingham, where I arrived in about five hours by rail road; travelling
without the least fatigue. It is quite wonderful how distances are
shortened by this invention since I was in England. My meeting with
our dear Sister[2] was, as you may suppose, most affecting For some
moments we were *clasped* in each others arms without speaking, our
hearts and eyes overflowing. I was glad there was no one by to see us
play the child. She is looking uncommonly well; freshened and plumped
up rather than withered by years. It delighted me to see her so, for I
had feared I should see marks of the marring hand of time. Marianne[3]
was at home, and soon came in. You would be much pleased with her.
She ⟨is qu⟩ has a charming intelligent countenance, and is a noble
hearted, disinterested and most companionable little being. Her countenance somewhat resembles Henrys. In a little while I felt once more
quite at home at the Shrubbery, ensconced in the easy arm chair in which
I used to lounge. The weather was delightful, and the look out of the
drawing room windows on the lawn more lovely than ever, for the shrubs
and trees have grown and multiplied since I have been here
  In the evening I was at Matildas.[4] She is looking very well though,
since the birth of her little girl she is said to be thinner than before. I
was much pleased with her husband;[5] he has a frank amiable countenance; and they appear to be living most happily together. William Van
Wart[6] is my delight and is I think, the flower of the flock. Full of life,

activity, good spirits and good humour; combining the good qualities
of both his parents. He is the life of the house whenever he enters it.
I drove over with him in his little fancy gig to his establishment; about
two miles off, commanding a sweet prospect. He has four boys:[7] very
fine children; though the eldest, which was called after me, is in a sad
precarious state of health and I fear will eventually fall a victim to
calomel; ⟨which⟩ with which he was dosed about five years since, and
which has completely pervaded his system. The second boy, William,
is one of the handsomest, sprightliest, most engaging children I ever
saw, and promises to be the father over again. Williams wife[8] appears
to be a most intelligent cultivated woman. I saw some drawings by her
in quite a superior style, and several likenesses she had taken of the
family, some in water colours and others on ivory that would not dis-
credit a regular artist. George whom I left a boy and who is now a
manly fellow, taller than his father, ⟨to?⟩ pleased me almost as much as
William. He appears to be perfectly worthy and considerate, very
affectionate; with a dash of peculiarity and humour. He is quite domestic
in his habits and pleasures; and indeed our dear sister has great reason
to feel happy in the domestic circle which surrounds her. Mr Van Wart
seems to have weathered these hard times without being the worse for
wear, though his hair is grayer than when last I saw him. He has given
up the intention of visiting the United States this spring: and I am in
some hopes of having him as a companion to France; having to meet
a Spanish customer there on business.

While I was in London I attended the levee to be presented. I know
the great interest you take in the young Queen[9] and that you will
expect some account of her. She is certainly quite low in stature, but
well formed and well rounded. Her countenance, though not decidedly
handsome is agreeable and intelligent. Her eyes light blue with ⟨long⟩
light eye lashes, and her mouth generally a little open, so that you can
see her teeth. She acquits herself in her receptions with great grace and
even with dignity. Prince Albert[10] stood beside her; a tall, elegantly
formed young man, with a handsome prepossessing countenance. He
is said to be frank, manly, intelligent and accomplished; to be fond of
his little wife, who in turn is strongly attached to him. It is rare to see
such a union of pure affection on a throne.

I experienced a very kind reception at court; was warmly welcomed
by many members of the diplomatic corps, though most of them were
strangers to me; but I met several of my old acquaintances among the
Ministers: Lord Aberdeen, Sir Robert Peel[11] &c who were very cordial
in their recognitions; and seemed to be in high good humor at having,
themselves, got once more into office.

Among the most gratifying meetings with old friends during my brief sojourn in London, I must mention those with Mr Rogers[12] and with Leslie.[13] Mr Rogers was quite affected on meeting with me, (it was at a dinner party at our Ministers, Mr Everetts) The old man took me in his arms quite in a paternal manner. He begins to shew the marks of his advanced age, though he still goes out to parties and is almost as much in company as ever. Leslie is occupied in painting a picture of the Royal christening.[14] His picture of the Coronation[15] has been the making of him. He has more orders for paintings than he can execute.

⟨May 9th. I remained in Birmingham but two days, as it was a mere preliminary visit⟩

May 9. *Little Cloisters, Westminster Abbey*. I returned to town on Saturday after passing two days in Birmingham, intending to pay it another and a longer visit before I leave England. I am here ensconced in the very heart of this old monastic establishment, with an old friend who keeps bachelors hall in one of the interior buildings connected with the Abbey. My host is Mr James Bandinel[16] of the foreign office, with whom I became acquainted during my former diplomatic residence in London. He is a peculiar character; a capital scholar a man variously and curiously informed; of great worth, kindness and hospitality. His quarters in the old abbey are a perfect "old curiosity shop," furnished with all kinds of antiquities and ⟨od⟩ curiosities. Quaint old furniture: the walls hung with ancient armour; weapons ⟨from⟩ ↑of↓ all ages and countries: curious pictures &c ⟨&c Shelv⟩ Cases and shelves of old books in every room. The entrance ⟨th⟩ to this singular and monkish nest is through the ⟨cloisters,⟩ vaulted passages and the long arcades of the cloisters, ⟨past⟩ over the tombstones (inserted in the pavements) of the ancient abbots which I have mentioned in the Sketch book,[17] and past that mural monument with a marble figure reclining on it which frightened Sarah so much that evening when she was brought to the Abbey unexpectedly by Mr Storrow. I have repeatedly passed through these cloisters and ⟨past⟩ ↑by↓ that monument at midnight on my way home from a party, and on one occasion the Abbey clock struck twelve just as I was passing. How strange it seems to me that I should thus be nestled quietly in the very heart of this old pile that used to be so much the Scene of my half romantic half meditative haunts, during my scribbling days. It is like my sojourn ⟨amon⟩ in the halls of the Alhambra—Am I always to have my dreams turned into realities! May 13th. I have kept this letter by me several days but have been unable to add a word, such is the hurry of engagements, visits, calls, notes &c &c in this overwhelming metropolis. I have neither rest by day nor sleep by night and am almost fagged out. I ⟨wa⟩ had hoped to enjoy some delightful quiet in this glorious seclusion in the heart of the cloisters, but the claims of the world follow me here and keep me in continual agitation. Last Sunday it is true I had a delicious treat in hearing the Cathedral service performed in a noble style; with the chaunts of the quire and the accompanyment of the organ: but, excepting this, I have seen nothing of the Abbey excepting to pass to and fro, by night and day through the cloisters, making the vaults and monuments echo with my footsteps at midnight.

I have ⟨b⟩ not been able to call on many of my old friends, but have met some of them on public occasions. Many of the literary folks I met at an anniversary dinner of the Literary Fund,[18] at which Prince Albert presided. Here I sat beside my friend Moore the Poet,[19] who came to town to attend the dinner. He looks thinner than when I last saw him, and has the cares and troubles of the world thickening upon him as he advances in years. He has two sons,[20] both had commissions in the Army. The youngest has recently returned home broken in health, and in danger of a consumption. The elder, Tom, has been rather wild; and is ⟨returning⟩ on his return from India, having for some unknown reason, sold his commission. The expenses of these two sons bear hard upon poor Moore: and he talks with some despondency of ⟨his⟩ the likelihood of his having to come upon the Literary Fund for assistance. The literary Fund Dinner was very splendid, and there was much dull speaking from various distinguished characters. I had come to it with great reluctance, knowing that ⟨I⟩ my health would be drunk; and, though I had determined not to make a speech in reply, yet the very idea of being ⟨obl⟩ singled out and obliged to get on my legs and return thanks ⟨kept me in⟩ made me nervous throughout the evening. The flattering speech ⟨of Sir Robert Inglis[21]⟩ by which the toast was preceded and the very warm and prolonged cheerings by which it was received, instead of relieving, contributed to agitate me, and I felt as if I would never attend a public dinner again, when I should have to undergo such a trial.

I believe I told you in a previous letter of the public dinner that had been intended me at Liverpool.[22] I have since received an invitation to accept a public dinner at Glasgow, which of course I declined; indeed ⟨nothing⟩ the manifestations of public regard which I have continually experienced since my arrival have been quite overpowering.

Last Evening I was at the Queens grand Fancy ball;[23] which surpassed in splendor and picturesque effect, any courtly assemblage that I ever witnessed or could imagine. The newspapers are full of details of this magnificent pageant, and I must refer you to them for particulars; for the whole is a scene of bewilderment in my reccollection. There were at least two thousand persons present all arrayed in ⟨rich⟩ historical, poetical or fanciful costumes, or in rich military and court uniforms. A kind of scheme was given to the whole by making it the representation of the visit of Anne of Brittany[24] (the character sustained by the Duchess of Cambridge)[25] to the Court of Edward III[26] (Prince Albert) and his

Queen Philippa[27] (Queen Victoria) The respective Sovriegns had all their courtiers & attendants in the costumes of the times, faithfully executed after old ↑historical↓ paintings & engravings—There was a reality mingled with the fiction of the Scene. Here Royalty represented Royalty, and nobility represented nobility: many of the personages present, played the parts of their own ancestors; their dresses being faithfully copied from old ↑family↓ paintings; by Vandyke[28] and other celebrated persons. There was no tinsel, nor stage trumpery on the dresses and jewels: all was of the richest materials; such as the characters represented would have worn; and there was on all sides a blaze of diamonds beyond any thing I had ever seen: The Saloons of the Palace were of great Size, so that there was ample room for display; and nothing could surpass the effect of the various groupes processions &c or the Splendor of the assemblage in the throne room where Albert and Victoria, as Edward & Philippa[29] were seated in state, receiving the homage of the brilliant throng.

I had a very favorable situation in one part of the evening, near the Royal party, when the different quadrilles ↑each in uniform costumes↓ danced before them. The personage who seemed least to enjoy the scene seemed to me to be the little queen herself. She was ↑flushed and heated and↓ evidently fatigued and oppressed with the state she had to keep up and the royal robes in which she was arrayed; and especially by a crown of gold, which weighed heavy on her brow and to which she was continually raising her hand to move it slightly when it pressed upon her brow. I hope and trust her real crown sits easier. Prince Albert looked uncommonly well [in] [MS torn] his costume. He would have realized the idea you have no doubt formed of a prince from all that you have read in fairy tales. He came up to where I was standing and held some little conversation with me. He speaks english very well, and his manner is extremely bland and prepossessing.

The Shrubbery. May 16th. I was interrupted in my letter and had to abandon it. Yesterday I made my escape from London in spite of a host of tempting invitations—and came off here, glad to get a little repose. I arrived wearied, exhausted, rheumatic (which I have been ever since my arrival on the Coast of England) and ↑yesterday afternoon and↓ all last evening could do little else than sleep; to make up for nights of broken rest. To day I feel quiet and refreshed: though still I feel the lingerings of rheumatic pain in my left shoulder and arm: I trust to get rid of it when I get out of this humid climate. Hector Ames[30] will come to Birmingham by the way of Oxford, Stratford on Avon & Warwick, in company with a Mr Lee[31] of Boston a connexion of the Storrows, who came out in the same ship with us—We shall all leave this together towards the end of the week, for Southampton to embark for France

I am very much pleased with Hector. He is an amiable, intelligent, quiet little fellow, whose company will be a great comfort to me.

Give my love to "all bodies"—I will write again soon.

Your afft brother, W. I.

ADDRESSED: Mrs Daniel Paris / Care of Ebnr Irving Esq / *Tarrytown* [*not in WI's hand*] / New York / ⟨Great Western⟩ POSTMARKED: NEW-YORK / JUNE / 7 DOCKETED: Washn. Irving to Mrs. Cath R. Paris. Birmingham / Engd. May 7. ↑to 16th.↓ 1842.

MANUSCRIPT: Va.–Barrett. PUBLISHED: PMI, III, 195–99, 201–3 (in part).

1. WI wrote "the."
2. Sarah Van Wart.
3. The Van Warts' fourth child and older daughter.
4. The Van Warts' fifth child and younger daughter.
5. Charles Aylett Kell.
6. William (d. 1868) was the Van Warts' third child.
7. These were Washington Irving (b. January 23, 1836), Wilfred, Harry, and Oscar Irving.
8. The former Rosalinda Bond.
9. Victoria (1819–1901), daughter of Edward, duke of Kent, and Victoria Maria Louisa of Saxe-Coburg, was crowned queen on June 28, 1838, after the death of William IV. Knowledgeable in constitutional principles, she exerted influence on governmental policy despite her youth.
10. Albert (1819–1861), the youngest son of the duke of Saxe-Coburg-Gotha, married Queen Victoria on February 10, 1840. He was given the title of consort in 1842 and of prince consort in 1857. Although his official role was largely ceremonial, he frequently influenced the queen's decisions with his practical advice.
11. Sir Robert Peel (1778–1850), whose public career had begun in 1811 as undersecretary for the colonies and continued with only brief interruptions for the rest of his life. At this time he was prime minister, the head of the Conservative party.
12. Samuel Rogers (1763–1855), with whom WI had been intimate in the 1820's.
13. Charles R. Leslie, an expatriate American artist. For other details, see WI to Eliza Leslie, December 20, 1839.
14. Leslie had actually begun *The Christening of the Princess Royal* (Victoria Adelaide Mary Louise [1840–1901]) in 1841. See Leslie, *Autobiographical Recollections*, pp. 321, 323.
15. *The Queen Receiving the Sacrament after the Coronation, June 28, 1838* was followed by a portrait of the duchess of Sutherland in her coronation robes. See Leslie, *Autobiographical Recollections*, pp. 311–15, 325, 359–60.
16. James Bandinel (1783–1849) was a clerk in the British Foreign Office with whom WI was well acquainted while he was secretary of the U.S. legation.
17. In the beginning of his essay, "Westminster Abbey," WI described the cloisters.

18. The Literary Fund Society, established in 1790 to provide for the needs of needy and unfortunate authors, held its fifty-third anniversary dinner at Freemasons' Hall on May 11, 1842. For details about the gathering, see London *Times*, May 12, 1842; and George P. Putnam, "Recollections of Irving," *Atlantic Monthly*, 6 (November, 1860), 601–2.

19. Thomas Moore (1779–1852), the Irish poet, was a friend whom WI had known well in London and Paris in the 1820's.

20. Thomas Lansdowne Moore (1818–1846) and John Russell Moore (1823–1842). The younger son died on November 23, 1842, of tuberculosis, and Thomas joined the Foreign Legion in Algiers, where he died in March, 1846. See Howard Mumford Jones, *The Harp That Once—A Chronicle of the Life of Thomas Moore* (New York, 1937), pp. 314–18.

21. Inglis (1786–1855), who represented Oxford University in the House of Commons from 1829 to 1853, was active in learned societies such as the Literary Club, the Society of Antiquaries, the Royal Society, and the Royal Academy. For other details, see WI to Inglis, September 23, 1836.

22. See WI to Thomas Todd, May 5, 1842.

23. This spectacular event was attended by all the nobility, the socially prominent, and the distinguished persons in London. A full report, including descriptions of the costumes and lists of the guests, covers five and one-half columns in the London *Times*, May 11, 1842. For other details, see the *Times*, May 9 and 11, 1842.

24. Anne of Brittany (1477–1514) had married Maximilian of Austria on December 19, 1490; but when Charles VIII invaded Brittany, she was forced to marry him. After the death of Charles she married Louis XII on January 8, 1499.

25. Princess Augusta Wilhelmina Louisa (d. 1889), who had married Adolphus Frederick (1774–1850), the seventh son of George III, in 1818.

26. Edward III (1312–1377) assumed the throne when he was fifteen and reigned for fifty years.

27. Philippa of Hainault (1314?–1369) married Edward III, her cousin, on January 30, 1328, at the age of fourteen.

28. Anthony Van Dyck (1599–1641) was the official painter at the English court during the last ten years of his life. His portraits of English courtiers were numerous. For a list, see *Bryan's Dictionary of Painters and Engravers* (London, 1905), II, 110–14.

29. In 1842 Sir Edwin Landseer (1802–1873) was commissioned to paint *Queen Victoria and Prince Albert in Costume* (as Philippa and Edward III). The painting is reproduced in Winslow Ames, *Prince Albert and Victorian Taste* (New York, 1968), opposite p. 46.

30. Ames, whom WI had chosen to be a member of the Legation staff in Madrid, was the son of Barrett Ames of New York. Irving Van Wart had married Sarah, Hector's sister, in 1839. See WI to Sarah Van Wart, March 26, 1839.

31. Henry Lee, Jr. (1817–1898), son of prominent Boston merchant and economist Henry Lee (1782–1867), had sailed on the *Independence* with WI to England. See *Journals of WI*, III, 196, 199, 200.

1417. To Walter Buchanan

[May 8, 1842]

My dear Sir,

I regret that it will not be in my power to accept your kind invitation for either Tuesday or thursday evening next. My visit in town is a mere flying one and is limited to the present week during which my time is already completely engrossed by engagements.

With many thanks for your kind wishes which I beg to reciprocate, I am,

Yours very faithfully
Washington Irving

Little Cloisters. / Westminster Abbey / Sunday Morng.

ADDRESSED: Walter Buchanan Esq / 2 Sussex Place / Hyde Park Gardens
    STAMPED: T. P / Charles S. West
MANUSCRIPT: Va.–Barrett.

Walter Buchanan and WI had met in Munich on October 13, 1822, and WI also saw him in London on September 7, 1824. At that time Buchanan lived at 33 Mark Lane. See *J&N*, III, 43, 393.

The date has been determined by the perpetual calendar and WI's reference to Little Cloisters.

1418. To Charles Bristed

Little Cloisters, Westminster Abbey / May 10th. 1842

My dear Charles,

I was grieved at receiving accounts from Mr Murray of your indisposition, and your letter[1] gives me the more uneasiness, finding there is such disagreement, as to its nature, among the various physicians you have consulted. As they must evidently be prescribing in the dark, I would be cautious about taking any violent remedies, that, in case of being wrong, might operate powerfully on your system; and would rather trust to diet and quiet. ⟨If you⟩ You say the journey to Paris injured you. It is plain therefore that fatigue and excitement should be avoided. Any severe application to study I should think would prove likewise injurious. As the beautiful season for the country is coming on, I should suggest a residence at some of the pleasant watering places, where there was agreeable scenery; and where, without entering into the dissipation, you might amuse yourself as a looker on; and might have the recreation of easy walks and drives.

Your Grandfather[2] was in his usual health when I last saw him, though daily growing feebler. He prevailed on Mr Cogswell to remain with him by offering to set the Library immediately on foot under his direction and to make him librarian with a liberal salary. I thought Mr Cogswell right in accepting his offer; indeed, though I should have been most happy to have had Mr Cogswell with me, I should never have suggested the thing to him had not I been expressly solicited to use my influence ⟨by M⟩ for his appointment by Mr Legare; the Attorney General of the U S. who was making interest in his favor with others of the Cabinet. Mr Alexander Hamilton Jr son of Mr James Hamilton has been appointed in his place.

I shall remain in London only for the present week; ⟨as⟩ if you can come up to town for a day I shall be most happy to see you. You will find me staying with a friend, Mr Bandinel—Little Cloisters Westminster Abbey.

> I am my dear Charles / Very truly & affectionately yours
>   Washington Irving

Charles Bristed Esqr

P. S. Your friend Mr Mills[3] has just returned to London and resides No 3. New Street Spring Gardens.

DOCKETED: Washington Irving Esq. / May 10. 42
MANUSCRIPT: SHR.

Charles Astor Bristed was the son of the Reverend John and Magdalen Astor Bristed and grandson of John Jacob Astor. At this time he was studying at Trinity College, Cambridge, from which he graduated in 1845. For other details, see WI to Bristed, September 28, 1840.

1. This letter has not been located.
2. John Jacob Astor.
3. Frank Mills was an English dramatist and scholar with whom WI stayed and traveled in 1824. See WI to John Howard Payne, June 2, 1824. When Bristed went to England in 1840, WI provided him with a letter of introduction to Mills. See WI to Bristed, October 1, 1840.

1419. To Sarah Storrow

Little Cloisters, Westminster Abbey/ May 10th. 1842

My dear Sarah,

I received your most welcome letter[1] two or three days since while I was at Birmingham[.] I am now in the midst of the hurry and turmoil of London distracted with a crowd of occupations and engagements and wishing myself, a thousand times, away from this scene of splendid din and confusion. You ask if I am not changed by my new situation— Most lamentably in point of comfort. After my quiet life at sweet little Sunny Side I feel myself almost unfitted again to cope with the turmoil of society, and especially of the great world; and; on first arriving in London, hesitated for a time about taking the plunge, ⟨[*unrecovered*]⟩ Indeed ⟨I⟩ my Spirits ⟨for a⟩, almost sank with a kind of apprehension and dismay, and I cast a longing look to the quiet little home I had left behind. However, I have breasted the current, have been to court, met with many of my old friends and experienced a most cordial reception on all hands. I shall remain in town until the end of this week; attend the Queens grand fancy ball on Thursday, eat a diplomatic dinner or two, then pay another visit of a few days to the Shrubbery, and then set off for France[.] I hope to be in Paris in about a fortnight— Need I tell you my dear, dear Sarah how happy I shall be to see you once more; and how delighted I shall be to take your little daughter[2] in my arms! My heart throbs at the very thought of it.

I shall come at once to your residence; but I have young Hector Ames with me who accompanies me to Spain and will form one of my household. I wish to have him near me: perhaps Mr Storrow can procure a snug nestling place for him in the neighborhood. If Alexander Hamilton, who is the Secretary of the Legation, should come out from the United States in time (and I partly expect him by the Great Western)[3] he and Hector can take an apartment together: otherwise I do not wish Hector to be far from me, as he is a young traveller and ⟨cannot⟩ speaks French very imperfectly. I find him a capital little fellow: correct, manly, quiet and gentlemanlike. He will be quite a comfort to me in my isolated Situation

By the date of my letter you will see that I am quaintly lodged; in the very heart of the old monumental pile of Westminster. An old friend of mine, Mr Bandinel, a veteran of the Foreign office, has monastic quarters here which he has fitted up like a real monk-barns, with all kinds of antiquities and curiosities, and ⟨th⟩ lives here more cosily and luxuriously than did ever any one of the old Abbots. He insisted upon my taking up my quarters with him, and here have I and Hector been ensconced for several days; surrounded by old furniture, reliques, armour, weapons; old books and every thing odd and curious. Our entrance is through the Cloisters into which Mr Storrow took you one night by surprize, ⟨and⟩ I have repeatedly passed through them at midnight, and one night the Abbey clock struck twelve just as I passed that mural monument with a figure reclining on it, that caused you such a fright. Our windows look out upon a green lawn, shaven like velvet, shaded by lofty trees, with rooks sailing and cawing about them, and partly surrounded by Gothic edifices. I hear the pealing of the organ as I go to a[nd] [*MS torn*] fro through the cloisters, and last Sunday heard the cat[he]dral [*MS torn*] service chaunted in glorious style; being accommoded with a dignified seat in one of the prebendary stalls. All this is worthy of being placed beside my residence in the Alhambra.

I am writing this in extreme haste Let me hear from you, and tell me whether my coming to your residence will not put you to inconvenience now that you have such an addition to your family. If it will in the least, say so frankly, and let Mr Storrow take an apartment for me in a hotel. I want nothing *grand*, merely *genteel*: for I have no idea of attempting to show off on my limited salary; part of which I shall have to devote to keeping up the *home establishment*

With kindest remembrances to Mr Storrow I am my dear Sarah ever most affectionately Your uncle.

W. I.

ADDRESSED: à Madame / Madame Storrow / aux Soins de Mr T. W. Storrow / Rue de Faubg Poissonniere / Paris / J Bandinel   POSTMARKED: Mai / 12 / 1842 // [*unrecovered*] 15 // [*unrecovered*] E   DOCKETED: *May 10th. 1842*
MANUSCRIPT: Yale.

1. This letter has not been located.
2. Catharine Paris Storrow, who was born on March 12, 1842.
3. The *Great Western*, a newly commissioned steamship, had begun her transatlantic crossings on April 2, 1842, sailing alternately to Bristol and to Liverpool. See NYEP, April 29, 1842. Hamilton was not on the published list of passengers departing from New York at this time.

1420. To D. M. Corkendale

Little Cloisters Westminster Abbey / May 11th. 1842

Sir,

I have the honor to acknowledge the receipt of your letter of the 5th. instant;[1] which, having been addressed to me at Liverpool, has but just come to hand, and which informs me of the desire of a number of gentlemen of Glasgow that I should visit their city during my sojourn in this country and accept of a public dinner.

I beg you to assure those gentlemen that I feel duly sensible of this very distinguished and flattering testimonial of their favorable opinion and most kind intentions, but that the very brief time I have to remain in this country, and the many engagements and occupations by which it is already engrossed, will not permit me to accept the high honor they would confer on me

I am, sir, very respectfully / Your obliged & humble Servt
Washington Irving

D. M Corkendale Esqr / &c &c &c

MANUSCRIPT: Huntington.

1. This letter has not been located.

1421.   To William H. Freeman

Birmingham. May 18th. 1842

William Henry Freeman Esq / United States Consul. Neuvitas, Cuba.
Sir

I have to acknowledge the receipt of ⟨your⟩ a Bill of Exchange for Four Pounds Sterling, on the house of the Ness & Browns ⟨the⟩ Liverpool, ↑remitted by you↓, to defray the expenses of your Exequater &c. As some little time may elapse before my arrival at Madrid I have written to Mr Vail, our ⟨consul there⟩ charge d'affaires there, to ⟨apply for your Exequatur⟩ ↑take the necessary steps in the matter↓ and to forward your commission to you.

I am sir, / very respectfully / Your obt Servt
Washington Irving

DOCKETED: To. / Wm Henry Freeman / concerning his Exequatur / May 18th. 1842.
MANUSCRIPT: NA, RG 84.

William Henry Freeman, who was nominated as U.S. consul for Nuevitas, Cuba, on December 19, 1841, and accepted the appointment on February 10, 1842, held the post until 1863. See Hasse, *Index to U.S. Documents*, III, 1747.

1422. To James Kenney

Edgbaston May 18t. 1842

My dear Kenney,
   I regret extremely that I did not receive your note[1] during my brief
visit to town. I know of no one I should have rejoiced more to take again
by the hand. This I must now defer until some future and more
quiet visit to England. My present visit is too hurried and agitating
to be really satisfactory. I was glad to extricate myself from London
where I was kept in a constant fever. I set off immediately for the
Continent and, after passing a short time in Paris will make the best
of my way to Madrid. If I can be of any service to you there command
me: when I next come to England I will beat up your quarters at Park
Terrace or wherever else you may be nestled.
   Ever my dear Kenney

Yours most truly
Washington Irving

James Kenney **Esqr**

Manuscript: Andrew B. Myers.
   James Kenney was an English writer whom WI had first met in 1823.

   1. This note has not been located.

1423. To Aaron Vail

Birmingham May 18, 1842

My dear Sir,
   I have received a letter from Mr William Henry Freeman recently
appointed consul of the United States at Neuvitas, Cuba, remitting me
a bill of Exchange for four pounds, and requesting me to apply to the
Spanish Government for his Exequator. As some little time will elapse
before my arrival at Madrid and as he is anxious to be *en regle,* I will
thank you to take the necessary Steps in the matter, and to forward his
commission to him at his post. I will account to you for the expenses
on my arrival.

I am my dear Sir / Yours ever very faithfully
Washington Irving
Aaron Vail Esqr / Chargé d' affaires of the U S. / Madrid.

ADDRESSED: Aaron Vail Esqr / Charge d'Affaires of the / United States / Madrid /
    Via France   POSTMARKED: [unrecovered] / 10.R / BAYONNE / 25 / MAI /
    42 / 1. MADRID 1. CAST. [unrecovered] / 28? / MAY / 1842 / [unrecov-
    ered] May 20th.   DOCKETED: W. Irving / 18 May 1842 / recd — 28 — /
    ansd. 28 —
MANUSCRIPT: Andrew B. Myers; NA, RG 84 (copy).

1424. To Sarah Storrow

Birmingham May 20th, 1842

My dear Sarah,

I shall embark tomorrow evening in the Southampton Steamer for
Havre, where I shall pass a day with friend Beasley[1] then proceed by
Steamer to Rouen & St Germain, so as to reach Paris on Tuesday.[2] I
wish quarters to be provided for Mr Ames[3] close at hand, otherwise he
will be very lonely. He is quite young, unaccustomed to travel, and
knows but very little of the French language. I wish to have him therefore, very much with me. Perhaps there may be a good boarding house
frequented by Americans, where he will have company and may find
companions to go the rounds of Paris with him.

Your affectionate Uncle,
Washington Irving

MANUSCRIPT: Yale.

1. Reuben Beasley, the American consul in Le Havre, was a friend of WI and
Peter Irving from the early 1820's. They had invested in a Seine River steamship company, with disastrous results.

2. May 24.

3. For other mention of Ames, see WI to Sarah Storrow, May 10, 1842.

1425. To Sarah Irving

Paris, May 29th. 1842

My dear Sarah,

I thank you a thousand times for your most acceptable and interesting
letter of the 25th. of April.[1] It was just like yourself, so kind and considerate. I did not expect it from you, and yet I do not know why I
should not, for it was just the thing that one like yourself, so studious
of every thing that could give happiness to others, would be likely to do.

You need not apologize for the style of your letter, it is exactly the kind of letter I like to receive; written for the sake of the reader, not the writer; to give welcome intelligence not to shew off fine periods. Always write in that way, and your letters will always give delight. You have placed dear little Sunnyside before me, with all its inmates and concerns and, while I was reading your letter I was at home among you all, as in a dream. Would to God I was so in reality; for there is no spot on earth where I shall be as happy as there. Do go on, my dear little girl, from time to time to give me such budgets of home news, and never fear being too particular. Every thing ⟨about⟩ ↑concerning↓ the house, the family, the farm, the neighborhood is full of heart felt interest to me. I have noted all that you say about the bank, the garden, the poultry &c. and it gives me both pride and pleasure to hear that Jenny is turning out such a fine cow; as you know I value myself upon rearing her. It is a great gratification to me to hear that your father takes such interest in the management of the place. I know of no ⟨hea⟩ sweeter and healthier occupations than those about such a choice little place, where the useful and the beautiful in rural life are combined. I am sure his residence at Sunnyside will both prolong and sweeten his existence. I have him continually in my minds eye, living quietly and cheerily ⟨in that?⟩ surrounded by you all in that little rural paradise, and the picture is a constant source of heartfelt gratification to me.

I have written from time to time to your aunt[2] giving some account of my movements; which letters must generally serve for you all, for ⟨in the⟩ I have now but little liesure, and quietude of mind to write letters, and have many to write on matters of business. My visit to Europe has by no means the charm of former visits. Scenes and objects have no longer the effect of novelty with me; I am no longer curious to see great sights or great people, and have been so long accustomed to a life of quiet that I find the turmoil of the world becomes irksome to me. Then I have a home of my own, a little domestic world, created in a manner by my own hand, which I have left behind, and which is continually haunting my thoughts, and coming in contrast with the noisy, tumultuous, heartless world in which I am called to mingle. However, I am somewhat of a philosopher and can accommodate myself to changes; so I shall endeavor to resign myself to the splendor of courts and the conversation of courtiers, comforting myself with the thoughts, that the time will arrive when I shall once more return to Sweet little Sunnyside, and be able to sit on a stone fence and talk about politics and rural affairs with neighbor Ferkel and uncle Brom.[3]

I have now been four or five days a guest with *Sarah Paris*[4]⟨;⟩—it seems strange to be domesticated with her under her own roof instead of under mine. You will have heard ere this from the Constants how happily she is fixed: and how pleasantly she lives. Her little establishment is quite a picture, and goes on with great order and quiet and a proper economy. Mr Storrow is an excellent manager, and Sarah proves herself a very good housewife; though indeed housekeeping here seems attended with but little trouble. Sarah is looking extremely well; much fresher and more blooming than when she left us. Her little daughter is already a pet of mine. She is a pretty child for one of her *months* (I had almost said *weeks*) and promises to be very sage and discreet, for she never laughs. She has blue eyes like Sarah, a small mouth like Mr Storrow, and a nose between the two, so now you have a perfect idea of her features.

I hope you have had ⟨all⟩ the carriage and other vehicles neatly repaired and fitted up, so that you may all drive about the country to your hearts content, ⟨during the beautiful⟩ whenever the weather is favorable. Tell Eliza ⟨to⟩ I am expecting a letter from her. I know letter writing is no task to her; for she used to keep up a most active and copious correspondence ⟨with⟩ from the Seminary with Helen. If you all knew how acceptable letters are to me from home; and especially from the Cottage; and how interesting the merest gossip about domestic affairs and the every day life of Sunnyside is to me, I am sure you would all conquer your repugnance to letter writing and scribble me an occasional line. Your very mention of Julia and Marys new bonnets has been delightful to me. It has presented the dear darling girls before me, prettily arrayed, as they always are—and even now while I write about them I feel my heart in my throat and the tears in my eyes. My dear Sarah you do not know how precious you all are to me, and how much my heart dwells in the home I have left behind.

Give my love to all the household. Tell Kate to find out the subject of the book which she accuses her father of writing in my room. Give my kind remembrances to Mammy and to Mary Gilhuly. I came away without bidding them good bye; lest you should all discover that I did not intend to come back to the Cottage before my embarkation. God bless you my dear Sarah. Your aff Uncle

W. I.rving[5]

ADDRESSED: Miss Sarah Irving / Sunnyside Cottage / Tarrytown   DOCKETED: Washn. Irving to Sarah Irving. Paris May 29 1842 / T. / S. Cot. MANUSCRIPT: Grinnell Morris.   PUBLISHED: PMI, III, 204–5 (in part).

In the upper left corner of MS page 1 is written "Sunny Side June 21 1842." This probably indicates when the letter was received.

1. This letter has not been located.
2. See WI to Catharine Paris, May 3 and May 7, 1842.
3. WI's nickname for Ebenezer Irving, whom he sometimes called "the Brahmin."
4. WI may be punning here in speaking of the former Sarah Paris now living in

Paris. He often used a second name to distinguish between relatives having the same first name, as in "Helen Pierre" for the wife of Pierre M. Irving and "Helen Treat" for the wife of John Treat Irving, Jr.

5. Apparently WI originally signed the letter with his initials and then added the remainder of his surname after the period.

1426. To Catharine Paris

Paris, May 29, 1842.

* * * Hitherto, since my arrival in Paris, I have been living very quietly, avoiding all engagements, that I might pass my time as much as possible with Sarah; but now I shall have to launch in some degree into society. I have to make diplomatic calls in company with our Minister, General Cass,[1] and these will lead, more or less, to various engagements. Fortunately, the fashionable season is over; the royal family are absent,[2] and there is less call for visits of ceremony and crowded entertainments. Still I feel a mortal repugnance to launching into the stream of public life, and I cling as long as possible to the quiet shore I am about to leave. I endeavor to conform to our old family motto, *Sub sole sub umbra virens* (flourishing in the sun and in the shade);[3] but I think, upon the whole, I am more calculated for the shade.

My predecessor, Mr. Vail, expects me early in July, and is anxious to leave Madrid with his family before the intense heats of summer. I have made a kind of half arrangement, by letter, with Mr. Vail, by which I shall take up my quarters with him when I arrive, and pretty much take his establishment, carriage, furniture, and servants off his hands. * * * I shall thus have a home at once on my arrival, without being subjected to the loss of time and trouble, the bother, and perplexity, and cheatery which I would otherwise incur in forming an establishment. I mention this to you because I know you are anxious on this point.

Published: PMI, III, 205–6.

1. Lewis Cass (1782–1866), who was a general in the War of 1812 and Jackson's secretary of war from 1831 to 1835, was U.S. envoy extraordinary and minister plenipotentiary to France from October 24, 1836, to November 12, 1842. He served in the U.S. Senate from 1845 to 1857, except for an interval in 1848 and 1849 when he was the unsuccessful Democratic candidate for president.

2. Louis Philippe (1776–1850) and Queen Marie Amelie (1782–1866) were staying at the royal residence at Neuilly. See WI to Catharine Paris, June 10, 1842.

3. A photograph of this motto and the family coat of arms on one of WI's watch fobs is to be found on the title page of Butler, *WI's Sunnyside* (1974 ed.).

1427. To Sarah Van Wart

Paris, June 8th. 1842

My dear Sister,

I thank you for your kind and most acceptable letter of the 3d. inst.[1] which reminds me of my own remissness in not writing sooner to you after my arrival in Paris; but I am kept in such continual agitation and hurry of mind from the rapid succession of scenes and events, and have my time so much cut up by engagements and interruptions of all kinds that I can find scarce a moment of liesure or composure of thought for letter writing.

I arrived at Havre ↑at an early hour on↓ the Sunday morning after I left you, having had a very smooth voyage across the channel. I passed the day at the delightful little half rural retreat of my friend Beasley which is situated in a garden on the descent of the hill over-looking Havre and the Surrounding extent of land and sea. I staid there until Monday morning, ⟨when⟩ Hector being quartered there with me. We then ascended the Seine in a steam boat to Rouen: passed a night there, and the next day proceeded by steam boat and rail road to Paris where we arrived on Tuesday evening. My visit to my excellent friend Beasley, and my voyage up the Seine, however gratifying in other re-spects, were full of melancholy associations; for at every step I was reminded of my dear, dear brother Peter,[2] who had so often been my com-panion in these scenes. In fact he is continually present to my mind since my return to Europe, ⟨and⟩ where we passed so many years to-gether and I think this circumstance contributes greatly to the mixture of melancholy with which of late I regard all those scenes and objects which once occasioned such joyous excitement. There is one little quiet conventual garden, with ↑shady↓ walks and shrubberies and seats, behind the old gothic church of St Ouen at Rouen,[3] which used to be his favorite resort during his solitary residence in that city, and where he used to pass his mornings with his book, amusing himself with the groupes of loungers, and of nursery maids and children. I felt my heart completely give way when I found myself in that garden—I was for a time a com-plete child. My dear, dear Brother: as I write the tears are gushing from my eyes—

I am residing with Sarah in her sweet little home; which is very prettily furnished, and very comfortably conducted. She is happily situated and seems to be quite happy. Her infant is quite a pretty child and very healthy, and you may suppose what an addition she is to the domestic happiness of the mother. For some days after my arrival I endeavored to keep quiet and to avoid invitations, but they are multiplying upon me and I find it will be impossible for me to keep much longer out of the whirl of—Society. It is true this is the dull season at Paris when every body, that can afford it, takes refuge in the country, but there is always society enough at Paris to consume ones time and interrupt ones leisure. I have been presented to the King and to some members of the royal family, at the rural palace at Neuilly, a short distance from Paris.⁴ The reception had none of the State and ceremony of a presentation at the British Court; but was much more ⟨free⟩ kind and gratifying. It is twelve years since I last say the King⁵ (it was at the time I accompanied Henry on his wedding visit to Paris) He shews the signs of age and care ⟨be⟩ and has lost something of his noble erect deportment; in conversation he is frank, friendly and remarkably full of correct information as to ⟨the⟩ passing ⟨histor⟩ events in all parts of the world.

I have felt the same disinclination at Paris as at London, to la[u]nch⁶ myself into the great tide of public and fashionable life, but I am getting from shore in spite of myself; and find myself in grand saloons and grand company when I would fain be at home ⟨in⟩ with Sarah and [*several lines clipped out to remove the signature on the reverse side*] met with in society is the Marquis Brignolli,⁷ Sardinian Ambassador He has always been associated in my mind with my romantic sojourn at Genoa when I was about twenty one years of age. He was then a year or so younger than I, and I saw him play the part of Orosman in a translation of Voltaires Tragedy of Zaire. It was at a beautiful little theatre at his mothers ⟨country⟩ villa at Sestri de Ponenti, a few miles from Genoa. He was an elegant young man and played the part with a grace and tenderness and fire that seemed to win the hearts of all the ladies present, and especially of the beautifu[l] [*MS torn*] Signora Rivarolla⁸ who played the part of Zaire. Alas! I found t[he] [*MS torn*] young and elegant Brignolli a grey headed man of some seven and fifty, with daughters and grand daughters. He still however is a fine looking man, and is universally extolled for his amiable and excellent character. We are in a fair way to become sociable —though he of course has none of the romantic associations with me that I have with him.

Tell Mr Van Wart I wish him to procure for me the following articles. Covers and warmers of rich plated ware for a service of twelve persons. 6 plated candlesticks. 4 doz table knives 1 doz small do. carving knives and forks (he will know the proper kind & numbers)—Those to be packed up and sent by the earliest opportunity to his correspondent in Spain; ⟨with⟩ letting me know in time that I may apply for an order for their admission free of duty.

Give my love to all the *households*. Sarah sends her love to you all and wishes she had Marianne here to pass some time with her. When

I go there will be a very nice bedroom vacant whenever Marianne chooses to occupy it. I hope in this pleasant season of the year you will make occasional visits to my dear Will's delightful little abode. I hold it in sweet reccollection, and all its inmates especially that fine little fellow "Will the weaver," who cannot walk for jumping. I am glad to hear that little Irving[9] continues to improve in health; poor dear little fellow; it will be a heartfelt delight for me when I revisit England to see him as gay, and as active as his brother[10]

[close and signature cut out]

ADDRESSED: Mrs Henry Van Wart / Care of H Van Wart Esqr / Birmingham
MANUSCRIPT: Va.–Barrett.   PUBLISHED: PMI, III, 203–4.

1. This letter has not been located.

2. Peter Irving (1771–1838) had lived in Rouen and Le Havre in the 1820's and 1830's before his return to New York.

3. This plot was formerly part of the dormitory of the abbey of St. Ouen on the north side of the church. See Karl Baedeker, *Northern France* (Leipzig, 1905), p. 57.

4. The royal palace of Neuilly, built north of the Bois de Boulogne in 1755 for the count of Argerson, became Louis Philippe's favorite residence. During the Revolution of 1848 a mob burned the palace, and the park was subsequently parceled out into building sites. See Karl Baedeker, *Paris and Environs*, p. 159; and *Dictionnaire Géographique et Administratif de la France*, 7 vols. (Paris, 1899), V, 2945. WI was presented in the evening of June 4, 1842. See *Journals of WI*, III, 209–10.

5. WI had attended the coronation of Louis Philippe in Paris on August 9, 1830. See WI to Louis McLane, August 9, 1830.

6. WI wrote "lanch."

7. Antonio Brignole-Sale (1786–1863), whom WI had first seen in 1806 acting in Voltaire's *Zaïre* in a theater at his mother's estate near Genoa. See *J&N*, I, 123.

8. Anna Maria Gasparda Vicenza Pieri, Marchesa Brignole-Sale (1765–1815) was noted for the breadth of her cultural interests and for her liberal political views. See *J&N*, I, 121–23; and WI to William Irving, December 25, 1804.

9. Invalid son of William Van Wart. See WI to Catharine Paris, May 7, 1842.

10. Wilfred Van Wart.

1428.   To Catharine Paris

Paris, June 10, 1842.

My dear Sister:

A few days since, I drove out, in the evening, with our Minister, **General Cass**, to Neuilly, one of the royal country residences near Paris, to be presented to the King.[1] Neuilly is situated in the midst of an English park, through which we had a pleasant drive. I observed sentinels stationed here and there about the park—a precaution taken in consequence of the repeated attempts upon the life of the King. Louis Philippe, I am told, is extremely annoyed, in his rides on horseback about the park, at finding himself thus under perpetual surveillance. He says he is almost as badly off as Napoleon at Longwood,[2] who could never find himself out of sight of a sentinel.

A suite of saloons on the ground floor of the palace were lighted up. Very little formality is observed in these country receptions. Passing through a number of domestics in the entrance hall, we found our way from one chamber to another, until we came to where the company were assembled in a central saloon. The Queen and Madame Adelaide[3] (sister to the King) were seated, with several ladies, at a round table, at work. The King was conversing by turns with gentlemen who were standing in groups round the room, some few of whom (General Cass and myself among the number), who were there on ceremony, were in court uniforms. The King was simply dressed in black, with pantaloons and shoes. I am thus particular in noting his dress, knowing your curiosity with respect to royalty, and lest you should suppose that kings and queens are always in long velvet robes, with golden crowns on their heads. I experienced a very kind reception from the King and Queen and Madame Adelaide, each of whom took occasion to say something complimentary about my writings. The King has altered much since I last saw him (which was in 1830, when he took the oaths of office). Age may begin to weigh upon him, but care, no doubt, still more. He is less erect than he used to be, and at times stoops considerably. How different from what he was when I first saw him,[4] nearly twenty years since—as the Duke of Orleans, in hussar uniform, mounted on a superb horse, in a public procession, the admiration of every eye. Still he is a fine-looking man for his years, and appeared to be in good health and good spirits, laughing heartily with some of those with whom he was conversing. In his conversation with General Cass and myself, he spoke of American affairs, and showed himself to be minutely observant of all that was passing in our country, and of the state of its relations with its neighbors in Canada, Texas, and Mexico. I am told he keeps a vigilant eye upon the newspapers, and thus informs himself of what is going on in all parts of the world. I am sure this will recommend him to the good opinion of our worthy brother, the present Laird of Sunnyside [whose devotion to the newspapers nearly excluded all other reading].[5]

The Queen, who is a most excellent, amiable person, is pale and thin, with blue eyes, and hair quite white. Nothing can be kinder than her manners. Her life is an anxious one. The repeated attempts upon the life of her husband, and even of her sons, have filled her with alarm, and I am told she is in a state of nervous agitation whenever they are absent on some public occasion of ceremony. She is a devoted wife and mother, a perfect pattern in the domestic relations of life. The King's sister, Madame Adelaide, is a women of more force of character; resembles the King in features, possesses vigorous good sense and great ambition. She is said to take great interest in public affairs, and in the stability of her brother's throne.

* * * * * * * * *

June 14th.—I had intended to write something in this letter every day, but I have been so much taken up by the usual demands of society, and so oppressed by the heat of the weather, that I have found it impossible to do so. Two or three days since, Mr. Storrow, Sarah, and myself dined at the country seat of Mrs. Welles,[6] and passed the evening delightfully strolling about the grounds. The day after to-morrow we intend going to Versailles, to pass two or three days there. * * *

I shall be glad to get out of Paris into the country. The weather is uncommonly warm, and, in spite of all my holding back, I have got launched into society, and find myself obliged to dine out almost every day. Yesterday I dined at the British ambassador's (Lord Cowley, brother to the Duke of Wellington).[7] The dinner, however, was very pleasant. Lady Cowley[8] I knew some years since, in England. I was treated most cordially. General Cass dined there also, and Mr. Rumpf,[9] son-in-law to Mr. Astor, besides other persons of my acquaintance. In the evening I was at a magnificent fête given by our countryman, Colonel Thorn,[10] on the occasion of one of his daughters' marriage with a French baron.[11] You know the history of Colonel Thorn, and the stand he has taken among the old French noblesse by dint of his wealth. His fête was really magnificent. His hotel[12] was brilliantly lighted up, the extensive gardens fancifully illuminated, and singers and musicians stationed among the distant groves, who occasionally regaled the company with concerted pieces of instrumental music, or romantic choruses and glees. The whole was one of those fairy scenes that would have enchanted me in my greener years of inexperience and romance; but I have grown too wise to be duped by such delusions, so I sagely came away just as the thoughtless throng were beginning to dance. It is wonderful how much more difficult it is to astonish or amuse me then when I was last in Europe. It is possible I may have gathered wisdom under the philosophic shades of Sleepy Hollow, or may have been rendered fastidious by the gay life of the cottage; it is certain that, amidst all the splendors of London and Paris, I find my imagination refuses to take fire, and my heart still yearns after dear little Sunnyside. This letter, I trust, will find you up there, and must answer for the household, for I have not time to write any more. Give my love to all the girls. I will not name any one in particular, lest it might appear like giving a preference; and God knows I love them all with all my heart. Oh! what would I not give to be once more among them.

PUBLISHED: PMI, III, 206–9.

This letter may have been incorrectly dated by PMI. According to his journal, WI dined at Lord Cowley's on June 13 and attended the fete at Colonel Thorn's in the evening. See *Journals of WI*, III, 216.

1. For other details see WI to Sarah Van Wart, June 8, 1842; and *Journals of WI*, III, 209–10.

2. The name of the farm at which Napoleon spent his exile on St. Helena. See August Fournier, *Napoleon the First, A Biography*, trans. Margaret Bacon Corwin and Arthur Dent Bissell (New York, 1903), pp. 730–31, 736, 737.

3. Adelaïde, Princesse d'Orléans (1777–1847), a trusted adviser to her brother, urged a conciliatory approach in affairs of government.

4. WI had seen him on September 27, 1824, on a cold, rainy day during the king's entry into Paris. See *J&N*, III, 399.

5. The bracketed passage was added by PMI.

6. Probably Mrs. Samuel Welles, wife of an international banker whom WI had known during his residence in Paris in the 1820's. See *J&N*, III, 206; and *Journals of WI*, III, 212–23.

7. Henry Wellesley, Baron Cowley (1773–1847) had been British ambassador to Spain from 1811 to 1822, to Vienna from 1823 to 1831, and to Paris in 1835. He retired with the change of the ministry but was reappointed and served from October, 1841, to 1846.

8. Georgiana Charlotte Augusta (d. 1860), eldest daughter of James Cecil, 1st màrquis of Salisbury.

9. Count Vincent Rumpff, a Swiss diplomat and acting minister of the Hanseatic Free Cities to France, had married Eliza Astor (1801–1838) on December 10, 1825. See Harvey O'Connor, *The Astors*, p. 463; and Porter, *Astor*, II, 1043.

10. Colonel Herman Thorn was a wealthy New Yorker who had lived in Paris for many years and traveled throughout Europe. He attracted attention because of his beautiful daughters and his lavish entertainments.

11. Miss Thorn had married Baron Pierre at the Church of St. Roque on June 7. See *Journals of WI*, III, 213.

12. Thorn lived in the Hotel Monaco, Rue de Varennes, Faubourg St. Germaine. See *Journals of WI*, III, 211.

1429. To Henry Van Wart

Paris, June 12th. 1842

My dear Brother,

In a letter to the "Missus" the other day[1] I mentioned a few articles which I wish you to procure for my Madrid Establishment: I have some apprehension that I may not have stated them correctly so I now repeat the order Richly plated covers and warmers for a service of twelve persons

Six plated *chamber* candlesticks
4 doz table knives
1 " Small do.

The proper number of carving knives & forks Forward them to your correspondent in Spain and advise me of the house to which you send them and of the time of Shipment

While upon *business* let me request you to attend to a small washing bill of three or four shillings which I neglected to settle with your house maid—Pay the same and charge it to me.

I am waiting for the arrival of Mr Hamilton, my Secretary of Legation, that I may proceed to Spain—The extreme heat of the weather renders it impossible for me to enjoy Paris and makes the invitations by which I am beset extremely irksome. Beside I long to get to my post, form my establishment and feel settled. Still I should pass my time pleasantly here in Sarahs charming little house, if I could have command of my time and of myself; but I have the curse of notoriety clinging to my footsteps which makes existence in cities a perpetual task and toil to me.

I am scrawling this in a brief interval of liesure Give my love to my dear Sister and all the households.

Your affectionate brother
Washington Irving

Henry Van Wart Esqr

ADDRESSED: Henry Van Wart Esq / Birmingham / England.   POSTMARKED: Paris /
    12 / JUIN // I / 15 JU 15 / 1842 // BIRMINGHAM / JU 15 / 1842
MANUSCRIPT: NYPL—Seligman Collection.

    1. June 8, 1842.

1430. To Helen Irving

[Paris, June 26, 1842]

My dear Helen:

If you knew with what avidity and relish I devoured your *half* letter,[1] you would immediately sit down and write me a whole one. * * * The merest gossip about home and its everyday concerns would be more prized by me than the finest turned periods. The accidental mention you make in your letter about the green sodded bank before the cottage, and about Julia and Mary in their new bonnets and dresses, has presented home pictures that speak at once to my heart.

    * * * I have been living as quietly as I could for some time past, in Sarah's pretty little establishment, trying to keep out of the turmoil of

the great world; for my desire has been not to *mount the Minister*, if possible, until my arrival in Spain, having no great relish for the pageantry of courts, or the thronged saloons of fashionable life; but I am drawn into the vortex occasionally in spite of myself,[2] so am kept in a half-drowned state, neither one thing nor t'other; neither enjoying repose nor dissipation; like a poor drenched Yankee fisherman whom I once met with, shivering, and drying himself before a fire in a little seashore inn at Martha's Vineyard, and who, tired of being neither fish nor flesh, wished he was "clever-*ly* dead." The fact is, I am spoiled by the life I have led at Sunnyside, and have not, during the whole time that I have been in Europe, had one of those right-down frolicksome moods that I have enjoyed at the cottage; but, indeed, they would not be becoming in diplomatic life. I shall therefore put by all my merriment until my return home, and will endeavor, in the mean time, to be dignified and dull.

* * * I am, my dear Helen, your affectionate uncle,

Washington Irving

PUBLISHED: PMI, III, 211–12.

1. This letter has not been located. PMI (III, 211) indicates that it was a postscript to his letter of May 31, 1842.

2. According to his letters and journals, WI was involved in social engagements of various sorts during his stay in Paris. These include: May 31, guest of François Pierre Guillaume Guizot; June 4, dinner with Colonel Thorn; June 6, visit to Mrs. Welles at Suresnes; June 7, marriage of Miss Thorn to Baron Pierre and dinner later with Sir Henry Lytton Bulwer; June 13, dinner with Lord and Lady Cowley and the evening at Colonel Thorn's fete in honor of his daughter's marriage; June 14, dinner with Colonel Charles Richard and Lady Mary Fox; June 15, dinner with Mr. and Mrs. Greene; June 16, dinner with Mr. and Mrs. Ellis; June 27, attendance at the soiree of the duchesse de Caze; and June 29, dinner with Baron Rothschild.

1431. To Pierre M. Irving

Paris, June 26, 1842

My dear Pierre:

I have just received your most welcome letter of May 31st,[1] and have read it with great interest. I thank you heartily for your kind attention to my pecuniary affairs, and am well pleased with the investment you have made.[2]

* * * I am delighted with the account you give of your nest at the bank.[3] * * * I presume the iron safe which you extol as such a "con-

venient fixture," must have become necessary to hoard up the bags of money you are now accumulating. * * *

* * * Since I begun this letter, Alexander Hamilton and Carson Brevoort[4] have reached Paris, and have brought me a thousand interesting details about home. Being now joined by my household, I shall set forward for Spain as soon as possible, though I suppose they will want a little time at Paris to fit themselves out. I am anxious to be at my post, to have my establishment formed, my books and papers about me, and to get settled. The restless life I have led for some months past has grown extremely irksome, and the continual shifting of the scene, and of the *dramatis personae,* distracts my mind without interesting me. I am too old a frequenter of the theatre of life to be much struck with novelty, pageant, or stage effect, and could willingly have remained in my little private *loge* at Sunnyside, and dozed out the rest of the performance.

Do write often, and let me know all about your own concerns, and the concerns of those around you. My heart dwells among you all at home, and my thoughts are continually reverting thither.

Your affectionate uncle,
Washington Irving

PUBLISHED: PMI, III, 210–11.

1. This letter has not been located.
2. The nature of this investment has not been ascertained.
3. WI is alluding to PMI's position as government pension agent for the Bank of Commerce. See WI to PMI, November 19, 1841.
4. James Carson Brevoort (1818–1887), son of WI's friend Henry Brevoort, had attended school in Switzerland and studied engineering in Paris. He assisted his uncle James Renwick on the Northeast Boundary Survey in 1838. After spending a year in the U.S. legation in Madrid with WI, he traveled for another year in Europe and returned to New York in 1844.

1432. To Henry Brevoort

Paris, July 1st 1842

My dear Brevoort,

I have barely time to scribble a few lines in the office of the Legation here, in reply to your letter by Carson.[1] I am delighted to have him with me and shall endeavor to do all that you wish respecting him. My heart warms toward him, not merely on his own account, but ↑also↓ on your own. He seems like a new link in our old friendship, which commenced when we were both his age or even younger, and which I have ⟨f⟩ always felt as something almost fraternal. Hamilton I perceive has already taken a strong attachment to him ⟨;⟩. ⟨t⟩ The other member of my diplomatic family, Hector Ames, is an excellent little fellow; quiet ⟨yet⟩ modest, yet manly and intelligent. I think they will all agree well together and form a very pleasant *état major*.

As they require some little time to fit themselves out I shall linger some eight or ten days longer at Paris; but I am anxious to get to my post and relieve my predecessor Mr Vail; who wishes to get to the mountains with his family, for the health of his children. I am desirous also of forming my establishment and feeling myself once more settled. The unsettled life I have led for some months past begins to be extremely irksome. I have enough to do to bother me, yet ⟨not⟩ no settled occupation to interest me. My mind is perplexed by arrangements for my domestic establishment, and solicitude about my new career, and with all this I am harrassed by the claims of society, which, with all my exertions, I cannot fight off. Paris & London are terrible places for these kinds of claims, which cut up ones time, disturb ones quiet, and render life a continual round of empty toils. I am amused with the solicitude of our friend Thorn on my account, who thinks I am turning my back upon fortune, and ruining my prospects in life by neglecting to follow up the friendships proferred me in Saloons. He could restrain his feelings no longer a few evenings since, at an evening party where the Duchess of Grammont[2] had sought an acquaintance with me and held me for some time in very amiable conversation. On leaving her Thorn took me aside and implored me to leave a card the next day ⟨at⟩ for the Duchess and at the same time read me a most affectionate lecture on my neglect of this piece of etiquette with respect to [var]ious [*MS torn*] other persons of rank. He attributes all this to my excessive modesty: not dreaming that the empty intercourse of Saloons with people of rank and fashion could be a bore to one who has run the rounds of society for the greater part of half a century, and who ⟨has⟩ likes to consult his own humours and pursuits.

I shall endeavor, when fixed at Madrid, to strike out some line of literary research and occupation for Carson according to your wish—In the mean time he will ⟨be⟩ be seeing continually new places, new people, and new customs and usages—at least new to him

At a moment of more liesure I will write to you more fully Remember me most kindly to Mrs Brevoort and the young folks.

Yours ever my dear Brevoort
Washington Irving

ADDRESSED: Henry Brevoort Esqr. / ⟨Fifth Avenue⟩ / ⟨New York⟩ West Point . N. Y.
MANUSCRIPT: NYPL—John Winslow Collection.   PUBLISHED: PMI, III, 213–14
   (in part); LIB, II, 238 (in part).
The original address has been cancelled and the forwarding address added by
another hand.

1. This letter has not been located.
2. Rosalie de Noailles (1767–1852) was the wife of Théodule, marquis de
Grammont (1766–1841) and sister-in-law of the marquis de La Fayette (1757–
1834). See André Maurois, *Adrienne ou La Vie de Mme de La Fayette* (Paris,
1960), "Tableaux Généalogique. I. Famille De Noailles" (no pagination).

1433. To Catharine Paris

Paris July 7th. 1842

My dear Sister
   Since last I wrote to you I have received your letter of June 1st.[1] which
was to have come by Mr Hamilton, but did not reach him in time. It is
twelve days earlier than the letter ⟨la⟩ previously received from you, yet
it seems to me not the less interesting for every line from home is precious to me. I feel deeply, my dear Sister, your attentive affection in
writing so often and such long letters to me. Your letters too, are just such
as I like to receive, full of ⟨daily⟩ particulars of the daily life at the Cottage
and of the domestic concerns of those I love. How climates go by con-
traries; you complain in your letters of suffering from unseasonable ⟨heat⟩
↑cold↓ ⟨while we⟩ at the very time that we in Paris were oppressed and
rendered almost incapable of action by excessive heat.[2] I do not know
when I have been more unnerved by hot weather than during some part
of my present sojourn in Paris It rendered me absolutely good for
nothing. The weather of late ha[s] [*MS torn*] been tempered by occasional showers and at times is really delightful.
   Sarah has no doubt kept you informed of our domestic movements
The little babe grows finely. It begins to take notice of things an[d]
[*MS torn*] persons; and to laugh and talk and crow; ⟨as it⟩ in nursery
langu[age.] [*MS torn*] It is really a very pretty child; ⟨and⟩ I find it
winning upon me day by day, and we are growing more and more sociable. It promises to be a very healthy child. The english nurse who has
charge of it, is faithful to her trust and appears to understand well the
management of children. Sarah is looking well and is in good health. Mr
Storrow intends taking lodgings in the country a few miles from Paris
for part of the Summer, which will be very refreshing for both mother and
child; after ⟨this⟩ enduring so much hot weather as has prevailed of late.
The hot weather is very oppressive in Paris. ⟨from⟩ The air ⟨here⟩ loses

its freshness and elasticity from the reflected heat from such an immense region of White walls and white pavements, and from the great sunburnt plains that surround the city. There is the want of the daily sea breeze and the frequent showers that temper hot weather in our climate. Yet in general the summer heat in Paris is much less than with us, only when it prevails for several days together the air seems to become dead like that ⟨su⟩ round a brick kiln.

⟨I [*unrecovered*] We expect to⟩

I have fixed on Monday next ↑(July 11)↓ for my departure from Paris. The articles purchased by Mr Storrow for my establishment were sent off yesterday; but as they go by heavy conveyances they will not reach Madrid until some time after I do. I have hired a commodious carriage and shall ↑travel↓ post to the Spanish frontier; where I shall determine whether to proceed further in the same manner, or to take the Diligence; which is reccommended to me as more expeditious, comfortable & secure in that country. I have engaged as courier the same man that travelled with Gabriel[3] and his family an Italian named Louis; and who bears an excellent characte[r.] [*MS torn*] I shall stop a couple of days at Bordeaux, where I renew old friend[ships] [*MS torn*] with the Guestiers, Johnsons &c. Beasley is there on a visit to his old father in law and he writes me that my ⟨arrival there is⟩ visit is anticipated in the most cordial manner by those excellent people, in whose hospitable circle our dear brother Peter and myself have passed so many happy days.

I look forward to experiencing great satisfaction from the society of the young gentlemen who form my diplomatic household. It really appears to me that I could not have been better off for companions in their relative positions. Alexander Hamilton is full of life, activity and intelligence; with great self possession ⟨and⟩ ↑an↓ excellent address, and a delightful disposition. Young Brevoort is highly cultivated with a fine taste in the arts; both he and Hamilton are skilful with the pencil; Brevoort has also a turn for different departments of natural history. He is withal, extremely modest, and of the gentlest and most attaching disposition. Little Hec[tor] [*MS torn*] is a capital little fellow, pure in principle ↑fine in temper↓ and right minded. They all are *gentlemen* in appearance; habits; principles and deportment. All are intelligent ⟨and⟩ in their pursuits, and I really believe free from all unworthy taint.

July 10th. I had intended to make this a very long and particular letter, but I have so little time or mood for writing in this bustling metropol[is] [*MS torn*] that I must let it go without more addition. Tomorrow we set off from Paris Instead of Louis the Courier (who could not accompany me into Spain) I have engaged a coloured man, a mulatto ↑Benjamin Gowein[4] an American↓ who has served for several years in our Legation ⟨at⟩ in Russia & has been repeatedly in Spain. He has excellent recommendations for honesty, sobriety & intelligence and his looks & deportment are in his favor. I engage him by the month, as footman & valet; to form part of my establishment at Madrid; where I should be in want of precisely such a person ⟨Having⟩ as Mr Vail takes one of his servants with him, which ⟨leaves⟩ would leave a vacancy.

I shall find it hard parting with Sarah and her dear little ba[by.] [MS torn] You cannot think how the little creature has already wound herself round [my] [MS torn] heart. It is indeed, & partiality apart, a beautiful and a most engaging [little?] [MS torn] being, and daily growing more and more winning and interesting

Give my love to all the household.

Your affe[ctio]nate brother [MS torn]
[W]ash[ing]ton Irving [MS torn]

ADDRESSED: Mrs Catharine Paris / Care of E. Irving Esq / Tarry town / New York.
    POSTMARKED: NEW-YORK / AUG / 2 ·
MANUSCRIPT: Yale.

1. This letter has not been located.
2. A report from a correspondent in Paris described a long drought which had affected the harvest. See London *Times*, June 27, 1842.
3. Gabriel Irving and his family had gone to Europe early in January, 1841. They sailed for the United States near the beginning of July. See WI to Sarah Storrow, July 31, 1842.
4. Benjamin Gowein, a mulatto from South Carolina, had been a servant of Henry Middleton (1771–1846) when he was minister to Russia. See WI to Catharine Paris, July 20, 1842.

1434. To William H. Seward

Paris 11 July 1842

My dear Sir

Although much hurried in preparing for my departure for Madrid I feel too deep an interest in the success of Mr Brodheads mission[1] to Europe to think of leaving Paris without testifying to the intelligence activity and perseverance with which, as far as it has come under my eye, he is executing the task he has undertaken, and without urging that prompt measures be taken, at the next session of our State legislature, to provide sufficient funds for the thorough and effectual accomplishment of this important historical enterprize

Mr Brodhead has had great success thus far in his researches. In Holland a very valuable amount of Historical information has been obtained. In England, through the courtesy of Lord Aberdeen he has had ⟨full⟩

free access to an immense number of the New York books of Records in the State Paper Office; the French government also, has been equally liberal, and has allowed him to examine all the Canada papers in the Archives of the Colonies. Besides these there are other repositories of Historical materials both here and in England to which access may doubtless be obtained. The opportunity is now afforded of enriching our Albany ⟨Archives⟩ ↑records↓ with documents so long beyond the reach of our historians and for which they have looked in vain to our archives; and we have an intelligent and indefatigable agent in the field, warm in the pursuit; acquainted with the ground, and who, if properly backed, can effect more in a little while, than others hereafter would be able to accomplish in years. Unless the legislature however, make at once a sufficient appropriation for procuring copies of the invaluable papers now put within our reach, this ⟨whole⟩ ↑noble↓ undertaking may be paralyzed, or at best but partially accomplished[.] I know that it cannot be carried into full effect without considerable expense; but I cannot estimate the value of the documents we have now an opportunity of procuring by any pecuniary standard. The State is abundantly rich in means and resources; and this is a matter of high concernment to State dignity and pride that ought not to admit of parsimonious calculations. The richer a state becomes in historical facts and mementos, the higher spirit of patriotic pride does it excite in its inhabitants. and the Stronger hold does it take upon their affections. Beside, this is not a matter which concerns the present age alone, it has reference to future time and concerns the honor of the state through future generations. It is to secure the deep foundations of our early history on which its after superstructure is to rest; and I feel satisfied there is no state in this great confederation whose early history is ⟨more⟩ fraught with themes of more varied character, exciting interest and instructive lesson. ⟨I trust therefore⟩ I will not permit myself to believe, therefore, that there is a citizen of this great "Empire state," above all, one who is native born, who, ⟨will⟩ through petty pecuniary considerations, will limit or curtail the operations of one of the most patriotic and enlightened undertakings ever set on foot by its government.

I beg you to excuse the crudeness, yet urgency with which I write in a hurried moment of preparation; but, as a *New Yorker* who loves the very soil of his native State, I cannot write coolly on this subject.

                    Believe me my dear Sir / Yours very respectfully & truly
                                                      Washington Irving

His Excellency / Governor Seward.

ADDRESSED: His Excellency / Governor Seward / New York.
MANUSCRIPT: University of Rochester Library.

1. John Romeyn Brodhead (1814–1873), who graduated from Rutgers in 1831, was attached to the U.S. legation in Paris, where his relative, Hermanus Bleecker, was chargé d'affaires. Brodhead spent three years searching in the archives of Holland, England, and France for materials relating to the early history of New York. The documents which he collected were translated and edited by E. B. O'Callaghan and published in eleven volumes as *Documents Relating to the Colonial History of the State of New York* between 1856 and 1886. His *History of the State of New York* (vol. 1, 1853; vol. 2, 1871; vol. 3, incomplete) was a synthesis of his extensive researches in foreign archives.

1435. To Sarah Storrow

Bordeaux July 16th. 1842

My dear Sarah,

We arrived here about Six OClock last evening after a very pleasant journey. The showers which took place the first night after our departure[1] cooled the air and laid the dust, and travelling for a couple of days was truly delightful. Indeed our carriage was so spacious; and there was such a current of air produced by the rapidity of our motions, that we suffered very little from heat throughout the journey. Some part of the country through which we passed, especially that along the Loire was beautiful[;] a great part, however, was level and monotonous. You would have been delighted however, with some of the places at which we stopped. Orleans has some fine old streets of aristocratical looking houses shut up within ⟨a⟩ courts; and has a fine cathedral[.][2] I was especially pleased with Poitiers,[3] a fine old warrior place on a hill; its walls and battlements turned into beautiful promenades overlooking a fresh green valley, with the Vienne[4] gleaming through it. I think the scene from the public promenade looking over the valley about sunset one of the finest things I have seen in France. The ⟨old⟩ cathedral and old churches of Poitiers[5] also are admirable. Angouleme was another of those stopping places that delighted me.[6] It stands also on an eminence and its old walls and bulwarks are turned into public promenades. I never took a stroll about these venerable places without wishing you were by my side, I met with so many things that I know you would have relished.

I have been very well pleased with my young travelling companions. Hamilton is always on the alert; full of good spirits and good humor;— and undertakes to make all the arrangements at the Hotels &c. Brevoort is Cashier, and an excellent one he is. I find him a most agreeable companion in exploring ⟨the⟩ antiquities &c from his knowledge of all the varieties of architecture, his correct taste and his varied and accurate information. Hector is a quiet little fellow that sits in his corner of the carriage and says nothing: he is however very observant. I believe I have made a good hit in my man Benjamin. He is an experienced travelling servant; knows the roads, the Inns; the usages &c—he is sober, quiet and attentive and conducts himself in the most respectful and respectable manner.

As is the case generally with our anticipations of pleasure in this world, I am disappointed in the enjoyment I had promised myself among my friends in Bordeaux. Beasley whom I calculated on finding here left town yesterday morning with old Mr Guestier,[7] to pass eight days with the latter at his chateau in Medoc. My valuable friend Peter Guestier the younger[8] is absent from town somewhere in the interior. Nathaniel Johns[t]on,[9] Mrs Guestiers[10] brother is confined by indisposition at his place in the country—I mean, this day to drive out to Floirac, to see Mrs Guestier; and also to visit old Mrs Johns[t]on,[11] at her retreat in the country. The absence of all the gentlemen, however, is a sad disappointment.

Thus my dear Sarah, I have given you an account, as I promised, of myself and my movements; that you may feel relieved from all anxiety about my health and welfare. I never felt better; and, in this mode of travelling, I could travel from Dan to Beersheba ⟨and f⟩ without feeling the worse for it.

And now my dear Sarah, a word about yourself. This second parting with you has been a hard trial to me; but I feel consoled by the idea that, being on this side of the Atlantic, our separation will not be very long. I shall be able to procure leave ↑of absence↓ now and then, to visit those of my family who are within reach; and when I next visit Paris it will be with a mind less embarrassed by cares and calculations than it was during my recent visit. I shall long to see your dear little infant again and to mark what progress she has made in intelligence. I never met with a little creature of her age that so completely took hold of my heart. I have her in my thoughts continually, with all her little looks and ways. It almost grieves me to think that I should part from her before she is capable of knowing or caring for me However, I trust one day or other we shall become great friends

—I have just received a note from Mrs Guestier written yesterday, before my arrival. The arrival of my trunk by Diligence had given notice that I would soon be here. She invites me in the kindest manner to come out and take up my quarters at Floirac: this, however, I shall not do, but I shall see as much of her and her family as possible during my sojourn in Bordeaux; which will be until Tuesday next.

Farewell my dear Sarah. Give my kindest remembrances to your excellent husband; to whom I feel deeply indebted for all his attentions and kind services during my sojourn in Paris Kiss my dear little Miss Maam—God bless her!

and believe me ever / most affectionately your uncle

Washington Irving

MANUSCRIPT: Yale.

1. WI and his party had left Paris on July 11 and spent the night at La Boule d'Or in Orléans. See *Journals of WI*, III, 217.

2. The Gothic cathedral of Ste. Croix, destroyed by the Huguenots in 1567, was rebuilt between 1601 and 1829, with a florid facade by Jacques Gabriel III (1667–1742). See Karl Baedeker, *Northern France*, pp. 270–71.

3. WI reached Poitiers, 180 miles southwest of Paris, on the evening of July 13 and stayed at the Hôtel de France. See *Journals of WI*, III, 218.

4. Poitiers is on the Clain River, a tributary of the Vienne.

5. The cathedral, St. Pierre, was begun in 1162 but not consecrated until 1379. Ste. Radegonde, built mainly from the eleventh to the thirteenth centuries; Notre-Dame-la-Grande, dating from the end of the eleventh century; St. Porchaire (mainly sixteenth century); and Ste. Hilaire, founded before the sixth century and rebuilt in the eleventh and twelfth centuries, are other churches in Poitiers. See Karl Baedeker, *Southern France, Including Corsica* (Leipzig, 1907), pp. 5–7.

6. WI arrived at Angoulême at 7:00 P.M. on July 14. He stayed at the Hôtel de la Porte. See *Journals of WI*, III, 218.

7. Daniel Guestier (1755–1847), a wine grower who had been WI's host on earlier visits to Bordeaux and the Chateau de Batailley in the Médoc region. See *J&N*, III, 528.

8. Pierre François Guestier (1793–1874), son of Daniel Guestier. His sister was married to Reuben Beasley, U.S. consul at Le Havre. See *J&N*, III, 212.

9. Nathaniel Johnston (1804–1870). See *J&N*, III, 528. WI always omits this *t* in the surname.

10. Anna Elizabeth Johnston (1801–1873), daughter of William Johnston (1770–1821), married Pierre Guestier in 1818. See *J&N*, III, 527.

11. Suzanne Gledstanes (1773–1853), whom William Johnston had married in 1797. See Young, *WI-Bordeaux*, p. 86.

1436. To Sarah Storrow

Bordeaux July 19th. 1842

My dear Sarah

I wrote to you a few days since rather dubiously about my visit to Bordeaux, from the absence ⟨of⟩ and indisposition of some of my friends: my visit, ⟨h⟩ notwithstanding, has proved delightful. Mr Guestier returned from his country tour, Mr Nathl Johns[t]on was sufficiently recovered to ⟨see company⟩ give me a most hospitable reception, and I

have been passing my time in this wide family connexion, at their beautiful country seats, feeling ⟨mor⟩ as if I were among relatives rather than
friends. Nothing could exceed the affectionate welcome which I have
experienced from them all. My excellent friend old Mrs Johns[t]on, who
always showed such a regard for ⟨your⟩ my dear brother Peter, received
me with a warmth and kindness that melted my very heart. I had not
⟨hoped⟩ expected to find her still alive and ⟨what⟩ and was rejoiced to
see her looking very much as when we parted, above sixteen years since.
I sat beside her at dinner yesterday at her beautiful country seat of
Lescure, where your uncle and myself have so often partaken of her
elegant hosptiality. ⟨She⟩ The ⟨gi?⟩ establishment is now kept up by her
son Nathl Johns[t]on, who reside[s][1] there all the year round. She passes
her summers with him but has her house in town.

Floirac, however, is the place of places—It is the country retreat of Mr
Peter Guestier, the younger, about three miles from Bordeaux; on the
brow of a woody hill, ⟨to⟩ which you ascend by zig zag ⟨road⟩ carriage
road, through groves and shrubberies. The house is on a natural terrace;
laid out in the English style; ⟨with noble trees;⟩ with groves and clumps
of trees; ⟨and⟩ thickets of ⟨an⟩ ornamental shrubs; ⟨and⟩ masses of
flowers &c. From this terrace there is an immense prospect that might almost rival that of Richmond hill.[2] A rich valley spreads far and wide below
you; with every variety of culture; vineyards, orchards, gardens, groves,
meadows and fields of grain; with villages, hamlets and country seats,
some on the plain emburied in trees, others brightening on the crests of
the hills, the Garonne pours its noble stream through the centre of the
prospect; with here and there a light sail gleaming upon it; and at a
distance is seen the noble city of Bordeaux; with its grand cathedral and
lofty spires.[3] It is indeed an enchanting spot, and if any thing ⟨th⟩ could
rival the lovely scenery around the house, it would be the domestic happiness and worth that reigns within. My dear Sarah how often I wished
that I had you with me to make you acquainted with this most estimable
family. I found my dear Mrs Guestier in excellent health, and looking
very much as when I left her, between sixteen and seventeen years since.
Time certainly has not dealt roughly with her. She was surrounded by a
family of daughters,[4] some of them born since I was here, two whom I had
left mere children were now women grown; one of them married, with
her husband[5] seated beside her, in whom I recognized her former cousin,[6]
whom I had left a boy. I had a joyous *family dinner* there, in which we
sat down about twenty to table. I believe their dinners are seldom less
numerous; for their house is a complete gathering place of the family
connexion. Mr Hamilton & Mr Brevoort dined there with me—as to
Hector he had to stay home and nurse a cold which has troubled him
throughout our journey, but from which he is now recovered. Our moon-

light drives home ⟨from⟩ were lovely—I never shall feel satisfied my dear Sarah until I have you with me at Bordeaux and make you acquainted with these excellent people. You will be charmed with their mode of life; where there is such a mixture of cordiality, good taste, good breeding and hearty enjoyment. Bordeaux too is a splendid city, and the environs beautiful. The vintage is the time to see this part of France in perfection, ⟨whe⟩ it is the season of abundance and festivity. I feel as if I were tearing myself again from home in parting with my Bordeaux friends; but I have promised that my next visit to them shall be ⟨a⟩ much longer.

This afternoon about 4 O Clock we set off for Bayonne in the Diligence. I have taken the Coupe and part of the interior. We shall travel all night, and reach Bayonne tomorrow afternoon. The weather has cooled and I anticipate a comfortable journey. I have written on to have like places secured for me in the Diligence that parts from Bayonne for Madrid.

I shall not have time to write home until I arrive at Madrid, so you must write to your mother about my welfare and my whereabouts.

Remember me most kindly to Mr Storrow ⟨Give a⟩ Kiss my dear little Miss Maam for me, and tell my good friend Elizabeth not to let the little woman ply the bottle too hard during this hot weather.

God bless you, my darling Sarah, / Your affectionate uncle
Washington Irving

MANUSCRIPT: Yale.

1. WI omitted the bracketed letter.

2. The terrace at Richmond Hill, located south of the Thames west of Wimbledon Park, provided a spectacular view of the river.

3. The cathedral of St. André, begun in the middle of the twelfth century and largely completed by the fourteenth century, was first examined by WI on his visit to Bordeaux in 1804. He recorded his impression in his journal on July 12, 1804. See *J&N*, I, 40–42.

4. In his journal for July 16, WI wrote: "drive out in the evening to Floirac to visit the Guestiers—Mr. Guestier absent. Find Mrs G at home with her son-in-law, Wash: [Pierre-François-Jean-Scott] Phelan, who married her daughter Minna, and Mr. ———, who married her niece, Miss Lorton [Lawton]—numerous family— four born since I was here." See *Journals of WI*, III, 219. The other daughters have not been identified.

5. The married daughter is Minna (Wilhelmina-Anna-Nathaline), whose wedding to Pierre Phelan occurred in April, 1842. According to Young, WI was using the intimate family name given to young Phelan by his parents as a token of their respect and admiration for WI himself. See Young, *WI-Bordeaux*, p. 106.

6. Since Bernard Phelan, the father of Pierre, had married the sister of Pierre Guestier, Marie-Elizabeth (1789–1879) on September 25, 1806, the newlyweds were first cousins. See Young, *WI-Bordeaux*, p. 105.

1437. *To Catharine Paris*

Bayonne, July 20th. 1842

My dear Sister

Here I am in the frontier town of France with the Pyrenees in view which I shall be traversing in the course of the day. My journey from Paris hither has been very pleasant. From Paris to Bordeaux I came post, in a very comfortable carriage The weather, for the greater part of the time was temperate in consequence of refreshing showers, so that we did not Suffer from Sun or dust. We stopped at several fine old historical places, such as Orleans, Tours, Poitiers & Angouleme. My fellow travellers are excellent companions, young and fresh and buoyant, and we get on joyously together. I have picked up a most valuable servant at Madrid,[1] a Mulatto named Benjamin Gowien, native of South Carolina, who came out with Mr Middleton,[2] when he went Minister to Russia, remained with him ten or twelve years, and has been travelling about Europe in various capacities for twenty four years past. He speaks most of the European languages fluently; is a capital travelling servant, and indeed a valuable servant at all points. Steady, quiet, respectful and trustworthy. In a word he suits me exactly and since I have had him he takes such good care of me that I feel as if there is no need of taking care of myself. I shall retain him as footman and valet at Madrid; where he has already been three times and made himself well acquainted with the language and with the customs of the country[.] I write particularly on this point, as I know you will feel some solicitude about my personal comforts. I passed ⟨ab⟩ between four and five days at Bordeaux among my excellent friends the Guestiers, Johns[t]ons & Bartons.[3] I was received by them as if I were one of their family connexion. That good old lady Mrs Johns[t]on, the great friend of our dear brother Peter, I found still in good health, though complaining of advanced age. My heart was full on meeting with her, for I thought of the many happy hours I had passed in her company and under her hospitable roof ⟨[*unrecovered*]⟩ with our dear brother. The good old lady received me with the warmest affection, and talked in the kindest and most touching manner about past times. My sojourn at Bordeaux was indeed full of heart felt reccollections, for here my dear Brother was constantly by my side enjoying the cordial intercourse with these excellent people, who all cherish the kindest remembrances of him. Indeed who ever knew him without loving him. For my own part never have I felt his loss more deeply than since my return to Europe, where every step I take recalls him to my mind, ⟨[*unrecovered*⟩] and recalls something he has done or said; some happy observation, some tasteful remark some delightful pleasantry from him whose whole life was was an exemplification of every excellence.

At Bordeaux we took the Diligence; securing the best places; ⟨and⟩ we left Bordeaux at 4 Oclock in the afternoon, travelled all night and arrived here at 4 Oclock the ↑next↓ afternoon; again favored by the weather. A timely shower having cooled the air and laid the dust. It was yesterday afternoon that we arrived, and this morning at 11 O clock we set off in the Diligence for Madrid, having again secured the "Coupée["] and part of the ⟨[unrecovered]⟩ "interieur,"i e, the best places. We shall be five days on the road to Madrid Stopping every night. The weather today is cool and fresh showers having fallen in the night; and I look forward to accomplishing the journey with a degree of comfort hardly to be expected in these sultry climates at this season of the year.

I scrawl this letter in great haste during preparations for departure. Give my love to all at the Cottage

I will write again when I arrive at Madrid

> Your affectionate brother
> Washington Irving

Mrs Daniel Paris / New York

MANUSCRIPT: SHR.   PUBLISHED: PMI, III, 215–16 (in part).

1. Someone else has canceled "Madrid" and written "Paris" above it.

2. Henry Middleton (1770–1846), a South Carolina planter who served in the state house of representatives from 1802 to 1810 and as governor from 1810 to 1812, was a Democratic representative to the U.S. Congress from 1815 to 1819. In 1820 he was appointed minister to Russia, a position he held until 1830.

3. Hugh Barton (1766–1854), who married Anne Johnston (1771–1842) in 1791, was a partner with Daniel Guestier in the wine merchandising firm of Barton and Guestier. See Young, WI-Bordeaux, pp. 98–99.

1438. To Sarah Storrow

Bayonne July 20th. 1842

My dear Sarah,

I enclose a letter hastily scrawled to your mother. It must serve for yourself to let you know how I have got on so far. I am in capital health & good spirits and all the better for the journey. When you have read the enclosed seal it up & send it to Mr Ledyard[1] to be forwarded

Kind remembrances to Mr Storrow and kiss little Miss Maam for me.

I would give fifty centimes to be able just now to kiss her myself and receive one of her "killin looks"

Your affectionate uncle
Washington Irving

PS   I am in the midst of people who look half French half Spanish, and speak a jargon composed of Spanish, Basque, French & the lord knows what all[.] I have just seen a Spanish lady pass my window in mantella & pasquins ⟨[unrecovered]⟩ the sight made my heart jump

MANUSCRIPT: Yale.

1. Henry Ledyard (1812–1880), the chargé d'affaires at the U.S. legation in Paris, had been appointed by Lewis Cass in 1836 and remained there until 1845, when he returned to the United States and settled in Detroit, Michigan.

1439. To Catharine Paris

Madrid, July 25th. 1842.

My dear Sister,
    I write you a brief line merely to apprise you of my arrival in Safety at the end of my long journey. I wrote to you from Bayonne,[1] when on the point of crossing the frontier. I left Bayonne at 11 OClock on thursday last,[2] in the Diligence for Madrid, we were four days making the journey, stopping for a few hours three of the nights, we travelled all last night, and reached here this morning (Monday) at Seven OClock[.] I have been unexpectedly favored by the weather almost ever since I left Paris. Though in Midsummer the heats which had previously been excessive have been moderate for the greater part of the way, and ⟨S⟩ in Spain, where I most expected to suffer I have travelled quite comfortably; and feel in no wise fatigued by my journey. At the Diligence office I found Lorenzo, my head servant or butler, and Antonio my cook (lately servants of Mr Vail and highly reccommended by him) waiting to receive me and to conduct me to my home. The young gentlemen of my diplomatic family went to a hotel until I could recconnoitre my establishment. I found the house[3] in good order and commodious. Juana (late handmaid to Mrs Vail, now my housekeeper) shewed me through the rooms. Benjamin, my valet, who had travelled with [me][4] from Paris brought my trunks to the house, and I at once found myself at home. The young gentlemen have since been here, chosen their rooms, ⟨f⟩ and are to bring their luggage in the course of the day. Until my china

ware, linen, &c &c arrive from France we have to make shift by hiring bedding, table furniture &c but we shall all feel delighted to be under our own roof and settled. I like the appearance of my new servants, especially Lorenzo and Juana; ⟨they are⟩ their countenances, deportment and mode of dressing themselves are highly in their favor and I make no doubt I shall find them to answer to the high reccommendations of Mr Vail with whom they have resided ever since he has been here. My cook, Antonio, who is a Greek; is said to be excellent in his art; he is not very brilliant in appearances, but as he will be among pots & kettles, it is not of much moment. When I have been here a few days and had time to look round me I will write you more particularly.

I found your letter of May the 26th. waiting for me here and one from brother E. I. of May 29th. also one of May 26 from my precious darling little Mary[5]—God bless her—how could I complain in one of my letters that none of the girls write to me, and here was this long letter from my dear dear little Mary waiting at Madrid for me. I have not read any of these letters ↑yet,↓ for I have not had time ⟨I⟩ as I am hurried by a thousand things, and am anxious to write to you, to Sarah, and to Sister Van Wart, to let you know of my having made this long anxious journey in perfect health—Beside I cannot allow myself to read these precious letters from home in a hurry[.] I will banquet on them by and bye, and will answer all, when I get over my present flutter and agitation[6]

It seems strange to me to find myself all at once the master of a new house; walking from room to room all having the look of a long established abode; strange servants running at my call and bowing to me with profound respect. My own chamber, which is a very spacious one is already all in order, my trunks all emptied and their contents neatly arranged by Benjamin in the various drawers & presses, and every thing has ⟨the⟩ ↑an↓ air as if I had been master here for a long time past[.] I must now finish this hurried scrawl to begin others—Give my love to all my dear household at the Cottage, and speak a kind word for me to my neighbors. Hamilton will write by this opportunity to his family and will be more particular than I have time to be. I feel very happy in my nice diplomatic family.

Your affectionate brother
Washington Irving

ADDRESSED: Mrs. Daniel Paris / Care of E. Irving Esqr / Tarrytown / New York. POSTMARKED: WASHINGTON CITY D. C. / AUG 21   DOCKETED: Washn. Irving to Mrs. C. R. Paris. Madrid (Spain) / July 25. 1842 / F. Sep. 17. / S. Oct 27

MANUSCRIPT: Yale.   PUBLISHED: PMI, III, 216–17 (in part).

In the upper left corner of MS page 1 is written "Wednesday Aug 24/42," apparently the date when the letter was received by Mrs. Paris.

A copy of the first eleven lines of the transcription with two parallel diagonal lines through it is preserved at Yale.

1. See WI to Catharine Paris, July 20, 1820.
2. Thursday, July 21.
3. WI lived at the hotel of the Duke of San Lorenzo in the Calle de Alcalá, no. 112 Plazuela de la Villa until mid-September, when he moved to the palace of the marques de Mos in the Calle de las Infantas. See STW, II, 142, 373; and WI to Catharine Paris, July 30, 1842.
4. WI's omission.
5. These letters have not been located.
6. This entire paragraph in the manuscript is covered by two intersecting diagonal lines, crossing it out.

1440. To Sarah Storrow

Madrid, July 25th. 1842

My dear Sarah,

I scrawled a mere line to you from Bayonne, inclosing a letter for your mother. I left Bayonne the same day, Thursday at 11 O clock. Had a pleasant journey through the Pyrenees, & the Basque provinces, and a dreary one across the naked Sterile plains & mountains of Old and New Castile; but, being unexpectedly favored by moderate weather, accomplished the whole journey with very little inconvenience. We stopped a few hours on three of the nights to snatch a morsel of sleep; travelled all last night and arrived here this morning Monday: at seven Oclock; in good health and spirits. I found Lorenzo, my Major domo, and Antonio, the cook, waiting at the Diligence office to receive me, and was at once conducted to Mr Vails late residence, which he had vacated but yesterday. My trunks have been brought here, Benjamin has already emptied them, arranged all their contents in commodes and clothes presses; my spacious bed room is in complete order, and I already feel at home. My young gentlemen who on arriving had gone to an inn are to have their trunks brought here this afternoon; and ⟨sl⟩ tonight we all sleep in our new home. This is truly delightful, after tossing about ⟨the⟩ through such a long journey.

I like the appearance of the servants. Lorenzo who is to be head servant is a very good looking fellow, well dressed, and of ⟨a⟩ most engaging manners and deportment. Juana, who from ladys maid is promoted to Housekeeper is likewise good looking and most respectable in her appearance. My cook, Antonio, a Greek, looks a little of the companionship of pots and kettles, but I am told he is a capital fellow in his profession. ⟨It was the⟩ The habitation, which is one part of a huge Spanish house, is convenient, though rather far from the public walks. It will do excellently well at all events for the present. It seems strange for me to walk through these great Spanish chambers, and to find myself suddenly the lord of the establishment, with Spanish servants bowing round me—I have written by this opportunity to your Mother & your Aunt Van Wart as I k[n]ow [MS torn] you will all be anxious to hear of me at the end of this arduous journey—I scrawl in haste to be in time for the mail—When I am more settled and at leisure I will write more fully. My affectionate Remembrances to your husband and a thousand loves to my dear little Miss Maam

Your affectionate uncle
Washington Irving

MANUSCRIPT: Yale.

1441. To Catharine Paris

Madrid July 30th. 1842

My dear Sister,

I wrote you a hasty line on my arrival here, ⟨to⟩ ↑(on Monday 25↓) to let you know that I had safely accomplished my long journey[.] I have since been busily employed arranging my diplomatic and household concerns. I am completely installed in the late residence of Mr Vail and shall probably continue to reside there for some time to come, as it is not easy to find ⟨a more⟩ a ⟨hab⟩ suitable habitation in that part of the city which I should prefer. I am in one wing, or half, of the hotel of the Duke of San Lorenzo; the opposite wing is occupied by Mr Albuquerque[1] Brazilian Resident Minister who married one of the Miss Oakeys of New York, so that we have a very pleasant and intelligent countrywoman for near neighbor. We are not far from the Royal library and the Royal palace.[2] Every morning the horse guards and the foot guards pass under our windows, each with a noble band of music, going to relieve guard at the palace. It is quite an animating sight. ⟨The furniture⟩ I have taken Mr Vails furniture off his hands and he has put it at very reduced prices. It is as good as new, the sofas & chairs never having had the covers off more than three or four times, so that they retain all their freshness and lustre. The furniture was made under Mr Vails eye by a French cabinet maker in New York, and is of the best workmanship and materials. The

Sofas & chairs are mahogany and Silk. Those of the grand saloon are watered silk of a cream color, with crimson ⟨satin⟩ Sattin Stripes, those of the Smaller saloon the same kind excepting that the silk has blue satin stripes. There are rich window curtains of the same materials to match the furniture. The carpets are Brussels for the large saloon & Wilton for the Smaller Other articles of furniture are in similar style. The carriage was built in New York; it is very genteel and commodious; almost as good as new, and much lighter and more elegant than those generally seen in Madrid. I am, therefore, very neatly set up and on very moderate terms.

I have made Benjamin my butler or upper servant; as I found he best understood the business and had the most judge[me]nt. [Ms torn] He appears to ⟨understand⟩ manage the house extremely well. Lorenzo is footman or valet. Juana is house maid and has charge of the linen, &c &c. Antonio is cook; ⟨[unrecovered]⟩ the young gentlemen have made a page or tygee of a nephew of Lorenzo, a boy whom they keep to loiter in the antechamber run their errands &c. Such is my household, as I have no horses yet I have not engaged a coachman: though I have bespoken a trusty one who is well reccommended. Carson Brevoort keeps the accounts of the establishment and enquires into all the expenditures; so that I hope to get on comfortably without being much fleeced. Our household is a very cheerful and pleasant one, and my young companions acquit themselves very amiably

The other morning as I was seated in the saloon conversing with a gentleman, the servant announced the Duke de Gor.[3] In a moment I was in his arms. You may remember that this was the nobleman with whom I was so intimate at Granada, ⟨who⟩ at whose house I was so often a guest; and who with his children made me frequent visits in the Alhambra. He is now resident with his family in Madrid. I cannot express to you how rejoiced I was to see him. He is a most estimable character in every respect. One of the *Moderados*,[4] and therefore not exactly in favor with the party in power. He is a leading man, however, in all public institutions, and the Duchess is at the head of many of the charitable institutions. The Duke gave me anecdotes of my friends in ⟨Madrid⟩ ↑Granada↓. Mateo,[5] on the strength of my writings, is quite the Cicerone of Granada & the Alhambra. Dolores and her husband[6] reside else where. The lovely little Niña[7] the daughter of the old Count, she who was quite my admiration and delight, is dead. She was married as I have related in some of my writings, to the young Marques del Pulgar,[8] and lived happily having two or three children—but died in childbed. The Duke was accompanied by a young gentleman whom he recalled to my reccollection as little Nicholas, alias el Rey Chico, who, a very small boy, had chased bats about the vaulted halls of the Alhambra

I have since returned the Dukes call and found the Duchess at home; who gave me a most cordial reception. She summoned her children to see me. One, a young lady about seventeen, was a romping little girl in the Alhambra the others had been born since I left Spain The oldest daughter of the Duchess,[9] who had been one of my visitors, is now married to a Spanish nobleman who resides at Bayonne, on the French frontier, ⟨not being ab⟩ being obliged to leave Spain on account of politics. I anticipate much pleasure from renewing my intimacy with the Gor family.

An Evening or two since I had my audience of the Minister of foreign Affairs the Count Almodovar,[10] who received me in the most courteous manner, expressing his satisfaction at my being sent to this court. I delivered him an official copy of the Presidents letter to the Queen,[11] and requested that a day might be assigned for me to present the original to the Regent. The day after tomorrow (Monday) at one O'clock is appointed for the ceremonial. Mr Albuquerque (hitherto charge d'affaires) will present his letters of credence as resident Minister at the same time. This ceremony over, I shall be a regularly accredited Minister, & will then make my visits of ceremony to the ⟨other ministers⟩ heads of departments and the gentlemen of the diplomatic corps. I am curious to have this presentation that I may have an interview with Espartero the Regent,[12] who certainly is one of the most remarkable men of the age. I have as yet only seen him one day in public, on the Prado where I was pleased with his ⟨appearance⟩ ↑soldier like↓ air and manly deportment.

I am scribbling this letter after dinner to go by the Estafette[13] of the French Embassy which departs this evening. I shall send it ⟨to⟩ open to our dear Sarah in Paris that she may read it and transmit it to you. I have not time to write to her at present.

I begin to feel at home, and shall feel still more so in the course of a few days, when my books and papers arrive and I get at work. I foresee I shall have plenty of liesure for literary occupation here, and I trust I shall turn it to advantage. ⟨I again⟩ I repeat that I am highly pleased with my diplomatic household. The young gentlemen conduct themselves well, are extremely amiable, agree together most harmoniously, so that, altogether, we form a very snug family.

I have received ↑a↓ letter today from brother E. I dated June 29th.[14] giving me many most interesting anecdotes about home and all its dear inmates. I shall write to him immediately. I am rejoiced to hear that Mrs Constant[15] has a little daughter. I trust the event will have a happy influence on her health and spirits. I had a letter a day or two since from our dear Sarah, who I am glad to find is enjoying the country air at ⟨Fontainbleau⟩ ↑St Germain↓, with her darling infant; who I declare to be one of the most precious little fairies I have ever known. I would speak more of her but that I know ⟨this will⟩ ↑that it would↓ meet Sarahs eye and make her vain.

I am scrawling almost in the dark and must conclude. Give my love to all the dear inmates of the Cottage.

Your affectionate brother
Washington Irving

ADDRESSED: Mrs Daniel Paris / Care of E. Irving Esqr / New York.
MANUSCRIPT: Yale.   PUBLISHED: PMI, III, 217–19 (in part).

1. José Francisco de Paula Cavalcanti de Albuquerque was Brazilian resident minister to Spain from 1842 to 1851. See Raul A. de Campos, *Relações Diplomaticas do Brasil* (Rio de Janeiro, 1913), pp. 68–69.

2. The Royal Library, founded by Philip V, contains 100,000 volumes and 5,000 manuscripts. It is located in the northeast corner of the Royal Palace. See Karl Baedeker, *Spain and Portugal* (Leipzig, 1913), p. 96.

3. The duke of Gor, who lived in Granada in 1829 when WI was staying in the Alhambra, had, as WI indicates, graciously befriended him and opened his library and his home to him. See WI to Prince Dolgorouki, June 15, 1829; and to Peter Irving, June 13 and August 4, 1829.

4. One segment of the Carlists, the liberal or constitutional party, sometimes called "royalist," though not supporters of Queen Isabella II or her mother, Queen María Christina. The Carlists had roughly three divisions: the Moderatos (equivalent to the English Tories or Conservatives), the Progresistas (Whigs), and the Escultados (Radicals). See Elizabeth W. Latimer, *Spain in the Nineteenth Century* (Chicago, 1897), p. 247.

5. Mateo Ximenes had been WI's valet, guide, and companion at the Alhambra during his stay there in 1829. Mateo used his association with WI to establish himself as the leading tour guide for the Moorish palace. See WI to Sarah Van Wart, October 24, 1838; and to Sarah Storrow, January 5, 1843.

6. Dolores was one of WI's attendants at the Alhambra. She married her cousin Manuel, who was a doctor. See WI to Sarah Van Wart, October 24, 1838.

7. WI's affectionate name for Carmen, the daughter of the count of Luque who was sixteen at the time of WI's residence in the Alhambra. WI sketches the girl and her father in "Visitors to the Alhambra." See *The Alhambra* (London, 1832), II, 7–14.

8. Hernando del Pulgar, marques of Salar, whom WI had met on visits to the duke of Gor's home in 1829. With Pulgar's cooperation and assistance WI was able to examine the family manuscripts for details about his illustrious ancestor who fought with Ferdinand and Isabella against the Moors. See WI to Peter Irving, June 13, 1829.

9. Dolores, the eldest daughter of the duke of Gor, was nine years old when WI met her in 1829. See Hellman, *WI Esquire*, p. 208; and PMI, II, 384.

10. General Ildefonso Diéz de Rivera, Count Almodóvar (1777–1846) had distinguished himself at Trafalgar fighting against Nelson in 1805. He fled to France until the death of Ferdinand VII because of his liberal ideas. He was a friend of Espartero's and from 1834 to 1840 was a deputy in the Cortes from Valencia and president of the Congress; in 1836 he was minister of war and in 1837–1843,

president of the Senate. At the fall of Espartero he returned to private life. See *Enciclopedia Universal Ilustrada*, IV, 850.

11. María Isabella Luisa (1830–1904), elder daughter of Ferdinand VII and María Christina, was invested at her baptism with the order of María Luisa and proclaimed successor to the Spanish throne when her father issued a Pragmatic Sanction setting aside the Salic law which excluded females from ruling. This action prompted Carlos, Ferdinand's brother, to try to seize the throne for himself. See Peter de Polnay, *A Queen of Spain* (London, 1962), pp. 20–27, 60; and Bowers, *Spanish Adventures of WI*, pp. 139–40.

12. Joaquín Baldomero Hernández Álvárez Espartero (1793–1879), a pious low-born radical and soldier, rose to power after the 1836 revolution. By 1839 he was the most powerful of the generals, devoted to the welfare of his troops. As commander in chief of the army he forced Queen María Christina to dismiss the Moderado government and annul the new municipal law. From October, 1840, to May, 1841, he headed an interim regency and then became sole regent until he was deposed by the Supreme Junta of Barcelona on June 29, 1843. Having been defeated in battle by Narváez on July 23, 1843, he embarked for England on July 30, 1843. On August 13, 1843, he was stripped of all his honors and titles. See Raymond Carr, *Spain, 1808–1939* (Oxford, 1966), pp. 175, 179–83, 219–27.

13. The express courier.

14. This letter has not been located.

15. One of WI's neighbors near Sunnyside. See WI to Catharine Paris, March 22, 1838; and to WI's six nieces, February 4, 1840.

1442. To Sarah Storrow

Madrid, July 30th. 1842

My dear Sarah,

I received a day or two since your delightful letter of July 20th. and ⟨yesterd⟩ this morning one from Mr Storrow enclosing a letter from New York.[1] I will answer your letter in the course of a day or two; at present the reading of the enclosed must Suffice.

I am glad to ⟨fi⟩ hear, that little Miss Maam is at St Germain. I believe all that you say about the improvement in her looks, though I almost feel as if I should wish her always to look exactly as she did when I used to dandle her in my arms at Paris—God bless her—and her Mamma.

Your affectionate uncle
Washington Irving

ADDRESSED: Madame / Madame Storrow / aux Soins de Mons. T. W. Storrow / 4 Rue de la Victoire   POSTMARKED: 2 me Dist. / 94 1/2 / 15c/ [*second postmark unrecovered*]   DOCKETED: July 20th 1842
MANUSCRIPT: Yale.

1. This letter has not been located.

1443. To Count Almodóvar

Legation of the United States, / Madrid 2nd. August 1842.

The undersigned Envoy Extraordinary and Minister Plenipotentiary of the United States of America has the honor to communicate to his Excellency Count de Almodovar, First Minister of State and of Foreign Affairs of Her Catholic Majesty, the original Commission of Mr Gurdon Bradley,[1] appointed Consul of the United States for the Port of Mayagues in the Island of Puerto Rico, and by direction of his Government, requests that his Excellency will cause the corresponding Royal Exequatur[2] to be issued, recognizing Mr. Bradley in his official character.

The Undersigned avails himself of this opportunity to offer to Count de Almodovar the assurances, of his most distinguished consideration.

Washington Irving

MANUSCRIPT: NA, RG 84 (letterbook copy); NA, RG 59 (copy).

The text of this letter is taken from a copy enclosed with despatch no. 1 to the secretary of state, August 2, 1842.

1. Gurdon Bradley of Connecticut was nominated as U.S. consul for Mayaguez, Puerto Rico on May 14, 1842. He was recalled in 1845. See Hasse, *Index to U. S. Documents*, III, 1747.

2. An official sanction by the host country authorizing a foreign consul or commercial agent to perform his duties.

1444. To T. M. Rodney

Legation of the United States / Madrid Augt. 2nd. 1842

T. M. Rodney Esqr. / Consul of the U. States—Matanzas—

Sir:

An application was made by Mr. Vail late Charge d'Affaires, for an Exequatur in your case on the 12th. of May last.

The Regulations of the Spanish Government, on this subject require that an Inquiry should in the first place be made at the Port, for which the Consul is appointed as to his character &c, and upon a favorable report being made in answer thereto, The Exequatur is granted by the Authorities here—The representation made heretofore against these delays, which in the cases of Ports in the Colonies are increased by two voyages across the Atlantic, have not been successful in obtaining a remedy.—So soon as your Papers are received, They shall be forwarded to you without delay.

> I am, Sir Respectfully / Your obdt Sert
> Washington Irving

MANUSCRIPT: NA, RG 84 (letterbook copy).

Thomas McKean Rodney (1800–1874), son of Caesar A. Rodney of Wilmington, Delaware, had prior diplomatic service as secretary of the American legation in Buenos Aires while his father was U.S. minister to Argentina and as consul general at Havana. He served as consul at Matanzas, Cuba from 1842 to 1845 and from 1849 to 1853. Later he was active in Republican politics. See Henry C. Conrad, *History of the State of Delaware* (Wilmington, 1908), III, 868; J. Thomas Scharf, *History of Delaware, 1609–1888* (Philadelphia, 1888), I, 205; and Hasse, *Index to U.S. Documents,* III, 1419, 1746.

1445. To Daniel Webster

Legation of the United States. / Madrid 2nd August 1842.

No. 1. / The Hon: Daniel Webster. / Secretary of State of the U. States. Washington.

Sir,

I arrived in this City on Monday last July 25th. when I received every possible attention from Mr. Vail to assist me in entering upon the business of my mission; accompanied by that Gentleman I had an audience on Wednesday evening July 27th. of Count Almodovar, First Minister of State and of Foreign Affairs to whom I delivered the Copy of my letter of Credence addressed to the Queen; and understood from him that the Original would have to be presented to the Duke of Victoria[1] as Regent; Though my written Instructions specified that the letter was to be delivered to the Queen yet verbal intimations at Washington had given me to understand that I might use my discretion in the matter: I therefore signified to Count Almodovar my acquiescence in the arrangement, and my wish that an early day might be appointed for the Ceremonial— I must observe that my interview with the Count was extremely friendly and satisfactory.

I had an audience of the Regent yesterday at one o'clock, at his Palace of Buena Vista,[2] when I delivered to him the Original letter for the Queen accompanied by the following observations, which I expressed as well as I could in Spanish:

"I have the honor to deliver into the hands of your Highness as Regent of this Kingdom, a Letter from the President of the United States of

America accrediting me as Envoy Extraordinary and Minister Plenipotentiary to this Court:

In presenting this letter I do but echo the sentiments of the President, in accompanying it with assurances of the high respect and regard of my Government, for the Sovereign of this Country; for its political institutions and for its People; of its Sincere desire to draw more and more closely the ties of amity, which so happily exist between the two Nations; and of its ardent wish that Spain under her present Constitutional form of Government, administered with Wisdom, Firmness and Patriotism, may open for herself a new career of prosperity and glory.

Your Highness will permit me on my own part to express the extreme satisfaction I feel in being appointed to a Mission the sole object of which I trust will be to promote mutual good understanding and good will, between my own Country and a Country for which I have ever entertained the highest consideration."

As I was aware that this presentation from the recent difficulties with the French Mission[3] would attract attention, and that the expressions of my address might be subject to comment, I endeavoured to word it cautiously with reference to my Instructions, and to the Spirit of the Conversations I had had with the members of my Government—My letter gave me no authority to pay any direct compliment to the Regent; I therefore used none, though I endeavoured to convey the general feeling of good will towards the actual Powers directing the affairs of this Nation, which I knew to pervade the Cabinet at Washington. The reply of the Regent was in the following words.

"Agradesco en el fondo de mi Corazon la Seguridad de los votos que el Presidente de los Estados Unidos manifiesta en favor de mi Reina y de mi Patria. Correspondo al digno Sucesor del immortal Washington, interesandome por su gloria y por que se afiancen cada dia mas la libertad y prosperidad de los Estados Unidos. Tambien me es Sumamente grato que seais vos Señor Ministro Plenipotentiario el encargado de transmitirme los sentimientos de vuestro Gobierno."[4]

I was exceedingly pleased with the appearance and Manners of the Regent. He has an open, frank, soldierlike air, and his demeanour was manly and courteous.

I had subsequently an audience of the Queen[5] at the Royal Palace where I was presented to her in my official capacity by the Count Almodovar and found her attended by her "Aya" or Governess Madame Mina[6] Widow of the general of that name, and by her Guardian the excellent Arguelles.[7]

I have found the Archives of the Legation in excellent order, and cannot refrain from testifying to the admirable manner, in which Mr. Vail appears to have conducted the affairs of this Mission, to the respect and good will he has inspired in the different members of the Spanish Government, with whom he has had dealings, and in the Public generally, and to his very amiable and gentlemanlike conduct towards myself, ever since I have been appointed to this Post: I feel that he has left me a difficult task to follow him in the punctual and efficient discharge of the duties of the legation.

I forbear to attempt any notice of Public Affairs in this Country (in this Country) in this Despatch My very recent arrival, and the hurry of arrangements incident to it, prevent my collecting any information worth communicating, and indeed the Despatches of Mr. Vail have kept you sufficiently informed on this subject.

I had the honor on the 1st. instant to receive your Despatch No. 3, enclosing the commission of Gurdon Bradley.—I have complied with its directions in relation to the Exequatur of Mr. Bradley as you will perceive by the enclosed Copy of my application.

I am Sir, / With great respect / Your obdt Sert.
Washington Irving

MANUSCRIPT: NA, RG 59.   PUBLISHED: Bowers, *Spanish Adventures of WI*, pp. 144–45 (in part).

Only the signature is in WI's handwriting.

1. Along with prince of Vergara, this was a title held by Joaquín Baldomero Hernández Álvárez Espartero.

2. This was the former palace of Prince Godoy near the Prado and the Retiro on Calle de Alcalá and now the location of all the Spanish ministries except that of foreign affairs. See Karl Baedeker, *Spain and Portugal*, p. 63.

3. Since Louis Philippe was determined not to acknowledge Espartero's regency, Narcisse-Achille, comte de Salvandy (1795–1856), French minister to Spain, refused to present his credentials to anyone but Queen Isabella. When his audience with the queen was denied, he vested authority in his chargé d'affaires and left Madrid in January, 1842. As WI indicates in the first paragraph, he was more tactful; he used his discretion and presented his letter of credence to the regent, who then arranged for the audience with Queen Isabella. See Bowers, *Spanish Adventures of WI*, p. 142; STW, II, 137; WI to Catharine Paris, September 2, 1842.

4. Translation: "From the bottom of my heart I am grateful for the assurance of the good wishes that the president of the United States manifests in favor of my queen and my country. I should like to reciprocate (the wishes) of the worthy successor of the immortal Washington, expressing my hope for the glory of the United States and for its liberty and prosperity to become firmer day by day. I am also most highly pleased that you, the minister plenipotentiary, are charged with transmitting to me the sentiments of your government."

5. María Isabella Luisa was proclaimed queen on October 24, 1833, with her mother designated as regent. See Peter de Polnay, *A Queen of Spain*, p. 28.

6. Juana María de la Vega, Countess Espoz y Mina (b. 1805) was a shopkeeper's daughter who had married General Francisco Espoz y Mina (1781–1836),

a liberal and a guerilla leader in the north of Spain. As governess, Countess Mina zealously guarded Isabella from what she considered bad influences and came into conflict with the queen-mother. When Espartero fell as regent, Countess Mina was removed as governess. See Edgar Holt, *The Carlist Wars in Spain* (London, 1967), p. 68; and Peter de Polnay, *A Queen of Spain*, pp. 63, 70–71.

7. Agustín Argüelles (1776–1844), one of the most brilliant orators in the Cortes and a man of liberal political opinions, had been forced into exile by Ferdinand. Recalled from exile, he helped construct the constitution of 1837 and helped to implement it by working with Espartero and serving as Isabella's tutor. See Bowers, *Spanish Adventures of WI*, pp. 145–47, 158; Raymond Carr, *Spain, 1808–1939*, p. 211; and WI to Catharine Paris, September 2, 1842, and December 10, 1842.

1446. To Count Almodóvar

Legation of the United States. / Madrid 3d. August 1842.

The Undersigned, Envoy Extraordinary and Minister Plenipotentiary of the United States of America has the honor to represent to his Excellency Count de Almodovar, First Minister of State and of Foreign Affairs of Her Catholic Majesty that Charles Griswold native of the United States but at present residing at Manilla under temporary permission of the local authorities and acting as clerk in the highly respectable House of Russell and Sturgis[1] is desirous of remaining there for an indefinite period:—As the objects of his residence are of a meritorious and useful kind, the undersigned, at the request of his highly respectable connexions, has the honor to solicit the necessary license[2] from the Spanish Government, for the said Charles Griswold to remain in the Philippine Islands:

The Undersigned takes this occasion to renew to Count de Almodovar the assurances of his very distinguished Consideration.

Washington Irving

Manuscript: NA, RG 84 (letterbook copy).

1. It is possible that WI was referring to Russell Sturgis, a shipping merchant in New York. No partnership of Russell and Sturgis has been located, though firms such as Sturgis, Roe, and Barker, and Sturgis, Bennett & Co. did operate in New York. See Scoville, *Old Merchants of NYC*, II, 293.

2. It is not clear whether WI means a personal visa or a commercial license.

1447.   To Mary Irving

Madrid Aug 3d 1842

My dear Mary

xxxxx

Your letter[1] was quite a surprise ↑and a delightful one↓ to me, for I had scarcely expected to receive one from you; and yet I do not know why you should not write as well as talk to me; it is but talking with the pen instead of the tongue; and you know I always listened to you with pleasure. Besides letter writing is a truly lady like accomplishment, and you could not have a better correspondent, ↑than myself↓ to exercise it upon, for no one could be more indulgent. But your letter needs no indulgence. I have read it over and over, my dear little girl, and have recalled you in every line, and the reading of it has done my heart good. Only think how precious it is to me, here, in my isolated position, without a relative near me, to have these communications of affection directly from the hands and hearts of those I love. I feel the value of these interchanges of affection more now than in former ⟨years⟩ periods of life, for as the world at large has less and less power to interest and delight me and I feel myself growing more and more indifferent to the scenes of gaiety and grandeur in which I am obliged to mingle, I cling the more dearly to those heartfelt home dwelling ties of kindred love which have formed the happiness of my recent years. My dear little girl, your picture of my happy little home at Sunnyside, with the honey suckles and cluster roses clambering about it and the Tartarean honey suckle under my window, with the Cat bird building its nest in it and singing in the neighboring Acacia tree, has filled my heart to the very brim, and nearly made it run over at my eyes. Take care that that worthy little bird is never molested; cherish it for my sake. I think with you that sweet little Sunnyside is one of the "most darling little places in the world" and it is a constant source of enjoyment to me to picture you all to myself, happily nestled there.

xxxx   I am residing, as my letters have already informed the family, in a part of the Hotel or Palacio of the Duke of San Lorenzo; where I have a suite of spacious handsome rooms and a wilderness of nooks and corners, and dark corridors and crinkum crankums, such as abound in old Spanish houses, The walls are covered with large gloomy pictures of saints and scripture events; several of which glare on me at night from different parts of my huge bed room." xxxx "What I miss most of any thing is the delightful verdure to which I have been accustomed. I want cool, shady walks, and the sight of green fields. Here the public walks have trees, but not a blade of grass is to be seen. The Retiro, that public garden in which during my former residence in Madrid I used to take delight, is parched up by the late drought; and as to the country around Madrid, the moment you step beyond the walls you behold naked sun burnt wastes, as far as the eye can reach, without a tree or even shrub. For rural recreations Madrid might as well be situated in the midst of one of the desarts of Africa. The house in which I reside also, is so situated that I must traverse a great part of the narrow and hot streets of the City to get at the public walks. xxxx I am very fortunate in having such an agreeable household of young gentlemen. ↑Indeed I should have been badly off without them↓ They are great company for me and agree together most harmoniously—Alexander Hamilton will make a first-rate diplomatist: he is so clear, intelligent and self possessed and has such affable engaging manners. He is the life of the house; always in good spirits and animated in conversation. Carson Brevoort, modest and quiet, is full of knowledge and acquirement; he regulates the household, keeps the accounts and keeps an eye to the expenditures. He and Hector Ames are continually together, and Carson has recently been giving Hector lessons in drawing.

As soon as the boxes and trunks arrive with our books & papers, and the China ware, linen, glass &c that I purchased in Paris I shall feel completely fixed; and as the visits of ceremony will be over in ↑the course of↓ a very few days we shall soon be able to cut out ⟨and⟩ for ourselves regular occupations and then I trust the household affairs will go on like clock work. xxxxxx I am glad to hear that ———[2] has regained his situation at the Navy Yard. When next you see him tell him from me, to be "true to himself" for every thing depends upon his good conduct. He has excellent qualities, and if he takes pains with himself, and marks out for himself a strict line of upright and honourable conduct, his path through life will be prosperous and pleasant; and I will endeavour all in my power to make it so. Above all he must guard against being led away by idle helter skelter companions, however inviting their companionship may seem. He must have an *honourable* pride in respect to his expenses; regulating them by his purse, however slender that may be; and must never be ashamed to acknowledge himself poor. There is nothing degrading in poverty when it is unattended by meanness. I never was prouder in my life, nor mingled more respectably in society than when excessively pinched in purse—But I made ⟨it⟩ a rule never to borrow money and never to run in debt—when I could not afford eighteen pence I dined for a shilling, and was not ashamed the world should know it. [*end of MS*]

MANUSCRIPT: Va.–Barrett (copy).

The copyist indicated omissions by the use of "x x x x" throughout.

1. This letter has not been located.
2. This blank was left by the copyist. WI may be referring to Washington, Mary's brother, for whom WI had solicited a commission in the Marines in March, 1842. See WI to Daniel Webster, March 22, 1842.

1448. To Catharine Paris

Madrid, August 3d. 1842

My dear Sister,

The day before yesterday I had my audience of the Regent, Espartero duke of Victoria, to present to him my original letter of credence, from the President to the Queen. I was accompanied by Mr Vail, who went to take leave, and by Alexander Hamilton as Secretary of Legation. We were in diplomatic uniform. The Regent resides in a very spacious palace called Buena Vista formerly belonging to The Prince of the Peace. It has an elevated scite, with terraces in front: so that it might resist an attack and maintain a respectable defense; an important consideration in the ↑residence of the↓ present Military head of this government; who is surounded by dangers and the object of incessant machinations. We passed by centinals posted at the entrance and in various parts of the palace and were introduced into an anteroom of spacious dimensions, with busts of Espartero in two of the Corners, and a picture of him in one of his most celebrated battles. Some of his officers & aids de camp were in this room, as well as Mr Cavalcanti de Albuquerque, Charge d'affaires of Brazil, who came to deliver letters of credence as ⟨Mi⟩ Resident Minister. After a little while we ↑(Mr Vail Hamilton & myself)↓ were ushered into an inner Saloon ↑at one end of↓ which Espartero stationed himself, with Count Almodovar, Minister of State, on his right hand[.] I advanced and read in Spanish a short address[1] stating that I ⟨deliv⟩ had the honor of delivering the letter of the President to the Queen, into his hands as Regent of the Kingdom, and expressing the sentiments of respect and good will entertained by my government for the Sovereign of this country for its institutions & its people; its desire to draw still closer the bonds of amity which exist between the two nations, and its ardent wish for the prosperity & glory of Spain under its present constitutional form of Government. I concluded by expressing my own feelings of gratification in being appointed to a mission the only object of which I trusted, would be to cultivate the relations of good will between my own country and a country which I had ever held in the highest consideration. My address was well received and the Regent replied in a manly, frank, cordial and courteous manner, responding to the expressions of national good will, and ending with some complimentary expressions to myself. I then introduced Mr Hamilton as Secretary of Legation; after which Mr Vail having taken leave of the Regent with ⟨some⟩ mutual expressions of respect & good will, we retired to the ant[e]room[2] to make way for the Brazilian Minister.

It being signified to us that the Queen would receive us at the Royal Palace we drove thither, but had to wait some time in the apartment of Count Almodovar, the Queen being at that time taking a sulphur bath, which she takes frequently on account of a cutaneous complaint.[3] After a while we had notice that she ⟨h⟩ was prepared to receive us. We accordingly passed through the spacious court, up the noble stair case, and through the long suites of apartments of this splendid edifice, most of them silent, & vacant, the casements closed to keep out the heat, so that a twilight ⟨reigned seemed throught⟩ ↑reigned throughout↓ the mighty pile, not a little emblematical of the dubious fortunes of its inmates. ↑It seemed more like traversing a convent than a palace↓ I ought to have mentioned that on ascending the grand staircase we found the Portal at the head of it, opening into the royal suite of apartments, still bearing the marks of the midnight attack upon the Palace in October last,[4] when an attempt was made to get possession of the persons of the little Queen and her Sister,[5] to carry them off, that their presence might give strength and authority to the party of the Queen Mother ⟨who⟩ ↑⟨Queen Maria Christina,[6] now at Paris⟩↓ on any contemplated insurrection or invasion of the country to regain the authority which she had abdicated. The marble casement of the doors had been shattered in several places, and the double doors themselves pierced all over with bullet holes, from the musquetry that played upon them from the Stair case during that eventful night. What must have been the feelings of those poor children ⟨hearing from⟩ ↑⟨on⟩ listening↓ from their apartment to the horrid tumult, the outcries of a furious multitude, and the reports of fire arms, echoing and reverberating through the vaulted halls and spacious courts of this immense edifice; and dubious ⟨what might be⟩ whether their own lives were not the object of the assault.

After passing through various chambers of the Palace ↑now silent and sombre, but↓ which I had traversed in former days, on grand court occasions in the times of Ferdinand VII, ⟨and which were then⟩ ↑when they were↓ glittering with all the splendor of a Court, we paused in a great Saloon, with high vaulted cieling encrusted with florid devices in

porcelain, and hung with Silken tapestry, but all in dim twilight like
the rest of the Palace. At one end of the Saloon a door opened to an
⟨interminab⟩ almost interminable range of other chambres, through which
at a distance we had a glimpse of some indistinct figures in black. They
glided into the Saloon, Slowly and with noiseless step. It was the little
queen, with her governess Madame Mina, widow of the general of that
name, and her Guardian, the excellent Arguellos, all in deep mourning
for the Duke of Orleans.[7] The little Queen advanced some steps within
the Saloon and then paused; Madame Mina took her station a little
distance behind her. The ⟨Queen Queen who⟩ ↑Count Almodovar then
introduced me to ⟨her⟩ ↑the Queen↓ in my official capacity and she received with a grave and quiet welcome expressed in a very low voice.↓
↑She↓ is nearly twelve years of age & is sufficiently ⟨g⟩well grown for
her years. She has a somewhat fair complexion; quite pale, with bluish
or light grey eyes; a grave demeanor but a graceful deportment. I
could not but regard her with deep interest, knowing what important
interests depended upon the life of this fragile little being, and ↑to↓
what a stormy and precarious carreer she might be destined. Her solitary
position also, separated from all her kindred, ⟨but⟩ ↑except↓ her little
sister, a mere effigy of royalty in the hands of states men; and surrounded
by the formalities and ceremonials of state, which spread sterility round
the occupant of a throne. I must observe, however, that the little Queen
and her sister are treated with great deference and protecting kindness;
that in Madame Mina, and in the upright, intelligent and kind hearted
Arguelles they have the best of guardians. I was sorry that the Queen's
sister was not present as I was desirous of having a near view of her
having heard her much spoken of for her beauty; she is also of a more
healthful constitution than the queen. As I was retiring from the presence
chamber I was overtaken by Arguelles; who accosted me in the most
cordial manner, reminding me of our having met in London, at the time
of my return from Spain, when he was in a state of exile. I had not
reccollected the circumstance; though I well remembered having heard
him often spoken of during my former residence in Spain, as one of the
best spirits of the Nation. He promised to call upon me; and I look
forward with interest to cultivating an intimacy with a man, who holds
⟨so important a trust⟩ in his hands ⟨an important⟩ ↑a sacred↓ trust so
important to the future destinies of Spain. He and Espartero are men
I felt extreme interest in seeing. Espartero is a fine manly soldierlike
fellow, with a frank deportment, a face full of resolution and intelligence
and a bright, beaming black eye. He was dressed in full uniform with
various orders. He has before him a grand carreer if he follows it out
as he has begun, and is permitted to ⟨complete his⟩ carry it to a successful termination. I am inclined to think his ambition of the right kind and

that he has the good of his country at heart. If he can conduct the affairs of Spain through the storms and quicksands that beset his Regency; if he can establish the present constitutional form of government on a firm basis, and, when the Queen arrives at the age to mount the throne, resign the power into her hands, and give up Spain to her, reviving in its industry and its resources, peaceful at home and respected abroad; he will leave a name in history to be enrolled among the most illustrious of patriots.

I cannot but feel a deep interest in the fortunes of this harrassed, impoverished, depressed, yet proud spirited and noble country, and a most earnest desire to see it relieved from its troubles and embarrassments, and re-established in a prosperous and independent stand among the nations.

—I was interrupted in my letter by a visit from the Bishop of ⟨Toledo⟩ Cordova & Toledo,[8] the Patriarch of the Indias. It was a visit of ceremony, I having sent my card to him after I had been presented to the Regent. The Bishop came in his robes, attended by his Vicar and made me a long and very friendly visit. He holds the diocese of Granada also, and, will one day be primate of Spain, should the Pope take the Kingdom once more into his holy keeping. The Bishop is an intelligent affable and very conversable old gentleman; and, having read my works, was particularly communicative about those subjects of Spanish history antiquities &c, about which I had treated. I was happy to hear from him that pains are taking at present to put the Alhambra in a state of repair, and to restore many parts that have been falling to decay. After conversing with me for some time he enquired after Alexander Hamilton, and appeared to be acquainted with the name and reputation of his grandfather. I sent for Hamilton with whom he likewise had considerable conversation and then took leave of us with many kind expressions. Indeed I must say from every person with whom I have had any intercourse since my arrival I have experienced the most marked respect and cordial good will all claim me as an acquaintance from my writings, and all welcome me as a "friend of Spain."

I am looking for the arrival of my books and papers which were forwarded from New York to Cadiz. As soon as I receive them I shall ⟨be⟩ set to work at my life of Washington, and foresee that I shall have abundant liesure here for literary occupation. In the mean time I shall go on with other literary matters that I have in hand, and trust that my present residenc[e][9] in Spain, like my former one, will be highly favorable for the exercise of the pen. The climate seems to suit me, and to capacitate me for ⟨literary⟩ intellectual labor. The air is pure, elastic and invigorating. I am not debilitated by the heat of summer, for there is no humidity in the atmosphere. Now while I am writing in my room at eleven Oclock in the morning the temperature of my chamber is delightful; though no doubt the action of the sun out of doors is powerful—

As I shall send this letter open to Sarah I shall leave the rest to be filled up by her. For household particulars I refer you to a letter written by this same opportunity to my darling little Mary. With love to all,

Your affectionate brother
Washington Irving

Mrs. Daniel Paris

Madrid. Aug 13. This letter having been detained a week by missing the courier of the French Embassy, I shall add a few lines before sending it off—I have just received yours of June 23,[10] which came by the way of Havre. You can have no idea how delightful your letters are to me; giving me such a perfect picture of my dear little home and all its inmates. You express a desire to know every thing concerning my establishment. I have already spoken of it in my letter to Mary. I have concluded to remain in the apartments formerly occupied by Mr Vail; being a part of the family residence of the Duke San Lorenzo. The apartments are Spacious; the whole mansion has a highly respectable appearance: ⟨and⟩ the Saloons are to be newly painted & papered and various alterations made ⟨to adopt the whole to⟩ which will render the whole very handsome & convenient. My servants, after upwards of a fortnights trial, continue to please me; every thing goes on quietly orderly and comfortably, and my little diplomatic family is an amiable and a cheerful one. I have not yet set up my carriage not having been able to procure good horses. I have engaged a good coachman; whose term of service & wages will commence as soon as he can find horses to suit me.[11]

Since I began this letter the Duchess of Victoria, wife to the Regent has returned from a country excursion. I have made her my visit as Minister and am highly pleased with her. She [is][12] a worthy partner of the elevated fortunes of her gallant husband.[13] She will soon commence her weekly Soirees, which will bring the diplomatic ⟨court⟩ ↑corps↓, and the Court people together, and enable me to look round me in Society. In some future letter I will give you a little sketch of ⟨the⟩ Spanish affairs and Spanish characters in high places that you may be able to form some distinct idea of the actual Situation and Government of Spain, which must be all bewilderment to you

Your affectionate brother
WI.

MANUSCRIPT: Yale.   PUBLISHED: PMI, III, 220–24 (in part).

1. For the text of WI's remarks and Regent Espartero's response to them, see WI to Daniel Webster, August 2, 1842.

2. WI omitted the *e*.

3. Isabella was afflicted with ichthyosis, an ailment which caused the skin to be dry and scaly. See Peter de Polnay, *A Queen of Spain*, pp. 55–56.

4. On October 7, 1841, a group of officers, led by Diego de León, attempted, on orders from María Christina, to kidnap the queen, but her halbardiers, commanded by Colonel Dulce, repulsed the attack and foiled the attempted abduction. See de Polnay, *A Queen of Spain*, pp. 64–67.

5. Infanta Luisa Fernanda (1832–1897).

6. María Christina Fernanda de Borbon (1806–1878) was the fourth wife of Ferdinand VII and queen regent from 1833 to 1840. In 1840 she resigned her regency and went to France, returning to Spain in 1843 when Isabella was declared of age. María Christina reentered politics but was later (1854) again forced into exile because of her scheming and her scandalous behavior. See de Polnay, *A Queen of Spain*, pp. 19–28, 59–69, 88–91, 162–72.

7. Ferdinand, duke of Orléans (b. 1810), was the eldest son of Louis Philippe and Marie Amélie, who was the sister of María Christina. The duke, who had died as a result of a fall from a carriage, was Queen Isabella's first cousin. See Alexandre Dumas, *The Last King of France, Being a History from the Birth of Louis Philippe in 1773 to the Revolution of 1848*, trans. R. S. Garnett, 2 vols. (London, 1915), II, 176.

8. Juan José Bonel y Orbe (1782–1857), who was ordained in 1805 and successively held the bishoprics of Ibiza, Málaga, and Córdoba, had been made patriarch of the Indias in December, 1839, and confessor to the queen in October, 1840. See *Diccionario de Historia Eclesiastica de España* (Madrid, 1970), I, 273, 617; II, 1048.

9. WI ran off the page before completing the word.

10. This letter has not been located.

11. A section in the middle of the page about 2½ inches high and extending the width of the page has been cut out.

12. WI omitted the bracketed word.

13. WI's admiration for the wife of Espartero was to increase as he watched her at public functions and as she expressed her solicitude during WI's illness. See Bowers, *Spanish Adventures of WI*, pp. 174–75, 179–80.

1449. To Count Almodóvar

Legation of the United States / Madrid August 4th. 1842

The Undersigned, Envoy Extraordinary and Minister Plenipotentiary of the United States of America has the honor to represent to his Excellency Count de Almodovar, First minister of State, and of Foreign Affairs of Her Catholic Majesty, that the officers of the Customs, in this City have declined to deliver without first inspecting them, a Trunk and other Baggage addressed to this Legation, and to solicit that an order may be issued for their delivery without examination.

As several Trunks and Boxes containing his Personal Effects are expected to arrive within two or Three Weeks, The Undersigned begs leave to suggest, in order to avoid the necessity of repeated Applications of this character, that a General order be issued for their delivery.

The Undersigned takes this occasion to offer to Count de Almodovar, renewed assurances of his very distinguished Consideration.

Washington Irving

MANUSCRIPT: Archivo de Ministerio de Asuntes Exteriores (Madrid); NA, RC 84 (letterbook copy).

1450. To Sarah Storrow

Madrid Aug 4th 1842

My dear Sarah,

I enclose with this two open letters for your Mother & for Mary Irving, which, after you have read you will seal up and forward. I must make my letters for home answer in this way, for yourself occasionally; it will save me the repetition of many items of intelligence, and enable me to keep you all *au courant de mes affaires* without the necessity of my writing so voluminously as I should otherwise have to do; and which would be extremely inconvenient, when I came to exercise my pen, (as I soon shall) in literary labors. My letter to Mary will give you a picture of my domestic establishment. In consequence of my arrangement with Mr Vail I have at once been put in possession of a home; and, though but a week has lapsed since my arrival in Madrid, every thing goes on regularly and pleasantly. You would have been quite amused to see me bestirring myself like a veteran housekeeper: looking into every hole and corner; ordering & arranging every thing; reforming abuses; putting a stop to wastes & extravagances, and exacting scrupulous order, punctuality & cleanliness. I have succeeded in several respects. My house is conducted with quiet; my meals are served ⟨with⟩ precisely at the hour specified, and as to cleanliness: though it would not pass muster with a Dutch housewife, yet I have attained to a degree quite notable in Spain.

—Benjamin has just brought in the papers & letters by the mail, and among the latter I find one from you dated 27 July.[1] I cannot express to you how welcome it is—I feel the value of letters here, more than I have done any where else. I am so cut off from all my friends & connexions. I am glad to find you are so well pleased with St Germain and also that it meets with the approbation of little Miss Maam. It also gives me no small pride and pleasure to hear that the little woman has actually laughed aloud—as I value myself upon being the first to teach her to laugh at all. I really believe had I not taken pains with her in that respect during my sojourn in Paris she would have remained a grave little personage all her life ⟨only⟩ crying occasionally. I will not talk any thing more about her at present, lest it should get to her ears and make her vain.

I was sure you would like Mr Lee; he is a most agreeable intelligent gentleman like young man and a first rate travelling companion. When you see him give him my kindest regards and tell him I shall be most happy to hear from him. Hector who used to go "Sight seeing" with him desires to be particularly remembered to him and would be delighted to play the part of Cicerone for him and shew him the wonders of Madrid.

When you see the Jones's[2] too, remember me to them most cordially. I shall be glad to hear particulars of their sojourn in Paris, and how they get on, and how they are pleased. I did not think they would relish London, but I feel persuaded they will find much to interest and delight them in Paris.

You are curious about the little Queen and her sister. The inclosed letter to your mother will give you some particulars about them. I feel a great interest in them; isolated as they are, at such a tender age, Surrounded by dreary magnificence, and by the political and military precautions incident to the present position of this government. They have, however, kind and excellent people about them under whose care they will be likely to be better instructed than ↑they would have been↓ in the ordinary routine of a Spanish Court. Every evening they drive out in a carriage drawn by six horses; ⟨h⟩ followed by another in which are their attendants, and escorted by a troop of horse—In this state they repair to a portion of the Retiro or Royal park. Separated from the rest and devoted to their recreation, or they drive up and down the Prado; a public promenade. I have given your mother ⟨a pi⟩ an account of my presentation to the Queen in the Royal palace. It was one of the most impressive scenes I ever went through, from past associations with the place and from the peculiar situation of its present occupants. The poor little Queen, in her black habiliments, and her few attendants, gliding noiselessly like a shadow through the silent and twilight apartments of that great edifice, and looking so pale and almost melancholy! God protect the poor innocent little being through the perilous carreer that is before her.

I begin to feel now more *en regle* than I have done ⟨for⟩ ever since my appointment. Having formed my establishment; presented my letters of credence, and made my visits of Ceremony I feel installed in my official station and begin to realize that I am actually a Minister; for I could not habituate myself to the thought while living in my usual simple informal way. My household establishment too, goes on comfortably. My servants appear to be good ones, and the young gentlemen of the legation are every thing I could wish.

Give my kind remembrance to Mr Storrow and my thanks for his letter inclosing one from New York.[3] Let me know all that you hear interesting from home; kiss little Miss Maam abundantly for me and write to me soon.

> Your affectionate uncle
> Washington Irving.

P.S—I leave a page or so in your mothers letter for you to fill up—You may also write something in Mary's to the girls.

ADDRESSED: À Madame / Madame Storrow / aux Soins de Mr. T. W Storrow / ⟨[unrecovered]⟩ / 17 Rue du faubourg Poissonniere / a Paris   DOCKETED: August 4th 1842
MANUSCRIPT: Yale.   PUBLISHED: Simison, Keogh Papers, pp. 189–92.

Above the address is written "No. 1."

1. This letter has not been located.
2. Probably WI's neighbors and friends from the Tarrytown area.
3. These letters have not been located.

1451. To Charles Callaghan

Legation of the United States / Madrid 5th. August 1842

Charles Callaghan Esq. / Philadelphia.
Sir,

I have received your letter of June 25th. in relation to the claimants under the Spanish Indemnity Certificates.[1]

With the disposition to do every thing in my power to forward the just claims for Indemnity of American Citizens, I regret that I cannot comply with the requests contained in your letter, not being at liberty to act under any other Instructions than those from the Department of State, to which also, I can alone report any measures, which may have been taken upon this subject.[2]

> I am, Sir, your obdt Sert.
> Washington Irving

MANUSCRIPT: NA, RG 84 (letterbook copy).

1. A convention for the settlement of claims was ratified by the United States on May 15, 1834, and by Spain on July 23, 1834, and provided for the payment of the equivalent of $600,000 to the United States. The certificates were apparently issued against this sum. See Moore, *International Arbitrations*, V, 4533–47.

2. WI was observing the stipulation that U.S. citizens making claims must initiate action with a petition filed with the secretary of state. See Moore, *International Arbitrations*, VI, 609.

1452. To Messrs. Peters & Co.

Legation of the United States / Madrid 5th. August 1842.

Messrs Peters & Co. New York
Gentlemen,
Your letter of May 21st.[1] asking for information in regard to the Spanish Indemnity Certificates was received on the 2nd. Instant at this Legation.

The claims of American Citizens under the Treaty to which you allude, have been very earnestly presented to the attention of the Spanish Government by Mr. Vail late Charge d'Affaires—I regret that I am not authorized to comply with your request to be informed as to the movements of the Government of Spain in relation to these Certificates, and can only refer you to the Department of State which can exercise on these points a discretion not allowed to the Foreign Ministers of the United States.

I am very respectfully / Your Obdt Sert
Washington Irving.

MANUSCRIPT: NA, RG 84 (letterbook copy).

John Peters & Co., commercial merchants located at 57 South Street, is listed in *Longworth's Directory for 1841–42*, p. 558.

1. This letter has not been located.

1453. To Gurdon Bradley

Legation of the United States. / Madrid 9th. August 1842.

Gurdon Bradley Esqr. / Consul U. S. for the Port of Mayagues
Sir.
Under direction from the Secretary of State I applied on the 2nd. Instant for your Exequatur. The Rule adopted by the Government of

Spain on this subject will I am afraid cause a very considerable delay in granting it.

As you have been informed by the State Department that the Exequatur cannot be delivered or forwarded to you until the Spanish Fees of office are paid I would suggest that you should (as is done in other cases to avoid delay) direct your Agent in this City to make the payment as soon as he receives notice from this Legation that the Exequatur is ready for Delivery.

> I am Sir respectfully / Your Obdt Sert
> Washington Irving.

MANUSCRIPT: NA, RG 84 (letterbook copy).

1454. To Daniel Webster

> Legation of the United States / Madrid August 10th 1842.

No. 2. / The Hon. Daniel Webster. / Secretary of State of the United States Washington.

Sir

I have the honor to enclose the Accounts and Vouchers of this Legation for the Quarter ending this day, shewing a balance of $43.28 in favor of the United States, carried to their credit in the next account: The Accounts will be made up at the close of September, to coincide with the division of the year, suggested in the Instructions from the Department.

As no direct opportunity offers for more than a month, I also transmit herewith a letter for Mr. Gurdon Bradley informing him of the application for his Exequatur.

> I am Sir, with great respect / Your Obdt Sevt.
> Washington Irving

P. S. I enclose also a short statement of the first quarters Salary and outfit.

> W. I.

DOCKETED: Rec Sept 20 / Mr. Markoe
MANUSCRIPT: NA, RG 59.

Only the signature and postscript is in WI's hand.

1455.   To Sarah Storrow

Madrid, ↑Friday.↓ Aug. 12th. 1842

My dear Sarah,

I wrote you a brief letter last week, enclosing others for your perusal addressed to your Mother & to Mary Irving. This pacquet ought to have gone by the Courier of the French Embassy, last Saturday, but was sent to the office too late, it will reach you therefore at the same time with this letter, which goes by the Courier of tomorrow—I have just received your letter from St Germain (no date)[1] acknowledging the receipt of my first letter from Madrid;[2] and giving me an account of your having witnessed the funeral of the Duke of Orleans; and met with the Jones Family. The funeral must have been very grand and imposing; and from the peculiar circumstances of the case, calculated to awaken sympathies seldom felt on witnessing ⟨the⟩ ↑royal↓ obsequies. ⟨of⟩ the effect of this death upon Louis Phillip must have been stupendous. It seemed like an awful visitation from heaven to humble human pride, and ↑to↓ confound ⟨to⟩ at one blow, the whole scheme of worldly prosperity and agrandisement, of one of the sagest and most fore seeing of monarchs. No death in Europe could have struck so completely on the general pulse of political affairs; what will be its ultimate effect no one can foresee, but it will materially change the policy of nations. There is no royal family in the world, moreover, in which a death of one of its members could carry more desolation, from the affinity which they have ever maintained in their habits, tastes and sympathies with the fresh and simple habitudes of common life. Amidst all the pomp and ceremonial of royalty they have loved each other with true bourgeois affection—I feel most especially for the Queen; who is a mother in all the tenderness of the word. Little did I think, when I looked with no ordinary interest on her amiable countenance ⟨ever⟩ pale and emaciated with care, and her Silver hair, Silvered more by anxiety than age, that so soon another sorrow, more overwhelming than any hitherto sustained, was to bow her towards the grave.

I have little to add about affairs in Madrid in addition to what you will find in the letters written last week. The warm weather which still prevails keeps me very much at home, excepting when I have to make or return visits of ceremony. By keeping my windows closed, and having thick walls between me and the Sun, and Spacious apartments, I pass the day comfortably enough; and sometimes do not go out even in the evening; excepting it is to pay a visit in the other wing of this great mansion, to my fair neighbor & country woman Madame Albuquerque, whom I find extremely amiable and conversible. To day we all dine with

Mr Albuquerque, and shall meet at his table some of the diplomatic corps, and some of the court dignitaries—As I have no horses yet, and it is rather a long warm walk ↑from my residence↓ through the town to the public walk of the Prado, I sometimes about sun set, take an airing on the public parade or terrace in front of the Royal palace, which is not far distant from my dwelling. The palace is built ↑on the confines of the city↓ along the edge of a steep descent into the valley of the Mansanares³ along the Terrace runs a parapet commanding an ⟨vast⟩ extensive view over the valley, with ⟨unrecovered⟩ the Mansanares gleaming from among avenues & groves of trees; vast naked hills and plains beyond; and the Guadarama Mountains⁴ in the distance. On this parapet Hamilton and myself occasionally take our seat; watch the setting of the sun behind the Guadarama Mountains, and as we gaze on their purple outlines boldly marked on the pure evening sky; talk about home, and the glorious sunsets ⟨and blue hu⟩ of the Hudson and the purple outlines of its Western hills—In fact the more I think of home the more it assumes the tints and colorings of romance to me; and I deck out sweet little Sunnyside with all the ideal charms the imagination of the lover bestows upon his absent mistress. You tell me you have received "a long delightful letter from your mother giving you all the news of dear little Sunnyside"—why did you not transcribe a part, if not the whole of it; every scrape of a pen concerning home is delightful to me. I beg you will be more communicative in this respect next time.

I continue to get on very comfortably with my Spanish household. The servants are regular and attentive, and answer to the good character given of them. My young gentlemen form a very pleasant family.

The Duchess of Victoria, wife to the Regent, who has been absent at one of the Royal Country Seats returned to town a few days since, when I paid her a visit accompanied by Mr Hamilton. I was very much pleased with her. She is one of the handsomest women I have seen in Spain; about twenty eight years of age; a fine brunette, with black hair, fine dark eyes; her person well shaped though a little inclining to embonpoint; her manners extremely affable, graceful and engaging. She sustains the elevated station to which she has been raised by the gallant and patriotic achievements of her husband; with native dignity and propriety. The old nobility have, (who are like the ancient Noblesse of the Faubg St Germain with respect to Louis Philip,) affect to look down upon the duchess as a parvenue; and she has been falsely represented as ⟨the⟩ the daughter of some obscure tradesman of Legroño. She is, however, the daughter of a military officer; and whether she derived it from nature, or has acquired it by cultivation, has certainly one of the most pleasing and ⟨gra⟩ easy and graceful modes of receiving company that I have ever witnessed at any court. I take great interest in Espartero; who is a frank, open, manly fellow, with direct good sense and I firmly believe patriotic purpose; and it delights me to find him so well suited in a partner to share his dignities and grace his station. As soon as the weather grows cooler the Duchess will ⟨have⟩ ↑resume↓ her Soirees which I am told are well attended. I shall be glad of the opportunit⟨ies⟩y they will give me to gain a nearer and more familiar knowledge of the Regent and his spouse.

I am looking anxiously for the arrival of my packages from Paris containing my china ware, linen &c &c, that I may complete my establishment; having to make shift for the present by hiring various articles for household use. I am desirous also for the arrival of my books and papers; that I may resume my literary avocations and turn my abundant liesure to account.

Yesterday I had a visit from Mr Aston[5] the British Minister, who has just returned from a visit to La Granja.[6] He was extremely friendly and off hand in his manner and I think we will become very sociable.

Among my various visitors was ⟨Sign⟩ Senor Escalente, one of the principal officers of Government; a very agreeable accomplished man, who among his various offices has been Governor of Granada. He expressed himself very handsomely about my writings respecting that city, and told me he was in England when my "Alhambra["]"[7] was published, and that he had translated parts of it as an exercise. Indeed I find that little work continually acting, as a passport for me to the good graces of the Spaniards.

I am glad that you have my amiable friend Mrs Thorndike as a neighbor at St Germain. She is a lovely woman in character manners and person. You could not have a *safer* companion. The piquant society of Mrs Ledyard[8] also will give quite a zest to your little circle. I was very much amused with her conversation in Paris, and there was a real honesty in her satire whenever she chose to exert it.

Does little Miss Maam follow up her equestrian exercises upon the Donkeys?—You cannot think how that little fairy dwells in my thoughts— I am continually recalling her looks and caprices, her glances of the eye, curlings of the lip and sulky mumblings of her fists—It is quite ridiculous to think so much about such an "exceedingly abundantly little small child" but I cannot help it. I really am haunted by her.

I hope you will give me further anecdotes of the progress of the Jones' family, though I confess I cannot help feeling a strong dash of concern for them. I reccollect all their kind good qualities and regret to see them launching off from the Safe shore of home and domestic life and drifting among the whirlpools and quicksands of Paris society. I fear they will have various causes hereafter to lament their aspirations after the Aristocratic scenes of Europe. When next you see them give them my kindest remembrances and best wishes—and my sincere advice that thcy make no home or abiding place but in their own country.—But upon second thought it is ⟨a⟩ useless and impertinent to volunteer advice in other peoples concerns; so you need not deliver it.

You tell me "you are almost affraid you will weary me with your repeated letters & have no doubt you often write of things I care nothing about—" My dear girl never ⟨utter⟩ ↑write↓ such another sentence—You could not ⟨fell⟩ feel and think what you write, and must have felt and known that your letters could not be too frequent for me; nor their contents trivial. Indeed, ⟨if bef⟩ before the receipt of your last I had bėen looking day after day for a line from you; ⟨expe⟩ in reply to the one I had written on my arrival. I beg you to write to me as often as you can, and never to regard the importance or triviality of ⟨the⟩ what you write. Cut off as I am from all conversation and personal intercourse with those I love their letters are my most precious solace.

With kind remembrances to your husband and many Kisses to my dear little Kitty

> Your affectionate uncle
> Washington Irving

Remember me kindly to the Thorndikes, Ledyards &c

Aug. 13. I have just recd. a letter from your mother dated 23d. June.[9] It is as usual crowded with precious anecdotes and details of home life at dear little Sunnyside. I read it over and over, until my heart is in my throat and my eyes full of tears; they are delicious tears however, for I ⟨read⟩ meet with nothing but pictures of domestic happiness and sweet rural enjoyment. She says old Mrs Renwick[10] had paid the cottage a visit. "She went round the place and admired how much every thing was grown and improved. The ivy has grown very thick and beautiful and will in a few years cover the whole side of the cottage. I think every thing more luxuriant than usual this year. We have had fine summer weather for a few days past and I have walked out under the trees and surveyed the exceeding beauty of the whole scene. I think my health is improving since I came in the country[.] I am always better in summer." and again—⟨all matters are going on comfortably⟩. I have just come up ⟨from⟩ ↑after↓ breakfast Kate has been singing some of her plaintive songs for me which I love to hear. Julia and our dear little Mary have been arranging the flowers for the centre table. All matters are going on comfortably. The morning is bright and lovely and for a long time before the family were stirring I was admiring from my windows the exceeding beauty of all around. There are more birds than I have ever known, singing sweetly. The little wren has taken possession of her house. Brother Ebenezer, Kate Charlotte and myself went for a drive yesterday above the old church.

I enjoyed it exceedingly. I have not strength to go far but I think I shall soon be able to take the round of my favorite drive Sawmill River. The carriages are all in very nice order, and my old friend has been nicely refitted with an extension top, looking like a new carriage."

———————

Yesterday Mr Albuquerque gave a diplomatic dinner in the other wing of the Mansion, in compliment to my arrival. ⟨The who⟩ Nearly the whole diplomatic corps (which ⟨at p⟩ is not very numerous just now) was present and I became acquainted with my confreres. Count Almodovar, Minister of State, and two or three other dignitaries of the government were likewise guests. The dinner was a very handsome one; but Albuquerques apartments are not as spacious as mine, and what with the number of persons and lights; ⟨and⟩ the narrowness of the dining room and the heat of the weather; it was rather a melting affair. After dinner Mr Aston the British Minister took Hamilton & myself in his carriage to the theatre, introduced us into his box, and after the theatre was over we adjourned to his house and took ices. I was much gratified with commencing my acquaintance with him in so social a style, and from his evidently friendly disposition and his frank pleasant manners, I anticipate that we shall become quite intimate. His Secretary, Mr Scott,[11] whom I used to know at Bordeaux, is absent with his wife at La Granja, but has sent me the most cordial messages. I am pleased with the French Charge d'Affaires the Duke de Glucksburgh.[12] Son of the Duke de Caze. He is amiable & gentlemanlike and appears disposed to be on a very friendly footing.

By the bye I ought to mention that my visit to the theatre with the British Minister was the first I had made, since my arrival, to any place of amusement; the warm weather having deterred me. I saw part of an Italian opera and a grotesque Italian ballet. There is an indifferent Italian company playing at a circus which has been fitted up for the purpose and another indifferent one playing occasionally at one of the Theatres; but it is expected we shall have a very respectable one in the Autumn—

When the weather is cooler I shall be a frequent visitor to the operas, such as they are; being able always to find much to relish in the music even though the singing be indifferent.

MANUSCRIPT: Yale.   PUBLISHED: LFSS, pp. 47–48 (in part).

1. This letter has not been located.

2. Written on July 25, 1842.

3. The Manzanares River, which begins in the eastern slopes of the Guadarrama Mountains, flows about fifty-five miles in a south-southeasterly and eastern direction and empties into the Jarama River about eleven miles southeast of Madrid. See Leon E. Seltzer, ed., *Columbia-Lippincott Gazetteer* (New York, 1970), p. 1144.

4. The Guadarrama Mountains rise northwest of Madrid, extend about 120 miles

northeast, and separate Old Castile from New Castile. See Seltzer, *Columbia-Lip-pincott Gazetteer*, p. 727.

5. Sir Arthur Ingram Aston was a wealthy Englishman whose cordial friendship and hospitality WI enjoyed during his early months in Madrid. See Bowers, *Spanish Adventures of WI*, pp. 166–67, 174.

6. La Granja at San Ildefonso about seventy miles northwest of Madrid was a royal palace and gardens built by Philip V in the eighteenth century. See Karl Baedeker, *Spain and Portugal*, pp. 120–22.

7. WI omitted the bracketed quotation mark.

8. Matilda Frances Cass, daughter of Lewis Cass, was married to Henry Ledyard on September 19, 1839. Ledyard, who worked in the U.S. legation in Paris from 1836 to 1845, became acquainted with Miss Cass while her father was U.S. minister to France. See Frank B. Woodford, *Lewis Cass, The Last Jeffersonian* (New York, 1973), p. 198.

9. This letter has not been located.

10. Jean Jeffrey Renwick (1774–1850) was a longtime acquaintance whose son James had been a close friend of WI's. For other details, see WI to Henry Brevoort, May 15, 1811.

11. Probably Newton Scott (b. 1810), son of Harry Scott, the British consul at Bordeaux whom WI met in 1825–1826. See Young, *WI-Bordeaux*, pp. 107, 109.

12. Louis Charles Élie Décazes, duke of Glücksberg (1819–1886) was the son of the well-known French statesman, Élie Décazes.

1456. To Catharine Irving

Madrid, August 15th, 1842

My dear Kate,

I yesterday received your letter of the 8th July[1] which was a most agreeable surprise to me as I had supposed you too much occupied with your own affairs to find leisure or mood for letter writing. You need none of you fear being anticipated by your father or by any one else in domestic news; for you all relate somethings that the rest have ommitted; or place things, already related, in a different light; and indeed I have such a relish for everything that relates to home that I can read the same news over and over again with never ceasing interest and gratification. If you all knew what beautiful enjoyment your unaffected, unpretending, simple narratives of domestic life and domestic affairs give me, I am sure your kind good hearts would feel amply repaid for all the labour of the pen.

In letters sent off a day or two since to your Aunt and your sister Mary,[2] I have given so many details of myself and my affairs that I have little more to communicate. Indeed now that I have gotten over the ceremony of delivering my credentials and paying and receiving visits of ceremony, I have dropped into a completely quiet, monotonous kind of life, and shall so continue until the summer heats are over.

I rarely stir out of the house until evening and sometimes not even then; passing occasionally a couple of days without going abroad. The heat here is of a dry parching kind owing to the rarity of the atmosphere; for Madrid, from its great elevation, on the vast table land of Castile, breathes a thin mountain air. By ten o'clock in the morning the streets are all like ovens, and a dull, parching heat prevails until late in the evening; especially this summer which has been unusually sultry. I find the only recourse is to keep all my windows closed, and to remain quiet, in the thinnest summer raiment. As my apartments are spacious and lofty I in this way get through the day without suffering from the heat, but I feel the want of exercise and the absence of all refreshment in the atmosphere. Having been accustomed to the groves and streams and grassy banks of sweet little Sunnyside and the enlivening breezes from the Tappen See, I am less fitted for these parched regions where the city has the temperature of a brick kiln and the country the aspect of a desert. However, the summer heats will soon be past, and I shall then be able to go about, take exercise, and hunt up the resources of Madrid. As yet I have been but once to the theatre; but calculate upon the Italian opera as a great standby in cold weather. We are now beginning to have fine moonlight nights, and I occasionally sally forth about ten o'clock at night and repair to the esplanade before the royal palace (not far from my residence) which overlooks the broad valley of the Manzanares and the sunburnt regions away to the Guadarrama mountains. There I take my seat on the parapet with some of my young diplomatic household; and we enjoy the temperate night breezes rising from the valley; and talk about home and distant friends. The valley of the Manzanares rises north and south like the Hudson; the constellation of the [unrecovered] bears from us just as it does from the cottage; so, with the aid of fancy which is ever ready to lend me a hand, I conjure the dimly lighted landscape into a [unrecovered] of home, and the Guadarrama mountains into the romantic line of heights beyond the Hudson. The only thing that dispells the illusion is when I turn round and behold before me the vast palace, with its colonades and columns all sleeping in the moonshine.

It is a great source of solace to me, in this expatriated state to have about me companions from our common home and circle of relatives and friends. We have so many sympathies and topics of interest common to each other. You would be amused to see, when the mail arrives with a budget of letters from home, what an exchange of anecdotes and gossip takes place among us, and what a fund of [unrecovered] conversation is afforded. My choice of Hamilton as a secretary was a very fortunate one. He is a bright, intelligent, entertaining companion; of most amiable disposition and gentlemanlike manner and is indeed the life of the house. In an official capacity he is clear, quick and comprehensive and calculated, I think to make a first rate diplomat. Indeed altogether I feel quite proud of my diplomatic household. My young gentlemen live together in perfect harmony and make my house quite a pleasant one.

Today Mr. Hamilton and myself take a sociable dinner with Sir Aston the British Minister—who has made the most frank advances toward a cordial acquaintance and whose house I fancy I shall find one of the pleasantest resorts. We are to meet there a son of the Marquess of Northampton[3] and two other young Englishmen who have somehow or other made their way across the Pyranees. It is quite rare to meet with other English or American travellers at Madrid.

Today I expect the arrival of my china, glass, linen, etc. etc from Paris having been more than a month on the way. I shall then get my [*unrecovered*] in order; having had to make shift hitherto by hiring articles of household use, table linen, plates, knives, and forks etc., by the day—not an unusual mode in Spain, where many live from year end to year end in this hand to mouth manner.

Your account of Mr. Minturn,[4] and of his obliging manner of turning his carriage into an omnibus for the accomodation of the neighborhood coincides exactly with my idea of that most generous, kindhearted man; whose great delight is to do good and disperse happiness. I was sure the Minturn family would prove most excellent neighbors.

And now my dear Kate before I finish let me say one thing—and bear it in your mind. Your father writes that the stocks in which you and your sister have money invested have paid no dividend. This must make no difference in your allowance. Sarah has full authority to draw on my resources for the deficit—as to yourself, *I set no limits to your allowance.* In your position you will naturally incur various expenses. I authorize and *enjoin upon you* to get from Pierre M. Irving in my name whatever money you may stand in need of. You must think of me in these months as a parent, and act accordingly and so God bless you my dear and excellent little woman.

Your affectionate uncle
Washington Irving

MANUSCRIPT: Dr. Robert S. Grinnell; transcription at SHR.

1. This letter has not been located.

2. See WI to Catharine Paris and to Mary Irving, both August 3, 1842.

3. Spencer Joshua Alwyne Compton, second marquis of Northampton (1790–1851), had four sons: Charles (1816–1864), who became third marquis; William (1818–1877), who became fourth marquis; Spencer Scott (1821–1855), and Alwyne (1825–1906).

4. Probably Robert B. Minturn (1805–1866), a partner in Grinnell, Minturn & Co. with his brother-in-law, Moses H. Grinnell. Perhaps following Grinnell's example, Minturn maintained a summer residence in the Tarrytown area.

1457. To Eliza Romeyn

Madrid. Aug 16th. 1842

My dear Eliza,

I am writing to so many of you about the same time, that I apprehend I shall be harping pretty much upon the same string, yet if I do not answer all your letters just now, while I have a little liesure, I may fall into a fit of procrastination; for in a short time I shall receive my books and papers, which are slowly on the road, and after their reception I shall be so much occupied in ↑my↓ literary tasks that I shall have but scanty mood and liesure for correspondence

Having no news to tell you that is not in ⟨oth⟩ the other letters to the family, I shall give you a picture of the routine of one day, which will serve pretty much for a specimen of every day in the week. I rise about five oclock, that I may have a good start of the Sun, which rules like a tyrant throughout the day. Throwing open the doors and windows of my chamber, to admit a free current of the morning air, I occupy myself reading & writing until about eight Oclock. At this time the distant sound of military music gives notice of the troops on their way to relieve guard at the Royal palace. In a little while the horse guards pass under my window, with a band of music on horseback, performing some favorite march or military air. I watch and listen as they prance down the street between spacious dwellings of the Nobility, and turn into the passage leading to the palace; by this time another band of music comes swelling from a distance and the foot guards approach in quick step to some glorious march or waltz—by the time these have disappeared I am summoned to breakfast, which is always a lively meal with us. While we are seated at breakfast we again hear the strains of military music and the troops come back from relieving guard: reversing the order of their march: the foot guards coming first and the horse guards afterwards. This pageant which invariably takes place at the same hour every morning is a regale of which we never get tired. ⟨[*unrecovered*] bre⟩ On our breakfast table are laid the Madrid gazettes, which seldom contain any thing of peculiar interest. Shortly after breakfast arrives the mail, with Paris and London papers; which occupy us some time reading and discussing news. Should the mail bring, as it sometimes does, a pacquet of letters for the different members of the household, giving us the news and gossip of home there is a complete scene of excitement, each hurrying over his letters and calling out, every moment, some piece of intelligence, or some amusing anecdote. This over, we separate to our different corner and pursuits; exchanging visits occasionally as circumstances may require or harmony dictate. The ⟨wind⟩ front windows of my apartments look

into one of the main streets; ⟨lead⟩ traversing the city from the Prado or
public walk to the Royal palace, so that every movement of consequence
is sure to pass through it. Immediately opposite some of my windows is
a small square, with the Ayuntamiento or town hall on one side; and a
huge mansion on the other, in a tower of which Francis I.[1] is said to have
been confined when a prisoner in Madrid. In the centre of this square is
a public fountain; thronged all day and until a late hour of the night by
water carriers, male & female servants, and the populace of the neighborhood all waiting for their turns to replenish their kegs ⟨and⟩ pitchers &
other water vessels. An officer of police attends to regulate their turns;
but such is the demand for water in this thirsty climate at this thirsty
season, that the fountain is a continual scene of strife, and clamour. The
groupes that form around it, however, in their different costumes are
extremely picturesque. My day, during this hot weather, is chiefly passed
in my bed room, which I likewise make my study. It is lofty & spacious,
about thirty feet by twenty two; the heat of day is shut out as in the
rest of the house and just sufficient light admitted to permit me to read &
write. Indeed a kind of twilight reigns throughout a spanish house during the summer heats. At five O'clock we dine, after which some take a
siesta, or lounge about until the evening is sufficiently advanced to take
a promenade, either on the Prado, or on the Esplanade ⟨whi⟩ in front of
the Royal palace. Such is the dull heat however that occasionally lingers
in the streets, that I frequently remain at home all the evening; taking my
seat in the balcony of my rooms, where I can catch any night breeze that
is stirring, ⟨then⟩ and can overlook the street. Between nine and ten a
running footman gives notice by the sound of a bugle ⟨that the of [unre-
covered] & for Royal⟩ of the approach of the Queen, on her return from
her evenings drive in the Retiro and on the Prado. Next come three or
four horsemen in advance: then the Royal carriage, drawn by six horses,
in which are the little queen and her sister and their Aya or governess
Madame Mina; as the carriage is an open barouche and passes immediately under my balcony I have a full view of these poor innocent little
beings, in whose isolated situation I take a great interest. Mounted attendants ride beside the carriage and it is followed by a troop of horse,
after which comes another carriage and six, ⟨containing persons⟩ with
those whose duties bring them in immediate attendance upon the persons
of the Queen & princess. After this cortege has passed by I continue in
my balcony until a late hour, enjoying the ⟨raising breezes of the night
which⟩ gradually cooling night air, which grows more and more temperate until towards midnight when I go to bed. Such is the routine of
most of my days during this hot weather: occasionally varied by ⟨the
necessity of making⟩ a sultry visit of Ceremony in the course of the day;
or a stroll late in the evening to the Prado, or the Esplanade about the

Palace. While I am thus cooped up among hot streets and hot walls, without the sight of a green tree or a blade of grass you are enjoying the rural quiet, ⟨and⟩ the green banks and delightful shades of Sunnyside—if you could only be here a little while in these arid regions you would know how to appreciate the freshness and verdure by which you are surrounded. However, the heats of summer will soon be over, and as soon as the weather is temperate enough for me to walk the streets in comfort, I shall be able to take exercise and to visit the places of interest and curiosity. I have as yet been but once to the Royal museum of paintings, but it was like a peep into a gold mine The collection was one of the very best in Europe when I was here before; but such treasures have been added to it of late years, that, to my mind, it surpasses all others that I have seen. This of itself will be an inexhaustible resource to me.

Aug 17. Yesterday Mr Hamilton & myself took a sociable dinner with Mr Aston the British Minister, who is a most agreeable person and disposed to be extremely sociable. We met at his table a young English nobleman Lord Compton,[2] son of the Marquis of Northampton,[3] and a Mr Swinton[4] & Mr Campbell, who are travelling with his lordship. ⟨They⟩ ↑Lord Compton & Mr Swinton↓ are amateur painters and intend to remain some little time here making sketches of some of the masterpieces in the gallery. We had a very pleasant dinner. The travelling party were delighted with their rambles about Spain, and considered it a fortunate incident that they had been robbed by banditti among the romantic mountains of Ronda.[5] Write to me as often as you feel disposed—your letters are just such as I delight to receive

Your affectionate Uncle—
Washington Irving

ADDRESSED: Mrs Eliza Romeyn / care of Ebenr Irving Esqr / New York.
MANUSCRIPT: Va.–Barrett.   PUBLISHED: PMI, III 225–28 (in part)

Eliza Romeyn (1801–1887), WI's niece and the daughter of Ann Sarah Irving and Richard Dodge, was residing temporarily at Sunnyside in the summer of 1842. See PMI, III, 224.

1. Francis I (1494–1547), king of France after 1515, had led a retaliatory force into Italy against Charles V and Charles, duke of Bourbon, and was captured at Pavia on February 24, 1525. He was removed to Madrid and held captive there from July 20, 1525, until March 17, 1526.

2. Charles Douglas, Lord Compton.

3. Spencer Joshua Alwyne Compton, who became second marquis of Northampton in 1828, was an intimate of Walter Scott. He was president of the Royal Society from 1838 to 1844.

4. Probably James Rannie Swinton (1816–1888), a painter who had studied at the school of the Royal Academy in 1840. After traveling in Italy and Spain from 1840 to 1843, he returned to London to become a fashionable portrait painter.

5. Ronda is built on the site of an old Roman town in the mountains about forty-four miles east of Cadiz. See Karl Baedeker, *Spain and Portugal,* pp. 437–39.

1458. To Count Almodóvar

Legacion de los Estados Unidos. / Madrid 17 de Agosto 1842.

Exmo. Sor.

Tengo la honra de remitir a V Exo. la adjunta lista de los articuols y efectos, que he dispuesto introducir del extrangero para el uso de mi casa afin que V. E. se sirva mandar se expedian las competentes ordenes para que me sean entregados los 7. Bultas que acaben de llegar a esta Aduana, fines ignorando yo las leyes vigentes, sobre este particular me han hecho presente que Sin una orden expresa del Ministerio de Hacienda no podra effectuarse dicha entrega.

Appro vecho esta occasion para reiteras a V. E. los sentimientos de la alta consideracion con que tengo la honra de Ser de V. E. Su atento, Segmo Servidor. Q. B. S M.

Washington Irving

Exmo. Sor. / Conde de Almodovar. / Premer Secretario del despacho de Estado &c &c.

Lista.

Caxo:

W. I. 1	Dos Velones con globos de Cristal y otros adherentes.
W. I. 2	Mantelera y ropa de Cama.
W. I. 3	Dos. Docenas Vasos de Cristal. Ocho " Copas para vino de varios clases. 1½ " Carafas &c. 2 Doz. Enguagatorias.
W. I. 5	Un par Candelabras doradas.
W. I. 6	Un Juego do Porcelana blanca.

W. I.   }
   7   }   Un Juego de Porcelana blanca dorada.

W. I.   }
   8   }   Un Juego de Porcelana para pastro.

MANUSCRIPT: NA, RG 84 (letterbook copy).
WI omitted "4" in his list.

Translation:
I have the honor to remit to your excellency the adjoined list of the articles
and items which I have had sent from abroad for the use of my house, in order
that you can issue the necessary orders to have these seven packages, which have
just arrived at the customs office, delivered to me; for since I did not know the
current laws about this matter, they informed me that without an express order
from the ministry of finance this delivery cannot be made.

I take advantage of this opportunity to repeat to your excellency the feelings
of high consideration with which I have the honor to be of your excellency the
humble servant who kisses your hand.

                                                          Washington Irving.

His Excellency / Count Almodovar / First Secretary of the Ministry of State &c &c.

                                        List.
Case:

W. I.   ) Two oil lamps with crystal shades and other effects.
   1   )

W. I.   ) Table and bed linens.
   2   )

) Two dozen crystal vases.
W. I.   (Eight dozen wine glasses of various classes.
   3   (1½ dozen carafes &c.
) 2 doz. finger bowls.

W. I.   ) One pair of gold candelabras.
   5   )

W. I.   ) One set of white porcelain.
   6   )

W. I.   ) One set of gilded white porcelain.
   7   )

W. I.   ) One set of dessert porcelain.
   8   )

1459. To Daniel Webster

(Private)

Madrid. Aug 17th. 1842

My dear Sir,

Understanding that strenuous efforts are making to have Mr Beasley[1] displaced from his situation as Consul at Havre, I feel it a duty both to him and to the Government to speak a word on the subject. I feel myself called upon, in this respect, from the peculiar advantages which an unreserved, and I may say almost fraternal, intimacy with Mr B. for upwards of twenty two years, has given me for knowing his character and conduct: an intimacy which owes its duration and[2] its closeness, solely to a conviction of his sterling worth and his undeviating integrity. In this long intimacy I have had ⟨repeated⟩ ↑constant↓ occasions to witness his intelligent, efficient, upright and straightforward conduct as a public officer: and in more than one instance his judicious, independent and indeed intrepid stand in questions of difficulty and delicacy pertaining to individual and national rights. I have witnessed also with proud satisfaction the high respect which he had acquired, by such conduct, both for his office and himself, from the public authorities and from the most respectable inhabitants of Havre. It is true, a certain resolute integrity in the discharge of his duties, an honest scorn of trick and chicanery and a somewhat abrupt mode of checking arrogant pretensions and assumptions may have rendered him unpopular with some Masters of vessels, who would prefer a consul of a more convenient, conniving and accommodating character; ⟨but⟩ I have seldom known a consul of independent conduct and[3] stern integrity who was a favorite with Sea Captains. I am convinced however, that the most respectable and long established Masters of vessels in the Havre trade will unite in the opinion I have given of Mr Beasley.

Of the intelligent services which he has rendered to our diplomatic concerns from his intimate knowledge of France and its affairs, I believe abundant proofs exist in his occasional correspondence with our government at home and our Missions abroad: in fact I am sure I need refer you to no surer testimonys of the able and upright discharge of his official duties than to the different persons who have held the legation at Paris, especially Mr Rives, or to General Cass himself, the actual Minister

I have been more immediately prompted to this expression of my opinion of Mr Beasley and his official conduct from hearing that an article has recently been published in the Havre papers, signed by

several Captains of vessels, charging Mr Beasley with frequent absence
from his post and neglect of his duties. I would only observe, from my
own knowledge, that the moment siezed upon for this public attack,
was when Mr Beasley was suddenly summoned to Bordeaux, by the
dangerous illness of his worthy father in law,[4] whose very advanced
age made his recovery doubtful, and between whom and Mr Beasley
there exists the strongest attachment. I leave to your own generous mind
to determine what wieght is to be given to such an attack *so timed*.
I will only add that when Mr Beasley happens to be absent from his
office the duties are faithfully and competently discharged by Mr Taylor
who has acted as ↑head clerk or↓ Vice Consul for upwards of twenty
years.

I trust my dear Sir, you will excuse this intervention on my part, but
I could not silently suffer a man to be misrepresented and undermined,
whose official services were so valuable to the Country, when I thought
an honest word from myself might put his character and conduct in a
right light.

Believe me ever with the highest regard

Very faithfully yours
Washington Irving

Hon. Daniel Webster / &c &c &c

DOCKETED: *Private*. / Washington Irving. / 17th. Augt., 1842.
MANUSCRIPT: Harvard.

1. Reuben Beasley was U.S. consul at Le Havre from 1816 to 1845. The attempt
to remove him at this time was obviously unsuccessful. See Hasse, *Index to U.S.
Documents*, I, 101.
2. WI repeated "and."
3. WI again repeated "and."
4. Daniel Guestier (1755–1847) was the father of Jenny-Adelaide Guestier Beasley. See Young, *WI-Bordeaux*, pp. 61–62; and *J&N*, III, 212.

1460.   *To Obadiah Rich*

Legation of the United States / Madrid Augt. 19th. 1842.

O. Rich Esq. / Consul of the U. States—Mahon.
Sir,
Your letter of the 24th ulto. asking for Information in the case of
Gabriel Fronti has been received at this Legation

You state that Mr. Fronti became in 1826, a naturalized Citizen of
the United States and remained there until the year 1835, when he

removed again to his Native Country where he has resided with slight exeception since that time; that he has purchased Property there and that he claims the Protection of an American Citizen with the Spanish Authorities

The Questions involved in your letter and the case of Mr. Fronti are among the most difficult and perplexing which can arise under the law of Nations; Each case of Citizenship lost or acquired by Domicil is to be decided, upon the facts connected with it; the object being in each to ascertain from an examination of the Acts and declarations of the Party what are his real motives and intentions in fixing his domicil—It would be impossible therefore to come to a correct decision upon the slight statement furnished in your letter—It appears that Mr. Fronti after living 10 or 12 years in the United States returned to his Native Country where he has now resided since 1835, a period of seven years, and the rule of ↑Law↓ clearly established on this point, and particularly in our Courts in the case of the "Dos Hermanos" 2nd. Wheat. p. 76.[1] is that the native character easily reverts and that it requires much fewer circumstances to constitute a domicil in the case of a Native Subject, than to impress the National character on one who is originally a Foreigner.

Here is an after residence of seven years by Mr. Fronti in the place of his birth; a longer time than is required under the laws of the United States to make a Citizen of a Foreigner; In addition to this you mention that he has purchased property at Mahon, which if done in his own name, would be exercising a right only allowed to a native Citizen: It would appear therefore that while he is taking advantage of his native character, to enjoy the rights of a Spanish subject, he is also claiming the exemptions and privileges of his adopted american Citizenship; a double character which finds no favor or Support from International Law: The rule in these cases is that if any hardships result from the conflicting claims of Native and acquired allegiance they are properly to be charged to the Person whose acts have given rise to them; and that he takes the advantages of his acquired Citizenship "cum onere."

It is not necessary therefore in the present case to go into the Question of Perpetual Allegiance, since the Party appears by his own acts to have excluded himself from claiming the protection of the American character—If however he can shew to my satisfaction that by overt acts and expressions or by other convincing proofs his long residence in Mahon is to be reconciled with an intention constantly kept in mind of returning to the United States, and with the outward maintenance of the American character; If he can shew that in acquiring property there he has not availed himself of his renounced rights as a Spanish native born Subject, I will do all in my power to procure for him the rights and immunities which would belong to him as a Bona fide American Citizen

I am respectfully. / Your Obdt Sevt.
Washington Irving

MANUSCRIPT: NA, RG 84 (letterbook copy).

Obadiah Rich (1783–1850), with whom WI lived upon his arrival in Madrid in 1826, was a collector of works of early Spanish history and literature. Rich, who opened his library to WI to gather material for his biography of Columbus, served as U.S. consul at Port Mahon in the Balearic Islands from 1834 to 1845. See Hasse, *Index to U.S. Documents*, III, 1398, 1747.

1. Henry Wheaton, "The Dos Hermanos-Green Claimant," *Reports of Cases Argued and Adjudged in the Supreme Court of the United States, February Term, 1817*, II, 76–96; reprinted in Stephen K. Williams, *United States Court Reports* (Rochester, N. Y., 1926), II.

1461.   To Count Almodóvar

Legation of the United States / Madrid August 24th. 1842

The undersigned Envoy Extraordinary and Minister Plenipotentiary of the United States had the honor on the 17th. Instant to address a note to Count Almodovar, First Minister of State and of Foreign Affairs of her Catholic Majesty requesting an order for the delivery of Seven Boxes containing articles destined for his personal use and which were actually in the Custom House of this City. The note was accompanied by a list specifying the contents of the Boxes:

The Undersigned had already felt aggrieved by certain Circumstances of a disrespectful kind, experienced by one of the Gentlemen attached to his Legation from the Officers of the Custom House, and by a threat of delay in the delivery of his Effects; He therefore waited with some anxiety for a reply to his Note. Upwards of a Week has elapsed but no such reply has been given; in the Mean time The Undersigned is daily suffering great inconvenience and incurring expence from the detention of articles indispensable to the daily use and the entire arrangement of his domestic Establishment. Under these Circumstances he trusts ⟨that⟩ he will not be deemed importunate if he again applies to Count Almodovar for an order for the prompt delivery of his Effects, after they shall have been subjected to such scrutiny and such duties as may be required by the Circumstances of the case or the Usages of this Court.

The Undersigned cannot refrain from observing that in passing through

England and France on his way to Spain, though he was entitled to no privileges in those Countries, yet in respectful consideration of his Official Character, his Effects were immediately passed at the Custom Houses free of all examination.[1] It is only since his arrival in this Country, to the Court of which he is accredited that his effects have been subjected to vexatious delays and Suspicious precautions, totally inconsistent with the delicacy and Courtesy universally observed towards Diplomatic Agents and by none, it is believed, more fully experienced than by the Members of Foreign Legations in the United States.

The Undersigned avails himself of this occasion to renew to Count Almodovar the assurances of his most distinguished consideration.

Washington Irving

MANUSCRIPT: NA, RG 84 (letterbook copy); Archivo de Ministerio de Asuntes Exteriores (Madrid).

1. Usually diplomats had their personal and diplomatic baggage passed through customs without inspection or delay. For further discussion of the practice, see John Bassett Moore, *A Digest of International Law*, IV, 675–76. On March 16, 1843, WI was still protesting to Count Almodóvar that his household effects had not arrived. Probably the delay stemmed in part from the unsettled political situation in Spain at this time.

1462.   To Count Almodóvar

[August 27, 1842]

The Undersigned Envoy Extraordinary and Minister Plenipotentiary from the United States of America, has the honor to request that His Excellency Count Almodovar First Minister of State and of Foreign Affairs of her Catholic Majesty will have the goodness to cause the necessary orders to be given for the free admission of the Effects comprised in the accompanying list, designed for the personal and Household use of the Undersigned

As some of these articles are actually on the way from Cadiz and will ↑soon↓ be here; especially the Cases of Books and private papers, of which the Undersigned is hourly in want, the Undersigned would most respectfully request His Excellency Count Almodovar that there may be as little delay as convenient in granting the requisite order.

The Undersigned avails himself with pleasure of this opportunity to renew to Count Almodovar the assurances of his very distinguished consideration.

Washington Irving

Madrid Augt. 27th. 1842. / His Excellency. / Count Almodovar. / &c &c &c.

List of Effects.
2 Carriages
4 Horses
3 Cases of Harness and Saddling
4 Cases of Sugar
4 Cases of Candles
2 Cases of Glass ware
2 Cases of Cutlery
2 Cases of Porcelain
2 Cases of Plated Ware
2 Cases of Bronze and gilt Articles
11 Cases of Household furniture
5 Cases of Linen, Silk cotton and other Stuffs for household furniture
2 Cases of Carpets
6 Cases mens clothes
1 Case Livry
2 Cases of Boots and shoes
2 Cases of Kitchen Utensils
1 Case of Stationary, Sealing wax and other articles for Office use
2 Cases of Soaps and perfumery
2 Cases of Tea
6 trunks and cases of books, manuscripts &c
1 Small Case of Wine
3 Barrells of Wine
1200 Bottles of Wine
100 Bottles of liqueurs
6 Doz ↑packs of↓ playing Cards
5000 Cigars

MANUSCRIPT: NA, RG 84 (letterbook copy); Archivo de Ministerio de Asuntes Exteriores (Madrid).

1463.   *To James S. Calhoun*

                Legation of the United States / Madrid August 27th. 1842.

James J. Calhoun Esqr / Consul U States Havana.
Sir;
    I herewith forward to you by way of New York your Exequatur received a few days since from the office of Foreign Affairs together with

your original commission from the President of the United States.

I have also to acknowledge the receipt of your letter of June 1st. in relation to the case of Captain Straw:[1] From the records of the Legation it appears that an unsuccessful application has already been made by Mr. Vail: I shall however address another Note to the Minister of Foreign Affairs in his behalf, founded upon the Statement contained in your letter, which I hope may meet with better Success.

> I am Sir respectfully / Your obdt sevt
> Washington Irving.

MANUSCRIPT: NA, RG 84 (letterbook copy).

James S. Calhoun of Georgia was nominated as U.S. consul to Havana on July 16, 1841. See Hasse, *Index to U.S. Documents*, III, 1745.

1. Captain Love Straw, master of the *Sarah Ann Alley*, was arrested and jailed in Havana in 1838 on a charge of stealing money from the trunk of a passenger on his ship. For a summary of the case, see WI to Count Almodóvar, October 4, 1842.

1464. To William H. Freeman

Legation of the United States. / Madrid August 27th. 1842.

Wm. H. Freeman Esq. / Consul. U. States.—Nuevitas.
Sir.

I herewith forward to you by way of New york your Exequatur recieved two or three days ago from the Office of Foreign Affairs, and the Original Commission signed by the President of the United States.

> I am Sir. respectfully / Your obdt Sevt.
> Washington Irving.

DOCKETED: Hon. Washington Irving / Minister Plenipotentiary / Court of Madrid / 27 Augt 1842
MANUSCRIPT: Va.–Barrett; NA, RG 84 (letterbook copy).

William H. Freeman of Pennsylvania was nominated as consul for Nuevitas, Cuba, in February, 1842. He resigned in 1843 and accepted an appointment almost immediately as consul for Curacao. See Hasse, *Index to U.S. Documents*, I, 645; III, 1720, 1747.
Only the signature is in WI's handwriting.

1465. To Daniel Webster

Legation of the United States. / Madrid August. 27th. 1842

No. 3 / The Hon: Daniel Webster. / Secretary of State of the U. States—
   Washington.
Sir.

I understand that Mr. Pablo Anguera[1] who is at present acting as our
Consular Agent at Barcelona, has made application for the Consulship of
that Port; This office is virtually vacant, Mr. Leonard who was appointed
to it more than two years since—having never presented himself to be
installed. I take the liberty therefore of recommending Mr. Anguera as a
Person extremely well fitted for the place: I have had opportunities of
knowing his character and course of conduct for many years past; he
having had extensive commercial transactions with some of my relatives
who have confided largely in his honor, intelligence, and punctuality in
business, and have never found him wanting. He holds a most respectable
station in public opinion in Barcelona and my predecessor, Mr. Vail, who
is now at that city on his way to France, speaks highly of his aimiable
and obliging deportment and pronounces him "in all respects a fit
depositary for the Consular honors"—It would give me much Satisfaction
therefore should my representations have any effect in procuring him the
Appointment.

I have but little news to offer of a Political nature. The Government
relieved from its immediate fears of Foreign machinations and internal
Conspiracies[2] seems to have a breathing Spell. Still it is obliged to keep
up a powerful army, which is at once its strength and its weakness: for
that army must be punctually paid to keep it in good faith and good
humor; so that, while it rallies round the Government, it exhausts the
Treasury.

The finances are indeed in a lamentable Condition.[3] The high duties,
which were expected, while they protected Domestic Manufactures, to
produce a large revenue have given rise to a system of smuggling which
overspreads and demoralizes the Country, and defrauds the Government
of the anticipated revenue: It is impossible however to get a reduction
of those duties: Whenever it is attempted the Cry is raised, That it
would ruin the Manufactories and that 30,000. manufacturers would be
turned destitute upon Society to become "facciosos" and ladrones. Attempts are making however to cut up the contraband System. To this
end the armed force employed to scour the Country in pursuit of
Smugglers, and which has generally played booty with them, is now to
receive a military organization, to be subjected to Courts Martial and
all the other regulations observed in the Army. Thus they are lopping at

the branches, instead of cutting at the root of this evil which over-shadows the land. Still the measure as far as it goes, will be very bene-ficial.

Efforts have been making also to trample out the Smould'ring Sparks of Sedition which exist in various parts of the Country, in the shape of prowling bands of what they term latro-facciosos, that is to say robber-factionists; who have been partizans during the rebellion and are public marauders, robbing villages and laying travellers under contribution. It has hitherto been found impossible to extirpate them, having so many friends among the people, and being able to evade or corrupt the slow process of law. A kind of Lynch law however has lately been put in force against these ruffians by General Zurbano,[4] who commands in Catalonia where they most abound. Wherever he has detected them he has caused them to be instantly shot, without waiting for the forms of law: he has adopted the same treatment with those guilty of harbouring or abetting them, and has even threatened like punishment to captured travellers who should ransom themselves from the hands of robbers; who were making this an important branch of their nefarious maraudings.

His measures have been exclaimed against in Spain and elsewhere as sanguinary and atrocious; and the Ministry has been assailed for authorising them—but they have been efficacious—Robberies are at an end in Catalonia: those persons who had been carried off in hopes of ex-tracting a ransom, have been suffered to return home and the roads are travelled in safety. The good effects of these measures begin to be acknowledged, and it is thought they will be adopted in other parts of the Country which are still infested by robbers. Spain is a Country accus-tomed to violent remedies and scenes now and then to require a political sangrado.

The Country, however, notwithstanding the long Civil War, through which it has Struggled is really in a much better condition than I had expected to find it. There is a general air of Improvement in its Cities; industry and enterprise are reviving; the People seem better off—indeed it is the Government chiefly that is poor. The reforms that have taken place during the late political revolutions have benefited the great masses of society. They have got rid of a standing army of monks and are re-lieved from the oppressive imposition of tithes. The sales of the Convent and church lands though they have mainly enriched Capitalists have also been of general benefit. There are more small Proprietors than for-merly; The cutting down of the "Mayorazgos" or entails also though its effect will be more slow, is already breaking down the overgrown estates of the Nobility and tending to equalize Conditions. The People at large who are quick witted and sagacious, perceive the advantages they are enjoying, are becoming more and more attached to their constitutional form of Government, and anxious for a continuance of peace, that it may be confirmed and Strengthened: One thing the government has to guard against is the zeal of some of its own adherents, men who, it is true, desire nothing but salutary reform but who are for pushing it forward too rapidly, eager to accomplish every thing during the two years minority of the Queen, while they have the power of reform in their hands, lest, when she comes to the throne, still immature in Judgment, she should be operated on by adverse influences.

There has been some talk of late of the dissolution of the present Cortes; and of changes in the Cabinet.[5] Meetings are held by the Coalition, which ejected the late Ministers, to organize opposition to their Successors. The leaders of that Coalition[6] were disappointed at not being chosen to seats in the Cabinet, and represent the present Incumbents as deficient in the political Science, energy of action, and above all the financial talent requisite for the management of affairs of State during the present crisis. A great part of the Members of the Coalition, however, are satisfied of the honesty, patriotism and good intentions of the present Ministers and are disposed to give them a fair trial. With these differences of opinion in its ranks, The Coalition may be considered at present neutralized, and the present Cortes is likely to continue, and the Ministers to keep their places, at least until the next meeting of the Chambers.

The Department has already, I believe been informed by Mr. Vail, 'that the Papers and Public Documents forwarded by way of Cadiz, do not in general reach the Legation until after two or three months delay, and even then at a great expense, Permit me therefore, to suggest, that for the future they should be sent by the Havre Packets, to the care of our Consul at that Port, or the Legation of the United States at Paris.— A copy of the Census and returns recently published by order of Congress and particularly the documents relating to our Commerce, would be of great service, should an opening present itself for the formation of a commercial arrangement, in relation to our intercourse with the Spanish West India Islands.

I am Sir very respectfully / Your Obdt. Sevt.

Washington Irving

DOCKETED: Rec. Oct 17 / Mr Markoe [*top of MS page 1*] / No. 3. W Irving, Madrid. 27 Augt. 1842 [*top of MS page 8*]

MANUSCRIPT: NA, RG 59.   PUBLISHED: Hellman, *WI Esquire*, pp. 280–83.

Only the signature is in WI's handwriting.

1. Pablo Anguera, a friend of Henry Van Wart's, had been a merchant in Havana. See PMI, III, 347. He apparently functioned intermittently as an unofficial representative of the United States at Barcelona until 1850. From then until 1857 he was U.S. consul. See Hasse, *Index to U.S. Documents*, III, 1744.

2. See *El Castellano*, August 8, 1842.

3. The disastrous state of Spanish finances was discussed in a front-page editorial in *El Castellano*, August 22, 1842.

4. Martín Zurbano (1788–1845) was a smuggler who joined the Liberal cause and terrified the northern provinces of Spain from the mid-1830's onward. As WI observes, he dispensed justice without recourse to normal legal procedures. See Christiansen, *Military Power*, p. 109. For reactions to Zurbano's methods and activities, see *El Castellano*, August 10, 12, 17, and 22, 1842.

5. See the front-page editorial in *El Castellano*, August 24, 1842.

6. The cabinet formed in 1841 included, among others, Antonio González (1792–1876), premier; Facundo Infante (1790–1873), minister of the interior; García Camba, minister of marine; and Evaristo San Miguel (1785–1862), minister of war. On May 29, 1842, Ramón Rodil (1789–1853) became premier and also assumed the duties of the minister of war. He did not have the support of the Progressives in the Cortes, and the unrest which WI mentions continued, with outbursts of violence in Barcelona in the fall of 1842. See Carr, *Spain, 1808–1939*, pp. 221–22; Christiansen, *Military Power*, pp. 107–15; WI to Daniel Webster, November 5, 1842. Many specific details of Spanish political turbulence during Espartero's regency are set forth in WI's despatches to the State Department in the months to come.

1466. To Sarah Storrow

Madrid *May* [August] 29th. 1842[1]

My dear Sarah,

It is now nineteen days since I received a letter from you and it seems a long long time. You will think me *exegiant* but in fact the receipt of letters is at present one of my greatest gratifications. I have been spoiled for bachelor life of late years by living continually in the bosom of a family surrounded by affectionate beings who cherished me: and I cannot as formerly, content myself with the isolated lot of a "Wanderer and a sojourner,"[2] unless I know and feel by the frequent receipt of letters that the chords of sympathy which link me to those I love are still vibrating. Therefore do scribble me a line frequently, however brief, if it be only to tell me that you and yours are well and happy.

I have been very much confined to the house since my arrival in Madrid by the heat of the weather. I am distant from the public walks, the places of amusement and the residences of the diplomatic corps, to walk ⟨th⟩ to them through crowded streets, which even late in the evening ⟨re⟩ have the dull heat of a brick kiln, is paying too dear for either recreation or society, ⟨as I⟩ and as yet I have been unable to procure carriage horses, so that my carriage remains idle in the coach house, and I inert in the saloon. I have some prospect now, however, of procuring a house,[3] in a different part of the city, near to the public walks, the gallery of paintings, the theatres and the Diplomatic Corps, and then I shall lead less of a hermit life. I have lately resumed my pen which has been a great resource to me. The ⟨Summer⟩ intense summer heats are now over, ⟨we have⟩ for a week past we have had cool evenings and mornings; and I now can venture out at midday.

Tell Mr Storrow the boxes containing the China glass, linen &c reached Madrid nearly a fortnight since: whether in good order or not I cannot say, for I have not them yet in my possession. Such are the official formalities and delays in this most procrastinating of all countries, that, though ⟨on my⟩ a Ministers effects are entitled to pass free of duty, mine are not yet delivered to me; and I have from day to day to hire every article of table furniture, toilet & bed linen &c &c, while my own articles of the kind are locked up in a custom house in my neighborhood. I expect, however, to get them in the course of the present day.

My household affairs go on smoothly and quietly, excepting that my Major Domo Benjamin has been taken down by an attack of *pulmonia* or pleurisy, one of the most dangerous maladies of this place. I ⟨toke⟩ put him immediately in the doctors hands; had him bled and leeched and succeeded in checking the complaint which had got under alarming head way. He is now sufficiently recovered to leave his bed. He is a steady, quiet and, I believe, faithful, servant and I set much store by him.

Since I wrote to you last I have had a long letter from that little "black diamond" Kate.[4] I need not tell you how welcome it was. She gave me an account of their fourth of July. Edgar Amanda and sonny[5] were with them; Uncle Natt & Oscar[6] and Mr Jones and his children were among their ⟨visitors⟩ days visitors. "We say[7] the Drecone[?][8] go by in the morning with Mr Bowdoin Mr Schuyler and some of the ladies. They gave each of the neighbors a salute as they passed by. Mr Bowdoin says he is coming soon to take us out. We are quite delighted with our new neighbors the Minturns; we spent an evening there last week and we had them here to tea last evening. I think Mr Minturn must be one of the best men in the world for I am sure his very face shows it. Last Sunday when we returned from Dobbs ferry church it rained very fast and he sent home a waggon load of people to Mr Archers—He takes every body to the boat and brings every one from it; so that he has quite got his name up in the country already. Mrs Minturn improves very much upon acquaintance; we like her extremely. We agreed last evening to go over the river with them; and another to go to Mrs Van Cortlandts, She is very well acquainted with her. ⟨Mr Constant⟩ I suppose you know that Mrs Constant has a little daughter. Mr Constant called here yesterday with Miss Johnson and he says that it is probably the finest child in the world not even excepting Sarah Paris', for he has seen them both."[9]—

I have already told you of my having a fair country woman for neighbor, in the other end of the huge house in which I am quartered. Madame Albuquerque (formerly Miss Oakey of New York) wife of the Brazilian Minister. I find her very affable and agreeable; and it is quite a resource to have a female friend who has so many sympathies in common with me. As her husband has recently had promotion from charge d'affairs to resident Minister I consider him fixed for a time at this post; so that I may count upon Madame Albuquerque as an intimate during my residence in Madrid.

On the receipt of this letter I beg you will instantly sit down and write me a reply. Tell me about my darling little Miss Maam, how she comes on; whether she has been cut shorter about the skirts; whether she continues to cultivate the talent at laughing which I first developed &c &c. I fear by the time I see her she will have grown and improved so much that I shall not like her half as well as in the days of her baby hood.

With kind remembrances to your husband

Your affectionate Uncle
Washington Irving

ADDRESSED: à Madame / Madame Storrow / aux Soins de Mr T. W. Storrow / 17. Rue du Faubg Poissoniere / à Paris
MANUSCRIPT: Yale.

1. WI wrote the month as "May," but the context clearly indicates that it is August. In a letter to Mrs. Storrow on September 11, 1842, he states that he misdated it as August 27. Actually he used the wrong month, not the wrong day as he thought.

2. This may be WI's variant of Genesis 23:4.

3. In September WI moved to an apartment in the palace of the marques de Mos on the Calle Victor Hugo. See Bowers, *Spanish Adventures of WI*, pp. 160–62; STW, II, 142–43.

4. Catharine Irving, Ebenezer's daughter, who was living at Sunnyside. The reason for WI's use of the epithet has not been ascertained.

5. Edgar Irving, his wife Amanda, and their son Washington (1835–1910).

6. Nathaniel Paulding (1776–1858) was the brother of Julia Paulding Irving (1768–1823), who was the mother of Oscar Irving (1800–1865).

7. WI probably meant to write "saw."

8. Probably the name of a yacht or boat.

9. Jones, Bowdoin, Schuyler, Minturn, Archer, Van Cortlandt, and Constant were friends and acquaintances of WI in the Tarrytown area. The Constants had visited Sarah Storrow in Paris earlier in the summer of 1842.

1467.   To Alexander Burton

Madrid August 31. 1842

My dear Sir,

I have received with great pleasure, your letter of the 22d instant and thank you for the very friendly expressions and kind congratulations which it contains and which are in unison with the hearty hospitality I experienced in your bachelor establishment in Cadiz in former days.[1] Should you come to Madrid I beg you will make my house your home and let me try to pay off a little of my debt in kind.

The parcel of news papers to which you allude found its way here through the post office a day or two since. The postage came to nearly four dollars, which, considering Newspapers do not, like wine, improve by age, was somewhat dear. I have advised Mr Miller[2] to find a cheaper channel for the transmission of *old news*.

I thank you for your hint about the six months limitation of diplomatic privilige but I had already guarded against it by sending in a list of articles which will probably cover all my wants during my residence here A list of this kind ↑which must be passed before the expiration of the six months↓ is filed at the Custom House accompanied by the order for free admission, and holds good for an indefinite period; the articles ordered from it, being ticked off as they enter. I have some articles on ⟨my⟩ the way to Madrid, which came through your port; but, not knowing whether or not ⟨they⟩ you were yet resident in Cadiz, I availed myself of the proferred services of another house, and they have accordingly been forwarded by your friend and neighbor, Mr Harmony[3] ("whose name," if I reccollect right "is not Harmony, it is Ximenes") I shall corre[ct] [*MS torn*] this procedure hereafter and give you all the trouble in my power. In the mean time believe me very truly

Your obliged friend
Washington Irving

Alexander Burton Esqr

ADDRESSED: Alexander Burton Esqr / Consul of the United States / Cadiz   POST-
    MARKED: [*unrecovered*] / 31 / Ag / 1842   DOCKETED: Washington Irving /
    Madrid 31 Augt. 1842 / Ansd. 20 Octo
MANUSCRIPT: HSP.

Alexander Burton of Pennsylvania was nominated as U.S. consul to Cadiz in 1824; he held the post until 1856. See Hasse, *Index to U.S. Documents*, III, 1745.

At the bottom of the address leaf is written, in another hand, "Ogden D. Wilkinson call / Alex Burton sect."

1. WI had stayed with Burton at Cadiz in April and September of 1828. See **WI** to Alexander H. Everett, April 15, 1828; PMI, II, 305–9, 342–43; and STW, I, 333, 341.

2. Probably John Miller, who was employed as U.S. despatch agent from 1832 to 1842. See Hasse, *Index to U.S. Documents*, II, 1088.

3. WI calls him a "rich old bachelor merchant, Peter Harmony (alias Ximenes) of Cadiz." See WI to Sarah Storrow, July 18, 1841.

1468.   To Catharine Paris

Madrid, Sept 2d. 1842.

My dear Sister,

In ⟨this⟩ the letter last received from you dated July 19th.[1] you give me as usual a world of news from the *cottage*. I will in return give you a little history of the *Palace*. I know you like to hear now and then what is going on in the grand world, and from your little sheltered country nook to "take a peep at royalty." So I will perform the promise I made you in a former letter, to give you an inkling of Spanish politics, that you ⟨might⟩ ↑may↓ understand the present ⟨situation⟩ ↑state↓ of this harrassed country, and of its poor little Queen and her sister, whose isolated situation I am sure must interest you

Spain having long experienced the evils of an absolute monarchy, where the will of the monarch was supreme law, has made repeated struggles to establish a constitutional form of government such as is enjoyed in England and France; where the power of the king is limited and controled by the constitution, and where the people have a voice in affairs through elective chambers of legislation. It succeeded in forming such a constitution in 1812, with the approbation of its sovreign Ferdinand VII,[2] ↑who was↓ at that time detained by Napoleon in France. The constitution was overthrown by Napoleon who placed his brother Joseph[3] on the throne. At the downfall of Napoleon Ferdinand regained his throne; but, false to the nation, he refused to restore the constitution; persecuted those who had supported it, and reigned absolute monarch. A revolution in 1820[4] was the consequence, the constitution was again proclaimed, and Ferdinand again swore to support it, declaring that in opposing it he had acted under the influence of bad advisors. A French army, sent by Charles X.[5] again trampled down the constitution and replaced the faithless Ferdinand in absolute power, which he exercised for the remainder of his worthless life. At the time of my former visit to Spain he was on the throne, and the French troops which had placed him there still lingered in the country. The liberties of Spain seemed com-

pletely prostrate and many of her most enlightened, virtuous and patriotic men were in Exile.

In 1829 Ferdinand married for his fourth wife Maria Christina[6] sister
of the King of Naples,[7] and niece of the present Queen of France.[8] By
her he had two daughters, his only children. In 1833 being low in health
without prospect of recovery, he became anxious to secure the succession
to the throne to his own progeny; but here arose a difficulty. By long
usage the *Salique* law of France, which excludes females from the exercise of regal authority, had become ⟨adopted⟩ naturalized in Spain:[9] according to this the Kings eldest brother Don Carlos,[10] being next male
heir, would inherit the crown. Ferdinand, however, supported by the
opinions of men learned in the law, revived the old Spanish law of succession, which made females equally ⟨competent⟩ ↑entitled to inherit↓
with males, and quoted the reign of the illustrious Isabella of glorious
memory as a case in point. ⟨Two parties⟩ The question agitated the country even before the death of Ferdinand. Don Carlos insisted on his rights,
and had a strong party in his favor composed of many of the aristocracy
who knew him to be an absolute monarchist, and by the monks and a
great part of the clergy, who knew him to be a bigot. ⟨Under his reign
they anticipated the⟩ The Queen Maria Christina of course stood up for
the rights of her infant daughter, and her cause was the popular one,
having all the *liberals*, or those who were anxious for a constitutional
government, in its favor.

Ferdinand died in 1833, and, in conformity to his will and testament
his eldest daughter, then but three years of age, was proclaimed Queen
by the name of Isabella II, and her mother, Maria Christina Queen
Regent, to exercise the royal authority in the name of her daughter, until
the latter should be fourteen years of age; when according to Spanish
law, she is of age to ascend the throne. Maria Christina was likewise
constituted guardian to the Queen during her minority.

Don Carlos immediately raised the standard of rebellion, and here commenced the modern "War of Succession" which desolated Spain for seven
years.[11] The liberals rallied round the standard of the Queen Regent, and
for a time she was exceedingly popular. Indeed never had a woman a better opportunity of playing a noble part as a mother and a sovreign, but
she proved herself unworthy of both characters. ⟨Her⟩ What first impaired
her popularity with the liberals was the opposition which she manifested
to all their plans of salutary reform; to this it was suspected she was
secretly instigated by her uncle Louis Philip, King of France, who, though
his own power originated in constitutional reform, has constantly been
hostile to constitutional reform in Spain.

Another deadly blow to the popularity, and indeed respectability of
the Queen Regent, was an unworthy ⟨passion⟩ connexion which she

formed not very long after the death of her husband, with one of the royal body guards named Muñoz,[12] whom she subsequently advanced in rank and fortune. This scandalous connexion it is said was ultimately recconciled to ideas of decency by a private marriage; though such a marriage was not valid in point of Spanish law, and if promulgated would have incapacitated her from acting as Regent, or as guardian to the Queen. ⟨Disgusted with her conduct⟩ The effect of this connexion in fact was to render ⟨the Queen Regent neglectful of her public duties⟩ ↑Maria Christina remiss in the exercise of her high office as Regent,↓ and what was still worse, neglectful of her sacred duties to her legitimate children; and the little Queen and her sister ⟨had to look⟩ ↑were left↓ to the interested and venial services of the attendants about a court, ⟨for that instruction and care which ought to have been⟩ to supply the want of the vigilant tenderness of a mother.

At length in 1836 a popular movement wrung from the fears of Maria Christina, what it was impossible to obtain from her gratitude or her sense of justice, and she was compelled to ⟨sign⟩ restore the constitution of 1812.[13] From this time it is thought she contemplated the probability of a retirement from Spain. She had already amassed great property from her yearly allowance of two millions of dollars. This was ⟨sended⟩ sent out of the Kingdom; as were large sums arising from the sale of every object under her control that she could convert into money. Muñoz her minion who formerly appeared every where with her in public, had for some time ⟨kept out of⟩ ceased to make himself conspicuous, but it was known that she had lavished much of her wealth on him and his family, and that her children by this degrading union had alienated her thoughts from her regal offspring.

At length in 1839 the civil war was brought to a close and Don Carlos driven from the Kingdom. A patriot general, Espartero, had risen to great popularity and influence by his successful campaigns, and was now commander in chief of the army, which idolized him and virtually controller of the politics of the Kingdom. By this time Maria Christina had made herself an object of popular distrust, and she gave a finishing blow to ascendancy by signing an act vesting the appointment of all municipal officers in the Crown; thereby violating one of the grand principles of the constitution and ⟨in a manner making the⟩ restoring in a great measure the absolute power of the throne.[14] This rash measure she was ↑secretly↓ prompted to by the French Minister resident at this Court:[15] ⟨yet she did not venture to sign the act until she repaired to Barcelona where⟩ but before signing the act she repaired to Barcelona, under pretence of taking the royal children there for sea bathing, but in fact to get the support of General Espartero and his victorious army; who were quartered in that city. Maria Christina miscalculated on her own reputed powers of persuasion, and on the *persuasibility* if I may use the term of Espartero. That General remained true to the popular cause and warned her against the consequences of the act she contemplated. She disregarded his advice and his remonstrances and signed the act. The consequence was a burst of indignation from all parts of Spain; under the appalling effects of which, and the public obloquy of her connexion with Muñoz, she abdicated the regency and retired from Spain,[16] leaving her royal children to their fortunes. The little Queen and her sister, then of the respective ages of ten and eight years, were ↑re↓ conducted in state by Espartero to Madrid, ⟨where they ↑and replaced a↓⟩ ↑where they↓ were received with acclamation, ⟨and he lodged⟩ ↑replaced in their usual residence↓ in the royal palace, and surrounded with the usual state and ceremony accorded to their rank and station. The office of Regent being vacant by the abdication of Maria Christina, Espartero was elected[17] and has hitherto discharged the sovreign duties with great integrity. Maria Christina having also forfeited her claims to the guardianship of the Queen and her sister, that important trust was confided to Don Augustin Arguellos, one of the most intelligent, upright and patriotic men of Spain; who for his lofty principles suffered exile under the perfidious Ferdinand, and with whom I became acquainted in England during his honorable exile. A kind of maternal care has likewise been exerted over the children by the Countess Mina,[18] widow of a patriot general. She fills the station of Aya or governess, and is a woman of amiable character and unblemished virtue. ↑Their education is superintended by Quintana,[19] one of the most learned men of the Kingdom.↓ The royal children, therefore, are more likely to be well educated and trained up in pure principles under the persons of worth who now have charge of them than they were under the former misrule of a corrupt and licentious court. They are treated too with mingled respect and tenderness; still they cannot but feel their isolated situation; without a mothers care, ⟨or the m⟩ and separated from all their kindred. This no doubt is one cause of the extreme affection they are said to evince for each other; always addressing each other by the most endearing epithets, and by those tender diminutives which are so touching in the Spanish language. (Such as Hermanita, for hermana, sister &c) The Queen I am told is never gratified by any attention or any present unless ⟨she has⟩ ↑her sister receives↓ something of the kind; and I observe that when they are in public they are generally dressed alike. The queen is of a delicate constitution, and somewhat grave cast of character; with ⟨a countenance⟩ sometimes a melancholy expression of countenance. Her little sister is healthful, lively and, as I am told, for I have never seen her near by, quite pretty.

Maria Christina, on leaving Spain, repaired to the Court of France, where she was received with great distinction; ⟨by⟩ and where she has since resided, countenancéd and favored by Louis Philip and his Queen; the latter of whom, as I have before observed, is her aunt. Her residence at ⟨the⟩ Paris and in its vicinity has become the focus of all kinds of machinations against the constitutional government of Spain. Her immense wealth gave her the means of fomenting insurrections, and the relics of the rebel armies, and the ↑rebel↓ generals and nobles ejected from the Kingdom, have lent themselves to her plans. Louis Philip is accused, and with apparent justice, of having countenanced ⟨and pr⟩ her and secretly promoted her plans in the hope of encreasing the power of his family by effecting a match between one of his sons and the little Queen. The consequence of all these plots beyond the Pyrenees was an insurrection in the north of Spain in the month of October last, when General O Donell ↑(a Spaniard in spite of his name[)]↓ siezed upon the citadel of Pamplona and proclaimed Maria Christina Queen Regent The most nefarious part of this plot was an attempt to get possession of the persons of the little Queen and her sister and bear them off to the rebel army, so as to give it the sanction of the royal presence. To promote this plan immense sums had been spent in Madrid, to corrupt the soldiery and the people about the palace, and the evening of the 7th. of October was the time appointed for the attempt. The royal palace stands on the confines of the city, ⟨alo⟩ on the brow of a steep descent sweeping down into the valley of the Manzanares; it overlooks the open country towards the Cuadarama Mountains, which is so lonely in the very vicinity of Madrid that ten minutes gallop from its walls takes you into scenes as savage and deserted as any of Salvator Rosas.[20] The palace is guarded every night by a body of troops, and is capable of a powerful defence; but the troops who were to mount guard that night were mostly under the influence of Generals Concha and Leon, who ⟨were⟩ had been gained over to the conspiracy. Concha was an artful man, related by marriage to Espartero, so that in this affair he was guilty of a double treason. Leon was a brave, warm hearted, weak headed fellow, who from his popularity with the soldiery was made use of as a tool. It was a dark tempestuous evening when the attempt was made. A part of the armed force was left to guard the avenues of the Palace, and Concha and Leon with a number of their followers entered the main portal, rushed up the grand staircase and expected to gain immediate entrance through the door ⟨at the head⟩ leading into the Queens suite of apartments; being guarded merely by a band of eighteen veteran halbardiers. To their astonishment they met with a vigorous repulse from these gallant fellows, ⟨who after a discharge⟩ and several of the assailants were shot down. ⟨The [unrecovered]⟩ Repeated attempts were made to force an entrance, but were uniformly repelled with loss. The Halbardiers ensconced them-

selves within the apartment, and fired through the woodwork of the door
the moment they heard ⟨step⟩ footsteps at the head of the staircase. In
this way the door became completely riddled with bullet holes which
remain to this day, and ⟨the stair case⟩ many of the assailants were slain
and wounded. In the mean time the situation of the poor little Queen and
her sister may be ⟨im⟩ more easily imagined than described. The repeated
discharges of fire arms which reverberated through the courts and halls
of the palace; the mingled shouts and curses, and groans and menaces
which accompanied the attack, joined to the darkness of the night and
the howling of the storm, filled their hearts with terror. They had no one
with them but their Aya or governess Madam Mina and some of their
female attendants, excepting their poor singing master, who was as much
frightened as any of the women. ⟨Uncertain of⟩ Ignorant of the object
of this attack and fearful that their own lives were menaced the poor
children gave themselves up to tears and outcries. ⟨especially the prin-
cess⟩ The Queen threw herself into the arms of her governess, crying
"Aya mia—(my dear aya) ⟨what⟩ ↑who↓ are they?—are they rebels: What
do they want ⟨f⟩ of me?["]—The princess was ⟨still⟩ in convulsions in
the arms of an attendant, ⟨crying out what is all this⟩ making the most
piteous exclamations.—It was with the greatest difficulty that the governess was able to soothe them into some degree of calmness. The noise of
fire arms continued; attempts were heard to force a door leading through
a private passage: two or three musket balls broke the windows of the
apartment ⟨and⟩ but were stopped by the inside shutters. In the midst
of these horrors the poor little princess, trembling and sobbing called to
one of the ladies in attendance, "Inez, I wish to say something to you—
Inez, I want to pray!" The wish of the innocent ⟨little being⟩ ↑child↓
was gratified; they all knelt down at the couch of the Queen and prayed;
"and I felt relieved" says Madame Mina in her narrative of this eventful night, "I felt relieved by the tears which I shed on contemplating the
situation of those two innocent beings, who, full of fervor, directed their
supplications to heaven to protect and deliver them from a peril, the
extent of which no one knew so well as I."—The clamour of the attack
subsided, the firing became less frequent. The attendants now spread
mattresses for the Queen and her sister in a corner of the apartment where
they would be safe from any random shot, and the poor little beings
exhausted by the agitation and fatigue they had suffered, at length fell
asleep.

The gallant defence of the handful of halbardiers effectually defeated
this atrocious attempt. They kept the assailants at bay until assistance
arrived. The alarm spread through Madrid. The regular troops and national guards assembled from all quarters: Espartero hastened to the
scene of action, and the palace was completely surrounded. Concha and

Leon seeing the case was desperate left their followers in the lurch and consulted their own safety in flight. They spurred their horses to the open country, but .Concha being in ordinary dress, returned unobserved, concealed himself in Madrid and ultimately escaped out of the Kingdom. The heedless Leon, being in full generals uniform was a marked object. He was discovered and arrested at some distance from Madrid, and though great interest was made in his favor, was ultimately shot.[21]

I am told that it was quite an affecting sight to witness the joy of the poor little Queen and her sister in the morning when their protectors thronged about them and assured them that all danger was over. Arguellos,[22] their guardian, assured me that he never experienced any thing more moving than when, on entering their appartment they ran up to him and shewed him the musket balls that had penetrated their chamber. At eight oclock in the morning they shewed themselves on a balcony of the palace, accompanied by Espartero, to satisfy the public of their safety. The troops passed in review before them and the air rang with shouts of gratulation. It appears that ⟨one of the assailants had it in⟩ in this infamous attempt one of the assailants of the palace was to have siezed the person of the queen and have borne her off before him on horseback. Think of this fragile little being of a delicate constitution, borne off in the grasp of a ruffian, ⟨amidst⟩ ↑gallopping↓ in a tempestuous night, down steep and rugged roads, and exposed to the volleys of fire arms that would have been discharged after the fugitives. Some think that there was a plot within a plot, and that in pretending to serve the cause of Maria christina, there were desperate partizans of Don Carlos, who intended to sacrifice the ⟨lifes of the⟩ lives of these innocent children in this chance medley affray, and thus clear off all claimants between him and the crown.

The result of this brutal attempt has been to throw complete odium on the cause of Maria Christina, to confound the enemies of the constitution, and to strengthen the hands of government. The insurrection in the provinces was speedily put down. Maria Christina hastened to disavow all share in the conspiracy; but proofs are ⟨to⟩ ↑too↓ strong against her; and the French government stands ⟨charged⟩ ↑chargeable↓ with at least connivance The stand which England has taken of late in the matter, and the declaration of ministers in parliament that they would not quietly permit the hostile interference of any foreign power in the affairs of Spain[23] has had a happy effect in checking the machinations of France. Spain now enjoys a breathing spell, and I hope may be enabled to regulate her internal affairs and recover from the exhausting effects of her ⟨long⟩ civil wars. The little Queen is now nearly twelve years of age; in about two years more her minority will terminate, and with it the regency of Espartero. I hope while the power still remains in his hands he may be enabled to carry out his proposed plans of reform and to ⟨place⟩ ↑confirm↓ the constitutional government so that it may not easily be shaken.

The details I have here given you will account to you for the deep interest I took in my first audience of the Queen. I passed through the door way at the head of the stair case opening to her apartment, and ↑⟨where the⟩↓ saw the ⟨marble endings of the⟩ vestiges of the attack in the shattered marble door cases, and the pannels of the doors pierced by innumerable balls[.] I have already given you an account of my interview, when I beheld the little Queen ⟨and⟩ in deep mourning for the Duke of Orleans, looking so pale, and moving noiselessly like a shadow, with a train of shadows after her, through the twilight salons of the great silent palace.

I cannot express the deep sympathy and tender concerns ⟨I⟩ with which I contemplate these two little beings whenever I behold them in public; surrounded by state and grandeur, yet so perfectly isolated. Every evening ↑as↓ they drive home from the prado, they pass ↑immediately below my balconies↓ in an open carriage drawn by six horses and guarded by a troop of horse. They have their worthy Aya or governess in the carriage with them. They are generally dressed alike. I watch for their passing and I feel my heart swell at the sight of them. Great heavens how much their mother has to answer for! How unworthy she has proved herself of her great trusts—how worthy a sister she has proved herself of the *Duchess de Berri!*[24]

⟨My sketch of Spanish affairs has⟩

The foregoing sketch will I trust enable you to form an idea of the position of Spanish affairs, and to take an interest in any particulars about this Court which I may hereafter have to relate. You will understand that Spain is now a constitutional monarchy, having its ⟨representative⟩ Cortes or representative bodies of legislature consisting of a senate and chamber of deputies; and that, until the Queen is fourteen years of age Espartero (Duke of Victory) holds the reins of government, ⟨in her⟩ as Regent, in her name. He is a soldier of fortune, who has risen by his merits and his services, and been placed in his present elevated situation by the votes of the Cortes. From all that I have seen and heard of him I believe him honestly disposed to uphold the present form of government, and to administer it for the real good of the nation.

You will now understand something of the jealousy and ill will that exists between this country and France; and of the failure of the Embassy of Mr Salvandy, which made so much noise last winter. However as the last affair may have escaped your notice, and as you and I are now embarked in Diplomacy I will call your attention to it.

⟨At the time of⟩ ↑After↓ the abdication and departure of Maria Christina from Spain, ⟨disposed to Louis Philip⟩ the French Government,

⟨to⟩ by way of slight, suffered itself ↑for a time↓ to remain unrepresented ⟨by⟩ ↑at↓ the Spanish court excepting by a temporary charge d affaires, whereas it has usually maintained a full Embassy at Madrid. At length ⟨the⟩ Louis Philip, finding that he was exciting the indignation of the Spanish people against himself, and increasing their antipathy to his nation, determined to send an Ambassador. Mr Salvandy ↑a man of conspicuous talents;↓ accordingly appeared at Madrid with a brilliant train but here a difficulty arose: his letter of credence was addressed to the Queen, and he was instructed to deliver it *into her hands.* ↑He demanded an audience of her for that purpose↓ It was objected on the part of the Spanish Government that the Queen, being yet a minor, was ⟨not competent to⟩ disqualified by the constitution from the performance of any public act; that a Regent had been appointed to whom, under that constitution, the regal power had been delegated, and who, in the name and stead of her Majesty, and at his own palace would receive Mr Salvandy and from his hands the credentials of which he was the bearer. The ambassador refused to deliver his letters at any other place than at the Royal palace, or into any other hands than those of the Queen herself; though he observed the Regent, if he thought proper, might be present at the ceremonial. The Spanish government repeated its objections and, the ambassador wrote to Paris for new instructions. The court of France approved of what he had done, and instructed him to persist; Louis Philip doubtless being disposed to pass a slight upon the constitutional government, and to pass by the Regent, as not being the actual head. The ambassador again ⟨[*unrecovered*]⟩ demanded an audience of the Queen, ⟨and again met with a refusal⟩ adding that if he were refused he should require his passports, take down the French arms from ⟨embas⟩ the front of the Embassy, and withdraw with the whole embassy from the country. The Spanish government stood firm; ⟨[*unrecovered*]⟩ the matter was discussed and argued on both sides but the Spaniards were not ⟨to be disposed to suffer any⟩ ↑to be argued into the admission of any↓ slight or indignity to the ↑constitutional↓ Regent of their own election. Mr Salvandy ⟨to⟩ after several days of fruitless discussion at length demanded passports for the Embassy, which were immediately granted, and he left Madrid with his retinue the same night: he moderated so much of his diplomatic threat, however, as to leave the Escutcheon of the French arms standing over the gate of the embassy; and ⟨one of the gentlemen of his suite⟩ ↑his↓ Second Secretary, as charge *des* affaires, to take temporary care of the affairs of the Mission—otherwise, a complete departure would have been tantamount to a rupture between the two nations.

You will now understand why some little importance was given to my arrival as Minister at this court. There was a curiosity to know how I would act with respect to the delivery of my credentials. My written instructions were to present the presidents letter of credence *to the Queen*; but from conversations with the government at Washington before my departure I understood that I might regulate my conduct by circumstances. As it is a principle with us, therefore, to deal always in our diplomacy with the actual government of a country I made no hesitation in delivering my letter into the hands of Espartero, at ⟨h⟩ an audience given at his palace, specifying in my address that it was from the President to the Queen and delivered into his hands as Regent of the Kingdom. You have no doubt seen the bad translation of my address, as the government was careful to obtain from me a copy of it ⟨that⟩ for publication; as it was the first time a foreign Minister had ⟨been accredited⟩ presented his credentials since the Regency of Espartero. It was considered also as a precedent, and indeed the resident minister of Brazil,[25] who presented his credentials at the same time, but after me, and who is rather opposed to the present form of government, told me he should not have presented his letter of credence to Espartero unless I had broken the way and set the example. Whether France will get over her pique and make a step towards reconciliation with Spain by sending a full mission and authorizing her representative to acknowledge Espartero as the legitimate head of the government by delivering the letter of credentials into his hand is yet to be seen. The conduct of France towards Spain of late years has been anything but fair and magnanimous; and Louis Philip, in manifesting such hostility to the constitutional forms of the government, and such a disposition to discountenance Espartero, the constitutional depositary of the Regal power, seems singularly to have forgotten the history of his own elevation.

And now, having discussed these royal and diplomatic themes I find it impossible, my dear sister, to descend to subjects of ordinary import, so shall conclude for the present, with a promise of giving you scme further anecdotes of courts and King, Queens in my future letters, finding these matters are so much to your taste. I would observe, however, that ↑as↓ this letter is really meant merely for your private amusement I do not wish it to be shewn about; a minister ought not to be gossiping about diplomatic affairs. Keep it therefore *strictly among yourselves, in the family*. and so God bless you!

Your affectionate brother
Washington Irving

Mrs Catharine R Paris.

MANUSCRIPT: Star P. Myles.   PUBLISHED: PMI, III, 232–44 (in part).

1. This letter has not been located.

2. Ferdinand became king on the abdication of his father, Charles IV, in 1808; but Napoleon forced Ferdinand to restore the crown to his father on May 5, 1808. Charles then gave it to Napoleon; and Ferdinand, compelled to renounce his rights as heir on May 10, was detained at Valençay, where he remained until 1814. In March, 1814, he returned to Spain as king.

3. Joseph Bonaparte (1768–1844) was on the Spanish throne from May, 1808, until 1813, but his sovereignty was very unsteady since his position was not endorsed or supported by the Spanish people.

4. This revolution was led by an impulsive liberal soldier, Rafael del Riego (1785–1823) and dissident army officers with little civilian support. See Raymond Carr, *Spain, 1808–1939*, pp. 128–29.

5. The French expedition was commanded by Louis Antoine, duc d'Angoulême (1775–1844), eldest son of the Comte d'Artois (1757–1836), who was to become Charles X in 1824.

6. Ferdinand's first three marriages were childless. In 1802 he married Maria Antonia de Borbón Sicilia (d. 1806); in 1816, Maria Isabel de Braganza y Borbón (1797–1818) of Portugal; in 1819, Maria Josefa Amalia (1803–1829).

7. Ferdinand II (1810–1859) was king of Naples from 1830 until his death.

8. Maria Amélie (1782–1866), the wife of Louis Philippe.

9. The Salic law was introduced by Philip V (1683–1746) in 1713. Although the Cortes had reinstated female inheritance in 1789, Charles IV (1748–1819), Ferdinand's father, had not publicized the action, so it was generally assumed that the Salic law was valid until 1830.

10. Carlos María Isidro de Borbón (1788–1855), who was four years younger than Ferdinand. WI's use of "eldest" is somewhat confusing.

11. The military forces of Don Carlos fought in various parts of Spain during this period and kept the country in a state of turmoil. Gradually under the leadership of Generals Léon, O'Donnell, Zurbano, and Espartero the forces supporting María Christina defeated the soldiers and guerillas of Don Carlos, and she was firmly established as queen regent. See Martin Hume, *Modern Spain* (London, 1923), pp. 306–62; and Edgar Holt, *The Carlist Wars in Spain*.

12. Agustín Fernando Muñoz (1808–1873), a soldier of the royal guard who secretly married María Christina a few months after Ferdinand's death. In order to remain queen regent, María Christina could not remarry until Isabella attained her majority at the age of fourteen, so she did not publicly acknowledge Muñoz as her husband until 1844, when he was made duke of Riánzares. See Peter de Polnay, *A Queen of Spain*, pp. 33–40, 90–91.

13. On August 13, 1836, María Christina, under great pressure from dissident soldiers, was forced to accept the Constitution of 1812 as the instrument of government. See Holt, *The Carlist Wars in Spain*, pp. 145–47.

14. María Christina had hoped to gain Espartero's support for the Municipality Bill, passed by the Cortes on June 4, 1840. When he refused, she signed the bill anyway on July 18, 1840. See Christiansen, *Military Power*, pp. 95–97.

15. The Marquis Gueuilluy de Rumigny was French minister to Spain in 1840. See *Almanach de Gotha pour l'Année 1840* (Gotha, 1840), p. 221.

16. On October 14, 1840, María Christina left Spain for Marseilles to begin her exile in France. See Holt, *The Carlist Wars in Spain*, p. 200.

17. Over the protests of antimilitarist deputies who supported a three-man regency, Espartero was able to convince the Cortes to appoint him sole regent,

and he assumed the post on May 10, 1841. See Christiansen, *Military Power*, p. 104.

18. For details about Argüelles and Madame Mina, see WI's letter of August 3, 1842.

19. Manuel José Quintana (1772–1857) was a poet, dramatist, and literary critic who opposed French interference in Spanish politics. Queen Isabella designated him national poet in 1855.

20. Rosa (1615–1673) painted numerous landscapes and gloomy forest scenes filled with wild, picturesque details which in the nineteenth century were called "romantic."

21. WI had alluded to some of these activities in his letter of August 27, 1842, to Daniel Webster.

22. WI here meant Agustín Argüelles.

23. The British Parliament, on March 4, 1842, had reports of assurance from the French government not to support revolutionary activities in Spain. It also expressed British support of the Spanish government in power. See London *Times*, March 5, 1842.

24. Caroline Ferdinande Louise (1798–1870), widow of Charles Duke de Berry, who tried to place her son on the French throne. After forming a liaison with a Neapolitan marquis, Lucchesi-Palli, she lost her political credibility.

25. Cavalcanti de Albuquerque. See WI to Catharine Paris, July 30, 1842.

1469.   To Sarah Storrow

Madrid, Sept 2d. 1842.

My dear Sarah,

My last letter from you was dated about a month since. I have written repeatedly to you and have inclosed several open letters addressed to members of the family at home, for you to read and forward. These letters were sent by the courier of the French Embassy. I begin to fear, from receiving no letter from you acknowledging their receipt, that there must be some irregularity in the transmission of letters, one way or the other. Have these letters been delivered to you?—perhaps the absence of Mr Ledyard from Paris may occasion delay in the letters forwarded through his hand. Answer this letter by mail, & frank it to the frontier. Your long silence gives me a little anxiety about yourself—Are you well? is your dear little child well? are you all well? do write to me immediately.

I have long delightful letters from home; they are exceeding kind in writing to me so often. One dated July 19 & 21. is from your mother;[1] written in good spirits and almost pleasant vein. She is quite delighted with the peeps I have given her of foreign courts, having a little relish for royalty so I have just written her a voluminous letter of three sheets, giving her anecdotes of Spanish affairs and a history of the little Spanish princesses but I fear to forward so important a document by the usual channel, being at present doubtful whether my letters do not miscarry.

Your Mother appears to be quite enjoying herself at the Cottage and to be more and more in love with the place and its beautiful environs. What a lucky hit it was my building that little mansion which proves such a precious family retreat for old and young. It was indeed a ↑real↓ blessing snatched out of the midst of unsubstantial speculations.

I shall change my quarters in the course of a ⟨f⟩ week or two having at length found a· habitation to suit me.[2] It is part of a huge house, recently repaired, repainted and fitted up so as to be as good as new. It is near the public walks; the foreign legations and all places of pleasant resort. The windows look into a garden and some of them command an extensive prospect. I shall be better accommodated in respect to sleeping rooms; ⟨than at⟩ servants chambers and offices than at present. Shall be in a quieter and more airy situation; and enabled to take more exercise than at present. And I shall, if any thing, be at a cheaper rent. It is ⟨all⟩ ↑more↓ important at Madrid, to have a pleasant residence, than elsewhere; one is so much at home, and has so few sources of pleasure abroad. The house belongs to the Marques de Mos, who will inhabit a small wing of it. It is in the Calle des Infantas,[3] which being anglicised is "the Street of Princesses!"—think what a neighborhood I must have. My great regret at leaving my present residence is that I shall ⟨have⟩ lose the neighborhood of Madame Albuquerque; who I find a most agreeable acquaintance, and towards whom I feel strongly drawn as my countrywoman and townswoman.

I enclose a note from the post office at Paris informing me of a letter to my address detained there for want of ˋbeing franked. I wish Mr Storrow to do the needful in the matter and forward it to me

Kiss my dear little Miss Maam for me; if[4] find her grandmamma is extremely fearful she will get the name of Kitty, you will therefore be careful how you call her though I believe she runs more risk of getting from you the very unpoetical name of "puss cat."

Your affectionate Uncle
Washington Irving

Mrs Sarah P Storrow

P S. Mr Storrow must charge all postages incurred in my correspondence to my account; and ⟨have⟩ I shall some time hence get him to send me a memorandum of what he paid for use for postages while I was in paris as well as the items incurred subsequently that I may use it as a voucher in making up my accounts with government; With this understanding you can send your letters to me direct, without troubling Mr Ledyard to forward them. I reccommended that channel merely to save you the expense of franking.

ADDRESSED: a Madame / Madame Storrow / Aux Soins de Mr T W Storrow / 17
    Rue du faubg Poissonniere / à Paris   POSTMARKED: MADRID [unrecovered] /
    3 / SET. / [1842?] / [unrecovered] / PARIS [unrecovered] / [unrecovered] /
    SEPT / 42   DOCKETED: September 2d 1842
MANUSCRIPT: Yale.

1. This letter has not been located.
2. WI had mentioned the prospect of changing his quarters in his letter of
August 29, 1842, to Sarah Storrow.
3. Actually the building extended along Calle Victor Hugo and overlooked Calle
de las Infantas. See Bowers, *Spanish Adventures of WI*, p. 161.
4. WI probably intended to write "I."

1470.   To Helen Irving

[Madrid, September 4, 1842]

* * *

It seems to me as if I did not half enough appreciate that home when
I was there, and yet I certainly delighted in it; but the longer I am away,
the more the charm of distance gathers round it, until it begins to be all
romance. I sometimes catch myself calculating the dwindling space of
life that's left to me, and almost repining that so much of the best of
it must be passed far away from all that I hold most dear and delightful;
but I check such thoughts, and recollect how much there is around me
to interest and exercise my mind.* * *
* * *

I must confess the more I get acquainted with the present state of
Spanish politics and the position of the Government, the more does the
whole assume a powerful dramatic interest, and I shall watch with great
attention every shifting of the scene. The future career of this gallant
soldier, Espartero, whose merits and services have placed him at the
head of the Government, and the future fortunes of these isolated little
princesses, the Queen and her sister, have an uncertainty hanging about
them worthy of the fifth act of a melodrama.* * *

PUBLISHED: PMI, III, 245–46, 231.

Although PMI quotes the second passage without giving a date, its details and
context suggest that it might be a part of the dated letter.

1471. To James Bandinel

Madrid Sept 5t. 1842

My dear Bandinel,

I have been intending to write to you ever since my arrival at this place, but hitherto have not found leisure or rather mood; my mind being occupied and bothered with the thousand shifts and contrivances one is driven to, on first arriving in this capital, to get tolerably fixed and to make ones self tolerably comfortable.

I shall now in the course of a few days, be established in quarters somewhat to my mind, in a situation near to the public walks and places of resort, and near to your Embassy; which I rather think will be my great resort for social intercourse.

Your Minister Mr Aston has taken me by the hand on my arrival in the most frank and cordial manner; I am greatly pleased with him and with his diplomatic household, and think we shall all get on well together.

I am most heartily rejoiced to find that there is a probability of the affairs in negotiation between our two countries being adjusted in an amicable and satisfactory manner.[1] I felt some little apprehension your government, like the public at large, might form a wrong idea as to the boundary line from the report and representations of a certain Mr Featherstonhaugh,[2] and so be inclined to insist pertinaciously on claims which our people were satisfied were unfounded. This Mr Featherstonhaugh I have had my eye on ever since his first arrival in the United States between thirty and forty years since. His carreer has been very much that of an adventurer and a charletan—full of pretension, destitute of solid merit. A few years since he was employed in some jobs by the United States to make some surveys in the western country, on which he assumed the title of "United States ⟨Geological Surveys⟩ Geologist," ⟨a title⟩ though he had no authority to do so nor was there such an office under our government. While at Washington he toaded Mr Fox[3] who reccommended him to Lord Palmerston as a fit person to be employed on the momentous survey of the disputed territory. His report has proved like every thing else he has ever done, specious and fallacious.

The country in dispute has been diligently and toilfully surveyed within a year or two, on the part of our government, by my friend Professor Renwick accompanied by several engineers with whom I am well acquainted all persons thoroughly to be relied upon. One of the young gentlemen attached to my legation,[4] who has received a first rate mathematical education, accompanied the surveyors. A voluminous report was made for Congress, with maps, sketches of the country, peoples and ↑barometrical↓ elevations of the mountains &c all made on the most accurate scientific principles. This report was not finished in time to be published by Congress, but has been seen by Lord Ashburton[5] and doubtless has influenced him in his negotiations. It completely exposed the careless or ignorant inaccuracies, or wilful discrepancies in the report of Mr Featherstonhaugh.

I am scrawling this in haste as the morning is far advanced and your Courier goes off at Midday—Give my kind remembrances to your son, and, if ever you find time for a scrawl to a friend let me hear from you

Yours ever my dear Bandinel / Most faithfully
Washington Irving

P.S. A gentleman by the name of Christmas[6] was here a day or two since and brought a letter from your son to Mr Ames. I did not see him until the day before his departure on an excursion to the Escurial, Segovia &c. but hope to see more of him on his return to Madrid.

James Bandinel Esq / &c &c &c

DOCKETED: *W Irving—Sept 5 / 42 /* Ans Oct 3 from Lyme
MANUSCRIPT: NYPL—Berg Collection.

1. The northeastern boundary between the United States and Canada as stipulated by the Treaty of 1783 had never been formally established, and various earlier attempts ended in failure. The British appointed Lord Ashburton to renegotiate the boundary, and the Webster-Ashburton Treaty was signed at Washington on August 9, 1842.

2. George William Featherstonhaugh (1780–1866), an English-born surveyor who prepared a geological survey of the western United States for the War Department, had been appointed to the boundary commission by the British. After the settlement he was appointed British consul for the French departments of Calvados and Seine.

3. Henry Stephen Fox (1791–1846), who was British minister plenipotentiary to Washington, was largely responsible for the success of the negotiations culminating the Webster-Ashburton Treaty.

4. James Carson Brevoort. See WI to PMI, June 26, 1842.

5. Alexander Baring, first Baron Ashburton (1774–1848), who had been president of the Board of Trade under Sir Robert Peel and raised to the peerage in 1835, was the principal British negotiator in the boundary dispute.

6. Probably Henry Christmas (1811–1868), afterward Noel-Fearn, a clergyman, editor, and numismatist, was a member of the Royal Society, the Royal Society of Antiquaries, and the Royal Academy of History of Madrid. He edited the *Church of England Quarterly Review* from 1840 to 1843 and from 1854 to 1858, the *Churchman* from 1840 to 1843, and the *British Churchman* from 1845 to 1848.

1472. *To Pierre M. Irving*

[Madrid, Sept. 5, 1842]

My dear Pierre:

I have written so many family letters, of late, relative to myself and my Madrid concerns, of all of which you will probably learn the contents, that I have little to say to you on that head, not being able, like Paganini,[1] to play a thousand variations on one string of my fiddle.

I find my home resources are drying up in various quarters, by the cessation of my arrangement with booksellers, the non-payment of dividend on stocks, &c. I trust, however, you have the ways and means to keep my home establishment on the usual footing.* * * Get all my funds, as soon as you can judiciously, out of these fluctuating stocks, and invest them safely, even though at less interest. I cannot afford to risk more losses for the chance of extra profits.* * *

I shall soon be comfortably settled in new quarters, with my books and papers about me, and shall then open a literary campaign, which I shall have ample leisure to prosecute, and which, I trust will furnish me with the ways and means to abridge my absence from home, for I am anxious to pass as much as possible of the evening of my days among my relatives and friends at sweet little Sunnyside.* * *

PUBLISHED: PMI, III, 245.

1. Niccolo Paganini (1782–1840) was a virtuoso Italian violinist and composer.

1473. *To Ebenezer Irving*

Madrid, Sept. 8th, 1842.—

* * * I observe that Lea & Blanchard decline the arrangement I proposed.[1] I presume, therefore, the source of income from that quarter is effectually dried up for the present. * * *

PUBLISHED: PMI, III, 228.

1. In light of suggestions from Lea & Blanchard WI had proposed to them that his present contract, due to expire in May of 1842, be extended for two years, after which the payments would be increased to $2,500 per year and continued for seven additional years. WI also proposed to provide new and revised editions and new collections of stories and sketches from earlier published writings. See WI to Lea & Blanchard, March 10, 1842.

1474. To Julia Grinnell

Madrid, Septr. 9th. 1842.

My dear Julia,

I have long been intending to write to you, but have had so many letters from the family to answer, as well as letters of business from all quarters, that I have not been able to find time. I am glad to learn that you are so well pleased with your country retreat.[1] I reccollect the place well; having visited it occasionally in my frolicking and dancing days; when it was the seat of great hospitality. One of the pleasantest balls I ever attended was in that mansion, at which divers respectable old ladies of the present day sparkled as belles. Had I passed this summer at my cottage I should have been delighted to drive across the country occasionally and make you a visit. The intermediate country is beautiful. If it should be my happy lot once more to find myself at dear little Sunnyside, I hope you may yet be tenants of the Hammond homestead; in which case I certainly shall be among your country visitors; though I should much prefer to have you more immediately in my neighborhood.

Helen has written me a very pleasant account of a fourth of July visit which she and Pierre paid you; she says you are delighted with the place because it is roomy and airy for ⟨her?⟩ your children with fine grounds for them to play in; and Mr Grinnell, because it is easy of access from the city and can accommodate just as much company as he chooses to bring—On the day in question it appears he had a *revenue cutter full.*

Helen tells me that the children enjoy themselves extremely: that Siss is growing quite tall and shews a decided taste for country life. That Bub[2] is as happy as possible, improves in his looks every day and is one of the sweetest little fellows in the world. I should like to see the joyous little fellow with a Whole lawn before him to frolick upon. I have no doubt he ⟨carries on⟩ and Siss carry on the Steam boat and rail road business on an enlarged scale. By the bye I suspect the stout hearted little man has grown too strong for Siss to manage, and must have thrown off the yoke of petticoat government, under which he was already restive before my departure.

The constant writing about all these home concerns and home scenes makes my heart yearn continually after the home I have left behind; and prevents me from identifying myself very readily with the scenes around me and the new home in which, for some indefinite time to come, my lot must be cast. The residence for several years, in the bosom of a family where all appeared like my own children, has awakened strong paternal feelings that make it hard for me to resume my old habits of bachelorhood. However, I humbly trust that I shall gradually degenerate into the characteristics and habitudes proper to my position

I hear excellent accounts from my folks at the cottage of their neighbors the Minturns; I was sure that family would suit them. Mr Minturn[3] has already made himself known, and of course valued, throughout the neighborhood. I have always felt the highest esteem and most cordial regard for him, and my feelings of good will have been still more quickened by a simple testimonial to his goodness in one of the letters of your poor uncle E. Irving: who seems quite won by his manner towards him—"so kind and considerate, more so than I am accustomed to from those not of my household. I am aware that it is troublesome to converse with, or attempt to entertain a person whose hearing has failed as mine has, and therefore I do not look for much attention on this score, but it is ⟨cheering to⟩ gratifying to be cheered occasionally by a passing remark; it shews that I am not yet looked upon as a mere cypher."

It is, in fact, in such little matters, so unthought of by the great mass of mankind, that the heart of true benevolence is shewn. I am tenderly alive to every thing connected with the comfort and enjoyment of my poor infirm brother; and I beg you, when you see Mr Minturn, you will tell him what a grateful chord he has touched upon in my feelings, ⟨but this⟩ by what after all was but the spontanious dictate of his own goodness.

Farewell my dear Julia. God bless you and yours, and keep you all well and prosperous and happy. Remember me most cordially to your good husband and believe me ever

Your affectionate uncle
Washington Irving

Mrs Julia Grinnell.

MANUSCRIPT: Yale.   PUBLISHED: PMI, III, 249 (in part).

1. PMI (III, 248–49) identifies the residence as "the former homestead of Abijah Hammond, at Throgg's Neck, on the East River, a country retreat about fourteen miles from the city of New York." See also J. T. Scharf, *History of Westchester County*, II, 15.

2. Irving (1839–1921), the Grinnells' second child.

3. Robert B. Minturn (1805–1866) was a partner of Moses H. Grinnell in the shipping firm of Grinnell, Minturn and Co.

1475. To Sarah Storrow

Madrid Sept 10th. 1842.

My dear Sarah,

Your letter of Sept 1.[1] received the day before yesterday was quite a relief to me for I began to be uneasy from your long Silence, first, lest my letters to you, and through you to the family had miscarried, and secondly, lest ⟨you⟩ all might not be well with you. Do not suffer so long a time to elapse again without dropping me a line, however brief.

I have no letters from home since last I wrote excepting one from your uncle dated Aug. 4th.[2] Your mother and all were well and enjoying themselves. The neighborhood had been visited, however, by one of the heaviest falls of rain that has occurred in many years. The lane as usual has been torn up, and rendered for a time impassable with carriages. Mrs Jones' Eastern piazza which is nearly even with the ground was inundated with mud and water which poured into the area and filled the Kitchen and basement rooms to the depth of a foot setting every thing afloat.

I see you are persuading yourself that I am to visit Paris the coming winter. My dear girl it is out of the question. It will be some time yet before I get fairly at work with my pen, and once engaged I have a long task before me to make up for the months that have elapsed since I was interrupted by my diplomatic appointment. ⟨A literary e⟩ For any important literary enterprize I require, to get my mind in order, to have it undisturbed by any project of change of place; and to ⟨carry it on successfully I⟩ keep it in order, that I should remain on my working ground. On my contemplated literary campaign depends much of the ease and comfort of my after life. If I can succeed in preparing some productive writings for the press, I may be able to get once more a head, and gradually secure the wherewithal to return home and pass the evening of my days among those who love me. My resources at home have dried up so much, and are growing so scanty, that I shall have to keep an eye upon my individual expenses, as well as to exert my pen, that I may take care of those dependent upon me, and, if possible, provide for the future. You must not, therefore, hold out any pictures of pleasant visitations which I cannot realize, ⟨and which may set⟩ ↑both on account of the money & time they would cost; but the idea of which↓ might serve to render me discontented with the isolated life which I have made up my mind to lead, until I have accomplished my task.

Your account of the infatuation of the poor Jones's[3] is really melancholy. I have a strong feeling of good will to them, from their really kind and good qualities and cannot but regret to see them, through their unlucky passion for titles and the *Grande Monde*, exposing themselves to the duping of ⟨titled⟩ the crackd nobility and fashionable fortune hunters of Paris. Do not join in any censorious comments on their foibles; reccollect they have always manifested a kind regard for you.. ⟨It will be Fo⟩ For you, however, in your quiet and appropriate style of living, to keep up any thing like intimacy with them, in the false position in which they are placing themselves, would be an inconvenience to you both; you are right, therefore, in not attempting it, but in subsiding for the time into an amiable acquaintanceship.

You ask if Mr Aston the British Minister has a wife: he has not, but Mrs Scott, wife to one of the gentlemen of the legation, does the honors of the Embassy. She is pretty, and affable, and excels as prima donna in the private theater of the embassy. We are on very sociable terms, as her husband is from Bordeaux, where I knew him when he was a stripling. Madame Albuquerque, however, is my dependance for female society. She is amiable, intelligent and conversable, and a perfect lady in appearance and manners. I regret extremely that my approaching change of residence will take me from her immediate neighborhood.

Your account of my darling little Miss Maam delights me—but then— she will be so much grown and improved before I shall see her that she will not be the same child. I hope you indulged Elizabeth in the pink Scarf for her. You must not be jealous my dear Sarah, but I feel at times as if I should almost be as glad to see that child as to see yourself. It is wonderful how the little creature managed to get hold of me; and yet at times she used me abominably—but, like poor Cuddy Headrig,[4] I have been always doomed to be under female influence.

How I should have liked to pass my time with you at S⟨an⟩t Germain instead of Paris; it would have been quite a different kind of visit. You must have had a very pleasant Summer there. Your account of Mrs Ledyard (the elder) and the Surveillance she has established upon the ⟨movement⟩ progress of the Jones family, has amused me much; ⟨she⟩ it will afford her a little variety, after her observations of the Thornes. She is a woman of acute good sense, and a quick perception of the absurd, which she has the talent of putting in the most striking and ridiculous light; but I really do not think her ill natured, nor mischievously satirical—at least I have never heard her indulge severity where it was not called forth by some feeling of ⟨scorn for⟩ well merited scorn, that rather bespoke elevated notions in herself.

Give my kind remembrances to your husband and kiss my dear little Kate for me

Your affectionate Uncle
Washington Irving

MANUSCRIPT: Yale.

1. This letter has not been located.
2. This letter from Ebenezer has not been located. WI had responded to it on September 8.
3. Mrs. Colford Jones and her daughter Helen were romantically involved with the duke of Breteuil and his son. See WI to Sarah Storrow, December 24, 1842.
4. A dull plowman in the service of Lady Bellenden (character in Walter Scott's *Old Mortality*).

1476. To Sarah Storrow

Madrid, Sept. 11th. 1842

My dear Sarah,

I wrote to you yesterday by the courier of the French Embassy, and this morning I have yours of September 4th.[1] in reply to one I wrote on the 27th. of august but misdated the 29th. I reproach myself, my dear Sarah, with having expressed myself in such a manner as to have awakened your kind solicitude about me and your apprehensions that I am suffering from depression of spirits. I do at times feel sensibly my separation from those I love, but this is more than compensated by the deep indwelling satisfaction arising from the knowledge that my temporary separation is enabling me to contribute to their comfort and enjoyment. Every letter from home, presenting me a picture of domestic happenings, which, but for my present position, might have been interrupted, makes me feel that I am living to some purpose.

My present plan of life is full of regular occupation, that keeps me generally in a state of cheerfulness. Tomorrow I begin arrangements in my new quarters, into which I shall move in the course of two or three days. Then I shall open all my household articles from Paris most of which are yet boxed up—I shall have all my books and papers, which have arrived from Cadiz, about me; I shall then feel completely fixed and at home; in a delightful habitation in a pleasant quarter, where I have public promenades close at hand, to take exercise whenever I have a spare half hour. I shall then embark fairly in my literary undertakings, and, once embarked, time will pass rapidly with me.

I wrote to you yesterday about this anticipated literary campaign; but not in as bright spirits as I ought to have done. I really look forward to it with great confidence and animation, as one that will give me ⟨great⟩ delightful occupation, and will change my whole pecuniary position. I am fortunately placed for a good spell of intellectual exercise. I shall have abundant liesure: the climate here always has seemed favorable to my system; the pure light air of this elevated region seems to clarify my mind and capacitate me for a great deal of mental labor. When I was here before I wrote more in the same space of time than at any other period of my life and that without weariness of the brain, and I seem as if I am capable of doing as much at present. A few months of occupation may put me so far on in the works I have in hand, that I may then afford myself holiday; and have the wherewithal to enjoy it. My only wish at present is to keep my mind undisturbed by any plans of pleasure or prospects of change of place, that may prevent it from settling down fixed and composed to the broad tasks before me. ⟨These once accomplished⟩

You speak of a letter which you wrote to me on the 24 August. I have never received it. I received one from you without a date, but which must have been written about the 1st August, as it reached me on the 8th. The next received from you was dated Sept 1²—an interval of a month—I apprehend some letters may have miscarried which have been sent ⟨to⟩ through ⟨a⟩ our legation at Paris, as Mr Hamilton, who receives most of his letters through that channel has long been without any. probably Mr Ledyards absence from Paris may have caused some derangement; or some servant employed to put the letters in the post office may have neglected to frank them. Hereafter ⟨write to me send your frank⟩ send your letters to the office and frank them yourself; and let Mr Storrow keep an account of the postage which I will settle with him and charge to my contingent fund

I wrote a long "diplomatic" letter to your mother a few days since.³ three or four sheets full, closely written, giving her a simple, but I trust, pretty clear and correct account of Spanish political affairs, especially as they bore on the situation of the little Queen and her sister, in whose peculiar fortunes I thought she would feel interested. As I felt at the time some doubt whether my other letters had reached you in safety I ⟨forbore to⟩ sent this despatch by the British Ambassadors courier, to our Dispatch Agent in London. I think when your mother receives it she will put on her largest pair of Spectacles. Your mother says she likes to have a "peep now and then at royalty." I think I have given her a broad Stare.

I thank you for all your delightful particulars about little *puss cat*— do not fear to be minute about her. I am rejoiced to find she has got into short skirts and is no longer playing bird of paradise with a long ⟨tail⟩ bothering tail. I presume the first tidings of this joyful event must have been given in the non received letter of Aug. 24th. Give her my sincere congratulations on this important curtailment of her train. I think now that you have docked off such a material item of expense, you can well afford to give her the pink scarf which Elizabeth petitions.

I shall look forward to your next for an account of the merry gathering

↑of Americans↓ you are to have at St Germain where you expect to
meet the Ledyards, Jones, &c I should be amused to hear Mrs. Ledyards
comments which are usually so spicy.

Give my kind remembrances to Mr Storrow Kiss little Miss Maam—and
believe me my darling Sarah ever your affectionate uncle

Washington Irving

ADDRESSED: Madame / Madame Storrow / aux Soins de M. T. w Storrow / 17.
Rue du Faubg Poissonniere / à Paris   POSTMARKED: Madrid. Sept. 11
MANUSCRIPT: Yale.

1. This letter has not been located.
2. This letter has not been located.
3. Dated September 2, 1842.

1477.   To Charlotte Irving

Madrid, Sept. 16, 1842.

My dear Charlotte:

Your letter of July 28th[1] reached me three or four days since, and
brought me a world of intelligence. First of all, your first appearance at
the Tarrytown and Dobbs' Ferry *soirées*, held that evening at Mrs.
Sheldon's,[2] at which, I trust, you produced a proper sensation. Then the
invasion of Sunnyside, by sea, by a roving *piragua*, fitted out at the port
of Yonkers, and manned by Edgar and a desperate crew of ladies and
gentlemen. Then the invasion by land, by Mrs. ———[3] and Mrs. ———'s
mother, and Mrs. ———'s sister and Mr. ———'s mother—no, Mr ———'s
aunt, and a Miss P., who was staying with Mrs. ———. And then the influx of all the ———s and of all the Dr. ———s. And then a second invasion
by sea, of all the Hamiltons in the Dream, and the carrying off of half
the garrison of Sunnyside to Rockland Lake and the mountains; and
then the great party at Mr. ———'s, given to Mr. and Mrs. ———, to which
Mrs. ——— did *not* think herself invited, but to which she afterward found
she *was* invited, and which turned out a most delightful party. Guide
us and keep us! what an eventful period of history we live in! Why, my
dear Charlie, if matters go on at this rate, I shall find Sleepy Hollow wide
awake by the time I come back.

And now, my exceeding good and very dear little woman, I will try to
give you, in return for your very agreeable letter, some little inkling of
my Spanish home and its affairs. I have just changed my residence, and
have taken the principal apartment in a great Spanish house belonging
to a bachelor nobleman named the Marquis de Mos, who has a bachelor's

nest in one wing of it. I have such a range of *salons*, that it gives me quite an appetite to walk from my study to the dining room. Then the windows of the *salons* all face the south, and look into a little dilapidated garden, in the centre of which is an old, half-ruined marble fountain, with gold fish swimming about in it, and a superannuated triton in the middle, blowing a conchshell, out of which, in his younger days, there no doubt rose a jet of water. My own private apartment, consisting of a bedroom and study, is in one end of the building. My bedroom formerly served as an oratory or chapel to the mansion. It is a small octagon room, rising to a little cupola or dome, with little windows in the top, about fifteen feet from the floor, by which the chamber is lighted. These windows catch the first rays of the rising sun, and, as the oratory is prettily painted of a delicate pink, yellow, and pale green, and as the centre of the dome is gilded, the whole becomes beautifully lighted up. You have no idea what a splendid waking up I have sometimes in the morning. I don't think "glorious Apollo," with his bedchamber of sun-gilt clouds, has much the advantage of me.—* * * * My study is immediately adjacent to the oratory; one window overlooks the garden of an old convent, and has a fine view of the Regent's palace, and the distant groves of the Retiro.

* * * * * * *

I have experienced a kind of home feeling of enjoyment since I have got into this house, that I have not felt before since my arrival in Madrid. My other residence was excessively noisy, and abounded with inconveniences, so that I could never feel at home in it; indeed, the very idea that I should remove as soon as I could find a house more to my mind, kept me unsettled and comfortless. Now, I trust, I am fixed for the whole of my sojourn in Madrid, and I consider myself singularly fortunate in finding in this uncomfortable metropolis so pleasant an abode.

PUBLISHED: PMI, III, 246–48.

1. This letter has not been located.
2. A Tarrytown neighbor.
3. This and succeeding blanks for proper names were editorial changes made by PMI.

1478. *To Sarah Storrow*

Madrid, Sept. 17th. 1842

My dear Sarah,

I enclose a letter for Charlie,[1] which I leave open that you may read it, as it gives an account, in somewhat of a rough style, of my present abode, and I should be sorry to have to write it over again. ⟨You⟩ I wish this letter to be sent to Mr Ledyard in time to be forwarded in the bag that goes by the Boston Steamer.

You will see by this letter that I am fixed very much to my mind in my new habitation, and I cannot express to you what a cheering effect it has had upon my feelings. I now really feel as if I can content myself for a time at Madrid and enjoy my usual state of cheerfulness. I am near to every ⟨thing that is⟩ source of recreation, and in the neighborhood of the Prado. I can almost hear the music of the opera from my window, for the theater is within three minutes walk of my house. For two or three nights I have been up until a late hour, strolling up and down my apartments ⟨and ha⟩ lit up by moon light, or leaning from the balconies ⟨that⟩ which look into the garden. The whole house is bright and cheerful; well lighted and well ventilated without a single dark dirt hole that a Spanish servant can take advantage of. ⟨My⟩ The furniture appears to great advantage and when I get down my ⟨curt⟩ rich carpets and get up my handsome window curtains (of poplin with satin stripes) I shall be quite fine for Madrid. The candalabras which Mr Storrow purchased for me form very pretty ornaments in the principal saloon and are much admired. The china, glass &c have all come in good order and will do admirably

Am I not gossipping like some old dame of a housekeeper? But really this change from a rather gloomy, and a very noisy house, into an abode so bright, so quiet, so almost rural, has brushed off a cloud of sad and weary fancies that at times overshadowed me; and enabled me to look round with enjoyment on the present, without casting back a repining eye to the distant and the past.

I had a very pleasant letter from your mother dated July 29th.[2] They have really had gay times at the Cottage and the girls appear to have enjoyed themselves very much. The Minturns are quite popular in the neighborhood and enter with true spirit into every party of pleasure. There have been pic nics at Rockland Lake and at the Croton Dam; and parties at the Sheldons and the Jones, & the Hamiltons. Your brother Irving was absent on an excursion to the Western part of the State. His letters your mother says were full of the freshness and joyousness of youth on a first excursion. He was enchanted with the great lakes and only wanted to go on to the far far west. Your mother goes on to say "Mr Constant expects to bring Mrs Constant and his little daughter up this week. They are both very well and the little baby one of the finest in the world. I shall call to see Mrs Constant very soon as I have a very great interest in little babies; my mind dwelling on them continually. I have just returned from my daily walk down to the stone steps then on the top of the wall under the trees, until I came to the spring. It is perfectly delightful under those trees, so cool; I must have a seat fixed there that I may sit and enjoy the ripple of the water, so quiet and so lovely."

This walk is entirely new; the wall she speaks of is the one made to protect the bank from being washed away; the bank is now all sodded and I am told adds greatly to the appearance of the cottage from the water. ⟨I had in⟩ The walk has been made since my departure, but according to my directions. I had intended to have seats placed along it.

I wish Mr. Storrow to call at the Galignanis and tell them that their paper[3] has not reached the legation regularly of late. I have received none for several days past. Mr Vail subscribed until October, after which time I wish it to be continued in my name. It is a paper I value very much and am anxious to have it punctually.

Farewell my dear, dear Sarah; give my kind regards to your husband and a kiss to my ⟨gr⟩ little great niece Miss Maam.

Your affectionate uncle
Washington Irving

ADDRESSED: Mrs T W Storrow / 17 Rue Faubg Poissonniere / a Paris
MANUSCRIPT: Yale.

1. WI to Charlotte Irving, September 16, 1842.
2. This letter has not been located.
3. *Galignani's Messenger* was an English-language newspaper published by John Anthony and William Galignani, prominent booksellers and the foremost publishers of English books in Paris.

1479. *To Count Almodóvar*

Legation of the United States / Madrid. September 24th. 1842.

The Undersigned, Envoy Extraordinary and Minister Plenipotentiary of the United States, has the honor to call the attention of Count Almodovar, First Minister of State and of Foreign affairs of Her Catholic Majesty to the case of Mr. Michael Drawsin Harang,[1] an American Citizen, which has already been a subject of correspondence with Her Majesty's Government.

It appears that, Luis Alexander Harang the father of the Applicant, was a Native of Louisiana, and Citizen of the United States: In consequence of the Royal Cedula or Decree of 10th. Augt. 1815, holding out inducements to Foreigners, as well as Spaniards, to settle in the Island of Porto Rico, by offers of gratuitous grants of land, and various privileges, he removed to that Island, purchased land there with the funds which he had brought with him; cultivated with his own means and Industry a Sugar plantation, and after Having amassed considerable property died at New York in 1835, bequeathing his property among his Children.

After his death his son Michael Drawsin Harang in his own behalf, and in virtue of a Power of attorney from his Coheirs, sold the property lying and being in the Island of Porto Rico, with the intention of conveying the proceeds out of the Island; when the Intendente interfered and exacted a *derecho de extraccion* or duty of exportation of 15 per cent upon the gross amount of the sales: the proceeds of which duty, amounting to near eleven Thousand Dollars, were gathered into the Royal Treasury.

Against this exaction Michael Drausin Harang protested; His father having been a Citizen of the United States, and his property bequeathed to his Heirs exempted from all *derechos de extraccion* according to the 11th. article of the Treaty of 1795.

The Intendente maintained the Justice of his exaction by alledging that Luis Alexander Harang, in accepting the Royal Cedula of Augt. 10th. 1815, and its benefits subjected him Self to its consequences; among which was this duty of extraccion of 15 per cent, on any property he might devise:—and further that, in becoming, a *Naturalized Subject of Spain*, he had forfeited the protection of the 11th. article of the Treaty of 1795, which only extended to Citizens of the United States.

· At this point the matter rested when last brought before this Government.

In reply Michael Drausin Harang observes, that his father, Luis Alexander Harang, when he migrated to the Island of Porto Rico, never accepted the Royal Cedula; that is to say, the grants and benefits held out in it, as a lure to Colonists; and, in not accepting these, he did not subject himself to "all the consequences" of that decree. The most prominent inducement held out in that Cedula was the gratuitory grant of land to any Spaniard or Foreigner, who would settle on the Island and Cultivate it; The said land to be assigned out in portions according to the number of the Colonists family and of his Slaves, and the assignment to be entered into the Register of Population, with the name of the Colonist, the day of his admission, the number of the Individuals of his Family &c.

Luis Alex: Harang neither asked nor received any such grant of lands: Had he done so, a Record thereof would exist in the Register of Population; and an authenticated Copy of it, would no doubt have been produced by the Intendente to support his assertion. But no such record exists—Mr. L. A. Harang purchased land with his own funds which he had brought with him; He cultivated and improved it at his own expense, and by his unassisted means and Industry; so far therefore from being a beneficiary of the Royal or Colonial Government, and of course, subject to pay for the benefits received, he was in this respect a benefactor of the Island.

Then, as to his becoming a Naturalized subject of Spain.—The article 12th. of the Royal Cedula says "The first five years of the establishment of Foreign Colonists in the Island being past, *and they then obliging themselves to remain permanently in it,* all the rights and privileges of naturalization will be conceded to them, as well as to the children they have brought with them, or which may have been born to them in the Island; that they may consequently be admitted to the honorable employs of the republic and the Militia &c.

Now Mr. Michael Drausin Harang expressly declares that his father never, either at the time of his arrival at the Island, or during his residence there, did or contemplated any act to divest himself of the character of a Citizen of the United States, or to acquire the character and rights of a Naturalized Subject of Spain. This point on which the Intendente rests the main stress of his Justification ought to have been substantiated by Documentary Evidence. The mere residence in the Island for any number of years, could not make him a Spanish subject, without some overt act or declaration on his part; nor could the Royal offer of Naturalization render its acceptance obligatory; a Specific formality was necessary, *The Declaration of an Intention to remain permanently in the Island.* If such declaration had been made for the purpose of obtaining Naturalization Some record of it must exist, and ought to have been produced to maintain this vital ground of defence on the part of the Intendente: No such proof is furnished and Mr. Michael D. Harang declares that the archives of the Secretaria of the Island of Porto Rico have been diligently searched but no evidences of his Father's naturalization or even domiciliation can be found—In fact he went to the Island merely at the time when the decree of Augt. 10th. 1815, threw the door open to Foreigners; he availed himself of the general license of the Decree, without accepting its specific Grants and benefits; and incurring the consequent obligations; He lived and died *a Citizen of the United States,* and as such his heirs claim for his Estate the rights Secured by the following paragraph of the 11th. Article of the Treaty of 1795 "And where on the death of any person holding real estate within the territories of the one party, such real estate would by the laws of the land, descend on a Citizen or subject of the other, were he not disqualified by alienage, such subject shall be allowed a reasonable time to sell the same, and to withdraw the proceeds without molestation and exempt from all rights of *detraction* on the part of the Government of the respective States."

The Government of the United States after maturely examining the case, are of opinion that the duty of fifteen per cent has been wrongfully exacted on the property of the deceased Luis Alex. Harang, a Citizen of the United States. and ought to be refunded, with damages for detention to his Heirs; they are convinced that Her Majesty's Government will concur with them in this opinion, when they have investigated the case, and they have instructed the Undersigned to use his utmost exertions in procuring a Speedy adjustment of a claim, where so much injury has already been caused by delay.

The Undersigned avails himself of this occasion to renew to Count de Almodovar, the assurances of his distinguished consideration.

                                                            Washington Irving

His Excellency / Count Almodovar / &c &c &c

Manuscript: NA, RG 59; NA, RG 84 (letterbook copy).

A copy of this letter was enclosed with WI's despatch no. 4 to Daniel Webster, October 8, 1842.

1. The Harang case was the subject of extensive correspondence between the American and Spanish governments, beginning in February of 1839 and continuing intermittently until March 26, 1853, when William L. Marcy, then secretary of state, refused to accept the interpretation of Article 11 of the 1795 Treaty which had formed the basis of the Harang claim. See Hasse, *Index to U.S. Documents*, I, 732–34.

1480. *To Sarah Storrow*

                                                    Madrid, Sept. 26th. 1842

My dear Sarah,

Since I last wrote to you I have recd. your letters of the 24th. August and 12th. of September[1] The former I presume had loitered in the post office at Paris until it was franked. I now have, I believe, received all the letters you have written to me. I would not have missed your letter of Aug 24th. for a great deal. It was full of most agreeable and interesting details; though I was a little uneasy to find little Miss Maam beginning so early to flirt with the red coats. I fear her head will be turned with the attentions of the gay world on the Terrace at St Germains.

I am getting quite at home in my new dwelling, which is indeed a very pleasant one. Tomorrow I give my first dinner, which will be to Mr Aston and the gentlemen of the British Embassy,[2] and Mr Albuquerque, the Brazilian minister. The party if all come, will consist of ten persons; a number which, if I can help it, I will never exceed. I mean that my dinners shall be in a pretty, but, not pretentious style, well cooked, well served, and, I hope, well relished. Tell Mr Storrow the china, glass &c have all arrived in admirable order having been capitally packed. There was but one article broken: a plate; which had been broken by a nail driven in too far in closing the box. I am very much pleased with every thing he has purchased for me. I was sure I could not do wrong in trusting to his taste. My silver articles have also arrived, with my books, from New York; and now I only want my plated ware and cultery,[3] which have just reached Cadiz, to ⟨render⟩ fit me out completely. My Establishment, I assure you, is a very creditable one for a bachelor, but I wish I had a few female moveables to grace and enliven it. I get on very well all day, for I am constantly occupied; but, when evening comes, I miss my dear little coterie of nieces that I have been accustomed to have round me. ⟨Then I feel⟩ I am not in the humor to ⟨great⟩ go out much in the world in quest of society; and Madrid is not a place where a stranger readily forms sociable intimacies. I have in fact no sociable visiting places excepting the British Embassy and Mr Albuquerques. The latter is my great resource. I am drawn to Madame Albuquerque from her being a countrywoman and a townswoman; but, in fact, I find her very amiable, intelligent and ladylike; ⟨and⟩ she takes a most kind interest in my affairs, and has been of great assistance to me in regulating my domestic concerns. Her husband is ⟨a⟩ very gentlemanlike and friendly and she has two pretty little girls that will become quite pets of mine. I regret extremely that my removal to the opposite side of the City puts us at a distance from each other.

28th.   Since writing the foregoing I have received yours of the 19th.[4] I cannot express to you, my dear Sarah, how acceptable these letters are to me. This frequency of correspondence at a few days distance, lessens the feeling of separation and absence; it is keeping up as it were a conversation across the Pyrenees. It ought not to be much of a task for you to write to me, you need only talk about yourself and your concerns, and especially about little Miss Maam and you are sure to interest me.

You would have been amused yesterday to see the fuss of preparation for my *first dinner*, that great event and era in housekeeping. Some furniture had yet to come home; some finishing off to be done by masons and painters; some articles to be provided the want of which had not been discovered until the last moment. Every one in the establishment: Secretary, attachées, domestics, hangers on, all were occupied and not the least part of the difficulty was to spur on the Spanish mechanics and workmen who of all beings of their class are the most dilatory and procrastinating. A marble slab, supported on iron brackets, had to be put up in one of the saloons to sustain a clock. The job had been put off from day to day until the very morning of the day I was to ⟨have⟩ ↑give↓ my dinner. With the utmost difficulty I then got the mason at work. He finished the job but to my dismay, defaced a great part of the wall which was painted in fresco. A painter was summoned who was occupied ⟨esp⟩ in the neighborhood. It was impossible for him to take the job in hand at that moment. ⟨His⟩ It was twelve Oclock; his men ⟨even⟩ had to dine—Well, but when they have dined?—Ah, Señor, then they must take their Siesta! —I offered to pay double, treble price—all in vain. The men could not be put out of their routine of eating and sleeping. But their Siesta would be over by half past two-Oclock and then the work should certainly be done. I had to submit; fortunately the painter kept his word—His men came refreshed with food and sleep and my wall was finished just in time to get the clock mounted before the company arrived—Every thing else was likewise arranged by the last moment, and the eventful dinner went off very successfully.

It was served on a round table; set out in the modern style the dessert ⟨set⟩ placed on the table and the meats brought in, ready cut up, and handed round to the guests by the servants. Thanks to your husband's good taste my china & table furniture had a very pretty appearance. My cook proved himself a good artist; the dishes were well cooked and nicely served up; and were highly approved. Benjamin was a first rate butler and was ably supported by Lorenzo, and by two or three hired aids de camp. Upon the whole the guests seemed to be very well pleased with their entertainment and I humbly trust will be encouraged to come again. Dinners like this, social, tasteful yet unpretending I can afford to give with tolerable frequency; they are of the kind that gives the most pleasure; and I am determined to give no dinners of parade.

You ask me whether Madrid is an expensive place. It certainly is not a cheap one. Every thing you have to buy is dear; still there are not so many obligations and temptations to Expense as in most other capitals My first year of course will require a great out lay of money to set up my establishment, but next year I trust to be able to live so much within my income as to be able to contribute to expenses at home; or to lay up something for the future. I must regulate my expenses carefully, however, to do so.

You wish to know whether my young gentlemen like Madrid. I can hardly say. They do not find it a very gay nor sociable place; but they occupy themselves studying the language; visiting the galleries of painting, & the museums; ⟨the⟩ and there is sufficient of national peculiarity in every thing around them to furnish subjects of curiosity and observation. Alexander Hamilton I think is the most disappointed. He is fond of society and especially of ladies society, and anticipated much delight among the dark eyed Señoritas of Spain. ⟨with this(?)⟩ As yet he has not been able to make the acquaintance, or at least the intimacy of a single one; the society of young ladies being quite taboo'd to young gentlemen in this country. His romance, therefore, is completely at fault; and he looks back with repining to the flirtations he was accustomed to enjoy in the United States. He is of a bright buoyant nature, however, and takes things with great good humour, though with a little humorous lamentation.

He has projected a tour of four or five weeks to Granada and other parts of Andalusia and I have agreed that Carson Brevoort and Hector Ames shall accompany him. They all want to visit that part of Spain, and ought to visit it, and it is a ⟨pitt⟩ pity they should not go together; to take care of each other, and have the advantage of good company. I shall feel somewhat lonely in my great apartment during their absence; but I trust by that time to be completely engrossed by literary occupations. They will set off in the early part of October.

The arrival of the Mott[5] family in Paris is quite an event; and bodes no good to the Jones dynasty. I shall be extremely anxious to hear how the campaign opens between these great rival powers and beg you to keep me minutely informed—"We certainly live in a most eventful period of history" Give my kind remembrances to Mr Storrow. Kiss little puss cat for me

Your affectionate uncle
Washington Irving

ADDRESSED: Madame Storrow /aux Soins de M. T. Storrow / 17. Rue du Faubg
    Poissonnière / à Paris
MANUSCRIPT: Yale.

1. These letters have not been located.
2. These included Newton Scott, Henry Valentine Jerningham, and Loftus Otway. See *Almanach de Gotha pour l'Année 1842* (Gotha, 1841), p. 293.
3. WI's spelling.
4. This letter has not been located.
5. Dr. and Mrs. Valentine Mott traveled extensively in Europe. In a letter of December 1, 1841, to Sarah Storrow, WI had mentioned a feud between Mrs. Jones and Mrs. Mott.

1481. To Sarah Irving

Madrid, Sept. 28, 1842

My dear Sarah,

I have again to thank you for a very acceptable letter dated July 31st and August 7.[1] Your letters are perfect little Sunnyside gazettes, giving me all the interesting news of the cottage and the neighborhood. I am glad to learn that your summer has passed away gaily and sociably. The Minturns are quite an acquisition to the neighborhood and the return of the Constants must have had an enlivening effect. I find by my last letters, you were on the point of giving a party at the cottage. I shall look to my next letters for an account of it.

I recently received my books and papers that were forwarded from America, and with these the articles of silver that were put up by you at the cottage. I now only want some plated ware and cutlery, which are on their way from England, to fit me out completely. All my china, glass, linen etc. purchased at Paris came here in perfect order. They were all purchased by Mr. Storrow and are credit to his judgement and good taste. They are simple but elegant.

My house being now tolerably arranged and my table furniture arrived, I yesterday gave my first dinner. My guests were the British Minister, the gentlemen of his legation, Mr. Alberquerque, the Brazilian Minister who married Miss Oakey. We sat down ten persons to table, a number I will never exceed if I can help it, as I wish my dinners to be lively and social, not formal and ostentatious. My round table made a very pretty show, the dessert being set out in the centre, and the meats brought in dish by dish, ready cut up, and handed round to the guests according to the modern fashion. My man Benjamin proved himself a first rate butler and my cook won laurels. The whole repast was considered a very successful first attempt.

In a recent letter to Charlotte,[3] I gave a particular description of my dwelling, accompanied by a map. That you may hereafter understand any household anecdotes better, I must tell you that the first saloon is yellow; the second or grand saloon green and the third or interior saloon pink, the walls being painted in fresco in these colours. The two first saloons are my state apartments, furnished with the furniture purchased by Mr. Vail; which is very handsome, yet simple; of mahogony and satin striped poplin; curtains to match and rich carpets. The pink saloon is our favorite family gathering place. It is extremely cheerful with very wide casements to the floor, opening into the broad glassed verandah; which would make a first rate conservatory. This will be a capital winter room, enjoying so much sunshine. The verandah will answer, like the cloisters of a convent, for exercise within doors. This room is plainly furnished for daily use and has two or three lounging chairs beside some quaint old-fashioned pieces of furniture that I have picked up in holes and corners. In this room I have my dinner table set out, when I have company; the meats being brought through the corridor which you will observe in the plan, passing between the saloons and bedrooms. I ought to have told you, in giving the plan of the house, that the kitchen is upstairs; the communication from it opening into the outer antichamber or waiting room. I am giving you quite a homey housckeeping letter, but I know that these are details in which you will take interest. I will dismiss this subject by saying that my suite of apartments is nearly one hundred and eighty feet in length .

I shall soon have my apartment all to myself for a time, as Mr. Hamilton and Mr Brevoort intend making a tour of four or five weeks in the South of Spain, and I have consented that S . . . .[3] may accompany them, as it will give him an opportunity of seeing that interesting part of Spain in good company. They will set off in the course of a week or ten days. I shall feel their absense; but I expect in the course of a few days to become completely occupied with my literary tasks and then I can get along very well alone. In fact it is only in the evenings that I feel the want of society, having been accustomed at home to have you all around me when my days occupations were over. At such times I feel my absence from dear little Sunnyside.

I am fortunate in having good servants. Benjamin is trusty and careful. He has charge of the china, plate, household stores, wine, etc. and I have every reason to believe him strictly faithful. Juana, the house maid, is in a manner the house keeper, has all the linen under her charge and attends to keeping it in order, having it washed, delivering it out for household use, etc. She also keeps all my own linen in nice order. She is a very respectable and very nice-looking girl, always well dressed. She has a very pretty room to herself, which had been intended in the construction of the house, for a dining room, and is finely painted in fresco with landscapes, etc. It is quite her pride and delight. (Lorenzo), the valet or footman, is invaluable. He has been with my two predecessors Mr. Eton and Mr. Vail, and is a complete diplomatic servant; and faithful in all things. Under these functionaries my house goes like clockwork.

Tell Eliza I have received her letter and will answer it soon. As I am about to become very much occupied with my pen in literary labour, I shall not be able to keep up so frequent a correspondence as heretofore, but I am sure you will all excuse me and will not wait for my replies before you repeat those letters which are so interesting and cheering to me during my absence.

I must work, that I may provide the ways and means of coming home and living amongst you once more; but when I really work with my pen, my correspondence has to stand still, or at least to be kept up very irregularly.

Give my love to all the household. I hope your Aunt has received my very long diplomatic letter.

Your affectionate uncle
Washington Irving

Oct. 1 . I have rec'd / Your aunts letter of Aug. 20th.

MANUSCRIPT: Robert S. Grinnell; typescript copy in SHR.   PUBLISHED: Butler,
    WI's *Sunnyside*, p. 24; (1974 ed.), p. 52.

1. These and other letters from relatives mentioned in this letter have not been
located.
2. See WI's letter of September 16, 1842.
3. This may be a reference to Hector Ames, who was a member of the legation
staff. See WI to Sarah Storrow, September 26, 1842, for other references to Hector's accompanying Hamilton and Brevoort on the trip.

1482. To Julia Grinnell

Madrid Sept. 30th. 1842

My dear Julia,

I have just received your delightful letter of Aug 25[1] which was
indeed most welcome. I wrote to you not long since, in hopes of drawing
from you a letter in return, but you have kindly anticipated me. I can
easily imagine your satisfaction with your country residence;[2] I know
the old mansion well, and the delightful country in which it is situated;
with its splendid advantages of water. I should think it would just hit
Mr Grinnells fancy; and hope he may find loose spending money enough
in his pocket to buy it; after he has put by that small provision in a cup
board, for Bub and Siss, which I have heretofore suggested to him.
Tell him not to "cast all his bread upon the water"[3] in the shape of ships,
however ship shaped they may be, but to anchor a little upon land, in
fast property. I like your idea of Lord Ashburton and Mr Webster
shaking hands, as ⟨a stern orn⟩ an ornament for the stern of the new
ship to be called after the former; perhaps the effect might be
heightened if you could bring in the boundary line, running across his
Lordships toes.

I am delighted with the treaty; it has been negotiated in a fine spirit
on both sides and is a great achievement for Mr Webster. He has
remained in the Cabinet to some purpose; and now, if he thinks proper,
may retire with flying colours;[4] yet I should be loth to see such a statesman retire from the management of our affairs. What successor will give
us such state papers—Who would have managed our ↑Mexican↓
correspondence in such style? Would to god he could remain in with
satisfaction to himself and have a good majority in Congress to back him.

I have just got myself settled in a pleasant habitation, which I think
will be my home during my residence in Madrid. It is spacious, as all
Spanish houses are, but quiet and clean, which are rare qualities in

Madrid mansions. I have just given my first dinner, not such feasts as you give in New York, one of which would exhaust a Madrid market, but in a pretty French style and to a small party; never if I can help it intending to exceed the limits of a social round table. I have indeed to play the Ambassador on a cautious scale, and to keep down my pride that I may "provide for my family;" fortunately there is no rivalry in expense in ·the diplomatic Corps at Madrid; the British Minister being the only one that entertains; and his immense fortune putting competition out of the question. I find him ⟨c⟩ very frank and cordial; and we are already on the most social terms.

I have had some brooding spells of home sickness since my arrival in Europe, but they are gradually wearing away, and I am now about to enter upon a carreer of literary occupation that will effectually dispell them. My letters from home, while they at times make me long to be among the scenes of rural enjoyment which they depict, impress me with a deep and grateful sense of the providential nature of my present position. I find from them that my former sources of subsistence ↑are↓ gradually drying up; and that, had I not received when I did, my present appointment, I should have been reduced to harrassing embarrassments, and forced to break up that delightful little rural establishment, which is such a happy nestling place for the family. These reflections lift up my spirit again to its proper level, and at times make my heart glow with affectionate gratitude to those whose friendship placed me where I am. Need I say that formost among these is your own noble hearted husband.

Mr Grinnell, in his appendix to your letter, says that Mr Webster enquired particularly after me and expressed much interest in my mission—As yet my mission has called for but little exertion of diplomatic skill, there being no questions of moment between the governments, and I not being disposed to make much smoke where there is but little fuel. If any question of difficulty or delicacy should arise, however, I will task my abilities, such as they are, to the utmost, to prevent Mr Webster from finding his confidence misplaced. I have been very quiet ever since my arrival in Madrid; getting my domestic affairs in order, and making myself acquainted with the complicated and entangled state of Spanish politics, but I shall now gradually take my stand in the diplomatic circle and endeavor that it shall be an unobtrusive but a firm one. I feel deeply interested in the present situation of Spain. I have a very favorable opinion of Espartero, the Regent, and am extremely anxious that he should be able to carry out his plans and wishes, which I firmly believe are for the honor and prosperity of his country. The situation of the little Queen, also, awakens my deep sympathy; I hope the poor child may not get under the influence of the bad advisors who surround her mother, and be induced when she comes to the throne, to do any thing inimical to the present constitutional form of government; any attempt to impair which would produce another reaction, fatal to herself and to all the old nobility of Spain. You see I am getting quite into a political vein; but I cannot help reccollecting that I am writing to the wife of an Ex Congressman and the mother of a *future politician*.

By the way, talking of Bub, I find by your letter he is breaking out in a new place ⟨and⟩ taking to a row boat and becoming a ferry man. I begin to fear Bub is too much of an *at all*, and will grow up a universal genius; his future course is quite problematical—your husband fears he will be *sly*!

You mention Mr & Mrs Henry Grinnell[5] as your neighbors across the water and your visitors on moonlight nights. I wish you would remember me most kindly to them. I reccollect with peculiar pleasure the evening visit I once paid them in company with your husband, and how much I was interested by their family circle. I am disposed to think well of Mrs Henry Grinnell from her being the sister of Mr Minturn, who I think one of the best men in the world—

With affectionate remembrances to your husband I am my dear Julia

> Your affectionate uncle
> Washington Irving

ADDRESSED: Mrs Julia Grinnell / care of M H Grinnell Esqr / 6. College Place / New York
MANUSCRIPT: Yale.   PUBLISHED: PMI, III, 249–51 (in part).

Above the first line of the address is stamped "SHIP."

1. This letter has not been located.
2. WI had mentioned the Hammond homestead in his letter of September 9, 1842, to Julia Grinnell.
3. Ecclesiastes 11:1.
4. Webster, who became secretary of state when William Henry Harrison assumed the presidency, remained in the post until May 9, 1843.
5. Henry Grinnell (1800–1874) was a businessman interested in geography and exploration. He married Sarah Minturn in 1822.

1483. To Count Almodóvar

Legation of the United States / Madrid October 4th. 1842

The Undersigned, Envoy Extraordinary and Minister Plenipotentiary of the United States has the honor to solicit the attention of His Excellency Count Almodovar, First Minister of State, and of Foreign Affairs of Her Catholic Majesty, to the case of Love Straw,[1] an American Citizen of the State of Maine, at present in confinement at Havanna for a criminal offence.

It appears that this individual in August 1838, while master of an American trading vessel, "The Sarah Ann Alley" bound to Havanna, purloined from the trunk of a passenger a large sum of money. For this offence he was arrested at Havanna, and thrown into Prison to await his trial.

On the 9th. November 1840. Mr. Vail, chargé d'affaires of the United States at this Court, applied under instructions from his Government, for an act of clemency on the part of Her Majesty's Government, towards the Said Love Straw, at that time, as he supposed, Still awaiting his trial in the prisons at Havanna. He represented ↑(in a letter to his Excellency Don Joachim M. Ferrer,[2] First Minister of State & Foreign↓ [Affairs][3] that a strong memorial had been made to the Government of the United States, from persons who had known Love Straw from his childhood, bearing testimony to his uniformly fair character and good conduct, excepting in the present instance; representing the great affliction caused by his imprisonment to his family and connexions and especially to his Wife, reduced to abject poverty by his confinement; suggesting that he had already suffered punishment adequate to the nature of his Crime, and entreating the Government to intercede in his behalf. This memorial was signed by a number of the most respectable Inhabitants of Maine, as well as by the very persons, who had been aggrieved by the offence of the delinquent. The Memorial was transmitted to the General Government by the Governor of the State of Maine, who expressed strong sympathies in the case, from knowing the family of Straw, and the distress of his devoted wife.

In consequence of these representations, and of the high sanction under which they were made, The President of the United States, though convinced of the guilt of the accused, had been induced to instruct Mr. Vail to present the case "*informally*" to the notice of the Spanish Government, and to ask in behalf of Captain Straw that measure of indulgence and mercy which might appear consistent with the ends of Justice. Mr. Vail concluded by suggesting that the said Love Straw be released from further prosecution, on condition of leaving the Island, and never returning to it, or to any part of the Spanish Dominions.

To this letter a reply was given on the 24th. November, by his Excellency Don. J. M. Ferrer, stating that he had that day, made the proper communication to the Captain General of Havanna, to the end that, if no obstacle presented, he should give orders for the liberation of the said Love Straw.

The communication of Mr. Ferrer, however, has been of no avail. Before it reached Havanna and indeed before Mr. Vail made his application, it would appear that Love Straw, after nearly two years painful confinement, was brought to trial, found guilty, and sentenced to six years imprisonment.

The Undersigned has now the honor to represent to his Excellency Count Almodovar, that the same reasons for lenity towards this delinquent, which existed in 1840, and which produced the humane recommendation of Mr. Ferrer for his release, still exist, with this additional circumstance, that, beside the long confinement he endured in waiting for his trial, and which Mr. Ferrer seems to have agreed was sufficient punishment, he has since been two more years in prison; so that his confinement from the time of his arrest to the present date has been upwards of *four years.* In fact, if he serve out the time to which he is sentenced, his whole term of imprisonment, instead of *Six*, will amount to about *Eight* years. Even if orders were now issued to set him at liberty, before they could be carried into effect, he would have suffered between *four and five years* of confinement.

As, from satisfactory testimony, It appears that the said Straw is no hardened offender, but a man, who in a moment of weakness, has yielded to strong temptation, and lapsed, in a solitary instance, from a uniform course of good conduct, the Undersigned leaves it to the humane[4] consideration of Count Almodovar whether the salutary ends of Justice, which, while they punish, seek to reform, have not already been attained by the pains and degradations inflicted upon this individual; and whether the sufferings of a meritorious and devoted Wife, reduced to penury and wretchedness by his confinement, may not be allowed to plead strongly in mitigation of that punishment, in which she is compelled to participate.

If such should be the sentiments of His Excellency Count Almodovar, the Undersigned would most respectfully suggest, that the same lenity heretofore exercised by his Excellency Mr. Ferrer, be again extended to this individual, and a similar order be forwarded with as little delay as convenient, to the authorities at Havanna for his liberation; an act of clemency which will be properly appreciated by the Government of the United States.

The Undersigned renews to His Excellency Count Almodovar, the assurances of his most distinguished consideration.

(Signed) Washington Irving
His Excellency. / Count Almodovar / &c. &c. &c.

MANUSCRIPT: NA, RG 59; NA, RG 84 (letterbook copy).

A copy of this letter was enclosed with WI's despatch no. 4 of October 8, 1842, to Daniel Webster.

1. On August 27, 1842, WI had acknowledged a letter from James S. Calhoun concerning this case.

2. Joaquín Maria de Ferrer y Cafranga (1777–1861), who was a representative in the Cortes from Guipuzcoa in 1836, helped to draft the Constitution of 1837. Later he was one of the governing group before Espartero was made regent.

3. The copyist omitted the bracketed word and the closing parenthesis. Neither parenthesis is found in the letterbook copy.

4. The copyist wrote "humance."

1484. To Edward Everett

Madrid Octr 7th. 1842

My dear Sir,

I received a few days since your letter of Sept. 10th.[1] relative to the claim of Mrs Elmes as relative and heir of the late General Sarsfield.[2] As this lay properly within the province of the British Minister I spoke to him on the subject before having any communication with the Spanish Government. As soon as I mentioned the case he said Mrs Elmes had written to him in the matter and had sent him a statement or memorial. This he had presented to the Regent who had appeared to take an interest in the application, and said the document should be immediately transmitted to the proper tribunal. Mr Aston observed to me that he believed the difficulty in the case to be to ascertain whether Genl Sarsfield did or did not die intestate. If he had left a will it was believed that a young man named Shelley[3] would be found named in it as his heir; if he had died intestate Mrs Elmes, proving herself to be the nearest relative, would inherit. As several years had now elapsed since Genl Sarsfields death, and no will had been produced, it was probable that there had been none, or that it had been destroyed with his other papers.

I asked Mr Aston if he had any objection to my speaking to the Spanish government on the subject; he replied that, on the contrary, he would be glad if I would do so, as an application on my part might have even more effect than on his; being less a matter of official duty and more likely to be prompted by the merits of the case. From the whole tenor of my conversation with Mr Aston I am satisfied Mrs Elmes does him injustice in supposing that he has been inattentive to the purport of her letter; though in the multiplicity of his occupations, he may have neglected to answer it.

Yesterday morning I called on Count Almodovar Minister of State and of Foreign affairs and introduced the subject. He expressed himself kindly in the matter; spoke with warmth of the memory of Genl Sars-field and assured me that he would give the Subject his attention. I left a memorandum with him to keep the matter in his mind.

When I have an opportunity I will speak to the Regent also; who cherishes the memory of Genl Sarsfield; and will stir up Mr Aston in the cause, with whom I am on very cordial terms.

After all, however, I would not have Mrs Elmes to build very sanguine hopes upon all these promises and professions. Every man high in place in Spain has at this moment more than he can attend to in maintaining his own political existence, nothing is more tedious than all suits in law ⟨and⟩ ↑or↓ Equity in this country, and nothing more difficult than to establish any claim, however, just and obvious, where the restitution of money is in question.

With kindest remembrances to Mrs and Miss Everett,[4] I am my dear Sir

Yours ever very truly
Washington Irving

His Excellency / Edward Everett / &c &c &c

MANUSCRIPT: Va.–Barrett (also draft copy).

1. This letter from Everett, then serving as U.S. minister to Great Britain, has not been located.
2. Pedro Sarsfield (1779–1837), who was viceroy of Navarre and governor of Pamplona, was a general in the war of independence until he was assassinated during an ultra-republican insurrection in Pamplona. See Thomas Humphrey Ward, *Men of the Reign* (reprint ed., Graz, 1968), p. 792.
3. Possibly Ricardo Shelley (1811–1855), who was a brigadier general in 1837 and held a political post in Barcelona in 1843. See Christiansen, *Military Power*, pp. 101, 124.
4. Charlotte Gray Brooks, who married Everett in 1822, and probably Charlotte, his second daughter, who was presented to Queen Victoria in June, 1843. See London *Times*, June 30, 1843.

1485. To Sarah Storrow

Madrid, ⟨S⟩ Octr. 8th. 1842.

My dear Sarah,

I received the day before yesterday your letter of ⟨Sept. 8th.⟩ Sept 27th. & 29th.[1] by which I find you are once more in town. It must have been hard parting with the pure sweet air, the noble terraces and fine umbrageous walks of St Germain. I thank you for your extracts from your mothers letter. I likewise have had a delightful one from her, since I wrote to you, quite tinctured with the rural feeling she says "I wish you could see how beautifully my window is adorned with Clematis and Honey suckle in full blossom, the white and scarlet intermingled; they are trained all round my window and a little humming bird comes every day and nestles among the blossoms"—Is it not consolatory in our separation, to receive these little pictures of home dwelling happiness which they are enjoying at dear little Sunnyside." I declare to you I feel more and more the value of that little spot every time I receive these accounts of the influence it has upon the well being and enjoyment of those I love. In this way I continue to receive heart felt pleasure from it even during my absence; beside indulging the sweet hope that I shall one day or other return to it, and find it improved in beauty. When I look back upon the time we all lived together there, though my mind was occasionally overclouded with worldly cares, yet it seems like one of the sweetest dreams of my somewhat dreamy life; It was one of those portions of my life in which I have been conscious, at the time, of my happiness. It has however, almost spoiled me. I have been so accustomed to have beings around me with whom I was connected by the tenderest ties of domestic affection, that it makes my present bachelor life at times inexpressibly barren, and joyless. In fact I never was meant for Bachelor life—I have always an amount of disportable domestic affection on hand that seeks an object. I must have some one at hand to love—I think if I had little Miss Maam with me ↑just now↓ I should perfectly idolize her.

I am glad to hear Mr Lee is again in Paris, and still more, that he is coming to Madrid. I shall be most happy to see him here; and to do every thing in my power to render his visit to Spain satisfactory Tell him he must not anticipate much pleasure in this country. It is rather a melancholy country in aspect as well as fortunes. A great part of the interior of the peninsula is naked and dreary, and looks like a desert. Madrid too, offers less *agremens*[?], than almost any other capital of Europe. The whole country must be regarded historically and poetically. It is clothed with romantic associations and the people are peculiar in all their habitudes as well as in their costumes. But a stranger from the gayer, ⟨and⟩ more polished ↑and luxurious↓ countries of Europe has much to tolerate in coming to Spain. I see it much more in its positive light than I did sixteen or seventeen years since, when my imagination still tinted and wrought up every scene. I am at times affraid that these involuntary tintings of my imagination may have awakened expectations in others with respect to this country, which the reality will disappoint; and that they will concur with an English traveller in the South of Spain in pronouncing me "the easily pleased Washington Irving."[2] Would to God I could continue to be "easily pleased" to the end of my carreer. How much of a life chequered by vicissitudes, and clouded at times by sordid cares, has been lighted up and embellished by this unbought trickery of the mind. "Surely" says the bible "a man walketh in a vain shadow and disquieteth himself in vain—"[3] but this has not been the case with me—Shadows have proved my substance; and from them I have derived many of my most exquisite enjoyments; while the Substantial realities of life have turned to shadows in my grasp. When I think what revelry of the mind I have enjoyed; what fairy air castles I have built—*and inhabited*—when I was poor in purse; and destitute of all the worldly gear on which others build their happiness; when I reccollect how cheap have been my most highly relished pleasures; ⟨who⟩ ↑how↓ independent of fortune and of the world; how easily conjured up under the most adverse and sterile circumstances; I feel as if, were I once more on the threshold of existence, ⟨I would say⟩ and the choice were given me I would say, give me the gilding of the imagination and let others have the solid gold—let me be the "easily pleased Washington Irving," and heap positive blessings on others, until they groan under them—

—What a raphsody I have run into!

The day before yesterday I gave another little round table dinner of ten persons. My guests were the ⟨Pur⟩ Portuguese and Brazilian ministers and the chargé d'affaires of Mexico, Belgium, Holland,[4] and France: the latter is the Duke de Glucksberg, Son of the Duke Ducaze; a very agreeable young man. The dinner went of[f][5] very well; my people all acquitting themselves admirably under the discipline of the Sage Benjamin.

You would be amused with my Major Domo Benjamin, who has grown very stately in his office and looks down with something of contempt on the other servants. One reason is that he cannot speak Spanish; which is a secret mortification, as he prides himself on a variety of tongues. "I dont want to know their language"—he says—"I dont keep company with them—when I wants company I goes to the English Embassy!"

⟨In superintending the porters who moved our furniture he got out of patience with them.⟩

In speaking of them once to Mr Brevoort he stygmatized them as a set of Lazaronians.

"Lazaroni, you mean Benjamin," said Mr B—

"Aye, thats the Italian, Sir" said Benjamin with a very learned air, "but I put it into English."

I find the good effect, however, of his holding himself aloof from the other servants. There is no colleagueing—and, while his own immediate department is kept in excellent order, he maintains a respected sway over the whole establishment. Thus far my establishment has gone on very well, and I hope will continue to do so—

When I sat down to write this letter I did not think I should be able to fill my sheet, I was so little in the mood and had so little to say; but I feared if I did not write ⟨or⟩ there would another long interval elapse without hearing from you—Do not wait for letters from me; but drop me a line every few days—no matter how brief it is—I never in my life looked out so anxiously for family letters.

I am sorry to hear that Genl Cass[6] is about to resign and return home; as you had formed so agreeable an intimacy with his family, and liked him so much. Ledyard I presume will remain as charge d'affaires, and I have no doubt, should he choose to continue in Diplomacy, for which he is well fitted, he would get some other post, on a new minister being appointed.

When you see the Joness' remember me kindly to them. I hope they may conduct themselves prudently and cautiously and not be betrayed into vain attempts at display, or be duped by fortune hunters. ⟨The Motts⟩ I shall be curious to know how the Motts open the campaign. I presume they will ⟨alli?⟩ be backed by the Tuilleries, in which case Mrs Mary Jones will have no other alternative than to throw herself into the arms of the old noblesse, and declare royalty a parvenu—

With kind remembrances to Mr Storrow and a thousand loves to little Miss Maam

Your affectionate uncle
Washington Irving

MANUSCRIPT: Yale.

1. This letter has not been located.

2. This exact phrase has not been found in any of the contemporaneous travel accounts. Thomas Roscoe calls WI an "agreeable modern chronicler," but his intended meaning is complimentary, not pejorative. See *The Tourist in Spain. Granada* (London, 1835), p. 249.

3. Psalms 39:6.

4. The Portuguese minister was Guillermo di Lima; the Brazilian minister was Cavalcanti de Albuquerque; the chargé d'affaires for Mexico, Ignacio Valdivielso, for Belgium, Charles Comte de Marnix; for Holland, Eduard, Baron Sirtema van Govestins (1797–1871). See *Almanach de Gotha pour L'Année 1842*, p. 293; and Bowers, *Spanish Adventures of WI*, p. 241.

5. WI omitted the bracketed letter.

6. Lewis Cass was the U.S. minister.

1486. To Daniel Webster

Legation of the United States /Madrid 8th. October 1842.

No. 4. / The Hon Daniel Webster, / Secretary of State of the
U. States. Washington.

Sir.

I had the honor to receive on the 12th. ulto. despatch No. 4. from the
Department, enclosing a copy of a confidential letter, to the Captain
General of the Island of Cuba, and one from Mr. M. D. Harang dated
at New Orleans, on the subject of his claim upon the Spanish Government.

In relation to the latter, I made an informal application, to the office
of State for a copy of the Royal Decree, under which the authorities of
Porto Rico acted; and soon after I had procured it, I addressed on the
24th. September, a note to Count Almodovar, Minister of State, of which
the enclosed is a Copy: to this I have as yet received no answer. After
a careful examination of the Treaty of '95 and the provisions of the
Decree above referred to it appears to me very doubtful, whether the
case of Mr. Harang can be supported under the Stipulations of the
Treaty; Still the reasons heretofore assigned by the Spanish Government for their refusal to make restitution do not appear to have much
force, and are mainly founded on the presumption that Harang, the
father, was a naturalized subject of Spain; of which no proof is adduced,
and which is totally denied by his heirs.

I likewise enclose a copy of a letter addressed on the 4th. Instant to
Count Almodovar in behalf of Captain Love Straw, for a mitigation of
his punishment; it having been represented to me by Mr. Calhoun,
Consul at Havanna, that the former application made by Mr. Vail under
instructions from the Government, had not produced the desired effect.

I also enclose the accounts of the Legation from the 10th. of August,
when they were last furnished, up to the 30th. of September inclusive,
in order to comply with the directions, as regards the fiscal divisions of
the year, pointed out by the Instructions from the Department; In future
they will be forwarded regularly at the close of each quarter.

I am, Sir, very respectfully / Your Obdt Sevt.
Washington Irving

MANUSCRIPT: NA, RG 59.

Only the signature is in WI's handwriting.

1487. To Sarah Storrow

Madrid Oct. 10th. 1842

My dear Sarah,

I have just received your letter dated 3d & 4th.[1] It came most opportunely, to cheer me during a long blustering storm which has kept
me to the house for two days past; ⟨and⟩ it was a perfect Sun beam. I
should have liked to accompany you to the Ray[2] party! I envy you
those little American gatherings, made up of familiar faces. I have quite
lost all relish for new acquaintances and hanker after old friends, and
society that smacks of home. When you see Mrs Colford tell her I take
it very kind of her that she admires my little pet niece. I should like
in return to give her a word or two of really friendly advice to guard
her against launching away, with her young family, ⟨among⟩ ↑into↓
the false and treacherous society of needy fashionables in Paris. The
reccollections of home give me a kind interest in the welfare of this
really amiable but most misjudging family; and I regret to see them,
unskilful pilots as they are, casting themselves loose from the safe
anchorage of home, to drift among foreign quicksands and whirlpools.
I fear they will never get back safe to port.

When you see Mrs Ledyard tell her I will most thankfully receive and
dutifully answer any letters with which she may favor me; though I
fear I shall have little to offer her, from this somewhat triste capital,
in exchange for the animating news of Paris. Perhaps however, some
little revolution may turn up; in which case I will make the most of it for
her entertainment.

You want to know how I warm my apartments. There is but one
fireplace in the whole establishment, and that is in the great saloon.
We made a fire there last evening for the first time, and found it quite
cheering. The pink Saloon, however, which is the innermost one, is our
family gathering place, and is really delightful. It opens by great glass
folding doors (or casements) into the Verandah; ⟨the Sun⟩ so that it,
in a manner has double windows. The Sun shines into it for the greater
part of the day so that it will scarce need any fire excepting early in
the morning, and in the evening. I intend having a French Stove put up
in it. I have partly furnished this room with old quaint articles of furniture, picked up in holes and corners, for a mere trifle, which I have
had painted up and varnished until they look quite picturesque. Here we
have our lounging chairs; and here we gather to read the papers; or at
night to assemble round the table lit up by one of the carcil lamps which
Mr Storrow purchased for me. This Saloon is my dining room when I

⟨give⟩ have company to dinner. Mr Hamilton intends to have a small stove in his bed room; but the rest of us will have our rooms warmed occasionally by braseros; which the servants know well how to manage, and which I have, during my former residence at Madrid, found quite sufficient. For my own part I am not very sensitive to cold, and as yet have felt no need of fire. Indeed I prefer the freshness of a cool apartment; and ⟨even⟩ find it much more favorable to mental exercise and application. The robe de chambre too, which I bought in company with you on the Boulevard, is a soft, flexible delightful wrapper, and quite guarantees me against all chilliness. We have no "damp rooms"—this mountain climate is too dry to admit of humidity For a great part of the year iron will scarcely rust here in the open air. What are most to be guarded against here are inflammatory colds; caused by the sudden and sharp blasts from the Guadarama Mountains; which attack the lungs; produce *pulmonia* or pulmonary inflammation and some times hurry off the patient in the course of three or four days. The Spaniards are therefore very careful to wrap themselves up when they go abroad in cold weather, and especially at night; and I shall not fail, of course, to follow their example. You know I am a good hand at taking care of myself.

The day after tomorrow, or rather tomorrow night, my three young gentlemen take their departure for Andalusia to be gone four or five weeks. I shall miss them very much, but shall endeavor to apply myself to my literary tasks, on which, as yet, I have not been able to engage myself effectually; when once thoroughly occupied in this manner I can play the hermit very contentedly.

You ask me how I would like an appointment to Paris. Such a thing my dear Sarah is out of the range of probability: nor do I wish it. It might enable me it is true, to live among my friends and to assemble round me some of my family; but a mission in Paris is full of annoyances. The minister has to be gentleman usher to all kinds of American travellers, who are anxious to have a vulgar peep at court. His narrow appointment is strained to the utmost to keep up a meagre establishment; and his time and spirits are still more taxed by the incessant claims of Society. It requires a heavy purse and a light heart to carry on comfortably the missions of Paris and London; or a passion for the bustle and parade of the great world, which I have not. I should delight in Paris so long as I could enjoy it as a spectator, but ⟨I should⟩ it is too huge a Scene for a quiet man like myself to enter upon as an actor.

Give my kind regards to Mr Lee but tell him not to spoil my little niece by flirting with her. Indeed I begin to feel alarmed at these early indications of the young lady of a disposition to coquetry.—I must beg you not to call her Katie.

With affectionate remembrances to your husband
I am my dear Sarah yours affectionately

Washington Irving

ADDRESSED: Madame / Madame Storrow / aux soins de M. T. W Storrow / 17.
    Rue du Faubg Poissonnier / à Paris
MANUSCRIPT: Yale.

1. These letters have not been located.
2. Possibly Mrs. Richard Ray, widow of a member of the mercantile firm of
Boggs, Sampson, and Thompson. After her husband's death she spent most of her
time in Europe. See Scoville, *Old Merchants of NYC*, IV, 215–16.

1488.   To John Wetherell

Madrid. Octr. 11th. 1842.

My dear Wetherell,
    Mr Hamilton, Secretary of the Legation of the U States and Messrs.
Brevoort and Ames, attached to the same, will pass two or three days at
Seville in the course of a tour in Andalusia; let me ask for them your
kind attentions.
    With kind remembrances to Mrs Wetherell to your sister and such
of the household and of old associates as may still be about you;
and with hopes of seeing you some day or other in Madrid
    I am my dear Wetherell

Yours ever very truly
Washington Irving

John Wetherell Esqr/&c &c. &c..

MANUSCRIPT: SHR.

John Wetherell was an English tanner, merchant, and antiquarian in Seville.
WI had met him there in 1828. See STW, I, 334.

1489.   To Prince Dmitri Ivanovitch Dolgorouki

Madrid, Oct 18h 1842

My dear Dolgorouki,
    You certainly are one of the most faithful, longsuffering and indulgent
of friends still to write to me[1] notwithstanding my neglect to answer your
previous letters. But I am reforming as a correspondent, and henceforth,

I trust, you will find me more punctual in my replies. In fact I had grown quite indolent and self indulgent in my happy little retreat on the banks of the Hudson, and needed something to rouse me into action. This most unlooked for appointment to the Legation at Madrid has completely drawn me out of the oblivious influence of Sleepy Hollow, and thrown me once more into the midst of the busy world and its concerns.

And here I am, on our old campaigning ground, where we first became acquainted; but either I or the place is greatly changed, for we seem to be quite strange to each other. I miss all my former intimates. Navarette,[2] grown old and infirm, has been absent from Madrid ever since my arrival. ⟨The⟩ I look with an eye of wistful reccollection at the house once inhabited by the D Oubrils;[3] which was my familiar and favorite resort. It is undergoing great repairs and alterations, to become the residence of some Millionaire who has made a fortune by Speculation. How often I recall the happy, happy hours I have passed there, and summon up the reccollections of that most amiable and interesting family. Years have passed without my learning any thing concerning them. Can you give me any information. I understand Mr D Oubril is Minister at Frankfurt, the children of course are all grown up, some perhaps married. When I was recently in Paris I heard from an American gentleman, that he had been acquainted with Miss Bolvilliers.[4] ⟨when at⟩ who, with her mother was at Florence. Have you seen her lately—and how is she? My return to Europe after such a long absence is full of half melancholy reccollections and associations. I am continually retracing the scenes of past pleasures and friendships and finding them vacant and desolate. I seem to come upon the very footprints of those with whom I have associated so pleasantly and kindly, but they only serve to remind me,— and *mournfully* to remind me,—that those who made those footprints, have passed away.

What would I not give to have that House of the D Oubrils once more inhabited by its former tenants; just as they were when I was here in 1825.[5] I long for such a resort; I long for such beings in whom I can take interest and feel delight. Madrid is barren, barren, barren to me of social intimacies. The civil wars, the political feuds and jealousies, seem to have cut up society and rendered the Spaniards unsocial except in their own peculiar tertulias and cliques: besides, I am not one to forage at large in general society, my intimacies are generally few and cherished.

I can give you but little intelligence of the gay world that used to assemble at the Soirees of Madame D'Oubril. If you may remember I ⟨seldom⟩ mingled generally as a mere spectator, and seldom took sufficient interest in individuals to bear them in distinct reccollection. Where I have done so I do not find the reccollection ⟨very⟩ productive of present satisfaction. Time dispells charms and illusions. You remember how much I was struck with a beautiful young woman, (I will not mention names) who appeared in a Tableau as Murillos Virgin of the Assumption.[6] She was young, recently married, fresh and unhackneyed in society, and my imagination decked her out with every thing that was pure, lovely, innocent and angelic in womanhood. She was pointed out to me at the theatre shortly after my ↑recent↓ arrival in Madrid. I turned with eagerness to the original of the picture that had ever remained hung up in *sanctity* in my mind. I found her still handsome, though somewhat matronly in her appearance, seated *with her daughters* in the box of a fashionable nobleman, younger than herself, rich in purse but poor in intellect; and who was openly and notoriously her *caviliere Servante*. The charm was broken—the picture fell from the wall—She may have the customs of a depraved country and licentious state of society to excuse her; but I can never think of her again in the halo of feminine purity and loveliness that surrounded the Virgin of Murillo. ⟨*The canceled sentence of two lines is unrecovered.*⟩

And so you have got my fellow traveller of the American wilds, and buffalo hunter of the prairies, Count Portales,[7] in your neighborhood. When next you see him remember me to him most cordially. Many, many pleasant scenes have we had together. He was full of talent, and had wonderful aptness at any thing he turned to; but he seemed careless of turning his talent to account. He was a perfect prodigal and squanderer of his intellectual riches, ⟨or rather he took no heed or⟩ and quite fitful and capricious in the use of them. Time and experience, and the mingling with public affairs must no doubt have had great effect in maturing his mind and bringing ⟨him into⟩ his talents into a proper channel. He is capable of making a distinguished figure in the world if he will do himself justice.

And now my dear Dolgorouki let me hear from you again, & before long. I envy you your beautiful residence at Naples; which is one of the lovely spots of earth that must unquestionably have dropt from the Sky. Would that I could exchange for it the sterile vicinity of Madrid.

Believe me ever yours most truly

Washington Irving

DOCKETED: reçu à Neapolis / le 3. Novr. 1842. / Ad. 19.
MANUSCRIPT: Yale.   PUBLISHED: PMI, III, 251–54 (in part); Hellman, *WI Esquire*, pp. 268–69.

Prince Dolgorouki (1797–1867) was now Russian minister to the court of the Kingdom of Naples. He and WI had been close friends and frequent traveling companions in Spain between 1826 and 1829. See Bowers, *Spanish Adventures of WI*, pp. 36–38.

1. Dolgorouki's letter has not been located.

2. Martín Fernández de Navarrete (1765–1844) collected and published the documents relating to Columbus's voyages of discovery. WI used them when he prepared his life of Columbus.

3. Pierre D'Oubril (1774–1847) was Russian minister to Spain when WI lived there from 1826 to 1829. Catherine D'Oubril, his wife, welcomed WI into their home as an intimate of the family. See WI to Madame D'Oubril, February 1, 1827; and Bowers, *Spanish Adventures of WI*, pp. 30–35.

4. Antoinette Bolviller was a niece of Madame D'Oubril and a member of the D'Oubril household in Madrid.

5. WI is wrong in his date. He did not arrive in Madrid until February 15, 1826. See STW, I, 299.

6. Madame Alkanisas. For details about this tableau, see WI to Dolgorouki, January 22, 1828.

7. Count Albert-Alexandre de Pourtalès (1812–1861), along with Charles Joseph Latrobe (1801–1875), accompanied WI on the trip into Indian Territory west of the Mississippi made by Indian Commissioner Henry Ellsworth (1791–1861) in 1832. For further details, see *On the Western Tour With Washington Irving: The Journals and Letters of Count de Pourtalès*, ed. George F. Spaulding (Norman, 1968).

1490.   To Catharine Paris

Madrid, Oct 18th. 1842.

My dear Sister,

My young house mates Hamilton, Brevoort and Ames, ⟨f⟩ left me about a week since on a tour in Andalusia, to be gone four or five weeks; and here have I since been living in solitary dignity, pacing my great empty saloons to the echoes of my own footsteps. The weather, however, is beautiful, like our own autumnal weather; with an atmosphere as transparent as chrystal, a fine buoyant temperature and splendid sunshine. The moon shines down at night over the tree tops of the garden into the long casements ↑of the saloons↓ and lights up my apartments most romantically; and I am sometimes, until a late hour, pacing the long glazed balcony or Veranda that adjoins my study, and recalling the moonlight nights on the Hudson, at sweet little Sunnyside. I cannot say that, though alone, I have felt very lonely. The greater part of my time is completely occupied by study, literary tasks and correspondence, and in this fine weather, at this mellow season of the year, I can pass a great deal of my leisure in quiet rambles by myself, and in pleasing though half melancholy reveries on the past, which begins to supply the place of my early habit of *castle building*.

I have ↑formed↓ no intimacies here as yet, excepting at the British Embassy, and with the Albuquerques, (the Brazilian minister who married one of the Miss Oakeys of New York) with the rest of the Diplomatic circle, which is at present very narrow. I am on friendly terms, but we only see each other occasionally; and as to Spanish society; it is so cut up by the feuds engendered in the late civil wars and by political intrigues and jealousies, that there is but little disposition to entertain strangers; neither in fact is there much attraction for strangers in circles which are entirely engrossed by their own topics and affairs. Fortunately I do not crave much society, and have found the dissipation and hospitality of other capitals quite harrassing to me; I am well pleased, therefore, with the ⟨state of some absence of⟩ somewhat unsocial state of Madrid, which leaves me so much of the golden liesure that I delight in.

The change in my residence, also, has had a very material influence on my feelings. My present mansion is so spacious, bright, cheerful and quiet, and affords me so much ⟨[unrecovered]⟩ room to move about in, that I scarcely need go abroad for exercise and recreation. My servants now perfectly understand my habits and wishes, and the rules I have laid down for my establishment, and every thing goes on with order and regularity. The Sage Benjamin fills his station of Butler and Major Domo with great dignity and selfsatisfaction He is a great amusement to me, and sometimes, when he is waiting on me at my solitary meals, we have long conversations. He never presumes on this familiarity but is always highly respectful. Yet he delights in an opportunity to display his knowledge of the world, and to talk of the countries he has seen. He has in fact been a perfect Gil Blas. He has been in our navy during the last war; he has served in a privateer; he was Butler to Mr Middleton for twelve years, when Minister in Russia, he has been steward in an English gentlemans Yacht, and as he says, *yotted* about the Mediterrancan for a year or two; he has travelled in Italy, in Greece, among the Turks and, for ought I know, among the Hottentots, and speaks (after a fashion) as many languages as prevailed at the tower of Babel. All his testimonials speak of his perfect sobriety and integrity; and I have every reason to be satisfied of their correctness. An instance of this poor fellows fidelity deserves to be particularly mentioned; it was what first reccommended him to my confidence. He was travelling about two or three years since with a young gentleman of Boston, of the name of Lawrence, who fell ill and died at Pau in the Pyrenees. Benjamin attended him sedulously in his illness, and on his death had him buried, as he says, "*very comfortably*" ⟨[unrecovered] deceased⟩ Among the effects of the deceased beside clothing were various trinkets of ⟨some⟩ value: a watch, and upwards of a thousand dollars in money. The police at Pau would have taken possession, but Benjamin stoutly resisted; had an inventory taken and every thing sealed up, and wrote to the American

Consul at Bordeaux for advice what to do with the effects. The Consul
declined to interfere; whereupon Benjamin wrote to the Consul at Paris.
Finally he had all the effects of the deceased packed up and carefully
transmitted to his family in Boston; who I believe have never made the
faithful fellow any return for his fidelity. Such is my man Benjamin:
and I find ⟨him⟩ every thing that he has charge of in first rate order.
He prides himself upon his integrity. He is rather dry and authoritative
with my other servants, whom he considers too ignorant to associate with
him. ↑He takes care however to put upon them the hardest part of the
work.↓ His intimacies he says are among the servants of the French and
English Embassies, among whom he is received with great respect. He
is quite a diplomatic personage.

Lorenzo, the valet & footman, of whom I have repeatedly spoken to
you, continues to prove a first rate servant, attentive to all his duties,
intelligent ↑hard working↓ and thoroughly trust worthy. Juana the
house maid and housekeeper, ⟨continues?⟩ perfectly answers to the good
character given of her by Mr & Mrs Vail. She keeps herself and every
thing about her in nice order; and my linen is as carefully attended to
as ever it was at Sunnyside. I had for a long time, ⟨some⟩ doubts about
my cook, Antonio, a Greek; very skillful in his art, but, like all experienced
European cooks, prone to fleece his employer. I have brought him down
however both in wages and expenditures and reduced him to reasonable
grounds; ⟨and⟩ so that I have concluded to keep him. I have to give
dinners occasionally, and unless one has a good cook here, it is necessary
to hire assistance for the day as well as to get extra dishes from the
French cooks; ↑both↓ at exhorbitant prices—I have thus given you another
peep at my domestic establishment about which you occasionally express
some solicitude. Be assured every thing is regulated with the strictest
consideration of what is required, on the one hand by my situation, and
on the other hand by my circumstances.

Oct 19. I have just received a letter from Alexander Hamilton dated
Saturday Oct 15.[1] at Granada, where he and his companions had arrived
safely the night before. He complains of a "great lack of adventures."
"plenty of soldiers in the Sierra Morena but no robbers;" ["] patrolling
parties on foot and horseback with picturesque 'corps de garde' on wild
points of rock, to shew us that there had been suspicion of thieves in
these regions."—"We have all been delighted with the Alhambra and
⟨have⟩ from an early hour this morning until a short time since (it is now
½ past 4) we have been rambling through it and the Generalife. It is
repairing and generally with very good taste, and no doubt, in comparison with the state in which you found it, it is in excellent preservation.
The trees, the walks all shew care and good taste. The Governor himself
acted as our Cicerone, but as he shuffled about in a marvellous old coat

and slippers, seemed a most unworthy successor of the doughty Governor
Manco. Your friend Dolores with her husband lives somewhere in the
direction of Valencia: Tia Antonia is lingering yet about her old haunts,
and I have been promised an interview. Mateo, escaped from the galleys,
where his father or brother is yet confined, lives in retirement, probably
under ground in one of the many rabbit holes about this old place[.]"
I am grieved to say that my old factotum Mateo has been under
⟨sentence⟩ ↑inflection↓ of the law for some three years past for some
awkward circumstance concerning the death of a man

"We picked roses and ate delicious figs from the tree at the foot of
the tower of the three sisters; while above us the Sierra Nevada shewed
its head, whitened with a snow storm of last night. In the Generalite after
enjoying the view we attacked the fruit and made great havoc among
the grapes, figs and pomegranates. Our guide, a funny French man,
who swears he fought at Victoria and of course accounts in every way
but the true one for ⟨the⟩ each defeat of his countrymen, desires to be
recalled to your memory, as the happy individual who blacked your
boots when you first arrived at the Hotel de l'Epee, and also was
honored with the commission to purchase the Album for the Alhambra.
He seems so well acquainted with various little particulars that I must
believe he does not exaggerate on these points."—

The young travellers were to leave Granada for Malaga on the 17th.
thence to proceed by steamboat to Gibraltar where they would remain
until about the 26th. and then turn their faces towards Cadiz and Seville.
The evening of the day when they wrote the letter they were going to
a Gypsy ball—"Where," says Hamilton, ["]the prettiest and most graceful
Gitañas (gypsies) of Granada are to dance for our amusement; it being
well understood that we pay the Fiddler."

If you see any of the Hamilton family you may give them this chapter
of Alexanders travels.

Oct 21. I have received a letter today from Sarah dated the 15th. inst.[2]
I am accustomed to look every week for a letter from her and am seldom
disappointed. It is an inexpressible comfort in my present isolated state,
to have these communications, at short dates, from one of the family.
The freshness of the dates make me feel as if we were near to each other,
and I forget the weary miles and mountains that intervene.

A storm of wind and rain has kept me pretty much at home for a day
or two past; but the Sun is again shining gloriously and I intend to
take one of my long solitary rambles. ⟨I cannot tell you⟩ I cannot express
to you how much this place is connected with the reccollection of our
dear brother Peter. Here we were incessantly together; and the absence
of varied amusements, or of much intercourse with society, made us
depend upon each other for our social enjoyments. Every walk about the

place and its environs brings him to my mind, and the conversations we have had together. I have got accustomed now to these mementos, and feel a melancholy pleasure in ⟨recalling⟩ tasking my reccollection to call up and connect parts of the conversations that have passed between us. I seem for the time to hold him in companionship. There is one of our favorite haunts, however, that I have only once revisited. It is the Retiro, a kind of park which was often the scene of our rambles. It was at that time in beautiful order; with groves and shrubberies and shady walks. I sought it shortly after my arrival but found it had been neglected and suffered to go almost to ruin. Many of the trees and shrubs had perished for want of being watered, and every thing looked desolate. I do not know when I have felt such dreariness of heart as on this occasion. I hastened to leave the place and never have put my foot in it since.

Octr 22d. The letters have just arrived which came out by the Great Western; but there is not one for me. This is quite a disappointment. It seems a long time since I have heard from the Cottage; but I believe I have been spoiled by the attentive correspondence you have all hitherto kept up. I presume even now some letters are on the way for me by some Havre Packet which always arrive later than those by the Steamers

Give my love to all at the Cottage. This letter must serve for all.

Your affectionate brother
Washington Irving

ADDRESSED: Mrs Daniel Paris / Care of E Irving Esqr / New York. / p. Steamer / via L.pool & Boston // per Steamer du 4. Novembre / de Liverpool pour Boston   POSTMARKED: PA[*unrecovered*] // [*unrecovered*] / 1 / NOV / 42 // [*unrecovered*]   FRANKED: *W. Irving*   DOCKETED: Washn. Irving to Mrs. Paris / Madrid oct. 18 1842
MANUSCRIPT: SHR.

1. This letter has not been located.
2. This letter has not been located.

1491. To John Wetherell

Madrid, October 18, 1842

I wrote you a few days since,[1] for the purpose of introducing three young gentlemen of my legation, Mr. Hamilton, Secretary of Legation and Mr. Brevoort and Mr. Ames, Attaches, who are making a tour of Andalusia. Mr. Hamilton is a grandson of our famous Genrl. Hamilton. .... their departure has left me in the wing of a large Spanish mansion like a shrimp in the empty claw of a lobster.... You tell me that your mother has been presented with a great grandson: by whom pray? ... not I trust by one of your children.... You ask me about my own movements; for many years I made none having bilt for myself a snug little cottage near Sleepy Hollow, on the banks of the Hudson; which I stocked with young nieces, like a dove cote, and lived there the happiest of old bachelors, and very much like a pere de famille.... In an evil hour however the Government having got information, somehow or other, that I had wonderful talents for diplomacy, though in a latent state, threw the bait of an Embassy to Madrid, like a gilded fly into my quiet retreat, and drew me out like a trout, ... so here I am hanging by the gills at Madrid very much like a fish out of water.... I have seen Quintava[2] but once.... He returned my call and we had some interesting conversation....

PUBLISHED: *Sale of the Collection of William F. Gable* (New York, 1923), part 3, item 434; Anderson Art Galleries, May 24, 1911, item 92.

Since the two catalogs quote different parts of the letter, the text is a composite of passages in both sources.

1. See WI to Wetherell, October 11, 1842.
2. Probably a mistranscription of "Quintana." WI may be referring to Manual José Quintana (1772–1857), who had served as Queen Isabella's tutor.

1492. To Sarah Storrow

Madrid Oct 21. 1842

My dear Sarah,

I felt confident this morning early that I should receive a letter from you by this days mail, and I have not been disappointed. Your letter[1] is the more welcome as I have received none from home for some time past, and when there is any long intermission I begin to feel as I fancy Elijah did ⟨whe⟩ in the wilderness, when the ravens were slow in bringing him his provant.[2] I am writing a letter to your mother,[3] which I shall leave open for your perusal. You will find in it an extract from a letter written by Alexr Hamilton from Granada. I was glad to hear that my young travellers had got on so far without mishap, as a circumstance that occurred just after their departure put me a little on the alert. They set off at midnight, and the next morning early one of the Escopeteros, or musqueteers who guard the Diligence made his appearance at the Legation and stated that he had had the small inconvenience to kill a man in a quarrel about four leagues on the road, and that the young gentlemen advised him to apply to me for protection. As he brought no letter from the young travellers the servants refused to disturb me and sent him to seek protection else where. As Hamilton makes no mention of this circumstance I presume either that it did not take place, or that he and his companions were asleep in the diligence at the time.

I do not feel the solitariness of my situation so irksome as you appear to imagine. My young gentlemen certainly make the house lively for me; but there are times when it suits my humor to be alone; and such has of late been the case. At such times, in the interval of occupation, I give free scope to my old habit of day dreaming, and enjoy the spacious solitude of my saloons, ⟨which⟩ the silent walls of which echo to my footsteps. I am more prone to those moods in early spring time, and in the mellow days of Autumn. I have been accustomed for a considerable portion of my life to live much alone, and ⟨have⟩ am enabled to while away days together quite independent of society. Indeed it is not in general the mere absence of society that makes me feel lonely; it is the absence of those who are peculiarly dear to me: those who are linked to me by kindred ties, which with me are all powerful—above all, I feel the absence of my "womenkind;" who of late years have been the great sweeteners of my domestic life. No male society can make up for the lack of them. I think if I had even little "Miss Maam" here I could be content—but I should spoil her. By the way I cherish the notion I have taken to that child, because it is a new affe[c]tion[4] that has unexpectedly sprung up in my heart, and shewn me that its sensibilities are not worn out. I fear, however, it is "the last rose of summer."[5]

Still, when the "silver cord"[6] which binds us to existence is gradually loosening, it is gratifying to find a new link forming where others have given way. I sometimes feel so indifferent to the things that once excited and interested me that I begin to fear the apathy of age is coming over me, and that the days are approaching in which I shall say "there is no pleasure in them,"[7] I am glad, therefore, when any new throb tells me that my heart is still alive.

One thing which has contributed greatly for these few days past to my enjoyment, is the Italian opera As I have before told you, it is but three minutes walk from my dwelling. Hitherto the pieces given & the company have not been sufficiently attractive: but recently they have procured a very good tenor and have brought out the beautiful opera of Lucia di Lammermoor.[8] This opera is now my delight. A few steps take me from my lounging chair at home to a comfortable seat at the Theatre: I sit and enjoy the music without any thing to interrupt my attention, and return home with my thoughts and feelings all in tune, and am sure to have sweet quiet sleep and pleasant dreams.

I am really sorry to hear of the beginning of the troubles and per-plexities of the Jones's. If William gave his mother anxiety in New York he will give ten times more in Paris. Mrs Colfords considerate attentions to you are characteristing[9] of her. She likes to do kind offices, and I believe she and all of them, always had a sincere regard for you. I am sure you will not join in any of the satyrical gossip that they are likely to provoke.

22d. I am quite disappointed. The letters by the Great Western[10] have arrived; lots of them for the young gentlemen of the Legation but not one for myself—This puts me out of mood for any more letter writing So with kind remembrances to Mr Storrow and kisses to little Miss Maam—whose head I presume is quite turned with her pink satin bonnet, not to mention her having for the first time got into shoes and stockings. I am my dear Sarah

> Your affectionate uncle
> Washington Irving

MANUSCRIPT: Yale.

1. This letter has not been located.
2. For the story of Elijah and the ravens, see 1 Kings 17:6.
3. This letter has not been located.
4. WI omitted the *c*.
5. Thomas Moore, "The Last Rose of Summer," stanza 1.
6. Ecclesiastes 12:6.
7. Ecclesiastes 12:1.
8. Gaetano Donizetti's *Lucia di Lammermoor* was first performed in Naples in 1835.
9. WI probably intended to write "characteristic."
10. WI is probably referring to the departure of the *Great Western* from New York on September 28. See NYEP, September 29, 1842.

1493. To Thomas M. Rodney

Legation of the United States / Madrid Oct 28th. 1842

Thomas M Rodney Esq

Sir,

I herewith forward to you by the way of New York, your Exequatur received a day or two since, and your original commission, signed by the President of the United States.

It is customary for newly appointed consuls to remit the amount of fees and expenses ($18[.]25) to the Legation which has to apply for the

Exequatur, and it is the practice to permit the Exequatur to remain in the State department of the Foreign government until such remittance arrives understanding, however, from Mr Alexander Hamilton the Secretary of this Legation, who is now temporarily absent, that he had met your wishes in some arrangement on the subject, and trusting to be remunerated through him for expenses incurred, I have concluded to forward the exequatur without delay.

> I am Sir, very respectfully / Your obt Servant
> Washington Irving

MANUSCRIPT: SHR; NA, RG 84 (letterbook copy in WI's hand).

For other details about Rodney, see WI to him, August 2, 1842.

1494. To Sarah Storrow

Madrid, Oct 28th. 1842

My dear Sarah,

I received yesterday your letter of the 21st.[1] and though I fear I have nothing to say worth writing down, and am a little crowded with correspondence, the ⟨French⟩ Courier of the French Embassy setting off this afternoon at 5 O clock, instead of tomorrow Saturday evening at 10, yet as a letter will cost no postage I will not let the courier go without a line to you. I have just received a letter from my young travellers, dated from Gibraltar,[2] where they were enjoying themselves greatly. They were soon to leave ⟨th⟩ for Cadiz where they expected to remain until the 31st. after which Seville would detain them for two or three days. I presume they will be home again in about ten days.

[You] [*blot on MS*] complain of ⟨having⟩ receiving no letters from home, but I think you must have received some just after making the complaint, as ⟨some⟩ ↑two↓ came lagging on to me, at the same time with yours, which were dated early in September, and sent by a Havre Packet. I received none by the Great Western. These letters[3] shew that every thing is going on cheerfully at Sunnyside. One is from my dear little Mary; giving accounts of pic nics and Soirees; in which the Minturns figure very popularly. The tableaux at Mrs Minturns seem to have been very successful—Charlotte figured in one as a young girl standing at a glass putting flowers in her hair and Angelica Hamilton[4] as a nun reproving her. In another was one of the Mr Delano's[5] as a Turk and Julia as a slave standing with a fan in her hand. Then they have given a Soirée at Sunnyside; where there was waltzing and quadrilling and all seemed well pleased—It has been quite a gay, visiting summer at Sunnyside.

In a letter from your uncle dated Sept 7th.[6] he says ["][7] I took a drive yesterday afternoon with Sister Catharine, Eliza Romeyn and my 'bonnie Kate' round the Saw Mill tour by Mr Howlands, I was glad to find that Sister Catharine was able to take so long a drive with very little fatigue, and to enjoy the ride too."—This will shew you whether you hear from your mother or not, that she is well, and is enjoying herself. All my accounts from home speak of the freshness and beauty of the country, in consequence of frequent showers.

As I have told you in a former letter, you must not suppose I am suffering from loneliness in the absence of the young members of my household. I have a great faculty for living alone, and have a variety of modes of either occupying or whiling away my time ⟨that⟩ so that there is never an hour hangs heavy on my hands. It is never the mere want of society that makes me melancholy—Society often jars those ↑half melancholy↓ moods, which if left to take their course, have something almost voluptuous in them; but which jarred and interrupted become nervous and irritable. It ⟨have pass⟩ is a long time since I have had such a space of liesure completely to myself, and I have enjoyed a part of it exceedingly, though quite alone. It has been quite a luxury for me to take a long idle stroll, outside of the walls and seat myself by some deserted fountain, with the yellow leaves of autumn rustling down from the surrounding trees, and there pass an hour or two enjoying ⟨the⟩ a kind of phantasmagoria of the mind, summoning up ⟨old⟩ past scenes and the images of those that are far away. I ⟨feel⟩ am sometimes of the advice of the poor hard working negro, who, being asked what he would do to kill time, if he were free replied, "Me sit in de Sun, Massa, and let time kill he self!"

And then, as I told you in my last, the opera has become a great resource to me, and every night or two I have the delicious music of Lucia de Lammermoor to send me to my pillow in harmony with myself and in good humor with all the world. When you see Mrs Colford Jones tell her how much I am indebted to her for making me familiar with the music of that opera. I have thus been able to appreciate it on the very first time that I heard it at the theatre, whereas it generally takes two or three hearings to be able to feel and understand the beauties of one of those great musical compositions.

Tell the Jones' that Madame Albuquerque desires to be remembered to them; she often speaks of them, and in very kind terms. She is my main resource here; I find her a perfect lady in appearance, manners and character; and we are on the most cordial terms.

I shall attend to your advice about making myself cosy and comfortable, and will immediately have a fire place constructed in my favorite lounge the pink room. The weather, however, has not as yet been such as to require fires, especially for me, who delight in a fresh atmosphere, and am not apt to suffer from cold. I will have fires lighted, however, for your sake.

Give my darling little Kate a Kiss and tell her it is from me—I am sorry to hear she is growing so fast. I wish I could find her as I left her, with her killing glances and her fists in her mouth.

Give my kind remembrances to Mr Storrow. The draft of 100 francs was drawn at the request of Carson Brevoort, for some humble friend of his mothers. Mr Storrow "did right" in paying it.

Your affectionate uncle
Washington Irving

MANUSCRIPT: Yale.

1. This letter has not been located.

2. This letter has not been located.

3. None of these letters written in September by WI's relatives have been located.

4. Probably the sister of James A. Hamilton, WI's neighbor, and the aunt of Alexander Hamilton, the secretary of WI's legation in Madrid.

5. Probably Franklin (1813–1893), the son of Warren Delano, a Massachusetts merchant. In 1844 Franklin married Laura (1824–1902), the daughter of William B. Astor. See Harvey O'Connor, *The Astors*, p. 74.

6. This letter has not been located.

7. WI neglected to insert the opening quotation marks.

1495. To Count Almodóvar

Legation of the United States / Madrid Oct. 29th. 1842

The Undersigned, Envoy Extraordinary and Minister Plenipotentiary of the United States of America, has the honor to transmit herewith to his Excellency Count Almodovar, First Minister of State and of Foreign affairs of Her Catholic Majesty the Commissions of Mr P Pon,[1] and Mr John R Cooke,[2] appointed Consuls, by the President of the United States; the former for the Port of Barcelona, and the latter for the port of Xibara, in the Island of Cuba; and the undersigned, by direction of his government, requests that his Excellency will cause the Corresponding Exequaturs to be issued.

The undersigned begs to continue to his Excellency assurances of his distinguished consideration

Washington Irving

MANUSCRIPT: NA, RG 84 (letterbook copy); NA, RG 59 (copy).

A copy of this letter was enclosed with WI's despatch no. 5 to Daniel Webster, November 5, 1842.

1. Paul Pon was nominated as U.S. consul for Barcelona on August 29, 1842, a post he held until 1846. See Hasse, *Index to U.S. Documents*, III, 1744.

2. John R. Cooke was nominated as U.S. consul for Xibara, Cuba, on August 29, 1842; he held the post until 1843. See Hasse, *Index to U.S. Documents*, III, 1749.

1496. To Ebenezer Irving

[October ?, 1842]

* * * You give me a sad account of my literary harvest; everything behind me seems to have turned to chaff and stubble, and if I desire any further profits from literature, it must be by the further exercise of my pen. * * * If I can have one good course of literary occupation, I may produce another profitable crop, though I cease to be very sanguine of profit.

* * * I have all my books and papers now around me, and am about to set to work. I find I have no copies of the Crayon Miscellany, containing the Tour on the Prairies, the Legends of the Conquest of Spain, and Abbotsford and Newstead Abbey. I wish you would send me a set of each. * * * You may send them by the captain of any ship bound to Cadiz, and direct them to the care of Alexander Barton,[1] Esq., Consul of the United States at that port.

PUBLISHED: PMI, III, 229.

1. PMI's mistranscription of "Burton."

1497. To Sarah Storrow

Madrid, Novr. 5th. 1842

My dear Sarah,

I am glad to find by your last letter received the day before yesterday, that you have had long letters from your mother. I thought you would.

I have likewise received two delightful letters from her, one dated 15th. the other the 29th. of September,[1] written in a most cheerful, and at times quite poetical vein. "We have had a week," says she [,"][2] of the most delightful weather, for which our Autumns are peculiar. Yesterday I strolled up the bank and seated myself on the settee under the trees. The atmosphere was perfectly delicious, so soft and dreamy; the river like glass with numerous sloops gliding slowly with the tide, the trees on the opposite shore just slightly tinged with the first appearance of autumn. We afterwards took a drive through Sleepy Hollow, Brother Ebenezer, Mary, Charlotte and myself. It was just weather suitable for such a drive and we enjoyed it exceedingly. The country is still fresh from the frequent rains we have had all summer. I think every thing around the cottage has grown wonderfully this summer. You would see a great change; the ivy is looking beautiful, and over the roof and the creeper is very luxuriant. We have plenty of squirrels, but very few birds left"

I give you these extracts though I presume they are very much like what you have in your letters; but I am gratified to find your mother writing in such a vein, and retaining such fresh feelings for the beauties of nature. My heart fills too at these little home pictures of Sunnyside and its inmates; and I feel thankful to god that I am enabled to keep up such a little paradise on earth for the enjoyment of those I love.

My young Diplomats have not yet returned. I had a letter from Hamilton dated on ⟨Saturday⟩ ↑Monday↓ last Oct 31.[3] They were all weather bound at Cadiz, but, as soon as they could, would set off for Seville and thence home. I shall look for them in the course of a day or two. In the mean time I am too busily occupied to feel lonely; having for some days past had official business to attend to and despatches to write.

Your account of your little evening gathering was quite gratifying. How I should have enjoyed it! I observe the admiration of the Jones'; for little Kate has quite won the mothers heart—"You hope to see them often during the winter in this quiet way." I really hope my dear Sarah that you will do so; and that they will continue to have their social feelings unvitiated by the fashion and dissipation of Paris, and be able to appreciate a quiet fireside like yours.

I have recently met with an old Madrid intimate. When I was here in 1825[4] I became acquainted with a young Irish officer a lieutenant in the Spanish Service, named De la Saussaye. He had come here from Naples under the patronage of the ⟨Spanish⟩ ↑Neopolitan↓ princess wife to the Infante Don Francisco.[5] De Saussaye was a handsome accomplished young fellow; well received in society, and had a very pretty talent for painting. He became intimate with your Uncle and myself and with Wilkie when here. The last I saw of him was at Barcelona as I was on my way to England. His ↑regiment↓ was stationed there and he was amusing himself in his soldiers quarters, painting a landscape to present to the princess. I heard nothing of him for years and used often to think what had become of this young soldier of fortune during the vicissitudes and civil wars of Spain. Shortly after my arrival in Madrid I ⟨receive⟩ was surprised by a letter from him.[6] He was a Brigadier general in the Spanish Service; had ↑military↓ command of a district, with his head quarters at Segovia; had been Knighted by Queen Victoria for his gallant services in the British legion in Spain and was now Sir Richard de la Saussaye. He urged me to come and see him at his military ⟨station⟩ Alcazar at Segovia; if not he would endeavor to come for a day or two to see me at Madrid. He has recently arrived here, having a congé for a year, to enable him to visit his family and friends in England. Yesterday I gave him a dinner; inviting some of the Diplomatic corps with whom he was acquainted. The dinner I assure you was a very pretty one and went off well; and I was complemented on having a good cook and a good *Cave*, two of the fundamental points of diplomacy. I would, observe, ⟨here⟩ however, that excepting Mr Aston and myself none of the Diplomatic corps here give dinners; at least ⟨I have been invited to⟩ none have been given since I have been here excepting an extraordinary one given to me just after my arrival by Mr Albuquerque. I do not intend to give them frequently, and I shall always limit myself to my round table of ten, which seems ⟨always⟩ to ensure a lively and social repast. I found De Saussaye still a handsome fellow of about forty years of age: full of Spanish anecdote of the most characteristic kind. I am told he quite distinguished himself by his personal bravery during the Civil wars and that he is a favorite of the Spanish soldiery.

I will send the letter which you wish, for Mr Lee, but am prevented from doing so at once by a whimsical reason. I have forgotten his Christian name,[7] and must wait until Hector returns to inform me of it. I am glad he is on such Sociable terms at your house for he is a young gentleman for whom I have a high regard

I did not think, when I began this letter, I should be able to fill the sheet, having so little to say, and being so fagged with diplomatic writing; but when I once begin to gossip with you upon paper my pen runs on and I am surprised to find how much I make out of nothing.

I had lately a letter from my friend Prince Dolgorouki,[8] who is at present Secretary of the Russian Legation at Naples. He said he was determined to try once more to draw a reply from me, now I was once more in Europe. I felt how culpable had been my neglect of one who has been so true and persevering in his friendship, and wrote him immediately a reply which I trust will convince him that my feelings towards him are still unaltered.

I had likewise a letter within a day or two from your aunt Van Wart,[9] in which she expresses her gratification at a pressing invitation you had given for Marianne to make you a visit. I am glad you made that invitation, but regret to find times are so hard and discouraging at Birmingham that your aunt doubts whether they can afford to let Marianne avail herself of it. I hope and trust that affairs will soon begin to brighten, and green things once more appear on the face of the earth, which seems to have become quite sterile. For my own part, if I had not fortunately been cast upon diplomacy, I do not know what would have become of me and mine; all my other resources for the present being nearly dried up. I had hoped before this to have become completely launched in my literary tasks, but some how or other I have not yet been able to enter into them with spirit; and recently have had to attend to diplomatic matters. It is comforting to think, therefore, that I have "Uncle Sam" to take care of me, and I hope the good old gentleman will not "let go of my hand" until I am once more able to take care of myself; if that will ever be.

I begin to habituate myself once more to Madrid and to find resources sufficient for my simple wants. The Opera of late has become quite a stand by, and I have found an agreeable intimate in the Belgian charge d affaires the Count de Marnix;[10] a worthy, amiable, kind hearted man frank and friendly in his manners; who lives in my immediate neighborhood and visits me occasionally of an evening, or proposes a visit together to some theatre. I assure you I quite *take to him.* I need not your advice to make frequent visits to Madame Albuquerque. I assure you she is my great comfort. I resort to her on all occasions for council in household matters, or in social concerns. She has been three or four years in Madrid and has become aquainted with its people and its habitudes. Her two little girls, also, are great friends of mine and always rejoiced when I make my appearance.

And now, my dear, when you have finished this letter sit down and write me a reply and be as egotistical as I have been. Tell me all about yourself and about "bonnie little Kate." I have her before me, waking with surprize and staring from between her blue curtains at the fine ladies who were admiring her. I am affraid Kate will be spoiled.

Give my kind remembrances to Mr Storrow, and believe me my dear Sarah

                                        Most affectionately your uncle
                                                Washington Irving

MANUSCRIPT: Yale.

1. These letters have not been located.
2. WI omitted the bracketed comma and punctuation marks.
3. This letter has not been located.
4. WI again erred concerning the time of his arrival in Spain (1826).
5. Francisco de Paula Antonio de Borbón (1794–1865), brother of Ferdinand VII, was married to Carlota Luisa de Borbón (1804–1844), daughter of François I, king of the Two Sicilies, and sister of María Christina, the queen mother.
6. This letter has not been located.
7. Henry Lee, Jr. of Boston had sailed to England with WI on the *Independence* and had dined with him in London. For other details see WI to Sarah Storrow, August 4, 1842.
8. This letter has not been located.
9. This letter has not been located.
10. Count Charles de Marnix was the Belgian chargé d'affairies at Madrid. See WI to Sarah Storrow, October 8, 1842.

1498. To Daniel Webster

Legation of the United States / Madrid November 5th. 1842.

No. 5. / The Hon. Daniel Webster. / Secretary of State of the / U. States. Washington.

Sir,

I had the honor to receive, on the 28th. ult. despatches No 6 & 7 from the Department of State, the former enclosing the commissions of Mr. P. Pon and Mr. John R. Cooke,[1] as Consuls for Barcelona in Spain, and Xebara in Cuba, and the latter enclosing a copy of the treaty lately concluded with Lord Ashburton. The enclosed copy of my application to the Minister of State will Shew that I have complied with the instructions relative to the Consular commissions.

I enclose likewise a note from Count Almodovar, received in reply to my application in favor of the claim of Michael Drausin Harang;[2] a reply which, according to the slow process of Spanish investigations, does not promise a speedy decision of the question.

I have received and forwarded, via New York, the Exequatur of Thomas M. Rodney,[3] Consul for Matanzas in the Island of Cuba.

Political affairs here are rising to fever heat as the time for the opening of the Cortes approaches, and powerful preparations are making to displace the present Cabinet. You may recollect that the actual Ministers came into office uncalled for by any party; being selected by the Regent, with one exception, from the Senate, much to the disappointment of the ultra exaltados, and of certain active leaders in the Cortes, who had contributed to unseat their predecessors, in the hopes of being chosen in their stead. The consequence has been, that the actual Ministry has not hitherto had the Support of any party, and at present is the object of attack from all quarters. The Constitutional party itself has long been broken up into divisions of conservatives, progressives and republicans, with intermediate Shades in favor of particular men or measures; while the moderados, or absolutists, take advantage of these feuds in the constitutional ranks, to attack the Regency itself and the whole scheme of the existing government.

All these discontented elements have recently been formed into a formidable coalition against the present administration, but threatening the very basis of the public tranquility.[3] The pretext has been a commission appointed by the government to revise the laws respecting the press, and to prepare some plan to be submitted to the Cortes, for correcting the licentiousness in which it has recently indulged. This has been denounced as a high-handed attempt to check the freedom of opinion and annihilate the liberty of the press.[4] The *Eco del Comercio*, a paper hitherto of the progressive party, but recently gained over to the interests of the Infante Don Francisco,[5] has Sounded the alarm and proposed a coalition of all parties to resist this flagrant invasion of their rights. All the public papers excepting three,[6] which are in the employ of government, have responded to the call, and a kind of manifesto has been published in which they pledge themselves, however they may differ on minor questions, to Stand by each other in defending the Sanctity of the press and resisting every infringement of the Constitution. In all this, there is a vast deal of solemn farce, but it will have its effect on the nation; while under cover of it a thousand petty plots and interests are at work. It would be difficult and indeed unprofitable to unravel the complicated web of intrigues and cross-purposes, woven over the whole Surface of public affairs in this country and impeding every effort for the general good; a few of the principal, however, are worth noticing.

The minority of the Queen is made a fruitful Source of political agitation. The absolutists are anxious to abridge it as much as possible; to get her from under the guardianship and tutelage of Arguelles and the other champions of Constitutional government; the exaltados would fain prolong it until her mind should be matured, her education advanced, her habits and opinions formed in consonance with the existing institutions of the country, and until those institutions should have had time to take root and be completed. With these views, attempts have been made and are Still making, in various parts of the country, and especially at Barcelona, to set on foot a movement in favor of restoring the Constitution of 1812; according to which the minority of the Queen would only be completed with her eighteenth year.

These attempts are clamorously denounced by the absolutists, who make no Scruple of attributing them to the underhand management of Espartero himself, in the design of prolonging his regency, if not of ultimately possessing himself of the sovereign power. It is in vain the government have publicly and indignantly repelled such insinuations, and declared the determination of the regent and the ministry to maintain the Constitution of 1837 and the limits of the royal minority thereby defined. The enemies of Espartero persist in asserting that whatever may be his public professions, his secret wishes are such as have been represented. He has Suddenly, say they, been elevated from the ordinary ranks of life into the dazzling proximity of the throne; he has drunk deep of the intoxicating draught of almost regal power; it is impossible that he can look forward with complacency to descending after two short years, from his brilliant elevation, and retiring to the modest and monotonous obscurity of Logroño.

Whether Espartero is really visited by any of these flutterings of ambition I have not had opportunities from personal observation, of forming an opinion. Those who know him intimately assure me that he is sincere in his professions and honest in his intentions: little skilled in intrigue; more of the Soldier than the Statesman, and indebted to his bravery and good fortune, rather than to artful management, for his political elevation. Prone to sink into apathy on ordinary occasions,[7] to let things take their course; and to appear less in intellect than those about him; but to be roused to action by questions of exigency or danger, and then to shew all the fearless energies of a man worthy to command. I rather apprehend that at such moments of sallying energy, the prompt Soldier now and then needs the warning voice of the wary Statesman, to keep him from trampling involuntarily over the boundaries of the constitution.

The marriage of the youthful queen is another topic of political perplexity, prematurely agitated and kept in a State of agitation both at home and abroad; certain reverend crowned heads and grey diplomatists, in neighbouring countries, being wonderfully anxious to provide a Suitable match for this child, Scarce entered in her teens. The better thinking of the Spanish nation would fain keep the mind of the youthful Sovereign unagitated by a theme so unsuited to her years; and they claim the right of judging for themselves what alliance would be best, for the interests of the nation; recalling, moreover, what Spain has experienced of the fruits of powerful matrimonial alliances in the disastrous ascendancies of the houses of Hapsburg and Bourbon. They are not Suffered, however.

to rest in quiet on this Subject; various young princes of different lines being spoken of from time to time as being agreed upon by foreign powers:[8] and one at this moment being said to be on the point of visiting this Court *incog,* like a prince in fairy tale.

In the mean time a native candidate is Started, near at home, but one, for various reasons equally unwelcome to the government. This is the Duke of Cadiz,[9] Son of the Infante Don Francisco de Paula: a youth of about twenty years of age. His mother, the Princess Luisa Carlota, sister of Maria Cristina is a woman of an ambitious, intrepid and designing character. She has long endeavoured in various ways to gain power into her immediate branch of the family; such as to have her husband appointed guardian to the queen, or advanced to the regency. Her favorite project now is to bring about a marriage between her son and the young queen. The government, however, is wary of her, and her political intrigues when in Madrid last Summer produced an intimation from high quarters that it would be adviseable for the health of Don Francisco and his family that they should pass the hot Season at some watering place. They have accordingly passed some of the recent months in the northern parts of Spain, courting popularity, and really gaining favor; the people being pleased with the unusual sight of some of the Royal family circulating familiarly among them. Don Francisco, especially, has pleased the lower classes, being a man of easy temper, familiar habits, somewhat plebeian appearance, and a great amateur of bullfights and other gross amusements in which the populace delight. His wife, meantime, carries on her scheme among people of higher intellect and pretension, and takes care to bring forward her son conspicuously as a native born Spanish prince, devoted to the country and the nation. The reception they have met with at Saragossa, that ancient & important Strong-hold of Arragon, has encouraged the princess to develope her project more boldly. Crowds have assembled under the balconies of the princely residence, serenading the family; hailing the Duke of Cadiz as one of the hopes of the nation, and coupling his name with that of the youthful queen, in Songs and acclamations. These have been carefully reechoed throughout the Kingdom in gazettes under the pay or the influence of Don Francisco, and are represented as the enthusiastic expressions of public feeling. The consequence has been another intimation from head quarters that it is expedient for Don Francisco and his family to leave Saragossa; and that their intended return to Madrid for the winter will be dispensed with.

All this would be mere diplomatic gossip, of little interest, did not every thing connected with the minority and marriage of the young queen bear upon the vital politics of the nation and affect the future destinies of Spain; and were not the whole policy of the country a game of trick and hazard.

Among various charges of arbitrary and unconstitutional conduct brought against the administration is the kind of Lynch law exercised by General Zurbano towards the *latro-facciosos*, or Seditious robbers of Catalonia.[10] It is probable that, in the exigencies of the case, knowing the province to be menaced with irruptions of refugees and robbers from the french frontiers, the general has been clothed by the government with those old fashioned discretionary powers, usual under the ancient regime; for the Spaniards have not yet become accustomed to the Somewhat slow operations of constitutional machinery, and are apt, in moments of emergency, to push the machine aside and resort to the rough but prompt measures of despotic rule. The apologists of General Zurbano, however, declare, that many of the charges against him are false, and others exaggerated; and that his rough exercice of power has been honestly directed and productive of the most beneficial effects. A recent act of the General has brought the government into Somewhat of a dilemma. He is charged with having ejected a worthy old Frenchman named Lefevre, from a convent in which he had established a manufactory; with having taken possession of the Same as quarters for his troops, and with having accompanied the ejection of the occupant with personal violence. The french government have seized upon this as a matter of national import; being irritably disposed in the present state of their diplomatic relations with this ⟨country⟩ ↑government↓, and well inclined to make the most of any subject of complaint against a country towards which they have been so much in the wrong. Strong letters I am told have been passed to the Spanish government, by the french diplomatic agent, at this Court, demanding explanation or redress for this outrage on the rights and person of a french subject; but as yet no reply has been given. The Spanish government require time to examine thoroughly into the circumstances of the case. The friends of general Zurbano alledge in his defence that when Lefevre hired the convent of the public authorities it was with the understanding that he Should vacate it on receiving timely notice of its being wanted for public purposes. That he received four months notice that it would be wanted for General Zurbano's troops. That he neglected to attend to such notification. That General Zurbano finding him Still in possession gave him some further days of grace, but on his failing to avail himself of them, ordered the edifice to be cleared of his effects:—that thereupon the gallic spirit of the occupant being roused, vented itself in such terms as to provoke a Sudden movement of the General, before which Lefevre found it prudent to retreat with Some precipitation. It is added that the general utterly denied having touched the respectable person of the worthy but vociferous gaul, but claims no merit of forbearance, as it was only, he says, in consequence of his retreating so rapidly as to be out of the reach of his foot.

Such is one of the petty subjects recently woven into the serio-comic tissue of diplomatic cross purposes between this country and France, and to which, if public papers and private rumors may be believed, the latter is inclined to attach Serious importance. In the mean time General Zurbano, instead of being disgraced is clothed with new trusts, being appointed Inspector of the Custom houses of Catalonia; under the late provisions for the detection & suppression of abuses and frauds in the collection of the revenue. This gives him complete control, for the time being, of every Custom house that he may visit; with powers to examine books, papers and individuals. He is said to be not much versed in accounts, but it is hinted that in the various phases of his fortune he has had some practical experience in contraband, and knows where to look for delinquencies; it is added that he will in all probability, look into the accounts with a pen over his ear but a sabre under his arm.

The policy of the government with respect to this man appears to be one of mere expediency. To retain him in Catalonia during the present feverish time, where the terror of his name and the promptness of his hand may keep that restive and seditious province in check; and it is probable all decision as to his alledged misdeeds will be avoided, and he will be continued there until the present crisis is past,[11] and the "Cotton question" which is again coming up, has been disposed of.

I have thus ventured to give a rough sketch of some of the political affairs of this country as far as I can make them out, being as yet but new to the ground and Surrounded by mystery and ledgerdemain. If I have not treated some of them with the gravity they may be thought to deserve, it is because it is impossible always to look on with solemnity where so much of the petty is mixed up with the grand; where princes are playing such a paltry game, and where the patriotism that has sprung up with the constitution is overlaid by the old fashioned trickery of the days of Gil Blas.

The administration is now bracing itself up and preparing with dubious heart, for the tempest that awaits it in the coming Cortes. Its great reliance is upon Calatrava[12] the Minister of Finance, who is prepared to lay before the Cortes at the opening of the session a scheme of finance, which, if adopted, will, he feels assured, relieve the nation from its present exigency and gradually extricate it from all its difficulties. Affairs, he says, have arrived at a crisis. The expenditures are three years in anticipation of the resources of the country and yet the treasury is empty. *There is a mere alternative between a financial and a social revolution.*

His scheme contemplates the former, and among other important measures will include a reduction of the tariff and a more liberal policy generally in respect to commerce: should his scheme be rejected he will resign; though it is added, that should Ministers meet with the same opposition that they experienced in the last session, the Cortes will be dissolved.

In my interviews with members of the present Cabinet I had forborne to touch upon our commercial relations thinking the time unpropitious after the defeat of the cotton question in the last Cortes; and the Ministers too likely to be transient in office. Understanding however, the liberal policy in commerce about to be recommended, I have recently brought up our own claims to participate in the benefits of the contemplated reform. I have spoken generally on the course of our trade both with the Colonies and the mother country, as burthened and impeded by prohibitions, differential duties and countervailing regulations, and as capable of great augmentation under proper laws; but I have particularly adverted to the tobacco monopoly, knowing it to have come under the consideration of recent Cabinets, and to be a fruitful cause of that contraband system which is the bane of the peninsula, and which the government at present, seems so anxious to put down. It is needless to repeat here the facts and arguments used on this subject, and which have been used so repeatedly with former Cabinets. I have found them generally admitted by those with whom I have conversed; and Count Almodovar has recently assured me that a free trade in tobacco was one of the measures under consideration with Mr Calatrava, in the financial scheme which he was preparing.

I shall look to the opening of the budget with some solicitude. Should the scheme of Mr Calatrava be such as has been represented, and should it be favorably received by the Cortes, I shall entertain a Sanguine hope that our Commercial relations with Spain may eventually be put upon the footing so long desired by our government. I fear, however, the present Ministry is not sufficiently strong to carry out any plan of reform, however salutary, especially one to which so many interests, legitimate and illigitimate are opposed, but that they will fall, under the tempest of opposition conjured up against them, with the consolation of falling in the support of a great question, for which the world will give them credit.

I am Sir, very respectfully / Your obt Servant
Washington Irving

DOCKETED: No. 5 W. Irving. Madrid. 5 Nov. 1842 / [*page 1, upper left*] Rec Dec 12 / Mr Markoe

MANUSCRIPT: NA, RG 59.   PUBLISHED: Hellman, *WI Esquire*, pp. 284–92; STW, II, 149–50 (in part).

Only the complimentary close and signature are in WI's handwriting.

1. See WI to Count Almodóvar, October 29, 1842.

2. See WI to Count Almodóvar, September 24, 1842.

3. See WI to Rodney, October 28, 1842.

4. Freedom of the press had been proclaimed in the Constitution of 1837, but the government's heavy-handed suppression of it produced local coalitions of opposition progressives and moderates. See Raymond Carr, *Spain, 1808–1939*, p. 225; and Edgar Holt, *The Carlist Wars in Spain*, p. 172.

5. Francisco de Paula (1794–1865), the youngest brother of Ferdinand VII, was not in the line of succession for the Spanish throne because it was reasonably certain that his father was Manuel Godoy (1767–1851), minister of Charles IV and lover of Queen María Luisa. See Holt, *Carlist Wars*, p. 26.

6. The *Eco del Comercio* presented the leftist interpretation of the news, while the *Correo Nacional* reflected the conservative views and the *Heraldo*, the Moderado position. See Christiansen, *Military Power*, p. 172. A proposal for a newspaper coalition is found in *Eco del Comercio*, October 25, 1842. *El Heraldo, La Posdata, El Castellano, El Peninsular, El Trono*, and *El Católico* had joined the journalistic league against the government. See *Eco del Comercio*, October 27, 28, 1842. The newspapers supporting the ministry of Count Almodóvar included *La Iberia, El Espectador, El Patriota*, and *La Gaceta*. See *Eco del Comercio*, October 30, November 2, 4, 6, 1842.

7. Espartero suffered from a "cyclothymic mental condition." "His long periods of bed-ridden and querulous torpor, punctuated by phases of galvanic and hysterical energy, might be taken to indicate either manic-depression or schizophrenia; his condition was aggravated by a weak bladder." See Christiansen, *Military Power*, pp. 99–100.

8. Among the possible husbands being considered for Isabella, in addition to the duke of Cadiz, were Enrique, the duke of Seville (1823–1870), Isabella's first cousin; Carlos Luis (1818–1861), son of Don Carlos and also Isabella's first cousin; the duke of Aumale (b. 1822) and the duke of Montpensier (1824–1890), sons of Louis Philippe; Prince Leopold of Saxe-Coburg (b. 1824), Queen Victoria's cousin; and the count of Trapani (1827–1892), brother of Queen Mother María Christina and Isabella's uncle. See John D. Bergamini, *The Spanish Bourbons* (New York, 1974), pp. 221–23; Holt, *Carlist Wars*, pp. 201–3; and Peter de Polnay, *A Queen of Spain*, p. 97.

9. Francisco de Asís (1822–1902), duke of Cadiz and Isabella's first cousin, was regarded in some quarters as an effeminate, feeble homosexual who was incapable of fathering an heir to the throne. At the same time Luisa Carlota, his mother, hoped to marry another son, Enrique, the duke of Seville, to Luisa Fernanda, Queen Isabella's sister. If the queen did not produce an heir, her sister's children would assume the throne of Spain. See de Polnay, *A Queen of Spain*, p. 97; and Bergamini, *The Spanish Bourbons*, p. 226.

10. Martín Zurbano, who enforced the death penalty upon smugglers in Catalonia, was also accused of terrorism and extortion. See Christiansen, *Military Power*, p. 109. For other details, see WI to Daniel Webster, August 27, 1842.

11. See WI to Webster, August 27, and December 10, 1842.

12. José María Calatrava (1781–1847), a lawyer who had been president of

the Council from August, 1836, to August, 1837, and a progressive opponent of Espartero as sole regent, headed a commission in 1842 which drew up a proposal imposing an *ad valorem* duty of twenty-five percent on British goods and granting corresponding advantages to Spanish wines and spirits. See WI to Webster, December 2, 1842; Christiansen, *Military Power*, pp. 66, 70; and Holt, *Carlist Wars*, p. 147.

1499. To Count Almodóvar

Legation of the United States / Madrid Novr 8th. 1842

His Excellency / Count Almodovar /First Minister of State &c &c &c
Sir

In consequence of the conversation which I recently had the honor to hold with your Excellency, in which you informed me of the intention of Her Majestys Government to propose at the approaching Session of the Cortes, some important changes in the regulations of commerce, I am induced to throw a few observations on paper on the state of the commercial relations of the United States with Spain, merely for the purpose of calling the attention of your Excellency to a more extended examination of the subject.

For many years past the government of the United States has desired to place these relations on a more free and liberal footing and to establish the same by treaty stipulations; being persuaded that these, while they inspire confidence, promote cordiality in the intercourse between nations. These wishes of the government of the United States, though frequently urged through its diplomatic agents at this Court have never been met, in like spirit by the Spanish government; and the international trade, being left to be regulated by the separate legislation of each country, has been subjected to every change that either has thought proper to introduce into its commercial code. The consequence has been continual fluctuation and uncertainty. Discriminating duties on the one side have been answered by countervailing regulations on the other, until, in this disastrous competition, though an equality of terms has been kept up, and neither has been able long to have the advantage of the other, the whole trade has become laden with burthens and restrictions that embarrass its operations and stint it of half its growth.

This is lamentably the case with the trade between the United States and Her Majesty's Colonial possessions. I especially allude to the Islands of Cuba and Porto Rico, concerning which I happen to have more immediate means of judging.[1] In looking over such statistical tables of this trade as I have at hand I find the imports into the United States from these possessions averaging for three years the annual amount of

$14.138.188; nearly as much as Spain herself imports from the whole world. The exports from the United States to those possessions, during the same time, averaged yearly *$6.869.104*. The duties arising from this trade must be one of the richest sources of revenue to the Spanish crown, and may induce a belief that, to be so productive the trade must be well regulated; yet I am assured by those well acquainted with the subject, that this golden stream of revenue is scanty to what it would be, were the channels of traffic through which at present it in a manner forces its way, were cleared of all obstructions. The rapid increase in the population and culture of those islands since they were first thrown open to foreign commerce, shews to what they are capable. They have the United States at hand for their best customer; the consumption of their produce, if unchecked by impolitic regulations would keep pace with the growing wealth and rapidly increasing population of that immense country; while the United States, from its boundless resources could furnish them in return with all the necessaries of life in never failing abundance and on the cheapest terms. The proximity of their respective marts, also, allow of those prompt operations and quick returns of capital, so profitable in commerce. Such is the trade between the United States and the Spanish Antilles; one of the most mutually beneficial and generously productive in the world; capable, under more liberal auspices, of being carried to the highest pitch of commercial productiveness; and, as such well worthy the most benignant and indulgent eye of Her Majestys government.

The trade of the United States with Peninsular Spain is in a sad state of decline, sinking under the prohibitory and protective system. The new Spanish tariff is even more unfavorable to foreign commerce than the previous one; almost all the principal articles of produce of the United States continue as before excluded. Tobacco, rice, breadstuffs, manufactures of cotton, leather, wood &c are either prohibited or taxed with duties that amount to exclusion. What is the consequence of this long continued policy? Ports that were once the well frequented marts of the commerce of the United States, are now almost entirely deserted by the flag of the republic. I will venture to mention a few instances which I have been able to gather in my hasty preparation of this paper. At Bilbao, where I observe in 1816 Seventy nine vessels of the United States, registering 8.299 tons, were fully laden and discharged, the average for four years ending with 1841 has been but two vessels and *341* tons, and in that period *none* have taken away cargoes.

In Barcelona no vessel of the United States has been seen for years. Some few Spanish vessels come there with cotton from ports of the United States, but have to touch at Cuba or Porto Rico by the way. The trade of the United States with Alicant, once so flourishing, has dwindled into insignificance. From 1810 to 1820 there used to be large importations into that port of tobacco, fish, flour, rice, staves, spars &c whereas now, in consequence of high tariffs and differential duties, there is but a limited trade in fish and staves; while the exports of wines, brandy barilla, fruits &c are reduced to insignificant quantities. The number of Ships of the United States arriving there in four years, ending with 1841 averages but four a year; and but one Spanish ship has cleared out for the United States in that time.

Cadiz, once so enriched by American commerce is now little more than a port of transit. The whole amount of merchandize landed there from United States shipping in four years past does not much exceed $800.000. The trade is reduced to the exchange of a few staves for salt; both articles of little pecuniary importance. "If the duties were moderated and the prohibitions taken off," says an old and experienced resident at the place, the merchandize now sent from the United States to Gibraltar would come direct to Cadiz and Malaga; but if nothing is done in favor of commerce at Cadiz, this beautiful city and port perhaps the best situated for foreign trade of any in Europe, will ere long be reduced to a mere fortress and the port serve only as a station for ships of war.

Malaga, which is at present the port where our commerce still lingers, complains equally with the rest of the embarrassments produced by the prohibitive and protective System. During four years prior to 1842 the exports from Malaga direct to the United States, were about $5.000 000. (not more than $1.200 000 a year) and yet this is the emporium of American trade in the Peninsula, affording wines and fruits for which there would be a vast demand; but I find the produce of the United States, permitted to enter in exchange for these five millions, did not amount to more than four hundred thousand dollars. No trade can prosper where there is so little reciprocity.

Neither does Spanish Shipping appear to be much benefited by the present regulations. Those Spanish ships that go from Malaga to the United States belong principally to Catalonia, where they commence their lading with some articles of the produce of that province; complete it at Malaga, with the productions of Andalusia, and proceed to the southern ports of the United States: unable however, in the present shackled state of the trade, to bring back the produce of the United States, direct, they go to Cuba or Porto Rico for the produce of those islands, or for cotton, which may have been conveyed there in American shipping; and thence return to Catalonia. When such is the disadvantage under which the national flag labors, that it cannot return home direct with the produce of the country to which it trades, how much more must be the embarrassment occasioned to the flag of the United States.

In the recent conversation with your Excellency, to which I have already alluded, I was particularly gratified to hear you say that among the measures which the Minister of Finance had under consideration in digesting his plan of commercial reform, was that of allowing a free trade in tobacco. I earnestly hope this measure may be carried into effect; I know of none that would have a more beneficial influence on the trade between the two countries or would give a severer blow to that system of contraband which is the curse of the Peninsula, and which Her Majesty's government manifests such a creditable anxiety to put down.

By reference to Statistical tables I find that the export of tobacco from the United States to Gibraltar in 1838 was 5998 Hogshead (about six millions of pounds) which of course was intended to be introduced into the Peninsula. In the same year the United States shipped direct to Spain 757 Hhds. for Government contract. Here were 6757 Hhds of United States tobacco brought into Spain in that year, while the amount of the same kind of tobacco which passed through the Royal fabrics is estimated at about two thousand hogsheads, or two millions of pounds: of course there must have been about 4775 hogsheads introduced from Gibraltar by contraband, beside what may have been smuggled in from other quarters. It stands to reason that 3.000.000 lbs of tobacco, which I am told is about the amount annually issued by the royal fabrics is but a small proportion of what is used by a nation of Smokers, and pays duty to the Crown.

Now though a larger amount of revenue may apparently accrue from the two thousand hogsheads, or 2.000.000 lbs of United States tobacco manufactured and sold under the royal monopoly, than would from the whole quantity admitted under duty; yet your Excellency will bear in mind the deductions to be made from this amount for the emmense expense in protecting this monopoly: the number of custom house troops kept in pay with all their accommodations and appurtenances; the vast number of useful hands and ingenious heads diverted from honest and productive labor to knavish pursuits; the vast number of useful hands lost to profitable labor in pursuing them, and the bribery and corruption and general demoralization to which the tobacco monopoly gives rise.

Had this monopoly the merit of being protective of any popular branch of industry or manufacture, like the protective duties on cottons, which nevertheless, and wisely, there seems a disposition to lighten, it might in some degree be tolerated; but the tobacco monopoly protects nothing—in fact it benefits nothing, but the smuggler and those whom he bribes. It is an attempt to raise revenue without regard to the morals of the nation, and in this it falls short of its aim. Government does not derive from it the revenue that it would from a free trade under reasonable duties; for we are not to form our estimate of what would be the amount of duties arising from the aggregate quantity that now, legally and illegally, finds its way into the peninsula. A free trade, by lowering the price would immeasurably increase the consumption of the article and consequently present a vastly greater surface from which to collect duties. Such, I believe, to be almost invariably the case on the cessation of the prohibitive and protective systems. I have an instance under my eye shewing how the commerce in this very article is affected by high and low duties. In Ireland for five years ending in 1798, when the duty on tobacco was eight pence per pound; the annual consumption was 7.337.217 lbs In 1828, when the population of Ireland had fully doubled, and consequently there ought to be twice the consumption of tobacco, say, 15.000.000 lbs. a five years average was again taken; when instead of an increase, the yearly consumption had shrunk to 3.972.703 lbs.—the reason was that in the interval *the duty had been raised to three shillings a pound.*

The same effects were produced in England by high duties on this article, and Mr Poulett Thompson,[2] one of the ablest financiers of the kingdom, gave it as his opinion that, if the duty were reduced to one shilling or one shilling and sixpence per pound "the public would be greatly served and the smuggling put down.["]

The increased quantity of tobacco used in the peninsula, like that of any other production of the United States, would correspondingly increase the means of purchasing the wines, oils, silks, fruits and other products of the country and encrease the use of them in the United States.

The commerce between the United States and Spain is well worthy of her cultivation; for it is a genial commerce, interfering with no honest interest; dealing in exchanges of produce; encouraging the agriculture and manufactures of the country, and the balance of it always inclining in favor of the peninsula.

The United States is a young country of vast consumption and constantly increasing demand. It seeks the produce and manufactures of all parts of the world. The enterprize of its merchants is well known. Wherever there is an advantageous foothold for commerce, however inhospitable the clime, there will be found the American Merchant, and wherever he appears he is the harbinger of commercial wealth. Yet it is an ominous fact that, in this country, so favored by nature, possessing as has well been observed "a genial climate, an active population, a soil of boundless fertility; a sea coast of great extent, numerous harbors, the noblest colonies ever enjoyed by any nation and boundless treasures of the precious metals," not two Merchants of the United States, unconnected with some official employment from their government, are resident, and the ships of the Republic are gradually disappearing from the ports.

I must again claim the indulgence of your Excellency for the crudeness of these suggestions, which are somewhat hastily thrown together merely to call attention to the commercial relations between the two countries, when collateral interests seem to be coming under consideration. Should they be so fortunate as to promote a closer examination of the subject by Her Majestys ministers, who have such ampler experience and more extensive means of information in the premises than I can pretend to, my purpose will be attained.

> I have the honor to remain /with assurances of the highest
> consideration / Your Excellencys most Obt Servt
> Washington Irving

MANUSCRIPT: NA, RG 84 (letterbook copy); NA, RG 59 (copy).

Another copy, in WI's hand, enclosed with despatch no. 6 to Daniel Webster, November 11, 1842, is used as copy-text.

1. WI alluded to this question in his letter of November 5, 1842, to Daniel Webster.
2. Charles Edward Poulett Thomson (1799–1841), first Baron Sydenham and Toronto, was president of the Board of Trade from 1834 to 1839 and governor-general of Canada from 1839 to 1841.

1500. To Count Almodóvar

Legation of the United States / Madrid Novr 10th. 1842.

The Undersigned Envoy Extraordinary and Minister Plenipotentiary of the United States, has the honor to communicate to his Excellency Count Almodovar &c that on the 22nd. of November 1841, Mr. Vail, then Chargé d'affaires of the United States at this Court, enclosed to his Excellency Don Antonio Gonzales,[1] then first Minister of State &c the commission of Mr. Orlando S. Morse[2] appointed Consul of the United States for the Port of St. Johns in the Island of Porto Rico and requested that the corresponding Exequatur might be issued—He received a reply dated 26th. of the same month, stating that the requisite preliminary information has been asked of the Colonial authorities.

The Undersigned, however has received a letter from Mr. Morse, dated at Washington the 29th. September last, stating that he had just returned from the Island of Porto Rico and that a few days before leaving the Island he had had a conversation with the Governor,[3] who assured him he had received no information on the subject of his appointment up to that period. Mr. Morse added that he had therefore applied at the State Department at Washington for the intervention of Government in the premises. The Undersigned has in consequence received instructions from his Government to make representation to her Majesty's Government of this circumstance and to urge the prompt recognition of Mr. Morse.

The Undersigned cannot but hope there will be no further procrastination in this case, as it would be hard that in addition to the long suspence to which all american Consuls in Spanish Colonial Ports are subjected by the precautionary regulations of her Majesty's government, so much complained of, Mr. Morse should suffer upwards of a years delay through some official neglect in executing those regulations.

The Undersigned takes this occasion to renew to his Excellency Count Almodovar the assurance of his high consideration.

Washington Irving

MANUSCRIPT: NA, RG 84 (letterbook copy); NA, RG 59 (copy).

Another copy was enclosed with despatch no. 6 to Daniel Webster, November 11, 1842.

1. Antonio González (1792–1876), who was appointed prime minister by Espartero, served from May 22, 1841, to May 29, 1842. See Christiansen, *Military Power*, p. 169.

2. Orlando S. Morse of Virginia was nominated as U.S. consul at San Juan, Puerto Rico on April 4, 1842; he resigned in 1845. See Hasse, *Index to U.S. Documents*, III, 1748.

3. General Santiago Méndez Vigo (1790–1860), who had distinguished himself in the war for independence, was serving as governor of Cuba.

1501. To Count Almodóvar

Legation of the United States / Madrid Novr. 11th. 1842.

The Undersigned, Envoy Extraordinary and Minister Plenipotentiary of the United States of America has the honor to represent to his Excellency Count Almodovar, First Minister of State and of Foreign Affairs of her Catholic Majesty that for more than twenty years past, The Ships of War of the United States have had free access to the Navy Yard or arsenal at Mahon, with the use of the workshops for the purpose of making repairs, and of the storehouses or Almacenes, for depositing Spare articles not required on board; That it is very rare that the Ships of any other nation make use of the same; still less the Ships of Spain; so that, were it not for the Americans the Navy Yard would be entirely deserted: The only return required of the latter has been to keep the premises in proper repair which they have done.

It is represented to the Undersigned, however that since the present "Commandante de Marina" has been in office at Mahon, difficulties are continually occurring and the use of the Almacenes, and workshops, is granted with great reluctance, and in some instances refused; The Commandant alledging that he has no authority from his Government to allow it, and that, whatever may have been the practise of his Predecessor, he can grant no facilities without an order from the Minister of Marine.[1]

As the Undersigned is satisfied there can be no disposition on the part of her Majesty's Government to interrupt or abridge any of the friendly accomodations heretofore yielded at Mahon to the Marine of the United States he trusts his Excellency Count Almodovar will take the requisite measures to have the same continued, on the same footing, and under the same stipulations as formerly.

The Undersigned takes this occasion to repeat to his Excellency Count Almodovar, the assurance of his high respect and consideration.

Washington Irving

MANUSCRIPT: NA, RG 84; NA, RG 59 (letterbook copy).

Another copy was enclosed with despatch no. 8 to Daniel Webster on November 26, 1842.

1. Dionisio Capaz, who became minister of the marine after Andrés García Camba moved to the War Ministry on October 20, 1842, succeeded Camba as war minister on November 20, 1842, and held the post until May, 1843. See Christiansen, *Military Power*, pp. 168, 171; and *Almanach de Gotha Pour L'Année 1843*, p. 332.

1502. To Daniel Webster

Legation of the United States / Madrid 11th. November 1842

No. 6. / Hon Daniel Webster / Secretary of State / Washington.

Sir

I have received within a day or two your despatch No 8. dated September 29th. calling my attention to the delay in respect to the Exequatur of Mr Orlando S. Morse. I immediately addressed a note on the Subject to the Minister of State, a Copy of which I enclose.[1]

In my last despatch dated the 5th inst. I mentioned the scheme of finance said to be in preparation by Mr Calatrava, embracing important reforms in the system of trade, and the conversation which I had held with Count almodovar on the subject. As I had great doubts of the permanancy of the present Cabinet, and of its power to carry any important scheme into operation, I did not intend, for the present, to take any particular step as to our commercial relations with this country; but to content myself with watching the course of affairs. Finding, however, that England and Belgium were pressing their tariff negotiations, and that commercial treaties with those powers were at least matters of public rumor I thought it adviseable to bring forward in a more formal manner our own claims to the consideration of Ministers in any plan of commercial regulations they might be concerting; and especially to insist upon the tobacco trade, as being at least equally entitled to reform with the trade in Cottons.

I accordingly passed a note to the Minister of Foreign affairs, a copy of which is inclosed.[2] It was prepared somewhat hastily, but the time for operation was brief. To be "a word in season"[3] it was necessary that it should be spoken at the moment.

I am not very sanguine of any thing important being at present effected in this matter and I think it probable the great cotton question will again experience a defeat in the Cortes. There are strong interests—legal and illegal, manufacturing and smuggling that will raise another storm of opposition; and the powerful coalition again reorganized will endeavor to defeat every measure of ministers, good or bad, in the effort to drive them out of office. Modifications of the laws of trade, however, and treaties of commerce are topics daily getting more and more in favor, and must occupy the attention of any cabinet that may succeed. A crisis is evidently at hand; and unless the whole system of finance be reformed every thing must be thrown into chaos.

I shall be happy to receive any further and more particular instructions the government may think it expedient to give in view of the possibility of a commercial arrangement; and any statistical documents and information that may bear upon the subject.

Before concluding I cannot but advert to a statement recently published in the daily papers giving the statistics of the Cabinet and the unparralleled number of changes that have taken place within the last few years. It gives a startling idea of the interruptions to which an extended negotiation with this government must be subjected. It appears that, within the last eight years, there have been *forty two* changes in the department of War; *twenty five* in that of the Marine and so on with the rest. This consumption of ministers is appalling. It is true the lowest number of changes occurs in the department of State, with which one would have to negotiate, but even here it is *nineteen;* which is at the rate of nearly two ministers and a half per annum.[4] To carry on a negotiation with such transient functionaries is like bargaining at the window of a rail road car, before you can get a reply to a proposition the other party is out of sight.

> I remain Sir / Very respectfully / Your Obt Servt
> Washington Irving

DOCKETED: Recd 28 Decr. [*upper left corner, page 1*] / No. 6. W. Irving. Madrid. 11 Nov. 1842
MANUSCRIPT: NA, RG 59.   PUBLISHED: PMI, III, 384–85 (in part); STW, II, 150–51 (in part).

This letter is in WI's handwriting.

1. See WI to Count Almodóvar, November 10, 1842.
2. See WI to Count Almodóvar, November 8, 1842.
3. Proverbs 15:23.
4. For the changes in prime ministers and ministers of war, see Christiansen, *Military Power*, pp. 168–71.

1503.   To Helen Irving

Madrid, Nov. 12, 1842

My dear Helen:

I did not intend to write to you by this opportunity, for I am fairly fagged out with letter writing by this courier, having, besides scribbling to friends, to send long despatches to Government; but I cannot suffer your long, delightful letter[1] to remain unacknowledged, though, at present, I scrawl but a line of thanks. My dear Helen, you cannot imagine what a rich treat such a letter from home is to me. It fills my heart to the very brim, and with the very best of good feelings; and then, your details about sweet little Sunnyside—God bless my dear little cottage!—what a treasure of comfort and enjoyment it is to me! Every letter from it or about it gives me such a picture of true, innocent, home-dwelling happiness, and of such joyous meetings and gatherings together of those I love, that I feel for a time as if I had just heard a strain of delightful music, which is one of my purest of earthly pleasures. I had just been reading and answering one of Pierre's, wherein he had given a most indignant account of a charge made upon me, in a *Lady's Magazine,* of having puffed my own works.[2] Don't tell Pierre, but absolutely he had put himself in such a passion on the subject, that I found all the indignation appurtenant to the matter was done to my hand, so I retained the smoothness of my temper without a wrinkle. As authorhood seems to be getting down in the world, and I have taken to the company of kings and queens and regents, and others of "the quality," I begin to think I'll give out that I am not the Washington Irving that wrote that farrago of literature they are occasionally cutting up, and that I have never followed any line of life but diplomacy, nor written anything but despatches. I certainly began life at the wrong end; it is only recently I have discovered what I was cut out for. However, don't mention it; people might think me vain. * * *

* * * And now, my dear Helen, as this letter was a perfect impromptu, totally unpremeditated, I must close it, to attend to other correspondents. I will take some other occasion to answer your long letter more at length; in the mean time, I beg you forthwith to sit down and write me such another one. And do, I again charge you, tell me everything that is pleasant and prosperous about yourself and Pierre; and tell Pierre not to take it so much to heart, if they make any further attacks upon that poor-devil author who has scribbled under my name.

Your affectionate uncle,
Washington Irving

PUBLISHED: PMI, III, 270–71.

1. This letter has not been located.
2. For details, see WI to Pierre M. Irving, November 12, 1842.

1504.   To Pierre M. Irving

Madrid, Nov. 12, 1842

My dear Pierre:

I have just received your letter of October 6th,[1] enclosing an article from *Graham's Magazine,*[2] charging me with writing laudatory notices of my own works for the Reviews, and alluding especially to the *Quarterly.* The only notice I ever took of any of my works, was an article which I wrote for the *Quarterly Review* on my Chronicle of the Conquest of Granada.[3] It was done a long time after the publication of the work, in compliance with the wishes of Mr. Murray, who thought the nature of the work was not sufficiently understood, and that it was considered rather as a work of fiction than one substantially of historic fact. Any person who will take the trouble to read that review, will perceive that it is merely *illustrative,* not *laudatory* of the work, explanatory of its historical foundation. I never made a secret of my having written that review; I wrote it under the presumption that the authorship of it would become known to any person who should think it worth his while to make the inquiry. I never wrote any other article for the *Quarterly Review* excepting a review to call favorable attention to the work of my friend and *countryman,* Captain McKenzie (then Slidell), entitled "A Year in Spain, by a Young American,"[4] and another review, for the same purpose, of a work of my friend and *countryman,* Mr. Wheaton, at present Minister at the Court of Prussia. This last article, though written for the *Quarterly Review,* did not appear in that publication, but was published in the *North American Review.*[5] The work of Mr. Wheaton which it reviews, was, I think, the History of the Northmen. These are the only articles that I am conscious of having ever written for the *Quarterly,* or any other European Review. I have never inserted in any publication in Europe or America a puff of any of my works, nor permitted any to be inserted by my publishers when I could prevent it; nor sought to procure favorable reviews from others, nor to prevent unfavorable ones where I thought they were to be apprehended. I have on all occasions, and in every respect, left my works to take their chance, and I leave them still to do the same. My present reply to your inquiry is only drawn forth by a charge that would affect my private character; though I hope *that* is sufficiently known to take care of itself on the point in question.

I understand a kind friend[6] has recently been vindicating me against attacks made on me in the *Southern Literary Messenger,* on the subject of my Life of Columbus.[7] I have never read those attacks, having been assured there was nothing in them that called for reply, and not being disposed to have my feelings ruffled unnecessarily. I understood they mainly charged me with making use of Mr. Navarrete's work without giving him due credit. Those who will look into my Life of Columbus, will find that in the preface I have cited the publication of Mr. Navarrete as the foundation of my work, and that I have referred to him incessantly at the foot of the pages. If I have not done so sufficiently, I was not aware of my "shortcomings." His work was chiefly documentary, and, as such, invaluable for the purpose of history. As my work was not a work of invention, I was glad to find such a store of facts in the volumes of Mr. Navarrete; and as I knew his scrupulous exactness, wherever I found a document published by him, I was sure of its correctness, and did not trouble myself to examine the original. My work, however, was made up from various sources, some in print, some in manuscript, all of which, I thought at the time, I had faithfully cited. Those who wish to know Mr. Navarrete's opinion of the work, will find it expressed in the third volume of his collections of documents, published after the appearance of Columbus, in which his expressions are anything but those of a man who felt himself wronged. I can only say, that I have never willingly, in any of my writings, sought to take advantage of a contemporary, but have endeavored to be fair in my literary dealings with all men; and if ever you hear again of my having practised any disingenuous artifice in literature, to advance myself or to injure others, you may boldly give the charge a flat contradiction. What I am as an author, the world at large must judge. You know what I am as a man, and know, when I give you my word, it is to be depended upon.

* * * * * *

Your affectionate uncle,
Washington Irving.

P.S.—This letter is written in great haste on the spur of the moment, to go by the courier that sets off for Paris to-day. I have not yet read Helen's long letter, from which I promise myself a perfect treat. The foregoing letter is, of course, not intended for publication, but you may use it as "authority," quoting from it what you think proper. I must expect attacks of this and other kinds now. I have been so long before the public, that the only way to make anything now out of me is to *cut me up*. However, I shall follow the example of Sam Williams, whilome American banker at London, who, when his ship was sinking at sea, sprang on board of another one that had run foul it, and was saved. As literature is sinking under me, I shall cling to diplomacy.

PUBLISHED: PMI, III, 267–69.

1. This letter has not been located.
2. In a review of the *Critical and Miscellaneous Writings of Sir Walter Scott* in *Graham's Magazine*, 21 (October, 1842), 218–19, the anonymous critic, possibly Rufus W. Griswold, comments on Scott's puffing his own writings with notices placed in magazines and then continues, "Washington Irving has done the same thing, in writing laudatory notices of his own works for the reviews and like Scott, received pay for whitewashing himself. We do not imagine that in either case there was any great injustice in the self-praise, but certainly Mr. Murray should not have been solicited to pay the 'guinea a page' " (p. 219). Apparently as a result of pressure from PMI, *Graham's* retracted its earlier assertion in its December issue, p. 344.
3. 43 (May, 1830), 55–80.
4. 44 (February, 1831), 319–42.
5. 35 (October, 1832), 342–71.
6. Probably Lewis Gaylord Clark, editor of the *Knickerbocker Magazine*. In its issues for July and August, 1842 (pp. 97, 197–205) the charges of Severn Teackle Wallis (1816–1894), the writer for the *Southern Literary Messenger*, were answered

but not to his satisfaction, for he responded with a repetitious rebuttal in the November issue. This, in turn, brought a further reply from the *Knickerbocker* in December (p. 586), which was followed by still another comment from the *Southern Literary Messenger*, 9 (January, 1843), 13–14. Wallis was a brilliant young Baltimore attorney with a deep interest in Spanish history and literature. In 1843 he was accorded the rare distinction of being elected a corresponding member of the Royal Academy of History of Madrid. He is identified as the author of the articles attacking WI's use of Spanish sources in Benjamin B. Minor, *The Southern Literary Messenger, 1834–1864* (New York, 1905), pp. 85, 91, 97. See also J. Thomas Scharf, *History of Maryland*, III, 366.

7. In the *Southern Literary Messenger*, 7 (March, 1841), 231–39, WI was charged, as he suggests, with using Navarrete's collection of documents without sufficiently acknowledging his indebtedness. When WI ignored the allegation, Wallis again renewed the charge with the comment that "we are bound to infer, that our distinguished countryman has preferred the quiet disparagement of a judgement by default, to the notoriety of a verdict, after a fruitless contest" (*Southern Literary Messenger*, 8 [May, 1842], 305 [entire article covers pp. 305–17]). In the *Messenger* for November, 1842 (7, pp. 725–35) Wallis responds to defenses of WI in the *Knickerbocker Magazine* for July and August, 1842, by repeating and expanding the arguments set forth in March, 1841 and by stating, "We think . . . that we have succeeded in establishing beyond successful controversy, our two original positions: first, that Mr. Irving is deeply and vitally indebted to Navarrete; and secondly, that he is far from having made that free acknowledgment, which candor and a just self-regard would seem to have rendered imperative" (p. 734).

1505.   To Sarah Storrow

Madrid, Novr. 12th. 1842

My dear Sarah,

I received three days since your letter of the 2d.[1] and feel very much obliged to you for writing to me so frequently [.] I wish I could conjure up something amusing or interesting to write to you in return; but my life here is somewhat monotonous; and those with whom I ⟨do⟩ associate you know and care nothing about. Indeed for two weeks past I have been very much at home, fagging at diplomatic business, having to make researches and treat about subjects quite foreign to my usual range of inquiry; as well as to prepare and copy out my notes to this government and my despatches to the government at home. However, I am always happiest when most occupied, and I have hardly known how time has flown, though I have sometimes not been out of the house for two and three days together. I have got through with my task and feel like a school boy who has mastered a difficult lesson.

I am every moment looking for the arrival of my young gentlemen, who come in the diligence that arrives this morning between ten and eleven. My last accounts from them was from Seville, where they were enjoying themselves mightily; being very much fêtcd by a family with whom I was intimate during my residence there,[2] and to whom I gave them letters.

I have a delightful letter from our dear Kate,[3] written in charming spirits. Speaking of the poor little Queen of Spain, of whom I had written some account she says "I wonder if she would not like to change her situation for a nice little cottage on the Hudson? I am sure she would be a great deal happier." Kate reminds me of a little poor devil barber named Cox[4] who used to dress your grandfathers wigs. He was deploring the fate of Louis XVIth "Ah Mr Irving! how much better it would have been to have left the poor King live and sent him out of the country. He might have come over to New York and set up a nice little grocery shop!" Poor Cox! He was a great dram drinker, and ↑this↓ greatest object of envy was the man who kept a grocery shop in his neighborhood, with whom he spent all his sixpences for rum toddy.

I have been interested of late by long conversations with my old friend de Saussaye. He is a man of talents and observation and has ⟨ha⟩ led a life of vicissitude and adventure. When quite a young man, having a small fortune, he travelled about to see the world, and was noticed by the royal family at Naples; where he became a favorite with the princesses. When at Florence he received letters from home informing him of the failure of a banker in whose hands was all his property. He was penniless. He immediately sought a ↑military↓ situation in foreign service. The Duchess de Berri[5] interested herself in his favor and reccommended him to her Sister the Princess Luisa Carlota wife of the Infante Don Francisco. He came on here and ⟨was⟩ received the commission of Ensign in the royal guards. Then it was that we became acquainted He has been in the Spanish Service ever since: and as I before told you, has risen to the rank of Brigader General, and military governor of Segovia: beside being knighted by Queen Victoria for his gallant services in the British legion.[6] I am told he has repeatedly signalized himself by his bravery. He is a favorite with the soldiery; consulting their comforts; avoiding exposing them to unnecessary dangers; but, whenever there then is any peril to be encountered, putting ⟨th⟩ himself at their head. This is what soldiers like in a commander. He is author of a work on Spain which I believe you have read as I used to have it ⟨in⟩ at Sunnyside—It is called Madrid in 1835:[7] and has as a frontispiece a view of the Prado.

—The young travellers have just arrived covered with the dust of travel, but brimfull of spirits and the house is quite alive with them. The servants are hurrying about in every direction and Juana is in perfect extacies, partly because the young Señoritos have all arrived home safe and partly because they have brought her a fine new shawl!

You tell me Mr Lee has given up the idea of coming to Spain this winter, but may possibly visit it in the Spring. Tell him the Spring is the very time to make the visit. I did not like to discourage him from coming in the winter, lest it might derange his travelling plans; but the winter is no time to visit this part of Spain. He may pass from Italy in the Spring to Valencia, or Barcelona by Steam boat; touch in the same way at the different Mediterranean ports and so on to Gibraltar; then go to Seville; Granada, and thence come to Madrid. From hence go to Lisbon & then shape his course as he pleases. At any rate, Spring is the beautiful season for the South of Spain, and a genial season ⟨all⟩ in all parts of the peninsula. I shall not send the letter for Col Thorn, as you say he has no respect for the Colonel or his family and would merely go there as a matter of curiosity. It would not be right to introduce a person to the hospitalities of the Colonel under such circumstances. Give my kindest regards to Mr Lee when you see him and tell him not to omit coming to Spain in the Spring

I have just received a long letter from Helen dated Oct 5th.[8] ⟨I w⟩ it is two sheets full, closely written. I have just read a page and half and put it by as a bonne bouche after I have dispatched my letters by the courier. I inclose a letter open to Pierre M Irving, in reply to a long one ⟨on⟩ about a paltry attack on me in an American magazine, which put honest Pierre in a great rage; but never ruffled my tranquility, as I happened to be ⟨send⟩ able to give a complete contradiction.

I must conclude, for I have other correspondence to finish by the Courier. The reason you get my letters generally on Saturday or Sunday is that a courier goes off ⟨from hence⟩ every Saturday for Paris from the French Embassy; which gives all the legations an opportunity of sending letters & dispatches so far free of postage. The Courier generally arrives in Paris on the following friday or saturday.

I am glad to find by your letter that little puss cat is "alive and *kicking*," though I am sorry to hear she kicks her shoes and stockings off. She shews her spirit early.

With kind remembrances to Mr Storrow

Your affectionate Uncle
Washington Irving

Do go and see my passion. Lucia di Lammermoor the first time it is represented.[9]

In sending my letters to New York put them all under one Envelope; directed either to Pierre M Irving, or to E Irving. The pacquet, arriving by ship at New York pays but 6 cents postage as *one letter;* no matter how many are within

ADDRESSED: Madame / Madame Storrow / aux Soins de Mr T W. Storrow / 17 Rue de Faubg Poissonniere / à Paris

MANUSCRIPT: Yale.

1. This letter has not been located.

2. Possibly John Wetherell. See WI's letter of October 11, 1842, to him.

3. This letter has not been located.

4. Possibly David Cox, who had a wig shop next door to the King's Arms Tavern at the corner of Broad and Dock Streets. See Esther Singleton, *Social New York under the Georges* (New York, 1902), p. 176; and W. Harrison Bayles, *Old Taverns of New York* (New York, 1915), pp. 114, 116.

5. Caroline de Bourbon, the duchess de Berry (1798–1870), a niece of Queen Marie-Amélie of France, had tried unsuccessfully in the 1820's to secure the French throne for her son, count de Chambord. For other details, see WI to Edward Livingston, June 29, 1831.

6. The date of de la Saussaye's knighting has not been ascertained. Edgar Holt asserts that only General George de Lacy Evans was knighted for his work with the British Legion. See Edgar Holt, *The Carlist Wars in Spain*, p. 166. For details about the activities of the British Legion in Spain, see Holt's study, especially chapters 8, 12, and 14. As WI suggests, de la Saussaye had been in the Spanish army for many years. He was attached to the Quarter-Master-General's Department of the British Legion on March 16, 1836, and was a member of the Royal and Military Order of St. Ferdinand of the British Legion. See Alexander Somerville, *History of the British Legion and the War in Spain* (London, 1839), pp. 665–66.

7. *Madrid in 1835. Sketches of the Metropolis of Spain and its Inhabitants, and of Society and Manners in the Peninsula*, by a Resident Officer, 2 vols. (London, 1836).

8. This letter has not been located.

9. At this point, at the bottom of the page, WI wrote "(*turn over*)", to advise Sarah to look on the other side of the page.

1506. To Paul Pon

Legation of the United States / Madrid November 13th. 1842

Paul Pon Esqr. / Consul of the United States. Barcelona.

Sir:

Your letter of the 5th. Inst was yesterday received at this Legation.

I have to inform you in reply that under instructions from the Department of State, I applied on the 29th. Ultimo,[1] for the usual Exequatur in your case.

It is the practise for the Consul, according to the directions of the Department to place in the hands of his Agent or correspondent in this City the amount of the Fees $18 25/100 which are to be paid upon the delivery of the Exequatur.

I am, Sir very respectfully, / Your Obdt. Servant.
Washington Irving.

MANUSCRIPT: NA, RG 84 (letterbook copy).

1. See WI to Count Almodóvar, October 29, 1842.

1507. To George Read

Legation of the United States. / Madrid November 14th. 1842.

George Read Esq. / Consul of the United States. Malaga.

Sir:

I have to acknowledge the receipt of your letter of the 2nd. inst, with the accompanying documents relative to the case of John Johnson,[1] an American Sailor, stabbed by a Spaniard named José Illesca y Torralva on the 28th. August last. I observe with great satisfaction, the zeal and activity you have displayed in investigating the case, and bringing it before the proper authorities; and your kind attention to the medical treatment and the personal comfort of your suffering countryman

I do not see that any further steps are necessary in procuring the punishment of the delinquent: His case is in the regular course of legal adjudication; The Spanish Authorities have shown no neglect or indifference in the cause, and the sentence of ten years confinement in the Presidio, is no doubt a severe punishment in Spanish eyes, for a Wound given in the course of an affray which had originated in a "Wine Shop."

I have likewise to acknowledge the receipt of your letter of the 5th. inst, giving me several interesting facts concerning the state of American trade in Malaga and enclosing the representation to the Cortes from the Municipality relative to the necessity of liberal commercial arrangements. I had just passed a note to the Spanish Government, on this very subject, in preparing which I was greatly benefited by your former communications to this legation; the facts you now furnish me will be valuable in any further communication I may have to make, and I shall feel greatly obliged to you for the "condensed Statement of the trade" you promise to send at the end of the year.

The other suggestion in your letter, will be attended to when a proper opportunity presents.

I remain, Sir, / Very respectfully / Your Obdt Sevt
Washington Irving.

MANUSCRIPT: NA, RG 84 (letterbook copy).

George Read of Pennsylvania was nominated as U.S. consul for Málaga on January 16, 1839. See Hasse, *Index to U.S. Documents*, III, 1746.

1. See WI to Count Almodóvar, November 14, 1842.

1508. *To Obadiah Rich*

Legation of the United States. / Madrid November 14th. 1842

O. Rich Esqr. / Consul of the United States—Mahon.

Sir,

I received on the 7th. inst your letter dated October 15th. informing me of the difficulties and restraints which the Ships of war of the United States experience in the accustomed use of the Navy Yard of Mahon since the arrival of the present "Commandante de Marina."

I have addressed a note to Count Almodovar the First Minister of State on the subject,[1] and trust the matter will be satisfactorily arranged.

Very respectfully / Your obdt Sevt.
Washington Irving.

Manuscript: NA, RG 84 (letterbook copy).

1. See WI to Count Almodóvar, November 11, 1842.

1509. *To Catharine Irving*

Madrid Nov 15th. 1842.

My dear Kate,

Your letter of Oct 1.[1] reached me a few days since and gave me a very sunshiny account of affairs at pleasant little Sunny Side. I thus enjoy by reflection the bright days which pass at that brightest of little homes. My present home is enlivened by the return of the young travellers from their tour in Andalusia which has been a very satisfactory one, excepting that they have not been robbed, at which they appear rather disappointed; ⟨it⟩ ↑an adventure with robbers↓ being looked upon as essential to the interest and romance of a tour in Spain. They have a world of travelling anecdotes to relate about Granada, and Malaga, and Gibraltar and Seville which make our repasts quite instructive as well as convivial. They are all in fine health and spirits, and, from their good tempers, good sense, good breeding and perfect harmony, make a very pleasant household.

You seem to pity the poor little Queen, ⟨?so?⟩ shut up with her sister,

like too[2] princesses in a fairy tale in a great, grand dreary palace, and
"wonder whether she would not like to change her Situation for a nice
little Cottage on the Hudson." Perhaps she would Kate, if she knew any
thing of the gaieties of Cottage life: if she had ever been with us at a
pic nic; or driven out in the Shandry dan,[3] with the two roans and James
in his slip shod hat for a coach man; or *yotted* in the Dream:[4] or sang
in the Tarrytown choir; or shopped at Tommy Deans:[5] but poor thing,
she would not know how to set about enjoying herself. She would never
think of appearing at church without a whole train of the Miss Manns
and the Miss Forkels and the Miss Dearmans[6] as maids of honor, nor
drive through Sleepy Hollow, except in a coach and six with a cloud of
dust and a troop of horsemen in glittering armor. So I think Kate we
must be content with pitying her and leaving her in ignorance of ⟨com-
parative⟩ the comparative desolateness of her situation.

  The last time I saw the little Queen was about ten days since, at the
Opera, with her sister. Espartero, the Regent, sat on her right hand.
She is fond of theatricals and appeared to take great interest in the
performance. She is growing fast, and will soon be quite womanly in
her appearance. I cannot say that she is ↑strictly↓ handsome, for which
I am sorry, on account of your Aunt: but you may console the latter
by assuring her that the queens sister is decidedly pretty enough to
answer her notions of a princess. I shall give your aunt another diplomatic chapter on Royalty and its concerns as soon as I can find liesure
from my diplomatic communications to government; but she must not
let it get to Mr Websters ears how communicative I am to her on these
subjects: He may not feel disposed to admit her into our secrets.

  As your Aunt expresses some solicitude about my winter quarters,
tell her I have put up a very nice French Stove or fire place in ⟨the⟩
our family gathering place the pink Saloon; which ⟨was⟩ is now a
delightful winter room; having the Sun shining into it all day; and the
glazed verandah or gallery in front. The travellers among other articles
of *provant* which they bought at Gibraltar, have brought home an
ample supply of green and black tea; so that we shall establish our tea
table for the winter evenings: a ⟨[*unrecovered*]⟩ cosey domestic meal unknown in this country and which we have hitherto neglected—In short, we
mean to make ourselves very comfortable. I do not know whether I have
mentioned in any of my letters to home, that we have an Italian Opera
house immediately in our neighborhood—absolutely within *two* minutes
walk of our house. The company in general is but tolerable, but has recently been improved by an excellent tenor who is likewise a good ⟨tenor⟩
↑actor↓ and a very good looking man. The prima donna also ⟨is⟩ has a
good voice and method: so that I manage to enjoy the performances
greatly. *Lucia di Lammermoor* is the opera now in the course of repre-

sentation and, whenever it is performed, is sure to draw me from my comfortable lounging chair at home to an almost equally comfortable seat in the theatre. It is a great resource to me. The opera just mentioned is full of delicious music. I had become familiar with it by hearing it often at the Mrs Jones's; perhaps it has won upon me more from bringing up reccollections of home, and associations of thought with the "widow and the fatherless", which ⟨Mary⟩ ↑your Sister↓ Mary will understand—

I am affraid, my dear Kate, from ⟨one passage of⟩ some observa[tions] [MS torn] in one passage of your letter, that you are all practising too much economy in your expenses. I should be vexed and mortified if this were the case. Before leaving home I made some general regulations in this respect, founded upon a calculation of what I could freely afford. Experience of my expenses abroad proves that calculation to be correct. so I beg that none of you will economize unnecessarily. As for you my dear Girl, I again repeat, circumstances may call for various expenditures on your part, I enjoin it upon you therefore, *as you love me,* do not stint yourself in any thing befitting your situation as *a lady.* Pierre has my instructions to answer all your drafts and I shall consider it a proof of your love for me and your confidence in my affection, if you make them freely. And now God bless you, my excellent, noble hearted little girl. I can never enough express how deeply I feel the affection I have experienced and ↑daily↓ ⟨still⟩ experience from you all⟨,⟩ ⟨which⟩ ↑It↓ constitutes the great happiness of my life.

Give my love to all the family—affectionately your uncle

Washington Irving

ADDRESSED: Miss Catharine Ann Irving / Care of E Irving Esqr / Tarrytown — / ⟨New York⟩ / Westchester Co. / N. Y.   POSTMARKED: NEW-YORK / DEC / 26

MANUSCRIPT: Virginia Morris Biddle (Mrs. Nicholas Biddle).   PUBLISHED: PMI, III, 255–57 (in part); and J. T. Scharf, *History of Westchester County,* II, 238 (in part).

1. This letter has not been located.
2. WI inadvertently wrote "too" instead of "two."
3. A chaise with a hood.
4. Probably WI's facetious expression for sailing in a local boat.
5. Dean (d. 1873) was proprietor of a store at the southwest corner of Broadway and Main Streets in Tarrytown. See J. T. Scharf, *History of Westchester County,* II, 205, 238.
6. Apparently these are young ladies from the Tarrytown area.

1510.   To Pierre M. Irving

Madrid, Nov. 17, 1842

My dear Pierre:

I wrote to you, a few days since,[1] in reply to your letter concerning the attack upon me in *Graham's Magazine*. As that reply was written hastily, I may not have been precise in one or two particulars. The review of the Conquest of Granada was written nearly, if not quite two years after the publication of the work, and after it had been very favorably noticed in several periodical publications. As I before observed, it was written in compliance with the wishes of Mr. Murray, to state the historical nature of the work; my use of the soubriquet of Fra Antonio Agapida, and the occasional romantic coloring, having led many to suppose it was a mere fabrication. I did not ask or expect any remuneration from Mr. Murray, but he sent me the sum he was accustomed to pay for similar contributions to his Review, and I did not hesitate to accept it, the article, in fact, being written for his benefit. Perhaps it would be as well to have the review republished in the *Knickerbocker*, and then the public will be able to judge whether or no it is "laudatory."

While I am upon these literary matters, I will furnish you with a fact or two in my literary life in Europe, which may enable you to reply to any similar charges that may be brought against me. In the early struggle of my literary career in London, before I had published the Sketch Book in England, I received a letter from Sir Walter Scott,[2] inviting me to Edinburgh to take charge of a periodical publication, holding out the certainty of a liberal sum per annum, with other incidental advantages. Though low in purse and uncertain in my prospects at the time, I declined accepting the invitation, fearing it might implicate me in foreign politics.

When I was in Spain, I was offered, by Mr. Murray, £1,000 per annum to conduct a magazine which he had in contemplation, I to be paid, *in addition*, for any articles I might contribute.[3] This I declined, because it would detain me in Europe, my desire being to return to the United States. Mr. Murray likewise offered me a hundred guineas an article for any article I might write about Spain for the *Quarterly Review*.[4] I refrained from accepting his very liberal offer. As I mentioned in my former letter, I contributed but two articles to his *Review*—one explanatory of the historical grounds of my Chronicles of Granada, and the other a review of my friend McKenzie's "Year in Spain, by a Young American."

I do not recollect having written for any other reviews or magazines in Europe, and I again repeat, I never in any way sought to "puff" my works, or to have them puffed. I always suffered them to take their chance, and always felt that I was favored beyond my deserts.

* * * I have, of late, been so much occupied in diplomatic business, that I have not had time to attend to the Life of Washington. Indeed, I have not done much at it since I have been here, but I shall soon take it earnestly in hand. I found it necessary to give up literary matters for a time, and turn my thoughts entirely into the subjects connected with my station. The statistics of trade about which I have had to occupy myself, are new to me, and require close attention for a time to master them.

PUBLISHED: PMI, III, 272–74.

1. See WI's letter of November 12, 1842.
2. For details about this offer to edit an anti-Jacobin weekly, see Scott to WI, November 17, 1819; WI to Scott, November 20, 1819; and Scott to WI, December 4, 1819, all quoted in PMI, I, 439–45.
3. WI outlines Murray's proposal in a letter to Ebenezer Irving, October 16, 1828.
4. In his journal for October 12, 1828, WI noted Murray's offer. See PMI, I, 346.

1511. To Catharine Paris

Madrid Novr 20th. 1842

My dear Sister,

I presume you are by this time desirous for another peep at royalty; so I'll give you an anecdote or two about the palace. You are aware that the Queen, according to the present constitution (of 1837) is a minor until 14 years of age; when she takes the reins of government in her own hands. Until then Espartero (Duke of Victory) exercises the Supreme authority as Regent, in her name. Until then, also, she, with her sister,[1] is under the tutelage or guardianship of Don Martin Arguelles. This is one of the most estimable men in Spain. He was one of the patriots who declared the Constitution in 1812. He has been true to the liberties of Spain through all the vicissitudes of the last thirty years; sometimes in the Ministry, sometimes in prison, sometimes in exile; but never has any one been able to charge him with a dishonorable act. I first met with him in England, when he was an exile during an interval of despotic rule. It is singular that ↑the man,↓ whom, for his patriotism Ferdinand once confined for six years in the dungeons of a Spanish fortress on the coast of Africa,[2] now has the guardianship of Ferdinands daughter. And I am told by persons in whom I have confidence, that he exercises his trust in the most exemplary manner. He has reformed various abuses in the palace; suppressed frauds in the royal expenditure; surrounded the queen and princess, ⟨with pers⟩ as far as he has had the control, with persons of virtuous character and conduct, and watched over their welfare with a truly paternal care. In this he has been seconded by ⟨Madame⟩ ↑the Countess de↓ Mina, their Aya or Governess, a woman of the most unblemished character, ↑widow of a patriotic general, and made a countess since his death.↓ All this, however, has ⟨giv been a cause of⟩ given great umbrage to the "Moderados" or high aristocratical party, among which are the grandees and others of the proud Spanish nobility, the partizans for absolute rule. They have been accustomed to see all the posts about the Royal person and royal household monopolized by their order; and are outrageous at seeing them given to persons who have nothing but merit to reccommend them. In consequence of the appointment of Madame Mina all the ladies of the nobility who held situations in the royal household, resigned; and the little queen ⟨in consequence⟩ was not able, at her last birthday, to hold a ⟨public general bes⟩ Besamanos or drawing room, for want of ⟨the usual retinue and⟩ ↑ladies in↓ attendance to ↑make up her retinue.↓ What has added to the annoyance of the old nobility is that Madame Mina has been made a grandee of Spain; which of course places her in the highest rank: they content themselves with saying she may call herself Grandee, but no one will think her such: Government may give her rank, but it cannot give her ancestry. Though the nobility have deserted the palace they keep an eye upon it and comment with scorn and bitterness upon every thing that takes place there. According to their representations, and the representations of the newspapers ⟨in⟩ ↑under↓ their influence; you would suppose the little Queen and her sister under the most rigorous restraint, and that Arguelles exerted a tyrannical authority over them out of vindictive reccollection of what he had suffered from ·their father. He is styled in the papers a "rancorous and vindictive old man," whereas he is one of the Kindest hearted beings imaginable, and, ↑I am told,↓ indulgent almost to a fault. The best proof is that the queen and her sister manifest the warmest attachment to him. In like manner there are constant attempts to destroy public confidence in Espartero; by insinuating that he is anxious to prolong the minority of the Queen, according to the constitution of 1812 which extends her minority to her 18th. year, whereas by the present constitution ⟨of 1837⟩ it expires with her 14th. year. It is impossible, they say, for Espartero, after having been suddenly raised to almost regal state and power, to return after two short years, to ordinary life; he wishes to prolong the term of his power; perhaps to render it *permanent*. ⟨It is⟩ These insinuations have been made so frequently and under such various forms that Espartero has felt himself obliged repeatedly to declare his intention of adhering loyally to the constitution of 1837, and to resign the power into the hands of the Queen at the expiration of her fourteenth year: and those who are in his intimacy and confidence, assure me that he is sincere in his declarations; that he ⟨is impatient⟩ is weary of the restraints and responsabilities of his situation and that he looks forward with impatience to the time when he will be able to lay down his charge and retire to his estate at Logroño there to amuse himself with agricultural and ⟨other⟩ manufacturin[g]³ schemes, which are among his day dreams. I am inclined to believe him a frank, honest man; he certainly is a brave one.

But to return to the little Queen. Yesterday was her Saints day: the day of St Isabella: this is more observed in Catholic countries than a birthday. A kind of Besamanos was got up for the occasion. At two Oclock the Queen was to receive congratulatory deputations from the Senate and the ⟨house of⟩ Chamber of Deputies and at 3 Oclock the Corps Diplomatic. ⟨When the deputation of grave Senators arrived⟩ As usual the deputations of the two legislative bodies had prepared speeches for the occasion ↑copies of↓ which had been communicated before hand, that the little queen might be provided with suitable replies. When the deputation of grave Senators arrived they were met in the ante room by the worthy Quintana; preceptor to the Queen. He whispered to them that the poor little Queen, agitated by the idea of the approaching ceremony, had quite forgot the speech which had been prepared for her; ⟨and⟩ he begged them, therefore, to dispense with it, and not to notice her agitation. ⟨In fact she must have had the terror In fact the poor little⟩ In fact she must have had the terrors of a school girl ⟨that⟩ who has forgotten her task at the awful hour of examination; for when the Senators entered they saw by her eyes that she had been crying; and there were yet some lingering sobs. Would you think it? This simple and natural scene, which speaks for itself, has been gossipped about in the noble circles and promulgated in the press, as evidence that the queen ⟨had been⟩ was driven to sobs and tears by the tyranny of those about her, seeking to compel her to make ↑a↓ speech ⟨of⟩ contrary to her feelings and opinions.

It was about an hour afterwards that the Diplomatic Corps had their audience. I was accompanied by Mr Hamilton & Hector Ames; Mr Brevoort, not having a uniform provided, staid at home. We ascended by the grand stair case; the scene of the ⟨night⟩ memorable night attack on the palace in October last year. The door at the head of the Stair case still remains pierced and shattered by innumerable balls; and several windows of the royal apartment bear traces of that outrage. The Palace, however, had not ⟨that⟩ ↑the↓ twilight gloom that prevailed on my visit last summer; when the windows were closed to exclude the heat. Now daylight was admitted into all the chambers and saloons. We assembled in the throne room; an immense Saloon, magnificently furnished;

the walls covered with crimson velvet; the lofty vaulted cieling beautifully painted in fresco, representing the inhabitants and productions of
all parts of the Spanish Empire; which at the time of the painting ⟨con-
tained⟩ extended into every climate and quarter of the world. I reccollected the Saloon of old; having frequently been there when I attended
court during the reign of Ferdinand. While, as usual, we were gossipping
in groupes, awaiting the signal to enter the presence chamber; it was
intimated to us that as the queen was extremely young, and unaccustomed
to these ceremonials, it would be embarrassing for her to find something
to say to each of us, as is customary with royalty on such occasions; and
that it would be better for us to say something to her.

Shortly afterwards the folding doors at the ⟨low⟩ upper end of the
saloon were thrown open and the "Introductor of Ambassadors" ushered
us to the royal presence. We had to traverse an intermediate Saloon, and
in the one beyond, immediately opposite the entrance, stood the little
queen: her sister on her left hand, Espartero the Regent in uniform on
her right, the Countess de Mina in attendance behind her, and some few
officers of the Court ranged beyond the Regent. As we traversed the intervening saloon in full view of the royal party I saw Espartero ⟨telling⟩
↑designating to↓ the Queen each member of the Diplomatic corps, to
guide her in the part she had to act. I wish I could tell you the dresses
of the little Queen and her sister as I know you and the girls will be
curious on this point, but really I forgot to notice them. They were white,
however, and silken, and I have since been told they wore beautiful diamonds and emeralds. Having made our bows on entering we ranged ourselves, according to precedence, along one side of the room. As we are
now on diplomatic matters I must acquaint you with the order of precedence in diplomacy, In former times ↑it was↓ a subject of constant disputes and heart burnings, and ⟨often⟩ occasionally of duels. At present it
is adjusted by a simple rule. Every one takes precedence according to his
official rank, and the date of his residence at the Court. ⟨Thus the ambassador who has been longest at the Court takes precedence of the
other ambassadors; the minister who has been longest ⟨resident⟩ pre-
who in their turn precede ministers resident; who precede Chargés d'Affaires &c The ambassador who has been longest at the Court precedes the
other ambassadors; the Minister who has been longest ⟨resident⟩ precedes the other ministers, and so on. Ambassadors are the representatives not merely of their respective countries but of the *Sovreigns* of that
country: As we are a Republic and have no Sovreign, we have no Ambassadors. The minister plenipotentiary is our highest diplomatic representative. At present there are no ambassadors at the Spanish Court. Mr
Aston, the English Minister Plenipotentiary has been ⟨here⟩ ↑accredited↓
the longest, and takes the lead; then comes Count Lima the Portuguese

minister; then myself; then the Chevalier de Albuquerque, ⟨Bra⟩ Resident Minister from Brazil & so on After we had taken our stand there was a pause; when Madame Mina whispered something to the little Queen and her sister, who thereupon bowed to us all. There was another pause; when, upon the prompting of Espartero, the little Queen, ⟨and⟩ ↑followed by↓ her sister, set forth on ⟨their⟩ ↑her↓ awful journey along the diplomatic line. I believe at first I felt almost as much fluttered as herself. I entered so much into the novelty and peculiarity of her task; a mere child having to give ⟨and⟩ audience to the official Representatives of nations. Mr Aston first addressed her: she had been accustomed to see him on other occasions, and that ⟨fact⟩ served to put her more at her ease. It was the same case with Count Lima, and by the time she had finished with him she began to smile. You will want to know what discourse I held with her, as my turn came next. I do not know whether I ought to impart these diplomatic conversations with royalty; as these are the verbal links that connect the destinies of nations. However, for once I'll venture confiding in your secrecy. I had been so interested in contemplating the little sovreign that I had absolutely forgotten to arrange any thing to say; and when she stood before me I was, as usual with me on public occasions, at a loss. However, something must be said, so I expressed my regret that my ignorance of the Spanish language rendered it so difficult for me to address her as I could wish. "But you speak it very well," ⟨sh⟩ said she, with a smile and a little flirt of her fan. I shook my head negatively. "Do you like Spain?" said she; "very much," replied I; and I spoke sincerely. She smiled again; gave another little clack of her fan; bowed, and passed on. Her sister followed; she had not the womanly carriage of the queen, being still more the child. I told her I hoped she had been pleased at the opera, where I had had the honor of seeing her a few nights before. She said "Yes, she liked the theatre—" and then glided on after her sister. When they had passed down the line they returned to their places and again, on being prompted, bowed to us; upon which we made respectful reverences and retired; taking care as we withdrew, not to turn our backs upon royalty. ⟨Such,⟩ I have thus, my dear Sister, given you another peep into court scenes, and shewn you the petty machinery of the Great world. I can imagine you smiling in the serene wisdom of your elbow chair, at this picture of a row of dignified diplomatic personages, some of them well stricken in years, and all of them sage representatives of governments, bowing with profound reverence and conjuring up nothings, to say to a couple of little girls. However, this is all the whipt syllabub of diplomacy; if I were to take you into one of our conferences with ⟨some⟩ cabinet ministers then you would know the solid wisdom required by our station—but this department of our official functions is a sealed book!

And now that I have had a second interview with the little Queen you will want to know more about her when seen near at hand. I must tell you then that my whole impression is of a more cheerful kind than at my first audience. I then passed through twilight halls and shadowy silent saloons; with the ⟨strong impress⟩ vivid idea, fresh in my mind, of the violent scenes that had recently taken place there, menacing the safety of these innocent helpless children—I found the little queen clad in mourning, which added to the surrounding gloom, seemed characteristic of her fortunes. Now the palace was enlivened by cheerful day light, and the Saloons had resumed their regal splendor. The little queen too was clad in white, and no longer looked like a mere shadow of royalty. But— to be particular—She is well grown for her years; and well formed inclining to fullness rather than the contrary; with extremely well shaped arms. Her countenance, though not handsome, is agreeable; she has light hair and light eyes; which are somewhat unusual in Spain. Her general health I should think from her appearance to be excellent; but she is unfortunately troubled with a complaint of the skin which gives it a rough and somewhat *mealy* look. In consequence of neglect on the part of her mother it was suffered to confirm itself and become obstinate—It is probable, however, that with the assistance of baths which she now takes frequently, she will out grow it. She will then become quite what is called "personable." Her Sister has dark hair and dark eyes; and, though it is said she has lost her colour and ↑much of↓ her good looks within the last year, she is quite pretty. I think she will grow up very handsome. She is said to be of a sprightlier turn than the queen; but the latter, if she begins to think for herself, and to cast a thoughtful eye upon the past, the present and the future, has enough to give a grave cast to her character. Novr. 25. Since I wrote the foregoing one of those popular paroxysms has occurred to which this unfortunate country is subject. An insurrection has taken place in Barcelona.[4] This is the next city in importance to Madrid. It is the capital of the province of Catalonia; the most active and industrious province in Spain. The Catalans are to Spain what the New England people are to the United States. Wherever money is to be made there is a Catalan. They are pushing, scheming, enterprising, hardy and litigious. Catalonia is one of the most restless and insubordinate of the Spanish provinces, and frequently the seat of political disturbances. It borders on France, and is infested by ⟨bands of the ↑bands↓⟩ half robber half rebel ⟨factions⟩ bands, the remnants of the factions of the civil wars which lurk about the French frontiers. ⟨Catalonia has also m⟩ There is a small but busy party of Republicanos, also, at Barcelona, who would gladly ⟨put an end to the present⟩ pull down the present form of government, and establish a republic. ⟨Then there is⟩ Catalonia also has a strong manufacturing interest ⟨that has⟩ having many cotton manufactories. This has taken the alarm at the rumor of a proposed commercial treaty with En-

gland for the introduction of her cotton goods at a lower rate of duties.
So that there is a mixture of various motives in the present convulsion;[5]
and the whole has been thrown in a ferment by the intrigues of foreign
agents who seek ⟨to⟩ the confusion of Spain and the downfall of its constitutional government The present insurrection seems to have broke out
suddenly and accidentally; some trifling affray with custom house offices
having been the spark which has set the combustible community in a
flame. There has been fighting in the streets, as in the famous "three days
of Paris,"[6] ⟨↑The regent↓⟩ and the troops have been obliged to evacuate
the city; but hold it closely invested. The Regent set off from Madrid
Some days since for the ⟨Sci⟩ Scene of action,[7] and troops are concentrating upon Catalonia from every direction, in the mean time Madrid is
full of rumors, and reports, that insurrections are breaking out in other
provinces; but I believe as yet ⟨the Sedition is confin⟩ the insurrection is
confined to Barcelona; and I think it probable it will be suppressed without much difficulty.

The departure of the Regent was a striking scene. All the uniform companies or national guard of Madrid, consisting of several thousand men,
well armed, equipped and disciplined; paraded in the grand esplanade of
the Prado in the neighborhood of the Regents palace of Buena Vista.
They really made a splendid appearance; and the air resounded with
military music, several of the regiments having complete bands. ⟨The
day was⟩ It was a bright sunshiny day. About two oclock the Regent
⟨made his⟩ sallied forth from Buena Vista at the head of his staff. He ⟨was⟩
is a fine martial figure, and was arrayed in full uniform, with towering
feathers, and mounted on a noble grey charger with a flowing mane and
a long silken tail that almost swept the ground. He rode along the heads
of the columns saluting them with his gauntleted hand, and receiving
cheers wherever he went. He stopped to speak particularly with some of
the troops of horse men; then returning to the centre of the Esplanade,
he drew his sword, made a signal as if about to speak, and in an instant
a profound silence prevailed over that vast body of troops, and the
thousands of ↑surrounding↓ Spectators. ⟨that⟩ I do not know that ever I
was more struck by any thing than by this Sudden quiet of an immense
multitude. The Regent then moved slowly backwards and forwards with
his horse, about a space of thirty yards, waving his sword and addressing
the troops in a voice so loud and clear that every word could be distinctly
heard to a great distance. The purport of his speech was to proclaim his
determination to protect the ↑present↓ constitution and the liberties of
Spain against despotism on the one hand and anarchy on the other; and
that as on a former occasion, when summoned away by distant insurrection, he ⟨left⟩ confided ⟨in⟩ to the loyalty of the national guards the protection of the peace of the capital and the Safeguard of their young and

innocent Queen. His speech was responded to by enthusiastic acclamations from the troops and the multitude; and he sallied forth in martial style from the great gate of Alcala.

I must note, to complete the Scene, that just as Espartero appeared ⟨s⟩ issued forth from Buena Vista and rode slowly down the Prado between the columns of the troops, a Solitary Raven came sailing ⟨heavily over head⟩ ↑down the course of the public promenade↓; passed immediately above him and over the whole line of troops, and so flitted heavily out of sight. This has been cited, even in the public papers, as a bad omen; and some of the superstitious say Espartero will never return ⟨safe⟩ to Madrid. I should not be surprised, however, if the omen had been prepared by some of the petty politicians with which this capital abounds: and that the Raven had been let loose just at this opportune moment However, with this portentous circumstance I will close my letter; especially as I have just recieved despatches from government, which, with the stirring events of the day, will cut out plenty of occupation for me

With love to all

Your affectionate brother
Washington Irving

P.S.   I have just recd. Pierre M Irvings letter of Oct. 31.[8] pr Brittania Steamer, and find there are letters on the way from you & brother E.I. which will come by the Havre Packet of 1st Nov.

DOCKETED: Washn. Irving to Mrs. Paris. Madrid. Nov. 20. 1842.
MANUSCRIPT: Yale.   PUBLISHED: PMI, III, 257, 259–61 (in part); LFSS, pp. 49–50 (in part); STW, II, 152 (in part).

1. For other details about Arguelles, see WI to Catharine Paris, August 3, 1842.

2. At Ceuta. Actually Arguelles was sentenced to serve for ten years as a common soldier there. See Elizabeth Wormsley Latimer, *Spain in the Nineteenth Century* (Chicago, 1897), p. 105.

3. The final letter runs off the page.

4. On November 13 a minor affray broke out between workers and officials who were trying to levy taxes on the wine the laborers wished to bring into the city. The incident was exploited by Republican extremists, and the next day the city was at the mercy of organized workmen who proclaimed the independence of Catalonia from Madrid until the reestablishment of a government to protect their industrial and agricultural interests. The captain-general, Antonio Van Halen (1792–1858), proclaimed a state of siege, the city gates were closed on November 16, and the leaders of the Republican party were arrested. See WI to Daniel Webster, November 26, 1842; London *Times*, November 26, 1842; H. Butler Clarke, *Modern Spain* (Cambridge, 1906), pp. 182–83; and Raymond Carr, *Spain, 1808–1939*, pp. 224–25.

5. For the development of Catalan industry and general sources of dissatisfaction,

see WI to Daniel Webster, August 27 and November 5 and 22, 1842; London *Times*, November 26 and 29, 1842; and Clarke, *Modern Spain*, pp. 180–81.

6. July 12 to 14, 1789, the three days which culminated in the fall of the Bastille in Paris. See Jacques Godechot, *The Taking of the Bastille* (New York, 1970); and Georges Lefebvre, *The French Revolution from its Origins to 1793*, trans. Elizabeth Moss Evanson (New York, 1962), I, 123.

7. Espartero left for Barcelona on November 21. See WI to Daniel Webster, November 22, 1842; and London *Times*, November 29, 1842.

8. This letter has not been located.

1512. To Daniel Webster

Legation of the United States. / Madrid November 22nd. 1842.

No. 7. / The Hon: Daniel Webster. / Secretary of State of the U. States—Washington.

Sir

Since I had the honor of sending my last despatch, the Cortes has opened its session, and the Ministers have been defeated in the election of officers;[1] Olozaga,[2] the coalition Candidate for the Presidency of the Congress being elected by a large majority. Ministers did not take this however, as a signal to retire, but resolved to fight their battle on the great questions of financial reform. Calatrava, the Minister of Finance accordingly brought forward his budget shewing a deficit for 1843, of about 20 millions of dollars, to remedy which he proposed, among other measures, that the Cortes should authorise the Government, to contract for a loan of 30 millions of Dollars; hypothecating for the payment of the interest, and reimbursement of the principal, all the revenues and contributions of the State; *and especially the increased revenues of the Customs under a new and improved system of duties, which the Cortes for the benefit of commerce and industry ⟨may⟩ ↑might↓ adopt.*

This had in view a treaty of commerce with England,[3] which, I am told, was in a state of advancement, for the introduction of her Cotton manufactures at reduced duties: she for the better security of reimbursement, to have the right of collecting the duties in her own ports, prior to embarkation, giving a certificate of the goods having paid such duties. On the above part of Calatrava's scheme, all parties were prepared for a violent conflict, when [all][4] of a sudden news arrived of a formidable insurrection at Barcelona.

The immediate cause of this outbreak appears to have been accidental; but the populace of Barcelona, at all times excitable, have of late been in a general state of uneasiness and irritation, caused it is said by the rigorous hand held over them by Government; by the rough and at times unconstitutional measures of General Zurbano in suppressing Sedition contraband and robbery; and by the apprehended "Cotton Treaty" with England, which they deprecate as the downfall of their manufactures. Politics are also adduced as having their share in the popular commotion; The republicans taking an active part in the hope of subverting the Monarchy. Though as usual, a Junta has been formed to conduct every thing on system, no leading principles have been proclaimed, and the motives and objects of the Insurrection are left to conjecture. It appears to have been a general and spontaneous rising of the populace something like that of the "three days" in Paris. Barricades have been formed in the streets, missiles hurled from the windows and even women and children have mingled in the affray. The troops after ineffectual efforts to maintain the mastery of the City have been driven out with heavy loss; some who lingered in the Citadel having been obliged to capitulate and to retire after surrendering their arms.

At the same time with these tidings came rumors of seditious intentions in Saragossa to make a "pronunciamiento" in favor of Don Francisco, at the head of a regency of three: These however have not since been confirmed.

On receiving news of the insurrection The Regent with characteristic promptness resolved to repair immediately in person to the scene of danger. The Congress of deputies, postponing all party discussions, in this moment of urgency, concurred almost unanimously in voting an address to the Regent, assuring him of their Support, and assistance in all measures for the public tranquility "within the circle of the laws and the Constitution."

Yesterday Espartero took his leave in military style of all the National Guards assembled in the Prado. He made them an address, professing his determination to maintain the Constitution of 1837, against despotism on the one hand and anarchy on the other; and he confided as on a former occasion to their patriotism, loyalty, and valor, the protection of the City and of their youthful Queen.

His address was received with animated acclamations and he departed amidst the cheerings of the multitude.[5] He will proceed first to Saragossa, where he will remain some four or five days to secure the tranquility of Aragon and to collect forces; thence he will proceed to Valencia and so on to Catalonia. In the mean time troops from Madrid and from various other parts will be concentrating on the scene of insurrection.

The accounts received late last night from the government[6] are considered as encouraging to the hope of a speedy suppression of the insurrection. It appears to be local. Saragossa and Valencia about which fears had been entertained remain quiet. The troops though drawn out of Barcelona, were stationed under Generals Van Halen and Zurbano in the neighbourhood, and are constantly receiving reinforcements, while none of the soldiery had deserted. Some Spanish vessels of war were anchored off the City; Monjuich; a Fortress which commands Barcelona[7] had commenced a bombardment of it; and on the departure of the Government express a deputation from the Junta headed by the British and French Consuls were holding a parley with Van Halen to prevent the City from being destroyed.

I give you what appears most to be depended upon of the various reports in circulation. If this insurrection be speedily put down it may strengthen the hand of Espartero and increase the public confidence in the sincerity of his professions concerning the Constitution of 1837, and the limited minority of the Queen. In the mean time all legislation on the great cotton question is interrupted, and the project of the British Treaty sleeps in the Portfolio of Calatrava.

An important schism is hinted at, as likely to take place in the ranks of the Coalition. Olozaga was written to, while in Paris, and the offer made of electing him to the Presidency of Congress, on condition that in the event of overturning the present Ministry he would consent to be placed at the head of the new Cabinet. He agreed by letter to the arrangement; but now it is said, draws back being unwilling to take upon himself the conducting of a cabinet without money; and that consequently would be as ephemeral and unpopular as those that had proceeded.

I have just been informed that by virtue of a decree left behind him by the Regent, The Cortes were prorogued indefinitely to day.

I am Sir very respectfully / Your Obdt Sevt.
Washington Irving

DOCKETED: Recd. 28 Dec. [*upper left corner of page 1*] / No. 7. W. Irving. Madrid. 22 Nov. 1842

MANUSCRIPT: NA, RG 59.

Only the signature is in WI's handwriting.

1. The Progressives, led by Salustiano Olózaga (1805–1873), Joaquín María López (1799–1855), and Manuel Cortina (1802–1879), had decisively defeated Espartero's ministry in the Cortes in May, 1841. When Olózaga refused to form a coalition cabinet, Espartero, in defiance, appointed as premier Ramón Rodil (1789–1853), who had no support in the Cortes. Prorogation was soon found necessary, and in November, 1842, the regent and his ministry were obliged by law to face the Cortes. Olózaga's election as president of the lower house was an act of direct

hostility against Espartero. See H. Butler Clarke, *Modern Spain*, p. 179; and Raymond Carr, *Spain, 1808–1939*, p. 222.

2. Salustiano Olózaga had been civil governor of Madrid in 1835, a member of the Cortes which drew up the 1837 constitution, and Espartero's ambassador to France in 1840. See Clarke, *Modern Spain*, pp. 16, 135, 179.

3. See *El Castellano*, November 22, 1842.

4. WI omitted the bracketed word.

5. Accounts of Espartero's speech and departure are reported in *Eco del Comercio*, November 21; in *La Gaceta*, November 22; and in *El Castellano*, November 21, 1842.

6. See reports and discussions in *El Castellano*, November 21 and 22, 1842.

7. Montjuich is a crest rising 575 feet above Barcelona in the southern sector. At its summit was a fortification which commanded the city and provided quarters for up to 10,000 men. See Karl Baedeker, *Spain and Portugal*, p. 245; and Martin Hume, *Modern Spain* (London, 1899), p. 370.

1513. To Sarah Storrow

Madrid, Novr. 26th. 1842.

My dear Sarah,

The arrival yesterday of your letter of the 18th. instant reminded me that a preceding one[1] remained unanswered; but I have been much occupied of late and my attention called off from domestic duties by public affairs. I enclose for your perusal a long letter which I have written to your mother[2] as a sequence to one which I wrote to her some time since, containing a sketch of Spanish politics and court anecdotes, as they relate to the little queen. I find the subject interests her, as I thought it would. Spanish history has at all times born the air of romance, and does so especially at this moment, when the fortunes of the little queen and her sister are connected with it. I shall pursue these themes from time to time in my letters to your mother, as it will be carrying on a living historical romance for her gratification, and I know no one ⟨whom⟩ ↑more fitted by↓ quick intelligence; ⟨and⟩ nice sensibilities and kindling imagination, to enjoy such picturings of real yet romantic life. I have had no letter from her since my long one above mentioned; her reply ⟨[has?]⟩ is on the way, by the Havre packet of the 1st Novr. ⟨I find by your letter however⟩ Her letters are a great delight to me: she writes frequently, and with a clearness of thought ⟨and⟩ vivacity of feeling and simple beauty of expression, that shew how remarkably she retains the "verdure of the Soul."

As you will see by the latter part of my letter to your mother, and as you must know by the public papers, Spain is threatened with one of its periodical combustions. The last news from Barcelona is that forty eight hours were given for it to lay down its arms and ⟨submit⟩ return to its allegiance or be bombarded. I hope to hear, this evening, that the insurrection is at an end and the city restored to quiet; but in this inflammable country, where the elements of discord are so varied, and industriously disseminated in different provinces there is always danger that when a flame breaks out in one place it will spread to others. There are continual intrigues and plots going on also in the Capitol, which though petty in their nature, often break out into popular tumults. Espartero, however, is popular with the national guard, which form the protection of Madrid, and I trust the quiet of the city will be maintained during his absence. I am much pleased with the manner in which he travels; pushing on, in a post chaise, ahead of all his ⟨military⟩ troops, without escort, accompanied merely by his aid de camp or secretary, and throwing himself singly and unarmed among the people of the towns and villages. This frank fearless confidence is appreciated as it ought to be; and he is received by the populace with perfect enthusiasm.

I am sorry to find by your last letter that you have been nervous and out of Spirits—you attribute it to the effect of Dickens novel; but you must have been in a nervous state to be so affected by a novel. When you feel yourself in such moods you must taboo all dismal works of fiction; the best ⟨remedy⟩ recipe to restore the tone of your spirits is exercise in the open air. It seems little Kate too has been giving way to her sensibilities. I hope you did not leave Dickens novel[3] lying in her cradle.

I dont think from the tone of your preceding letter, an intimate intercourse with the Jones family is likely to contribute to your enjoyment; I would advise you therefore, as I before suggested, to slacken it off; ⟨into⟩ but gently and amiably. The sphere and style in which they appear ambitious to move might render an intercourse inconvenient to both; however kind your feelings toward each other. Do not however suffer yourself to think, and above all to speak of them with asperity. Reccollect that towards you ⟨they⟩ and yours they have always manifested esteem and exercised kindness; and reccollect also that all that can really be laid to their charge are foibles not vices, and a too great desire to captivate the admiration of a heartless and sneering world. I only regret that they are not aware how worthless is the fashionable ⟨circle they are⟩ notoriety they are striving after and how surrounded by pitfalls.

My little household is completely in the winter establishment. We have our cosey evening fireside; and as the young gentlemen have brought home a supply of tea, with backgammon boards, chess men &c there are means of diversifying the evening very pleasantly.

Give my love to little Kate and tell her if she makes another lip and
a queer mouth at Mr Beasley Ill never forgive her.

Your affectionate uncle
Washington Irving

ADDRESSED: Madame / Madame Storrow / aux soins de Mr T. W. Storrow / 17
   Rue du Poissonniere / à Paris
MANUSCRIPT: Yale.   PUBLISHED: Simison, *Keogh Papers*, pp. 192–95.

1. These letters have not been located.
2. WI to Catharine Paris, November 25, 1842.
3. *The Old Curiosity Shop* was Dickens's latest novel at this time. Some of its
scenes could possibly have prompted Sarah's depression.

1514. To Daniel Webster

Legation of the United States. / Madrid November 26th. 1842.

No. 8. / The Hon: Daniel Webster. / Secretary of State of the U. States—
   Washington.

Sir.
   I have the honor to acknowledge the receipt of your despatch No. 5.
dated August 29th. which only reached me yesterday; having been
detained in London until an opportunity occurred of Sending it by
private hand, to save the postage on so voluminous a pacquet, and under
the idea probably that it contained merely Newspapers or printed
documents. On casting my eye over the despatch and its accompanying
documents, I regret extremely this detention, and the further delay
that may occur in obtaining and forwarding the desired information
from this Government, as to its authorization of the claim proposed by
the Chevalier D'Argaiz;[1] Count Almodovar the Minister of State, being
confined to his bed by illness, and the Cabinet in a state of perturbation,
caused by the insurrection of Barcelona, and its attendant circumstances.
I shall lose no time however in executing your instructions in the
premises.
   The last accounts from Barcelona represent that City as organizing
itself for an obstinate resistance; its affairs are at present in more responsible hands. The "popular Junta directiva" which had for a time
the entire sway is said to be composed of men without character or
standing; some of them strangers. The principles they proclaimed were
sufficiently comprehensive. "A Union of all liberals—The downfall of Es-

partero and his Government—constituent Cortes or assemblies; the regency if continued, to consist of more than one person—the Queen to be affianced to none but a Spaniard—Justice and protection of the National industry."

A "Junta consultation" has now been nominated; acting with the former, but embracing several of the richest, and most respectable inhabitants. Some of them it is Said declined to Serve, and others Serve under a degree of Compulsion: order, however, is maintained in the interior of the City; and it keeps up an air of quiet defiance though immediately under the threatening guns of Monjuich.—Van Halen has declared his intention to bombard it, unless, it should resume its allegiance within eight and forty hours.[2] The French consul[3] has protested against such measure, but Van Halen seems disposed to disregard his protest. The City will probably hold out to the verge of extremity in hope that the insurrection will extend to other parts of the province, and break out in other provinces of the Kingdom; but though feverish symptoms have manifested themselves in Valencia and elsewhere, they have been speedily quieted without bloodshed: The Regent, who travels without escort, throwing himself with frank and fearless confidence into the midst of the People, is every where received with enthusiasm; troops are concentrating upon Catalonia from various directions; there is every probability therefore, that the first fire from the Fort of Monjuich will bring the City to a capitulation.

I have the honor to enclose a copy of a note recently passed by me to the Minister of State on the subject of the occasional occupation by our Ships of War of the Arsenal and Navy Yard at Mahon.

I have the honor to remain / very respectfully / Your Obdt Sevt.

Washington Irving

Docketed: Recd. 28 Jany. / No. 8. W. Irving, Madrid. 26 Nov. 1842
Manuscript: NA, RG 59.

Only the signature is in WI's handwriting.

1. Pedro Alcántara Argáiz was Spanish envoy extraordinary and minister plenipotentiary to the United States from September 26, 1836, to January 2, 1844.

2. See *El Castellano*, November 26, 1842.

3. Ferdinand, vicomte de Lesseps (1805–1894), the French consul general in Barcelona, was acting under orders from Guizot's government to foster disturbances in the city, with a view to toppling Espartero's regency and restoring María Christina to power. See H. Butler Clarke, *Modern Spain*, pp. 179, 183–84; and WI to Daniel Webster, January 9, 1843.

1515. To Count Almodóvar

Legation of the United States. / Madrid November 29t. 1842

The Undersigned Envoy Extraordinary and Minister Plenipotentiary of the United States of America has the honor to communicate to his Excellency Count Almodovar First Minister of State and of Foreign Affairs of Her Catholic Majesty the original commission of Mr Robert. B. Campbell,[1] appointed Consul of the United States for the Port of Havana in the Island of Cuba; and by direction of his Government requests that His Excellency will cause the corresponding Royal Exequatur to be issued recognizing Mr. Campbell, in his official character.

The Undersigned takes the opportunity to renew to his Excellency the assurances of his most distinguished consideration.

Washington Irving

MANUSCRIPT: NA, RG 84 (letterbook copy).

1. Robert Blair Campbell (d. 1862), who had represented South Carolina in the U.S. Congress from 1823 to 1825 and from 1833 to 1837, was appointed U.S. consul at Havana on September 22, 1842, and served until July 22, 1850. He later replaced Thomas Aspinwall as U.S. consul at London, serving from August, 1854, to March, 1861.

1516. To Count Almodóvar

Légation des Etats Unis / Le 2 de Decembre 1842.

M. Irving Envoyé Extraordinaire et Ministre Plenipotentiaire des Etats-Unis d'Amerique, a l'honneur de presenter a son Excellence Monsieur Le Comte Almodovar, ses félicitations sur le retablissement de sa sante et de prier son Excellence de vouloir bien lui indiquer le premier jour; ou elle se trouvera assez retablie pour lui accorder une entrevue sur des affaires importans.

Mons. Irving saisit avec plaisir cette occasion pour offrir a son Excellence Mons. Le Comte Almodovar les assurances de sa consideration tres distinguée.

Son Excellence
Mons. Le Comte Almodovar/&ca. &ca. &ca.

DOCKETED: En 4 se le contesto que seria recibido al dia siguiente: a mediodia en casa del S. C. ("On the 4th he was advised that he would be received the next day at noon in the home of the Count.")

MANUSCRIPT: Archivo de Ministerio de Asuntes Exteriores, Madrid.

Translation: "Mr. Irving, envoy extraordinary and minister plenipotentiary of the United States of America, has the honor of offering His Excellency Count Almodovar his felicitations for the return of his health and would His Excellency please indicate when would· be the first opportunity he might be disposed to grant him an interview concerning important matters.

It is with pleasure that Mr. Irving takes advantage of the occasion to extend His Excellency Count Almodovar the assurances of his most distinguished consideration."

1517. To Alexander Burton et al.

Legation of the United States. / Madrid Decr. 2nd 1842.

Circular.

Alexr: Burton Esqr. Consul Cadiz.

George Read	do.	Malaga.
M: de Aguirre.	do.	Bilbao.
O. Rich.	do.	Mahon.

Pablo Anguera. Consular Agent. Barcelona

Sir.

By a decree of the Regent of this Kingdom, dated Saragossa the 26th. Ulto. and just communicated officially to this Legation, a blockade is declared of the Port of Barcelona and the adjacent Coast, from the River Besos to Llobregat both included; to commence on the 8th Inst.[1]

I am, Sir, respectfully / Your Obdt Sevt.
Washington Irving

MANUSCRIPT: NA, RG 84 (letterbook copy).

Maximo de Aguirre was nominated for the post of U.S. consul at Bilbao in 1834. He apparently held it until 1862. See Hasse, *Index to U.S. Documents*, I, 18; III, 1745.

1. The decree was published in *La Gaceta* and *El Castellano* on December 2, 1842.

1518. To Daniel Webster

Legation of the United States. / Madrid December 2nd. 1842.

No. 9. / The Hon: Daniel Webster. / Secretary of State—Washington.

Sir

By a decree of the Regent of this Kingdom dated Saragossa November 26th. and just communicated officially to this Legation, a Blockade is declared of the Port of Barcelona, and the adjacent Coast, from the river Besos to ↑the↓ Llobregat,[1] both included; to commence on the 8h. inst:

I have the honor to enclose a copy of the Decree, and of the instructions and regulations issued by the Minister of Marine for the carrying of it into effect.

I am, Sir, very respectfully / Your Obdt Sevt.
Washington Irving

DOCKETED: Recd. 28 Jany. / Mr Markoe
MANUSCRIPT: NA, RG 59.

Only the signature is in WI's handwriting.

1. These rivers were, respectively, on the northern and southern outskirts of Barcelona.

1519. To Daniel Webster

Legation of the United States. / Madrid December 5th. 1842

No. 10. / The Hon: Daniel Webster. / Secretary of State of the United States—Washington.

Sir

Count Almodovar, the first minister of State, being sufficiently recovered from his Indisposition to attend to business I had an interview with him this morning on the subject of the difficulty which had occurred in respect to the semi-annual payment of interest due 14th. August, on the debt owing by Spain to the United States.[1]

On stating the case, the Count assured me that the Spanish Government had never for a moment thought of suffering the claim arising in the case of the Amistad[2] to interfere with the punctual payment of the interest in question; and that he had no doubt the payment had been made long since.

It would appear ⟨from what he said⟩ that ⟨a game of cross purposes ha⟨d⟩s arisen in this matter from some petty arrangement contemplated by⟩ the Chevalier D'Argaiz,[3] who expecting a final answer from you on the 15th. August, relative to the claim for indemnification in the case of the Amistad and that there would be a payment to be made to the Spanish claimants resident in Cuba; had written to that effect to the Intendente of the Island,[4] advising him to stay his hand in the remittance of the interest, as it might be an accomodation to all parties to pay it into the hands of the indemnified claimants. It was in consequence of this letter that the Intendente wrote you the letter of the 23d. July; so that neither he nor M. Argaïz were acting in consequence of any instructions from the Spanish Government.—Such is the explanation given to me of this part of the case.

On receiving the letter from the Chevalier D'Argaiz The Intendente wrote to the Government at Madrid for instructions. Subsequently however, when he had received your letter, he consulted with the Captain General of the Island of Cuba, and it was determined between them, that the payment of the interest should be made at once without waiting for instructions; and it is presumed by the Count Almodovar that it was so made—The Intendente, however, wrote to the Count, informing him of this determination, and hoping it might be approved by Government. Before that letter reached Madrid, the Government in consequence of the previous letter on the subject, had written to him, ordering him to make the payment without fail or delay; and in no wise to mingle the matter with that of the Amistad.

A few days after sending off this letter, Count Almodovar received a despatch from the Chevalier D'Argaïz enclosing all the correspondence which he had recently had with the Government of the United States; as this correspondence included your letter to the Chevalier D'Argaïz informing him that you had written on the subject to the Diplomatic representative of the United States at Madrid; Count Almodovar delayed his reply to the Chevalier until he should receive a communication from me; which he had been continually expecting.

I explained to him the reason of my being so long in making the communication; my instructions having been three months on the road; and expressed my great satisfaction at the explanation I had just received, which was entirely in comformity[5] with what has been expected by you, from the honor and good faith of the Spanish Government.

Count Almodovar still seemed nettled that there should have been any doubt of the intentions of the Spanish Government most scrupulously to fulfil its engagements: and expressed some chagrin also that you had not given the answer promised to be furnished to the Chevalier D'Argaïz on the 15 August, to the claims for indemnification in the case of the Amistad; as it kept the claimants out of the property of which they had so long been deprived. He said as the subjects were totally distinct you might have gone on with your correspondence in respect to the Amistad without regard to the question of the payments.

I replied that if he would regard your correspondence attentively, he would find that all the present cross purposes had arisen entirely from the want of a little frankness on the part of the Chevalier D'Argaïz. That you were actually engaged on the promised reply, when you were led, by the letter of the Intendente of Cuba to suppose that the Chevalier D'Argaïz had interposed the pending claim of the Amistad in the way of the regular payment of interest. That, exceedingly surprised, you had written to the Chevalier to know whether he had been instructed by his Government to do so; but that he had evaded replying to the enquiry, making a reply dependant on your answer to the Amistad claim. This want of frankness threw a doubt over the matter, which you were exceedingly unwilling to indulge, and obliged you to Seek from the Government at Madrid that information which was withheld by its representative at Washington. In the mean time you felt yourself authorised until such information were obtained, to pause in your correspondence respecting a claim which apparently was to be intruded so much out of place.

Before leaving him Count Almodovar requested that I would pass in the form of a note the communication I had been instructed to make, that he might reply in the same manner.

In connection with this subject, permit ↑me↓ to suggest that this Legation be furnished with a Series of the Reports of the Supreme Court: It is quite unnecessary to call your attention to the great advantage of such a collection to all future Ministers of the United States, but I may mention that the Decision of the Supreme Court in the case of the Amistad,[6] which has given rise to this question between the Governments, is to be found, neither among the papers lately transmitted by the Department,[7] nor among those previously existing in the Archives of the Legation.

I have the honor to acknowledge the receipt of Despatch No. 9. from the Department enclosing the Commission of Mr. Robt. B. Campbell, as Consul of the United States for the Port of Havana, and to state that in compliance with its directions I applied on the 29th. ulto. for the usual royal Exequatur in his case.

I am Sir, very respectfully / Your Obdt Sevt.
Washington Irving

DOCKETED: Recd. 28 Jany.
MANUSCRIPT: NA, RG 59.

Only the signature is in WI's handwriting.

1. The Convention for Settlement of Claims, signed at Madrid on February 17, 1834, and proclaimed on November 1, 1834, established the semiannual payment of $15,000 at Paris. Only four of these payments were made, in 1835 and 1836. On April 2, 1841, a secret arrangement was made by the Spanish government whereby "the Treasury of Cuba shall pay . . . annually sixty thousand dollars" to discharge this debt and accrued interest. These annual payments made up in a few years the arrears of interest, and thereafter $30,000 was paid annually. See *Treaties and Other International Acts of the United States of America,* ed. Hunter Miller, 7 vols. (Washington, 1933), III, 810–22, especially p. 821.

2. In June, 1839, the Spanish schooner *Amistad* bearing African slaves sailed from Havana to Principe. The slaves mutinied and killed the captain but were brought to Long Island Sound, where they were discovered on August 26, 1839. The Spanish minister demanded total restoration of the vessel, cargo, and slaves under Article IX of the United States-Spanish Treaty of 1795. The U.S. district attorney decided that if they had been transported as slaves from Africa in violation of the act of Congress of March 3, 1819, the Africans should be returned to Africa. On January 23, 1840, the district court awarded the vessel and cargo to their lawful owners and directed that those claiming to be native Africans be returned home. The U.S. Supreme Court upheld the decision except that it ordered the Africans to be freed. Spain demanded total indemnification, and on February 27, 1843, President Tyler suggested a refund of the amount of salvage as proof of good faith. A convention was finally signed at Madrid on March 5, 1860, when Spain agreed to pay the "Cuban Claims" while the *Amistad* was to be submitted for arbitration. On June 27, 1860, the Senate declined to exchange ratification, and the claim was never settled. See Moore, *A Digest of International Law,* V, 852–54, STW, II, 363.

3. For Argaïz's diplomatic tactlessness, see WI to Daniel Webster, November 26, December 6, 1842; January 9, 1843; and to A. P. Upshur, March 2, 1844.

4. Gerónimo Valdés y Sierra (1784–1855) was governor-general of Cuba until September, 1843. See WI to Daniel Webster, March 10, 1843; and to A. P. Upshur, March 2, 1844.

5. The copyist misspelled the word.

6. After Spain appealed the district court decision, the Supreme Court upheld the lower court ruling, except to order the freeing of the Africans. See Moore, *A Digest of International Law,* V, 853–54.

7. For Webster's correspondence on the *Amistad* affair, see *The Writings of Daniel Webster* (Boston, 1903), XII, 65–79; and XIV, 403–4.

1520.   To Count Almodóvar

Legation of the United States / Madrid December 6th. 1842

The Undersigned Envoy Extraordinary and Minister Plenipotentiary of the United States of America has the honor to communicate to his

Excellency Count Almodovar, First Minister of State and of Foreign affairs of Her Catholic Majesty the purport of a verbal communication which he had the honor to make to his Excellency yesterday, and of which His Excellency required a written statement.

On the 3d. of June last, the Secretary of State of the United States wrote to the Intendente of the Island of Cuba, suggesting the expediency of remitting the Semi-annual interest, under the treaty of 1834, which would fall due on the 14th. of August in bills payable in Newyork, as had been done with the previous instalment.[1]

On the 15th. of August the Secretary received a reply in which the Intendente expressed his willingness to comply with the arrangement but added "Siento decir a V. E. que en el entre tanto no reciba contestacion del Mro. plenipotentiario de mi nacion en esa no me es permitido efectuar el giro, porque pende al parecer el arreglo de un ajuste en indemnizacion que se reclama, pero esto no obstante, hoy mismo me dirigo al Exmo Sñor Ministro de Estado en Madrid pidiendole instrucciones, y a la vez al refirido plenipotenciario, con el fin de que acuerde por Medio de V. E. con el Gefe Supremo de esa Republica, el total de la indemnizacion pedida, y como ha de discontarse"[2]

This passage of the letter struck the Secretary of State with extreme surprise. The pending claim for indemnification alluded to, the presumed to be one respecting the Schooner Amistad, about which he was at that moment writing a letter to the Chevalier D'Argaïz. He suspended his correspondence about the Amistad, and wrote to the Chevalier D'Argaïz informing him of the reply of the Intendente, and making of him the following enquiry.

"I have the Presidents directions to lose no time in inquiring whether you have been instructed by your Government to signify in any way to the Intendente of Havana that these payments falling due under the last arrangement between the United States and Spain, and intended as a means of enabling Spain more easily to fulfil her solemn treaty obligations, are to be suspended, or abated, or in any way affected by the pendency of the claim presented by you in the case of the Amistad."

The reply of the Chevalier D'Argaïz to this enquiry was as follows.

"I have the honor to state to you in answer to your said note, that, even supposing me to have received instructions from Her Majesty's Government those [instructions] could not be carried into effect until I knew the resolution which the Government of the United States might adopt on the claim which I have pending in the name of Her Majesty in your Department, and on which I expected an answer on the 15th. Instant. You Sir, will easily conceive how disagreeable it is to me to be without the means of giving you fuller explanations"

This refusal of the Chevalier D'Argaïz to furnish the required explanation left the Secretary of State in a painful dilemma; he could hardly suppose that the Chevalier D'Argaïz could on his own responsibility have taken so extraordinary a step as to interpose an unsettled and unacknowledged claim in the way of a payment due under the solemn Stipulations of a treaty; yet it was still more difficult to believe that he could have been authorized to such a Step by instructions from his Government. Under these Circumstances the Secretary of State felt compelled to apply to her Majesty's Government at Madrid for that information in the premises which its representative at Washington declined to furnish.

In applying for this information the Undersigned was instructed to say that the Government of the United States never would consent that such a claim as that proposed by the Chevalier D'Argaïz (whether such as the Government of the United States might or might not eventually allow) should interfere to prevent the payment by Spain of interest on a debt guaranteed by solemn treaty, or should be deducted from, or in any manner connected with such payment; and the Undersigned was instructed to add that the Government of the United States hardly believed the Spanish Government intended, or had authorised its representative at Washington to suggest such a measure.

Such is the purport of the verbal communication which, by order of his Government, The Undersigned had the honor to make yesterday to his Excellency the Count Almodovar; and he was most happy to learn from his Excellency in reply that the Government of the United States was justified in its unwillingness to impute this intrusion of the claim of the Amistad, and this suspension of the payment of interest to any instructions from the Spanish Government; and that the whole misunderstanding had arisen from some petty financial arrangement suggested by the Chevalier D'Argaïz to the Intendente of Cuba, as to balancing the amount of interest about to fall due in that Island, with an amount of indemnity expected to fall due from the United States Government, about the same time at Washington.

It is only to be regretted that the Chevalier D'Argaïz did not deem it expedient to make this simple explanation of his interference in the payment of the interest, when the inquiry upon the subject was addressed to him by the Secretary of State in August last; as it might at once have put an end to any misunderstanding as to the feelings and intentions of either Government.

The Undersigned avails himself of this occasion to renew to his Excellency Count Almodovar the assurances of his most distinguished Consideration.

Washington Irving

MANUSCRIPT: NA, RG 84 (letterbook copy); NA, RG 59 (copy); Archivo de Ministerio de Asuntes Exteriores, Madrid.

Only the signature is in WI's handwriting.

1. For other details about the Spanish-Cuban-United States problem, see WI to Daniel Webster, December 5, 1842.

2. Translation: "I regret to say to your excellency that until I receive an answer from the minister plenipotentiary of my country in that [country] I am not permitted to effectuate the draft (payment), because apparently the arrangement of a settlement in indemnity which is being claimed is pending. Nevertheless, this very day I am writing to the most excellent minister of state in Madrid, requesting instructions, and, at the same time to the aforementioned plenipotentiary to the end that he may come to an agreement, through your excellency, with the supreme head of that Republic on the total of the requested indemnity and how it must be discounted."

1521. *To Count Almodóvar*

Legation of the United States. / December 8h. 1842.

The Undersigned Envoy Extraordinary and Minister Plenipotentiary of the United States of America has received with the greatest satisfaction the intelligence communicated to him by his Excellency Count de Almodovar of the submission of Barcelona to the government of Her Majesty and the reinstalment of the legitimate authorities in their respective functions.[1]

The Undersigned will immediately communicate this gratifying intelligence to his Government, which takes the liveliest interest in every thing that concerns the prosperity and happiness of Spain.

The Undersigned avails himself of this occasion to renew to his Excellency assurances of his highest consideration.

Washington Irving

MANUSCRIPT: NA, RG 84 (letterbook copy).

Another copy was enclosed with WI's despatch No. 11 of December 10, 1842, to Daniel Webster.

1. Upon arriving in Barcelona on November 29, Espartero refused the moderate terms of capitulation the city proposed and sent away its deputation unheard. Treating the city as collectively guilty, he ordered cannon to bombard it. The gates were closed, and during Van Halen's bombardment on December 3 a violent faction plundered and terrorized respectable citizens. Van Halen entered the city the next evening, and Espartero, holding the city guilty, imposed a £12,000 fine to repair the citadel of Monjuich. See Raymond Carr, *Spain*, p. 225; H. Butler Clarke, *Modern Spain*, pp. 182–83; London *Times*, December 3, 8, 13, 1842; WI to Daniel Webster, November 20 and December 10, 1842; and *El Castellano*, December 7, 1842.

1522. To George Read.

Legation of the United States / Madrid 8th. December 1842.

George Read Esqr. / Consul of the United States—Malaga.

Sir

Your letter of November 18th. has been received at this Legation.[1]

After carefully examining the language of the Resolution of the Senate, to which you refer,[2] it appears to me that the word "Cost" is to be considered as equivalent to "Market value" during the months specified, and that the information is sought probably with reference to impost duties—you are aware that whenever a duty is laid ad valorem, in our Tariffs, the Courts of the United States have decided that the "Market value" of the article at the port of shipment, into which the expense of transportation &c &c, enters; and not the mere cost to the manufacturer or producer is the basis upon which the duty is ↑to be↓ calculated.

I am, Sir, with respect / Your Obdt Sevt.
Washington Irving

Manuscript: NA, RG 84 (letterbook copy).

1. See WI to George Read, November 14, 1842.
2. On August 9, 1842, President Tyler vetoed the Large Tariff Bill, but the Senate passed a Modified Tariff Bill on August 27, section 3 of which specified that "the ad valorem rate of the duties . . . shall be estimated . . . to the actual cost, if the same shall have been actually purchased, or the actual value, if the same shall have been procured otherwise than by purchase, at the time and place when and where purchased or otherwise procured, shall be added ten per centum on such cost or value." See Senate, *Congressional Globe*, 27th Cong., 2d sess., pt. 11, pp. 679, 733, 761–62, 786, 944.

1523. To Catharine Paris

Madrid Decr. 10th. 1842.

My dear Sister

I received a few days since your letter of the 27th. October;[1] brimfull as usual of domestic news. Your letters are written in a clear distinct hand, and with a degree of mental vivacity and vigor that ⟨speak⟩ afford the most satisfactory evidence of your well being. I hope, however, you do not overtask yourself in writing to me so frequently and copiously, as you have other correspondents to attend to on this side of the Ocean. I am glad you have taken up your winter quarters again at Mrs Thomas's They appeared to suit you and to be very comfortable and the family of the house to be kind and attentive. You have become accustomed to each other also, and that has a great effect in producing a home feeling. I beg you to remember me kindly to Mrs Thomas and tell her how happy I am that you are in such good hands.

My last letter ended I think with the departure of the Regent to quell the insurrection in Barcelona. He travelled in his own fearless style: pushing on in a post chaize ahead of his troops and without escort, ⟨attended⟩ ↑accompanied↓ merely by an officer or two of his staff; and threw himself frankly among the people in the towns and villages; who shewed their sense of this confidence in their loyalty; receiving him every where with acclamations. After his departure Madrid was full of rumors; insurrections were said to be breaking out every where; the downfall of Espartero and of the existing government was confidently predicted: and there were not wanting factious people and factious prints to endeavor to blow this ⟨head⟩ Sudden flame into a general conflagration. Thus far, however, they have been disappointed. Madrid has remained quiet under the guardianship of the National guards; and ⟨though⟩ the insurrection did not extend beyond Barcelona. That factious city has once more been brought into submission to the government, but not until it had suffered a bombardment of several hours.[2] As yet we have no particulars of the damage done but it must have been considerable: and I fear we shall hear of Severe punishments inflicted upon those who have been most active in exciting this rebellion. Barcelona has sinned so often in this way that it is deemed necessary to treat it in the present instance with rigor. The bombardment, though repeatedly threatened, and the day and hour assigned; was put off from day to day and hour to hour, in the hope that the insurgent city would surrender; but a band of desperados had got the upperhand who refused to submit excepting on such terms as it would have been degrading to the government to grant.

And now to turn to a more agreeable Subject. Ill give you a word or two about your little friend the Queen in whom you take such great interest. A few days since the Corps diplomatique received invitations to attend an evening anniversary meeting of the Liceo,[3] a numerous and fashionable society instituted for the cultivation of literature and the fine arts, on which occasion gold medals and other prizes were to be distributed by the queen ⟨f⟩ to such as had excelled in the various departments. The meeting was held in an immense and lofty saloon in

what was formerly a ducal palace: at one end of which is fitted up a
⟨be⟩ very pretty stage with scenic decorations, where the members of
the Liceo have amateur theatricals. The Saloon was crowded on our
arrival with a brilliant assemblage of both sexes. ⟨Front⟩ seats were
⟨assured⟩ reserved for the Diplomatic Corps immediately in front of
the stage; while on their left, and on the right of the stage, was a raised
Dais richly carpeted, with two chairs of state, forming a kind of throne
for the queen and her sister.

After some time the arrival of the little sovereign was announced, and
every body rose; ⟨while I saw⟩ the ladies mounted on chairs and benches
to get a fair view of royalty, and many a beautiful Spanish face with
dark flashing eyes was to be seen peering anxiously over the heads of
the crowd. The little queen and her sister attended by their Aya or
governess, Madame Mina, and one or two ladies and officers of the
royal household, and escorted by a few of the faithful halberdiers ⟨pas⟩
advanced along a passage left in the centre of the Saloon, saluting the
company to the right and left in very gracious style. They then ascended
the dais, took their seats in the Chairs of State while a halberdier with
his musket, stood posted like a Statue on each side. The distribution of
the prizes was a very pretty ceremony. The Duke of Ossuna[4] the richest
grandee and greatest Dandy in Spain, and really a tall elegant man
about thirty years of age, officiated as master of ceremonies, being
president of the Lyceo. He placed in her majestys hands the prize to be
distributed; the person to receive it, in two instances a young lady, was
conducted up to the foot of the throne. After receiving the prize the
candidate kneeled and kissed the queens hand, and then took a seat with
the other successful candidates on the lefthand side of the stage immediately opposite to the throne. After the prizes had been distributed we
had some vocal and instrumental ⟨fr⟩ music from Amateurs, ↑members↓
of the Society; and the evenings entertainment concluded with a
sprightly comedy admirably played by Amateurs. The little queen and
her sister conducted themselves with great grace and decorum, not
laughing more than it was becoming for a queen and a princess royal
to laugh, yet evidently enjoying the whole scene mightily During the
last act of the Comedy however her little majesty began to yawn behind
her fan, and to shew evident signs that it was past her usual bed time;
whereupon the actors hurried forward with their parts with such rapid
volubility that I could scarcely understand a word. The curtain fell.
Her Majesty rose, bowed ⟨graciously⟩ ↑gracefully↓ to the assemblage
and then retired; nodding graciously to the right and left as she passed.
I saw her and her sister mount into their carriage amid a blaze of torch
light and whirl off followed by a clattering and glittering troop of horse.

I have told you in my last letter[5] of the malignant falsehoods told about the worthy Arguellas, the Queens guardian, with respect to her difficulty about delivering her speech on the day of her receiving the legislative deputations at her Besamanos;[6] the same venemous disposition to slander was evinced on the present occasion. One of the opposition news papers[7] asserted that the Liceo having prepared a raised dais or throne, with chairs of State for the Queen and her sister, Arguellas, in his levelling disposition to degrade royalty, had ordered ⟨↑that↓⟩ the whole ⟨to⟩ ⟨↑should↓⟩ be taken away ⟨and the queen⟩ so that the queen was left to take her seat on a common chair on a level with the rest of the Audience. A contradiction to this falsehood appeared in one of the government papers. What was the consequence; a formal ⟨and impudent⟩ repetition of it the next day; with various aggravating additions. This was meant to have effect at a distance, for so impudent a lie could have no effect in Madrid, since a crowded assemblage of the first people of the city were witnesses of its falsity. This, however, will give you an idea of the profligate attempts great and small that are continually making to throw odium upon the worthy and well meaning personages to whom the care and the virtuous education of the "Royal orphans" ⟨is entrust⟩ are entrusted.

We are now getting on towards the middle of December, but as yet we have had no appearance of ice; there has been occasionally a hoar frost in the morning on the roofs of the houses; but ⟨many of⟩ the days are generally bright and sunny; the fields are ⟨still⟩ all green, and the weather has often the soft balmy feeling of Spring. For my own part I never suffer from cold here, and if it were not for two or three roasting months of mid summer, I should have nothing to say against the climate. There is a purity and lightness in the atmosphere quite exhilerating, and I find it a climate in which I can go through a vast deal of close mental application without weariness of mind or body.

You ask me ⟨about⟩ whether I have furnished myself with horses. I have never been able to meet with a pair to suit me. It is extremely difficult to get carriage horses in Madrid. Several have been brought to me, but all had some inexcusable defect. I have a man looking out for a pair and it behoves him to do so diligently, as he is to be my coachman as soon as I have horses ⟨to dr⟩ for him to drive, but as yet his search has been unsuccessful. As I have no ladies in my family, and as there are scarcely any public occasions on which an equipage is necessary at Madrid, now that there is no regular court, I do not feel the want of a carriage *officially*. When it is necessary to turn out I can hire a good pair of horses for the occasion, and then the carriage I purchased of Mr Vail makes a very good appearance. Still I shall complete my establishment in this respect as soon as I can find horses worth buying.

Give my love to "all bodies" and tell them I will write to them all very soon. I expect letters tomorrow by the great Western,[8] as I see she arrived in England about ten or eleven days since.

Your affectionate brother
Washington Irving

MANUSCRIPT: Yale.   PUBLISHED: *Yale Review*, 17 (October, 1927), 100–02 (in part); PMI, III, 262–63; LFSS, pp. 50–53 (in part).
ADDRESSED: Mrs Daniel Paris / care of E. Irving Esq / New York.

1. This letter has not been located.
2. Although Van Halen delayed his plan to bombard the city on November 28, Espartero ordered the cannon to be used. Reports of the damage varied from "trifling in proportion to the number of shells [812] thrown" to over 400 houses destroyed. See London *Times*, December 3, 14, 1842; and H. Butler Clarke, *Modern Spain*, p. 183.
3. The Liceo was a public salon founded in 1836 by Don José Fernández de la Vega for the cultivation of literature and art. In essence a public debating and literary society, it extended the intimate family tertulia to "the most varied classes of cultivated society" and aimed to provide a national and literary revival for Spain. By this time its 600 members were meeting at the palace of Villa Hermosa at the corner of the Prado. It soon closed. See Bowers, *Spanish Adventures of WI*, pp. 167–69; and Raymond Carr, *Spain*, pp. 207–8.
4. Téllez Girón y Beaufort (Pedro de Alcántara) 11th duke of Ossuna, duke of Infantado (1810–1844) was a great patron of the arts and literature.
5. See WI to Catharine Paris, November 20, 1842.
6. A formal reception or levee at which guests show their respect by kissing the sovereign's hand.
7. See *El Castellano*, December 1, 1842.
8. The *Great Western* had arrived at Liverpool from New York on November 29. See London *Times*, December 1, 1842.

1524. To Sarah Storrow

Madrid Decr 10th. 1842

My dear Sarah,

I enclose a letter for your mother[1] which must also serve for yourself as I have no time to write another. I have been so full of diplomatic business of late and have had such a diplomatic correspondence to keep up, that I have not been ⟨up⟩ able to write so frequently to the family as formerly. My literary tasks, too, have for two months past been entirely interrupted. However I shall have more liesure bye & bye and then will put my pen in its old track.

Your late letters[2] have not been written in your usual good spirits and your last speaks of your suffering indisposition and depression of spirits in consequence of a severe cold accompanied by deafness. I am daily looking out for a letter from you giving me better accounts of yourself; and am every day disappointed at the mail bring[ing]³ me nothing from you. I do not wish to task you my darling girl; but whenever you give me bad news about yourself, let me have a line however brief, as soon as you feel brighter or better.

I was quite amused of your account of that little baggage Kate with her doll, of which she had already knocked off the nose. I have a singularly craving desire to see that child. If she were here I think she would be the perfect delight of my life but as Juliet says of Romeo, "I should spoil her with much cherishing"⁴

I must conclude and send this off

[end of MS]

MANUSCRIPT: Yale.

1. See WI to Catharine Paris, December 10, 1842.
2. These letters have not been located.
3. WI omitted the bracketed letters.
4. WI's variation of *Romeo and Juliet*, II, 2, 184.

1525. *To Daniel Webster*

Legation of the United States. / Madrid December 10th. 1842.

No. 11. / The Hon: Daniel Webster. / Secretary of State of the United States—Washington.

Sir,

I have the honor to enclose copies of official notes between Count Almodovar, and myself on the subject of the submission of Barcelona to the Government.

The City held out longer than was suspected, and only yielded at last to a severe bombardment.¹ This destructive measure though repeatedly threatened, and the time notified was deferred from day to day and hour to hour, until the forbearance of the Regent was made a matter of taunting scoff and ridicule by the Coalition prints of Madrid. The same papers are now loud and foul-mouthed in their abuse of him for the harsh measures he felt ultimately compelled to adopt;² but indeed there is a licentiousness of language indulged here by the opposition press in Speaking of the Government that far exceeds the excesses of our free press in the United States. It is lamentable to see also how all patriotic feeling is lost in the violence of parties, and how opposite factions coalesce in their efforts to fan a partial flame into a general conflagration.

In the present instance the hopes and wishes of the Agitators have been disappointed. The Insurrection has been confined to Barcelona, and though slight attempts were made to get up agitations in other parts of the country, they were promptly checked, and the general tranquility of the Kingdom maintained. This shews that the present Government rests upon a firmer basis than its enemies had supposed, and that the nation at large is desirous of order and repose.

Great efforts will be made to cast odium upon Espartero for the bombardment of Barcelona, and for the rigorous punishments with which the Insurgents are menaced; but the Catalans are not favorites throughout Spain, and their turbulent Capital has so often troubled the tranquility of the Nation by its seditions that the public seem disposed to acquiesce in the policy of a castigation that may serve as a warning to it in future. Beside, the Spanish Public is exceedingly tolerant of strong measures, and accustomed to those severe remedies, incident to what may be called a national state of intermittent revolution. It is thought, therefore, by some of the connoisseurs in Spanish politics, that this abortive insurrection, and the prompt and vigorous manner in which it has been quelled will tend to strengthen the hands of Government.

How the affair of Barcelona will operate upon the Cotton Question is yet to be seen—The influence of England with the Government certainly increases on every recurrence of these national outbreaks from the friendly countenance and efficient aid it ever seems disposed to render to those in power: and it has shewn strong sympathy with the government in the present instance; having ordered ships of war round from Gibralter with provisions for the Garrison of Monjuich.

What it gains with the Government, however, it is likely to lose with the people. The Spanish public ever quick to imbibe the most absurd suspicions with respect to Strangers, have been assured that English Intrigues in favor of the cotton trade[3] and hostile to Spanish manufactures are at the bottom of the troubles and disasters in Catalonia; rumors have been circulated that at the time of the bombardment, the British Ships of War fired upon the town, and an opposition paper insidiously remarks; that the same day on which news arrived at Madrid of the batteries of Monjuich being opened upon this rich and *manufacturing* Capital of Catalonia, intelligence was received that a treaty of commerce between Spain and England had been signed in London!

A strong representation has recently been made to the Cortes by the municipality of Malaga on the subject of the necessity of more liberal commercial arrangements with other countries and especially with the United States: instancing the decline of our trade with that place in consequence of high duties and restrictive measures. This comes opportunely though I much doubt ↑of↓ any thing beneficial being done at present with respect to our relations; on the Contrary I am sorry to find our tobacco trade[4] likely to suffer from the disposition of the Spanish Government to foster the growth of tobacco in Manilla. The tobacco of that Island which was formerly introduced without success on account of its inferior quality, has been much improved in cultivation and is now found to answer extremely well for popular use when wrapped in the low priced Havana tobacco, called "Vuelta de arriba." A partner of a British House at Madrid, therefore, which has for several years past taken contracts of the Spanish Government to furnish its fabrics with tobacco of the United States, informs me that they have been unable to get a contract for the present year; the Government having determined to supply itself with tobacco the growth of Manilla.

> I remain Sir / Very respectfully / Your obt Servt
> Washington Irving

DOCKETED: Recd. 28 Jany. / Mr Markoe [upper left corner, page 1]
MANUSCRIPT: NA, RG 59.   PUBLISHED: Hellman, WI Esquire, pp. 292–95.

Only the complimentary close and signature are in WI's handwriting.

1. For other details of the bombardment, see WI to Catharine Paris, December 10, 1842.

2. See Eco del Comercio, November 29 and December 3, 1842.

3. For other aspects of British interest in the cotton trade, see WI to Daniel Webster, August 27, November 5, and December 24, 1842; and Eco del Comercio, December 3, 1842.

4. On the tobacco question, see WI to John C. Calhoun, June 8, 1844.

1526. To Sarah Storrow

Madrid Decr. 12th. 1842

My dear Sarah,

I have just received your letter of the 6th. inst.[1] which arrived just as I had taken up my pen to write to you; having again got into a little fit of uneasiness on your account. Your two last letters had not been written ⟨in⟩ ↑with↓ your usual cheerfulness and spoke of indisposition, depression of spirits &c The night before the last, after I had sent off a letter to you, in which I had spoken on the subject and so fixed it more strongly in my mind, I had a distressing dream about you, which haunted me all yesterday and contributes to make me very nervous and uncomfortable. I watched for the arrival of the mail and when it came and brought no letter from you I concluded you must be too ill to write. I began a letter to you, but found it would run into the dismal vein, so I threw by my pen, postponed writing until this morning, and sallied forth to take the air. Do not suppose I am a believer in dreams; ⟨but⟩ the scenes and images they present to the mind are but the fitful and distorted reflections of[2] ⟨how⟩ circumstances or thoughts that have passed over it in wakeful moments; and often take their tone and colouring from the state of the body. I have been a little fagged of late by close study of some diplomatic questions, and the preparation of papers ⟨to be⟩ and letters for this government and the government at home, and I went to bed rather nervous the night before last, and got up Still more nervous yesterday; so that I was in a mood for dreams and shadows to have an effect upon me. However a good deal of exercise in the open air yesterday, and a cheerful visit to my friend Madame Albuquerque and her two little "princesses," quite put me in tone again. Your letter by this mornings mail has set my heart at rest; though it still represents you as being under the doctors hands. Thank god you are not seriously ill, though still uncomfortably so. Your last letter is the only one I have received from you in which there is not a word about darling little Kate[.] I beg you will never omit to mention her hereafter, if it be only to put her in a parenthesis.

You must not take all for granted that you see in French papers[3] about Spanish affairs. ⟨There is a disposition⟩ Many of the articles that appear in them are extracted from the opposition papers of Madrid, which paint every public event in the blackest colours and endeavor to throw odium upon the Regent and the Ministers and doubt upon the stability of the present government. The ⟨gov⟩ French government too is unfriendly to the constitutional government of Spain, and would gladly ⟨as it has⟩ see a change even though it should cost the country another civil war. Indeed the ⟨late⟩ recent insurrection in Barcelona has been ascribed to French agency and the secret subsidies of Maria Christina, though I no more believe this, than the opposite assertion which ascribes it to the intrigues of England to destroy the cotton fabrics of Catalonia! England and France are political rivals for the ascendancy in Spain, and the Peninsula is ⟨to them like a⟩ their political chess board; let us trust, however, that they both play an honorable game. Still this will account to you for the exaggerated tone in which every popular disturbance in Spain is spoken of in the French ministerial papers.

The insurrection in Barcelona has been bad enough, there is no doubt, and it has been put down in a lamentably distructive manner; but the quiet that has been maintained throughout the rest of Spain shews that it was a local out break; and that the government is more firmly seated than its enemies had supposed. During this period of popular anxiety Madrid has remained tranquil under the guardianship of its national guard, and every thing goes on as usual. Should there ever really be a popular commotion here you need not fear for my personal safety. There could be no cause of hostility to me; I am not one who goes abroad in riotous times in quest of adventures; and the house of a diplomatic representative is Sacred even from the intrusion of the authorities; while the national arms above the portal are respected even by the rabble.

You will hear and read a great deal against the Regent Espartero, concerning this affair of Barcelona and concerning his conduct generally in the management of the national affairs. As far as I ⟨can⟩ have had an opportunity of judging of him[4] he is an open, frank, well meaning man; more of the Soldier than the Statesman; but sincerely disposed to uphold the present constitution; to protect the throne of the little queen, and to give up the reins of government into her hands when her minority is finished. He has a difficult part however to play. He is surrounded by Enemies from without and from within, whose schemes of power depend upon his downfall & who endeavor ⟨to⟩ ↑in every way↓ to drive him to some ⟨act⟩ high handed act that may destroy his popularity. Even the present unbridled licentiousness of the press that taunts him in every way, by misrepresenting his motives and actions, by branding him with the names of tyrant, Nero &c &c, is indulged in the hope of irritating him to an attempt to check the liberty of the press, which would be at once be[5] made a watch word for a popular outbreak. I hope ⟨that he will have calmness and judgement⟩ ↑and trust he will have discernment↓ sufficient to see through these machinations and calmness and self command to disregard them. On his steadfast and upright administration of the power confided to his hands, appears to me to depend the present welfare of unhappy Spain. His fall would produce immediate confusion.[6]

I am scribbling this in the midst of a little domestic hubbub, as I am going to give a dinner today to some of my diplomatic associates; especially those of the British legation; as I am deeply in arrears to Mr Aston who is continually inviting me to his house, and who in fact is most frank & cordial on all occasions. To cope with him however is out of the question; beside his ample salary he has a large private fortune and can afford to keep open table.

My dinner ⟨will far⟩ will exceed the usual number, as there will be twelve at table; but I was some how or other obliged to ask as many. The dinner is more especially given to the Danish Chargé d'Affaires, M Dal Borgo di Primo[7] who has just returned to Madrid after a congé of nearly a year. He is a veteran in years and in diplomacy, being about seventy, and having passed a great part of his life in office. He is however, young in spirits, full of gaiety and good humor, and during the twelve Years that he has been stationed here has made himself a universal favorite of man woman and child.

I have got on very pleasant social terms with my fellow diplomats, to which my occasional dinners have much contributed. There is a good deal of good fellow ship in diplomacy; the members of a Corps being thrown together on foreign posts, where they have many topics of common interest and common sympathy among themselves and stand in a manner detached from the community around them. Mr Astons house is a great rallying place where some of us often come together. One is received there on the easiest and most cordial footing, and Mrs Scott[8] does the honors of the house with great amiability.

I have received a letter this morning by a Packet ship, from your Uncle E. I. dated Nov. 6.[9] but yours from your mother by the Great Western must be later. I thank you for your extract from it. Your dear mother is repeatedly expressing concern in her letters about my having such a heavy family to take care of. She ought to know that it is this which spurs me on to cheerful activity of mind and body and gives an interest to existence. Had I only myself to take care of I should become as inert, querulous and good for nothing as other old bachelors who only live for themselves, and should soon become weary of life, as ⟨I⟩ indeed I have been now and then, when every thing went smooth with me and I had only to think of my own enjoyment: but I have never felt such real interest in existence, and so desirous to live on, as of late years, since my life has become important to others: and I have never felt in such good humor with myself as since I have began[10] to consider myself a '*pere de famille*.' God knows I have no great idea of bachelor hood, and am not one of the fraternity through choice—but providence has some how or other thwarted the warm wishes of my heart and the tendencies of my nature in those earlier seasons of life when tender and happy unions are made; and has protected me ⟨from⟩ in those more advanced periods when matrimonial unions are apt to be unsuited or ungenial: but I have often repined at my single state and have looked forward with doubt and solicitude to the possibility of an old age solitary, uncherished and unloved. Thank god; I now feel differently. The years I have recently passed at home, and especially at my blessed little cottage, in the bosom of a family; with young hearts growing up round me and clinging to me, make me confident that there are those who will cling tenderly to me to the last, and bear kindly with me, even when I may cease to be almost any thing but a burthen. When I think of the ⟨at⟩ affection lavished upon me by my kindred, I am but too happy to do any thing in my power to prove how deeply I feel and how heartily I return their love.

But I must conclude, for the magisterial Benjamin[11] claims the very table on which I am writing to convert it into a sideboard.

Give my kind regards to Mr Storrow and many Kisses to little Miss Kate and her doll.

Your affectionate uncle
Washington Irving

ADDRESSED: Madame / Madame Storrow / No 4. Rue de la Victoire / à Paris.
MANUSCRIPT: Yale.   PUBLISHED: *Yale Review*, 17 (October, 1927), 102–5 (in part); LFSS, pp. 53–56 (in part).

1. This letter has not been located.
2. WI wrote "of" twice.
3. France openly supported María Christina in opposition to Espartero, and there was widespread suspicion that France intended to invade Spain as soon as possible and to create disruption and unrest. See London *Times*, December 2, 5, 14, 1842. An article on the "Anglo mania" prevalent in Paris appeared in the London *Times*, December 19, 1842. See also WI to Daniel Webster, November 26, 1842.
4. WI's romantic image of Espartero as a glamorous soldier blinded him to Espartero's moments of extreme ruthlessness as a military leader, to his erratic periods of torpor and phases of hysterical energy, and his overwhelming conceit. Although apparently honest, he lacked experience and penetration and so failed as a statesman. See Christiansen, *Military Power*, pp. 99–100; H. Butler Clarke, *Modern Spain*, pp. 166, 185, 190, 258; and Raymond Carr, *Spain*, pp. 183, 221.
5. WI repeated "be."
6. For Espartero's subsequent fall and exile, see WI to Catharine Paris, January 12 and August 10, 1843.
7. Olinto dal Borgo di Primo, Maria Emilio de Gasparo d'Andrea Giusti (1775–1856).
8. The wife of the secretary of the British Legation and hostess for it.
9. This letter has not been located.
10. WI probably intended to write "begun."
11. WI's butler and servant. See WI to Sarah Storrow, July 16, 1842.

1527. To Ebenezer Irving

[Madrid, December 21, 1842]

I have been much interrupted in my literary occupations for the last two or three months, by the necessity of applying my mind to the examination of some subjects connected with my diplomatic duties, and of preparing rather voluminous papers. Within this week or two past, however, I have been able to add a few chapters to my history.[1]

PUBLISHED: PMI, III, 274.

1. Probably WI means his life of George Washington. In a letter to Sarah Storrow on October 20, 1851, WI observed that he had begun the biography nine years earlier.

1528. To Daniel Webster

Legation of the United States / Madrid December 21st. 1842

No. 12 / The Hon: Daniel Webster, / Secretary of State of the United States—Washington.

Sir.

I have the honor to enclose a note which I passed to the Government about a fortnight since, on the subject of my conversation with Count Almodovar relative to the cross purposes in regard to the semi-annual payment of the interest in Cuba.[1] As I furnished the note merely at the request of Count Almodovar, and as the circumstances of the case had been satisfactorily explained by him in our conversation I did not think it necessary to express myself so emphatically with the pen, as I had, under your instructions, by word of mouth. I have delayed sending a copy of my note, hitherto, in the hope of being able to send a Copy of a reply at the same time; but none has yet been received, probably in consequence of the recurring indisposition of Count Almodovar.

Nothing of political importance has occurred Since my last despatch. The opposition papers are full of violent tirades against the Government,[2] and personal abuse of Espartero, for the measures taken in the suppression of the insurrection at Barcelona; but I do not think the Nation at large coincides with them in their views of the affair, or is deceived by their exaggerations. Barcelona is restored to a stern tranquility, under military rule, but the punishments inflicted on the Insurgents have so far been less severe than was anticipated. The Country remains quiet; but is full of uneasiness and anxiety; looking doubtfully to the future.

The Cabinet shrouds itself in mystery, partly from its own feebleness and indecision, and partly from the certainty of meeting with violent opposition at every move. Finding that it could not command a majority in the present Cortes and that its conduct in the recent events would be made the subject of vehement attack it has determined to dissolve that body; and I am privately informed that the decree, accompanied by a Manifesto, has been forwarded to the Regent for his signature. In the mean time, how the Government is to get on for some months to come, without any legislative provision of the Ways and Means; with an acknowledged deficit, enormously increased, and daily increasing through extraordinary military expenses, and with all its plans of finance thrown on the wind, is one of those questions which would drive one to despair any where but in Spain; where the Government, like individuals, has an inscrutable secret of subsisting without money.

By the last accounts from Barcelona, the Regent was to leave that place

this day for Valencia on his way to Madrid, where he is expected to arrive
towards the end of the month.

I am, Sir, very respectfully / Your Obdt Sert.

Washington Irving

DOCKETED: Recd. 28 Jany. / Mr Markoe [*upper left corner, page 1*] / No. 12. W.
Irving. Madrid. 21 Dec. 1842
MANUSCRIPT: NA, RG 59.

Only the signature is in WI's handwriting.

1. See WI to Count Almodóvar, December 6, 1842.
2. *El Heraldo* and *El Corresponsal* were loudest in their attacks.

1529. *To Ebenezer Irving*

[Madrid, Fall, 1842]

I mentioned, in a former letter, my wish that you would have an iron
railing put around the grave of our dear brother Peter, and a gravestone
within, with a simple inscription of his name, age, date of his birth, &c.
Have honeysuckles and shrubs planted inside of the inclosure, that they
may, in time, overrun it. I had intended to have his remains transported
to a family vault or burying ground which I contemplated establishing
at the old Dutch Sleepy Hollow church. * * * Even now, perhaps, it
might be as well to buy of the widow Beekman[1] a few yards square of
the woody height, adjacent to the north end of the burying ground, and
have it enclosed with a paling for the family place of sepulture. * * * I
think a family burying place, with a gate opening into the main burying
ground, would be preferable to a vault. If this should be determined upon,
it would not be necessary to put up the iron railing above mentioned,
as our dear brother's remains might be conveyed to the above-mentioned
place. Think of all this, and carry it into effect. It is a thing that lies near
my heart. I hope, some day or other, to sleep my last sleep in that favorite
resort of my boyhood.

P. S.—You do not mention, in any of your letters, whether neighbor Forkel
has still the superintendence of Mrs. Jones' property. I like to hear occasionally how all my country neighbors are coming on—the Manns, the
Forkels, the Ackers,[2] &c. Give a kind word to them occasionally in my
name. They have always proved good neighbors to me.

PUBLISHED: PMI, III, 230.

1. Cornelia Van Cortlandt Beekman (ca. 1752–1847) was the widow of Gerard

G. Beekman (ca. 1746–1822), who owned between 750 and 900 acres of land in Westchester County. See J. T. Scharf, *History of Westchester County*, II, 285–86. WI subsequently developed the burying ground of the Sleepy Hollow Church for the Irving family.

2. The Acker family owned the farm next to the Van Tassel farm, of which Sunnyside had been a part. WI had bought "Wolfert's Roost," named after Wolfert Acker, from Benson Ferris (1794–1882), who was married to Maria Acker (1797–1881). See Scharf, *History of Westchester County*, II, 233–34.

1530. To Fitzhenry McReady

Legation of the United States. / Madrid December 23d. 1842.

Fitzhenry McCready Esqr. U. S. Consul Baracoa. Cuba—
Sir
I have the honor to enclose your Exequatur, and original Commission received this day from the Department of State and of Foreign affairs.

I have received from Mr. Vail the fees on the Exequatur, which had been forwarded to him.

I am, Sir, respectfully / Your obdt: Sevt:
Washington Irving.

MANUSCRIPT: NA, RG 84 (letterbook copy).

Fitzhenry McReady of New York was nominated as U.S. consul for Baracoa, Cuba, on February 3, 1841. He resigned early in 1843. See Hasse, *Index to U.S. Documents*, III, 1744.

1531. To Orlando S. Morse

Legation of the United States / Madrid December 23d. 184[2].[1]

Orlando. S. Morse Esqr.—Consul St Johns.
Sir
I have the honor to enclose your Exequatur and original commission received yesterday from the office of State—They are forwarded by the Spanish Vessel "Apollo" advertised to sail in a few days for Porto Rico.

I have drawn on Frederick Rudolph of Cadiz for the fees on the Exequatur in compliance with his letters of advice to this Legation.

I have to acknowledge the receipt of your letter of September 29th. but the previous one to which you refer written in June last, has not yet been received.

I am, Sir, respectfully. / Your Obdt Sevt
Washington Irving.

MANUSCRIPT: NA, RG 84 (letterbook copy).

Orlando S. Morse of Virginia was nominated as U.S. consul for St. John's, Puerto Rico on April 4, 1842. See Hasse, *Index to U.S. Documents*, III, 1748.

1. The copyist had mistakenly written "1843." The letter is found in the letterbook between copies dated December 8 and December 23, 1842.

1532. To Sarah Storrow

Madrid Dec 24th. 1842

My dear Sarah,

I am endeavoring not to feel uneasy at having received no letter from you since that dated the 6th. which represented you as still indisposed. The illness of Mr Ledyard, however, will cause now and then a little fluttering of anxiety[.] I hope you take care to have yourself vaccinated at proper intervals. Tomorrow (Sunday) I shall look with confidence for a letter in reply to mine ↑(of the 10th)↓ which you must have received a week since

I have myself been a little out of order with a cold; but have cured myself by taking holyday and plenty of exercise in the open air in weather resembling our beautiful October weather in America. Our Winter, so far, has been very mild: no frost in the ground, and glorious sunshine.

Tomorrow we all eat our Christmas dinner at the British Embassy where Mr Aston has promised us orthodox mince pies. My servants have a regale at home according to Spanish custom, on which occasion I shall allow them champagn wine—a great treat in Spain. They are faithful good servants and entitled to indulgence. The magisterial Benjamin I have no doubt will preside with great dignity on the occasion.

I have a letter from your mother dated 22d November,[1] crowded full of matter as usual. If I did not know that letter writing is an occupation which fills up her time satisfactorily I should be fearful she overtasked herself; she writes so often and so minutely. But she is in fact quite *a young woman*, notwithstanding her years and infirmities

Your uncle E. I. writes that they have reports that Mrs Colford is to Marry the Duke de Breteuil[2] and her daughter Helen the dukes son, the Count de Breteuil. I presume these are false reports; though I should not be surprized if mother & daughter and all the family should be sought after by the impoverished nobility as they have money and are not deficient in style. I hope they may not make unhappy connexions. I shall always be glad to hear any thing good concerning them—or even whimsical—provided it is not ill natured. They may make their way pleasantly and happily in France; but I confess I fear for them. The carreer they seem ambitious of entering is one that must necessarily separate them more and more from their old friends and connexions; from their country people and their country.

For your own part, my dear Sarah, make it a rule never to keep up close intercourse with those Americans in Paris who aim at moving in the aristocratical circles; but do it candidly and good humoredly; alleging that your own quiet course of life is on level ground, and that it is inconvenient to drive along it, with one wheel occasionally tilting up on a bank. I think Mrs Ledyards plan is a good one never to visit folks who live in the Faubg St Germain—Receive all visits from such persons frankly and kindly, return them merely by cards.—never find fault with their plan of life, but say that would not accord with yours.

The american aspirants hanging on to the skirts of French aristocracy appear to be increasing in number and forming I fear, rather a whimsical future in Parisian society.

In casting my eye back upon what I have written I fear it may be construed into harsh censure of the Jones family. I do not mean it, in its force, to apply to them. I feel for them ⟨a⟩ real kindness and regard; I should be ungrateful did I not, considering the warm friendship I and mine have ever experienced from them. But I see that their very friendship in their present position might become ⟨inconvenient⟩ full of inconveniences to you, and I wish to suggest to you a line of conduct that may relieve you from the irksomeness of intimacy without giving reasonable grounds of offence.

I must conclude this letter, to send it off by the Courier. I feel that it is a stupid one, but my head is muddled with various occupation and I have been fagging all day on matters of business. Let me hear a great deal about my darling little Kate. How she looks, and how she dresses and how she amuses herself and how she treats company and how she treats her doll. With kind regards to Mr Storrow, ever my dear Sarah most affectionately your uncle

Washington Irving

Manuscript: Yale.

1. This letter has not been located.
2. Achille Charles Stanislaus Émile Le Tonnelier, count de Breteuil (1781–1864) was a French politician who was, as WI suggests, interested in Mrs. Colford Jones for her money.

1533. To Daniel Webster

Legation of the United States /Madrid December 24th. 1842.

No. 13. / The Hon: Daniel Webster, / Secretary of State of the
U. States—Washington.

Sir,

Having had reason to suspect that, in the negotiation going on between the English and Spanish Governments, the latter were disposed
to make one of the conditions of the treaty that the deposit of Tobacco
at Gibraltar should be broken up, I took occasion this morning to have
a frank conversation with Mr. Aston on the subject. He acknowledged
that such a condition was suggested by the Spanish Government, but
with the express understanding that it would be preparatory to, if not
simultaneous with, the opening of a free trade in Tobacco, admitting
the foreign article into the ports of Spain at quite a moderate duty; and
subjecting it subsequently to an excise. This he said was the idea of
Mr. Ferrer, one of the Committee appointed to treat with him, and of
Mr. Calatrava the Minister of Finance, they being convinced that
Government would be a gainer in point of revenue, besides putting a
Stop to the pernicious system of contraband. I am aware, from other
sources, that such views are entertained by those Gentlemen.

I told Mr. Aston that I had apprehended the Spanish Government
might desire to break up the deposit, so that they might keep up their
system of monopoly and favor their Manilla and Cuba tobacco to the
exclusion of that of the United States; and I observed that, should the
British Government, in seeking favor for its cotton trade, grant a condition that might impede a liberal modification of our tobacco trade, it
would be considered a very ungracious act in the United States. He
assured me that if such condition were acceded to, it would only be
with the understanding already mentioned. He added that the whole
result of their negotiation was as yet quite uncertain.

I have thought it adviseable to report this conversation promptly to
you; as I observe the possibility of the before mentioned condition being
urged by the Spanish Government, has been hinted at in the English
Papers, and might meet your eye.

In the course of our conversation Mr. Aston observed that the operation of our Tariff on the Spanish Trade in dried fruits &c, began to be
very sensibly felt, and he thought it would be a strong inducement for
them to grant an open trade in Tobacco, if we would agree to lower
our duties on their fruits. I told him that would all come into consideration in any liberal arrangement that might take place between the two

countries; but that Spain had no reason to complain of high duties on our part, when, ↑by similar exactions,↓ she was almost excluding our produce from her ports.

I have within a day or two received the Exequaturs for Mr. O. S. Morse Consul at St Johns Porto Rico, and Mr. Fitzhenry McCready, Consul at Baracoa Cuba, and have forwarded them to those gentlemen,

I am, Sir, very respectfully / Your Obdt Scvt.
Washington Irving

DOCKETED: Recd. Feby 22 / recd. feb. 22 Mr Markoe [upper left corner, page 1] / No. 13. W. Irving Madrid. 24 Doc. 1842
MANUSCRIPT: NA, RG 59.   PUBLISHED: STW, II, 154 (in part).

Only the signature is in WI's handwriting.

1534. To Daniel Webster

Legation of the United States. / Madrid January 1st. 1843.

No. 15. / The Hon: Daniel Webster. / Secretary of State of the U. States—Washington.

Sir,
I have the honor to enclose my accounts and vouchers for the 4th. Quarter of 1842, ending December 31st.; shewing a balance in favor of the United States of $95.59, which will be carried to their credit in next account.

I am, Sir, with great respect / Your obdt Sevt.
Washington Irving

DOCKETED: Recd. 22 Feb. [upper left corner, page 1] / [unrecovered] to Mr Stubbs [center left margin, page 1]
MANUSCRIPT: NA, RG 59.

1535. To Sarah Storrow

Madrid Jany 5th. 184⟨2⟩ ↑3↓

A happy New Year to you and yours, my dear Sarah, and many happy ones to follow it. Your recent letters assuring me of your improved

health and that precious little Kate is as "bright as a bird" have relieved
me from a lurking uneasiness that I could not drive out of my thoughts.
My heart yearns toward you when I read your letters. Oh how delighted
I should be to be able to able[1] to make a dash across the Pyrenees and
pay you a visit in Paris, but such a thing is out of the question at present,
and may be for a considerable time to come. Various private considerations ⟨will render⟩ ↑make↓ it adviseable for me to remain quiet, and
official considerations are multiplying to ⟨fix⟩ ↑render↓ me stationary
at my post. We are here on a kind of political ⟨or⟩ volcano, which
though in a state of quietude at present, or only rumbling and smoking,
may at any moment burst ⟨into a⟩ forth with an eruption. Symptoms all
around us are threatening and portentous, and every thing is plot and
mystery. At such a time a diplomatic agent must be at his post, and
be on the alert to watch the course of events and to keep his government
informed of any thing may affect its interests.

I do not wonder that you are shocked at the affair of Barcelona,[2]
and disposed to think hardly of Espartero for the measures he has taken
to suppress the insurrection: you would not have a womans feelings
if you did not. But you must not believe all that you read in the newspapers, nor suffer your judgement to be affected by the colouring they
give to this event. I will endeavor in some future letter to give you a
key to the mysteries of Spanish politics, which are full of trick, intrigue
and falsehood. My heart aches at times for this unhappy country which
seems doomed to be kept in a state of confusion by foreign intrigue and
domestic treason. As far as I have been able to judge I am inclined to
think well of Espartero, and to believe that his professions are sincere
and his intentions honest; but the poor man is surrounded by pitfalls
dug by treacherous hands; ⟨and I am⟩ and has not the wiley head of a
Statesman to guard against them. If he were as wary a politician as he
is a brave soldier, the destinies of the country would be safe in his
hands. As it is, I believe him to be faithful among the faithless, ⟨and⟩
that he is disposed to stand by the throne of the little queen according
to his engagement, and that he is, at present, the only safeguard between
it and a state of anarchy.

You must be aware of the Spanish factions[3] that lurk within the territories of France, ⟨the remnants of the⟩ reliques from the Civil wars,
and refugees of all kinds, who are continually carrying on plots against
the actual government of Spain, and employing agents to stir up commotions and seditions. The insurrection in the north of Spain ⟨last⟩
the autumn before last, and the attack on the Royal palace for the purpose
of carrying off the little queen and her sister, ⟨was no⟩ formed one of
their grand attempts, which failed:[4] I believe the insurrection at Barcelona to be another. As early as last April it was stated in a newspaper

that this ⟨faction⟩ Spanish faction beyond the pyrennes intended to send in emissaries and armed bands to *stir up an insurrection in Barcelona,* with a view to throw the country into a general state of anarchy, or, failing in that, to provoke some severe measure on the part of the government, which might be made use of to render it unpopular with the nation and with foreign powers. I *made a note of this prediction at the time and it now lies before me.* The recent events at Barcelona are in strict accordance with it. An *insurrection has taken place*—the ⟨mea⟩ prompt measures of Government have presented it from extending and producing a general state of anarchy—and now *those measures are made matters of accusation against the government.*

As all the private accounts I have of the character of Espartero represent him as neither sanguinary nor despotic, but rather a good tempered and kind hearted man, we will endeavor to see what can be said on his side of the question. When he arrived before Barcelona it was in open rebellion. The populace had risen upon the Military and driven them from the city with heavy loss; had formed a revolutionary junta and proclaimed their intention to put down the regent and the existing government. The city had been summoned to return to its allegiance by a certain time under pain of bombardment. It persisted in rebellion, trusting that other parts of the country would rise and the *general state of anarchy* take place. The arrival of the Regent produced no favorable effect, the insurgents refused to submit except on terms which the government could not grant without degradation. The bombardment was postponed from day to day and hour to hour, until the forbearance of Espartero became a matter of taunt and ridicule to the very newspapers which are now so vociferous against the ⟨act⟩ ↑measure↓ which they tried to pique him to ⟨[unrecovered]⟩ adopt. The bombardment at length took place, ⟨and⟩ the city was subjugated, and ever since that time the papers have been full of invectives against the Regents cruelty.

A bombardment, of course, is a very terrible affair.[5] It makes a great noise in itself, and a still greater noise in the newspapers, but what was to be done? The insurrection must be quelled, and that promptly, or the whole country might be thrown in combustion.

The *city might have been invested and reduced by famine,* say some. But the regent had not the means of investing it by sea; it could therefore receive supplies and reinforcements by Ships, of which there were abundance in the harbor ready to aid the insurgents. A reduction by investment is moreover a slow process: before it could produce effect other parts of the country might rise in rebellion and the government forces might find themselves between two fires. Granting it could be carried into effect; have you an idea my dear Sarah of the *quiet* process of a reduction by investment and famine. It makes no noise, like a bombardment: it causes no carnage; it falls lightest upon the ⟨rebels in⟩ soldiery in arms, for they are the strongest in the city and can ⟨lay the⟩ wrest from the peaceable inhabitants the last morsel of provisions— it injures no property; demolishes no houses; but it enters silently into the domestic dwelling and there ⟨a⟩ produces its pining and wasting ravages. It falls upon the peaceful, the helpless, the aged, the infirm; upon women and upon children. It is accompanied by the most agonizing ⟨of⟩ and protracted of domestic miseries God help the poor city that is subdued by the quiet process of famine!

The city might have been carried by assault say others. That is to say, the soldiery, who had been expelled from the city, and whose feelings were still exasperated by the reccollection of their comrades shot down by their sides from doors and windows, or crushed by missiles hurled upon them by women and children, might have battered the walls by cannonry, and entering, might have subjugated the place by grape shot, musquetry and the bayonet—for such is the process of carrying a place by assault. Louis Philip adopted this plan when he sent his son the Duke of Orleans to reduce the revolted city of Lyons.[6] What was the result. The fighting lasted for many days; it went on from street to street and house to house. The Streets were swept with grape shot; houses ↑in which the insurgents fortified themselves↓ were cannonaded, under-mined and blown up: the bayonet did its horrid work, tenfold more savage and destructive than that of gunpowder. I am affraid to say how many thousands of lives were sacraficed in that awful scene of carnage. Yet no one accused Louis Philip of *cruelty*. It was known that the prompt and effectual suppression of an insurrection, even, with blood shed ⟨may⟩ ↑might↓ be a merciful measure; saving a country from the wide spreading horrors of a civil war.

A bombardment, as I am assured by military men; and by others who have been in places which have suffered one, is by no means so disasterous in effect as it is formidable and alarming in appearance. It is more distructive of property than of life and generally brings a city to terms before either have suffered severely. Notwithstanding all the ⟨suf an⟩ terrible pictures drawn in the papers of Barcelona in ruins and its helpless inhabitants destroyed, private letters state that but few houses have been destroyed, or seriously injured and that the loss of life has been quite inconsiderable. ⟨Indeed I have heard of but one death by a bomb shell; though numbers have been wounded.⟩ ↑(Official returns, just received give seven killed and thirty wounded.)↓

This, my dear Sarah, is the candid view I have taken of this lamentable affair; in which I do not as yet see cause to tax the Regent with tyranny nor blood thirstiness Nor ⟨had his⟩ have his measures since the surrender been cruel or vindictive, as it was predicted they would be. But fourteen of the insurgents have been put to death after a military trial,[7] at which even the opposition papers admit, several fiscal personages of high respectability assisted. Of these fourteen ten were soldiers who had twice deserted and turned against their own commanders; none were persons of note; all had been active among the miscreants who held the city in terror.

As to the accounts ↑given↓ of this affair both in the French and English papers,[8] they are to be taken with great caution. Spain is a country in which both of these powers are striving for the ascendancy. English writers see the hand of Louis Philip in every plot set on foot by the Spanish factions beyond the pyrenees; and French writers see sordid schemes of English traffic at the bottom of all their interference in the affairs of the Peninsula.[9] The English have, of late, had the advantage in the game by supporting the constitutional form of government at present in operation, and by befriending the Regency of Espartero; they have, therefore, great influence with those in power. The policy of Louis Philip is adverse to Espartero and his government,[10] being aware that so long as they have ⟨the⟩ sway his wish with respect to the hand of the youthful queen for a prince of the House of Bourbon, and his desire to restore the French ascendancy in the affairs of the Peninsula are not likely to be gratified.

As I believe Louis Philip to be an upright and just man, I acquit him of the machinations against the internal peace of Spain with which English writers have charged him, but I do not wonder that he feels in no wise favorably disposed towards Espartero; ⟨and⟩ that he is inclined to construe rigorously every measure of his government, and to take quick offense at every thing on his part that may seem to bear upon French interests or French dignity. It is not at a French tribunal, therefore, that questions touching the conduct and policy of Espartero are to be decided.

All these matters are for your private reading my dear Sarah; I may be mistaken in my views, for as yet I am a novice in these scenes of political intrigue and may ultimately discover Espartero not to be the well meaning man that at present I think him. While 1 do entertain such a belief, however, I cannot but look with some interest on his arduous struggle in which at times it appears to me he has almost as much to fear from the counsils of his friends as from the machinations of his enemies. As long as he stands faithfully by the throne of the little queen, who has my strongest sympathies, I shall wish him well; if I thought him faltering in the least, in his fidelity to her I should give him up. I ought to say, also, in his fidelity to the constitution, but my romantic feelings went in the advance of my political. Beside, I consider her safety as linked with that of the constitution. If the latter were subverted we should have another scene of wild confusion, in which the Sceptre of the little queen might be trampled under foot.

And now to turn to smaller matters. I have lately been highly gratified by letters from my old Squire of the Alhambra Mateo Ximenes, and Miguel Jose Molina formerly the cousin but subsequently the husband of the bright eyed Dolores.[11] It seems that Mateo heard of my being "Ambassador" at Madrid from some travellers to whom he was shewing the lions of Granada. He immediately posted off with the intelligence to Dolores and her husband, who reside in a village near Granada, where Miguel is practising medicine. The news seems to have caused great joy among the worthy people, and produced a letter from Miguel,[12] full of affectionate expressions on the part of himself, of Dolores and of their aunt who is living with them, and inclosing one of my old visiting cards, to shew that they had treasured up the smallest memento of me. They had been displaced from the Alhambra by a change in the government, much to the grief of both, but especially of Dolores. They had four children, three girls and a boy. Two of them, however, were unfortunately born deaf and dumb, which honest Miguel attributes to the chagrin experienced for a long time by poor Dolores at being ejected from her favorite abode. I shall reply to the letter immediately.

The letter from Mateo is a scrawl that cost me as much pains to decypher as if it had been an Egyptian obolesk. I find he still inhabits the ˙Alhambra—officiating as Cicerone at a small hotel that has been established within the walls. I believe I told you some time since that Mateo had been in confinement for being concerned in a murder—a crime which I never should have suspected him of spirit enough to commit. I have since learnt that it was his son who had killed a man in a quarrel and been confined for it; but that the affair ⟨sh⟩ had thrown a shadow over the fortunes of Mateo.

Your last letter shows the Jones family to be in a state of disappointment with respect to their hopes of a brilliant entree in French Society. It may prove really beneficial to them. What a pity they could not content themselves with seeing all that was instructive, interesting and delightful in Europe, and returning home cultivated in taste, enriched in thought and stored with agreeable reccollections for the rest of their lives—How erroneous for Americans to come to Paris not to *see* but to be *seen*.

I shall be glad to hear that they are cured of their error, and are cultivating and gaining the good graces of their countrymen—You say you believe they intend to Separate—I hope these two sisters hitherto inseparable are not falling asunder.

God bless you my dear Sarah. I do not know when I shall be able to write you another long letter. My correspondence is getting completely the upper hand of me and numbers of letters are remaining unanswered, while those I do answer consume my time and prevent my attention to my literary tasks: which have been long neglected. With kind remembrances to Mr Storrow and kisses for darling little Kate whom I would give all the money in my pocket to see rolling and tumbling on the carpet. I am my dear Sarah

affectionately your uncle
Washington Irving

P.S. I see our friend ⟨the⟩ General Cass has his banner up for the presidency—Success to him!

ADDRESSED: a Madame / Madame Storrow / aux Soins de Mr. T. W Storrow / 17. Rue de Faubg Poissonniere / à Paris
MANUSCRIPT: Yale.   PUBLISHED: Simison, *Keogh Papers*, pp. 195–204; STW, II, 160 (in part).

In the year in the dateline the "2" has been canceled and the "3" added in pencil.

1. WI inadvertently repeated "to able."
2. WI is referring to the bombardment of Barcelona on December 3, 1842, and its subsequent occupation under martial law (until February, 1843). See Christiansen, *Military Power*, p. 113; H. Butler Clarke, *Modern Spain*, p. 183; and WI to Daniel Webster, December 12, 1842.
3. Among the 4000 refugees who left Spain in 1841 were Colonels José Gutiérrez de la Concha (1809–1895); Manuel Gutiérrez de la Concha (1808–1874); Fernando Córdova (1809–1893); General Angel García y Loigorri, duke of Vistahermosa (1805–1887); Manuel Bretón, count de la Riva y Picamoxons (1780–1859); Major Francisco Lersundi (1817–1874), and General Ramón María Narvaéz (1799–1868). Among those known to be associated in exile with María Christina were General Leopoldo O'Donnell (1809–1867); Francisco Martínez de la Rosa (1787–1842), and Count de Toreno (1786–1843). With General Juan de Pezuela (1810–1906), Louis Philippe, and María Christina, they plotted against Espartero. See Clarke, *Modern Spain*, p. 184; Edgar Holt, *The Carlist Wars in Spain*, p. 201; Martin Hume, *Modern Spain*, p. 371; and Christiansen, *Military Power*, pp. 111–12.
4. For details about this attempted kidnapping on October 7, 1841, see Peter de Polnay, *A Queen of Spain*, pp. 64–67.
5. Reports of the damage inflicted on Barcelona varied widely, from only a few buildings to 400 houses. See London *Times*, December 20, 23, 1842; and Clarke, *Modern Spain*, p. 183.
6. On November 21, 1831, 400 silk workers in Lyons gathered to persuade other workers to strike in favor of a tariff to improve their economic situation. The National Guard charged, killing eight workers; and fighting continued until 7:00 P.M. the next night. The duke of Orleans entered the city on December 3, took possession, disarmed the workers, disbanded the National Guard, and declared the city

in a state of siege. See *Le Moniteur Universel*, November 25, 29, 30, December 5, 1831; and Alexander Dumas, *The Last King of France*, I, 383–86.

7. Some reports stated that thirteen men were executed. The London *Times* (December 20, 1842) cited the *Diario* of Barcelona of December 15 as listing the names of fourteen men who had died since December 4; seventy-four were sentenced to ten years of hard labor in the presidio; seven were sentenced to six years; two, to two years; and fifty-five were discharged. See London *Times*, December 20, 22, 23, 1842; and Clarke, *Modern Spain*, p. 183.

8. WI may have seen the article, "The French Press and the Bombardment of Barcelona," in the London *Times*, December 15, 1842.

9. Since the Peninsular War the Spanish Constitutional or Liberal party had turned to England for support, while the Absolutists and the Moderates had striven for a close alliance with France. From 1836 the success of the Radicals had increased English influence in Madrid, with the result that the presence of Sir George Villiers, the British minister, was strongly felt in all that concerned representative and constitutional government. Aston was also reported to have given orders to Espartero, and it was feared that a commercial treaty might be signed to gain further English support for Espartero's government. Primarily, England sought political stability in Spain; there had been pro-Christina support in England since the volunteer British Legion had fought for her. Palmerston, who had sent a British squadron to Bilbao against the Carlists, also intervened during the Carlist War to help with mediation in April, June, and August of 1839. See Clarke, *Modern Spain*, pp. 133, 156, 182; Raymond Carr, *Spain*, p. 155; de Polnay, *A Queen of Spain*, p. 72; Holt, *The Carlist Wars in Spain*, p. 166; and Hume, *Modern Spain*, p. 387.

10. Louis Philippe, María Christina's champion, was prevented from invading Spain on her behalf because of the Quadruple Alliance. However, he openly worked for her restoration by intriguing in Spain and by his lavish expenditure of French money. Greatly fearing revolution, he attempted to dampen the liberal tendencies appearing in the Spanish government with the encouragement of the English. See Clarke, *Modern Spain*, p. 170.

11. Miguel and Dolores were children of different brothers of Maria Antonia Sabonea, the old seamstress who had lived under a staircase in the Alhambra during WI's stay there. See STW, I, 363, 365.

12. This letter and the one from Mateo, mentioned in the next paragraph, have not been located.

1536. To Daniel Webster

Legation of the United States./ Madrid January 9th. 1843.

No. 14. / The Hon: Daniel Webster. / Secretary of State of the U. States—Washington.

Sir.

I have the honor to enclose a copy of the reply of Count Almodovar, First Minister of State &c, to my note of the 6h. December on the subject of the interference of the Chev: D'Argaiz in the regular payment of the instalment of interest by the Intendente of Cuba.[1] My despatch No. 10, will have anticipated the purport of this reply. I trust the whole matter in question has been long since adjusted.

I have also to acknowledge the receipt via Cadiz of a Box containing Several volumes of Public Documents extending to the close of the 1st. Session of the 27th. Congress.

Since I last had the honor of writing to you the Regent has returned to Madrid, and made his entry in Military Style; His reception certainly was cold; and, though the municipal authorities and the various bodies of National Guards have since waited upon him in form, and greeted him with the warmest demonstrations of attachment and devotion, it is evident the events of Barcelona have had some effect upon his popularity. It could hardly be otherwise considering the falsehoods and exaggerations concerning those events, which have been industriously propagated through the opposition Papers,[2] and the false colourings given to the conduct of the Regent in the affair; who is held up as a perfect Nero.

From all that I can learn, I am inclined to consider the affair at Barcelona, the result of the ill concerted plots and intrigues of the refugee faction in France, which are every now and then producing partial explosions in this Country. The Province of Catalonia from its contiguity to France; from the turbulent character of its population; and from their political discontents, has been a favorite field of operation for the refugees. Early last spring it was stated in a public newspaper that the Carlist and Christino *facciosos* in their plan of operations had stationed a committee at Toulouse for the purpose of promoting disturbances in Catalonia. They were to send in bands of desperadoes to plunder and harrass the province, and emissaries to endeavor to stir up insurrection at Barcelona; the idea was either to throw the whole country into a state of anarchy and civil war, or at least to provoke severe measures on the part of Government, which might be made matters of accusation against it, and diminish its popularity at home, and its credit abroad.

I made a note of this statement at the time[3] and events have apparently corroborated it. Catalonia has been harrassed by bands of desperadoes, and the prompt and rough measures of General Zurbano to extirpate them have been made the theme of vehement invectives against the Government: An insurrection has been stirred up in Barcelona, and the mode in which it has been checked, and prevented from throwing the country into a state of anarchy, has been held up as an act of cruelty and despotism on the part of the Regent.

Now as far as I have had an opportunity of judging of the character of the Regent he is neither cruel nor despotic, nor does it appear to me that he has resorted to measures that were not warranted by the exigencies of the case. A bombardment is a noisy process, terrific to eye and ear; but I doubt whether the insurrection could have been put down and the threatened anarchy of the country prevented as promptly and effectually and at as little cost and bloodshed, by any other mode within the competency of the besieging force. Notwithstanding the lamentable pictures given in the opposition prints of Barcelona in ruins, I am told the damage done to houses and public edifices, is likely to be very speedily repaired,[4] and that the loss of life according to official returns is quite inconsiderable.

You will observe that France and England, those great rivals for ascendancy in the peninsula, have become somewhat mixed up in this affair, and that their official Gazettes have been suffered to advance criminating assertions which the respective Governments now find it their policy to contradict or unsay.

Louis Philippe, also has left himself deeply aggrieved in the person of his consul Mr. Lesseps, whose miscellaneous intermeddlings in the affair of Barcelona have brought upon him the charge, by the Political chief of the City, of promoting the insurrection.[5] The French Monarch has Shewn his full and lively faith in the immaculate purity of his Consul by instantly clothing him with unwonted honors and decorations before the accusations against him were examined. He has since been endeavoring to draw from the Spanish Government a public apology for this alledged outrage upon his Agent—The matter has been for some time in negotiation, the French Chargé d'affaires having had repeated interviews with the Minister of State, and making verbal demands of the required atonement. The Spanish Government on the other hand stands on the reserve; declining to reply to any thing but a specification in writing of the wrong done, and the satisfaction required.[6] In the mean time it has caused the matter to be closely investigated, and, while it disclaims all idea of implicating the Government of France in the late affair at Barcelona, it has forwarded to it documents, Sufficient, as it thinks to prove, that the French Consul has in several respects exceeded the bounds of his duties and privileges, and has merited a reprimand rather than a reward on the part of his Government. Such, I am told is the present position of this affair. I expect that the echoes of the bombardment of Barcelona, which have been so noisy for a time in the Paris and London press will gradually die away in the softening reverberations of Diplomacy.

If the effect of this whole affair has been to diminish the popularity of the Regent, it has on the other hand increased his military power. There is no longer a talk of reducing the army; on the contrary it has been augmented during the late agitation, and been distributed in every part of the Country where seditious movements were to be apprehended. The disaffected, also, have been disarmed: and the national Militia wherever suspected of disloyalty have been disbanded. It is to be hoped that the plots and seditions which beset his path; the intemperate attacks of the press; and the idea of being undermined in his popularity, may not drive him to rely too much upon his Military power, and to adopt those "Strong Measures" recommended by some of his injudicious friends and to which his enemies are evidently endeavoring to pique him. I trust for his safe guard in this respect, partly to the honesty of his intentions, and partly to the vis inertia of his nature, which in general induces him "to let things take their course". I am also pleased to hear some of his warm adherents express their fears that, as on former occasions; he will neglect the present opportunity of "making a stand" and causing his Government to be *felt* and respected.

Finding that nothing was to be expected from the existing Cortes but violent attack and opposition and not choosing to submit his actions to the arbitrament of a majority formed by a coalition of various parties, and representing no general sentiment or opinion of the nation, he has dissolved the legislative bodies, and appealed to the ballot box.[7] The ensuing election will be arduous and important. The Moderados or Monarchists, composing the old nobility and people of wealth, who since the revolution of September 1840, have refused to vote or to take any part in public affairs, treating the present Government as an usurpation, are now talking of entering the lists again. Some even suggest the policy of making terms with Espartero, and giving a conditional sanction to his Government, lest by keeping aloof too long, they sink into complete political insignificence, or provoke further measures subversive of their interests. These suggestions, I am told, have within a few days past, produced almost a schism among the leaders in the Moderado Camp.

Under present circumstances, the English Influence by dint of being exercised a little too openly and actively with the Government, has lost ground with the public: the coalition press has identified the much talked of treaty of commerce with the calamities of Barcelona: and the sempiternal "cotton question" is likely again to be hung up for future negotiation.[8] In consequence of a rumor that it might be carried into effect without waiting for the sanction of the Cortes, the Heraldo,[9] the Thersites of the coalition, declares, that the Independent Press will protest, not merely against any treaty of commerce whatsoever, celebrated without the requisites and solemnities provided in the fundamental code, but also against any mercantile arrangement, made under the influence of transient personal interests, contrary to the interests of the nation.[10] A commercial treaty it adds, concluded by General Espartero, would be an "infamous and lionlike bargain, in which to secure his domination, he would put at the disposition of England the future industry, the prosperity, and even the political existence of our Country. Patriotism and decorum, compel us to show to England, or to any other nation that desires to enter into mercantile negotiations with Spain, that we will not consent that they treat with one who represents nothing; with an odious and exotic power, whose agrandisement is founded on the ruin of the nation; In fine—we oppose ourselves formally to the celebrating of any treaty of commerce in the *Head Quarters of Buena Vista.*"[11]

This will give you some idea of the dictatorial tone of the coalition press, which is setting itself up almost as a separate Government; and will shew you the hostile feeling it is stirring up against the Cotton question.

> I have the honor to remain / Very respectfully / Your Obdt Sevt.
> Washington Irving

DOCKETED: Recd 22 Feb [*upper left corner, page 1*] / No. 1⟨9⟩4. ↑14↓ W. Irving. Madrid. 9 Jany. 1843
MANUSCRIPT: NA, RG 59.   PUBLISHED: STW, II, 153, 376 (in part).

Only the signature is in WI's handwriting.

1. WI included both a copy of Almodóvar's letter in Spanish and the following English translation of it:

Palace December 24th. 1842.
Sir.   I have the honor to acknowledge the receipt of your note of the 6th instant, in which, with regard to the subject of our conference of the preceding day, you declare yourself instructed to state that the Government of the United States will never consent, that a claim such as that proposed by Her Majesty's Minister Plenipotentiary at Washington (whether that claim be admitted by the Government of the Union or not), should be interposed to arrest the payment of the interests accruing on a debt guarantied by a solemn treaty; or that the[re] should be deducted from, or in any manner connected with, the said payment; and that the Government of the United States could not persuade itself, that Her Majesty's Government, would have authorized its representative at Washington, to adopt such a measure.

In answer I have to inform you (as I had the honor to do verbally in the conference above referred to) that the facts in this case are really these: the Intendant of the Island of Cuba learned from Her Majesty's Minister Plenipotentiary at Washington that the Honourable Secretary of State and foreign affairs of the United States had promised to answer his note respecting the claim on account of the Schooner Amistad before the 15th of August. That day was the time of payment of the second instalment of the interests on the debt acknowledged by Spain to be due to the United States: and as from the ⟨spirit of⟩ justice and righteousness of the claim, on the part of Her Majesty's Government, on account of the Schooner Amistad, (as often demonstrated by Sr Argaiz in the notes addressed by him, to the Secretary of State of the United States on this subject, which need not be here examined) Her Majesty's Minister could not expect that the promised answer would be other than satisfactory, the Intendant of Cuba thought proper to suspend the payment of the said instalment, on the grounds that the amount of the expected indemnification might be deducted from the sixty thousand dollars, and thus the drawing of bills of exchange for the said amount of the indemnification might be avoided.

Hence arose his answer to the letter addressed to him by the Secretary of State, requesting him to remit bills on New York for the amount of the second instalment of the interests on the debt, as he had done with regard to the first instalment. So far however was this answer from being the result of instructions from Her Majesty's Government, that on the 24th of September, and before the receipt of the account of this circumstance from Washington, the proceeding of the Intendant was disapproved by His Highness the Regent of the Kingdom, and that officer was instructed to make payment of that instalment, without delay. It is to be presumed that this has been already done, as on the 28th of September, the Intendant of Cuba, gave notice that he was about to make the payment, ↑he↓ having adopted that course agreeably to the spirit of honour of the Government, even before he had received the order above mentioned.

I hope that these explanations, the fruit of the desire which animates Her Majesty's Government to maintain the frank and amicable relations which hold Spain and the United States together, for the advantage of both countries, will be sufficient to convince you Sir and the Government which you so worthily represent, of the sincerity with which in this as in every other case Her Majesty's Government has acted and does act, and that it has viewed this incident with regret.

2. On January 2, 1843, *El Castellano* attacked *La Gaceta* for flattering Espartero and misrepresenting the nature of his reception upon his return to Madrid on the preceding day. The correspondent for the London *Times* reported (January 11, 1843) that "The reception of Espartero by the people was cold, and little or no enthusiasm was manifested by the troops or national guards." See also London *Times*, January 12, 1843.

3. See WI to Daniel Webster, November 26, 1842.

4. The effects of the bombardment were not always apparent from the streets. Many of the bombs fell inside the houses, destroying the roofs, floors, and interior walls while leaving the exterior walls undamaged. See *El Castellano*, January 9, 1843.

5. However, many foreigners thanked Lesseps for his help to them during the bombardment. See *El Castellano*, January 2, 1843; London *Times*, January 14, 1843. For other details about Lesseps, see WI to Daniel Webster, November 26, 1842.

6. See *El Sol*, January 3, 1842; London *Times*, January 13, 1843.

7. Espartero dissolved the Cortes on January 3 and scheduled elections for February 27, 1843. See *El Castellano*, January 4, 5, 1843; London *Times*, January 12, 1843. In many areas the elections were not held until March 2 and 3. See London *Times*, February 27, March 6, 8, 9, 13, 1843.

8. The association of the treaty and the bombardment of Barcelona is men-

tioned in *El Castellano*, January 2, 1843, which quotes a statement published in *Archivo Militar*.

9. The *Heraldo*, a Moderado paper founded in 1842 and edited by Luis Sartorius, count of San Luis (1820–1871), was one of the leading newspapers in Madrid in the 1840's. After the fall of Espartero it supported the new regent, General Narváez. See Christiansen, *Military Power*, pp. 120, 172; *Enciclopedia Universal Illustrada*, LIV, 655. The file of *El Heraldo* for 1843 is missing from the Hemeroteca Municipal in Madrid.

10. On January 3, 1843, thirteen editors of the independent newspapers issued a declaration opposing a treaty between Spain and Great Britain. For the text, see London *Times*, January 12, 1843; see also London *Times*, January 13, 1843.

11. The palace which was the seat of Espartero's government.

1537. To T. W. C. Moore

Madrid, Jany 10th. 1843

My dear Sir,

I have suffered your very kind and welcome letter[1] to remain a long time unanswered but really I have been ⟨for⟩ of late so occupied in a variety of ways as to put me quite behind hand in my correspondence. I have received very unfavorable news by my last letters of the state of Mr Astors health:[2] I am told he is confined to his bed. I hope however to hear by my next that his illness has been but temporary When you next see him I wish you would remember me to him most kindly. If you should find time to drop me another line let me know all about the old gentlemen and the little coterie which used to frequent his house and enliven his table. I should like exceedingly to be once more present at those pleasant meetings. I am happy to hear that Cogswell ⟨and⟩ Mrs Sewall ↑and Miss Oxenham↓[3] are still with him—I beg you to remember me to them all.

I am wearing my way into the traces of diplomacy and beginning to feel at home at Madrid[.] I am on very special terms with my confreres of the diplomatic corps and find some very pleasant companions among them. In September last I moved from the quarters I had inherited from Mr Vail and took up my residence in the house of the Marquis de Mos at the bottom of the Calle de las Infantas, which had been newly fitted up and painted, and where I am very pleasantly accommodated in the neighborhood of the Prado and within easy distance of all the places of public resort. I took all Mr Vails furniture off his hands as well as his carriage and servants, so that I was at once completely set up. Should you revisit Madrid I shall be happy to give you further proofs of Antonio's culinary science[4] which you were the first to extol to me.

Of the public affairs of Spain you will be able to inform yourself from
the public papers, making the usual allowance for exaggerations, false
colourings and downright lies, with which it appears to me the Spanish
papers abound. The country continues to suffer its casual paroxysms
and rough remedies; so that ⟨there⟩ between the desease and the doctor
the patient ⟨is⟩ has a hard time of it. If you had specified in your letter
any subject of a public or private nature about which you desired
information I should have had great pleasure in endeavoring to furnish
it. I sh⟨ould⟩all always be happy here or elsewhere to [be] of any
service to you.

Believe me, my dear Sir, with great regard

Yours very truly
Washington Irving

T. W. ↑C↓ Moore. Esqr

P.S. I shall be most happy to have another chapter of ↑real↓ home
affairs whenever you can find liesure. Your letter was a perfect little
chronicle

ADDRESSED: T. W. ↑C↓ Moore Esqr / ⟨149 Barrord[?] Street / New York⟩ / To care
    Messrs. M. Hoffman & Co. / New Orleans / L. A   POSTMARKED: NEW YORK
    FEB 23.
MANUSCRIPT: Yale.   PUBLISHED: STW, II, 160 (in part).

Thomas W. Channing Moore was a New York friend of WI's.

1. This letter has not been located.
2. John Jacob Astor, now seventy-nine years old, had been in ill health since
1835. He seems to have suffered from nothing more than a lifetime of overwork
and the complications of old age. See Porter, *Astor*, II, 1116.
3. Miss Oxenham was Astor's grandniece, the granddaughter of his brother George
Peter (1752–1813). She had come from London to care for him. See Porter,
Astor, II, 1026–29.
4. Antonio was WI's cook who was dismissed a few months later for dishonesty.
See WI to Sarah Storrow, June 10, 1843.

1538.   To Irving Paris

Madrid Jany 10th. 1843

My dear Irving,

I should have replied sooner to your very acceptable letter of Oct 24th[1]
but have been much occupied of late by various concerns. Indeed political events have been thickening upon us so as to require incessant at-

tention among diplomatic agents to collect correct information for their respective governments; for you must know that in this country of plots and revolutions every fact is so overlaid by mysteries, misrepresentations and down right lies, that to get at the ⟨so⟩ truth requires almost the miraculous optics of that worthy personage of yore renowned for seeing into millstones.[2]

You have doubtless read accounts of the late insurrection at Barcelona; which ⟨has been⟩ the French and English papers have clamoured up into an affair of European importance; you must take these accounts with great deduction; each nation giving a coloured view of the affair, and seeking to charge the other with nefarious interference in the matter. Those two nations are incessantly playing a game for ascendancy in the peninsula and are excessively suspicious of each others intentions and watchful of each others movements. England has the advantage at present by openly befriending the Regent and the constitutional form of government, and has great influence ⟨in⟩ with Espartero and his cabinet; while Louis Philippe feels that as long as Espartero and the actual government have sway, he has no chance of controling the affairs of Spain. A knowledge of this fact and of the shrewd and persevering policy of the French monarch wherever he has a favorite object in view, has induced many to suspect him of countenancing, if not promoting the schemes set on foot by the Carlists, Christinos and other Spanish refugees in ⟨Spain for⟩ ↑France↓ for throwing this country into confusion and overturning its present government. Louis Philippe is extremely sensitive on the subject, and hence the high and angry tone he has taken in demanding satisfaction from this government for the charges made against his Consul in Barcelona of being active in promoting the insurrection; a ⟨matter⟩ ↑demand↓ which [is] still undergoing diplomatic negotiation.

Though I acquit Louis Philippe of all unworthy participation in this matter I have no doubt that the insurrection ↑at Barcelona↓ was brought about like the insurrection in the North ⟨last⟩ in the autumn of 1840 and the attempt to carry off the little queen, by the plots and intrigues of the Spanish refugees in France. ⟨I have reason to⟩ I met with an intimation many months since in a public paper, published last Spring: that such an insurrection would be attempted in the hope either of throwing the country into a state of anarchy and civil war or to provoke some strong measures on the part of the Regent and his government that might be made use of against them. The insurrection has failed; but the other object has been attained. Espartero resorted to the "strong measure" of a bombardment, and it is now denounced as an act of cruelty and barbarism. I do not consider it in such light. It was necessary to put down the insurrection *promptly* or the whole country might have bccn again plunged into a civil war. A revolted city in arms cannot be subdued without bloodshed. A bombardment is the noisiest and most terrific mode, and the very terror it excites is apt to render it more promptly efficacious than others; while it really occasions less human suffering and loss of life than either investment and famine, as some have suggested, and an assault of arms as has been suggested by others. A reduction by famine carries sufferings and death into every household; an assault by arms involves the horrible carnage of grape shot, musquetry and the bayonet. Louis Philippe reduced the revolted city of Lyons by assault; the fighting from street to street and house to house lasted for several days; and many thousand lives were sacraficed. The Bombardment of Barcelona has demolished a few houses and damaged others but I am told the destruction of property is nothing so serious as has been represented while the official returns are said to give seven killed and twenty six wounded. The [unrecovered] [MS torn] since the reduction of the place have [never] [MS torn] been [unrecovered] [MS torn] by any unjust severity though the opposition paper[s] [MS torn] had predicted the most sanguinary vengeance. In fact he is not a cruel nor a despotic man and, if left to discharge the duties of his office tranquilly I believe would act ⟨with⟩ up, with strict faith, to all his professions and engagements, but he has military power at command, and ↑if↓ factions within and without the country go on to beset his path with plots and pitfalls; if a licentious press persist in villifying his character and should succeed in undermining his popularity, he may be driven to exercise that power in a manner and degree not at present within his wishes or intentions.[3] However, all these political topics I shall treat further of, in my next diplomatic letter to your mother[4] to whom ↑in the mean time↓ I beg you to communicate this letter as something by way of lunch.—With affectionate remembrances to "all bodies" Your affectionate uncle

Washington Irving

ADDRESSED: Irving Paris Esqr. / New York.
MANUSCRIPT: Va.–Barrett.

1. This letter has not been located.
2. See John Lyly, *Euphues and His England*, in *The Complete Works of John Lyly*, ed. R. Warwick Bond, 3 vols. (Oxford, 1967), II, 64.
3. WI had touched upon many of these points in his letters of January 5, 1843, to Sarah Storrow, and of January 9, 1843, to Daniel Webster.
4. See WI to Catharine Paris, January 12, 1843.

1539.   To George Ticknor

Madrid, Jany 11th. 1843.

My dear Ticknor,

I have two letters from you, June 25th and October 29th. to answer,[1] and if I have not answered them sooner it is only because I have had so many calls upon my time and my pen since my residence in Madrid as to render it impossible for me to be punctual in Correspondence.

Mr Gayangos[2] has not yet arrived here; when he comes I shall attend to your wishes in facilitating his researches, advancing funds &c[.] I was very much pleased with what I saw of him ↑in London↓ and shall be most happy to renew my acquaintance with him here. Any thing I can do to promote your literary enterprises, or to serve you in any other respect during my residence in Spain you may frankly command with the assurance that it will be giving me pleasure.

I am glad to hear Prescott is so near ⟨the⟩ finishing his Conquest of Mexico. I shall be impatient to read the work. I was very much gratified with making his acquaintance just before my departure from the United States. He is one of those ↑few↓ authors who do not disappoint in personal intercourse the high expectations they raise by their works. I beg when you see him you will remember me most kindly to him. Tell him I have just received his letter[3] respecting the suit of Mr Tudor,[4] whose interests I shall immediately attend to.

Excuse the hastiness of this mere scrawl. It is made in a moment of hurry when I am endeavoring to prepare a number of letters for a Courier about to depart. I feared to postpone it to a time of more liesure when I might ⟨m⟩ write more fully and satisfactorily, as a letter postponed is apt never to be written.

Ever my dear Ticknor / Yours very faithfully
Washington Irving

Geo Ticknor Esqr / &c &c &c

MANUSCRIPT: Dartmouth College Library.

1. These letters have not been located.

2. Don Pascual de Gayangos y Arce (1809–1897) was an editor, writer, and student of Arabic language and Moorish history who acted as scribe in Spain for Ticknor and Prescott. After he returned to Madrid in February, 1843, he and WI met frequently. See STW, II, 115, 364, 381.

3. This letter has not been preserved.

4. Frederick Tudor (1783–1863) was a Boston merchant who shipped ice to the tropics. He carried on a lengthy and fierce fight with his agent in Havana for control of the business there. In a letter of February 11, 1843, to Daniel Webster, WI mentioned a law suit between Tudor and John W. Damon.

1540. To Catharine Paris

Madrid. Jany 12th. 1843.

My dear Sister,

As you and I are so completely launched on the diplomatic line, I shall give you a few more notes about Spanish politics, which in fact must serve for the family fire side; for I shall have to give up writing multifarious family letters or I shall never get on in literary labour.

Notwithstanding the boding raven which hovered over Espartero on his sallying forth from Madrid on his expedition to Malaga, and which was considered by many a fatal augury: he has returned in safety and made his military entry on New Years day. I must say, however, that his reception was rather cold, and shcwed that the popular feeling towards him had been affected by the measures taken for the suppression of the insurrection; or rather had been affected by the misrepresentations and false colourings of the opposition papers.[1] In a letter to your son Irving[2] I have just given my notions on the subject; and have acquitted the Regent of all cruelty or unnecessary severity in the measures he adopted. ⟨In⟩ I believe ⟨it was⟩ those prompt measures saved the whole province of Catalonia from being thrown into confusion, and prevented the insurrection from extending to other parts of the Kingdom. In fact the insurrection at Barcelona I have no doubt was another of those plots hatched in France by Spanish refugees, for the subversion of the present government, similar to the one which was the subject of my former ⟨letter⟩ diplomatic letter.[3] The French government has been charged with instigating this insurrection through its secret agents. I do not believe the insinuation; but I am convinced Louis Philippe would be glad ⟨to⟩ of any event that produced the downfall of Espartero and the constitutional government.

As I find my former letter on Spanish politics has interested you all, and gave you more distinct notions of the affairs of this country, and as there is in fact a vast deal of political romance in them, especially as they are connected with the fortunes of the little queen. I shall ⟨give you a⟩ endeavor to give you a more complete key to the subject. though in so doing I may repeat some of the observations of my former letter. These letters, of course, are merely for the use of the family circle. In my former letter I did not go far enough back to give you the origin of opinions, prejudices and passions which agitate Spain at the present day: ⟨I⟩ and of the pretensions to interfere in Spanish affairs set up by other nations.

Spanish politicians of the liberal party declare that their constitutional struggle within the present century is but an attempt to revive old rights and popular institutions of which they had been deprived for centuries by *foreign influence*. As early as the twelvth century, say they, we had our *Cortes* or legislative assembl⟨y⟩ies, in which deputies from the towns, boroughs and villages, *representatives of the people*, took their seats beside the nobles and the clergy.

Our cities, towns and even villages had their municipal rights and privileges secured to them by charters from the crown: they were governed by their own magistrates and ayuntamientos or corporations, elected by themselves, they marched to battle under their own leaders and their own standards, and woe to anyone, even the monarch himself, who should dare to invade their chartered rights. Such was Spain, say they, before she passed under foreign domination. She was in the advance of all the rest of Europe in *representative legislation*.

In 1496 Ferdinand and Isabella[4] sought to strengthen themselves by foreign alliances. Their second daughter Juana the Simple,[5] was married to Philip Archduke of *Austria*.[6] The issue of this marriage was Charles V.[7] who inherited the throne in 1516, and was the first of the line of Spanish sovreigns of the house of *Austria* or *Hapsburg*. ⟨He brought a⟩ This dynasty continued nearly two hundred years and was distinguished for a time by foreign conquest and false glory, but was marked say the Spaniards with the decline of the popular institutions of the nation and was destructive of the national prosperity and intelligence.

Charles IId[8] the last of this line died without children in 1700: he bequeathed the crown, which he had no right to do, to Philip of Anjou,[9] grandson of Louis 14th. of France. Philip also claimed the crown as being a descendant from Juana the Simple. The title of Philip was disputed by other claimants of the house of Austria, but was powerfully supported by France, and hence arose the famous *War of the Succession*[10] at the commencement of the last century, which, for thirteen years, agitated all Europe and desolated the fairest provinces of Spain. Philip maintained his seat on the throne and with him commenced the Spanish dynasty of the *House of Bourbon*, which, say the Spaniards, was still more fatal to the national independence and national institutions than that of the house of Austria. The court of France assumed to dictate to that of Spain as being the oldest branch of the house of Bourbon and *the strongest* of the two. There was a continual struggle on the part of the Spanish cabinet against this dictation of the cabinet of the Tuilleries but all in vain. Spain became little better than a dependence upon France and its feeble princes of the Bourbon line ⟨was⟩ ↑were↓ completely under the control of the French Ambassadors, who figured like masters at the court of Madrid. It was thus, under the Bourbon ascendancy that France acquired the habit, and the fancied right of dictating and intermeddling in the affairs of Spain which she seems disposed to exercise at the present day—During this ascendancy the old Cortes or representative assemblies had entirely disappeared: the monarchy had become *absolute*.

As we approach our own ⟨day we find⟩ ↑times we come to↓ Charles IV[11] one of the most worthless of the Bourbon line of Spanish sovreigns. He was in fact a mere sportsman, and left the reigns of government in the hands of one Godoy,[12] a minion and paramour of the profligate queen Maria Louisa,[13] and through her influence raised to the title and dignity of Prince of the Peace.[14] The insolence and rapacity of this favorite, the abuses and corruptions of his administration & the extravagance and profligacy of the court roused the popular indignation; Charles IV was compelled to abdicate in favor of his son Ferdinand VII who in fact promoted the downfall of his father by his own conspiracies— Charles with his Queen retired to France where he appealed to Napoleon against his son, protesting that he had abdicated his crown through compulsion.

Ferdinand appointed a junta at Madrid to conduct the government during his absence and hastened to France to plead his cause with Napoleon. The latter profited by these domestic quarrels, and, having father and son within his power, obtained from them the cession to him of their rights to the crown of Spain, which he forthwith made over to his brother Joseph.

Ferdinand, who had conspired against his father proceeded in that course of duplicity which has marked his character. While he publicly and formally ceded his rights to the Emperor, he sent off a *secret express* dated 5th of May enjoining the junta whom he had left ⟨be⟩ in command to oppose the entrance of the French into Spain, ⟨and⟩ to *assemble the Cortes* and to make preparations for the defence of the Kingdom and of his rights. Having given these *secret* orders, he, on the 12th of the same month, by open proclamation, absolved the Spaniards from their oath of fidelity to his dynasty and exhorted them to conform to the disposition of the Emperor Napoleon.

The junta, who understood this double dealing obeyed the *secret* commands of the Captive monarch. They resumed with alacrity their old popular institutions so long trampled down by foreign domination, and revived the *Cortes* or legislative assemblies In these Cortes sat some of the wisest and purest patriots of the country. Here first came forward the good Arguelles of whom you have often heard me speak, and who has sustained a character for integrity and truth that has undergone all kinds of trials. These men went on to digest the old political forms and institutions of the country into a constitution more in unison with the lights of the age and the improved system of legislation. Thus was formed the constitution of 1812.[15] The men who formed it remained true to the liberties of their country and the rights of their captive king through all the trials of the peninsular war—resisting the invasion of Napoleon and the usurpation of his brother Joseph.

When Ferdinand was restored to his country and throne in 1814, while he was yet on his way to Madrid, and uncertain how he might be received by those who still held the power, he published a decree declaring his ⟨intention⟩ determination to abide by the constitution which had been framed in his absence and that his intentions were "not those of a tyrant and a despot, but of a King and the father of his country." How did he fulfil his promise? As soon as he felt himself secure he assumed despotic power: he dissolved the Cortes, he arrested the patriots of the constitution who had adhered to him in exile some he confined in convents and fortresses, others he banished; and others he hurried off to dungeons on the coast of Africa where they languished six years Among these was the good Argüelles, the *present guardian of the queen.*

For six years the popular liberty was again trampled down, and the constitution abolished. The nation made several ineffectual struggles, at length in 1820 it succeeded by a violent effort in restoring the Constitution.[16] *Ferdinand again swore to adhere to it.* The patriots were released from prison, recalled from Exile: Arguelles was drawn from his six years dungeon in Africa and offered a seat in the cabinet, as minister of the interior. He refused to accept it. Ferdinand with hypocritical fervor displayed a copy of the constitution. "I have sworn to it freely," cried he, ["]and with all my heart. I will observe it and cause it to be observed scrupulously." Arguelles trusted to his word and his oath and became a minister. An engraving was published of this scene in which the confiding patriot was deceived by the traitor King. In three years from that Ferdinand aided by France had again trampled the constitution under foot, and Arguelles was in exile.

Supported by the armed intervention of France Ferdinand reigned absolute until his death in 1832; one of the most faithless and brutal of the Bourbons. You will now understand the ancient and inherent spirit of independence and the love for the popular institutions of early times, which have been at the bottom of the modern revolutions of Spain, and which render ⟨the⟩ Spaniards so opposed to foreign intervention.

Ferdinand, as I shewed you in my former letter had but two children both daughters, offspring of his third and last wife Maria Christina of *the house of Bourbon,* ⟨daughter of⟩ a royal princess of Naples and niece of the wife of Louis Philippe. By the salique law which had been introduced into Spain from France no female could succeed to the throne: but Ferdinand revoked this law before his death, restored the old Spanish law of succession and made his infant daughter Isabella IId heir to the crown. I have shewn you how her title was contested by her uncle the Infante, (or Prince Royal): Don Carlos, and defended by her mother, Maria Christina˜ who acted as Regent during the minority of her daughter and how another *War of Succession* took place, which distracted unhappy Spain for nearly seven years. In this war the cause of Maria Christina and her daughter was countenanced and aided by France and England, the liberal party too ranged on her side and obtained from her a restoration of the constitution; which underwent some important modifications in 1837. Still the civil war was protracted to the misery and impoverishment of the kingdom. At length a successful commander appeared in the person of General Espartero. He was of humble but decent parentage, born in Granatula, a village of La Mancha had been patronized by the monks and sent to receive a military education at a military school at Cadiz, where he proved but an indifferent student. He rose, however, by bravery and good fortune in the wars in Spanish America and came back to Spain with rank and reputation. His bravery and good fortune were again signalized in the Civil wars of the peninsula: he drove the pretender Don Carlos from the Kingdom, succeeded in bringing the rebel commanders to terms and by a treaty of peace and reconciliation secured the allegiance of the whole nation to the throne of the youthful Isabella. I cannot do better than to give you the words of an eloquent Spanish writer (Marliani)[17] on this subject "The hour of reconciliation of the Spaniards had struck Every one felt the need of repose. The fortunate Genl. Espartero, after having combated the insurrection for six years, had the glory to disarm it. His word was the sole gage which the enemy demanded, to surrender. He gave it as a soldier; as a good Spaniard; as a good citizen. As a soldier— for he was generous after shewing himself of ↑an↓ admirable bravery; as a good Spaniard—for he declared to Colonel Wylde,[18] an English commissary that he wished foreigners to interfere as little as possible in the pacification; and as a good citizen—for he knew how to respect the omnipotence of the representatives of the nation on the subject of *Fueros.*" "(chartered rights)" His popularity was now unbounded. He was idolized by the Army; rewarded by the government with all kinds of orders and honors and with the title of the Duke of La Victoria; but hailed by the nation with the still nobler title of Pacificator of Spain. I have shewn you in my former letter[19] how the Queen Regent Maria Christina, impaired her great popularity and lessened her dignity in the eyes of the nation by a low ↑and gross↓ connexion, sanctioned, it is said, by a *tardy* marriage. I have shewn you how she lost the confidence of the liberals by tampering with the constitution: and how, under the advice of the Moderado's, or absolute monarchists, and of the French Ambassador, she made a bold attempt upon those *fueros* or chartered rights, so jealously treasured by the people. This shewed her ignorance of Spanish institutions and of the

Spanish character—By a royal decree the municipal law was to be altered;
⟨and⟩ the elective franchise taken away and municipal offices to be in
the gift of the crown. As I shewed you in my letter she did not venture
to launch this perfidious decree until she had repaired to Barcelona,
where she trusted to be supported by Espartero and the Army. Espartero remonstrated with her but in vain. The decree was launched. The
effect was instantaneous. Not a town, not a village but was up in arms for
the defence of its chartered rights. The storm of indignation broke upon
the Queen Regent from every part of the Kingdom She sank before it:
abdicated the regency and retired from the Kingdom.

In this exigency when the Country was almost with out a government,
and in danger of another civil war every eye was turned to Espartero
as the person most likely from his popularity with the army and the
people to centralize the feelings of parties and to give the government
that unity and strength so important to public tranquility. He was accordingly elected Regent by the Cortes. In this capacity [he][20] was ⟨[un-
recovered]⟩ to exercise the sovreign power in the name of Isabella II.
during her minority, which according to the revised constitution of 1837,
ceases when she is fourteen years of age, which will be in October 1844.
He has now been two years in the Regency. His enemies have assailed
him with all kinds of plots and have heaped upon him all kinds of slanders. They accuse him of ambition: of intending to restore the Constitution of 1812, by which the minority of the queen, and of course his
Regency, would be extended to her 18th year: and even of aiming at absolute dictatorship, if not ⟨the⟩ absolute sovreignty. As far as I can judge,
however, he means well. With a great military force at his command he
has never ⟨abm⟩ made an ambitious use of it and so far has been true to his
engagements and loyal to the throne of the little queen. I regard his conduct with intense interest and hope he may not be made to swerve from
the straight forward course either by foe or friend. He appears to me to
be the only safe guard between the little queen and anarchy. And now to
come to the little queen herself. Do you know that, though scarce entered
in her teens, her hand has already become as much an object of rivalry
as the hand of any princess in fairy tale?[21] Louis Philippe early fixed his
eyes upon it, for one of his sons, as a means of providing for his family,
⟨of⟩ and of continuing the ascendancy of France and the dynasty of the
Bourbons in the Peninsula. England, suggested a prince of the House of
Cobourg, with which its own Royal line was linked by matrimonial ties;
Austria spoke up for one of its Archdukes; at one time, during the civil
war the eldest son of Don Carlos was suggested, as a mode of uniting the
claims to the crown; and recently a son of the Infante Don Francisco,

another cousin of the youthful queen has been brought forward by his mother, who is sister of Maria Christina, and likewise of the house of Bourbon, as a candidate for the hand of the little Isabella. Spain however claims the right of acting in the matter for itself and dreads any further matrimonial alliances with powerful lines that may again usurp ascendancy in her affairs. France, notwithstanding, keeps up her pretensions to dictate in the affair and Louis Philippe has openly declared that the marriage of the little queen with any other than ⟨the⟩ a prince of the house of Bourbon will be considered by France as a sufficient cause of war. You will ask why France is so desirous of an ascendancy on the Peninsula. I will endeavor to shew you; though I believe I have already explained it in my letter to Irving. France is a warlike nation, and has warlike neighbors. She has to keep a strong military frontier towards the north, that region of warrior powers with whom she has so often been at deadly strife It is important, therefore, that Spain, her immediate neighbor on the south, should either be *friendly* or be *weak*; hence she seeks to secure her by matromonial alliances to get a complete control over her, or else to break down her strength and render her harmless. You have now a key to the policy of Louis Philippe in seeking the hand of the little queen for one of his sons: to his hatred of Espartero whom he knows to be opposed to his wishes: and to his hostility to the constitutional form of government in Spain of which he dreads the invigorating effects on the character and prosperity of the nation.

The policy of England, on the contrary, is to strengthen Spain; to make it independent of France to render it a jealous and formidable ↑neighbor↓ of the latter, pressing upon it with a military frontier ⟨so as⟩ and acting as a check upon it in its wars with other nations. Thus Spain is a kind of political chess board on which these two nations are playing for mastery. ⟨Spain⟩ ↑France↓ had an advantage in the game while Maria Christina was in power and exercised the Regency; when she left the country the Bourbon ascendancy departed with her. Louis Philippe received her at his court; withdrew his countenance from Spain, affected to consider the country in a state of anarchy and Espartero as a kind of usurper, and ⟨for⟩ by his representations prevented the northern powers from sending diplomatic representatives to Madrid so long as the queen should be in her minority and Espartero in power. Hence his refusal to let his Ambassador, Mr. Salvandy, deliver his credentials into the hand of the Regent as head of the government; in consequence of which that gentleman returned to Paris with a sleeveless errand and France has no representative at this court but a young Secretary of Legation acting as a Charge *des* affaires.

sionally weave in characters and incidents as they rise before me: and

All these things have latterly given England the upper hand and enabled her to play an open game. ⟨It⟩ Her interest accords with her professions It is her policy to uphold the Constitution and to sustain ⟨the⟩ Espartero in the Regency. She has repeatedly aided Spain in her constitutional struggles, and last spring, when it was supposed France meditated some hostile movement, she declared in parliament that she would never passively permit the armed interference of any foreign power with the present political institutions of Spain. You will now perceive what caution must be observed in weighing the charges of both England and France against each other with respect to the affairs of the Peninsula. French writers declare that the whole object of England is to check the rising manufactures and industry of Spain, to make it a mere market for her own manufactures and ⟨a⟩ to reduce it to the state of Portugal; which say they is little better than an English colony.

English writers on the other hand, see the hand of Louis Philippe in all the plots and insurrections set on foot by the refugee factions within his dominions. His object, say they, is to produce such a state of anarchy that the country may appear to foreign nations and even to its inhabitants, incapable of extricating itself from its perplexities and woes, so that he may appear justified in the eyes of the world in marching an army across the Pyrenees, restoring Spain to tranquility and giving it a settled government.

These mutual criminations of French and English writers are strikingly apparent in treating of the late affair at Barcelona. The accounts of both parties are to be taken with great deductions, but you will especially understand why the French papers are prone to take such prejudiced views of the conduct of Espartero.

I have thus, at the risk of repeating things already said in my former letter, given you a more complete though still a brief map of Spanish politics, because I find you all so much interested in the subject, and because there is more real romance about it than about any thing else in modern history. The fortunes of this bold soldier thus suddenly elevated to almost regal power: the part he has yet to play in this complicated and eventful drama: the fortunes of the little queen and her sister, at the hazard of conspiracies, insurrections and civil war; all these will crowd the brief term that yet remains of the minority with circumstances of intense interest, and will make her accession to the throne, if haply she attains to it, an eventful crisis in Spanish affairs. All th⟨i⟩ese scenes in which I am mingling and likely to mingle, will hereafter form one of the romantic epochs ⟨of⟩ in the history of this country

As I have now given you the ground work of the story I will occawill take occasion to depict more at large, some of the circumstances and scenes which I have merely touched upon in my general sketch. I am glad you take care of these letters, for they will serve me hereafter as reccollections; as I keep no journal of passing events. You have repeatedly expressed your anxiety that I would ⟨keep⟩ take care of myself and keep myself warm both within doors and without during the winter. As yet I can hardly say we have had winter. There is no frost in the ground though the thermometer is some times at night a little below the freezing point. The days are bright and beautiful with sunshine as warm as in our month of October. The fields around Madrid are green; and there are green vegetables growing in the convent garden opposite my study window. The pink saloon which is our family gathering place, and in which I at present have my writing desk, is open to the South and so warm from the sunshine that there is no need of fire at midday.

I have received your letters of Nov 22d. and Decr 13.[22] which as usual are full of interesting family news You have the true mode of letter writing: putting down every day ⟨the⟩ something of family chit chat.

Give my affectionate remembrances to Mr Paris. I am happy to find his situation gives him such cheerful occupation

Your affectionate brother
Washington Irving

DOCKETED: Washington Irving to Mrs. Paris. / Madrid Jany 12. 1843.
MANUSCRIPT: Va.–Barrett; Yale (copy, in part).

1. As an example, Nicomedes Pastor Díaz, editor of *El Sol*, was tried on January 7, 1843, for criticizing Espartero's conduct in Barcelona, but he was absolved by the jury. See *El Castellano*, January 9, 1843.

2. See WI to Irving Paris, January 10, 1843.

3. See WI to Catharine Paris, November 20 and December 10, 1842.

4. Ferdinand (1452–1516) and Isabella I (1451–1504), who began their reign in 1474 and united the kingdoms of Aragon and Castile in 1479, conquered the Moors and sponsored the first voyage of Columbus in 1492.

5. Juana (1479–1555), who became queen of Castile at her mother's death in 1504.

6. Philip (1478–1506), who was the son of Emperor Maxmilian (1459–1519) and Mary of Burgundy.

7. Charles (1500–1558) was king of Spain from 1526 to 1556 and Holy Roman Emperor from 1519 to 1556.

8. Charles II (1661–1700), son of Philip IV (1605–1665), became king of Spain in 1665; his mother, Mariana of Austria, was regent for ten years.

9. Philip, Duke of Anjou (1683–1746), the grandson of Louis XIV, was named by Charles II a month before his death as his successor to the throne.

10. The War of Spanish Succession (1701–1713) was fought to determine

whether the House of Bourbon or the House of Hapsburg should dominate the Spanish Empire with its wealthy holdings in the New World. The Treaty of Utrecht was concluded by France, England, Holland, Prussia, Portugal, and Savoy on April 11, 1713, and signed by Spain on July 13, 1713.

11. Charles IV (1748–1819), the second son of Charles III (1716–1788) and Maria Amelia of Saxony, was king of Spain from 1788 to 1808, when he abdicated in favor of Ferdinand VII, who in turn was replaced by Joseph Bonaparte.

12. For Manuel de Godoy, see WI to Catharine Paris, August 3, 1842.

13. Maria Louisa of Parma (1751–1819) dominated her good-natured, simple-minded, weak husband, Charles IV.

14. Godoy received this title because of his successful negotiation of the Peace of Basel, which ended the war with France in 1795. See H. Butler Clarke, *Modern Spain*, pp. 10–11.

15. The purpose of this constitution was to limit the despotism of the Spanish monarch and to establish a division of powers based on a contractualist political theory. See Clarke, *Modern Spain*, pp. 16–25; Raymond Carr, *Spain*, pp. 92–97; and WI to Catharine Paris, September 2, 1842.

16. For other details, see WI to Catharine Paris, September 2, 1842.

17. Probably Manuel Marliani (d. 1873), a politician and writer who later went to Italy and involved himself in the annexation of the Piedmont. He was the author of *Histoire Politique de l'Espagne Moderne* (Paris, 1840).

18. William Wylde was the leader of the British Legion, which fought with the Cristino armies in the 1830's against Don Carlos. See Edgar Holt, *The Carlist Wars in Spain*, pp. 80, 90, 162, 187–88.

19. See WI to Catharine Paris, September 2, 1842.

20. WI omitted this word.

21. For other details about the widespread concern over Isabella's marriage, see WI to Daniel Webster, November 5, 1842.

22. These letters have not been located.

1541. To Sarah Irving

[Madrid], January 13th, 1843

* * * Your information that Mr. ——— had given Mrs. ———[1] a two-story house in Broadway, gave me great satisfaction; but when you added that the mantelpieces were of wood, it went to my heart. However, let us hope for the best. If the young couple really love each other, they may manage to have a happy fireside in spite of the mantelpiece; and who knows but the old gentleman's heart may soften toward them before his death, and he may leave them a marble mantelpiece in his will. Miss ———,[2] on the contrary, who married according to his wishes, has been rewarded, I am told, with a three-story (I am not certain that it is not a *four*-story) house. These two instances of the matrimonial fortunes of two sisters, my dear girl, should be held up as warnings to young ladies disposed to enter the connubial state, not to give away their soft

and tender hearts without first consulting the harder hearts of all the old gentlemen they may happen to be related to. For my own part, I should take it in great dudgeon, if any of you girls at the cottage should throw yourselves away upon any agreeable young gentleman, without his first gaining the affections of your father and myself; though I trust I should not go to the length of condemning you to a wooden mantelpiece.

I thought of you all at dear little Sunnyside on Christmas day, and heartily wished myself there to eat my Christmas dinner among you. I hope you kept up Christmas in the usual style, and that the cottage was decked with evergreens. You must not let my absence cause any relaxations in the old rules and customs of the cottage; everything must go on the same as it did when I was there.

[His own Christmas dinner he had eaten at the British embassy, where, he remarks,][3] "we had the good old Christmas luxuries of plum pudding and minced pies, and our repast was a very pleasant one."

PUBLISHED: PMI, III, 275–76.

1. The context suggests that the names omitted by PMI are John Jacob Astor and Louisa Kane. See Porter, *Astor*, II, 1042; and WI to Sarah Storrow, July 11, 1841.

2. Eliza Langdon (1818–1899) had married Matthew Wilks on October 3, 1842. See Harvey O'Connor, *The Astors*, p. 77; and London *Times*, January 5, 1843.

3. Bracketed passage added by PMI.

1542. To George Read

Legation of the United States– / Madrid January 13h. 1843.

George Read Esq. / Consul of the United States. Malaga

Sir,

I have received with much pleasure your letter of the 7th. Instant, covering the consular returns of the course of trade for the Port of Malaga for the year 1842:

It is upon such full and ample statements as those you have furnished, that the chief reliance can be placed for inducing the Government of this Country to enter into an arrangement with that of the United States, by which the commerce & wealth of both nations may be augmented, and the present injurious restrictions, upon the exchange of their peculiar productions, modified or removed:

It is to be regretted, in the interest of the public service, that your course in this respect is not more generally followed.

Your communication to the State Department accompanying a former letter was forwarded by the last Courier, to the United States.

I am, with respect / Your Obdt Sert.
Washington Irving

ADDRESSED: Seña Don Jorge Read / Consul de los Estados Unidos / de America. / *Malaga.* / España.   POSTMARKED: [*unrecovered*] / EN 2 / 1843 / 1. / SPAIN.   DOCKETED: 1843 / Legation U S. / [*MS torn*] / Recd. 17th. do. / Ansd.

MANUSCRIPT: NA, RG 84 (also letterbook copy).

Only the signature is in WI's handwriting.

1543. To Sarah Storrow

Madrid Jany. 15th. 1843.

My dear Sarah,

I have just received your letter of Jany 1st. to 7th.[1] full of pleasant details. I inclosed to you yesterday letters for home, among which was a voluminous letter to your mother. I ⟨h⟩ was too much fagged by letter writing to add one for yourself.

I beg you not to make any excuses for taking up so much of your letters with little Kate and her vagaries. She is my perfect little pet and I read over and over every thing about her and her dolls; and have her completely before my eyes; though I always think of her exactly as she was when I left her. I dare say you and I are both very foolish about that child, but we must bear with one anothers *faiblesse.*

You were looking for accounts of our christmas dinner at the British Embassy, but it had nothing to distinguish it from other dinners ↑of↓ which we frequently partake there; excepting havind[2] minced pies & plum pudding—the ordinary fare being *à la Francaise.* Mr Aston & myself are on the most frank and cordial terms of intimacy and see each other continually. He is ⟨an⟩ intelligent, manly, straightforward and good tempered, and quite above the old fashioned formalities, mysteries and finesse of diplomacy. Indeed I have formed very agreeable intimacies among my fellow diplomats which quite enliven my residence in Madrid. General society here offers very few resources being so much cut up ⟨and⟩ by political feuds. I cannot say I regret it, as I have more time to myself, and am not harrassed by invitations and engagements of all kinds as at Paris and London. There has been but one grand ball in the fashionable world this winter; which was given by the Countess Montijo,[3] one of the leaders of the Ton; it was very crowded and very animated and all the elite of Madrid was there, filling a large suite of Saloons and chambers. I had never seen the countess and was surprised, therefore, on making my bow to be received by her with the warmth and eagerness of an old friend. She explained it by letting me know that she was the wife (at present widow) of the Count de Theba[4] (subsequently Montijo) whom I had known at Granada, and who had often spoken of me with the greatest regard. I instantly reccollected the Count: a gallant fellow; full of intelligence and animation, but who had been sadly cut up in the wars: having lost an eye and been crippled in a leg and a hand. At the time I knew him in Granada the Countess was absent, but he had a family of little girls, mere children, about him. The Countess took me to another room where was a miniature of the Count ⟨st⟩ such as I knew him, with a black patch over one eye. She subsequently introduced me to the little girls,[5] now young ladies; fashionables of Madrid. Throughout the evening the Countess was extremely attentive to me, and to Mr Hamilton whom I had introduced to her: and made me promise to see her often; which I feel well inclined to do, as she and her daughters speak English, and their house is reputed to be one of the most agreeable resorts of Madrid.

Yesterday I had a visit from Don Ignazio Pinzon descendant of the Pinzons, companions of Columbus. He was a young gentleman studying law at Seville during my residence there, and gave me the letter of introduction to his father which procured me such kind attentions on my "pilgrimage to Palos."[6] I was extremely glad to see him as you may well suppose: and asked him many questions about his family. His good old father[7] died in 1836, after a long life full of goodness and kindness. His funeral was the most numerously attended that ever had been known in Moguer. All ranks and all parties attended. The Shops were shut up: the very laborers of the fields suspended their ⟨labors⟩ ↑toils↓ to follow the remains of this really good old cavalier to the grave. The family have sold the Hacienda or estate at Palos, where the old gentleman and myself spent a day together. At present they reside in Moguer, where Don Gabriel (a ↑mere↓ youth at the time of my visit) now resides, and inherits all his fathers love for ⟨the country, for⟩ hunting, shooting and all other country sports.

Jany 21. This letter has been lying by me several days untouched for I have had one of my spells of inaction of the pen, when I sally forth and take exercise, and endeavor to get myself in order for the next writing fit. When I resume my pen I trust it will be to resume my literary tasks, which have been sadly interrupted.

For three days past we have been without mails from Paris, and it[8] the morning of the fourth day is now far advanced, and still no letters nor newspapers. This is occasioned, I am told, by the state of the roads in France, and the Swelling of the rivers by wintry Storms. The failure of the mails for a day or two makes a gap in existence in this isolated place, where we ⟨are constantly looking for⟩ ↑depend upon↓ intelligence from the other parts of the world to keep us informed of the moves in the great game of life, of which we seem to be mere distant spectators. However, we have a game of our own going on here, which promises to thicken in interest, and to involve some desperate hazards.

We shall have a box coming from Paris soon, with clothes for Mr Hamilton and articles of stationary &c for the Legation. If you have any thing to forward to me, such as books or pamphlets, send them to Mr Ledyard before the 20th. February, and he will have them put in the box.

With kind remembrances to Mr Storrow and many Kisses to my darling little Kate.

Yours my dear Sarah most affectionately
Washington Irving

MANUSCRIPT: Yale.

1. This letter has not been located.

2. WI probably intended to write "having."

3. Maria Manuela Kirkpatrick (1794–1879) was the daughter of William Kirkpatrick a Scottish-born American citizen who was appointed U.S. consul at Málaga in 1791. In 1817 she had married Don Cipriano Guzman Palafox (1786?–1839), count of Teba and after the death of his elder brother, marques of Montijo. See Harold Kurtz, *The Empress Eugénie, 1826–1920* (Boston, 1964), pp. 5, 6, 316; and Philip W. Sergeant, *The Last Empress of the French* (Philadelphia, n.d.), pp. 4, 7, 10.

4. In 1834 he became count of Montijo, duke of Peñaranda. He was permanently maimed and crippled in various military campaigns. See Kurtz, *The Empress Eugénie*, pp. 7–8, 20–21; and Sergeant, *The Last Empress of the French*, p. 17.

5. The two children whom WI met were Francesca (or Paca) (1825–1860), the future duchess of Alba, and Eugenia (1826–1920), the future wife of Napoleon III and empress of France. See Kurtz, *The Empress Eugénie*, p. 153.

6. For other details, see WI to John Wetherell, May 13, 1830; WI to Alexander H. Everett, August 20, 1828; and *Diary 1828–1829*, pp. 48–50.

7. Juan Fernández Pinzón.

8. WI inadvertently added this word.

1544. To Count Almodóvar

Legation of the United States / Madrid January 23d. 1843.

Mr. Samuel McLean[1] having been appointed Consul of the United States of America for the *Port of Cien Fuegos in the Island of Cuba, and such other parts as shall be nearer thereto than to the residence of any*

*other Consul or Vice Consul of the United States within the same alle-
giance,* the Undersigned Envoy Extraordinary and Minister Plenipotentiary of the said United States has the honor to enclose Mr. McLean's
commission, and to request that his Excellency Count Almodovar, First
Minister of State and of Foreign affairs of her Catholic Majesty will
cause the corresponding exequatur to be issued recognizing Mr. McLean
in his official character.

The Undersigned avails himself of the occasion to offer to his Excellency assurances of his highest consideration.

Washington Irving.

MANUSCRIPT: NA, RG 84 (letterbook copy).

1. Samuel McLean of Washington D.C. served as U.S. consul at Cienfuegos
in 1843 and 1844. See Hasse, *Index to U.S. Documents,* III, 1745.

1545. To Madame Albuquerque

[Madrid, January 24, 1843]

My "great devil" Antonio is at your command, and is instructed to wait
on Mr. Albuquerque today for his orders. As your note makes no mention
of the arrival of your brother[1] I presume he is lingering among the belles
of Cadiz or Seville.

I hope you have recovered from the effects of the dance the other
evening.[2]

PUBLISHED: W. R. Benjamin, Autographs, *The Collector,* no. 854, p. 7.

The printed transcription spells the name of the recipient as "Albaquerque."
In reality, she was the former Miss Oakey of New York City and wife of the
Brazilian ambassador in Madrid at the time WI was U.S. minister. The description in *The Collector* suggests that the letter was written between 1826 and 1829
on WI's first visit to Spain, but the perpetual calendar establishes the year as 1843,
a date corroborated by WI's allusion to Antonio, his cook at that time.

1. Daniel Oakey, the son of Daniel Oakey, a New York merchant whose business was located at 140 Pearl Street. See *Longworth's Directory of New York for
1841,* p. 477.

2. This sentence was a postscript, according to the description in *The Collector.*

1546. To Catharine Paris

Madrid Feb 6. 1843.

My dear Sister,

I have again to thank you for another letter[1] from your unwearied pen; full, as usual, of interesting domestic details. It has come most opportunely to enliven me during a confinement of several days to the house, by indisposition, the consequence of a cold. I cannot but smile at one question in your letter—whether *we have sleighing at Madrid*? For the greater part of this winter the thermometer has rarely been below the freezing point except at nights: and we have had long spells of bright, warm sunny weather as in the month of June. The public promenades have been crowded; the company walking or sitting in groupes *in the shade*, as in Summer time. I have enjoyed it greatly; having, in consequence of too much sedentary and mental occupation, been obliged to give myself complete holy day for a time; but this soft weather played me a trick. You must know that this brilliant beautiful climate of Madrid[2] requires to be as much watched as our little chestnut horse. We are here in an elevated region of table land, two thirds as high as the Catskill mountains; with broad sunny plains around us. & a powerful sun overhead; we breathe a thin pure subtle air, to me exquisitely enlivening, but irritating to the nerves and quick to produce inflammation; while we have the Guadarama mountains near at hand, for many months of the year covered with snow, from which come nimble airs and searching blasts, apt to take one napping, or catch him at the turn of a corner when off his guard. Indeed from these opposite effects of the Sun and the air, we have two climates in every street, on the sunny and shady sides of the way. As you walk in the one your outer garments are a burthen: as you cross into the other, you gather your cloak about you. The Spaniards, brought up to this climate, are perfect epicures in this matter. We walk out "to take the air"—A Spaniard in winter walks out—*para tomar el Sol*—to take the Sun. The lower orders bask in the sun shine. You see them strewed along in groups: sitting and lying at the foot of the walls on the sunny sides of the streets. As long as there is sun shine the Spaniards are out of doors; the streets are full, the promenades are crowded, but as soon as the sun sets, or the sky clouds up, every one skulks home and sits muffled up in a corner or dozing over a *brasero*.[3]

As I delight in fine weather I enjoyed this spell of summer warmth and sunshine mightily; taking long walks into the neighborhood of the City; the fields being all green as in Spring time, and the landscape as soft and balmy and vapoury, as in ⟨th⟩ our latter part of May. I fancy I got chilled while in a perspiration, by sitting down on the summit of a hill to enjoy a beautiful view of the Guadarama Mountains, and the perfidious breeze which came blowing from them. I was the same night taken by the throat by a sharp cold: struggled with it for a day or two, and then sent for Dr Murta, a worthy, intelligent Irish physician, who attends upon the British Embassy. By his aid I have got the better of the enemy and to morrow shall sally forth again. I shall, henceforth, be more distrustful of these hypocritical freaks of the Madrid winter: which now and then cheats you into security with ⟨the⟩ a warm summer smile and then stabs you to the heart with an icicle.

My worthy and dignified Major domo Benjamin has twice been taken down by this climate; being some what weak in the chest. The first time I was really alarmed for him: he had a violent attack of *pulmonia*, or inflammation of the lungs and nothing ⟨but⟩ saved him but copious bleeding & leeching &c under the direction of an excellent Spanish Physician—Not long after the worthy physician himself was hurried off by the same complaint.

The second attack of Benjamin was the "Spanish cholic" as it is called —another inflammatory complaint. Of this he was cured by Dr Murta. I have had him well taken care of in each instance; and have looked to his comfort and and⁴ good treatment myself.

Notwithstanding these exceptions, I consider this a fine healthful climate to one of my make and constitution: it only requires that one should keep an eye on its skittish freaks; as I used to do on the little chestnut horse—The purity and elasticity of the air have a bracing effect, and enable me to apply myself to mental and sedentary occupations, much more than I could do in other climates without injury to the health.

Feb. 11. Since writing the foregoing I have completely recovered from my indisposition and have been out two or three times: but the weather has become raw and wintry; with rain and flurries of snow, melting as they fall: so that I have kept pretty much to the house.

We have been enlivened by the arrival of an American, (a rare occurrence in Madrid) Mr Daniel Oakey of New York, brother of Madame Albuquerque. We had him and Mr & Mrs Albuquerque to dine at the Legation a day or two since; and ⟨enjoyed a⟩ had quite an American dinner; talking over home and all its concerns. You have no idea how delightful it is to meet with a fellow countryman on this side of the Pyrenees; those barriers which seem to sever us from all the world. Mr Oakey remains here two or three weeks longer, during which time my young folks will be hunting the lions with him about Madrid and parts adjacent. Carnival⁵ is just commencing and I expect they will have gay times.

The day before yesterday I recieved a long letter from the Cottage from my good little Sarah⁶ giving me a budget of pleasant intelligence. Every thing seems to go on well in that peaceful little abode—May the blessing of heaven ever rest upon it!

God bless you my dear Sister

Your affectionate brother
Washington Irving

DOCKETED: Washn Irving to Mrs. Paris / Madrid Feb. 6. 1843.
MANUSCRIPT: Yale.

1. This letter has not been located.
2. The mean annual winter temperature at Madrid is about 43 degrees, but it occasionally drops to 10 degrees. In the summer the average temperature is about 76 degrees. As WI notes, the Guadarrama Mountains to the northwest of the city cause sudden variations in temperature. See Karl Baedeker, *Spain and Portugal*, pp. 58–59; and Richard Ford, *A Hand-Book for Travellers in Spain*, 3 vols. (Carbondale, 1966), III, 1076.
3. A fireplace or hearth.
4. WI repeated "and."
5. In 1843 Lent began on March 8. In the weeks before its start the people often engaged in riotous festivities and merrymaking.
6. This letter has not been located.

1547. To John Miller

Legation of the United States / Madrid February 11th. 1843.

John Miller Esqr. / Agent U. S. Legation—London.

Dear Sir:

I have received your account in duplicate for postage &c paid by you on account of this Legation during the last quarter.

I enclose a check on Messrs Rothschild & Sons for the amount £12..4..3, payable to your order at sight.[1]

Very respectfully / Your obdt Sevt.
Washington Irving.

MANUSCRIPT: NA, RG 84 (letterbook copy).

1. The following copy of WI's draft was included in the letterbook:

Enclosure
Legation of the United States. / Madrid February 11th. 1843.
£12..4..3.
At sight please to pay John Miller Esqr. or order, twelve pounds. four shillings.

and three pence Sterling and charge to the United States on account of the Contingent Expenses of this Legation.

Washington Irving.

Messrs N. M. Rothschild & Sons. / Bankers U. S. London.

1548. *To Sarah Storrow*

Madrid, Feb 11th. 1843.

My dear Sarah,

I received some few days since your letter of Jany 31st.[1] which came to me most welcomely during a weary confinement to the house by indisposition—of which the inclosed letter to your mother[2] makes mention. I had really longed for a letter from you, and never welcomed one more heartily.

I thank you for your entertaining account of the wedding festivities; which, whatever you may think of your epistolary powers, presented the scene to me with graphic effect. I beg you to give me more such details of ⟨your a⟩ the scenes in which you mingle, and give them in your own off hand unpretending manner. You hit the mark when you least suspect it.

I am writing despatches today and therefore have to be brief with my private letters—Besides, I have recently felt the effect slightly, of overtasking myself with ↑the↓ various exercises of the pen, and have had to give myself complete relaxation—So I trust you will take the enclosed letter to your mother instead of one to yourself, and when you have read it forward it to her, with some additions of your own to make it more welcome. Do not however let ⟨my⟩ the brief & unsatisfactory nature of my letter prevent you from writing to me promptly and fully You do not know how precious your letters are to me—I will repay them by copious replies when I have more time and mood for letter writing. Give my kind remembrances to Mr Storrow and kiss my darling little Kate for me

Your affectionate uncle
Washington Irving

Manuscript: Yale.

1. This letter has not been located.
2. Probably WI's letter of February 6, 1843.

1549. To Daniel Webster

Legation of the United States / Madrid February. 11th. 1843.

No. 16 / The Hon: Daniel Webster. / Secretary of State of the U. S—
Washington.

Sir:

I have the honor to acknowledge the receipt of your despatch No. 10.
which, being forwarded by the way of Lisbon, was upwards of two
months in reaching me; whereas letters forwarded via *London* or *Havre*
generally come to hand within a month.

I shall attend to your instructions in endeavoring to see strict justice
done in the law suit between John. W. Damon and Frederick Tudor[1] and
to prevent either party taking the other by surprise. I must observe,
however, that letters from highly respectable sources in the United States,
such as Mr. William H. Prescott of Boston, and Mr. Alexr: H. Everett,
formerly Minister at this Court, represent Mr. Tudor as being decidedly
the aggrieved party.[2] Mr. Everett was personally cognizant of the details
of the suit, in its progress through the Colonial Courts of Cuba.

The application for an Exequatur for Mr. Samuel McLean, appointed
Consul for the port of Cien Fuegoste, was made by me on the 25th.
January.[3] I have since received the draft of P. Harmony & Co. on F. X.
Harmony Cadiz for $18.25 forwarded through the Department of State
by Mr. McLean to defray the expenses of procuring his Exequatur.

My despatch No. 14. gave you, as far as I could understand it, the state
of the negotiations between the French and Spanish Governments on the
subject of the indignities which Louis Philippe conceived he had sustained
in the aspersions thrown upon the conduct and character of his Consul,
for his intermeddlings in the late affair of Barcelona. I am happy to
inform you that these negotiations are drawing to a close.

For a time the French Government made vague and verbal demands
for a general atonement or apology. The Spanish Government declined
answering any but written and specific demands; at the same time forwarding what it conceived to be sufficient proofs of improper conduct in
various instances on the part of the Consul and requesting his removal.

Within a few days the French Government has given in its ultimatum;
for the first time making its demand in writing, and reducing it to one
specific point—An official letter of the 3d. December last from Gutierrez
the "Political" Chief[4] of Barcelona, to the Minister of the Government of
the Peninsula, at Madrid, in which he charges the French Consul with
having been instrumental in fomenting the insurrection, by causing the
disembarcation of the Rebel Junta from the French Shipping in the

harbor—This letter was published in the Madrid Gazette (The Government paper) on the 8th. of December.[5]

In presenting the note demanding an apology the Duke de Glucksberg, French Chargé des Affaires, signified that, unless it were furnished within eight days, he was instructed to demand his passports.

Now it appears that, however much the Spanish Government may think itself aggrieved by the general intermeddlings of the Consul, yet it has failed to collect proofs of his delinquency on this Specific point. It would appear that the charge was hastily made by Gutierrez, then in the Camp before Barcelona, on rumors brought by fugitives from the City; and his letter to the Minister at Madrid, was published in the Government Gazette with equal want of consideration.

The Spanish Government has consequently felt itself obliged, in the Gazette of the ninth instant,[6] publicly to declare this charge, thus hastily made and inconsiderately published, to have been disproved on diligent investigation. Such a declaration, it is said, the Duke de Glucksberg had previously signified, would be accepted by the French Government as a sufficient atonement. Gutierrez was sometime since removed from his official post in Barcelona, which was considered at the time as a concession made to irritated French feeling. No such concession, I am told, is likely to be reciprocated; The French Government manifesting a determination to continue its consul, Mr. Lesseps at Barcelona, however his general conduct may have appeared exceptionable in the eyes of the Government of Spain, and however his residence at the port in question may be irksome to it. The only instance in which a disposition is shown to yield to the solicitations of this Government, is in removing to some distance from its frontier certain refugee leaders, who have been most active and efficient in stirring up troubles within its territories.

In the mean time faction flourishes in this Country.[7] Money is lavishly distributed by unseen hands feeding sedition and subsidizing a licentious press. Every measure of government is impeded. The turbulent population of Barcelona is daily instigated to new outbreaks, and is only kept down by the iron hand of military rule, and though the punishments inflicted upon those most active in the late insurrection have been moderate in number, considering the gravity of the case, and though the greater part of the contributions have been remitted, yet the City remains like a half:extinguished Volcano; ready at any moment for another eruption.

I enclose with this despatch a copy of a manifesto just issued by the Regent, intended no doubt to have an effect on the approaching election.[8] He has been driven to this by the virulent and incessant attacks upon him by the press; misrepresenting his character and conduct and attributing to him motives and aims which he indignantly, and I believe honestly, disclaims.

In the mean time, until the election be decided, it is useless to attempt to carry on any business with this Government: the general affairs of the Country being very much interrupted and neglected. It remains to be seen whether the next Cortes will present a majority according in principles, and representing the popular will; out of which the Regent may be able to form a cabinet capable of carrying on the Government; or whether it is to present another overpowering coalition of factions,— if the latter, we shall be one long stride nearer to chaos.

I am, Sir, very respectfully /Your Obdt Sevt.
Washington Irving

DOCKETED: Rec Mar 23d / mr Markoe
MANUSCRIPT: NA, RG 59.

Only the signature is in WI's handwriting.

1. Damon was probably Tudor's agent in Havana. See WI to George Ticknor, January 11, 1843.
2. These letters have not been located.
3. WI erred in the date. See his letter to Count Almodóvar, January 23, 1843.
4. This same phrase is used by Víctor Balaguer to describe Don Juan Gutiérrez. See *Historia de Cataluña y la Corona de Aragón* (Barcelona, 1863), V, 699.
5. See *La Gaceta*, no. 2984, December 8, 1842.
6. Actually the letter of Espartero, dated February 9, 1843, appeared in *La Gaceta* on February 10, 1843.
7. For details, see *El Castellano*, January 12, 17, 20, 25, 31, February 2, 1843.
8. The three and one-half page printed document in Spanish is preserved with this despatch. The elections were scheduled for February 27, 1843, but some of them did not take place until March 2 and 3. See WI to Daniel Webster, January 9, 1843.

1550. To Pablo Anguera

Legation of the United States / Madrid Feby 14th. 1843.

Pablo Anguera Esqr.

Sir.

I have to acknowledge the receipt of your letter of the 9th. Inst, expressing your surprise at the appointment of Mr. Pon as Consul at Barcelona and your hope that my letter in your favor to the Government might have the effect of nullifying that appointment. I regret with you that my letter should have arrived after the appointment had been made; but whatever effect it might have had previously, it certainly can have none in reversing an appointment made no doubt on sufficient grounds.

In compliance [with]¹ instructions from the Department of State I applied for an Exequatur for Mr Pon on the 29th. October last: but as yet none has been issued. I attribute this delay on the part of the Spanish Government to its extreme caution in respect to any new Consular appointments in the present critical state of Barcelona.

I am sure I need not tell you, for your individual guidance during the time you may continue in office, that it is the especial policy of our Government, expressly enjoined on its agents, that, whatever may be their private opinions and feelings, they *officially* observe a strict neutrality in the political affairs of the Country to which they are accredited; and never interfere *officially*, either by name or in person, in public matters, but when it is absolutely necessary for the protection of the national interests confided to their charge.

I would further observe that throughout the late disturbances at Barcelona, I have been the only Diplomatic representative at this Court who has received no information of the course of affairs from the Consular Agent of his Government resident at that port, I have been obliged therefore to look to other sources for the facts which it was my duty to communicate from time to time to my Government.

I am Sir / very respectfully / Your Obdt Sevt
Washington Irving

MANUSCRIPT: NA, RG 84 (letterbook copy).

For other details about Anguera, see WI to Daniel Webster, August 27, 1842; and PMI, III, 347.

1. The copyist omitted the bracketed word.

1551. To George Read

Legation of the United States / Madrid Feby. 15th. 1843.

Geo. Read Esqr / Consul of the U States Malaga.

Dear Sir,

I received this morning your letter informing me that a person by the name of Ignacio Figueroa had announced himself at Adra as having been appointed by me Vice Consul of the United States at that place.

I have made no such appointment and do not know the individual in question.

I remember on a visit to Adra in 1828, passing a very agreeable evening at the house of a very worthy and respectable gentleman of the name of Kirkpatrick[1] a relation I presume of the Mr. Kirkpatrick of whom you make mention.

Very respectfully / Your Obdt Sevt
Washington Irving

Manuscript: NA, RG 84 (letterbook copy).

1. WI had visited William Kirkpatrick at Adra on March 24, 1828, on his trip through Andalusia. See *Journal 1828*, p. 43. At this time WI apparently was not aware that Kirkpatrick was the father of the Countess Montijo, whose ball he had described in his letter of January 15, 1843, to Sarah Storrow.

1552. To Sarah Storrow

Madrid. Feb 24th. 1843

My dear Sarah,

I received some days since your letter without a date, giving me a very amusing account of the Jones Ball——I had just written the above when I received your delightful letter of the 17th.[1] How comforting how delicious these letters are to me—I would indeed, have enjoyed your charming little soiree—it was just the kind of party that I delight in—Your accounts of the Jones family interest me. I am glad to hear that the Baron Tropbriand is likely to make so good a husband, and to have so favorable an influence over the manners of the family. You are passing a happy winter, and it rejoices my heart to think so—But my dear Sarah, let me ask you, as Hamlet says, to "absent yourself from happiness a while"[2] now and then, and write me more such letters, without waiting for a reply—at some future time I will repay you abundantly—At present I have to throw by my pen and to give up all occupation—I have foolishly overtasked myself and must abide the penalty. After the cold which confined me to the house for some days, came on a herpetic attack, similar to that brought on me about twenty years since, by too much application to the pen. It first siezed me by the ancles & lamed me. and afterwards attacked other parts of my body. I have been lying on a Sofa for nearly a fortnight—endeavouring to amuse myself with light reading. The weather has been incessantly raining so that I have only twice been able to get an airing in the carriage—I have however, excellent servants, a good physician and have begun a course of baths which I trust will in a little while make me myself again—These attacks are not dangerous, but very tormenting. The evil with me is that I am obliged to forego all close mental occupation; as that was the cause of the malady. This is the first letter I have written for many days.

I shall be most happy to receive the promised letter from Mrs Ledyard; though I know not when I shall be able to reply to it.

Kiss my dear little Kate, and continue to tell me all about her—Her very fits of passion and her quarrels with dolls & teaspoons are amusing to me—Give my kind remembrances to your good husband

God bless you my dear Sarah / Your affectionate Uncle
Washington Irving

ADDRESSED: Madame / Madame Storrow / 17. Rue de Faubg Poissonniere / a Paris
MANUSCRIPT: Yale.

1. These letters have not been located.
2. WI's variation of *Hamlet*, V, 2, 358.

1553. *To Eliza McCloud*

Legation of the United States. / Madrid February 25h. 1843.

Mrs. Eliza McCloud

Madam

I received in the latter part of December your letter in relation to your claim upon Don Enriqu-Bayo for services rendered and money loaned to him during his visit to the United States in the year 1839.

Soon after the receipt of your letter I employed Mr. John Merino, a gentleman connected with the Legation to visit Mr. Bayo's mother, and obtain if possible the payment of your claim.

By the enclosed letter from Mr. Merino you will see that the family of Mr. Bayo are not at present in a situation to repay you, and that he himself is absent from the City and has been prevented by illness from entering upon the duties of an office to which he has been appointed. I also enclose a note from his mother Mrs. Henry.

I hope that Mr. Bayo will be enabled in time to satisfy a debt which has such strong claims upon him, and shall have much pleasure in forwarding to you any sums which I may receive for this purpose.

I am respectfully / Your Obdt Sevt.
Washington Irving

MANUSCRIPT: NA, RG 84 (letterbook copy).

1554. To Catharine Paris

Madrid March 4th 1843

My dear Sister,

I wrote to you about three weeks since[1] when recovering as I thought from an indisposition the consequence of a cold. That indisposition was immediately followed by an attack of Herpes; an inflammatory disease of the skin, similar to that which I experienced about twenty years since, but much more virulent—as that was confined to the legs whereas this has extended to every limb, indeed to the whole body. It is the result as in the former instance of having overtasked myself—and taken too little exercise. But I had many tasks literary diplomatic & Epistolary to cope with and was anxious to get a head so fagged way for three or four months incessantly until I deranged my system. It is fortunate that the effects took this course—as, had they attacked the head the consequences might have been disastrous indeed. The complaint under which I labor though ⟨t⟩ annoying and obstinate is not dangerous, and is to be conquered by patience, perseverance and medicated baths; but I am obliged to give my mind complete holyday & renounce all mental occupations as they irritate the complaint. So dont expect to hear much from me for some time to come, but I hope you will all write to me—for letters from home are perfectly balmy Yesterday I received a delightful one from my dear little Mary[2] which had a most cheering effect. It brought Sweet little Sunny side and all its dear inmates before me and gave me a variety of pleasant domestic details Today I received a long and excellent letter from David Davidson[3] informing me of his having been advanced to the post of Book keeper—of the reform and regularity of his fathers family—and of his visit to the Cottage—in which he gave a faithful account of ⟨[*unrecovered*]⟩ every horse, cow dog, chicken &c—It was quite a treat to me.

For some few days past I have passed most of my time in bed as I find the pressure & confinement of clothes very troublesome. My servants are very attentive. Lorenzo is perfectly invaluable—The young gentlemen are very amiable and do all they can to amuse me—Mr Hamilton reads a great part of the day to me—I must conclude to send off by the courier. I have gone into particulars of my case lest you might hear of my being unwell and fancy I was in danger

Give my love to all bodies

Your affectionate brother
W. I.

DOCKETED: Washn. Irving to Mrs. Paris / Madrid March 4, 1843
MANUSCRIPT: SHR.

1. Probably WI's letter of February 6, 1843.
2. This letter has not been located.
3. This letter has not been located.

1555. To Count Almodóvar

Légation des Etats Unis. / Madrid le 7. Mars 1843.

Le Soussigné Envoyé Extráordinaire et Ministre Plenipoténtiare des Etats Unis d'Amerique a l'honneur de faire Savoir a son Excellence Monsieur Le Comte d'Almodovar Premier Ministre d'État et des Affaires Étrangères de sa Majesté Catholique, qu'il vient de recevoir de son Gouvernement des depeches et instructions Sur un Sujet qui lui parait de quelque importance et qui, sans doute, ne sera pas sans intéret pour le Gouvernement de Sa Majesté Catholique.

Le Soussigné, se trouvant dans l'impossibilité d'avoir avec Son Excellence Mons le Comte d'Almodovar une conversation en personne, par suite d'une indisposition assez grave, qui le retrent au lit, prie son Excellence de vouloir bien accordes une entrevue a Monsieur Hamilton, Secretaire de Légation qui passerait chez son Excellence Monsieur le comte d'Almodovar au jour et a l'heure qu'elle voudra bien lui indiquer.

Le Soussigne prie son Excellence Monsieur Le Comte d'Almodovar, d'agreer les assurances de sa plus haute considération.

Washington Irving.

MANUSCRIPT: NA, RG 84 (letterbook copy).

This copy is in WI's handwriting.
Translation:
"The undersigned, envoy extraordinary and minister plenipotentiary of the United States of America, has the honor to make known to his excellency, Count Almodóvar, minister of state and foreign affairs of her Catholic majesty, that he has just received from his government despatches and instructions on a subject which appears to him of some importance and which, doubtless, will not be without interest for her Catholic majesty's government.

"The undersigned, finding it impossible to have a personal conversation with his excellency, Count Almodóvar, owing to a somewhat serious illness which forces him to bed, prays that his excellency will agree to grant an interview with Mr. Hamilton, secretary of the legation, who would call on his excellency at the day and hour he would indicate to him.

"The undersigned begs his excellency to accept his assurances of his highest consideration."

1556. To Daniel Webster

Legation of the United States. / Madrid March 10th. 1843.

No. 17 / The Hon: Daniel Webster. / Secretary of State of the United
States. Washington.

Sir.

I had the honor to receive on the 4th. Inst. Despatch No. 11, from the
Department, enclosing a Copy of the private and confidential letter ad-
dressed by the Department to Mr. Robert. B. Campbell,[1] Consul of the
United States at Havana, and Document No. 35 respecting the Sandwich
Islands.[2]

Having been attacked by a severe disorder which for more than a
month has confined me to the house, and during the past week to my bed,
without a prospect of a very speedy recovery, I was induced, by the importance of the matter connected with the letter to Mr. Campbell; and
which did not admit of delay, or of being made the subject of a communication in writing, to apply to Count Almodovar for an interview
in favor of the Secretary of Legation; and accordingly, after a careful examination of the Archives of the Legation and several conversations with
me on this subject, Mr. Hamilton passed this morning by appointment
to visit the Minister at the Department of State.

Explaining to Count Almodovar in a few words that I was prevented by
indisposition from having the honor of a personal interview, he went on to
state that the Government of the United States, deeply interested in
every event that might affect or alter the present condition of the Island
of Cuba, had received from a source entitled to credit information of
alleged plots and conspiracies which had for their object, an insurrection of the Creoles and Slaves; the expulsion of the Spaniards from the
Island and the establishment of a black military republic on the ruins
of the existing government. He mentioned the statements in regard to
the agents of the abolition Societies; their offers of Ships of War, and the
aid and protection of a great naval power; and concluded by saying that
tho' the Government of the United States did not place much reliance
upon these statements, yet taken in connexion with notorious occurrences,
they were induced to investigate the foundations on which they rested,
and at the same time to give notice of their existence to the Government
of Her Majesty, in order that by a frank interchange of information and
views upon a subject, in which they had a common interest, steps might
be taken (if necessary) to prevent the accomplishment of designs affecting the peace and prosperity of both Countries.

In reply Count Almodovar mentioned that he had some days before, received a despatch from Her Majesty's Minister in Washington,[3] containing the substance of this information, as well as full and circumstantial reports from the Governor General,[4] and local authorities of the Island in corroboration of the Statements furnished to the Government of the United States: That this subject had naturally received the careful consideration of Her Majesty's Government, and that instructions had been forwarded to Her Majesty's Minister at Washington, and to the authorities of the Island, to take the necessary measures to put down, and punish severely any attempts at revolt which might be made; That the military and naval force of the Island was in good condition, and the fortifications at strong points had been strengthened and increased: Finally, that the Government of Her Majesty did not at present entertain serious apprehensions in regard to the Island; while at the same time it was deeply sensible of and grateful for the kind offers of assistance made by the Government of the United States through Her Majesty's Minister at Washington, and their own representative at this Court, and in case of need, would avail itself with pleasure of the aid of the United States to defeat attempts which the two nations were alike interested in suppressing.

I avail myself of a private opportunity tonight to send off this brief account to the care of the Legation of the United States at Paris; and shall immediately transmit to the Department any further information which I may be able to procure on this subject.

The Ministry have obtained a complete triumph in this City in the elections of Senators and Deputies to sit in the Cortes which meet on the 4th. of April next.[5] The returns from the peninsula generally are not yet sufficiently authentic to enable me to form an opinion as to which side the majority will incline.

I am, Sir, very respectfully / Your Obdt Sevt.
Washington Irving

DOCKETED: Recd. 21 April / Mr. Markoe
MANUSCRIPT: NA, RG 59.   PUBLISHED: Manning, *Diplomatic Correspondence*, 331–32 (in part).

Only the signature is in WI's handwriting.

1. Webster had written to Campbell to verify allegations made in a letter from a high-placed Cuban that the British, being thwarted in their attempts to eliminate slavery in Cuba, were prepared to bring ruin to the island by fomenting insurrection of the slaves and offering them independence, and that white Cubans and Spaniards there preferred to have American intervention and occupation of the island to continued British agitation. Through Hamilton, WI communicated to Count Almodóvar that the United States "never would permit the occupation of [Cuba] by British agents or forces upon any pretext whatsoever; and that in the

event of any attempt to wrest it from [Spain], she might securely rely upon the whole naval and military resources of [the United States] to aid her in preserving or recovering it." See John Bassett Moore, A *Digest of International Law*, VI, 450–51.

2. This document related to United States recognition of the Hawaiian Kingdom as a sovereign government. For details concerning Webster's action, see Moore, A *Digest of International Law*, I, 476–78; and *Treaties and Other International Acts of the U. S. A.*, ed. Hunter Miller, V, 600–02.

3. Pedro Alcántara Argaïz was the Spanish minister in Washington.

4. Lieutenant-General Gerónimo Valdés (1784–1855) was governor-general of Cuba from 1841 to September of 1843. See Hugh Thomas, *Cuba, or the Pursuit of Freedom* (New York, 1971), p. 202, 207.

5. In Madrid the Ministerialist slate of ten candidates—Argüelles, Mendizábal, A. González, Beroqui, Angulo, Acevedo, J. Mendez, A. Santos, Sánchez Ocaña, Lorente—won easily over the Progresista and Moderado slates. See *El Castellano*, March 4, 1843. Election results from outlying areas trickled in throughout the rest of the month. See *El Castellano*, March 7, 16, 17, 18, 20, 21, 31, 1843.

1557. To Count Almodóvar

[March 16, 1843]

El Señor Irving Ministro Plenipotenciaro de los Estados Unidos besa las manos al Exmo Señor Conde de Almodovar y tiene la honra de poner en el conocimiento de S. E. que todos los efectos señalados para el uso de su casa, e incluidos en la lista con fecha de 27 de Agosto del año pasado; no han llegado todavia en esta corte.

El Señor Irving por esta razon pide con respeto que S. E. se sirva mandar expedir las ordenes necessarias extendiendo el tiempo para la libre entrada de los efectos incluidos en dicha lista; y entretanto aprovecha gustoso esta ocasion para ofrecer al Exmo Señor Conde de Almodovar las seguridades de su distinguida consideracion.

Washington Irving
Legacion de los Estados Unidos / El 16 de Marzo de 1843

Exmo Señor / Conde de Almodovar / &c &c &c

DOCKETED: Marzo 19/1843 / Dejado á Hacienda / para que por aquel / Minsterio se expidan / las ordenes correspondientes / sirbiendose transladarlo / a este Ministerio para / conocimiento de Mr. Irving / fecho ("March 19/1843 / Left at the Exchequer so that said Ministry can issue the corresponding orders and advise this Ministry for Mr. Irving's information. done")

MANUSCRIPT: Archivo de Ministerio de Asuntes Exteriores, Madrid; NA, RG 84 (letterbook copy).

Only the signature is in WI's handwriting.
Translation:

"The minister plenipotentiary of the United States sends his warmest regards to the most excellent Count Almodóvar and has the honor of advising his excellency that none of his household effects included in the list of August 27 of last year have yet arrived in Madrid.

"For this reason Mr. Irving respectfully requests that his excellency be so kind as to issue the appropriate orders extending the deadline for the effects included in said list; and meanwhile he gladly takes advantage of this occasion to offer the most excellent Count Almodóvar the assurances of his distinguished consideration."

1558. To Señor de Barzanallana

Legacion de los Estados Unidos / Madrid el 22 de Marzo de 1843

El Señor Irving Ministro Plenipotenciario de los Estados Unidos B. L. M. al Exmo Señor Director General de Aduanas, y tiene la honra de poner en su conscimiento que hallandose en la actualidad detenido en la cama por una enfermedad bastante grave, El Señor Hamilton Secretario de Esta legacion pasara a visitar al Señor Director General para tratar de un asunto de alguna importancia, a las dos de la tarda de este dia, si conviene tal hora al Señor de Barzanallana.

El Señor Irving aprovecha esta ocasion para ofrecer al Señor De Barzanallana las seguridades de su distinguida consideracion.

Washington Irving.

Exmo Señor. / Director General de Aduanas. / &ca &ca &ca

MANUSCRIPT: NA, RG 84 (letterbook copy).

Translation:

"Mr. Irving, minister plenipotentiary of the United States, sends his respects to his excellency director general of customs and has the honor of informing him that finding himself actually detained in bed by a somewhat serious illness, Mr. Hamilton, secretary of this legation, will visit the director general in order to deal with an affair of some importance, at two in the afternoon today, if such an hour is agreeable to Señor de Barzanallana.

"Mr. Irving takes this occasion to offer Señor de Barzanallana the assurances of his most distinguished consideration."

In the left margin of the letterbook is the following note: "In regard to Barque Empress but not sent, as orders to free the vessel had been already forwarded by the Director General"

1559.   To George Read

Legation of the United States. / Madrid. 22nd. March. 1843.
George Read. Esqr. U. S. Consul. Malaga.

Sir.

I have to acknowledge the receipt of your letter of the 13th. Instant, with the accompanying documents, in relation to the case of the American Barque "Empress".[1]

Arrangements had been made for an interview on this subject with the Director General of the Customs this day, to represent to him the hardship of this case; but having already received copies of the Documents, he had, as I am just informed, promptly given orders for the liberation of the vessel, which were forwarded by the Courier of yesterday.

For this friendly act, I have already taken occasion to offer my thanks; and I cannot close this letter, without expressing to you also, my sense of the activity and zeal you have manifested in the protection of the interests confided to your charge.

I am, respectfully / Your Obdt Sevt.
Washington Irving

P. S. Since writing the above, your second letter of the 17th. Instant, with the accompanying Documents has been received: Representations will be promptly made without delay to the Government of Her Catholic Majesty, which will, no doubt adopt such measures as the circumstances of the case may appear to require.

W. I.

ADDRESSED: Señr. / Don Jorge Read / Consul de los Estados Unidos / de America. / Malaga . Espana.   POSTMARKED: Madrid / 1 / [*unrecovered*] 1843 / 22 Mar 1843. / Mala[ga] / 3 [*unrecovered*] 1843 / ANDAL. B.
MANUSCRIPT: NA, RG 84 (also letterbook copy).

Only the signature is in WI's handwriting.

1. For a full statement of the problem relating to the *Empress*, see WI to Count Almodóvar, March 27, 1843.

1560. To George Read

Legation of the United States. / Madrid March 24h. 1843.

George Read Esqr. U. S. Consul, Malaga.

Sir,

After an examination of the Archives of the Legation and particularly your correspondence, with my predecessor, Mr. Vail, it appears to me that there may exist a misconstruction of the provisions of the Royal Arauncel in relation to the duties on Codfish, by which an important discrimination is made against American cured fish, in favor of that of England and France.

As the Araunccl or Tariff provides that vessels, coming direct from the Fisheries shall be subject to a certain rate of duty, which is increased by about one fourth, when they do not proceed direct; and as the Ports in Newfoundland and Labrador, are considered as Fishing Ports, while those of Maine or Massachusetts are not; it is evident that the English or French vessel, fitted out from any of the former, with a differential duty of one fourth in its favor, can utterly exclude from the trade vessels of the United States, sailing from the Ports of the above States.

This distinction (if it exist) is clearly unfounded, and could not have been intended by the framers of the law; and in order that the proper construction of the terms of the Arauncel may be established, I have to request that you will address the following interrogatories to the Intendente or Chief of the Customs at your port, in such manner that his answers may be laid (if requisite) before the Director General in this City.

1st. What rate of duty would be demanded on the Cargo of an American Vessel, fitted out from Eastport, Machias, Portsmouth, or any other port of Maine or Massachusetts, and proceeding direct from the Fisheries with a Cargo of Codfish to the Port of Malaga?

2nd. Would any discrimination be made between the case of An American Vessel, proceeding direct from any of the Ports mentioned, and an English Ship coming also direct from a port of Newfoundland?

The following Questions can be answered by yourself.

1st. Has any American Vessel arrived at the port of Malaga, laden with Codfish, in whole or in part within the last five years, and if so, what duties were demanded on the Cargo?

2 At what price, can the fish arriving in English vessels, be profitably sold in your port, and what is the average of this price?

3 Can you state, approximately what quantity of F[ish] [MS torn] is

imported annually into the Port of Malaga [in] [*MS torn*] English vessels?

You will oblige me by procuring the answ[ers] [*MS torn*] to these interrogatories as soon as possible and transmitting them with any other information on this subject, which may come within your knowledge.

I am, Sir, Respectfully / Your Obdt Sert.
Washington Irving

ADDRESSED: Señr. / Don Jorge Read / Consul de los Estados Unidos. / en *Malaga*.
   POSTMARKED: [*unrecovered*] / 1843 / 1 / C[?]STLA[?] / 1.
MANUSCRIPT: NA, RG 84 (also letterbook copy dated March 23, 1843).

Only the signature is in WI's handwriting.

1561. To Robert B. Campbell

Legation of the United States. / Madrid March 25h. 1843.

Robert B. Campbell Esqr. U. S. Consul–Havana

Sir,
   I herewith forward to your[1] your Exequatur received two or three days since from the office of State, and your original Commission signed by the President of the United States–They are sent by the Spanish Government packet, which sails from Cadiz on the 1st. of April:
   The draft, in duplicate, on a Banker in this city for the payment of the fees on the Exequatur, has been duly received.

I am respectfully / Your Obdt Sevt.
Washington Irving

MANUSCRIPT: NA, RG 84 (letterbook copy).

   1. The copyist probably intended to write "you."

1561a. To Catharine Paris

Madrid ⟨Feb⟩ ↑March↓ 25. 1843

My dear Sister,
   I wrote to you about three weeks since,[1] informing you of my indisposition, suffering under a severe attack of herpes, or inflammation of the

skin. Since then I have been miserably ill; having taken cold in the course of my medicated baths which struck the complaint inwards and produced a derangement of the system, accompanied by fever, total loss of appetite &c, and confining me helplessly to my bed. My Irish physician called in the aid of an experienced Spanish physician, & by bleeding and careful treatment they have succeeded in conquering the fever; restoring the stomach to its functions and leaving nothing but the original complaint to contend with. I now begin to sit up part of the day and am able to relish light food; but as you may suppose am much enfeebled and reduced. My illness has been aggravated by the harsh, wet and chilly weather; which has prevailed during the whole time & which ⟨t⟩ in this subtle climate has great influence over an invalid. The Season however is in my favor. ⟨The⟩ Spring is about to burst forth in all its beauty and I hope in the course of a few days to be well enough to take daily drives in the carriage. I have a most excellent, devoted, intelligent Servant in Lorenzo who watches over me and nurses me as if I were a child. He sleeps in my room every night, and in fact is my best Doctor. Juana also has proved herself most kind, attentive and efficient—as to Benjamin, he has shewn himself the complete "old Soldier"—pursuing his usual routine of duties, but taking none of the extra toil and care occasioned by my illness.

The young gentleman of the Legation have been all that I could wish—passing a great part of the time in my room, reading to me by the hour and doing every thing they could to alleviate the evils of my situation. Hamilton especially has attended to me with incessant assiduity and with a womans kindness. I cannot speak too highly of his conduct.

It will take me some time no doubt, to conquer this irksome malady—but I shall be daily gaining strength, and shall be able to drive out, to amuse myself by light reading, and to receive visits occasionally from my friends—⟨for⟩ to whom, for some time past, I have been denied.

While in this state of illness and suffering my spirits have been sadly affected by news of the illness of our dear Sister, about whom I feel great anxiety: but hope to hear accounts of her convalescence. I received also, yesterday a letter from Pierre M Irving,[2] relating the conduct of that miserable animal Phil Paulding.[3] I feel deeply for poor Kate—yet there is a consolation in the idea that she has escaped a connexion with such ⟨an⟩ a selfish drivelling dolt, who really seems to have something of mental imbecillity mingled with his meanness. In fact, whatever affection she may have felt for him must soon be completely superceded by contempt. But enough of these melancholy themes—I hope & trust my next letter will be more cheerful—

This is quite an exertion for me—and I have two or three other letters to write—after which I must again renounce the pen for a while—

for I dare not risk much mental exertion in my present debilitated state the least excitement producing irritation in my complaint.

I received lately a sweet letter from my dear little Mary, and delightful ones also from Helen and Eliza.[4] I hope they will write again without waiting for replies from me—

Give my affectionate regards to "all bodies" and tell Julia Grinnell I am glad to hear such "beautiful" accounts of her little Fanny.[5]

God bless you my dear Sister

Your affectionate brother
Washington Irving

DOCKETED: Washington Irving to Mrs. Paris / Madrid. March 25. 1843.
MANUSCRIPT: Harriet Paris Philips.

1. See WI to Catharine Paris, March 6, 1843.
2. This letter has not been located.
3. For other reactions to Philip Paulding's behavior, see WI to Sarah Storrow, April 13, 1843.
4. These letters have not been located.
5. Fanny Leslie Grinnell, daughter of Moses and Julia Grinnell, was born on September 23, 1842.

1562. To Sarah Storrow

Madrid, March 25th. 1843.

My dear Sarah,

Since last I wrote to you I have been wretchedly ill. A cold which I took in the course of my medicated baths, struck the complaint inwardly and produced fever and sad derangement of my system. For nearly three weeks I have been confined to my bed, almost helpless. Suffering under a slow fever &c.

I have ⟨had⟩ both an Irish & Spanish physician and by their careful treatment the fever has been conquered. I am beginning to sit up a little, and my appetite is gradually returning to me; but I am much enfeebled & reduced. I have now nothing but my herpetic complaint to contend with—which I hope gradually to cure—The season will be in my favor as soon as I can venture out—

The young gentlemen of my legation have been most kind & attentive to me; reading to me by the hour; for I was unable to read myself—Alexander Hamilton ⟨has⟩ above all has exerted the most unremitting attention and kindness—seeking in every way to alleviate my Sufferings—I can not speak too highly of his amiable and affectionate assiduities

Lorenzo has proved himself a perfect jewel. He sleeps every night in my room and watches over me with the most faithful and devoted vigilance—

Juana too is kind, attentive and efficient. The "faithful Benjamin" has proved himself rather an "old soldier" taking as little extra care and trouble as he possibly could—

I scrawl this with difficulty—I have received two or three letters from you[1] since I last wrote—If you knew what a solace they were, you would write oftener and fuller—

God bless you and yours—

Kiss Kate for me—

Your affectionate uncle
Washington Irving

MANUSCRIPT: Yale.

1. These letters have not been located.

1563. To Count Almodóvar

Legation of the United States. / Madrid March 27th. 1843.

The Undersigned Envoy Extraordinary and Minister Plenipotentiary of the United States has the honor to present to His Excellency Count Almodovar, First Minister of State and of Foreign Affairs of Her Catholic Majesty the following statement of a recent occurrence at Malaga, to which the Undersigned would respectfully solicit the earliest attention of His Excellency.

It appears that the Barque "Empress" of New York of more than 200 Tons burthen, Captain Moses Townsend, arrived at the Port of Malaga, on the 3d. Instant, and that on being visited by the Health Commission, the Captain stated he was from Gibraltar in ballast.

Immediately on landing, the Captain visited the Consignees of the vessel, and stated to them that he had on board some barrels of rosin as ballast, and other articles shipped at Gibralter for New York: Finding that his technical use of the word "*ballast*" to denote that his vessel was "*light*", or without Cargo might be misinterpreted, he immediately made the necessary correction at the Health Office (Junta de Sanidad) and an entry of the circumstance was accordingly made in the Register of that office.

On presenting his Manifest at the Custom House the next day within the time required by law, it was refused; and the "Administrador" shortly after proceeded to visit the vessel, and to mark and Seal (prescintar y sellar) the goods on board in order to disembark and deposit them in the Custom House.

At this stage of the proceeding, the Consul of the United States interposed and wrote to the Intendente protesting against the landing of the goods: In reply the Intendente stated, that after examining the case, he believed that there was bad faith on the part of Captain Townsend in not presenting, as laid down by Article 3d. of the Instructions of the Custom House, a note of the Cargo, when required by the Resguardo, and that altho he, the Intendente *had referred the case to His Asesor de Rentas, who had given an opinion favorable to the Captain,* he should nevertheless take upon himself the responsibility of renewing the order to land the goods, and detain the vessel until he could consult the Direccion de Aduanas at Madrid.

In answer to this letter the Consul offered to prove by the Health Commission itself that *no officer of the Resguardo had visited the vessel on arriving*; that no note of the Cargo had been required; that the Captain (who visited Spain for the first time) had corrected the mistake as to the word "ballast" in the report to the "Junta de Sanidad" as soon as he was made aware of it, and finally the Consul urged that inasmuch as the legal advisers of the Intendente had given an opinion favorable to the Captain, the vessel ought not to be subjected to a vexatious detention and unlading, especially as a return Cargo to the United States was waiting to be Shipped.

The Consul also applied to the Commandant General, Judge Protector of Strangers, who in reply stated, that he had referred the case to the Señor Asesor del Juzgado, who gave his opinion, supported by that of the fiscal letrado, that "there was no ground for the unlading and detention of the Empress," (no hay merito para la descarga y detencion de la Empress) and that a copy of this letter from the Commandant General had been furnished to the Intendente.—I have the honor to enclose a copy of this letter from the Commandant General with the legal opinions, to your Excellency.

Notwithstanding the opinions of the Commandant General and three officers of the law against him, and the offer to prove by the Health officers that no note of the cargo had been asked on arrival, and that therefore, there could be no intention to defraud the revenue, or conceal the cargo, the Intendente persisted in detaining the vessel, until he forwarded his views of the case to the Direccion General in this city. The Consul also forwarded to this Legation copies of all the Documents: These, the Undersigned was on the point of presenting to the Director General, when he was informed that that officer upon the statement of the Intendente, had immediately with a promptitude and intelligence which do him the highest credit, given orders for the liberation of the vessel.

Here the matter might have rested, and the injury so promptly redressed by the Directer General of the Customs might have called for no further notice, had not the Intendente thought proper to add to his already rude and arbitrary proceedings, further acts of needless violence, insulting to the flag of a friendly power, and menacing to the lives and property of those, whom it ought to have protected. Instead of waiting for the decision of the Director General, on the representations which had been forwarded by both parties; he persisted in his design of unlading the vessel. The United States Consul interposed and stated that the goods on board were necessary as ballast, and their removal would endanger the safety of the Ship; He at the same time proposed that the Hatches should be Secured, and the keys delivered to the Intendente, and offered to guarantee on his own responsibility that nothing should be unladen from the vessel, nor should she leave the port, until an answer should be received from Madrid:—It was of no avail; the Intendente gave notice that on the 14th. Instant he should proceed to use force (if necessary) to take the cargo out of the vessel: The Consul thereupon applied to the Commandant General who answered with another copy of the opinion of his legal Counsel, requiring that the case should be heard before the Juzgado de Guerra and in the mean time that the discharge of the goods should be suspended; failing which, he, the Commandant General should protest against the acts of the Intendente and make the proper representations to the Government.

Regardless of all these contrary opinions and of every respectful proposition of the American Consul, the Intendente persisted in his violent and arbitrary career as if he were acting against a suspicious rover of the seas, instead of a respectable and well known ship of a friendly power; a regular trader to the port: on the 14h. of this month a boat with armed Carabineers proceded to the ship; The Intendente calling out to them from the mole, in presence of a numerous throng, *to fire upon the crew*, should they make any resistance!; a needless order, since no resistance was intended as the Intendente had been repeatedly assured in writing by the Consul. No resistance in fact was offered; the vessel was seized; the flag of the United States which had been spread over the hatches, in hope of inspiring respect, was stripped away; The hatches were broken open, and a part of the Cargo landed; it being impossible to land the whole, without peculiar risk of the overturning of the vessel.

The American consul now lowered the insulted flag of his Country seeing that it gave no protection against arbitrary violence, and the

Captain and crew abandoned the Ship. In consequence however of her dangerous and exposed situation the Consul afterwards replaced the Captain and crew as Ship keepers to preserve her for any parties interested.

The Undersigned submits this statement founded on official documents with as few comments as possible; in fact, it needs none, but will speak for itself to the quick intelligence and high sense of justice of Count Almodovar—He will perceive that the original detention of the vessel was a vexatious, unfriendly and self willed proceeding on the part of the Intendente, opposed almost unanimously by the other officers of the port; protested against by his superior; especially counselled against by the legal advisers, and condemned immediately and without hesitation by the Director General of this City.

He will perceive that the subsequent harsh and violent seizure of the vessel was not necessary for the protection of the revenue; the Consul of the United States having offered every precaution and guarantee on his personal responsability to maintain the ship, in her actual condition until the decision of the authorities at Madrid could be known.

He will perceive too, the gross, violent, and insulting mode of Seizure; in open day, before the whole town; by armed men under the direction of the Intendente with orders to fire on the crew in case of resistance.

What serious consequences menacing to the friendly relations of both countries might have ensued from the execution of that rash order, had any of the crew of the American vessel, irritated by the parade of force, and by what they considered a violation of their flag, been provoked to offer the slightest resistance, the Undersigned will leave to the consideration of Count Almodovar.

As to the damages which may be caused to American Citizens, or other parties in interest by reason of the detention and unlading of the vessel, the Intendente by rejecting (Separandose de) the legal opinion of his asesor de Rentas, has made himself, and will assuredly be held responsable for the same.

But this is not a mere question of pecuniary damages; nor does it merely concern the owners of the vessel. It is a case in which national insult has been mixed up with individual injury, and therefore calls for some measure of national redress.

The Undersigned is confident that the quick sense of honor, and of what is due to their own dignity, will cause Her Majesty's Government to see the matter in this light, and that the friendly feelings, which he is satisfied it reciprocates with his own Government will make it prompt and eager to discountenance a transaction, so hazardous to the amicable relations happily existing between the two Countries. He is confident that it will be eager to vindicate the character of its commercial regulations, in the eye of the world, from the stigma of this act of arbitrary violence, unusual in the intercourse of civilized nations.

What expiation on the part of the delinquent officer will be a sufficient atonement for his insulting conduct to a friendly flag, the Undersigned will not pretend to specify—He leaves it to Her Majesty's Government to determine whether it can trust the controul of one of its most important Marts of commerce, in the hands of a man capable by a wilful abuse of power to embroil the peaceful relations of the Country and to banish every friendly sail from the port, over which he so arrogantly pretends to domineer.

The Undersigned takes this occasion to renew to His Excellency the assurances of his most distinguished consideration.

(Signed) Washington Irving

His Excellency / Count Almodovar / &ca. &ca. &ca.

MANUSCRIPT: NA, RG 84 (letterbook copy); NA, RG 59 (copy).

A copy of this letter was enclosed with WI's despatch no. 18 of April 1, 1843, to Daniel Webster.

1564. To Charles R. Leslie

Madrid, March 28, 1843

... Mrs. William Van Wart, wife of one of my Birmingham nephews, has really a very superior talent for painting in water colours and surprised me, when I was last in England, by the excellence of some of her productions. The present hard times render it important for her to turn her talent—to profit—she is—preparing drawings for exhibition and sale in London but will require the advice and countenance of some person of experience and 'authority' in the art of bringing them advantageously before the public. Will you be that person—for the sake of old friends and 'auld lang syne.' I cannot say more—as I am writing from a sick bed, having been confined—for nearly two months by a distressing illness—The writing of this letter is an effort which nothing but my solicitude on the subject enables me to make. . . .

PUBLISHED: Catalog 109, pp. 14–15, of Robert K. Black, 109 Lorraine Avenue, Upper Montclair, New Jersey 07043.

Charles R. Leslie was a well-known painter of American origins who had made a reputation for himself in England.

1565. To Paul Pon

Legation of the United States. / Madrid March 30h. 1843.

Paul Pon Esqr.—U. S. Consul—Barcelona

Sir.

I have the honor to forward to you, your Exequatur received a few days since from the State Department and your original commission signed by the President of the United States: The fees on the Exequatur have been paid by Mr Lefevre of this city.

As the town of Barcelona seems to be peculiarly liable to political agitations; and has recently passed through a Severe crisis of this character, it may be well to remind you that it is the settled policy of the United States to recognize in every country of Europe, the existing Government, and to abstain from all interference, direct or indirect, in their domestic policy: This; which is the rule generally for all their Agents or representatives, applies especially to the Consuls of the United States, who are considered by their Government, as Commercial Agents solely; whose duty it is in the event of revolutionary attempts, to protect, as far as in them lies, the lives and property of American Citizens; to refrain from giving the sanction of their official names, or character to the acts of any party; and in all cases in which it may be necessary to appeal to the Government, by which they are recognized, to address themselves for that purpose to the Diplomatic representative of the United States— These points you will find Stated at length in your instructions from the Government; but the recent occurrences at Barcelona, have induced me to bring them, thus particularly to your notice.

I am, Sir, respectfully / Your Obdt Sevt.
Washington Irving

Manuscript: NA, RG 84 (letterbook copy).

1566. To Catharine Paris

Madrid April 1. 1843.

My dear Sister,

I wrote you a few lines about a week since, merely to let you know the State of my health; and I now do the same, for the same purpose.

I am still confined to the house but am slowly recovering from my tedious and harrassing complaint. I sit up for a great part of the day and am able to walk up and down the glass gallery. Next week (this is saturday) if the weather is fine, I hope to be able to drive out occasionally in the carriage. This will have an effect in getting up my spirits which have been much depressed, and, in that way have retarded my cure.

I am daily and anxiously looking for further accounts from Birmingham about the state of the health of our dear Sister. The news of her illness was quite a shock to me.[1] I hope however to hear that she is recovering from this alarming attack

I am well attended and well taken care of—The long storms which ⟨h⟩ succeeded that treacherous spell of fine weather in mid winter, have at length ceased; and spring is tardily awakening the Season will now be in my favor.

Give my love to all bodies / Your affectionate brother
Washington Irving.

Mrs Danl Paris

ADDRESSED: Mrs Daniel Paris / care of E Irving Esqr / New York.
MANUSCRIPT: Yale.

1. When WI visited Birmingham in 1844, Sarah Van Wart was partially paralyzed. Apparently she had had some difficulty by the time of this letter by WI. See STW, II, 179, 382; and WI to Catharine Paris, August 30, 1844.

1567. To George Read

Legation of the United States. / Madrid April 1st. 1843.

George Read Esqr.—US. Consul. Malaga

Sir

Your letter of the 27th. Ulto. acknowledging the receipt of my first communication, in relation to the Barque "Empress," was received yesterday.

On the 27th. of March, I passed to Count Almodovar a note containing a statement of the improper conduct of the Intendente at Malaga, based upon the documents you had forwarded to the Legation, and received yesterday a reply, stating that it had been referred to the Ministro de Hacienda to whose department it belonged: The official Gazette, however of this morning publishes a decree of the Regent dated 30th. Ultimo, removing from office the Intendente, D. Alejo Benito de Gaminde, and appointing provisionally in his place the Intendente of Alicante,[1] of whom I hear a very favorable character.

This prompt redress on the part of the Spanish Government cannot fail to be duly appreciated by our own; will remove, I hope, from the minds of our Countrymen, the irritated feelings which have been excited by this unpleasant affair, and induce them to act on any future occasion with the same prudence and discretion, which have marked their conduct in this case; convinced as they must be, of the disposition of the highest authorities to do them ample justice in any difficulties with the subordinate officers.

It may be well to communicate the substance of this note to the Captain of the Empress, in order that any unfriendly impressions which the knowledge alone of the detention and harsh treatment of this vessel, must cause in the United States, may be removed by the additional intelligence of the speedy punishment of the offending officer.

> I am, Sir, respectfully / Your Obdt Sevt.
> Washington Irving

ADDRESSED: Señor. / D. Jorge Read / Consul de los Estados Unidos. / de America. / *Malaga.*   POSTMARKED: 13 / I / MADRID / I / CASTL[*unrecovered*] / 2 Apr. 1843
MANUSCRIPT: NA, RG 84 (also letterbook copy).

Only the signature is in WI's handwriting.

1. Manuel de Elizaicin. See *La Gaceta*, no. 3098, April 1, 1843.

1568.   *To Daniel Webster*

Legation of the United States / Madrid April 1st. 1843.

No. 18. / The Hon: Daniel Webster, / Secretary of State of the United States—Washington.

Sir.

I have the honor to enclose a copy of a note passed to the Spanish Government on the 28th. ultimo on the subject of the outrageous treatment of the Barque Empress of New York by the Intendente of the Port of Malaga —Within two days, I received a reply from Count Almodovar, stating that my communication had been referred to the "Ministro de Hacienda" to whose department it belonged. It now appears by the Official Gazette of this morning that a decree was made by the Regent on the

30th. of March, appointing the Intendente of Alicante to the post of this delinquent officer, previously removed from office.[1] This remar⟨qu⟩↑k↓able and very unusual promptness on the part of this Government, whether due to my official note, or springing from their own sense of duty, indicates a friendly disposition towards us, which I shall consider it my duty to acknowledge properly, as soon as it is officially made known to me.

The Cortes will be opened with great state on Monday next:[2] as far as I can learn there will be a majority in the chamber for the Constitutional Government, but not for the actual Ministry: In the last Cortes, a Coalition of parties expelled from power the Gonzalez Cabinet;[3] but their leader having declined to form a new Ministry upon the invitation of the Regent, he Selected for his Ministers, moderate men of different parties. In the present Congress there are supposed to be 103 members opposed to the former coalition, 61 in their favor, and 18 doubtful: The greater part of the members opposed to the coalition are understood to be in favor of Espartero, as the representative of a Constitutional Government, against the efforts of other factions, but not the present Cabinet[4] which will probably be dissolved; indeed a Courier has already been despatched to General Sancho,[5] the Spanish Ambassador in London, inviting him to return and form a new Ministry.

There will be violent opposition and stormy discussion in the house: The Infante Don Francisco who had been kept aloof from Madrid, has managed to get himself returned as a Deputy from Saragossa, and entered the City two days ago in great style. He himself, however, possesses very little energy or character, but his wife Louisa Carlotta is a scheming, ambitious, intrepid, woman, anxious to bring about a marriage between their son and the little Queen; and there is an unprincipled, dangerous man Count Parsent, who is always with them, supposed to be the paramour of the Princess, and who has great influence with the lower orders: This arrival will complicate still more the difficult question of the Queen's Marriage, which will probably be one of the agitating topics before the chambers, and thus Madrid is likely to be a scene of new intrigues from that quarter.

Jerome Napoleon,[6] a son of the Ex-King of Westphalia has been here for some time past: he was favorably received by the Regent, and has had a private audience of the Queen: It is thought that he is a new candidate, and one that would not be unacceptable to the Government— He is about twenty two years of age; bears a strong resemblance to his Uncle the late Emperor, and is well spoken of as to his moral and intellectual qualities.

I am still confined to the house by indisposition but am slowly recovering: I am so reduced however by this long confinement, that I may find it necessary to visit some watering place, or make some journey to recover my health. I shall not do so, unless compelled by circumstances: In case, I have to absent myself from my post, I will have the satisfaction of knowing that in leaving it in charge of Mr. Hamilton, I confide it to a person, who by his intelligence, and apt and prompt discharge of business, is fully competent to carry on the affairs of the Legation.

I have the honor to acknowledge the receipt of Despatch No. 12, from the Department, enclosing the documents of Madame de Viar,[7] whose claim, I shall in compliance with your instructions urge upon the favorable consideration of the Spanish Government.

Since my last communication, the Exequaturs of Messrs Campbell, and Pon, Consuls at Havana and Barcelona, have been received and forwarded with the original commissions to these gentlemen respectively.

I transmit also to the Department in order that it may be more surely conveyed to her, the enclosed letter to Mrs. M. Cloud, containing the result of an application made in her behalf in relation to a claim against a Spanish Citizen.

I am, Sir, / very respectfully / Your Obdt Sevt.
Washington Irving

DOCKETED: Recd. 6th May. / mr. Markoe
MANUSCRIPT: NA, RG 59.　PUBLISHED: Hellman, *WI Esquire*, pp. 295–97; STW, II, 154 (in part).

1. Manuel de Elizaicin replaced Benito Alejo de Gaminde as Intendente of Alicante. See *La Gaceta*, April 1, 1843.

2. The preparatory meeting of the Cortes took place on April 2, with the formal opening on April 3, 1843. See *El Castellano*, April 3, 1843; and *La Gaceta*, April 3, 1843.

3. The cabinet of Antonio González, which served from May 22, 1841, to May 29, 1842, included González as minister of foreign affairs, Evaristo San Miguel as minister of war, Facundo Infante as minister of the interior, José Alonso as minister of justice, García Camba as minister of marine, and Pedro Surra y Rull as minister of finance. See *Almanach de Gotha pour l'Année 1842*, p. 292; and Christiansen, *Military Power*, pp. 105, 169.

4. Ramón Rodil's ministry held office from May 29, 1842, to May 9, 1843, and included Count Almodóvar as foreign minister, Rodil as minister of war, Torres–Solano as minister of the interior, Tomás Zumalacárregui as minister of justice, Capaz as minister of marine, and José María Calatrava as minister of finance. See *Almanach de Gotha pour l'Année 1843*, p. 332; and Christiansen, *Military Power*, p. 169.

5. Vicente Sancho (b. 1784), who was minister to Great Britain, had served as premier from September 12 to October 3, 1840. See *Almanach de Gotha . . . 1843*, p. 392; and Christiansen, *Military Power*, p. 169.

6. Napoleon Joseph Charles Paul (1822–1891), the youngest child of Jerome Bonaparte's second marriage, spent the spring and summer in Madrid but apparently was not a serious contender for Isabella's hand. Because he often signed his name as Napoleon Jerome, he is sometimes confused with his older brother Jerome

Napoleon Charles (1814–1847). See Edgar Holt, *Plon-Plon, The Life of Prince Napoleon* (London, 1973), pp. 15, 37–39.

7. Juana de Viar, daughter of José Ignacio de Viar, who had been Spanish consul general to the United States and had died in Philadelphia in 1818, was married to James Keefe, an American. She was trying to obtain funds from her father's estate, a claim which had been repeatedly rejected by the Spanish government. See Mrs. Keefe to WI, February, 1843 (NA, RG 59).

1569. To Count Almodóvar

Legation of the United States. / Madrid April 6th 1843.

The Undersigned Envoy Extraordinary and Minister Plenipotentiary of the United States, has the honor to acknowledge the receipt of the note of His Excellency Count Almodovar, First Minister of State and of Foreign affairs of Her Catholic Majesty acquainting him with the decree of His Highness the Regent removing from office the Intendente of Malaga; and with the judicial proceedings in progress for the further punishment of that officer for the outrages committed upon the United States vessel "The Empress."

The Undersigned had already communicated to his Government with sentiments of the most lively satisfaction, the very prompt measures taken by Her Majesty's Government in this matter; so indicative of a high sense of Justice, and of pure and honorable faith; and he will have great pleasure in transmiting to his Government this note of His Excellency, which cannot fail to prove highly gratifying; containing as it does still further manifestations of that amicable feeling reciprocated by Her Majesty's government with the Government of the United States.

The Undersigned renews to His Excellency on this occasion the assurances of his very distinguished consideration.

(Signed)   Washington Irving.
His Excellency / Count Almodovar / &ca &ca. &ca

MANUSCRIPT: NA, RG 84 (letterbook copy); NA, RG 59 (copy).

Another copy of this letter was enclosed with WI's despatch no. 19 to Daniel Webster, April 6, 1843.

1570.   To Daniel Webster

Legation of the United States / Madrid April 6th. 1843.

No. 19. / The Hon: Daniel Webster. / Secretary of State of the United States—Washington.

Sir,

I have the honor to enclose a copy of the reply of Count Almodovar to my note complaining of the conduct of the Intendente of Malaga, in the affair of the Barque Empress. By this you will perceive that the Government not content with dismissing the Intendente from office, intend to institute legal proceedings against him for his misconduct.[1]

This affair has excited much attention here, and the uncommonly prompt and thorough measures adopted by this Government, have occasioned great surprise; especially as the Intendente is a person of much political influence and importance and had rendered many services to the existing government.—Besides the evidence which it furnishes of a very friendly disposition towards ↑us;↓ it affords a proof on their part, of an awakening sense of the importance of reviving the languishing trade between the United States and the peninsula: whose decline has very sensibly affected the prosperity of the Wine and Fruit Districts of Malaga: From indications lately furnished by the higher officers, and assurances, which it is understood have been given by the Regent to the representations from that quarter, I am not without hope that an opening may be afforded to place our trade on a better footing; but to establish this, some modication[2] will be expected on our part in regard to their wines and fruits.

I cannot omit calling the attention of the government to the tact and discretion, which have been exhibited by Mr. Read, our Consul at Malaga throughout his correspondence in relation to the Empress; to his efforts it has been chiefly owing that the current of public feeling has been so strongly directed in our favor; as has been shown almost unanimously by the articles in the public prints.

I also enclose a copy of my note, of this date, in reply to the communication of Count Almodovar.[3]

I am, Sir, very respectfully / Your obdt Sevt.
Washington Irving

Docketed: Recd. 6 May / Mr. Markoe / No. 19. W Irving. Madrid — 6 Apl. 1843—
Manuscript: NA, RG 59.

Only the signature is in WI's handwriting.

1. See *El Castellano*, April 1, 1843.
2. The copyist probably intended to write "modification."
3. See WI to Count Almodóvar, April 6, 1843.

1571. To George Read

Legation of the United [States] [*MS torn*] / Madrid
Apri[l 7th. 1843.] [*MS torn*]

George Read Esq. U. S. Consul Malaga—

Sir,

Your two letters of the 29th. March; one relating to the duty on Codfish, and the other to the barque Empress; as well as your subsequent communication of the 31st. also referring to the Empress, have been received at this Legation.

As at the date of your last letter you were not yet aware of the removal of the Intendente D. Benito Alejo de Gaminde, and the appointment of his Successor, I have not thought it necessary to make any further application to the Government, presuming that the new incumbent will without delay take the requisite measures to undo the work of his predecessor, and replace the vessel and her Cargo in their original condition.

For greater certainty however the subject was mentioned two days since to the Director General of the [Custom]s [*MS torn*] when he announced that he had received information [of the] [*MS torn*] detention of the Cargo; but that the orders already given [to the] [*MS torn*] new Intendente had probably before this time removed [all] [*MS torn*] difficulties.

I hope that this unpleasant affair has now been brought to a close; as far at least as it concerns the injuries to the Citizens of the United States— In a communication from the Minister of State of the 2nd. Instant I am informed that the Government are preparing to institute legal proceedings against the Intendente before the Supreme Tribunal of Justice:

I congratulate you, in conclusion, upon this happy result, to which your exertions have in a great degree contributed; and to which I have had the pleasure of calling the attention of our government, in the terms which I consider they have merited.

I am Sir respectfully / Your obdt Sevt.
Washington Irving

ADDRESSED: Señor / Don Jorge Read / Consul de los Estados Unidos. / *Malaga.* / España   POSTMARKED: 5 / Malaga / 11 Apr / 1843 / [*unrecovered*] DAL II
MANUSCRIPT: NA, RG 84 (also letterbook copy).

1572. To Daniel Webster

Legation of the United States. / Madrid April 8th. 1843.

No. 20. / The Hon Daniel Webster. / Secretary of State of the United States—Washington.

Sir.

I have the honor to enclose the accounts and vouchers of this Legation for the first quarter of 1843; showing a balance in favor of the United States of $94.89 which will appear to their credit in next account:

I also transmit a printed Copy of the Regent's Speech at the opening of the Cortes.[1]

I am, Sir, with great respect / Your Obdt Sevt.
Washington Irving

DOCKETED: Recd. 14 May / Mr. Markoe
MANUSCRIPT: NA, RG 59.

Only the signature is in WI's handwriting.

1. Espartero delivered his address on April 3, 1843.

1573. To Gurdon Bradley

Legation of the United States. / Madrid April 10th. 1843.

Gurdon Bradley Esqr.—U. S. Consul Mayagues.

Sir.

I herewith forward to you your Exequatur received this day from the Department of State; and your original Commission signed by the President of the United States.[1]

Your letter of the 18th. August last was duly received and the proceeds of the draft enclosed in it will be applied to the payment of the fees.

I am Sir respectfully / Your obdt Sert
Washington Irving.

MANUSCRIPT: NA, RG 84 (letterbook copy).

1. WI had requested Bradley's exequatur on August 2, 1842. See WI to Count Almodóvar, August 2, 1842.

1574. To Sarah Storrow

Madrid, April 13. 1843

My dear Sarah,

I yesterday received yours of the 5th.[1] and feel most sensibly all the kind solicitude you express about the state of my health. I am happy to inform you that my general health has much improved of late. I have had no return of fever and am gradually regaining my appetite. My original malady is also abating so that I hope before long to be able to resume my usual habits & occupations and once more to enjoy existence, which for sometime past has been a burthen to me. I have lately been able to drive out once and sometimes twice a day, and this has had a most beneficial effect. For two days past however I have been kept to the house by bad weather: which rather throws me back. Carson Brevoort left us the day before yesterday for Italy; he will make a tour of a few months and be in Paris sometime in the Course of the Summer on his way home. I was extremely sorry to part with him for he was every way estimable and amiable. Mr Hamilton & Mr Ames, left me at the same time to pass three or four days at Toledo during the ceremonies of Holy Week: so these last two dreary, rainy days I have been quite alone. The prospect of a tolerably speedy cure, however, keeps me in good spirits. and I have excellent attendance in my faithful and devoted Lorenzo; who in fact is doctor, nurse and every thing to me

The visit to Paris which you urge upon me would be no doubt beneficial as well as agreeable; but I have many considerations, which I cannot now enter upon, to render it at present quite unadvisable.

I am happy to hear both from you and from letters from Birmingham that my dear Sisters health is improving[.] I received tidings of her alarming illness and of the base conduct of that contemptible animal Phil Paulding[2] about the same time, when I was confined to my bed, and you may imagine their effect upon me.

You of course have had from your mother an account of the Paulding affair. I feel rejoiced that our dear Kate has escaped a union with such a miserable wretch. I can hardly persuade myself that he is not under the influence of some mental alienation[.] I find from letters recd. two days since ⟨from⟩ ↑by↓ Alex Hamilton, that some fortnight previous to Phils letter to your uncle breaking off the connexion, the gentleman had sent a present of Dr Channings works to Mary Hamilton[3] accompanied by a letter which I presume must have been a declaration. She was astonished and ⟨infor⟩ incensed and handed the letter to Geo Schuyler[4]—The latter was in a furious passion. He wrote to Phil telling him that nothing could justify him in writing such a letter to Miss Hamilton but the circumstance of his engagement with Miss Irving being at an end and demanded to know whether or not such were the case, *that he might know what course to take.* I presume this demand of Schuyler threw the craven scamp into a fright, and forced from him that letter to your uncle renouncing the engagement. The latter part of Mary Hamiltons letter to her brother states that Phil was overwhelmed by the universal reprobation of his conduct and according to the last accounts was lying on his bed with some one to bathe his head

I am happy to hear that Kate conducts herself nobly on the occasion. She of course must have felt greatly shocked at being so deceived in the man on whom she had placed her affections,—but the contempt inspired by his conduct and by the recent development of his character must have extinguished all affection.

Writing is still rather a task to me so you must excuse this miserable Scrawl. Tell Mr Storrow I have recd his letter giving a statement of my account which I will attend to. Remember me affectionately to him and kiss my darling little Kate for me.

Your affectionate uncle
Washington Irving

MANUSCRIPT: Yale.

1. This letter has not been located.
2. On December 1, 1841, WI had reported with satisfaction the engagement of Ebenezer's daughter Catharine to Philip Paulding, a Tarrytown neighbor and son of General William Paulding. See WI to Sarah Storrow, December 1, 1841.
3. The sister of Alexander Hamilton, Jr. and daughter of WI's Tarrytown neighbor, James Alexander Hamilton.
4. George Lee Schuyler (1811–1890) was married to Eliza Hamilton, Mary's sister. Schuyler, later devoted to yachting, was one of the owners of the *America* when it won the world's championship in 1851. See New York *Times*, August 1, 1890.

1575. *To John Miller*

Legation of the United States / Madrid April 18th. 1843.

John Miller Esqr. / Agent U. S. Legation—London.

Dear Sir.

I have received your account in duplicate for postage &c, paid by you on account of this legation during the last quarter.

I enclose a check on Messrs Rothschild & Sons for the amount ↑(£8.7.10)↓ payable to your order at sight[1]

I am very respectfully / Your Obdt Sevt.
Washington Irving.

MANUSCRIPT: NA, RG 84 (letterbook copy).

1. The following enclosure was copied into the letterbook:

Legation of the United States. / Madrid April 18th. 1843.
£8. 7. 10.
At sight to to pay John Miller Esqr. or order eight pounds, seven shillings, and ten pence sterling and charge to the United States on account of the contingent expenses of this legation.

Washington Irving.

Messrs N. M. Rothschild & Sons / Bankers U. S. London.

The copyist repeated "to" in line 3.

1576.   To Sarah Storrow

Madrid, April 22d. 1843.

My dear Sarah,

I received a few days since your most kind & affectionate letter[1] expressive of such solicitude for my health. I am happy to say that my general health is daily improving and that I have reason to hope for a speedy relief from the particular malady which has so long tormented me— Within a few days I have been able to get out of the carriage and take little walks in the fields and meadows, and these snatches of country air and country exercise have had a wonderful effect on my health and spirits. I have discovered some ⟨t⟩ pleasant meadows studded with ↑groves↓ and with thickets of hawthorn, along the banks of the Manzanares about two miles from Madrid—I had no idea there was any thing so really rural in the vicinity of this sterile city. For the two last days I have driven there with Madame Albuquerque and her little girls, and we have passed two or three hours in the meadows, ⟨[unrecovered]⟩ ↑strolling along the river,↓ amusing ourselves with the children who were delighted with this outbreak into the country and were running about, gathering flowers & making garlands. The hawthorn was just beginning to put forth its fragrant blossoms; the trees were full of nightingales—while at a distance, gleaming through vistas of the groves, were the Guadarama mountains covered with snow. Think of the effect of such a scene, and of having such pleasant society around me, after nearly three dreary months of illness confinement, and solitary rumination. I this day for the first time have been enabled to put on bottines,[2] and now shall daily take ⟨again⟩ exercise on foot, which will soon put me in tone again. I find however, that it does not do yet to task my mind—A process of calculation in making up my accounts immediately produces a slight irritation of the system. I shall have to keep holy day for a time and amuse myself—Fortunately the beautiful season of spring is opening delightfully—and I find my carriage a great resource, in conveying me to the few pleasant country spots there are in the vicinity of Madrid. I intend to get a general order to admit me into the grounds of some of the Royal country seats, where I may pass a day occasionally ruralizing; and we are concocting little pic nic parties. Now if I had you and Kate here, what a time we should have in the meadows among the flowers and nightingales! My young horses about which you express some anxiety, are as gentle as lambs: yet they are fine spirited looking little animals. The Spanish horses are, in general, remarkably gentle and docile—though apparently full of fire.

I am looking daily for letters from home by the Steamer of the 1st. inst. I had a letter from your uncle E. I dated 8t March.[3] Kate ⟨was⟩ and Sarah were passing a month in town with Julia Grinnell. Kate acquits herself admirably—She and Charlotte will pass part of the summer at Geneva, with their brothers—

Give my kind remembrances to Mr Storrow: and Kiss that heady high minded little woman Kate for me

Your affectionate Uncle
Washington Irving

ADDRESSED: Madame Storrow / 4. Rue de la Victoire / à Paris
MANUSCRIPT: Yale.

1. This letter has not been located.
2. High boots which partially cover the legs.
3. This letter has not been located.

1577. To Count Almodóvar

Legation of the United States. / Madrid April 24h. 1843.

The Undersigned Envoy Extraordinary and Minister Plenipotentiary of the United States of America has the honor to communicate to His Excellency Count Almodovar, First Minister of State and of Foreign Affairs of Her Catholic Majesty the original commissions of Mr. Franklin Gage and of Mr. John Hartman[1] appointed respectively Consuls of the United States for the Ports of Cardenas and Baracoa in the Island of Cuba; and by direction of his Government requests that his Excellency will cause the corresponding royal Exequaturs to be issued recognizing Messrs Gage and Hartman in their official characters.

The Undersigned takes the opportunity to renew to His Excellency the assurance of his most distinguished consideration.

Washington Irving.

MANUSCRIPT: NA, RG 84 (letterbook copy).

1. These men were nominated for their consulships on March 2, 1843, but there is no record that they received their exequaturs. On February 26, 1847, James Buchanan wrote to Romulus Saunders (WI's successor at Madrid) that S. M. Johnson, U.S. consul at Matanzas, Cuba, had appointed Franklin Gage as consular agent. See Hasse, *Index to U.S. Documents*, III, 1744–45; and *The Works of James Buchanan*, ed. John Bassett Moore, 12 vols. (New York, 1960), VII, 228.

1578. To Alexander Burton

Legation of the United States. / Madrid April 24th. 1843.

Alexr. Burton Esqr. . / Consul. U. S. Cadiz.

Sir.

I have to acknowledge the receipt this morning of your letter of the 18th. Inst, with its enclosures in relation to the claims upon you for War and other extraordinary contributions

In consequence of your letter of October last alluding to this subject my attention was called to the provisions of our treaties with this Government, and especially to the 19th. Article of the treaty of 1795[1] and the result of this examination was an entire concurrence in the opinion expressed by my predecessor Mr. Vail that "your exemption from such charges cannot admit of a doubt."

Under these circumstances I consider your right to resist the payment of these contributions, and all attempts to levy the same upon your property to be perfect; and shall lose no time in placing before this Government your claims to these exemptions, founded upon the very explicit terms of the treaty and the documents with which you have furnished me.

I am, Sir, respectfully / Your Obdt Sevt.
Washington   Irving.

MANUSCRIPT: NA, RG 84 (letterbook copy).

1. The Treaty of Friendship, Limits, and Navigation was signed at San Lorenzo el Real on October 25, 1795. Article 19 states: "Consuls shall be reciprocally established with the privileges and powers which those of the most favoured nations enjoy in the ports where their consuls reside, or are permitted to be." The main concerns of the treaty were with establishing the boundaries between the Spanish possessions in North America and the southern United States, with navigation rights on the Mississippi River, and with storage rights for the United States at New Orleans. See *Treaties and Other International Acts of the U. S. A.*, ed. Hunter Miller, II, 318; John Bassett Moore, *A Digest of International Law*, V, 849–55; and WI to Count Almodóvar, April 26, 1843.

1579. To Count Almodóvar

Legation of the United States. / Madrid April 26th. 1843.

The Undersigned Envoy Extraordinary and Minister Plenipotentiary of the United States has the honor to solicit the attention of His Excellency Count Almodovar, First Minister of State and of Foreign affairs of Her Catholic Majesty to the following case relating to the United States Consul at Cadiz.[1]

It appears that this officer has been required by the Constitutional Ayuntamiento of the City to pay a sum of about three thousand reals of vellon on account of War and other extraordinary contributions and has received notice that in case of refusal or neglect to pay the same within eight days a sentinel will be placed at his door, and the amount levied by a seizure and sale (embargo y venta) of his property.

The Consul relying upon the provisions in his favor contained in the treaties between the two Governments, and upon the renewed assurances of the Diplomatic Representatives of the United States at this Court that he was under the treaties rightfully exempt from such contributions has hitherto refused to make the payments demanded, and has applied to this Legation for the protection to which he considers himself entitled.

The Undersigned after a careful examination of the treaties and documents referring to this subject is satisfied that a brief statement and explanation of the grounds upon which this exemption is claimed will be sufficient to satisfy the penetration and discernment of Count Almodovar of the justice of this claim and to induce his Excellency to take the necessary measures to protect the Consul from this exaction

The treaty of 1795 between His Catholic Majesty and the Government of the United States framed as the preamble declares "to consolidate on a permanent basis the friend ship and good correspondence happily prevailing between the two parties" in its 19th. Article provides for the establishment of Consuls in the following words "Consuls shall be reciprocally established with the privileges and powers which those of the most favored nations enjoy in the ports where their Consuls reside or are permitted to be"[2]

To attempt by argument or illustration to add strength or clearness to what is here so plainly established as the intention of the two Governments would be uselessly to occupy the attention of Count Almodovar—. From this short article, confirmed by the 12th. article of the subsequent treaty of 1819 between the same governments it is manifest that the Spanish Consuls in the ports of the United States and the Consuls of the United States in the ports of Spain are reciprocally entitled and may lay claim to, whatever privileges or exemptions shall be accorded to any other, the most favored nations:—It then only remains to be ascertained whether the consuls of other Nations are exempted from the payment of these extraordinary contributions.

Of the fact that the Consuls of England, France and Portugal are so exempt by virtue of treaty stipulations Count Almodovar is undoubtedly well informed; but the undersigned in order to establish clearly the position he has taken considers himself bound to present to His Excellency's notice, the accompanying copy of a note from the Secretary of State of Her Catholic Majesty to the Minister of Her Britannic Majesty at this Court under date January 14th. 1837. He also takes the liberty to refer His Excellency to the Royal order of September 27th. of the same year to establish the exemption of French Consuls.

In addition to the explicit terms of the Article of the treaty which has been cited, and which renders any further proof unnecessary, the Undersigned might have relied on the 7th. Article of the Treaty of 1795, which declares that "the subjects or citizens of either party, their vessels, or effects, shall not be liable to any embargo or detention (embargo o detencion) on the part of the other for any *military expedition* or other public or private purpose whatever"—It happens that the expression in the treaty; "embargo" is the same as that made use of by the Commission for the levying of the war contribution, in their notice to the Consul to make the payment; thereby placing the solemn stipulations of a treaty in direct, and even literal, opposition to the recovery which they seek to enforce.

The Undersigned is too well satisfied of the desire of Count Almodovar (so clearly shown on a late occasion) to maintain the friendly relations of a political as well as commercial character happily existing between the two countries to doubt his disposition to secure to this Consul of the United States all the immunities to which he is entitled.[3] This Officer has exercised his functions at the port of Cadiz for a quarter of a century; has during that period regularly paid all the ordinary contributions; and has now only appealed to this Legation against the exaction of these extraordinary taxes; after having remonstrated in vain with the subordinate officers, who threaten him with the compulsory measures of military coercion and the forced sale of his property.

In conclusion the Undersigned will express the hope which he is assured he feels in common with His Excellency that the necessary measures may be taken in time to prevent any unpleasant collisions.

The Undersigned renews to His Excellency the assurances of his most distinguished consideration.

(Signed) Washington Irving.

DOCKETED: With M. Irving's No. 21.
MANUSCRIPT: NA, RG 84 (letterbook copy); NA, RG 59 (copy).

1. The U.S. consul at Cadiz was Alexander Burton.

2. For the text of this treaty, see *Treaties and Other International Acts of the U. S. A.*, ed. Hunter Miller, III, 15.

3. In a letter of April 18, 1843, to WI, Burton stated that the Cadiz authorities had tried to make him pay for an earlier war contribution in 1840 but he claimed exemption for the United States under Article 7 of the 1795 Treaty, which was similar to an exemption granted to England, France, and Portugal (letter in NA, RG 59).

1580. To Sarah Storrow

Madrid April 29. 1843

My dear Sarah,

I received yesterday your most kind & welcome letter[1] which I am sorry I cannot reply to more at length, but since last I wrote, giving an account of my two days revel in the meadows among nightingales & flowers there has been a change of temperature, and harsh winds from the Guadarama mountains which have had an effect on my sensitive frame, and given me a most uncomfortable week. My hands are at this moment so inflamed that writing is irksome to me. Still my general health continues good, and I hope by patience and perseverance, ⟨to⟩ gradually to get the better of this harrassing malady which unfits me for every thing, It must take time however—

I received this morning a very acceptable letter from your mother[2] written in good spirits. Her health continues good, and she appears to enjoy her residence in town.

I wish when you write home you would mention the state of my health; for I cannot write another letter today—Say that my general health is daily improving; and that I have nothing to b⟨i⟩attle with but this malady; which, though it now & then turns upon me, is gradually giving way. The Season has been against me. The Spring has been wet & cold; and even now it is blustering and raining: but the settled warm weather must soon commence, which will be all in my favour.

I will write to you again in the course of a few days: when I have the complete use of my hands. Their inflamation is temporary occasioned by the application of remedies

With kindest remembrances to Mr Storrow and a dozen kisses to my dear little Kate

Your affectionate Uncle
WI.

MANUSCRIPT: Yale.

1. This letter has not been located.
2. This letter has not been located.

1581. *To Catharine Paris*

Madrid May 6th. 1843

My dear Sister,·

I have to thank you for your long and interesting letter of 22d. March.[1]
I wish I could make a better return than mere thanks, but as yet I am
incapable of letter writing, my malady still clinging to me and unfitting
me for every thing. I am happy to say however, that it is gradually
yielding to incessant remedies, which are almost as irksome as the
disease. When the weather becomes settled ⟨into⟩ and warm I have no
doubt I shall get on more rapidly; but the seasons have been against
me throughout my indisposition The treacherous spell of Summer
weather in midwinter which first put me out of order by giving me a
cold has been succeeded by an uncommonly cold and wet spring; which
is extending even into the month of May, and which has a sad influence
over my debilitated and sensitive frame. However, we have occasional
fine days by which I profit. I drive out every day; and take the country
air, and occasionally I have the company of my amiable & charming
friend Madame Albuquerque and her lovely children: ⟨who are and we
have⟩ when we repair to the groves and meadows on the banks of the
Manzanares; which at present are sprinkled with flowers, fragrant with
the hawthorn, and alive with nightingales in full song. This family is my
great comfort & resource here. I have taught them all to call me uncle,
so that when among them I have a feeling of home.

It is good always in the midst of our afflictions to ⟨comf⟩ console ourselves with the idea how much worse matters might have been under
other circumstances. This malady which totally unfits me for all literary
exertions, was brought upon me by overtasking of the mind. Suppose I
had remained in America and it had been brought upon me there, by the
Literary tasks in which I was disposed to engage with all my powers—
what would have been my situation? Without income to meet ⟨the⟩ current expenses, and all the sources of future profit suddenly dried up, I
should have been driven to dispair. At present, though I am incapable
of working, I can think, and can direct others; I can manage to carry on
the business of the Legation, which just now is light—and my income
goes on and enables me to take care of every body. This is the consideration which brings comfort to me in the midst of my dreary malady.

Carson Brevoort left us nearly a month since. We have had letters from him² ⟨since he⟩ while travelling. He appears to be enjoying his tour greatly[.] I was very sorry to part with him, for he is a most amiable and estimable young man.

I have written a longer letter than I thought I should have been able to do, & must conclude with love to all in town and country

Your affectionate brother
Washington Irving

ADDRESSED: Mrs Daniel Paris / care of E. Irving Esqr / New York / pr Steamer / via Boston   POSTMARKED: BOSTON Mas / JUN / 19   DOCKETED: Washn. Irving to Mrs. Paris / *Madrid May 6. 1843* [*upper left corner, page 1*] MANUSCRIPT: Yale.   PUBLISHED: STW, II, 159 (in part).

At the bottom of page 4 Sarah Storrow added the following note: "I have just received this letter my dear Mother, which I shall send to Mr. Ledyard to forward. I will write you by the Boston Steamer. You find Uncle is gradually improving. I am glad to hear this, as by my last letter he had been more indisposed again. Mr Storrow and Kate join in much love. Ever your affectionate daughter / Sarah"

1. This letter has not been located.
2. This letter has not been located.

1582. *To Daniel Webster*

Legation of the United States. / Madrid May. 9th. 1843.

No. 21. / The Hon: Daniel Webster. / Secretary of State of the U. States— Washington.

Sir.

I have the honor to enclose a copy of a note which I addressed to the Minister of State on the 26th. ulto.; and to which I have as yet received no answer: this is owing rather to the unsettled state of affairs at this moment than to any difficulty belonging to the question itself, as the language of the treaty on this point is too precise and clear to admit of a doubt as to the exemption claimed for our Consuls.

The Chamber of Deputies after being employed nearly four weeks in the examination of the qualifications of its members was finally constituted on Sunday April 30th. and by an overwhelming majority the opposition candidate Mr. Cortina¹ was at once elected to the presidency. The vice presidents and Secretaries were also without exception Selected from the members of the opposition; and the Ministry on the same day, after this unequivocal proof of the hostility of the popular branch of the Legislature resigned their posts: The Regent accepted their resignations and since that time they have only been holding over until the appointment of their Successors:

This has proved no easy task; since now after an interval of nearly nine days the question although very much advanced, cannot be considered entirely settled. In obedience to the principle of representative Government, the Regent without delay called upon Mr. Cortina to form a Cabinet, and this gentleman accepted the mission; but after two days consumed in useless efforts to reconcile the various fractions of the legislature, he signified to the Regent ↑that↓ he must abandon all further efforts for the present—Notwithstanding the election of Mr. Cortina to the Presidents chair by so large a vote, it appears that this vote did not indicate the strength of his party in that body; but was rather the result of an arrangement, and that after pulling down the existing ministry the parties who had united for that purpose solely were now ready to contend among each other for the prize of their victory.

M. Olozaga,[2] another prominent leader, and last year president of the Chamber was then called upon by the Regent to form a Ministry: He too after an effort of two or three days in turn acknowledged that he could not make any combination which would command a majority in the Legislature and upon his failure the Regent next addressed himself to M. Lopez;[3] a distinguished orator, and the head of a considerable party. M Lopez has now been occupied three days in the arrangement of a Cabinet, and has reached such an advanced stage that the names of the members who are to compose it are given (with one or two exceptions) on very good authority—The Cabinet thus formed will be of a very heterogeneous character, and it seems doubtful whether the discordant materials of which it is framed will be able for any length of time to hold together, and carry on the Government.[4] In this interval the country continues in a feverish excited state, and rumors of plots reach us from all quarters. It is to be hoped for the interest and tranquillity of the nation that this "Ministerial Crisis" may not be much further prolonged.

I have the honor to acknowledge the receipt of Despatch No. 13. from the Department enclosing the commissions of Messrs Franklin Gage and John Hartman as Consuls of the United States for the ports of Cardenas and Baracoa in the Island of Cuba, and to state that in compliance with its directions, I applied on the 24th. ult: for the usual royal Exequaturs in their behalf.

I am Sir, very respectfully, / Your obdt Sevt.
Washington Irving

DOCKETED: Recd. 22 June / Mr. Markoe [upper left corner, page 1] / No. 21. W. Irving. Madrid. 9 May 1843 —

Manuscript: NA, RG 59.

Only the signature is in WI's handwriting.

1. Manuel Cortina (1802–1879) of Seville, who ranked second only to Olózaga in influence in the Progressive party, was elected president of the lower chamber of the Cortes. See Christiansen, *Military Power*, p. 119; and H. Butler Clarke, *Modern Spain*, p. 184.

2. Salustiano Olózaga. See WI to Catharine Paris, November 22, 1842.

3. Joaquín María López (1797–1855), an orator and lawyer in the Progressive party, had served in Calatrava's ministry (August 15, 1836–August 17, 1837) as minister of the interior. See Raymond Carr, *Spain*, p. 222; and Christiansen, *Military Power*, p. 168.

4. The López ministry, which served from May 10 to 20, 1843, consisted of López as premier; Manuel María de Aguilar, minister of state; Francisco Serrano, war; Joaquín de Frías (1783–1851), marine; Mateo Miguel Ayllón, finance; and Fermín Caballero, interior. See *Vida militar y política de Espartero*, 3 vols. (Madrid, 1845), III, 137; and *La Gaceta*, May 5, 6, 8, 1843.

1583. *To Joaquín de Frías*

Legation of the United States. / Madrid May 11th. 1843.

The Undersigned Envoy Extraordinary and Minister Plenipotentiary of the United States of America has the honor to acknowledge the receipt of the note by which His Excellency Don Joaquin de Frias informed him that His Highness the Regent of the Kingdom had confided to His Excellency the management ad interim of the Department of State.[1]

The Undersigned in offering to His Excellency his congratulations on this distinguished mark of confidence on the part of the Executive is most happy to reciprocate in the fullest manner the kind and friendly sentiments which are expressed not only towards the Government which he has the honor to represent, but to himself personally and he begs leave to assure His Excellency that no efforts will be wanting on his part to promote and foster the amicable relations which are now existing between the two governments.

The Undersigned takes the opportunity to convey to His Excellency the assurances of his most distinguished consideration.

Washington Irving.

Manuscript: NA, RG 84 (letterbook copy).

Joaquín Fernández de Velasco de Frías (1783–1851), an aristocrat who had served as premier for two and one-half months in 1838, had been minister of war in Espartero's cabinet from January 10 to May 21, 1841. See Christiansen, *Military Power*, p. 169.

1. The appointment of Frías was announced in *La Gaceta*, May 10, 1843, and in *El Castellano*, May 10, 1843.

1584. To Arthur MacCulloch

Legation of the United States. / Madrid May 12th. 1843.

Arthur McCulloch Esqr. / Vice Consul U. S. Alicante.

Sir

In answer to the request contained in your letter[1] I have to state that it is very questionable whether the power to grant leaves of absence to Consular Agents for any length of time belongs to this Legation; applications for such indulgences being usually made to the Department of State.[2]

I have great pleasure however, in expressing my conviction that, in consideration of the shortness of your contemplated absence, and the fact, that the affairs of the consulate will in the interval be intrusted to competent hands, your wishes may be gratified without fear of objection from the Department of State.

I am, Sir, respectfully / Your Obdt Sevt
Washington Irving.

MANUSCRIPT: NA, RG 84 (letterbook copy).

1. MacCulloch had written to WI on May 7, 1843 (NA, RG 59).
2. MacCulloch had indicated that his business partner in Alicante, Thomas Carey, who served as Belgian vice-consul, would attend to MacCulloch's duties as U.S. vice-consul during his brief absence.

1585. To Olegario de los Cuetos

Legation of the United States. / Madrid May 22nd. 1843.

The Undersigned Envoy Extraordinary and Minister Plenipotentiary of the United States of America has the honor to acknowledge the receipt of the note by which His Excellency Don Olegario de los Cuetos informed him that His Highness the Regent of the Kingdom had confided to His Excellency the management ad interim of the Department of State.[1]

The Undersigned begs leave to offer his sincere congratulations on this distinguished mark of the confidence of the Executive and at the same time to reciprocate most cordially the friendly sentiments manifested in His Excellency's note.

The Undersigned avails himself with pleasure of this first opportunity to convey to His Excellency the assurances of his most distinguished consideration.

Washington Irving.

MANUSCRIPT: NA, RG 84 (letterbook copy).

Olegario de los Cuetos (d. 1844) was a Progressive party stalwart who was asked to assume temporary direction of the Ministry of State in the cabinet of Gomez Becerra, which was in power from May 20 to June 29, 1843. See Christiansen, *Military Power*, p. 170; and H. Butler Clarke, *Modern Spain*, pp. 185–86. In a letter of May 21, 1843, Olegario de los Cuetos had informed WI of his assuming the responsibilities of the Ministry of State (NA, RG 84).

1. The appointment of Olegario de los Cuetos was announced in *La Gaceta*, May 22, 1843, and in *El Castellano*, May 22, 1843.

1586.   To Daniel Webster

Legation of the United States. / Madrid May 24th. 1843.

No. 22. / The Hon: Daniel Webster, / Secretary of State of The U. States
‧ —Washington

Sir

The Lopez Cabinet which I had the honor to announce to you as nearly formed at the date of my last despatch, (May 9th.) has been short lived; and the doubt which I had expressed of its duration has been realised after an existence of ten days only.

From the first there appeared in it few elements of stability: the members of the new Ministry were not united upon any fixed principles of political action and the majority upon which they counted, was to be made up of various fractions which had been held together for a time by their opposition to the former cabinet.

Under these circumstances their remaining long at the head of affairs seemed doubtful, but their course towards the Regent soon determined their fate.

The first measure of importance presented to him for his approbation was a general law of amnesty to date back from the convention of Vezgara; that is, from the conclusion of the Civil war with Don Carlos.[1] Of course, the effect of this decree could not be to heal the deep wounds which had been caused by that conflict, and from which the nation is still suffering; but on the contrary to raise up perhaps new difficulties (and it is alleged that it was framed for that purpose) by calling back to the country the men who, within the last two years, had plotted to overturn the government of Espartero; who had excited revolts; who had attempted to carry off the young Queen, and had even with the same object, sought to take the life of the Regent: these men; Espartero's bitterest enemies were to be received again after expiating by a short exile, their share in insurrections for which so many others had paid with their lives: Notwithstanding his objections to such a partial measure, and one which seemed rather aimed at himself than having in view the good of the Country, the Regent was prepared to give to it his assent.

Within a day or two the Ministry presented itself at Buena Vista with a list of removals, comprising it is said, some 30 or 40 officers, friends of the Regent, and in confidential military posts about his person, from very high to lower stations, and forming the channel through which he directs the Military force of the Country. At this point Espartero paused, and taking up the list stated his willingness to remove any individual against whom specific and sufficient cause ↑were↓ alleged, but that, failing in this, he should continue them in their posts—The Ministers, unable to convince him of the propriety of these changes, at once tendered their resignations, which he at first refused to accept; having considered the matter, however, during the night he gave them notice the next morning that he consented to their retiring and appointed, as the leader of a new Cabinet, the President of the Senate M. Gomez Becerra.[2]

The announcement of the fall of the Lopez Cabinet and the choice of a successor caused great excitement in the Chambers, and gave rise to a most stormy debate: The new Minister was received with outcries from the galleries, and amid disorder on the floor: after a short and tumultuous session a decree of the Regent was read adjourning the legislative bodies to the 27th. Inst, and the President of the new Cabinet was treated with indignity by the populace as he drove off from the open square in front of the Palace of the Deputies. It was thought expedient that night to have the troops in readiness in their quarters and strong detachments at exposed points, but the public tranquility was not impaired, and the excitement has been since subsiding—The public attention is fixed upon the termination of the interval which has been created to organize and establish the new Government.—All the posts are filled save the Ministry of Foreign Affairs. The names are thus given officially in the Gazette.[3]
President of the Council. Minister of Justice—Gomez Becerra.

> of the Treasury—M Mendizabal[4]
> of Marine—M. de los Cuetos
> of the Interior—M. de la Serna[5]
> of War—M. de Hoyos.[6]

These are moderate men, of course well inclined to the Regent but without, I believe, much prospect of obtaining a majority in the Cortes— a dissolution or at least a prorogation ↑of which↓ would seem to be inevitable.

The causes of the late difficulties are represented in a widely different light according to political sympathies: The friends of Espartero declare that the chief object of the late cabinet through their short career was to overturn the government of the Regent and that, with this view, they were to receive the support of the motley and various factions opposed to him. That the attempt would be made either by forcing upon him the most unpleasant and obnoxious measures, to induce him in disgust to throw up the reins of government, or, by removing his supports, and undermining his influence with the army, gradually prepare the way for a coup de main. As corroborating this they state as a fact that the names of a Regency of Three, representing the different parties to the league were already circulating among its members and that under co⟨l⟩ver of a plan of amnesty and reconciliation a dangerous blow was to be struck at the the Regent to be followed by the destruction of all his friends under the pretext of removing improper influence.

The Regent's enemies on the other hand complain most loudly that after a Cabinet had been formed, with great labor and difficulty, to carry on the government in a constitutional manner with the cooperation of the Chambers, he has sacrificed it to his affection for his friend and his determination to maintain a military rule: That his professions of respect for the Constitution are plainly insincere, and that his object is to get rid of the legislative bodies in order to rule by the sword alone—In opposition to the charge made against their party of being under the French influence they urge the subjection of Espartero to England, and the constant and undisguised interference at Buena Vista of the British Ambassador, to whom they say the late changes are to be chiefly attributed, he being well aware that he could not procure the assent of the late Cabinet to his commercial treaty.[7]

Between these charges and recriminations the truth I am induced to believe inclines towards the former statements—I am convinced of the disposition of the Regent honestly to carry on the government according to the Constitution and laws, but I fear that the efforts of his enemies will drive him to the wall, and place him in a position wherein he cannot act constitutionally—Already he seems approaching such a point; since, to go ↑on↓ with the present Chamber is impossible, and the result of a new election would not probably change in any great degree its political character.

Amid this conflict and confusion of parties and passions the Constitution is continually appealed to by all, but rather as a weapon of offence, and a stumbling block to their adversaries than as the rule and guide of their own conduct—From my observation thus far I am led to fear that it is inapplicable in its present form, to the condition of the nation, and that a long series of years and education ⟨is⟩ ↑will be↓ necessary, in order that they may grow up to the capacity of enjoying it.

I regret to say that the indisposition to which I alluded in a former despatch and which has confined me to the house for about four months still continues though with less violence and I am strenuously urged by my physician to avoid the heat of a Spanish summer in my present reduced condition. I may find it necessary therefore towards the close of the next month to repair to the Pyrennees or some temperate part of France until the return of cool weather; leaving the legation in the hands of Mr. Hamilton in whose ability and whose attention to business, as I before observed, I have the fullest confidence.

I am, Sir very respectfully / Your obdt Sevt.

Washington Irving

DOCKETED: Recd. 22 June. / Mr. Markoe [upper left corner, page 1] / No. 22. W. Irving. Madrid. 24 May. 1843 —

MANUSCRIPT: NA, RG 59.   PUBLISHED: STW, II, 154–55 (in part).

Only the signature is in WI's handwriting.

1. This document of surrender was signed by General Rafael Maroto (1783–1847), the leader of the rebellious army of Don Carlos, on August 3, 1839. See Edgar Holt, *The Carlist Wars in Spain*, p. 189; and Martin Hume, *Modern Spain*, p. 355.

2. Alvaro Gómez Becerra (1771–1855), who had been minister of justice in Mendizábal's cabinet in 1835–36, formed a new ministry which functioned from May 20 to June 29, 1843. See Christiansen, *Military Power*, p. 170.

3. See *La Gaceta*, May 20, 21, 1843.

4. Juan Alvarez Mendizábal (1790–1853), a shrewd financier who had served as count of Toreno's finance minister in 1835 and succeeded him as premier (September 14, 1835–May 15, 1836), later held the financial post in Calatrava's cabinet (August 15, 1836–August 17, 1837). See Christiansen, *Military Power*, p. 168; and H. Butler Clarke, *Modern Spain*, pp. 113–18.

5. Pedro Gómez de la Serna (1806–1871) was a lawyer and writer. See *Enciclopedia Universal Ilustrada*, XXVI, 558.

6. Isidoro de Hoyos y Rubín de Celis (1793–1876) was a general and a senator from Asturias. See *Enciclopedia Universal Ilustrada*, XXVIII, 489.

7. WI had informed Webster of various aspects of the commercial negotiations with Spain in his letters of August 27, November 5, December 10 and 24, 1842.

1587. To Sarah Storrow

Madrid May 25. 1843

My dear Sarah,

I have recd. two or three letters from you[1]—which remain unanswered; but letter writing is difficult to me. I am struggling on with his miserable malady which still clings to me and incapacitates me for every thing: but which I trust is gradually yielding You must make your Summer arrangements without reference to me. I cannot promise to come on: though, should circumstances warrant it, nothing would give me greater delight. I should rejoice to pass some time with you at Havre, near my dear friend Beasley and in the neighborhood of the Greenes,[2] but I ⟨can⟩ dread Paris.

I have to scrawl this line on returning from a drive, ⟨to⟩ the French Courier goes at 5 Oclock, and it is now half past four.

Give my affectionate remembrances to Mr Storrow & kiss my darling Kate for me.

Your affectionate Uncle
Washington Irving

P.S   Thank Mr Corbin[3] for the extracts of letters, for me. I reccollect him perfectly well; one of the most Gentlemanlike Americans that frequented our Legation at London. I am glad you have such agreeable intimates as Mr & Mrs Corbin.[4]

Hector leaves me in a few days to return home. He will go to Barcelona & Marseilles & thence shape his course to Paris

ADDRESSED: Madame / Madame Storrow / Aux soins de M. T. W. Storrow / No. 17
    Rue du Faubourg Poissonniere / Paris
MANUSCRIPT: Yale.

1. These letters have not been located.
2. Friends with whom WI socialized in Le Havre in the fall of 1823 and in late June and early July, 1825, and in Paris in August, 1824, and the summer of 1825. See *J&N*, III, 224-26, 383, 385-87, 496-500.
3. Probably Francis Porteous Corbin (1801-1876), who was educated in France and England.
4. Probably Agnes Rebecca Hamilton (1801-1893) of Philadelphia who married Corbin in 1825.

1588. To Sarah Storrow

Madrid, June 3d. 1843.

My dear Sarah,

I wrote to you about a week Since[1] in reply to your letters proposing that I should come on to Paris &c. I am affraid my letter was a very triste one, for I was suffering under a wretched dejection of spirits which afflicted me for several days; caused in some measure by the obstinacy of my malady, and no doubt operating to aggravate it. Since then there has been a favorable change both in my complaint & my feelings. The weather has become genial, and that has had its effect; I [have][2] been able not merely to drive out, but to walk out a little: to visit my friends, go to the opera &c and these have all operated to make quite a different man of me. I now look forward to more cheerful times, and trust soon to have conquered the chief inconveniences of my malady—but I have had a dreary time of it.

My doctor urges me to leave Spain for the hot months, and others concur in the same advice; but I am loth to quit my post for any length of time in the critical state of Spanish affairs. A Civil war may break out, and I may find it difficult to get back again. Beside, if I leave Madrid for any length of time I must break up my establishment, sell my horses &c &c as I could not afford to keep an establishment going on here and in America and to travel into the bargain now that my literary resources are dried up. These and other considerations deter me from taking a step which must so completely unsettle me. I wrote, however, some time since to government mentioning my long & continued indisposition, and the possibility that I might be compelled to seek a change of air and to travel for the restoration of my health; in which case I should leave the legation in the hands of Mr Hamilton.

I have no intention of visiting any watering place in the Pyrenees: if I should have to take natural mineral baths I would rather go to Enghein[3] in the neighborhood of Paris, where I would be near you: but I hope soon to be well enough to dispense with baths. You must not, however, make any of your arrangements dependent upon mine—my plans and movements are at the mercy of circumstances—instructions from home; events *in* Spain: changes in my own state of health &c. Should I come on I will find you out wherever you are and would rejoice to join you and Kate any where in the Country—But Paris and all its dissipations; and visitations and botherations are a perfect horror to me in my present "weak and low condition"

Hector Ames sets off in about a week for Barcelona, on his way homeward Via Paris. He expects to embark at Havre early in July.

My man Benjamin sets off about the same time for Paris direct: I having no longer occasion for his services. He ⟨has had his⟩ is honest, and capable; but he has had his head turned by being Major Domo, and has been above all household work; and above all, has been very negligent during my long indisposition; leaving all the extra trouble and care to fall upon the faithful Lorenzo; whom I have ↑now↓ put at the head of my household; and who I should take with me in case I came into France

As I still write with some inconvenience You must excuse this scrawl, which I fear you will hardly decypher. I will write to you again soon, by which time I trust my mind will be made up as to my plans for the summer—at present it is rather in confusion.

Give my affectionate remembrances to Mr Storrow & Kiss little Miss Kate for me.

Your affectionate Uncle
Washington Irving

P S   I beg you to mention to nobody the possibility of my coming on to Paris. In case I should visit it; which is very uncertain, I should like to do it as quietly as possible

Manuscript: Yale.

1. WI to Sarah Storrow, May 25, 1843.
2. WI omitted the bracketed word.
3. Enghien-les Bains, a suburb eight miles northwest of the center of Paris, is noted for its cold sulphur springs. See *Columbia-Lippincott Gazetteer of the World*, p. 577; and Karl Baedeker, *Paris and Its Environs*, p. 430.

1589.   To Olegario de los Cuetos

Legation of the United States. / Madrid June 6th. 1843.

The Undersigned Envoy Extraordinary and Minister Plenipotentiary of the United States of America, respectfully solicits the early attention of His Excellency Don Olegario de los Cuetos, First Minister of State and of Foreign affairs ad interim of Her Catholic Majesty to the accompanying extract of a letter from the American Consul at Mahon.[1]

That Consul states that several parcels of letters forwarded by the United States Consul at Marseilles[2] for the American Squadron at Mahon were deposited in the post office at that place; but that upon being applied for, the post master refused to deliver them except upon the payment of 10 reals vellon for the single letters, and more in proportion for the heavier ones.

As it appears that the postage on these letters had been paid to Marseilles, and that they had been brought from Marseilles, to Mahon in a transient vessel without any expense whatever to Her Majesty's Post office Department it is evident that, under the provisions of the royal order of June 20th. 1832, no postage could rightfully be demanded, save perhaps a few cuartos for the expense of distribution.

The order to which the Undersigned has referred provides that all letters brought to Spanish ports by foreign vessels for the carriage of which nothing was paid by the post-office Department, should be distributed and transmitted by the Department free from other charges than such as are paid upon the correspondence mailed at the place of landing; and that the charges paid upon the ultra marine correspondence, or Sea postage, should be laid upon such correspondence only as was brought by Spanish vessels employed on that service

The unjust, and, since the promulgation of that order, unlawful exactions of the post-masters at various ports in regard to letters brought by sea, without expense to the royal treasury gave rise to a correspondence of some length on the part of the predecessor of the Undersigned Mr. Vail, and has it is believed, been complained of in succession by several of the Representatives of the United States: Under these circumstances it is with regret that the Undersigned is compelled to bring to your notice a case of such an exorbitant charge without any adequate service rendered and he doubts not that your Excellency will lay the matter promptly before that department to which it belongs, in order that the provisions of the royal order cited, may be fully enforced.

Even upon the supposition that the letters in question had been brought by a vessel in the service of the post office Department, it would seem improbable that the sea-postage on a single letter from Marseilles to Mahon should amount to the Sum of 10 reals vellon.

The Circumstance that the port of Mahon is the rendezvous and dépôt of the United States Squadron in the Mediterranean[3] and that letters are continually arriving for the American officers on that station seems to furnish an additional reason that the cases in which sea-postages may be exacted, as well as the various rates which may be charged, should be carefully ascertained.

The Undersigned has the pleasure to offer to His Excellency the assurances of his most distinguished consideration.

Washington Irving.

MANUSCRIPT: NA, RG 84 (letterbook copy).

1. From Obadiah Rich's letter of May 18, 1843 (NA, RG 84).
2. D. C. Croxall of New Jersey served as U.S. consul at Marseilles from 1830 to 1850. See Hasse, *Index to U.S. Documents*, III, 1722.

3. Even after the Tripolitan War the Barbaries continued to be restive, so the United States established a depot and repair docks at Port Mahon in the Balearic Islands and sent a squadron of its best ships to the Mediterranean each year. See Fletcher Pratt, *The Navy, A History* (New York, 1941), pp. 220, 223.

1590. To Stephen Pleasanton

Legation of the United States. / Madrid June 7th. 1843.

Stephen Pleasanton Esqr. / 5th. Auditor of the Treasury—Washington.

Sir,

I beg leave to recommend to your early attention the accounts which have been transmitted from this Legation up to the end of the month of March or the first quarter of 1843: They have been made up regularly at the close of each quarter, with the exception of that of the 10th. of August which was owing to the circumstance that the date of my appointment did not coincide with the divisions of the year suggested in the instructions from the Department.

Tho I am under the impression that all the charges contained in these accounts are strictly within the line of established precedents, yet as nearly a year has elapsed since the first were rendered, I am desirous that they should be examined and audited; or that any objections which might exist should be stated in order that the charges may be explained and supported before the vouchers referring to them shall be mislaid or lost.

As these accounts are in themselves so simple and involve so few items, I have thought it probable that they may have been settled, but that the notification of the settlement had not yet been forwarded to me.

I am with respect / Your obdt Sert
Washington Irving.

MANUSCRIPT: NA, RG 84 (letterbook copy).

Stephen Pleasanton (d. 1855) of Delaware was fifth auditor of the Treasury from 1817 to 1855. For other details see WI to Pleasanton, January 14, 1830. The fifth auditor handled diplomatic and consular accounts, as well as those of the Department of State and the Bureau of Internal Revenue. See Ben: Perley Poore, *The Political Register and Congressional Directory* (Boston, 1878), p. 626.

1591. To Sarah Storrow

Madrid June 10th. 1843

My dear Sarah,

I am looking daily for letters from you to know what you determine upon for the summer. I am sorry I can give nothing definite as to my own plans, as they must depend upon circumstances over which I have no control. I have been improving much in health within the last fortnight; and am able to go out a little on foot; to pay visits &c which contribute greatly to promote cheerfulness. The day before yesterday I dined at the British Embassy—the first time I had dined out for upwards of four months; but the dinner quite deranged me, and I have not yet quite got over it. I feel every day sensible how much I have been pulled down by this long & harrassing indisposition. . Fortunately the weather is temperate and the usual Summer heats have not yet set in.

Hector Ames leave[s][1] this in three days for Barcelona, & will be in Paris early in July. I feel sorry to part with him: he is a most correct worthy little fellow and has conducted himself in the most unexceptionable manner.

My man Benjamin set off for France this morning with Mr Scotts[2] family, who are to give him a lift as far as Bayonne, after which he must find his own way to Paris. I have dismissed him on account of his heartless conduct during my long malady: when he left every thing to be done for me to my good faithful Lorenzo. In fact Benjamins head was turned by thinking himself Major domo of an embassy, and he was above all menial occupation: gadding about continually to the other legations. He is a capable Servant and perfectly honest, but he is an arrant *old soldier* and will work no more than he can help.

I have placed Lorenzo at the head of my establishment; taken a woman cook of his reccommendation in place of the Greek Cook I had before employed;[3] who regularly cheated me. Lorenzo now makes all the purchases & settles all the bills and the consequence is that my household expenses have shrunk about one third.

I must be brief, as I have to write another letter by this courier, and the time is nearly expired. Give my affectionate regards to your husband and kiss darling little Kate for me

Your affectionate uncle
Washington Irving

P. S. Mr Storrow sent me some time since an ⟨af⟩ account of postage, and of money paid to Gagliani[4] for his paper. I wish him to send me *duplicate* receipts of Galignani—and duplicate accounts of so much due to himself for letters franked and forwarded to the legation. Our Government is very strict and requires vouchers for all our expenditures. I wish him to send these under cover to Mr Alex Hamilton Secy of Legation, so that they may reach here before the 1st of next month when the quarters accounts of the legation have to be made up & forwarded.

There is no need of specifying the number of letters, but say merely. US. Legation at Madrid—To T W Storrow Dr for ⟨letters⟩ postage & letters ↑franked &c↓—so much.

ADDRESSED: Madame / Madame Storrow / aux soins de Mr T. W Storrow / 17 Rue de Faubg Poissonniere / à Paris
MANUSCRIPT: Yale.

1. WI omitted the bracketed letter.
2. Newton Scott, the secretary of the British legation in Madrid, was the son of Harry Scott, the British consul in Bordeaux and an old acquaintance of WI's. See WI to Sarah Storrow, August 12, 1842.
3. For WI's initial reaction to Antonio, the cook, see his letter to Sarah Storrow, July 25, 1842.
4. William and Anthony Galignani were booksellers in Paris who published books in English. They also issued *Galignani's Messenger,* a daily newspaper in English to which WI is doubtless referring. See *A Famous Bookstore* (Paris, 1920), pp. 11–13; and Giles Barber, "Galignani's and the Publication of English Books in France from 1800 to 1852," *The Library,* 5th ser. 16 (1961), 269.

1592.   To Obadiah Rich

Legation of the United States. / Madrid June 11th. 1843.

O. Rich, Esqr. / U. S. Consul—Mahon.

Sir.

Your letter of the 18th. May[1] in relation to postages was received on the 31st. Ulto.

Upon examining the files of the Legation, it appeared that the last communication upon this subject, from the Spanish Government, was a note from M. Gonzalez under date of Decr. 31st. 1841. to Mr. Vail, enclosing a copy of the royal order of 1832 to which you refer—I send you herewith a copy of that order.

On the 6th. Inst, I passed a note to the Minister of Foreign affairs[2] in which I represented to him the exorbitant charges on sea letters made by the Post-Master at Mahon, and urged the enforcement of the royal order above alluded to: To this note an answer was received yesterday informing me that the subject had been referred to the Minister of the

Interior,[3] in order to the adoption of such measures as might be necessary

I am with respect / Your Obdt Sevt.
Washington Irving.

MANUSCRIPT: NA, RG 84 (letterbook copy); NYPL—Seligman Collection (copy).

1. Rich's letter to WI is preserved in NA, RG 84.
2. See WI to Olegario de los Cuetos, June 6, 1843.
3. Pedro Gómez de la Serna. See WI to Daniel Webster, May 24, 1843.

1593. To Alexander Burton

Legation of the United States / Madrid June 16th. 1843.

Alexr. Burton Esqr. / Consul U. S.—Cadiz

Sir.

I have hitherto delayed a reply to your letter of May 8th.[1] and to those which preceded it, in relation to the war contributions, in the expectation of receiving an official communication from this Government on the subject.

I addressed a note on the 26th. of April, within two days after the receipt of your first letter,[2] to the Minister of Foreign affairs, in which I quoted at some length the provisions of the treaty to show the illegality of the attempt to levy upon you these extraordinary contributions and urged that steps should be promptly taken to relieve you from the coercive measures adopted by the local authorities: Some days having elapsed without receiving an answer, Count Almodovar was applied to verbally and an assurance was received that the subject should be attended to on the following day: the next day however, the Ministry of which Count Almodovar was a Member left office, and the state of affairs since that period must be too well known to you, to require any further explanation of the delay.

Informal applications have been made in the interval, and assurances of the same character have been given, that the case shall be finally settled within a short period, and I have reason to believe that in the meantime orders have been issued to suspend all proceedings against yourself, or your property.

I am, with respect / Your Obdt Sevt
Washington Irving.

MANUSCRIPT: NA, RG 84 (letterbook copy).

1. See Burton to WI, May 8, 1843, in NA, RG 84.

2. Burton had written to WI on April 18, 1843, and again on April 27, 1843 (NA, RG 84).

1594. To George Read

Legation of the United States / Madrid June 16th. 1843.

George Read Esqr. / Consul. U. S.—Malaga.

Sir.

I have received with pleasure your Several letters of the 5th., 7, and 9th. Inst[1] containing information of the late occurrences at Malaga.[2]

Should any serious commotion occur in the city itself, you will, I feel confident, take all the measures within your [power][3], to protect American Citizens and their property; at the same time adhering to the prudent line of conduct, which you have hitherto maintained: If cases should arise in which after due consideration, you may not think it consistent with the principle, which our Government has so frequently declared, of non-interference in the affairs of other nations, to unite in the course adopted by the other Consuls resident in Malaga, you should not hesitate to separate yourself from them, in obedience to the established policy of the United States.

I am, respectfully / Your obdt Sert.
Washington Irving

MANUSCRIPT: NG, RG 84; NYPL (copy).

1. These letters are preserved in NA, RG 84.

2. Civilian unrest in Málaga, a center of liberalism, had flared up in late May with the establishment of a junta supported by the military forces. Among the leaders were General José Cabrera and Brigadier Torremejia, who demanded the return of the López ministry which had held power from May 10 to 20, 1843, and was to regain control for five months beginning June 29. The junta dissolved itself on June 6, but another composed of respectable merchants was formed. When General Alvarez entered Málaga on June 14, this group fled temporarily but resumed power shortly afterward when most of Spain broke into revolt. See London *Times*, June 12, 19, 20, 23, 26, 28, 1843; and George Read to WI, June 5, 7, 9, 12, 1843.

3. The copyist omitted the bracketed word.

1595. To Sarah Storrow

Madrid June 17th. 1843.

My dear Sarah,

I wrote to you a few days since and have since received a letter from you, which lets me know that another is on the way,[1] in the care of a Mr Sumner.[2] Your last letter says nothing of your plans for the summer; but, by the drift of some part of it I am inclined to think Mr Storrow has abandoned the idea of going out to America this Summer. I shall look anxiously to be better informed in your next—

I am doing well, as regards my complaint. It ceases to harrass and shackle me—I can visit, and can walk out a little: though I still sally forth generally in the Carriage. I am regaining appetite, strength and spirits and hope, before very long, to be myself again.

I can make no plans as to travelling. Affairs here are in a crisis, and will remain so for some ten days or a fortnight yet, by which time it will be determined, I think, whether the Regent will be able to keep his ground against the coalition formed to pull him down & against the insurrections stirred ⟨of⟩up in all parts of the country.[3] If he falls, matters will very likely be in a state of chaos and anarchy for a time until a new government is formed. I am inclined to think he will weather the present storm; but he is likely to have a tempestuous time during the remainder of his Regency.

In ⟨such⟩ the present unsettled and uncertain crisis, when civil war is threatening in various parts of the country; and when insurrection may break out in the Capitol, I do not feel inclined to absent myself from my post, unless my health should absolutely require it. As I said, a couple of weeks will probably enable me to form some judgement of the ⟨probability of⟩ course events are likely to take; and whether I can venture to absent myself for a little while without the risque of finding the government demolished before my return.

I have had charming letters from home: from your mother & from the family at the Cottage.[4] The only drawback in the pleasure they give me is the intense longing they create to find myself once more at dear little Sunnyside

Give my affectionate remembrances to Mr Storrow; and half a dozen kisses to little passionate imperious Kate.

Your affectionate uncle
Washington Irving

MANUSCRIPT: Yale.   PUBLISHED: Simison, *Keogh Papers*, pp. 204–5.

1. These letters have not been located.

2. George Sumner (1817–1863), author, traveler, and student at Heidelberg and Berlin, was to succeed Alexander Hamilton as secretary of the legation. WI aided Sumner in his researches in Spanish libraries and archives by providing him with letters of introduction. See WI to Don Fermín Caballero, September 6, 1843; to Don Olegario de los Cuetos, June 19, 1843; and to Sarah Storrow, July 23, 1843, and April 6, 1844.

3. Revolts and unrest occurred in Málaga, Granada, Lérida, Barcelona, Valencia, Reus, Tortosa, San Felipe de Jativa, and Castellón. See *El Castellano*, May 29, 30, June 10, 12, 13, 17, 1843.

4. These letters have not been located.

1596. *To Olegario de los Cuetos?*

Legation des Etats Unis / Madrid le 19. Juin 1843.

Non-officiel

Monsieur le Ministre.

Un citoyen distingué des Etats Unis[1] etant occupé en ce moment a rediger l'histoire de la Louisiane m'a eté fortement recommandé pour obtenir des renseignemens relatifs a l'ancienne colonie de la Louisiane, pendant qu'elle à eté sous la domination Epagnole (de 1766 a 1803) et se composant de la correspondance entre le Gouvernement de Sa Majeste Catholique et les Gouverneurs ou Intendants de la Colonie. Etant informé que toutes les pieces relatives a cette colonie se trouvent dans le Ministère des affaires Etrangères, Je m'addresse pour cet objet a Votre Excellence.

Comptant sur la bienviellance du Gouvernement de Sa Majesté pour un objet dont la seul but est dans l'interet de la literature et des coinnoissances utiles de fournir des materiaux pour Servir a l'histoire d'une portion interessante des Etats Unis, je prie Votre Excellence de vouloir bien lui preter votre appui, en donnant la direction convenable a la liste ci-jointe des points speciaux sur lesquelles, les renseignemens me sont demandés; et j'ose vous prier, en outre de vouloir bien mettre M. Hamilton Secretaire de cette Legation en rapports personels avec l'officier chargé de la conservation de ces documents, dans le but de lui demander verbalement quelques autres informations d'une nature moins specifique, mais toujours ayant trait au meme sujet.

Je suis Monsieur, avec la plus parfaite consideration, de Votre Excellence

Le très obeissant Serviteur.
Washington Irving.

MANUSCRIPT: NA, RG 84 (letterbook copy).

Translation:

"A distinguished citizen of the United States being occupied at this moment in writing a history of Louisiana has been strongly recommended to me for the purpose of obtaining information relative to the old colony of Louisiana, while it was under Spanish control (from 1766 to 1803) and consisting of the correspondence between the government of his Catholic majesty and the governors and intendants of the colony. Being informed that all materials relating to this colony are found in the Ministry of Foreign Affairs, I address myself to your excellency for this object.

"Counting on the kindness of her majesty's government for an object whose only purpose is in the interest of literature and useful knowledge to furnish materials to serve for the history of an interesting part of the United States, I ask your excellency to grant him your assistance in giving suitable direction to the attached list of special points of which information is requested of me; and I venture to ask you, besides, kindly to send Mr. Hamilton, secretary of this legation, into personal contact with the officer entrusted with the care of these documents, for the purpose of asking him about some other information of a less specific nature, but still dealing with the same subject."

1. WI is probably referring to George Sumner, mentioned in his letter of June 17, 1843, to Sarah Storrow.

1597.   To Catharine Paris

Madrid, June 21st 1843.

My dear Sister

I have again to thank you for kind and cheering letters,[1] full of precious home details. I am sorry I can make but such poor returns; but, though my malady has ceased in its virulence I find writing still irksome to me, and indeed am prohibited by my physician from indulging in it. It is a ⟨hard⟩ great privation and reduces me to a state of idleness foreign to my habits and inclinations. The Doctor would also, if he could, put a stop to my almost incessant reading, as he thinks that any fixed attention for a length of time wearies the brain and in some degree produces those effects on the system which originated my complaint: but I cannot give up reading, in my otherwise listless state. He has been very urgent for me to travel, ⟨as much⟩ not merely for a change of air, but because the Succession of Scenes & incidents amuses without fatiguing the mind and thus operates healthfully upon the system. I have been recovering so much of late, however, that I hope to be able to dispense with this part of his advice, and to continue at my post. I should be loth to leave it in the present critical state of the Country; when insurrections are breaking out in various parts of the Kingdom and Spain is once more threatened with civil war.

My illness has prevented me from giving you a detail of the political

events of the country; which have of late assumed an alarming aspect.
A coalition of various factions (opposite in their views and doctrines,
and no one of them of sufficient magnitude to form a majority) has
united in ⟨the⟩ a vehement attempt to pull down the Regent and put
an end to the existing Government. ⟨Should the⟩ For this purpose insurrections have been stirred up in various parts of the country;[2] and
latterly in Barcelona, that old seat of rebellion.[3] To day, the Regent
sallies forth from the capital to put himself once more at the head of
his troops and endeavor to quell these insurrections.[4] I heartily pray for
his success, for should he fail, and should he be ejected from power, a
fearful state of anarchy would ensue. The very coalition ⟨which⟩ now
combined against him would break into warring factions, each striving
for the ascendancy, and we ⟨should⟩ ↑might↓ have civil war of the worst
kind.

—I have just returned from attending a levee held by the Regent ⟨for⟩
at 12 Oclock: preparatory to his departure. He made a frank & manly
address to the Diplomatic Corps:[5] declaring his disposition to cultivate
cordial relations with all countries, but particularly with those who had
representations at this court & who recognized the Constitution of Spain,
the throne of Isabella II and his Regency. His loyal devotion to the
⟨throne⟩ constitution & the throne and his Sole & uniform ⟨ab⟩ ambition
to ⟨s⟩ place the reins of Government in the hands of the youthful queen
on the 10 of October 1844 when she should have completed her minority;[6]
and to ⟨give her⟩ place under her command a peaceful prosperous &
happy country: but he expressed at the same time his determination to
resist every attempt to throw the country into a state of anarchy; and
to defend the throne of Isabella and the constitution of 1837 like a
good soldier.

At four Oclock a general review of the National Militia takes place
in the Prado, as on a former occasion, when the Regent, as before, will
no doubt make them a speech,[7] confiding the Safety of the city and of
the youthful Queen and her sister to their patriotism and loyalty. At 5.
Oclock he takes his departure. I cannot but feel that he sallies forth,
this time, with much more doubtful prospects than in his former expedition against Barcelona. The spirit of rebellion is more widely
diffused;[8] and is breaking forth at various points. A few days, ⟨will⟩
or a very few weeks at farthest, will decide his fate; and determine
whether he is to maintain his post and keep up some form of government for the remainder of the minority of the Queen (about 15 months
& ½) or whether his power, if not himself is to be annihilated and every
thing for a time thrown into chaos.[9]

In these critical times, when every thing threatens a tempest, I feel
more and more solicitude about the little Queen; whose fortunes are

so much at the mercy of events. I lately had a most interesting conversation about her with her guardian the good Arguelles. He speaks English very fluently, though with something of an accent, and always mentions the little Queen and her sister as "thece two yong ladies—" giving a sharp sound to the S, as if it were a C. According to his account every hour of their time is most profitably employed in the study of languages; of history, geography, mathematics, and the acquisition of various accomplishments. He extols the amiable disposition of the little Queen; the total absence of all pretension or superiority in her intercourse, not merely with her sister, but with some of the young people, (daughters of the Camaristas)[10] & others of the household, who occasionally join in her amusements. He ⟨mentioned the⟩ dwelt on the charitable disposition of the Queen & her sister. Their monthly allowance for spending money, instead of being laid out on finery, or play things; is devoted to private charities. When they walk out petitions are often presented to them and applications made for relief. They take note of all these and cause them to be enquired into—Once a month they have their settling day: when, like two little women of business, all these claims are canvassed: they look personally into each case; decide on its merits, and determine what sum shall be dispensed to the applicant. I am told it is quite interesting and touching to see the manner in which they acquit themselves ⟨i⟩on this occasion.

Since my partial recovery I have seen the little Queen two or three times in public. She has grown very much of late and really begins to look somewhat womanly. I am told her opening of the last Cortes,[11] when she went in State ⟨and took her⟩ ↑passed up through the Center of the Senate chamber escorted by the Regent, her train borne by ⟨h⟩ ladies in waiting, and took her↓ seat alone on the throne, was quite charming. It was observed that her eyes were continually turning to a Tribune on one side of the ⟨hall of⟩ Senate Hall, in which was seated her little Sister; it was the only time they had ever been separated.

—On Sunday evening last. I attended the Soiree held weekly at the Regents: it was the only one I have been able to attend for upwards of four months: but I was anxious to go to it, as it would be the last before the departure of the Regent. It was thinly attended and I remarked a general gloom on the faces of those attached to the Regent, or whose interests were connected with his fortunes. The Regent himself did not appear, being engaged in a cabinet council. The Duchess[12] was pale, and had a dejected air, complaining of head ache. I rather fear it was heart ache, for she feels their hazardous position and the "pitfalls which surround them. ["] She is an amiable and a lovely woman: and her dejected air rather heightened her beauty in my eyes. I had not seen her since my illness and I had to thank her for many kind enquiries she had made after my health: sending one of the Dukes aids de camp for the purpose. It will be a joyful hour for her I am convinced, when the Duke lays down his Regency and returns to the quiet & security of private life. It is said she will accompany the Duke on his present expedition; rather than remain alone, in the magnificent palace of Buena Vista; exposed to the vicissitudes and hazards of this critical juncture. Certainly if any evil should befal the Duke in his expedition her situation here would be painful and precarious—I have not been able to ascertain, however, whether she accompanies him or not. I doubt whether she will go immediately. She may rejoin him, some days hence.

I have scrawled a longer letter than I had any idea of accomplishing & must conclude. Tell Eliza Romeyn, Sarah Irving &c &c that I have received their letters[13] giving me most acceptable cottage news and beg them to write on, without waiting for replies. I cannot write letters at present—indeed I *must* not. Every thing concerning dear little Sunnyside is interesting to me. My heart dwells in that blessed little Spot; and I really believe that when I die I shall haunt it: but it will be as a *good spirit*, that no one need be affraid of. Though I cannot enjoy its delights in person at present, I enjoy them at second hand, by the accounts given by others. When I think of America my thoughts all center there; and I believe that, even ⟨if⟩ though exiled from it; a great portion of my actual enjoyment in life, is hearing and thinking about it; picturing it in my thoughts, dreaming about it; and flattering myself with the hope that I shall return and end my days there. In the mean time, thank God it is a happy house for my dear brother and his family.

> Ever my dear Sister / Most affectionately your brother
> Washington Irving

MANUSCRIPT: Yale.   PUBLISHED: PMI, III, 277–81 (in part); STW, II, 155 (in part).

1. These letters have not been located.

2. The Moderates and Republicans united against Espartero exploited the sudden indignation of the people at the Regent's decree dissolving the Cortes on May 26, 1843. Widespread denunciations of him and demonstrations in favor of Isabella and the Constitution of 1837 followed. After May 23, pronunciamientos spread throughout the Andalusia, culminating in the rebellion of Seville on July 17. On June 8, the Supreme Provincial Junta was installed at Sabadell in Catalonia; it declared the province independent of Espartero and on June 29 appointed General Francisco Serrano (1810–1885) as universal minister. Early in June Moderates and Progressives at Seville, Valencia, and Barcelona declared against the regent. A secret society, the Spanish Military Order, founded in Paris by Leopoldo O'Donnell (1809–1867), and Ramón María Narváez (1799–1868), worked throughout the army with the hope of restoring Christina. Many resigned their commissions, while those retaining their command were only watching events. See WI to Daniel Webster, May 9 and 24, 1843; George F. White, *A Century of Spain*

and Portugal (London, 1909), p. 226; Raymond Carr, *Spain*, pp. 225–26; and H. Butler Clarke, *Modern Spain*, p. 187.

3. Espartero's breach with Barcelona radicalism dated from the Junta of Vigilance of October, 1841, and widened with his bombardment of the city in November, 1842. On June 6, 1843, Barcelona named a new junta, and on June 12 an insurrection broke out in the city. At this point Juan Prim (1814–1870), the Catalan general and politician, took charge, and on June 13 the Barcelona garrison, under General Valdes, declared for the insurrectionary junta. See WI to Catharine Paris, November 20, December 10, 1842; and to Daniel Webster, December 10, 1842; to the secretary of state, June 22, 1843; Carr, *Spain*, pp. 225–26; and London *Times*, June 15, 16, 19, 26, 1843.

4. Espartero hesitated in Madrid until June 21, when his cause was already virtually lost. With five to six thousand men he left to take post at Albacete. Similar small movements rather than campaigns followed. The only sure support of his government was his personal following among the Ayacucho generals, the Progressives who preferred him to forces dominated by Moderates and the Madrid militia. See White, *A Century of Spain and Portugal*, p. 226; and Carr, *Spain*, p. 225.

5. This address echoed Espartero's earlier speeches, which had included an apologetic manifesto denying that he wished to prolong the Regency (June 13, 1843) and an address to the National Guard (June 15, 1843). See *El Castellano*, June 20, 1843; London *Times*, June 23, 24, 26, 1843; and *Vida Militar y Política de Espartero* (Madrid, 1845), III, 755–56.

6. Isabella was declared of age on November 8, 1843, although by the constitution she was not legally so until her fourteenth birthday in 1844. See Martin Hume, *Modern Spain*, p. 375; and White, *A Century of Spain and Portugal*, p. 228.

7. "Proclamation of the Regent." See London *Times*, June 28, 1843.

8. Generals Martín Zurbano and Antonio Seoane (1791–1870), marched from Lerida for Barcelona. However, since their men seemed disposed to revolt, they retired toward Saragossa. Francisco Javier Azpiroz (1797–1868), elected captain-general of Valladolid by its junta, marched to Madrid; Narváez hurried from exile, was joined by men sent to oppose him, and marched to Madrid. At the end of July Zurbano and Seoane also reached the capital. On July 22 at Torrejon the armies refused to fight, and Madrid opened its gates to them. Although General Van Halen had occupied Cordova and bombarded Seville, the news from Madrid caused all of his forces to desert him. See White, *A Century of Spain and Portugal*, pp. 226–27; and Clarke, *Modern Spain*, p. 188.

9. WI's fears were confirmed as in the case of Barcelona, whom Francisco Serrano had promised to aid in their aims with the central junta at Madrid. Serrano had hidden the Royalist and reactionary character of the revolution, while he divided the Liberal opinion by proclaiming the López ministry. When Serrano failed either to aid them or to listen to their delegates, the city revolted and other areas of Catalonia became defiant. Prim besieged the city for six weeks, bombarding it into submission in November and ending serious civil strife in Spain for several years. See White, *A Century of Spain and Portugal*, pp. 227–28; and Clarke, *Modern Spain*, p. 188.

10. That is, the maid of honor to the queen.

11. Probably after the formation of the ministry headed by Gomez Becerra on May 20, 1843. See Christiansen, *Military Power*, p. 170.

12. The duchess of Victoria, wife of Regent Espartero.

13. These letters have not been located.

1598. To the Secretary of State

Legation of the United States / Madrid June 22nd. 1843.

No. 23. / The Hon: / The Secretary of State of the U. S—Washington.
Sir,

Since the date of my last despatch (May 24th.) the political affairs of Spain have gone on from bad to worse, until we are threatened with that state of anarchy and civil war, which appears to have been the persevering aim of secret influences both within and without the Country.

The regent finding the Cortes completely under the domination of a coalition of factions, of distinct and opposite principles, but momentarily combined by a spirit of hostility to the existing government, dissolved that body and again appealed to the nation by a new election. The Coalition thwarted in their plans of effecting the downfall of the regent by the measures of the Lopez Cabinet, have carried their plots into the provinces, and by means of agents, emissaries and the liberal expenditure of gold, supplied by unseen hands, have stirred up insurrections in various parts of the kingdom.[1] The most formidable is in Catalonia, headed by Colonel Prim,[2] an ex-deputy of the Cortes; of fiery spirit and great activity; who has declared for the immediate majority of Isabella IInd.

These multiplied insurrections have assumed such a formidable character, that the regent has found it necessary once more to take the field, and accordingly sallied forth yesterday for Valencia, which is in a state of insurrection,[3] and where the populace have murdered Camacho,[4] the political chief in the public streets. Prior to his departure the regent held a levee, in which he made a frank and manly address to the Diplomatic Corps, stating the situation in which he was placed, the loyalty of his feelings and intentions, and his hope that while Spain continued to shew the highest respect for the national rights and independence of other powers, she would receive in turn the same consideration for her own.

He afterwards held a review of the National Guard, by which he was received with much enthusiasm; and as before, on setting out on similar expeditions, confided the city and the youthful Queen to their protection.

I have forborne to weary you with a detail of the tissue of intrigues and machinations which have been carried on here for some weeks past and which have ended in producing this general confusion. Happily our position with respect to this country renders such details of small importance to us. I will only say that as far as I have had an opportunity of getting at the truth, through the cloud of falsehood and misrepresentation in which every thing is enveloped, I retain a favorable opinion of the Regent and a belief in the sincerity of his professions, and regard the recent parliamentary opposition and the present outbreak in various parts of the country as the result of an unholy alliance of factions banded together by a hatred to the party in power; and which after having effected the downfall of the latter, would be cutting each others throats in the struggle for ascendancy.

As yet I believe the Regent has the main part of the army and of the National Guards attached to him; he has generals in the field marching upon the insurgent points; he will soon be himself in the scene of action, and a short time must determine whether he will be able to maintain himself in power or whether his regency must give way to anarchy and confusion.

As yet no Minister of Foreign affairs has been appointed under the new Ministry; the Minister of Marine[5] acting ad interim in the Department of State; this circumstance and the confusion and disorder incident to the present condition of the Country have prevented me from pressing officially the settlement of one or two subjects which are pending: Informal and verbal applications have been made however to which the enclosed paper is the answer: It will be perceived that the case of the United States Consul at Cadiz[6] may be considered as settled in favor of the exemption from War Contributions claimed for him in my note of April 26, to which no official answer has yet been received: In my despatch No. 21, I had the honor to forward a copy of this note to the Department.

I am, Sir, very respectfully / Your Obdt Sevt.
Washington Irving

DOCKETED: No. 23. W. Irving. Madrid 22 June 1843 / Recd. 20 July
MANUSCRIPT: NA, RG 59.

Only the signature is in WI's handwriting.

1. For other details, see WI to Catharine Paris, June 21, 1843.

2. General Juan Prim (1814–1870), a soldier-democrat and champion of the Radicals, rose rapidly from a humble birth to become a general and a count by 1843 and captain-general of Puerto Rico by 1847. He was elected deputy for Tarragona in 1841. Having vainly supported the Catalan grievances against Espartero's failure to suppress smuggling in Catalonia and remembering the bombardment of Barcelona, he called, on May 23, 1843, for the Catalans to rise up against Espartero. See Raymond Carr, *Spain*, pp. 223, 228; and Christiansen, *Military Power*, p. 113.

3. The insurrection broke out in Valencia on June 11, 1843. Narváez and Manuel de la Concha were eagerly welcomed by the Valencia junta and adopted a coalition program consisting of the López ministry, the constitution of 1837, and the Liberal union. Narváez then headed north, and after a successful skirmish at Teruel he advanced to join Azpiroz and camp outside of Madrid until the latter entered the city on July 23, 1843. See London *Times*, June 19, 1843; and H. Butler Clarke, *Spain*, p. 188.

4. Miguel Antonio Comacho, governor of Valencia for ten years, was murdered (*El Castellano* for June 15 labels his death a suicide), although the captain-general of the city, Juan de Zavala (1804–1879), was loyal to Espartero. See London *Times*, June 19, 1843.

5. Olegario de los Cuetos.

6. Alexander Burton.

1599.   To Sarah Storrow

Madrid June 24th. 1843

My dear Sarah,

I yesterday received your letter of the 15th inst:[1] ⟨by⟩ ↑from↓ the tenor of which I conclude that Mr Storrow does not go out to the UStates this summer. I can give no idea ⟨of⟩ as to my own plans: they must depend on the Course of public affairs here, which at present is in a very critical state. Espartero is once more in the field, to endeavor to put down the rebellion which is breaking out in various parts of the Country. I cannot leave my post at a time when the country is menaced with anarchy and Civil war. I am happy to say that my health is daily improving; the Summer thus far is temperate, so that I am gaining strength to support the heats of July and August; and I am getting freed from this malady which has so long harrassed me. Still I am rather listless, and incapable of mental application; and begin to fear I shall contract lazy habits by this long indulgence in perfect idleness[.] I can hardly recognize in myself, so listless and inert, the being that six months since was in an incessant state of mental activity. Oh! if I could but once more be myself again and have two or three years of health of mind and body, to carry out my plans and close my literary carreer; then I should be content to throw down my pen and idle away the remnant of life that might be allotted me; for then I should have provided for the well being of those dependent upon me. This long fit of illness, and the mental inactivity ⟨which attendant⟩ consequent to it, have sadly marred my plans and changed my prospects. Still, I trust I have a fund of health and good spirits yet in reserve and that I shall yet be able to get a good deal of cheerful work out of myself.

Yesterday I had a young gentleman of New York to dine with me, a Mr Austin;[2] he is an acquaintance of Mr Storrows and will call on you on his arrival in Paris, where he will be ⟨some⟩ within a few days after the receipt of this letter. I had Mr & Madm Albuquerque to dine with me also, so that we had a little American party; and I enjoyed it greatly. Madame Albuquerque is my great resource. She is in the place of a niece to me, and indeed calls me uncle. Her children are great pets of mine.

I perfectly reccollect Miss Johnson (now Madame Hacquet) She was in Paris under the care of an aunt. I reccollect her marriage and am sorry it has not proved a happy one. She must prove quite an agreeable acquaintance. Remember me to her kindly.

I am daily looking for letters from Hector, who will find himself in the midst of insurrection at Barcelona. However, his passport and his official character will form a protection for him and he will have an opportunity of seeing a little of life. Hamilton & myself get on very cosily together. He is an excellent companion; cheerful, animated, amiable and full of intelligence & information.

Your account of that little "varment woman" Kate gives me an intense desire to see her[.] I am affraid she will get past all her "baby accomplishments" and be a perfect "little limb"[3] before we meet. Still I think I can tolerate a great deal of unruliness in her; as she is the only child I could ever take in my arms and fondle when it was crying.

God bless her and you my dear Sarah. Give my kind remembrances to Mr Storrow

Your affectionate Uncle
Washington Irving

ADDRESSED: Madame / Madame Storrow / aux Soins de Mr T. W. Storrow / 17. Rue de Faubg Poissonniere / à Paris
MANUSCRIPT: Yale.   PUBLISHED: STW, II, 159 (in part).

1. This letter has not been located.
2. Perhaps a son of Daniel Austin, a New York merchant with a business at 10 Old Slip; or of George Austin, a dry goods merchant at 166½ Broadway. See *New York City Directory for 1843–44*, p. 22.
3. A mischievous person (*OED*).

1600.   To Sarah Storrow

Madrid, June 27th. 1843

My dear Sarah,

The critical state of Spanish affairs, and the indifferent state of my own health have made me give up all thoughts of travelling for the present; but as Mr Hamilton has likewise been out of health lately and is in great need of change of air, and as an agreeable opportunity presented for him to make an excursion to the Pyrenees I have advised him to embrace it. He accordingly sets off this night for Bayonne: from whence he will visit some of the watering places in the Pyrenees, where there are some of his New York intimates, and I presume he will be back here towards the end of July. After which, if my health still requires it, and nothing occurs to render it inexpedient, I may make an excursion. I cannot, however, hold out any strong probability on the Subject.

I apprehend that Mr Hamilton will meet with some interruptions in his route, as the whole country is getting into a State of insurrection. His passports & his diplomatic character however, will protect him, and he seems rather desirous of adventure. I shall miss him very much for he is a delightful companion, and has come more and more upon me the more I have known him, but I could not bear that he should pass the whole year in the monotonous life of Madrid, ⟨without⟩ and thought an excursion of the kind he is about to make would refresh and invigorate his mind as well as his body.

We are in the midst of plots conspiracies & insurrections and know not what a day may bring forth.[1] The Regent is on his way to one part of the Kingdom which is in a state of insurrection, in the mean time insurrections are breaking forth in other quarters. Many predict that he will never return to Madrid; but so they predicted last year, when he sallied forth to put down the insurrection at Barcelona. For my part, I never expect to see Spain enjoy tranquility and a settled form of government during the time I may sojourn in it, and fear I may have to witness some sanguinary scenes of popular commotion. I have looked upon Espartero as the only man likely to maintain the country in a tolerable state of tranquility during the Minority of the little Queen; but I now doubt if he will be able to keep up against the combination of factions bent upon his destruction. A few days will determine his fortunes.

I have not heard from Hector Ames since he left here; though I find, by drafts made by him on our Banker, that he was in Barcelona on the 19th. He seems as much inclined to taciturnity with the pen as with the tongue. He must be in Paris by the time this letter arrives. Should he be in want of money, I will thank Mr Storrow to furnish him with the needful and take his drafts upon his father.

I am getting on very well; though it takes always a tedious time to get rid of maladies of the kind I have to struggle with. The weather has as much effect upon me as upon a barometer; and this season has been uncommonly capricious. It favors me in one respect, that we have none of the usual fervid heats of Summer; ⟨but⟩ which might debilitate me; but the cloudy, windy & occasionally chilly weather irritates my system. However, I trust in another month to be superior to these influences

Give my affectionate regards to Mr Storrow and Kiss dear little good-fornothing Kate for me

Your affectionate Uncle
Washington Irving

Docketed: Washington Irving to Mrs. S. Storrow—Paris / Madrid June 17. 1843. Manuscript: Yale.   Published: PMI, III, 281–82 (in part).

1. For comment on the unstable political situation, see *El Castellano*, May 22, 24, 26, 1843.

1601. To Hugh S. Legaré

Legation of the United States / Madrid. July 9th. 1843.

No 24. The Hon. Hugh S. Legare / Secretary of State (ad interim) / of the United States. Washington.

Sir,

I had the honor a few days since to receive your despatch of the 9th.[1] of May, giving me the intelligence of your appointment (ad interim) as Secretary of State. It will give me great satisfaction, in the discharge of the duties of my post, to have to correspond with one for whom I have ever entertained such high respect and regard.

In my despatch of June 22d I gave a brief view of the political affairs of Spain. Since that date they have hastened on with encreasing rapidity to that state of chaos which I have long apprehended. I forbear to attempt an analysis of what has been a tissue of plot and counter plot. Indeed the falsehood and misrepresentation with which every thing is overlaid in political affairs renders it almost impossible to get at the truth. The insurrection, however it may have originated in corruption and intrigue; has spread to all parts of the country. In many places it is on the mere surface of society; got up by a handful of busy bodies, or confined to the military, but in others it has assumed a popular form and taken a deeper root. The national jealousy with respect to foreigners has been shrewdly wrought upon, by the Secret agents of French ascendancy. They have given the party in power the name of the Anglo Ayacuchos faction,[2] and have spread the belief that, suborned by English gold, they were ready to sacrafice national independence and national industry, to the grasping avarice and love of rule of Great Britain. It is really surprising how rapidly and extensively a bitter anti anglo feeling has been engendered within the last few months, and how much it has aided the views of the insurgents.

The insurrection, as I have ⟨before⟩ ↑heretofore↓ shewn, is ↑the result of↓ a temporary agglomeration of various parties. Among the leaders are men who have figured in former insurrections and been obliged to fly the country; but who have hurried in from France to "ride in the whirl wind and direct the Storm."[3] Among those are some of the very men who made the night attack on the Royal Palace for the purpose of carrying off the youthful Queen.[4] The insurrection is organizing itself, forming a provisional government at Barcelona, issuing decrees in the name of the queen; denouncing Espartero and all who may adhere to him, and declaring all his acts since the 28th of May last, null and void.

In the mean time Espartero remains at Albacete in a state of apparent inactivity, ⟨[*unrecovered*]⟩ ↑which, whatever may be the motive,↓ is certainly injuring his cause at a distance. His friends say, that he is waiting to be joined by Soane, Zurbano,[5] and Enna[6] with their troops, when he will be in sufficient force to strike a decided blow. They persuade themselves that delay is breeding discord in the heterogeneous ranks of the insurgents and giving time for jealousies to break out between their leaders; who are discordant in their political principles, and individually selfish in their aims.[7] I doubt, however, whether the common feeling of hostility to Espartero will not prove sufficiently strong to hold them together until they have effected his downfall. In fact a few days may decide the fate of the Regency. While Espartero is lingering at Albacete, held apparently in check by the insurgents of Catalonia and Valen⟨t⟩cia, an army collected from various places of Leon and old Castile is marching upon Madrid, under the command of General [Azpiroz][8] and threatens to be here in the course of a week. Popular rumor states it to be 15.000 strong: but more reliable reports estimate it at 4000 effective men. No doubt cooperation is expected from within the city; in which there are at present scarce any regular troops; though there is a great force of national guards. It is apprehended that one object of the advancing army will be to get possession of the person of the young Queen and thus to give a death blow to the Regency of Espartero.

Such is the extraordinary crisis to which affairs have arrived; and which is in hourly hazard of some tragical catastrophe. I lament to say, that, taking a deep interest in the honor and prosperity of this country, I look forward with gloomy apprehensions to a State of anarchy that must long prevent the dawn of happier days.

> I am Sir, / very respectfully / Your obedient Servant
> Washington Irving

Docketed: Rec. 21 Augt. / Mr Markoe [*upper left and center, page 1*] / No. 24, W. Irving. Madrid. 9 July 1843–
Manuscript: NA, RG 59.   Published: STW, II, 150–51, 153, 156, 376 (in part).

Unknown to WI, Legaré had died on June 20, and Abel P. Upshur, the secretary of the navy, had assumed the post of secretary of state (ad interim). Upshur, who became secretary of state on a permanent basis on July 24, 1843, continued in the position until he was killed in a gun explosion on the *Princeton* on February 28, 1844.

1. Daniel Webster had resigned as secretary of state on May 8, 1843.
2. A major faction in the Spanish army and in Court politics since 1836, the Ayacuchos were a group of generals around the marquess of Rodil who were responsible for deposing Pezuela, the captain-general of Peru. They were also

suspected of having sold out in their surrender before Ayacucho in 1829. Many supported Espartero as regent and remained in moral isolation after the unpopular execution of Diego de León for his October, 1841, attack on the Royal Palace to which WI alludes in the next paragraph. Continued opposition to their government appointments was central to the founding in Paris of the Spanish Military Order and to the May, 1843, insurrections. See Raymond Carr, *Spain*, pp. 217, 220–22, 225–26; H. Butler Clarke, *Modern Spain*, pp. 187–88; and E. Christiansen, *Military Power*, p. 83. See *El Castellano*'s quotations from *El Espectador* on this topic on June 27, 28, 1843.

3. Joseph Addison, "The Storm," (1704), line 91.

4. For other details, see WI to Catharine Paris, September 2, 1842.

5. See WI to Catharine Paris, June 21, 1843, for details about Martín Zurbano and Antonio Seoane.

6. Manuel Enna (d. 1851), who had served as military governor in various areas of Catalonia, had laid siege to Teruel but was forced to retreat when attacked by the troops of Narváez between July 3 and 7. See London *Times*, July 13, 15, 17, 1843.

7. Another device used by the government was a decree permitting only *La Gaceta*, *El Espectador*, *El Patriota*, and *El Centinela* to send their issues through the mails. *El Eco del Comercio*, *El Castellano*, *Fray Gerundio*, *El Heraldo*, *La Posdata*, *El Católico*, *El Reparador*, *El Archivo*, *La Revista de España y del Estrangero*, *El Gío Fidel*, and *La Revista de Madrid* signed a statement protesting their exclusion. See *El Castellano*, July 1, 1843.

8. Although WI did not fill in the name, despatches indicate that General Francisco Javier Azpiroz was moving toward Madrid at this time. See London *Times*, July 15, 20, 22, 1843. WI confirms the identity of Azpiroz in his despatch to Legaré on July 22, 1843.

1602.   *To Olegario de los Cuetos*

Legation of the U States / Madrid July 10th. 1843.

His Excellency / Don Olegario de los Cuetos / First Minister of State and / of Foreign Affairs ad interim
Sir,

I have the honor to acknowledge the receipt of your Excellencys note of the 4th inst. informing me that a royal pardon will be graciously extended to Captain Love Straw,[1] a prisoner in Havanna for robbery, on condition that this act of ↑grace↓ be previously approved by the party or parties aggrieved.

As the aggrieved parties reside beyond Seas (I believe in the United States) much time would be lost, and the humane intent of the pardon be impeded, if their consent had previously to be verified at this court. I would respectfully suggest, therefore, that a conditional pardon be forthwith forwarded to the Authorities at Havana, to go into effect on the production of satisfactory proof of the aforesaid consent. I shall write immediately to the United States to have such consent obtained, properly authenticated according to legal form, and transmitted to the Audience at Havana.

I have the honor to remain, with the highest consideration

Your Excellencys obt Servt
Washington Irving

––––––––

N. B. Letters dated July 20th were written to Governor John Fairfield[2] of Maine, and the Hon Albert Smith[3] member of Congress from the same who had sought the intervention of the Government of the United States in favor of Straw—apprising them of the conditional pardon and the necessity of procuring and forwarding documentary proof of the consent of the aggrieved parties—a letter of same date to the same effect, was also sent to Daniel Deshon Esqr. of Boston; the person who had been robbed by Captain Straw.

MANUSCRIPT: NA, RG 84 (letterbook copy).

The letter is in WI's handwriting; the appended note is in a secretary's handwriting.

1. WI had first applied to Count Almodóvar on October 4, 1842, for a pardon for Captain Straw.

2. For details about Fairfield, see WI's letter of July 20, 1843.

3. Albert Smith (1793–1867) had represented Maine in the U.S. Congress from 1839 to 1841. At the time of this letter he was serving as American commissioner working out the boundary between Maine and Canada under the terms of the Webster-Ashburton Treaty.

1603.   To Maximo de Aguirre

Legation of the United States / Madrid July 11. 1843.

Maximo de Aguirre Esq. / Consul of the U States / Bilbao.

Sir,

I have to acknowledge the receipt of your letter of July 5th. informing me of your having unwillingly been appointed first "Alcalde Constitutional" in the Provisional Ayuntamiento just formed in Bilbao. I fully understand the difficulties and delicacy of your position and appreciate the honorable motives which induce you to offer the resignation of your post as consul of the United States. Whether such resignation will, or will not, be accepted by the Secretary of State I cannot foresee, but, in the mean time, I beg you to continue in the discharge of the duties of the Station, as I doubt whether they can be confided to worthier hands.

I shall retain your Exequatur in my possession for the present, in case of any emergency, though I apprehend none; and I shall take occasion, personally and verbally, to explain the circumstances of the case to the Government.

As to your suggestion that I should make a claim for the restitution of two thousand dollars, heretofore exacted from you as an arbitrary fine, by a military commander, I would observe that this is not a moment to urge such a claim with any chance of success; it had better remain, therefore, for future consideration and action

I am Sir, / Very respectfully / Your Obt Servt
Washington Irving

MANUSCRIPT: NA, RG 84 (letterbook copy)

This copy is in WI's handwriting.
Maximo de Aguirre was appointed U.S. consul for Bilbao in 1834. See Hasse, *Index to U.S. Documents*, III, 1745.

1604.   To Sarah Storrow

Madrid July 14th. 1843.

My dear Sarah,

I have just received your letter of the 8th[1] by which I find that the valiant Hector has arrived safely at Paris, after his adventurous journey. I have no news recently of Mr Hamilton, who must be enjoying himself in the Pyrenees. The letters I have written to him I have reason to believe have been intercepted on the road by the insurgents.

We are here in the midst of confusion and alarm. I speak of the city & the people; for, as to myself, ⟨I⟩ my mind is as tranquil and almost as stagnant as a mill pond. A singular kind of Rebellion is going forward. ⟨[*unrecovered*]⟩ Armies marching & counter marching about the Countr⟨ies⟩y; City after City declaring itself in a state of insurrection—but as yet no fighting. An insurgent army ↑under General Espiroz↓ has been hovering about Madrid for several days; another ↑(under Genl Narvaez)↓ is marching from a different direction to cooperate with it; and Government troops ↑under Genl Soane & Zurbano↓ are pushing in from a distance to aid in the defence of the place. In the mean time the City is declared in a State of siege,[2] and placed under martial law; The gates are closed, ⟨ad⟩ & guarded; and we are thus shut up within the walls. The day before yesterday I was sitting in my room writing when I was attracted to the window by an uncommon bustle & confusion of voices in the street. I looked out and saw men women & children scampering in every direction; as far as the eye could reach there was the same hurry scurry movement, hither & thither. I summoned Lorenzo and asked the reason. He told me there was "a revolution!" It appears the "general" or alarm had been sounded: which is only done at moments of imminent peril; summoning every one to his post. The word was circulated that the enemy ↑(an advanced guard of the Army of Genl. Aspiroz,)↓ were at the "Puerta de hierro" or Iron gate;[3] Which crosses the main road about ↑half↓ a league from the city gate. In a little while the national guard, or militia, were issuing from every hole & corner, hastily equipped & hurrying to their posts; women were gathering their children home, like hens gathering their chickens under their wings on the sight of a hawk. Before long there were eighteen thousand men under arms within the City. all the gates were strongly guarded: the main Squares were full of troops; with cannon planted at the entrances of the streets opening into them. The shops were all shut up; and the streets in general, deserted and silent; all those not on duty keeping as much as possible within doors. At night the whole city was illuminated; as is generally the case when any popular movement is apprehended; so that an enemy may not have darkness to favor his designs.

I was advised not to stir out; as one may get involved in tumults, at such times. I kept at home all day, but in the evening I could not resist the desire to see something of a city in a state of siege, and under an alarm. I accordingly sallied forth in my carriage and drove to the Prado. Instead of being crowded by the fashionable world it was full of troops; there having been a review of the national guard. I alighted & walked among them; they seemed all to be in high spirits. There were but two carriages beside my own, on the drive, usually so crowded. I drove from gate to gate, ⟨but⟩ of this end of the city—all closed & guarded. As the night advanced I drove through most of the principal streets. The houses were illuminated from top to bottom: few people were walking in the streets; but groupes were gathered about every door: ⟨and⟩ troops were patroling in every direction, and in the main squares: which formed military posts: both officers and men were bivouacking on the pavements. The appearance of a solitary carriage rumbling through the streets attracted universal attention, but no one offered to molest me. I drove to Madame Albuquerques; took tea there and returned home about 11 Oclock. I never saw Madrid under more striking and picturesque circumstances.

⟨This morning⟩

Yesterday was comparatively tranquil but this morning the ↑"General" or↓ alarm has been given at 6 Oclock. The Enemy has approached a different gate of the City; and there is news ⟨the⟩ that Genl Narvaez and his troops are at Guadalajara,[4] a few leagues distant. The City is again under arms; I presume the shops are shut up; but I have not as yet been out of the house. The greatest evil I have as yet experienced is the cutting off the supply of butter & cows milk for my breakfast; both coming from the Royal dairy beyond the puerta de hierro or Iron gate.

As the government has prohibited the circulation of the opposition papers by the mail they have all ceased to publish: the government papers themselves are very scanty of intelligence. So that we are left in a state of ignorance of passing events; and are at the mercy of rumour; which fabricates all kinds of stories of plots; conspiracies to carry off the queen: to blow up the powder magazines &c &c &c.

Contradictory reports prevail also with respect to the Regent: ⟨some say⟩ who by last accounts was in La Mancha.[5] Some say he is on his march back to Madrid others that he is going to Cordova: others to Granada, to quell the insurrection in Andalusia. Some say his troops are in a high state of enthusiasm: others that they are deserting him—Every report has its counterreport: so that one is reduced to mere conjecture.

I had looked forward to such a state of things: and I look forward to one still worse; when the hostile parties come to blows. ⟨Should⟩ There may also be perplexing questions for Diplomatists: should the invading armies get possession of the Capital, and of the person of the young Queen. The Question may then arise "where is the actual Government—? and which party is to be considered legitimate.["][6] You will now understand why at such a crisis, a diplomatic agent should not be absent from his post.

We have no regular troops in the city but a large force of national guards—and of the national militia from the neighboring villages. Some feel great confidence in their maintaining the safety of the city; others doubt their being willing to fight, seeing that the invaders are their countrymen My idea is that if Soane & Zurbano arrive in the neighborhood with the force they are said to have, the ⟨f⟩ invaders will have to retreat, or to make battle. Should no such Succour arrive I should not be surprised if, after a few days, the city should make terms; ⟨and⟩ acknowledge the insurgent authority,—and that a new ↑temporary↓ government should suddenly be organized here—how long to last it would be useless even to conjecture—

I am scrawling this hastily to be sent off by the French Courier—I doubt letters going safely at present by the mail; as the insurgent cities through which it passes are eager to get at news from the capital. As I have no time to write to your mother send her this letter when you have done with it. It will help to keep up the thread of Spanish affairs I have given her.

I miss much the delightful companionship of my dear Hamilton; whom I have learnt to prize more & more, the more I have known him. But I trust he will be here again before long with renovated health and happy spirits[.] I am much cheered by the society of Mr Sumner; who dines with me almost every day; and is very intelligent & conversable My health is daily improving and I am gradually getting freed from the malady which has so long clung to me. The weather continues generally cool for the Season; and I find my large saloons very pleasant and airy for Summer.

I have received Mr Oliffes book;[7] it is as sweet as Spanish sweetmeats; in which there is sometimes an attempt even to sweeten honey.

Tell him "I have not had time or mood to write to him, being very much ↑occupied and very much↓ of an invalid; but that I feel he has done me more than justice in the kind way in which he has dished up his morsels from my works—" I think that will do—

Let me hear of your plans and your whereabouts—I can make none for myself at present, as you must perceive—Give my kind regards to Mrs Ledyard and the young Ledyards.

With affectionate remembrances to your husband & Kisses to Kate

Your affectionate uncle
Washington Irving

DOCKETED: Washn. Irving to Mrs. Sarah Storrow. Paris. / Madrid July 14, 1843
MANUSCRIPT: Yale.   PUBLISHED: PMI, III, 282–87.

1. This letter has not been located.
2. See *La Gaceta*, July 12, 1843.
3. This gate was on the northwestern edge of Madrid. See Richard Ford, *A Hand-Book for Travellers in Spain*, III, 120.
4. Guadalajara is about thirty miles northeast of Madrid.
5. Espartero is reported as being at Albacete, Balazote, Bonillo, Valdepeñas, Santa Elena, and Bailén. See *La Gaceta*, July 7, 9, 12, 13, 14, 15, 1843.
6. WI omitted the bracketed quotation mark.
7. Charles Oliffe had prepared *Extracts from the Complete Works of Washington Irving* (Paris, 1843). See *Bibliographie de France*, no. 11 (March 18, 1843), p. 137, item 1330.

1605.   *To Sarah Storrow*

Madrid July 18th. 1843

My dear Sarah,

I have just learnt that a French Courier is about to set off from the French Embassy & I hasten to scrawl you a line by it; as letters by the

Mail are apt at the present moment to be intercepted and you may be anxious to hear from me during these warlike times. I wrote to you about four days since, giving you some account of the critical state of affairs in this city. Since that time we have been in a state of siege; the enemy at the gates; the whole body of national guards &c under arms; the main streets barricaded; ⟨at this⟩ every house illuminated at night; the streets swarming with military men; the shops shut; the publication of the newspapers suspended; and the public ear abused with all kinds of lying rumors. There has been brisk firing of musketry about some of the gates and an occasional report of a cannon; but the besiegers calculated upon disaffection & treachery within the walls; ⟨and that⟩ upon a pronunciamento in favor of the insurrectional government, and upon the gates being thrown open to them. They therefore came without artillery. Thus far they have been disappointed. The national guards have remained firm and true; and have kept up a brisk fire whenever the enemy made any demonstrations. One of my windows commands a view of one of the city gates and its vicinity; and I could hear every discharge, and at night could see the flash of the guns. It has been extremely interesting to me; and fortunately I have ⟨been⟩ so far recovered from the lingerings of my malady that I could go all about on foot, and witness some of the Striking scenes presented by a city in a state of siege and hourly in apprehension of being taken by assault. Troops were stationed in the houses along the main streets; to fire upon the enemy from the windows & balconies should they effect an entrance: and it was resolved to dispute the ground street by street; and to make the last stand in the Royal palace where were the Queen & her sister, and where the Duchess of Victory (wife of the regent) had taken refuge, her own palace being in one of the most exposed parts of the city. apprehending that the lives of the ⟨Royal⟩ Queen & her sister might be exposed to extreme hazard as much in the defence as in the attack; the diplomatic corps addressed a note to the govt. urging the most scrupulous attention to the safety of these helpless little beings: and offering to repair in a body to the palace, and remain there during the time of peril.[1] Our offer has been declined; the Ministry thinking the safety of the Queen and her sister sufficiently secured by the devotion of the inhabitants of Madrid &c—

Last ⟨night⟩ evening it was confidently reported that there would be a grand attack at various points in the course of the night: and many were in a great state of alarm. I had returned home ⟨lat⟩ at a late hour and had just got into bed, when I found a note lying on ⟨my⟩ the table beside my bed, which proved to be from Mrs Weiswieller; the young and beautiful bride of Mr Weiswieller,[2] a connexion and representative of the Rothchilds; who arrived here recently from England, and whose residence was in the main street leading from the gate that would be attacked. ↑She

requested permission to take refuge in my house,↓ It was already twelve
Oclock, but I hastily dressed myself again and repaired to the residence
of Mr Weiswieller, escorted by Lorenzo. Groupes of soldiers ⟨&⟩ with
centinels were stationed at every corner. I found Mr & Mrs Weiswieller
in much anxiety, he having received ⟨fr⟩ what he considered certain intelligence that the attack would take place about four Oclock in the
morning.

I offered every accommodation my house would afford: and after much
deliberation, it was determined that on the first alarm of the attack they
should repair to my residence. This being settled I returned home but did
not get asleep until between one & two oclock. This morning I awoke
about four: there was the sound of a drum in the street & the report of
two or three distant shots. I ⟨prepared to⟩ thought the attack was about to
commence & prepared to rise; but all remained quiet, and there was no
further alarm.

It appeared that instead of attacking, the enemy had drawn off in the
night. They had heard of the approach of the forces under Genls Soane
and Zurbano in one direction, and of a smaller force ↑(about 3000 men)↓
under Genls Iriarte[3] and Enna in another direction. ⟨They had⟩ General
Narvaez therefore has marched to encounter Soane & Zurbano; and General Aspiroz to encounter Iriarte & Enna: should they vanquish them they
will return upon Madrid; which in such case will ⟨like⟩ ↑probably↓ capitulate. Should Soane & the others be successful, the Regents government
will be strengthened in Madrid. ↑Should they fail, his government will be
overthrown.↓ However this present contest may end, I look upon it as
but the commencement of another series of conflicts and struggles for rule
that will desolate unhappy Spain. Espartero has been the only man that
has presented, for many years, calculated to ⟨unite the feelings of the
[unrecovered]⟩ be a kind of Keystone to the arch; but his popularity has
been undermined, and whether he be displaced or not: I fear he will no
longer have power and influence sufficient to prevent the whole edifice
falling to ruin and confusion.

I scrawl this in great haste and have no time to write to any of the family: you must forward it therefore to your Mother that it may let all at
home know that I am *safe* and mean to continue so—whatever storms may
prevail around me. I have just recd a letter from Hamilton[4] dated from
Laubonne in the pyrenees where he is suffering from Rain and snow, but
has found enjoyment in the society of some American friends. He will be
much grieved at being absent from Madrid in these stirring and eventful
times.

My health is continually improving, and I think the excitement of the
last two or three days has been of great service to me. Yesterday I was on

my feet from ten Oclock in the morning until twelve or one at night; and, though much fatigued, feel all the better for it.

Give my affectionate remembrances to your husband & Kiss darling little Kate for me

Your affectionate uncle
Washington Irving

DOCKETED: Washn. Irving to Mrs Sarah Storrow. Paris / Madrid July 18. 1843. MANUSCRIPTS Yale.. PUBLISHED: PMI, III, 287–90 (in part).

WI transcribes the date of the letter as July 13, 1843.

1. WI, who prepared the note on behalf of the other diplomats in the beleaguered city, was later accused of being manipulated by either the French chargé d'affaires or the British minister. In reality he was thinking of the safety of Isabella during these troubled hours. For WI's later explanations, see his letters to Mrs. Paris, August 10, 1843, and to Henry Brevoort, November 26, 1843. The Madrid newspapers did not notice the diplomats' efforts. The text is preserved in WI's handwriting in the letterbook of the legation in Madrid (NA, RG 84): "Note passed to the Government by the Diplomatic Corps, during the Siege of Madrid in July":

"Les soussignés membres du Corps diplomatique accredité aupres de Sa Majesté et de son gouvernement ayant appris q'une attaque est projeté contre cette Capitale et prenant en consideration la situation exceptionelle dans laquelle S. M. et son auguste soeur se trouvent croient de leur devoir au nom de leurs gouvernements respectifs, d'exprimer au gouvernement de S. M. leur vif desir que dans quelque conflit que puisse arriver la sureté personnelle de la reine et de sa soeur soient l'objet des plus grands égards.

"En consequence des sentiments ci-dessus exprimés les soussignés offrent de se rendre aupres de S. M. au moment ou leur presence pourrait y etre utile. Ils ne doutent nullement que cette declaration qui leur est commandée par leur devoir aussi bien que par leurs desirs ne soit apprecies par le Gouvernement se S. M. C. en meme temps qu'il restera entendu qu'il n'ont ete mis dans la presente declaration que par le vif et respectueux interet qu'ils portent a la sureté de la Reine et de son auguste soeur."

The note is signed by the members of the diplomatic corps.

2. Weismuller, whose name WI had garbled as Weiswieller, had represented the Rothschild interests in Madrid as early as 1836 and had advanced funds from these bankers for support of the British Legion in Spain. See Bertrand Gille, *Histoire de la Maison Rothschild* (Geneva, 1965), I, 253, 257.

3. Martín Iriate (b. 1799) was a radical general who had served in 1837 as military governor of Pamplona. See Christiansen, *Military Power*, pp. 102, 187.

4. This letter has not been located.

1606. To John Fairfield

Legation of the United States / Madrid July 20. 1843
His Excellency / John Fairfield / Governor of Maine.

Sir,

I have the honor to inform you that a pardon has at length been obtained for Capt Love Straw, imprisoned in Havana for having embezzled money of the owner of his vessel;[1] and in whose behalf you made an application to the United States Government about three years since.

The pardon is conditional and requires the approbation of the party or parties aggrieved, I presume there will be no difficulty in obtaining such approbation from the owner of the vessel. It must be authenticated in legal form and forwarded to the "Audiencia" at Havana* to which the pardon will likewise be forwarded, to go into effect on the receipt of the before mentioned document.

I remain Sir / Very respectfully / Your obt St.
Washington Irving

[*In left margin*:]* PS It can be forwarded to our Consul at Havana: who can lay it before the "Audiencia."

Letters to the effect of the preceding one were at the same time sent to the Hon Albert Smith, Member of Congress from Maine, who made application to Govt in favor of Capt Straw: and to Danl Deshon Esqr of Boston one of the owners of the vessel—

MANUSCRIPT: NYPL—Emmett Collection; NA, RG 84 (copy in WI's handwriting).

John Fairfield (1797–1847) was twice governor of Maine, in 1839 and 1840, and from 1841 to 1843. He resigned in December, 1843, to become U.S. senator, a post he held until his death.

1. See WI to Olegario de los Cuetos, July 10, 1843.

1607. To Hugh S. Legaré

Legation of the United States / Madrid July 22. 1843.

No 25. / The Hon. Hugh S. Legare / Secretary of State / &c &c &c
Sir,

Since the date of my last despatch Madrid has been in a state of Siege. The insurgent troops from Leon and old Castile[1] under General Aspiroz took a position on one side while a superior force under General

Narvaez, who had managed to out manoeuvre or out march the regents generals, invested it on the other   They had brought no artillery and evidently calculated on a cooperation from within, expecting that a *pronunciamento* would take place, and the gates be thrown open to them; or, at least, that the City being defended merely by the National ⟨na⟩ Guards, would soon surrender. In this expectation they were disappointed. The militia behaved admirably. Martial law was proclaimed on the 10th. inst. On the 12th. the whole population seemed under arms, and twenty thousand men, well equipped, were at the orders of the Captain General of Madrid.[2] The gates were barricaded, batteries planted commanding the approaches to the city, trenches digged and breastworks thrown up in the principal streets; troops stationed in the houses on each side to fire from the upper windows and every preparation made to defend the city street by street and step by step; and to make the last stand at the palace

For three days and nights the siege continued, ↑with much skirmishing about the gates;↓ the city holding out in the hope of relief from troops under Generals Soane, Zurbano and Iriarte which were known to be on the march for the capital. Aware of their approach the besiegers repeated their summons to surrender, with threats of a general attack and ↑of↓ rigorous terms in case the place were carried by storm. Their summons and threats had no effect.

Apprehensive that, should the city be carried by storm the lives of the youthful queen and her sister might be endangered by the defense being pushed to an extremity, and the palace used as a citadel; the Diplomatic Corps addressed a note to the government, urging the utmost caution with respect to the safety of the Royal children, and offering to repair in person to the palace and be near the queen at any moment their presence might be deemed useful. This offer was respectfully declined.

Two days since the besieging troops, finding the advancing forces of the Regency were near at hand, drew off to a distance of two or three leagues, where they took up a position   General Iriarte has since reached Madrid with about three thousand men, but sallied forth this morning to co operate with Generals Soane and Zurbano, who, with a large force and considerable train of artillery are close upon the army of Narvaez ↑and are confident of Success.↓ Tidings are incessantly expected of a battle decisive of the fate of the capital.

July 23d. The question is decided. The armies met yesterday morning; a few shots were exchanged when a general embracing took place between the soldiery, and the troops of the Regency joined the insurgents. General Soane and a son of Zurbano[3] were taken prisoners: as to Zurbano himself, he contrived to escape and arrived in Madrid in the evening attended merely by three aids de camp. The city was overwhelmed with astonishment. The members of the Cabinet resigned their functions, excepting Mendizabel: the municipal authorities have taken the management of affairs and have sent out deputations last evening and this morning to treat for terms. The last deputation has not yet returned. The main point of difficulty is the demand of Narvaez that the whole national guard shall be disarmed. This may occasion some trouble; and some scenes of violence: Narvaez, however, has the power at present to impose his own terms, but will doubtless be influenced by leading men of his party within the city, who will be cautious not to exasperate the populace.[4]

I consider this blow as decisive of the political fortunes of the Regent. Other troops from various points are marching upon the capital; where the insurgents will soon concentrate a force of between thirty and forty thousand men. The insurrection is too wide and general to be quelled by any troops the Regent can collect. He is at present in Andalusia; seeking it is said to bring that rich province into obedience. Others think he is desirous of making his way to Cadiz; from whence, in case of extremity, he may embark and save himself by sea. On hearing of the signal defection of the army and the capture of the capital it is thought he will either resign, or endeavor to leave the kingdom.[5]

I shall keep this despatch open until the last moment, to give any further tidings that may arrive.

A tárdy pardon has at length been granted by this government to Captain Love Straw, a prisoner in Havana for having embezzled money on board of his own vessel, and for whom intercession was made, according to instructions from the government of the United States nearly three years since. The pardon is on condition that the party or parties aggrieved approve of the same. I have requested that, to save time, the pardon be forwarded to the Audiencia at Havana, to take effect on the approbation of the aggrieved party being properly authenticated   It will be necessary to obtain such approbation have it authenticated according to legal form and forwarded to our Consul at Havana, to be laid before the Audiencia

I am Sir, / Very respectfully / Your obt Servt

Washington Irving

DOCKETED: Recd. 23 Augt. [*upper left corner, page 1*] / No. 25. W. Irving. Madrid. 22 July 1843—
MANUSCRIPT: NA, RG 59.   PUBLISHED: Hellman, *WI Esquire*, pp. 297–300; STW, II, 156, 376–77 (in part).

1. Areas of northern and central Spain.
2. Evaristo San Miguel (1785–1862), who had been minister of war in the González cabinet, was captain-general of the province of Madrid. See Christiansen, *Military Power*, pp. 169, 192.
3. A report in the London *Times* for July 27, 1843, corroborates WI's statement that Zurbano's son was captured by the insurgents. His first name is not given.

4. Decrees reinstating the López cabinet and making Narváez captain-general of Madrid were issued, and an editorial stated that a political change had taken place. See *La Gaceta*, July 24, 1843.

5. WI's speculations were close to the regent's actual movements. Espartero left Spain from Cadiz and went to London on a British ship. See H. Butler Clarke, *Modern Spain*, p. 189; and Martin Hume, *Modern Spain*, p. 372.

1608. To Sarah Storrow

Madrid, July 23d. 1843.

My dear Sarah,

I wrote to you about four days since giving you some account of our state of Siege. Yesterday we were hourly in expectation of tidings of a battle in the neighborhood, between the invading army which had drawn off to the distance of three or four leagues, and Generals Soane & Zurbano who were approaching with a formidable force of troops of the Regency. Towards evening news came that the armies had met; that the troops of the Regency had gone over to the insurgents; that General Soane was prisoner—In the Evening Zurbano entered the capital a fugitive; followed by merely three aids de camp. All is confusion and suspense here. The members of the Govt. have resigned: the Municipal authorities have sent out deputations to treat with Narvaez for terms. He insists on disarming the national guards; which may occasion some trouble & scenes of violence.

I consider the political career of the Regent at an end and that he will either be compelled to resign or to leave the Kingdom. He is down in Andalusia; endeavoring to quell the insurrection in that province; but the insurrection is too widely spread to be subdued. He may make his way to Cadiz; make a stand there, and if driven to extremity embark and save himself by sea.

I have quite a God send in Mr Sumner; who just now supplies the place of Mr Hamilton. Like him he is intelligent, amiable and very companionable. I have attached him to the Legation and he ⟨acquits⟩ plays the part of Secretary.

Give my affectionate regards to Mr Storrow and Kisses to Kate

Your affectionate Uncle
Washington Irving

MANUSCRIPT: Yale.   PUBLISHED: Simison, *Keogh Papers*, pp. 205–6.

1609. To Joaquín de Frías

Legation of the United States / Madrid July 25th. 1843.

His Excellency / Don Joaquin de Frias / &c &c &c
Sir.

I have the honor to acknowledge the receipt of your Excellency's note of the 24th. Inst, informing me of your having resumed the Ministry of the Department of Marine and (ad interim) of that of state, according as the same was formerly confided to you in the name of Her Majesty the Queen by a decree of the 9th. of May last past.[1]

Permit me to reiterate my sincere felicitations for the distinguished honor which has again been so worthily bestowed; and appreciating in their full value the assurances which your Excellency is pleased to give me that you will take a pleasure in drawing closer and closer the bands of amity which unite our respective governments, I pledge myself to use my most strenuous exertions to promote so worthy and desirable an object.

In the mean time I profit by the present occasion to reiterate to your Excellency the assurance of my high consideration

Washington Irving.

MANUSCRIPT: NA, RG 84 (letterbook copy)

1. See *La Gaceta*, July 24, 1843.

1610. To Joaquín de Frías

Legation of the United States. / Madrid July 25th. 1843

His Excellency / Don Joaquin de Frias

Sir,

I have the honor to acknowledge the receipt of your Excellency's note of the 24th. Inst; in which you have thought proper to communicate various facts and observations relative to the political state of the country and to the origin of the actual government of Her Majesty the Queen; as well as to intimate the line of policy which that Government proposes to pursue in its exterior relations.

Deeply impressed with the importance of the communication I shall lose no time in complying with the wishes of your Excellency by transmitting the same to my Government.

In the mean time I will have the honor to continue my communications with your Excellency according as may be required by the mutual interests of our respective countries.

I take this occasion to renew to your Excellency assurance of my distinguished consideration.

Washington Irving

MANUSCRIPT: NA, RG 84 (letterbook copy).

1611. To Hugh S. Legaré

Legation of the United States / Madrid July 25th. 1843.

No. 26. / The Hon. Hugh S Legare / &c &c &c
Sir,

My last despatch was sent off the day before yesterday; since then ↑the↓ city has surrendered, and has been taken possession of by the invading armies, which have arrived from various points, and ↑have↓ entered, to the number of between forty and fifty thousand men. The national guard has been desarmed; and troops are stationed in every part of the city. The revolutionary government, now styling itself the government of the nation, and acting in the name of the Queen Isabella II, has entered upon its functions. It is chiefly composed of the Lopes Cabinet;[1] formed by a decree of the Regent dated the 9th. of May last. The brief time allowed me before the departure of the courier by which this despatch will be forwarded, does not ⟨allow⟩ ↑permit↓ me to enter into particulars

The different members of the Diplomatic corps have received notes from Don Joaquin de Frias, Minister of Marine and (ad interim) of Foreign affaires, ↑one,↓ informing them of his re-entering on the descharge of the duties of those departments, as confided to him by the decree of the 9th. of May last; another giving them a brief account of the origin and intentions of the actual government—Some of the Diplomatic Corps have determined to abstain from opening regular communications with the government until they can receive instructions from their respective governments. I have felt my situation to be different from theirs; partly on account of the distance I am placed from my government, and the time that must elapse before I could receive instructions and partly from the general policy observed in our diplomatic concerns; to treat always with the government *de facto*, without enquiring into its political history or origin. I have consulted however with one of the corps diplomatic, whose position is in many respects similar to mine, and who is a person of great judgement and integrity, I mean Mr Valdevielso,[2] the Mexican Minister.

He agrees with me in considering the government of the Regent as virtually at an end; and the government just established at Madrid, so powerful in its armed force; so extensively acknowledged and obeyed throughout most parts of the Kingdom, and above all, possessing such a tower of strength in the person of the Queen, that it may be fairly esteemed the government *de facto*. We have, therefore, replied to the notes of Señor Frias opening communications with him as the minister of the departments of which he has charge. I have the honor to enclose a copy of the second note of Señor Frias,[3] before alluded to, illustrative of the political state of the country and of the origin and views of his government.

> I have the Honor to remain / Very respectfully / Your Obt Servt
> Washington Irving

DOCKETED: Recd. 25 Septr. Mr. Markoe. / No. 26. W. Irving. 25 July. 1843–
MANUSCRIPT: NA, RG 59.   PUBLISHED: Hellman, *WI Esquire*, pp. 300–301; STW,
II, 158 (in part).

1. For the members of the López cabinet, see WI to Webster, May 9, 1843. Espartero had dismissed these ministers and had asked Gómez Becerra to form a new government which continued until June 29, 1843. See Christiansen, *Military Power*, p. 170.

2. Ignacio Valdivielso (1805–1861) became envoy extraordinary and minister plenipotentiary from Mexico to Spain in 1842. He held the post for two years, went to Rome on another diplomatic mission, and then returned to Madrid until 1846. His tour of duty in Spain roughly parallels WI's.

3. WI's enclosure included copies of the Spanish text and its translation, which follows:

Palace July 24th. 1843.

Sir—In my communication of this day, I had the honour to inform you, that I had again been charged *ad interim* with the Department of State. I now propose to add some observations, respecting the political state of the country, and the ends proposed by the Government of our Lady the Queen, in her foreign relations, in order that you, by becoming well informed on ↑both↓ these points, may afford a sufficient and exact idea of them to your Government.

Without entering into a long examination of previous acts and causes, it is not to be denied, that the Provinces having risen up against the Government of the Duke of Victory, the Peninsula was in a critical situation, and a social dissolution was impending. The prudence of the Spaniards, and their love and respect for the Queen and the political motivations, were from that moment the correctives by means of which the risks of so dangerous a state of things could be opposed. In effect, a Supreme Junta of Safety was organised at Barcelona, the authority of which was acknowledged, and which, for finding no means more certain for re establishing order, by inspiring confidence among the people who had ⟨[*unrecovered*]⟩ proclaimed the ministry which had been appointed on the 9th of May of this year, regarding that Ministry as the representative of the political principles which had been set forth, with universal applause, in the Co-legislative bodies.

This measure obtained the explicit and spontaneous assent of all the provinces, which had had time to express their opinions; so that the title of the existing Ministry rested upon the vote of the Nation, solemnly and spontaneously expressed. This idea, as was to be expected ↑has↓ smoothed all obstacles, calmed all discontent, blunted the arms of the small portion of the army, which continued to fight against the general will, and finally gave ↑to the Ministry of the 9th of May, reinstated at Barcelona,↓ a free and peaceful entrance into the Capital of the Kingdom, and allowed it to offer its homage to the Queen. The Queen's Government therefore flatters itself, that all difficulties are ↑now↓ overcome, the opinion of the people being proclaimed, the administrative action being concentrated, and the fear that new ↑and↓ painful scenes may again disturb the rest of the Spaniards, being disapated.

In this state, and with the resolution to sustain by the strong hand, the Empire of the Law in the interior, the Queen's Government can do nothing more important, than to fix its attention on the relations which that ↑Lady↓ wishes to maintain, with the nations her friends and allies. To that end, she will endeavour to strengthen those relations, by all the bonds of political and commercial, which are compatible with the advantage and interests of her subjects. She will neglect no means, which may secure to foreigners in her dominions, the protection and considerations inseparable from the genius and character of the Nation; and may enable them to find all the guarantees promised to them by treaties and special laws.

These are therefore the facts and the observations which My Lady the Queen and the Council of Ministers, charge me to communicate to you, in order that you may, if you think proper, make them known to your Government: in the hope that your Government will not for a moment refuse to ⟨follow⟩ pursue the former friendly relations, in which it now is with her Majesty's Government, and that in the mean time you will not hesitate to honour me with your communications, and ⟨with [*unrecovered*] business⟩ to treat ↑with me↓ on the matters which may occur.

I avail myself of this occasion to repeat to you Sir the assurances of my distinguished consideration

Your Most Obede Svt
Joaquin de Frias

1612. To Sarah Storrow

Madrid, July 29th. 1843.

My dear Sarah,

It is upwards of twenty days since the date of your last letter, and this interval of Silence is somewhat provoking, as I am anxious to know your arrangements as to a summer residence, and whether Mr Storrow goes out in the Great Western.[1]

I have now a commission for you to perform on behalf of my fair friend Madame Albuquerque. She has suddenly made up her mind to make a brief visit to Paris for the purpose of having an interview with the great Brewster, the dentist She leaves her[e] on Tuesday next, accompanied merely by her femme de chambre—Theres resolution for you!—As she has no correspondents in Paris, I engaged that you should see Mr Brewster and ⟨secur⟩ make an arrangement for her. I received a note from her this morning in which she says "I shall feel deeply obliged if your niece Mrs Storrow will interest herself sufficiently in a stranger to her to ask of Brewster an hour for me on the 9th. of August[.] I shall be in Paris on the 8th. when I shall take the liberty of writing a line to Mrs Storrow to know if the dentist can comply with my wish. Should he be engaged on the 9th. I shall be glad to avail myself of his first liesure hour. I should prefer any hour between 9 and 12 oclock in the morning but should those hours not suit Brewster he can name his time.

As soon as *that dreaded visit* is over I shall lose no time in waiting on Mrs Storrow, with whom I already feel half acquainted—"

—Madame Albuquerque will return to Madrid almost immediately— as she goes to Paris merely for the above purpose.

You will see by the newspapers, that the Regents sway is at an end; though he is still engaged in military operations in Andalusia. These will no doubt be brought to a close as soon as tidings reach there of the defection of the troops of the Regency in the neighborhood of Madrid; and of the occupation of the capital by the insurgent forces. The new government growing out of the insurrection styles itself the "Government of the Nation["] and acts in the name of the youthful queen. As, however illegitimate its origin, it possesses the main power and sway, and˙has likewise the person of the queen to sanction its acts, I consider it the government *de facto,* and ⟨as such⟩ have therefore officially acknowledged it: such being the rule with our government in its diplomacy.

The excitement I felt during the state of siege, and the fatigue, and ⟨the⟩ exposure to which I subjected myself, for I could not keep within doors: brought on a slight bilious attack; and that brought on an access of my malady, from which I had nearly recovered: so for some days past I have been again an invalid, and can only sally forth in the carriage. I trust, however, in a very little while to get over this ill turn and to be once more in the high road to health. ⟨The⟩ Mr Hamilton has not yet returned, as I wrote to him not to hurry himself if he found himself very pleasantly situated. I expect him in the course of three or four days. In the mean time Mr Sumner obligingly assists me whenever I have any official business to be attended to.

I have written to you two or three times lately during the Siege—I hope you have transmitted the letters to your mother; who otherwise will be without accounts of me during these warlike times.

After Mr Hamiltons return I shall determine whether circumstances will permit me to leave my post. You perceive what an important question has just occurred; whether or not the legation should acknowledge the actual govt. I should not have liked to subject Mr Hamilton to the responsibility of deciding such a question. I believe the Mexican Minister and myself are the only two of the Diplomatic corps that have fully recognized it. The rest, though many of them were strongly in favor of the insurgent party, waited for instructions from their Governments— But the Mexican Minister & myself consulted together, our positions being similar—both representatives of Republics—both at a great distance from our govts. and both authorized ⟨to⟩ by our national policy, to treat with whatever we should consider to be the *Govt de Facto*. We agreed therefore upon the same course of conduct, in answering the official note from the Minister of State ↑of the new Govt↓ informing us of his appointment—

I do not consider the affairs of Spain ⟨if any⟩ likely to be tranquilized by this revolution in government. On the contrary.; the moment that Espartero is completely put down and they have done with warring against him, I look for violent feuds and struggles for ascendancy among the leaders of opposite parties, who have been leagued together to destroy him. I hope, however, the recently established government may prove strong and durable enough to ⟨get⟩ bring the distracted affairs of the country into some degree of order.

With affectionate regards to Mr Storrow and kisses to the limb—

> Your affectionate uncle
> W.I.

MANUSCRIPT: Yale.   PUBLISHED: Simison, *Keogh Papers*, pp. 206–9.

1. The *Great Western* sailed from Liverpool for New York on Saturday, August 5, 1843. See NYEP, July 14, 1843.

1613. To Paul Pon

> Legation of the United States. / Madrid July 31st. 1843.

Paul Pon Esqr. / Consul of the United States / Barcelona
Sir,

I have duly received your letter of the 13th. Inst.[1] It will be a sufficient reply for the present to the main purport of its contents for me to inform you that considering the provisional government recently established in Madrid and acting in the name of Her Majesty Isabella II, as the government de facto of the Kingdom, I have already according to the general policy of our Govt. entered into the usual relations with it.

> I am Sir, respectfully / Your Obdt Sevt.
> Washington Irving

N. B. Notes were sent to the other consuls apprising them of the above fact.

MANUSCRIPT: NA, RG 84 (letterbook copy)

1. In his letter Pon reported on military movements in the area of Barcelona and on the English and French naval vessels outside the harbor (NA, RG 84).

1614. To George Read

Legation of the United States / Madrid July 31st. 1843

George Read Esqr, / Consul of the United States, / Malaga.
Sir,
Considering, under all the circumstances of the case the provisional government, recently established at Madrid and acting in the name of her Majesty Queen Isabella IId. as the government *de facto* ↑of the Kingdom,↓ I have, according to the general policy of our Government, entered into the usual relations with it.

I am Sir / Very respectfully / Your obt St
Washington Irving

ADDRESSED: George Read Esqr / Consul of the United States of America / Málaga.
      POSTMARKED: 9 / 1 / CASTI[*unrecovered*] / 2 / Aug / 1843
MANUSCRIPT: NA, RG 84.

Read had written to WI on July 17 and 19, 1843, reporting on various commercial and military matters affecting the Malaga area (NA, RG 84).

1615. To Secretary of State

Legation of the United States / Madrid Aug 3d. 1843

No 27. / The Hon / The Secretary of State of the / United States—
Washington

Sir,
Intelligence through the public papers which will reach you at least as soon as this Despatch, will give you particulars of the catastrophe of Espartero's regency. The intelligence of the reverses at Madrid reached his camp while pressing the Siege and bombardment of Seville.[1] A dissolution of his army seems almost immediately to have taken place. He hastily raised the siege and retreated towards Cadiz, but, being

deserted by most of his troops, and finding he was likely to be headed by a force under General Concha, he made for the little port of St Marys, nearly opposite Cadiz, from whence he with the chief part of his suit, was conveyed by a Spanish Steamer on board of a British Ship of war;[2] the yards of which were manned and a salute of twenty one guns fired on his entering on board. From thence he will probably issue some manifesto to the Spanish nation.[3]

The closing campaign of Esparteros carreer has certainly been unfortunate. An ambiguity has hung about his movements; which has perplexed his best friends; an inactivity[4] in times of gathering peril; an apparent want of decision, and an absence of concerted plan. The bombardment of Seville, too, is exclaimed against as an act of barbarism, particularly as it was continued after intelligence of the loss of the capital had time to reach his camp and to shew him that his cause was hopeless.

His friends explain all the ambiguities and cross purposes in his military movements by alledged treachery on the part of General Seoane on whom he depended as upon a second self; and who they affirm, was false to him from the very outset of the campaign, disconcerting all his plans, and who finally gave up his army and betrayed the capital into the hands of Narvaez.

As to the bombardment of Seville, say they, it was undertaken while Madrid was considered secure; and was justified by the exigencies of the case, the prompt reduction of Seville being important to the subjugation of Andalusia. It was protracted longer than it would have been had the Regent received news of the reverses of Madrid in due time; but the despatches sent to him were all intercepted, and the tidings reached his camp circuitously and by chance, two days later than they ought to have done. These explanations, however, will have little effect, for some time at least, in obviating the load of calumny and execration his enemies are heaping upon his name; nor will he now have any opportunity of proving the sincerity of his reiterated declarations of his intention to uphold the constitution and the throne of the youthful queen, and to surrender the reins of government into her hands on the 10th. of October 1844. It is one of the singular reverses and transitions characteristic of the political affairs of thes country, that its legitimate ruler, at one moment a popular idol, and the favorite of the army; is at the next, by a successful rebellion, and by the desertion of his troops obliged to fly for his life; driven an exile from its shores; his justifiable defence of the constitution and the throne committed to his charge, construed into a crime against the nation, and that he should be branded as a traitor and a rebel by those who have sucessfully rebelled against him!

It remains to be seen how the coalition which has risen to power upon his downfall, will cohere; now that the object of common hostility is removed. Most heartily do I wish, for the sake of Spain, that a government may be formed capable of carrying on the affairs of the nation in a durable and prosperous manner, but I fear there are too many elements of discord in a state of fermentation to permit such an event. There are already three rival generals in the capital, each watching with jealousy the honors accorded to the others.[5] There are opposite factions each claiming the merit of the recent victory and grasping at the lions share of the spoils. The country is in a general state of disorganization; every provincial junta arrogates to itself almost sovereign powers: some already begin to dictate to the capital and to question the authority of the provisional government. Barcelona, that political volcano is again heaving and murmuring with internal fires; the army is demoralized; it is broken up into seperate legions having provincial interests and prejudices, and provincial leaders; the desmembered troops of the Regency also are roving about and will soon fill the country with robbers and *facciosos*. A stern discontent and silent uneasiness prevail in the capital; the ⟨citi⟩ inhabitants see with humiliation and chagrin bands of rough soldiery, and Catalan guerrillas, who look like demi savages, roaming about their streets with triumphant air, while their national guards, the legitimate defenders of the city are disarmed. There is a "fearful looking out"[6] for future feuds and bloody dissensions; and many who have been great sticklers for national independence begin to talk of an armed intervention from abroad, as the only means of rescuing the country from a state of anarchy and maintaining it in tranquility.

There is a strong party in favor of immediately declaring the queen of age; others, desirous of respecting in some small degree the forms of the constitution, propose the creation of a provisional regency to continue until the 10th of October 1844; or, at least the postponement of all action in the premises until the Cortes can be convoked. An assembly of the Cortes for the ensuing 15th of October has been called by the government, when, beside the question of the queens majority, that of her marriage will probably come under discussion. This is in fact the European question of Spain, in which the various powers will take more or less interest, but which will be a matter of jealous rivalship between France and England. The latter power has certainly been outmanaged of late by her great rival, in the struggle for ascendancy in the peninsula, and having been represented as the adviser and protector of Espartero, will feel mortified by his downfall. She will therefore have a watchful and an angry eye on every future movement of France towards Spain and it will need the profoundest skill of Louis Philippe to carry his favorite scheme into execution without an open rupture with his irritated neighbor.

I have the honor to enclose a note recently received from the Spanish government announcing and explaining the resignation of Don Augustin Arguelles of the post of tutor to the Queen and Princess, and the provisional nomination in his place, of the venerable General Castanos the Duke of Bailen.[7]

I have but just received Dispatch no 14 dated the 20th of April last, announcing the change in the diplomatic banking house to take place on the 1st. of July last—I have already drawn for the quarters salary due on that day, on the house of the Rothschilds, but trust my draft will be protected by the Barings.[8] The despatch in question came in the centre of a bundle of news papers, sent via Cadiz, and was of course three months and a half in reaching me. I would again suggest that despatches might always be sent by mail, either by way of England or through our Consulate at Havre

I remain Sir / Very respectfully / Your Obt St
Washington Irving

DOCKETED: Recd. 6 Sept / Mr Markoe [*upper left corner, page 1*] / No. 27. W. Irving. Madrid, 3 Aug. 1843
MANUSCRIPT: NA, RG 59.   PUBLISHED: Hellman, *WI Esquire*, pp. 302–5; STW, II, 157, 158 (in part).

This letter is in WI's handwriting.

1. Espartero was shelling Seville from July 21 to 25, when he raised the siege of the city. The bombardment continued until July 27, even after Espartero had left for Cadiz. See London *Times,* August 2, 5, 7, 10, 1843.

2. On July 30, Espartero took refuge on the *Malabar,* a British warship of seventy-two guns, which sailed from Cadiz on August 1. See *La Gaceta,* August 3, 1843; and London *Times,* August 16, 1843.

3. In his manifesto of July 30, Espartero declared that he was never a perjuror, had never violated the constitution, and wished happiness for Spain. See London *Times,* August 17, 1843. The full text of his address is printed in *Vida militar y política de Espartero,* III, 797.

4. For discussions of Espartero's lethargy, see Christiansen, *Military Power,* pp. 99–100, 113, 115.

5. Azpiroz and Narváez entered Madrid on July 23, and Prim followed the next day. See H. Butler Clarke, *Modern Spain,* p. 188.

6. See Hebrews 10:27.

7. Francisco Javier Castaños, duke of Bailén (1758–1852) had first distinguished himself by defeating the French at Bailén in 1808. See Raymond Carr, *Spain,* p. 106; Martin Hume, *Modern Spain,* pp. 138–40; and *La Gaceta,* July 29, 1843.

8. Baring Brothers and Company was an international banking house founded in 1779. Alexander Baring, first Baron Ashburton (1774–1848) negotiated the boundary settlement between the United States and Canada resulting in the Webster-Ashburton Treaty of 1842.

1616. To Sarah Storrow

Madrid Aug 7th. 1843

My dear Sarah,

Since I wrote last to you I have received a letter from Mr Hamilton[1] dated at Cauterets[2] in the Pyrenees, where he is likely to be detained for perhaps three or four weeks, by indisposition. This disconcerts my travelling plans for the present, and will oblige me to weather out the midsummer heats at Madrid. Fortunately my apartments are spacious and airy; & by keeping to them all the day and only ⟨going⟩ ↑driving↓ out in the cool of the Evening, I get on very tolerably. I am regaining my health daily and shall soon be as well in all respects as I was before this transient relapse. I must say this letter of Mr Hamiltons has caused me a disappointment, for I was hourly expecting him, and intended immediately to prepare ⟨f⟩ to set off the moment I was in travelling condition— ⟨I have⟩ He expresses great regret at his detention and anxiety to return, and is solicitous about the state of ⟨h⟩ my health. I have written to him enjoining it upon him not to hasten his return nor to set out on a journey during these summer heats, until he is completely fitted to bear the journey. He is of a delicate, irritable constitution and I would not have him run any risks.

I wrote to you in my last in behalf of Madame Albuquerque. Just after I had sent my letter I received yours telling me of your having removed to lodgings at Versailles. I immediately wrote to Brewster[3] direct, begging him to reserve a day for Madame Albuquerque, I hope it may have the desired effect. I want you to see Madame Albuquerque during her brief stay in Paris and ⟨that you⟩ and to take Kate to see her. She will tell you all you may want to know about me, as I see her almost every day. And I particularly want her to see you & Kate, (now that my chance of seeing you is defferred) that she may bring me personal accounts of you.

I must finish this hasty letter to send it in time for the Courier.

Your affectionate uncle
W. I.

MANUSCRIPT: Yale.

1. This letter has not been located.
2. Cauterets is a French village in the Pyrenees near the Spanish border known for its hot sulphur springs.
3. Sarah Storrow's letter to WI and his to Dr. Brewster have not been located.

1617. *To Catharine Paris*

Madrid, August 10th, 1843.

My dear Sister,

I have not been able to keep up the thread of my diplomatic correspondence with you of late, but have requested Sarah to send you some
⟨hast⟩ letters hastily scrawled off to her which will give you a glimpse
or two of the scenes of warfare and confusion of which I have been a
witness. I felt extremely interested and excited; and, having regained
the use of my legs, I could not keep at home, but sallied out with as
much eagerness as, when a boy, I used to break bounds and sally
forth at midnight to see a fire. The consequence has been a relapse in
my malady, from which however, I am nearly recovered. I do not know
any thing more striking than the picture, or succession of pictures furnished by the city at night—The streets lit up by torches and lantherns
placed in every window and balcony of the tall houses: centinels at
every point; patrols of footsoldiers with gleaming guns & bayonets: or
of horsemen with tramping steeds, glittering helmets & sabres, or lances
with fluttering pennons: the squares full of troops, bivouacked on the
bare ground, with their muskets stacked behind them; the grand
portal of every house presenting a groupe of the inhabitants of the
different apartments from the cellar to the garret; all gathered round
the door, listening to the distant report of firearms from the Skirmishers
at the city gates; and frightening each other with doleful prognostications. My residence is not very far from the Gate of Alcala, about which
most of the skirmishing took place, I could see the flash of firearms
from my window, and was often woke up by the report of them in
the night.

I see the French and English papers[1] have published incorrect accounts
of an interposition of the Corps diplomatique in relation to the safety of
the little queen & her sister in case of the city being carried by Storm.
I am represented by some as having prepared a note under the direction
of the French charge d'affaires, by others as having prepared it in concert
with the British minister. The fact is I prepared one according to my
own conception of what would be likely to meet with the concurrence
of both parties, whose disagreement was likely to defeat the whole
measure. The intervention was in consequence of preparations being
made to convert the Royal palace into a citadel where, in case the city
were carried by assault, the last desperate stand was to be made—and
in consequence of a declaration of that fanfaron[2] Mendizabal, who had
the control of affairs, that if pushed to the utmost he would Sally forth
with the queen & her sister in each hand, put himself in the midst of the

troops, and fight his way out of the city. I looked upon this as empty swaggering, but I knew not how far the defence might be pushed, or to what dangers the poor little queen & her sister might be exposed, by those who might seek to Screen themselves behind the fancied sanctity of their persons. I entered, therefore, into the remonstrance of the Diplomatic corps solely on account of the royal children. I was for protesting against any EXTREME *either of attack or defence* which might put their persons in imminent jeopardy; knowing that the protest of the diplomatic ↑corps↓ would be promulgated and would reach the besieging army: with the leaders of which ↑the objections of↓ a part of the Diplomatic corps would have influence: while that of ⟨[*unrecovered*]⟩ another part, would have an effect upon the leaders of the defence. I had, however, as I before observed, to modify the whole note, as the British minister would only protest against the *attack*, while the rest of the diplomatic corps objected to omitting the word defence. I suggested the idea of offering to repair to the palace and be near the queen in any moment of danger; which was adopted and incorporated in the note. Our offer was declined, fortunately events obviated the necessity of the measure. My only view in joining in the measure, as I before observed, was, as far as our interference could have effect, to prevent the poor little Queen and her sister from being personally exposed to the dangers of any ruffian contest between warring and desperate factions. I am happy to say the storm has passed away, and they are at present safe.

The day before yesterday we had one of those transitions of Scene and circumstance to which the melodramatic politics of this country are subject. Poor Espartero, as you will learn from the public papers, has been completely cast down and driven out of the country—Notwithstanding all the obloquy heaped upon his name by those who have effected his downfall,[3] I still believe him to have been loyal in his intentions towards the crown and the Constitution—but of this no more for the present. Those who were lately insurgents now possess the power; have formed themselves into a provisional government, ⟨and⟩ occupy the capital and carry on the affairs of the country in the accustomed manner, at the public offices. Their great object now is to declare the Queen of age as soon as possible; so that there will be no need of a Regency, and that they will be able to act immediately in her name and by her authority. Some were ⟨for⟩ of opinion that the government (or cabinet of ministers) ought to declare her so instantly, as authorized by the wish of the nation, expressed in the various juntas and pronunciamentos, but others objected that this would be unconstitutional; the Cortes only could by its vote abbreviate the minority of the Queen but declare her of age to govern, and before the Cortes only could she take the necessary oaths, on assuming the reins of government. It was determined, therefore, to defer the measure until the meeting of the Cortes in October next;[4] but in the mean time to have a ⟨solemn⟩ ↑grand↓ cere- monial in presence of all the dignitaries of the Kingdom and the Diplo- matic Corps, wherein the measure should be reccommended in an address to the Queen and concurred in by her: and thus a solemn pledge given to the nation that ↑the Cortes concurring,↓ the minority would cease ⟨in Oct⟩ and the Queen begin to reign in her own person, in October. Accordingly, the day before yesterday ↑at 5 oclock in the afternoon↓ I was present at another imposing scene at that theatre of political events the royal palace I have given you two or three ↑rather gloomy↓ scenes there already, connected with the story of the little Queen—I will now give you one of a different character. As the ⟨las⟩ recent change of affairs has been one in which the moderados, or ⟨the⟩ Aristocracy, have taken great part a complete change has taken place in the affairs of the palace. Arguelles; Madame Mina[5] and all the of- ficial characters elevated into place about the royal person, by former revolutions, are now superseded, and the ⟨no⟩ old nobility who stood aloof, and refused to mingle at court with people who had risen from the ⟨mass of the people⟩ ranks; now surround the throne and throng the saloons of the palace. As my carriage drew up at the foot of the vast and magnificent stair case, at the upper landing place of which the the[6] hottest of the night attack on the Royal palace was carried on, I observed hosts of old aristocratic courtiers in their court dresses thronging the marble steps; like the angels on Jacobs ladder,[7] excepting that they were all ascending—none descending. I followed them up, to this higher heaven of royalty. I paused for a moment at the great portal opening into the royal apartments: the marble casings ⟨of the⟩ still bear marks of the shattering musket balls; and the folding doors are still riddled like a sieve—Mementos of that fearful night when this sacred abode of royalty and innocence was made the scene of desperate violence. Now all was changed; the doors thrown open gave access to an immense and lofty anti sala where we passed through lines of halbardiers and court servants all in new and bright array. All the anterooms were swarming with courtiers, military and civic officers and clergy in their different costumes. The magnificent hall of the ambassadors; which at our last audience of the little queen, was almost empty and silent; was now absolutely crowded. I have already mentioned this hall to you. It is of great size, very lofty; the ceilings painted with representations of the various climes and realms of Spain in her palmy days when the sun never set on her dominions. The walls are hung with crimson velvet; relieved with rich gilding—The chandaliers are of chrystal—All the furni- ture is sumptuous. On one side of the saloon, just opposite the centre windows, is the throne, on a raised dais and under a superb canopy of velvet.

In this Saloon, as I observed, were congregated an immense throng: old and new courtiers; many of the ancient nobility who had kept out of sight during the domination of Espartero, but who now crept forth to hail the dawn of what they consider better days. Here were too, many of the generals and officers who had figured in the recent insurrection, or who had hastened back from exile, to come in for a share of power. Here was Narvaez who lately held Madrid in Siege; here was Aspiroz ⟨who likewise⟩ his confederate in arms: here was O Donnel[8] the hero of the insurrection of 1840,[9] connected with the night attack on the palace—In short, it was a complete resurrection and re-union of courtiers and military partizans, Suddenly brought together by a political *coup de theatre.*

For a while all was buzz and hum like a bee hive in swarming time, when suddenly ⟨there⟩ a voice from the lower end of the saloon proclaimed *La Reina, la Reina* (the Queen! the Queen) In an instant all was hushed; a lane was opened through the crowd and the little Queen advanced led by the venerable General Castaños, Duke de Bailen, who has succeeded Arguelles as tutor and guardian; her train was borne by the Marchioness of Valverde, a splendid looking woman one of the highest nobility, next followed her little sister, her train borne by the Duchess of Medina Celi,[10] likewise one of the grandees: Several other ladies of the highest rank were in attendance. The queen was handed up to the throne by the duke of Bailen, who took his stand beside her: the Duchess of Valverde arranged the royal train over the back of the ⟨large⟩ chair ↑of state↓ which forms the throne: so that it spread behind the little queen something like the tail of a peacock. The little princess took her seat in a chair of State ↑on the floor↓ a little to the left of the throne: the duchess of Medina Celi behind her and the other ↑noble↓ ladies in waiting ranged along to her left ↑all glittering in jewels and diamonds.↓ A little further off, likewise in a chair of State was Don Francisco, the queens uncle, and beside him, stood his son the Duke of Cadiz, who is one of the candidates for the hand of her little Majesty. I had now a good opportunity of seeing this youth. He was in a hussars uniform; and a much better looking stripling than I had been led to suppose him. As I know I am now on a diplomatic theme that will be peculiarly interesting to you—good republican as you are—I wish I could detail to you, learnedly, the dresses of the little queen and her sister, which, as usual, were alike. I know ⟨there was a⟩ ↑the body and skirt were of↓ beautiful brocade, richly fringed with gold; ⟨and⟩ there was abundance of superb lace; the trains were of deep green velvet; the queen a kind of light crown of diamonds, in which alone she differed from the princess: they both had diamond pendants and necklaces; and diamond ornaments in their side locks—The little queen looked well: she is quite plump, and has grown much. She acquitted herself with wonderful self possession: considering that she was thus elevated individually in the midst of such an immense and gorgeous assemblage and the object of every eye. Her manner was dignified and graceful. Her little sister, however, is far her superior both in looks and carriage. She has beautiful eyes: an intelligent countenance; a sweet smile and promises to be absolutely fascinating. Her looks and her winning manners she is said to inherit from her mother. She seemed to be in fine spirits; indeed both of the Sisters appeared to enjoy the Scene. It was the **first time** that the little Queen had been surrounded by the aristocratical splendors of a court. I know that you will simpathize with her—(good republican as you are) and therefore I dwell on these details.

When the Queen had taken her seat the cabinet ministers took their stand before the throne and one of them read an address to her stating the circumstances that made it expedient she should be declared of age by the next Cortes and should then take the oaths of office. As the little queen held her reply, ready cut and dry, in a paper in her hand, she paid but little attention to the speech; but kept glancing her eyes here and there about the hall; and now and then towards her little sister; when a faint smile would appear stealing over her lips, but instantly repressed. The speech ended, she opened the paper in her hand and read the brief reply which had been prepared for her. A shout then burst forth from the assemblage of *Viva la Reina!* (Long live the Queen). The venerable Duke of Bailen, taking the lead as tutor to the Queen, then bent on one knee and kissed her hand—The Infante Don Francisco and his son, gave the same token of allegiance—The same was done by every person present, excepting the Diplomatic Corps. They also knelt and kissed the hand of the princess, and some kissed the hand of Don Francisco, but those were his partisans. As the crowd was great this ceremonial took up some time—I observed that the Queen and her sister discriminated greatly as to the crowd of persons who paid this homage—distinguishing with smiles and sometimes with pleasant words, those with whom they were acquainted. ⟨all this being⟩ It was curious to see Generals kneeling and kissing the hand of the Sovereign, who but three weeks since were ⟨besieging her capital;⟩ in rebellion against her government, besieging her capital and menacing the royal abode where they were now doing her homage.

This ceremony over the Queen and her sister took their stand in a balcony in front of the great hall of ambassadors, under a rich and lofty silken awning. The high dignitaries of her court attended on her—The ladies of the court were in a balcony on one side, and the Diplomatic corps in one on the other; and every window of the royal suite of appartments was thronged by persons in court dresses or uniforms. The whole effect, in that magnificent palace, was remarkably brilliant. A vast throng was collected in the great square before the palace. In a little while ⟨the⟩ martial music was heard ⟨from the⟩ and ⟨her own troop the⟩ General Narvaez with his staff escorted by a troop of horse, came advancing under an arch way on the opposite side of the Square. In fact the whole army that had lately besieged the city now came marching in review before the palace; shouting *vivas* as they passed beneath the ⟨balcony⟩ royal balcony. It was really a splendid sight; one of those golden cloudless evenings of this brilliant climate when the sun was pouring his richest effulgence into the vast square, round which the troops paraded. Here were troops from various parts of Spain; many of them way worn and travelstained,—and all burnt by the ardent sun under which they had marched. The most curious part of this military spectacle was the Catalan legion—men who looked like banditti rather than soldiers—arrayed in half arab dress; with mantas, like horse cloths, thrown over one shoulder: red woolen caps: and hempen socks instead of shoes— They are in fact little better than banditti—a fierce turbulent race as are all the Catalans.[11] I remained for a great part of an hour witnessing the passing of these insurgent legions which were recently overrunning the country and menacing the capital: but which, by the sudden hocus pocus of political affairs, are transformed into loyal soldiers, parading peacefully before the royal palace and shouting vivas for the Queen—This is the last act I have witnessed of the Royal drama, and here I will let fall the curtain:—thanking you (good republican as you are) for the profound attention ↑with which↓ you have ⟨paid⟩ honored my exhibition.

Aug 11. After writing the foregoing I drove out yesterday to pay visits of ceremony to some of the persons who have suddenly been brought into official station by the recent change of government. ⟨One of these was the Marchioness of Valverde⟩ I must observe to you that, in this great revolution of court affairs, the ladies of the aristocracy who formerly held places in the royal household and about the persons of the Queen and her sister, have all been reinstated. The Marchioness of Santa Cruz[12] ↑one of the most intelligent and accomplished of the old nobility↓ has again been made Aya or Governess of the Queen and her sister, in place of Madama Mina. She is at present in France, but in her absence the Marchioness Valverde the next person of the Royal Household, officiates in her stead.

I accordingly paid an official visit to the Marchioness. You may like to see the interior of a Spanish house. On driving up to the great portal my servant ascertained from the porter that the Marchioness was at home and "received." I accordingly alighted and ascended the great

staircase, the porters bell giving notice of a visitor. The door of the antechamber was opened by a footman; my entrance roused two or three
other domestics, who, according to Spanish custom were sleeping on
benches about the antechamber. I passed through a suite of rooms; in
one I was startled by the screams and vociferations of parrots of all
sizes perched about the room; ⟨the⟩ My entrance to the next was disputed
by a legion of Spanish and other pet dogs—I felt like the prince in the
fairy tale in quest of the singing tree and dancing waters,[13] who is beset
by menacing cries at every step, but like him I pushed on resolutely,
and attained unharmed to the cabinet or boudoir in which the Marchioness was ensconced. I was accompanied by my good friend and
colleague the Mexican Minister,[14] who being like me the representative
of a Republic accords with me on most points of diplomacy. We met
with a very amiable reception from the Marchioness, whose manners
are both elegant and affable. Our conversation with her would have
delighted you—good republican as you are, being chiefly about the little
Queen and her sister and the internal affairs of the palace. I soon perceived that, under the new regime every thing is to be put on a different footing in the Royal household. More of Royal state and style
and the etiquette of a court will be introduced; while every attention
will be paid to render the Queen and her sister contented with the change
of persons and affairs, and to encrease their importance in the eyes of
the public. The recent ceremonial at the palace was suddenly determined
upon, and had to be got up in four and twenty hours. The reappoint-
ments in the Royal household were instantly made that the Queen might
have ladies of the nobility about her on the occasion. In the hurry and
confusion of preparation one of the most amusing difficulties was the getting ready a state dress for the Queen. ⟨Such a⟩ Having had no high ceremonials of the kind for a long time, the Royal wardrobe was in a state
of destitution.[15] There was one beautiful dress of rich brocade, but it
was found the little Queen had completely outgrown it. Nothing else,
however, presented that could be got ready in time, so they managed ⟨to
make a shift with it on⟩ to alter and lengthen it with deep fringes so as
to make it answer the purpose—

As there is no longer ⟨an⟩ apprehensions of the Queen and her sister
being carried off, a greater scope is to be given to their recreations.
Tomorrow they set off for the Pardo,[16] a royal country seat a few miles
from Madrid. Here they will be able to take country air and exercise.
They will be accompanied by some of the Royal household and a number
of the dignitaries of the Kingdom, and the day after tomorrow the
Queen gives a banquet to the cabinet ministers. The little Queen is quite
delighted with this influx of life and splendor, ⟨and⟩ into her late gloomy
court; and urged ⟨she⟩ her guardian the old Duke of Bailen to let her

give a ball. He represented to her that the weather was too hot for
dancing and that most of the nobility were out of town—that such a
thing might do in the month of October—"Well then, ["]¹⁷ replied the little
Queen—"you promise me that there shall be a court ball in October"—
The venerable old Duke was too kind and gallant to say nay—In a word,
a gayer court is anticipated under the reign of the youthful Queen than
Spain has witnessed for many a year; for that of Ferdinand VII in its
brightest days was but a gloomy one. I hope this sudden gleam of sunshine in the Royal palace may prove lasting; but this is a country of
sudden and sad reverses; the elements of discord are already at work
in the ranks of the triumphant party: and there are threats of new
discontents and insurrections in the distant provinces. The sooner the
Queen is declared of age and placed in full exercise of the sovreignty,
and the sooner the question is settled whom she is to marry, the better
will it be for the security of her throne and the tranquility of Spain; for
those two questions are at the root of all the political agitations.¹⁸

As I know that you ⟨take a⟩ have romantic associations with everything
respecting the little Queen and her sister I will give you a pleasing
anecdote concerning them. The princess, who is a very animated intelligent child, has a great passion for letter writing—Supposing that the
late ceremony was to invest her sister with full powers of Sovreignty
and make her Queen outright she thought it proper to address her a
letter and make her a present on the occasion. All this was done secretly
and by way of surprize. The following is a rough translation of the letter
but it loses all its naivete and sweetness in our stiff language.

"My ⟨well⟩ ↑dearly↓ beloved sister: thou canst not imagine the delight
I feel on thy taking the reins of government; and all Spaniards will
rejoice, for they love thee with all their hearts and thou also must love
them well"

I love thee with all my heart, as thou knowest, and if at any time I
have [been] wanting in any thing towards thee, pardon it in me, as I
⟨know⟩ now understand it, and henceforth will endeavor to please thee
in every thing.¹⁹

I hope thou wilt like the little present I give thee; I could have wished
it had been most beautiful, as thou deservedst, for thou art very beautiful
and very amiable; but as I could not buy any thing, lest any one else
should know it, I give thee this pin of the letter F. which signifies
Felicity for the country and the Queen.

                    Adieu for the present my beloved little sister / Thy sister
                                                                Lucia Fernanda²⁰
Madrid Aug 8, 1843.

The meaning of the sentence marked thus X is that she fears she may in times heretofore been deficient in points of duty and deference toward her *as her Queen*, but now, understanding their relative positions, she will ⟨henceforth⟩ ↑endeavor to↓ conduct towards her accordingly. The present was a diamond pin selected from among her own jewels; not venturing to buy any thing lest her intended surprise should be defeated.

Before I conclude let me say a word or two about that most amiable and excellent woman the Duchess of Victory. I have always esteemed and admired her, but never so much as since her great reverse of fortune. During the Siege as the palace of Buena Vista was near the point of attack she took refuge in the Royal palace. Since the capitulation of the City, ⟨and⟩ the occupation of it by the insurgent armies and the formation of the provisional government, she retired to the house of ⟨her⟩ ↑an↓ aunt in the centre of Madrid. Here I visited her and found her still attended by some faithful friends. I found her calm, self possessed and free from all useless repining or weak lamentation. In fact she was in a far better state of mind than when I saw her at her Soirees at Buena Vista, surrounded by something like a court, but harrassed by doubts and forebodings. She said her conscience was clear: she had never been excited by her elevation as the wife of the Regent, and trusted her conduct had always been the same as when wife of a simple general—She felt no humiliation in her downfall. She spoke of the charges made against her husband of grasping ambition; artifice; love of power—He, said she, whose habits were so simple; whose desires so limited; who cared not for State and less for money; whose great pleasure was to be in his garden planting trees and cultivating flowers—It was a matter of pride and consolation to her she added, that they left the Regency poorer than when they entered it. I was pleased to see that she spoke without acrimony of those political rivals who had effected the downfall of her husband; but ⟨of⟩ ↑with↓ deep feeling of the conduct of some who had always professed devotion to him, who had risen by his friendship and who had betrayed him— ["]²¹ This said she is the severest blow of all; for it destroys our confidence in human kind. I could not but admire the discrimination of her conduct with respect to the two great leaders of the present government, General Narvaez, ↑(Commander in Chief) ⟨who was always a bitter enemy of her husband⟩; and Serrano ↑(the Minister of war)↓ ⟨once his friend.⟩ They both sent her offers of escort, and of any other service and facility. As to General Narvaez said she he has always been the ⟨open and⟩ avowed enemy of my husband, but an open and frank one; he practised nothing but what he professed; I accept his offers with gratitude and thanks; as to Serrano, he professed to be my husbands friend; he rose by his friendship and favors, and he proved faithless to him—I will accept nothing at his hands and beg his name may not again be mentioned to me"

The Duchess has set off for England by the way of France, and an escort was furnished her by Narvaez to protect her on her journey through Spain. I have no doubt she will be well received in England and will feel a tranquility of mind there, to which she has long been a stranger—"Oh" said she, drawing a long breath, "how glad I shall be to find myself once more at complete liberty: where I can breathe a freer air, and be out of this atmosphere of politics, trouble and anxiety."

I must now bring this long letter to an end hoping you will not expect another of the same length for a long time to come. As I mentioned in the beginning of this letter I am nearly recovered from the lingering effects of a relapse in my complaint occasioned by fatigues and exposures during the time of the Siege. Mr. Hamilton is about on an excursion to the Pyrenees; but detained there by indisposition from which he is recovering. I have written to him not to hasten his return but to give himself time for complete recovery. In the mean time I have given up for the present, all thoughts of an excursion into France.

Give my love to all the household & the extensive family connexions.

Your affectionate brother
Washington Irving

MANUSCRIPT: Yale.   PUBLISHED: PMI, III, 291, 292–302 (in part); Hellman, *WI Esquire*, pp. 270–71 (in part); STW, II, 162 (in part).

1. For the account of the actions of the diplomats in Madrid, see London *Times*, July 26, 1843.

2. Braggart or blusterer.

3. The López ministry denounced Espartero as a traitor and stripped him and his friends of all their honors and titles. See Martin Hume, *Modern Spain*, p. 374; H. Butler Clarke, *Modern Spain*, pp. 189–90; *Vida militar y política de Espartero*, III, 795; and *La Posdata*, August 5, 1843.

4. The Cortes was scheduled to meet on October 13, with new deputies and senators chosen at elections beginning on September 15. See *La Gaceta*, July 31, 1843.

5. In its gossip column *La Posdata* (July 25, 1843) brought in allusions to *Don Quixote* when it referred to Madame Mina as "La Dueña Dolorida" and to Argüelles as "Zapatero Simon," the tutor who tried to commit suicide when he was removed from his tutorship.

6. WI repeated "the."

7. See Genesis 28:12.

8. Leopoldo O'Donnell, duke of Tetuan, Count Lucena (1809–1867), a supporter of María Christina, was exiled from 1840 to 1843. During that time he trained a revolutionary military force which returned to Spain in 1843. See Christiansen, *Military Power*, pp. 111, 190; and Hume, *Modern Spain*, p. 367.

9. This uprising brought Espartero into power and caused María Christina to leave Spain at Valencia under the protection of General O'Donnell. See Clarke, *Modern Spain*, pp. 360–64; and Christiansen, *Military Power*, pp. 97–98.

10. Wife of one of the members of the council named in Ferdinand VII's will to aid the regent. WI had visited the palace of the Duke of Medina Coeli in

Seville in 1828. See Hume, *Modern Spain*, p. 299; and *Diary 1828–1829*, p. 9.

11. "The men [of Catalonia] wear loose cloth or plush trousers of dark colours. . . . These trousers come so high- up to the armpits that they are called *breeches*. . . . The gay silken Spanish sash, *faja*, is, however, indispensable. Their jackets are very short, and hang in fine weather over their shoulders. . . . they wear a *gorro*, or red or purple cap . . . the end either hangs down on one side or is doubled up and brought over the forehead" (Richard Ford, *A Hand-Book for Travellers in Spain*, II, 694).

12. Wife of one of the Moderate generals supporting María Christina, the marchioness had been Isabella's nurse in infancy and later the first lady of her bedchamber before Espartero dismissed her. See Peter de Polnay, *A Queen of Spain*, pp. 20, 63.

13. This story is told by Scheherazade during the 671st to 681st nights of the *Arabian Nights*. See *Supplemental Nights to the Book of the Thousand and One Nights*, ed. Richard F. Burton ([London, 1886]), III, 323–44.

14. Ignacio Valdivielso.

15. Even later, when María Christina returned to the palace, she found that Isabella's wardrobe consisted of "eighteen shirts for day wear, twelve night-dresses, twelve vests, twelve pairs of drawers, twenty pairs of stockings, thirty-six napkins, nineteen pairs of sheets, one quilt, thirty handkerchiefs and one dozen camisoles." See de Polnay, *A Queen of Spain*, p. 90.

16. Originally a hunting lodge built in 1543 by Charles V nine miles northwest of Madrid, it was refurbished by Charles III in 1772. See Karl Baedeker, *Spain and Portugal*, p. 107; and Federico Carlos Sainz de Robles, *Madrid, crónica y guía de una ciudad impar* (Madrid, 1962), pp. 549–53.

17. WI omitted the bracketed quotation marks.

18. Madrid newspapers disagreed about the manner of handling the question of Isabella's majority. *El Castellano* and *La Posdata* (both August 10, 1843) felt it should be treated as a separate issue, while *El Eco del Comercio* (August 10, 1843) argued that it should be related to the marriage question.

19. WI had placed an X in the left margin of this paragraph, beside the words "I have [been] wanting. . . ." He refers to it following Luisa Fernanda's letter.

20. Luisa Fernanda's letter was printed in *El Castellano*, August 12, 1843.

21. WI omitted the bracketed quotation marks.

1617a. To David Davidson

Madrid Aug 12th. 1843

My dear David,

A harrassing and protracted indisposition of several months, which unfitted me for all exercise of the pen has prevented an earlier reply to your letter of the 17th. of January last.[1] I do not know when I have received a letter that gave me more heart felt satisfaction; as it proved to me that you were continuing in the practice of those upright and honorable principles, and that faithful and disinterested line of conduct that originally won for you my entire confidence and my affectionate regard, and which induced me to reccommend you in the most unqualified terms to your present employers.[2] I am happy to find that they have not been disappointed in you; and I am sure you will go on to make yourself more and more worthy of their approbation and good will. It is a great advantage to you to be with strict men of business who expect each one in their employ to do his duty; and, much as I feel obliged to Mr Wiley[3] for having first taken you on trust, on my mere word, I am sure he would not have shewn the growing confidence with which he has since honored you; had you not merited it by your good actions. As you well observe "such confidence is more to be valued than any salary."

I thank you for your lively picture of the Cottage and all its residents both indoors and out of doors. I had received from the family ↑an↓ account of your visit; which was very gratifying to the whole household. I hope you will be able to repeat your visit there in a more favorable season of the year. My heart dwells in that blessed little spot, and it will be the happiest day of my life when I am able to return there.

As I mentioned in the beginning of this letter I have had a long and harrassing illness which commenced at the beginning of last February and ⟨from⟩ the lingering effects of which ⟨I⟩ still hang about me; though I am nearly recovered. I hope to be able to make a journey early in the Autumn and that it will entirely re establish my health

I am very much pleased to hear such good accounts of your father[4] and family, and trust that his prospects will improve with the return of busy and prosperous times. I beg you to present him with my respects— and my best wishes.

Let me hear from you occasionally, and tell me of all your plans and prospects; do not fear being too minute in your letters, every thing respecting you is interesting to me; and, wherever I am, I shall always have a guardian eye to your welfare.

Present my kindest remembrances to Mr Wiley and believe me my dear David

> *[complimentary close and signature clipped from the letter]*

Mr David Davidson.

ADDRESSED: Mr. David Davidson / Care of Messrs. Wiley & Putnam / New York
MANUSCRIPT: Ralph M. Aderman.

1. This letter has not been located.

2. As the address indicates, Davidson was working for Wiley & Putnam, booksellers in New York. The directory for 1844–45 lists him as an accountant at 39 John Street, with his residence in Jersey City. WI had arranged for his employment in Wiley & Putnam's "retail department, with a salary of $200 a year...." See WI to Sarah Storrow, September 1, 1841.

3. John Wiley (1809–1891), publisher and bookseller who was in partnership with George P. Putnam.

4. Samuel Davidson (1786–1863), who was born in Badenoch, Scotland. Information received from Iris M. Esterbrook, February 22, 1981.

1618. *To Sarah Storrow*

⟨Paris⟩, ↑Madrid↓ Aug 13 [1843]

My dear Sarah,

I enclose a letter for your Mother[1] which is left open for your perusal & to serve in place of a long letter to yourself. A letter received two or three days since from Alexander Hamilton[2] represents him as still suffering from indisposition though anxious to return to Madrid. I hope and trust my letters to him will prevent his setting out before his physicians think him in perfect condition to travel. I do not expect to see him here for some time, ⟨yet⟩, and for the present have given up all my travelling plans. My health continues to improve and I have nearly got over the effects of my late relapse, though I have still to be extremely sparing of pedestrian exercise. My cheif recreations are a drive out in the evening, and then a couple of hours at the opera; where we have a very fair troupe and a succession of the most popular operas. This is my grand resource and, in fact, the Great Sweetener of my present monotonous existence

Mr Sumner still remains in Madrid and takes a tête a tête dinner with me daily; giving me assistance occasionally in the Secretary ship of the legation.

I am anxious to hear from you and to learn how you are pleased with your residence at Versailles and how Mamselle Kate conducts herself. I hope you have seen Madame Albuquerque—I shall endeavor to scribble a line to her by this courier—Kiss Kate for me

Your affectionate Uncle
Washington Irving

ADDRESSED: Madame / Madame Storrow.
MANUSCRIPT: Yale.

The year is written in pencil in another hand.

1. See WI to Catharine Paris, August 10, 1843.
2. This letter and the one to Madame Albuquerque mentioned in the last paragraph have not been located.

1619. To the Secretary of State

Legation of the United States / Madrid Aug 19, 1843.

No 28 / The Hon / The Secretary of State / Washington
Sir,

In my last I mentioned that there was a strong disposition on the part of some of the ruling party immediately to declare the youthful Queen of age. This was particularly the wish of Narvaez, Captain General of the district, and in fact the military head of the government; a man strongly inclined to exercise military sway. Indeed he had determined that the declaration should take place on the 7th. inst. and be celebrated in military style, having arranged a review of the whole army to pass under the balconies of the royal palace and hail the youthful Isabella as Queen. This measure was objected to by Mr Lopes and others of the Cabinet as unconstitutional, the Cortes alone having the power to make such a declaration and to receive from the Queen the necessary oaths. A warm dispute ensued which was with difficulty settled by compromise, and the adoption of a half way measure. According to this the review was postponed till the 8th. on which day in presence of all the public authorities, the state functionaries, and the diplomatic corps, assembled at the royal palace the Queen was addressed by the Cabinet Ministers, announcing to her that it was the wish of the nation she should be declared of age by the next cortes; before which body she would take the necessary oaths, until which time they would conduct the government in her name.[1]

The Queen having in a short reply signified her concurrence; received the homage of all the Spaniards present; and afterwards was hailed as Queen by the troops as they passed in review before the palace. This half way measure however, has proved very unsatisfactory to those of the ruling party who are for prompt and vigorous action in the government.

The great political question, however, is the marriage of the Queen; It is already producing disunion in the Cabinet and the "league."[2] A grand division is said to be taking place. on one side report Marshalls Serrano, Minister of War, Narvaez, the Military chieftain; all the Moderados, together with the influence of Maria christina and of the Tuilleries. On the other side are arrayed Lopez, Caballero and aillers[3] of the Cabinet; the republicans, many of the progresistas; with the influence of Don Francisco.[4] This last division counts upon the discontented in Catalonia, Aragon and the Basque provinces; and will probably be joined by the Ayacuchos or partizans of the late Regent. This party will be for reforms in the Constitution; modifying if not

entirely abolishing the Senate, which is decried as by its subservient
intervention enabling the government to defeat the intentions of Congress. It will likewise be for abridging the royal power, especially in
regard to the frequent dissolution of the Cortes. The great aim of this
party at present however, is the marriage of the Queen; which it is
urged should be settled by the next Cortes. Their candidate is the Duke
of Cadiz the son of the Infante Don Francisco; whom they hold up as
most likely to sustain the independence and promote the prosperity of
the country being a native born Spaniard and a liberal.

The other party, having other interests, and a foreign alliance in view,
are desirous of postponing the question of the marriage, ostensibly on
account of the extreme youth of the Queen, but probably to gain time
for the maturity of their plans.

In the mean time there is a growing jealousy and sensitiveness on this
subject; as is apparent from the reports and alarms, which begin to be
circulated with respect to the movements of the Queen and the designs
of those about her. She and her sister have been taken within a day
or two to La Granja[5] one of the royal Sitios or country residences, for
the benefit of air and exercise. It has been whispered by some that she
has been taken there to have private interviews with some emissary
from her Mother, Maria Christina relative to an alliance with one of
the sons of Louis Philippe. Another report inserted in one of the papers,
was, that she was to be spirited away to the Basque provinces, out of
the reach and control of the people of Madrid, and within the influence
of French policy. The last rumor, which I heard from the mouth of an
ex minister was that on the 25th. instant, Narvaez was going to have
her proclaimed of age *by the army* at La Granja having detached five
thousand troops there for that purpose. She was then to form a new
cabinet and to be affianced to a prince of her mothers choice.

Such are some of the reports which abound in this idle and gossipping
capital; and which serve to shew the feverish state of the public mind.
In fact the capital and the whole country are in an anxious and distracted state, and ready for new commotions. Secret societies are forming
among the discontented and the factious military, emissaries are dispatched by them to all parts of the Kingdom, to foment new disturbances
and to be ready to take the lead in any new outbreaks; and great efforts
will be made to get up a counter revolution.

At present the youthful queen is the only rallying point of national
feeling and she will continue ↑to be↓ so, as long as she continues politi-
cally unbiased and insignificant; but the moment her minority ends,
and, as queen, she favors either party, that moment she will become
an object of hostility, and her very throne may be shaken in the violent
convulsions which are likely to arise. Already in one of the public meet-

ings in which the abridgement of the Royal powers was discussed it was observed by one of the ultras, that he would be content with the taking away of the Royal veto,[6] but he would be much better pleased with the taking away of the Queen. I dwell on this subject because on it hinge the destinies of the country for a long time to come. The judicious and satisfactory espousals of the queen are all important to the tranquility of the country. It is to be hoped this agitating question may be disposed off amicably in the next Cortes; but between this and the 15th of October next is a critical space of time, ↑in this country of events and reverses↓; and many apprehend that there will be out breaks in various provinces sufficient to prevent an election.

I am Sir / Very respectfully / Your obt Servt
Washington Irving

Docketed: Recd. 22d. Septr. / Mr. Markoe
Manuscript: NA, RG 59.   Published: Hellman, *WI Esquire*, pp. 305–8; STW, II, 162 (in part).

This despatch is in WI's handwriting.

1. The queen's remarks provoked discussions in the Madrid newspapers of August 10, 1843. See WI to Catharine Paris, August 10, 1843, n. 18.

2. WI is probably referring to those who were united in opposition to Espartero's regency. Apparently there was no league in a formal sense.

3. For other details, see WI to Daniel Webster, May 9, 1843.

4. On August 12 a group was formed to advocate the marriage of Isabella to Don Francisco, the duke of Cadiz. See *El Castellano*, August 15, 1843.

5. La Granja, a royal palace built by Philip V, is about forty-three miles northwest of Madrid. See Karl Baedeker, *Spain and Portugal*, pp. 120–22.

6. According to the Constitution of 1837, the Spanish monarch had the power of absolute veto and was empowered to summon, suspend, or dissolve the Cortes, with the stipulation that if the crown did not call the Cortes every year, the chambers would convoke themselves on December 1. See Martin Hume, *Modern Spain*, p. 339. On August 19, 1843, *El Castellano* discussed the program of *El Eco del Comercio* for abridging royal power.

1620. To Sarah Storrow

Madrid, Aug 23d. 1843.

My dear Sarah,

I have just received your letter of the 14th. & 16th.[1] giving me an account of the visit of my charming friend Madame Albuquerque It was indeed a most obliging act in her, pressed as she must be for time, to make an expedition to Versailles to see you; but she is a noble hearted woman and full of energy and devotion in her friendships. I hope you will have carried into effect your idea of going to Paris to have another interview with her. I shall welcome her return now with double delight, as she will bring me personal accounts of you and of that little virago Kate, who, by your letter must have been in one of her hoity toity humors during the whole visit. By the way, I cannot tell you how I long to see that little baggage; and every account you give of her towring passions and deadly affronts only amuse me and encrease my desire to see her.

I have no accounts of Mr Hamilton since the 11th. when his friend Mr Livingston[2] wrote that Hamilton had taken a place in the Diligence to return, but had experienced a relapse and been obliged to give it up, and that he then knew not when he would be fit for the journey. His physician, however, says his case is not attended with the least danger.

Even if I should be able to put my much talked of visit in Execution I doubt whether I now shall be able to join you before your return from Versailles; as you limit your sojourn there to the 20th. September. I deeply regret the circumstances which have defeated my summer plans, both on their own account and on account of their effects.

As I mentioned in my letter of yesterday, the Midsummer heats of Madrid, of which you express such apprehension, have been infinitely more supportable than I had anticipated. Last summer I had to endure them in a house badly calculated for the hot season; where there was not good ventilation, and where the windows looked upon a Street glaring with sunshine and heated like a furnace. This summer my saloons look into a garden; the air steals in from among trees; the bed rooms on the opposite side of the house face the north and look into a shady street; my apartments are spacious and lofty, and by closing some windows and opening others, ⟨and by⟩ ↑maintaining a mere twilight and↓ leaving open interior doors opening upon a long paved corridor, I manage to keep up a pleasant temperature and to have a free circulation of air. After sunset the heats immediately subside and then it is very agreeable and refreshing to take a drive—⟨four or five times⟩ In fact I am so reduced in flesh by my long indisposition that I am not so sensible to heat as formerly; and, instead of *melting* as I used to do at this season of the year, and as I did while in Paris, I have not had a complete persperation this whole summer. There is some comfort in this, whatever may be the cause. My great resource as I have told you, is the opera;[3] which we have almost every evening. The troupe is very respectable and we have a succession of the most popular operas; ⟨Fort Fort⟩ and as, fortunately, I am more of an amateur than a connoissieur, I ⟨continue to⟩ manage to derive a vast deal of enjoyment from these performances. They are in fact the sweeteners of my other wise somewhat insipid existence—I speak of my existence as insipid only in reference to my present condition; when my protracted indisposition prevents me from engaging in any of those intellectual pursuits and animating occupations, which usually ⟨make time appear⟩ crowd existence with excitement and make time appear too short. However, these will all come again within my reach, and then Madrid will be quite a different place to me.

You tell me to "burn all the scrawls you have written to me at Madrid and you will try to write better in future." I beg my dear Sarah you will not try to do any such thing; but continue to write as you always have written, naturally and without effort. It is this which makes your letters so delightful to me—I feel that they are unstudied and sincere—could you have seen the effect of the first letter I received from you during the severe crises of my illness. I had been for several days confined to my bed; ↑in a helpless state↓ reduced by ↑fever and by↓ bleeding; ⟨helpless,⟩ until my very heart had given way and become as weak as a childs. I felt lonely and homesick; it seemed an age since I had heard from any of my friends; I turned ⟨anxiously⟩ ↑an anxious eye↓ to Lorenzo every morning as he brought in the mail, but turned from him peevish and disheartened when I saw nothing but newspapers. I felt *vexed with you,* for it seemed to me as if you ought to have known that I was ill and ought to have written. At length came a letter from you. Lorenzo handed it to me with exultation. I was so miserably weak in spirits that I could not command myself but siezed it from him, and Kissed it and burst into tears—I do not know when I have been so weakhearted and broken down in spirits as I was about that period. It shows what a shock my constitution had sustained, for my heart, when I am in health, is a pretty stout one, though it plays me many tricks. ———

———Aug 28. I enclose with this a long letter to your mother left open for your perusal—⟨and⟩

Your affectionate uncle
WI.

MANUSCRIPT: Yale.   PUBLISHED: STW, II, 160 (in part).

At the lower right bottom of page four, inverted, are the words "a week or."

1. These letters have not been located.

2. Jasper Livingston, son of WI's friend Brockholst Livingston, was Hamilton's successor as secretary of the Madrid legation in 1844. Livingston's letter has not been located.

3. WI had earlier commented upon his enjoyment of the opera. See WI to Sarah Storrow, October 21, 1842.

1621. To Catharine Paris

Madrid Aug 25th. 1843.

My dear Sister,

In compliance with your Republican taste for Royalty I proceed to give you another peep into the palace, and a view of the little Queen in her present state of (perhaps transistory!) splendor. Some days since notice was sent to the different members of the Court, the Corps diplomatic &c that a grand Religious ceremony would take place in the chapel of the Royal palace where high mass would be performed with pontifical state and solemnity, by the Cardinal, Patriarch of the Indias,[1] after which a grand Te Deum would be chanted in honor of the recent events. On this occasion her Majesty was to attend seated in state on a throne; a circumstance which had not occurred at any ceremony of the kind since the time of Isabella of glorious memory, no Queen having swayed the Sceptre of Spain in her own right since that time.

On the day appointed the palace was thronged with civil military and religious functionaries all in grand costume. I took up the Minister of Brazil and his secretary on my way to the palace, and we were set down at the foot of the great marble Staircase so often mentioned to you. It was again thronged with courtiers in their embroidered dresses, hastening to pay their devotions to the throne rather than to the altar. We passed up the splendid staircase and along a glazed gallery surrounding the great interior court of the palace; a kind of alley being formed by two rows of halberdiers all in new uniforms. The chapel is in the back part of the palace. It is of Octagon form, with lofty arches and alcoves; sumptuously gilded, and the high altar and the cielings decorated with fine paintings. The chapel was already crowded. Benches had been placed for the official characters, religious, civil and military, who were for the most part in their places; there was a great throng of ladies, who, however ↑not being on court duty, but mere spectators↓ were generally arrayed in black, with veils or mantillas attached to the backs of their heads; the usual dress of ladies on attending mass. In the lofty recesses of the arches were small galleries, or rather windows low and long, looking down into the chapel, and sufficient to accommodate several spectators—All these were thronged with heads ⟨of⟩ mostly of youthful persons, females of the royal household and their friends & relatives; eagerly gazing down upon the splendid scene. ⟨The grand altar was⟩ Notwithstanding the brilliant day light that glanced through, and was reflected by the gilded arches, the grand altar was lighted up by waxen tapers of great size. ⟨and was⟩ The dignitaries of the church were seated on each side of it. At a little distance on the right of the altar was the throne prepared for the youthful Isabella. It consisted of a Sumptuous chair of State, elevated on a platform covered with ⟨a⟩ Rich carpet; and under a lofty canopy of damask, on which, behind the Royal chair, were wrought the arms of Spain. On the same platform, a little to the left of the chair and between it and the grand altar, facing the latter, was the royal *prie Dieu* or praying desk, covered with a mantle of damask, with a damask cushion for the Queen to kneel on, whenever the Sacred ceremonies required genuflexion. Fortunately ⟨the⟩ a front bench facing the throne was assigned to the diplomatic corps, and as I happened to be at the head of the corps on that occasion, I was seated almost immediately opposite to the queen, which enables me to gratify you with this minute discription.

For a while all was suspense; the seats still vacant kept gradually filling up; and the throng of ladies, crowded in recesses, now and then grew rather insurrectional; taking possession of benches reserved for personages of the court and attendants, upon the queen ⟨I amused myself with from⟩ whence they were with some difficulty ejected by officials appointed to keep order. During this time I amused myself with scanning the magnificent scene; with noticing the pretty and picturesque young female heads, peeping down from the galleries and windows; with admiring the dark flashing eyes of some of the ladies in ⟨mantillas⟩ veils and mantillas and the restless movement of their fans so expressive of their own restless and excitable spirits; while not a little amusement did I derive from the crowd of veteran courtiers, in court dresses that ⟨have⟩ had weathered many a political storm in this Revolutionary country, and which, like their owners, were much the worse for wear. In fact men are so often turned in and turned out of office by the ⟨rapid chan⟩ frequent and sudden changes in this government, that they and their coats are worn threadbare and limber as rags. Scarce a man about court, I might almost say about the streets, ⟨what⟩ ↑but↓ has ⟨not⟩ been, or is, or expects to be a Cabinet Minister or other high functionary; and I am careful now to pull off my hat to every dabbler in politics, however shabby his looks or low his condition, as I do not know but by a sudden turn of the wheel, I may have to treat with him about affairs of State. I was at a private concert last winter at which were present the Duchess of Victory and several persons high in office. A ⟨pers⟩ foreigner, long resident in Madrid, was speaking of the political reverses to which this country is subject. You see these persons ⟨said he⟩ ↑there↓ present, said he, who appear firmly seated in power and popularity; nothing is more uncertain than their position. On a sudden you may find them fugitives beyond the Pyrenees; and their places occupied by persons now in exile—I smiled at the suggestion. Scarce six months have elapsed and it has come to pass!—but I am forgetting the Royal chapel.

There was the swell of military music from the great ⟨gallery⟩ Court of the palace; a bustle was heard in the gallery; the folding doors of the Chapel were thrown open, and the Queen was announced. She was preceded by officers of the Court; chamberlains &c &c—and led by her guardian the venerable Duke de Bailen; her train as on a former occasion, was borne by the Marchioness of Valverde; the train of her Sister the little princess was borne by the Marchioness of Alcanizes, one of the most beautiful women of Spain. Then came the Infanta Luisa Carlotta,[2] aunt to the Queen & princess, and wife to the Infante Don Francisco— with the princess her daughter;[3] Then came Don Francisco himself, with his son the Duke of Cadiz, one of the candidates for the hand of the youthful Queen. Then came a train of nobles and attendants of both sexes "too tedious to mention." The little Queen ascended the throne and took her seat in the chair of State. Her ladies in attendance ranged themselves to her right on a bench assigned them; and beyond them were ↑seated↓ the Grandees of Spain. The Infante Don Francisco and his son the Duke of Cadiz took their seats in chairs immediately to the right of the throne. The Queens little sister, her Aunt Luisa Carlota, and the daughter of the latter, ⟨to the⟩ repaired to the royal tribune, where the Queen & royal family sit on usual occasions. It is in a deep recess formed by an arch immediately opposite the grand altar, and is separated from the rest of the Chapel by a screen or window of plate glass. Before I go a step further I must say something of the dress of the Queen: but that is always a difficult matter with me, not being learned in these matters. It was of magnificent lace over a skirt of white ↑satin↓ or brocade; her train was scarlet velvet, deeply bordered or embroidered with gold. She wore a ⟨splendid⟩ ↑brilliant↓ circlet of diamonds round her head, to which was attached a splendid white lace veil. A broad ribband of some distinguished order, but of which I am not courtier enough to know, was worn over one shoulder—there were other decorations and jewels which I do not distinctly reccollect; but I think I have mentioned enough to deck her out in Regal style. The ceremony (⟨,⟩ mass, music Te Deum &c), lasted about two hours and was conducted in very grand style. ↑The Patriarch of the Indias is a man of most venerable appearance and he was assisted by a number of Church dignitaries in their Sacerdotal robes.↓ The music was excellent, and had a fine effect, resounding among the lofty vaults and arches of the chapel. In fact ⟨it⟩ th⟨e⟩is union of religious and royal pomp displayed in roman Catholic ceremonial, and monarchical pageant is one of the most striking exhibitions that human ingenuity has devised and I never saw it presented with more effect than on the present occasion; where the sovreign was a virgin queen in her innocent and tender years, for the first time occupying a Royal throne beside the altar, which no Queen had occupied for centuries. You would have been charmed (good republican as you are) could you have Seen the dignified yet Simple grace with which the little Sovereign conducted herself—seated thus alone, ⟨and⟩ elevated in the midst of a great assemblage, ↑and officiated to by venerable prelates of the highest order↓ But she is quite womanly both in her appearance and deportment—Though not quite thirteen years of age she looks to be fifteen at least, and acquits herself with wonderful propriety and self possession. She improves too, daily in her appearance, and on this occasion looked quite handsome. It was a beautiful sight to see her at various parts of the service, rise from her chair, advance to the Prie Dieu and kneel down at it, with her prayer book; her long train extending behind her across the throne. It was a subject for a painter. When the ceremony was over she descended from the throne; was joined by the Royal Cortege and retired from the chapel in the same state in which she had entered; bowing to the Corps diplomatic and to the different functionaries as she passed.—Thus have I given you another picture of the little Queen at this present moment, when a gleam of Sunshine sheds its splendor about her throne: how fleeting and deceptive that gleam may be; and what fearful gloom may follow it who can tell! Never have I witnessed any scene of human pomp and ⟨outward⟩ ↑seeming↓ prosperity with a deeper misgiving of the heart that all was hollow and precarious, on what quicksands all political power rests in this country is evidenced in the sudden manner in which the Regency and all the State and grandeur and apparent popularity of Espartero ↑have↓ passed away. But a few months since, he stood beside the throne, apparently the protector of the youthful Queen, and possessed of almost Regal sway—at present he is an Exile! Who shall say that the throne itself is secure, when such convulsions suddenly sweep away all those who surround it? As yet the Queen has her extreme youth, and her freedom from political bias in her favor. ⟨Her very want of⟩ She has all the poetical interest of Royalty (in her) to reccommend her to the popular feeling; but the moment she is declared of age and assumes the Reins of government she becomes a different being—and to which ever party or interest she inclines she becomes an object of hostility to all the rest. The great question of her marriage is one that is now threatening, ⟨to⟩ not merely to throw the country into commotion, but to agitate the political circles of Europe; but before this can be settled plots and conspiracies are likely to take place and ⟨bloody⟩ ↑deadly↓ feuds to break forth, that may fill this capital with alarm and make it the theatre of sanguinary scenes. Heaven grant that my forebodings may not take place; ⟨and⟩ ↑Heaven grant↓ that the government may acquire solidity and be conducted on sound ↑constitutional↓ principles; that the little Queen may be well and happily married and seated on a secure and prosperous throne, ⟨But the [unrecovered] of that takes a [one line unrecovered]⟩ I consider, under all circumstances, a constitutional monarchy the best form of government for Spain in its present state of knowledge and improvement, and I believe it is the form desired by the great mass of the people; but there are some bigots in politics who would fain restore an absolute monarchy and zealots who would hurry every thing into a wild democracy. One of the latter made a startling speech in a recent political meeting, wherein reforms in the Constitution were proposed abridging the power of the crown and taking from it the *Veto.* I shall be satisfied said this ⟨demagogue⟩ ↑Loco Foco↓[4] if you do away with the *Veto*—but I should be much more satisfied if you would do away with the *Queen!* This is the first ↑time↓ such an idea has been uttered—it appears to have met with no concurrence—but ⟨in⟩ such a voice heard from the midst of the present revolutionary agitations is portentous.

And now, my dear Sister, I will conclude this long chapter of politics and court ceremonial—which is only meant for the meridian of the Cottage and should not stray beyond the domestic circle of dear little SunnySide. But I know these peeps at the great world ⟨be⟩ will be relished by you all in your quiet retirement. I fear, to be sure, that I may turn the heads of my nieces with these descriptions of the little Queen and her Royal state; her diamonds and brocades and Regal robes; and that they may be sighing now and then to go to Tarrytown church in long velvet trains and diamond coronets; and have Doctor Creighton[5] officiate to them in pontifical state and ceremony, like the Patriarch of the Indias—but let them reccollect that they have a safer seat on the Sofa than the little Queen on her throne; that the Cottage, if it has not the pomp, is at least free from the perils of the palace, and that they reign without dispute over the whole empire of SunnySide.

It is upwards of a fortnight since the date of my last accounts from Mr Hamilton; and I am at a loss to know whether he is on his way to Madrid or is still detained in the Pyrenees. My Summer tour, of course, is given up, though I may make an excursion in the early part of the Autumn; being still hampered by the lingerings of ⟨th⟩ my malady, which my physician thinks a change of air and the refreshment of travel would entirely remove.

I recently received your letter of July 19 & 20, written from the Cottage and treating of honeysuckles, humming birds and trumpet creepers. Oh! my dear Sister, how sweet and refreshing these letters are to me; bringing that blessed little spot full before my eyes, and ⟨showing⟩ presenting you all to imagination happily nestled there, enjoying the simple delights with which you are surrounded. I have my good brother, too, frequently before me; "out all day," as you say, "over looking the men and sometimes working with them" and enjoying that health and good spirits which accompany rural occupation—at least the rural occupation of *gentlemen agriculturalists*.

God bless you all, and keep you all hearty and happy!

Your affectionate brother
Washington Irving

MANUSCRIPT: Yale.   PUBLISHED: *Yale Review*, 17 (October, 1927), 105–10; LFSS, pp. 57–65; STW, II, 162–63 (in part).

1. Juan José Bonel, bishop of Cordoba and Toledo. For other details, see August 3, 1842.

2. Luisa Carlota (1804–1844), daughter of Francis I of Naples.

3. Probably Isabella (1821–1897), the eldest of Carlota's eleven children.

4. A group of radical New York Democrats opposing the regulars in the party in the late 1830's.

5. The rector of Christ Church, Tarrytown, from 1836 to 1865.

1622. To John Miller

Legation of the United States / Madrid September 1st. 1843

John Miller Esqr. / Agent. U. S. Legation London. /

Dear Sir

I have received your account in duplicate for postage &c paid by you on account of this Legation during the last quarter.

I enclose a check on Messrs Baring Brothers & Co. for the amount £1⟨0⟩1:4:10 payable to your order at sight.

Very respectfully / Your Obdt Sevt
Washington Irving

MANUSCRIPT: NA, RG 84 (letterbook copy).

The following was included with the letter.

Enclosure
Legation of the United States / Madrid Septr. 1st. 1843.

£11.4.10.

At sight please to pay John Miller on order, eleven pounds, four shillings and ten pence sterling and charge the same to the United States on account of the contingent expenses of this Legation.

Washington Irving.

Messrs. Baring Brothers & Co.
Bankers U. S. London

1623. To Joaquín de Frías

Legation of the United States. / Madrid Septr. 4th. 1843.

The Undersigned Envoy Extraordinary and Minister Plenipotentiary of the United States has great satisfaction in acknowledging the receipt of the note of His Excellency Don Joaquin de Frias informing him of the appointment of Don José Ruiz de Arana[1] to the post of Introducer of Ambassadors, in union with the Marquis of Ceballos, Conde del Asalto;[2]—and appointment which from the well known urbanity, courtesy and experience of Don José Ruiz de Arana cannot but prove highly acceptable to the whole diplomatic corps.

The Undersigned avails himself of this occasion to offer to His Excellency Don Joaquin de Frias the assurances of his most distinguished consideration.

Washington Irving.

MANUSCRIPT: NA, RG 84 (letterbook copy).

1. José Ruíz de Arana, duke of Baena, was later one of Queen Isabella's lovers and was thought to be the father of her daughter, María Isabel Francisco (1851–1931). See Peter de Polnay, *A Queen of Spain*, p. 146; and Aronson, *Royal Vendetta*, p. 71.

2. Possibly Francisco de Ceballos y Vargas (1814–1883), an adjutant of General Evaristo San Miguel and an opponent of Espartero. See *Enciclopedia Universal Ilustrada*, XII, 789.

1624. To John Wetherell

Madrid Sept. 4th. 1843

My dear Wetherell,

Permit me to reccomend to your acquaintance and civilities my friend and countryman Mr George Sumner who proposes to make a short sojourn in your city in the course of his tour through Spain. Any attentions you may find it convenient to pay him will be gratefully considered by

Your assured friend
Washington Irving

P S. My kindest remembrances to your Sister and nieces.

ADDRESSED: John Wetherell Esqr / &c &c &c / Seville.
MANUSCRIPT: SHR.

1625. To Fermín Caballero

Madrid 5 de setiembre de 1843.

El Señor Irving Ministro Plenipotenciario de los Estados Unidos besa las manos al Exmo Señor Don Fermin Caballero y tiene la honra de poner en su conocimiento que el Señor Don Jorge Sumner, un ciudadano de los Estados Unidos, distinguido por sus conocimientos desearia visitar el Archivo de las Indias en Sevilla para examinar y hacer copiar algunos documentos.

Siendo esto un objeto en el interes de las literatura el Senor Irving espera de la bondad de S. E. que se sirva mandar expedir las ordenes oportunas para la examinacion indicada.

El Senor Irving aprovecha esta ocasion para ofrecer el Exmo Señor Don Fermin Caballera, las seguridades de su distinguida consideracion.

Washington Irving.

MANUSCRIPT: NA, RG 84 (letterbook copy).

Fermín Caballero was a political economist and journalist who served in the original cabinet as minister of the interior. See WI to Daniel Webster, May 9, 1843; H. Butler Clarke, *Modern Spain*, pp. 184–85; and Pierre L. Ullman, *Mariano de Larra and Spanish Political Rhetoric* (Madison, 1971), p. 89.

Translation:

"Mr. Irving, minister plenipotentiary of the United States, greets Don Fermin Caballero and has the honor of making known to him that the gentleman Don Jorge Sumner, a citizen of the United States distinguished by his knowledge, would like to visit the Archive of the Indias and have some documents copied.

"This being a purpose in the interest of literature, Mr. Irving hopes from the kindness of his excellency that he would direct that the appropriate orders for the indicated examination be issued.

"Mr. Irving takes this opportunity to offer to His Excellency Don Fermin Caballero the assurances of his distinguished regard."

1626. To Sarah Storrow

Madrid, Septr. 6. 1843.

My dear Sarah.

When this reaches you I shall probably be on your side of the Pyrenees. I leave Madrid at Six Oclock tomorrow morning in the carriage of the British courier; which, accidents apart, will deposit me in Bayonne in the Course of Saturday next.[1] I shall then determine in what way to travel and by what route: which will depend in some measure upon the condition in which I arrive at Bayonne and the manner in which I have stood this first part of my journey. I may loiter a little, or may take a circuitous route; but will probably be with you in a few days after the receipt of this letter. I hope still to find you at Versailles, and would prefer infinitely sojourning there than at Paris. I come as an *invalid* and having suffered the ills mean to claim the privileges of the character and to excuse myself from all visiting and fête-ing. I do not wish you to say any thing of my intended visit.

Lorenzo left here the day before yesterday in the Diligence to await my arrival in Bayonne; there being no place for him in the Couriers carriage which only takes two persons. I shall want quarters for him either in the house where you have apartments, or in the immediate vicinity so that he can be at hand to wait upon me.

I ought to have mentioned before, that Mr Hamilton arrived home a few days since; in far better health and looks than I had anticipated. His arrival has brought sunshine into the house. I leave the legation in his charge, and feel great satisfaction in confiding it to such competent hands.

Kiss Kate for me and tell her *I* hope soon to kiss her myself—

God bless you / Your affectionate Uncle
Washington Irving

MANUSCRIPT: Yale (paragraphs 1 and 2); NYPL—Berg Collection (remainder of letter).   PUBLISHED: STW, II, 163 (in part).

1. September 9, 1843.

1627.   To A. P. Upshur

Legation of the United States. / Madrid September 6th. 1843

No. 29. / The Hon: A. P. Upshur, / Secretary of State of the U S— Washington.

Sir,

I had the honor a few days since to receive your despatch dated June 24th, informing me that the President had been pleased to charge you with the duties of the Department of State *ad interim.*[1] It will give me great satisfaction, Sir, in the execution of my official duties, to cooperate with you in promoting the interests of our Common Country.

Since the date of my last despatch nothing of especial moment has occurred in the political affairs of this Country; though every thing continues to wear a threatening aspect. The rupture of the recent and triumphant league[2] has become complete, and the factions are daily be-

coming more and more embittered against each other. The division in
the Cabinet continues, and is promoted by a division in the councils of the leading moderados; the older and more experienced are
for proceeding with great caution; for conciliating popular favor by
an appearance of lenity in the exercise of power; and of adherence to
the Constitution: the young moderados however flushed with recent
success, are for high handed measures; for an intolerant policy towards
the vanquished; in a word, for a strong government. They are continually
sounding the alarm of plots and conspiracies and endeavoring to have
the Capital declared in a state of siege; that the sword may become
supreme and Narvaez be military dictator. A really moderate and constitutional part of the Cabinet has hitherto served as a check to these
hot-brained councils; but there are apprehensions that this part will
ultimately be forced to resign; and that the Government will be precipi-
tated into a course of policy calculated to bring on another, and a far
more dangerous popular Explosion. The attention of all parties is now
fixed upon the approaching elections, which take place on the 15th.
Instant: Should the Ministry obtain a majority, and be able to maintain
tranquillity until the meeting of the Cortes on the 15th. October, there
will be some prospect of consolidating the present state of affairs.

In letters written some weeks since to the Department I intimated the
probability that I should be obliged by the state of my health to try the
effects of travel and a change of climate; being strongly urged to do so
by my physicians. The critical state of affairs, however, in this country
made me unwilling to leave my post, and I have accordingly continued
here through the summer. I am still troubled with the lingerings of a
malady which has harassed me more or less for seven months past a
great part of the time confining me to the house, if not to my bed. I
am told that a change of air is indispensable to my perfect recovery.—I
have therefore determined to make an excursion of a few weeks into
France, leaving the legation in the hands of the Secretary Mr. Hamilton,
of whose perfect competency to the duties of the situation I have already
expressed my opinion to the Government.

I enclose the accounts and vouchers of the legation for the 2nd. quarter
of 1843; exhibiting a balance in my favor of $31..02; which in the next
account will be carried to the debit of the United States.

I also forward an extract from a Gibralter paper containing the circumstances connected with the loss of the U. S. Steam frigate Missouri.[3]

I am, Sir, very respectfully / Your Obdt Sevt.
Washington Irving

P. S.
I would observe that the despatch acknowledged at the commence-

ment of this letter being forwarded via Cadiz was as usual, a long time on the way. It came like a former one envelopped with old newspapers: Had the Despatch and the newspapers been sent severally *by mail* via England or Havre, they would have reached me much sooner and at *less expense*, than by the apparently favorite way of Cadiz.

W. I.

DOCKETED: Recd. 6 oct / Mr. Markoe [*upper left, page 1*] / No. 29. W. Irving. Madrid. 6 Sept. 1843.
MANUSCRIPT: NA, RG 59.

Only the signature is in WI's handwriting.

1. Upshur was interim secretary of state from June 24 to July 24, 1843, after which he served as secretary until his death on February 28, 1844.
2. The overthrow of Espartero was accomplished through a coalition of Progressives and Moderates. The López cabinet, which represented the Progressives, was replaced by the short-lived (November 24–28, 1843) ministry of Salustiano Oló-zaga. For details, see Raymond Carr, *Spain*, pp. 227–30.
3. The ten-gun steam frigate *Missouri*, one of the first steam vessels in the American navy, was launched in the New York Navy Yard on January 7, 1841, and commissioned early in 1842. It burned at Gibraltar on August 26, 1843, after a crewman broke a demijohn of turpentine which ignited and destroyed the ship. See *Dictionary of American Naval Ships*, 5 vols. (Washington, 1959–1970), IV, 390–91.

1628. To Alexander Hamilton

Bayonne, Saturday 8 Sept [1843]

My dear Hamilton
  I arrived here about 3 oclock this afternoon in such good order that I have determined to continue on with the worthy courier to Bordeaux leaving Lorenzo to follow me in the Diligence.
  The weather has been fine and the drive through the mountainous provinces splendid. I have felt already the effects of green landscapes and soft genial airs, and the sight of the sea and the breath of the sea breeze have quite vivified me. I never enjoyed any scenery more than the mountains last night by the light of a full moon. Give my kind remembrances to Madame Albuquerque & family.
  Tell Juana to take good care of the house and not to go to the door without a gun on her shoulder.

Affectionately yours
Washington Irving

P. S. When you send the fee to the Doctor let it be two ounces *in gold*

It is more professional and will account for my sending them that particular amount—being the sum prescribed by Dr. Murta.[1]

MANUSCRIPT: Lehigh University.   PUBLISHED: *American Literature*, 35 (May, 1963), 172.

1. The physician for the British embassy in Madrid. See WI to Catharine Paris, February 6, 1843.

1629.   To Sarah Storrow

Bordeaux ↑Monday↓ Sept 11th. 1843.

My dear Sarah,

I left Madrid on thursday morning last, in the carriage of a British courier. We travelled day and night and arrived in the course of Saturday at Bayonne. Finding myself in good condition and none the worse for travelling I continued on with him the same evening and arrived at this place the next afternoon (Sunday) The journey has agreed wonderfully well with my general health; but I have to ⟨lay by⟩ pause a little to allay a slight irritation in my legs. I want also to pass a little time among my Bordeaux friends[1] after which I shall resume my journey; posting along liesurely in a light carriage which I have hired.

As I may reach Versailles without touching Paris ⟨I wish⟩—and as I do not know in what part of the place you are quartered I wish you would leave your address at that Hotel adjoining the Royal Gardens,[2] where we put up on our Visit. I shall ⟨stop⟩ ↑call↓ there to enquire for you[.] I hope you will retain your apartments at Versailles. I would vastly prefer visiting you there than at Paris.

I must tell you that I have thus far enjoyed my journey extremely. I do not know when scenery had a more vivifying effect on my feelings than in passing from the dreary parched wastes of the Castiles, to the green mountains and valleys of the Basque provinces. The nights were superb—a full moon lighting up splendid mountain scenery.—the air bland & fresh and balmy, instead of the parching airs of Madrid. The first sight of the sea too, and the inhaling of the sea breeze, brought a home feeling that was quite reviving You cannot imagine how beautiful France looks to me; with her orchards, and vinyards, and groves and green meadows, after naked sterile Spain—I feel confident I shall return from this excursion with a stock of health and good spirits to carry me through the winter.

God bless you—tell Kate to put on her best looks, best cap and best temper against I arrive, which will be in a few days.

Your affectionate Uncle
Washington Irving

MANUSCRIPT: Yale.   PUBLISHED: PMI, III, 303–4 (in part).

1. The Guestiers and the Johnstons. See WI to Sarah Storrow, July 16 and 19, 1842.

2. Probably the Reservoir Hotel (Hôtel des Réservoirs). WI had stayed there on his visit in June, 1842. See *Journals of WI*, III, 216–17.

1630.   To Catharine Paris

Versailles, Septr 16—1843

My dear Sister,

Sarah tells me that she forwarded you my letter written to her from Bordeaux[1] informing her of my arrival at that city on my way hither. I left Bordeaux on Wednesday morning last and posted hither, travelling day and night and arriving here yesterday (Friday) about three Oclock. I have stood the journey well and find myself daily gaining strong in health; and have no doubt that a little repose here will entirely free me from the lingerings of my malady. I found Sarah looking extremely well —fuller in person and fresher than when I last saw her; and her little girl a picture of health. I have barely time to give you this morsel of intelligence as the clerk is waiting to take this letter to Paris, being the last day for writing by the Steam Packet.

I need not tell you what a joyful meeting it has been to Sarah & myself. I am sure this visit will effect my perfect restoration.

———Our cheerfulness is dashed however by the sad intelligence just received, of the death of poor Susan Storrow[2]—Sarah has this moment learnt it by a letter received from Mr Storrow—

Give my love to all at the Cottage

Your affectionate brother
Washington Irving

ADDRESSED: Mrs Daniel Paris / care of E. Irving Esq / New York
MANUSCRIPT: Yale.   PUBLISHED: PMI, III, 304 (in part).

1. On September 11, 1843.
2. Henry Van Wart, Jr. had married Susan Storrow (b. 1807).

1631. To Catharine Paris

Versailles, Septr. 18th. 1843

My dear Sister,

I scrawled a hasty line to you a day or two since, to go by the Boston Steamer, and now scribble another, almost as hastily, to send by the Great Western. In fact the state of inaction which generally follows a long journey and a state of excitement, quite indisposes me at present for letter writing, yet I know you will be anxious to hear from me by every opportunity now that I am with Sarah. As ⟨I⟩ you will have been informed by previous letters, I travelled day and night from Madrid to Bordeaux, in the carriage of a British cabinet messenger. At Bordeaux I remained two days, partly to repose and partly to see my good friends the Guestiers and Johns[t]ons. I hired a convenient travelling carriage at Bordeaux, for two months, and posted on day and night for this place; leaving Bordeaux at eight Oclock on Wednesday morning and arriving here at about three Oclock, Friday afternoon: rather rapid travelling; but I was eager to get to the end of my journey and be at rest. I drove up to the door of Sarahs residence just as she was setting out with her nursing maid and little Kate for a walk. It was but the day before that she had received my letters, one from Madrid and one from Bordeaux apprising her of my being on the way to visit her; for I forebore to write until the last moment lest something should turn up to prevent the journey. She was of course rather surprised and was somewhat overcome by my so prompt appearance. However she soon became tranquillized and our meeting was a most joyful one. For my own part, after so long a separation from kith and kin, and so much time passed in loneliness and sickness, it is a heartfelt gratification to be with ⟨some of my own⟩ one kindred in heart as well as blood; and to find myself once more within the verge of the family circle. The lingerings of my malady; irritated a little by travelling, still deprive me of the free use of my legs, ⟨and⟩ keeping me pretty much to the sopha, and preventing my sallying forth except in carriage; but a few days of repose will, I trust, be sufficient to remedy these lurking evils; in the mean time I find sufficient to occupy and enliven me in the society of my dear Sarah and her child. As I told you in my recent letter Sarah is looking extremely well; having gained both in flesh and freshness since we parted. Kate is really a fine child; and for healthy looks and sound constitution may vie with Julia Grinnells children; Sarah having observed pretty much the same course of diet and treatment ⟨that⟩ adopted by Julia. By the way, I am glad to hear from all quarters accounts of the beauty of Julias last child,[1] ⟨I am⟩ and to hear likewise that her other children continue to thrive; ⟨Helen tells me that⟩ little Julia[2] I am told is a sweet little girl. I think she will grow up of a calm placid disposition while glorious little Bub[3] will be full of fire and frolic. However—it is ⟨not⟩ easier to read the stars than prognosticate the future characters of children: but I am a firm believer in *good stock* and that these children are by both sides of the house.

But to return to little Kate about whom you are most interested. She is a very amusing child: somewhat touchy; and of a hundred moods in a minute, but to me, pleasant in them all. She is a perpetual source of entertainment to me; and ⟨Sarah⟩ we became instantly on the most sociable terms.

Sarah has very pleasant apartments here, and intends to tent in them until the end of the month. This will give me an interval of complete repose before entering Paris.

The day of my arrival here I received (via Madrid) your letter dated 3 to 6th. of August; as usual, ⟨f⟩ a complete budget of family news. I fear your letter by the Great Western has gone to Madrid; in which case I shall not receive it until nearly a fortnight hence. I find by subsequent accounts that you have had a heavy fall of rain, which as usual has torn up the lane and carried away its paltry bridges. I trust the neighbors have patched all up again in the usual way so as to last until the next inundation. The labor and expense wasted upon building cheap bridges in that lane would have been sufficient to construct solid and spacious bridges ⟨that would have⟩ capable of lasting until doomsday—

I am scribbling against the grain and against the mood which must serve as an excuse for this scrawl; but I could not let the Great Western depart without a letter.

Love to all the kindred

Your affectn brother
Washington Irving

ADDRESSED: Mrs Daniel Paris / care of E — Irving Esqr / New York.   POSTMARKED:
NE[W-YORK] / OCT / 8 // [*unrecovered*] DELIVERY
MANUSCRIPT: Va.–Barrett.   PUBLISHED: PMI, III, 304 (in part).

1. Fanny Leslie Grinnell, who was born on September 23, 1842. She died on May 14, 1887.
2. Julia Irving Grinnell (1837–1915).
3. The Grinnells' second child, Irving (1839–1921).

1632.   To J. Carson Brevoort

[Versailles, September 19, 1843]

My dear Carson,

I have received your card and am looking for your promised visit. You will find me at home at any hour of the day, for I am still somewhat of an invalid and keep to the house. We dine at half past five, and I trust you will stay to dinner.

Yours affectionately
Washington Irving

Versailles. Sept 19 [1843] / Place d'Armoir No 7.

Manuscript: SHR.

J. Carson Brevoort, son of WI's old friend, Henry Brevoort, had been traveling in Europe after leaving the staff of the U.S. legation in Madrid.

1633.   To Aaron Vail

Versailles, Sept 20th 1843

My dear Sir,

I am extremely sorry that the lingerings of a long indisposition oblige me to keep quiet after my recent journey, and prevent me from coming to Paris to have the pleasure of seeing you and Mrs Vail previous to your departure.

I send this by Lorenzo who is desirous of seeing a little more of you both and who entertains for you the most grateful attachment. I have found him every thing that you represented; and he has proved a most devoted and kind hearted attendant upon me during my long and harrassing malady. Juana too has conducted herself in the most satisfactory manner and I have left the establishment and Mr Hamilton under her charge.

I trust you have found by your bankers account that I have paid what I owed you for furniture carriage &c[1] excepting about sixty dollars, which I have left standing until I shall have settled for the painting which is undergoing repairs, and which will be finished in the fullness of (Spanish) time. Whatever ballance may remain due I will remit to you through my agent in the United States

Give my kindest remembrance to Mrs Vail,[2] and, with warmest wishes for your prosperity & happiness, believe me sincerely

Your friend
Washington Irving

DOCKETED: W. Irving. / 20 Sept 1843 / ansd — 20 — / Miscellaneous / abroad /
from July 1840 / to / September 1843.
MANUSCRIPT: Va.–Barrett.

1. WI had purchased these items in Madrid from Vail, who had been U.S.
chargé d'affaires.
2. In 1835 Vail had married Emilie Salles, daughter of a prominent New York
merchant.

1634. To Edward Everett

Versailles Sept 24th. 1843.

My dear Sir,

I am here on an excursion for the benefit of ⟨the⟩ travel and a change
of air in the hope of conquering a malady with which I have been
afflicted for seven or eight months past; but which still confines me very
much to the house.

I take the liberty of presenting to you Mr Carson Brevoort, who has
been attached to my Legation. He is son of Mr Henry Brevoort of New
York, and is a young gentleman of whose merits I cannot speak too
highly. He will pass but a short time in London and is desirous of turning
that time to the greatest advantage in acquainting himself wih various
objects connected with the arts and sciences. Any facilities you may be
able to afford him will be well bestowed and will be considered as
favors by
My dear Sir,

Yours most faithfully
Washington Irving

P. S. I beg you will present my kind remembrances to Mrs & Miss Everett.

MANUSCRIPT: MHS.

At this time Everett was U.S. minister to Great Britain.

1635. To Charles R. Leslie

Versailles, Sept 24th. 1843.

My dear Leslie,

I have taken leave of absence from Madrid, for a Visit to France in
search of health; being still harrassed by the lingerings of a malady

which has afflicted me for nearly eight months past. I am passing a little time here with My Niece Mrs Storrow; after which I shall return to my post.

This letter is for the purpose of presenting to you Mr Carson Brevoort, son of my old friend Henry Brevoort Esqr of New York. He has been attached to my legation & has resided nearly a year with me at Madrid. He is a young gentleman of real merit and has both taste and feeling for the arts. His stay in London will be brief— ⟨any⟩ I wish you would give him any facilities in your power to turn his time to the most advantage

Remember me kindly to Mrs Leslie and to the young folks and believe me ever

Yours most affectionately
Washington Irving

Charles R Leslie Esq / Pineapple Terrace / Edgeware Road.

ADDRESSED: Charles R Leslie Esq R A. / Pine apple Terrace / Edgeware Road.
MANUSCRIPT: NYPL—Berg Collection.

On the left side of the address fold running vertically in another hand is written "Aux soins / de M. Henry Ledyard / Chargé d'Affaires / des Etats Unis / Paris."

1636. *To Ebenezer Irving*

[Paris,] Sept. 30, [1843]

We came to Paris the day before yesterday, but I have not yet been out of the house. I am gradually, however, getting over this transient access of my complaint, and hope in a few days to be again able to go about on foot. I intend consulting the ablest physician on the subject. I am anxious to get well, so as to be able to return to Madrid before the cold weather sets in. I do not like to be away from my post in these critical times. * * * I have full confidence in the ability of Alexander Hamilton to carry on the ordinary business of the legation, but questions may arise, and claims to sovereignty between warring parties in these revolutionary times, in respect to which I wish to take upon myself the responsibility of deciding.

PUBLISHED: PMI, III, 305.

1637. To Catharine Paris

Paris Octr. 12th. 1843.

My dear Sister,

I wrote to you between two and three weeks since, from Versailles, shortly after my arrival[.] I remained there nearly a fortnight; still fettered by my malady, which obliged me to keep to the house except-ing when I could drive out in a carriage. I enjoyed however, some delightful drives in company with Sarah and the babe, through the magnificent parks and pleasure grounds of the palace, and about the neighboring country, where there is some of the most lovely scenery that I have seen in France. I would especially note a beautiful valley several miles in length with a small stream wending through it—which put me in mind occasionally of the Saw mill river[1] valley; excepting that it was wrought into a softer and more complete state of cultivation, and studded with venerable villages, and stately villas with their ornamented grounds.

I have now been two weeks in Paris, but am still confined very much to the house excepting when I go out in a carriage. The least exercise on foot produces an irritation of the malady, which still lingers about my ankles, and thus retards my cure. Indeed I begin to think it will yet take a considerable time effectually to conquer it; and that I shall have to return to Madrid before my cure is completed. My general health however is good, my appetite excellent and I am growing as "stout a gentleman" as formerly. My time passes pleasantly in the house having the "babe" as a play mate; and a delightful one she is I can assure you. She is very intelligent for so young a creature, and has a thousand winning and amusing ways. We now understand each other perfectly and have a great many jokes together. She relishes ⟨and humours⟩ my jokes greatly ↑and enters into the spirit of them completely↓ which makes me think she has a quick perception of wit and humor. Every day I drive out with Sarah and the child, in the Champs Elysees, the Bois de Bologne ⟨and⟩ &c Sarah is looking extremely well. I think she has improved greatly both in looks and substantial health since her residence in Paris. She is more the woman, in looks, character and deportment; a general improvement to be expected from her change of condition, and the cares, duties, ⟨and⟩ occupations and intercourse arising from it. She appears to enjoy the respect and good will of the Americans resident in Paris, and to hold just the position among them, that was to be wished. Her house is a well regulated, respectable and happy one. She has good servants, who serve her with fidelity and affection and her little child is the delight of her life. With all these advantages and with an excellent husband, calculated and disposed to render every thing pleasant around her, her lot may well be considered a happy one; and the certainty of all this cannot but operate to console you, my dear sister, under your long separation.

A recent letter from Marianne[2] gives favorable accounts of the convalescence of our dear Sister—When I left Madrid I had some thoughts of extending my tour so as to make a brief visit to Birmingham, though it would be stretching the licence I have already given myself, in leaving my post without specified permission from head quarters—The obstinate lingerings of my malady, however, and its disposition to recur upon the least irritation oblige me to give up all idea of the kind; and to endeavor by quiet and by careful treatment, to prepare myself for the journey back to Madrid, which must be made before cold weather.

Sarah received a letter from you a day or two since, giving as usual a budget of cottage news. I have likewise received one of the regular despatches from brother Ebenezer[3] full of details of the business of the farm. You cannot concieve how interesting and gratifying these letters are to me; though at times they make me half home sick. ⟨[*4½ lines unrecovered*]⟩ Only let me once more recover perfect health and the use of my pen and I shall go ahead bravely.

With affectionate remembrances to "all bodies"

Your affectionate brother
Washington Irving

DOCKETED: Washn. Irving to Mrs. Paris. / Paris Oct 12. 1843.
MANUSCRIPT: Va.–Barrett.   PUBLISHED: PMI, III, 305–6 (in part); Hellman, *WI Esquire*, p. 271 (in part).

1. A stream in Westchester County near Sunnyside.
2. The daughter of Henry and Sarah Van Wart.
3. This letter has not been located.

1638. To Pierre M. Irving

[October 13, 1843]

I am leading a very quiet life in the very centre of all that is gay and splendid. My obstinate malady, which still clings to me just sufficiently to fetter me, prevents my sallying forth excepting in a carriage, so that I pass most of the time in the house. Last night, however, I managed to visit the opera, and saw Grisi[1] in Norma. She is one of the finest actors I have ever seen, quite worthy of being classed with the Siddonses,[2]

Pastas,[3] &c. I had scarcely expected ever again to have seen such a glorious combination of talent and personal endowment on the stage.

Published: PMI, III, 306

1. Giulia Grisi (1811–1869), who was born in Milan, was renowned for her interpretations of Bellini's operas, especially *I Puritani* and *Norma*. WI probably saw her at the Théâtre des Italiens in Paris, where she was engaged from 1832 to 1849. See *Grove's Dictionary of Music and Musicians*, ed. Eric Blom, III, 816.

2. Sarah Kemble Siddons (1755–1831) was a popular English actress who played for many years at Drury Lane and Covent Garden. Her most famous role was that of Lady Macbeth. Her son Henry (1775–1815) was associated with the Edinburgh Theatre.

3. Giuditta Pasta (1798–1865), who made her debut on the Italian musical stage in 1815, was acclaimed for her interpretations of Bellini's *La Sonnambula* and *Norma*, which were written for her. See *Grove's Dictionary of Music and Musicians*, VI, 587–88.

1639. To John Miller

Legation of the United States / Madrid October 15th. 1843.

John Miller Esqr. / U. S. Despatch Agent—London.
Dear Sir,

I have received your account in duplicate for postage &c, paid by you during the last quarter on account of this legation.

I enclose a check on Messrs Baring, Brothers & Co. for the amount. £9..4..3., payable to your order at sight:

The irregularity in the receipt of "The Times" still continues; but I suppose it is now to be attributed entirely to the inefficient arrangements of the Spanish post office.

Very respectfully / Your Obdt Sevt.
Washington Irving

Manuscript: MHS; NA, RG 84 (letterbook copy).

The NA version, which includes a copy of the sight draft, has been used for copy-text. Although signed with WI's name, this letter was prepared and sent by Alexander Hamilton.

The following was included with the letter.

Enclosure
Legation of the United States, / Madrid October 15th. 1843.

£9..4..3.

At sight please pay John Miller or order nine pounds, four shillings and three pence sterling and charge the same to the United States on account of the contingent expenses of this Legation.

Messrs Baring Brothers & Co. Bankers. U. S. London.

Washingon Irving.

1640. To Sarah Storrow

Bordeaux, Nov. 24th. 1843.

My dear Sarah,

My journey hitherto has been very comfortable. I found the accommodations in the Malle poste[1] excellent; though I had not the *little Stool* so much insisted upon. My carpet bag however, supplied its place completely and enabled me to stretch my legs as well as if I had one of your sofas to repose on. I slept well, and arrived here between nine and ten this morning in very, good order. I have experienced none of the irritation in my system that I had anticipated from the journey; still I am on the point of taking a vapor bath as a preventive. The baths, here I am told are very good.

The chicken you ordered to be put up for me was a fortunate supply as we did not stop to take any refreshment until the following evening at Poitiers.

I find the Guestier family is in town, but I have not seen them as yet; nor shall see them until after my bath.

I hope the Baby missed me; though I much doubt it, for she is a pebble hearted little woman. Give her a kiss however for me, and endeavor to keep her in mind of me for a few days at least.

With kind remembrances to Mr Storrow I am my dear Sarah

Your affectionate uncle
Washington Irving

Docketed: Washn. Irving to Mrs. Sarah Storrow. Paris. / Bordeaux Nov. 24 1843.
Manuscript: Yale.

1. The mail coach.

1641. To Henry Brevoort

Bordeaux Nov. 26th. 1843.

My dear Brevoort,

I received your most kind and welcome letter some short time before leaving Paris,[1] and should have answered it immediately, but I was in one of those moods when ⟨I dont⟩ my mind has no power over my pen.

Indeed I have long owed you a letter[2] and have intended to write to you; but correspondents ⟨have⟩ multiplied fearfully upon me, and my pen was tasked diplomatically and otherwise, on my arrival at Madrid to such a degree as to fag me out, and to produce the malady which has harrassed me for nearly a year past. I am now on my way back to my post after between two and three months absence. I set out in pursuit of health and thought a little travelling and a change of air would "make me my own man"[3] again; but I was laid by the heels at Paris by a recurrence of my malady, and have just escaped out of the Doctors hands sufficiently recovered to get back to my post; where I hope, by care and ⟨qu⟩ medical treatment to effect my cure.

This indisposition has been a sad check upon all my plans. I had hoped, by zealous employment of all the liesure afforded me at Madrid, to accomplish one or two literary tasks which I have in hand; and thereby to encrease my pecuniary means so as to enable myself by and bye to return home and live in quiet in the bosom of my family. A year, however, has now been completely lost to me; and a precious year at my time of life. The Life of Washington; and indeed all my literary tasks have remained suspended; and my pen has remained idle; excepting now and then in writing a despatch to government or scrawling a letter to my family. In the mean time ⟨my⟩ the income which I used to derive from farming out my writings has died away; my monied investments yielded scarce any interest; and I really do not know what would have become of me and of those dependent upon me, if Uncle Sam had not in a critical juncture taken me under his wing and made me a diplomatist! However, thank God, my ⟨capacity for wo⟩ health and with it my capacity for working are returning. I shall soon again have pen in hand and hope to get two or three good years of literary labor out of myself—times are improving in America; and with them may improve the landed property which I hold—I may again find some bookseller to take a lease of my published works; and thus, by hook and by crook; may be enabled to return home and spend some few years with my kindred and friends before I die.

Carson will give you an account of diplomatic and household affairs at Madrid. I was extremely sorry to part with him, but I could not advise him to stay, where there was no carreer nor regular pursuit opening to him. I found him all that you represented him. Pure; amiable, intelligent, variously informed and accomplished, and of the strictest principles. He is a youth whom it is impossible to live with intimately and not become attached to. His only defects are want of energy and perseverance, and a too great diffidence of himself.[4] These prevent his undertaking great things, or following out his enterprises when undertaken. He has been highly esteemed by such persons here as became acquainted with him—among them some men of science. Indeed wherever he gives himself a chance of being known he will be appreciated: and when once he has gained a friend he will never lose him.

I do not know whether you speak in jest or earnest about the popular view of my conduct on the occasion of the diplomatic intervention for the safety of the little Queen during the late Siege of Madrid.[5] My conduct was dictated at the time by honest and spontaneous impulse, without reference to policy or politics—I felt deeply for the situation of the Queen and her sister and was anxious that ⟨they should⟩ their persons should be secured from the civil brawls and fightings which threatened to distract the city and invade the very courts of the Royal palace. In all my diplomacy I have depended more upon good intentions and frank and open conduct than upon any subtle management. I have an opinion that the old maxim *"Honesty is the best policy"* holds good even in diplomacy!

Thus far I have got on well with my brother diplomatists; and have met with very respectful treatment from the Spanish government in all its changes and fluctuations. I have endeavored punctually to perform the duties of my office and to execute the instructions of government, and I believe that the archives of the Legation will testify that the business of the Mission has never been neglected[.] I have not suffered illness to prevent me from keeping every thing in train; and indeed my recovery has been retarded by remaining at my post during the ⟨popular⟩ revolutionary scenes of last summer though urged by my physicians to spend the hot months at the watering places in the mountains. I do not pretend to any great skill as a diplomatist; but in whatever situation I am placed in life, when I doubt my skill I endeavor to make up for it, by conscientious assiduity.

While I was in Paris in driving out one day with my niece in the Champs Elysees we nearly ran over my old friend Rogers.[6] We stopped and took him in. He was on one of his yearly epicurean visits to Paris to enjoy the Italian opera and other refined sources of pleasure. The hand of age begins to bow him down, but his intellect is clear as ever, and his talents and taste for society in full vigor. He breakfasted with us several times and I have never known him more delightful. He would sit for two or three hours continually conversing and giving anecdotes of all the conspicuous persons who have figured within the last sixty years; with most of whom he has been on terms of intimacy. He has refined upon the art of telling a story until he has brought it to the most perfect simplicity—where there is not a word too much nor too little; and where every word has its effect. His manner too is the most quiet, natural and unpretending that can be imagined. I was very much amused by an anecdote he gave us of little Queen Victoria and her nautical vagaries. Lord Aberdeen[7] has had to attend her in her cruisings very much against his will; or, at least, against his stomach You know he is one of the gravest and most laconic men in the world. The Queen one day undertook to reconcile him to his fate. "I believe my lord["] said she graciously, ["][8] you are not *often* sea sick—"—"*Always* madam," was the grave reply—"But—" still more graciously, "not *very* sea sick,"— with profounder gravity—"VERY Madam!" Lord Aberdeen declare[s][9] that if her Majesty persists in her cruisings[10] he will have to resign.

I rejoice to hear of Mrs Brevoorts improved health and think you are right, should you find the sea coast of Long Island ⟨ag⟩ favorable to the healths of your family, to set up a retreat there. You might build a very pleasant summer lodge at a cheap rate; and I ⟨have⟩ can say from experience that a man has ten-fold ↑more↓ ⟨the⟩ enjóyment from any rural retreat that belongs to himself than from any that he hires as a temporary sojourn.

Give my kind remembrances to Mrs Brevoort and to all the young folks, and believe me my dear Brevoort

Ever most affectionately yours
Washington Irving

MANUSCRIPT: NYPL—Seligman Collection. PUBLISHED: PMI, III, 307–10 (in part); LIB, II, 241–48.

1. See Henry Brevoort to WI, October 18, 1843 (NYPL). Published in LBI, II, 130–40.

2. See Brevoort to WI, December 28, 1842, in LBI, II, 121–29.

3. WI's variation of Congreve, *The Way of the World*, II, i, 561.

4. In his letter to WI, Brevoort had observed that Carson "assures me that he has imbibed a little brass, which is a material indispensable to his success in this country, where impudence is at a high premium" (LBI, II, 130–31). Because of this statement WI probably felt justified in criticizing young Brevoort.

5. Brevoort noted that WI's action "has added immensely to your diplomatic fame among your *admiring* countrymen; besides stirring up the ambitions of becoming Ministers among yr. literary contemporaries Bancroft Sparks Cooper &c...." See LBI, II, 139; and WI to Sarah Storrow, July 18, 1843, and to Catharine Paris, August 10, 1843.

6. Samuel Rogers, the English banker and poet whom WI had last seen in London in early May, 1842. See WI to Catharine Paris, May 7, 1842.

7. George Hamilton Gordon, Lord Aberdeen (1784–1860), whom WI had known during his secretaryship at the U.S. legation a dozen years earlier, was the current British foreign secretary.

8. WI omitted the bracketed quotation marks.

9. WI omitted the bracketed letter.

10. The British nation had presented Victoria with the yacht *Victoria and Albert*, launched on April 25, 1843. Lord Aberdeen had accompanied her on a trip to visit Louis Philippe at the Chateau d'Eu in September of 1843. See Cecil Woodham-Smith, *Queen Victoria, Her Life and Times* (London, 1972), pp. 239, 243.

1642. To Sarah Storrow

Bordeaux Nov 26th. 1843

My dear Sarah,

I have now been part of three days in Bordeaux and find myself none the worse for my late journey: on the contrary I am in capital condition; if any thing better than in the last two days I past in Paris.

Yesterday I partook of a family dinner with my excellent friends the Guestiers where I found myself surrounded by members of the family whom I had once known as children, but who were now married and had children of their own. Nothing could exceed the kindness and affection by which I am treated by these worthy people: I need not say, therefore, I feel quite at home among them, and enjoy myself in the most heartfelt manner. To day I dine with old Mrs Johnston, Mrs Guestiers mother, and one who was a great friend of your Uncle Peter. It will be another family dinner of the kind I delight in. Tomorrow (Monday) I set off at Midday for Bayonne; having taken ⟨the⟩ as before, the interior of the Malle Poste. I have written to a gentleman at Bayonne to Secure the Spanish Malle poste for me the first day it should be vacant; so that I hope to experience very little delay in the rest of my journey.

You will have read, no doubt, in Galignani an account of the Malle Poste being robbed ⟨between ab⟩ near Aranda,[1] about half way between Madrid and Bayonne, but you must not let it make you uneasy on my account. That robbing makes my journey the more secure, as the robbers always remain quiet a long time after an affair of this kind: while the government is roused to greater activity in guarding against their depredations. I had intended, had I travelled post in a private carriage, to have taken a Strong guard for two or three posts each side of Aranda as it is a neighborhood noted for scamps and vagabonds. When I came on, in September, with the British courier, we passed through there in the night; and for the post previous to arriving at Aranda, he was unable to procure a guard. He was in a great worry all the way and drew a long breath when we drove safe into Aranda. He told me his postillion had been fired upon in that neighborhood about a year before, and that they only escaped robbing by lashing the horses into a gallop. At present that neighborhood will be cautiously quiet ; ↑the police will be in quest of the robbers↓ and the guard of the Malle post will be doubled in the suspicious places.

We have had rainy weather ever since our arrival in Bordeaux; but to day it has held up. Yesterday morning, while arranging my rooms Lorenzo observed. "es mala tiempo Señor para la Niña; no puede Salir pasearse—" "It is bad weather for the child, sir, she cannot go out to walk." I did not know at first what he meant, but I found he was speaking of *Baby*. "Jamas["] said he, "ha viste niña mas bonita: —nunca— nunca—" ["]I[2] have never seen a prettier child—never—never." It was quite a speech for the modest silent Lorenzo, who rarely ⟨spat[?]⟩ speaks to me unless spoken to—but he seemed to feel what he said, and I liked him all the better for it, as I have no doubt you will. The good fellows heart seemed full on our leaving Paris; and after we had travelled some time in silence he could not help telling me, with evident feeling, that the women kind of your house hold—the *doncellas*,[3] as he termed them, shed tears when he ⟨came away⟩ parted with them.

Nothing can exceed the quiet, unobtrusive, but watchful and assiduous attentions which this faithful ↑fellow↓ pays me while travelling: and indeed at all times. He seems to be actuated by affection as well as a high sense of duty.

Kiss my dear little Kate for me. Keep her in mind of the Uncle who watched so anxiously over her improvement. Alas! who will there be to *bang*[4] her now I am away! I already begin to pine after her; and absolutely would rather see her act that scene over again with Madame Hacquets[5] Italian grey hound, than see Grisi in the finest scene of Norma.

Give my affectionate regards to your good husband.

Ever my dear Sarah / Your affectionate Uncle
Washington Irving

DOCKETED: Washn. Irving to Mrs. Sarah Storrow. Paris / Bordeaux, Nov 26. 1843. [*written upside down on bottom of page 4*]
MANUSCRIPT: Yale.

1. Aranda de Duero in Burgos province is about seventy-five miles north of Madrid.
2. WI omitted the bracketed quotation marks.
3. Girls or maidens.
4. "A bounce" (*OED*).
5. An acquaintance of Sarah Storrow's whose marriage had turned out badly. See WI to Sarah Storrow, June 24, 1843.

1643. To Sarah Storrow

Bayonne ↑(Tuesday[)]↓ Nov. 28th. 1843

My dear Sarah,

Thus far I have come on very comfortably and find myself very well. This precaution of having the Malle poste all to myself enables me to arrange every thing so as to stretch my limbs and put myself at my ease

I leave this in the Malle poste in about three hours time and expect to be in Madrid on thursday evening

Give my kind remembrances to Mr Storrow Kiss the darling for me—

Your affectionate uncle
Washington Irving

ADDRESSED: Madame / Madame Storrow / 4 Rue de la Victoire / à Paris   POST-
    MARKED: BAYONNE / 28 / NOV / 43 / ([*unrecovered*])   DOCKETED:
    November 28th. 1843
MANUSCRIPT: Rush Rhees Library, University of Rochester.

1644. To Sarah Storrow

Madrid Dec 1—1843.

My dear Sarah,

I arrived here safely last night at midnight; roused the house, and was received with half hysterical laughing and crying by the simplehearted Juana; who had feared I would be devoured alive by the robbers. My journey was comfortable; having the Coupée of the Malle poste to myself I made a sofa of the seat on which I stretched myself; while Lorenzo made a luxurious seat of a well stuffed carpet bag & sat with his back to the door. where he slept profoundly—We had a couple of Escopeteros or musquateers to guard the Malle poste through the robber region, both of whom went to sleep—I followed their example; and we all slept our way through the scenes of peril without being molested.

I as yet feel no bad effects from my journey; ⟨and⟩ though I have the same lingerings of my complaint that I had at Paris, and which it will take some time yet entirely to eradicate. But I have time & leisure before me and shall give the enemy no rest until I have completely expelled him—This is written at a gallop to save the post, and give you ⟨the⟩ news of my safe arrival. I will write to you again in the course of a day or two—

With kind regards to Mr Storrow and kisses and bangs to dear little Kate

Your affectionate uncle
Washington Irving

MANUSCRIPT: Yale.

1645. To Sarah Storrow

Madrid, Dec. 2d. 1843

My dear Sarah,

I will thank you to search in the Room I occupied in your house for a pacquet ⟨of⟩ ↑containing two↓ dispatches from the U.S. Govt. in the Shape of a very large letter. Inclosed in it ↑also↓ was a Commission for a Consul at Neuvitas in Cuba—&c It may have fallen behind the bed; or Commode—Or it may be somewhere in the saloons. I missed it before my departure but presumed Lorenzo had packed it up in one of the trunks. The loss of it embarrasses me sadly. If you find it send it to me immediately by Mail. Have a good rummage for it—Look in the books &c &c—If after well searching the apartment you cannot find it write me word, as I must immediately write to the department of ⟨the⟩ State for copies of the dispatches—which will be rather mortifying—

I still remain very well after my journey, notwithstanding that I have been obliged to be a good deal about: paying visits; attending the chamber of Deputies &c—We are in the midst of extremely critical times, as you will perceive if you read attentively the articles in the French papers on Spanish affairs; which just now are well worth your attention. You will see that what I apprehended has come to pass, a complete Schism at head quarters among the leaders of the Successful party—Olozaga, who a few days since was at the head of the Cabinet[1] and at the Queens right hand, was dismissed the evening before my arrival and stands charged with having extorted a decree (dissolving the Cortes,) from the little Queen, in a violent and most insulting manner. He endeavors to exculpate himself; and in so doing implies falsehood and deceit on the part of the Queen The rest of the Ministers have resigned & seem inclined to take part with Olozaga—Affairs are getting more and more complicated here; and threaten a convulsion, and I am deeply concerned to see the poor little Queen drawn into the vortex of political dissension. Her situation is full of peril and uncertainty.

I write in extreme haste. The evening is advanced and I wish to save the mail—

Remember me kindly to Mr Storrow and Kiss my dear little Kate. Oh how I should like to have her on my lap, playing her evening game of high jinks

Affectionately your uncle
Washington Irving

MANUSCRIPT: Yale.   PUBLISHED: Simison, *Keogh Papers*, pp. 209–10.

1. Salustiano de Olózaga, who succeeded Joaquín María López as prime minister on November 24, 1843, tried to strengthen his power by obtaining a decree to dissolve the Cortes from Isabella. His pressure tactic failed, and he was dismissed on November 28, 1843. See H. Butler Clarke, *Modern Spain*, pp. 193–96. For further details from WI, see his letter to A. P. Upshur, December 8, 1843.

1646.   To Luis González Bravo

Legation of the United States / Madrid December 4h. 1843.

The Undersigned Envoy Extraordinary and Minister Plenipotentiary of the United States has the honor to acknowledge the receipt of the note of His Excellency Don Luis Gonzalez Bravo conveying the information of his having been appointed by Her Majesty. Minister of State and of Foreign Affairs.[1]

While congratulating His Excellency on this distinguished mark of Royal esteem and confidence the Undersigned assures him of the high satisfaction he shall experience in entering with him in official correspondence and vying with him in efforts to promote and strengthen the bonds of amity which so happily exist between the two Nations.

The Undersigned avails himself of this occasion to offer to His Excellency Don Luis Gonzalez Bravo assurances of his high consideration.

Washington Irving

MANUSCRIPT: NA, RG 84 (letterbook copy).

Luis González Bravo (1811–1871), formerly a political extremist and a vituperative newspaper editor who attacked the government, was now a conservative who held the balance of power between the two major factions and wished to govern on his own terms. See Carr, *Spain*, p. 228; Clarke, *Modern Spain*, pp. 194, 196; Latimer, *Spain in the Nineteenth Century*, pp. 260, 264; and Christiansen, *Military Power*, pp. 119–21, 170.

1. González Bravo's appointment was reported in *La Gaceta*, December 2, 1843.

1647.   To Luis González Bravo

Legation of the United States. / Madrid December 4th. 1843.

The Undersigned Envoy Extraordinary and Minister Plenipotentiary of the United States has the honor to acknowledge the receipt of the letter of His Excellency Don Luis Gonzalez Bravo, First Minister of State and of Foreign affairs dated December 1st. enclosing a certified copy of

the Act of the Solemn declaration of Her Majesty relative to the transaction of the 28th. November.

The Undersigned will lose no time in transmitting this important document to his government and in informing it at the same time of the loyal
determination expressed by His Excellency to respond faithfully to the
high confidence reposed in him and to maintain intact the prerogatives of
the Throne and the Sanctity of the royal person.

The Undersigned takes this occasion to renew to His Excellency the
assurance of his high consideration.

Washington Irving.

MANUSCRIPT: NA, RG 84 (letterbook copy).

1648.   To A. P. Upshur

Legation of the United States. / Madrid December 8th. 1843.

No. 33. / The Hon: A. P. Upshur. / Secretary of State of the U. S.—
Washington.

Sir,

The important events which were succeeding each other so rapidly in
this country induced me to hasten my return to my post, before a complete cure had been effected of the obstinate malady which has so long
afflicted me. I accordingly arrived in this city after a rapid journey on
the Evening of the 30th. and just in time to witness one of the most
threatening paroxysms of the intermittent revolution by which this country is so frequently convulsed. A brief notice of the course of events during the short interval which has elapsed since the date of the last despatch
may serve to throw light on the present critical state of affairs.

The despatch of Mr. Hamilton dated November 25th. announced the
formation of Mr. Olozaga's Cabinet, and the two difficult questions; one
relating to the National Militia; the other to the municipalities which
had been left to it as a legacy by the provisional government. Mr. Olozaga's first act was a decree suspending the reorganization of the Militia[1]
which gave great satisfaction to the Moderado party, and offended in an
equal degree the *Exaltados* or ultras. His next step was a decree in the
same sense suspending the law relative to the municipal bodies.[2] These
measures produced a slight popular tumult, which, however, was easily
quelled and the Ministers appeared to have Secured the support of all
lovers of order and good government. On the second day of their administration a third decree was issued restoring all the honors and grades

which had been granted by Espartero,[3] up to the time of his embarkation on board of the Malabar, considering that as the actual termination of his regency. If the first two measures of the new Ministry had pleased the Moderados and Conservatives, the last which seemed equally founded in justice and enlightened policy produced a storm of abuse from the same party, being viewed only in a party light without regard to the principles of reconciliation and legality on which it was based.

In the midst of the angry commentaries to which this measure gave rise, the public was astounded on the morning of the 30th, November by the appearance in the Gazette of a royal decree, dismissing Mr. Olozaga from office; and still more by an article in the "Heraldo" the leading paper of the Moderados charging that Minister with having on the evening of the 28th. by peremptory and even personal violence compelled the youthful Queen to sign a decree, without date, by which he was empowered at any moment to dissolve the Cortes.

I arrived at Madrid just at this juncture: The City presented a singular scene; It was the commencement of three days of public rejoicing. The Houses were decked out with tapestry; there were illuminations by night; games dances spectacles and parades by day; fountains were running with wine and milk and the streets thronged by the populace in their holyday garbs; all in honor of the recent accession of the youthful Queen to the throne; while at that very moment the political world was agitated by an occurrence, the effects of which might shake that throne to its foundations. In contrast to the gay throngs of the populace might be seen dark knots of politicians muffled in their cloaks and holding mysterious conversations at every corner; while the legislative halls and the streets and squares in their vicinity were filled by anxious crowds watching the course of affairs, and contributing to the general agitation by their factious clamours.

Each hour produced its event. The other members of Mr. Olozagas Cabinet gave in their resignations and their places were occupied ad interim by Mr. Luis Gonzalez Bravo, who for the time being acted as Universal Minister. His elevation to such a post and to immediate proximity with the youthful Queen drew much scoffing and censure upon the Moderados: His connexions were said to be low; his wife had been an actress; some of his relations were actually on the stage; for himself he had formerly been an Editor of a scurrilous paper in which Maria Christina the mother of the youthful Queen had been assailed in the grossest manner and stigmatized in Capital letters with the vilest appellation, which can be given to a woman. and this, cried the liberals is the man chosen by the Aristocracy as prime Minister, and placed by the side of our Virgin Queen[4]

The first act of Mr. Gonzalez Bravo was seemingly unadvised and has certainly been productive of disastrous consequences. The Queen had made a declaration before certain of the principal dignitaries of the state of the circumstances of the scene of ministerial violence in which her signature to the decree of dissolution was said to have been extorted from her by Mr. Olozaga—Her declaration had been reduced to writing and duly witnessed; and it was expressly directed in the latter part of it, that it should be deposited in the Archives of State. Mr. Gonzalez Bravo, however, apparently on his own impulse read it before the Chamber of Deputies and thus brought the subject immediately into discussion in that disputatious assemblage; placing the Queen in a manner in litigation with her degraded minister.

Mr. Olozaga of course stood on the defensive denying the acts of constraint and violence imputed to him; intimated that in making the statement the youthful mind of the sovereign had been swayed and biassed by a "camarilla" or knot of both sexes who surround her and sought to govern her; and that the whole was a palace intrigue with a view to his downfall

The ex-ministers and the other leaders of the progresista party some of whom had been jealous rivals of Mr. Olozaga now joined in his defence; the coalition was declared at an end and political warfare was declared between the Moderados and the progresistas. The discussions growing out of this subject have been personal and acrimonious, the auditors have taken sides in the controversy and every inflammatory period uttered on the floor has produced hisses or shouts from the crowded galleries.[5]

The discord thus commenced in the Palace and the legislative halls soon spread into the streets; there were tumults even on the days of rejoicing. A crowd in front of the town hall cried "Viva Espartero"; "death to Narvaez"; "death to all Traitors," and while some hailed the name of the newly enthroned Queen others shouted for the "Sovereign people". The tumult was not appeased without bloodshed and the loss of life. The quiet of the Capital however has hitherto been maintained by the strong measures of Narvaez, who has pickets of troops stationed at various points; and makes the bayonet glitter in every street. In the mean time emissaries have been despatched by both parties to the provinces, to influence the public mind on these agitating subjects. The Moderados who flatter themselves that the nation is eminently monarchical, call on all true Spaniards to rally round the throne of their youthful and insulted Queen; while the progresistas hold up Ologaza as a political martyr; sacrificed to a scheme of the Moderados to bring constitutional Monarchy into disrepute and to restore the reign of absolutism. In a few days the provinces will begin to act back upon the Capital; and we shall probably hear of fresh pronunciamientos and disturbances and cries for a Central Junta, which is almost equivalent to cries for a republic.

The Moderados are evidently determined on strong measures, and having the army at their command are disposed to rule by the sword, while the progresistas calculate on the enduring and irresistible force of the public will. Every thing seems to portend another general convulsion; and fears are entertained that it will be more fierce and sanguinary than the last.

Let events go as they may a fatal blow has been struck to the popularity of the youthful Queen, and with it, to the stability of her throne. I had always apprehended that she would lose a share of her general popularity in coming to the throne and taking a part in public measures; but had no idea of seeing her so soon an object of party odium. While some degree of restraint and decorum is observed in parliamentary discussions, some of the vindicators of Olozaga out of doors charge her with arch-falsehood and deceit; others with being a mere Manikin in the hands of designing courtiers; while all identify her with the Moderado party and seek to destroy the weight and influence of her name.

I have the honor to enclose a copy of the declaration of the Queen which has been furnished by Mr. Luis Gonzalez Bravo; who begs me to assure my government that he is determined to merit the high honor conferred on him by Her Majesty in the confidence she had placed in him and that he hopes to be able to maintain inviolate the prerogatives of the throne and the sanctity that should surround her royal person.

> I am, Sir, / Very respectfully / Your Obdt Sevt.
> Washington Irving

DOCKETED: Recd. 30 Jany. [*upper left corner, page 1*] / No. 33. W. Irving–Madrid.
     8 Dec. 1843
MANUSCRIPT: NA, RG 59.   PUBLISHED: STW, II, 164, 165 (in part).

Only the signature is in WI's handwriting.

1. When Narváez entered Madrid, he disarmed its militia, promoted sympathetic officers, and remitted two years of service for enlisted men, actions which were reversed by Olózaga when he became prime minister. See H. Butler Clarke, *Modern Spain*, pp. 191–92.

2. On June 4, 1840, the Cortes had passed a bill abolishing the election of local mayors and substituting the appointment of those chosen by the central government. See Clarke, *Modern Spain*, pp. 160–61, 196; Christiansen, *Military Power*, pp. 95–97, 121; Raymond Carr, *Spain*, pp. 180–81; 220–21; and *La Gaceta*, November 29, 1843.

3. During his brief term Olózaga had revoked the titles and honors bestowed by Espartero. These were quickly restored by González Bravo. See Clarke, *Modern Spain*, p. 197; and *La Gaceta*, November 27, 1843; and *El Castellano*, November 28, 1843.

4. WI's summation of Madrid gossip about González Bravo is echoed by Madame

Calderón de la Barca: "...a Deputy, called González Bravo, who when still young had edited an infamous paper called the Guirigay, in which he had spoken of Queen Christina in terms which no woman or Queen could ever forgive. Moreover his wife is the sister of the celebrated actress, Mathilde Díaz, and of Romea the actor, and was herself an actress. Imagine this man, who is clever and pushing, and is a good speaker, suddenly finding himself Minister of State! without the slightest experience, without any knowledge of forms or of the etiquette of a court, and what is of more importance, totally inexperienced in affairs" (Madame Calderón de la Barca to W. H. Prescott, January 8, 1844, in *The Correspondence of William Hickling Prescott, 1833–1847*, ed. Roger Wolcott [Boston, 1925], p. 431; and Elizabeth W. Latimer, *Spain in the Nineteenth Century*, p. 265).

5. The debate in the Cortes over Olózaga's action lasted seventeen days and resulted in his impeachment. See Peter de Polnay, *A Queen of Spain*, pp. 85–86; and Clarke, *Modern Spain*, p. 196; and daily résumés in *El Castellano*.

1649. To Catharine Paris

Madrid, Dec. 10th. 1843.

My dear Sister,

I received yesterday your letter dated about the middle of last month.[1] It was extremely gratifying to me for I was longing for domestic news from home and your letters always place home completely before me. I have not time to write you a long letter for I have been writing dispatches to Government and am fatigued; and the Courier is soon to set off.

I arrived safe in Madrid about ten days since after a somewhat rapid journey; but I had the mail carriage to myself and was enabled to make myself comfortable. On approaching Spain I heard of the mail having been robbed between Bayonne and Madrid, and the passengers extremely maltreated, and was advised not to go on until I could be well escorted; but I knew that ↑high way↓ robberies seldom occurred twice in any neighborhood unless at long intervals; so I pushed forward. It had been advertized that the mail would be doubly guarded in consequence of the late robberies, but the promise was not fulfilled. We passed through the robber region in the night, with only two Musqueteers to guard the carriage; both of whom went to sleep. As I did not care to keep watch myself and alarm myself with shadows, I arranged myself comfortably and fell asleep likewise; and continued napping through all the dangerous part of the road.

I arrived at Madrid just in time to witness the three days of public rejoicing for the ↑young queens↓ accession to the throne. ⟨of the⟩ ⟨th⟩ All the houses were decorated the balconies hung with tapestry; there were triumphal arches; fountains running with milk and wine; games, dances, processions & parades by day. Illuminations and Spectacles at night; and the Streets were constantly thronged by the populace in their holyday garb. At this very time, however, an occurrence had taken place that threatens to blight the popularity of the poor little queen and ↑even↓ to shake the stability of her throne. On the evening previous to my arrival she had suddenly dismissed the prime minister, Mr Olózaga from office; and as a reason for this dismission alle⟨d⟩ged, before a number of the first dignitaries of the Kingdom; that he had by peremptory means and even by personal violence, compelled her to sign a decree dissolving the Cortes. You will see a full account of all this in the public papers, which I reccommend to your earnest perusal. It has lighted a flame in the country which it will not be easy to extinguish and which may lead to civil war. The Minister stands on his defence,—denies the violent conduct imputed to him and asserts that the statement of the Queen has been dictated to her by a camarilla or clique of ⟨fem⟩ male and female courtiers who surround her, and that the whole was an intrigue intended for his downfall. As he is a leading chief of the progresista party they have all espoused his cause. It has occasioned a violent schism between the Moderados and Progresistas: that is to say the Aristocrats and liberals: and every thing threatens new convulsions. The Moderados have the government at present; and are determined to maintain their sway by military means: ⟨the⟩ General Narvaez is with them and under his military vigilance the capital gleams with the bayonet as in time of war. The worst is the poor little Queen is mixed up with their political feuds— her statement is disputed. She is charged by some with falsehood and deceit; by others with being a mere puppet in the hands of the Moderados—I feel extremely anxious for her and look with a boding eye towards the future; which seems lowering with storms and troubles.

I have brought back with me to Madrid the lingerings of my malady; but trust with care and patience to free myself entirely from them before long—I write in extreme haste as you must perceive by the way in which this letter is scrawled.

Love to all bodies

Your affectionate brother
W I.

ADDRESSED: Mrs Daniel Paris / Care of E. Irving Esq / New York / Pr "Emerald"
  POSTMARKED: [*unrecovered*] / 25 / DEC. / 1843 //   FORWARDING STAMP:
  T. B. Grenade / Havre:
MANUSCRIPT: Va.–Barrett.   PUBLISHED: PMI, III, 310–11 (in part); Hellman, *WI Esquire*, p. 272 (in part).

1. This letter has not been located.

1650. To Maximo de Aguirre

Legation of the United States. / Madrid December 16th. 1843.
Maximo de Aguirre Esqr. / Consul of the U. States—Bilbao.

Sir

I enclose a copy of a despatch recently recently[1] received from the
Secretary of State by which I am happy to see that he concurs with me
in the view I took of your conduct during the recent political crisis; and
is desirous that you should continue in the exercise of the consular duties
at Bilbao.[2]

I have to acknowledge the receipt of your letter of the 19th. ulto., in
which you allude to the recovery of the "two thousand and odd dollars
unjustly and violently extorted from you; and request my official interference in claiming from the Spanish government restitution."[3] Having
just returned from an absence of nearly three months, during which great
changes have taken place in the Spanish Cabinet, I have not yet entered
into those personal relations with the members of the government which
would afford the most favorable occasions for presenting your claims.—
I cannot however forbear expressing to you frankly my opinion, that after an examination of the circumstances, I concur in the view taken by
my predecessor Mr. Vail of the impropriety of an *official* interference in a
case which concerns you chiefly in your character of a Spanish Subject.—I hope nevertheless that the present government may be induced
to look with a more favorable eye than their predecessors upon the justice of the appeal you have made.

I am Sir respectfully / Your Obdt Sevt
Washington Irving.

P. S. I enclose also the Exequatur which you so frankly placed at my disposal[4]

W. I.

Manuscript: NA, RG 84 (letterbook copy).

1. The copyist repeated "recently."
2. Aguirre had tendered his resignation to WI on July 5, 1843. See Aguirre to
WI, July 5, 1843 (NA, RG 84).
3. General Zurbano had put Aguirre in jail when he refused to pay a fine of
$2,000 for his alleged part in the Bilbao insurrection of October, 1841. Aguirre
subsequently paid it under duress and requested that it be returned to him. See
Aguirre to WI, July 5, 1843 (NA, RG 84).
4. Aguirre had enclosed his exequatur in his letter of resignation.

1651.   To Luis González Bravo

Legation of the United States / Madrid December 16th. 1843.

The Undersigned Envoy Extraordinary and Minister Plenipotentiary of the United States has the honor to communicate to His Excellency Don Luis Gonzalez Bravo, First Minister of State and of Foreign Affairs of Her Catholic Majesty the original commission of Mr. William Hogan[1] appointed Consul of the United States for the port of Nuevitas in the Island of Cuba; and by direction of his government requests that His Excellency will cause the corresponding royal Exequatur to be issued recognizing Mr. Hogan in his official character.

The Undersigned avails himself of this occasion to renew to His Excellency the assurance of his most distinguised consideration.

Washington Irving.

MANUSCRIPT: NA, RG 84 (letterbook copy).

1. Possibly William Hogan (1792–ca. 1875), a lawyer, translator, and land developer in upstate New York. He served as U.S. consul at Nuevitas only during 1844. See Hasse, *Index to U.S. Documents*, III, 1747.

1652.   To Samuel McLean

Legation of the United States. / Madrid December 16th. 1843.

Samuel McLean Esqr. / U. States Consul—Cienfuegos.
Sir,
    I herewith forward to you your Exequatur received this day from the Department of Foreign Affairs, together with the original commission signed by the President of the United States.

    The draft on Mr. F. X. Harmony of Cadiz forwarded through the State Department has been applied to the payment of the fees on the Exequatur.[1]

I am with respect / Your Obdt Sevt.
Washington Irving.

MANUSCRIPT: NA, RG 84 (letterbook copy).

1. WI had written to McLean on January 23, 1843, concerning the fees for the exequatur (NA, RG 84).

1653. To Henry P. Sturgis

Legation of the United States. / Madrid December 16th. 1843.

Henry. P. Sturgis Esqr. / Consul of the U. States—Manila
Sir
I herewith forward to you, your Exequatur received this day from the
Department of Foreign Affairs, together with the original commission
Signed by the President of the United States.
The draft on Messrs Bertodano & Co. of this city enclosed in your for-
mer letter will be applied to the payment of the fees on the Exequatur.
Your letter of 22nd. March has been recieved at the Legation.

I am Sir very respectfully / Your obdt Sevt
Washington Irving

MANUSCRIPT: NA, RG 84 (letterbook copy).

Henry P. Sturgis of Massachusetts was nominated as U.S. consul for Manila and
the Philippines in May, 1843. He resigned in 1845. See Hasse, *Index to U. S. Documents*, III, 1746.

1654. To Sarah Storrow

Madrid, Dec 20th. 1843.

My dear Sarah,
I am a little in arrears to you in letter writing; but I have been so
much Occupied since my return that I have had but little time for correspondence. Your cautionary letter addressed to me at Bordeaux reached
me at Madrid; after I had run the gauntlet and passed through the robber region unmolested. I have since received other letters[1] from you,
and likewise the missing despatches; the sight of which made my heart
leap for joy.
I found Mr Hamilton in good health and good looks on my return. He
has conducted the legation extremely well during my absence; and gave
it up into my hands in complete order. Mr Livingston has appartments
at no great distance from the Legation and dines with us frequently. He
was much dismayed at the discomforts of the country on his first arrival; but is ⟨more recon⟩ at present more reconciled. He is a close attendant on the Cortes to ⟨improve⟩ ↑perfect↓ himself in Spanish, of which
he has already an intimate knowledge. He is a very gentlemanlike young

man; of a distinguished air; acquits himself well in Society and is *making his way*. I am altogether much pleased with him

Juana was highly pleased with her work box, and still more with the idea that I had thought of her while in Paris. She has had the easy chair covered with the chintz I brought from Paris and it now makes a distinguished figure in my drawing room and is a most luxurious lounge for me. I have not had either of the dressing gowns made up yet; one being intended for summer and the other being superfluous at present, Juana having put my old one in excellent repair.

I have been making great changes in the arrangement of my house; removing the furniture from the first Saloon to my favorite room the pink Saloon; which I had hitherto made a kind of half Study, half Sitting room; with ordinary furniture. Being now carpeted; curtained and well furnished; it makes a very handsome room for reception; and is a luxurious winter room. The windows of it open into a covered and glazed Verandah; which might answer for a Conservatory; and the warmth is so genial that there is no need of fire excepting ↑early↓ in the mornings; and after sun set. All my Saloons look to the South and have ample sunshine in winter. The following is the range of my main chambers or saloons

Pick Up Artwork ~~~~~ ....

The furniture which was in the pink Saloon is transferred to the yellow Saloon; which a mere Saloon of passage The best furniture is now in the two last Saloons, and gives the whole establishment a much better appearance as well as a more comfortable arrangement. I have also changed my dining room and fitted it up more commodiously. These changes have been made ⟨by⟩ ↑at↓ the suggestion and under the superintendence of my kind friend Madame Albuquerque. I have now a very comfortable winter habitation.

The weather since my return has been for the greater part of the time very fine and temperate; more like spring time than winter. ⟨As soon⟩ The damp rainy weather which prevailed while I was in Paris followed me to Bordeaux; and even accompanied me while among the mountains; but as soon as I reached the plains I emerged into Spanish sunshine, and have enjoyed it almost ever since. It is really a blessing in this country and compensates for many discomforts which one has to endure.

I was cordially welcomed back, by my brother diplomats and really had a home feeling in finding myself once more among them. I miss my old Crony Mr Aston,[2] however, sadly; and fear it will be difficult to

Supply his loss. The Count De Bresson[3] has arrived and I have become acquainted with him. He appears to be a frank, worthy, up right man and I dare say we shall be on the most friendly footing. At present he seems perfectly aghast at the ⟨comfortless⟩ Strange and comfortless aspect of every thing around him and, at the wild chaotic character of Spanish politics; where as yet every thing is perplexity and contradiction to him. He looks back with a heavy heart to Berlin; where he had lived for twelve years, in the happiest manner, and from whence he has been so suddenly whirled to this half ⟨b⟩ Barbaric capital. I am likewise much pleased with the Countess de Bresson;[4] who [is][5] amiable and unaffected. I think I shall find their house, which is within three minutes walk of my residence, a very agreeable resort.

The diplomatic circle has likewise been enlarged by the accession of The Prince & Princess of Carini;[6] The former as Minister Plenipotentiary from Naples. I have not had an opportunity of judging of the Prince, who may very easily be better than he looks; being certainly not much like a Prince of fairy tale. He however is quite affable and seems disposed to be agreeable. The Princess is handsome; with very fine eyes; and an animated manner. I am disposed in her favor by her reminding me in the cast of her countenance and the expression of her eyes of Rebecca McLane.[7] Mr Hamilton was also struck with the resemblance.

We have here also Mr Calderon[8] (formerly Minister to the U States) and his lady;[9] ⟨who⟩ ↑The latter↓ recently wrote a very lively work on a residence in Mexico; which I reccommend to your perusal. She is originally Scotch; but has resided for some time in the United States. I am highly pleased with her—She is intelligent, sprightly and full of agreeable talent. I fear, however, she will not remain here long as Mr Calderon is likely to be appointed to some diplomatic post. Madame Calderon is a constant correspondent of Mr Prescott. By the bye she has just lent me a copy of his Conquest of Mexico, in sheets.[10] I have read a great part of the Introductory chapters treating of Aztec &c antiquities manners, customs &c and am deeply interested in it

You wish some light with respect to recent events in Spanish politics; especially, I suppose, as to the affair of the little Queen & Mr Olozaga. I have no time however to give any at present. I shall be writing to your Mother soon, and then will endeavor to give my cloudy ideas on ⟨the⟩ ↑a↓ subject, which is so beset with doubts and contradictions. I am sorry to say that, between friends and foes, or rather between the parties in and out of power, the poor little Queens popularity is in a very hazardous condition and threatens to be blighted in the very blossom. I am affraid she will be mingled up in the new political feuds which are engendering; and which threaten to have tenfold rancor to those which have gone before them. If you reccollect I said before I left Paris, that I apprehended further political convulsions in Spain; but that they would originate in the Capital, in the head of the Government, ⟨and⟩ in the rivalries and schisms of the leaders who had just risen to power. These schisms have taken place ⟨more⟩ sooner and more completely than I had anticipated. The ⟨s⟩ coalition that put down Espartero is completely broken up: and many of those who were false to him, and rose to station in the government through their false hood, are now thrown out by their coadjutors, and are seeking to league themselves with the Esparteristas in forming a new coalition and setting on foot a new revolution. Such are the continual changes and contradictions which render the politics of this wretched country ⟨a riddle and⟩ a tissue of confusion and a matter for scoffing. I begin to despair of any regeneration for the prosperity and dignity of Spain.

As you will wish to know something about the state of my health, I can only say it is about the Same as when I was in Paris. My general health is good; but I am Still hampered by this obstinate malady; which clings to me in spite of every remedy, and which it will still, most probably, require much time and patience completely to eradicate. I begin to doubt whether I shall get rid of it without a visit next year to the baths in the Pyrenees.

Do not be affraid of being too particular in writing about my dear little Kate. I read those parts of your letters over and over, and have the little baggage completely before me. I cannot express how much at times I miss her; and how it would cheer my evenings to have a gallop with her up the Champs Elysees with the little dog barking after us. I think the evening gallop did both of us good and made us both sleep the sweeter.

Farewell my dear Sarah. Give my kind remembrances to Mr Storrow and kiss darling little Kate for me.

Your affectionate uncle
Washington Irving

MANUSCRIPT: Yale.   PUBLISHED: PMI, III, 311–12 (in part); Simison, *Keogh Papers*, pp. 211–15; STW, II, 164, 166–67 (in part).

1. These letters have not been located.

2. Sir Henry Bulwer (1801–1872), who had been British attaché in Berlin, Vienna, The Hague, and Brussels and chargé d'affaires in Constantinople and Paris, had replaced Aston during WI's absence. See Bowers, *Spanish Adventures of WI*, p. 211. He "arrived [in Madrid] with a train of men and women and birds and monkeys, filling it is said 14 carriages. He is deeply marked with the small pox, and his face is half a yard long, not content with which, he wears his hair like a tuft of feathers, which makes it longer" (Fanny Calderón de la Barca to W. H. Prescott, January 8, 1844, in *Correspondence of William Hickling Prescott, 1833–1847*, ed. Wolcott, p. 432).

3. Charles-Joseph, count de Bresson (1798–1847), who had served earlier as

French minister to Hannover and Munich, was French minister to Berlin from 1831 to 1843.

4. Louise de Comminges-Guitant, Bresson's second wife.

5. WI omitted the bracketed word.

6. The Carinis, according to Madame Calderón, were "rather an ignoble couple, with a suspicious air of *parvenus* about them . . ." (Fanny Calderón de la Barca to W. H. Prescott, January 8, 1844, in *Correspondence of . . . Prescott*, p. 432). See also *El Castellano*, December 2, 1843.

7. Rebecca McLane (b. October 2, 1813) was the eldest daughter of Louis McLane, with whom WI had been on intimate terms a decade earlier.

8. Angel Calderón de la Barca (1790–1861), who had served as Spanish minister to the United States from 1835 to 1839 and to Mexico from 1839 to 1841, was to return to the United States as minister from 1844 to 1853.

9. Frances Erskine Inglis (1804–1882), a Scotswoman who had immigrated to the United States and had taught school on Staten Island and in Boston and Baltimore, had married Calderón in 1838.

10. In October, 1843, Prescott had sent Calderón the proof sheets of *The Conquest of Mexico*. See Prescott to Fanny Calderón de la Barca, October 15, 1843, in *Correspondence of . . . Prescott*, p. 399.

1655. To Edward Everett

Legation of the United States. / Madrid December 23d. 1843.

My dear Sir,

Your letter dated 30th, November,[1] and which you evidently expected would find me in Paris, did not reach me until yesterday: I immediately attended to its contents.,—Mr. Hamilton the Secretary of Legation called on one of the under Secretaries of State and after a little preliminary conversation which served to interest the Secretary in the matter stated to him the wish of this legation to obtain copies of "all the documents brought forward by Spain in 1790 in her controversy with England about Nootka,"[2] specifying a desire that they should comprise the "treaties, demarcations, takings of possession, and the most decided acts of sovereignty exercised by the Spaniards in these stations from the reign of Charles II, and authorised by that Monarch in 1692."— Mr. Hamilton at the same time gave him a memorandum in writing to the same purport.

The Secretary promised that the necessary researches should be made, and that within Eight days we might expect a list of all the documents found. When this is done, I shall attend to procuring copies.[3]

I forward by the French Courier addressed to the care of Mr. Ledyard in Paris; a copy of the voyage of the Spanish Schooners, Sutil y Mexicana, in 1792;[4] for which that gentleman had written in your behalf.

I am, my dear Sir, / Very truly yours,
Washington Irving

His Excellency / Edward Everett

MANUSCRIPT: MHS; NA, RG 84 (letterbook copy). Manning, *Diplomatic Correspondence: Canada*, III, 840.

Only the signature is in WI's handwriting.

1. Everett's letter requesting details about Spanish documents concerning the Nootka controversy with Great Britain was prompted by discussions about the Oregon boundary question (NA, RG 84).

2. Nootka Island, off the west central coast of Vancouver Island, was the site of the Spanish seizure of an English vessel in 1789. The incident nearly caused an armed encounter between the two powers, but Spain backed down and acknowledged that that area of the Pacific ocean should be open to British shipping and fishing vessels. See *The Cambridge History of British Foreign Policy, 1783–1919*, ed. A. W. Ward and G. P. Gooch, I, 197–201.

3. On January 15, 1844, WI reported to Everett that the Spanish archives did not contain the documents he had requested (NA, RG 84). A thorough study of the Nootka controversy reveals that 169 pages of documents were copied from the Archivo Historico Nacional in Madrid and 262 pages from the Archivo General de Indias in Seville. See W. R. Manning, "The Nootka Sound Controversy," *Annual Report of the American Historical Association* (1904), pp. 279–478, esp. p. 472.

4. *Relacion del viage hecho por las goletas Sutil y Mexicana un 1792, para reconocer el Estrecho de Fuca* (Madrid, 1802).

1656. To A. P. Upshur

Legation of the United States. / Madrid December 23d.1843.

No. 34. / The Hon: / A. P. Upshur. / Secretary of State of the U. States. Washington.

Sir,

I have to acknowledge the receipt of Despatch No. 19. from the Department, in relation to the case of Consul Aguirre of Bilbao, and have thought that the best disposition, which could be given to the subject, was to forward to the Consul a copy of that communication; at the same time returning to him the Exequatur, which had been enclosed to the Legation.

The Despatch No. 20, enclosing the commission of W. Hogan, appointed Consul of the United States for the port of Nuevitas in the Island of Cuba, has also been received and its directions complied with as will appear by the enclosed copy of my application for an Exequatur in his behalf.

I have the honor to enclose the accounts and Vouchers of the Legation for the third quarter of 1843, showing a balance in favor of the United States of $2.71, which will be carried to their credit in next account.

I am Sir with great respect / Your obdt sevt.
Washington Irving

DOCKETED: Recd. 11 Feby. / Mr. Markoe
MANUSCRIPT: NA, RG 59.

1657. To Julia Grinnell

Madrid Decr 29th. 1843.

My dear Julia,

I have long been in debt to you for your delightful letter of August 4th.[1] but I am sure you will excuse this tardiness in one who is ↑so↓ completely untuned for all exercise of the pen by a long protracted malady. Your picture of your old rural abode at Throgs neck,[2] and of the children rambling about the grounds with their little rustic companions, is quite captivating and makes me still more regret ⟨the⟩ my exile from all those home scenes which are my delight. I am glad to find that you continue your admirable system with your children,[3] which I have always considered well calculated to produce the desired effect "sound bodies, well developed organs, senses perfected by exercises and stamina which will enable them in future life to study or labor with energy and without injury" Let others aim at making their children precocious prodigies, intellectual wonders; and wear out their organs of thought, and enfeeble their constitutions by early overtasking of the mind, and confinement of the body; I will always bet in the long run, on those who have had a happy untasked child hood, with simple wholesome diet and plenty of frolick in the open air. ⟨Wants you [unrecovered] you to a society⟩ I am happy to find, also, that your system, while it has such excellent effects on your own children, is benefiting other branches of the family, who have wisely adopted it. Sarah Storrow has followed your example and the consequence is that her little girl is one of the healthiest and most cheery children I have ever known. Irving Van Warts good little wife had like wise adopted it, before I left the United States, and I am told her two boys[4] continue to be pictures of health. Thus, my dear Julia, you bid ⟨likely⟩ ↑fair↓ to improve the whole stock, beside adding to it your own little prize specimens. By the bye I am told your little Fanny is the flower of your flock, quite a little beauty, and as engaging as she is beautiful. I do not wonder that she should "hold the key of her fathers heart."

I perfectly agree with you in your idea of Pierre and Helen.[5] Never was there a better suited union. I feel deeply my separation from them, they both seemed to take the place of others dear to my heart, whom I had lost and deplored. Pierre came to ⟨be⟩ my side when I was grieving over the loss of my dear brother Peter, who had so long been the companion of my thoughts; and I found in him many of the qualities which made that brother so invaluable to me as a bosom friend. The same delicacy of feeling and rectitude of thought; the same generous disinterestedness; and the same scrupulous faith in all confidential matters: while Helen in the delightful variety of her character; so affectionate, so tender; so playful at times, and at other times so serious and elevated; and always so intelligent and sensitive continually brought to mind her mother;[6] who was one of the tenderest friends of my child-hood, and the delight of my youthful years. God bless and prosper them both! and it gives me joy to think that they are prospering; and that Pierre is effectively taking root and thriving in his native city.

Your account of the wonderful additions and attractions in the house in College place quite astonishes me. Grinnell certainly must have the bump of Constructiveness Strongly develloped; particularly in that department of architecture which appertains to dining rooms, butlers pantrys and wine cellars. I have no doubt that, in consequence of his encreased facilities, he now gives two dinners where he formerly gave one; though that can hardly be as he formerly, ⟨gave⟩ in general, gave one dinner and a half per diem, the latter being smuggled into the house hold economy under the name of a supper. I think it was a wonderful instance of self ⟨det⟩ ↑denial↓ in him to give you up his *junior wine cellar* for a store room. God bless his bounteous heart! I have no doubt that, had he been in the place of his great name sake, of holy writ, when he smote the rock there would have Spouted out wine instead of water[7]

I understand by late letters from home, that you have give[n] [*MS torn*] the girls at the Cottage kind invitations to visit you occasionally during the winter. I thank you on their behalf, my dear Julia; and I thank you on my own account, for this attention to my little flock. I constantly fear that my absence from home must abridge their oppor-tunities of enjoyment; which I was always studious to multiply as far as my slender means afforded. I think, too, my presence made the long winters less tedious and monotonous in the solitude of the country. A visit now and then to town will help them through the winter months and keep them from being too much shut up from the world. Would to God I could return and be once more with them. My heart yearns for home, and as I have now probably turned the last corner in life and my remaining years are growing scanty in number, I begrudge every one that I am obliged to pass separated from my cottage and my kindred.

And now farewell, my dear Julia, Give my most affectionate remembrances to your good husband, and believe me ever most truly,

> Your affectionate uncle
> Washington Irving

ADDRESSED: Mrs Julia I. Grinnell / College Place / New York.   ENDORSED: 8th. January. / Havre packet
MANUSCRIPT: Yale.   PUBLISHED: PMI, III, 312–13 (in part).

1. This letter has not been located.
2. For details about this homestead, see WI to Julia Grinnell, September 30, 1842, and PMI, III, 248–49.
3. The Grinnell children were Julia (1837–1915), Irving (1839–1921), and Fanny, who was born on September 23, 1842.
4. Ames and Irving, twin sons born on January 20, 1841.
5. Pierre M. Irving had married his first cousin Helen Dodge on October 10, 1836.
6. Ann Sarah Irving Dodge (1770–1808).
7. See Exodus 17:6.

1658. To Sarah Storrow

Madrid Decr. 31t 1843.

My dear Sarah,

I have been looking out for a few days past for a letter from you; not that I have a right to expect such frequent correspondence, but because, in my isolated situation, letters from any of the family are precious to me.

I have nothing new to write about. Spanish political affairs have become distasteful to me; they are so full of intrigue, falsehood and meanness. Olozaga, the Ex Minister, has fled to Portugal;[1] which is considered by his enemies as proof of the truth of the charges made against him by the Queen. His friends say nothing at present in his defence. My own idea always has been that, accustomed in his preceding situation as Tutor, to treat the little Queen with undue familiarity he continued it as Minister; and on her declining to sign the decree dissolving the Cortes, he became somewhat peremptory, considering it the opposition of a froward child; or that she was acting under the secret instigation of a clique of palace intriguers, who wished to disconcert his plans. ⟨I can⟩ and effect his downfall. I doubt whether the little Queen was aware at the time of the extreme indecorum and breach of Royal dignity, ⟨and she⟩ of this conduct, or that her ire was kindled until afterwards informed of the flagrancy of the act. Poor child! She has indeed need of a Mother, or some other sincere and experienced guardian at hand, to council her amid the deceits and stratagems and perils by which she is surrounded. I have not seen her since my return. There have been no court ceremonials; and I was prevented by indisposition from attending a public distribution of prizes at the Liceo, at which she presided. Indeed I have seen little of any thing or any body for some time past: leading much such a life as I did in Paris, confined to the house excepting when I drive out in the carriage. The opera is my chief resource. At first I could not but be struck with its inferiority to that at Paris; but in a little while I became accustomed to ⟨the⟩ it, and ceased to draw comparisons. One consolation is that, if inferior, it is vastly cheaper.

I have arranged my house very comfortably for the winter. The pink saloon, (now transformed to a yellow one by being newly papered) is fitted up with [some]² of the best furniture; curtains & carpet; and is really one of the most delightful winter rooms I have ever inhabited. It has broad & high windows descending to the floor and opening onto a Verandah enclosed with glass like a conservatory. The Sun shines into it throughout the day, so that there is no need of fire excepting early in the morning & in the Evening. As the Room is spacious & lofty and the Verandah likewise, ⟨it is⟩ the air is never close or confined; yet has always ⟨a rea⟩ quite a Summer temperature. I am boasting very much of this Saloon; but to me who has to pass so much of his time within doors it is a great comfort to have such a luxurious chambre to lounge in.

I miss you and Kate amazingly when I take my solitary drives. They are apt to be a little dreary and are taken more as medical prescriptions than as agreeable relaxations.

I dined a few days since at the French Ambassadors; the only guest beside myself was Count Marnix,³ the Belgian Charge d'affairs. The young gentlemen attached to the Embassy, ⟨and⟩ of course form the diplomatic family. I am much pleased with the Countess de Bresson; she is well bred amiable and unaffected. The poor Count has not yet got over his profound distaste for his new situation. He sees the dark side of every thing; ⟨and⟩ continually recalls with lamentations his happy abode at Berlin; and, in his reccollections of the flesh pots of Egypt,⁴ refuses to console himself with the Quails and Manna[5] that are to be met with even in this wilderness.

I am happy to hear that a part of the Jones family have got back safely to Paris and beg you to remember me kindly to them.

I hope you continue to take occasional drives with Mrs Hacquet, and that Kate and Lolo[6] are as good friends as ever.

This is the last day of the year. I hope tomorrow will ⟨t⟩ usher in a happy and prosperous year to you and yours and with this fervent wish will conclude

Your affectionate Uncle
Washington Irving

MANUSCRIPT: Yale.   PUBLISHED: Simison, *Keogh Papers*, pp. 215–17.

1. Olózaga was reported as seen at Talavera on December 15 and at Torralba a few days later. See *El Castellano*, December 19, 21, 1843. In Lisbon Olózaga stayed with Mr. Southern, a British agent. See *El Castellano*, January 6, 1844.
2. WI wrote "since."
3. Charles-Gustave-Ghislain-Marie, count of Marnix (1807–1862), who served in Madrid from 1841 to 1847.
4. See Exodus 16:3.
5. See Exodus 16:13–15.
6. Little Kate's dog.

1659. To Luis González Bravo

Legation of the United States. / Madrid January 2nd. 1844.

Mr. John. K. Cooke[1] having been appointed Consul of The United States of America for the port of Trinidad de Cuba; The Undersigned Envoy Extraordinary and Minister Plenipotentiary of the United States has the honor to enclose Mr. Cooke's commission and to request that his Excellency Don Luis Gonzalez Bravo, First Minister of State and of Foreign Affairs of Her Catholic Majesty will cause the corresponding Exequatur to be issued recognizing Mr. Cooke in his official character.

The Undersigned avails himself of the occasion to offer to His Excellency assurances of his highest consideration.

Washington Irving

MANUSCRIPT: NA, RG 84 (letterbook copy).

1. Cooke's name had been withdrawn on December 28, 1843, and S. McLean was nominated on January 4, 1844. However, he resigned on January 17, 1844. See Hasse, *Index to U.S. Documents*, III, 1748.

1660. To Sarah Storrow

Madrid, Jany 7th. 1844

My dear Sarah,

I am again longing for a letter from you: your last was[1] very brief being written while you were suffering from a head ache. Your next I hope will be written under better auspices. You will say I am very exigeant, and I am half affraid that I am: but family letters are such a treat and consolation to me that I cannot help being greedy of them. Madame Albuquerque says my visit to Paris has done me a good in one respect: that I am less content with Madrid since my return, but in fact I am at times disheartened by the continuance of my malady; which obliges me to abstain from all literary occupations, and half disables me ⟨from⟩ ↑for↓ social intercourse. If I could only exercise my pen I should be quite another being: as then, besides being agreeably employed, I should be looking forward to an improvement in my pecuniary means and of course an abbreviation of the term of my separation from kindred & friends. I do not know that my malady is worse than while I was in Paris; but I have not equal means of cure at hand. I distrust the baths and I distrust the Physicians in this comfortless country, and pursue only such remedies as I have satisfactorily proved to be alleviating if not effective. I question whether I shall get rid of this blighting malady until I am enabled to visit the baths in the Pyrenees early in the next Summer.

I am preparing to ↑give↓ a diplomatic dinner; which is something of an undertaking in my present nerveless condition. The Count de Bresson has now been here for nearly a month; the Prince Carini Minister from Naples has likewise been here some time and Mr Bulwer has been here a week. Then there is a Minister from Chili, accredited last Summer, who has never dined with me. All these must be feted and feasted without further delay, and I have accordingly ordered my cook to get his coppers and saucepans in order and prepare to take the field. I wish the affair were well over, or that I were more in heart to cope with it. I have not seen so much of the French Ambassador as I intended, ↑not↓ having been in visiting trim or mood lately. What I have seen of him and his lady I like decidedly. Mr Bulwer and myself have exchanged calls repeatedly; but some how or other, have not yet met. I understand he has made up his mind to be pleased with every thing and every body at Madrid, which is excellent policy; but I much doubt whether ⟨t⟩his long habitudes of luxurious life and highly cultivated Society in the polite capitals of Europe, will not call for the constant exercise of diplomatic ⟨toleration⟩ ↑complacency and↓ self command.

He has commenced judiciously by cultivating a courteous and friendly intercourse with the Count de Bresson.

Notwithstanding Mr Ledyards prognostics, I have been much pleased with Madame Calderon. It is true I have not been able to see much of her; and on the first visit I was in a loquacious mood and *did most of the talking myself*: not a very usual thing with me with strangers. I have just read her Life in Mexico which gives a most lively and no doubt accurate picture of life, manners, population and scenery in that country. It came in time just as I had finished reading Prescotts "Conquest of Mexico," with which I have been deeply interested and highly pleased. I believe Madame Calderon is making observations and gathering materials for a work on Life in Madrid,[2] at least so it is hinted, and I hope it is true. Her position in political and social society here give her admirable opportunities.

And now write to me all about yourself and your own little domestic world; above all, about my little playmate Kate, who is continually present to my mind in my lonely hours; would to god I had her here to enliven them! Have you been to the opera lately? Have you seen Grisi in Anna Bolena[3]? It must give fine scope for her powers. I reccollect Pasta in it, who ⟨was⟩ gave it admirably. Have you seen more of Brambilla;[4] and how do you like her? She haunts my reccollection with a charm almost equal to that of Grisi; so delightful was she the two last times I saw her; and I am continually calling her to mind ⟨in⟩ as the gay young coxcomb in Marie de Rohan; and the kind of ballad which she sang with such spirit and effect.

Do you drive out occasionally with Madame Hacquet [?] I beg you to remember me kindly to her when you see her. How I should enjoy a drive ⟨up⟩ ↑in↓ the Champs Elysees with you & Kate in the Snug little carriage I had while in Paris. I am much of the opinion of Lorenzo who says "a mere promenade in Paris is worth all the sights and fetes of Madrid." By the way, the constant wish of the honest fellow is that he may see Paris once more before he dies. I am happy to say he has returned home unspoiled by his travels and takes care of my house and my concerns with his accustomed attention and fidelity. Under his supervision every thing goes on well and at much diminished expense.

I hope Eliza[5] continues to have charge of Baby and that your household is as harmonious as when I was with you. I miss Elizas cheerful musical voice early in the mornings when she used to be busy about little Miss Maams toilette.

God bless you & yours / Your affectionate uncle

W. I.

ADDRESSED: Madame / Madame Storrow / aux soins de Mr T. W Storrow / 17.
Rue de Faubg Poissonniere / à Paris
MANUSCRIPT: Yale. PUBLISHED: PMI, III, 314–15 (in part); STW, II, 167,
168 (in part).

1. This letter has not been located.

2. Madame Calderón apparently did not remain long enough in Madrid to collect impressions for a volume similar to her *Life in Mexico*, which was published in Boston and London in 1843, although in 1856 she brought out *The Attaché in Madrid; or, Sketches of the Court of Isabella II*. In early March of 1844 she reported that her husband had been appointed Spanish minister to the United States, with his departure scheduled for later in the month. See Fanny Calderón de la Barca to W. H. Prescott, March 8, 1844, in *Correspondence of William Hickling Prescott, 1833–1847*, ed. Wolcott, p. 449.

3. Donizetti's opera, *Anna Bolena*, was first performed in Milan on December 26, 1830, with the first Paris performance on September 1, 1831, at the Théâtre des Italiens with Giuditta Pasta singing the lead. See *International Cyclopedia of Music and Musicians*, ed. Oscar Thompson (New York, 1964), p. 73; and Herbert Weinstock, *Donizetti and the World of Opera in Italy, Paris, and Vienna in the First Half of the Nineteenth Century* (New York, 1963), pp. 325–27.

4. Marietta Brambilla (1807–1875), an Italian contralto who made her debut in London in Rossini's *Semiramide* in 1827. She was in the premiere of Donizetti's *Maria de Rohan* at the Théâtre des Italiens on November 14, 1843. See Weinstock, *Donizetti*, pp. 364–65; and *Grove's Dictionary of Music and Musicians*, ed. Eric Blom, VI, 587–88.

5. Probably the Storrows' nursemaid.

1661. To George Read

Legation of the United States. / Madrid January 12th 1844.

George Read Esqr. / U. S. Consul—Malaga.

Sir,

I have received your letter of the 5th. instant, enclosing a copy of the returns for the last six months, from which I regret to observe that the trade to the U. S. continues on the decline. Amid the existing restraints and difficulties under which it labors, nothing but a return of the strong and vigorous prosperity of the United States, which defies all obstacles, can restore it to its former condition.

It gives me great pleasure to be informed of the flattering acknowledgement of your services, which you have received from the Department of State: from the many opportunities I have had to judge of your conduct, I know that it was well deserved; and in my communications with the Department on this subject, I only expressed myself in the terms, which your active but prudent course naturally suggested: I hope you may long continue to Serve your country with equal Success and zeal, and,

am, Sir, / Very respectfully / Your Obdt Sevt
Washington Irving.

MANUSCRIPT: NA, RG 84 (letterbook copy).

1662. (deleted)

1663. To Edward Everett

Legation of the United States. / Madrid January 15th. 1844.

My dear Sir,

The application for Documents in relation to the North-Western Territory referred to in my letter of 23d. December last has not, I am sorry to inform you met with any success: The answer which was delayed beyond the period first mentioned was received only two days since, and was in substance to the effect that after a diligent search, none of the documents or papers mentioned in the note furnished to the Department of Foreign Affairs could be found among the archives of State.

A similar application made two months Since met with the same result; and the explanation then given was that on the removal of the Court from Seville to Cadiz in the year 1823,[1] a vessel laden with documents having been sunk in the river Guadalquivir, many files of official papers in the Department of Foreign affairs had been lost.

I procured for you from the Hydrographical Bureau here a copy of the voyage of the Spanish Schooners Sutil and Mexicana in 1792, which was forwarded by the French Courier to Mr. Ledyard two weeks since.

I am, my dear Sir, / with sincere respect, / Yours very truly,
Washington Irving.

His Excellency / Edward Everett / &ca. &ca. &ca.

MANUSCRIPT: NA, RG 84 (letterbook copy). Manning, *Diplomatic Correspondence: Canada*, III, 842.

1. On March 20, 1823, Ferdinand VII had moved the government from Madrid to Seville when pressed by French troops. Under similar pressures the court was moved from Seville to Cadiz in June, 1823. See H. Butler Clarke, *Modern Spain*, pp. 65–71; Raymond Carr, *Spain 1808–1939*, pp. 139–40; and Martin Hume, *Modern Spain*, pp. 230–45.

1664.   To John Miller

                    Legation of the United States. / Madrid January 15th. 1844.
£7.9.8.

At sight please pay John Miller or order. Seven pounds, nine shillings
and Eight pence sterling and charge the same to the United States on
account of the contingent expenses of this legation.

                                                           Washington Irving.
Messrs Baring, Brothers & Co.
Bankers of the U. States—London.

                    Legation of the United States. / Madrid January 15th. 1844.

John Miller Esqre. / U. S. Despatch Agent—London

Dear Sir,
    I received this morning your account in duplicate for postage &c paid
by you during the last quarter on account of this Legation.
    I enclose a check on Messrs Baring Brothers & Co. for the amount
£7.9.8 sterling payable to your order at Sight.

                                              Very respectfully. / Your obdt Sevt.
                                                           Washington Irving.

Manuscript: NA, RG 84 (letterbook copy).

1665.   To Sarah Irving

                                                    Madrid, Jany 19th. 1844.

My dear Sarah,
    I have to thank you for your letter of Novr. 25: which had all the flavor
of dear little Sunnyside about it. It gives me great satisfaction to find that
all things go on smoothly and pleasantly at the homestead; but they
could hardly do otherwise under such excellent management. I am
looking for accounts of the Christmas holydays, and trust to hear of the
cottage being duly dressed with evergreens, and that you all danced to
your hearts content: though it grieves me that I could not be there to
have my annual waltz. The account of Mary the cooks marriage to
Michael the gardner is certainly a very eventful chapter in the chronicles

of the Cottage. I now shall look forward with confidence ⟨for⟩ ↑to↓ that match which Helen Pierre used to predict for Mauncey; but ⟨which⟩ the very mention of which ⟨excited⟩ ↑⟨[unrecovered]⟩ used to excite↓ such indignation in Charlie.[1] I hope you all will make your contemplated visits to Julia Grinnell in the course of the winter; it will serve to break up the monotony of the season—though, for my part, if I could only be in my little cottage, looking out from its snug warm shelter upon the broad expanse of the Tappan Sea, all brilliant with snow and ice and sunshine, I think I should be loth to leave it for the city—but then what would suit a philosophic old gentleman, who has seen enough of the world and grown too wise for its gayeties, would hardly be to the taste of a bevy of young ladies for whom the world has still some novelty.

As you and I always talk over household affairs I must tell you how I passed my Christmas. My diplomatic family now consists of Mr Hamilton, and Mr Jasper Livingston attached to the Legation. The latter is a son of the late Brockholst Livingston of New York: in whose office I once read law. He is an extremely genteel young man; highly prepossessing in his appearance and manners, and politely accomplished. There happened to be two Americans in Madrid Mr Delaplaine of New York and Mr Partridge of Baltimore. These formed my dinner party both for Christmas and New Year day. We had no ladies to grace and enliven the table, or to dance with us in the evening; but it ⟨f⟩ had some thing of a home feeling that we were all Americans. Had I been well enough I should have asked Madame Albuquerque and Madame Calderon, the latter being half an American; but I was still too much of an invalid to play the gallant host. I must not omit to tell you that, under the directions of Mr Hamilton my cook succeeded in getting up some capital mince pies on these festive occasions, and served these up with a sauce boat of brandy sauce, in blue blazes, that would have horrified the temperance society.

Since these little Social repasts I have had to give a diplomatic dinner in consequence of the accession of the French Ambassador and the Ministers of Great Britain and ⟨Eng⟩ Naples to our diplomatic corps. This was an arduous undertaking for one in my half disabled condition; but I have a kind friend in Madame Albuquerque; who acts the part of a niece towards me, and who came and superintended the whole arrangement of my table, and my apartments. You must know that by her advice, and under the suggestions of her good taste, I have made quite a change this winter, in the arrangement of my rooms; if you look to the plan I once furnished Charlie you will understand it. The pink saloon, which used to be ⟨[unrecovered]⟩ half sitting room, half study, and furnished in an ordinary style, is now my saloon of reception; being newly papered, ⟨[unrecovered]⟩ with sunshiny yellow paper, and ↑decked out with↓ the blue silken furniture and curtains that used to figure in the first (or yellow) saloon It makes a delightful winter ⟨salo⟩ room; the large folding windows which descend to the floor, opening into the great glazed Verandah: which is like a conservatory. In the bright sunny winter days we need no fire in this room excepting ↑early↓ in the mornings, and after sun set; and the thermometer often rises to 70. This arrangement has given an air and a reality of comfort to my establishment which it wanted before in the winter season: and the furniture which appeared to but little advantage before, in the first saloon, which was a mere passage room, now gives my reception room a decided air of [?] elegance.

[At] [MS torn] my diplomatic dinner I had the Count de Bresson, Ambassador of France, Mr Bulwer the British Minister: the Prince de Carini, Minister from Naples; the Duke de Glucksburg the Prince de Broglie[2] and others of the Diplomatic Corps, with the Duke de Gor & others of the Spanish nobility. The dinner went off better than I had anticipated, and I felt greatly relieved in mind when it was over, but so fatigued in body; or rather so worried in my limbs from having to be so much on my legs, that I ⟨had to⟩ was almost knocked up for a day or two. I have now, however, got over the effects; and, as I decline all invitations and shall give no more big dinners, I shall be able to remain quiet and attend to my slow, but gradually advancing recovery. I cannot at present take exercise on foot, but I daily drive out in the carriage. I have a pair of excellent young horses, coal black. I wish you had as good and handsome a pair at the Cottage. My domestic concerns are under the management of Lorenzo, the best and most faithful of servants, under whose superintendence every thing goes on regularly, and at much less expense than formerly.

Thus my dear Sarah, I have given you a detail of my housekeeping, knowing it to be so much in your line; and only ask in return that you will give me further accounts of the internal affairs of the Cottage; which I regard as peculiarly under your charge.

Give my love to all its dear inmates and believe me ever my excellent little girl, Your affectionate uncle

Washington Irving

ADDRESSED: Miss Sarah Irving / Care of E. Irving Esqr / ⟨New York⟩ ↑Tarrytown↓ /
      Westchester Co / N Y — POSTMARKED: [NEW-]YORK / FEB / 21
MANUSCRIPT: Sarah Grinnell Metzger.   PUBLISHED: PMI, III, 315 (in part).

1. Charlotte Van Wart Irving, Sarah's sister and Ebenezer's youngest daughter.
2. Jacques-Victor-Albert, duc de Broglie (1821–1901), after completing his studies of law, entered diplomacy in November, 1843, as second secretary of the French legation in Madrid. After about five years of service in Madrid, London, and

Rome, he retired to devote himself to the writing of history. See Dominique de Broglie, *Les Broglie, leur histoire* (Paris, [1972]), pp. 148–57.

1666. To A. P. Upshur

Legation of the United States. / Madrid. January 19th. 1844.

No. 35. / The Hon: A. P. Upshur, / Secretary of State of the U. States.

Sir,

In my despatch No. 33, I noticed the critical state of affairs growing out of the introduction before the Cortes of the declaration of the Queen, accusing Mr. Olozaga, the ex-minister of state, of outrageous conduct towards her, in compelling her signature of a decree dissolving the Cortes. The violent altercations rising out of the subject for some time convulsed the house, and agitated the public mind; while they completely dismembered the already shattered coalition.[1] A loyal address to the Queen, on the part of the Congress of Deputies, in consequence of her declaration of "the deplorable events of the evening of the 28th. November," after Several days of animated discussion, in which the leaders of the progresista party came out in Support of Mr. Olozaga, was voted by a large majority; thus showing that the Ministers still held possession of the house. A Commission was appointed to examine into the circumstances of the case, and to determine whether there were grounds for criminal proceedings against Mr. Olozaga; an investigation solicited by himself. Before, however, the commission had time to make a report, or even to enter upon the business, the Cortes was suddenly and indefinitely suspended. This was immediately after a session in which the Ministry were assailed by a crowd of interpellations, each involving or threatening to involve prolonged discussions; and in the course of which Mr. Gonzalez Bravo, the Minister of State, was severely attacked, and had twice the lie given him by his late coadjutors. The reasons given for thus abruptly suspending the Cortes were, that there was evidently a plan to impede all business by incessant interpellations, and that the Ministry were determined to set on foot, by decree, certain laws long required by the exigencies of the nation, but constantly lost in the discussions of the chamber; and it was added that, after these laws were decreed, the Chambers would be reassembled, and these intermediate transactions submitted to their arbitrament, in the hope of a bill of indemnity. It is said, however, that a main object in suspending the Chambers was to get rid of the Olozaga question, which, if investigated, threatened to lead to revelations of palace Secrets, and of diplomatic transactions when Mr. Olozaga was Serving the coalition at the Court of the Tuilleries:[2] Indeed Mr. Olozaga had more than once hinted, in the course of his recent speeches, that he stopped short in his defence, and forbore entering upon matters or producing documents which might be forced from him if urged to extremity. It is certain that the abrupt suspension of the Cortes, when the Ministry apparently had a large majority; when various important subjects were pressing for consideration; and when even the ways and means had not been voted; surprised and displeased many even of the Moderados, who may not have been initiated into the secret motives of the Cabinet. About the same time the secret flight of Mr. Olozaga to Portugal occasioned scarcely less surprise, after the confident tone and manner which he had maintained in the Cortes, and it was triumphantly adduced by the Moderados as a proof of consciousness of guilt and craven fear of punishment. A letter from Mr. Olozaga,[3] just published, however, declares that he was reluctantly and with difficulty brought to adopt this precaution of Safety in consequence of the threats of his enemies, the urgent advice of his friends and the circumstance of finding himself repeatedly in personal peril, being watched and waylaid. That immediately on his arrival in Portugal he had addressed a letter to the commissioners stating his readiness to return the moment their commission was regularly opened and that his presence was deemed necessary.

Since the suspension of the Cortes the Bravo Ministry have proceeded with a kind of mongrel policy; constantly professing orthodox principles but committing *unavoidable* Sins. They declare themselves convinced that the great majority of the nation is with them, but in the mean time they are filling up and reorganizing the army; keeping it well clad, well fed, and well paid,[4] and stationing it about the kingdom; evidently depending upon it as their main support. They are cultivating, too, the good will of the clergy, knowing that, notwithstanding its impoverishment and decline, this is still a powerful agent in influencing the lower classes. They are making a sweeping change in offices great and small throughout the kingdom, and generating a new, and as they hope, loyal class of employès. They have revived, with some modification, the decree concerning ayuntamientos,[5] passed by the Cortes in 1840, but condemned by the people, and which was the stumbling block of the regency of Maria Christina. By this they hope to centralize the civic power and prevent future pronunciamientos.

The Ministry, however, have just received an ominous check in the recent election held in the city and province of Madrid to replace several deputies who had been appointed to office. The opposition placed the name of Olozaga at the head of their list, and carried their whole ticket by a large majority. The reelection of Olozaga, by electors residing in the capital and its neighbourhood, under the very walls, as it were, of the royal palace, is hailed by the progresistas as the triumph of public opinion and individual right over Court intrigue and the prestige of the throne. The moderados decry it as a scandal, impugning the veracity of the youthful Queen and attacking the Monarchical principle. The effect that these elections at the capital may have on other elections throughout the kingdom is a matter of alarm to the Ministerialists. By the multiplicity of recent appointments, between forty and fifty seats have become vacant on the ministerial side of the house. Should the elections be adverse, as is apprehended, the Ministry will lose its majority in the Chamber. In view of such a probability there is already talk of a dissolution of the Cortes; this would be avoiding one evil by plunging into another, but such is the sad, make-shift nature of Spanish politics.

The great want of the Moderado party is a concentration of talent and moral worth in the Cabinet[.] Unfortunately the men of commanding respectability of the Moderado party shrink from responsability. Some of them, like Martinez de la Rosa,[6] accept places of honor and profit which take them abroad, out of the reach of party collisions, and thus weaken the ranks at home; but in general they look ahead to the possibility of further revolutions, and fear to undertake any political charge which may bring upon them future proscription and exile. Thus the affairs of the country are left to the management of adventurous, aspiring and too often unprincipled politicians, who have every thing to gain and nothing to lose; and who are destitute of the respect and confidence of the nation

Among the signs and portents of coming evils are said to be jealousies among the leading military men: Narvaez, who is an able and intrepid soldier, and a man of energy and address, exerts great influence in the Cabinet and the palace, and has been decried as a kind of military dictator. His celebrity and the honors that have been heaped upon him, have awakened the jealousy of the Generals Concha, and Serrano, who consider themselves equally efficient in rearing up the present government; but who find themselves completely eclipsed by their late coadjutor. This, it is suggested, may lead to fatal schisms at head quarters; if not to a change of the military dictatorship.

I have thus given a few of the elements of discord which are at work to prolong the distractions of this unfortunate country. To enter into a minute detail, where every thing is intrigue, falsehood and inconsistency, would be a perplexing and an unprofitable task.

The Queen Mother, Maria Christina is expected here in the course of next month.[7] It is diligently given to understand that she comes merely on a visit to see her daughters; that she intends to take no part in political affairs, and that, if any thing, her tendencies would be to uphold the constitution in its purity. The youthful Queen certainly stands in need of such a friend and counsellor as a mother of judgment, virtue, and experience might prove; but it is doubted whether the arrival of Maria Christina might not revive former hostilities, excite additional rancor and add to the perils of the throne. Her arrival, too, at a time when the decree of the Ayuntamientos is forced upon the nation contrary to the popular will, may again identify her with that hazardous attack upon those municipal rights of which the Spaniards are so tenacious.

Among other rumors it is said that the Moderados, feeling their own weakness as a party, and observing that the ranks of the opposition are swelling by the coalition of various factions, are inclined to make a league with the Carlists, on the basis of the marriage of the Queen with the eldest son of the Pretender.[8] Such a league might give them a temporary accession of strength, but it would again arouse the bitter animosity of the late civil war. Such a marriage, too, made under such auspices, though it might settle the question of succession to the throne, might awaken hostility to the throne itself, and might hurry the opposition party into the revolutionary extreme of republicanism.

In this critical state are affairs at present; in a lulling pause between political convulsions: but experienced lookers on dread further and more violent paroxysms, and lament that these continual shocks and changes lead to no definite good; but threaten national exhaustion and decline.

Since my last political communication the French Ambassador, the Count de Bresson, and Mr. Bulwer the British Minister have arrived here. The Ambassador has a difficult and delicate part to perform; being much looked to by the dominant party and his government being deeply committed in the present state of affairs; and being obliged to act under the watchful eye of a public, jealous of foreign interference, and cautioned against french ascendancy. A man of probity and intelligence, and sincerely disposed to do what is right, the Ambassador appears to be completely confounded and dismayed by the political chaos before him and at a loss how to proceed. Mr. Bulwer has an easier task. He is cool and self possessed; regards the tissue of perplexities before him, as one in which his government has no responsability, and, while he professes general good will, seems disposed to remain a looker on while others puzzle through the game they have commenced.

I would observe that a perfect good understanding and friendly intercourse prevails between the rival diplomatists.

While there has been such a liberal sharing out of honors and offices, the place of Minister Plenipotentiary to the United States remains vacant. Mr. Calderon de la Barca who is here, has been talked of for the appointment. He would be much pleased to have it, and I should think his appointment would be acceptable to our government. It has been hinted to me, however, that Mr. Gonzalez Bravo holds the place in reserve, as a provision for himself, in case the course of events should render it expedient for him to retire from the Cabinet.

A despatch, not numbered,—in order No. 18,—and dated August 7th. 1842, was not received until the 29th. December last; having been forwarded in a bundle of Newspapers by way of Cadiz. Its directions in relation to Mr. Cooke's commission as Consul at Trinidad were complied with on the 2nd. January, by an application for the usual exequatur in his behalf.[9]

I have the honor to enclose the accounts and vouchers of the Legation for the quarter ending December 31st. 1843, by which there appears a balance of $14.16, against the United States, which will be carried to their debit in the next account.

I am, Sir, / Very respectfully / Your obdt Sevt.

Washington Irving

Docketed: Recd. April 19/11 / Mr. Markoe [top of page 1] / No. 35. W. Irving, Madrid, 19 Jany. 1844

Manuscript: NA, RG 59.   Published: STW, II, 167, 171 (in part).

1. The coalition which overthrew Espartero was made up of members of the left who wanted to bring back the López cabinet and the Progressives and members of the right who wanted to eliminate leftist soldiers from controlling the army. See Christiansen, *Military Power*, p. 116.

2. Olózaga had served as minister to France between 1840 and 1843.

3. See *El Eco del Comercio*, January 19, 1844.

4. Low pay was a frequent cause of military unrest and insurrection. See Carr, *Spain 1808–1939*, p. 226.

5. This provided for appointment of the mayors of municipalities by politicians of the central government, thus reducing the local autonomy. See Christiansen, *Military Power*, p. 95.

6. At this time Martínez de la Rosa was Spanish minister to France. See London *Times*, January 19, 1844.

7. She returned to Spain to rejoin her daughters on April 4, 1844. See Peter de Polnay, *A Queen of Spain*, p. 89. *El Castellano* (January 19, 1844) printed a report from Paris that María Christina would return to Spain in the early days of February.

8. Carlos, count de Montemolín (1818–1861), Isabella's first cousin. See Aronson, *Royal Vendetta*, pp. 49–50.

9. See WI to Luis González Bravo, January 2, 1844.

1667.   To Pierre M. Irving

[Madrid,] January 20, 1844

* * * I feel sadly the loss of the past year, which has disconcerted all those literary plans I formed on leaving home. However, I still hope

the opening year, or at least a part of it, may be more profitably employed.

Give my love to my dear Helen, whose letters are perfect balm to me when I am in a moody fit, as I am apt to be sometimes, when my cure does not go on as well as I could wish. I will write to her before long, so beg her to send the answer in advance.

PUBLISHED: PMI, III, 315–16.

1668. To Catharine Paris

Madrid Jany 20th 1844

My dear Sister,

I believe it is now a year since I concluded a fagging course of literary application by writing a letter to you; after which I threw by the pen to indulge in a relaxation which I felt was necessary. I threw it by too late, as I had laid the foundation of that malady which has ever since harrassed me, and made the past year a literary blank to me. I have brought the malady back to Madrid with me, and, in consequence of being obliged, for some time after my return, to be too much on my legs, I have had somewhat troublesome attacks of it. I once more trust, however, that I am in the way of gradually getting clear of it; and mean to keep quiet and avoid every thing that may retard my cure.

The public papers will have shewn you that the entrance of the poor little Queen upon her reign has been the commencement of troubles. Mr Olozaga, the Minister of State, and one of the leading men of the coalition that overthrew Espartero; was suddenly dismissed from office, and accused by the Queen with having, when alone with her in her cabinet, treated her in an arrogant and imperious manner, insisting on her signing a decree dissolving the Cortes, and actually bolting the doors and preventing her leaving the room until she had so given her signature. This accusation has produced a prodigious effect in the political world. Mr Olozaga has defended himself in the Chamber of Deputies declaring that the Queen signed the decree voluntarily, ⟨and⟩ that the accusation was dictated to the Queen by a ⟨knot⟩ Camarilla, or knot of court intriguers, who surround her, and that the whole was a Palace intrigue, designed to produce his downfall. The whole party of Progresistas, who had been in league with the Moderados, broke from the coalition and espoused the side of Mr Olozaga; and the members of the cabinet who were of that party, resigned their posts and came out in defence of the fallen minister. A commission was appointed to examine into the circumstances of the case and to ascertain whether there were grounds for criminal proceedings against Mr Olozaga;

in the mean time, ⟨finding himself⟩ the latter secretly fled to Portugal; declaring by letter that he did so in consequence of finding himself waylaid and threatened with assassination, but that he was ready to return and appear before the commission whenever the investigation should be ⟨of⟩ commenced and his presence required.

The misfortune of all this is, that it places the veracity of the Queen in the ballance with that of a subject; and that the public seem inclined to decide in favor of the latter: since, in a recent election to supply vacancies in the chamber of deputies, ↑⟨the [unrecovered]⟩↓ Mr Olozaga has been placed at the head of the list of opposition candidates, and elected by a large majority. This is hailed as a great triumph by the progresista party; but it appears to me ominous to the throne, and shews that the prestige which so lately surrounded the youthful Queen, is already impaired by party rancor.

My idea is that this famous scene in the cabinet of the Queen has not been fairly stated by either party; each having perhaps unconsciously, given it an after colouring. A jealousy evidently existed between Olozaga and those in the Palace who were daily about the Queen. He suspected them of seeking his downfall. When the Queen hesitated to sign the decree dissolving the Cortes he no doubt supposed ↑that↓ she acted, not from her own judgement or inclination, but from the instigations of others, his enemies. Accustomed in his former office as tutor, to treat her with great familiarity, and to look upon her as a child, rather than as his sovereign; ⟨he now exacts that⟩ and vexed that his present measures of state policy should be impeded by the mere wilfulness of an inexperienced girl; he probably became authoritative and peremptory, like a tutor ⟨with his⟩ enforcing a necessary task upon his pupil, and the Queen acquiesced as a matter of course; without, probably, feeling outraged by his dictatorial conduct.

It may not have been until afterwards, when her palace advisors, ⟨informed her of the⟩ exclaimed against the dangerous nature of the decree which she had signed, that, ⟨she⟩ like a child, she sought to excuse herself by saying Mr Olozaga made her sign it; and then was made aware by those experienced courtiers, of the terrible infraction of sovereign dignity perpetuated by Mr Olozaga and of the gross outrage she had unconsciously sustained. Of course, she then saw the whole ⟨mat⟩ affair in a different light; her ire was kindled, and ↑in↓ her subsequent accounts facts were colored and exaggerated by her feelings. Such would commonly be the case with the statements of a child under similar circumstances; and after all the poor little Queen, though the Cortes has solemnly declared her of age, is but a child. I cannot explain this matter to myself in any other manner, without thinking either that the little Queen has been guilty of a wanton and unprofitable falsehood,

or that Mr Olozaga has acted like a *fool* as well as a brute. I have no
great opinion of Mr Olozagas principles or manners. He has been a
shifting, intriguing politician, and during his elevation to ⟨a place⟩
office, which brought him in immediate proximity with the Sovereign,
he displayed a forward, and, at times, jocose familiarity, which shewed
he was unaccustomed to the etiquette of courts, ⟨and⟩ unconscious of
the high decorum and almost sanctity which should surround the royal
person, and incapable of the dignified ↑yet modest↓ self command and
self respect proper to a statesman in his elevated position: he is, however, a shrewd, able man, and could scarcely have been *intentionally*
guilty of such an outrage upon the Royal will and dignity, as might be
inferred by a rigorous view of his conduct in this transaction; he probably was not aware of the construction ⟨that⟩ of which his conduct was
susceptible, nor thought that while he was exercising the authority of a
tutor on a ⟨wilful⟩ refractory pupil, he, as a Minister, was outraging the
dignity of a Sovreign.

You now see what ↑in↓ a critical situation the poor little Queen is
placed by being declared of age. She has now to exercise the functions
of a Sovereign, while her mind is immature; her character unfixed;
when she has no one at hand of talent integrity and distinterested devotion, to whom she can look for council; ⟨and⟩ when she is surrounded
by court flatterers and court intriguers of both sexes, and when even
her ministers are faithless. Already she is becoming an object of party
hostility, though it is not openly avowed; and the late triumphant re
election of Olozaga, in thus returning him ↑to the Cortes↓ to confront
his sovereign, as it were, in her own capital, before the charges against
him are investigated, shews the disposition of the opposition party to
prejudge the case in his favor. As I observed before I draw from this
election a sad presage of the future fortunes of the Queen. Her mother,
Maria Christina, is expected to return to Madrid in the course of February or March; professedly to make a visit to her children, without any
intention of interfering in politics. The poor little Queen is certainly
in want of such a friend and councellor as a mother of Maria Christinas
age and experience might prove, and I sincerely hope that the latter may
be able to guide and guard her during her very immature years; but
I fear the return of the queen mother will revive old hostilities against
herself and extend them to her daughter. ⟨The question⟩

We have had ⟨an⟩ important additions to the diplomatic circle. The
Count de Bresson, Ambassador of France. Mr Henry Lytton Bulwer
(brother of the novellist)[1] minister from G Britain and the Prince de
Carini, Minister from Naples. I am very much pleased with the Count
de Bresson. He appears to be an upright, intelligent straight forward
man; more of a German in his appearance and manners than a French-

man, probably from having resided upwards of twelve years at Berlin. He is tall, and stout in proportion, and of frank, grave, sincere deportment. He has been highly reccommended to me by our Berlin Minister Mr Wheaton,[2] who has known him for twenty years, and all that I have seen of him confirms the reccommendation. He is thoroughly in the confidence of Louis Philippe, and considered one of his ablest diplomatists, and it shews the sagacity of that most sagacious of monarchs, to send a ⟨S⟩ man of such experience and such a reliable character to conduct French diplomacy at this court during the present critical times. I consider his presence here as contributing much towards the security of the spanish throne

Count de Bresson has strong American feelings: having during his youth been attached to the French Legation at Washington and passed some years in the United States where he married (his first wife) a daughter of Judge Thompson of New York.[3] His present wife, to whom he has been married about two or three years, is ⟨a⟩ very amiable and pleasing in appearance and manners: ⟨with⟩ and quite domestic in her feelings. They live within three minutes walk of my house; and are disposed to be very friendly. I have no doubt, that, as soon as I am in visiting condition I shall see them frequently.

Mr Bulwer, the representative of John Bull, is as little fitted to be the representative of such a burly personage as possible. He is a genteel looking man, but excessively thin, pale and emaciated; having the appearance of man who has been withered and wasted by the artificial life of saloons; "a man who has been knocking about the world by candle light" as was well observed of him. He looks to me like a pencil sketch nearly rubbed out. He has talent however and address; is quiet and observant: cool and almost listless in his manner: moving about noiselessly like a cat and like a cat having a *patte de velours*[4] with a concealed claw, ⟨ready to be⟩ slightly unsheathed now and then, just enough to let you know that he could scratch if ⟨pos⟩ need be. He sets out with an apparent determination to ⟨be⟩ make himself popular: professing himself pleased with every thing and every body; yet he cannot help, now and then, in his cool quiet way, letting slip a satyrical word or two, ⟨that⟩ ↑which↓ shew to me how he could clapper claw if he chose. We are on very good terms: he having paid me marked attentions when I was in Paris the year before last,[5] on my way to Madrid. I trust to find in him an amusing acquaintance; but he can never supply the place of my frank, cordial, generous hearted friend Mr Aston.

The Prince de Carini I have as yet seen but little of. He certainly is not as handsome as a prince in fairy tale, but he appears to be social, good humored and conciliating in his manner. He has brought with him a young wife; ⟨Fren⟩ a parisian, rather handsome, with remarkably fine eyes; and for whom I have conceived a favorable opinion from her resembling Rebecca McLane. The ladies, here, criticise her severely as deficient in the true *haut ton* of the Faubourg ⟨San⟩ St Germain, the true test of Parisian aristocracy. She, however, is young and joyous; appears delighted with her rank: with the official station of her husband, talks of her jewels, and of her child, a little prince of a few months old whom she left behind in Italy but intends to have brought on as soon as he is old enough to bear the journey While the other newly arrived members of the diplomatic circle are complaining of the comfortless character of their habitations though among the best in Madrid; the Princess who is really most miserably lodged, expresses herself perfectly satisfied. "Upon my word," said one of the young French diplomatists, ["]if the Princess finds her lodgings tolerable I should not be surprised if she should think her husband handsome."[6] For my part, from all the cavilling that I have heard about the princess, I am disposed to feel a great good will toward her, and shall certainly seek to know more of her when I resume my intercourse with society. I am pleased to find, from a private conversation with her husband, that he thinks her perfection.

So much for politics and gossip—for domestic affairs I must refer you to a letter written to little dame Sarah at the cottage, and must now conclude with "love to all bodies"

Your affectionate brother
Washington Irving

ADDRESSED: Mrs Daniel Paris / Care of E. Irving Esqr / New York.   POSTMARKED:
[*unrecovered*] / FEB / 19
MANUSCRIPT: Va.–Barrett.   PUBLISHED: PMI, III, 316–19 (in part).

1. Edward George Earle Lytton Bulwer, First Baron Lytton (1803–1873) was a prolific historical novelist.

2. Henry Wheaton was the U.S. minister to Prussia.

3. Bresson had married Catherine Livingston Thompson in 1830. Her father was Smith Thompson (1768–1843), a jurist who was associate justice of the U.S. Supreme Court from 1824 until his death.

4. "Velvet paw."

5. WI had met Bulwer, then secretary of the British legation, at a reception given by Louis Philippe on June 4, 1842, and subsequently dined with him on June 7. The two men met socially in Paris on several other occasions. See *Journals of WI*, III, 210, 213, 216–17.

6. WI omitted the bracketed quotation marks.

1669. To Sarah Storrow

Madrid Jany 21. 184(3)4

My dear Sarah,

I received a few days since your letter of the 9th. inst. which I confess
I had been looking for with some impatience. In fact I had been much
depressed in spirits, as perhaps my last letters evinced; being harrassed
by an access of my tormenting malady; which when it recurs at present,
after such a long course of assiduous treatment, almost drives me to
despair. At present I am again better, and, as usual, my hopes and
spirits are again lifted up; to be again, perhaps, cast down. I fear I am
growing miserly over the remnant of existence, and cannot bear to have
any of the few years that remain to me wasted as the last has been. I
hope this year I may live more to the purpose; other wise, it is a heavy
tax to pay for mere existence.

I must refer you to the enclosed letters to your mother & Sarah
Irving, for details about public and private affairs. To your mother
I only write about courts and queens and princes; but to little Dame
Sarah I give an account of household matters

Let me have a budget about Kate. Have you got a larger crib for her
to romp in in the evenings; does she take her usual gambol before
going to bed. Has she ⟨learnt⟩ ↑cut↓ any new teeth or learnt any new
capers; does she begin to string words together; and does she quarrel
about her bread & butter as much as ever. I am sure you might write
a long letter about her, and I will assure you I should read and re read
every word of it. Give her a kiss and a *bang*; and tell her Unty sent
them; I think she will reccollect me best by the latter.

When you see Mrs Mary Jones[1] tell her I congratulate her on the
birth of her *grand* daughter; and be sure to lay an emphasis upon
"Grand"; for you know Mrs Mary delights in every thing that comes
under that ⟨apellation⟩ ↑classification↓. Tell her that, though the child
is but a baroness in her infancy I have strong hopes that she may grow
up to be a duchess.

With kind remembrances to Mr Storrow

Your affectionate uncle
Washington Irving

ADDRESSED: Madame / Madame Storrow / No 4 Rue de la Victoire / a Paris
MANUSCRIPT: Yale.

1. Probably the Mrs. Jones who married the duke of Breteuil at the time her
daughter married his son, the count of Breteuil. See WI to Sarah Storrow, September 10 and December 24, 1842.

1670. To Luis González Bravo

Legation of the United States. / Madrid January 25th. 1844.

The Undersigned Envoy Extraordinary and Minister Plenipotentiary of the United States has the honor to solicit the attention of His Excellency Don Luis Gonzalez Bravo, First Minister of State and of Foreign Affairs of Her Catholic Majesty to certain circumstances in the Quarantine Regulations of the Canary Islands. According to these regulations as at present interpreted and enforced, all vessels arriving from the United States from the 1st. of June to the end of November are obliged to perform a quarantine of observation of eight days; while vessels from England and other parts of Europe are admitted to *immediate pratique*.[1] Now the trade of the United States with the Canary Islands is carried on from the ports of Norfolk, Baltimore, Philadelphia, New york, and Boston; *Ports as healthy as those of England.* From ports south of Norfolk; which might be considered suspicious, there is no trade with the Canaries. Another grievance sustained by Ships from the United States, is that, whatever may be their port of destination in the Canaries, they are obliged to perform their quarantine at *the port of Santa Cruz in the island of Trinidad.*

The effect of this last regulation is often very injurious: If vessels were permitted to perform their quarantine in the port of their destination, they might be securely harboured and during the time of quarantine, be permitted to land the unobjectionable parts of their Cargoes; thus expediting the time of their departure. Being sent to Santa Cruz however they lose the whole term of quarantine, and the time of going thither and returning; besides incurring the risks of the Sea and of being obliged to anchor in an open roadstead.

The Undersigned will barely instance two cases, one, the Brig Sarah Deering which sailed from New york the 16th. October 1842, *with a clean bill of health certified by the Spanish Consul.* She arrived at her port of destination in the Island of the Grand Canary, but was ordered to Santa Cruz to perform the quarantine of observation. Here she was obliged to anchor in very deep water, near a ledge of rocks, and was blown out to Sea with the loss of her anchors. The detention and delay thus occasioned affected the fortunes of her voyage and caused her ultimate Shipwreck.

Another vessel the Isaac Franklin arriving 16th. October 1843, at Orotava[2] from Norfolk in Virginia with a Cargo of staves and *with a clean bill of health signed by the Spanish Consul,* was ordered to Santa Cruz for 8 days quarantine. She likewise was blown out to Sea; and her detention was at least thirty days, at an expense of fifteen dollars a day.

These are only two cases which happen to come within the knowledge of the Undersigned, but which he cites as instances of the losses and embarrassments caused to vessels of the United States by these regulations.

The Undersigned would observe that the Canary Islands are dependent upon Foreigners for the Sale of their produce; and particularly upon vessels from the United States. The latter are their best customers for one of the staple articles of produce of the Islands, Barilla.[3] A liberal and enlightened policy, therefore, would dictate every facility and accommodation to such ships in their traffic with the island; and more especially at present, when the general trade of the Canaries is in a very paralyzed state, and needs the fostering care of government to revive and invigorate it.

The Undersigned is informed that these vexatious regulations do not emanate from the general government at Madrid, but arise from the misconstructions or misapprehensions of its ordinances by the provincial Junta of Sanidad of Sta. Cruz; made, it is hinted, with a view to monopolize, for that port, all the trade of the islands. He is informed that the general ordinance of the Junta Suprema de Sanidad at Madrid, dated 28th. December 1835, specifies as subject to the quarantine of observation, all vessels from *the Antilles and the Gulf of Mexico*; and that this, by forced construction on the part of the provincial Junta, is made to apply to all vessels of the United States, however northern and healthy the latitudes whence they may come.

The object of this application on the part of the Undersigned, therefore, is most respectfully to solicit, that these regulations, whatever may be the quarter in which they have originated, may receive the early attention of Her Majesty's Government, and be either repealed, or so modified, as to meet the interests of the various ports of the Islands, and to relieve the ships of a friendly nation, from impediments and losses to which the ships of other Nations are not subjected.

If Her Majesty's Government should See fit to continue to enforce the quarantine of observation, the Undersigned would suggest that the ports of the United States should be discriminated which come under its provisions; and that vessels, with clean bills of health, from unquestionably healthy latitudes, should be exempted from its embarrassments, and, like those from England, be admitted to immediate pratique.

The Undersigned would also solicit, that all vessels of the United States, subject to quarantine, should be permitted to perform it at the port of their destination.

The Undersigned has been encouraged to urge this application at the present moment by observing the awakening attention and zeal on the part of Her Majesty's government, to place the various interests of the Kingdom on a liberal and prosperous footing; and he feels satisfied that Her Majesty's Government will be well disposed to relieve from all unnecessary embarrassments the Commercial intercourse with a nation which has ever cherished for Spain the sincerest amity.

The Undersigned avails himself of this occasion to offer to His Excellency renewed assurances of his distinguished consideration.

Washington Irving.

MANUSCRIPT: NA, RG 84 (letterbook copy).

Another copy was enclosed with WI's despatch no. 36, February 6, 1844, to A. P. Upshur.

1. "Permission or license granted to a ship to hold intercourse with a port after quarantine or showing a clean bill of health" (*OED*).

2. A town on Tenerife in the Canary Islands.

3. A maritime plant which, when burned, produces an alkaline powder used in making soda, soap, and glass.

1671. To Luis González Bravo

Legation of the United States / Madrid January 30th. 1844

The Undersigned Envoy Extraordinary and Minister Plenipotentiary of the United States had the honor a few days since to solicit the attention of His Excellency Don Luis Gonzalez Bravo, First Minister of State and of Foreign affairs of Her Catholic Majesty to certain circumstances in the administration of the quarantine laws in the Canary Islands. The Undersigned now begs leave to call His Excellency's attention to another circumstance in the administration of those laws.

According to recent regulations of the Government of the United States there will constantly be a Squadron of vessels of war cruising upon the coast of Africa.[1] It is highly desirable that these Ships should have free access to the Canary Islands, as a healthful resort during these arduous cruisings; and as places where they may obtain provisions and where bills of exchange for the supply of funds may be favorably negotiated.

With a view to such accommodations, Commodore Perry,[2] the Commander of the Squadron visited the port of Santa Cruz last June in his flag ship, the Macedonian,[3] recently from New york; but to his surprize was obliged to perform a quarantine of 8 days. as this was a regulation never exacted from English Ships, in a like State of health, and as he understood it was not authorised by any orders from Madrid; he was constrained to attribute it to some local unwillingness on the part of the authorities to receive visits from United States ships of war.

He was strengthened in this supposition by the conduct of the public functionaries, four of whom he waited upon, on obtaining pratique, yet not one of whom returned his call. What made this official neglect of etiquette the more remarkable was that, the anniversary of the independence of the United States, occurring about this time, he fired three national salutes on the occasion.

As the Undersigned is persuaded that it is the wish and intention of Her Majesty's Government to facilitate in every way the friendly intercourse of the two nations, and, as the advantages which must accrue to the trade of the islands themselves from the furnishing the supplies to a considerable squadron, and the negotiation of the funds for their payment,—are obvious; he is convinced that this impediment thrown in the way of American ships of war in their visits to the Canary islands, and this instance of official disrespect to the Commander of the United States Squadron and consequently to the flag of the nation can only have originated in some local interest and jealousy.

He is satisfied moreover that he has merely to point out these facts to the intelligent mind of his Excellency Don Luis Gonzalez Bravo, to have their recurrence promptly obviated, and to procure for the vessels of war of the United States such facilities and such courteous reception in the ports of the Canary Islands, as are due to the vessels of a friendly power, and as are extended to the ships of other Nations.

The Undersigned is happy to avail himself of this occasion to offer to His Excellency the assurance of his distinguished consideration

Washington Irving.

MANUSCRIPT: NA, RG 84 (letterbook copy).

Another copy was enclosed with WI's despatch no. 36, February 6, 1844, to A. P. Upshur.

1. The African Squadron was patrolling against ships picking up slaves for sale in the Western hemisphere. See Fletcher Pratt, *The Navy, A History*, pp. 222–23, 230.

2. Matthew C. Perry, who had been WI's neighbor in the Tarrytown area a few years earlier.

3. The *Macedonian*, a thirty-six-gun frigate placed in service in 1836, was assigned to the West India Squadron and also cruised along the western coast of Africa as a deterrent to Caribbean pirates. See *Dictionary of American Naval Fighting Ships* (Washington, 1969), IV, 179–80.

1672. To Luis González Bravo

Legation of the United States. / Madrid January 31st. 1844.

The Undersigned Envoy Extraordinary and Minister Plenipotentiary of the United States, has the honor to acknowledge the receipt of the note of His Excellency Don Luis Gonzalez Bravo, First Minister of State and of Foreign affairs of Her Catholic Majesty, informing him of the sudden and untimely death of Her Royal Highness, The Infanta Doña Luisa Carlota.[1]

The Undersigned will hasten to communicate this melancholy intelligence to his government; which, ever taking a deep interest in every thing concerning the royal family and the government of Spain, cannot fail to condole with them, over this afflicting and unlooked for deprivation.

The Undersigned avails himself of this occasion to renew to His Excellency the assurance of his distinguished consideration.

Washington Irving.

MANUSCRIPT: NA, RG 84 (letterbook copy).

1. González Bravo's note of January 29 informed WI of the demise of Luisa Carlota (b. 1804) at 5:00 P.M. of a severe attack of the measles which had lasted only two days (NR, RG 84). See also *La Gaceta* and *El Castellano*, January 30, 31, 1844. More details of her death and the funeral arrangements are given in *El Castellano*, February 1, 1844.

1673. To Luis González Bravo

Legation of the United States. / Madrid February 2nd. 1844.

The Undersigned Envoy Extraordinary and Minister Plenipotentiary of the United States, has the honor to acknowledge the receipt of the note of His Excellency Don Luis Gonzalez Bravo, First Minister of State and of Foreign affairs of Her Catholic Majesty dated February 1st. accompanied by a Gazette of the same date, containing the decree of the Minister of Marine,[1] ordering the blockade of the port of Alicant[2] in consequence of revolutionary movements.

The Undersigned will not fail communicating this important intelligence to his government; and in the mean time avails himself of this occasion to renew to His Excellency Don Luis Gonzalez Bravo the assurrance of his distinguished consideration.

Washington Irving.

MANUSCRIPT: NA, RG 84 (letterbook copy).

1. The minister of marine was named Portillo. See London *Times*, February 1, 1844.

2. For details, see *El Castellano*, February 1, 6, 1844.

1674. To A. P. Upshur

Legation of the United States / Madrid February 6th. 1844.

No. 36 / The Hon A. P. Upshur,
    Secretary of State of the U.S—Washington.

Sir,

The Court of Spain has suddenly been put into mourning by the death of the Infanta Maria Carlota, wife of the Infante Don Francisco and Aunt of the Queen. It took place before the public were aware of her illness, and was the consequence of a combined attack of pulmonia and measles, which hurried her out of existence in the course of two or three days in the 39th. year of her age. She was a woman of strong passions and ⟨great⟩ ↑restless↓ ambition; and her schemes and intrigues for the advancement of her immediate family, and especially for the marriage of her son, the Duke of Cadiz, with the young Queen, have tended much to complicate and embroil the affairs of Spain. The failure of these plans; and the odium, impoverishment and neglect they had brought upon herself are said to have exasperated her feelings and to have produced an absolute fever of the mind which immediately preceded her illness and probably contributed to render it fatal.

An insurrection has recently broken out in Alicant, headed by one Colonel Pantaleon Bonet or Boné,[1] formerly a *faccioso* or semi political robber, recently a commander of Carabiniers in the service of the revenue. This worthy entered Alicant on the 29th. January with between three and four hundred men, horse and foot, as if on an enterprize against smugglers; but in the course of the night surprised the castle as well as the barracks; obliged the garrison to capitulate and imprisoned the civil and military authorities and other persons of note. A Junta of Government was then formed with Bonet as President and a proclamation issued denouncing the actual ministry as originating in falsehood and deception, and as basely begging the support of the Carlists: and vowing never to lay down arms until the Constitution was reformed; ending with the words "down with the Ministry, the *Camarilla*, and the law of Ayuntamientos in the name of *the Sovereignty of the people*.["] A circular was also directed to the Ayuntamientos ↑of the province↓ calling for their co-operation.

On receiving intelligence of this affair, Government instantly fulminated a set of decrees of unwonted severity. Alicant was placed under martial law: All insurgent officers and subalterns, whether of the army, the militia, or the navy, were ordered to be shot *"on the sole identification of their persons"*: All troops in rebellion and refusing to return instantly to their allegiance were to be decimated; all citizens, leaders in the insurrection, were likewise to be shot; Alicant was declared in a state of blockade, and vessels of war and troops were ordered thither: At the same time the press was strictly forbidden to republish the proclamation of the insurgent Junta. Equally prompt measures were taken to detect cooperation at head quarters. Tidings of the insurrection having reached Government by express, in anticipation of the mail, the Ministers took possession of the post office and seized the letters from Alicant on their arrival. Among them, it is said, were several inculpating persons of note. Several important arrests took place the same night. Among these was Cortina the deputy from Seville;[2] a man of great popularity and influence in Andalusia, one of the most formidable leaders of the progresista party, and lately a strenuous supporter of Olozaga: Madoz[3] also one of the most active and prominent of the progresista deputies and of great influence in the Asturias.

Several arrests of less note were made[4] and others would have taken place but that, as usual among the hide and seek politicians of this Capital during a crisis, all who considered themselves under the evil eye of government, fled or hid themselves, until the affair should blow over. Among those who narrowly escaped was Lopez, recently so famous as the head of the coalition Cabinet which overturned Espartero. His lodgings were searched, but he was fortunately, it is said, "passing the night with a friends wife."

It is worthy of note how short lived has been the triumph, and how complete the fall of the progresista leaders, who last summer leagued with the Moderados to overturn the regency and effect the downfall of their quondam associate, Espartero. Scarce six months have elapsed and they have been ejected from transient rule by the very moderados whom they helped up into power. Olozaga, so lately at the head of the Cabinet is, like Espartero, degraded, proscribed and driven to take refuge in foreign parts; Cortina is in prison; Lopez, the temporary mirror of patriotism, whose very name was a watchword for the coalition; has absconded, no one knows whither; to escape from those who returned from exile under his own act of amnesty. This may be poetical justice, but it is the poetical justice of a melodrame; these changes and reverses would be considered too sudden and improbable for the regular drama. In Spain, however, truth outruns fiction.

As to the insurrection in Alicant, it has been attributed to mercenary,

as well as patriotic, motives; Boné and his myrmidons are said to have
been bribed by British Gold, furnished by a club of conspirators nestled
in Gibralter. Such, at least, is the insinuation in the government papers.
The true version probably is, that it is partly the result of a great
smuggling enterprize, originating in Gibralter. A number of smuggling
vessels were hovering about the coast at the time; and the moment the
Bonet Junta had the sway in Alicant an immense amount of British cotton
goods were landed free of duty. Similar contraband operations, originating in Gibralter, have, ↑heretofore,↓ been connected with similar
patriotic outbreaks at Malaga, and it has generally been found that,
after a great inundation of smuggled goods has taken place, the patriotic
paroxysm subsides.[5]

Such it was presumed would be the case in the present instance;
and, it is thought, that Ministers gladly availed themselves of the opportunity to give, at a cheap rate, a severe and salutary lesson to the
nation, and to put a stop to those pronunciamientos, which, through
too much lenity in government, have become a ready and favorite recourse of the public on all occasions.

The insurrection, however, is not confined to Alicant, but has likewise
broken out in Carthagena, against which rigorous measures have also
been adopted.[6] An instance of the determined severity of government
has been shown in the treatment of persons taken in insurrection in a
small place near Alicant, named Alcoy.[7]—A royal decree was immediately issued ordering that they *should be shot*. The Junta at Alicant
had declared that every death thus inflicted on their partizans should be
revenged by the death of five of their prisoners. The royal decree orders
that no heed should be given to such menaces; and adds that should
any loyal subjects be thus sacrificed they would have the consolation of
suffering in the cause of their country!

Ministers are evidently acting on the maxim that to maintain power
they must exercise power; so far their measures, though at time[s][8]
startling and arbitrary, have been effective. Having suspended the Cortes
they get on by ordinances, and, for the time being, exercise an almost
absolute rule. They have recruited and reorganized the army and put
it on a superior footing; they have paralyzed the militia; they have
decreed an all pervading police similar to that of France, and they have
sapped the independence of the Ayuntamientos formerly the sturdy
bulwarks of the popular will. In the mean time they no longer talk of
reassembling the Cortes, nor of looking to it for a bill of indemnities.
Some of the Moderado party look with apprehension at these measures
and fear they are pushed with too much precipitancy; but others declare that the party have nothing to hope from a half way policy;
that their safety lies in energy and decision. The present Minister of

State, Gonzalez Bravo, is active, prompt and resolute, and at the same time cool and self possessed. Narvaez is all efficient in military affairs; he has maintained the peace of the Capital through a perilous crisis, by his military measures, and seems to think that the peace of the kingdom is to be maintained in like manner. According to his policy the army is the government.[9]

The French Ambassador has frequent and long interviews with the Ministers. He is an upright, intelligent, judicious man and his councils, I have no doubt, would go towards restraining the impetuousity of the Cabinet and inculcating that measured, but firm and sagacious policy, by which Louis Philippe has been so successful in tranquilizing France. He seems, however, to look upon the political affairs of the Country as in a desperate State beyond the reach of remedy.

I have the honor to enclose copies of notes recently passed to the Spanish Government on the subject of certain quarantine regulations in the Canary Islands. By a reply from the Minister of State, I learn that the first of these notes has been referred to the Minister of the Interior[10] for his consideration and action.

I also enclose a copy of the decree of blockade of Alicant.

I am, Sir, / very respectfully / Your obdt Sevt.
Washington Irving

February 9th. The delay of the courier which takes this despatch allows me to add a few items. Since writing the foregoing a royal decree has extended the blockade to the whole coast from Alicant to Carthagena inclusive.[11] Another decree has put the whole kingdom under martial law until the insurrection is at end. In consequence of this domination of the sword the opposition papers have suspended their publication. Their last numbers contained furious and inflammatory articles on the subject of the royal decree ordering the insurgents captured at Alcoy to be shot; this decree having been so injudiciously worded as to signify it as the express wish and command of the Queen. This is another instance wherin the present Cabinet, in its eagerness to avail itself of the Queen's name, has given a severe blow to her popularity and compromised her future fortunes.

By accounts received yesterday the insurgents of Alicant have been defeated; some slain and many more taken prisoners. Boné was wounded but escaped.[12] It is thought the insurrection in that quarter will be suppressed; but much solicitude is felt for the general tranquility of the Country and the stability of government.

I shall again, I fear, have to ask the indulgence of government to permit me to absent myself from my post, for a short time in the course of the coming Spring or early in the summer, for the purpose of visiting some watering place, or seeking a change of climate for the restoration of my health; being still harrassed by the lingerings of a malady which has afflicted me more or less for a year past, and to which the climate of Madrid seems to be particularly unfavorable.

Very respectfully
W. I.

DOCKETED: Recd. 25 March. / Mr Markoe
MANUSCRIPT: NA, RG 59.   PUBLISHED: STW, II, 172–73 (in part).

Only the signature and the inserted "heretofore" in paragraph 6 are in WI's handwriting.

1. For details about Bonet and his activities, see *El Castellano*, February 2, 3, 1844.

2. Manuel Cortina (1802–1879).

3. Pascual Madoz (1806–1870), who came from the northwestern part of Spain.

4. Among others arrested were Garnica, Garrido, Verdú, Arquiága, and Lérin. See *El Castellano*, February 1, 1844.

5. The London *Times* for February 14, 1844, noted that Bonet's chief supporters were smugglers. "Perhaps, indeed, the whole movement on the coast is more connected with the admission of foreign calicoes and woolens than with the subversion of the Government, and in the present state of Spain these insurrections are the most convenient mode of opening the ports of the country to foreign trade."

6. The Alicante uprising broke out on February 2 and that at Cartagena soon thereafter. By February 6 both towns were blockaded. See *La Gaceta*, February 4, 6, 1844.

7. The fighting at Alcoy took place on January 29. Narváez ordered Federico Roncali, count of Alcoy (1800–1857) to shoot seven officers who had fought with the insurgents there. See Christiansen, *Military Power*, p. 121; and *El Castellano*, February 7, 1844.

8. The copyist omitted the bracketed letter.

9. Once the January and February rebellions had been suppressed with military force, Narváez became the champion of law and constitutional methods of government. See Christiansen, *Military Power*, p. 121.

10. Penaflorida was minister of the interior. See London *Times*, February 10, 1844.

11. See *La Gaceta*, February 7, 1844.

12. Bonet was reported as on his way to Alcoy. See *El Castellano*, February 8, 1844.

1675. To Joshua Bates

Madrid, Feb.. 9th. 1844

My dear Sir,

The address of Sir Arthur Aston, G. C B. is Aston Hall, Preston Brook, Cheshire. Dr Murta resides with him and manages his Estate.

We are in the midst of critical and uneasy times here; with insurrections breaking out which the government is endeavoring to put down with a strong hand. The whole Kingdom is under military law; which appears to be the only kind of law that can be enforced in Spain. I hope these measures may be efficacious in producing tranquility; but, I am sorry to say, I doubt more than I hope.

I am still some what of an invalid; or rather, though my general health is good I am troubled by the lingerings of a complaint in the ankles which confines me to the house unless when I drive out in the carriage.

Give my kindest remembrances to Mrs Bates[1] and believe me ever

Very truly yours
Washington Irving

Joshua Bates Esqr / &c &c &c

MANUSCRIPT: SHR.

Joshua Bates (1788–1865) was a senior partner in Baring Brothers, the banking firm. He was one of the founders of the Boston Public Library, which opened in 1854.

1. Mrs. Bates was the former Lucretia Augusta Sturgis.

1676. To James S. Buckingham

Madrid Feb 9th. 1844

Sir,

I have the honor to acknowledge the receipt of your letter of Decr 19th. informing me of my being elected an honorary member of the British and Foreign Institute.[1]

I beg you, Sir, to communicate to that association the deep and grateful sense I entertain of the honor and the privileges thus conferred upon me; and that you will accept, for yourself, my sincere acknowledgements for the very courteous and flattering language in which you have conveyed the information

I am Sir / Very respectfully / Your obliged
Washington Irving

J. S. Buckingham / Resident Director &c &c / London

MANUSCRIPT: SHR.

James Silk Buckingham (1786–1855), author and traveler, edited the Calcutta *Journal* from 1818 to 1823 and the *Oriental Herald and Colonial Review* from 1824 to 1829. He wrote numerous books on his travels in Palestine, Arabia, Persia, and other areas of the Near East, as well as three works on the United States in 1841 and 1842.

1. Buckingham founded the British and Foreign Institute in Hanover Square in 1843. Ridiculed in *Punch* as "Literary and Foreign Destitute," it lasted only four years. See *Dictionary of National Biography*, III, 202.

1677. To Moses H. Grinnell

Madrid. Feb. 9th. 1844

My dear Grinnell,

I promised the Count de Bresson, the French Ambassador at Madrid, to procure him a supply of American Sperm candles which are his admiration. As you are a New Bedford man[1] you ought to know where the article is to be had in perfection. I wish you would have 500 lbs. shipped by the first opportunity to the French Consul at Cadiz, with letter of advice of the same. The boxes to be directed, "For the Count de Bresson; Ambassador of France, at Madrid." and send me an account of the same.

I have had very satisfactory accounts of the encreasing and flourishing state of your family, and hear that your last production[2] is decidedly an improvement of all that preceded it. I have also heard much of your architectural achievements in that wonderful house in College place, and that you have made as great a *bustle* behind it as can be displayed by the greatest belle in New York.

I am living a quiet life here in Madrid, though in the midst of plots, and insurrections. I am still kept very much to the house by the remains of an obstinate malady which has worried me for a year past, and to which the climate of this place seems decidedly hostile. I wish you had interest at Washington and could get the folks there to shift me to either of the German courts that should become vacant. I might there regain my health entirely, and resume those literary pursuits which now are suspended; and on which I depended so much for my future pecuniary resources.

God bless you my dear Grinnell. Give my love to Julia; remember me cordially to your brother and to Mr Minturn[3] and believe me ever

affectionately yours
Washington Irving

ADDRESSED: M H Grinnell Esq / 6. College Place / New York.   POSTMARKED:
BOSTON / March 22nd / Steamer
MANUSCRIPT: Yale.   PUBLISHED: STW, II, 198–99 (in part).

1. Grinnell was born and educated at New Bedford, Massachusetts, one of the
chief American whaling ports in the early nineteenth century.
2. Fanny Grinnell, born in 1842. For other details, see WI to Julia Grinnell,
December 29, 1843.
3. Henry Grinnell and Robert B. Minturn were also partners in Grinnell, Minturn
and Company.

1678. To Catharine Paris

Madrid, Feb. 9th. 1844

My dear Sister,
   I received a few days since your letter dated from the 22d. to 29th
of December:[1] in which you talk of the possibility of your undertaking
a voyage to France in the Spring, to rejoin Sarah: and hope for my
concurrence—You have that, my dear Sister, in any plan which you
may consider conducive to your comfort and well being: but I will not
venture to give advice in the matter. A voyage to France in one of our
fine packet Ships is without fatigue, and, provided one does not suffer
too much from sea sickness, may be made with advantage to the health
even of the frail and feeble. From Havre to Paris the travelling is now
very commodious by Steam boat and rail road: there is nothing, therefore, to deter you on these heads. How you might be able to accommodate yourself, however, to the manners, customs and habitudes of
a country where every thing would be strange to you, and with the
language of which, also, you had scarce any acquaintance, would be
quite another consideration. ⟨In the United States⟩ The very novelty,
which makes every thing in a foreign country agreeable to a young
person, renders it ⟨I⟩ irksome to an old person, as clashing with long
established habitudes. In the United States you have your homes and
your resorts to which you are accustomed and which are accustomed
to you. You are surrounded by a little world of family connexions, ready
to cheer and take care of you in case of sickness. You have nieces at
hand who would be at your bed side and be with you day and night
in case of need. All these are important considerations for one at your
time of life[2] and with your precarious health. In being with Sarah you
would have but herself to look to; and she has now various claims upon
her time and attentions which would prevent her being your constant
and devoted chamber companion as she was formerly. You would need
to bring such a companion with you. These things I suggest for your

consideration. Were I resident in Paris instead of Madrid I could obviate these things and arrange every thing to your hearts content; but at present I can only give good wishes; and can again assure you that, whatever course your feelings and inclinations may lead you to adopt, you have my hearty concurrence.

The Spanish Court has recently been put into mourning by the sudden death of the Infanta Louisa Carlota, wife to the Infante Don Francisco, and aunt to the Queen She was a women of strong passions and restless ambition. For some time past she had been scheming and intriguing to effect a marriage between her Son the Duke of Cadiz and his cousin the youthful Queen, and had embroiled herself with all parties and impoverished her husband and herself in the prosecution of her plans. Their failure mortified her pride and exasperated her temper; and of late she had been extremely ungracious in looks and manners. Her illness was preceded by a kind of fever of the mind. "I know not what is the matter with me," said she to one of her attendants; ["]wherever I am and wherever I go I am in a constant state of irritation; at the theatre; on the Prado, at home, it is still the same, I am in a passion (*je m'enrage*)."[3] In this state of mind she was attacked by measles and *pulmonia* (a kind of inflammation of the lungs) which acting upon an extremely full, plethoric habit, hurried her out of existence in the course of two or three days, and in the 39th. year of her age. The body lay in state for three days; and the populace were admitted to see it according to Spanish custom. I called to inscribe my name on the list of visitors, as is the etiquette; and suffered myself to be carried by the throng through a suite of rooms decked out with escutcheons, funeral hatchments, lighted tapers and files of mute attendants. The corpse was on a bed of State, ⟨deck⟩ ↑and↓ arrayed in a Gala dress, white brocade & gold, with a royal coronet; ⟨I⟩ the face livid and bloated with disease. I have given you, my dear Sister, some pictures of royalty in its grandeur: ⟨yo⟩ here you have it brought down to the dusty level of mere mortality. But a few days previously I had beheld this proud hearted princess walking the prado with her family with ⟨haughty⟩ ↑sullen↓ and almost disdainful air, scarce noticing the salutations of the well dressed throngs which bowed with uncovered head as she passed. Here she was, on her bed of death, exposed to the gaze of the unmannered populace; ⟨who⟩ ↑some of whom↓ even whispered jests to each other, and sneered and laughed as they criticised the corpse and the funeral pageant!

We are again in the midst of popular commotions. Insurrections have broken out in Alicant and Carthagena and Government are taking strong measures to nip them in the bud. The whole kingdom is put under martial law; all political offenses are to be tried by military tribunals; and all officers and subaltern officers taken in rebellion, are to be shot on the mere identification of their persons. The government is evidently determined to rule by the sword. Unfortunately some of these sanguinary decrees are worded as if ⟨de⟩ proceeding from the immediate will and wish of the Queen: who, poor child, is little conscious of the force and nature of the papers she is signing. They have produced a great sensation, and I fear will contribute to involve the innocent little Queen in the party odium which the opposition is endeavoring to excite against the government.

Important arrests have taken place of persons suspected of participation in the new conspiracies. Among these are some of the political leaders who were active last summer in effecting the downfall of Espartero; and who are now proscribed by their late confederates whom they helped up into power; Such is the continual succession of plot and counterplot in this unhappy country. It is probable the strong measures taken by government will check the present insurrection, and that the Moderados (or aristocratical party) may maintain ⟨themselves⟩ the Sway for a time—if not, their case will be desperate; for these strong measures have awakened the most deadly enmity in the opposition, and a new revolution I fear would be sanguinary and vindictive in the extreme. I fear, too, it would be disastrous for the poor little Queen.

I must conclude my letter, having others to write by the present courier. My general health is good, and I am gradually conquering the remains of my malady; which, however, disputes the ground inch by inch as it retreats.

With love to the families—

Your affectionate brother
Washington Irving

MANUSCRIPT: Yale.   PUBLISHED: PMI, III, 320–22 (in part); STW, II, 172 (in part).

1. This letter has not been located.
2. Mrs. Paris, born in 1774, was seventy years old.
3. WI omitted the bracketed quotation mark.

1679.   To Sarah Storrow

Madrid, Feb 10th. 1844

My dear Sarah

I did not intend to write to you this ⟨morning⟩ week, for your correspondence of late has been so scanty, and I have so many others to write to, that I thought it high time to put you upon allowance. Your letter

of the 3d.[1] received yesterday, however, has mollified me, and has induced me once more to take pen in hand but I will not promise to be so
forgiving hereafter but will make my correspondence at least as meagre
as your own.

Colonel Winchester and his regiment arrived here some time since,
passed some days in Madrid and then took up their line of March for
Andalusia. I gave them a dinner, and procured for them admissions to
⟨the⟩ see the royal palace & visit the public institutions; ⟨and⟩ Mr Hamilton was very attentive to them and I trust they departed satisfied with
the legation. For a few days past we have had here Captain Newton,[2]
late commander of the Frigate Missouri (burnt at Gibralter) and his purser Mr Price;[3] both Americans of the right stamp. The[y][4] dined with me
two or three days since and are to dine with me again tomorrow: in
the mean time Hamilton & Livingston are shewing them the lions. It is
extremely agreeable to have countrymen of their appearance, deportment
and qualifications dropping in upon us in this out of the world place.

You seem to take an interest in my ⟨diplom⟩ sketches of the diplomatic circle and want to hear more about the Princess. I have not
seen any thing of her since I wrote that letter to your mother. I called
upon her but she was out. I heard her pulled to pieces, however, by a
Spanish marchioness, who would not admit a word in her favor. ⟨She
denied⟩ This was in conversation with another lady; who expressed a
great regard for the princess, but was obliged in candor to admit, one
by one, all the censures of the Marchioness. They both (being handsome
women) agreed that the princess had no pretensions to beauty. I ventured humbly to suggest that the Princess had fine eyes—"Fine eyes!
poogh; what are fine eyes in Spain where they go begging about the
Streets?"—I had not another word to say. The Marchioness summed up,
however, by the greatest crime of the Princess: *she was positively fond
of her husband,* a crime almost unheard of in high life in Madrid. She
illustrated this by some over tender speeches made by the Princess to
her husband in Society; and some fond ↑& rather mawkish↓ reproaches
to him for having been absent from her a whole evening; which were
given with a provoking humor and mimickry that ⟨seized⟩ compelled me
to laugh in spite of my secret predilection for the Princess. It was, ungenerous, however in the Marchioness to attack the poor princess on a
point on which she herself was so secure; since no one can accuse her of
⟨loyalty⟩ ↑devotion↓ to her own husband, though she is said to be full
of loving kindness to all man kind beside.

The more I see of the De Bressons the more I like them. They are very
domestic, and perfectly frank, unpretending and friendly. Madame De
Bresson ⟨has⟩ is rather handsome; with an open, engaging, truth like
expression of countenance They both appear to me to have more of the

German kindliness and friendliness than of the French *politesse*: or rather the latter has been warmed up and enriched by residing in Germany and acquiring German benevolence. Of Mr Bulwer I see nothing. He has dined with me once and has asked me to a sociable dinner with him, which I had to decline on account of indisposition. He has been part of the time unwell, and I can only visit in carriage: so, with, I believe, mutual disposition to be on civil sociable terms, we as yet have seen but little of each other.

He set out with a determination to sail smoothly ⟨in⟩ over the troubled water of Spanish politics and avoid all the shoals and quicksands which disturbed the navigation of his frank open hearted predecessor: he has, however, in spite of his coolness and caution got into repeated scrapes. He gave a snug dinner to ↑Gonzales Bravo↓ the Minister of State and two others of the Cabinet; without knowing that the two last held the first in utter contempt as a renegado and an upstart, and that, though leagued in the cabinet, they were bitter enemies in private life.

He gave a dinner to the good Arguelles and two or three others of the leading men of the Regency,[5] and the government newspapers were instantly out upon him for ⟨fet⟩ feasting political leaders who were in open opposition to the government to which he was accredited. So poor Bulwer, like the man with his ass in the fable, in attempting to please every body, has, so far, pleased no body.[6]—The fact is, he has launched out too soon; he should have taken a little more time to make himself acquainted with the intricacies of Spanish society, which are as perplexing as the ⟨new⟩ rocks and shoals: and eddies, and counter currents and whirlpools of our own Hell gate. The only person in Spanish Society that I have heard to speak well of him was the Marchioness, aforesaid, who after she had demolished the poor princess broke out in praises of Mr Bulwer who had twice visited her, and was so polite and agreeable that he had quite made a conquest of her: her female friend hinted to me, after she had gone, that it was a very easy conquest on which Mr Bulwer need not plume himself.

We are now, as you will perceive by the papers, under Martial law; in consequence of new insurrections. The present government is determined to rule by the sword; and to check all insurrections in the bud. Royal decrees have been issued ordering that ⟨all⟩ the officers & subalterns of all forces taken in rebellion shall be shot, on the mere identification of their persons: and that the same shall be done to all citizens taking a lead in insurrection. Unfortunately these decrees have been so worded as if it was the express will and wish of the Queen that these sanguinary orders should be ↑rigorously↓ carried into effect. This has caused vehement tirades from the opposition press, and will, I fear, tend to distroy the prestige of the Queens name, which is already on the decline: though of course the poor child knew nothing of the force and tendency of the decrees she was signing. I feel more and more apprehensive of the future destinies of this innocent little being: and fear, that, ⟨in⟩ should another revolution take place, which the opposition are evidently laboring to bring about, she may be involved in the fortunes of the Moderado party, towards whom the most vindictive measures will probably be enforced. I heartily wish she had ⟨her⟩ had her mother Maria Christina by her side ever since the declaration of her Majority: she is lamentably in want of such a friend and guardian, to protect her from the ⟨in⟩ rash expedients of Ministers; who, in seeking to avail themselves of the influence of her innocent name, are blighting that name in its very blossom.

I beg you to give my kind remembrances to Mrs Ledyard but to entreat her to send me no more messages about the widow. That, contained in your letter of yesterday, set me dreaming about her last night and I was surprised to find what a vivid reccollection I entertained of her and of the beautiful dress in which she figured at her last ball in New York. I cannot get her and that dress out of my mind all this blessed day—I believe the dress came from Paris. Tell Mrs Ledyard, who I know has a touch of ↑womanly↓ pity in her nature, that it is cruel to trifle with the feelings of a poor forlorn Bachelor in my desolate situation, far from all the womankind who once garrisoned my house and ⟨made⟩ ↑formed↓ a body guard around me. Tell her, what's more, that a Spanish nobleman ↑of great taste & fashion,↓ who were⁷ at Mrs Ledyards balls last season, says they were decidedly among the most elegant and recherchés in Paris, and tell her I have no doubt, those of this season will be still more stylish: and tell her finally that I only wish *I was well enough to dance at them.*

I have written home for leave of absence in the ⟨an⟩ course of the early part of the year; that I may visit some watering place and effect a complete cure of this malady which still troubles me, though in a very diminished degree, and to which the climate of Madrid seems very hostile. The misfortune is that it at present is seated in the ancles and consists of a tendency to become inflamed if I am much on my legs: I am therefore in a manner fettered and can mingle but little in society, nor stir abroad excepting in a carriage.

I am glad to hear Kate is making such progress in talking; though I think it scandalous in her to be such a tell tale and to complain to all the world of the process I took to correct her faults and improve her manners. I shall look to your next letter to ample accounts of her.

Whenever, you wish to forward any letters to me free of postage or any thing else that might form a small pacquet, send them to the Bureau des Affaires Etrangeres before 4 Oclock on Saturday: ⟨directed to⟩ and have them delivered to Mr de le Rea, who has charge of the Spanish department. They will then come by the courier in five days. I wonder Mr Ledyard does not avail himself of this mode of forwarding letters &c to Madrid.

I think now I have written you a longer letter than you deserve; and when I tell you that, by a British courier of yesterday I sent several letters home, beside a long dispatch to Government, I am sure you will think that you have your full share. In fact my correspondence takes up all the time and mind I can afford to my pen; and I shall have to give the greater part of it up, if I wish to prosecute any literary labor.

Give my kind remembrances to Mr Storrow and kiss darling little Kate for me

Your affectionate uncle
Washington Irving

ADDRESSED: Madame / Madame Storrow / No. 4. Rue de la Victoire / à Paris
MANUSCRIPT: Yale.   PUBLISHED: Simison, *Keogh Papers*, pp. 218–23; STW, II, 167–68, 170–71 (in part).

1. This letter has not been located.
2. John T. Newton (1793–1857), who entered the U.S. Navy in 1819, was promoted to commander in 1827 and to captain in 1837. From 1848 to 1852 he was in charge of the Pensacola Navy Yard.
3. Rodman M. Price (1816–1894) was appointed purser in 1840. He later served on the *Cyane* on the western coast of Mexico and as naval agent in California from 1848 to 1850. Upon his return to New Jersey he was elected to Congress (1851–1853) and to the governorship (1854–1857).
4. WI omitted the bracketed letter.
5. The London *Times* (February 12, 1844) found fault with Bulwer for having invited Argüelles, Ferrer, and Tejada, who were intimate friends of Olózaga, now in exile.
6. WI is probably referring to Aesop's fable of "The Miller, His Son, and Their Ass." See William Ellery Leonard, *Aesop and Hyssop, Being Fables Adapted and Original, With Morals Carefully Formulated* (Chicago, 1912), pp. 95–97.
7. WI probably intended to write "was."

1680. To Luis González Bravo

Legation of the United States. / Madrid February 28th. 1844.

Mr. Samuel McLean[1] having been appointed Consul of the United States for the port of Trinidad de Cuba The Undersigned Envoy Extraordinary and Minister Plenipotentiary of the United States has the honor to enclose Mr. McLean's commission and to request that His Excellency Don Luis Gonzalez Bravo, First Minister of State and of Foreign Affairs of Her Catholic Majesty will cause the corresponding exequatur to be issued recognizing Mr. McLean in his official character.

The Undersigned avails himself of this occasion to renew to His Excellency the assurance of his distinguished consideration

Washington Irving.

MANUSCRIPT: NA, RG 84 (letterbook copy).

1. McLean had been serving as U.S. consul at Cien Fuegos. See WI to Count Almodóvar, January 23, 1843, and to González Bravo, January 2, 1844; Hasse, *Index to U.S. Documents*, III, 1748.

1681. To Sarah Storrow

Madrid Feb 29. 1844

My dear Sarah,

Your letter of the 19th.[1] has put me very much out of humor with myself since I find that, while I was murmuring at the scantiness of your recent correspondence, you were suffering under a long indisposition, and kindly concealing it from me lest it should cause me uneasiness: and that even the letters which I received so thanklessly, were written at the cost of additional pain and debility. My dear, dear girl, what an ill return have I made for such, true and considerate affection; but we men are always inferior to your sex in these matters. I am sure, however, you will forgive my unreasonableness when you know it only proceeds from my affection for you, and the pain I feel [at][2] our being so widely separated: which can only be alleviated by frequent correspondence.

We are about to have stirring times here, on the arrival of the Queen mother; which will probably take place in about a fortnight. The little Queen and her Sister will go to the Royal Sitio or country residence of Aranjuez[3] to meet her, and all the court, and the Corps Diplomatique are expected to go there likewise. All the hotels, houses and apartments at Aranjuez are already engaged The Albuquerques, in company with the Prince and Princess of Carini and some others of the diplomats have taken a large house containing various separate appartments; and have promised me a nestling place. They have taken it not merely for the present occasion which will last but four or five days; but for the ⟨Se⟩ *temporada* or spring visit which the Queen proposes to make there in May, and which will last for six weeks or two months. It has always been the custom for the Spanish sovreigns to make these visits in the Spring and Summer, to the Royal Sitios of Aranjuez; La Granja & the Escurial;[4] in which the court accompanies them. It is rather troublesome and expensive to the Diplomatic corps: but I shall not make the visits in *extenso*;

but ⟨merely go an remain make my [*unrecovered*]⟩ remain for the most of the time in Madrid; repairing to the Sitios only when there is some particular fete or ceremonial. Indeed I look forward with a little solicitude to these court festivities; and especially to the *besa manos*, or levees; where the corps diplomatique has to be in the royal presence for upwards of three hours; standing all the while. I shall ⟨avoid⟩ excuse myself as often as possible; for I am still too infirm to support such fatigue; or rather, my ankles remain in too irritable a condition.

We have had a gay marriage in high life; a daughter of the Marchioness of Montijo,[5] with the young Duke of Alva;[6] immense wealth on both sides. The brides trousseau is said to have been worth six hundred thousand francs!—I have been unable to attend any of the fetes given on the occasion; as I cannot keep long enough on my legs for evening parties.

I shall make careful enquiries as to the comparative merits of watering places before I determine upon my course for the summer. I am affraid the waters of Enghien are not sufficiently efficacious: those of the Pyrenees are unquestionable. It will not do for me to fail in my next campaign; my expedition for the summer must be effective. To continue on in my present state is to moulder away existence. Indeed, if I only lived for myself, I would rather die than live in such a blighted condition

I have just had letters from home of a very cheerful tone: affairs appear to be generally brightening. I had a letter from your mother dated 29 Jany.[7] and presume you have likewise heard from her. She appears to be comfortably fixed this winter, and to receive continual visits from the different members of the family, which serve to render her room cheerful. Julia, Mary and charlotte were on a visit to Julia Grinnel; who was about to give a ball; from which they were anticipating much pleasure. Dear simple hearted little creatures; how little it takes to make them happy. Charlotte had received a present of a beautiful dress from her friend Helen Jones, in which she would probably figure on this occasion. By the way, I think you are quite right in declining the invitations to the Jones', and in refraining from visiting them on their receiving days. They have chosen a totally different circle of Society from that in which you move, and one in which you could not venture occasionally without feeling yourself a stranger, undervalued perhaps; and *out of tune* with those around you. Your true plan is to choose your intimates among the well informed and well bred of your own country, in this you will consult not only your enjoyment, but your respectability. Do not, however, suffer yourself to speak, nor if possible to think harshly of the poor Jones's. They are really kind hearted people at bottom, and I believe have a sincere regard for you; but they are carried away by their mania for pleasure, finery and fashion. I hope they may not wreck their happiness in the pursuit.

I shall shortly lose my friends the Calderons; whom I shall much regret, for I ⟨we⟩ are[8] on very sociable terms and I am quite pleased with them. Mr Calderon is appointed Minister Plenipotentiary to the United States.[9] I have become acquainted through them, with a young lady, native of Havanna, Leocadia Zamora;[10] who promises to be a charming addition to the small circle of my intimacy. She is very handsome, very graceful and amiable, but what is to me her great charm, she sings divinely; having ⟨naught but⟩ a delightful voice, ⟨and⟩ cultivated by the instructions of the best masters. She sings for me all the finest airs from the current Italian operas, and delights me almost as much as Grisi or Persiani.[11] Is not this a veritable God send!

Give my kind remembrances to Mr Storrow. Kiss my darling little Kate for me, and write ⟨me at⟩ more about her than you have of late—

Your affectionate uncle
Washington Irving

MANUSCRIPT: Yale.   PUBLISHED: Simison, *Keogh Papers*, pp. 223–26.

1. This letter has not been located.
2. WI wrote "it."
3. About thirty miles south of Madrid on the Tagus River, Aranjuez was a summer residence of Spanish monarchs since the time of Ferdinand and Isabella. See Karl Baedeker, *Spain and Portugal*, pp. 123–25.
4. The Escorial, or Escurial, located twenty-seven miles northwest of Madrid, combines palace, monastery, and the tombs of many Spanish rulers. See Baedeker, *Spain and Portugal*, pp. 108–14.
5. María Manuela Kirkpatrick, countess of Montijo, whom WI had met in January, 1843, was the mother of María Francisca de Sales Portocarrero Palafox (1825–1860).
6. James Louis Francis Paul Raphael (Stuart FitzJames), eighth duke of Berwick and fifteenth duke of Alba (1821–1881) was married to María Francesca on February 14, 1844. See *El Castellano*, February 14, 1844.
7. This letter has not been located.
8. WI apparently canceled the wrong word.
9. See the announcement of Calderón's appointment in *El Castellano*, February 28, 1844.
10. Leocadia Zamora, member of a wealthy Cuban family, was the toast of Madrid in 1844. She later entered a Carmelite convent and withdrew from the world. See Bowers, *Spanish Adventures of WI*, pp. 249–52.
11. Fanny Tacchinardi Persiani (1812–1867) was a popular Italian coloratura soprano. See *The International Cyclopedia of Music and Musicians*, ed. Oscar Thompson, p. 1611.

1682. To A. P. Upshur

Legation of the United States. / Madrid March 2nd. 1844.

No. 37. / The Hon: A. P. Upshur. / Secretary of State of the U. S. Washington.

Sir,

I have the honor to acknowledge the receipt of despatches Nos. 21 and 22, which came to hand the evening before last, the contents of which shall have prompt and full attention.

As to the recall of Mr. Argaiz[1] I would observe, that I had previously received no information on the subject, either from my own or from this government, but had learnt it from another quarter, and had been left to conjecture as to the circumstances connected with it. In respect to ↑the policy of the United States regarding↓ the island of Cuba, I had taken occasion to have that full and frank conversation with Mr. Gonzalez Bravo, the present Minister of Foreign Affairs, which this legation is instructed to hold with each succeeding Spanish government. I was quickened to this by fresh reports of plots and insurrections in the Island, and by some surprise expressed in a Ministerial paper, at the avowal of Mr. Ingersoll,[2] in the United States House of Representatives[3] of a readiness to go to war with England on the subject of Cuba. ↑In the conversation alluded to↓ Mr. Gonzalez Bravo expressed himself aware that the interests and feelings of the Spanish and United States Governments were identical on most subjects connected with negro slavery; and that our policy was fair and friendly towards Spain in regard to her West India Colonies; and he appeared to be much gratified by my avowal of the determination of our government to maintain Spain in the possession of Cuba ↑by force of arms, if necessary,↓ and to consider it a cause of war for any other power to attempt to possess itself of the Island. He expressed no apprehensions about the present state of Cuba, but on the contrary, a full confidence that the vigorous measures, which the Spanish government were about to take, would be efficacious in putting the island in a state of security.

In consequence of the receipt of your instructions I shall take an early opportunity to have another conversation with Mr. Gonzalez Bravo on this subject, and on that of the recall of Mr. Argaiz. On the last I had some conversation last evening with a person who is likely to be well informed. He observed that, it was not in consequence of the application of Mr. Argaiz to the government of the United States for armed assistance to frustrate the sinister designs of another power against the island, that he was recalled; but for other and previous circumstances. It is true, he said, the government had considered his application to the United States precipitate and uncalled for, and made with a view to atone for past devotion to Espartero by a striking exhibition of zeal in the cause of his successors. It had also been displeased with his irregular proceeding in communicating the fact by letter to the second person in command in the island of Cuba, instead of ↑to↓ the first (Genl. Valdez)[4] as though he thought the latter in league with the enemy. The consequence had been contradictory rumours and suspicions in the Island. one party asserting the grasping intentions of the English upon Cuba, and another, in which was the British Consul,[5] asserting the design of the United States to send vessels of war to take possession of the island.

Though these circumstances, as I said before, ⟨was⟩ ↑were↓ alleged by my informant as displeasing to the Spanish government and considered as gross blundering, yet they were not, he repeated, the real cause of Mr. Argaiz' recall. This had been determined upon by the Cabinet of Mr. Frias,[6] in consequence of a series of blunders and cross purposes; which proved him in the estimation ↑of the cabinet↓ incompetent to his station. Among these were, his mismanagement of the affair of the Amistad; ↑and↓ his intermeddling in the payment of the instalments from Cuba, so as to produce a temporary misunderstanding between the governments, and to detain a large amount of money in his hands, or rather in the hands of his bankers, if not to his own emolument, at least to the disadvantage of the American Creditors.

Much of his diplomatic inefficiency was attributed to his residing at a distance from Washington and thus being out of the way of getting accurate information; besides suffering himself to be too much influenced by a young and inexperienced member of his legation. On the whole, it was said, he was a well meaning man, but little fitted for diplomacy, and that on returning home he would probably be provided for in some other way. My informant added that the expression, on the part of the United States, of a prompt disposition to render military aid, called out by the unnecessary application of Mr. Argaiz; instead of awakening distrust, had given much satisfaction to the Spanish government.

Such is the amount of information I have just received on this subject. I give it to you as I heard it; but shall pursue the inquiry in other quarters. I am satisfied however, from all that I can judge of the present tone of feeling of the actual Cabinet, and of the people at large in respect to England; there is no danger of any views she may have with regard to the island of Cuba, meeting with encouragement in this quarter.

In relation to the case of Mr. Aguirre, Consul of the United States at Bilbao, who I find has applied to you to authorize official interposition in his behalf, for the recovery of a fine imposed upon him, I will briefly state for your consideration the circumstances as they appear from the documents on file in the legation

In consequence of revolutionary attempts in the month of October 1841, a fine was imposed on the town of Bilbao. Mr. Aguirre, as a Spanish subject, possessed of property in the town, was called upon to contribute his proportion of the fine. This he refused to do on the ground of his official position as Consul of the United States, and applied to Mr. Vail my predecessor, for his interposition. Application was in consequence made, *unofficially*, by that gentleman to the Spanish government, but without success. Mr. Aguirre then urged him to make an official and direct appeal to the government. Mr. Vail stated in reply that Mr. Aguirre's character as a Spanish subject did not authorize him to adopt such a measure, as it could only be applied in the case of an American Citizen; that Mr. Aguirres exequatur in express terms, separated the foreign consul from the Spanish subject, granting to one all such prerogatives as are essential to the discharge of his functions; but retaining the other in undiminished subjection to all national and municipal burthens, obligations and liabilities; and, finally, that this just and obvious distinction had been taken by the Spanish Minister in his correspondence on the subject.

Here the matter rested until Mr. Aguirre requested my *official* interposition in his behalf. I remarked in reply under date of 16th December last, that I concurred with the view of his case taken by Mr. Vail, and did not consider myself authorised by the circumstances, to make it the subject of official communication to the Spanish government, but that I would make an unofficial representation in his favor. I accordingly did so, about a fortnight since, which was as early as I thought judicious in the agitated state of public affairs. The Minister's answer indicated a disposition to give the matter a favorable consideration; and I intended shortly to call it again to his attention.

Since the receipt of your despatch, I have again reconsidered the case, in connexion with the correspondence, and the exequatur of Mr. Aguirre, and am, if possible, more thoroughly convinced than before of the correctness of Mr. Vails views, and of the course he adopted. It is obvious that the fine imposed applies to Mr. Aguirre in his position of Spanish subject, totally unconnected with the discharge of his functions as Consul, and the exequatur in his case, differing from those of Consuls who are citizens of the United States, expressly reserves all his liabilities and obligations as a Spaniard, and guards, with great caution, against the interposition of any official immunities of his consular character. Thus the very document on which Mr. Aguirre founds his claim, decides the case against him.

However wide a construction may be given to the immunities and privileges of Consuls, they can never be made to extend to a case in which a government, while recognizing in one of its own citizens, an agent of a foreign power, makes it an express condition that he shall remain subject to all previous obligations.

You observe in your despatch, that the government of Spain, it is understood, has "admitted the wrong" done to Mr. Aguirre, "and thereby tacitly acknowledged the justice of his claim for reparation." I can find no such admission in the records of the legation; and am convinced, if such were really made, that it acknowledged the fine, as an act of extortion exercised on a subject, a case with which officially I could have nothing to do.

To conclude, as you have left this matter to my judgment, to take such steps in it as *I may think proper,* I shall proceed to execute my original intention, viz, to write to Mr. Aguirre, recommending him to make a written statement of his case, presenting all his just claims for indemnification, from his government, and to forward it to me. I will then present it to Mr. Gonzalez Bravo, accompanied by such informal recommendation to favor, as my knowledge of the circumstances of the case, and of the character and conduct of Mr. Aguirre will justify me in making. I only regret that this gentleman has thought it necessary or expedient to trouble you in a matter in which this legation has never been slow nor unwilling to render him all proper assistance.

Despatch No. 23 from the Department, enclosing the commission of Mr. McLean as Consul for Trinidad de Cuba, has been received, and its directions complied with by an application on the 28th. February for the usual exequatur in his behalf.

Though the official announcement has not yet appeared in the Gazette, I learn from good authority that Mr. Calderon de la Barca, has been a second time appointed Envoy Extraordinary and Minister Plenipotentiary to the United States. As this gentleman proposes to visit England on his way to his post, two or three months will probably elapse before his arrival in Washington.

> I am, Sir, / Very respectfully / Your obdt Sevt.
> Washington Irving

DOCKETED: Recd. April 24/44 / Mr. Markoe
MANUSCRIPT: NA, RG 59.   PUBLISHED: STW, II, 183 (in part); *Diplomatic Correspondence,* 335–37 (in part).

Only the signature is in WI's handwriting.

1. Pedro Alcantara Argaïz was recalled as Spanish minister to the United States on January 2, 1844. For other details about Argaïz and his activities, see WI to Daniel Webster, November 26, and December 5, 1842.

2. Charles Jared Ingersoll (1782–1862) was the chairman of the Foreign Af-

fairs Committee on the U.S. House of Representatives at this time.

3. For debate on the Cuba question between Ingersoll and John Quincy Adams, see Senate, *Congressional Globe*, 28th Cong., 1st sess., p. 79.

4. Gerónimo Valdés. For other details, see WI to Daniel Webster, March 10, 1843.

5. David Turnbull, an active abolitionist, went to Havana as British consul in 1840 and began agitating for the freeing of the Cuban slaves. Late in 1842 he was arrested for trying to organize a slave revolt and was expelled from the island. See Hugh Thomas, *Cuba, or The Pursuit of Freedom*, pp. 201–04.

6. Frías was prime minister from September 6 to November 27, 1838. See Christiansen, *Military Power*, p. 169.

1683. To Maximo de Aguirre

Legation of the United States. / Madrid March 3d. 1844.

Maximo de Aguirre Esqr. / Consul of the U. States. Bilbao.

Sir,

Between two and three weeks since thinking the time favorable, I took occasion, unofficially to call the attention of Mr. Gonzalez Bravo, first Minister of State to the subject of your fine, and dwelt strongly on every circumstance of the case which I thought entitled you to redress from your government. Mr. Gonzalez Bravo appeared to be favorably impressed by the statement; said he knew you and knew your character to be such as I had represented it; and promised me to give the matter the earliest possible attention.

A few days after I received a despatch from the Department of State at Washington to the following effect "The case of Mr. Aguirre United States Consul, has already been laid before you by himself,—who submitted it I presume with a view to your official interposition in his behalf. It is the wish of the Department that you would examine into the circumstances of this case, and take Such steps as may be proper to aid the consul in obtaining redress from the government of Spain; which it is understood has admitted the wrong; and thereby tacitly acknowledged the justice of his claim for reparation,—provided there exists no good reason, of which the Department is ignorant, for withholding such interposition.["][1]

I have accordingly reexamined the circumstances of the case, and see nothing in it to alter the opinion heretofore expressed to you, that it is not one in which I can properly make an *official* interposition. I have stated the grounds of my opinion in my reply to the Department, and as they are the same with those of Mr. Vail, with which you are fully possessed, it is needless here to repeat them.

"All such steps as *may be proper*" to aid you in obtaining redress from your government I will take with pleasure; but I cannot *properly* take any one out of the limits of my official privileges. As mere verbal applications, however much they may impress at the time, are liable to be forgotten in the press of affairs; I would suggest to you to make a written application to your government for redress; stating all the circumstances of the case. Send this to me and I will present it unofficially and accompany it with my own good word and good wishes, expressed as forcibly as I am able.

I am, Sir, respectfully / Your Obdt Sevt.
Washington Irving.

MANUSCRIPT: NA, RG 84 (letterbook copy).

1. WI omitted the bracketed quotation marks.

1684. *To Joseph Cullen*

Legation of the United States. / Madrid March 4th. 1844.

Joseph Cullen Esq. / U. S. Consul—Teneriffe.

Sir,

I have duly received your communication on the subject of the quarantine regulations in the Canary Islands, but the agitated state of affairs here and the frequent changes of the Cabinet discouraged me from taking any official step in the matter. On the 25th. January last however, I passed a note to Mr. Gonzalez Bravo, First Minister of State, placing the evils and abuses of the present quarantine system in those islands in as strong a light as I could, and soliciting the repeals and modifications which you suggest. In reply Mr. Gonzalez Bravo informed me that my letter had been referred to the Minister of the Interior for his consideration and action in the premises.

I hope the application may have a beneficial effect; but in the exigencies of the times and the multiplicity of affairs pressing upon the attention of the Ministers, much delay in these matters of minor importance is to be apprehended.

I also in a Second note made a special remonstrance as to the quarantine imposed upon our ships of war in the ports of the Canary Islands, as complained of to me by Commodore Perry. I shall be happy to hear from you should any favorable change take place in these vexatious regulations.

I am, Sir, respectfully / Your obdt Sevt.
Washington Irving.

MANUSCRIPT: NA, RG 84 (letterbook copy).

Joseph Cullen was U.S. consul at Teneriffe from 1835 until his death in late 1846 or early 1847. See Hasse, *Index to U.S. Documents*, III, 1748.

1685. To Matthew C. Perry

Legation of the United States./ Madrid March 4th. 1844

My dear Commodore.

Ill health, which has made me rather irregular in my correspondence, has prevented an earlier reply to your letter of July 5th. 1843,[1] complaining of the quarantine imposed upon our Ships of war in the Canary Islands, and of the want of courtesy towards you on the part of the authorities in not returning your official visits.

I have made a written representation of these circumstances to the Spanish Government, and trust it will be effective.

Wishing you pleasant and prosperous cruizings and all manner of prosperity.

I am, my dear Commodore, / Ever very truly yours.
Washington Irving.

Commodore M. C. Perry. / Commanding African Squadron.

MANUSCRIPT: NA, RG 84 (letterbook copy).

1. In this letter (NA, RG 84) Perry set forth the arguments which WI used in his official note to González Bravo on January 25, 1844.

1686. To Sarah Storrow

Madrid, March 8t 1844

My dear Sarah,

I was agreeably surprised yesterday, while at dinner, by the receipt of your letter of the 2d. inst.[1] This is the first you have sent by the French Courier, and, being promptly delivered, reached me, as you perceive, in five days. I thank you for giving me so many particulars about my darling little Kate. They place her completely before my eyes and amuse me extremely. I find she is a true Parisian in her love for dress, but console myself with observing that she still keeps up her literary taste and pores over those valuable volumes which I gave her.

In your next I expect to hear of your having received a visit from

Capt Newton & Mr Price² as I gave them a letter ⟨to y⟩ of introduction to you. I was much pleased with both of them, but especially with the Captain, who appeard to me a naval officer of the highest merit.

In a little while after the receipt of this letter you may look for a visit from Mr Jasper Livingston, half brother to Mrs Ledyard,³ and attached to this legation. He left Madrid yesterday, in the Malle Poste, and will arrive in Paris nearly about the time with this letter, which goes to day by the English Courier. Mr Livingston will be able to give you as much news as you desire, about me, as I saw him almost every day, and he was almost an inmate in my house. I have been more and more pleased with him the more I have known him. He is a gentleman in appearance, mind, and manners, well instructed & well informed. He speaks Spanish with correctness and even with elegance; and has been well received and highly respected in Spanish Society. I expect him to return to Madrid in the course of May, or early in June, and to continue in the legation. In fact, as Hamilton has made up his mind to return home in May or June, I have written to the Government, urgently soliciting the appointment of Mr Livingston⁴ in his place, and hope my application may be successful. From the familiar opportunity I have had of becoming acquainted with his qualifications I think he would perfectly suit me as Secretary of Legation. Perhaps it may be as well to say nothing on this subject for the present, lest other applications should be made for the office, which might throw difficulties in the way of Mr Livingstons nomination.

I shall regret extremely to part with Alexander Hamilton. We have lived most happily together. He is an animated, intelligent, delightful companion, and has been the life of my house. In official matters too, he has shewn himself highly competent; and carried on the business of the Legation with great tact and judgement during my absence. For the kind sympathy he has ever manifested towards me during my long and harrassing malady I never can be sufficiently grateful. It will be a great consolation to me, however, in parting with him, if I can have his place supplied by so worthy a successor as Mr Livingston; one too, to whom I have become so familiarly accustomed. Hitherto I have been very fortunate in the members of my Legation. They have all been gentlemen in appearance, principles and deportment, and have contributed greatly to the respectibility of the mission.

The little Queen and her sister set off the day before yesterday for Aranjuez, to await the arrival of their mother.⁵ The Court Diplomatic Corps &c are all flitting after them. I shall delay my departure until the last moment: it being extremely uncomfortable for me to be absent from home at this season of the year, and in my present unfortunate plight. ⟨In s[?]⟩ I shall make the excursion in my own carriage, accompanied by Mr Valdivielso the Mexican Minister, who ⟨sh⟩ sends his horses ahead, to act as relays. I am to have a room in the apartment of the Albuquerques: who have joined with the Carinis, and others of the Diplomatic circle, in taking a large house for the season. I expect to be absent but three or four days; but feel as if they will be *long* ones.

I was much pleased with your account of the Washington birth night ball and should really have liked to be there (health permitting). I should be sorry should Col Thorn attribute my not calling on him last summer to any prejudice or intentional slight. It would be a great want of kindness and courtesy in me to indulge in any thing of the kind, for his conduct towards me has always been decidedly hospitable and gentlemanlike. I avoided calling on him, as I did upon all whose positions in Society made their houses somewhat conspicuous resorts, merely because I was an invalid, and wished to live quiet and retired and entirely out of the vortex of Society. Under any other circumstances I should consider it a very unjustifiable neglect in me, on arriving at Paris, not to call on a gentleman from whom I had received and accepted such civilities.

Among my few intimates here I do not know that I have ever mentioned to you Mrs O'Shea[6] wife of my banker. Her husband[7] is an Irishman and has lived here many years. I knew him, when I was in Madrid in 1825. He has made a large fortune and ⟨lov⟩ lives in hospitable and handsome style, entertaining the best society of Madrid. They occupy the apartments I had on first coming to Madrid, in the opposite wing of the house to that occupied by the Albuquerques. Mrs O'Shea is an English woman; of good understanding and the kindest and most amiable manners. She ⟨has⟩ suffered deep affliction in the loss of one of her children upwards of a year since, ⟨which h⟩ and though recovered from the poignancy of it, has still a mixture of melancholy in her manners that renders them soft and interesting. We are growing to be great friends.

I had a delightful treat two evenings since on the singing of the fair Leocadia Zamora; who sang for me several of my most favorite airs; so that, invalid and blighted as I am, you see I have still some social enjoyments within my reach.

Give my kind remembrances to Mr Storrow and kiss the darling little baggage for me

Your affectionate uncle
Washington Irving

Manuscript: Yale.

1. This letter has not been located.
2. For details, see WI to Sarah Storrow, February 10, 1844.

3. Perhaps WI erred and meant Mr. Ledyard, whose mother was Susan French Livingston.

4. WI's recommendation was accepted. Livingston was nominated as secretary of the U.S. legation in Madrid on April 22, 1844, and was commissioned on June 14, 1844. See Hasse, *Index to U.S. Documents*, III, 1834.

5. See *La Gaceta*, March 7, 1844.

6. Sabina O'Shea became one of WI's closest friends during his last year in Madrid. She occupied a place similar to Madame Pierre D'Oubril during his earlier residence there. For WI's letters to Mrs. O'Shea, see Penney, *Bulletin NYPL*.

7. Henry O'Shea operated H. O'Shea and Co., a Madrid banking firm. See Penney, *Bulletin NYPL*, 62 (December, 1958), 629.

1687. To Maximo de Aguirre

Legation of the United States. / Madrid March 12th. 1844.

Maximo de Aguirre Esqr. / U. S. Consul, Bilbao.

Sir,

I have duly received your letter of the 8th. instant by which I am happy to see that you are likely to have the money refunded to you which was extorted by Generals Alcala and Zurbano.[1]

It was needless for you to recapitulate the circumstances of your case. I believe they were perfectly understood both by Mr. Vail and myself and we both interfered in the matter as far as our official privileges permitted.

The obvious distinction,—again and again pointed out to you by this lègation,—between your case and that of Consuls *not* Spanish subjects cannot be more clearly shown than in the language of your own exequatur: You will there find that the Spanish government, (mediante que &c,)[2] considering that you are a Spanish subject; declares that you shall not enjoy all the privileges of Consuls who are foreign citizens; but shall be subject to all your obligations and liabilities (civil and criminal) as a Spaniard. Compare this with the exequatur of the Dutch Consul,—if, as I suppose he is a Dutch Citizen,—and you *must* see the wide difference between the two cases.

You are a Spaniard; He is not. Your government has a right to refuse absolutely to acknowledge you as Consul; and in giving you an Exequatur, can limit your rights and privileges according to its will: This has been done, and the United States, or any other government, in similar circumstances must either acquiesce in these conditions or appoint one of its own citizens to whom they do not apply.

Mr. Vail acted upon the distinction which he explained to you: In the matter of the fine which was levied upon you as a Spaniard he would not interfere *officially*; but on being informed that a Centinel had been placed at your door, and the access to the Consulate obstructed, he on 1st. Decr. 1841, made a formal complaint to this government and demanded that these restrictions should be removed. The latter was an infringement of the rights Secured in the exequatur, as "prerogativas anejas a su officio";[3] the former, viz, the fine, was one of the "cargas a que esta sujeto como subdito Español,"[4] and was expressly excepted from your official privileges.

If, instead of being Consul only, you were the representative of the United States at this Court, and at the Same time a Spaniard, you would continue,—unless this government should make an exception in your favor, —subject to all your duties and liabilities as a Spaniard. This is a well established principle of international law, and, if it applies in the case of a Minister, how much more strongly in regard to a Consul, who is *not* a public minister, and has in general a right to those immunities only which are ⟨reserved⟩ ↑granted↓ in his Exequatur

I have again for the last time explained this matter to you so fully, on account of the strange way in which you have compared your case with that of the Dutch Consul, between whom and yourself there is, as I have already said, this wide difference: He is not a Spaniard; you are. Should any doubt still exist, I must ask you to read his Exequatur, and your own together, and observe the distinction which your government has made between you.

I shall communicate the purport of your letter to the Department of State and am,

> Very respectfully / Your obdt Sert.
> Washington Irving.

MANUSCRIPT: NA, RG 84 (letterbook copy).

1. Felix Galiano Alcalá, marqués de Piedras Attas (1804–1862) and Martín Zurbano (1788–1845).
2. "intervening by virtue of."
3. "privileges connected with his office."
4. "obligation upon you as a Spaniard."

1688. *To Mary Irving*

Madrid, March 15t. 1844

My dear Mary,

I am told you want me to write you again, "if it is only a few lines." So my dear good little girl I will give you a small letter, which is all

I can afford for the present, having to write not merely to your aunt in New York but to "Uncle Sam" at Washington, who generally expects pretty long letters.

We are on the eve of great fetes and ceremonies to greet the arrival of the Queen Mother, who is on her way once more to embrace her children. I wish you could be here to enjoy these sights and festivities; ⟨th⟩ I think they would delight you. They are rather thrown away upon me; I am not well enough to enter into them with spirit—and then I have grown so wise!

I was a few mornings since on a visit to the Duchess of Berwick.[1] She is the widow of a grandee of Spain, who claimed some kind of descent from the royal line of the Stuarts. She is of immense wealth and resides in the most beautiful palace in Madrid (excepting the royal one.) I passed up a splendid staircase and through halls and saloons without number all magnificently furnished, and hung, with pictures and family portraits. This Duchess was an Italian by birth and brought up .in the Royal family at Naples. She is the very head of fashion here.—Well— this lady, of almost princely state, will be one of the ladies in waiting on the little Queen, when she receives her mother. She will stand be- hind the Queen at the foot of the stair case of the Royal palace, and perhaps bear her majestys train—Think of that my dear—think how grandly these little queens of thirteen years of age are waited upon.

This Duchess of Berwick, or Duchess of Alva as she is sometimes called, for these Spanish grandees have sometimes half a dozen titles, is quite a remarkable person. When she married the Duke of Berwick, or Alva, he was supposed to ⟨be worth⟩ ↑have a revenue of↓ about seven hundred thousand dollars a year. The Duchess, having been royally brought up, spent money accordingly. After a while it was found that in consequence of bad management of the Dukes estates, they did not yield above one hundred and fifty thousand dollars a year, and the young couple had ⟨run in⟩ contracted a debt of about two millions of dollars. The Duke ⟨was⟩ had no hand for accounts, and would have gone on plunging more and more into debt, but the Duchess took the management of affairs into her own hands. She investigated the condition of their various estates; changed the administrators of them; made some of the property more productive; and, without sacraficing any becoming style in living, ↑has↓ managed to pay off nearly the whole debt, and to restore the revenue to its original amount. The management of a princely estate of the kind requires a perfect counting house and various clerks; and such is the variety of sources of revenue, from lands, houses & stocks &c &c that they have never been able to get at a perfect idea of the state of their affairs. Such my dear Mary, is a peep into the interior of the mansion of one of the first grandees of Spain.

A grand wedding took place shortly since between the eldest son of the Duchess (the present Duke of Alva, about 22 years of age) and the daughter of the Countess of Montijo another very rich grandee. The corbeille, or wedding presents of the bride amounts to one hundred and twenty thousand dollars, ↑all in finery.↓ There were lace handkerchiefs worth a hundred or two dollars only to look at; and dresses the very sight of which made several young ladies unwell. The young Duchess is thought to be one of the happiest and best dressed ↑young↓ ladies in the whole world. She is already quite hated in the beau monde.

After all this magnificent detail I shall expect in return an account of cousin Julias ball, and how you all enjoyed yourselves and how you were all dressed. Between you and I I would not give little Sunny side for the grandest Dukes palace in Spain, and as to the bride and her fine dresses, when you and Julie get on your spring dresses and spring bonnets I should not be affraid to challenge a comparison

And now my dear little girl, I have scribbled for you a very rigamarole letter, but it was the best I could furnish in this hurried moment. I hope it may find you, bright and happy at our dear little cottage, where it will be the happiest moment of my life once more to join you

Give my love to all the family and believe me ever, my dear, dear Mary

Your affectionate uncle
Washington Irving

MANUSCRIPT: Robert Stone Grinnell.   PUBLISHED: PMI, III, 322–24 (in part).

1. Rosalia Ventimiglia Moncada (1798–1868) was the widow of Carlos Miguel Stuart Fitz-James, the seventh duke of Berwick and the fourteenth duke of Alba (1794–1835).

1689.   To ———

[March 15, 1844]

. . . . for the return of the Queen Mother; who is making her way slowly through the country, praying at every shrine and altar and having to listen and reply to loyal speeches from the Alcalde of the smallest pueblo. I hope her return may have a beneficial effect on public affairs and strengthen the throne of the little queen; but every thing in this country is full of uncertainty; and at the mercy of plots and pronunciamentos. The government at the present [*several words unrecovered*]. . . . my[1] existence is bound up.—whereas who or what is there in Madrid that you care about? I hope, however, that this letter, such as it is, will draw out a reply from you, and that you will not be rigid in requiring par value for your letters.

Yours ever very truly
Washington Irving

MANUSCRIPT: Va.–Barrett.

This fragment is the top portion of a holograph letter written on both sides of the page. Below the signature in another hand is written "The above is from a letter dated Madrid March 15. 1844."

1. The verso of the fragment begins with this word.

1690.   To Catharine Paris

Madrid, March 16. 1844.

My dear Sister,

We are preparing for great ceremonies and festivities on the arrival of the Queen Mother, who has lately entered from France and is slowly making her way to the capital, to be restored to her children. The little Queen and her sister departed from Madrid some time since, to meet her mother on the road, according to Spanish usage. The meeting is to take place a little beyond the Royal Sitio, or country residence of Aranjuez, between that place and Ocaña.¹ A temporary structure has been put up in the road for the purpose. The corps diplomatique and all the court and nobility are invited to attend on the occasion; and ⟨the⟩ Aranjuez is already crowded. This place is about twenty seven miles from Madrid, Situated in a narrow valley watered by the Tagus. It is a small town or rather village, ⟨composed⟩ ↑in which are some indifferent hotels, and large barracks of houses, and↓ which is almost deserted excepting when visited by the Sovereign in the Spring. The Royal palace is spacious, but not magnificent. The great attractions are delicious gardens; with shady walks & bowers, refreshing fountains and thousands of nightingales. Also noble avenues of trees, and fine shady drives. All these render it a paradise in this arid, naked country. And you come upon it by surprize; after traversing dreary plains for it lies sunk in a narrow green valley ⟨carve⟩ scooped out of the desert by the Tagus. As I have not yet sufficiently the use of my legs to enjoy the gardens and promenades I shall not go to Aranjuez this time, until the day before the queen is expected to arrive. I may pass some time there later in the season however, when the trees are in leaf and the Nightingales in Song, and when the court will make a sojourn there of several weeks. At present I shall go there in my carriage accompanied by my good friend Mr

Valdivielso, the Mexican Minister, who will send his horses ahead so as to form relays. I shall take Lorenzo with me. I have a room secured for me in a house taken for the season by the Albuquerques, the Prince & Princess of Carini and two or three single gentlemen of the diplomatic Corps.

The return of the Queen Mother is quite an event in the Royal Romance of the Palace; and the circumstances of her journey have really ⟨an⟩ touching interest for me. She returns by the very way by which she left the Kingdom in 1840, when the whole world seemed to be roused against her and she was followed by clamor and execrations. What is the case at present. The cities that were then almost in arms against her, now receive her with fetes and rejoicings. Arches of triumph are erected in the streets; *Te deums* are chanted in the cathedrals; processions issue forth to ⟨receive he⟩ escort her; the streets ring with shouts and acclamation; homage and adulation meet her at every step; the meanest village has its ceremonial of respect, and a speech of loyalty from its alcalde. Thus her progress through the Kingdom is a continual triumph. You will ask is not her heart lifted up and her head elevated by this triumphant reverse. Poor soul! quite otherwise. She has learnt, by sad experience, the shallowness and falseness of all this 'mouth honor' The last few years have been years of severe trial to her. You may read it, they say, in her looks and manners. Though but between thirty and forty years of age, her hair is already grey; and though yet in the heyday of life, her spirit seems subdued. ⟨Instead of being always ab⟩ Her journey seems more a pilgrimage than a triumphant progress. At every stage instead of exulting in the homage lavished upon her, she seeks the chapel and the shrine, prostrates herself before the altar and passes hours in prayer and humiliation. All this is perfectly sincere; she is in fact becoming almost a devotee; but it is the result of deep mental suffering. She still retains the amiableness of disposition, and the benignity of demeanor for which she was always remarked; for she is evidently one of those natures which sweeten and soften under affliction. She has had her errors, and great ones, but does not this humiliation and contrition of the heart atone for them. And then ↑the idea↓ that she is making her way through a Kingdom that was hostile to her and that still abounds with lurking enemies and hidden dangers, merely to take once more her children to her heart, has something in it to me extremely affecting. I shall take a deep interest in witnessing her restoration to her children. The poor little Queen and her sister are full of eagerness and anxiety on the subject, and must suffer from the delay which the Queen Mother experiences at every step of her journey.

The Meeting, as I have said, will take place on the road between Aranjuez and Ocaña: they will then proceed together to Aranjuez. The little Queen will then return to Madrid to give her mother a ceremonious reception in the Royal Palace. This will be ⟨an⟩ ↑another of the↓ imposing spectacles which that splendid edifice will furnish to this historical romance. The little Queen will descend with her court to the foot of the magnificent stair case leading up from the Great marble courts and halls to the Royal apartments. There she will receive her mother with the grandeur of a queen, but the reverence of a daughter.

That same stair case was the scene of the memorable night attack, when an attempt was made to carry off the little Queen and her sister. Is not this Royal palace a most dramatic and eventful pile!

Your affectionate brother
W I.

ADDRESSED: Mrs Daniel Paris / Care of E. Irving Esqr / New York.   POSTMARKED: [*unrecovered*] // [*unrecovered*]
MANUSCRIPT: Yale.   PUBLISHED: PMI, III, 324–25 (in part); STW, II, 174–75 (in part).

1. A village about eight miles southeast of Aranjuez.

1691. To Sarah Storrow

Madrid March 16. 1844

My dear Sarah,

I have again a letter[1] from you by the French Courier, which reached me in five days. You see what a quick conveyance this is, and one by which you may send a letter of any size free of postage.

I hope in your next to have an account of your breakfast to Capt Newton & Mr Price, and of babys breakfast to her young friends. I hope she had a high chair, in which to take the head of the table. I would have given much to have been one of the guests.

You want to know something more about the beautiful and gifted Leocadia Zamora. If you have seen Mr Livingston he probably ⟨ha⟩ may have told you something about her, as he is acquainted with her. She is a native of Havanna; where her father[2] held a post under government. He now resides in Madrid, where, at the request of government, he is preparing a work for the press on the Statistics of Spanish colonial commerce &c[3] Leocadia and a brother compose the old gentlemans ⟨f⟩ family at present, but he expects soon to be joined by his wife and two young daughters, who are in France, and he has a daughter married in England. Leocadia has been in the United States, in England, and in different parts of the continent, has received instructions from the best masters and has seen much of society. For one so handsome, so gifted and that has been so much admired, she is singularly void of affectation and pretension. She is frank, affable and animated; quick and apt in the varied application of her talents: and seems to do every thing *con amore*, that is to say, for the love of the thing itself. When she is in the mood for singing, she seems, like a bird, to be excited by her own melody, and to revel in the music. ⟨She is⟩ The first evening I passed at her house we had a succession of *Tableaus Vivants*, got up by her and two or three young friends in very beautiful style; though there were no persons present but the Calderons, Alexander Hamilton and myself. In arranging the tableaus a door at one end of a saloon was made to form the frame of the picture and a small stage was placed behind: enclosed by drapery. I suggested to Leocadia that this might be used as a little theatre,[4] in which she could give airs and even scenes from operas; with infinitely more effect than when standing at the piano. She caught the idea at once, and two or three evenings since made her first assay: the Calderons and myself forming the audience. She gave us the scene from the opera of Romeo & Juliet, where Juliet is in her bridal dress.[5] Her singing master, who is also teacher to the Queen, accompanied her on the piano. It was perfectly beautiful. She was dressed in character; and gave the delightful and affecting air with a grace an[d][6] expression worthy of an accomplished actress ⟨& which⟩ Her countenance is extremely expressive and her eyes are as fine for the stage as Fanny Kembles. In the course of the evening a young gentleman came in, a Mr Arcos, who used to perform in the amateur operas at the British Embassy. He is a splendid tenor, with a voice almost equal to Rubini's.[7] It was his first visit to Leocadias, having met with her in company a few evenings before. They sang several duets together, and their young fresh voices harmonized most admirably. I have not had such a musical treat for a long time. Mr. Arcos has a brother (at present in Paris) who is as fine a bass as he is a tenor, and who used take the lead in the operas at the Embassy. I hope he will return to Madrid before long, and then I shall not regret the opera at Paris. ⟨It is quite a⟩ I am quite a privileged auditor, and a sopha is placed where I may recline in comfort, and enjoy these treats. It is an additional comfort that the residence of the *prima donna* is but a few minutes walk from my quarters. I think I have now said enough about Leocadia Zamora. You know I am *fanatico per la musica*, but if I say any thing more you will think it is the musician and not the music that charms me.

The Queen Mother is making slow progress through the Kingdom and will not be at Aranjuez under eight or ten days; I am therefore postponing my departure and endeavoring to get myself in a State to endure the fatigues of court ceremonies. I shall avoid them as much as possible;

but the meeting of the Queen Mother and the royal children is an event not to be regarded with indifference

I have received a note from Madame Albuquerque who has ⟨alread⟩ been at Aranjuez upwards of a fortnight. She has a room all ready for me and urges me to come. The Carini's, are in the same house with her, and form part of the diplomatic commonwealth quartered under the same roof. Madame Albuquerque writes in very favorable terms of the Princess Carini, whom she finds extremely good natured and friendly: and with whom she gets on ⟨in⟩ most harmoniously. I have just discovered that our government allows the expenses of the Minister at this court, when he is obliged to follow the sovreign to the Royal Sitios or country residences. This is quite a discovery; as it will enable me to pass part of the Spring and the early part of the Summer at Aranjuez, La Granja &c, where there are delightful gardens, refreshed with fountains and full of nightingales. I dreaded the expense and meant to make my visits very brief; when absolutely compelled to go, by business or etiquette.

Give my kind remembrances to Mr Storrow and many kisses to Kate.

Your affectionate uncle
Washington Irving

ADDRESSED: Madame / Madame Storrow / No 4 Rue de la Victoire / à Paris
MANUSCRIPT: Yale.

1. This letter has not been located.
2. José María Zamora y Coronado (1785–1852) was a magistrate and director of the Royal Economic Society of Havana before coming to Madrid.
3. The study was somewhat broader than WI suggests: *Biblioteca de Legislacion Ultramarina en forma de diccionario alfabetico*, 6 vols. (Madrid, 1844–1849).
4. Above the comma WI placed a dash.
5. Probably Bellini's *I Capuletti ed i Montecchi* (1830).
6. WI omitted the bracketed letter.
7. Giovanni Battista Rubini (1795–1854) was an Italian tenor who scored great successes in the operas of Rossini, Bellini, and Donizetti. He retired in 1845 with an immense fortune. See *International Cyclopedia of Music and Musicians*, p. 1849.

1692.   To William R. King

Madrid March 21. 1844

My dear King
    This will be handed you by Dr Alfaro[1] of Madrid a gentleman of highly cultivated talents and amiable manners and who, possessed of an ample fortune, is devoting himself to Scientific studies and pursuits with the

most liberal views. He is accompanied by his wife, a lady of New York and sister to the wife of Mr Aaron Vail[2] our former representative at this court. It is their intention to pass a few months at Paris and then return to take up their residence in this city. Any attentions You may find it convenient to pay them will be esteemed as favors conferred on myself.

Should the Minister who is to succeed me at this Court pass through Paris, he may find it of advantage to become acquainted with Dr Alfaro; who will be able to give him that kind of information most important to a Stranger arriving for the first time in Spain

Every my dear King / Yours very faithfully
Washington Irving

His Excellency / William R King / &c &c &c

Manuscript: SHR.

William R. deV. King (1786–1853), who had served as a U.S. congressman from North Carolina from 1811 to 1816 and as a U.S. senator from Alabama from 1819 to 1844, was appointed minister to France earlier in 1844 to forestall French and British intervention in the American annexation of the Republic of Texas.

1. Probably Nicolas de Alfaro, who had written *Tratado de colera-morbo* (Barcelona, 1832) and *Tratado teorico-practico de enfermedades cutaneas* (Madrid, 1840).

2. Aaron Vail had married Emilie Salles of New York.

1693. To Catharine Paris

Madrid, March 23d. 1844

My dear Sister,

I have just received your long letter of Feb. 25 to 29th.[1] and feel how kind it is in you to give me such frequent budgets from home. Your letters are full of matter; and being written from day to day give me an every day peep into domestic affairs. I have a letter also from Pierre M Irving, giving me a very satisfactory statement of my affairs, which he has managed with great judgement. He is an invaluable friend and Standby, on whom I feel that I can rely with the most entire confidence, as he serves me through affection, not interest. He comes next to my dear brothers in that full communion of heart and soul which is the invincible bond of Kindred.

I must now give you a chapter of the Romance of the Palace. I set off the day before yesterday for Aranjuez, to be present at the meeting of the little queen and her mother. I started at six oclock in the morning in my carriage, with old Pedro the coachman, and my faithful Lorenzo.

Mr Valdevielso the Mexican Minister accompanied me: having sent on his four horses to be stationed on the road as relays. We had a beautiful morning & enjoyed our drive to the old village of Val de Moro,[2] where we left Pedro and the horses to await our return, and took the first pair of Mr Valdevielsos horses with his coachman. With these we drove to Aranjuez, not finding occasion to use the second relay: which followed us. We arrived at Aranjuez at half past eleven, and found the meeting was expected to take place about five oclock in the after noon, about three miles from Aranjuez, on the road to Ocaña: a royal tent having been put up for the occasion. Aranjuez was crowded with company—All the nobility from Madrid, ⟨with⟩ The Military; & official characters of all sorts not to mention office hunters and the countless crowd that courts the smiles of royalty. Every vehicle at Madrid had been engaged at high prices to bring on the multitude; every lodging good or bad at Aranjuez had been taken up before hand. I had comfortable quarters with my good friends the Albuquerques, and found myself the inmate of quite a diplomatic common wealth, occupying a huge house hired for the occasion. It was two stories high, built round a square court yard. You may imagine the size of the Spanish houses when I tell you that in this were accommodated the French Ambassador and his lady, with two young gentlemen of the Embassy: The Albuquerques and their family. The Prince and Princess di Carini; the Count Marnix ⟨Charge⟩ Belgian charge d'affaires. Mr. D'Albergo, charge d'affaires of Denmark; The Mexican Minister and myself—and that each family had a distinct apartment to itself, with sitting rooms, antechambres &c. We all dined together, and a pleasant dinner we had: while throughout the day and evening Madame Albuquerques Saloon was a general resort. Here I had a comfortable Sofa to lounge upon, and was quite petted by the good people. This gathering together of the diplomatic corps had indeed a most sociable agreeable effect. We seemed like one family. I ⟨beg⟩ became great friends with the Princess Carini, who is full of good humor, and good spirits and disposed to take the world cheerfully. Her husband was quite the life of the house: ever ready for any thing that may ⟨present⟩ amuse: a man of varied talent: a musician a painter &c &c. I do not wonder that his little wife is fond of him notwithstanding his ugliness.

In the course of the afternoon I drove out with Mr Valdevielso to the place where the Royal meeting was to take place. The road was full of carriages & horsemen; hastening to the rendezvous, ⟨which⟩ and was lined with Spectators, seated by the road side in gaping expectation. The Scene of the Rendezvous was quite picturesque. In an open plain, a short distance from the road, was pitched the Royal tent; very spacious, and decorated with fluttering flags and streamers, three or four other tents were pitched in the vicinity, and there was an immense assemblage of

carriages; with ⟨troops of ca⟩ squadrons of cavalry; and crowds of people
of all ranks from the grandee to the beggar. We left our carriage at a
distance from the tent and proceeded on foot, to the Royal presence. The
impatience of the little queen ⟨would⟩ and her sister would not permit
them to remain in the tent: they were continually sallying forth among
the throng of courtiers, to a position that commanded a distant view of
the road of Ocana, as it sloped down the side of a rising ground. Poor
things, they were kept nearly a couple of hours in anxious suspence.
Twice there were false alarms. The young princesses (daughters to the
Deceased Infanta) having preceded the queen mother several miles).[3] At
length the royal cortege was seen descending the distant slope of the
road; escorted by Squadrons of lancers: whose yellow uniforms, with
the red flag of the lance fluttering aloft—made them look at a distance
like a ↑moving↓ mass of fire and flame As they drew near the squadrons
of horse wheeled off into the plain and the royal carriage approached.
The impatience of the little Queen could no longer be restrained. Without waiting at the entrance of the tent to receive her royal mother according to etiquette she hurried forth, through the avenue of ⟨solid?⟩
guards, quite to the road; where I lost sight of her amidst a throng of
courtiers, horseguards &c &c. There the Mother and her children were
locked in each others embraces, with a fullness of feeling that defied all
etiquette. A few minutes afterwards I saw them as they passed into the
tent—the queen mother in the middle, ↑clasping↓ ⟨with⟩ the hands of her
children; her face varying with conflicting emotions. As to the little queen,
she was sobbing with joy and the tears were streaming down her cheeks.
The reception of the queen mother was quite enthusiastic. The air resounded with acclamations. As she passed into the tent I saw many
throw themselves on their knees and kiss ⟨th⟩ her hands: others, stern
soldiers too, absolutely wept like children. Much of this enthusiasm may
have been false, or interested, but much evidently came from the heart.
The queen mother was much beloved by those who had personal occasion
of knowing her amiable qualities: beside, ⟨many of the⟩ the Old nobility
⟨look on⟩ who have long been cast down and dispirited, and surrounded
by doubt and danger, look upon the return of the Queen Mother as the
triumph of their cause, and the harbinger of happier and more prosperous
days. God send it may prove so! It was quite affecting to see the meetings of some of the court party with those of their kindred and friends
who had returned with the queen from a long exile.

After witnessing this meeting I hastened back to Aranjuez to dine and
get some repose before the reception of the corps diplomatique, which
was to take place at the Palace at half past nine Oclock. We were received in plain clothes; the queen mother wishing to avoid the necessity
of putting on a Court dress. The Royal palace was illuminated, and was

surrounded by a crowd. We were received in a very beautiful saloon, furnished in the style of "the Empire" that is to say, the classic style prevalent during the reign of Napoleon. Our diplomatic circle has quite increased of late, since the Queen has been recognized by different courts. The Ambassador of France takes precedence in it, from his diplomatic rank: then come the ministers &c according to the date of their residence, first the Portuguese Minister then myself, then the Mexican Minister &c—The little Queen entered the room, followed by her mother and her Sister and the Minister of State. The Ambassador of France made her a congratulatory address in the name of the Corps—to which she read a brief, written reply—She then, followed by her Mother & Sister, passed along the line, addressing some words of course to each member of the diplomatic corps: after which, the royal party curtsey'd themselves out of the room.

I was, as you may suppose, extremely interested by the appearance of the Queen Mother. She does not, at present, resemble any of the pictures I have seen of her. She is thinner. Indeed, she has the appearance of one somewhat worn by care and anxiety: yet she has a benignant expression of countenance, a most engaging smile, and a deportment full of kindness and affability. The little Queen was all radiant with joy. I told her I had seen her in tears that day and that I hoped she would have frequent cause to shed such happy tears.

Such is a hurried account of this most interesting meeting. I was glad to get to bed that night, for my poor ↑ancles↓ fairly ached with having to be so much on my legs that day. The next morning Mr Valdivielso and myself returned to Madrid, as did most of the diplomatic corps; so as to be ready to see the royal entrance in the Capital. It will take place between three and four Oclock this afternoon, and I will keep my letter open to give you a word or two about it. The original plan was for the little Queen to precede her mother by a day or so, so as to be ready to receive her at the palace, according to royal etiquette; but when once the mother and children found themselves together it was impossible for them to separate, and so it was determined they should all come on together this day. I was amused to hear of the little Queens difficulty ⟨to⟩ as assuming rank and state with her mother. She begged to know of her mother whether they might not go on together. It is not for me to say, replied Maria Christina—You are the Queen now—and you are to say when and how it is to be—So in entering the carriage the little Queen could not be prevailed upon to ⟨take⟩ seat herself on the right side of her Mother (the place of State) until the latter told her that these points of etiquette must be observed.

I was amused too, to observe her, on entering the Saloon where she gave us audience, drawing back to let her mother take the lead; and the latter repeatedly giving her a gentle touch and motioning her forward with a smile. As she began her movement along the diplomatic line her mother watched her with a fond yet half anxious eye, ⟨it⟩ to see how her young, inexperienced child would play the queen. She did it however, very well: indeed she acquits herself with much self possession on these occasions. She is growing quite womanly: and is almost as tall as her mother. Her figure is full; but her complexion is ⟨sa⟩ pale, and I fear her constitution is not a strong one.

Aranjuez is not yet in its beauty. The trees are not in leaf; and there is an air of dilapidation and neglect about the place. A little later however, when the groves and avenues and gardens are all verdant and blooming and the Nightingales in song, it will be a delightful change from the dreary nakedness of Madrid Scenery.

It is thought the court will go there in April to pass some weeks there: in which case the diplomatic corps will for the most part, take up their quarters there. ⟨I shall⟩ If so I shall pass some time there; and am promised an apartment in the house occupied by the Albuquerques &c[.] I am happy to find that our government bears the ⟨expen⟩ extra expense incurred by its ministers in accompanying the Court in its Summer visits to Aranjuez. La Granja, the Escurial &c—Indeed it would be a hard case to subject them to expenses of the Kind, incurred in no other court. Under such circumstances, these summer visits to the 'Sitios' or Royal country residences, divirsify the monotony of Madrid life—

I have just returned from witnessing the ⟨entry of⟩ entrance of ⟨the⟩ Queen Christina: but have no time to give particulars, as it is dinner time & the courier is about to depart. There was a great parade of military and the streets were filled with a countless multitude. The Queen Mother sat in an open carriage on the left hand of her daughter The houses were all decorated with tapestry hung out of the windows and balconys. The reception of the Queen by the populace was not very animated; She is popular with the Moderados, that is to say, the aristocracy—

I must close my letter abruptly with love to "all bodies"

Your affectionate brother
Washington Irving

MANUSCRIPT: Yale.   PUBLISHED: PMI, III, 326–31 (in part); STW, II, 174–75 (in part).

1. This letter and the one to PMI have not been located.
2. A town about fifteen miles south of Madrid, midway on the road to Aranjuez.
3. WI did not include an opening parenthesis.

1694. To Sarah Storrow

Madrid, March 23d. 1844

My dear Sarah,

I enclose a letter to your mother which must serve instead of an ample one to yourself. I received your last letter on thursday at Aranjuez not long after my arrival; it having come on there ⟨in the⟩ with the Courier to the Ambassador. You see how promptly letters come to hand by the Ambassadors bag; and then you need not mind how large a pacquet of letters you make up.

I am much pleased with your account of the two breakfasts: to Capt Newton, and to little Kates play mates. Capt Newton is well worthy of the good opinion you express of him.

When you see Mr Sumner I beg you to remember me to him and tell him that I have continually had the intention of answering his ⟨in a⟩ letters, but have been so pressed by my various correspondence, and incommoded by ⟨th⟩ my ill health, that my intention has remained unexecuted. I really have received two or three very agreeable and interesting letters from him from various parts of Spain; and do seriously intend to answer them, whenever I can find time, but I am much tasked by my correspondence and indeed a little too free indulgence of my pen lately has I think produced a temporary irritation of my complaint. I beg you to be civil to Mr Sumner when you meet him.

With kind remembrances to your husband and many kisses to the little limb,

Your affectionate uncle
W. I.

Manuscript: Yale.

1695. To Pierre M. Irving

Madrid, March 24, 1844

My dear Pierre:

I have received your letter of the 29th February,[1] containing the account current and the statement, both of which are highly satisfactory. I am glad to find that you have concluded the Green Bay transfer, and raked twenty-one hundred dollars for me out of the ashes and cinders of that once sanguine speculation.[2] It is so much money that will yield me interest during my lifetime, instead of producing a possible profit after my death. I trust my other investments will turn out more productive, but shall be glad to get them in such a train as to yield me income. I watch with an anxious eye the gradual growth of my productive funds at home. * * *

The cruel malady which has afflicted me for nearly fourteen months past, has marred those literary plans on which I calculated so sanguinely when I set off upon my mission. I have lately resumed my pen, and occupied myself occasionally with revising some of my works for a new edition; but I have to exercise the pen sparingly, as I find literary excitement produces irritation in my complaint. My correspondence, too, is a heavy tax upon my pen, and occupies most of the time I can venture to devote to it; yet I cannot give it up; it is the only mode I have now of keeping up an intercourse with my family and friends. * * * * *

I need not say how much I am delighted with the work.[3] It well sustains the high reputation acquired by the History of Ferdinand and Isabella. * * * * * * * * *

I doubt whether Mr. Prescott was aware of the extent of the sacrifice I made. This was a favorite subject, which had delighted my imagination ever since I was a boy. I had brought home books from Spain to aid me in it, and looked upon it as the pendent to my Columbus. When I gave it up to him, I in a manner gave him up my bread, for I depended upon the profit of it to recruit my waning finances. I had no other subject at hand to supply its place. I was dismounted from my *cheval de bataille*, and have never been completely mounted since. Had I accomplished that work, my whole pecuniary situation would have been altered. * * * When I made the sacrifice, it was not with a view to compliments or thanks, but from a warm and sudden impulse. I am not sorry for having made it. Mr. Prescott has justified the opinion I expressed at the time, that he would treat the subject with more close and ample research than I should probably do, and would produce a work more thoroughly worthy of the theme. He has produced a work that does honor to himself and his country, and I wish him the full enjoyment of his laurels.

The plan I had intended to pursue was different from that which he has adopted. I should not have had any preliminary dissertation on the history, civilization, &c., of the natives, as I find such dissertations hurried over, if not skipped entirely, by a great class of readers, who are eager for narrative and action. I should have carried on the reader with the discoverers and conquerors, letting the newly explored countries break upon him as it did upon them; describing objects, places, customs, as they awakened curiosity and interest, and required to be explained for the conduct of the story. The reader should first have an idea of the superior civilization of the people from the great buildings and temples

of stone and lime that brightened along the coast, and "shone like silver."
He should have had vague accounts of Mexico from the people on the
seaboard; from the messengers of Montezuma.[4] His interest concerning
it should have increased as he went on, deriving ideas of its grandeur,
power, riches, &c., from the Tlascalans,[5] &c. Every step, as he accompanied the conquerors on their march, would have been a step develop-
ing some striking fact, yet the distance would still have been full of
magnificent mystery. He should next have seen Mexico from the mountains, far below him, shining with its vast edifices, its glassy lakes, its
far-stretching causeways, its sunny plain, surrounded by snow-topped
volcanoes. Still it would have been vague in its magnificence. At length
he should have marched in with the conquerors, full of curiosity and
wonder, on every side beholding objects of novelty, indicating a mighty
people, distinct in manners, arts, and civilization from all the races of
the Old World. During the residence in the capital, all these matters
would have been fully described and explained in connection with the
incidents of the story. In this way the reader, like the conquerors, would
have become gradually acquainted with Mexico and the Mexicans; and
by the time the conquest was achieved, he would have been familiar
with the country, without having been detained by long dissertations,
so repulsive to the more indolent class of readers.

My intention also was, to study the different characters of the *dramatis
personae*, so as to bring them out in strong relief, and to have kept them,
as much as possible, in view throughout the work. It is surprising how
quickly distinctive characteristics may be caught from a few incidental
words in old documents, letters, &c., and how the development of them
and the putting them in action gives life and reality to a narrative. Most
of the traits that give individuality to Columbus, in my biography of
him, were gathered from slightly mentioned facts in his journals, letters,
&c., which had remained almost unnoticed by former writers on the
subject.

However, I am running on into idle "scribble scrabble" about a
matter now passed away, and which I would not utter to any one but
yourself, who are becoming in a manner my father confessor. My plan
might have had an advantage in some respects; it might have thrown a
more poetical interest over the work; but the plan of Mr. Prescott is
superior in other respects; and I feel I never should have wrought out
a work so "worthy of all acceptation,"[6] as that which he has given to
the public.

PUBLISHED: PMI, III, 332–33, 143–45.

According to PMI (III, 146), this letter was marked "(Private)."

1. This letter has not been located.

2. John Jacob Astor had sold WI five shares of Astor's land in the Green Bay area for $4000. See WI to Peter Irving, February 16, 1836.

3. W. H. Prescott's *The Conquest of Mexico*, of which WI had just received a copy. He had read the work in the proof sheets which Prescott had sent to Calderón de la Barca. See WI to Sarah Storrow, December 20, 1843.

4. Montezuma (1466–1520), the Aztec ruler captured by Cortés.

5. Residents of Tlaxcala, an Indian district which refused to surrender to the Aztec Confederation. They joined with Cortés as his principal ally in the conquest of Mexico from 1519 to 1521.

6. See Timothy 1:15.

1696. To Sarah Storrow

Madrid, March 30th. 1844

My dear Sarah,

Your letter (including Julia Grinnels)[1] put in the Ambassadors bag on Saturday reached me on Thursday morning; you see what a prompt conveyance this is, beside costing nothing. It was an excellent idea of yours to forward Julias letter. I shall detain it a little longer, to read it once or twice again, and then return it to you. It is a most satisfactory, delightful letter. I feel deeply gratified by Julias attention to the girls, thus breaking their long monotonous winter by a six weeks visit to the City. Poor Girls; I have always regretted their too great seclusion at the Cottage; but have not had the means of obviating it.

I shall, as you may suppose, feel greatly the departure of Mr Hamilton, who is one of the cheerfullest, most amiable and intelligent of companions, but it is a consolation to me that he will be [s]ucceeded [*MS damaged by seal*] by a gentleman with whom I have had an opportunity of becoming well acquainted, and whom I know to be well fitted for the office. Mr Livingston, though apparently a fashionable man of society, is quiet and intellectual in his habits and pursuits: at least he has been so while at Madrid. He is sufficiently a man of business for all the business there is likely to be in this legation. He has been almost domesticated with me so that I have had an opportunity of judging of his companionable qualities, which are very satisfactory. His manners are excellent. I therefore think I ⟨am fortunate⟩ shall be fortunate if the government appoint him to the Secretaryship. It ⟨is⟩ ↑will be↓ a pleasure to me to have with me a son of Judge Livingston with whom I read law in my younger days. You know I hold greatly to these early reccollections

I find by your letter we are to have Mr & Mrs Deacon here in a short time. She will not be the first American lady to visit Madrid during my residence. For a few days past we have had a Mr & Mrs Cromwell[2] here. He is a lawyer from New York, ⟨we⟩ a pleasant looking, good humored fellow who has mounted a beard and moustaches, and been rattling about the world for some months past; Scouring Europe; visiting Greece, Constantinople &c &c with his wife, a pleasing, slight built, little American woman, ↑superior to her husband, as women often are,↓ who braves every hardship and danger with real manly spirit They dined with me the other day in company with Mr Weston, whom you spoke of sometime since in one of your letters as a clergyman, but also, by what we can gather from his conversation, has been a military man, a lawyer & perhaps half a dozen other things. He is a very agreeable, intelligent man, of the Boston School, and appears to have an old fashioned veneration for the Greeks and Romans. As he will remain here some little time longer I shall no doubt see more of him. Mr Cromwell and his wife set off tomorrow on their way to Paris

Two American Gentlemen called yesterday while I was out, but did not leave their names; they are to call this morning at One Oclock. I am inclined to think they are a Mr Jones and a Mr Parker of whom I heard lately from Malaga. Can this Mr Parker be any relative of Mrs Deacon, come here to meet her?[3]

In fact Madrid is becoming much more a place of visitation of the Americans than it used to be though still ⟨not⟩ an immeasurable distance behind Paris in this particular. Col Winchester, when he was here, told me that he was one of, I think, *forty six* presented at one time to Louis Philippe—What a task for a minister to have to present such a regiment! I never could stand it.

We have had a grand Besamanos (or Hand Kissing) at the Palace, (in honor of the Return of Maria Christina) and various entertainments at the Theatres, Churches &c, to which the Diplomatic Corps were invited.[4] I have had to absent myself from most of them in consequence of my persevering malady. I am now taking a course of baths at home, and, as usual, hope they will be effectual. If it was not for this *hope* which seems as persevering as the malady, I do not know what would become of me.

Our Spring is backward, not from Cold, but from drought. ⟨The⟩ Vegetation needs more moisture to bring it forth; and there has been very little rain for months past. My drives, therefore, in the neighborhood of the City continue to be somewhat dull and dreary; but I hope soon to find the Meadows along the Manzanares once more green; the groves in leaf, and the nightingales in Song. I doubt if the King who first made Madrid the court residence, has yet got out of purgatory for this monstrous evil inflicted upon the nation and its visitors. I hope he may be kept there as long as I am obliged to sojourn here—so theres christian charity for you.

I find Kate is still cutting teeth, and quarrelling with the last comer.

By the time this letter reaches you she will have got over the affair. She certainly has had a most favorable time with her teeth, and I am inclined to attribute it ⟨to s⟩ in some degree to the healthful course you observe in her diet and daily treatment. This will probably render light any other maladies incident to childhood, which she may yet have to undergo—It certainly will have a permanent effect on her constitution and her happiness—Give her many kisses for me: whom she must, by this time, have entirely forgotten.

With kind remembrances to your husband

Your affectionate Uncle
Washington Irving

Manuscript: Yale.   Published: PMI, III, 333–34 (in part).

1. These letters have not been located.
2. This may be Charles T. Cromwell, an attorney with an office at 5 Peck-slip and a residence at 107 East Broadway. See *Longworth's New York City Directory for 1841–42*, p. 202.
3. At this point WI placed an asterisk and wrote vertically on the fold between pages two and three the following: "I have since seen them. Mr Parker is brother of Mrs Deacon, Mr Jones is a fine handsome gentlemanly fellow from South Carolina They dine with me tomorrow"
4. The besamanos, together with parties at the theater and opera house and a Te Deum, were reported in *El Castellano*, March 27, 30, 1844.

1697. To George Sumner

[Madrid, Late March, 1844]

I have just received Prescott's "Conquest of Mexico." I had already perused it in proof sheets lent me by Mr. Calderon de la Barca. It is an admirable work and fully sustains the high reputation he acquired by his "Ferdinand and Isabella." It has the advantage, too, of being quite different as to the nature of the theme, so as to afford a variety in the exercise of his pen. I shall now look forward with confident anticipations of delight to the history of "Philip the Second" which he is about to undertake, and which will open a new field for his talent. The two works he has produced are signal triumphs for our literature, which will be repeated in every language of the civilized world.

Published: Rollo Ogden, *William Hickling Prescott* (Boston, 1904), pp. 148–49.

The date is determined from a similar reference to Prescott's book in WI's letter to PMI, March 24, 1844.

1698. To the Secretary of State

Legation of the United States. / Madrid April 2nd. 1844.

No. 38. / The Hon: The Secretary of State[1] / of the United States —
Washington.

Sir,

It was some time after the date of my last despatch, before the hurried state of the Spanish Cabinet, incident to the return of the Queen Mother, permitted me to have an interview with Mr. Gonzalez Bravo, Minister of State. When I had such opportunity I took occasion, according to my instructions (,) from the Department, to express in the strongest terms the high estimation of the government of the United States for the public and private character of the Chevalier D'Argaïz, and the regret with which the president had received the letters of his recall; and in eulogizing the vigilance and ability with which the Chevalier had availed himself of the "favorable interests" of the United States, I alluded especially,—as I was instructed,—to his conduct on a recent occasion with regard to the island of Cuba.[2]

And here, I cannot but notice how illy I was prepared by the Department to discuss this delicate point. I was instructed to dwell strongly on the eminent services rendered to his country by the chevalier; "especially on a recent occasion when this government had an opportunity of manifesting the sincerity of its friendship for Her Catholic Majesty, with reference to the Island of Cuba; not without some sacrifice on its part, which the importance of the crisis seemed to demand." Now with respect to all this important and delicate transaction, thus vaguely alluded to, this Legation has hitherto been left by the department completely in the dark; and all that it knows respecting the application of the Chevalier to our government for assistance and the consequent manifestations of friendship on our part, was communicated by *a member of the French legation at Madrid.*

In reply to my observations, Mr. G. Bravo, after admitting the general good character and good conduct of the Chevalier D'Argaiz, observed that, in the affair of Cuba, that gentleman had acted without especial, and quite beyond the limits of his general, instructions. That he had been precipitate and indiscreet, and had unnecessarily run the risk of compromising his government with the government of another nation; his application to the government of the United States having become known in the Island and having filled it with rumors of armed intervention on our part, and awakened the jealousy of the British Consul.

As I have observed, the vagueness of my information on this topic left me at a disadvantage in discussing it; I however made the best defence of the conduct of the Chevalier that my materials permitted, and dwelt on the unequivocal manifestations of active and effective friendship on the part of the government of the United States which his application had called forth, and which, I observed, ought to be highly satisfactory to Her Majesty's Government, as well as conducive to the tranquility of the Island.

Mr. Gonzalez Bravo made very full acknowledgements on this head, and assured me that the government was perfectly satisfied of the patriotism and good intentions of the Chevalier D'Argaiz and would give him convincing proofs to that effect on his return home.

From the course of my conversation with Mr. Gonzalez Bravo on this, and on a former occasion, and from all that I have been able to collect elsewhere, I am satisfied there is no ground for "uneasiness" or "suspicion" as to any sinister influence of England in the recall of the Chevalier D'Argaiz. I apprehend that it has been contemplated ever since the downfall of Espartero, of whom he was considered a partizan; and was a part of the general "turning out" of the office holders under the regency, to provide for adherents to the dominant party; and I think it highly probable he would have been recalled, had the affair of Cuba not occurred.

I repeat what I expressed in my last despatch, that I am satisfied nóthing is to be apprehended in this quarter, at present, from any machinations of England with regard to the island of Cuba. I do not apprehend any pecuniary pressure that would induce this government to concede to her a control over that Island. Indeed, any measure of the kind would be one of the most unpopular expedients the government could adopt, both from the jealousy of the public with regard to English interference of all kinds, and from the sensitive pride of the Spaniards respecting the few but precious relics left of their once splendid American domains.

With respect to the case of Mr. Maximo de Aguirre, our Consul at Bilbao, I find there is no need of any further application in his favor, as I learn from him, that, by an order of the Spanish government, the whole of the fines extorted at Bilbao by Generals Alcala and Zurbano, are to be refunded in monthly payments out of the revenue of the custom house of that city

I have had a tedious correspondence with Mr. Aguirre,[3] having had to explain to him, what had repeatedly been explained to him before, the peculiarities of his case as a Spanish subject officiating as a foreign consul; and proving to him, that, in all respects where his consular privileges had been interfered with, Mr. Vail had promptly and effectually remonstrated in his *official* capacity; but had properly made only *informal* representations where the circumstances of the case concerned the allegiance of Mr. Aguirre to the Spanish government.

Mr. Aguirre is at length brought to unwilling conviction on this head; but, finding the privileges and immunities of the consulship so short of his original conception, expresses his wish to resign the post, observing "that the United States offer no encouragement to consuls thus placed, to display much zeal in their service:" He adds however that he will continue his official assistance to Masters and Mariners until the American government finds opportunity to appoint a more Suitable servant in his place;[4] but intimates an intention to persevere in a course which he has observed ever since the indignities he experienced in his consular character in 1841; viz, "to decline all invitations to public ceremonies; and to cease the visits and courtesies to military and superior authorities in company with the consuls of England, France, Holland & Belgium—."

I trust the government may be able to find a successor to Mr. Aguirre willing to fulfil these more important duties of his office. I cannot but observe, however, the swelling ideas which foreign functionaries of this class are apt to entertain; and how difficult it is to make them understand that after all, a consul is but a mortal man, and subject to mortal laws.

Since my last notice of public affairs, the Queen Mother has arrived and taken up her residence in the Royal palace. It was apprehended that her return would produce great changes in the Cabinet; and the capital has of late days been full of rumors to that effect; but, I understand she expresses herself satisfied with the conduct of the present Ministers,[5] and well disposed to give them time to carry out their plan of policy. The latter have certainly acted with unwonted energy and hardihood, and aided by martial law, have carried into operation measures which less daring and more scrupulous statesmen would not have ventured to propose: They have altered the law of Ayuntamientos, or municipalities; disarmed the militia, reorganized the army; formed a civil guard similar to the gendarmerie, of France;[6] effected great financial contracts, and are now contemplating, it is said, the formation of a royal body guard of ten thousand men, similar to that disbanded by Espartero; the establishment of a censorship of the press; and the convocation of "Cortes Constituyentes" for the modification of the Constitution!

The insurrections of Alicant and Carthagena are at an end, and Boné and many of his fellow insurgents have paid for their treason with their lives; still, martial law continues and will probably be kept up until the Ministers have carried all their bold schemes into operation. There has lately been a sudden talk of a war with Marocco to avenge the death of a Spanish Consular agent:[7] The Ministerial papers were for a time vehement and voluminous on the subject, though it did not appear that they had clearly ascertained the circumstances of the case, or the gravity of the offen⟨s⟩ce. It is thought the Ministry were glad of something to occupy the public mind, and to find distant occupation for dangerous spirits of the army; who were growing factious in idleness. France, it is said, encourages this martial project; as it would favor her African enterprize; and prevent a more dangerous European neighbour on the Barbary Coast. The french papers have even talked of the policy of giving the Spaniards military aid in this new crusade; pretending to feel aggrieved by the death of the Spanish Consul; he having been by birth a Frenchman.

This war talk, however, though furious for a time, has rather cooled for some days past; there being doubts of the safety of detaching a large military force to a distance, under the command of ambitious officers; lest it might produce another military revolution.

I am Sir / Very respectfully / Your Obt Servt
Washington Irving

DOCKETED: Recd. 22 May. / Mr. Markoe [top of page 1] / No 38. W. Irving, Madrid. 2 Apl. 1844
MANUSCRIPT: NA, RG 59.   PUBLISHED: Manning, Diplomatic Correspondence, 337–38 (in part).

Only the complimentary close and signature are in WI's handwriting.

1. WI used this form of address because he had apparently heard of the death of A. P. Upshur but did not know the name of his successor. John C. Calhoun was appointed on March 6, 1844, and entered upon his duties on April 1, 1844.

2. On March 2, 1844, WI had reported to the State Department his earlier conversations with González Bravo on this subject.

3. See WI's letters of December 16, 1843; March 3 and 12, 1844.

4. Aguirre apparently continued in the post until the early 1860's. See Hasse, Index to U.S. Documents, III, 1745.

5. Ministers in the González Bravo cabinet included Manuel Mazarredo (1807–1857), war; Carrasco, finance; Luis Mayáns y Enriquez de Navarra (1805–1880), justice; Peñaflorida, interior; and Portillo, marine. See Christiansen, Military Power, p. 170; and London Times, February 1, 10, and April 4, 11, 1844.

6. This nonpartisan military group was designed to promote law and order without the corruption of earlier groups. See Raymond Carr, Spain, 1809–1939, pp. 233–34; and El Castellano, March 29 and April 1, 1844.

7. In February of 1844, Victor Darmon, a native of Marseilles who was Spanish consular agent at Maragon on the coast of Morocco, was dragged into the streets and killed. The Spanish government threatened to send an expeditionary force to Morocco, but, as WI suggests, this threat may have been an attempt to divert attention from domestic problems. See London Times, March 21, April 10, 1844; and El Castellano, March 26, 27, 28, 1844.

1699. To Sarah Storrow

Madrid April 6th. 1844.

My dear Sarah,

I have again a letter[1] from you by the French Courier; which came to hand as usual, on Thursday morning. Holy Week has been kept up with great pomp and solemnity in Madrid: there have been grand religious ceremonies in the Palace, superb music in the Royal Chapel; processions of the Queens & court to various churches &c—I however, have been obliged to absent myself from all; not being willing to encounter the fatigue nor to run the risk of taking cold, now that I am taking a course of baths. I take the latter at home, and have a snug little bathing room opening into my bed room. The baths appear to be very efficacious and give me hopes of at length conquering my malady.

Tomorrow I give a sociable dinner to the Calderons, who leave Madrid in the course of the coming week.

There is talk that the Court will go to Aranjuez ⟨toward⟩ in the course of this month, to pass several weeks there. If so I shall go there for a time, and take up my quarters in the house hired by the Albuquerques; Carinis and others of the Diplomatic Corps. I hope to be ⟨so⟩ sufficiently recovered to take exercise in the gardens and delightful promenades for which that place is noted.

I have seen nothing of my fair friend Leocadia since I last wrote to you. She gave a delightful soiree I am told, with beautiful tableaux vivantes, and *tableaux cantantes,* ↑among↓ the last her soliloquy in Juliet[2]—and the harp scene of Desdemona, in Otello,[3] ↑both↓ which I am told were exquisite, both as to singing and acting. Unfortunately I was not well enough to attend. I hope however to be indemnified on some future occasion.

We are to have two Italian Opera troupes here this season. One as usual in the Circo:[4] the other to alternate between the two theatres[5] which have hitherto given Spanish plays: so I shall be at no loss for music. It is true we have nothing on the Stage here to equal the first rate singers of Paris; but I have an accommodating palate, and, when I cannot get truffled turkeys and pates de Strasbourg I can reconcile myself to a Spanish *puchero.*[6] Beside, some of the singers here are very respectable; ⟨and⟩ the choruses are good and the orchestra performs its part very decently: so that upon the whole, a man like myself, who is amateur rather than connoisseur, can find wherewithal to make out a very good evenings amusement. We have a basso, here, Salvatori,[7] who is a *first rate* actor, and has been a first rate singer; ⟨though his vo⟩ but his voice is now a little worn. He was the original Belisario[8]—the part having been composed for him; and his performance of it is really noble.

I am glad you have seen Mr Livingston; and that you are pleased with him. You would not like him worse for knowing him better; for he has real worth which improves upon you as you become acquainted with him. I am satisfied he will be fully competent to all the business likely to come under his attention. You are right too in your opinion of Mr Sumner. He is extremely well informed and has seen a great deal of the world; and has an entertaining manner of relating what he has seen. I was too unwell last summer to do justice to his society; having to be for hours with him tete a tete almost every day, when I could not keep up conversation and at times could not enjoy it. I always found him most obliging and invariably good humored. I apprehend some injustice has been done to him by Americans, who exaggerate his mode of *getting on* in society, and are perhaps envious of his success. He certainly is enterprising and persevering in the matter; but his object is to see people of *merit* and *renown,* rather than people of *rank* and *fashion*; and whenever ⟨his⟩ he has made his way to them he has been able by his conversation to hold his ground. He must have a world of anecdote and curious remark in his common place book. Do not hesitate to encourage his visits, there is more instruction and amusement in his conversation than in that of half a hundred well bred, well dressed, commonplace americans.

I enclose a dainty letter confided to my care by the worthy Lorenzo: who seems to entertain a soft reccollection of babys lady of the bed chamber.

I would give any thing to pass one of these fine Spring mornings with you in the garden of the Tuilleries: with Kate racing after her big ball; and I would give still more to have you and her with me here—I should then content myself even with Madrid. Kiss the little darling for me— Remember me kindly to Mr Storrow

Your affectionate uncle
Washington Irving

ADDRESSED: Madame / Madame Storrow / No. 4 Rue de la Victoire / à Paris
MANUSCRIPT: Yale.   PUBLISHED: STW, II, 169 (in part).

1. This letter has not been located.

2. For other details, see WI to Sarah Storrow, March 16, 1844.

3. In the third act of Rossini's *Otello, ossia il Moro di Venezia* (1832) Desdemona sings "Assisa al pie d'un salice." See Stendhal, *The Life of Rossini,* trans. Richard N. Coe (New York, 1970), pp. 232–34.

4. El Teatro del Circo was a recently built theater in Madrid featuring musical performances. See Richard Ford, *A Hand-Book for Travellers in Spain,* III, 1181; and *El Castellano,* April 6, 1844.

5. Teatro de la Cruz (built in 1737 and seating 1,300) and Del Principe (built in 1806 and seating 1,200). See Ford, *A Hand-Book for Travellers in Spain*, III, 1181–82.

6. Stew or ordinary food.

7. Celestino Salvatori.

8. Donizetti's opera *Belisario* (1835–1836) had its premiere on February 4, 1836, at the Teatro la Fenice in Venice with Salvatori in the title role. See Herbert Weinstock, *Donizetti and the World of Opera in Italy, Paris, and Venice*, pp. 350–51.

1700. To Luis González Bravo

Legacion de los Estados Unidos / de America Madrid 8 de abril de 1844

Muy Señor mio

Con sumo sentimiento me he visto en la imposibilidad de concurrir a la mayor parte de las funciones que se han celebrado con el plausible motivo de la feliz vuelta de S. M. la Reina madre. Así es que V. me dispensará un particular favor, si, cuando la ocasion se presente, quiere manifestar a SS. MM. que mi falta de asistencia esta muy lejos de ser causada por la del mas profundo respeto hacia sus augustas personas o de verdadera simpatía por un suceso tan interesante por si mismo y del que tantos bienes debe prometerse la nacion; no reconsciendo otro principio que el mal estado de mi salud que pone fuera de mis facultades el asistir como descará á esas ceremonias publicas.

Rogando a V. sirva aceptar mis gracias anticipadas por tal obsequio, queda de V.

&ca. &c.
Washington Irving.

Exmo Señor D. Luis Gonzalez Bravo. / &ca. &ca. &ca.

MANUSCRIPT: NA, RG 84 (copy in WI's hand).

Translation:

"With the greatest regret I have found myself in the impossibility of attending the greater part of the ceremonies commendably celebrated on the occasion of the felicitous return of the queen mother. Thus you will accord me a particular favor if, when the occasion presents itself, you would declare to their majesties that my lack of attendance is quite far from having been caused by my [lack] of the most profound respect toward their august persons or of true sympathy for an event of such interest in itself and from which the nation can expect so much good; not recognizing any other factor than the bad state of my health which has put beyond my capacity my attending those public ceremonies as I had wished.

"Requesting that you deign to accept my thanks in advance for such kindness. . . ."

1701. To Sarah Storrow

Madrid April 13th. 1844

My dear Sarah,

Your letter of the 6th.[1] by the French Courier, reached me, as usual, on Thursday morning: on which morning I now regularly look for a letter from you. It is now Saturday the day of departure of the courier, and I cannot let it pass without answering you; though I am in a very indifferent mood for writing this morning. I am happy to tell you that I am ⟨improving⟩ advancing daily in the cure of my malady, by the use of baths, and hope, before long, to be entirely relieved from it. Yesterday I was at a very handsome and a very pleasant dinner given by the Albuquerques, at which several of the diplomatic corps were present. Madame Albuquerque continues to be a kind of substitute for my nieces. She always calls me uncle as do likewise her children, which gives me something like a home feeling when I am with them. We are kept in doubt whether the Court will go to Aranjuez this Spring or not. It certainly will not go until after the 27th. of this month, as that is the saints day of the Queen Mother,[2] on which there will be a grand Besamanos, at the Royal paseo in Madrid. Should the Court not go the Albuquerques intend going there for two or three weeks, as they have a house engaged for the season. In that case I shall pass a few days there with them, and enjoy myself in the beautiful gardens, among the green alleys, and fountains and nightingales. I look forward almost with a schoolboys anticipation to the time when I shall once more have the use of my limbs and be able to enjoy the recreations of the country.

The day before yesterday I had some delightful songs from the fair Leocadia; who has promised to sing for me whenever I will come to see her. She is meditating an improvement on the little ⟨dramatic⟩ Tableaux *cantantes*, which I first suggested to her. I am told those she gave on that evening when I was prevented by indisposition, from attending, were really admirable; and commanded the applause of some of the best society of Madrid who were present. What delights me with her is her frank, unaffected, unpretending manner, and the little consequence she assumes on account of those gifts and graces which nature has lavished upon her.

I had a lively little dinner party on Sunday last, consisting of Mr & Mrs Calderon with Miss McLeod[3] niece of Madame Calderon and Miss Virginia[4]—a niece of Mr Calderon— Mr Weston and Mr Gayangos[5] a Spanish Gentleman. As we were all well acquainted the dinner passed off cheerily. Madame Calderon is very intelligent, very good humored and always in good spirits; Miss McLeod (or Kate as she is commonly called) is also very agreeable: and Virginia is a little quiet & modest creature, with beautiful Spanish eyes; which seemed to have an effect upon the heart of the worthy Weston who had a long tete a tete conversation with her after dinner. He, however, ⟨f⟩ left her and Madrid a day or two afterward; and is by this time among the Pyrenees. We have never been able ⟨exactly⟩ to determine what he is: you represented him to me as a clergyman: and Hamilton discovered by his conversation that he had been a Soldier and a Lawyer. I fancy if a soldier it must be of the Church Militant here upon earth—At any rate he ⟨p⟩ has proved a very intelligent agreeable visitor: and I am always happy to See Such Americans at Madrid.

I am glad to find you continue to drive ⟨ab⟩ out with Madame Hacquet. She is quite a pleasant acquaintance for you, and one with whom you may feel the assurance of being valued. Your intimacy must also be extremely satisfactory to her. It is a great thing for a lady in her situation to have the friendship and companionship of one like yourself, so respectable in every respect. I beg you to remember me most kindly to her.

If Captain Funk is still at Paris give him my hearty reccollections and kind greetings; I apprehend however, he will have taken his departure before this reaches you.

In one of your letters you mention having seen the opera of the Puritani.[6] It is frequently performed here, and is one which this troupe gives with the most effect. It is a charming, romantic ⟨off⟩ opera; full of delightful music. I never get tired of it. It almost rivals Lucia[7] in my estimation.

The dish which Julia wishes you to procure for her is *round*—but I will return her letter to you by this Courier.

Kiss my darling little Kate for me; I hope she has done cutting teeth for the present, and able to enjoy the beautiful spring weather in the Garden of the Tuilleries

With kind remembrances to Mr Storrow

Your affectionate uncle
Washington Irving

ADDRESSED: Madame / Madame Storrow / aux Soins de M. T W. Storrow
MANUSCRIPT: Yale.

1. This letter has not been located.
2. María Christina was born on April 27, 1806. Probably her saint was Mariana of Jesus the Blessed (Mariana Navarra de Guevara, 1565–1624), "the lily of Madrid," who was beatified by Pius VI. Her feast day is April 27. See *The Book of Saints*, comp. Benedictine Monks of St. Augustine's Abbey, Ramsgate (New York, 1966), p. 469.
3. Catherine McLeod (b. 1826) was the daughter of Richmond Inglis, Fanny

Calderón de la Barca's older sister, who had been married to Alexander Norman McLeod. The couple separated, and Kate spent much time with her aunt. See *Life in Mexico, The Letters of Fanny Calderón de la Barca*, ed. Howard T. Fisher and Marion Hall Fisher (New York, 1966), p. xxvi.

4. Virginia De Lizane, called by her Aunt Madame Calderón, "a perfect Spanish beauty, though born and bred in London." See Fanny Calderón de la Barca to W. H. Prescott, October 8, 1843, in *The Correspondence of William Hickling Prescott, 1833–1847*, ed. Wolcott, p. 393.

5. Pascual Gayangos y Arce, a Spanish scholar and a friend of Ticknor and Prescott. For other details, see WI to George Ticknor, January 11, 1843.

6. Bellini's *I Puritani di Scozia* (1835), which was performed on December 15, 1843. See *La Gaceta*, December 15, 1843.

7. Donizetti's *Lucia di Lammermoor* (1835), based on Scott's *The Bride of Lammermoor*.

1702.   To John Miller

Legation of the United States. / Madrid April 16th. 1844.

John Miller Esqr. / U. S. Despatch Agent, London.

Dear Sir,

I received this morning your account in duplicate for postage &c paid by you, during the last quarter on account of this legation.

I enclose a check on Messrs. Baring Brothers & co for the amount £5.8.6½ payable to your order at sight.

Very respectfully / Your obdt Sevt.
Washington Irving.

Enclosure.

Legation of the United States. / Madrid April 16th. 1844.

£5.8.6½.

At sight please pay John Miller or order, five pounds, eight shillings and six pence halfpenny sterling and charge the same to the United States on account of the contingent Expenses of this legation.

Washington Irving.
Messrs. Baring Brothers & Co. / Bankers of the U. States—London.

MANUSCRIPT: NA, RG 84 (letterbook copy).

1703.   To Catharine Paris

Madrid April 17th. 1844

My dear Sister,

My last letter concluded with the entrance of the Queen & Queen Mother into Madrid. Various fetes and ceremonies civil and religious have since taken place in honor of the return of Maria Christina, I have been obliged to absent myself from most of them on account of my indisposition. I was present, however, at the *Besa manos* (or Hand Kissing) at the Royal Palace. This is the grand act of homage to the Sovreign and the Royal family. The day was bright and propitious. ⟨All the avenues to⟩ ↑The place in front of↓ the Royal palace was thronged with people waiting to see the equipages drive up; while the avenues were guarded by horse and foot, and ⟨military bands⟩ the courts and halls echoed with military music. On entering the palace, the grand stair case of the antechambers were lined with the officers, halbardiers, and attendants of the Royal household, and thronged with a gorgeous multitude, civil and military glittering with gold lace and embroidery. I made my way into the Hall of Ambassadors, where the throne is situated, and which I found already filled with grandees and high functionaries, and a number of the Corps diplomatique

I have already noticed this Hall in my former letters: it is very magnificent, though somewhat *sombre*, ⟨being⟩ the walls being covered with crimson velvet. It has a great number of ⟨mir⟩ large mirrors; immense chandaliers of chrystal; and the vaulted cieling is beautifully painted representing in various compartments, the people and productions of the various countries and climates of the Spanish Empire; as it existed before its dismembrement. The throne is on the side of the Hall opposite to the windows, just midway. It is raised three or four steps, and surmounted by a rich canopy of velvet. There were two chairs of state ⟨on this throne⟩ thus elevated, one on the right hand for the Queen, and on the left for the Queen Mother; at the foot of the throne, to the left, was a chair of State for the Queens sister. As every body is expected to stand in the Royal presence, there are no other seats provided. I began to apprehend a severe trial for my legs, as some time would probably elapse before the entrance of the Queen. The Introducer of Ambassadors, however, (the Chevalier de Arana)[1] knowing my invalid condition, kindly pointed out to me a statue at the ⟨upper⟩ ↑lower↓ end of the hall, with a low pedestal, and advised me to take my seat there until the opening of the Court. I gladly availed myself of the ⟨kind⟩ suggestion, and seating myself on the edge of the pedestal indulged myself in a quiet survey of the scene before me, and a meditation on the various scenes of the kind I had witnessed in this hall in the time of Ferdinand [V] II² and during the time of my present sojourn at this court; and in calling to mind the rapid vicissitudes which had occurred, even in my limited experience, in the gilded and anxious throngs which each in their turns have glittered about this ⟨chambre⟩ Hall. ⟨Now [*two lines unrecovered*]⟩ how brief has been their butterfly existence; how sudden and desolate their reverses. Exile, imprisonment, death itself, have followed hard upon the transient pageants of a court; and who could say how soon a like lot might befall the courtier host before me, thus swarming forth into sudden sunshine. They all seemed, however, secure that their summer was to last, and that the golden days of Monarchical rule had once more returned. The arrival of the Queen Mother has been regarded by the Aristocracy as the ⟨la⟩ completion and consolidation of their triumph. They have crowded, therefore, to do homage to the throne, and the Spanish Court has once more resumed something of its ancient splendor. Indeed I had never seen the Royal Palace so brilliantly attended; and the whole ceremonial had an effect even upon the French Ambassador, who has been slow to see any thing good at Madrid, but who acknowledged that the splendor of the Court quite surpassed his expectations.

After we had been for some time assembled the Queen was announced, and every one immediately ranged himself in order. The grandees take their station on the right hand of the throne; the Diplomatic Corps ⟨is⟩ forms a line directly in front of it; with the French Ambassador at the head. The Queen ⟨Moth⟩ entered first, followed by her mother, and the princess Royal, and a long train of ladies of the highest nobility magnificently dressed. The Queen & the Queen Mother took their seats on the throne; the latter on the left hand. The princess was seated in a chair of state to the left of the throne; and the ladies in attendance ranged themselves from the left of the throne to the ⟨upper⟩ ↑lower↓ end of the Hall Among them were some of the most beautiful ladies of the nobility they were all in court dresses; with lappets and trains; and as fine as silk, and plumes, and lace and diamonds could make them. ⟨I think if King Solomon had seen them⟩ I doubt whether even the lilies of the valley, though better arrayed than King Solomon in all his glory,³ could have stood a comparison with them. (I hope it is not wicked to say so.)

The little Queen and her sister were each dressed in white sattin richly trimmed with lace; they had trains of lilac silk; and wreaths of diamonds on their heads—The ⟨Queen⟩ only difference in their dress being the superior number of diamonds of the Queen—The Queen Mother had a train of asure blue, her favorite color—I like to describe dresses, having a knack at at, but I absolutely forget the rest of her equipments. The little Queen, who by the bye will soon cease to deserve the ⟨name⟩ ↑adjective↓ of little, looked rather full and puffy on the occasion; being perhaps too straitly caparisoned: the infanta too, looked pale, and, I was told, was in bad health. The Queen Mother on the contrary, was in her best looks: no longer fatigued and worn by a long and anxious journey, as when I saw her at Aranjuez; but cheerful and animated; with a countenance beaming with benignity. I think for Queenly grace and dignity, mingled with the most gracious affability, she surpasses any sovereign I have ever seen. Her manner of receiving every one, as they knelt, and kissed her hand; and the smile with which she sent them on their way rejoicing, let me at once into the secret of her popularity with all who have frequented her court.

I remained but a short time after the Besa manos had commenced. It was likely to be between two and three hours before the immense crowd of courtiers, clergy, military, municipality &c could pay homage; and it was impossible for me to remain standing so long. I beat a retreat, therefore, in company with the chargé d'affaires of Denmark, the veteran D'Albergo; a thorough going courtier, who had risen from a sick bed to be present on the occasion. I have since written a note to the Minister of State, requesting him to explain to the Queen & Queen Mother the cause of my absence from most of the Court ceremonies on the recent joyful occasion; and have received a very satisfactory note in reply,[4] with kind expressions on the part of the sovreigns. There is to be another grand Besamanos, on the twenty seventh of this month, by which time I hope to be sufficiently recovered from my long indisposition to resume my usual station in the diplomatic corps.

March[5] 20th.   I forgot to mention to you in giving my account in a former letter of the arrival of the Queen Mother; that the worthy Arguelles died the very morning of the day on which she entered Madrid. His health had been broken for some time, and the agitations through which he has passed of late may have hastened his end; which, however, was some what sudden.[6] He was a good man, a true patriot and an able statesman, but ardent and anxious as a politician. His life had been a life of trial and vicissitude; he had borne all kind of reverses of fortune: one time in power, another in exile or in prison, but through every trial he passed pure and unsullied. When he had the guardianship of the young Queen he was entitled to a salary of about seventy thousand dollars; he only accepted one tenth. ⟨He retired from office (on the When the present party effected the revolution and⟩ On the triumph of the Moderado party last year he retired from office poor. When he died but twenty two dollars were found in his house and he left debts to the amount of nearly five thousand dollars. He was faithful in his guardianship of the little Queen and her sister, and was strongly attached to them. He was represented by his political opponents as an enemy of the Queen Mother; but, though he may have disapproved of her political course when in power, he did justice to the amiableness of her character, and, in a conversation with me, lamented that she was seperated from her daughters, as her presence would have been of vast advantage to them; especially to the young Queen. When the Queen Mother was entering Madrid in State, in company with the little Queen and her sister, an officious courtier rode up to the carriage and ⟨congratulated⟩ announced to her with congratulations, the death of her enemy Arguelles. "Hush," said the Queen Mother "do not let the children hear you—*for they loved the old man!*" Poor Arguelles! few men who have figured in the political affairs of Spain for the last thirty years will leave so honest a name behind.

Since the Queen Mother has become re established in the palace she has begun essential changes in the regulations of the Royal household, which had fallen sadly into disorder; and it is said she contemplates important changes in the ⟨noble⟩ personages about the Queen. She sent lately for Madame Mina, who was aya or governess of the Queen during the time of Espartero, and whose elevation to that important post had given great umbrage to the old nobility and caused most of them to resign their posts in the palace. I am told the Queen Mother thanked Madame Mina in the handsomest terms for the kindness and devotion with which she had acquitted herself, and ⟨to which⟩ ↑which had been reported to her by↓ the little Queen and her Sister. ⟨had⟩ Madame Mina was their attendant & protectress on the famous night of the attack upon the palace.

I cannot but feel deeply interested for the Queen Mother. Her situation is full of peril and uncertainty, and she knows it, and is at times anxious and depressed. She is ⟨anx⟩ desirous to do right, but is fearful of committing errors or mistakes in the present critical times, when all is cabal and intrigue about her—She would willingly abstain from taking any part in political affairs; but it is impossible when the welfare of her children is connected with them, and when the Queen is so young and inexperienced. She has been taking measures lately to re establish the health of the Queen who has long been subject to a cutaneous affection: but who has had no one to control her diet, nor subject her to medical treatment.

It is now said that, on the 10th. of May, the Court will ⟨repair to⟩ ↑visit↓ some of the provinces, where the Queen may have the benefit of mineral baths. Should this plan be carried into effect it may produce a political crisis—Madrid is quiet at present, but it is full of stifled mischief and conspiracy which is only kept down by the stern exercise of military rule. I hope my apprehensions may prove groundless, but I fear further convulsions which may once more throw this unfortunate country into confusion. I have not time, however, to enter into the grounds of my apprehensions.

I am happy to tell you that I am getting on prosperously in my cure by the aid of baths, which I take at home. Indeed I expect, in a very little time, to be able to go about on foot, as usual; and only refrain from doing so at present, lest, by any over exercise, I might retard my complete recovery. When I drive out and notice the opening of Spring I feel sometimes almost moved to tears at the thought that in a little while I shall again have the use of my limbs and be able to ramble about and enjoy those green fields and meadows. It seems almost too great a privilege. I am affraid when I once more sally forth and walk about the streets I shall feel like a boy with a new coat, who thinks every body will turn round to look at him. "Bless my soul, how that gentleman has the use of his legs!"

I want some little excitement of the kind just now to enliven me: for Alexander Hamilton is packing up and preparing for his departure; which will probably take place in the course of three weeks. It will be a hard parting for me and I shall feel his loss sadly; for he has been every thing to me as an efficient aid in business, a most kind hearted attendant in sickness, and a cheerful, intelligent, sunshiny companion at all times. He will leave a popular name behind him among his intimates and acquaintances in Madrid; who have learnt to appreciate his noble qualities of head and heart. What makes his departure very trying to me is, that he is in a manner linked with my home, and is the last of the young companions who left home with me. God bless him! he will carry home sunshine to his family, and make his good mothers heart glad,

And now, with love to "all bodies" I must conclude.

Your affectionate brother
Washington Irving

MANUSCRIPT: Yale.   PUBLISHED: PMI, III, 330–31, 334–39 (in part); Hellman, *WI Esquire*, pp. 273–74 (in part).

1. For Arana, see WI to Joaquín de Frías, September 4, 1843.
2. WI omitted the bracketed numeral. He had been presented to Ferdinand VII on February 26, 1826. See WI to Charles R. Leslie, February 23, 1826.
3. See Matthew 6:28–29.
4. See Luis González Bravo to WI, April 9, 1844 (NA, RG 84).
5. WI should have written "April."
6. Agustín Argüelles (b. 1776) died on March 26, 1844. See *El Castellano*, March 26, 29, 1844.

1704. To Luis González Bravo

Legation of the United States. / Madrid April 19th. 1844.

His Excellency. / Don Luis Gonzalez Bravo,/ First Minister
of State and of Foreign Affairs.

Sir,
   A case containing books, wearing apparel and other effects introduced
for, and belonging to, members of this legation[1] being about to be
forwarded to the United States through the port of Malaga; and it being
desirable that it should be inspected and examined at the Custom House
in this city in order that,—being sealed and leaded,—it may not be subjected to unpacking and reexamination at the frontier; I have the honor
to request that Your Excellency will cause the necessary steps to be
taken to obtain from the Treasury Department an order to this effect.
   With sentiments of high respect and consideration

                                             I am, Sir / Your most obdt Sevt.
                                                      Washington Irving

MANUSCRIPT: NA, RG 84 (letterbook copy).

   1. These materials probably belonged to Alexander Hamilton, who had recently
resigned as secretary of the legation. Other members who had left included J.
Carson Brevoort and Hector Ames.

1705. To Henry O'Shea

                                                        [April 20, 1844]

My dear Sir,
   Will you make one of a small social party at dinner at my house,
tomorrow at half past six, and oblige

                                                    Yours very truly
                                                    Washington Irving
Saturday, April 20 [1844]

MANUSCRIPT: HSA.   PUBLISHED: Penney, *Bulletin NYPL*, 62 (December, 1958),
   616.

   The date is determined by the perpetual calendar.

1706. To Sarah Storrow

Madrid. April 20th. 1844

My dear Sarah,

I enclose a letter for your mother which must answer for one to yourself: as I have not time to write more. Yours[1] by the last courier was received in due time—You need be under no apprehensions about the baths I take at home: I never took any more completely secure against cold. Their effect upon my malady has been immediate and progressive and I now confidently look forward to being completely freed from it before long. You may easily suppose what a cheering effect all this has upon me, who have so long felt under a blight, and have almost given up society and all social enjoyment.

My movements this summer must depend upon leave of absence from government, and a Secretary competent to be left in charge of the Legation. If Mr Livingston should be appointed I should have no hesitation in confiding the Legation into his hands; after he had had a little time to inform himself of its routine and affairs. I want very much to make a visit to England and pass a little time with your Aunt; who is anxious to see me, and to whom I think, now that I am likely to be well, and that she has considerably recovered, a visit from me would be cheering and beneficial.[2] I could not have ventured upon a meeting last year, when we were both in such melancholy plight, but now my heart yearns for it.

Kiss my darling little Kate for me. I long to gallant her about the garden of the Tuilleries.

With kind remembrances to your husband

Your affectionate uncle
Washington Irving

P.S. I enclose a letter written by a young Belgian, Count Merode,[3] to his friend Count Marnix, charge d'affaires of Belgium, giving an account of his being robbed on the way to Seville. The Count Merode was a great favorite in our diplomatic and social circle, and passed the evening with me previous to his departure. Had Mr Livingston executed his original plan of visiting Andalusia this Spring, he would have travelled with Count Merode, and have been his companion in misfortune.

P. S. 2d. You had better forward the letter to your mother by a Havre Packet; to save postage in the United States

DOCKETED: April 20th. 1844
MANUSCRIPT: Yale.

1. This letter has not been located.
2. Sarah Van Wart had had a stroke. See WI to Catharine Paris, April 1 and October 12, 1843.
3. Frédéric François Xavier Ghislain, comte de Mérode (1820–1874), who had an illustrious military career as a young man, received the cross of the Legion of Honor for his services in Algeria. Later he abandoned his military activities, took ecclesiastical orders, and joined the staff of the Vatican States.

1707. To John C. Calhoun

Legation of the United States. / Madrid April 23. 1844.

No. 39. / The Hon: / The Secretary of State, / of the
    United States—Washington.

Sir
    Political affairs here wear a tranquil Surface under the domination of martial law; a schism however, is taking place between the leaders of the party in power, which gives great solicitude to those who wish the continuance of the present government.[1] Many of the older moderados, especially those of high aristocratic pride, are desirous of getting rid of Gonzalez Bravo, whose loyalty they distrust and whose origin they despise. They would form a cabinet from men of their own *creed* and their own *caste*; and would give Narvaez a place in it as Minister of War; in which case he would probably have the control. Gonzalez Bravo, however, is not disposed to relinquish the post which has raised him to such importance, and in which he really has acquitted himself with great spirit and ability. He is endeavoring to organize a little party of his own, formed of what is technically called the "Young Spain," and to set up General Concha in opposition to Narvaez. Narvaez is in favor at the Palace, and by his past services has secured the good will of the Queen Mother; though she apparently countenances Gonzalez Bravo, who pays assiduous court to her; the latter has the support of the French Ambassador, who at present has great influence at Madrid.
    As Narvaez and Gonzalez Bravo are the master Spirits of the actual government, an open rupture between them might shake the whole to its foundations; exertions therefore are made, by the considerate and experienced of the party, to prevent such a catastrophe, but there are so many young and hot heads at present in power, and there are such rivalries and jealousies at work, that it is next to impossible to maintain

that unity of purpose and of action requisite to carry out any great scheme of policy.

Since I last wrote to the Department the decree subjecting the press to great restrictions, has been promulgated,[2] and has been received with silent acquiescence. Some of the opposition papers are preparing to resume publication, subject to those restrictions. A decree is also in existence restoring to the clergy such of their confiscated lands as have not been sold. This measure is said to have been dictated by the religious feelings of the Queen Mother; and to have been strongly objected to by part of the Cabinet; from the embarrassment it might give to the Treasury, and the clamours it might awaken among the people. It is likely, therefore, to be held in reserve for the present.

Among the various reports got up by alarmists, is that of a combination forming between the Carlists and the liberals, to compel a match between the young Queen and the eldest son of Don Carlos; or to revive the pretensions of the latter to the throne. Numbers of Carlist *facciosos* have been arrested making their way into Spain from the French frontier; and some of them have been shot according to the prompt dispensation of martial law.

While jealousies and intrigues are formenting in the capital, and seditions have been but recently stifled in the provinces, the Court is projecting an expedition into Catalonia, on the 8th. of next month, to give the young Queen the benefit of a change of air, and a course of mineral baths, prescribed by physicians as necessary for the cure of a cutaneous malady with which she has long been afflicted. This project of the Court is regarded by many with great solicitude; apprehending that it may bring the present differences between the party leaders to a crisis and produce some explosion. They observe that it was precisely a journey of the kind, to the same region, and ostensibly for the same purpose (the health of the young Queen) that preceded the abdication and exile of Queen Christina, and the downfall of the Moderado party in 1840. Madrid, they say, is too dangerous a capital to be left to its own internal fires.

Mr. Calderon de la Barca, recently appointed Minister plenipotentiary to our Government, has just left Madrid for his place of destination, via France and England. I was desirous of having some further conversation with the Minister of State on the subject of Cuba, prior to the departure of Mr. Calderon; but have repeatedly been disappointed in seeking an interview; Ministers being so much engrossed at present by their own immediate interests and concerns, and the struggle to maintain their places. Indeed, Mr. Calderon himself has been unable to have a full explanation with the Ministry and has departed without his written instructions, which are to be sent after him. A proof how little clear knowledge prevails here with respect to our Country and its concerns, is, that in a conversation with the Minister Mr. Calderon was charged to inform himself diligently of occurrences in Cuba, from every vessel that arrived from that island at Washington;—the Minister having supposed Washington a Sea-port, in frequent intercourse with Havanna!

With such ignorance respecting us, it would not be surprising if the expressions drawn from our government by the application of the Chevalier D'Argaiz, with respect to the island of Cuba, should have inspired the Spanish Cabinet with some distrust as to our real motives. I am persuaded some such distrust has been felt, and I am apprehensive it may be fomented by England and France; both of whom (but especially the former) are jealous of our designs upon the island. I shall endeavor, whenever an opportunity presents, to remove any such doubt from the minds of Ministers and to impress them with the sincerity of our wish and determination to maintain Spain in the possession of the island.

Information, derived from an intelligent Spaniard, commercially connected with the Island of Cuba, gives an alarming picture of the state of affairs there.

It seems beyond a doubt that, under the new Captain General, O'Donnell,[3] slaves are again admitted in great numbers. Under Valdes, the former governor, who faithfully carried into effect the laws and treaties for the suppression of the slave trade, the traffic in a great measure declined, and many abandoned it, discouraged by the difficulties and losses attending its prosecution. These men have returned, or are returning to it under the present governor.

It is argued that the plantations and factories of Cuba cannot be kept up without fresh importations of Negroes; there not being a sufficient number born in the island to keep up the necessary supply; few women being imported excepting for household service. It is true, the introduction of a large number of African males in the present excited condition of the blacks is hazardous in the extreme; but the proprietors of the plantations and factories are chiefly Spanish Capitalists, and they reason on the selfish principle, that, if affairs continue as they are for a few years only, their fortunes will be made, and withdrawn from the island; with the fate of which they will then be disconnected.

The government of Spain appears to close its eyes to these dangers; and indeed could not, without timely and very urgent notice of troubles, send any considerable force for the protection of the island. The troops actually there are said to be about 20.000 men; one half of whom are regulars; the rest Militia. The Naval force consists of half a dozen vessels of various rates; the most efficient being two small steamers built some years since in the United States.

There is a general impression, among the planters, that the partial insurrections which occurred lately near Matanzas,[4] were the result of a plan which extended throughout the island; and which still subsists, awaiting a favorable opportunity to strike a decisive blow.

In concluding I must again express my regret that I have so little information from home to guide me in respect to this delicate and critical subject; and that I have been left entirely in the dark as to the circumstances of the negotiation of the chevalier D'Argaïz, which seems to have been so fruitful of doubts and jealousies. I feel this especially, whenever I have to converse with the Ministry here on the matter; fearing they may impute to a want of frankness that vagueness and reserve on certain points, which results from a want of full and accurate information.

I am, Sir, very respectfully / Your Obdt Sevt.
Washington Irving

DOCKETED: Recd. 20 May / Mr. Markoe [top of page 1] / No. 39. W. Irving. Madrid — 23 Apl 1844.
MANUSCRIPT: NA, RG 59; NYPL—Berg Collection (letterbook copy). PUBLISHED: STW, II, 386 (in part); Manning, Diplomatic Correspondence, 339–40 (in part).

Only the signature is in WI's handwriting.

1. See El Castellano, March 21, 22, and April 4, 22, 24, 1844.
2. On April 10, 1844, the queen and the marques de Peñaflorida signed the new press law, prompting adverse editorial comment from El Castellano. See El Castellano, April 11, 16, 17, 1844.
3. Leopoldo O'Donnell, one of Narváez's military rivals, was removed from the domestic scene by his appointment as governor of Cuba. See Christiansen, Military Power, p. 119.
4. This revolt at Triunvirato involved 400 slaves who wrecked five mills and burned the cane before being subdued. As a result, about 4,000 people in Matanzas were arrested, including 2,000 free Negroes. See Thomas, Cuba, The Pursuit of Freedom, p. 205.

1708.   To John C. Calhoun

Legation of the United States / Madrid April 27th. 1844.

No. 40. / The Hon: / The Secretary of State / of the United States— Washington

Sir,

I have the honor to enclose the accounts and vouchers of the legation for the 1st. quarter of 1844, showing a balance against the United States of $28.11; which will be carried to their debit in next account.

On the arrival of the Queen Mother, the Corps diplomatique proceeded by invitation to Aranjuez to witness the ceremony of the meeting of the Queens: I have included in my accounts, a small item for travelling expenses incurred on this occasion; according to what has been thought the uniform practise of this legation sanctioned by the Report of the Committee on Mr. Van Ness' case in July 1842[1]

> I am, Sir, / Very respectfully / Your obdt Sevt.
> Washington Irving

DOCKETED: Recd. June 11/44 / Mr Markoe
MANUSCRIPT: NA, RG 59; NYPL—Berg Collection (letterbook copy).

1. The Van Ness claim, which dragged on for many years, was withdrawn in 1857. See Hasse, *Index to U.S. Documents*, III, 1874.

1709. To Sarah Storrow

Madrid, April 27th. 1844

My dear Sarah,

I have barely time to scribble a few words this morning, having to prepare for the Besa manos (this being the birth day of the Queen Mother) which takes place at One Oclock.[1] I am happy to say my limbs are in such condition that I can now stand out the Ceremony, long as it may be. We have a bright beautiful day for it, and shall no doubt have an immense crowd at the Palace. I wish you could See the exterior and interior of the palace on one of these great fete days; the spectacle really is imposing, ⟨and⟩ the *local* is favorable, and the brilliant sunshine of Madrid gives great effect to the whole.

Your friends the Deacons have not yet reached Madrid. I have heard of them, at Malaga, skirting the Mediterranean coast of Spain; they were to go thence to Gibraltar, Cadiz, Seville & so up the centre of the country to the capital; where they will probably arrive about the 10th May. Mrs Deacons brother young Mr Parker is still here, and with his travelling companion Mr Jones, has dined twice with me. There are two other Americans here Mr Chouteau[2] & Mr Shaw[3] of St Louis; so that I have had quite American parties.

I have likewise given two Diplomatic dinners lately and shall give a third tomorrow. They are social unpretending dinners, of ten persons each. I make no parade, but take care to have every thing choice of its kind. I have a very good cook; and Lorenzo makes a capital Mayer domo; so that the whole goes off well, and without costing me the least trouble. Indeed no one could have a smoother domestic establishment than I have at present, never the least difficulty nor cross purpose. You will think I am quite "breaking forth"[4] with dinner parties; but in truth I have for a long time been so much depressed and out of social mood with my tedious malady that I feel quite in arrears; and one of the first impulses, on finding myself really getting better, was to call my friends about me and make good cheer—Three or four days since I drove to the Retiro with Madame Albuquerque and her children, and, for the first time in upwards of ⟨eighteen⟩ fifteen months, took a walk in the green alleys of that pleasant resort. It was almost too great a delight to find myself once more among trees and flowers, and to hear the birds singing around me.

The Court is seriously meditating an expedition to ⟨Cat⟩ the baths in Catalonia,[5] and a sojourn in some of the other provinces, for the health of the young queen. I do not know whether the Corps diplomatique will be invited or expected to accompany the Court; I believe it is at present a matter of discussion. I shall not go if I can avoid it without appearing particular, or wanting in proper respect; but if all the rest of the diplomats go I cannot well stay behind. This will, in some way or other, affect my arrangements for the summer; which are at present unsettled, and dependent on contingencies.

I had long letters by the last Steamer, full of pleasant news from home. Your mother wrote in very good spirits, and had passed a very comfortable satisfactory winter: you, however, have a letter from her by the same opportunity, and, of course know all that she has to say. I had a letter from Pierre[6] giving me an account of poor Helens having undergone the surgical operation.[7] Now it is well over she must have a load of silent disquiet taken off of her heart, which long has laid heavy there. Pierre says she is so elated that she can scarce think of any thing else. I suppose she will be like me ⟨with my⟩ on regaining the use of my legs; she will call in her friends to make merry with her.

Pierres letters are encouraging as to ↑the↓ influence the return of 'good times' is likely to have on my own scanty means. I fear, however, it will yet be a good while before I can realize much income from my property, and I do not see any likelihood of realizing Sufficient to enable me to return home and be independent of the fagging of the pen. Bachelor as I am, I have too large a family now to provide for: and, if it were not for *diplomacy*, I do not know what would become of us. However, as Theodore[8] says, 'the Heavenly father"[9] has ordered things wonderfully for us; so I am humbly thankful—and bless *Uncle Sam* into the bargain.

I have scribbled a longer letter than I had anticipated; and must now hasten to put on my diplomatic toggery and prepare to take the field.

I wish ⟨you⟩ when you tell me Kate has a new dress, you would tell me what it is, that I may have her little ladyship in my minds eye as she figures vain-gloriously before the glass. I suspect the Jones's have bitten her, some time or other, when they have pretended to kiss her, and that she will go mad on millenary and French dresses. However, dont say I said so, for it is a scandalous insinuation, and I take it all back.

With many Kisses to the vain little baggage and kind remembrances to Mr Storrow

Your affectionate uncle
Washington Irving

MANUSCRIPT: Yale.   PUBLISHED: PMI, III, 339 (in part).

1. See *La Gaceta*, April 25, 1844.
2. Probably Pierre Chouteau (1789–1865), whose father WI had met in St. Louis in 1832.
3. Henry Shaw (1800–1889) made a fortune in hardware in St. Louis. In 1840 he retired and traveled for ten years.
4. See Exodus 9:10.
5. WI noted in a letter of May 10, 1844, to Sarah Storrow that Isabella was visiting the baths of Caldas near Barcelona, a point confirmed by a report in London *Times*, May 17, 1844.
6. The letters of Mrs. Paris and PMI have not been located.
7. The nature of Helen's surgery has not been ascertained.
8. Theodore Irving, son of Ebenezer, was a clergyman.
9. WI used a single quotation mark before "the."

1710.   *To Helen Irving*

Madrid, April 28, 1844.

My dear Helen:
        * * * I have been rather lighthearted of late, at being in a great degree relieved from the malady which has so long kept me, as it were, in fetters. Yesterday I was at a *Besa manos*, or royal levee, at the palace, in honor of the birthday of the Queen Mother, where all the nobility and people of official rank have the honor of kissing the hands of the Queen and royal family; and though the ceremonial lasted between two and three hours, I stood through the whole of it without flinching. I have also taken a walk in the green alleys of the Retiro, for the first time in upward of fifteen months, and performed the feat to admiration. I do not figure about yet in the streets on foot, lest people should think me proud; I continue, therefore, to drive out in my carriage. Indeed, I endeavor to behave as humbly and modestly as possible under "so great a dispensation;" but one cannot help being puffed up a little on having the use of one's legs.

* * * In consequence of the flourishing accounts Pierre has lately written of the state of my investments, I have just given a succession of diplomatic dinners, and am looking forward with impatience to the arrival of an American party of travellers, to have a pretence for giving more. I am terribly afraid my purse will get ahead of me under Pierre's accumulating management, and I shall grow rich and stingy. However, I'll have a "hard try" for the contrary.

May 3d.—We have beautiful weather, and yesterday, for the first time in upward of a year, I took a walk on the Prado among all the gay world, and then seated myself under one of the trees, and looked on. The delightful temperature of the air, the sight of verdure, and the sound of fountains, made me feel quite young again, and I presume that was the reason why all the ladies looked so beautiful. I do not think I have seen so many pretty faces in the course of a morning since I was a young man. In fact, I have now and then thought that the world was growing old, and all the beauty dying out; but yesterday's walk in the Prado convinced me that I was mistaken.

* * * * * * *

God bless these surgeons and dentists! May their good deeds be returned upon them a thousandfold! May they have the felicity, in the next world, to have successful operations performed upon them to all eternity!

PUBLISHED: PMI, III, 340–41; Hellman, WI Esquire, p. 274 (in part).

1711. To Sarah Storrow

Madrid May 3d. 1844

My dear Sarah,

Word is just brought me that the French courier departs this evening, instead of tomorrow evening; I have, therefore, only time to scrawl a line, and inclose for your perusal a letter, already written, to Helen. When you see Mr Sumner beg him to present my kindest remembrances to Madame Villamil,[1] whom I shall seek out, the moment I arrive at Paris. I retain the most pleasant and friendly reccollections of her. My friend Moore[2] and his family occupied a cottage in the Grounds of Mr Villamils Villa of La Butte, close by St Cloud: and many a time on my visits to him I have partaken of Mr Villamils hospitality. Madame Villamil was most amiable and agreeable: she had a delightful voice, and great taste and skill in Music which rendered her house a charming resort. Get Mr Sumner to give you her address that I may know where to find her.

I am sorry to hear that Kate has such tantrums at times. You must spare no pains in conquering these little paroxysms of temper; though of course she will outgrow them as her reason strengthens; they will however, render her less docile and engaging during childhood. Such a temper requires much quiet, but persevering management. It must not be severely thwarted as that only irritates, nor must these wilful freaks of passion be indulged and yielded to. They should always be shewn to be utterly unavailing to effect the purpose aimed at. Never cede to passion any thing which you have previously refused. Always let her see that after giving way to a fit of passion she has some difficulty to retrieve your good graces. I have known a child cured of such freaks of temper by being undressed and put to bed when they occurred. I suspect Kate would soon recover her temper if stripped of her finery.

⟨I should think Versailles⟩

I shall be anxious to know where you pitch your tent for the Summer. Versailles will probably be as favorable a place as you can find, especially if the Walshes, Ledyards and Greenes are there. My summer movements are yet uncertain. I wait to know whether Mr Livingston will be appointed; and if so, to receive and induct him into office. I want to know also, what will be the summer arrangements of the Court here. Whether the Queen will go to any of the Sitios, or to Barcelona, and whether the Diplomatic Corps will be invited and expected to follow the movements of the Court—I hope not. Mr Hamilton is nearly ready to take his departure; which will depend upon the probable arrival of Mr Livingston here.

My cure is proceeding gradually, but, I believe, surely, so that I hope before long it will be complete.

Give my kind remembrances to Mr Storrow and kiss my darling little naughty Kate and tell her to grow a perfectly good little girl against I come to Paris

> Your affectionate uncle
> Washington Irving

ADDRESSED: Madame / Madame Storrow   DOCKETED: *May 3th. 1844*
MANUSCRIPT: Yale.

1. The Villamils were friends whom WI had met through Thomas Moore and seen frequently in Paris in 1823 and 1824. See *J&N*, III, 210 and passim.
2. WI had first met Thomas Moore in Paris on December 21, 1820. See *J&N*, III, 252.

1712. To Alejandro Mon

Legation of the United States. / Madrid May 5th. 1844.

Sir,

I have the honor to acknowledge the receipt of your Excellency's note informing me of the important changes which Her Majesty has been pleased to make in her Cabinet; among which I have the satisfaction to notice the appointment of Your Excellency as Minister of the Treasury with the charge *ad interim* of the Department of State and of Foreign affairs

I beg leave to offer Your Excellency my congratulations on such high marks of royal esteem and confidence, so worthily bestowed, and to assure you of the pleasure I shall feel in transacting with you such affairs as may come within the scope of my official duties.

I take this occasion to offer to your Excellency the assurance of my distinguished consideration.

Washington Irving.

His Excellency / Don Alexander Mon, / Minister of the Treasury & (ad interim) of State— / and Foreign Affairs.

MANUSCRIPT: NA, RG 84; NYPL—Berg Collection (letterbook copy).

Alejandro Mon (1801–1882), the new minister of the treasury and acting minister of state and foreign affairs, was a relative of Pedro José Pidal (1800–1865), the new minister of the interior. See Christiansen, *Military Power*, pp. 122, 189.

1713. To John C. Calhoun

Legation of the United States / Madrid May 6th. 1844

No. 41. / The Hon. The Secretary of State / of the U. States. Washington.

Sir,

The schism among the leaders of the dominant party, which I mentioned in my despatch No 39. April 23d. has ended in the dissolution of the Bravo Cabinet. It has fallen without any ostensible cause. The Ministers have been dismissed with encomiums and rewards. It is acknowledged ↑by the Moderado papers,↓ that they assumed the government at a moment of difficulty and danger; that they conducted themselves with courage and loyalty, and that their measures have been perfectly satisfactory to their party; all that has been alleged against them

is a falling off in their energy, and a tardiness in their action at a time
when the exigencies of the state called for unremitting vigor. It is evident that personal interests, and feuds, and prejudices lay at the bottom
of the affair. As a proof that they are not in disgrace with the government, Gonzalez Bravo has been appointed Minister plenipotentiary to
Portugal; and General Mazarredo, late Minister of War, has been made
Captain General of New Castile.

The fall of the Cabinet would seem to imply that French influence is not
so potent here as had been imagined, the Ambassador of France having
given strong support to Gonzalez Bravo. Indeed it is suggested that the
Ambassador may have injured his own cause by exerting himself too
openly in the national affairs. The Spaniards are excessively jealous of
foreign intervention. There is a point at which their pride takes the
alarm, and they become restive even under the friendly interference
of strangers, and begin to pique themselves upon "national independence." Such was the case when Mr Aston, the late British Minister, from
his great personal intimacy with the Ex Regent, and his Ministers, was
supposed to exert undue influence in Spanish politics; and such has recently begun to be the case with the French Ambassador, who has been
thought too assiduous and too much in favor at the palace, and in the
department of State. In both instances, I have no doubt, foreign interference and foreign influence have been over rated.

The task of forming the new Cabinet was assigned to General Narvaez; with the intimation that he should take a place in it, as president of
the Council and Minister of War. At first he professed a disinclination to
enter the Cabinet, alleging that he was most fitted for his actual position
in the Army; but his objections were over ruled. Some pretend that his
enemies have contrived to get him placed in this prominent and responsible situation in the hope that he may pursue a high handed policy and
commit errors productive of his downfall; or that, on the dissolution of
the Cabinet, which, in the ordinary course of Spanish events, cannot fail
soon to take place, he will remain without office, severed from the Army
and stripped of that military prestige which has hitherto rendered him so
formidable. I am told, however, that Narvaez is well aware of the perils
of his new situation and will be on his guard against them.

From the little opportunity I have had of testing popular report by
personal observation I am inclined to think General Narvaez honest,
though limited, in his political views; sagacious and practically experienced, but not extensively instructed or informed; of strong passions,
great courage and prompt and energetic action, a true Spaniard in his
national pride and his some what tumid notions of honor, yet free from
arrogance, and by no means deficient in courtesy in private intercourse.
He is loyally devoted to the Queen and the Queen Mother, and I believe,

however he may err in policy, he is patriotic in his intentions. I have been pleased with certain instances of independence in his conduct which have privately come to my knowledge. During the late schism, when it appeared likely he would gain the ascendancy, amicable advances were made to him by the diplomatic representatives of both France and England, in the hope of influencing him in his political course; but he civilly, though coolly stood aloof from both, and conducted himself throughout the crisis totally free from foreign influence, forming his cabinet on, what he concieved, true Spanish principles.

I am led to make these observations on the character and conduct of General Narvaez, from the important place he at present occupies in Spanish affairs. How long he may continue to occupy that place it is impossible to judge; reverses being so frequent and sudden in this government, where danger always keeps on a par with elevation, and where men apparently rise but to fall.

The new cabinet is superior in weight of character to the last, and more acceptable to the pride of the Moderados. The Marques of Vilhuma who is nominated to the department of state, is well spoken of for his integrity, intelligence and energy. It is not known whether he will accept, being at present in England, as Minister plenipotentiary; in the interim Mr Mon, Minister of the Treasury, will have charge of the department of State. The latter formerly figured in the Moderado Cabinet of Count Ofalia[1] and administered the public finances with acknowledged ability and integrity during the civil war. Don Pedro Jose Pidal, late president of the chamber of deputies, is minister of the government of the peninsula: he is a man of science and erudition and great rectitude of principle. Don Francisco Armero[2] Minister of Marine, is likewise highly spoken of. One member of the former Cabinet retains his place; Don Luis Mayans, Minister of Grace and Justice.[3] It is supposed he has made friends with some of the high dignitaries of the church, who are rapidly regaining influence, and to whom he has dispensed liberally, from the funds under his control, to defray their travelling expenses.

There is no doubt that the cabinet is a respectable one in point of character and talent; it remains to be seen how the members of it will work together. Its enemies predict that they will soon be at variance; four of them—Narvaez, Vilhuma, Mons and Armero, being men of high tempers, and each likely to indulge a strong individual will on any point of difference. It is to be hoped, for the tranquility of the country, they may falsify this prediction.

The first measure of the new cabinet is certainly of good augury, putting an end to martial law.[4] It is expected that a decree will soon be issued dissolving the present Cortes and ordering new elections, thus restoring affairs to their legal course. Great uneasiness and distrust having been lately produced by the rumor of an intended suspension of the sale of the church lands. Much pains are taken by the government papers to quiet the public mind on that critical and widely interesting subject; and to allay the apprehension that the Cabinet will be retrograde in its policy. The ministers, however, are loudly called upon to publish a manifesto declaring the line of policy they intend to pursue

I am Sir, / Very respectfully / Your obt Servt
Washington Irving

DOCKETED: Recd. June 3/44 — Mr. Markoe [top of page 1] / No. 41. W. Irving. Madrid. 6 May — 1844
MANUSCRIPT: NA, RG 59.   PUBLISHED: STW, II, 176 (in part).

This letter is in WI's handwriting.

1. Narcisco de Heredia, count of Ofalia (1777–1843) had been prime minister of Spain from December 16, 1837, to September 6, 1838. See Christiansen, *Military Power*, pp. 169, 180.
2. Francisco Armero y Peñaranda, marquis of Nervión (1804–1867).
3. These cabinet changes are reported in. *La Gaceta*, May 4, 1844.
4. See *La Gaceta*, May 5, 1844.

1714.   To Ebenezer Irving

[Madrid, Early May 1844]

Give my regards to General Morris,[1] and tell him he is quite welcome to my "Wife,"[2] which is more than most of his friends could say.

PUBLISHED: PMI, III, 341; Hellman, *WI Esquire*, p. 274 (in part).

1. George Pope Morris (1802–1864), who acquired his military title from his connection with the New York State Militia, had been founder and editor of the *New-York Mirror and Ladies' Literary Gazette* (1823–1842).
2. WI's story, "The Wife," from *The Sketch Book*, appeared in *Sands of Gold*, a collection published by Morris and N. P. Willis in 1844. See *A Bibliography of WI*, pp. 31–32.

1715.   To Alejandro Mon

Legation of the United States. / Madrid May 10th. 1844.

His Excellency / Don Alejandro Mon, / &ca. &ca. &ca.

Sir,

I have the honor to acknowledge the receipt of Your Excellency's note informing me of the intended departure of Her Majesty the Queen for Valencia and Barcelona,[1] in company with her august Mother and sister, and that Her Majesty has been pleased to leave to my own election the honor of accompanying her on the journey.

I cannot but feel deeply sensible of the very gracious and accommodating spirit of this notification and shall not fail to do every thing in the matter that shall appear to me most likely to be acceptable to Her Majesty; most consonant with that high respect I am at all times disposed to manifest towards her; and most calculated to promote the objects of my mission to her Court.

Availing myself of this occasion to renew to your Excellency the assurance of my distinguished consideration

I am, most respectfully / Your Excellency's, / Obdt Sevt.
Washington Irving.

MANUSCRIPT: NA, RG 84 (letterbook copy); NYPL—Berg Collection (letterbook copy).

1. The trip to Valencia was announced for May 20. See *El Castellano*, May 10, 1844.

1716.   To Sarah Storrow

Madrid May 10th. 1844

My dear Sarah,

Yesterday (thursday) was the usual day of the arrival of the French courier; of late I have got into the habit of expecting a letter on that day from you. The day passed away and none arrived and I went to bed quite disappointed. This morning, however, your letter of the 4th.[1] has been put in my hands; the courier having, probably, met with Some delay on the road. I am spoiled, my dear Sarah, by your frequent correspondence, it has become quite a necessary aliment to me, like my daily bread. I am now looking with impatience for letters from america in reply to my request for leave of absence and my reccommendation of Mr Livingston as Secretary of Legation. On the last subject however I cannot expect a reply for some little time yet. Mr Hamilton will leave me in the course of a few days; and expects to meet Mr Livingston at Pau. He will probably be in Paris about the 24th. inst. I feel great regret that I have to part with him; but, since he is to go, I wish him to set off in time to enjoy the fine Seasons in Paris and London. I can easily get on without a Secretary until a new one arrives.

Yesterday I received an official notice of the intended departure of the Queen, with her Mother and sister, for Valencia and Barcelona, for the purpose of taking the ⟨baths⟩ Mineral baths of Caldas near the latter place. It is left at the option of the Diplomatic Corps to accompany the Court in this migration; but as I believe all the *chefs* of the other missions intend to do so, I shall have to follow suite, or appear singular, if not remiss. The baths of Caldas would be full as beneficial for ⟨the⟩ my malady as those of the Pyrenees; but in fact I have so nearly conquered the last traces of the complaint by baths at home, that I scarce need any natural baths. However, if I go I shall take a regular course of them. Indeed I do not intend to desist from the treatment which I have found so efficacious until I get completely out of sight of the malady, and *round the corner*, so that there may be no chance of its overtaking me again.

I cannot tell you how cheering is this deliverance from my long state of thraldom. I yet use my newly recovered limbs but moderately; so as not to produce any heat or irritation; but every day makes me feel more secure of a complete recovery.

Mr and Mrs Deacon arrived here three or four days since and almost immediately called upon me. I assure you I was quite pleased to see them; American ladies are rare birds in Madrid. They had coasted the Mediterranean parts of Spain; been at the Alhambra, where they had sought out all my old haunts and met with some of my old dependents, had afterwards been at Gibraltar, Cadiz and Seville, and so came up through the centre of Spain to Madrid. It was a hardy tour for a lady of Mrs Deacons delicate frame; but she seems to have enjoyed it. Yesterday they dined with me. It was such an American gathering as I have not before seen at Madrid there being Mr & Mrs ⟨Parker⟩ Deacon, Mr Parker (her brother), Mr Jones of S Carolina, Mr Chouteau & Mr Shaw of St Louis, and Mr & Madame Albuquerque. We had a very pleasant, social dinner; at least it was so to me, and I hope my Guests were not less pleased. Mr & Mrs Deacon have gone this day to the Escurial, to return on Saturday evening. On Tuesday next they set off on their return to France. I trust you will see them when they return; do not let any little prejudice prevent you. Indeed endeavor as much as possible

in all your intercourse with ⟨society⟩ ↑the world↓, to avoid yielding to
petty ↑personal↓ distastes so as to neglect the regular courtesies of
Society. In these matters we are too apt to let the notions and prejudices
of others influence us; and to persuade ourselves that people are 'bores'
because others say they are so. Toleration is a grand ingredient of good
breeding, and that is greatly facilitated by acquiring a habit of looking
out for peoples good qualities instead of their faults. I really have
found sufficient companionable qualities in the Deacons to render the
few hours I have had occasion to pass in their society very pleasant.
But I do not pretend to set myself up as a standard in these matters.
I know I am "the easily pleased Washington Irving."[2] God forgive me
for the same!

This evening I am going to a little soiree at the house of my fair
young friend the gifted Leocadia. where we shall have some musical
tableaus, exhibited by her and two or three young ladies of her acquaintance. I anticipate great enjoyment.

Saturday May 10.[3] I passed a dissipated evening. In the early part I
went to the opera and saw the two first acts of my favorite Lucia de
Lammermoor and then repaired to the fair Leocadias— whom I found
already in full song. The party was small, but comfortably select; consisting of a few of the grandees; General Narvaez the military dictator
of the day, and some of the diplomatic corps. We had some charming
singing in the saloon, then a fine scene & duet from Norma, by Leocadia
and a niece of the Marchioness of Montija; they were dressed in character and performed on the little Stage formed for tableaux vivantes.
It was really quite a treat; they performed well, Sang better, and looked
beautifully. We had afterwards two or three charming tableaus; and I
returned home at One O'clock at night to dream of delightful music;
singing pictures and bright Spanish eyes. Decidedly Leocadias eyes
surpass those of Fanny Kemble. This morning at 11 Oclock I drive
out to ⟨the⟩ see the Royal country seat of the Pardo, a few miles from
Madrid in company with Madame Albuquerque and Hamilton

With kind remembrances to Mr Storrow and many kisses to the darling

Your affectionate uncle
WI.

MANUSCRIPT: Yale.   PUBLISHED: STW, II, 169 (in part).

1. This letter has not been located.
2. This phrase must have rankled WI. See WI to Sarah Storrow, October 8,
1842.
3. WI probably intended to write "11," which fell on Saturday in 1844.

1717.   To Henry Hallam

Madrid May 14th. 1844

My dear Sir

Permit me to present to you Mr Alexander Hamilton; who has been with me since my arrival in Spain as Secretary of Legation. He is grand Son of General Hamilton the associate of Washington and one of the founders of our Constitution; and he inherits much of the high intellectual qualities of his grandfather. Should you be curious about Spanish affairs and Spanish public characters; or about the political and Statistical affairs of the United States I know no one better able to give you correct information than Mr Hamilton. Reccommending him as every way worthy of any attention which it may suit your convenience to bestow upon him, I am, my dear Sir,

Yours ever very faithfully
Washington Irving

Henry Hallam Esqr / &c &c &c / London

MANUSCRIPT: Christ Church Library, Oxford.

Henry Hallam (1777–1859) was a historian of the Middle Ages whom WI had first met in John Murray's drawing room in 1820. See WI to James K. Paulding, May 27, 1820, and to Henry Brevoort, August 15, 1820.

1718.   To John Murray III

Madrid May 14th. 1844

My dear Sir,

Permit me to make you acquainted with Mr Alexander Hamilton, who has been with me ever since my arrival in Spain as Secretary of Legation. He is a young gentleman of high qualities both of head and heart; grandson of General Hamilton, the associate of Washington and one of the founders of our Constitution⟨,⟩. ⟨and⟩ Mr Hamilton is one whom I selected from all the young men of my acquaintance for the post which he has occupied, and in which he has acquitted himself with great ability. He is full of information concerning Spain and has a most agreeable manner of communicating it. I am sure you will be well pleased with his acquaintance.

Present my kindest remembrances to your Mother and Sisters and believe me ever

Yours very faithfully
Washington Irving

John Murray Esqr / &c &c &c

ADDRESSED: John Murray Esqr / &c &c &c / Albemarle Street.   DOCKETED: *May 14. 1844* / Irving — W

MANUSCRIPT: John Murray.

John Murray III (1808–1893), with whom WI had had earlier business dealings, took over management of the family publishing firm when his father died in 1843.

1719. *To Sarah Storrow*

Madrid May 15th. 1844

My dear Sarah,

The American party which was so recently assembled at my table is all dispersed. Some have gone to Andalusia; Mr & Mrs Deacon set off two days since for Paris and Alexander Hamilton set off last night in the Malle Poste for France in company with Mr Jones and Mr Parker.

The departure of Hamilton is a perfect bereavement to me. I had no idea how important he was to my comfort and enjoyment. He has so endeared himself to me by his kindness in Sickness; his generous sympathies on all occasions; by his honorable principles; his bright intelligence; his varied information, and his happy disposition that, while he was in the house I needed no other companions and he was almost always at home. And then the parting with him was in a manner parting with a portion of home; for he was the last of the three young companions ⟨linked⟩ who had embarked with me in my mission and were linked to me by home affinities. Today there is an inexpressible loneliness in my mansion, and its great saloons seem uncommonly empty and silent. I feel my heart choking me as I walk about and miss Hamilton from the places and seats he used to occupy. The Servants partake in my dreary feelings and that encreases them. Juana cannot speak of the *Señorit⟨a⟩o* without the tears starting in her eyes. He was beloved by them all, and with reason.

I am scrawling this because it is a relief to me to express what I feel, and I have no one at hand to converse with. The morning has been rainy but it is holding up and I shall drive out and get rid of these lonely feelings. To day I dine with the Albuquerques, of which I am glad.

All this will soon pass away, for I have been accustomed for a great part of my life to be much alone; but I think of late years, living at home, with those around to love and cherish me, my heart has become accustomed to look around for others to lean upon. Or perhaps I am growing less self dependent, and self competent than I used to be. However, thank God, I am getting completely clear of my malady, and in a train to resume the occasional exercise of my pen; and when I have that to occupy and solace me, I am independent of the world.

The Royal family and many of the dignitaries and officers of the Court set out on the 20th. for Valencia and Barcelona. I doubt whether I shall make a journey in that direction: as I find part of the Corps diplomatique remain here; and I do not wish to budge now that I am in the fair way of making a complete cure at home.

I am looking anxiously for letters from the United States, which must determine all my plans for the year. I doubt, however, whether I shall have any thing definitive until the letters arrive by the Steamer of the 1st May: which will not get here for eight or nine days yet. Mr Livingston I presume it at this time at Pau; ⟨now⟩ waiting to know whether he is appointed. Mr Hamilton will probably see him there. He will no doubt proceed on to Madrid the moment he receives official notification.

The home feeling has been strong upon me of late; partly no doubt from the ⟨affairs⟩ preparations for Hamiltons departure, and the idea that he was soon to return to the scenes and the friends who are so dear to me. I sometimes catch myself breaking out into ejaculations at my loneliness and my separation from all my Kith and Kin, but I instantly repress them and reccollect how great are the benefits that result from my exile. In general, however, cheerfulness preponderates; and if I had you and darling little Kate here to lavish those domestic feelings and affections upon, which are superfluous and even troublesome in my bachelor condition, I think I could make myself perfectly content. I do not think I was ever intended for a bachelor; certainly not for an *old* bachelor, for the older I grow the more I want women kind and children kind around me to give a zest to existence.

Tomorrow will be Thursday, when I shall look for a letter from you— my bright day in the week!—The sun is just come out and is shining brightly. So I'll go abroad and shake off all dull thoughts. Kiss my darling for me and remember me kindly to Mr Storrow.

Affectionately your uncle
WI.

Manuscript: Yale.   Published: PMI, III, 342–43; Hellman, *WI Esquire*, p. 274 (in part).

1720.   To Israel K. Tefft

Madrid May 17th. 1844

Dear Sir,

A long and harrassing indisposition of upwards of a year and from which I am scarcely recovered; has deranged all my correspondence and prevented my attending to many commissions of friendship; this I trust will be a sufficient apology for not having replied earlier to your letters of 18 June and 11 Jany last.[1]

You wish to have a research made in the Spanish archives for any documents which may exist relative to the hostilities between Florida and the provinces of S Carolina & Georgia in the time of Genl Oglethorpe.[2]

Persons at a distance have little idea of the difficulty attending researches in the Spanish archives. The government is loth to grant permission; and generally does so with great restrictions and for specific objects; this is especially the case of late, in consequence of great abuses of the privilege by a Belgian of the name of Gachard.[3] The research you wish to have made is rather vague and general; after documents which *may* exist. If such as you mention do exist they must be either in the Archives at Semancas,[4] or in those of the casa de contratacion at Seville.[5] If I could obtain permission from government for a rummage of the kind it would require time, and the attention of a person who could ↑go to those places and↓ make it his business: these archives being a perfect wilderness of documents. ⟨since a bond on would have to⟩

The research, therefore, even though it might be fruitless, would be attended with considerable expense. These matters I suggest for your consideration in the mean time I shall endeavor to learn by general enquiry, whether there is a probability of such a research being successful

I am Sir / Very respectfully
Washington Irving

I K Tefft Esq / &c &c &c

MANUSCRIPT: Georgia Historical Society.

1. These letters have not been located.
2. James Edward Oglethorpe (1696–1785), one of the chartering founders of Georgia, went to the area in 1733. In 1736 he built Frederica on the Altamaha River as an outpost against the Spanish. He later attacked the Spanish settlement at St. Augustine in 1740, and the Spanish retaliated by attacking Frederica in 1742.

3. Louis Prosper Gachard (1800–1885), keeper of the Archives of Belgium, was copying documents relating to the Spanish occupation of Flanders. He aroused the suspicions of the Spanish authorities, who, in turn, made another copy of each document and arranged for their immediate publication. See Pascual de Gayangos to W. H. Prescott, October 10, 1843; April 13 and November 11, 1844, in *The Correspondence of William Hickling Prescott, 1833–1847*, ed. Wolcott, pp. 395, 460, 516–17.

4. At Simancas, a town about seven miles southwest of Valladolid, is a castle containing the national archives of Spain with the exception of the documents relating to South America, which were transferred to the Archives of the Indias in Seville in 1783, and those relating to French diplomacy and the capture of Francis I, which were removed by the French in 1809. See Karl Baedeker, *Spain and Portugal*, p. 41; and Richard Ford, *A Hand-Book for Travellers in Spain*, II, 928–29.

5. This structure, designed by Juan de Herrera in 1585, houses the Archives of the Indias, which was founded in 1781. See Baedeker, *Spain and Portugal*, p. 397; Ford, *A Hand-Book for Travellers in Spain*, I, 378–79.

1721. *To Sarah Storrow*

Madrid, May 18 184⟨3⟩4

My dear Sarah,

I wrote to you on Wednesday last, by way of scribbling off a feeling of great loneliness on the departure of Alexander Hamilton. I have since kept myself busy, and so fought off the blue devils which were besetting me and am now getting into my usual humdrum vein. I am not so badly off as I was last year, when I was alone for many weeks during Hamiltons absence; and was suffering with my malady into the bargain. Now, thank heaven, the latter is nearly extirpated, and no longer disables nor annoys me and I can occupy and amuse myself with my usual pursuits. It was only the idea that Hamilton had gone *not to return*, that made his departure so painful to me: but I shall soon get accustomed even to that idea. In fact if I remain long at Madrid I shall get accustomed to do without attachments or enjoyments of any kind, and shall live as philosophically and negatively and selfishly as an oyster in his shell.

This evening I go, with several others of the Diplomatic Corps, to take leave of the Queen & Queen Mother &c who depart on Monday for Barcelona. I have concluded not to accompany the Court; as about one half of the diplomatic Corps remain at Madrid; and I prefer remaining here until I think my cure effected beyond the danger of relapse. When that is completed, I may repair for a short time to Barcelona; provided I have a Secretary of Legation to whom I can confide the mission during my absence; and provided there are no new outbreaks and pronunciamentos; which are apt to occur in the hot summer months when the blood of the Spaniards mounts to fever heat. Indeed there is sad croaking among politicians of all denominations; who seem to think we are on the eve of further convulsions. I hope they may be wrong in their prognostications; for the next political convulsion will probably be more violent and sanguinary than the preceding; the late events and reverses having engendered so much deadly hate and such ardent thirst for vengeance[.] I am wearied and at times heartsick of the wretched politics of this country; where there is so much intrigue, false-hood, profligacy and crime, and so little of high honor and pure patriotism in political affairs. ⟨What I have seen of⟩ The last ten or twelve years of my life, passed among sordid speculators in the United States, and political adventurers in Spain, has shewn me so much of the dark side of human nature, that I begin to have painful doubts of my fellow man; and look back with regret to the confiding period of my literary car⟨r⟩eer, when, poor as a rat, but rich in dreams, I beheld the world through the medium of my imagination and was apt to believe men as good as I wished them to be.

Your late letters give me pleasant accounts of your rural excursions in the neighborhood of Paris; and makes me long to be with you, help-ing Kate to gather butter cups and daisies and to chase butterflies. I am glad to find that your intimacy with Madame Hacquet continues, and that you take occasional drives with her. I have a very kind feeling toward her for "auld lang Syne" and beg you to remember me to her. I hope Kate and the little dogs continue on good terms.

Four days more will in all probability bring me letters from home to the first of May; decisive of my plans for the rest of the year. I am looking forward with great Solicitude.

I am anxious to know where you pitch your tent for the Summer. The account you give of the house formerly occupied by Genl Cass at Versailles is very promising; but beware of taking a house in company with another family, unless you have appartments (Saloons & all) entirely distinct. Indeed it is perilous for families to live under the the same roof. Friendships are always safest when kept up a little at a distance;—for, however discreet the heads of the families may be, the harmony may be interrupted by petty squabbles among the children or the Servants.

This is my second letter this week. I hope the two will procure one long one in reply; and that you will not leave it ⟨to S⟩ till Saturday, to write in a hurry—Tell me all about your Excursion to Fontainbleau.[1] I should like to drive about the old Forest with you, and look out for the Spectre Huntsman,[2] who, I presume, still haunts it.

Remember me affectionately to Mr Storrow—and give my dear little
Kate a Kiss for me.

Your affectionate uncle
Washington Irving

ADDRESSED: Madame / Madame Storrow / No 4. Rue de la Victoire / à Paris
MANUSCRIPT: Yale.   PUBLISHED: PMI, III, 343 (in part); Hellman, *WI Esquire*,
    p. 274 (in part).

1. Nearly fifty miles in circumference, the forest of Fontainebleau covers an area
of 42,500 acres. In its midst, about thirty-seven miles southeast of Paris, is the
palace of Fountainebleau, dating from the Middle Ages, a favorite residence for the
kings of France. See Karl Baedeker, *Paris and Its Environs*, p. 344.
    2. Shortly before his assassination Henry IV (1553–1610), king of France from
1589 to 1610, heard the noise of a hunt approaching and suddenly was confronted
by a huge, hideous black huntsman who shouted a warning and immediately disappeared. See Findlay Muirhead and Marcel Monmarché, *Paris and Its Environs*
(London, 1922), p. 358.

1722.   To John C. Calhoun

Legation of the United States / Madrid, May 21st. 1844

No 42. / The Hon / The Secretary of State / of the United States.
Washington.

Sir,
    The Queen, accompanied by her mother and Sister, departed yester-
day morning for Valencia and Barcelona, to avail herself of the mineral
baths of Caldas, near the latter city. The only member of the Cabinet
who formed part of the Royal Cortege, was General Narvaez, Minister
of War. The French Ambassador set off about the same time to accompany the royal family on the journey. Others of the Diplomatic Corps,
especially the Ministers of Great Britain and Naples, are about to follow
the court to Barcelona: as some of the corps however, remain for the
present at Madrid, I shall do the same; nor shall I make the journey
unless the objects of my mission appear to require it, or so many of the
diplomatic corps go, that it would seem singular to remain behind, and
might be construed into a want of proper respect and consideration for
the Queen and her court.
    The Marques of Viluma has accepted the post of Minister of State and
of Foreign affairs[1] and will proceed from England to Barcelona to present
himself before the Queen and take the oaths of office. Should he remain

with the Court at Barcelona the whole of the diplomatic corps will probably go there.

This Royal expedition to the sea ports of the Mediterranean has given rise to a variety of rumors of secret plans connected with the marriage of the young queen; all which are ridiculed as groundless by the court journals.[2] The journey, however, is generally considered impolitic in the present state of affairs, and at a time when the popular mind is so full of Suspicions.

The absence of the Court from the Capital and the consequent dislocation of the Cabinet will retard the despatch of public business, and will cause the measure dissolving the present Cortes and ordering elections for a new one, to be postponed. It is thought ministers are glad to avail themselves of this delay if they have not contrived it purposely, to gain time to arrange their future plan of operations, and to prevent their being goaded on to precipitate action or clamored at for inactivity; as was the case with the Bravo Cabinet. Though incessantly urged, they have as yet declared no line of policy, but the ministerial journals profess for them a determination to adhere to and support the Constitution and to act within the circle of the laws: it is evident however that they mean to strengthen the hands of government; and that the military spirit of Narvaez will enter largely into their councils.

The Chevalier de Argaiz arrived here a few days since and experienced a very favorable reception from the Queen and Queen Mother, as well as from the Cabinet. The letter of the President, and the cordial and respectful mention heretofore made of him by this legation, on the behalf of the President and cabinet, have placed the Chevalier in an advantageous footing at his court. I have no doubt that the full and fair explanations he is disposed to make with respect to our whole line of policy in regard to this country and its colonial possessions, will have the effect of putting all matters in their proper light.

I have had some little conversation in regard to the Island of Cuba, with Mr Mon the minister of the treasury; who acts, ad interim, as minister of State. He considers the tranquility of the island secure for the present; and the negro insurrection completely suffocated. It is almost useless, however, to agitate topics of the kind with these transient occupants of office; who seldom have time or inclination to make themselves acquainted with the details of the department momentarily confided to their superintendance. I look to have more ample communications with the Marques of Viluma when he enters upon the duty of his office

> I am Sir / Very respectfully / Your obt Servt
> Washington Irving

DOCKETED: Recd. June 21 — *Mr Markoe* [*top of page 1*] / No. 42. W. Irving.
  Madrid. 21 May 1844.
MANUSCRIPT: NA, RG 59.   PUBLISHED: Manning, *Diplomatic Correspondence*, 340–
  41 (in part).

1. See *El Castellano*, May 17, 1844.
2. See *La Gaceta*, May 16, 1844; and *El Castellano*, May 17, 1844.

1723.   To Sarah Storrow.

Madrid, May 24th. 1844

My dear Sarah,
  Yesterday (thursday) has passed without bringing me a letter from
you. I presume the courier of the French Embassy, instead of coming
direct to Madrid, goes at present to Barcelona, as the Ambassador has
accompanied the Court to that city: ⟨If⟩ your letter, therefore, if you
have sent one by the Courier, will not reach me for several days. Send
your letters hereafter by the post, until I give you directions otherwise.
  Hamilton is by this time ⟨with⟩ in Paris. I had a very acceptable letter
from him[1] from Bayonne, letting me know that he was safely over the
frontier. He will be able to give you a world of information about Madrid
life in general and our domestic life in particular. I miss him sadly—
sadly. His bright countinance and bright and happy spirit were sunshine
within doors, and his varied intelligence and information made him an
admirable companion. I have turned myself out of doors since his departure; and go to all kinds of sights and shows. and promenades, and
so keep myself from feeling lonely.
  I am looking every moment for the return of Pepe[2] from the Post
office with the morning mail; as I expect letters and papers from the
United States by the Steamer of the first of May, which I see has arrived.
This mail I trust will determine whether I am to have Mr Livingston
for a Secretary; and whether I shall have leave of absence this Summer.
  I see that a New Minister has been appointed for Paris. Mr W King
↑of Alabama[3]↓ who for many years has been in the Senate of the U
States. He is an old acquaintance of mine; a very gentlemanlike man. I
first knew him about the year 1817 when I was residing with your uncle
Peter in Liverpool. He was then on his way home from Russia having
been attached to the Legation in that Court.[4] He remained a week or
two at Liverpool, and dined alternately with us; with a Mr Kernan[5] of
Philada & Mr Haggerty of Virginia, So that we were every day the same
party of five; though at different houses. We supposed he would give a
good account of Liverpool on his return home, as a very hospitable

place, ⟨though there were⟩ ↑but with↓ *only five inhabitants.* I believe
he is still a bachelor[6]—in which case I should not be surprised if he
were an old one.

I have enjoyed myself greatly in the Retiro of late. It is such a delight
to be able once more to ramble about the shady alleys, and to have the
companionship of nightingales with which the place abounds at this
season of the year. There is a beautiful prospect too of the distant Guadarama mountains; seen rising above the tree tops; ⟨in be⟩ tinted with
hazy purple, and crowned with snow. The Retiro is one of the few
pleasant haunts that cheer the surrounding sterility of Madrid—Here
comes Pepe—and I see a large pacquet in his hand which must contain
the letters by the Steamer.

—I have just finished reading my letters, and am left in most tantalizing
ignorance and doubt on the subjects at this moment most important to
me. I have nothing from Govt. on the subject of my leave of absence,
or of the appointment of Mr Livingston. Indeed I have nothing from
government but a despatch inclosing a letter of condolence to the Queen
on the death of her aunt the Infanta Luisa Carlota—By the number of
this despatch there are three despatches which have not yet come to
hand and which have probably been forwarded by sailing packets. They
may contain replies on the points in question. I find Mr Hamiltons letters
have been forwarded to Paris. If he receives any information of importance he will no doubt communicate it to me immediately. I must
wait in *impatience.*

I am rejoiced to find by ⟨these⟩ my family letters that Mr Grinnell
has taken Mr George Jones' house for the present year: and that Mr
⟨Jones⟩ Minturn continues to occupy Mrs Colford Jones:—What delightful arrangements these will be for the cottage—I feel homesick at the
very idea! It will be a gay, social neighborhood; with gaiety of the right
kind. Grinnell will be a famous hand for Yachting with the jovial mariners
of Nevis. Tell Alexander Hamilton I envy him the merry cruisings there
will be this summer on the Tappan Zee.

I feel quite undecided about a journey to Barcelona but suppose I
shall have to go; especially as I have this letter of condolence to deliver
to the Queen. I shall wait, however, until I receive the despatches which
are on their way, and until I have a Secretary to take charge of the
Legation in my absence.

Give my kind remembrances to Mr Storrow and kiss my darling little
Kate for me—who I fear has quite forgotten the 'Unty' from whom she
receives so many remittances of the Kin⟨g⟩d

Your affectionate uncle
Washington Irving

MANUSCRIPT: Yale.   PUBLISHED: PMI, III, 343–44 (in part).

1. This letter has not been located.
2. Probably one of WI's Spanish house servants.
3. For other details, see WI to William R. King, March 21, 1844.
4. King had accompanied William Pinkney on a special mission to Naples and Russia from 1816 to 1818.
5. See WI to Peter Irving, September 20, 1817.
6. WI was correct. King never married.

1724.   To Sabina O'Shea

[Madrid, May 26, 1844?]

My dear Mrs O'Shea,

I return you the Journal des Enfans[1] with many apologies for detaining it so long from my friend Kickeys[2] library. I hope, in so doing, I have not interfered with the studies of that ingenious young hidalgo.

I have made several attempts to see you of late, but have not been able to get inside of your front door. Has your husband any hand in this? I trust not. I trust he has seen and read ⟨of⟩ enough of Spanish plays, which of course "hold the mirror up to nature,"[3] to know that when once a young fellow is determined to see a fine woman, all the husbands in the world cannot prevent him.

However, say nothing to him on the subject, as it might make mischief between us—I'll try again.

In the mean time believe me

Your devoted and not discouraged
Washington Irving

Madrid, May 26th [1844?]

ADDRESSED: Madame / Madame O'Shea / chez elle   DOCKETED: W — — Irving / May 26th.
MANUSCRIPT: HSA.   PUBLISHED: Penney, Bulletin NYPL, 62 (December, 1958), 616.

1. Probably issues of *Journal des Enfants*, a children's magazine published in Paris from 1832 to 1848 and resumed from 1855 to 1897. See *Catalogue collectif des périodiques du début du XVIIe siècle à 1939*, 4 vols. (Paris, 1969), III, 139.
2. One of several nicknames given to Henry George O'Shea (1838–1905), who later was a diplomat, a writer of poetry, drama, and travel books, a member of the Royal Academy of History, and president of the Society of Science, Art, and Literature at Biarritz. See Penney, *Bulletin NYPL*, 62 (December, 1958), 629.
3. See *Hamlet*, III, ii, 25.

1725. *To Alejandro Mon*

Legation of the United States / Madrid May 27th 1844

His Excellency / Don Alejandro Mon / Etc etc etc

The undersigned Envoy Extraordinary and Minister Plenipotentiary of the United States, has the honor to solicit the attention of his Excellency Don Alexander Mon, her Catholic Majesty's first Minister of State and of Foreign Affairs ad interim to a claim for indemnification on the part of Mr James Wood the head of a respectable American Mercantile house at Canary and for twenty years a respectable resident of that island

It appears that by a royal order of the 12th October 1841 a privileged or exclusive tariff was granted to the Canary Islands allowing them to import goods from all parts of the world at a fixed rate of duty. Mr James Wood from time to time imported goods in conformity to it in the month of *Feby 1843*; another American House did the same on the 1st of September of the same year. The Tariff therefore continued in force at this time, and no notice was given of any intention to alter it. On the *4th of September* Mr Wood on the reasonable confidence that this Tariff would be continued ordered another shipment of goods from the United States directed to the Islands. These goods arrived on the *31st of the following December* on the American Schooner Statesman. They were entered in the usual form, *landed for consumption in the Islands* and warehoused at the Custom House. On proceeding to dispatch them on the 26th of February, Mr Wood was surprised to find that duties were exacted on them conformably to the Tariff of the Spanish ↑Peninsula↓ dated at Madrid *31st August 1841*, orders having been recently received to enforce that Tariff in the islands so far as all Americans were concerned.

Now it appears that according to this peninsular tariff the duties on his goods amounted to *Eighteen hundred and one Dollars and fifty two cents* whereas according to the privileged tariff they would only have been *Seven hundred and seven dollars and 90 cents*. It appears also that the full duties were exacted on the whole cargo though a part of it was damaged; the reason given was that the master of the vessel had not endorsed on his Manifest, his protest against probable average[?], a formality before altogether unknown.

Mr James Wood applied to the Intendant for redress. He pleaded that the Spanish Govt had not given due notice of this sudden change of tariff otherwise the goods would not have been entered at the Custom House or would have been bonded *in transit*; and he represented that if the duties were exacted in the present case according to the new Tariff several of the articles such as Tea, Duck, Rosin etc would have to be abandoned, the duties exceeding their actual worth.

The reply of the Intendent was that the goods must pay duties conformably with the Peninsular tariff and that the exponent would have his recourse in applying to the Supreme Govt of Spain for indemnification.

In compliance with the request of Mr James Wood the undersigned now makes this application in his favour and he trusts that the plain statement he has made carries with it sufficient claims upon the principles of Justice and equity which characterize her Majesty's Govt. to gain for it prompt and *favorable* attention.

The undersigned takes the occasi[o]n[1] to renew to his Exy Don Alejando Mon the assurance of his distinguished consideration

Signed Washington Irving

MANUSCRIPT: NA, RG 84 (letterbook copy).

1. The copyist omitted the bracketed letter.

1726. To Alejandro Mon

Legation of the United States / Madrid May 29th 1844

His Excellency / Don Alejandro Mon / First Minister of State / and of Foreign Affairs (ad interim)

Sir,

On the 25th of Jany last I had the honor to address a note to her Majesty's Govt representing the unequitable and injurious operation of the quarantine regulations in the Canary Islands upon vessels coming from the United States Understanding that these regulations complained of continue in force I take the liberty briefly to revert to the matter and to recommend it to the consideration of your Excellency.[1]

The following are the regulations in question. *First* all vessels sailing from any port of the United States south of Boston after the 1st of June and before the 1st of November, are subjected at the Canary Islands to eight days quarantine of observation. This sweeping regulation comprehending within its scope many degrees of latitude and a variety of climates, lays its ban upon a number of important ports as healthy as those of England or of any part of Europe; yet the ships of the latter at whatever time of the year they may have sailed are admitted to immediate pratique. *Second.* All vessels arriving in the Canary Islands, whatever be their port of destination must proceed to Sa Cruz to perform their quarantine. This regulation in conjunction with the preceding one has greatly embarrassed the trade of the U. S. with the Islands causing much needless expense and loss of time and in one instance specified in my former note, a total loss of the vessel. To place its unequitable operations in a clear point of view I will observe that, if a vessel, sailing from an American port south of Boston between the 1st of June and the 1st of November should arrive at the grand Canary on the same day with a vessel from an European port, each having a clean bill of health, the American vessel having to proceed to Sa Cruz go through the sanitary ordeal of eight days and return, a process which occasionally consumes ↑nearly↓ a month, might not get back to the Grand Canary to enter upon the business of her voyage before the European ship had landed and disposed of her cargo, despatched her business and set sail for home. The simple remedy for such complaints would be

First. To put all the ports of the United States, *north of Cape Hatteras* on the same footing with regard to quarantine with the ports of Europe and the Mediterranean; that is to say, to admit all vessels coming from them to immediate pratique, provided always that they arrive with clean bills of health certified by the Spanish Consul or the collector of the Customs resident at the port of sailing

Second. To permit every vessel subject to quarantine to perform it at ⟨the⟩ her port of destination.

It has been intimated to me that exertions are ma⟨king⟩de by persons resident at Sa Cruz to keep up the vexatious regulations before mentioned as they tend to give their port a monopoly of the trade to the Islands and benefit a large class of function⟨n⟩aries by the profits arising from quarantine regulations. Such interested and selfish machinations if they really exist cannot escape the eye and the equitable provision of her Majesty's Government. It has also been suggested that in the administration of the sovereign decrees and ordinances in these islands, the local authorities frequently confound the U. S. with Spanish America in their application of the general term "the Americas." This misconstruction might easily be prevented by a more particular specification.

Referring to my former note for a more ample discussion of some points of this subject I have the honor to remain

With best respect / Your Exc's obt servt.
(Signed)   Washington Irving

MANUSCRIPT: NA, RG 84 (letterbook copy); NYPL—Berg Collection (letterbook copy).

1. On May 31, Mon acknowledged receipt of WI's note and indicated that he was referring it to the minister of the interior for action. See Mon to WI, May 31, 1844 (NA, RG 84).

1727.   To John C. Calhoun

Legation of the United States / Madrid June 1st. 1844

No 43 / The Honorable / The Secretary of State / of the United States. Washington.

Sir,

Since the date of my last despatch, May 21. I have received Despatches Nos. *29* and *30.* The former again calls my attention to the claim of Madam de Viar[1] on the Spanish Government; about which I had been instructed, in a former despatch, to interest myself. The latter contains a letter of condolence from the President to the queen on the death of her aunt the Infanta Luisa Carlota.

The papers in the case of Madam de Viar, forwarded to me some time since, consist of a Memorial to the Cortes, accompanied by certificates; the whole enclosed in an open letter to the Minister of State, requesting him to present the memorial in due form.

Ever since the receipt of those papers affairs here have been in an extremely agitated and unsettled state; with frequent changes in the cabinet,[2] and brief and tumultuous sessions of the Cortes. I was advised by persons well experienced in the chances attending suits at the Spanish court by no means to bring forward the quiet claim of Madam de Viar at such a moment; "it would be like casting it into a whirlpool."

Even now, though the matter is again pressed upon me, I am loth to move in it. Mr. Mon, who administers the Department of State *ad interim*, is also Minister of the Treasury, and is in all the agitation of a financial crisis; it is difficult to engage his attention to any thing but questions of finance: he will, also, leave the department of State long before the meeting of the legislative body to which the memorial is to be presented. I doubt whether I shall not best consult the interests of Madam de Viar by waiting until the Marques de Villuma[3] has been installed in office, and, perhaps, until the meeting of a Cortes is at hand. Her papers being then presented to the Minister and urged upon his attention, will run less risk of being buried in the ↑daily↓ accumulating mass of similar documents, in the department of State, or of being forgotten before the assembling of the Cortes. I shall, however, be determined by circumstances.

With respect to the letter of condolence to the Queen, her absence from the capital prevents the immediate delivery of it. Beside, I presume there must be a letter on the way from the President congratulating her upon her majority and her assumption of the government. I shall wait, therefore, for the arrival of Despatches, Nos. 25, 27, and 28, which have not yet come to hand, and in one or other of which, in all probability is the letter in question

I am Sir, / Very respectfully / Your Obt Servt
Washington Irving

DOCKETED: Recd. July 5 — Mr Markoe [top of page 1] / No. 43. W. Irving. Madrid — 1 June 1844
MANUSCRIPT: NA, RG 59; NYPL—Berg Collection (letterbook copy).

This letter is entirely in WI's handwriting.

1. For other details, see WI to Daniel Webster, April 1, 1843.
2. For the composition of the cabinet of Narváez, see WI to John C. Calhoun, May 0, 1844.
3. Villuma had not yet returned to Spain from England, where he had served as ambassador.

1728. To Sarah Storrow

Madrid (Saturday) June 1. 1844

My dear Sarah,

I am a long time without hearing from you. The letter which I presume you sent by the French Courier, this day two weeks, and which, in ordinary course, would have reached me this thursday before the last, has not yet come to hand, having gone by the way of Barcelona, and having to await the arrival of the Ambassador in that city. I hope to ⟨ha⟩ receive it tomorrow or next day. I fear Hamilton may have written to me from Paris by the same conveyance, as I have received no letter notifying me of his arrival there my last letter from him was dated from Bordeaux.

I am hoping soon to have Mr Livingston here. I find by a letter recd from him[1] some days since he had heard of his being nominated to the Senate, and I at the same time received & forwarded a letter written to him from New York, and addressed to him as Secretary of Legation; from which I conclude his nomination was confirmed. It is singular that in respect to two matters about which I was so highly interested, as the appointment of Mr Livingston & my leave of absence, I should have been left in such suspence, from the want of intelligence by letter in the due course of time. All that I know about Mr Livingstons appointment is at second hand, in a round about way, and by inference. The non arrival ⟨of⟩ also of dispatches from Government, which are certainly on the way, being anterior to others received, leaves me undecided about my own movements. I shall no doubt have to go to

Barcelona, but I cannot well do so until I receive those dispatches, one of which must contain a letter of ceremony to the Queen; which I must deliver in person.

I begin to feel doubts about my being able to visit you this summer. I fear my request for a leave of absence, which was made at the end of one of my dispatches, will be over looked, or forgotten: and I cannot, a second time, *take* leave, however my health may require it. It will be vexatious to have my routine of life broken in upon by this expedition to Barcelona, and not to be able to make the excursion upon which I have set my heart.

I am not in a writing mood and question whether I shall get in the vein immediately for writing to Hamilton. As you will probably see him soon after the receipt of this letter tell him that I do not think there is any probability of my arriving in England while he is there (as he seems to expect) Indeed ⟨I⟩ the chance of my seeing England any time this year is exceedingly dubious, though I am extremely anxious to pay your aunt a visit. A few days more must put an end to my suspense in regard to my Summer plans; as I must receive the letters which are behind hand, and others by the Steamer of the 15th–16th. of May, and in a few days, I trust, Mr Livingston will be with me. I have written to him to come on without delay, and to come at once to my house; where I can accommodate him and his nephew[2] until he has time to make his permanent arrangements.

I shall be anxious to hear whether or no you are to lose the Society of the Ledyards this summer. I presume it will depend upon the arrival of the new minister, Mr King: which may be delayed for some little time. It will be quite a loss out of your little circle of intimacy.

I had a very pleasant letter from Mr Grinnell[3] the other day who seems well pleased with having summer quarters in the neighborhood of the Cottage. It will be a merry neighborhood this summer.

I am writing in a very hum drum mood as ⟨you⟩ the tenor of my letter will show; but I would not let the week elapse without letting you hear from me. In fact this last week has been a dull and tedious one: every day looking for letters from my friends, and every day disappointed. I can hardly treat Pepe civilly every morning when he returns from the post office and brings me nothing but newspapers. Next week I trust will be more productive. Letters are the salt that seasons existence in Madrid;—at least *my* existence, which depends so much upon my family and friends to give it interest.

I was seated a few days since on the Prado when a lady came by with a little girl just about the age, and as I thought much of the countenance and air of Kate. I could have taken the little creature in my arms and folded it to my heart. My heart beat as I gazed at it, and I felt the tears

rising in my eyes. I hope to see that child again. It ⟨is⟩ ↑was↓ not dark
eyed and dark haired like Spanish children in general; and its mother
seemed to have dressed it with as much vain glory as another mother
that I could mention.

God bless you my dear Sarah. Give my kind regards to your husband
and kiss my own little darling Kate for me.

Your affectionate uncle
Washington Irving

P S. Do you ever see Mr Carter & his friend Mr Ritchie?[4]

ADDRESSED: Madame / Madame Storrow / No 4. Rue de la Victoire / *à Paris*
MANUSCRIPT: Yale.

1. This letter has not been located.
2. This nephew was thirteen years old. See WI to Catharine Paris, June 15,
1844, and to Sarah Storrow, June 9, 1844.
3. This letter has not been located.
4. Possibly William F. Ritchie (1813–1877), a Virginia editor for whom WI
had written a letter of introduction to Thomas Moore in 1833. See WI to Moore,
June 22, 1833.

1729. *To Sarah Storrow*

Madrid (Sunday) June 2d. 1844

My dear Sarah,

I was rejoiced this morning by the receipt of your letter of 27th. May;[1]
the very sight of your handwriting on the superscription made my heart
leap. There has been a sad break in my correspondence lately: or rather
I am more sensible of a little interruption from being somewhat lonely
of late, and from looking for letters to determine all my summer plans.
Your letter which came by mail; is dated on Monday last. I presume
you wrote to me, as usual, on each of the ↑two↓ preceding Saturdays
↑May 18 & 25↓; both of which letters have gone by the confounded
French Courier to Barcelona, and will not reach me for two or three
days yet to come. I fear Hamilton may have written to me from Paris
by the same round about medium.

I find by the tenor of your letter that you have taken apartments at
Versailles. I should be delighted to be there with you, and have no
doubt the little room you mention would be spacious enough for ⟨all⟩
my accommodation. ⟨Though⟩ I am wearied of the solitary spaciousness
of Saloons, and feel as if I could crib myself within a nut Shell,[2] if I
could only be among those I love. ⟨But I⟩

I have not the dismal reccollections of Versailles that you imagine. I reccollect with delight our beautiful drives through the soft rich valley watered by (I believe) the Baviere:[3] and other drives among wooded hills and among shady villas. I should be able, too, this year to be in the park with you and Kate, which would be a daily enjoyment.

I have a boding apprehension of late, however, that I shall be disappointed in my Summer excursion: perhaps this has been produced by the delay and the cross purposes in my correspondence, and the consequent state of suspence, acting upon a system a little sensitive by long indisposition and just now morbidly irritable from ⟨the⟩ wretched, wet, gloomy weather, so unusual in Spain at this season of the⟨s⟩ year.

It would seem by your letter⟨s⟩, that Mr Hamilton had not heard, for certain, of Mr Livingstons appointment. As he must have had letters of as late date as those received by Mr Livingston, the latter cannot ⟨of⟩ have heard of it either. I had presumed he had merely from the Superscription of a letter to him from New York, ↑(which I forwarded to him)↓ bearing the N York post mark 25 April, and addressed to him as Secretary of Legation. Until Mr Livingston is perfectly certain on this point he will not set out for Madrid. I cannot expect him therefore so soon as I had calculated. All this tends to embarrass me and to prevent my arranging my plans. As soon as Mr Livingston is comfortably fixed here, and inducted into office, I shall have to set off for Barcelona— all my after movements must depend upon my dispatches from Government, and whether I get leave of absence. As I mentioned in my last I apprehend, in the late deaths & derangements in our Cabinet, ⟨that⟩ the request I made may be overlooked or forgotten. In such case I cannot presume to give myself a congé.[4] A few days, however, must bring the lagging dispatches (which must have been written prior to the 10th. of April) and will set my mind at rest upon this point. My uncertainty once at an end I shall reconcile myself to whichever course matters may take. If I have no leave of absence I shall prolong my sojourn at ⟨Bayonne⟩ ↑Barcelona↓, and profit by the mineral baths in the neighborhood completely to exterpate the lurking remains of my malady.

I have written three letters to Mr Hamilton[5] since his departure, addressed to him at the Legation at Paris. I trust he has received them.

Remember me Kindly to Mr Storrow—& Kiss Kate for me.

Your affectionate uncle
W. I.

ADDRESSED: Madame / Madame Storrow / No 4 Rue de la Victoire / à Paris
MANUSCRIPT: Yale.

1. This letter has not been located.
2. See *Hamlet*, II, ii, 260.
3. The Bièvre is a small stream starting in the pool of Saint Quentin southwest of Paris and draining into a sewer near the Ghobelins manufactory.
4. A leave of absence.
5. These letters have not been located.

1730. *To Sarah Storrow*

Madrid June 3d. 1844

My dear Sarah,

I have this day received your two letters[1] sent by the French Courier, which have made the tour by the way of Barcelona. I have also received this morning, the expected dispatches from Government, which have been so long on the way. I have now all the dispatches that were due; but there is not a word in any on the subject of my request for a leave of absence. I fear, therefore, I must give up the hope of seeing you this year; which has been one of my constant and most cheering anticipations. It is a sad disappointment; but I will not dwell upon it.

I have received the congratulatory letter from the President to the Queen, and now only await the arrival and comfortable lodgement of Mr Livingston, to depart, with Lorenzo, for Barcelona. I expect to have some of the members of the corps diplomatique, for fellow travellers.

I have as yet ⟨not⟩ no certain intelligence of the appointment of Mr Livingston, but consider it as a thing of course, after his nomination to the Senate.

I have a hurried letter from my dear Hamilton[2] written the day after his arrival. He had had his first interview with you. How I envy him his long chat with you; and his interview with little Kate.

My dear Sarah I believe I almost feel the disappointment of not seeing Kate as much as that of not seeing you. The little baggage has fast hold of my heart Strings—Do not fancy I have a bad opinion of her temper. I know those little gusty natures are among the most kind, and affectionate and generous; and I never saw any freak of temper in Kate that did not pass away like a summer cloud, and leave all sunshine and blue sky behind it. God bless her! If I had her here to fold her to my heart, she might indulge in all the freaks and tantrums she pleased.

I am shocked to hear of the death of Miss Parker. What dismal tidings for her sister and brother[3] on their arrival—I wish when you see them you will remember me to them most kindly.

You tell me the Jones's are all thinking of returning to the United

States, and that Madame Tropbriand has lost her little girl. I fear their glittering dream of pleasure and excitement ⟨ha⟩ is at an end; and that they begin to prove how shadowy and unreal are the objects after which they have been striving. Will they find, however, their American home the same as when they left it? or will they have the same capacity to enjoy it? I doubt much whether their giddy carreer in Europe will not keep their heads spinning even after their return. They have my kindest and best wishes, mingled with mournful doubts. Wherever they go they will hardly take quiet and settled root; but will ↑probably↓ remain a transplanted family.

I grieve that you are to lose your kind friends the Ledyards, especially Mrs Ledyard the elder; who, where she once concieves a friendship is, I am convinced, sincere; and whose friendship is discriminating and, therefore, the more satisfactory and creditable.

I thank Mr Sumner for communicating my remembrances to Madame Villamil; and for forwarding me the note she wrote to him on the subject. I shall be most happy when I visit Paris to renew my intimacy with that lady and her family.

And now my dear Sarah I must close my letter, having to write others in reply to those this day received. My dear Sarah, my heart yearns toward you and your dear little one, and I feel that I have a sad, sad disappointment to struggle with.

Give my affectionate regards to your worthy husband and Kiss my darling Kate for me—

> Your affectionate uncle
> Washington Irving

Manuscript: Yale.

1. These letters have not been located.
2. This letter has not been located.
3. Mrs. Deacon and Mr. Parker, who had recently visited Madrid. See WI to Sarah Storrow, March 30, 1844.

1731. To John O'Shea

[June 7, 1844?]

My dear Don Juan,

I return you the bills of Exchg. signed. I know that nothing definitive has been arranged with Mr Mon. I wish merely to state in a paragraph of a despatch I am writing to my Government what is the nature of his ⟨contemplated⟩ *proposed* arrangement or project of financial reform:

but I wish to state it with technical correctness; being but indifferently versed in the fiscal vocabulary.

Yours very truly
W Irving

Friday, June 7th. [1844?]

MANUSCRIPT: HSA.   PUBLISHED: Penney, *Bulletin NYPL*, 62 (December, 1958), 617.

John O'Shea, the founder of the Madrid banking house bearing his name, was married to a beautiful Spanish lady, Isabel Hurtado de Corcuera. On his first visit to Madrid in 1826 WI was on intimate terms with them. This Mrs. O'Shea is often confused with Sabina, the wife of Henry O'Shea, of whom WI saw much during his last two years in Madrid. See Bowers, *Spanish Adventures of WI*, pp. 28–30; and Penney, *Bulletin NYPL*, 62 (December, 1958), 616, 629.

1732. To John C. Calhoun

Legation of the United States / Madrid June 8th. 1844

No 44. / The Honorable / John C Calhoun / Secretary of State of / the U States. Washington

Sir,

I have the honor to acknowledge the receipt of Despatch No 28 dated April 1st. but not received until the third instant, communicating the intelligence of your having received the appointment of Secretary of State. It will afford me great satisfaction, in the discharge of my official duties, to have to communicate with a person for whose talents and virtues I have ever entertained the highest respect.

In company with the despatch above mentioned I received Despatches Nos. 25 and 27, the former conveying the melancholy intelligence of the death of Mr Upshur and the temporary appointment of Mr Nelson[1] in his place; the latter enclosing a letter of congratulation from the President to the Queen on her majority.

These three despatches, of widely different dates, came *together*, via Cadiz; having apparently been detained until a vessel should sail for that port. I beg leave to dwell on this matter because an unfortunate predilection, which exists somewhere or other in the forwarding department, to send despatches by the way of Cadiz, has caused frequent, and occasionally embarrassing, irregularities and delays in the correspondence of this legation, and has been made the subject of repeated representations both by myself and my predecessors in office In the present instance the intelligence of the death of Mr Upshur has been *ninety five* days in reaching me; that of your appointment *Seventy two* days; and the congratulatory letter to the Queen *eighty two* days; arriving eleven days after the letter of condolence on the death of her aunt, written *forty two* days subsequently. I am also induced to specify these facts to account for what may have appeared inexactness and delay on my part, in not sooner acknowledging the receipt of those despatches

I beg leave to observe once more to the department, that the most Speedy, and by no means the dearest, channel by which to forward both letters and newspapers to this legation, is by the Steamers to England, addressed to the care of our Agent at London; they generally come to hand in from twenty two to twenty six days, and always within the month. The next best way is by the Sailing packets to Havre, addressed to the care of the American Consul.

The route via Cadiz should never be adopted unless for heavy parcels of books and documents; where delay is not important and where postage would be excessive

Having now both the letters of congratulation and condolence I shall, as soon as I can make the necessary arrangements, and leave the legation in proper hands, depart for the court at Barcelona, to deliver them personally to the Queen.

The government here is in the midst of a financial crisis. Mr Mon, the Minister of Finance, found on his accession to office an empty treasury, and all branches of the public revenue pledged to capitalists and loan contractors, so that nothing was left for the current expenses of the government which was virtually at the mercy of Speculators. He determined to attempt a reform by a recision of all existing contracts, giving due compensation to the interested parties. His first operation was with the tobacco contract; which, after some negotiation, the contractors consented to release. By this time a clamor had been raised by a set of political and financial black legs, who unfortunately beset this government and thrive on the embarrassments of the treasury. They charged Mon with meditating bankruptcy, and the non payment of the just claims upon the government, and intimated that he was under the secret influence of the Rothschilds[2] to whose grasping avarice he was disposed to sacrifice the Spanish capitalists. These Slanders had their effect even on honest minds, and expresses were sent off to the court at Barcelona, representing the schemes and motives of Mon in the most nefarious light.

After the expresses had departed the contractors, on sober second thought, appointed a committee to confer with Mr Mon, and ascertain his real intentions. In the first conference the minister succeeded in satisfying them that his plan of financial reform, while it would relieve the government from the Shackles which impeded all its movements and threatened a speedy bankruptcy, would provide for the complete protection of the interest of all parties concerned.[3]

A revolution instantly took place in favor of Mr Mon; he was cried up as the very man to extricate the country from its financial embarrassments, and other expresses were sent off, post haste, to Barcelona, to counteract all that had been rashly written against him.

Several meetings have since been held for the purpose of carrying out the views of Mr Mon, who proposes to give the contractors, in lieu of the Securities which they now hold, three per cent Stock at a conventional price. The advantage to the government would be; in the first place the total release of the pledged branches of the revenue; and, in the second, the payment of the creditors by an annual amount of interest, instead of the principal of the debt. Beside, the minister, no longer harrassed by claimants, and having the absolute control of the revenue, would be enabled to undertake reforms in the administration which, under present circumstances, are totally impracticable. The Capitalists and loan contractors would also find their advantage in the proposed arrangement, inasmuch as they could at any time dispose of the three per cent stock here, or in the foreign market. Nothing definitive has yet been done, but it is considered probable that the proposed plan will eventually be adopted. There are not wanting political croakers, however, who affirm that Mon is attempting too much; that there are too many venal interests and too powerful a phalanx of corruption arrayed against his plan of reform, and that his honesty and patriotism will ensure his downfall.

It is said, too, that he and his brother in law Pidal, are the only members of the Cabinet sincerely in favor of the Constitution; that the others affect to uphold it through policy, but are really undermining it; and that letters have been received from Paris, reporting ↑an↓ unguarded opinion uttered in that capital by the Marques de Viluma, that a constitutional form of government was unsuited to Spain.

All these circumstances weaken public confidence in the duration of the present Cabinet, and give rise to rumors of changes and removals.

A decree has been sent off by the Ministers in Madrid for the Queens approbation and Signature, dissolving the present Cortes and ordering an election for a new one.

I am Sir / Very respectfully / Your obt Servt
Washington Irving

P. S. All the Despatches from the Department to No 30 inclusive, have been received.

DOCKETED: Recd. July 5 Mr Markoe [*top of page 1*] / No. 44. W. Irving. Madrid —
8 June 1844.
MANUSCRIPT: NA, RG 59; NYPL—Berg Collection (letterbook copy).   PUBLISHED:
STW, II, 371 (in part).

This despatch is written entirely in WI's handwriting.

1. John Nelson (1791–1860), U.S. attorney general from 1843 to 1845, was acting secretary of state from February 29 to March 5, 1844.
2. The Rothschild interests in Madrid were represented by Mr. Weismuller,
whom WI had given protection in the U.S. legation during the attack on Madrid
in July of 1843. See Bowers, *Spanish Adventures of WI*, p. 186; and WI to Sarah
Storrow, July 18, 1843.
3. Mon issued three percent bonds to cover the existing debt and tried to balance income with expenditures in his reform of the fiscal structure. "Taxes were
evenly distributed and reduced to five chief headings: (1) a tax on agriculture;
(2) a tax on urban rents, manufactures, and commerce; (3) on octroi duty; (4)
a tax on land-registration, mortgages, and successions; (5) custom dues." These
measures were calculated to bring in £6,500,000 per year, enough for running
expenses and interest payments. See H. Butler Clarke, *Modern Spain*, pp. 198–99;
and *El Castellano*, May 30, 31, June 3, 4, 1844.

1733. To Sarah Storrow

Madrid June 9th. 1844

My dear Sarah,
   Mr Livingston and his little nephew arrived safe last evening and
have taken up their abode with me—which dispells the loneliness of my
house. I shall now prepare for my journey to Barcelona; which I apprehend will be rather uncomfortable from the heat of the weather.
Niether Mr Livingston nor myself have heard of the confirmation of
his appointment; ⟨though⟩ ↑but↓ we neither of us have doubts of it.
I have no newspapers by the last Steamer, and but one letter (from Pierre
M Irving[)].[1] He speaks of rumors of recalls of the Foreign ministers;
myself among the number. but attaches little importance to them.
For my own part I hardly think Mr Tyler would recall me, whom he
appointed; and for whose recall he could give no good reason that I
know of. If I were perfectly well and enabled to exercise my pen as
formerly I should scarcely regret it; but at present, that my literary
faculties are suspended, and that I have a family to support, my salary
continues to be important to the well being of others, as well as ⟨to⟩
myself—However, I will not suffer my mind to be disturbed by what
may be mere idle rumors.
   I have heard nothing from Hamilton since his note written the day
after his arrival in Paris; I presume he is now at London or on the way

there—I am looking daily for another letter from you but fear this interruption of the French ↑Diplomatic↓ Couriers will put an end to the regularity of your weekly letters.

I am writing a mere apology for a letter but the fact is I have been occupied for two or three days past writing dispatches and am rather fagged; and ⟨th⟩ my thoughts do not run copiously: when I feel more in the mood I will write a longer letter

Remember me kindly to Mr Storrow and give my darling little Kate a kiss for me; would to God I were at hand to give it myself.

Your affectionate uncle
Washington Irving

ADDRESSED: Madame / Madame Storrow / No 4. Rue de Victoire / à Paris
MANUSCRIPT: Yale.

1. This letter is not located. WI omitted the closing parenthesis.

1734. To John K. Cooke

Legation of U. S. / Madrid 11th June 1844

To John K. Cooke Esqre

Sir

Agreeably to instructions from the Dept of State I applied to the Spanish Govt July 2nd 1844 for your Exequatur as Consul of the U. S. for Trinidad de Cuba[1] It will be advisable for you to remit in time to your Agent in Madrid the fees demanded by the Spanish Govt on the delivery of that Instrument.

I am Sir / Very respectfully yours
(signed) Washington Irving

MANUSCRIPT: NA, RG 84 (letterbook copy); NYPL—Berg Collection (letterbook copy).

1. Apparently WI was unaware that Cooke had resigned and had been replaced by Samuel McLean, to whom he wrote on this same day. See Hasse, *Index to U.S. Documents*, III, 1748.

1735. To John R. Cooke

Legation of U. S. / Madrid 11th. June 1844

To John R. Cooke Esqre

Sir,

Agreeably to instructions from the Dept of State I applied to the Spanish Govt Oct 29th 1842 for your Exequatur as Consul of the U. S. for Xibera, Cuba.[1] It will be advisable for you to remit in time to your agent in Madrid the fees demanded by the Spanish Govt on the delivery of that Instrument.

I am Sir very respectfully yours
(Signed) Washington Irving

MANUSCRIPT: NA, RG 84 (letterbook copy); NYPL—Berg Collection (letterbook copy).

1. Apparently when Cooke went to Xibara, he was not permitted to assume the duties of U.S. consul. Although he was compensated for his actual service in 1842 and 1843, Cooke petitioned Congress for payment of expenses and losses incurred with the appointment. By the time of WI's letter he was no longer in the diplomatic service. See Hasse, *Index to U.S. Documents*, I, 411; III, 1749.

1736. To Franklin Gage

Legation of U. S. / Madrid June 11th 1844

To Franklin Gage Esqr

Sir,

Agreeably to instructions from the Dept of State I applied on the 24th April 1843 for your Exequatur as Consul for Cardenas. It has not as yet been granted, the Spanish Govt taking much time to make the customary enquiries. It will be advisable for you to remit in time to your agent in Madrid the fees demanded by the Spanish Govt on the delivery of that Instrument.

Very respectfully / Your obt servt
(Signed)   Washington Irving

MANUSCRIPT: NA, RG 84 (letterbook copy); NYPL—Berg Collection (letterbook copy).

1737. To John Hartman

Legation of the U. S. / Madrid 11th of June 1844

To John Hartman Esqre

Sir,

An application was made by this Legation to the Spanish Govt 24th April 1843 for your Exequatur as Consul at Panama, Cuba. As soon as it is received from the Spanish Govt it will be forwarded to you. Your bill of exchange on Sr Ulloa Ponce de Leon for the amount of fees has been received and the money collected and passed to your credit.

I am, Sir, / Respectfully your obt st
(signed)   Washington Irving

MANUSCRIPT: NA, RG 84 (letterbook copy); NYPL—Berg Collection (letterbook copy).

1738. To Samuel McLean

Legation of U. S. / Madrid 11th June 1844

To Saml McLean Esqre

Sir,

Application was made to the Spanish Govt on the 28th. Feby. 1844 for your Exequatur as Consul of the U. S. at Trinidad de Cuba.

It will be expedient for you to forward in time to your Agent in Madrid the fees exacted by the Spanish Govt on the delivery of the Exequatur.

I am Sir / Very respectfully your obt sevt
(signed) Washington Irving.

MANUSCRIPT: NA, RG 84 (letterbook copy); NYPL—Berg Collection (letterbook copy).

1739. To Marques de Viluma

Legation of the United States / Madrid 12th June 1844

⟨To His Exy the Marques de Viluma⟩ / ⟨First Minister of State etc⟩

⟨Sir⟩
    The ↑undersigned,[1]↓ Envoy Extry and Minister Plenipotentiary of the
U. S. has the honor to acknowledge the receipt of the note of his Excy
the Marques de Viluma conveying the information of his having entered
upon the discharge of his official duties as First Minister of State and of
Foreign Affairs.
    While congratulating his Excy on this distinguished mark of royal
esteem and confidence the undersigned assures him of the high satisfaction he shall experience in entering with him in official correspondence
and vying with him in efforts to promote and strengthen the bonds of
amity which so happily exist between the two nations
    The undersigned avails himself etc

(Signed) Washington Irving

MANUSCRIPT: NA, RG 84 (letterbook copy); NYPL—Berg Collection (letterbook
    copy).

    1. Only the inserted word, "undersigned," is in WI's handwriting.

1740. To Catharine Paris

Madrid June 15t. 1844

My dear Sister,
    It is some time since I last wrote to you. The Queen and her court
have departed for Barcelona, and the Royal palace is silent and deserted.
I went there with the Corps diplomatique, an evening or two before her
departure to pay her a farewell visit. As I know you delight in Royal
palaces and every thing belonging to them, and as I have described
former visits to this palace, I will give you a word or two about the
visit in Question. We went at half past nine. As it was not a visit of great
ceremony, the palace was not in its gala splendor. We ascended the
grand marble Stair case (famous in the memorable night attack) It
was soberly lighted by two or three large lanthorns; ⟨a sentinel was
placed⟩ here and there; was a centinel, a halbardier, or an officer of the
royal household. We passed through great Silent halls and lofty saloons,

all dimly lighted up, but gaining in shadowy grandeur what they lost in brilliancy. The great Saloon of Ambassadors, with its vaulted cielings; its deep crimson hangings, was only lit up by a few wax tapers on side tables; the rays of which were reflected in the huge mirrors, or Sparkled in the christal chandeliers; but ⟨were clouded in the⟩ could not dispel the pompous gloom of the vast apartment. The throne was vacant, and instead of the brilliant throng I had usually beheld here, there was only the Introducer of Ambassadors, preceding us to usher us into the presence chamber. After passing through two Saloons beyond, we arrived in the Anteroom to the apartment actually inhabited by the Queen. We had not been here long when the little Queen entered alone, from an inner room. She was simply dressed in grey silk, her hair drawn back from her face and forehead in somewhat of a chinese fashion. She acquitted herself with great self possession and amiableness, and ⟨by⟩ ↑in↓ the subdued light of the apartment, looked better than usual. She appeared to be quite animated with the idea of her approaching journey. We had afterwards an interview with the Queen Mother, who received us with her usual grace and affability. The whole reception was simple and without parade; there being only a lady or two in waiting in their ordinary dresses.

I am now preparing for a journey to Barcelona; where I have to go to deliver two letters from the President to the Queen. One congratulatory on her accession to the throne: the other of condolence on the death of her Aunt. They have been a long time on the way, and did not reach me until long after the Queens departure: otherwise I should have delivered them here, and have endeavored to dispense with this journey to Barcelona. It is a long journey to make in this hot weather and I fear I shall find Barcelona crowded and comfortable quarters not to be had.

Mr Livingston, who takes the place of Mr Hamilton, arrived here about a week since, with a nephew, a fine boy thirteen years of age. They have taken up their abode with me and h[ave] [MS torn] quite enlivened my house. I am looking every day for news from the United States of the confirmation of Mr Livingstons nomination as Secretary of Legation.

I have received no reply from government to my request for leave to make a tour for health, and have therefore given up all idea of seeing Sarah this year. My health, however, I am happy to say is almost entirely reestablished; having nothing but some slight lingerings of my old malady which I trust soon entirely to exterpate.

You will soon have Mr Hamilton among you all; who will give you much better accounts of all matters here, public and domestic, than I can do by letters.

Your last letter was written during an attack of influenza[.] I trust your next one will report you restored to health and enjoying yourself at Sunny side.

Ever my dear Sister

Your affectionate brother
W I.

ADDRESSED: Mrs Daniel Paris / Care of E Irving Esqr / New York. / for Packet Ship / to N York

MANUSCRIPT: Yale.   PUBLISHED: PMI, III, 345 (in part).

1741. To Marques de Viluma

Legation of U. S. / Madrid 16th of June 1844

To his Exy The Marques de Vilume / First Minister of State etc.

Sir,

The undersigned Envoy Extraordinary and Minister Plenipotentiary of the U. S. has the honor to solicit the attention of his Exy to the case of Michael Dauson Harang, ↑son of Lewis Harang↓ deceased who claims restitution of 10978 dollars wrongfully levied by the Intendant of Puerto Rico as derichos de Extraccion on the sale of lands of the defunct.

This claim was brought to the notice of her Majesty's Govt 26th ↑27th↓[1] of April 1841 by Mr Vail at that time Chargé d'Affaires and was still more fully urged by the undersigned in a note addressed Sept. 24th. 1842 to Ct Almodovar at that time First Minister of State. In reply Ct Almodovar observed that finding the claim to be pending before the tribunals of Puerto Rico he had ordered enquiries to be made in the matter, the results of which would be communicated to the undersigned. As a year and eight months have elapsed since that reply without any communication on the subject being made by her Majesty's Govt to the undersigned he trusts he will not be deemed importunate in respectfully requesting information in the premises [?] from his Excy and the Ms de Viluma at as early a period as his convenience may permit.

The undersigned avails himself of this occasion to renew to his Excy the Ms de V. the assurance of his distinguished consideration

(Signed) Washington Irving

MANUSCRIPT: NA, RG 84 (letterbook copy); NYPL—Berg Collection (letterbook copy).

1. This number is written in different ink.

1742. *To Franklin Gage*

Legation of U. S. / Madrid 17th June 1844

To Franklin Gage Esqre

Sir

I had the honor to write you a few lines on the 11th advising you to forward in time to your Agent in Madrid the fees demanded by the Spanish Govt on the delivery of your Exequatur. Since then your letter of the 23rd April has been recieved enclosing a bill of exchange on Don Juan Ml Calderon. The money has been collected and passed to your credit. As soon as the Exequatur is received it will be forwarded to you

I am Sir / Very respectfully your obt sert
(signed) Washington Irving.

Manuscript: NA, RG 84 (letterbook copy); NYPL–Berg Collection (letterbook copy).

1743. *To Francisco Armero*

Lega⟨t⟩cion de los E. U / Madrid 19 de Junio de 1844

Unofficial / Al Exmo Sr / El General Armero / Ministro de Marina, Commercio y Gobernacion de Ultramar

Tengo la honro de remitir a V. S. una proposicion del Senor Luttrell Jewett ciudadano de los Estados Unidos para el establecimiento de un Vapor en las isla de Puerto Rico. Creo de mi deber poner en su conocimento de Ud. que le acompaña una recomendacion muy poderosa de un miembro distinguido de nuestro Senado[1], a quien consta ser el interesado un comerciante respectabilismo e inteligente el cual ha visitado varias veces la isla y tiene relaciones en ella. Habiendole examinado me parece ser digne de la alta consideracion de V. S. y en conclusion le ruego se sirva proporcionarme una contestacion cuanto mas pronta le permitan las circunstancias à fin de que la pueda remitir a mi digno conciudadano.

Me aprovecho de esta primera ocasion para ofrecer a V. S. las seguridades de mi distinguida consideracion

B. L. M. de V. P. / su atento y seguro servidor
(signed) Washington Irving

Manuscript: NA, RG 84 (letterbook copy).

Translation:
"I have the honor of remitting to your lordship a proposal from Mr. Luttrell
Jewett, a citizen of the United States, for the establishment of a steamship in
the island of Puerto Rico. I believe that it is incumbent on me to inform you
that he has with him a very powerful recommendation from a distinguished member
of our Senate, who deems the person in question to be a most respectable and an
intelligent merchant who has visited the island several times and has relations
in it. Having examined him, he seems to me worthy of your lordship's high consideration, and consequently I beg you to be kind enough to provide me with an
answer as soon as circumstances allow, so that I may remit it to my worthy com-
patriot.
"I take the first opportunity to offer your lordship the assurance of my most
distinguished consideration"

1. George Evans (1797–1867), a prominent legislator and criminal lawyer from
Maine, was in the U.S. Senate from 1841 to 1847.

1744. To Pedro Pidal

Legacion de los Estados Unidos / Madrid 19 de Junio de 1844

Unofficial / El Exmo Señor / Don Pedro Pidal / Ministro de Gobernacion

Exmo Señor
Tengo la honra de rogar a Ud. se sirva expedir las ordenes par a que
se pueda copiar la segunda parte de los libros S 1 hasta 28 inclusivos de
la obra historica de Oviedo[1] la cual existe en la Real Academia de Madrid.
Se solicita dicha copia en favor de Sr. O. Rich por mucho tiempo
residente en esta Corte y quien tiene el derecho de reclamar esta
indulgencia de parte de la Academia habiendo esta por medio del
interesado logrado una copia de los libros S 9 a 48 de la misma obra.
Me aprovecho de esta primera ocasion etc. etc.

Washington Irving

Manuscript: NA, RG 84 (letterbook copy).

Translation:
"I have the honor of requesting you to expedite the orders for copying the second
part of books S 1 to 28 inclusive of the historical work of Oviedo which is in the
Royal Academy of Madrid.
"Said copy is solicited in behalf of Mr. O. Rich for a long time resident at this
Court and who has the right to claim this indulgence on the part of the Academy,
the concerned party having obtained a copy of books S 9 to 48 of the same work."

1. Gonzalo Hernández de Oviedo y Valdés (1478–1557) wrote *Historia generale
de las Indias* in 1535. WI had referred to the work in a letter to Thomas Storrow,
April 14, 1826.

1745. To O'Neil Bryson

Legation of the U. S. / Madrid June 24th 1844

Unofficial / To O'Neil Bryson Esqre

Sir

I have delayed answering your letter until I could obtain satisfactory and authentic information on the subject of your distinguished relative Arthur Duke O'Neil's will, a copy of which is now in my possession; you will see by the following extract that your claim, however well founded, has been urged too late as it is particularly specified "that the said tribes (meaning his irish kinsmen) will have a claim for the space of 70 years from the 12th day of May 1770 and if not so claimed the said Duke O'Neil allows the same to be forfeited to the Crown and charitable institutions of Spain."

I am Sir respectfully / Your obt servant
(signed) Washington Irving

MANUSCRIPT: NA, RG 84 (letterbook copy).

1746. To John C. Calhoun

Legation of the United States / Madrid 24th. June 1844

No 45 / The Hble John C. Calhoun, / Secretary of State Washington

Sir

I have the honor to acknowledge the receipt of Dispatch No 31 recalling my attention to the claim of Michael Drauson Harang. I have not lost sight of this claim since my correspondence with the Spanish Secretary of State on the subject in September 1842 but have not been able to procure any other reply to my enquiries than that the Government was waiting for information on the subject.

I have now addressed a note to the Marques de Viluma and hope the reply may be more explicit. It is difficult to give an idea, however, of the delays and evasions to which all applications of the kind are at all times subjected in the Spanish offices and more especially in the present agitated and revolutionary times. I believe, in general, I have fared better in my negotiations with the Spanish Government than most of my colleagues, some of whom complain bitterly that their personal applications are unavailing and their letters unanswered.

I received a reply some short time since to my complaint[1] of the Quarantine of eight days imposed upon the flag ship of Commodore Perry at the Island of Teneriffe and of the want of courtesy and due observance of the etiquette on the part of the authorities in not returning his official visits. In reply the Minister of State observes that the ship of Commodore Perry coming from the coast of Africa[2] was subjected to no other quarantine than that imposed upon all other ships in like predicament, whether foreign or national; and that as to the lack of etiquette on the part of the authorities they have since received an admonition "to observe the conduct required by the good harmony which happily subsists between Spain and the United States of America and which the Government of her Majesty is desirous to maintain." As the Minister in his correspondence intimated that the Quarantine laws connected with the Canary Islands were undergoing revision with a view to their melioration; I took occasion again to press upon the Minister the following modifications with regard to our trade

First. To put all the ports north of Cape Hatteras on the same footing with regard to Quarantine with the ports of Europe and the Mediterranean; that is to say, to admit all vessels coming from them to immediate pratique, provided always that they arrive with clean bills of health certified by the Spanish Consul or the Collector of the Customs resident at the port of sailing.

Second. To permit every vessel subject to Quarantine to perform it at her port of destination.

On the 27th of May last I made a written application on the part of James Wood an american merchant resident in the Grand Canary for indemnity for excessive duties wrongfully imposed upon a shipment of merchandize in consequence of a sudden change in the accustomed tariff without due notice thereof having been given in the Islands. A note in reply from the Minister of State dated 30th May informs me that this case has been submitted to the consideration of the Minister of Finance.

The four Cabinet Ministers who had remained in Madrid have suddenly departed for the Court at Barcelona.[3] Their departure has filled the Capital with uneasiness and given rise to a thousand rumors. A schism in the Cabinet is talked of on some important point of policy such as the dissolution and convocation of the Cortes, the marriage of the Queen, the restitution of the property of the Clergy, a modification of the Constitution etc. Every body apprehends a crisis. Viluma is represented as an absolutist; the Queen Mother is under apostolical domination and many affirm that the royal journey to Barcelona was a mere measure of policy to put the Court in a safe position in a Seaport and under the protection of the fortress of Montjuich preparatory to some Coup d'Etat which might convulse the Kingdom. . . These are mere specimens of a thousand contradictory rumors and surmises which distract the public mind in this city of idleness and political gossip. I may be able to give more accurate information after my arrival in Barcelona for which City I shall set out the day after tomorrow (the 26th inst) in company with the Brazilian Minister and the Danish Chargé d'Affaires, leaving the office of the Legation in the competent hands of Mr Jasper Livingston, whom I have made Secretary of the Legation pro tem, and who, I understand was nominated to the Senate for that post on the 22nd of April last.

I am Sir / Very respectfully / Your obedient servant.
Washington Irving

DOCKETED: Recd. 3 Augt. / Mr Markoe [*upper left corner of page 1*] / No. 45. W. Irving, Madrid. 24 June 1844

MANUSCRIPT: NA, RG 59; NYPL—Berg Collection (letterbook copy).

1. See WI to Luis González Bravo, January 30, 1844. Alejandro Mon had responded to WI's note on June 7, 1844 (NA, RG 84).

2. "In this there is an error, the ship was from the U. S. and bound to the coast of Africa" (footnote in MS).

3. These ministers were Mon, Hacienda; Pidal, Gracia y Justicia; Armero, Marina; and Mayans, Gobernacion. See *La Gaceta*, June 27, 28. They left Barcelona on July 4 and arrived in Madrid on July 8. See *La Gaceta*, July 8, 1844.

1747. To Joseph Cullen

Legation of the United States / Madrid 24th June 1844

To Joseph Cullen Esqr / U. S. Consul Teneriffe

Sir

Agreeably to your request I have presented the papers you forwarded to me last September at the "Oficinas de dendas publicas" where I was informed that a law having been passed in 1828 called "Costa de Cuenta," by the articles of which all debts were to be called in and settled previously to the year 1834 or after that period they would fall into the domain of "Dend Nacional" and would only be liquidated by the paper, which, in your communication, I am particularly instructed not to accept Its real value, I am credibly informed, at the present is about 6 per cent. It now rests with you to accept or reject this so called compensation. If you decide upon the former it will be necessary to have the certificate renewed as it must be presented within three months after date.

I received a communication lately from the Spanish Government in reply to mine on the subject of the Quarantine Regulations at the Canary Islands in which I am given to understand that that branch of the Quarantine regulations connected with the Canary Islands is undergoing revision and that in the meantime the existing laws must remain in operation.

The following are the modifications I have suggested with a view to this revision.

First. To put all the ports north of Cape Hatteras on the same footing with regard to Quarantine regulations with the ports of Europe and the Mediterranean that is to say to admit all vessels coming from them to immediate pratique, provided always that they arrive with clean bills certified by the Spanish Consul or the Collector of the Customs resident at the port of sailing

Second. To permit every vessel subject to Quarantine to perform it at her port of destination.

I am Sir / respectfully your obt sert
(signed) Washington Irving

DOCKETED: Recd. 10th July from Spanish Archives
MANUSCRIPT: NA, RG 84 (original and letterbook copy); NYPL—Berg Collection
  (letterbook copy).

1748.   To J. S. Dancher[?]

Legation of U. S. / Madrid 24th June 1844

Unofficial / To J. S. Dancher[?] / Counsellor at Law N. York

Sir,

I have been endeavoring to ascertain whether the claims of your client Mr P. O'Neil,[1] was lodged by my predecessor Mr Eaton,[2] as I was given to understand was Mr O'Neil's desire. Owing to the incessant changes of Ministry in this unhappy country it is a matter of considerable difficulty to obtain information or even an answer on any subject not personally interesting to the Minister. I hope, nevertheless, to be able to forward you before long correct information whether the claim was made in time or not. By the will you will probably remember, it is expressly set forth that the claims of all the Duke's irish kinsmen must be made within 71 years from the 12th May 1770 or the property will be allowed to go to the Crown.

MANUSCRIPT: NA, RG 84 (letterbook copy).

1. Probably a relative of O'Neil Bryson, to whom WI had also written on June 24, 1844.

2. John Henry Eaton (1790–1856), who had been secretary of war and governor of Florida during Jackson's administration, was U.S. minister to Spain from 1836 to 1840.

1749. To Luttrell Jewett

Legation of the U. S. / Madrid 24th June 1844

Unoffi[ci]al / To Luttrell Jewett Esqre

Sir,

I lost no time in forwarding your proposition relative to the establishment of a Steamboat at Puerto Rico to the Spanish Govt. To ensure it immediate attention, a matter at all times of extreme difficulty in this distracted country where ministerial changes are of such frequent occurrence, I had it translated into Spanish and enclosed with it a note from myself to the Minister of Marine[1] particularly requesting his careful and prompt examination of it. As soon as I receive an answer I shall forward it to you.

I am Sir respectfully. / Your obt servt
(signed) Washington Irving

MANUSCRIPT: NA, RG 84 (letterbook copy).

1. See WI to Francisco Armero, June 19, 1844.

1750. To Sarah Storrow

Madrid June 25. 1844

My dear Sarah,

I received two or three days since your letter of the 13th.[1] by which I find you are settled ⟨for the⟩ at your Summer quarters at Versailles. What I would give to be there with you! I am in the midst of the bustle of preparation for my journey to Barcelona. I set off tomorrow morning early, in Company with Mr Albuquerque (the Brazilian Minister) and Mr D'Albergo the Danish Charge d Affairs. We take the interior of the Diligence, and put our servants in the Rotonde. It is the ⟨only⟩ ↑most↓

comfortable mode of travelling between this and Barcelona, if any mode
may be called comfortable in this country. I take Lorenzo with me. How
long I shall remain at Barcelona is uncertain and will depend upon
circumstances after I arrive there. Two of the Diplomatic Corps who
have preceded me ⟨has p⟩ have promised to look out for a house where
several of us may live together and keep bachelors hall. When I get to
Barcelona I shall write to you ⟨and tell you all about⟩ at more liesure
and length.

I received a letter yesterday from your mother, written on her recovery from an attack of influenza; and written with her usual animation. She was to depart in the course of a few days for dear little Sunnyside and was anticipating health and refreshment of spirits from its
⟨delight⟩ sweet air, the sight of the trees and flowers and the singing of
the birds.

I too am anticipating benefit and enjoyment from Sea breezes and Sea
bathing at Barcelona; and mean to take the mineral baths of Caldas in
the neighborhood: so as completely to eradicate any lurking remains of
my malady.

I leave the office of the legation, and the see[i]ng over my household,
in the charge of Mr Livingston, from whom I am very sorry to part.
He suits me exactly. He is very quiet and domestic, passes almost the
whole of the day in the house, reading, writing & superintending the education of his little nephew; and in the evening we drive out ⟨, and visit
the⟩ together: and finish by a visit to the opera. I have certainly been
very lucky in my choice of Secretarys.

Farewell my dear Sarah, write to me soon and tell me every thing
about yourself, and Kate and her leghorn hat: Give my kindest remembrances to your worthy husband

Your affectionate Uncle
Washington Irving

MANUSCRIPT: Yale.

1. This letter has not been located.

1751.   To Sarah Storrow

Barcelona, June 30th. 1844

My dear Sarah,

I arrived here yesterday afternoon after a pretty hard journey of three
days and a half of almost constant travelling, having only twice an

opportunity of reposing ourselves from about four until ten in the evening, dining time included. A considerable part of our journey lay through very wild mountainous Scenery in Arragon and Catalonia; with old picturesque towns and villages a mixture of Moorish and Gothic, and people as wild and picturesque as their scenery. Much of the Country however, had the arid, sun burnt, desolate character so prevalent in the Spanish landscape. In the last two days of our journey we suffered very much from heat, but still more from dust, which in fact was intolerable the diligence at times was drawn by eight and even ten Mules, ⟨so⟩ clattering along far a head, and raising dense clouds of dust, which envelloped the diligence and entered on every side. A great part of the scanty intervals given us for repose was expended in endeavoring to cool and cleanse ourselves. I had very pleasant fellow travellers; my good friend Mr Albuquerque who is in every respect the Gentleman, and my good old crony D'Albergo di Primo, the Danish chargé d'affairs; one of the best tempered, kindest hearted, and gayest of human beings. A man who knows every body of all ranks and conditions, and whom every body likes. He is quite a character. His passion seems to be to please and to oblige. From his devotion to the Sovriegn and to the great he would pass for an arrant courtier, did not the same disposition to win favor and to oblige, extend to the humblest individuals. He is continually making presents to great and small rich and poor; and on our journey, when we occasionally walked through a village, he would dispense halfpence among the beggars and the children until we had a troop at our heels. He was in high good humour throughout the journey, and, when the heat and the dust did not absolutely render merriment a kind of "flying in the face of nature," he and I had a merry time of it.

We all arrived in Barcelona about five oclock in the afternoon covered with dust, and so "way worn and travel stained," that, had not apartments been fortunately engaged for us in the principal hotel I doubt whether any decent Landlord would have given us admission. After an hour or two spent in bathing and dressing, and another hour or so in dining, I had stretched myself on a Sopha and was fast asleep when I was roused by the Prince Carini, who had heard of my arrival and had come over, between the acts of the opera, to welcome me. The opera house is nearly opposite my hotel, so in a few moments I was in the princes box, ↑seated↓ beside my friend the little Princess who gave me a most cordial reception. The opera house is spacious and beautiful: far superior in size and style to any of the theatres of Madrid: the troupe is very good and the scenery, dresses &c excellent. Indeed there are two Italian operas ⟨Barcelona, June 30th 1844⟩ at Barcelona,[1] for the place is celebrated for its musical taste, but that at which I was present is the best and most fashionable. I found ⟨all⟩ there all the members of the diplomatic corps who had preceded me. The French Ambassador has a box furnished to him by the Municipality. I visited the box between the acts of the opera; and promised to dine with the Count and Countess de Bresson today. All that I have met seem delighted with the change from Madrid to Barcelona; and I do not wonder at it for this is really a very gay, animated city, beautifully situated with the Mediterranean spread out before it. It has the vivacity and somewhat of the air of a French town. The Rambla,[2] a broad public walk shaded by trees, which passes through the centre of the city and is cooled by the sea breeze, is like the boulevards: always thronged: with Cafés on each side. My windows overlook this promenade; and it was a most animated scene until past midnight: being a beautiful night with a full moon. There is also a noble terraced walk along the harbor,[3] looking upon the sea which is a favorite resort after dinner In a word, Barcelona, during the present residence of the court seems like some fashionable watering place; and, in witnessing the general animation and vivacity, one would hardly believe that it is the same city which within the last two years has been the scene of repeated tumults and been twice bombarded. As yet, however, I have only glanced at the City from the balcony of my window and from a box at the opera, The ills of a city are not to be discovered at theatres and public promenades.

I am happy to learn that the baths have had the most favorable effect on the malady of the little Queen. As I feel a strong sympathy with her as a fellow sufferer, as well as a general interest in her well being, I have hailed this news with great pleasure. Finding the baths of such service and the residence at Barcelona so favorable in other respects, it is probable the Queen will remain here until the end of September.

You will perceive by the papers that there has just been an important change in the Spanish Cabinet and that General Narvaez is now Minister of State as well as president of the Council.[4] As far as I can judge at the moment I am inclined to think that this change will be favorable in its effects; as the cabinet will adhere to the Constitution, but the government will be administred with vigor. As soon as the ⟨Cabin⟩ New Cabinet is arranged I shall seek an audience of the Queen to present the letters from the President, one of congratulations on her majority, the other of condolence on the death of her aunt. The circumstances of that audience will be another chapter in the "Romance of the palace," which I am dealing out to your mother by piece meal. By the way, I had began this letter merely for yourself, but it must serve for her likewise as I have not time to write another; when you have read it therefore, you must send it to her. I had nearly forgotten to tell you that my journey, notwithstanding the heat, dust, fatigue and want of rest to which I was exposed, has not produced that irritation in my system which I had apprehended. I have it is true some traces of my malady still hanging about me, but nothing of consequence. In some respects the journey has been of service to me; and I trust now to sea bathing, and to a slight course of the neighboring baths of Caldas, so beneficial to the Queen, to put me quite out of the reach of all relapse.

I hope soon to hear from you through the French courier, which comes direct from Paris to Barcelona.

Give my kind remembrances to Mr Storrow and kiss my darling little Kate for me

Your affectionate uncle
Washington Irving

MANUSCRIPT: Yale. PUBLISHED: LFSS, pp. 66–69 (in part); STW, II, 177 (in part).

1. These opera houses are the Gran Teatro del Liceo on the Rambla and the Teatro Principal in the Plaza del Teatro. See Karl Baedeker, *Spain and Portugal*, p. 230.

2. The Rambla, from the Arabic word for riverbed, was a promenade built on a former streamlet, on which the theaters, best shops, and post office were located. For details, see Richard Ford, *A Hand-Book for Travellers in Spain*, II, 716.

3. La Muralla del Mar, or the mole overlooking the harbor. See Ford, *A Hand-Book*, II, 725.

4. Narváez had become prime minister on May 3, 1844. See Christiansen, *Military Power*, p. 170.

1752. *To Marques of Viluma*

Legation of the United States / Barcelona July 1. 1844

His Excellency / The Marques of Viluma / First Minister of State / and of Foreign affairs,

Sir,

I have the honor to enclose Copies of two letters from the President of the United States of America to Her Majesty Queen Isabella the Second,[1] and will be much obliged to your Excellency if you will ascertain when it will be agreeable to Her Majesty to grant me an audience for the delivery of the originals

I am, very respectfully / Your Excellencys most obt St
Washington Irving

MANUSCRIPT: NYPL—Berg Collection (letterbook copy).

1. As WI had noted earlier, these letters contained congratulations on her becoming queen and condolences on the death of her aunt, Luisa Carlota.

1753.   To John C. Calhoun

Legation of the United States / Barcelona July 3d. 1844

No. 47. / The Hon. John C Calhoun / Secretary of State. Washington

Sir,

Agreeable to the intention expressed in my despatch No 45. I left
Madrid at day break, on the 25th. Ulto. for Barcelona, via Saragossa. I
travelled in the Dilligence in company with the Brazilian Minister and
the Danish charge d'affairs, and, after three days and a half of almost
unremitting travel, rendered excessively fatiguing by heat and dust and
rugged mountainous roads, I arrived in this city on the evening of the
30th.

I have since had an Audience of the Queen and have delivered ↑to
her↓ the two letters from the President. She has a much more healthful
aspect than when she left Madrid, and indeed, is in every way improved
in personal appearance. She acquires more and more a womanly deportment, and acquits herself with a dignity and self possession hardly to be
expected at her years.

I had also an Audience of the Queen Mother, who received me with
her characteristic grace and amiability, and expressed her friendly
hope that I had favorable accounts from the United States and that all
our affairs were prosperous

The Ministerial crisis from which so much was apprehended, or predicted, has ended in the resignation of the Marques of Viluma.[1] The main
point of policy on which he is said to have separated from his colleagues
was the immediate dissolution of the present Cortes and the convocation
of a new one; a measure which he considered as calculated to prolong
the agitations of the country, and to defer indefinitely the organic reforms so loudly called for; his idea apparently being to continue to legis-
late by decrees until the desired reforms were actually carried into operation. He is a man of elevated and honorable character, and of open
and courteous deportment, with whom it would have been a pleasure
to transact business; it is to be regretted, therefore, that his political
views would not allow him to continue in the cabinet. He has retired
with grace and dignity, and his resignation has been accepted with great
reluctance. He will be succeeded by General Narvaez, who will continue

to be president of the council. No official notice has yet been given of the appointment of the latter, but it is stated as certain. General Mazarredo, it is said, will again have the department of War. As he is the great friend and adherent of Genl. Narvaez, the latter may be considered as having both civil and military sway; his position, therefore, becomes of great importance, and he has the power of doing a vast deal of good and evil.

I have spoken in a former letter of the independent stand which he took with regard to foreign influence and interference, when he had to form a cabinet; I have not yet had an opportunity of judging whether during the recent crisis he has continued to adhere to this creditable line of conduct. I am pleased to find that he has declared in favor of a strictly constitutional course of policy, a contrary course having been apprehended from him. He will no doubt administer the government with vigor, and with somewhat of a military spirit; but, as long as he does so within the limits of the constitution, his energy will be benificial in the present state of Spanish affairs. I shall look with great interest to his course of conduct and hope he may have the capacity to act up to his situation, and the true ambition to gain for himself that honorable fame which is now within his reach.

> I am Sir, / Very respectfully / Your Obt St.
> Washington Irving

DOCKETED: Recd. 3 Augt. Mr. Markoe [top of page 1] /No. 47. W. Irving, Barcelona 3 July 1844
MANUSCRIPT: NA, RG 59; NYPL—Berg Collection (letterbook copy).   PUBLISHED: Hellman, WI Esquire, pp. 308–10.

This despatch is entirely in WI's handwriting.

1. Viluma, who had been Spanish minister to Great Britain, went to Barcelona to accept the position as minister of state and foreign affairs. Because of the differences of opinion mentioned by WI, Viluma resigned before exerting any influence in the office. See La Gaceta, June 10, July 5, 1844; and El Castellano, June 10, 24, 25, 26, 27, July 1, 5, 1844.

1754. To Ramón María Narváez

Legation of the United States / Barcelona July 4th 1844

His Excellency, / The Captain-General Ramon de Narvaez / President
of the Council / etc etc etc

Sir

I have the honor to acknowledge the honor of your Excellency's note[1]
informing me that her Majesty the Queen had accepted the resignation
of the Marques de Viluma and in the interim had confided to you the
Department of state.

I congratulate your Excellency sincerely on this new and distinguished
mark of royal esteem and confidence and on the still greater scope thus
offered you for the exercise of your energies and the illustration of your
patriotism. I trust the royal confidence will prove in the present instance
to have been most worthily reposed and I assure your Excellency it will
give me high satisfaction to transact such affairs with you as may concern the interests of our respective countries.

I avail myself of this occasion to offer to your Excellency the assurance
of my most distinguished consideration

(Signed) Washington Irving

MANUSCRIPT: NA, RG 84 (letterbook copy); NYPL—Berg Collection (letterbook
copy).

1. Narváez had written to WI on July 2, 1844 (NA, RG 84).

1755.   To Catharine Paris

Barcelona July 5th. 1844

My dear Sister,

I presume Sarah Storrow has forwarded to you the letter I wrote to her
on my arrival at this city,[1] giving ⟨an⟩ ↑some↓ account of my journey
from Madrid, through the wild, mountainous region of Arragon. It was
very fatiguing, very hot and very dusty; yet I am glad I have made it,
as it took me through a great part of what was a distinct Kingdom, before the marriage of Ferdinand with Isabella;[2] by which the crowns of
Arragon and Castile became united. We travelled almost constantly, day
and night; in some of the mountainous parts the dilligence was drawn
by eight and occasionally ten mules; harnessed two and two; with a

driver on the box; a Zagal, or help, who scampered for ⟨[unrecovered]⟩ a great part of the way beside the mules; thwacking them occasionally with a stick, and bawling out their names in all kinds of tones and inflections; while a lad of fifteen years of age was mounted on one of the leaders, to act as pilot. This lad kept on with us for a great part of the journey: how he bore the fatigue I can hardly imagine; and more especially the want of sleep, for we only paused about six hours each evening to dine and take repose. He, however, I found, could sleep on horseback; and repeatedly, when our long line of mules ⟨with⟩ ↑and↓ the lumbering dilligence, where winding along roads cut round the face of mountains, and along the brink of tremendous precipices, the postilion was sleeping in his saddle, and we were left to the caution and discretion of the mules. However, we accomplished our journey in safety, in defiance of rough roads and robbers and arrived here after three days and half of almost continual travel.

My first ⟨[unrecovered]⟩ care was to get into comfortable quarters; every Hotel being crowded, and all furnished apartments being taken up, since the arrival of the court. For a few days I was stowed away in a small room in the upper part of a hotel, and reccollected with regret my spacious and cool saloons at Madrid. While thus lodged I received a visit from a Mr or Don Pablo Anguera; who formerly acted here as American Consul, and who is an old customer and intimate of Mr Van Wart; having a mercantile establishment in Havanna, where he has made his fortune. He and his wife have resided for a couple of years in England, in the neighborhood of Mr Van Warts and have been extremely intimate with the family. Mr Anguera has also been in New York, and will be remembered by brother E. I. with whom he has had dealings. Finding I was so indifferently lodged nothing would suit this worthy man but I must accept of a part of his house: it was very spacious he said, and his family was very small—and I could have a distinct apartment entirely to myself. In fine, I was easily compelled to avail myself of his hospitality, and accordingly, here I am, most capitally accommodated. I have the front part of the house, which looks on the street, to myself; while the family occupy the apartments in the rear, which look on a very pretty garden, with fountains, statues &c—I have a spacious and beautiful Saloon, richly gilded; the cielings painted in fresco; the furniture fashionable and commodious: adjoining which is a cabinet, in similar style, where I write, receive visitors &c; and ⟨an ample⟩ ↑a noble↓ alcove, in which is a bed ample enough for the seven sleepers and so luxurious that, had they once been tucked into it they would have slept on until dooms day. Lorenzo has a room adjoining, so as to be completely within call—My breakfasts are served to me in the cabinet; and I dine with the family, or dine abroad as I may find pleasant or convenient. I find Madame Anguera a most amiable domestic person; full of kind reccollections of such of my friends as she has known; while Anguera has a hearty good humor, and a thorough disposition to oblige. They have three very fine children, two boys and a girl, whom I see when I visit the family part of the house. In a word, nothing could have been more *apropos*; and I could not have imagined a more pleasant and comfortable arrangement.

I am delighted with Barcelona. It is a beautiful city, especially the new part, with a mixture of Spanish, French and Italian character. The climate is soft and voluptuous; the heats being tempered by the sea breezes. Instead of the naked desert which surrounds Madrid, we have here, between the sea and the mountains, a rich and fertile plain; with ⟨gardens, villas &c [*unrecovered*]⟩ ↑villas buried among groves and gardens in which↓ grow the orange, the citron, the pomegranate and other fruits of southern climates. We have here too an excellent Italian opera; which is a great resource to me. Indeed the theatre is the nightly place of meeting of the diplomatic corps and various members of the Court; and there is great visiting from box to box. The greatest novelty in our diplomatic circle is the Turkish Minister,[3] who arrived lately at Barcelona on a special mission to the Spanish Court. His arrival made quite a sensation here, there having been no representative from the court of the Grand Sultan for more than half a century. He was for a time quite the lion: Every thing he said and did, was the theme of conversation. I think, however, he has quite disappointed the popular curiosity. Something oriental and theatrical was expected; a turk in a turban and bagging trowsers; with a furred robe, a long pipe, a ↑huge↓ beard and moustaches, ⟨and⟩ a ⟨ha harem⟩ bevy of wives and a regiment of black slaves—Instead of this, ⟨they [*unrecovered*]⟩ the Turkish ambassador turned out to be an easy, pleasant, gentleman like man; in a frock coat, white drill pantaloons; black cravat, white kid gloves and dandy cane; with nothing Turkish in his costume but a red cap with a long blue silken tassel. In fact he is a complete man of society; who has visited various parts of Europe; is European in his manners; and, when he takes off his turkish cap, has very much the look of a well bred Italian gentleman. I confess I should rather have seen him in the magnificent costume of the East; and I regret that that costume, ⟨is⟩ endeared to me by the Arabian Nights entertainment, that joy of my boyhood, is fast giving way to the levelling and monotonous prevalence of French and English fashions. The Turks, too, are not aware of what they lose by the change of costume. In their oriental dress they are magnificent looking men and seem superior in dignity of form to Europeans; but ⟨when they⟩ once stripped of Turban and flowing robes and attired in the close fitting, trimly cut modern dress, and they shrink in dimensions and turn out a very ill made race. Nothwithstanding his christian dress, however, I have found the Effendi a very intelligent and interesting companion. He is extremely well informed; has read much and observed still more, and is very frank and animated in conversation. Unfortunately his sojourn here will be but for a very few days longer. He intends to make the tour of Spain and to visit those parts especially which contain ⟨memen⟩ historical remains of the time of the Moors and Arabs. Granada will be a leading object of curiosity with him. I should have delighted to visit it in company with him.

I know all this while you are dying to have another chapter about the little Queen, so I must gratify you. I applied for an audience shortly after my arrival; having two letters to deliver to the Queen from President Tyler; one congratulating her on her majority; the other condoling with her on the death of her aunt. The next day, at six oclock in the evening, was appointed for the audience; which was granted at the same time to the members of the Diplomatic corps who had travelled in company with me and to two others who had preceded us. It was about the time when the queen drives out to take the air. Troops were drawn up in the square ⟨of⟩ in front of the Palace[4] awaiting her ⟨asp?⟩ appearance and a considerable crowd assembled. As we ascended the ⟨Sta⟩ grand staircase we found groups of people on the principal landing places, waiting to get a sight of royalty. ⟨I reccollected the Palace of old; where⟩ This palace had a peculiar interest for me. Here, as often occurs in my unsettled and wandering life, I was coming back again on the footsteps of former times. In 1829 when I passed a few days in Barcelona on my way to England, to take my post as Secretary of Legation, this palace was inhabited by the Count de Espagne[5] at that time captain general of the province. I had heard much of the cruelty of his disposition; and the rigor of his military rule. He was the terror of the Catalans, and hated by them as much as he was feared. I dined with him[6] in company with two or three English gentlemen,[7] residents of the place with whom he was on familiar terms. In entering his palace I felt that I was entering the abode of a tyrant. His appearance was characteristic. ↑He was about forty five years of age↓ of the middle size, but well set and strongly built, and became his military dress. He[8] face was rather handsome; ⟨but⟩ his demeanour courteous, and at table he became social and jocose; but I thought I could see a lurking devil in his eye and something hard hearted and derisive in his laugh. The English guests were his cronies and with them I perceived his jokes were coarse and his humor inclined to buffoonery. At that time Maria Christina, then a beautiful neapolitan princess, in the flower of her years, was daily expected at Barcelona, on her way to Madrid to be married to Ferdinand VII. While the Count and his guests were seated at table after dinner, enjoying the wine and segars, one of the petty functionaries of the city, equivalent to a deputy alderman,[9] was announced. The count winked to the company and promised a scene for their amusement. The city dignitary came bustling into the apartment with an air of hurried zeal and momentous import, as if about to make some great revelation. He had just received intelligence by letter, of the movements of the princess and the time when she might be expected to arrive, and had hastened to communicate it at head quarters. There was nothing in the intelligence that had not been previously known to the count, and that he had not communicated to us during dinner, but he effected to receive the information with great surprize; made the functionary repeat it over and over, each time deepening the profundity ⟨with wh⟩ of his attention; finally he bowed the city oracle quite out of the saloon and almost to the head of the stair case, and sent him home swelling with the idea that he had communicated a state secret and fixed himself in the favor of the count. The latter returned to us laughing immoderately at the manner in which he had played off the little dignitary and mimicking the voice and manner with which the latter had imparted his important nothings—It was altogether a high farce; more comic in the acting than in the description, but it was the sportive gamboling of a tiger, and I give it to shew how the tyrant, in his hours of familiarity may play the buffoon.

The Count d'Espagne was a favorite general of Ferdinand and, during. the life of that monarch, continued in high military command. In the civil wars he espoused the cause of Don Carlos and was charged with many sanguinary acts. His day of retribution came. He fell into the hands of his enemies; and was murdered, it is said with savage cruelty while being conducted a prisoner among the mountains. Such are the bloody reverses ⟨to⟩ which continually occur in this eventful country; especially in these revolutionary times.

I thought of all these things as I ascended the grand stair case. Fifteen years had elapsed since I took leave of the Count at the top of this stair case, and it seemed as if his hard hearted derisive laugh still sounded in my ears. He was then a loyal subject and a powerful commander he had since been branded as a traitor and a rebel, ⟨and⟩ murdered by those whom he had oppressed and hurried into a bloody grave. The beautiful young princess whose approach was at that time the theme of every tongue, had since gone through all kinds of reverses; she had been on a throne, she had been in exile; she was now a widowed queen, a subject of her own daughter; and a sojourner in this palace.

On entering the royal apartments I recognized some of the old courtiers whom ⟨we⟩ ↑I had been accustomed to see↓ about the royal person at Madrid and was cordially greeted by them, ⟨I was cordially greeted by them;⟩ for at Barcelona we all come together sociably as at a watering

place. The "Introducer of Ambassadors" (the Chevalier de Arana) conducted my companions and myself into a saloon, where we waited to
be summoned into the royal presence. I being the highest in diplomatic
rank of the party present, was first summoned. On entering I found the
little queen standing in the centre of the room and at a little distance
behind her, the Marchioness of Santa Cruz, first lady in attendance. Unfortunately I forgot to take notice how the Queen was dressed, and for
this time cannot give you accurate information on this important point.
I only know that she was dressed to ⟨drive⟩ take her evening drive; she
had a pinkish bonnet, with pinkish flowers, and altogether her whole
dress has left a kind of pinkish idea in my mind. She had even a slight
pinkish bloom in her face, which is usually pale. Indeed her whole appearance is improved; it is more healthful: she is growing more and more
womanly, and more and more engaging. The expression of her countenance was extremely amiable. She received me in a quiet graceful manner, with ⟨[unrecovered]⟩ ↑considerable↓ self possession expressing in a
low voice, the hope that I had made a pleasant journey &c This must
be the hardest task for ⟨the⟩ so young a creature; to have to play the
queen *solus*, receiving one by one the diplomatic corps, and beginning
the conversation with each. Our interview was brief. I presented my two
letters, expressed the satisfaction ⟨() which I (really) felt ()⟩ at seeing,
by her improved looks that the ⟨[unrecovered⟩] sojourn at Barcelona
had [been][10] beneficial to her &c afe[11] which I retired to give place to
my companions. We had afterwards, one by one, an audience of the
Queen Mother; who is looking very well, though I am told she is still
subject to great anxiety and frequent depression of spirits, feeling the
uncertainty of political affairs in Spain, and the difficulties and dangers
which surround the throne of her youthful daughter. Nothing could be
more gracious and amiable than her reception. Her smile is one of the
most winning I have ever witnessed; and the more I see of her the less
I wonder at that fascination, which, in her younger and more beautiful
days was so omnipotent, and which even now has such controul over
all who ⟨have frequent⟩ are much about her person.

I have conducted you ceremoniously into the palace, and have shewn
you the little queen on an occasion of ceremony. would you have a peep
in at one of the windows, and behold her majesty when she plays the
little girl. The palace at Barcelona is not isolated as at Madrid; one part
faces on a narrow street, with private dwellings opposite. A curious
lady ↑resident↓ in one of these, had a glance into the windows of ⟨the y⟩
a room where ↑were↓ the little queen and her sister. The infanta, not
having the cares of royalty upon her mind, was playing with her doll,
the little queen had book in hand, and was apparently endeavoring to
master some hard task that had been set her—until she threw it down

in despair and began to cry—Poor child—she already begins to feel the
tasks which royalty impose upon her

July 7th. Yesterday I made a ⟨p⟩ very pleasant excursion into the country, two or three miles from Barcelona, towards the mountains; to a little
rural retreat of the Brazilian Consul, ⟨Here we had a dinner⟩ who gave
a dinner to about twenty two persons, ladies and gentlemen, of the
corps diplomatic and the consular corps. It was a very handsome and a
very gay dinner. The Saloon ⟨[unrecovered]⟩ in which the table was laid,
looked out upon a garden with fountains; the rich plain; the city of
Barcelona in the distance and the blue mediterranean beyond: a splendid picture, seen under a southern sky and and[12] with the enjoyment of the
softest and most voluptuous temperature. The garden⟨s⟩ of the villa was
shaded by Fig trees, orange trees, citrons, and the hedges of the neighboring fields were of the aloes—Every thing looked and felt and
breathed of the sweet south. We returned for a great part of the way
to town on foot; the evening was so delicious. The more I see of Barcelona and its environs the more I am delighted with them—I must
bring this letter, however, to a close to send it off by the French courier, which departs this day.

God bless you my dear Sister—Give my hearts love to all the dear inmates of sweet little Sunnyside—

Your affectionate brother
Washington Irving

MANUSCRIPT: SHR.   PUBLISHED: PMI, III, 346–54 (in part).

1. See WI to Sarah Storrow, June 30, 1844.

2. In 1469.

3. The impending arrival of Fuad Effendi had attracted considerable attention
because it was rumored that he would be accompanied by six wives. His movements
were closely observed and reported in the press. See *El Castellano*, May 16, June
3, 11, 19, 21, July 2, 1844; and London *Times*, May 27, June 19, 1844.

4. Originally a cloth hall built in 1444, the building served as an armory from
1514 to 1652, when Philip IV converted it into a residence for his viceroy. It was
enlarged and modernized in the late eighteenth century, and in September, 1843,
its plaza was damaged in the bombardment of Barcelona. See Richard Ford, *A
Hand-Book for Travellers in Spain*, II, 732.

5. Carlos José Enrique de España (1775–1839). See STW, I, 501.

6. On August 17, 1829. See *Journals of WI*, III, 94–95.

7. WI, together with Richard de la Saussaye, an Irish officer in the Spanish
Royal Guards, Mr. Dedel, the Dutch minister at Madrid, Mr. Ryan, an agent for
the British consul, Ralph Sneyd (1800–1829), WI's traveling companion, and several Spaniards, dined with the count. See *Journals of WI*, III, 92–95.

8. WI probably intended to write "His."

9. WI has forgotten; in reality it was the Neapolitan consul. See *Journals of WI*,
III, 94.

10. WI omitted the bracketed word.
11. WI probably intended to write "after."
12. WI repeated "and."

1756. *To Sarah Storrow*

Barcelona July 7th. 1844

My dear Sarah,

I enclose a long letter to your mother left open for your perusal—As you may easily suppose, I have but little time to add any thing for yourself. I have received your two letters of the 21t and 26t of June.[1] The last a *double* one. I cannot tell you my dearest girl how much I feel this kindness on your part to write to me so frequently. But you must know how precious your letters are to me, and much I count upon them as ⟨a so⟩ some sort of solace for the regret of our protracted Separation. Next week I will write to you specially: in the mean time do not ccase to let me hear every thing about yourself and dear little Kate to whom give many Kisses on the part of

Your affectionate uncle / Washington Irving

ADDRESSED: Madame / Madame Storrow / 4 Rue de la Victoire / à Paris   DOCK-
ETED: *July 2d 1844*
MANUSCRIPT: Yale.

1. These letters have not been located.

1757. *To Ramón María Narváez*

Legation of the United States / Barcelona, July 8th. 1844

The Undersigned, Envoy Extraordinary and Minister Plenipotentiary of the United States of America, has the honor to acknowledge the receipt of the Note of His Excellency General Ramon Maria Narvaez, First Minister of State and of Foreign Affairs, ad interim, inclosing ⟨th⟩ Copies of the Ultimatum recently addressed by Her Majestys government to the Emperor of Marocco[1] and of the reply of that Monarch to the same; and informing the undersigned that Her Majesty had subsequently commanded her agent at Tangier to break off all communications with the Authorities of Marocco, and to Signify ↑to the Emperor↓ through the agents of France and England, that, unless the reclamations contained in the Seven articles in the Ultimatum were complied with ⟨within⟩ ↑in↓ the Space of fifteen days, the negotiation would terminate in war.

The Undersigned will lose no time in transmitting these documents and this important intelligence to his government.

The Undersigned avails himself of this occasion to renew to His Excellency Genl Narvaez the assurance of his distinguished consideration

W.I.

MANUSCRIPT: NYPL—Berg Collection (letterbook copy).

The entire letter is marked with a large "X", and the word "*cancelled*" appears vertically on the left margin.

1. Abd-al Rahmān (b. 1789/90) allied himself with Abd-al-Kādir against France and was defeated at the battle of Isly on August 14, 1844. The murder of the Spanish consular agent, Victor Darmon, endangered Abd-al Rahmān's relations with foreign governments. See *The Encyclopedia of Islam*, I, 84–85; and WI to John C. Calhoun, April 2, 1844.

1758. (*deleted*)

1759. To Ramón María Narváez

Legation of the United States. / Barcelona July 13th 1844

His Excellency / Captain General Ramon Ma Narvaez / ⟨Her Majestys⟩ President of the Council / First Minister of State & of Foreign Affairs. / &c &c &c

Sir,

The President of the United States having appointed Josiah Raymond Consul for the port of Manzanillo, in the Island of Cuba, I have the honor to enclose to your Excellency his commission, and to request that the Royal Exequatur may be issued to enable him to ⟨enter upon⟩ ↑discharge↓ the duties of his office

I avail myself of this occasion to reiterate to Your Excellency the assurance of my very high consideration

Washington Irving

MANUSCRIPT: NYPL—Berg Collection (letterbook copy).

1760. To Josiah Raymond

Barcelona 13th July 1844

Josiah Raymond Esqre

Sir

Agreeably to instructions from the Department of State I applied on the 12th inst. for your Exequatur as Consul for the port of Manzanillo in the Island of Cuba. It will probably take some months for the Spanish Government to make the customary enquiries previous to issuing that instrument. In the interim, to prevent further delay it will be advisable for you to remit to some agent in Madrid the fees exacted by the Spanish ⟨Govt⟩ offices on the delivery of the Exequatur.

Very respectfully / Your obt servant
(signed)   Washington Irving.

MANUSCRIPT: NA, RG 84 (letterbook copy).

Josiah Raymond of Massachusetts was nominated as U.S. consul for Manzanillo, Cuba on May 17, 1844. See Hasse, *Index to U.S. Documents*, III, 1746.

1761. To John C. Calhoun

Legation of the United States / Barcelona July 14th. 1844

No 48. / The Hon. / John C. Calhoun / Secretary of State, Washington

Sir,

I received the day before yesterday your despatch No 32. enclosing the commission of Josiah Raymond, as consul of the United States for Manzanillo in Cuba; and applied yesterday in form, for his Exequatur.

The documents which you forward relative to the claim of Michael Drausin Harang throw no new light on the case, which was discussed by me, to the best of my judgment, in a note passed to the Spanish government on the 24th. of September 1842; a copy of which was sent to your department. I was informed yesterday that I should soon receive a written answer on the subject.

I enclose a note, with its accompanying documents, recently received from the Minister of State, shewing the Situation of affairs between the Spanish government and the Emperor of Marocco; which appear fast verging into open war. I doubt however, that the Emperor of Marocco will venture to make a stand against Spain, backed by the powerful aid of France, or that the policy of England will permit such an event.

The Cortes has just been dissolved, and a new one called to meet on the 10th. of October. Ministers look with some solicitude to the elections about to take place throughout the country, knowing that political agitators are busy sowing the seeds of new conspiracies and commotions in various parts of the Kingdom. General Narvaez, therefore, is anxious to abridge the absence of the Queen from the capital, that the cabinet may be re-united at this critical juncture; and it is propable[1] the court will set out on its return about the beginning of next month.

The department of State is held by General Narvaez ad interim; the Marques of Miraflores[2] it is thought, will be appointed to it, as such is the wish of Narvaez. The latter will, then, remain Minister of War and President of the Council. He is, in fact, the potent and active Spirit of the government. A frank conversation which I recently had with him on the affairs of Spain, raised him in my estimation, as to his tact and his general capacity: and if he faithfully acts up to the feelings, and carries out the views which he therein professed, he may really render important service to his country; but he is surrounded with difficulties and dangers; he has open enemies, invidious rivals and faithless partizans: and he has foibles of which diligent advantage will be taken to work his down fall. The great chance in his favor is that he is aware of his danger but is undismayed by it.

I feel greatly obliged to the President for the leave of absence granted me for two months, for the benefit of my health. I am happy to say that I have nearly recovered from the herpetic malady which made me ask this indulgence. Still I am subject to slight returns of it if I indulge too closely in sedentary and mental occupation, and am desirous of escaping the dry and irritating heats of a Madrid Summer until my cure is completed. I shall, therefore, most probably, avail myself of the Presidents kind permission, when the Court returns to Madrid, to make an excursion into France; but shall be back at the Spanish capital, perfectly re established, I hope, in health, prior to the opening of the Cortes in October.

> I am Sir, / Very respectfully / Your Obt Servt
> Washington Irving

DOCKETED: Recd. Augt. 21. Mr. Markoe [top of page 1] / No. 48. W. Irving. Barcelona. 14 July 1844
MANUSCRIPT: NA, RG 59; NYPL—Berg Collection (letterbook copy).

This despatch is entirely in WI's handwriting.

1. WI used this spelling for "probable."
2. The Marques of Miraflores (1792–1872), a Liberal, did not succed Narváez

as prime minister until February 13, 1846, and then only for a period of about five weeks. See Christiansen, *Military Power*, p. 170.

1762. *To Sarah Storrow*

Barcelona, July 14th. 1844

My dear Sarah,

I have barely time to scrawl a line to say that I received a despatch from Government the day before yesterday, in which leave of absence for two months is granted me. I can't tell you how my heart leaped at the news. I shall remain here until the Queen returns to Madrid which, it is expected, will be about the beginning of August; when I will set out for France; and, before long, I trust, will fold you and my darling little Kate to my heart.

God bless you

Your affectionate Uncle
Washington Irving

P S. Say nothing of my coming, for the present. I wish to be very quiet

MANUSCRIPT: Yale.   PUBLISHED: STW, II, 178 (in part).

1763. *To John Miller*

Barcelona July 16th 1844

Mr John Miller / U. S. Dispatch Agt London. /

Dear Sir

I enclose a draft on Messrs Baring Brothers and Co payable to your order for £ 11.4.10½ being in payment of your acct incurred for postage of this Legation for the last quarter

Yours very respectfully
(signed)   Washington Irving

MANUSCRIPT: NA, RG 84 (letterbook copy).

1764.   To Pierre M. Irving

[Barcelona,] July 18, 1844

Yesterday I received my letters by the steam packet of the 15th of June, among which is a despatch from Government, granting me the temporary leave of absence for the benefit of my health which I had solicited. I shall avail myself of the leave of absence toward the end of this month, to make an excursion to Paris previous to returning to Madrid. I shall thus escape the dry, parching summer heat of the Spanish capital, be enabled, if necessary, to consult the French physician who attended me last autumn, refresh and recruit myself by a pleasant tour and complete change of climate, and return to Madrid early in the autumn, fully prepared, I trust, to enter with vigor upon my literary as well as my diplomatic occupations. I feel quite obliged to President Tyler for enabling me to make this pleasant and healthful arrangement, and hope, in return, that, if he should succeed in annexing Texas, it may become an apanage[1] in his family, for the benefit of his eldest son! However, this is a dangerous aspiration, and I beg you will not breathe it to any one but Helen.

By the same opportunity I have received the joint letter of yourself and Helen;[2] or, rather, her letter with your postscript crowded into holes and corners. * * * Your postscript, however, is worth its weight in gold, as you tell me you have sold my —— shares of —— stock for —— dollars a share. This is really so much money hauled out of the ashes. I shall now begin to think something may one day turn up for the girls, out of the dead and buried claim of Anaky Yanz.

Tell Helen this new and unlooked-for influx of wealth makes it indispensable for me to hurry to Paris, to prevent a plethora of the purse. Jupiter! how I will burn the candle at both ends when I get there! Don't tell your aunt, though, for I see she thinks I'm a wild, expensive young dog.

Your affectionate uncle,
W. I.

P. S.—I have written to Mr. Livingston, my Secretary of Legation, to have my old carriage vamped up and varnished, and a taller cockade put in Pepe's hat against I return to Madrid, for I am determined, now my pockets are so full, to strike out with unusual splendor. Not a word to your aunt, however.

PUBLISHED: PMI, III, 354–56; Hellman, *WI Esquire*, p. 275 (in part).

PMI prefaced the excerpt from WI's letter with the following:

"Eleven days after the date of the foregoing letter [WI to Catharine Paris, July 5, 1844], to which he refers me, with a hint that he should have to 'greatly retrench the epistolary prodigality of [his] pen,' and in reply to a letter in which I informed him of my having taken advantage of a miraculous resuscitation of some long-barren stock of his to sell it, he writes me from Barcelona as follows:"

1. An apanage normally is a provision made for the maintenance of the younger children of royalty. WI here facetiously applies the term to Robert Tyler (1818–1877), who served as his father's private secretary during his presidency.

2. This letter has not been located.

1765. To Sarah Storrow

Barcelona, July 21. 1844

My dear Sarah,

After the receipt of this letter you need not direct any more to me to this place as it is doubtful whether they would find me here There is a Grand Besamanos at the palace on the 24th. in honor of the Queen Mothers birthday, on which occasion I shall take my leave of the Queen, as ⟨I shall⟩ after that day I shall leave Barcelona as soon as I have received my letters by the Steamer of the 2nd July; by which I expect to hear of the confirmation of Mr Livingstons nomination. If these letters come in time, I shall depart in a Steamer which sets off for Marseilles on the 27th. If not I shall take the earliest opportunity afterwards. I may make some pauses ⟨on⟩ in the course of my route, so that it will probably be after the middle of August before I reach Versailles.

The Queen, with great reluctance, has at last fixed the day for her departure, which will be the 12th. of next month.[1] She has been much benefited in health by her sojourn here and is delighted with the place. The palace is to be newly fitted up and furnished at her expense in the prospect of another visit, which, it is said, she talks of making next year. An arrangement which would be extremely agreeable to all the Corps diplomatique.

You are surprised that she does not give up Madrid altogether and make this the Royal Residence. You must reccollect that though a Queen she is not an absolute one; and has to consult her cabinet and cortes; and there are many reasons that make it impolitic to change the seat of government, and above all to transfer it to a corner of the Kingdom. I hope, however, she will make occasional residences ⟨at⟩ for two or three months at a time at agreeable cities such as Barcelona, Seville &c, instead of going to the Royal Sitios of the Escurial; La Granja &c.

Two or three evenings since I was at a grand ball given by the Commanders of two French vessels of war in the harbor. The vessels, one of which was a steamer, were placed side by side, and so arranged by flags of every nation, as to make two grand Saloons in the form of tents. The company danced in one and supped in the other. The whole was arranged with great taste and went off in the pleasantest style.

To day I dine at a Torre, or country seat a few miles from the city where the American consul[2] gives a dinner, ⟨on⟩ to ⟨the⟩ some of the corps diplomatique and to the various consuls resident in this port. It is intended as a kind of fête to me; though I strongly urged the worthy little man not to put himself to such trouble and expense on my account, who am the last man in the world to care for compliments of the Kind; but he was not be dis[s]uaded.[3] I expect to see something like Balshazzars feast;[4] for the little man, who has made a fortune as an apothecary, knows nothing of entertaining and has probably never given a dinner in his life. He has ⟨put signed⟩ called in the assistance of a French fondist or Hotel Keeper on the occasion, who I have no doubt will lay earth air and sea under contribution in loading the table.

On the 24th. the day of the Besamanos, General Narvaez (the head of the cabinet) gives a grand diplomatic dinner in honor of the Queen Mother. This will probably be the last of the feasts and fêtes at which I shall "assist" previous to my departure.[5]

I am glad to hear that Mr King has been so well received and is so well pleased with Louis Philip. The more I consider the character and conduct of that monarch the more I am convinced he is one of the greatest ⟨monarchs⟩ sovreigns that ever sat upon a throne. Indeed the three great names of modern history, which rise far above all others, are Washington, Napoleon and Louis Philippe.

Give my kind remembrances to your good husband and Kiss my darling little Kate for me; whom, it is delightful to think I shall soon Kiss in person

Your affectionate Uncle
Washington Irving

ADDRESSED: Madame / Madame Storrow / 4. Rue de la Victoire / à Paris
MANUSCRIPT: Yale.

1. Reports of the queen's changing plans to leave Barcelona appeared in the newspapers. See *La Gaceta,* July 9, 29, 1844; and *El Castellano,* August 1, 1844.

2. Paul Pon was U.S. consul at Barcelona.

3. WI omitted the bracketed letter.

4. See Daniel 5:1–9.

5. WI's attendance at Narváez's state banquet was reported in *El Castellano,* July 30, 1844.

1766. To Ramón María Narváez

Legation of United States / Barcelona July 26th 1844

His Excellency / Captain General Narvaez / President of the Council /
First Minister of State and of / Foreign Affairs (ad interim)

Sir

Being about to avail myself of two ⟨l⟩ months leave of absence from
my post granted to me by the President of the United States, and my
Govt being solicitous that the business of the mission should not suffer
from my absence, I have the honor to inform your Excellency that I shall
leave the Affairs of the Legation in charge of the actual Secretary, Mr
Jasper H. Livingston, who I trust, will in his official capacity, receive the
same attention and respect which I have ever experienced from her
Majesty's Govt. I avail myself of this occasion to renew to your Excellency the assistance of my distinguished consideration

(Signed)   Washington Irving

Manuscript: NA, RG 84 (letterbook copy); NYPL—Berg Collection (letterbook
copy).

1767. To John C. Calhoun

Legation of the United States for Spain / Barcelona July 27th. 1844

No 49. / The Hon / John C Calhoun / Secretary of State. Washington

Sir,

I have the honor to enclose a copy of a note just received from the
Minister of State and of Foreign affairs, informing me that the modifications of the Quarantine laws of the Canary Islands, in regard to shipping
from the United States, which I suggested in a note to the Spanish government, dated the 25th. January last, having been approved by the
Supreme Junta of Health, orders had been issued to carry them into
immediate operation.

The modifications alluded to, as you will perceive on reference to my
former despatches were;

1st.   That all vessels arriving from ports of the United States north of
Cape Hatteras, and bringing clean bills of health countersigned by the
Spanish Consul resident in the port of departure, or the Collector of
the Same, shall be admitted to immediate pratique.

2d. That every vessel subject to quarantine shall be permitted to perform it at the port of her destination.

I am, Sir, / Very respectfully, / Your obt Servt.
Washington Irving

MANUSCRIPT: NA, RG 59; NYPL—Berg Collection (letterbook copy).

This entire despatch is in WI's handwriting.

1768. To Ramón María Narváez

Legation of United States / Barcelona July 27th 1844

His Excellency / Captain General Narvaez / President of the Council / &c &c &c

Sir

I have the honor to acknowledge the receipt of your Excellency's note of the 26th instant informing me that the modifications ↑of the Quarantine↓ laws of the Canary Islands in respect to vessels from the U. S., which I suggested in my note of the 25th Jan last have met with the approbation of the Junta Suprema de Sanidad and that orders have been issued to put them in immediate operation.

I cannot but express to your Excellency how much I feel gratified by this considerate attention to my representations the result of which, will, I trust, prove advantageous to both countries. I shall hasten to communicate the purport of your Excellency's note to my Govt to which, I am convinced, it will be highly satisfactory

I take this occasion to renew to your Excellency the assurance of my very distinguished consideration

(signed) Washington Irving

MANUSCRIPT: NA, RG 84 (letterbook copy); NYPL—Berg Collection (letterbook copy).

1769. To Paul Pon

[Barcelona, July 27, 1844]

My dear Sir,

I return you, with many thanks, your very pretty little tale of the Rose from the Generalife. I trust the rose was transfered to the bosom of the fair Prima Donna to whom it was given, and that the tale made its way to her heart and softened it towards the gallant consul, who, it would appear, was sighing at her feet. I should be very proud indeed if any thing I have written could have the effect of striking out such sparks of sentiment and setting combustible hearts in a blaze.

Pray can you send me by the bearer three or four sheets of fools cap paper, of the kind of which I send you a sample. I believe it is your official paper, as it is ours. I want to write a despatch to Government but have not a sheet of the regulation paper left

Very truly yours
Washington Irving

Barcelona July 27th. 1844

MANUSCRIPT: Va.–Barrett.

The recipient is determined from the reference in the second paragraph to the special foolscap paper used for writing official despatches. Paul Pon, who had entertained WI and other diplomats on July 21, was the U.S. consul at Barcelona.

1770.   To Catharine Paris

Barcelona July 2⟨7⟩8. 1844

My dear Sister

Tomorrow I embark in a Spanish Steamer for Marseilles, on my way to Paris. I leave this beautiful city with regret for my time has passed here most happily. Indeed one enjoys the very poetry of existence in these soft southern climates which border the Mediterranean. All here is picture and romance. Nothing has given me greater delight than ⟨little excursions I have made with⟩ occasional evening drives with some of my diplomatic colleagues to those little country seats or Torres as they are called, ⟨which⟩ situated on the slopes of the hills, two or three miles from the city; Surrounded by groves of oranges, ⟨and⟩ citrons ↑Figs, pomgranates &c↓ with ⟨gard⟩ terraced gardens gay with flowers, and fountains. Here we would sit on the ↑lofty↓ terraces, overlooking the rich and varied plain; the distant city gilded by the setting sun and the blue sea beyond. Nothing can be purer and softer and sweeter than the evening air inhaled in these favored retreats.

My sojourn has been rendered the more pleasant by the frank and unaffected kindness and hospitality of Mr and Mrs Anguera; whose house has been made a perfect home to me. They have three fine children, two boys and a girl who have been quite playmates to me, and have contributed to the home feeling I have experienced under their hospitable roof. They have made me promise that whenever I come to Barcelona I will come direct to their house and take up my abode there.

July 29. On board of the Spanish Steamer Villa de Madrid—At Seven O Clock this morning we left Barcelona; and have been all day gliding along a Smooth Summer Sea, in Sight of the Spanish Coast; which is here very mountainous and picturesque. Old ruined castles are to be seen here and there on the summit of cragged heights: with villages gleaming along the shore below them. The Catalonian coast is studded with bright little towns; the Seats of industry and enterprise for Catalonia is the New England of Spain, full of bustle and activity. We have as usual a clear blue sky over head; the air is bland and delightful; and the sea enlivened here and there by the picturesque Mediterranean vessels with their tapering latteen sails.[1] To night we shall have delightful sailing by the light of the full moon;;[2] a light which I have peculiarly enjoyed of late among the orange gardens of Barcelona.

On board of the Steamer we have a joyous party of Catalans; gentlemen and ladies; who are bound to St Filieu,[3] a town on the coast where there is to be held some annual fete. They have all the gaiety and animation which distinguish the people of their province: While I am writing at a table in the cabin I am sensible of the power of a pair of Splendid Spanish eyes which are occasionally flashing upon me, and which almost seem to throw a light upon the paper; since I cannot break the spell I will discribe the owner of them. She is a young married lady, about four or five and twenty. Middle sized; finely modelled; ⟨with round⟩ a Grecian outline of face; a complexion sallow yet healthful; raven black hair; eyes dark, large and beaming; softened by long eye lashes; lips full ↑and rosy red↓ yet finely chizzled, and teeth of dazzling whiteness. She is dressed in black as if in mourning. on one hand is a black glove; the other hand, ungloved, is small, exquisitely formed; with taper fingers and blue veins—She has just put it up to adjust her clustering black locks —I never saw female hand more exquisite—really if I were a young man I should not be able to draw the portrait of this beautiful creature so calmly——
—I was interrupted in my letter writing by an observation of the lady whom I was discribing. She had ⟨[unrecovered]⟩ caught my eye occasionally as it glanced from my letter toward her—"Really Señor" said she at length with a smile—"one would think you were a painter taking my likeness—" I could not resist the impulse—["]Indeed["] said I. ["]I am taking it—I am writing to a friend the other side of the world, discribing things that are passing before me, and I could not help noting down one of the best specimens of the Country that I had met with."[4] A little ban-

tering took place between the young lady, her husband and myself which ended in my reading off, as well as I could into Spanish the description I had just written down. It occasioned a world of merriment and was taken in excellent part. The ladys cheek for once mantled with the Rose; she laughed, shook her head and said I was a very fanciful portrait painter; and the husband declared that, if I would stop at St Filieu all the ladies in the place would crowd to me to have their portraits taken—my pictures were so flattering—I have just parted with them—The Steam Ship ⟨ca⟩ stopped in the open sea, just in front of the little bay of St Filieu; boats came off from shore for the party. I helped the beautiful original of the portrait into the boat and promised her and her husband if ever I should come to St Filieu I would pay them a visit. The last I noticed of her was a Spanish farewell wave of her beautiful white hand, and a gleam of her dazzling teeth as she smiled adieu — —— So theres a very tolerable touch of romance for a Gentleman of my years.

Having nothing worth discribing after the departure of my Spanish beauty I will put by my pen until after my arrival in Marseilles.

Marseilles, July 31t. I arrived ⟨y⟩ here yesterday morning about eight Oclock; after a beautiful ⟨nights⟩ sail by moonlight, which kept me a great part of the night on the deck.

⟨On landing in Marseilles I felt quite at a loss where to apply for information as to my mode of proceeding to Paris. I⟩

I entered the harbor of Marseilles between the forts[5] which guard it like two giants. Just without the port I recognized a little cove where I used to bathe when I was here just *forty* years since. I landed on the quay where I had often walked in old times. It was but little altered, but the harbor at that time was ⟨empty⟩ nearly empty, being a time of war: it was now crowded with shipping The city had nearly doubled in size; and had greatly improved in beauty, as have all European cities during this long peace. It is indeed a magnificent city; one of the Stateliest in France The Streets broad and regular. The houses built of a whitish lime stone; many squares; avenues and alleys of noble trees: public fountains &c. I felt perfectly a stranger in the place and knew not where to apply for information as to my route to ⟨p⟩ Paris; when I reccollected that Mr Fitch[6] of New York; my excentric friend; who ⟨a⟩ insisted on furnishing me occasionally with St Peray wine; had a house in this place and a brother resident here. I accordingly hunted him out and found him residing in one of the finest houses in the place. He received me most cordially; accompanied me to all the coach offices &c until I took ⟨my⟩ seats for Lorenzo and myself in a diligence to part the

next day for Avignon. Mr Fitch regretted that I was determined to part
so soon. ⟨He was⟩ His family were passing the summer at a retreat
in the country a few miles from town and unfortunately he was engaged
⟨with his⟩ with Mrs Fitch, to dine out that very day—

About an hour afterwards he called upon me. ⟨again⟩ He had seen the
gentleman with whom he was to dine who, learning I was in town, had
urged him to bring me with him—In fine—I was pressed into the dinner
party. In the afternoon Mr Fitch & his wife called in their carriage to
take me to the dinner. She is a native of Marseilles but speaks English
perfectly. ⟨The din⟩ On our way to the dinner I was told that it was
given by a bachelor named Marseilles; to a number of the ladies and
gentlemen of the place. It was ⟨given at⟩ to be given at a kind of banquetting house on the Sea Shore, not far from the city, a favorite resort
of the fashionable inhabitants, to have fish dinners. All the company excepting Mr Fitch & myself would be natives of Marseilles, and it would
be quite a Marseilles junketting party to endulge in Marseilles dainties.

It was indeed a most joyous amusing scene. The house was spacious;
with ⟨arca⟩ ↑a↓ noble dining saloon looking upon the Sea: ⟨sh⟩ fine terraces &c. The Sea came rippling and washing the sands within a short
distance of the house: we had a noble view of the city: its promontories,
and islands with towns and castles: and the blue Mediterranean; which I
never get tired of contemplating.

The dinner was excellent, a great variety of fish dressed in various
ways: with all the luxuries the market afforded: and abundance of the
fine fruits of this favored climate. As the party was composed of people
who had known each other from infancy, it was a very social, merry
one. In the course of the dinner the gentleman who gave it drank my
health, alluded to the circumstance of my sudden and unexpected arrival and made some very complimentary remarks about myself & my
writings: which ⟨was⟩ were cheered by the company: and, to my surprize,
I found I was quite an old acquaintance among them. This is one of the
few instances in which I have not found my literary notoriety irksome
to me. On the contrary, I was glad to find myself so much at home
among such pleasant people; and the cordial manner in which I was
treated throughout the rest of the evening made me feel as if I had
known them for years. I again passed a lovely ⟨eve⟩ moonlight evening
on one of those terraces which are characteristic of country architecture
about the Coast of the Mediterranean The drive home too was delightful; and as ⟨it⟩ we drove through the spacious moon lit streets of
Marseilles it ⟨seem⟩ looked like a city of palaces. Indeed many of the
houses are almost palaces in size and style; and the ⟨merch⟩ principal
merchants ⟨lit⟩ live like princes. I parted from my new friends with many

cordial expressions, and promised them, if the Spanish Court should make another sojourn at Barcelona next year, I would pay Marseilles a longer visit and accept of their proferred hospitality.

Lyons, August, 3d.   I left Marseilles on the afternoon of the 31st. for Avignon. I had taken the ↑whole of the↓ Coupe of the Dilligence. This is the front part; and is like a chariot, with glass doors and windows, and has places for three. There was therefore ample accommodation for Lorenzo and myself. We travelled all night, and early the next morning entered the ancient and picturesque town of Avignon.[7] Having visited it in former days and seen all its curiosities, I awaited only the departure of the Steamer, to continue my wayfaring: Still I had time enough to take another look at the old Castle where the Popes resided for nearly a century, ⟨when Avignon was⟩ ↑during which↓ the papal residence was transferred from Rome to Avignon. I took a peep also into the old church where once was the tomb of Petrarchs Laura—At an early hour I embarked in a Steamer of the Rhone and was two days and a half mounting that river from Avignon to Lyons; a distance not quite as great as from N York to Albany; but the river runs with the rapidity of a mill race; and the boats descend the same distance in eleven hours. I was delighted with the Scenery of the River. It is very varied; many parts wild mountainous and picturesque: Some parts resembling the Scenery of the Hudson; with the addition of old towns; villages, ruined castles &c

On board of the Steamboat I had a great pet in a little french girl about two years and half old, in which I fancied a resemblance to Sarahs little Kate. She was travelling with her father and mother; but soon took to me, and became quite my companion. It was a most engaging child and the resemblance I had fancied quite attached me to her, so that when we parted on arriving at Lyons I felt absolutely grieved. We arrived here early in the afternoon; and tomorrow morning we continue our course in another Steamer up the Saone to Chalons, where I have secured the Coupe of the Dilligence for Paris. Thus I shall make ⟨the g⟩ a great part of my journey by water; and in the part by land will be most comfortably accommodated

Versailles, Aug 9th.   I arrived here two or three days since; after accomplishing a most agreeable expedition by Sea and land from Barcelona. My voyage up the Saone was very pleasant, though not so interesting as that up the Rhone, the Scenery not being so striking. In the journey by Land from Chalons I passed through the valley of the Gonne: a soft, rich pastoral country where every thing bore the air of abundance In fact this route has carried me through some of the most interesting parts of France, and in a season when the folks were getting in their harvest and when the finest fruits were ripening.

On my arrival here to my surprise I found that twelve days before, Sarah had presented her husband with another daughter.[8] I had had no idea that such an event was pending: Mr Storrows recent letters to me[9] on the subject having reached Spain after my departure. I am happy to say our dear Sarah is getting on admirably. She begins to sit up, and is in good looks and good spirits. The infant I am told is a very fine child—for my own part I am no judge of these very small folks. Kate is in glorious health—a perfect picture. ⟨She⟩ I do not know whether she reccollected me, but she took to me instantly and we have ever since my arrival been almost inseparable. She is an admirable instance of the excellence of Julia Grinnells system of treating children; never out of order; always fresh, blooming, active, and full of enjoyment. I have just been out with her in the park where we have had a fine range together about the shady alleys and the green lawns.

You may well be satisfied, my dear Sister, with your daughters lot. She has a kind, attentive, affectionate husband; fine healthful children; a quiet happy home where her servants idolize her: a most respectable position in society; which enables her ⟨to⟩ on the most easy terms, to cultivate the friendship of the elite of her country people, who occasionaly reside at Paris; and by whom I am happy to observe she is highly appreciated.

—I have just received a letter from Alexander Hamilton,[10] written the morning after his arrival at home and informing me that he had already visited the Cottage and seen you all. How kind and attentive in him to write to me at such a moment: and to be so prompt in paying a visit to my dear little home—but he is full of kind and generous feeling and delights in contributing to the happiness of others. What a joy there must have been diffused through the household at Nevis on his return; and how his good mothers heart must have leapt for joy. He is just the kind of son to delight a mothers heart.

In the course of three or four days I shall set off for Havre to pay my worthy friend Beasley a visit. He has written to me ⟨to⟩ urging me to come down there before Captain Funck sails; that I may jollify a little with the magnanimous little captain, and with the Ledyards who are to embark with him. After passing a few days with honest Beasley and enjoying sea bathing, I shall cross to England and make the best of my way to the Shrubbery; or wherever else our dear Sister may happen to be; for I rather think she is at some watering place

Aug 13th.   I must close this long rambling letter to send it off in time for the Great Western. In the course of this morning I depart with Lorenzo by the rail road for Rouen where I shall arrive early in the afternoon. Tomorrow morning early I shall take passage in the Steam boat on the Seine, and in the course of the morning trust to find myself under the hospitable roof of my worthy friend Beasley.

The week I have passed here has been one of heartfelt pleasure; being so much with Sarah and her children—Kate and I are constant play mates. I have furnished her with dolls and picture books and polichinellos, and she is too generous to keep her play things all to herself; so I have had the full worth of my money out of them

—Give my love to all the Cottagers; as well as those at the "Square house"

Your affectionate brother
Washington Irving

DOCKETED: Sunnyside Sept 2 / 44 / To Mrs Cath R Paris 7 PM
MANUSCRIPT: Yale.   PUBLISHED: PMI, III, 357–61 (in part); Hellman, *WI Esquire*, p. 275 (in part); STW, II, 178–79 (in part).

1. Triangular sails suspended by a long yard at an angle of about 45 degrees.
2. WI repeated the semicolon.
3. San Filieu de Guixole, a town about forty miles northeast of Barcelona, the chief port for shipping Spanish cork. See Karl Baedeker, *Spain and Portugal*, p. 224.
4. WI omitted the bracketed quotation marks.
5. Fort St. Nicolas and Fort St. Jean. See Karl Baedeker, *South-Eastern France . . . Including Corsica* (Leipzig, 1895), p. 214.
6. Possibly William Fitch, who was a passenger on the *Remittance*, the ship on which WI returned to the United States in 1806. See *J&N*, I, 580.
7. For WI's earlier visit to Avignon, see his letter to William Irving, August 24, 1804; and *J&N*, I, 72–74.
8. Susan Van Wart Storrow was born on July 26, 1844.
9. These have not been located.
10. This letter has not been located.

1771.   To Sarah Storrow

Lyons Aug 4th 1844

My dear Sarah,

I would have been with you as soon as this letter if I could have got a place in the Malle Poste; but I shall arrive within a day or two after it. I have just come up the Rhone in a Steamer, and set off early tomorrow morning in a Steamer up the Saone to Chalons, whence I have secured the whole Coupé of a Dilligence for Paris. ⟨I s⟩ When I set out from

Barcelona I intended to loiter by the way and visit sundry places, but I am so impatient to see you and Kate that I cannot help pushing forward.

                                                        Your affectionate uncle
                                                        Washington Irving

P. S—on board of the Steamer I met [*end of MS*]

MANUSCRIPT: Yale.

1772.   *To Sarah Storrow*

                                                    [Havre, August 20, 1844]

Tell Mr. Storrow to send all letters for me in an envelope addressed to Mr. Van Wart. I do not want my name to appear in any way that may draw upon me invitations.

PUBLISHED: PMI, III, 361.

1773.   *To Catharine Paris*

                                        The Shrubbery. Edgbaston / Aug 30th. 1844

My dear Sister,

Here I am once more under the roof of our dear Sister. I left Havre upwards of a week since in a Steam Packet for London, where I arrived after a voyage of about 22 hours. I made no stop in London but proceeded immediately by rail road for this place. ⟨I found our dear Sister⟩ I had anticipated a very melancholy meeting with our dear Sister, expecting to find her a mere wreck, but was greatly surprised and rejoiced to find her looking as well as when I last saw her; in full possession of all her social powers, and, though still somewhat paralyzed in the limbs of the right side, yet enabled to walk about a little without assistance, to amuse herself with Knitting &c. Did she never recover to more health and strength than she possesses at present, she still would be able to enjoy life and the social intercourse with her family and friends: but she is daily improving in every respect and I should not be surprised if her recovery should prove almost perfect. She is very much in the open air, being wheeled about the walks of the Shrubbery in a Bath chair; which is somewhat like a childs Phaeton. In this way she takes exercise for hours in the course of the day; and occasionally gets out of the vehicle and walks a quarter of a mile at a time. Marianne is constantly with her.

Matildas cottage also adjoins the Shrubbery, and she and her children are frequent visitors. It is quite delightful to see Sister wheeled about in her chair with the little folk gambolling about her. Matilda has three very fine children.[1] The eldest and the youngest are boys; and sturdy boys they are. The middle one is a little blue eyed girl; with long yellow ringlets; and a dimpled smile, a little beauty, and a most engaging child.

a few days before my arrival William Van Wart and Rosa lost their little son Irving,[2] a most interesting child; but whose death had long been foreseen and was in fact, a relief. They have three very fine boys: handsome, frank manly little fellows and a lovely little girl; with dark eyes and flaxen hair: a little fairy.[3] I am told Rosa has written to you occasionally, in which case you must have perceived by her letters that she is quite a superior woman. She is indeed an admirable character: full of talent; excelling with the pen & the pencil and skilled in music, but with all most modest and unpretending. I have rarely met with a woman so perfectly calculated to win and maintain affection and esteem. In fact our dear Sister is eminently blessed in her domestic relations. She is surrounded by good and kind beings who idolize her and study in every way to promote her happiness. Marianne is a lovely character; one of the best of daughters and is never from her mothers side. Van Wart is all kindness and cheeriness. George, who resides at home, is a most worthy affectionate fellow. Tender and attentive in his conduct to his mother and sisters. William calls in almost every day, on his way to & from his house which is about three miles from town; and his visits are like gleams of Sunshine; while Rosa and her little ones come occasionally to pass the day.

As I slipt through London without making my arrival known to any one I have not been troubled with invitations or engagements but have been enabled to pass my whole time in the bosom of this Kind and affectionate family connexion; and I do not know when I have enjoyed more heartfelt satisfaction.

I am happy to say that the return of better times has been felt by Mr Van Warts establishment: which is at present in a prosperous state of activity. Indeed within the last Six months he has had a greater accession of new customers than he has ever had in the same space of time since he has been in business.

I think of remaining here about eight or ten days longer when I shall return to Paris to pass some little time with Sarah before I shape my course for Madrid. I have frequent letters from Mr Livingston, whom I have left in charge of the Legation, and who appears to discharge the duties of it in a very satisfactory manner.

I left my faithful servant Lorenzo at Mr Beasleys, at Havre, until my return; as he would be but a burthen in England, not speaking the language. He looked rather downcast at parting with me, but Beasley writes me that since my departure he consoles himself by playing the Guitar.

I recd. before leaving Havre your letter by the Steamer of the 1st August giving me pleasant accounts from the Cottage and most satisfactory accounts of your own health.

Give my love to all the household and the neighborhood

Your affectionate brother
Washington Irving

MANUSCRIPT: Yale.

1. Probably Robert Henry Van Wart Kell, Rosalind Kell, and Charles Van Wart Kell.

2. Washington Irving Kell died on August 16, 1844.

3. Wilfred, Harry, Oscar, and Alyce. For other details, see WI to Catharine Paris, May 7, 1842.

1774.   To Catharine Paris

Paris, Sept. 15th. 1844

My dear Sister,

I left Birmingham on Tuesday the 10th. after having passed nearly three weeks there. My whole time was passed in the domestic circle; and principally with our dear Sister. From all that I can judge of her case I doubt of her ever recovering perfectly; but think she will yet improve considerably. Even if she should never attain a better state of health than she has at present, she is quite well enough to enjoy life and to contribute to the happiness of her friends. I have no doubt that, if she were convinced she would never be freer from the effects of her malady than she is at present she would soon make up her mind to it, and settle into suitable habitudes; it is only the expectation of improving in health, ⟨that makes h⟩ and the constan[t][1] remedies she pursues, that keep her thinking of her malady and feeling herself an invalid.

As my visit to England was merely to pass some time at the Shrubbery, with our dear Sister, I stopped but a part of two days ⟨on my⟩ at London on my way back to France. The first day was passed in company with my old and valued friend Leslie, with whom I went around seeing sights, as we used to in days of yore, and a delightful day it was. The next day I devoted to visits of business, and to looking at some of the new parts of London, and at those parts which have undergone alterations. At Five Oclock in the afternoon I departed in the Rail road for Southampton; where I arrived at nine Oclock in the evening, just in time to take my passage in the Steam packet for Havre. The weather was soft and serene; the sea quiet as a mill pond; I slept on a settee on deck, under an awning and enjoyed as sweet and ⟨fr⟩ refreshing a nights rest as I have done in the open air on the prairies, as I lay on my couch I saw the sun rise splendidly from the sea. About seven oclock in the morning we entered the harbor of Havre. Almost the first person that caught my eye was my faithful Lorenzo watching the arrival of the ⟨b⟩ Steamer from the battlements of a fort which overlooks the mouth of the harbor. He did not know that I was to arrive in this steamer, but, I found, had been watching the arrival of every steamer for some days past. I made a signal to him, and the poor fellow leapd for joy on descrying me. He had been quite desolate at my having left him so long alone in Havre: though I found he was quite a favorite among Mr Beasleys servants and had been the magnus apollo of the kitchen. At half past ten oclock I took passage in the dilligence for Rouen; having as usual secured the whole of the Coupé, which enabled me to travel most commodiously. (We arrived about half past⟩ The day was superb, and the road passed frequently in sight of the Seine presenting some of the most beautiful prospects of land and water in France. We arrived at Rouen between five and six; where I dined and then took places in the rail road for Paris, where I arrived safely about half past ten; thus having accomplished the journey from London to Paris in less than thirty hours; stopping about three hours at Havre and an hour and half at Rouen; and arriving at my journeys end without feeling fatigued. Such is the rapidity and such the convenience of modern travelling.

I found all well at Sarahs. She is in excellent health: and in better looks than I have seen her for years. She is "plumping up" and is as fresh as a rose. She tells me that all her clothes have grown too tight for her and have to be let out. Mr Storrow too is in much better flesh and better looks than he was last year. The children are hearty as usual. The babe begins to acquire something like settled features and is as pretty as such non descript little beings usually are[.] Kate has learnt several ⟨Paris, September 15th. 1844⟩ new tricks and acquired several new oddities since I last saw her. She has of late become a great correspondent and at present is very busy writing a letter to her grand mamma.

I received yesterday a letter from Eliza Romeyn,[2] dated, July 23d. (upwards of seven weeks on the way) and begging me to answer it before I replied to one which brother E. I was writing at the same time. His letter however came to hand first; but I will answer hers as soon as I can find liesure.

Give my love to "all bodies"

Your affectionate brother
Washington Irving.

P. S. By the bye I have just heard that you are coming out in gay style; having recently been at a dinner party at Mr Constants. I expect to hear soon that you are practising the Polka for the next ball.[3]

ADDRESSED: Mrs Daniel Paris / Care of E. Irving Esqr . New York / *Via Angleterre*
    POSTMARKED: PARIS / 16 / SEPT / 44 // PAID / SEP 18 / 44 // [*unre-covered*] // PD
MANUSCRIPT: Va.–Barrett.

1. WI omitted the bracketed letter.
2. These letters from Eliza Romeyn and Ebenezer Irving have not been located.
3. This postscript is written vertically along the left margin of page 1.

1775.   To Henry Van Wart

Paris, September 16, 1844

I wish you to execute a small commission for my fair friend and country· woman, Madame Albuquerque, wife of the Brazilian Minister at Madrid, and one who acts the part of an affectionate niece to me there.

.   .   .   .

Tell George[1] I have not the Doctor's verses at hand to send him a copy. I swallowed them at a dose but cannot perceive that I am anything the better for them.

PUBLISHED: Maggs Bros. Catalogue 266, Easter 1911, item 369.

1. Van Wart's son and WI's nephew.

1776.   To Jasper Livingston

Paris, Sept. 25th. 1844

My dear Livingston
    I am accumulating a heavy debt of correspondence; not having answered your long and delightful letter of the 11th. nor your shorter one of the 14th. inst., and now having just received your budget of the 19th[1] full as usual of anecdote and remarks which put me quite in the current of Madrid life, I really do not know how to thank you enough for

such frequent and interesting correspondence, and only wish I could repay it in kind, but I am stagnant, absolutely stagnant, though in the midst of Paris. I have had something of a bilious attack recently, of which I had slight premonitory symptoms for some time past. It was. accompanied by a sharp return of my old malady and has confined me to the house for nearly a week. I am getting over it however, and as soon as I find myself in travelling condition, will set out on my route for Madrid. This indisposition however will retard my return; which I had hoped would be in time for the opening of the cortes, having a great desire to see the little Queen officiate on that occasion. I must give up that hope, and leave you to do the honors of the Legation in my stead. It is a great satisfaction to me to think the Legation will be so well represented.

My indisposition has been very inopportune on another account. Just as I was taken unwell I heard that Mrs. Carrol Livingston was at Meurice's.[2] I desired most earnestly to call upon her, but have not since been able to leave the house, and she has gone to Havre & in fact, embarked there. I doubt of her knowing that I was in Paris or she would probably have charged me with some commissions for Brocky,[3] which I would have been most happy to execute.

You must not be impatient at delays in receiving replys to letters addressed to the members of the Spanish cabinet; nor consider them as slights resulting from want of consideration & respect. The same delays occur in all cabinets, but are more incident to one like that of Spain; which is continually changing and is surrounded by revolutionary dangers. Think how many letters a minister must receive every day not merely from the various members of the diplomatic corps, but from all kinds of persons and from all parts of the Kingdom. How can he attend to all and answer all promptly? Think how many matters of vital importance are pressing upon his anxious thoughts—how can he at any moment turn from them to attend to some note about a distant concern, of vastly inferior consequence.

If you converse with the other members of the diplomatic corps you will find that your case is not singular; they all consider their correspondence neglected—in fact they none of them make proper allowance for the exigencies in which ministers are placed; but expect the latter to have equal time to answer every note, whether of business or ceremony, which they have such ample leisure to write. It is like expecting a drowning man, who is catching at straws, to take off his hat, return the salutation of the gentlemen who are quietly walking along the river bank and wish them a very good morning.

I regret extremely my absence from the amateur opera at [Caravancheles?][4]. The performance of the fair Leocadia[5] must have been a perfect gem. There is a charm too about a performance by such an artist quite distinct from the effects produced by the performance of hackneyed actors. An idea of something more choice and pure and sanctified. I think with all my vivid recollection of the Grisi in this part, I could be equally moved by the natural pathos and feeling of Leocadia.

I have heard with deep concern the sad loss sustained by the De Bressons.[6] It is indeed a most desolating blow and must plunge them in the deepest affliction.

I have been intending to write to Madame Albuquerque but my indisposition has prevented me. Tell her I have written to England to have the articles procured of which she is in want. I shall write to her soon, as well as to the excellent and indefatigable and omnipresent Dalborgo[7]—whom heaven preserve!

Yours with great regard
Washington Irving

PUBLISHED: *Hudson River Day Line Magazine*, 27 (September–October, 1914), 12–13.

1. These letters have not been located.
2. A fashionable hotel on the Rue de Rivoli frequented by English-speaking travelers. See Karl Baedeker, *Paris and Its Environs*, p. 3.
3. Probably Livingston's nephew who had accompanied him to Madrid.
4. The published transcription is "Caraboi . . . ils." The Caravancheles are two villages outside Madrid on the way to Toledo where María Christina created a villa, gave royal entertainments, and provided amusement for the courtiers. See Richard Ford, *A Hand-Book for Travellers in Spain*, III, 1186–87.
5. The published transcription is "Leocadra," but the context indicates that it should be "Leocadia," for Leocadia Zamora, the beautiful singer who greatly impressed WI.
6. The published transcription is "De Boissons," but WI is referring to De Bresson, the French ambassador. The nature of their loss is not clear. Possibly it was the death of an infant. Countess de Bresson gave birth to a child in June of 1845. See Penney, *Bulletin NYPL*, 62 (December, 1958), 618.
7. The published transcription is "Dalborjo," but the reference is to Olinto dal Borgo di Primo, the Chargé d'Affaires for Denmark.

1777. To William H. Prescott

Paris, Octr. 15th. 1844

My dear Sir,

I ought to have acknowledged long, long since, the receipt of your letter, with the accompanying copy of your History of the Conquest of Mexico; and I should have done so, had I not proposed to myself to give, in my reply some detailed observations on your work. Unfortunately the deranged state of my health, brought on by too close confinement among my books and papers, has obliged me, for nearly two years past, to abstain as much as possible from all literary occupation; and has produced such a morbid feeling in this respect that the least exercise of the pen becomes an undertaking. In this state of mind the meditated reply was postponed from day to day, week to week and month to month, until, as usual in epistolary postponements I became spell bound with regard to it. I am now determined to break the spell; and, by speaking out, however briefly, to release myself from the thraldom of this literary nightmare. To this effect I give up all all[1] further thought of ⟨discussing⟩ ↑a detailed discussion of↓ the merits of your work, indeed the opinions passed upon it by the public press both in America and Europe; and the applause and admiration which it has excited throughout the whole republic of letters, render any comment on my part superfluous. I can only say that you have fully answered the high expectations I had formed from the manner in which you had acquitted yourself in your admirable history of Ferdinand and Isabella; you have done full justice to the singularly poetic and romantic nature of your subject, without being seduced by it from the scrupulous verification of facts, and from ⟨and⟩ the sober gravity of Style which belong to History You have given to the world another work of which your country may well be proud, and which ⟨stands forth⟩ has already taken its rank as one of the noblest and most beautiful productions of modern literature.

I received some time since a letter from Lord Morpeth,[2] who takes the warmest interest in your literary renown, urging me to write a critique on your work for the Edinburgh Review; I regret that the same morbid state of mind which postponed my reply to your letter, obliged me to excuse myself from complying with his lord ships wishes. I had hoped that the Spanish public would receive a satisfactory translation of your history from the pen of Mr Calderon de la Barca; but the diplomatic mission of that gentleman interrupted his undertaking when just commenced. I then endeavored to get a young Spanish gentleman of literary talents, at Madrid, to undertake it; but he was deterred ⟨from⟩ ↑by↓ the magnitude of the work and the fear that, ⟨it⟩ in the present distracted state of Spain, it would not command sufficient sale to cover the expense. On my return to Spain I hope to find some translator more enterprising, if the work should not be already in the course of translation.

I rejoice to hear that you are about commencing the history of the Conquest of Peru and shall be happy to render you any service, while in Spain, in collecting materials. In the present dismantled state of my mind, I seem to be of but little use except to cheer others on in their more fortunate careers; but if, in my stranded condition, I now and then look with a wistful eye as you all sweep by me with favoring breeze and flowing sail, yet, from the bottom of my heart, I wish you all God Speed!

Ever my dear Sir most truly yours
Washington Irving

William H Prescott Esqr / &c &c &c

DOCKETED: From / Washington Irving / Paris. Oct. 15. 1844
MANUSCRIPT: Va.–Barrett; NYPL–Berg Collection (draft copy).

1. WI repeated "all."
2. WI had met Lord Morpeth on December 1, 1841, in New York during his American tour. See WI to Sarah Storrow, December 1, 1841.

1778. *To John C. Calhoun*

Paris October 16th 1844

The Hon. John C Calhoun / Secretary of State, Washington

Sir

I have duly received your despatches enclosing ⟨the⟩ copies of ↑the↓ letters from the department of State to our Ministers at Paris and Mexico[1] on the subject of Texas. I have read those two important documents with deep attention and with no common interest, and shall bear them in mind in any communications I may have to make or any conversations I may have to hold, in regard to the topics and views contained in them, in my diplomatic capacity.

In recent conversations with Mr Smith[2] the Texian Charge d'Affaires at the Court of France he assured me that he considered all likelihood of annexation at an end, and that the hope of it was generally given up in Texas. That they felt they would have to act for themselves, and rely upon themselves as an independent power, and that, under this conviction, instructions had been given him by his government. to ascertain whether there was a probability of opening diplomatic relations with the Spanish government, and establishing a direct and unembarrassed trade between Texas and the Island of Cuba. He wanted to know my opinion in the matter. I did not hold out any very encouraging prospects to him, in the present agitated state of Spain and the precarious situation of its government: indeed, I considered his whole conversation on the subject as intended merely to draw out my own views and feelings on the question of annexation[.] I cannot persuade myself that the Texians consider the case hopeless, seeing the encreasing popularity of the question in the United States

I have had conversations also with Mr. Jollivet, member of the chamber of Deputies and deligate for the Island of Martinique; who is earnestly prosecuting the scheme of organizing a coalition between the French and Spanish colonies, Brazil and the Southern parts of the United States to protect themselves from the abolition intrigues and machinations of England He finds much difficulty to contend with in France, several of the leading papers such as the Journal des debats, the Presse, the constitutionnel[3] &c being, as he says, in the pay of Antislavery societies in England or under the influence of British Diplomacy. He is endeavoring to interest the Spanish government in the Subject, and to that effect has just written a letter to M Martinez de la Rosa, who, while Ambassador at Paris, professed himself favorable to the measure. I have promised to take a copy of his letter and have it, safely delivered into the hands of Martinez de la Rosa.

I believe the actual government of Spain is very distrustful of the policy of England with respect to their West India possessions, and would gladly concur in any measure to counteract it; but should the progresista party come into power and the Esparterists once more have sway, the English influence would revive and might be detrimental to the colonial interests. England is endeavoring to regain the footing she has lost in Spain; and the good offices, such as they were, rendered by her minister Mr Bulwer in aiding to settle the difficulties between Spain and Marocco, are constantly placed in the strongest light to catch the public eye.

I have not numbered this letter as I do not intend it as a regular despatch. I regret that I have to date it from Paris having expected, before this time to have been at my post at Madrid. In availing myself of the two months leave of absence kindly granted me by the President, I extended my tour of health to England to pass some little time with a sister, now advanced in years, from whom I have long been seperated, and who, of late has suffered from a dangerous illness. After a visit of about three weeks I set out on my return, but had an attack of bile in Paris which brought on a temporary return of my herpetic malady; ⟨which⟩ and obliged me to have recourse to mineral baths. I am now nearly recovered and trust in the course of a few days to be able to resume my journey to Madrid.

I have felt it proper to make this explanation of my delay in returning to my post; lest the President should think I was heedlessly exceeding ⟨the term of⟩ my leave of absence, or was availing myself of his indulgence for purposes of personal gratification

> I am Sir, / Very respectfully / Your obt Servt
> Washington Irving

DOCKETED: Recd 6 Nov. / Mr. Markoe [*upper left corner, page 1*] / W. Irving,
    Paris. 16 Oct 1844.
MANUSCRIPT: NA, RG 59.   PUBLISHED: Manning, *Diplomatic Correspondence*,
    342–43.

The entire despatch is in WI's handwriting.

1. William R. King and Wilson Shannon (1802–1877), respectively.
2. Ashbel Smith (1805–1886), an M.D. from Yale who was appointed surgeon
general of Texas in 1837, was Texas's minister to England and France from 1842
to 1844.
3. *Journal des débats*, established in 1789 and owned by Louis-Marie-Armand
Bertin (1801–1854), supported Guizot, while *La Presse*, founded in 1836 by
Émile de Girardin (1806–1881), espoused a right of center position and was critical of Guizot. *Le Constitutionel*, founded in 1815, was left of center and supported
Guizot. See Irene Collins, *The Government and the Newspaper Press in France,
1814–1881* (Oxford, 1959), pp. 87, 88–90, 91, 97.

1779.   To Lady Rancliffe

[ca. October 26, 1844]

My dear Lady Rancliffe
    I regret extremely that I am engaged this evening, having to be pre-
sented to the King, but I will do myself the pleasure of waiting on you
tomorrow.

With great regard / Your obliged
Washington Irving

No 4. Rue de La Victoire

MANUSCRIPT: Brigham Young University Library.

Elizabeth Mary Forbes (d. 1852) was the wife of George Augustus Parkyns
(1785–1850), second Baron Rancliffe. WI had met the couple in Paris several times
between 1823 and 1825 and presumably renewed his acquaintance during a visit
to the Storrows in 1844. See *J&N*, III, 241, 305, 422, 513.
    The date is ascertained from WI's reference to a visit to Louis Philippe in a
letter to Mrs. Paris, November 2, 1844.

1780.   To Catharine Paris

Paris, Novr. 2d. 1844

My dear Sister,
    I am lingering in Paris longer than I had intended, ⟨but⟩ in hopes of get-
ting in good travelling condition by the aid of baths; for the teasing

remains of my malady still cling to me. I shall however set off in the course of three or four days on my long journey to my post.

Yesterday the two children were christened by an English clergyman. The little creatures behaved very well. Kate it is true was rather awed by the sight of the clergyman in his robe & surplice and cried a little when he took her in his arms and sprinkled water in his[1] face; but little Susan was as quiet as a lamb. The good old gentleman was charmed with their appearance and pronounced them beautiful children, and so they are. What is better, they enjoy the most perfect health, and give every evidence of pure and strong constitutions. I shall find it hard parting with Kate who is my constant play mate, and who is really one of the most amusing little beings I have ever known; full of whim and good spirits and with a thousand droll ways. You have, indeed, my dear Sister, reason to be satisfied with the lot of your child. Her life is a happy one: her house delightful; ⟨and⟩ she has a pleasant circle of american friends among whom she is very popular, and who give her the occasional variety of social intercourse without drawing her into dissipation. The general tenor of her life is quite domestic, and her chief happiness centres in her children. Mr Storrows business is very prosperous, and is constantly encreasing; and as he conducts it with great prudence there is every prospect of his realizing, in the course of a few years, a handsome competency. Sarahs health is excellent. She is much improved in looks within the last two years: and within the present year especially. She is fuller in person with a fine healthful complexion; and indeed looks as fresh and fair as when I first saw her on my return from Europe. Mrs Ledyard, however, has no doubt given you a full account of her, still I may ⟨be⟩ give ⟨he⟩ you a better idea of her by being able to compare her with what she has been. You used to complain of her falling off in appearance and "growing old;" you would not do so now if you were to see her. She is younger in looks and constitution than when she left America.

⟨I have nothing new to tell you⟩

I have been living so quietly for some time past that I have nothing new to tell you excepting a visit which I paid to King Louis Philippe about a week since. I made it in company with Mr King our Minister at this court, and Mr Wheaton, our Minister to Prussia, who is making a sojourn in this city. The Royal family were at St Cloud, a few miles from Paris. The King, while at the country seats, receives privileged visitors in the evenings; when they go in plain dress. We drove out to St Cloud in Mr Kings carriage. I thought of Napoleon[2] as we entered the gates and ascended the great marble stair case of this beautiful palace; for it was one of his favorite residences. The interior of the palace was brilliantly lighted up; we passed through spacious halls and antechambers and caught vistas through long galleries superbly painted & gilded; all contrasting with the partial gloom of the Royal palace at Madrid, on my last evening visit to it.

We found the Royal family in a lofty square chamber, at the end of one of the Saloons. As on my former visit, (in 1842)[3] the ⟨ladies of the were seat⟩ Queen & Madame Adelaide were seated at a round table, engaged in needlework, or embroidery; the beautiful young Duchess de Nemours[4] was likewise seated at the table, as were two or three ladies of rank. At another round table on the opposite side of the room were seated ⟨the⟩ two or three ladies of honor; the tea equipage was on the table, as in a private house. ⟨The⟩ Several gentlemen, some in military uniforms were in groupes about the room; The Duke de Nemours[5] was in one of the groupes, and the King was conversing with a diplomatic personage in the embrasure of one of the windows. The King was in Plain dress, and there was altogether an absence of form and ceremony. I paid my respects to the Queen and Madame Adelaide, both of whom reccollected me and my previous visit: received me very amiably ⟨desired to know⟩ enquired whether I was engaged on any literary work &c—The Queen is always pale and thin, but appears still thinner than when I last saw her. You may reccollect that it was but a few days after that visit that her son the Duke of Orleans[6] was killed by a fall from his carriage; a domestic blow which she has never ceased to deplore.

We had a long and varied conversation with the King. He appears to to be in excellent health and spirits and bears in his countenance and carriage the promise of a length of days. He converses very freely and copiously, and turned from one subject to another; varying his humor with his theme. He is fond of telling stories of his adventures in the back woods in America,[7] and gave us one or two in excellent style, laughing heartily. I was surprised to find how tenaciously he retains the names of places and persons; the relative distances; the nature of the country &c —&c. Our conversation must have lasted for upwards of half an hour; and was more like the frank social conversation of common life than the diplomatic communications between a King and Ambassadors. The King has been highly gratified by his late visit to England; and it has put him in wonderful good humor. He regretted that the ⟨Sea⟩ Ocean was so wide and the United States so far off, that he could not pay our country a visit with equal convenience. We assured him that if he did so he would ⟨receive⟩ experience a reception full as cordial, ⟨if not still more so,⟩ as in England if not still more so

I have been interrupted repeatedly while writing this letter and have no time to prolong it, as the pacquet must be made up for the post. Give my love to "all bodies." Tell Ebenezer to have the Kitchen range arranged to his liking; but above all not to postpone the sacred duty which I enjoined upon him in one of my letters

Your affectionate brother
W. I.

MANUSCRIPT: Yale.   PUBLISHED: PMI, III, 312–13 (in part).

1. WI intended to write "her."
2. Napoleon was proclaimed as first consul at St. Cloud on November 12, 1799.
3. WI was presented to Louis-Philippe on June 4, 1842. See WI to Sarah Storrow, June 8, 1842.
4. Victoria (1822–1857), daughter of Ferdinand of Saxe-Coburg-Gotha (1785–1851) and Antoinette de Kohary (1797–1862), married the duke de Nemours in 1840.
5. Louis, the duke de Nemours (1814–1896) was Louis-Philippe's second and oldest surviving son.
6. Ferdinand-Louis-Charles, duke of Orléans (1810–1842).
7. Louis-Philippe had sailed for Philadelphia from Hamburg on September 24, 1796. He visited Nashville and early in 1798 made a harrowing voyage of forty days down the Mississippi River in the dead of winter. See T. E. B. Howarth, *Citizen King, The Life of Louis-Philippe, King of the French* (London, 1961), pp. 87, 95, 99, 101, 102.

1781. To Sarah Storrow

Bayonne 15th. ↑November↓ 1844

My dear Sarah,

I write merely to let you know that I left Bordeaux at two Oclock yesterday in the Malle poste and arrived here at Six Oclock this morning, having made a very comfortable journey. My good friend Mr La Caze[1] of this place, to whom I had written, has secured me the Coupé of the Malle poste which departs at twelve oclock to day ↑(Friday)↓ for Madrid, ⟨so that in three days⟩ ↑and on Sunday evening about eight oclock↓ I shall be at the end of my journey. The weather for the last two days has been beautiful and there is every prospect of its continuing so. I am in very good travelling condition, and have just taken a warm bath which has made me "as cool as a cucumber."[2] So you see I am getting on most comfortably on this much dreaded journey.

Looking forward to early letters from you, giving me accounts of "all bodies" ⟨and⟩ I am, my dear Sarah, with kind remembrances to Mr Storrow, ⟨and⟩ many kisses to dear little good for nothing Kate and my respects to her proud little sister

Your affectionate uncle
Washington Irving

ADDRESSED: Madame / Madame Storrow / No 4 Rue de la Victoire / à Paris
MANUSCRIPT: Yale.

1. This may be Pierre Caze (1767–1849), whom WI had met in Bordeaux in
the winter of 1825–1826. See J&N, III, 549, 551–54, 557, 560–62.
2. See John Gay, "A New Song of Similies" (1727).

1782. To Francisco Martínez de la Rosa

Madrid 21st November 1844
El Excmo Señor / Don Francisco Martinez de la Rosa / Primer Ministro
de Estado

El infrascrito Enviado extraordinario y Ministro Plenipotenciario de los
Estados Unidos besa las manos de S. Ex Don Fo Mz de la Rosa y le ruega
se digne mandar expedir la real orden oportuna para la libre entrada
por la aduana de Irun de treinta y ocho docenas de botellas de vino.

El infrascrito ruega tambien a S. E tenga a bien mandar activen la
expedicion de la real orden solicitada el primero del corriente, para le
libre entrada de dos cajas de documentos destinados a los archivos de
esta Legacion.

El infrascrito aprovecha esta primera ocasion etc

(Signed) Washington Irving

MANUSCRIPT: NA, RG 84 (letterbook copy).

Translation:
"The undersigned envoy extraordinary and minister plenipotentiary of the United
States kisses the hands of His Excellency Don Francisco Martinez de la Rosa and
begs him to be kind enough to have the opportune order sent for the free entry
through the Irun customs of thirty-eight bottles of wine.

"The undersigned also begs your excellency to be kind enough to have the
dispatch of the royal order requested on the first of the current month activated,
for the free entry of two crates of documents destined for the archives of this
legation."

1783. To Sarah Storrow

Madrid, Nov. 23. 1844

My dear Sarah,
A morning or two Since the French ambassador entered my apartment,
bearing your most acceptable and delightful letter. He never made himself
so welcome. You did well to let so much of your letter be about darling
little Kate; you never can write enough to me about her. I cannot tell

you how the little creature has wound herself round my heart. The account you gave of her conduct after my departure; and her attempts to console you with the assurance that I would come again brought tears into my eyes. She certainly is a most intelligent little being, full of heart and soul. I think if I had her here I should perfectly idolize her; and should hardly be able to put her *in the closet*, let her be ever so naughty. I amuse myself continually in recalling her whims, and humors, and her mimickrys, for ·which last she is quite remarkable. I have laughed repeatedly at recalling her putting her doll in my arms to go *do do*, and ⟨the⟩ ↑her↓ authoritative air; ⟨and th⟩ and the motion of her hand and ↑the↓ hush! hush! when I attempted to speak or sing. I did not understand it at the time. I now find it must be a mimickry of Elizas manner of commanding silence when she was lulling the baby to sleep. What nursery gossip this is—but I[1] this letter is only meant for yourself, who are as foolish about Kate as I am. Dont repeat my nonsense to any one else.

I am happy to tell you that my ankles are ⟨f⟩ more free from irritation at present that they have been for months past; and yet I have given them severe trials. About two or three days after my arrival there was a Besa manos,[2] where I had to be on my legs for two or three hours, and in the evening a grand ball given by Genl Narvaez at which the queen and Royal family were present, and where I had to be again on my legs from ten oclock until three in the morning. I went home excessively leg weary and with the idea that I should be laid up for a week and put back for a month in my cure. No such thing—the next day my ankles were free from inflammation and have been improving ever since. I am convinced it was the humidity and chilliness in France and England that put me back repeatedly and retarded my cure. A complete change has taken place in my local malady since I have got into this dry climate and genial temperature and I now feel sanguine of soon getting completely rid of the enemy.

I shall not be able to write home by the steamer of the first; so I beg you to give your mother tidings of my safe arrival here and of my well being. I shall send her a pacquet by the Great Western, in which I will give her an account of the Besa manos; the grand ball &c as she delights in court fetes and ceremonials. We are likely to have a gay court this winter. A charming concert was given at the Palace just before my arrival, and preparations are making for a series of royal fetes there; ↑dinners,↓ concerts & balls. One is to take place in the course of a few days. Genl. Narvaez intends soon to give another ball[3]—not so crowded as the recent one, at which there were 1500 people. There will be balls and concerts given by the nobility—the French Ambassador—British Minister &c—in a word, if no political over turn takes place Madrid will present a scene of gaiety and splendor this winter that has not been witnessed in the course of the present century

If I were a younger man I should delight in all this; but I own I now look forward with a little apprehension to all this gaiety, and would prefer a quieter life. The cordial little circle of american friends at Paris ⟨is the⟩ would be far preferable to me ⟨than⟩ ↑to↓ all the splendors of a court and the dissipation of general society. Still there is something peculiar and piquant about the Spanish court and Spanish society, which for a time excites interest; and the fortunes of the young queen ⟨and her⟩ you know form a vein of romance in my eyes which throws a charm over all the affairs of the palace.

Farewell, my dear Sarah—when you receive this letter let Kate have a visit from her doll, and tell her she has just come from "Unty in Spain."

I hope to hear in your next of your evening at Mrs Fishers, and of all our American friends whom you have met there: particularly Mr King, Mr Martin[4] and Mr Kings nephew—

With many kisses to my dear little Kate and my respects to her proud sister

Your affectionate uncle
Washington Irving

PS: I wish to have the name and if possible the address of the French Upholsterer at Madrid, who furnished your appartment

MANUSCRIPT: Yale.

This letter was written on stationery bearing the letterhead, "Legacion de los Estados Unidos."

1. WI probably intended to cancel "I."
2. WI reached Madrid on November 17 and attended the besamanos and the ball on November 19. See WI to Catharine Paris, November 26, 1844; *La Posdata*, November 20, 1844; and *El Castellano*, November 20, 1844.
3. See report in *La Posdata*, November 28, 1844.
4. J. L. Martin was the secretary of the U.S. legation in Paris. See *Almanach de Gotha pour l'Année 1845* (Gotha, [1845]), p. 360.

1784.   To Catharine Paris

Madrid Novr. 26th. 1844

My dear Sister

I arrived in Madrid on the evening of the 17th. after a much more comfortable journey from Paris than I had anticipated, I travelled the whole way day and night, excepting that I made a pause of three days at Bordeaux to rest myself and to enjoy the society of my kind and hospitable friends in that beautiful city. The journey has not produced the irritation of my malady, which I had apprehended. On the contrary, since my arrival in Madrid the irritation which still hung about my ancles while at Paris has declined and I am in hopes of soon getting rid of it entirely. I am inclined to think it was kept up by the humidity and chilliness of the climate in France and England. Whatever may be wanting in Spain we at least have plenty of glorious sunshine here; which I find has a happy influence both on mind and body.

My return home was hailed with transports of joy by the whole household. Juana threw her arms round my neck old Pedro the coachman cut a most uncouth caper and I had much ado to avoid the embraces of the cooks aid de camp and the footboy. I found every thing prepared to make me comfortable for the winter; my bed room fresh papered, curtained and carpeted and looking so cosey, that, were I an old bachelor (which you know I am not,) I should have been tempted to nestle myself in it and give up the world until springtime.

I find Madrid quite grand and gay under the domination of the Moderados. The nobility and the wealthy are vying with each other in display, during this interval of political sunshine: and as many fortunes have been made by men in office and political speculators, all Madrid rattles and glitters with new equipages. One would hardly suspect from the luxury of the capital, that the country was so wretchedly impoverished. The court too, is more gay and magnificent than I have ever known it to be. There had been a grand concert at the Palace a few days before my arrival; and I came just in time for a Besamanos, at the palace, and a ball at General Narvaez' on the young Queens saints day. The Besa manos was crowded, and we were kept standing for a couple of hours, ↑in front of the throne,↓ while the immense throng passed one by one, ⟨to⟩ kneeling and kissing the hands of the Queen and Royal family. I have already given you some idea of the magnificent reception rooms of the palace. They were this day uncommonly brilliant, ⟨for⟩ from the gilded throng which poured through them in bright uniforms or rich embroidery. A long line of peeresses lined the saloon to the left of the Queen and the blaze of their diamonds *almost threw the sunshine into the shade!* During the ceremony a band of music stationed in a distant saloon, performed various pieces and airs from the most popular operas, and the effect of the music floating through these spacious and lofty halls was delicious. Whenever this band paused, ↑it was relieved by↓ another, stationed in the vast place in front of the Palace. I know you will want to know how the Queen and her mother & sister was dressed, and that is always the hardest part of my task. The ⟨Q⟩ young Queen and her sister were in white figured Sattin, with abundance of lace, and long trains of pink silk. They wore Tiaras, pendants and necklaces of diamonds; those of the Queen of course the most magnificent. The Queen-Mother was similarly dressed excepting that her train was of ↑light↓ blue silk. The young queen (I can no longer call her the *little* Queen) ⟨had⟩ ↑is↓ much grown: indeed she is now nearly as tall and as large as her mother; but I cannot say that she looks healthy. Her person is too full: her arms have a swollen look. She evidently is still subject to the cutaneous malady which has so long afflicted her. Her sister, the infanta, is likewise much grown. She is decidedly handsome, with a distinguished air and carriage; but she ⟨p⟩ is pale and does not appear to be of a strong constitution.

In the evening was the ball at the ⟨palace⟩ ↑Hotel↓ of General Narvaez;[1] at which the Queen and Royal family were present; a compliment rarely paid to a subject at this punctilious court. Though the ⟨pa⟩ Hotel of Genl Narvaez is of great size; built round an open court, with great saloons, yet it was excessively crowded, there being about fifteen hundred persons present. The General is of a swelling, magnificent spirit and does not regard expense; and certainly nothing had been spared to make this entertainment worthy of the Royal presence. An inner room, at the end of the principal saloon, was appropriated to the Queen and Royal family, with such of the Royal household as were in attendance on them; and to the members of the Corps diplomatique, who are expected to be near the Royal person. I had great difficulty in making my way through the crowded saloons to the Royal ⟨chambre⟩ presence. The young Queen ⟨was in⟩ had laid aside ↑her↓ state dress of the morning and was arrayed simply, but becomingly in white. Her principal ornament was a necklace of Six rows of pearls with a splendid diamond clasp. She was in high glee. Indeed I never saw a School girl at a school ball enjoy herself more completely. A Royal quadrille was formed in the saloon just in front of the presence chamber: in the first quadrille Genl Narvaez danced with the Queen. Count Bresson (the French Ambassador) with the Queen Mother; the Portuguese Minister with the Infanta: others of the diplomatic corps & of the Royal household, with the princesses, (daughters of Don Francisco)[2] the Princess Carini, The French Ambassadoress &c There were blunders in the quadrille which set the little Queen laughing; and queer old fashioned dancing on the part of the Portuguese Minister, which encreased her risability: she was at times absolutely convulsed with laughter; and throughout the whole evening shewed ⟨the⟩ ↑a↓ merriment ⟨of a⟩ that was quite contagious. I have never seen her in such a joyous mood, having chiefly seen her on ceremonious occasions, and had no idea that she had so much real *fun* in her disposition. She danced with various members of the diplomatic corps; and about four oclock in the morning, when she was asked if she could venture upon another dance; oh yes, she said, she could dance eight more if necessary. The Queen Mother, however, got her away between four and five. I was repeatedly asked to take part in the Royal Quadrille, but pleaded my lameness as an excuse; for I do not know whether my *years* would have been a sufficient apology where royalty was in question. I left the ball about three Oclock in the morning, and having been on my legs at that, and the Besa Manos, almost ever since one Oclock on the preceding day—I expected to be laid up with inflammation of the ancles. To my great surprise and satisfaction I have experienced no ill effects; and ever since the symptoms of my malady have been declining.

I have given you but the beginning of court gaieties. Tomorrow the Corps diplomatique are invited to a Royal dinner at the Palace, which I am curious to see,—having never been present on an occasion of the kind at this court. There is talk also of a succession of concerts and balls at the Palace; of another ball at Genl Narvaez,[3] and of other entertainments in the court circle—unless some conspiracy or insurrection should break out to throw every thing in confusion. Every thing is undertaken here with such a proviso; and a lady who was preparing for the grand ball of Genl Narvaez expressed her fears to me that we should all be blown up there; a plot having been discovered some months since to blow the general up at his lodgings. [*end of MS at Va.—Barrett*]

Novr. 29th.   The royal banquet on the 27th. was one of the grandest fêtes I have ever witnessed. The guests assembled at the palace, according to invitation, at half past six. It is difficult to give any thing like an adequate idea of these state ceremonials to one who has not a tolerable idea of the Royal palace, on which so much of their effect depends. It is the most magnificent palace ⟨that I have seen⟩ in Europe, as far as I have seen. Fancy an edifice ↑much↓ larger in front than our City Hall, and forming a square, ⟨[*unrecovered*]⟩ the sides and rear equal to the front; and all built round spacious interior paved courts. You may imagine then what great ranges of apartments it admits of. In fact only a portion of it is open and lighted up on each occasion, yet the suites of saloons and chambres thus thrown open are immense. On arriving at the Palace we ascended the grand and eventful staircase, so often mentioned in my letters; on each side ⟨were⟩ was a row of lacqueys, in royal livery, standing like statues on every second or third step, holding large flambeaux; with these were intermingled halberdiers, who struck the end of their halberds on the pavement ⟨as e⟩ in salutation, as each ⟨p⟩ guest of note passed by. The number of guests was upwards of a hundred; composed of the ⟨principal⟩ Cabinet ministers, the principal dignitaries of the government, the Diplomatic Corps, with their ladies, (such as had any) and the ladies in attendance upon the royal family. The company assembled in two ⟨of the⟩

↑contiguous↓ Saloons; and, being all in uniforms, made a brilliant appearance. The number of ladies was limited, being ↑as I observed↓ merely those of the Diplomatic Corps, and those in attendance on the Royal family; as, to venture beyond those limits, would have involved the necessity of innumerable invitations among the nobility to avoid creating jealousies and giving offence. All the places at table had been assigned according to strict etiquette and the laws of precedence. The Chief officer of the Queen Mothers household came round with a written paper on which was noted who were to take in the several ladies to the banquet room, and where each was to be seated. according to this arrangement the French ambassador, being the representative of a monarch, was to take in the Queen: the rest of the Diplomatic corps ⟨was [*unrecovered*⟩] succeeded according to their official rank and the date of their residence at the court; and it fell to my lot to take in the Princess de Carini, wife of the Neapolitan minister, and to take my seat on the left of ⟨the⟩ Queen Maria Christina. ⟨Herea⟩ I was well pleased with this arrangement as the Princess is very lively and sociable and we are great friends; but here a difficulty occurred; the princess was detained at home by indisposition— This occasioned a flaw in the order of precedence; but it was soon accommodated by substituting Madame Albuquerque, the next in diplomatic rank to the Princess de Carini, Nothing, as you may suppose, could have been more gratifying to me.

It was near eight Oclock before we were summoned to the banquetting room. In going to it we passed through a magnificent range of apartments: among others the great Saloon of the throne: all were brilliantly lighted, and ⟨I was⟩ you may imagine the effect of such a procession, through those vast and lofty chambers; of the various groupes of guards, domestics &c I never saw any thing more stately. The banquet was given in an immense hall of a quadrangular form, ⟨and⟩ with vaulted ⟨and paint⟩ cieling lofty as that of a church and painted with al↑l↓egorical designs. It is called the hall of the columns; from the noble pillars which sustain the vaults. The tables surrounded the hall thus   with openings on each side for the guests ⟨to⟩ seated within the circle to enter, and for the servants to go to and fro. The Queen was seated at No 1. and the Queen Mother at No 2. the guests arranged themselves on both sides of the tables (that is to say, outside and inside of the circle[)], ⟨according to it⟩ in the places assigned them. The distance across, from Queen to Queen, was about eighty or ninety feet. The table was splendidly set out; the vast hall lighted up by a great number of chandaliers; candelabras &c and the tables were served by a legion of Servants in rich court liveries; blue coats; with scarlet under clothes; ⟨all⟩ the coats, waistcoats and small clothes all decorated with broad gold lace. During the repast a band of music in an outer hall; performed favorite airs from the most fashionable operas. The band was composed entirely of wind instruments, and the effect was delightful: the music being softened by distance so as not to stun the ear nor ⟨interrupt⟩ drown conversation. My seat at table was to the left of the Queen mother, between her and Madame Albuquerque. ⟨On the other side of the⟩ Across the table just opposite me was the Queens sister, the Infanta, and next to her Genl Narvaez, who had brought her in. My position was most agreeable. The Queen Mother was extremely affable and conversed with that amiability and grace for which she is celebrated. The expression of her countenance as she converses is quite winning and her smile is fascinating, yet I would not have you suppose that she is mannered and artificial; nothing can be more easy, simple and natural than her whole deportment. She conversed alternately with the Portuguese minister who was seated on her right (being my elder in office) and myself; and as the ⟨d⟩ Repast lasted for nearly a couple of hours, you may easily suppose that I had considerable conversation with her. She amused me with an account of ⟨the⟩ a lesson the young Queen & the infanta had had in shooting at a mark. The fears of the latter on first handling fire arms, her crying, before she could be prevailed upon to pull trigger, and her subsequent hardihood; having succeeded in hitting a paper which was put up as a mark. I presume as the Queen and her sister have to attend reviews and military ceremonies where there is much firing of musquetry & cannon, it is thought advisable to accustom them to the Sound; and, indeed, in this country of plots, insurrections and revolutions, it behoves even princesses to know something of the use of fire arms. The young Queen and the Infanta have practiced riding on horseback since the return of their mother. I asked the latter if the Queen had courage on horse back: "Yes," said she, "if anything rather too much." I told her one could hardly have too much, as ⟨th⟩ in courage on horseback consisted safety.—I am told in fact that the little Queen is quite a bold rider and continually leaves her more timid sister behind.

In the course of conversation the Queen mother asked me whether I had been at Naples, and finding that I had we had much to say about that city; about Italy in general and when she learnt that I had been in Sicily; that cried she is my native country. I was born at Palermo. Having visited that beautiful city during the festivities of Carneval I retained a lively recollection of it and of its mercurial inhabitants.

In the midst of our Conversation there was a sudden alarm throughout the assemblage. The young queen was taken unwell ⟨and left the table⟩, rose from table and left the banquetting room. Every body started up; ⟨Some⟩ Genl Narvaez and several of the officers of the court and ladies in attendance hurried out; there was an anxious pause. The Queen Mother begged us all to resume our seats, she was sure it was nothing serious. After a time one messenger after another came hurrying back ⟨; the⟩

with intelligence to the Queen Mother, ⟨it was n⟩ the Queen was better: it was a slight inconvenience and had passed away. The fact at length came out; the little queen had been too tightly laced: They had endeavored to make a *fine figure* of her: She had borne with the ⟨in⟩ uncomfortableness as long as possible, but at length ⟨had to⟩ was nearly overcome and had to seek relief. The last messenger brought word that being put quite at ease in her dress she had entirely recovered. "Well" said the Queen Mother ↑smiling↓—"tell her to leave her dress loose, to put on a shawl and to come back." In a little while the young queen returned to the banquetting hall, not ⟨with a sha⟩ envelloped in a shawl, but free from the misery of a fine figure—It was nearly ten Oclock before we left the dining hall, when we adjourned to a distant saloon where coffee was served up; and where the Queen and the rest of the Royal family went about, conversing with the various guests. The young Queen was in high good humor, and conversed in a sociable way, quite different from the formal and vapid commonplace which takes place on more ceremonious occasions. In fact this banquet, and the ball of the other evening, have given me quite a familiar opportunity of seeing the Royal family in their natural characters, and have impressed me most favorably with respect to the young Queen. I have always heard her kind and amiable disposition extolled by those about her: but I had no idea she had so much real merriment of heart.

After remaining upwards of an hour in the withdrawing room; where as much easy conversation prevailed as at an ordinary evening party; the Royal family made their curtsies and retired; and the assemblage broke up; though not the least picturesque part of the evening was the breaking up; When the guests strolled in gilded groupes about those magnificent Saloons and stair cases; loitering and chatting, until their carriages should be announced.

Thus, my dear Sister, I have endeavored to give you a familiar idea of a Royal banquet, and the interior of a Royal palace. I am affraid, if any strange eye should peruse these domestic scribblings, I should be set down as one infatuated with courts and court ceremonials; but these are intended only for your eye my dear Sister, and for the domestic little circle of the Cottage; and to gratify that curiosity which those who live in the quiet and happy seclusion of the country, have to learn the reality about Kings and Queens, and to have a peep into the interiors of their abodes. I had nearly forgotten to tell you that on the present occasion the Queen and her sister were dressed in flowered brocade, with a white ground; and wore wreathes of roses and diamonds. The Queen Mother was in puce coloured velvet; with a band of diamonds round her head, and ⟨a small coronet of diamonds⟩ her hair gathered behind into a small ⟨&⟩ coronet of diamonds.

It was eleven oclock before we left the palace.

I must now conclude this most royal epistle—charging you not to shew all this gossipping about ⟨Kings &⟩ Queens and Royal palaces to any one out of the family circle—

I received yesterday your letter of the 28th. and 29th. of October[4] by which I find you are comfortably established in ⟨your⟩ the same winter quarters you had last year. I think you were right in removing to the city; where you have daily visits from friends and connexions, to keep you from feeling lonely during the seclusion of winter.

Give my love to "all bodies"

> Your affectionate brother
> Washington Irving

P S. I had nearly forgotten to tell you that my ankles continue in a very prosperous state; so that I trust I shall soon conquer the last lingerings of my malady.

DOCKETED: To Mrs Paris

MANUSCRIPT: Va.–Barrett (*MS p. 1*); Yale (*remainder of MS*).   PUBLISHED: PMI, III, 364–67 (in part); *Yale Review*, 17 (October, 1927), 111–14 (in part); LSS, pp. 70–75 (in part).

This letter was enclosed with WI's letter to Sarah Storrow, November 30, 1844. The first page of the manuscript dated November 26, 1844, was separated from the remainder of what WI wrote on that date, and the portion dated November 29 was separated from the earlier segment of the letter. At the center top of page 1 of the manuscript dated November 29 is written "[1844 / STW]," indicating that Stanley T. Williams had dated that part of the letter.

1. Located on the Calle de la Luna. See Bowers, *Spanish Adventures of WI*, p. 235; *La Posdata* and *El Castellano*, November 20, 1844.

2. The two older daughters of Francisco de Paula, the ones most likely to be at the ball, were Isabella (1821–1897) and Josepha (1827–1910). See Aronson, *Royal Vendetta*, genealogical chart on end papers.

3. It was held on November 27. See *La Posdata*, November 28, 1844.

4. This letter has not been located.

1785.   *To Francisco Martínez de la Rosa*

Madrid 28th November 1844

His Excy / Don Francisco Martinez de la Rosa / First Minister of State

Sir

I have the honor to transmit to your Excy the Commission of Patrick I. Devine[1] whom the President of the United States has appointed Consul for the Port of Sagua la Grande[2] in Cuba; and to request that the Regium Exequatur may be issued recognizing him as such.

I take this occasion to call the attention of your Excy to the usage of the Spanish Govt of levying certain fees of office on the emission of its Exequaturs. It is a usage at total variance with that of the U. S. which never exacts any charge whatever from the Consular officers of Spain or of any other nation, for similar documents nor for their promulgation through the journals which publish the official acts of Govt. As it is in the interest of two nations so cordially allied as Spain and the U. S., to maintain strict reciprocity in all things, the Government of the latter felt persuaded that it had but to point out the existence of this inequitable and vexatious exaction to have it instantly abrogated. Accordingly, in 1830, Mr Van Ness then Minister of the U. S. at this Court was instructed to make a formal application that this tax might cease. The reply of the Spanish Minister of State, was, the fees complained of were of "old established usage" and were tacitly submitted to by all foreign Consuls. The usage, therefore, has been continued and has become more and more irksome to the Govt of the U. S.; for, independent of the want of equity in the case, the tax thus levied, though small in amount is constantly productive of inconvenience to the U. S. in its arrangements with its Consular officers.

I am, therefore, instructed by my Govt to say that the reason given by the Govt of Spain for declining the application of Mr Van Ness is quite ↑un↓satisfactory and I am instructed furthermore, to protest against the continuance of an exaction petty and vexatious in its nature, derogatory to the well known courtesy and highminded policy of the Spanish Govt and totally inconsistent with the strict reciprocity which should be maintained between the two nations.

I have the honor etc

(signed) Washington Irving.

MANUSCRIPT: NA, RG 84 (letterbook copy); NA, RG 59 (copy, in part).

1. Patrick I. Devine of New York was nominated as U.S. consul for Sagua la Grande, Cuba on December 18, 1844, and rejected by the Senate Commerce Committee on January 27, 1845. See Hasse, Index to U.S. Documents, III, 1747.

2. A port on the northern coast of Cuba, about 150 miles southeast of Havana. The copyist used the spelling "Sagra" instead of "Sagua."

1786. To Sarah Storrow

Madrid, Novr. 30th. 1844

My dear Sarah—

I enclose a long letter for your Mother;[1] which must be my excuse for writing a short one to yourself. I received the day before yesterday your letter of the 23d. giving me anecdotes of our friends in Paris. Every thing relative to the cordial little circle of American friends which I left there is full of interest to me.

You say I "will smile and think you very changeable" in becoming pleased with Miss Fisher on further acquaintance. If I smile it is with real pleasure my dear Sarah at finding that you have acquired so amiable and agreeable a companion, and one who has ample liesure to be frequently with you; and I shall always be glad to find that You are prompt to change false impressions with respect to acquaintances, All I ask is that if you frequently experience such changes of opinion for the better on becoming acquainted with individuals, you will profit by that experience in combatting prejudices, lightly taken up, on superficial observation.

Miss Fisher is just the kind of acquaintance you want. She appears to be cheerful, intelligent and well bred. She is lady like in appearance and deportment. Being resident in Paris she will not prove an emphemeral acquaintance; and being single and unembarrassed by domestic cares, she can devote more time to an intimacy with you than a married lady can. I really think you are fortunate ⟨f⟩ on having so easy and agreeable a companion for your liesure hours and for your promenades; and I am sure you can make your intimacy very acceptable to her. I beg you to thank Mrs Henderson for her kind remembrances and to assure her that I shall not readily forget the brief but pleasant hours I have passed with her in Paris. I should regret them more deeply if I did not look forward to Renewing our Sociability when she She[2] becomes my neighbor on that beautiful farm which she intends to persuade her husband to purchase on the banks of the Hudson.

I regret that I did not make the acquaintances of your friends the Thurneystons while I was in Paris; since they seem so disposed to be friendly with you.

I feel disposed to like every body that likes you my dear Sarah; but in so doing I shall widely extend my circle of loving kindness; for I am sure that every body who knows you well will end by liking you. ⟨I should think⟩ I am pleased with your account of Mr Lutteroth; an old gentlemen of his stamp is one of the most genial companions imaginable. I hope you may have an opportunity of cultivating his acquaintance.

We are to have quite a Musical Season at Madrid this winter. ⟨The⟩ Operas are given as usual at the Circo, where we have had the two noble operas of *Nabuco* (Nebucadnezzar) and *Hernani*,[3] by Verdi, a new composer who promises great things, and whose music is full of ⟨[*unrecovered*]⟩ spirit, beauty, and grandeur. The troupe at this theatre has fallen off, but is to be recruited; ⟨al⟩ and Salvatori, an excellent base, and one of the best actors I have ever seen, is about to return to it. Then a rival troupe is about to open at the Theatre of the Cruz; report speaks highly of it. The tenor will be Moriani,[4] who I believe has been excluded from paris by the manoeuvres of Grisi.[5] That troupe commences with the beautiful operas of Lucretia Borgia[6] and Lucia di Lammermoor. Beside all this we are to have concerts at the palace where they are given in great style, in a magnificent apartment of the palace ⟨whe⟩ consisting of a Suite of eight rooms and Saloons—quite distinct from the great range opened at the late banquet.

I thought to scribble but a hasty line or two when I set down to this letter, and here I am on the fourth page—but I must conclude, as I have other letters to write by this "courier." I shall look forward to your next letter for an account of your French dinner at Mr Mandrons—and of your pedestrian expedition with Miss Fisher to the Legation. Before you write that letter you will have ⟨received⟩ learned the result of the presidential election;[7] which I expect to hear of in the course of a day or two. I shall be curious to know how it is received in the circle at Paris.

Keep my darling little Kate in mind of me if possible; but I fear I shall soon fade from her reccollection. Kiss her and dear little Susie for me, and with kind remembrances to Mr Storrow believe me most affectionately your uncle

Washington Irving

Do not fail to remember me most kindly to the Walshes—You must give me a particular detail of all the lions you see at their promised party. P.S. When you have read the letter to your mother enclose it open, to Birmingham, for your aunt to read it.

Manuscript: Yale.   Published: STW, II, 189 (in part).

WI wrote this letter on official stationery inscribed "Legacion de los Estados Unidos en España."

Above the dateline WI wrote the following directions: "Seal up the envellope directed to Mr Van Wart, and enclose that and the letter to E Irving in the envellope addressed to Mr Miller"

1. This is dated November 26 and 29.
2. WI repeated "She."

3. *Nabucco* or *Nabucodonosor*, a four-act opera by Giuseppi Verdi (1813–1901), was first performed in Milan on March 9, 1842. *Ernani*, based on Victor Hugo's drama, had its premiere in Venice on March 9, 1844. See David Ewen, *The New Encyclopedia of the Opera* (New York, 1971), pp. 469, 216.

4. Napoleone Moriani (1808–1878), who by 1840 was acclaimed the first tenor of Italy, was decorated with the Order of Isabella by the Spanish queen in 1846. See *Grove's Dictionary of Music and Musicians*, ed. Eric Blom, V, 892.

5. Giulia Grisi was the reigning opera singer at the Théâtre des Italiens in Paris at this time. See WI to Pierre M. Irving, October 13, 1843.

6. *Lucrezia Borgia*, a three-act opera by Gaetano Donizetti, was first performed in Milan on December 26, 1833. See Ewen, *New Encyclopedia of the Opera*, p. 390.

7. James K. Polk (1795–1849), the Democratic candidate for president, narrowly defeated Henry Clay, the Whig nominee.

1787. To the Director General of Customs

Madrid 3 de Diciembre de 1844

Al Señor Director Genl de Aduanas

Muy Señor mio: En vista de la proroga de mi franquicia concedidame por el Gobierno de S. M. (Q. D. G.) vengo a rogarle a Vd. se digne comunicarla a las Aduanas de Cadiz e Irun lo mas pronto que sea posible por encontrarse detenidos en dichos puntos varios efectos incluidos en mi lista.

Aprovecho esta ocasion para ofrecer a Vd. las seguridades de mi distinguida consideracion.

B. L. M. de Vd. / su mas ale sego servidor
(signed) Washington Irving

MANUSCRIPT: NA, RG 84 (letterbook copy).

Translation:
"In view of the extension of my exemption conceded to me by the government of her majesty (may God keep her) I beg you to be kind enough to communicate it to the Customs of Cadiz and Irun as soon as possible, as several effects included in my list have been detained at several points."

1788. To Sarah Storrow

Madrid Dec 6 1844

My dear Sarah,

Stormy weather among the mountains has detained the French Courier this week and has rendered "Kates Uncle" rather impatient for your weekly ⟨paper⟩ letter.[1] At length it has arrived and has been received with more than usual welcome. In fact I have been some what out of spirits for a few days past, and in such moods I feel the want of some affectionate heart at hand; and am apt to long for tidings from you and Kate. I have become habituated to the receipt of a weekly letter from you, and the failure of it would cause the most lively disappointment. I hope, therefore that you will continue to be punctual. I believe my visits to Paris do me no good. I find on my return to Madrid I am continually missing my home enjoyments in the Rue de la Victoire, and the cordial little "reunions" of my American friends.

I am delighted to find from Your letter that you have exchanged Such Social visits with Mrs. Ellis,[2] and that Your opinion of her coincides so completely with my own. I think you characterise her ⟨completely admirably [?]⟩ ↑truly,↓ as refined and lady like; free from pretension and remarkable for ⟨the simplicity⟩ her conversational powers; "making such admirable remarks with so much simplicity and ease" If you had seen as much as I have of the brilliant wits and celebrated talkers of Society, you would know the charm of such ⟨inf⟩ natural, unforced and unpretending gaiety, ⟨and⟩ good feeling and good sense as seemed united in the conversation of Mrs Ellis, and I was well pleased to find in the course of my acquaintance with her, a ⟨quiet⟩ gentle but settled feeling of religion which threw a quiet grace over her character. I do not know when I have met with a lady for whom, on so brief an acquaintance, I have concieved a sincerer or more respectful friendship. I trust I am not expressing myself in a tone of gallantry; which ⟨is⟩ would be quite incompatible with the high respect I have for Mrs Ellis. The election of Mr Polk to the presidency will continue Mr King at the French court. I hope Mrs Ellis will continue with him; we shall then have a Legation at Paris of which the Americans may well be proud

You must not suffer yourself to be grieved at the election of Mr Polk. From all that I can learn he is likely to make a very good president. He is well educated;[3] of highly respectable talents; experienced in public life,[4] ⟨and⟩ of most unexceptionable private character; and of amiab[le] [*MS torn*] and gentleman like manners. He has the advantage also of not being a hackneyed politician; but of coming fresh and unshackled before the public. The account Mrs Ellis gives you of his wife[5] I have heard confirmed from other quarters. She is said to be very handsome and well fitted to preside at the "White House."

I have a letter from Pierre M Irving by the last arrival who is anxious that I should prepare to return home; not that he thinks there is any likelihood of my being displaced by the new President but because he thinks (and with reason) that I would be happier among my friends. ⟨Tha⟩ And gladly would I return if I had the means of keeping up my little establishment at Sunny Side; but you know how the cruel malady under which I have suffered for nearly two years past has defeated all those literary plans on which I depended for the means of future support. I have now regained my health and am about to resume my literary occupations, and, if I am spared in office a year or so more, I hope to get my literary concerns in such a state of forwardness ⟨, that⟩ as to be able to return home with the means of providing for those dependant upon me—To return home now would be to return to a state of pecuniary anxiety and embarrassment ⟨;⟩.

I am happy to tell you that the lingering remains of my malady are gradually disappearing. I keep on however in the Steady observance of remedies and shall do so until I have "made assurance doubly sure"[6] and am in no danger of a relapse.

You want to know about my ↑female↓ intimates here. The kindest and those upon whom I most count are Madame Albuquerque and Mrs O'Shea; the latter is the wife of my banker; and a most amiable, gentle and kind hearted person she is, and very lady like. I have others who are very agreeable acquaintances; but with whom I am not on such cordial terms of intimacy. The fair Leocadia Zamora I have seen but once since my return; and that at Genl Narvaez ball: where I had not an opportunity of Speaking to her particularly—I have called on her without finding her at home; and, observing that she appeared to be very much launched in the gay world; I have not followed up the acquaintance as I have a horror of being thought to play the old beau to a young belle.

Social life is rather meagre with me in Madrid; at least I feel it so on returning from Paris. However, I have a great faculty at living alone; and, provided I have plenty of books, and the occasional resource of the Opera, I feel very independent of society. And yet you know I am very socially inclined; but then it is the society of cordial and genial beings that I crave.

I think I feel my separation from you and Kate more since my return from Paris this year than on either of the former occasions. My heart is continually yearning towards you and I am constantly calling up the reccollection of all that darling little creatures odd and amusing, and winning ways. God bless her! if I only had her in my arms at this moment how happy I should be.

Give my kind remembrances to Mrs Henderson and thank her for her friendly reccollections of me. I am glad to hear that she and Mr Henderson still talk of the place upon the banks of the Hudson, and hope that she and I may some day or another tend our sheep together in the pastoral glades of Sleepy Hollow.

I beg you will also remember me to Mrs Fisher who you say speaks so kindly of her. I wish I could have one of her social little American Soirèes here at Madrid.

I wish you would now and then get some little play thing for Kate and give it to her, as just ⟨arrived⟩ sent by *Unty* from Spain. Do keep me as long as possible in her reccollection: though I fear she already begins to forget how I look

God bless you my dear Sarah, Do not fail to write to me by every courier; ⟨and⟩ let your letters be as long as possible and fill them with all kind of Gossip about yourself your children, ⟨and⟩ your visits &c. I am glad your French dinner turned out so pleasant.

Your affectionate uncle
Washington Irving

MANUSCRIPT: Yale.   PUBLISHED: STW, II, 169 (in part).

1. This letter has not been located.

2. Mrs. Ellis was the niece of William King, the American minister in Paris.

3. Polk had graduated in 1818 from the University of North Carolina with honors in mathematics and classics; in 1820 he was admitted to the bar in Tennessee.

4. He had served in Congress from 1825 to 1838 and as governor of Tennessee from 1839 to 1841.

5. Sarah Childers (1803–1891), who married Polk on January 1, 1820, was one of the most popular first ladies.

6. See *Macbeth*, V, i, 83.

1789. To John C. Calhoun

Legation of the United States / Madrid 7th December 1844

No 56 / The Hble / John C. Calhoun / Secretary of State

Sir

I returned to this city a short time since much recruited in health and nearly freed from the malady which has so long harassed me. Since my return I have received your Excellency's Despatch *No 37* enclosing the commission of Patrick I. Devine.

In applying for the Royal Exequatur I have taken occasion to follow your instructions in protesting against the tax levied by this Government on similar documents. I enclose a copy of such part of my note as relates to the subject and shall follow up my written remonstrance by personal representations

You will have seen by the public papers that the late revolutionary attempts[1] in various parts of the Peninsula have been promptly quelled and rigorously punished. They do not seem to have been sympathised in by the people at large, who in fact, are tired and exhausted by past agitations and troubles and are desirous of peace at any price. The party in power rules with a strong hand and having the army at its command and having disarmed the national militia, feels confident of retaining its stern domination. Having managed the elections so as to ensure the almost unanimous vote in the parliamentary bodies, the measures of reform are nearly completed and will leave the Constitution so modified as vastly to increase the power of the Throne and to render the matrimonial question almost independent of the will of the Cortes.

By the way I have just received private information which if true will cause new perplexities as to this all important question. It is said that an arrangement formed under the auspices of the Queen Mother, had nearly been completed for the marriage of the young Queen with her uncle the Count Trapani;[2] that the Pope[3] had with much difficulty been propitiated and was about to grant the necessary dispensation, (the parties being within the forbidden bounds of Kindred) when the Austrian Ambassador suddenly interposed, and, in the name of his Sovereign "forbade the bans." The tidings of this untoward event, it is said, have completely disconcerted the plans of the Palace. The chances of Trapani are at an end: indeed, I am told, they had never received the countenance of Narvaez. It is added that a new candidate for the hand of the Queen will be brought forward in the person of the Archduke Frederick, nephew of the Emperor of Austria,[4] who, is said to be about twenty seven years of age, well educated and accomplished, of manly character and who has distinguished himself before Beyrout[?]. His pretensions, it is said, will receive the support of England. If this be true it will bring the diplomacy of France and England in arduous competition at this Court. From some recent symptoms the french influence would seem to be endangered with the ruling party. Spanish pride has been ruffled by certain articles in the french semi-ministerial paper⟨s⟩ the "Journal des Debats" strongly animadverting on the recent measures of the Spanish Government. Recriminations have appeared in the Ministerial journals of Madrid. The Heraldo particularly resents the remarks of the Journal des Debats on the military execution of the son and brother in law of Zurbano[5] and observes: "The Spanish Government ought to investigate whether the journal countenanced by the French Government speaks from its own inspirations or under the inspirations of others. If the first, contempt is all that is merited by language dictated by the most petulant arrogance or the grossest ignorance: if the second; this incident will serve to make our Government regulate its conduct according to the proofs of amity shown it. For our own part we are not accustomed to mingle with passion or acrimony in the affairs of our neighbors; we respect ourselves too much to repay, in the same money, the good offices of the Journal des Debats; but we feel assured that if the Spanish Press should meddle in so strange a manner in the acts of the French Government, and *should reveal certain transactions* ("brechos") and should be less circumspect and generous, in such case the damage received by our neighbors would be more serious than any that could be caused to us by the shots of the Journal des Debats. *If decidedly they throw us the gauntlet, they may be assured we will not suffer it to lie on the ground.*" The passages which I have underlined in the above extract are extremely significant, especially as they are said to have been written under the dictation of Genl Narvaez. They do not speak well for the cordial understanding between the two Governments. As far as our own interests are concerned it may perhaps be more to our advantage that the influence of France should predominate over that of England in the Peninsula; especially as it regards colonial questions; though it is much to be desired that Spain could be free from all foreign influence and have the independent management of her own affairs. Genl Narvaez continues to be the master spirit of the present Government. He is prompt, sagacious daring and domineering. Under his military rule Justice is more apt to make use of her sword than of her balance; the latter being considered too tedious of adjustment for the exigency of the times. The vigor with which he acts, however, and the severity with which he punishes political offences have created for him many deadly enemies among those opposed to him in politics; while the eclat with which he moves, lavish ostentation with ↑which↓ he lives and the degree of state with which he surrounds himself, create rankling jealousy and envy among ⟨his⟩ military rivals in his own party. He is, therefore, in continual danger from secret perfidy more than from open violence. His life has been repeatedly attempted[6] and almost miraculously preserved, while his death would be likely to throw all things here into confusion.

Various capitalists in Madrid interested in the prosperity of Cuba are attempting to arouse the attention of Government and of the public to the State of Affairs in that Island and of the Colonial Affairs of Spain in general. A weekly page of the Ministerial paper, the Heraldo, has been secured for the purpose; in which articles will appear calculated to set the statistics of Colonial Trade in a proper light. I have conversed with a gentleman who takes a leading part in the measure, and, who, having resided for some years in the United States is well affected to our country and well acquainted with the nature and extent of its intercourse with the Spanish Colonies. I have promised to furnish him with any information on the subject which I might meet with in American newspapers and public documents. I am in hopes that this may prove a favorable channel for conveying facts to the Spanish Government and people calculated to give them a right understanding of our commercial relations, to convince them of the loyalty of our intentions towards their colonial possessions and to put them upon their guard against the invidious policy of any other power.

I am respectfully / Your obedient servant.

Washington Irving

DOCKETED: Recd. Feby 22 — / Mr Markoe
MANUSCRIPT: NA, RG 59.   PUBLISHED: Hellman, WI Esquire, pp. 310–13.

Only the signature is in WI's handwriting.

1. Most of the unrest was occurring in Navarre and in the Barcelona area. See *El Castellano*, October 21, 22, 24, November 12, 16, 18, 28, 29, December 2, 3, 1844; London *Times*, October 7, 9, 26, November 5, 6, 8, 25, 27, December 5, 1844.

2. Francisco, Count Trapini (1827–1892) was the younger brother of María Christina.

3. Pope Gregory XVI (1765–1846).

4. Ferdinand I (1793–1875) was emperor of Austria from 1835 to 1848, a period dominated by the absolutist policies of Metternich.

5. An extant file of *El Heraldo* for this period has not been located. Benito Zurbano and an uncle named Martinez were shot on November 24, and his brother Feliciano was executed on November 29, 1844. See *El Castellano*, November 27, 28, 29; *La Gaceta*, December 3; *La Posdata*, November 26, 27, 1844; London *Times*, December 3, 4, 1844; January 29, 1845; *Annual Register of . . . 1844* (London, 1845), p. 269.

6. For a report of one attempt on the life of Narváez, see *El Castellano*, October 28, 1844; London *Times*, November 5, 1844.

1790. To [William R. King]

Madrid Decr 7. 1844

My dear friend & Colleague,

I congratulate you on the election of Mr Polk, as I know, independent of party predilections, You entertain for him sentiments of private esteem and friendship. From all that I can learn of him I trust he will make a good president. I am glad too that he ⟨ca⟩ will come into office, fresh and unshackled; ⟨with his⟩ withers unwrung by party struggles; and his spirit not bowed down by concessions to the vulgar and the ignorant. I doubt whether we have not a better chance for a fair and independent administration from a new man thus suddenly brought forward, than from old and hackneyed candidates, though of Superior abilities. One result of his election is peculiarly satisfactory to me. It will continue you in your post at Paris, which you fill so much to the satisfaction of your countrymen. I hope and trust you ⟨f⟩ will find it more and more to your ⟨lik⟩ taste the longer you occupy it.

I cannot, however, but feel for the defeat and disappointment of poor Clay; who, after the struggle of a life time, had seen the coveted prize snatched away, when it seemed within his grasp, and who has not breath left for another effort. Poor Clay! I cannot but reccollect him in the brightness and freshness of his early carreer when he was foremost among that glorious clique of young statesmen (such as Calhoun, Lowndes, Cheves[1] &c) who led us so gallantly into our last war with Great Britain. I had then a young mans enthusiasm for him and though I have since seen but little of him personally, and the difference of our pursuits has led us widely apart; yet I still retain somewhat of my early impressions concerning him, and whenever his image rises to my mind, it comes as it was in the days of his prime, clothed more or less with the romantic associations of my youth.

How does the winter climate of Paris agree with you? I fear you must suffer from your rheumatism. For my own part I believe the chills and humidity of Paris were injurious to me and retarded me in my convalescence The moment I entered the dry and sunny climate of Spain I began to improve; and I have now almost entirely freed myself from the last lingerings of the malady which held me so long in fetters. I wish you were here to enjoy the sunshine and fine weather of Madrid.

How go on all the affairs of your social circle? I envy you the pleasant gatherings of Americans which you enjoy in Paris. How sterile ↑to me↓ in comparison are the circles of Madrid, where all are strangers. I often recall with "melancholy pleasure" the astronomical evenings I passed with you in your ⟨box⟩ observatory at the opera; where assisted by that far seeing star gazer Mr Martin, we swept the higher regions with our telescopes and scanned all the heavenly bodies. Does the Bird of paradise still figure with full plumage in her nest: I have heard some vague report of her having lost her mate. If so I trust Mr Martin will have the gallantry to bear her consolation. Is the momentous question decided which threatened to shake your legation to its centre—viz. whether

Mrs. W—— was or was not a beauty. For my part I had as little doubt on the subject as if it regarded her husband.

I beg you to remember me most kindly and respectfully to Mrs. Ellis. It was a great matter of regret to me to leave Paris without taking personal leave of one whose amiable and estimable qualities had inspired so high a regard, and whom I might never see again.

Before I conclude I would ask you, if you should at any time meet with ⟨soluti⟩ documents relative to our trade with Cuba; and to our affairs connected with the slave question, that you would ⟨pass me⟩ have the kindness to transmit them to me when you have done with them.

Give my kind regards to Mr Martin and believe me very heartily and truly

Your friend
Washington Irving

P S. I inclose an article cut out of an American Paper relative to Mr Polk. I have prepared a notice of him for the Government paper here; placing his character in a proper light. The same should be done in Paris —London &c.—that at the outset of his carreer his character should be placed above the Calumnies which have been cast upon it by the British press ↑and which have been echoed even in this place.↓ This should be a matter of national pride, not of party feeling.

MANUSCRIPT: NYPL—Seligman Collection.

This letter is written on official stationery inscribed "Legacion / de los / Estados Unidos / en España."

1. Calhoun, William Lowndes (1782–1822), and Langdon Cheves (1776–1857) were all congressmen from South Carolina who vigorously supported the idea of war with Great Britain. See WI to Henry Clay, November 1, 1812.

1791. To Francisco Martínez de la Rosa

Madrid 19 de Diciembre de 1844

Al Exmo Senor Don F. M. de la Rosa / Primer Ministro de Estado

Muy Señor mio: Tengo el honor de solicitar de V. E. el Regium Exequatur para el Señor Wright (James J.),[1] cuya comision incluyo, nombrado por el Presidente de los Estados Unidos Consul en el puerto de Santiago de Cuba

Me aprovecho etc.

(signed) Washington Irving

MANUSCRIPT: NA, RG 84 (letterbook copy).

Translation:
"I have the honor of soliciting from your excellency the regium exequatur for Mr. Wright (James J.), whose commission I include herewith, named by the president of the United States consul in the port of Santiago of Cuba."

1. James Wright (d. 1846) of Ohio served from December, 1844, until his death about a year later. See Hasse, *Index to U.S. Documents*, III, 1748.

1792. To Sarah Storrow

Madrid. Decr 20th. 1844

My dear Sarah,

I received your letter of the 14th.[1] late last evening when I had given up all hope of its arriving on account of the badness of the weather; which for several days past has been as stormy here as it appears to have been throughout most parts of Europe. I have already read your letter over three if not four times, ⟨t⟩so you may imagine whether or not your letters have the ⟨ful⟩ power of interesting, which you seem to doubt. My dear Sarah, any thing from you, and about you is. full of interest to me, and the only fault I find with your letters is, that they are so short; but I should find the same fault if they were ten times as voluminous.

There is some postponement or delay in the anticipated festivities of the palace and the Court. I do not know whether any political reason is at the bottom of it, as this court is full of mystery and intrigue. In the meantime there is considerable social life in the diplomatic circle. Frequent dinners, and evening gatherings. Whist parties are held Mondays and Fridays at the French Embassy and Wednesday evenings at Mr O'Shea's the Diplomatic bankers. These are very pleasant gatherings as we are all well acquainted with each other. To day (Friday) I dine with the French Ambassador and pass the evening there. To morrow I give a Diplomatic dinner to the heads of the various missions, to Genl Narvaez, Martinez de la Rosa &c, after this dinner of ceremony I intend to give several social dinners,—round tables of a dozen—which are always the pleasantest. My china arrived a few days since, all in good order—

In preparing for a dinner party I miss Alexander Hamilton who used to take all the trouble of the arrangement off my hands and delighted in the occupation. Indeed I miss him continually in my household ⟨as we⟩ concerns and my fireside liesure of which he was the life. His bright happy spirit and animated intelligence used to spread sunshine around him.

Have you read in the papers of the enormous robbery at the bank of our old friend Mr Rogers?[2] I am in hopes, however, that measures will be taken by the Bank of England by cancelling the 1,000 £ bills, of which there were 30—to render the greater part of the amount stolen valueless in the hands of the robbers. It must have been a great shock to Mr Rogers; accustomed as he is to quiet unruffled life. The bank too was one of these quiet little, old fashioned, old gentlemanlike banks, that did business so snugly, and cautiously, and on so moderate a scale, that one had no idea there was steam enough in its boiler for such a "blow up"

You are right in distrusting the account of the insensibility evinced by the Young Queen in the supplication of the Mother of Zurbano.[3] Every thing is discolored here by party. She is amiable and kind hearted; at least so I am told by all those who are about her. ⟨The death of the⟩ She was fully disposed to ⟨pardon the⟩ grant the pardon applied for; but she had to yield to the policy of her Ministers; who ⟨we⟩ had just recieved news of the murder of an officer of the crown by the insurgents; and considered an act of rigor called for. ⟨A queen Sovreign has not always⟩ Sovreigns ⟨have⟩ ↑are↓ not always able to indulge their own will in such cases but have to consult the will of their cabinets. I think the execution of the prisoners a very unwise measure and calculated to cast unmerited odium upon the young Queen: but ministers here are surrounded by danger and conspiracy and think their safety depends upon ↑stern and↓ vigorous ⟨me⟩ action in punishing delinquents.

I am sorry to learn that the Americans begin to grumble at Mr King for not keeping open house for their accommodation; but it is what I expected. They think a minister is bound to waste his private fortune in giving them dinners and ⟨dances⟩. balls. They give Republican pay and demand aristocratic entertainment. Mr King, I am sure will attend faithfully to the *business* of his mission, and the *interests* of his country and his country men. As to those ↑idlers↓ who want a "*little dance*," let them take it in the ante chamber.

Decr 21. I had a very pleasant dinner yesterday at the French Ambassadors; at whose house I have always a cordial welcome. Mr Livingston & myself hurried away immediately after dinner to see for the second time at the theatre of the Cruz the opera of Lucrezia Borgia.[4] How often I thought of Grisi in the course of the opera and thanked her in my heart for having prevented Moriani from appearing on the Paris boards. What a treat she has unintentionally given us at Madrid. I was if possible, more charmed and touched by Moriani's singing and acting than the first time I saw him—He has wonderful requisites for the stage. Voice, countinance, person, intellect and action. I never witnessed such rapturous applause at Madrid as followed some of his scenes. The prima donna too, is an actress of the highest merit. She is tall, well formed, handsome, with a very expressive countenance, and plays with almost as much soul as Grisi. I do not know when I have had a purer treat at the theatre than last night. The same evening a new opera by *Verdi* was brought out at the Circo. "The Lombards in the first Crusade"[5] I am told it is splendid as to music, and was produced with great effect. So that you see we are "up to the ears" in Italian music here.

Today my house is topsy turvy, preparing for the Diplomatic dinner. My Kind friends Madame Albuquerque and Mrs O'Shea assist me with their counsels and with the loan of such things as may be wanting to fit my table out in proper style.

I was pleased to find by your letter that Miss Fisher had passed a day with you; and that you were to drive out occasionally with Mrs Ellis. You are fortunate in having two such acquaintances on such easy and social terms. I beg you to make my kind remembrances to them, and to let me hear all about them; but particularly about Miss Fisher.

I regret to hear such bad accounts of the health of the Walsh's, but hope before this reaches you they will have recovered from their colds and rheumatisms. I beg you to remember me kindly to them and to their beautiful little daughter.

Farewell—I must look to the affairs of my household—Would that this big dinner was over! Kiss my dear little Kate and Susy for me— I can easily believe that the latter is growing in beauty, and hope she may equal her sister in "grace and ⟨godliness⟩ goodliness." Does Kate still continue to walk "Hombod" occasionally. I fear she will lose all the accomplishments I taught her

Your affectionate uncle
Washington Irving

ADDRESSED: / Madame / Madame Storrow / No. 4 Rue de la Victoire / à Paris
MANUSCRIPT: Yale.   PUBLISHED: Simison, *Keogh Papers*, pp. 226–30.

1. This letter has not been located.

2. On November 23, 1844, £40,000 in Bank of England notes and gold was taken from the bank owned by Samuel Rogers, the English poet, *bon vivant*, and friend of WI. See London *Times*, November 26, 28, 1844; *Annual Register of . . . 1844* (London, 1845), p. 141.

3. The queen and the queen mother rejected the pleas of Zurbano's relatives, as WI suggests, for reasons of political expediency. See *La Posdata*, November 26, 27, 1844; London *Times*, December 3, 4, 1844.

4. See *La Gaceta*, December 20, 1844 for an announcement of the performance.

5. Verdi's opera *I Lombardi alla prima crociata* was first performed on February 11, 1843, at La Scala in Milan. See *Grove's Dictionary of Music and Musicians*, V, 368. For a long article on the operas then being performed in Madrid, see *La Gaceta*, December 23, 1844.

1793. *To John C. Calhoun*

Legation of the United States / Madrid 24th December 1844

No 57 / The Hble John C. Calhoun / Secretary of State

Sir

Since the date of my last I have received Despatch No 38 containing the commission of James J. Wright as Consul at Santiago de Cuba and have applied for his Exequatur.

The flour trade to Cuba has recently been made the subject of discussion in the Madrid papers[1] and will probably be brought before the Cortes. The inhabitants of Cuba wish that the duties on flour both from Spain and the United States should be reduced. The exporters of flour from Spain wish the reduction to be exclusively in their favor, pretending that the enormous difference which at present exists between the duty of two dollars and fifty cents per barrel on spanish and ten dollars per barrel on American flour is not sufficient to give the former an equal chance in the market. I forward three or four Madrid papers containing articles which have appeared on each side of the question. I have furnished some facts and hints for the writers in favor of American interests and shall watch the future course of the question. I transmit also this day's *Gaceta de Madrid*[2] containing the project of a law for the suppression of the slave trade made by the Minister of State in conformity to Treaty stipulations between Spain and Gt Britain and presented by him for the approbation of the Cortes.

I am, Sir, respectfully / Your most obedient servant
Washington Irving

DOCKETED: Recd—27 Jany. Mr Markoe
MANUSCRIPT: NA, RG 59.

Only the signature is in WI's handwriting.

1. See *La Posdata*, December 17, 19, 21; and *El Castellano*, December 20, 1844.
2. A clerk has added a note in the right margin: "Paper not recd."

1794. To Francisco Martínez de la Rosa

Madrid 26 de Diciembre de 1844

Al Excmo Señor Don F. M. de la Rosa / Ministro de Estado

El infrascrito Ministro Plenipotenciario y Enviado Extraordinario de los Estados Unidos tiene la honra de solicitar del Excmo. Señor Don F. M. de la Rosa, Ministro de Estado, el Regium Exequatur para el Sr. I. B. Lacey nombrado por el Presidente de los Estados Unidos Consul en el puerto de Nuevitas en la Isla de Cuba.
Aprovecha el infrascrito etc.

(signed) Washington Irving

MANUSCRIPT: NA, RG 84 (letterbook copy).

Translation:
"The undersigned minister plenipotentiary and envoy extraordinary of the United States has the honor of soliciting from the Honorable Señor Don F. M. de la Rosa, Minister of State, the regium exequatur for Mr. I. B. Lacey named by the president of the United States consul in the port of Nuevitas in the Island of Cuba."

1795. To Alexander Burton et al.

Madrid 27th. December 1844
Circular

Alexr Burton Esqre	Consul	Cadiz
George Read Esqre	"	Malaga
Paul Pon Esqre	"	Barcelona
Maximo Aguirre Esqre	"	Bilbao
Arthur Macculloch	"	Alicante
Joseph Cullen	"	Teneriffe

Sir,
It is desirable that this Legation be put in possession of the most detailed and accurate information of the Commerce between the U. S. and Spain during the present year of 1844.

I am Sir respectfully / Your obt servant
(signed) Washington Irving

MANUSCRIPT: NA, RG 84 (letterbook copy).

1796. To Francisco Martínez de la Rosa

Madrid 27th December 1844

His Excy / Don Fro M de la Rosa

Sir

I have observed for some days past a discussion in the public journals of the policy of altering the duties at present exacted on Spanish and foreign flours on being admitted into the Island of Cuba. As this is a question which vitally affects the trade of the U. S. with that Island it is one in which the Govt of the U. S. will naturally desire the earliest information in order to regulate its own action. I should be much obliged therefore to your Excellency if it would suit your convenience to let me know whether there is a probability of the subject being acted upon in the Cortes and to give me an intimation of what is likely to be the course of policy of her Majesty's Govt in the matter.

I remain very respectfully etc

(signed) Washington Irving

MANUSCRIPT: NA, RG 84 (letterbook copy).

1797. To Sarah Storrow

Madrid. Decr. 29 1844

My dear Sarah,

A thousand thanks for your long and delightful "rigmarole" letter;[1] which I have enjoyed the more highly from its being rigmarole; that is to say, written offhand from the thought and feeling of the moment; the only way a familiar letter should be written. I have read it over and over, as I do all your letters; for every line of them gives some pleasant information, or is stamped with the image of yourself. You cannot think what a delight your letters are to me. I look forward to them with anticipations of pleasure; and Thursday, when they generally arrive, is a bright day in the week to me.

I am gratified by the accounts you give me of your social meetings with Mrs Ellis, Mrs Henderson and Miss Fisher. You are fortunate in having such intimates. They will give quite a zest to your winter parties. I received a most cordial reply from Mr King to my letter; it was written in his own frank, sensible and gentleman like style; with a little touch, in one part, of that quiet humor which we have noticed in him. In reply to a question I put to him as to the state of the dispute about Mrs Wilsons beauty, he observes "the beauty of Mrs W is as much the subject of contest as ever, but I am convinced that Martin is jealous of the favor I have found in the eyes of the fair lady and that Mrs Ellis is envious of her superior charms—so I am determined not to be flouted out of my admiration—"

This is all very well, excepting as it regards Mrs Ellis, who, I think is brought in very ungraciously—but it is not given to all uncles ⟨like myself⟩ to know, like myself, how to appreciate a niece properly. By the bye, I should like to know more ⟨of th⟩ about the history of Mrs Ellis, and of that Uncle who cherished and brought her up. She certainly does credit to his care, for she is well bred and evidently well informed, with all the tone and manner of a person accustomed to be in easy intelligent Society. ⟨The⟩ And then the General[2] sending his son abroad under her care shews the confidence he has in her judgement. I think the General must be something of *a character,* as his brother the minister is—and I trust of the same generous stamp, a real cavalier. I was much amused with your detecting the treason of the Nephew who sat so demurely like Io in a corner, ↑in the box at the opera,↓ listening to the diplomatic ⟨discussions⟩ ↑conferences↓ of his Uncle, Mr Martin and Myself, as we gravely discussed the comparative beauty of the ladies. The villainy of this youth to make sport of such serious matters! But he has taken a leaf out of Mrs Ellis's Diplomacy, who makes no scruple to betray the table discussions of the Legation.

My last letter was written in the midst of preparations for my diplomatic dinner. The dinner went off extremely well. Mrs O Shea and Madame Albuquerque had looked in, to see that the table was well arranged. My cook gained great credit; my servants acquitted themselves well, and my wines were pronounced excellent. So that affair is happily accomplished.

On Christmas day I partook of a Sociable dinner of eight persons at the Albuquerques, and a very pleasant dinner it was.

On New Years day I am to dine with Genl Narvaez. It will be a diplomatic dinner with a ball in the evening; for the General does every thing in a grand style.

I received a few days since a letter from Pierre M Irving on the same subject mentioned by your Mother, the renting of the cottage &c—That must be left entirely to the wishes of the inhabitants of the cottage. If they find it lonely to be so many months of the year shut up in the country, ⟨they may⟩ and if your Uncle E. I. would like it, they may remove to the City; but it must not be through motives of economy, and at the sacrafice of inclination. If my health continues good and I am ⟨up⟩ able to continue my present exercise of my pen I trust in the course of the year to make a great change in my pecuniary resources and prospects; ⟨at any⟩ At the end of that time I shall be likely to know what I can afford and what I cannot afford for a continuance—and will then shape my expenses and my mode of living accordingly. In the interim it is not worth while to derange domestic affairs, for any temporary saving—which could not amount to much.

I have considered the cottage as a quiet retreat for your Mother & your uncle, and do not like to have it disturbed. I should not relish the idea too of your uncle, with his growing infirmities, being obliged to engage once more in the busy turmoil of the city. He seems to be happy where he is; and it is a source of happiness to me to think he is so. I regret, however, that the ⟨cott⟩ little modest domains of the Cottage are likely to be encompassed by the Rural retreats of the Jones's: who I am sorry to say, appear to have carried back a great deal of silly pretension and unfitting ostentation from Europe. I hope their bewigged and bepowdered coachman has been Snow balled.

You give me the first news of the marriage of William Irving.[3] The Silence of the rest of the family convinces me the match is a bad one. It could hardly be otherwise. Thank heaven there is but one more of your uncles sons to get married.[4] What a numerous and poverty stricken race are likely to be the descendants of Anaky Jants[?]![5]

Many Kisses to Kate and Susy / Your aff. uncle
Washington Irving

P.S. In a late letter I expressed a wish that Mr Storrow would procure and forward to me a pair of Gilt Candalabras; similar to those he purchased for me in 1842. They are for the Albuquerques. I wish to have them forwarded as early as possible; as the ⟨time⟩ term of my privilege to enter articles free of duty is drawing to a close.

MANUSCRIPT: Yale.

1. This and the other letters mentioned by WI in this letter have not been located.
2. Thomas D. King (1779–1854), a soldier from North Carolina.
3. William Irving (1811–1854), fourth son of Ebenezer, married Sarah Ann Mann of Boston in the summer of 1844.
4. Washington Ebenezer Irving (1822–1894), who was to marry Guadeloupe Gomez.
5. On the lower left margin of the fourth page appears the following canceled phrase: "P. S. In a late letter I".

1798. To Sarah Storrow

Madrid Jany 2d. 1845

A happy new Year to you and yours, my dear Sarah; and many happy ones to follow it. I have just received yours of the 28th.[1] in which you complain of not receiving your weekly letter. I wrote one, notwithstanding, on the saturday of the previous week. ↑(the 21st. December)↓ when in the midst of preparations for a diplomatic dinner, which I gave on that day. The servant may not have taken the letter to the French Embassy in time, in which case you will receive two letters this present week. I believe I have not missed writing every week since my return.

Yesterday I took my New Years dinner with Genl Narvaez, and a grand dinner it was.[2] We sat down forty persons to table, ladies and gentlemen. These were part of the Diplomatic Corps; all the Cabinet Ministers and various dignitaries of the Court, army &c. ⟨The dinner⟩ The banquet was given in excellent style. The General had ⟨g⟩ received a complete table service from Paris, very beautiful and ⟨in⟩ very tasteful. ⟨[unrecovered]⟩ His hotel was brilliantly lighted up, and the whole went off admirably. I was fortunately placed at table. I took in the Countess of Montijo; one of the leaders of fashion here, and a woman of intellect and talent. She speaks english well, and has always been very cordial towards me. I having been well acquainted with her ⟨hu⟩ ↑late↓ husband during my—residence in Granada. On the other side of me was one of the most beautiful young ladies I have Seen in Spain: Sister to the Duke of Riansaras (the husband of Queen Christina)[3] She is shortly to be married to the brother of the Minister of Marine.[4] I found her very amiable and pleasing in her manners and conversation.

Our dinner lasted until nearly nine Oclock and about half after nine company began to arrive for a ball. The assemblage took place in ⟨the⟩ a Suite of apartments on the other side of the hotel (which is built round a court.)

The whole royal family came to the ball; but not in the State in which they came to the generals former ball. This was a kind of impromptu on their part; done without ceremony; and the consequence was that there was less restraint and more pleasure. Before the ⟨ball⟩ dancing we had singing by several young ladies, amateurs, and I do not know when I have heard better amateur singing. The one, however, who carried off the palm was Leocadia Zamora. She sang exquisitely: with the truest feeling and the best taste and she looked charmingly. Indeed she has improved in her looks for some months past; the cool weather agrees with her. Every body was in raptures with her, while she received their applause in her quiet, unaffected manner; and with that absence of pretension which gives a charm to her talent. I wish my friend King could see and hear her, he who is so nice a connoisseur in female charms—I think she would charm away his rheumatism.

After the concert the dancing commenced with a quadrille ⟨by⟩ ↑the ladies of which were↓ the Queen & her sister—⟨l⟩ their cousins the two daughters of the Infante Don Francesco; the French Ambassadress, the Princess Carini: and one or two ladies of the Court. The Queen danced with Genl Narvaez. Her sister with the French ambassador The little Queen is one of the merriest dancers in the world. The moment she begins to dance she begins to laugh; and is in frolick spirits the whole time. I cannot speak much for her grace in dancing I think her heart dances better than her feet.

I merely waited to see this quadrille, and then made my way through the crowded saloons, and the anterooms filled with halberdiers: guards in cuirasses & helmets &c. to my carriage, and got comfortably home by half past twelve; rather fatigued; but very much pleased with my New Years entertainment.

Jany. 4th   Madrid is commencing the year in gay style. Tonight there is to be a dramatic & musical entertainment by a society of amateurs, at the Liceo,[5] at which the Queen and Royal family are to be present, and to which all the Corps diplomatique is invited. Tomorrow night there will be a grand ball at the Countess of Montijo's: and several other fetes are in perspective not to be behind hand I give tomorrow my second large dinner which I hope may go off as well as the first one. It will not be quite so diplomatic, but probably more gay and social.

I am glad you are taking French lessons. Take pains to make yourself well acquainted with the verbs. A little labour will save you a world of after embarrassment and annoyance. In the various scenes and circles of society in which I have been, and am still, obliged to mingle, I have continually felt the effects of not having grounded myself well in the grammer of the French language It destroys all ease and freedom in conversation and makes me stand aloof from persons with whom I should like to be in terms of cordial intimacy. It is too late for me now to remedy the defect: ⟨[unrecovered]⟩ it is not worth while, for the brief time I am yet likely to mingle with the world; but you have I trust many many years of social intercourse before you, a great part of which may be passed in society where the French language is the medium of conversation: take a little pains therefore to put yourself at ease in the language. Let your lessons turn upon the difficulties of the language; which after all are but few. It is wonderful what a small number of peculiarities they are which fetter our tongues and cause all our stumbling.

Poor King! how I feel for him having to appear at court with his long train of American would be courtiers, like a loco motive engine, doomed to conduct a caboose rout of rail road cars. I do not wonder he is nervous. I think if I were in his place I should lose heart on the eve of the presentation day and elope.

I want to know about Mrs Ellis ⟨presentation⟩ ↑reception↓ at Court— and likewise how she did the honours of presenting the American ladies. She never can fail to acquit herself well. She has a simple grace about her that bespeaks the lady, and fits her for every occasion.

You promise me that your next letter will be a long one. I hope you may keep your promise; but do not leave writing until the end of the week, write a part of ⟨the⟩ ↑a↓ letter in the middle of each week, and ⟨then⟩ finish it on Saturday and then ⟨it will be⟩ you will not be in such a hurry. You dont tell me half enough about Kate and her sister the little Hombod. How I should like to have passed the holidays with them; and to have played with Kate and Dolly and the bergere. My dear Sarah I cannot tell you how much I feel at times my separation from you and your dear little ones. I feel it more this year than I did the last; each visit to Paris makes me feel it more sensibly on my return to Madrid.

—I have been interrupted by the French Ambassador, who has just been in to see me on business, and must conclude abruptly with Kisses to Kate and Susy and kind remembrances to Mr Storrow

Your affectionate Uncle
Washington Irving

MANUSCRIPT: University of Pennsylvania Library.   PUBLISHED: *American Literature*, 25 (November, 1953), 355–58.

1. This letter has not been located.
2. See *La Posdata*, January 2, 1845.
4. María Christina's marriage to the corporal of her guard, Agustín Fernando Muñoz y Sanchez, by a bogus priest had occurred in 1833; the couple was married again in 1844 by the bishop of Cordova. In the same year he was made duke of Rianzares and a grandee. See Peter de Polnay, *A Queen of Spain*, pp. 36–37, 91; and Elizabeth W. Latimer, *Spain in the Nineteenth Century*, p. 251.
4. Señor Portillo. See WI to John C. Calhoun, April 2, 1844.
5. See *La Posdata*, January 6, 1845.

1799. To John Miller

Madrid 9th Jany 1845

To John Miller Esqre

Dear Sir

I enclose a draft on Messrs Baring and Co of London, payable to your order for £7.4.2 being in payment of your account incurred for this Legation for the last quarter

I am respectfully / Your obt servant
(signed) Washington Irving

MANUSCRIPT: NA, RG 84 (letterbook copy).

1800. To Sarah Storrow

Madrid Jany 10th. 1845

My dear Sarah,

Madrid has become quite a gay capital of late, and I am leading quite a dissipated life, in spite of myself. Operas, dinners, balls and amateur theatricals keep the fashionable world in continual excitement. We have had a play of Martinez de la Rosa's[1] performed by an Amateur company at the Liceo, at which the Queen and Royal family were present, and of course the Corps diplomatique, and tomorrow night we are to have an amateur concert at the same place, at which Royalty will likewise be present, and where there will be a raffle for various pretty articles, fabricated by the Queen & her sister and various ladies of the Court & the nobility, the whole being for the benefit of the sufferers by the fire at Granada last year. At this concert my fair friend Leocadia Zamora will sing.

At the Opera of the Cruz Moriani continues to draw crowds and to delight. ⟨He has f⟩ I have seen him three times in the opera of Lucrezzia Borgia, in which he both sings and plays admirably. You will no doubt see him some day or other at Paris; for he has an engagement in the Spring at London, from whence he will probably find his way to the ⟨Italian opera⟩ French capital in spite of Grisi. He came to Madrid on an engagement but for twenty performances. I can easily understand why the Singing of Mario[2] does not touch you. His voice is sweet but rather luscious; ⟨[*unrecovered*] he⟩ ↑his countenance↓ is handsome, but not intellectual; he wants warmth and expression both in singing and acting. I think Moriani would be more to your taste, he is so decidedly dramatic ⟨in⟩ and so full of passion and pathos. I think, like myself, you like the actor to be combined with the singer.

Since I last wrote to you I gave a dinner of twelve persons, which went off very pleasantly and I am to give another, of about the same number, the day after tomorrow. My servants acquit themselves extremely well, and my cook has acquired quite a reputation; so that the dinner parties are attended with ⟨not⟩ none of ⟨that⟩ the trouble and vexation which attend those where the domestic machinery does not work well. A few evenings since I was at a grand ball at the Countess of Montijos, where all the fashionable world was assembled, and where, meeting with two or three of my especial favorites, I loitered until quite a late, or rather an early hour. Next week we have a childs fancy ball at the house of my friend Mrs O'Shea where there will be a gathering of fashionables young and old; and a few evenings after we are to have a ⟨very [unrecovered]⟩ grand ball at the magnificent house of the Marques of Miraflores³— Can you recognize poor triste Madrid in the midst of all this gaiety?

I am delighted to hear of Kates holy day presents and flattered that she gives me a seat in her new carriage. I hope her new doll will not throw the old one in the shade. I beg you to keep my "dolly" quite in the reserve. Let her come now and then on a visit from "Unty" in Spain, to play with Kate whenever she has any new toys. I consider dolly as a kind of link between us to keep me in her reccollection.

Dear little Susy, and her first doll, all covered with bells! I have the dear little creature often in my minds eye, as I saw her once lying in your lap looking up earnestly and sweetly in your face as you bent over her, and seeming to try to understand what you were saying to her.

Why does not Madame Hacquets husband forward the papers to support his claim? By & bye something may turn up to prevent my rendering the assistance which is now in my power; and he may lose the best chance of having his claim attended to. Give my kind remembrances to Madame Hacquet, but do not tell her that I consider her husband one of the very poorest of poor devils.

I am looking forward to an account which you give me reason to expect in your next letter of the presentation at court of the long string of American gentlemen and American ladies, by friend King and his "lady bird" niece. Poor Mrs Ellis, I can fancy her with a whole string of ladies, like those little figures hand in hand cut out of white paper. However her task is the easiest, for our ladies really are superior to our gentlemen and look well and dress well and deport themselves well. As to Mrs Ellis herself, I shall be much mistaken if she is not highly appreciated by the Royal family. I think she is just the kind of person to please them. -

My paper is full, and I must conclude; hoping that your next letter may be more full of matter than the two last, which were rather meagre. Give my best love and kisses to my dear little Kate and to Sweet little Susy—and kind remembrances to Mr Storrow.

Your affectionate uncle
W. I.

Addressed: Madame / Madame Storrow / No 4. Rue de la Victoire / à Paris
Manuscript: Yale.

1. This was *El Español en Venecia*, published in 1843. See *La Posdata*, January 6, 1845.

2. Giuseppe Mario (1810–1883), a popular Italian operatic tenor, was the husband of Giulia Grisi.

3. Manuel Pando Fernández de Pineda, marques of Miraflores (1792–1872), a liberal politician who was to serve briefly as minister of state in February of 1846, was a courtier in opposition to strong military intervention. See Christiansen, *Military Power*, p. 124.

1801. To John C. Calhoun

Legation of the United States / Madrid 11th January 1845

No 58 / The Hble John C. Calhoun / Secretary of State

Sir,

I have the honor to enclose the accounts and Vouchers of this Legation for the Fourth Quarter of 1844 shewing a balance against me of $15.11 which will be carried to my debit in my next account.

In my contingent expenses for the first quarter of 1844 I charged my expenses in following the Court to Aranjuez to attend the meeting of the Queen and Queen Mother; to my present account I append a charge for my expenses in following the Court to Barcelona;[1] the motives for which journey will be perceived on reference to my Despatch No 44.[2] These charges are made in accordance with what appears to have been the uniform practise of this Legation sanctioned by the Report of the Committee on the case of Mr Van Ness in July 1842. I have not drawn for this last amount and would solicit an order from the competent authority for the adjustment of the same and likewise of the preceding charge, should there be any hesitation on the part of the fourth Auditer to allow it.

The Spanish Court now that the young Queen is established on the Throne, is about to resume its old custom of making sojourns during the summer months at the royal Sitios or rural residences and there is talk of another visit to Barcelona. On these occasions the presence of the Diplomatic Corps is expected for at least a part of the royal sojourn and is sometimes necessary for the despatch of business as the Sovereign is generally accompanied by some if not all of the Cabinet. These followings of the Court necessarily involve extra expenses which are allowed to the Diplomatic Agents by their respective Governments. There is not the same necessity for this Legation to comply rigidly with this custom, that there is for other Legations whose governments have closer relations and family alliances with the Spanish Throne; still it cannot be altogether neglected without an appearance of a want of respect and deference for the royal personage and Government. It would be well, therefore, for the Department to instruct this Legation how far it is expected to comply with this Custom and to what degree it may exercise its discretion according to circumstances, and it would be desirous for the Legation to be instructed on this point at as early a date as convenient in order to regulate its conduct in the coming season.

I am Sir / Very respectfully / Your obedient servant
Washington Irving

DOCKETED: Recd. July 22 — Mr Markoe [top of page 1] / No. 58. W. Irving. Madrid, 11 Jany. 1845
MANUSCRIPT: NA, RG 59.

Only the signature is in WI's handwriting.

1. WI spent about a month in Barcelona from late June to late July of 1844.
2. See WI to John C. Calhoun, June 8, 1844.

1802. To Catharine Irving

Madrid, Jany 11. 184⟨4⟩5

My dear Kate,

I have only time to say a few brief words in reply to your most welcome and affectionate letter of November 28th.[1] The long malady with which I have been afflicted, but which, thank God, I am now almost entirely clear of, having obliged me for nearly two years to suspend my literary labors, has disconcerted all my plans, so that I do not find myself in a Situation, in regard to pecuniary resources, to return home next Spring as I had originally intended. If I am not removed from office, therefore, I shall continue at Madrid for the present, but hope, if my health continues good, to get my literary affairs in ↑such↓ train, that at the end of a year or so I may return home without inconvenience.

As I begin to fear the residence at the Cottage, especially in the Winter months, is lonely and irksome to you all, I beg you will consult together, and adopt such other domestic arrangement, by removing to town, or otherwise, as may conduce more to your comfort and enjoyment. I have written to your father and to Pierre M Irving to the same purport, and you must hold a council of war among yourselves—All I ask is that you do nothing through motives of mere economy, but that you be guided ⟨merely⟩ entirely by considerations of domestic convenience and happiness.

You speak of John Manns' marriage. I presume it is the tall handsome young man with whom I used to sit and gossip occasionally in the workshop—I hope the match meets with the approbation of the Mann family, who you know are a little particular. Should you meet with the bride groom and it is not too long after the fair I beg you to give him my congratulations

I am writing this, my dear Kate, after having written a variety of letters to Government, ⟨and⟩ to persons in various directions and to different members of the family and I am quite exhausted, So I trust you will excuse its brevity—It is intended chiefly to speak to you on the important point of Your domestic arrangemen[ts] [*MS torn*], which ⟨as⟩ I ⟨look[?]⟩ leave entirely to be regulated according to what you shall all conclude for the best.

Give my love to all the inmates of the Cottage and do not cease to write to me; because I am compelled to be scanty in my correspondence If I could wield a dozen pens at a time and this poor worn out brain of mine would not grow weary, I would write to every one of you on every occasion

> Your affectionate Uncle
> Washington Irving

ADDRESSED: Miss Catharine A. Irving / care of P M Irving / Bank of Commerce / N York
MANUSCRIPT: SHR.

1. This letter has not been located.
2. A member of a neighboring family at Tarrytown. See WI to Ebenezer Irving, Fall, 1842.

1803. To John C. Calhoun

Legation of the United States / Madrid 18th January 1845

No 59 / The Hble / John C. Calhoun / Secretary of State

Sir

I have received Dispatch No 39 containing the commission of I. B. Lacey as Consul for Nueviatas[1] and have applied for his Exequatur. I have received no answer as yet to my note to the Minister of State protesting against the exaction of fees for Consular Exequaturs. Indeed in speaking subsequently to Mr Martinez de la Rosa on the subject he appeared to know nothing about it, so that he ↑either↓ had not read my letter or its contents had escaped his memory. He made a memorandum however of the matter and promised to attend to it. It was the same with the remonstrances addressed in writing by this Legation against the eight days Quarantine imposed on United States vessels although coming from northern ports. He knew nothing about the matter, made a memorandum and promised to attend to it. In fact he is quite inattentive and inefficient in official matters; his whole efficiency as a Minister lies in speaking in the Cortes; while he remains in the Ministry, therefore, all minor questions like the foregoing will be very liable to neglect.

The question of the duties on foreign and spanish flours introduced into Cuba[2] which I adverted to in my last dispatch continued for some time to be discussed with animation and warmth in the public journals, but has latterly died away. I have endeavored to learn from Ministers their intentions with respect to it, but they have avoided committing themselves. I am inclined to believe they are unwilling to meddle with it seeing it brings the interests of Cuba and the Peninsula into such angry collision. It may not therefore be brought before the Cortes at present. The project of a law relative to the ↑abolition of the↓ slave trade has awakened suspicions of British intervention and influence which have been quickened by articles in the public papers charging the British Cabinet with a covert policy in this matter. A few days since Mr Isturitz[3] took occasion in the Chamber of Deputies to enquire of Ministers whether the proposed law was the result of any recent communications on the part of the British Cabinet, in which case he should wish to have all such documents laid before the Chamber when the subject should be brought up.

The Minister of the Interior[4] would not say or not whether the Government had had communications on the subject but he would say that whatever they might have been, they had not been the motives of this law which had always been intended in compliance with treaty stipulations and had recently been rendered expedient by information collected in in[5] the Peninsula and in Cuba.

It is probable the law will be attacked by Mr Isturiz when it comes before the Chamber of Deputies. The same distrust of british agency and influence in the production of this law was manifested when a committee reported in its favor in the Senate. Some members refused to vote for the Bill so long as the the[6] intrusive policy of the British Government was permitted in the Spanish Colonies and a British ship of war suffered to remain in the harbor of Havanna as a negro receiving ship.

Mr Martinez de la Rosa exerted his eloquence to quiet these suspicions and to demonstrate how much the honor of Spain was committed in the case by her Treaties with Great Britain. He added that the receiving ship which gives such offence had been anchored in the port of Havannah with the consent of the Spanish Government on condition of being withdrawn whenever Spain should request it.

The sensitiveness of the Senate, however, still continued and was shewn when the penal clauses of the Bill[7] came to be discussed, for though there was no longer a question of trying offenders by a mixed commission, and though offences were to be judged by the resident authorities, still there was an apprehension that any investigations as to the property in slaves, whether these slaves were native born or imported from Africa and the date of their importation etc. might give rise to inquisitorial proceedings calculated to throw the whole island into confusion. A Senator, therefore, Señor Olavarrieta moved an additional clause providing against any such inquisition. It was opposed in an animated speech by Mr Martinez de la Rosa and a motion made to reject it but the motion was lost by a vote of 55 to 19. A proviso was consequently added to the penal clauses stipulating that "in no case and at no time can proceedings be instituted to disquiet or molest the proprietors of slaves under pretext of their (the slaves) origin." (Pero en ningun caso ni tiempo podra procederse para inquietar ni molestar a los propietarios de esclavos con pretesto de su procedencia.) When it is considered that the law in question has been brought forward and anxiously supported by Ministers, and that the Senate on most other questions have been completely at the beck of the ⟨Ministers⟩ Cabinet, it will be perceived by the vote thus given that the Spanish public is wide awake in every thing connected with Cuba and the Slave Trade and cautious of giving through motives of humanity any opening for foreign intermeddling in the interior affairs of their Colonies. In fact the Treaties concerning the Slave Trade entered into with G. Britain in 1817 and 1835 are felt as shackles by the nation. Even those con-

scientiously opposed to negro slavery begin to perceive how the efforts
to suppress it may be misapplied or mismanaged so as to produce great
evil. They are aware that the plea of philanthropy may be set up by
politic statesmen to sanction dangerous invasions of national rights as in
the fanatical times of the Crusades, the cross at the hilt of the sword
was made to sanctify the weapon, however mischievously it might be
used.

I have the honor to remain Sir / Most respectfully /
Your obedient servant
Washington Irving

DOCKETED: Recd. 21 March. / Mr. Markoe [top of page 1] / No. 59., W. Irving,
Madrid — 18 Jan. 1845.
MANUSCRIPT: NA, RG 59.

Only the signature is in WI's handwritiing.

1. I. B. Lacey of Virginia was appointed as U.S. consul for Nuevitas, Cuba in
December, 1844. See Hasse, Index to U.S. Documents, III, 1747.
2. For details, see El Castellano, December 20, 1844; La Posdata, December 17,
19, 21, 1844; January 7, 1845.
3. Xavier Istúriz (1790–1871), who was minister of state for three months in
1836, was a Liberal leader. For his speech, see La Posdata, January 10, 1845.
4. Pedro José Pidal.
5. The copyist repeated "in."
6. The copyist repeated "the."
7. See La Posdata, January 11, 1845.

1804.   To Sarah Storrow

Madrid, Jany 18th. 1845

My dear Sarah,
Your last letter,[1] though you say it was hastily written, was one of
the most delightful I have ever received from you. I have read it over
and over, and only find it too short, though it is twice as long as usual.
In fact the acquaintance I made ⟨with⟩ during my last visit to Paris with
the persons with whom you are in habits of intimacy make your letters
which speak of them extremely interesting to me. But in truth you are
uncommonly fortunate in your intimates this winter; Mrs Ellis, Mrs
Henderson and Miss Fisher, with their cordial disposition to be sociable,
are quite enough to render you independent of the rest of the world.
Your week had indeed been quite rich of Mrs Ellis. A long visit to her
in her room, an evening with her at the opera, a drive with her in the
Bois de Bologne! I hope you were perfectly sensible of your happiness.

The accounts you give me of her family are full of interest. What a capital character her uncle the General[2] must be—such a generous compound of manly and gentle qualities. I feel that if I knew him my heart would "cleave unto him."[3] The little anecdote you give me of his sons conduct on receiving a letter from him speaks admirably for the character of both. The son is worthy of the father. I regret extremely that I did not become more acquainted with this youth. Do give me any more particulars you may learn about the General and his family—and let me have something occasionally about my friend the Minister whom I look on as quite a character, and whom I prize greatly. By the way, let me know what is the christian name of Mrs Ellis. I hope it is a suitable one.

Since I last wrote I have been very dissipated The evening of the day when I sent that letter I was at an amateur Concert at the Liceo, where the Royal family and all the court circle were present. It was a benefit given for the relief of the sufferers ⟨f⟩ by the fire last year at Granada. My fair friend Leocadia Zamora was to have sung but her heart failed her and another lady took her place. We had a lottery in the course of the evening. The prizes were articles of needle work, embroidery, drawing &c some wrought by the hands of the Queen & the princesses, others by ladies of rank. I was not so fortunate as to draw a prize. The Concert was good, but too long. I came away ⟨before⟩ ↑as↓ the third part was commencing and it was already past one Oclock. ⟨At⟩ The next day I gave my third large dinner, which was the most animated and cheerful of the three. I had some of the Diplomatic corps, and several Spaniards of note with whom I am on social terms. The company were well acquainted with each other, and, though we were fourteen at table the conversation was general and lively. When I have a dinner of this size I have a double service—That is to say, two dishes of each kind one served round to the right the other to the left, so that no one is kept waiting long for each dish. ⟨I find my⟩ I am fortunate in my cook and in my other servants, so that my dinners are well cooked and well served, and I find have a very good name. My invitations certainly are always accepted.

On Monday last I was at a childs ball given by my excellent friend Mrs OShea. We had an assemblage of beautiful children, together with a large number of the fashionables of Madrid. I was delighted with the little folks, particularly with a little girl, the daughter of the Duke of Montemar, who did not appear to be much larger than Kate yet who danced the Polka to admiration. I think if Kate had seen her she would have taken her for a doll.

Two or three evenings afterwards I was at a grand ball given by the Marchioness of Miraflores at which all the high society of Madrid was present. The Miraflores hotel is one of the largest in Madrid; there were long Suites of rooms brilliantly lighted; but ⟨th⟩ as there are no grand Saloons the rooms were excessively crowded. The dresses of the ladies were greatly extolled, and there was a universal blaze of diamonds; for in old aristocracies like Spain ⟨the⟩ ladies are decked out in the hereditary jewels accumulated through many generations. I did not remain long at the ball, having lost my zest for such crowded assemblages and ⟨being⟩ having had sufficient entertainment for one evening in the opera of Lucrezzia Borgia, to which I had previously been, and in which for the third time I had witnessed the admirable acting of Moriani and the prima donna Tozzi.[4]

To night there is to be a grand concert at the Palace, where all the world will be assembled in Court dresses & uniforms; and where a magnificent suite of apartments, recently refitted, will be thrown open. I have never ⟨atten⟩ been present at a concert at the palace, but have heard much of the style of grandeur in which an entertainment of the Kind is given, and I can easily concieve it from the Spaciousness & magnificence of the local. The only draw back on my anticipation is that I understand the concert will be immensely long. We are invited at 8 Oclock and probably shall not get away from the palace until three in the morning!

You will ⟨Supp⟩ conclude from all these details of gaieties that I am a very gay fellow; but I assure you I am often, in the midst of these brilliant throngs, the very dullest of the dull. Unless there should be some one or other of my very few cordial intimates present to whom I can link myself, I am apt to gaze on [the][5] crowd around me with perfect apathy; and find it very difficult, and at times impossible to pay those common place attentions and make those common place speeches to scores of half acquaintances, required in the wide circulation of fashionable society. I have grown too old or too wise for all that; I hope those who observe my delinquency attribute it to the latter cause. How different my feelings are at these Court fetes and fashionable routs, from what they were at our cordial little American Soirees at Paris.

Tomorrow I take a cosey dinner with my friends the O'Sheas at whose house I always enjoy myself. In fact Mrs O'Shea and Madame Albuquerque are my great resources. They occupy the opposite ends of the same house (the Hotel of the Duke of San Lorenzo where I was quartered ⟨when I⟩ on my ⟨first⟩ arrival in Madrid) I see one or the other of them almost every day, and my carriage is almost daily standing for hours before the door. I consult them on all points of domestic economy and they are my counsellors in all things appertaining to the beau monde.

O'Shea is a warm hearted Irishman who has resided in Madrid for many years (he was here when I was here in 1825)[6] and has accumulated a large fortune by banking and by contracts with the Government. He is extremely hospitable and very charitable. It was but yesterday I heard of one instance of his charity which was, distributing soup three times a week to sixty poor persons in the barrio or quarter in which he resides. And when they have eaten their soup they have each a large portion of the puchero or meats of which it is made to carry home to their families. His wife is a woman you would love. She is truly feminine in her virtues and her deportment, and is prized by all who have the happiness of knowing her.

And now farewell—⟨yo⟩ in your last letter you crowded poor little Kate and Susy quite into a Corner. I hope they will have more space allowed them in the next. I want to hear more about Kate and her new carriage and Susy and her little doll covered with bells. Kiss them both for me. Give my kind remembrances to your husband.

Your affectionate Uncle
Washington Irving

P.S. I am very much concerned at the loss of that letter to you containing my first order for the Candlabras. It was sent, like all my other letters to you, by the Courier of the French Embassy—I have written to you, I believe, every week since my return to Madrid, and I believe the receipt of every letter has been acknowldged by you excepting of that one

ADDRESSED: Madame / Madame Storrow / No 4. Rue de la Victoire / à Paris
MANUSCRIPT: Yale.   PUBLISHED: PMI, III, 367–68; STW, II, 189 (in part).

1. This letter has not been located.
2. Thomas D. King. See WI to Sarah Storrow, December 29, 1844.
3. See Genesis 2:23–24.
4. This may be Adelaida Tossi. See José Subirá, *El teatro del Real Palacio (1849–1851)* (Madrid, 1950), p. 134.
5. WI omitted the bracketed word.
6. WI is in error about the date. He did not arrive in Madrid until 1826.

1805. To Sarah Storrow

Madrid Jany 25. 1845

My dear Sarah,

You hurry your last letter[1] to a close by saying that Miss Fisher has been in and talked away the time you had to devote to letter writing. I wont admit such an excuse another time. Tell Miss Fisher if she repeats the offence I shall *hate* her (as Kate Irving would say) however amiable and agreeable she may be.

I have just received pleasant letters from home and, among the rest, one from your Mother written in very good spirits. She had been much gratified by cheerful letters from you which had sent her to bed full of pleasant thoughts and feelings, and given her a Sweet nights rest. Let all your letters to her be in a cheerful vein, they are perfect hearts ease to her. I have a very agreeable letter from Alexander Hamilton, who is launched in the law and succeeds beyond his expectation. His family has moved into town for the winter so that he has the comforts of a home, instead of leading the life of a Bachelor upon town. He tells me that young Sheldon is "paying some small attentions" to Helen Jones and that the parents on both sides are looking on with complacency. It would be a ten times better match for her than any of the ⟨foreign⟩ ↑needy↓ continental counts and Barons by whom she was at one time in danger of being captivated. A favorable symptom as to the result of this affair is that Mrs Sheldon has of late quite omitted the Jones's in the excursive range of her tongue, though they have afforded ample scope for her Satirical animadversions. They have, in fact, turned the quiet, sober, modest establishment of very gentleman like personage George Jones, quite topsy turvy with their attempts at Parisian style: and powdered lacqueys, in crimson plush breeches and white stockings, announce all visitors with becoming emphasis. I trust, as in Paris, they give their titles. Mr Stock broker so and so. Mrs Sugar baker so and so. Mr Whole sale Dry good importer Wiggins &c &c &c In a little while New York will be little better than Paris travestied. I hope the Jones's will exhaust this freak in the city and not carry their second hand style up into the country, to balderdash the neighborhood of simple little Sunny side.

I am still, willy nilly, in the midst of gaiety at Madrid, which has of late become quite a dissipated capital. The concert at the Palace was very brilliant. A Splendid suite of apartments was opened, quite different from those of the banquet. We had some excellent amateur singing by ladies of fashion. Among others the fair Leocadia sang, but she was frightened and did not do herself full justice There was an excellent supper, and every thing was conducted in Royal style. There is soon to be a ball at the palace and also another banquet; there are to be fancy balls at General Narvaez, at the British Embassy; the Countess of Montijos &c. &c. in a word all the world is madding here. Independent of these grand fetes we have regular little diplomatic *reunions* three times a week—Mondays and Fridays at the French Embassy and Wednesdays at Mr O'Sheas, at which all the members of the diplomatic circle meet and many of the pleasantest people about the Court. They are very easy and Social; some playing at cards and others chatting. These with frequent dinner parties, and two opera houses, present amusement and dissipation enough for a far more festive person than myself. Indeed I find it difficult to cope with the part I am obliged to take in the game

I am glad to hear that my friend King got so well through the task of the presentation. Kit Hughes[2] was the very man to Stand by him on such an occasion. I am glad Mrs Ellis does not like great crowds, however fashionable; it accords with my idea of her ⟨character⟩ tastes and habits.

Do the Hendersons still talk of purchasing the Dutcher farm? I fear it will be all talk. What a delightful addition it would be to the social life at the Cottage to have such neighbors just within the reach of a pleasant ↑ten minutes↓ walk through our little skirt of wood and along the shore.

Your last two letters give me hardly any news about Kate and Susey. I beg you will not be so silent about those two respectable little personages. You can say nothing about them but what is interesting to me. Their looks, their dress, their play things, their very caprices. Tell me too every thing about yourself—your amusements, acquaintances &c Have you seen Macready—I observe he is quite the ⟨f⟩ rage in Paris. I consider him a manufactured kind of actor; wrought after various patterns; with more head work than heart work. Eminent in the absence of real eminences; ⟨yet⟩ with considerable talent ⟨and⟩ much experience —but very moderate genius

Your affectionate Uncle
W. I.

MANUSCRIPT: Yale.

1. This and the letters mentioned in the next paragraph have not been located.
2. Probably Christopher Hughes (1786–1849), who was secretary of the legation and chargé d'affaires in Sweden, Norway, and the Netherlands between . 1816 and 1845.

1806. To Sarah Storrow

Madrid, Jany [31, 1845][1]

My dear Sarah,

I received your letter of the[2] yesterday just as I was going to Court to attend a Besamanos, so I determined not to read it until my return home, that I might have liesure to enjoy it.

I thank you for taking my hint and giving me more gossip about those

precious little folk Kate and Susie. You cannot be too ample and minute
about them nor fear of praising them too much. You have no idea how
I dwell upon every particular concerning them, and how often and
often I read it over. I begin to think I have a little touch of dotage about
them; a sign of gathering years; but you I trust will excuse it and
indulge it.

Madrid continues to be gay and I to be dissipated but, for the most
part, I am dissipated *officially*, as I have to attend Court fetes of all
kinds, and dinners and balls given by personages in office. a few days
since we had a grand review of all the troops, to the Number of twelve
or thirteen thousand. What gave it peculiar eclat was that the young
Queen, for the first time attended the review as Commander in Chief.[3]
It was what Genl Narvaez has been persuading her to do for a year
past. She was mounted on a beautiful dun colored horse, ⟨which⟩ perfectly well broken, and was dressed in a blue cloth riding habit and
black beaver hat, quite ala l'Anglaise—with badges ⟨to shew that⟩ of
the Military rank of captain general. General Narvaez rode by her side
and she was followed by a brilliant cortege of general officers ⟨splendidly⟩
After which came the Royal carriages ↑one↓ containing the Queen
Mother & the Infanta, another the Infante Don Francisco and the princesses his daughters &c &c The little queen was in high spirits and greatly
delighted, and indeed the whole effect was charming.

I sallied out on foot to see the sight, and encountered the French
Ambassador and his wife, (the Count and Countess de Bresson) likewise
on foot. I joined them, and we had a famous trudge for two or three
hours, among the troops, through the crowd; ⟨on f⟩ along the Prado,
outside of the gates &c &c. The Countess is a capital hand for an expedition of the kind. She fears nothing, and is active and enterprising After
our perambulation we took our stand on ⟨th⟩ one of the balconies of the
British embassy to see the Queen receive the passing salute of the troops.
After which I took a Social dinner at the French embassy and finished
my evening at the Theatre of the Cruz, where I saw Moriani perform
admirably in the opera of Rolla or the Artist[4]—So there is one days
dissipation.

The next evening I was at a very brilliant ball at the Countess of
Montijos; which was pleasant to me from meeting there and having
a good deal of chat with my favorites Mrs O'Shea and the fair Leocadia.
I came away however, very early.

Yesterday was a Besa manos, being the birth day of the infanta.[5]
It was as usual a splendid ceremony, but from its ⟨so⟩ formality might
have been dull, had I not been in the neighborhood of Bulwer, and the
Prince Carini, who stand next to me in the Diplomatic line; and with
whom I had most amusing conversation; making our remarks upon the

oddities of the Court, and the odd figures which passed as it were in review before us. I took occasion when the young Queen came along the line to speak to us, to congratulate her on her first ↑Military↓ Sally. ⟨forth⟩ She told me that she relished it highly.

The Besa manos was followed by a Court dinner, but it was a small one, not more than *Seventy* at table. The Corps diplomatique did not attend. In the evening I was at a concert at the palace: not so thronged as the former one, nor so long, but very good. Moriani sang several pieces delightfully.

⟨The great⟩ What chiefly attracted my attention at the Besa manos and the Concert, was the re appearance of the Marchioness of Alcanizes;[6] who has for some time been in eclipse in consequence of being in deep mourning. When I was in Madrid in 1826.7. she was the belle. She had not long been married and was in the early freshness of her beauty. I reccollect her one evening at the Russian Ministers Mr. Oubril's forming a tableau vivant, representing Murillos picture of the Assumption of the Virgin It was a thing to fall down and worship. It has remained in my mind ever since. On my return to Madrid after an absence of fifteen years I found her still handsome, though matured in person. Last year she lost a favorite son and not long afterwards her lover the Duke of Ossuna;[7] to whom she had been attached for many years. She retired from Sight and only yesterday made her re appearance at court. Grief had left no traces on her face or form. Indeed She almost looked as beautiful as in her early years. She is very amiable, but is said not to possess acute sensibility. Hence the durability of her beauty; the soul does not wear and tear the body. At a distance she has something of the look of Grisi. The same classic head and bust, with the air and expression and suavity of one of the ⟨female⟩ pictures of Guido;[8] but she ⟨is⟩ ↑has a↓ rather more refined air than Grisi She has the same complexion and the Same brown hair. Hers is not the dark eyed, flashing Spanish beauty. Her eyes are blue or rather grey. Her head was splendidly and classically set off with a superb tiara of diamonds; and her hair gathered behind in a kind of coronet of [*end of MS*]

MANUSCRIPT: Yale.   PUBLISHED: *Yale Review*, 17 (October, 1927), 115–16 (in part); LSS, pp. 75–78 (in part).

A bracketed note at the top of page 1, "[1845? / STW]," indicates that Stanley T. Williams attempted to date this letter.

1. The letter can be precisely dated from WI's reference to the Infanta Luisa's birthday, which occurred on January 30, 1832. See John D. Bergamini, *The Spanish Bourbons*, p. 188; and *La Posdata*, January 24, 1845.

2. WI left a blank following "the." The letter has not been located.

3. For a report on the review of the troops, see *La Posdata*, January 28, 1845.

4. Salvatore Sarmiento (1817–1869), composer of many operas and religious works, brought out *Rolla* in 1841. A performance on January 23 was noted in *La Posdata*, January 24, 1845, but WI apparently saw a later performance not reported in the newspapers.

5. See note 1.

6. For WI's earlier reactions to the beauty of the marchioness, see his letters of January 22 and March 29, 1828, to Prince Ivanovitch Dolgorouki.

7. Pedro de Alcántara Téllez-Girón y Beaufort.

8. Guido Reni (1575–1642) was an Italian painter whose works are in many collections in England and on the Continent. WI may have seen his *Cleopatra, Portrait of a Girl*, and *Madonna à la Chaise Magdalen* in Madrid.

1807. To Sarah Storrow

Madrid Feb. 5th. 1845

My dear Sarah,

We are in the midst of Carnavel,[1] which, thank heaven, is a short one this year; for I am already jaded and sated with the share I have been obliged by my official station, to take in the dissipation of the court and of the court circle. Last evening I fairly came to a stand, and excused myself from going to a grand ball given by the Marchioness of Miraflores; the second she has given this season. It happened that none of my peculiar favorites were to be there, and I had not spirits enough to go through the task of making bows and talking common places in bad French and Spanish to hosts of people ⟨for⟩ ↑in↓ whom I took no interest, nor they any in me.

I was very well amused, however, at the fancy ball given a few evenings since by General Narvaez.[2] The Queen and all the Royal family were there. ⟨This is the Second time⟩ and the fete was of course very brilliant. After making my bow to the Queen and remaining in her neighborhood for a time, to see the Royal party dance a Quadrille, I made my way through the gay and gilded throng, into another Saloon, where I took my seat in a corner beside my amiable friend Mrs O'Shea, and by degrees we saw all the world pass, as it were, in review before us. The gentlemen were for the most part in diplomatic or military uniforms; but there were several very beautiful ⟨and cos⟩ and striking costumes among the ladies; and the Spanish countenance with its eloquent eyes, looks well in fanciful coiffures. One of the most picturesque and yet most simple costumes was that of my fair friend the Princess Carini. Though ⟨a french⟩ a parisienne she has quite an Italian face, with fine black eyes. She was in a kind of riding dress of antique form. A *juste a corps* (something like a short gown) of puce coloured velvet; trimmed with fur, a brocade skirt, and a grey low crowned broad brimmed hat, with a white feather lying along it and falling behind. something in this form³ ⟨large⟩ clusters of small black ringlets on each side and ⟨fa⟩ reaching almost to her shoulders; and a small riding whip in her hand. Her costume was no doubt suggested by the prince, who is an excellent painter and a 'universal genius;' and as she has a light good figure and something of a jaunty air it became her admirably.

I had intended to steal away from the ball at a very early hour, but my old Coachman Pedro mistook my orders or misunderstood my bad French and came at two Oclock instead of twelve. I however passed the interval very pleasantly.

Friday. 7th. I received yesterday your letter of ⟨the preceeding⟩ last week,⁴ which of course I had been on the look out for. I thank you for the particulars you give me about Kate and Susie; it gratifies me that the former has not forgotten how to "walk hombod," for I feared, during my long absence, she would lose all the accomplishments I had taught her. How few it is who know how to instruct children!—and indeed how few children are worth the trouble. Kate, however, is uncommonly quick and apprehensive; and I think if I had her a little while under my management and tuition I would turn her out one of the most curiously instructed children in christendom. Does she still manifest her taste for the toilette and figure about in newspaper caps and shawls?

Saturday, 8th. I am scribbling this letter piece meal, ⟨between⟩ in intervals of other occupations; having a good deal of writing to do just now in official matters, beside a continual task of the pen on my literary plans. Beside I have so little to write about here that can be very interesting to you. These Court fetes and fashionable Routes have a great sameness in them, and then you know nothing of the people around me— Whereas when you write you have but to let your pen run on about your children and your intimates, and I devour every thing with eagerness read your letters over and over again, and only find them too short.

I am in hopes your next letter will give me more about Mrs Ellis, whom, when you wrote your last you had not seen for some time. Let me know whether Mrs Henderson intends that her husband shall buy that farm—I am affraid she will let it get into other hands and then I shall never forgive her.

I am glad Miss Fisher continues ⟨to⟩ occasionally to pass a day with you. She is just the kind of companion to enliven your home and to heighten the pleasure of your promenades. Give my kind remembrances to her when next she visits you and tell her I commend Kate to her, to ⟨thank for⟩ ↑be taught↓ the *graces*. I can teach her the *airs*.

Your affectionate Uncle
Washington Irving

MANUSCRIPT: Yale.

1. The festivities before the start of Lent. Easter fell on March 23, 1845.
2. For a report on the ball, see *La Posdata*, February 3, 1845.
3. After this word WI drew a rough sketch of the hat and the feather.
4. This letter has not been located.

1808. To John C. Calhoun

Legation of the United States / Madrid 8th February 1845

No. 60 / The Hble John C Calhoun / Secretary of State

Sir

I have the honor to enclose a note just received from Mr Martinez de la Rosa Minister of State and of Foreign Affairs, by which you will perceive that the Spanish Government declines admitting foreign Consuls in any but four ports of the Island of Cuba viz *Havanna, Matanzas, Cuba* and *Trinidad*

This measure is taken no doubt on account of the intermeddling of foreign agents in the internal affairs of the Island[.] Mr Saml. McLean being the last person nominated by the President as Consul for the Port of Trinidad I have signified him to Don M. de la Rosa as the definitive candidate for the office.

I have received no reply from the Spanish Government as yet to my protest against the tax levied on Consular Exequaturs.

The penal law against the slave trade continues to be the subject of animated discussion in the Chamber of Deputies. It will finally pass, however, with the clause appended by the Senate to one of the articles for the protection of slaveholders in Cuba against any investigation as to their origin.[1]

The penal law has been thus suddenly brought up and pushed forward by Ministers in consequence of the urgent instances of England. The French Ambassador at first set countenance against it until Mr Bulwer informed him privately that he was instructed by Lord Aberdeen to leave Madrid if the law were not passed. After this intimation Count de Bresson recommended the passing ↑of↓ the law. Exertions will be made, however, to set on foot a negotiation for the repeal or modification of the right of visit which bears hard on Spanish pride and spanish sensibilities, and I am in hopes some steps will be taken by the Spanish Government in the matter. I trust also that a demand will be made for the removal of the Paston a British Three Decker anchored in the Harbor of Havannah ostensibly for the reception of liberated negroes and which one of the Deputies in the Cortes has quaintly and not unaptly compared to the wooden horse so unwarily admitted within the walls of Troy.

I have taken all the steps in this matter that the delicate nature of the question permitted, endeavoring to discriminate between what was due to the suppression of the Slave Trade and what was important for the pro-tection ↑of↑ the tranquillity↓ of the Island with which the tranquillity of of our Southern States is so closely connected. I am happy to find from a conversation with Don Martinez de la Rosa that the Spanish Cabinet are fully possessed of our policy with regard to their colonial possessions. In this they have been enlightened by ample representations made by the Chevalier Argaiz late Spanish Minister at Washington and by the recent correspondence of Mr Calderon de la Barca, who, from what fell from Mr Martinez de la Rosa, has placed the dispositions and characters of our Cabinet in the fairest point of view and inspired the fullest confi-dence in our friendship and good faith on the part of the Spanish Gov-ernment.

We have recently received in this Legation the case of books forwarded from the Department via Cadiz. In this are the 3rd, 4th, and 5th volumes of the American Archives.[2] The Legation was previously in possession of two *Second* volumes of this valuable work but the *first volume* is still wanting. The *4th volume* of the *Executive Documents* of 1842,43 is ↑likewise↓ wanting ↑and↓ the *1st volume* of Senate Documents.[3] There is now an excellent body of legislative and diplomatic history in this Legation amounting to about one hundred volumes and it is of peculiar value in this place where one is so cut off from the sources of information usual in other capitals. There is a want of book cases however in which to arrange and protect the books[.] Mr Livingston the secretary of this Legation has already made a representation on this subject. I would most respectfully suggest that permission be given to provide book cases for the purpose. Eighty or a hundred dollars would cover all expenses and would be within the limits of the contingent fund of this Legation.

I am respectfully Sir / Your most obedient servant
Washington Irving

P. S. In a preceding dispatch I suggested that American newspapers might be forwarded to Madrid via England[.] I have since found that they would be subject to heavy postage. I would advise therefore that *newspapers* be always sent *via Havre* to the care of the American Consul.

DOCKETED: Recd. 21 March / Mr. Markoe [*top of page 1*] / No. 60. W. Irving. Madrid — 8 Feb. 1845 —
MANUSCRIPT: NA, RG 59; NA RG 84 (letterbook copy and partial draft).

Only the signature is in WI's handwriting.

1. On March 4, 1845, the Cortes approved "The Law of Abolition and Repression of the Slave Trade," a measure designed to stop traffic in slaves but not concerned with the abolition of slavery itself. See Arthur F. Corwin, *Spain and the Abolition of Slavery in Cuba, 1817–1886*, Latin American Monographs, no. 9, Institute of Latin American Studies, University of Texas (Austin, 1967), pp. 84–85.
2. Peter Force began publication of these American documents in 1837 and by 1844 had brought out five volumes of the fourth series. A sixth volume followed in 1846. The first three series never appeared.
3. By "Executive Documents" WI probably meant the *House Documents* of the 27th Congress, 3d session, which met from December 5, 1842, to March 3, 1843. The messages and reports of the departments of the Executive branch were printed in House Documents, of which eight volumes were issued for this session of Congress. *Senate Documents* made up four volumes. See *Checklist of United States Public Documents, 1789–1909*. 3d ed. (Washington, 1911), p. 18.

1809. To Elisha K. Kane

Madrid 8th February 1845

My Dear Sir

I am most happy to inform you that in consequence of my personal and urgent application to the Minister of the Interior, the Council of Public Instruction has consented at length to the nomination of a special commission in Manilla for your examination.

I began to anticipate a very different result to my application, on being informed that an English physician of the name of Field had come all the way from Manilla to Madrid in order to pass his examination here. I made it however a personal thing with the Minister and at length have had the satisfaction to receive a note (which I enclose for your better guidance) informing me that an order would be issued to the Captain General of the Philippine Islands to nominate a commission of examination.

I presume you are aware that it is necessary to undergo this examination in the Spanish language

I beg, in conclusion, that you will always command my services in either my official or private capacity, and believe me ever very truly yours,

Washington Irving

ADDRESSED: Doctor Elisha K. Kane.
MANUSCRIPT: American Philosophical Library.

Only the signature is in WI's handwriting.

Elisha K. Kane (1820–1857), naval officer, physician, and explorer, had been medical officer to the China Mission of 1843–1844, headed by Caleb Cushing. Apparently Kane planned to return to the Far East, but he was assigned instead to the African Squadron of the U.S. Navy.

1810. To Francisco Martínez de la Rosa

Madrid 8th February 1845

His Excellency / Don F. M. de la Rose / etc etc

Sir

I have the honor to acknowledge the receipt of your Excellency's note of the 4th instant[1] informing me that her Majesty's Govt had deemed it expedient to admit foreign Consuls solely in four ports of the Island of Cuba, viz, Havanna, Matanzas, Cuba and Trinidad. I shall immediately transmit your Excy's note to my govt. In the meantime I would observe that the candidate definitively presented for the Consulship at Trinidad is Mr Saml. McLean.[2] If your Excy will take the trouble to refer to my note of the 19th Decr last you will find that it enclosed the commission of James I. Wright appointed Consul for Santiago de Cuba. There are consequently *two* commissions of Consuls instead of *one* as your Excy erroneously observes in his note of the 4th inst. to act upon.

I avail myself of this opportunity to call your Excy's attention particularly to this last named commission as the port of Santiago de Cuba being at this moment without a Consular Agent much and serious inconvenience is felt by American merchants trading with it and it would therefore be a great accommodation if the Regium Exequatur for Mr James I. Wright[3] could be expedited with the least possible delay.

In a note which I had the honor to address some time since[4] to your Excy I took occasion by order of my Govt. to protest against the tax levied in the offices of her Majesty's Govt in issuing Consular Exequaturs. No notice having apparently been taken of this protest I take the liberty of recalling it to your Excellency's attention trusting that a tax vexatious in itself, unexampled in the usages of other nations and totally at variance with the liberal practice of the American conduct towards spanish Consuls will only need the proper consideration of her Majesty's Govt to be immediately repealed

I have the honor to be etc
(signed) Washington Irving

MANUSCRIPT: NA, RG 84 (letterbook copy).

1. This note dealt at great length with the reasons for not approving U.S. consuls at other Cuban ports. The main reason was that commerce was insufficient to justify such an official representative (NA, RG 84).

2. Martínez de la Rosa had asked about the status of John Cooke, for whom an exequatur for Trinidad had also been requested (NA, RG 84).

3. On February 21, 1845, Martínez de la Rosa acknowledged that Wright's exequatur would be issued as soon as his papers were in order (NA, RG 84).

4. See WI to Martínez de la Rosa, November 28, 1844.

1811. To Francisco Martínez de la Rosa

Madrid 14 de Febrero de 1845

El Exmo Señor / Don F. M. de la Rosa etc

El infrascrito Ministro Plenipotenciario de los Estados Unidos saluda al Exmo Señor Don F. M. de la Rosa y tiene la honra de rogarle se sirva dar las ordenes oportunas para la exportacion por la Aduana de Cadiz de Treinta moruecos merinos a nombre del Señor Newbold[1] ciudadano de los Estados Unidos.

Aprovecho etc

(signed) Washington Irving

MANUSCRIPT: NA, RG 84 (letterbook copy).

Translation:
"The undersigned minister plenipotentiary of the United States greets his excellency, Don F. M. de la Rosa and has the honor to request that he cause to give the appropriate orders for the exportation from the Customs of Cadiz of thirty merino sheep in the name of Mr. Newbold, a citizen of the United States."

1. Possibly Richard S. Newbold, who married a daughter of Herman LeRoy of LeRoy, Bayard & Co., the New York shipping firm, and later served as U.S. consul at Trinidad. See Scoville, *Old Merchants of NYC*, I, 160; and Hasse, *Index to U.S. Documents*, III, 1149. He is mentioned in WI's letter to Sarah Storrow, February 14, 1845.

1812. To Sarah Storrow

Madrid. Feb. 14th. 1845

My dear Sarah

I received yesterday yours of the 7th.[1] which has given me great pleasure from ⟨the⟩ its treating so much of little Kate and Susie. How easy it ought to be for you to fill a letter to me. You have only to fancy you were talking with Mrs Henderson about your children, as you say you often do, and you would be in no want of a copious theme, of which I can never be tired. It must be so much more amusing and interesting now that Susie begins to take notice and play her part, and that Kate begins to act as an instructor and to teach her "baby accomplishments[.]" I cannot concieve a more delightful groupe than those two little folk at their gambols. It calls to mind Matilda and Marianne Van Wart, when they were about the same ages.

I must thank you too for your pretty picture of the fair lady of the Embassy[2] in her dress of rich black velvet with a lace ruffle, Seated beside an "immense fire in the Grand Saloon," Bless her gentle heart! I am glad to hear of her being for once in such comfortable quarters; for I have feared she would be chilled to death, with her delicate constitution, in that cold glassy house with French fire places. I am glad too that you continue to be on such cordial terms with her; She is much such an intimate as you had in Mrs James Paulding,[3] ↑having↓ the same social qualities regulated by the same ladylike propriety and grace. Such a companion is a pearl above all price.[4]

The amusements of our Carnival closed with a grand fancy ball at the Countess of Montijos; where I remained rather beyond my usual early hour of retiring. The most striking feature of the ball was a groupe of young folks ⟨of⟩ dressed as officers of the French guards in the time of the Regency, and ladies of that time who in a caprice of fashion adopted the same dress as far as it could be connected with female attire. You see instances of this semi male dress in old pictures The gentlemen of the groupe were in Scarlet Coats fitting close to the body with wide skirts. White underclothes with long black garters or spatter dashes reaching above the knees. The hair buckled stiff over each ear, queued behind and well powdered; and Small three cornered hats, edged with white feathers. The ladies had similar Military coats of Scarlet; rather short but full skirts and light bottines—Shoulder knots of ribbon; the hair buckled over the ears but clubbed behind & equally well powdered and the same kind of three cornered hats edged with white feathers. Two of the ladies were the daughters of Madame Montijo —viz the young Duchess of Alva and the Countess of Teba, a third was my fair friend Leocadie Zamora, who had very much the look of a *Mauvais Sujet* or roguish young page. Indeed you can concieve nothing more knowing and piquante than this groupe; especially the female part of it.

Young Astor[5] with his uncle Mr Armstrong,[6] of whose coming you gave me notice arrived here two or three days since and with them came Mr Newbold & Mr Edgar[7] of New York. about the same time arrived a Mr Ely[8] also of New York. quite an influx of Americans for Madrid. I had them all to dinner yesterday, with three or four agreeable persons to meet them, so that we had quite a pleasant dinner party. They all depart almost immediately for other parts of Spain, excepting Mr Armstrong and Mr Newbold, who intend to pass about a month here. We have now a gendarmerie[9] established throughout Spain, which has already been very efficient in apprehending and shooting robbers. The roads are therefore becoming more secure, and if the Country continues tranquil, under the active and energetic administration of Genl Narvaez, I shall not be surprised to see it over run by tourists.

My friend Madame Albuquerque has recently presented her husband with another son. The little fellow has been christened at the palace under the name of Fernando, the Queen Mother acting as Godmother. The nurse came home all glorious. She had been Nurse to Mrs OSheas children and by her reccommended to Madame Albuquerque. She told Mrs O'Shea that the Queen had spoken to her and smiled upon her. Oh Madame said she ⟨I⟩ After this I shall never take any other persons children to be christened—unless it should be some child of yours ⟨of⟩ or of Master Williams. The poor woman thinks herself nearly a grandee. She will talk of the palace and the queen and the Royal family for the rest of her life.

Pierre M Irving[10] tells me in a recent letter that he sent me by the same Havre packet a lithographed view of the Cottage. If it should come to your hands I wish you to forward it to me by the French courier.

And now with many kisses to my dear little Kate and Susie, and kind remembrances to Mr Storrow believe me ever

Your affectionate uncle
Washington Irving

MANUSCRIPT: Yale.

This letter is written on official stationery with the letterhead "Legacion / de los / Estados Unidos / en / España."

1. This letter has not been located.
2. Probably Mrs. Ellis, niece of the U.S. minister, William R. King. She served as hostess for her bachelor uncle.
3. WI does not remember accurately. Julia Irving Grinnell, not Sarah Paris, had been taken around in Washington by Mrs. James K. Paulding, "an invaluable guide and companion," who was the wife of the secretary of the navy. See WI to "My Six Nieces," February 4, 1840.
4. See Matthew 13:45–46.
5. John Jacob Astor III (1822–1890), son of William B. Astor. He had graduated from Harvard Law School in 1842.

6. Probably Robert Armstrong (1792–1854), brother of young Astor's mother, whom Polk had appointed as consul to Liverpool.

7. Probably William Edgar, who married Cornelia Le Roy, a sister of Mrs. Newbold. Edgar, son of William Edgar, a prominent New York merchant, conducted his business in Paris later in his life. See Scoville, *Old Merchants of NYC*, I, 160, 309.

8. Richard S. Ely (1818–1894), who worked in the St. Felix importing house, later lived in Paris and Liverpool, where he was engaged in banking and shipping.

9. The Civil. Guard was a military elite connected with the ministry of the interior rather than the ministry of war and designed to provide protection to the general populace. See Christiansen, *Military Power*, pp. 127–28; and Raymond Carr, *Spain*, pp. 233–34.

10. This letter has not been located.

1813. To Francisco Martínez de la Rosa

Madrid 17 de Febrero de 1845

Al Excmo Señor Don Francisco M. de la Rosa / etc etc

Muy Señor mio: Con fecha 31 de Marzo de 1838 dijo el Sr. Ministro de Gracia y Justicia oficialmente al Prte. del Supremo Tribunal de Justicia lo siguiente: He dado cuenta a la Reina Gobernadora de lo consultado por su Tribunal acerca de la autorizacion que por conducto del Ministro de los Estados Unidos solicita Filomena de la Rua y Josefa Wright para disponer de los bienes que tienen en España y considerando que estos interesados son actualmente ciudadanos de los Estados Unidos que segun las leyes de su pais se hallan ya en la mayor edad y que por la demas el tratado existente entre aquella Potencia que España autoriza a los ciudadanos de ambos Estados para disponer de los bienes que los del uno tengan en el otro se ha servido S. M. resolver que no existiendo como no existe la incapacidad de tierna edad no debe impedirse a dichos interesados la facultad que tienen en virtud de aquel tratado para enajenar los bienes que poseen en España sin mas limitacion ni formalidades que las que determinan las leyes respecto de los Españoles mayores de edad.

Tengo el honor pues de rogar à V. S. se sirva mandar se me provea de una copia autorizada en duplicado para los efectos que convengan por haber [*two words unrecovered*] extraviado dicha autorizacion y por no existir en esta Legacion copia alguna de ella.

Aprovecha etc

(signed) Washington Irving

MANUSCRIPT: NA, RG 84 (letterbook copy).

Translation:
"On the date of March 31, 1838, the minister of justice officially said to the president of the Supreme Tribunal of Justice the following: 'I have given an account to the queen regent of what has been consulted on by her tribunal[?] concerning the authorization which through the mediation [or channels] of the minister of the United States the request of Filomena de la Rua and Josefa Wright in order to dispose of the property that they have in Spain and considering that these interested parties are presently citizens of the United States who according to the laws of their country are already at the age of majority and that moreover the existing treaty between that power which Spain authorizes to citizens of both States to dispose of the good that those of one may have in the other, her majesty has resolved that in the case of there not existing—which in fact does not exist—the incapacity of tender age, the faculty which the interested parties have by virue of that treaty to alienate goods they possess in Spain without more limitations or formalities than those which the laws determine with respect to Spaniards of minor age must not be impeded.'

"I have the honor, then, to request your lordship kindly to order that an authorized copy be provided to me in duplicate to the effects that may be appropriate because [*words unrecovered*] lost said authorization and there not being in this legation any copy of it."

1814. To Franklin Lippincott et al.

Madrid 19 February 1845

Circular to Consuls in Cuba.

Franklin Lippincott[1]	— Cienfuegos
I. B. Lacey	— Nuevitas
Josiah Raymond	— Manzanillo
John R. Cooke	— Xibara
I. B. Devine	— Sagua la Grande.

Sir
I have just received from the Spanish Government information ⟨that⟩ ↑of↓ its having come to the determination not to admit Foreign Consuls in any port of the Island of Cuba excepting four, viz, Havanna, Matanzas, Santiago de Cuba and Trinidad.

I am Sir very respectfully / Your obt Servant
Signed: Washington Irving

MANUSCRIPT: NA, RG 84 (letterbook copy).

1. Franklin Lippincott of New Jersey was nominated on December 18, 1844, as U.S. consul at Cienfuegos to replace Samuel McLean, who was transferred to Trinidad de Cuba. The copyist erred in the initials of Patrick I. Devine. See Hasse, *Index to U.S. Documents*, III, 1745, 1747.

1815. To Catharine Paris

Madrid Feb. 19th. 1845

My dear Sister,

⟨I have⟩ If I do not write to you as frequently and copiously at present, as I used to do it is because, ⟨I⟩ now that I am enabled to resume my pen freely, I have to employ it in a variety of ways to make up for lost time, and above all in endeavoring to get my literary matters into a profitable train.

Madrid has been uncommonly gay this winter. The Aristocracy having got the government in their hands and feeling confident of continuing in power, have resumed somewhat of their old state and splendor. The Court has been quite magnificent, and we have had Several fêtes at the palace; given in truly royal style. The fêtes at the palace interest me more than any other. The grand historical pile in which they ⟨had⟩ are given, ↑(which for generations has been↓ the residence of the *Pharaohs* of Spain), and the Courtly pomp and ceremonial which characterize them, elevate them quite above the fêtes of ordinary life. I have been particularly pleased with two concerts[1] given at the palace; one wa[s] [*MS torn*] an amateur concert, at which several ladies of [the] [*MS torn*] court circle acquitted themselves in a manner that would have done credit to first rate Artistes. On these occasions an immense range of Saloons and chambers was thrown open, different from those in which the banquet was given or in which the *besa manos* are held. The concert was given in a splendid Saloon, where seats were provided for a great part of the Company; many however had to stand the whole time. ⟨and⟩ The seats ⟨provided for⟩ ↑assigned to↓ the Diplomatic Corps were in front, close to those of the Queen and Royal family; there was no stirring, therefore, from ones place. After the first part of the Concert, however, we all adjourned to a distant apartment fitted up in the style of a grotto, where tables were set out with a cold Supper, confectionary ices &c &c all which were taken Standing. Here the Queen and Queen Mother moved about the Court Circle, addressing a word or two to each person of note. When the company returned to the Concert room I did not return to my place, but passed through, to the range of apartments beyond. Here I enjoyed myself in my own way. Loitering about a long suite of magnificent rooms brilliantly lighted up; decorated with all the luxuries of art; hung with paintings of the great masters and with ↑historical↓ portraits. These I had, in a manner, all to myself for excepting here and there a domestic in Royal livery, or a couple of Courtiers who had stolen out to whisper Secrets in a corner, the whole range was deserted; All the embroidered throng had crowded into the concert room to be in the presence of Majesty. I wandered about therefore, musing and weaving fancies, and seeming to mingle them with the sweet notes of female voices, which came floating through the silken chambers from the distant music room. And now and then I half moralized upon the portraits of Kings and Queens looking down upon me from the walls; who had figured for a time in the pageants of this royal pile, but one after another, had "gone down to dusty death."[2] Among them was Ferdinand VII and his wife, Amelia of Saxony,[3] who had presided in this palace during my first visit to Spain; and whom I had often seen objects of the adulation of its Courtiers. Amelia, whose death knell I heard rung from the Cathedral towers of Granada at the time I was a resident in the Alhambra. Talk of moralizing among the tombs! you see one may moralize even in a palace and within hearing of the revelry of a court.

Beside the Royal fetes at the palace we have had fetes in the palace of Genl Narvaez, concerts and Fancy balls, at which all the Royal family were present. Three times this winter they have been present at balls given by the General; an honor rarely done by the Spanish Sovriegn to a subject. The General also got up a grand review of all the troops where the little Queen appeared on horseback, ⟨with⟩ at the head of a brilliant staff of general officers; and rode along the line, receiving the salutes. She was dressed in a riding habit of blue cloth, with a black beaver hat, and acquitted herself extremely well. She was quite delighted; even more so I believe than with the ball. General Narvaez rode by her side, in the Splendid uniform of a Field Marshall and on the other side was the Captain General of the province.

General Narvaez you percieve, is quite the Lord of the Ascendant.[4] There appears to be more court paid to him even than to the Sovreign. Wherever he goes he is the object of adulation not merely among men but among women. He is a great admirer of the Sex and received by them every where with smiles; and he has a quick, inflammable temper that makes men stand in awe of him. He is in fact a singular compound. Brave, high spirited, proud and even vain; generous to profusion, ⟨excess⟩ very punctilious; excessively sensitive to affronts, but passionate rather than vindictive, for though in the first moment of passion he is capable of any excess; yet when passion is past, he can forgive any thing but an insult. What has delighted me in him is his conduct to his Mother. A worthy old dame accustomed ↑and fitted↓ to figure in a country town: and where many a man in Narvaez situation would have left her. But he has brought her up from ↑Loxa in↓ Andalusia to court; put her at the head of his establishment; and made her share all his honors and distinctions ⟨with him⟩. Nay more: the Queen offered to confer a title upon him but he declined it, and begged it might be con-

ferred upon his mother; who accordingly is the Marchioness of Alta
Cañada You would be amused to see how the good motherly old lady
is courted by the highest nobility; and how she acquits herself on state
occasions, when in the Royal presence, every now and then glancing
her eye at her son, as if seeking a hint how to conduct herself.

While thus at the hight of power as a subject, and apparently basking
in the Sunshine of Royal favor, I look on the position of Narvaez as perilous in the extreme, and I should not be surprised at seeing him ⟨t⟩ suddenly toppled down by some unlooked for catastrophe. A schism has gradually taken place between him and the Queen Mother, which is daily
widening; though still they wear the external appearance of good will.
The Narvaez cabinet has pushed the reforms of the Constitution to a
great extent; so as to take a vast deal of the power out of the hands
of the people and invest it in the crown. ⟨It has recently brought
forward a measure also f to the⟩ It has stopped short, however,
of what is desired by some of the absolutists; who are for restoring an
absolute monarchy; and it has stopped short of the wishes of the Clergy.
During the Revolution the Clergy ⟨was⟩ were stripped of their immense
landed possessions, which gave the church such power in Spain; and
all the Convents of Monks, and most of those of nuns were suppressed.
a great part of the lands thus confiscated have been sold and resold
and have passed into the hands of persons of all ranks and conditions.
One great object of the Queen Mother since her return to Spain has
been to replace the clergy as much as possible in their former ⟨condition⟩
↑state↓. To this she is urged by the Court of Rome, and it is made
condition for her being received into favor with the Pope; receiving
absolution for her sins, and for her daughter Isabella II being recognized
↑by the Pope↓ as the legitimate Sovriegn of Spain. The Narvaez cabinet
in compliance with these views and wishes have suspended the sale
of the Church property and have determined that all that remained
unsold, should be devoted to the benefit of the Clergy.[5] This, however,
is not considered enough by a number of hot headed priests; who have
recently ⟨preached⟩ denounced from their pulpits all those who should
purchase, or hold property that had been wrested from the Church.
An alarm has spread through all ranks of society, as this ⟨threatened
to strike at the Root of the fortunes⟩ rendered all property ⟨secu⟩
insecure and threatened to unsettle Society. The Queen Mother, being
a little tender in Conscience and under the influence of some of the
most bigotted of the priesthood; is thought to incline to ultra monarchical
and apostolical measures.[6] Narvaez has come out bravely in opposition
to any measures of the Kind; and has declared his determination to
stand by the constitution as at present reformed; defending it equally
against absolute Monarchists ⟨on the one s⟩ and ultra Apostolicals on

the one side and Revolutionists, or radicals on the other. He says the Cabinet are all ⟨det⟩ strictly united, and determined to stand or fall together and he trusts upon the fidelity of the army to check any attempts at insurrection. Thus you see how critical a stand he takes. How full of danger. The whole Cabinet may be upset by a *Coup d'Etat* ↑brought about by the policy of the Queen Mother↓—or ⟨should⟩ Narvaez may be shot down by a secret enemy or rival, (as [he][7] had nearly been last year) or the army may be corrupted, as it was under Espartero—and then we shall have confusion and bloodshed. Even within these two days a conspiracy has been discovered in Vittoria[8] ⟨in the⟩ among the troops stationed there. And this days gazette gives the name of three Captains several lieutenants and about twenty sergeants arrested; of whom a number will no doubt be promptly shot. I ⟨shall⟩ feel great regret at seeing the Queen Mother under such sinister influence as I fear it will redound to her own injury and the injury of her daughter: and I sincerely and ardently hope that the present threatening symptoms may subside; and that the government may be able to carry on the affairs of the country in peace. Narvaez has great faults; but he has also great merits. He has risen to the level of his situation, and displays a tact and capacity in the various concerns of government quite beyond what was expected from him. He is extremely vigilant; prompt in action and possesses the true spirit of command. Altogether he appears to me to ⟨come nearer to the character of one⟩ be one of the most striking characters; if not the most striking, ⟨character⟩ that has risen to power in Spain during the long course of her convulsions.

And now my dear Sister I must close; for I have other letters to finish for this Courier. My health continues to be excellent; and every body congratulates me upon my healthy appearance. I hope this will hold, and that I may be able to get a good deal of work out of myself this year. I shall take care however not to over work myself, and shall take plenty of exercise in the open air.

Thank Irving[9] for me for his letter and his kind offer of services. I shall not hesitate to call upon him if ever I need them, for I know he is in all respects a most reliable person.

With affectionate remembrances to "all bodies"

Your affectionate brother
Washington Irving

ADDRESSED: Mrs Daniel Paris / care of E. Irving Esq / New York
MANUSCRIPT: Yale.   PUBLISHED: PMI, III, 368–69, 370–73 (in part); STW, II, 384 (in part).

1. These occurred on January 18 and 30, 1845. See WI to Sarah Storrow, January 18 and January [31, 1845].

2. WI's variant of *Macbeth*, V, v, 23.

3. Maria Josepha Amalia (1803–1829), Ferdinand VII's third wife, died in May, 1829. See John D. Bergamini, *The Spanish Bourbons*, p. 185.

4. For an assessment of Narváez in 1845, see Bowers, *Spanish Adventures of WI*, pp. 265–70.

5. Both Narváez and Martínez de la Rosa resisted the pressure to restore the lands confiscated from the church and sold, but they agreed to return unsold lands. See H. Butler Clarke, *Modern Spain*, pp. 201–2; *La Posdata*, February 10, 1845; and London *Times*, February·20, 24, and March 3, 1845.

6. See WI to James Buchanan, July 10, 1845; and STW, II, 186–87.

7. WI omitted the bracketed word.

8. The London *Times* for February 27, 1845, reports that Madrid papers of February 19 mention the discovery of a Carlist conspiracy in Burgos, but no specific mention is made of Vitoria; nor is the matter alluded to later.

9. This letter from Irving Paris has not been located. On April 19, 1845, WI wrote to his nephew asking for legal assistance for Spanish friends concerning property in the United States.

1816.   To Isaac Stone et al.

Madrid 19th Feby 1845

Circular to Consuls in Cuba

(2)	Isaac Stone[1]	Consul.	San Juan de los Remedies
(3)	William Hogan	"	Nuevitos.
(1)	{ Franklin Gage	"	Cárdenas.
	{ John Hartman	"	Panama.

Sir

After holding several applications for Consular Exequaturs in suspense for a long time the Spanish Govt. has recently signified its determination to admit Foreign Consuls in but four posts of the Island of Cuba viz. Havanna, Santiago de Cuba, Matanzas, and Trinidad. I have requested my agent in New York Mr Pierre Irving, Bank of Commerce, to pay your order (*in the case of Messrs Hartman (1) and Franklin Gage (1), the sum of Eighteen dollars and twenty five cents—in that of Mr Isaac Stone (2) Twenty one dollars and in that of Mr William Hogan (3) Three pounds fourteen shillings* Sterling) remitted by you to this Legation in anticipation of the fees exacted by the Spanish offices.

I am Sir respectfully / Your obt Servant
signed = Washington Irving.

MANUSCRIPT: NA, RG 84 (letterbook copy).

1. Isaac Stone was nominated as U.S. consul for San Juan de los Remodios, Cuba on December 18, 1844, and consented to on January 13, 1845. See Hasse, *Index to U.S. Documents*, III, 1747.

1817. To Messrs. Lombard and Whitmore

Madrid Feb. 21st 1845

Unofficial / Messrs Lombard and Whitmore / Boston

Gentlemen,

I have duly received your letter of December 16th and have attended to its contents.[1] On receiving the commission of Mr James I. Wright U. S. Consul for the Port of St Iago de Cuba I immediately sent it to the Spanish Dept of State and of Foreign Affairs and in my accompanying note urged the speedy grant of an Exequatur for the reasons alleged in your letter[.][2] I have since urged the same in a conversation with the Minister of State. I doubt however whether my representations will be availing. The Spanish Govt is extremely cautious as to the Consular Agents whom it admits into its Colonial possessions and especially into the Island of Cuba and has always taken time to write out to the place to which the Consul is nominated to enquire whether his appointment would be advisable Thus you see the Consul's name has to cross the ocean four times before he receives his Exequatur. The Spanish Govt has recently given another proof of its extreme caution in respect to foreign agents in Cuba, in declining to admit Consuls in any but four ports of the Island, namely, Havanna, St Iago de Cuba, Matanzas and Trinidad.

I shall take occasion to repeat my application in favor of Mr Wright.

I remain Gentlemen / Very respectfully / Your obt servant
signed = Washington Irving

MANUSCRIPT: NA, RG 84 (letterbook copy).

1. In their letter Lombard and Whitmore urged quick action on Wright's nomination as consul. "The American Trade at that port is large—Robt. G. Shaw Esq, P. S. Shelton Esq and ourselves are extensively engaged in said trade—as are also many of the first Commercial Houses in New York and Philadelphia—" (NA, RG 84).

2. See WI to Martínez de la Rosa, February 8, 1845.

1818. To Sarah Storrow

Madrid, Feb. 21st. 1845

My dear Sarah,

I was disappointed yesterday in receiving no letter from you; I console myself however with the idea that the Courier has been detained on the road by wintry weather, and hope to receive one today. I wrote yesterday to your mother; but had to send the letter direct by post to England; fearing it would be too late for the Steamer if I should send it through your hands. I fear at times that you feel this weekly correspondence a tax upon you; and yet, my dear Sarah, Seperated as we are, it is almost the only intercourse that we can have for the rest of life. For my part I grieve that I cannot devote my pen almost exclusively to the correspondence with my family and friends, and that I have so many other imperious claims upon it.

It is expected that the Court will go to Barcelona this year as early as ⟨the⟩ in the Month of May.[1] I have written to government to know whether it wishes me to follow the Court in its visits to the provinces. I have no inclination to do so, but wish to remain stationary this year (if I am permitted to remain in office) and to devote myself to my literary tasks. Now that I am able once more to exercise my pen, I have a vast deal of lee way to make up; and on this years labors will depend whether I am once more to be independent in my circumstances, or am ⟨to⟩ still to cling to office. I have had enough of diplomacy and of Court life, and if I had but to care for my single self, I would rather live on a morsel in some quiet corner, and indulge my own quiet tastes and humors, than banquet with Kings and Queens and figure in palaces. But such is the hardness of my lot. I have to be grand that others may be comfortable, and to revel in the palace that they may live Cosily in the Cottage.

Feb 22d Since I wrote the foregoing I have received your letter of the 14th.[2] which has been quite a treat. I am glad to hear that your ball went off so well; though I was sure ⟨I⟩ it would as the effect of parties of the kind depend very much upon the character of the Mistress of the house; and I think you have just the cordial genial kind of nature to make your guests feel at home—and poor little Kate and Susie I suppose, slept through the whole of it, little dreaming, poor "babes in the wood," ⟨of⟩ what capers their Mamma was cutting in the next room! You mention Madame de la Valette as being present, but you say nothing of the Greenes. Did they meet on this occasion? and if so, did my merry friend Mrs Greene laugh as heartily as usual?—I cannot concieve of Mrs Ellis in a white dress. I have only seen her in black; and I admired her so much in that, that I can hardly think she would look as well in any other. In her "rich black velvet," about which you rave, she must have been perfection. Did she dance?

I perfectly join with you in your admiration of Miss Tessiere, without having ever seen her. Her ⟨delight with⟩ admiration of Kate and Susie has quite won my heart, and convinced me that she must be a young lady of superior taste and observation.

You give me no account of my friends Mrs Henderson and Miss Fisher at the ball, this is a sad omission. Mrs Henderson is just the person to enjoy such a social party, and to add to its cheerfulness, and Miss Fisher ⟨is quite⟩ with her taste in dress and her graceful movement in the dance is quite an ornament to a ball room.

I think it a great pity you had not received your mothers letter in time to have adopted her hint and had Kate and Susie taught the Polka; they would have been the belles of the evening

I have been interrupted by the arrival of the mail and it brings me a letter from your mother[3] written in excellent spirits. She had received my letter giving her an account of Court gaieties, and says 'I have enjoyed your splendid ball at General Narvaez as I feel considerably acquainted with the Royal family and have quite an attachment to the young Queen, and princess. My reccollection of Queen Christina when in the zenith of her charms is ⟨quite⟩ ↑most↓ agreeable. Although a faulty character I think she has redeeming traits in the Strong affection she bears her daughters. She must be still a very fascinating woman. Your description of ⟨all⟩ the magnificence of the Royal banquet is really delightful. I enjoy it as I used to do the Arabian Nights when a little girl. In my secluded life it is quite an event to get one of those delightful letters, and for several days I am in Madrid mingling with the great and noble, treading magnificent saloons."

How gratifying it is to find your mother retaining at her period of life, ⟨those⟩ such lively sensibility, and such freshness of feeling. It is this which induces me to write her such long accounts of the little Queen and her court; where there is something of the interest of historical romance mingled with scenic splendor. I know the excitable imagination I am addressing and its power of multiplying the materials I furnish

Kiss my darlings Kate and Susie: you have no idea how the latter is rising in importance and gaining in interest with me.

Your affectionate uncle
Washington Irving

P.S.[4] Cannot you fold the print of the Cottage[5] neatly about the Size of this sheet of paper, enclose it in a stout envellope and send it by the French Courier?

ADDRESSED: Madame / Madame Storrow / No 4. Rue de la Victoire / *à Paris*
MANUSCRIPT: Yale.

1. Isabella, the queen mother, and the infanta left for Barcelona and the baths at the end of May. See Bowers, *Spanish Adventures of WI*, pp. 259, 261.
2. This letter has not been located.
3. This letter has not been located.
4. This postscript is written at the top of page 1, above the heading and salutation.
5. WI had mentioned this lithograph in his letter to Sarah Storrow, February 14, 1845.

1819.   To Samuel McLean

Madrid 22nd Feby 1845

Saml McLean Esqre / U. S. Consul, Trinidad

Sir

I herewith forward to you your Exequatur received this day from the Department of State together with the original commission signed by the President of the U. S. In consequence of representations made by me in obedience to instructions from our Govt her Majesty's Govt has consented to relinquish for the future the fees hitherto exacted on the delivery of Exequaturs.[1]

It has also determined not to admit foreign Consuls in any but four ports of the Island of Cuba, viz. Havanna, St Iago de Cuba, Matanzas and Trinidad.

I am respectfully / etc
signed—Washington Irving.

MANUSCRIPT: NA, RG 84 (letterbook copy).

1. See WI to Martínez de la Rosa, November 28, 1845.

1820. To Francisco Martínez de la Rosa

Madrid 23rd Feby. 1845

To his Exy / Don F. M. de la Rosa / etc etc

Sir

I have the honor to acknowledge the receipt of your Excy's note[1] accompanying the Regium Exequatur of Saml McLean and informing me that her Majesty the Queen has thought proper to order that this instrument should be issued without the exaction of any fees in just reciprocity of what is practised by the Govt of the U. S.[2] in regard to Spanish Consuls.

I feel highly gratified at the just view her Majesty has taken of this matter which however was to be expected from the honorable and equitable disposition which characterizes her Majesty's Govt.

It is with pleasure also that I received from your Excy the assurance that the Regium Exequatur will be extended to Mr Wright recently nominated Consul for St Iago de Cuba as promptly as expedient. As the usual process of collecting information in the Colonies and transmitting it to Madrid respecting the fitness of every Candidate for a Consulship involves the delay of two extra voyages across the Atlantic and as the Commerce of the U. S. to the port of St Iago de Cuba is likely to suffer for want of a Consul during the time required by these voyages I would respectfully suggest as a measure of expedition that the Exequatur be sent out at once to the competent authorities in the Island of Cuba, to be delivered to Mr Wright as soon as it shall appear to these authorities, on proper investigation that it is expedient to grant it to him

I am etc
Signed = Washington Irving

MANUSCRIPT: NA, RG 84 (letterbook copy).

1. See Martínez de la Rosa to WI, February 21, 1845 (NA, RG 84).
2. WI had emphasized this point in his letter of November 28, 1844.

1821. To Paul Pon

Madrid 24th Feby 1845

Paul Pon Esqre / U. S. Consul Barcelona.

Sir

I have duly received your two letters of the 21st Jany[1] one giving me a statement of the Trade of the U. S. to your port during the last year for which I am much obliged to you, the other stating what you suppose to be excessive charges for tonnelage etc on the American Corvette Nautilus.

On examin[in]g[2] I find that the dues exacted from the Nautilus are in conformity to the tariff of charges imposed in the port of Barcelona upon all foreign vessels excepting the French. These latter enjoy certain exemptions in consequence of Treaty Stipulations of long standing. I believe the old "facto de familia" between France and Spain and are reciprocated to spanish vessels arriving in France. This stipulation was violated in a few instances during Espartero's administration in regard to French vessels. The French Ambassador recently made a reclamation to the Spanish Govt whereupon the sums wrongfully exacted were refunded and the royal order issued a copy of which you enclosed to me. The difference between 8 rials per ton charged in the port of Barcelona and 1 rial per ton charged in Malaga and elsewhere is on account of the mole which has to be kept up at great expense in the former port and towards which foreign vessels have to contribute.

The charges on tonnage etc vary greatly in the different Spanish ports, according to circumstances They are local regulations of expediency or necessity with which the ⟨Spanish⟩ ↑General↓ Govt does not readily interfere

I am Sir / respectfully your obt servant
Signed = Washington Irving.

MANUSCRIPT: NA, RG 84 (letterbook copy).

A copy of this letter is enclosed with WI's despatch no. 61 to John C. Calhoun, March 4, 1845.

1. Pon's letters are preserved in the files of the Madrid legation (NA, RG 84).
2. The copyist omitted the bracketed letters.

1822.   To Francisco Martínez de la Rosa

Madrid 24th Feby 1845

His Excy / Don F. M. de la Rosa / etc etc

Sir

I had the satisfaction last summer to obtain from her Majesty's Govt a modification of the Quarantine laws of the Canary Islands with respect to vessels of the U. S. relieving from the eight days Quarantine of observation all such of the aforesaid vessels as should arrive with clean bills of health from any port north of Cape Hatteras.

I had hoped that this modification so beneficial to the Commercial in-

terests of both countries would have been extended to the ports of the
Peninsula and repeated notes have been passed to her Majesty's Govt
from this Legation urging the safety and policy of such a measure, showing that the American ports for which this exemption was solicited, were
as healthy as any in Europe and that all vessels arriving at such ports
from the Southern parts of the U. S. were subject to Quarantine.

I am sorry to find that these representations have hitherto been ineffec-
tive and that vessels from the healthiest parts of the U. S. and which
would be admitted to pratique in any other country of Europe are still
subjected on arriving in Spain to the useless vexations and expensive
delays and restrictions so judiciously abolished in the Canary Islands.

It is not my intention to dwell on a subject which has been repeatedly
discussed by this Legation[.] I would merely press it upon your Excellency's consideration as in accordance with that intelligent and increasing interest manifested by her Majesty's Govt in facilitating the operations
of Commerce. On reference to the previous communications referred to
of this Legation your Excellency will perceive that we ask for no exemptions and regulations that are not accorded by other nations the most
enlightened on the subject of Quarantines and the most intelligent in the
concerns of Commerce and that we ask for nothing which is not as much
to the interest of Spain as of the United States

> I am with great respect etc
> Signed = Washington Irving

MANUSCRIPT: NA, RG 84 (letterbook copy).

1823. *To Sarah Storrow*

Madrid Feb 27th. 1845

My dear Sarah,

It is Thursday morning, which generally brings me my weekly letter
from you; and as there has been no bad weather in the mountains to delay
the Courier I expect to receive one before dinner time. As it is Lent I
have no more fêtes to describe. Madrid is quiet, and I am well content
that these late revels are at an end. We have our little diplomatic Soirees,
twice a week at the French Ambassadors, and once a week at the O'Sheas,
which bring us together sociably and are very pleasant. On Saturday
there is to be a large dinner at Mr O'Sheas given to Genl Narvaez and
some of the other Spanish Ministers and to the chiefs of the Diplomatic
Corps. I am not fond of these great dinners, though all kind of parties

at the O'Sheas, are apt to be pleasant. You would delight in Mrs O'Shea; she is every thing that is kind, and cordial and gentle and lady like. I find her an invaluable friend, and only regret that I shall soon lose her for several months; as they go early in the season to pass the warm weather at Biaritz, near Bayonne, on the Sea Shore, where Mr O'Shea has built a pleasant Summer retreat. I shall miss the OSheas sadly.

My friend Madame Albuquerque has sufficiently recovered to sit up and receive visits. She is very proud of her babe, which is indeed a very fine child.

I continue busy with my pen, and am happy to find that my literary application is not attended with any return of my malady[.] I, however, am cautious not to apply myself too closely. The carriage is ready at a regular hour, when I break off, however, closely engaged, and sally forth for air, exercise and recreation

Do you ever drive out now with Madame Hacquet. You did not tell me whether she was at your ball or, not. I suppose not, as it was an American party where she would have found herself among Strangers. I wish she would shorten her poor devil husbands allowance and make him exert himself to get what is due to him. What a contemptible animal he must be, to hang on her for support. But I reccollect what a miserable animal he was as a lover; if in fact he ever was a lover, or any thing better than a mere fortune hunter.

Friday Your letter,[1] my dear Sarah, came yesterday as I expected; and came most opportunely; just as I was lounging on the Sopha, a little fatigued with working—It was quite a restorative. I should have liked to [have]² had some extracts from your ⟨letters abo⟩ American letters, giving me an account of my friend Georges³ arrival among his American relatives. I think they cannot but like him he is so truly amiable and worthy.

I had heard from America that Gabriel⁴ was about to make a short visit to Europe. I hope, poor fellow, it may benefit his health, which is but indifferent. It would, indeed, be a most desireable event for you that he should bring out his good little wife and his children, and establish himself for a time, in Paris or its vicinity

I hope you will give me a full account of Mr Kings ball. Poor Mr King! with his dancing "constituents." I dont envy him his position. You now see what petty cabals and cavillings an American Minister is subject to in Paris, from the swarm of idlers of his country, who infest that capital, and think him bound to consult their amusement and gratify their vanity. I wonder what congress would say if a Minister were to ask for an encrease of ⟨pa⟩ salary, or at least ⟨f⟩ ↑of the↓ contingent fund, to enable him to meet the expense of giving his country men dinners and balls in Paris; and yet how can he do it to their satisfaction on his actual salary? But they must have dances forsooth! and must be ushered into the diplomatic circle. By Jupiter I'd invite some dancing bears to meet them, and persuade them they were Russian diplomats. The fact is our Ministers are sent out to attend to business. They have the means of living decently as the business agents of a republic; but are allowed nothing for luxury and ostentation. The government, ⟨but⟩ by its very limited allowance. virtually discountenances all indulgence of the Kind.

I have not seen the letter of Mr Walsh[5] about the Consulate, and wish you would send me any newspaper which may contain it. I should be sorry to find him indulging in any unkind remarks about Mr Draper;[6] who always appeared to me to be a very worthy and kind hearted man.

I can believe all you tell me about little Susies being the most beautiful and the very best baby in the whole world. She is continually growing in my good graces without my seeing her; and I have quite a picture of her in my mind as she must be at present. I am sorry however, to find that Kates toilette is neglected and that you find it too troublesome to make her newspaper caps and scarfs. Dear, darling restless little Kate! if I were only with her I'd be delighted to make her newspaper dresses all day long. Her "whims and caprices" as [you][7] call them were a source of inexhaustable amusement to me; and I frequently find myself laughing out loud when some one or other of them comes across my mind. If I had her here, I think I'd neglect literature, diplomacy and every thing else, and pass my whole time in playing with her. I never met with a child that hit my humor more completely.

You must not connect me with any of your travelling or country plans for next Summer; not suggest any thing that may make me discontented with my residence in Madrid. I look upon this as; in all probability the last year I shall pass in Spain, and it is important for me to turn it to the ⟨first⟩ best advantage by as close literary application as my health and the duties of my office will permit. If I receive no instructions from the Government, therefore, to follow the Court in its visit, to the provinces, I think it likely I shall remain quietly in my quarters at Madrid, endeavoring to get my literary concerns into a State of forwardness. I have no time now to lose. I have much to do, with which the wellfare of others is connected, and I cannot hope, as formerly, for years of bodily activity and mental power. Now that my health is restored, therefore, I cannot spare months for recreation and travelling. In the early part of my literary carreer I used to think I would take warning by the fate of writers who kept on writing until they "wrote themselves down", and that I would retire while ↑still↓ in the freshness of my powers—but ⟨circum⟩ you see circumstances have obliged me to change my plans, and I am likely to write on until the pen drops from my hand.

Saturday, March 1. Tell Mr Storrow that the Candalabras have arrived in good order. They are exactly the same pattern with those he purchased for me in 1842 and are much admired. I am very much obliged to him for his kindness in executing the commission.

We are looking forward to strong reinforcements of our Italian troupes after lent. They have not ⟨the[?]⟩ been very brilliant of late; Moriani having departed for London, and the prima donna Tossi who used to perform with him, having been ill. Ronconi,[8] however, is to come here from Paris to the troupe at the Circo, and several other performers of note are spoken of. The opera and the ballet are quite the rage at Madrid and as Madrid ⟨is⟩ has become quite gay and prodigal of late, it presents a better mart for talent. One cause of this prodigality is the gambling spirit which has taken possession of this capital. I mean gambling in the funds. It pervades all classes, and influences all affairs. The highest functionaries of the Government indulge in it.[9] Purchases and sales of Stocks are made every day to the ↑⟨[*unrecovered*]⟩↓ amount of millions: ⟨in this way⟩ fortunes are suddenly made by speculators; who instantly set up their carriage ⟨and⟩ take their opera box; and live like beggars on horseback,[10] until some ↑bad speculation or some↓ sudden change in the funds sends them where beggars on horseback are proverbially said to go.[11]

For these two or three last days we have ⟨the⟩ had soft spring weather, and people begin to talk of ⟨excursions to the⟩ visits to Aranguez, which, in spring time, is the paradise of the Madridlanians[.] I ⟨[*unrecovered*]⟩ do not know whether the Court will go there this spring; I presume it will depend upon the time determined upon for the ↑royal↓ journey to Barcelona, which may take place as early as the month of May. I wish we had a Bois de Bologne in the neighborhood of Madrid to drive in—I feel sadly the want of agreeable drives now spring is coming on

Farewell my dear Sarah. Kiss the darlings for me and give kind remembrances to Mr Storrow.

Your affectionate uncle
Washington Irving

MANUSCRIPT: Yale.   PUBLISHED: STW, II, 190 (in part).

1. This letter has not been located.
2. WI omitted the bracketed word.
3. Possibly George Sumner, who had been living in Paris.
4. Gabriel, son of John Treat Irving.
5. Robert Walsh (1784–1859), editor and man of letters who served as U.S. consul in Paris from 1844 to 1851.
6. Apparently Draper was a clerk at the consulate.
7. WI omitted the bracketed word.

8. Either Giorgio Ronconi (1810–1890), an Italian operatic baritone who performed in Madrid and Barcelona between 1842 and 1847 or his brother Sebastiano (1810–1900), another baritone who appeared frequently in Spain. See *International Cyclopedia of Music and Musicians*, ed. Oscar Thompson, p. 1571.

9. Among the speculators was General Narváez, who, it was rumored, was using government funds for his gambling. See Bowers, *Spanish Adventures of WI*, pp. 267–71.

10. See Robert Burton, *Anatomy of Melancholy*, pt. 2. sec. 2, member 2.

11. "Set a beggar on horse-back, and he'll ride to the devil" (*Cobbett's Political Register*, XV, xii, 429).

1824. To Javier Quinto

Madrid 28 de Febo 1845

Al Señor Don Javier Quinto / Administrador Gl de Correos

Muy Señor mio: Las quejas repetidas que recibo de los Consules de mi pais establecidos en los puertos de la Peninsula sobre los postes escesivos en sus cartas procedentes de los Estados Unidos me ponen en la precision de acudir a vd. para que se sirva intervenir en unos abusos que son indignos de la buena administracion que con tanto afan ha introducido en ese ramo importante del servicio publico.

Èl Consul de Malaga me participa en una carta fecha 19 del corriente haberse visto obligado a pagar por una carta llegante de los Estados Unidos la cantidad exorbitante de 38 rs 30 ms vn. Hizo presente al Administrador que dicho cargo era ilegal y en abierta contravencion con lo dispuesto por la Real orden del 30 de Julio de 1832 por la cual cartas procedentes de los Estados Unidos no estan sujetas a pagar como ultramarinas. Pero sus representaciones quedaron burladas.

Seguro de que basta llamar su atencion celosa sobre estos abusos escandalosos para que no vuelvan a repetirse me abstendre de ocupar mas a Vd. de este asunto.

Estimaria[?] mucho tambien tenga vd. a bien mardarseme franca de una copia de la Real orden arriba citada.

Soy con la mayor consideracion etc

(signed) Washington Irving.

Copy of Royal order referred to in note to Don Javier Quinto, Page 149, 150. The original was sent to Mr Read U. S Consul Malaga 8th March 45

Royal Order.

Enterado el Rey N. S. del informe que la direccion nos ha dirigido con fecha 16 del mes ppo relativamente a la queja del Ministro de los E. U. sobre el excesivo poste que se carga en la Admn de Cadiz a las cartas y papeles que vienen de dichos Estados para la Legacion y Consules de aquel pais se ha dignado S. M. resolver por previsto genl que toda correspondencia llegada a los Puertos de España en buques extranjeros para cuya conduccion nada les abone la admn de Correos debera entregarse y remitirse por las respectivas Admnes de Correos sin exigir mas derechos que los que admiten las demas Correspondencias del pais en que fueran entregadas por los capitanes de los buques conductores y que solo se exijan se carguen los partes señalados para las correspondencias de ultramar cuando estas hayan sido conducidas en Buques Españoles destinado al objeto o ya por los de guerra o Mercantes, puesto que la Real orden en que la Direccion apoya su dictamen ninguna conexion tiene con los postes de cartas de que se trata y es mas bien por miras de politica que de interes el que se haya mandado que ni los capitanes ni los demas que componen la tripulacion y pasajeros pueden conducir ni entregar cartas ninjunas sino que todas deben remitirse por el primer bote de Sanidad que comunique con el barco conductor a la Admn de Correos para que esta les de el curso debido.

San Ildefonso 20 de Julio de 1832. El Conde de Alcudia
Addressed to Señores Directores de Correos.

Es Copia
Signed = Javier de Quinto

Manuscript: NA, RG 84 (letterbook copy).

Translation:
"The repeated complaints that I receive from the consuls of my country established in the ports of the Peninsula concerning the excessive postage charges placed on their letters proceeding from the United States place me in the obligation of resorting to you in order that you kindly intervene in abuses that are unworthy of the good administration which you have introduced with such zeal in that important branch of public service. The consul in Málaga informs me in a letter dated the 19th of this month that he has found himself obliged to pay for a letter arriving from the United States the exorbitant sum of 38 reales 30 maravedíes vellón. He brought to the attention of the administrator that such a charge was illegal and in open breach with what had been specified by the royal order of July 30, 1832, by which letters proceeding from the United States are not subject to payment as overseas letters. But their petitions were frustrated. Being certain that it is sufficient to call your zealous attention to these scandalous abuses so that they not be repeated, I shall abstain from occupying you further with this matter. I would greatly appreciate your sending me free of mail charges a copy of the abovementioned royal order."

Translation of the copy of the royal order:

"Our lord the king having been informed of the report that the direction has sent to us with the date of the 16 of this month relative to the complaint of the minister of the U.S. on the excessive mail charge levied in the administration of Cádiz on the letters and papers coming from said States for the legation and consuls of that country, his majesty has condescended to decree as a general provision that any correspondence arriving at the ports of Spain in foreign ships for whose conveyance the Postal Administration provides nothing will have to be delivered and remitted by the respective Postal Administrations without requiring any fees other than those which are allowed for the other correspondence of the country in which they had been delivered by the captains of the conveying ships and that it be required that the charges indicated for overseas correspondence be levied only when they have been conveyed by Spanish ships designated for this purpose, whether warships or merchant ships, since the royal order on which the direction bases its judgment has no connection with the charges in question and it is rather with a view to politics than to interest that it has been ordered that neither the captains nor others who make up the crew and passengers can take or deliver letters but that all must be transmitted by the first sanitation boat which communicates with the conveying ship to the Postal Administration so that the latter may give to them the proper course."

1825. To Francisco Martínez de la Rosa

Madrid 9 de Marzo 1845

Al Exco Senor Don F. M. de la Rosa / etc etc

Muy Señor mio:

Tuve el honor de dirigir a V. S. el 14 del mes proximo pasado una carta solicitando una real orden para la exportacion por la aduana de Cadiz, à nombre del Sr Newbold, ciudadano de los E. U. de treinta moruecos merinos.

Este caballero tiene vastas posesiones en el Estado de la Nueva York donde posee de los rebaños mas puros en los Estados Unidos; ha venido a España y se encuentra en este momento en Madrid esperando que consiga el permiso solicitado para marcharse a Extramadura en busca de los moruecos que desea esportar a fin de conservar en toda su pureza el rebaño de casta española que ya posee.

Estimaré mucho, por lo tanto, se de despacho a este asunto y se me avise, lo mas pronto posible del resultado de la solicitacion

Aprovecho etc

signed = Washington Irving.

N. B. No royal order was required: merely an *export duty*

MANUSCRIPT: NA, RG 84 (letterbook copy).

Translation:

"I had the honor of sending to your excellency on the 14th of last month a letter requesting a royal order for the exportation through customs at Cadiz of thirty merino rams in the name of Mr. Newbold, a citizen of the United States.

"This gentleman has vast holdings in the State of New York where he has one of the purest flocks in the United States; he has come to Spain and at this moment is waiting to receive the permission he has requested to leave for Estremadura in search of the rams he hopes to export in order to conserve the purity of the flock of Spanish stock which he now has.

"I would be grateful, therefore, if you would attend to this matter and notify as soon as possible regarding the outcome of the request."

1826. To John C. Calhoun

Legation of the United States / Madrid, March 4th 1845

No 61 / The Hon / John C. Calhoun / Secretary of State Washington.

Sir,

Since I had last the honor of addressing you[1] I have received and forwarded to Mr Samuel McLean his Exequatur as consul for Trinidad de Cuba.[2]

In a note from Mr Martinez de la Rosa,[3] Minister of State and of Foreign affairs, which accompanied the exequatur⟨e⟩, and a copy of which I enclose, he informs me that the fees hitherto exacted in the Spanish offices on issuing instruments of the kind, and against which, according to your instructions, I had protested, are discontinued.

Repeated applications have been made by this Legation to the Spanish government to have all vessels arriving at ports of the Peninsula, with clean bills of health, from any port north of Cape Hatteras, exempted from the eight days "quarantine of observation." A note recently received from the Minister of State,[4] and which I have the honor to enclose, will shew you that those applications have been ineffectual. I also regret to learn from our Consul in the Canary Islands,[5] that the modifications of the quarantine laws in those islands, granted in consequence of my representations, have been less ample than I had suggested, and than I had been led to infer, from a note of the Minister of State,[6] addressed to me while I was at Barcelona last summer. In fact it appears that the exemption from the eight days quarantine of observation is granted in those islands merely to vessels coming (with clean bills of health) from Philadelphia and ports to the northward: leaving all those from ports within the Chesapeak and south as far as the Oronoco, subject to the old sanatary ordeal. Neither does the new sanatery order contain any permission for vessels to perform their quarantine of observation at their port of destination; they are subject, therefore, as before, to be ordered for that purpose to the port of Santa Cruz.

These vexatious regulations may partly be the result of petty intrigues to promote local interests and accumulate official fees; but they may also be attributed in a great degree to the laxity of our own quarantine regulations. In reply to the argument I have repeatedly urged of the healthiness of our northern ports, I am told that those ports are in frequent and quick communication with ports to the South, considered unhealthy by the Supreme board of health of Spain; and that it is the practise for vessels from the south, bound for Europe, to touch at a northern port and take out a clean bill of health, which is readily procured. Such, at least, are the representations sent home by Spanish Consuls resident in our ports.

I received recently a letter from our Consul at Barcelona (Mr Paul Pon)[7] representing what he concieved to be excessive and irregular charges of Tonnage &c exacted in that port from the American Corvette *Nautilus*, and informing me that the French Government had resisted similar charges, levied on French vessels, and had obtained a royal order for restitution of sums thus exacted and exemption from similar charges in future.

I have enquired into the matter, and as the consul informs me that he has written to you on the subject, I enclose a copy of my reply to him;[8] in which I have informed him that the vessel was subjected to none but the usual port charges levied in Barcelona on all foreign vessels excepting the French; and that these are excepted in consequence of treaty stipulations granting like exemptions to Spanish vessels in French ports.

In the course of my inquiries I met with a tariff of the duties exacted in the several ports of the peninsula on vessels of 200 tons burthen; from which estimates may be made for vessels of different tonnage. As this document is not to be met with in any of the public offices of Madrid, but appears to be the result of private investigation, I have made a copy of it, which I enclose, for the use of the Department of State. As has been observed, French vessels are not included in the category of Foreign vessels, but, in almost every particular pay the same duties as those of Spain.

Great delays have hitherto taken place in obtaining royal exequaturs for our consuls appointed to ports in the Spanish Colonies, the government at Madrid requiring time to write to the colony and obtain information as to the expediency of the appointment, previous to issuing an Exequatur. To obviate these delays, and save the time required for two voyages across the atlantic I have suggested, in applying for an exequatur for Mr Wright, recently nominated consul for St Iago de Cuba, that the exequatur should at once be issued and forwarded to the proper authorities in Cuba, to be delivered to Mr Wright when those authorities should be satisfied, on proper investigation, that his appointment was expedient. I have just received a reply from Mr Martinez de la Rosa[9] approving of my suggestion, and assuring me, that, as soon as Mr Wright's Exequatur should be issued, it would be forwarded directly to the Captain General of Cuba, and advice given me of the same. I trust this will establish a precedent to be observed in like cases for the future.

It is expected that the Court will repair to Barcelona early in May, to sojourn there for a time on account of the Queens health. A part of the Cabinet and most of the Diplomatic Corps will either accompany the Court, or visit it during its sojourn. I requested, in a former dispatch,[10] to be instructed how to proceed in such cases; as these followings of the Court, peculiar, I believe, to Spain, necessarily involve extra expenses, which have been allowed by government to my predecessors, in conformity to general diplomatic usage. I hope to receive a reply on this subject in time. It appears to me that, if no peculiar affair of business should call for ⟨my⟩ ↑a lengthened↓ attendance there, a mere temporary visit, for the purpose of testifying respect to the Sovreign would be sufficient

> I remain Sir / Very respectfully / Your obt Servt
> Washington Irving

DOCKETED: Recd. 17 Apl. / Mr Markoe
MANUSCRIPT: NA, RG 59.
This despatch is entirely in WI's handwriting.

1. On February 8, 1845.
2. On February 22, 1845.
3. Martínez de la Rosa to WI, February 21, 1845 (NA, RG 84).
4. Martínez de la Rosa, February 26, 1845 (NA, RG 84).
5. Joseph Cullen to WI, January 20, 1845 (NA, RG 84).
6. Ramón María Narváez, July 26, 1844 (NA, RG 84).
7. Pon to WI, January 21, 1845 (NA, RG 84).
8. WI to Paul Pon, February 24, 1845.
9. Letter dated March 2, 1845 (NA, RG 84).
10. January 11, 1845.

1827. To Messrs. Lombard and Whitmore

Madrid 5th March '45

Messrs Lombard and Whitmore / Boston

Gentlemen,

Since the date of my previous letter (Feb 21) I have addressed a note to Mr Martinez de la Rosa, Minister of State, suggesting as a measure of expedition in the case of Mr Wright that, instead, of waiting until information could be collected in the Island of Cuba and transmitted to Spain as to the expediency of granting his Exequatur, the Govt should at once issue an Exequatur and send it to the competent authorities on the Island of Cuba to be delivered to Mr Wright as soon as, on proper investigation his appointment shall be deemed by these authorities expedient thus saving the delay of two voyages of documents across the Atlantic

I have just received a reply from the Minister of State[1] approving of my suggestions and assuring me that as soon as Mr Wright's Exequatur is issued, it will be forwarded directly to the Captain General of Cuba; and advice will be given me of the same. I trust therefore soon to hear that the document is on its way

I am Gentlemen / Very respectfully / Your obt servant
signed = Washington Irving

MANUSCRIPT: NA, RG 84 (letterbook copy).

1. Dated March 2, 1845 (NA, RG 84).

1828. To Sarah Storrow

Madrid, March 6th. 1845

My dear Sarah,

Thursday having arrived, I am on the look out for your weekly letter; especially as this one is to bring me ⟨the⟩ your bulletin of the ball at the Embassy. I hope my friend King has been sufficiently well to do the honors of his house with comfort to himself as I am sure he has done to the satisfaction of his guests. He has great advantage in having such a perfect lady to do the honors of his house. By the bye ⟨I se⟩ one of the newspapers last received from the United States mentions the probability of Mr Kings return home on account of ill health, and suggests the possibility of his having a place in Mr Polks cabinet. I presume, however, it is one of the groundless rumors of Washington.[1]

I received yesterday a long and very pleasant letter from Helen Pierre,[2] giving me the chit chat of the family; by which I find the girls from the Cottage have been making, by turns, long visits to town, so as to break in upon the monotony of winter. Charlotte has passed nearly the whole winter with Julia Grinnell, who has always shewn a great partiality for her. The others take up their quarters with Edgar and Amanda. Poor Edgar & Amanda! what kind hearted and affectionate beings they are. I shall endeavor to make some arrangement against next winter by which they may afford the girls a *pied a terre*[3] in town without suffering by their hospitality. Heavens! how I do feel at times the narrowness of my means, which continually cramps my efforts to do what I would wish to do.

Friday—Yesterday brought no letter from you; I suppose the courier has been delayed by bad travelling. The letter would have been uncommonly welcome, for the weather was wet and chilly so that I did not go abroad; and I was in no humor to busy myself with my pen at home; so I half read half moped the day away; listening to every step along the corridor in hopes that it might be Lorenzo with your letter from the French Embassy. I trust this day will be more fortunate. Whenever I am in a writing mood, time flies swiftly and the day appears too short; but when I am out of humor with pen ink and paper, as at present, the hours lag heavily and I feel that I am alone. What would I not give at such times for dear little Kate and Susie to be here with me and gambol about my saloons. I have ample play ground for them within doors. What a zest they would give to my lonely drives! I often think now that spring is about opening what a delight it would be to ⟨transport⟩ be able to transport my whole establishment to Paris, and to be able to drive out daily with you and the children to the Champs Elysee or the Bois— Here the means for such enjoyment are thrown away upon me. I have two carriages; for beside my large one, which I purchased of Mr Vail I have a very handsome coupé, built by Binder at Paris, which Mr Livingstons brother sent to him recently, and which I have taken of him at cost and charges. It is just the kind of pretty little Equipage which I heard you once admire and I would give the world to have you in it by my side. For my own part, these lonely drives are irksome to me; I take them as I would a prescription, and when Pepé comes every day to tell me the carriage is ready I am half inclined to ⟨send it⟩ order it back to the Coach house—but I think better of it and take my dose. Have I not in mind your constant exhortation, repeated in every letter, to take plenty of air and Exercise? You See how obedient I am.

Saturday. I am sadly disappointed. The French Courier arrived on Thursday, but has brought me no letter from you. I had certainly calculated on one this week as you had a theme provided by the Diplomatic ball, of which you promised to give me an account. I see by Galignani[4] that it was very brilliant, and that Mr King and *his Sister* Mrs Ellis did the honors of the house in proper style.

I wish when you seé Mr King you would enquire whether he received a Second letter which I wrote to him. As he has not replied to it, and as a former letter which I wrote to you and sent by the French courier never came to hand, I fear this too may have miscarried. ⟨I do not⟩ I wish you to say that it is not by way of exacting a reply from him that I request you to make the enquiry, for my letter was not of a nature to necessitate a reply; but simply because I wish to ascertain whether there is any uncertainty in sending letters by the French Courier in which case I should prefer the mail, whatever might be the expense

Farewell my dear Sarah, I have been for two days confined to the house by gloomy wet weather so unusual in Spain, and here is a third which promises to be as bad. A letter from you would have been a God Send. Do not disappoint me again

Kiss the darlings for me and remember me kindly to Mr Storrow.

> Your affectionate uncle
> W.I.

MANUSCRIPT: Yale.

This letter is written on official stationery with the letterhead "Legacion / de los / Estados Unidos / en / España."

1. WI was correct in his assessment. King returned to the United States in 1846 and was elected to the U.S. Senate. He served from 1848 to 1852, when he was elected as Pierce's vice-president.
2. This letter from Mrs. Pierre M. Irving has not been located.
3. Temporary lodging.
4. *Galignani's Messenger*, the English language newspaper published by John and William Galignani in Paris.

1829. *To Francisco Martínez de la Rosa*

Madrid 9th. March 1845

His Excellency / Don Francisco Martinez de la Rosa / Minister of State

Sir,

I have to acknowledge the receipt of your Excellency's note of the 20th Feby[1] informing me of the reasons given by the Supreme Board of Health for declining to exempt vessels arriving at ports of the Peninsula from ports of the United States north of Cape Hatteras from the eight days Quarantine of observation.

I learn also, with regret, from letters received from the U. S. Consul at the Canary Islands[2] that the recent ameliorations of the Quarantine Laws in these Islands have not been to the extent which I had been led to imagine from the note which I had the honor to receive from the Minister of State dated the 26th[3] of July last. In this note his Excellency observes—"I have just received a communication from the Minister of the Interior in which he informs me that having required from the Supreme Board of Health information relative to the reclamation of your Excy dated 25th Jany[4] last in which your Excy proposes certain modifications in the sanitary regulations observed in the Canary Islands, the Supreme Board finds your Excy's reclamation well founded and consequently has decreed that the proposed modifications shall be immediately put into practi⟨s⟩ce. I hasten to communicate this agreeable news to your Excy flattering myself that the facilities thus offered to commerce will increase the maritime relations between the Union and Spain."

The modifications indicated in my note were

First: That all vessels coming with clean bills of health from ports north of Cape Hatteras should be admitted to immediate pratique and: Second: That wherever Quarantine was exacted the vessel might perform it at the port of destination instead of being sent to Santa Cruz for the purpose.

Supposing from his Excellency's letter that these were to be put in "immediate practice," I immediately wrote information thereof to my Govt[5] and notice of the same was promulgated in the public papers throughout the Union.

I now find to my surprise that the modification is extended only to vessels coming from Philadelphia and ports to the northward, thus leaving all the ports of the Chesapeake and the important port of Norfolk though at all times perfectly healthy, still subject to this vexatious Quarantine of Observation.

I find also that the new modifications express no permission for vessels subject to Quarantine to perform it at their ports of destination; consequently they may, as formerly, be ordered to Santa Cruz for that purpose; the delay, expense and frequent risk of which arrangement, and its injustice to other ports of the Canary Islands, I had flattered myself, I had sufficiently pointed out in the notes which I had the honor to address to her Majesty's Govt[6] on the subject.

I cannot but apprehend that my Government will be much disappointed when it finds how far the facilities to commerce afforded by these recent modifications fall short of what it had been led to anticipate from the purport of the letter of the Minister of State[7] before cited.

As your Excellency in your recent note[8] gives me reason to infer that the whole sanitary system is under consideration and is likely to undergo further regulations, I cannot but flatter myself that the modifications of the Quarantine Laws in the Canary Islands may yet be carried to the full extent suggested in my former communications and that they may be ultimately extended to the Peninsula so that vessels arriving from the U. S. in Spanish ports may meet with the same reception which they experience in all the ports of Europe

It is a measure which I should hail as a happy augury of the gradual cessation of those various burthens and impediments which at present obstruct our commerce with her Majesty's Dominions and are rapidly banishing our vessels from her shores.

I have the honor / etc etc

Signed = Washington Irving

MANUSCRIPT: NA, RG 59 (copy); NA, RG 84 (letterbook copy).

The copy sent with WI's despatch no. 61 of March 4, 1845, has been used as copy-text because it has the Spanish passages from Narváez's letter translated into English. At the top of this copy on legation letterhead is "Copy of Despatch to the Minister of State / relating to Quarantine Regulations of / Canary Islands."

1. The copyist erred. The date should be "the 26th."
2. Letter from Joseph Cullen, dated January 20, 1845 (NA, RG 84).
3. Narváez to WI (NA, RG 84).
4. WI to Luis González Bravo, January 25, 1844.
5. WI to John C. Calhoun, July 27, 1844.
6. See note 4.
7. On July 26, 1844.
8. Martínez de la Rosa to WI, February 26, 1845 (NA, RG 84).

1830. (deleted)

1831. To Ramón María Narváez

Madrid March [10][1] 1845

His Excy. / Cn Gl Narvaez / Minister of War, President of the Council

Sir

I must trust to your Excy's indulgence in addressing you on a subject which may not strictly belong to your immediate Dept, but I am induced to do so from the quick perception which you you[2] have manifested in matters of general policy and the prompt and vigorous good sense ↑with↓ which you appear occasionally to strike to the heart of a subject. I speak this in frankness, not by way of flattery, but as an excuse for what might otherwise appear as an intrusion. Your Excy cannot be ignorant of the policy of the Govt of the U. S. in regard to the Island of Cuba. It is our earnest desire that it should be prosperous and tranquil and loyally attached to her Majesty's Govt. It is our disposition and our determination as far as lies in our power, to maintain it so. We do not profess to do this out of mere friendship for Spain, although there is no country with which our relations are of a more amicable kind, but we are prompted by considerations of interest. The welfare of Cuba is, in a great degree, identical with the welfare of the U. S.; every blow to the internal quiet and safety of that Island vibrates ⟨vibrates⟩ through the southern parts of our Union and awakens solicitude at our seat of Govt. One of the leading objects of my mission, is to attend to everything which may affect the interests of Spain and of the U. S. in connexion with the tranquillity and loyalty of that Island. It is in compliance with this duty that I have watched with some solicitude the discussion which has been going on for some time past in the public papers on what is called the "flour question" and which appears to me ↑to↓ have occasionally assumed something beyond mere commercial importance.

I do not mean to trouble your Excellency with the statistics of this question; still I will briefly state what appear to be the simple facts of the case.

Cuba draws her supplies of flour from Spain and from the U. S. The Spanish flour from a difference in the first price and from greater expense of transportation costs much more on arriving in the harbor of Havannah than the American flour; to cover the difference and to give the Spanish flour an equal chance in the market, a vast difference is made in the duties; the Castilian flour paying 50 rials per Barrel and the American 200. The result is that the price of flour is rendered excessively high on the market of Cuba. Of this the people of Cuba complain. They say that it is unjust to make them eat their bread at so dear a rate; for the purpose of yielding a profit to the people of another Province of ⟨Spain⟩ ↑the Kingdom.↓ They urge as a relief that the duties be entirely taken off Castilian flour and those on the American flour reduced to 100 rials. By this arrangement they say the price of bread would be cheapened and the spanish flour would have sufficient protection. The revenue also ↑would not↓ in the end be the loser; for at the present high rate of duty a great part of the American flour finds its way by contraband paying nothing to the Custom House, whereas a duty of 100 rials per barrel would be sufficiently low to prevent contraband and the Govt would then derive revenue from all the American flour introduced. The quantity imported also would be greater, the consumption of flour increasing with its cheapness, many eating bread who are now obliged to content themselves with plantains and other vegetable substitutes.

The flour merchants of Santander, however, urge that their flour should be duty free while 200 rials per barrel should ⟨be⟩ continue to be imposed upon American flour thus flattering themselves to obtain a monopoly of the market.

It is not however in a mere commercial point of view that I regard this question or that I present it to your Excellency. An excessive differential duty which might appear intended to drive our flour from the market, might not, it is true, be very kindly regarded by us; it might be considered in unison with other commercial measures on the part of Spain, the policy of which we have always doubted and which have contributed to prevent the commercial intercourse between the two countries from being as mutually and largely profitable as it might be; it might too lead to countervailing measures on our part. All these considerations, however, I waive. The flour trade is after all but a small part of the trade of the U. S. with Cuba and if checked at the Custom House might find its way ⌈as has⌋ been observed through other channels to the detriment of the revenue. But what gives this question importance in my eyes is the effect it seems to have on the public mind and public feeling in Cuba, and the tone which has been observed on both sides in the public papers in discussing it. In truth, as it regards the people of Cuba it is one of those questions which have ever been most fruitful of popular murmurs and discontents, for it concerns the *price of bread*. They complain that this common and indispensable element of life is rendered unreasonably dear to them for the purpose of swelling the revenue of Spain, and enriching the flour speculators of Castille. They complain too that while the latter have their deputies in the Cortes to urge their interests, they, the people of Cuba have no representatives in that body. That while the people of Castille are close a⟨re⟩t hand to send deputations to the Court and to plead their cause with Ministers they of Cuba are deprived of such advantage from the distance of their position The discontents thus manifested will be increased when they learn the manner in which this subject has been treated in the public papers of Madrid and especially by a member of the Cortes, who speaks disparingly of Cuba not as a *Province* but as a *Colony* and as a disloyal Colony too which affects independence. These appear to me to be dangerous words and dangerous suggestions and it ⟨was⟩ is with deep regret that I have seen them uttered in print by a person who from his position, I presume to have some weight in the community. Cuba ought not to be taunted with her isolated position; she ought not to be made to feel herself distinct from Spain, a mere colony, a mere source of revenue. She should be made to feel that Govt regards her as an integral part of the Kingdom and places her interests on an equality with those of its fairest provinces. Above all no doubt should be uttered of her loyalty; doubt and suspicion too freely expressed weaken fidelity and often produce the very evils they apprehend.

Your Excy may think I am regarding these discontents in too serious a point of view but I merely hold them up as growing evils to be sedulously guarded against in a general line of policy. I cannot but recollect that it was precisely discontents of this kind arising from taxes and duties, from being treated as mere colonies and from having no representatives in Parliament which gradually weaned the U. S. from the mother country and finally made them throw off allegiance to ⟨the Mother Country⟩ Great Britain. Such, I hope and trust will not be the case with Cuba, but everything which has a tendency to such an effect, everything which is likely to render her dissatisfied with the Govt of the Peninsula ought most studiously to be avoided. What gives the flour question more importance at the present moment than it would otherwise have is the accidental concurrence of other causes of public solicitude in Cuba. A general uneasiness has been produced among the inhabitants by the agitations of the Slave question and a great soreness and irritation by the foreign intrusions and machinations ↑to↓ which it has given rise. They are mortified at seeing their whole commerce under the surveillance and liable to the interruptions of British cruisers and at having a British floating citadel anchored in their principal port. These measures however they may be justified by circumstances bear hard on the pride and grieve the spirits of the People of Cuba⟨ns⟩ The late penal enactments by her Majesty's Govt against the Slave Trade though dictated by justice and an honorable fulfilment of Treaty Stipulations will add to the uneasiness of holders of slave property. Nor will it be one of the least subjects of chagrin to the inhabitants of Cuba to find, that, while Spanish Statesmen are making this generous concession, this species of self sacrifice to the dubious policy of Great Britain that power, by discriminating duties between free labor and slave labor sugar is artfully aiming to gain a preference for the productions of her own colonies, and, if possible, to drive the staple productions of Cuba out of the market.

I leave it to the quick discernment of your Excy to determine whether while these various circumstances are contributing to irritate the feelings alarm the fears and actually impair the means of the inhabitants of the invaluable Island it would be discreet in her Majesty's Ministers to turn a deaf ear to their prayer for an effectual measure of relief, by *which the price of their daily bread might be cheapened.*

I must again entreat your Excy's indulgence for these brief and imperfect suggestions,[3] which, as I before observed do not pretend to enter into the statistics of this question, but rather to regard it morally as connected with that general line of liberal and fraternal policy called for by the actual state of Cuba and calculated to conciliate the affections of its inhabitants and permanently to secure to the Crown its most precious possession beyond the Seas.

Renewing etc

Signed = Washington Irving

MANUSCRIPT: NA, RG 84 (letterbook copy); NA, RG 59 (copy). PUBLISHED: Manning, *Diplomatic Correspondence*, 343-46; STW, II, 185-86 (in part).

Copies of this letter and Narváez's reply of March 19, 1845, were enclosed with WI's despatch no. 62 of March 28, 1845, to John C. Calhoun.

1. The copyist omitted the bracketed date.
2. The copyist repeated "you."
3. On March 19, 1845, Narváez acknowledged receipt of "the luminous ideas and notable observations which your excellency brings forward in favor of the prosperity of the Island of Cuba" (NA, RG 59).

1832. To Sarah Storrow

Madrid, March 12th. 1845

My dear Sarah,

I received yesterday your most welcome letter of the 3d.[1] It was very kind and considerate of you to send it by the Mail instead of waiting for the next courier for I had felt quite blank without my weekly despatch from you. Your letter is full of interesting and amusing details. I am glad to learn that Gabriel[2] is safely arrived in Paris and under such good care as that of Dr De Kay;[3] I only regret that Gabriel could not have brought his family with him and taken some pleasant apartment either in Paris near the Garden of the Tuilleries or the Champs Elysèes, or in the neighborhood of the City. I thank you for your extract from the pleasant little letter from dear little Abby.[4] The removal of the family from the old residence in Chamber Street will be equal to the flight of Mahomet from Mecca. I think your aunt[5] ought thence forward to date every thing, as the Mahometans do, such and such a year of the *Hegira*.[6]

Your account of the ball at the legation is quite delightful. I was sure my worthy friend King would acquit himself like a prince and that the *gentle* and *genteel* Mrs Ellis would be every thing that was ⟨amiable and⟩ *graceful* and *gracious* (I hope this jingle of words falls pleasantly upon your ear). I am glad, for your sake, that she wore her dress of "rich black velvet," and I only wish that, when she cannot pay you a visit in person, she would send that dress in her stead. She may have looked better than usual in her long curls, but I cannot realize it. I cannot think of her otherwise than I was accustomed to see her, when I thought there was no need of improvement, though I now reccollect some one did insinuate that her mouth might be altered for the better—I *never* thought so.

You speak of a Miss Mac Tavish as the belle of the ball. She is the daughter of my old friend John Mac Tavish,[7] one of the early associates of Brevoort, Paulding the Kembles &c and myself. He was ⟨one of the⟩ a young Scot, originally of the North West Company of Canada; and was one of the handsomest and pleasantest young fellows of our intimacy; ⟨and⟩ ↑but↓ of late years one of the dullest of respectable elderly gentlemen. Her mother[8] was one of the Miss Catons[9] of Baltimore, a sister of Lady Wellesley She is still in Baltimore where her husband is British Consul.

You say nothing more in your late letters of that charming Miss Tessiere of Philadelphia, who *quite won your heart.* I am affraid she has not availed herself of the kind permission she wrung from you that she might come every day of the week, and Sundays into the bargain, to kiss Kate and Susie. I begin to think that after all, she is no great things—rather a *hombod.* By the bye I cannot forgive you for crowding Kate and that Stout gentleman who *walked hombod,* into a mere cross corner of your letter. I beg in your next you will give the little lady ample space to shew herself off to advantage. Your anecdote of her is capital. But to return to the ball.

The dresses of Mrs Henderson and Miss Fisher meet with my full approbation—and you know I am a critic in these matters. You were fortunate in having such a companion for the evening as Mrs Henderson who I should think apt at merry remark without being satirical. How much our enjoyment of a scene depends upon a good companion to share it with us. As to Miss Fisher, I trust the young gentlemen dancers had too good taste to leave much of her time at your disposal.

You say nothing of late of Mrs Corbin. I presume she was at the ball. I should think Corbin would be a prime councellor on such an occasion; having such a knowledge of Parisian style.

The worthy Secretary must have been in the seventh heaven. I have no doubt when he walked about the Saloons so softly *on the points of his feet* he fancied he was walking on the clouds, and feared he might fall through. As I saw by Galignanis paper that there were a number of the English at the ball I half hoped to hear from you that the "bird of paradise" had figured there. I think Mr King was bound in gratitude to send her an invitation after the infinite amusement she had furnished to his box at the Opera

I feel obliged to Mrs Ellis for having made you acquainted with young Jones. He is one of the very best specimens of our young countrymen that I have met with during my present residence in Europe; and the good opinion I formed of him while he was in Madrid was confirmed by the account given of him by Hamilton, with whom he travelled in company on returning into France.

Saturday. I was partly in hopes of a letter this week by the French Courier; but I presume your having written early in the week by the Mail prevented you—

My house is a little in a bustle preparing for another big dinner which I am affraid will be a dull one. It is given to the Venezuelan Minister[10] who has ⟨jis⟩ just joined our Diplomatic Corps and I have to make a kind of omnium gatherum company of persons not much accustomed to be together;

Give my affectionate remembrance to Gabriel when you see him. With many kisses for the two little women and kind regards to your husband

Your affectionate uncle
W I.

P S. You have never ascertained Mrs Ellis's christian name for me.

MANUSCRIPT: Yale.

1. This letter has not been located.

2. Gabriel Irving was to die on May 18, 1845.

3. James E. DeKay (1792–1851), who was born in Portugal, was a physician and naturalist who lived at Oyster Bay, New York.

4. The daughter of Gabriel Irving.

5. Mrs. John Treat Irving, Sr., who apparently had recently moved from the family home on Chambers Street in lower Manhattan.

6. WI alludes to Mohammed's flight from Mecca to Medina in 622, the date with which the Mohammedan calendar begins.

7. John MacTavish (ca. 1787–1852) in 1828 inherited the fortune of Simon MacTavish, his uncle and head of MacTavish, Frobisher & Company, the supply house of the Great North West Company. From 1835 he served as British consul for Maryland (letter from Mrs. Mary K. Meyer, Baltimore, Maryland, August 4, 1976).

8. Emily Caton (ca. 1793–1867), youngest daughter of Mary Carroll and Richard Caton, was married to John MacTavish in Montreal on August 15, 1816. Except for a brief sojourn in Montreal, the couple resided in Baltimore after their marriage (letter from Mrs. Mary K. Meyer, August 4, 1976).

9. The three older Caton sisters married into British aristocracy: Louisa (ca. 1791–1874) first married Sir Felton Bathurst Hervey and then the marquis of Caermarthen; Mary Ann (ca. 1787–1853), who married Robert Patterson of Baltimore (d. 1822), later became the wife of the marquis of Wellesley; Elizabeth (ca. 1789–1862) married Lord Stafford in 1836. See Carolina V. Davison, "Maximilian and Eliza Godefroy," *Maryland Historical Magazine,* 29 (March, 1934), 16.

10. This diplomat apparently never achieved official status, for he is not included among those listed in the *Almanach de Gotha.*

1833. To Francisco Martínez de la Rosa

Madrid 18 de Marzo de 1845.
Al Excmo Señor Don Francisco Martinez de la Rosa / Ministro de Estado

Muy Señor mio:

Es con el mayor sentimiento que me veo en la necesidad de incomodar à V. S. por una piolera como la que ahora me obliga a escribirle.

En la Aduana de Irun siguen detenidas una *silla* y una *gamarra* que habia mandado se reexportasen à Francia, pero el Administrador de aquella Aduana se opuso à la reexportacion sin una *real orden.* Por lo tanto no me queda otro recurso que el de rogar à V. S. se sirva dar las ordenes oportunas para que se efectúe. Aprovecho esta ocasion para renovar à V. P. las seguridades de mi mas distinguida consideracion

B. L. M de V. S. / Su mas atento seguro servidor
Washington Irving

DOCKETED: A Hacienda / fho 27 Mzo.
MANUSCRIPT: Archivo de Ministerio de Asuntos Exteriores, Madrid.

Only the signature is in WI's handwriting. The letter is written on stationery imprinted "Legacion / de los / Estados Unidos / en / España."

Translation:

"It is with great regret that I find it necessary to inconvenience your lordship for a trifle such as that which obliges me to write to you now.

"In the Customs at Irun there continue to be detained a *chair* and a *martingale* to be reexported to France, but the director of Customs there objected to their reexportation without a *royal order.* Therefore I have no other recourse than to beg your lordship to issue the necessary orders so that this may be done. I take advantage of this occasion to repeat to your lordship the assurances of my most distinguished consideration."

1834. To Sarah Storrow

Madrid, March 18th. 1845

My dear Sarah,

We are in the midst of the dullness of Holy Week; with the heavens wrapped in congenial gloom and a Succession of rainy days which almost make me think myself in Paris. It seems as if the Winter which has been covering the rest of Europe with snow, has crossed the Pyrenees and turned to rain. The good people of Madrid are quite in despair at being so long without their accustomed Sunshine. The only thing that is to diversify the week is the annual ceremony at the palace of the Queen washing the feet of the beggars. It will be celebrated this year with unusual pomp and solemnity, as the Queen Mother has a devout passion for religious ceremonies. I must confess, notwithstanding the divine origin of the ceremonial, it is one for ↑some of↓ the details of which I have but little relish. Every ceremony, however, in the royal palace, is striking from the grandeur of the *local.* The Corps diplomatique are expected to attend, in full dress, and an elevated place is assigned for us, from whence we shall have a commanding view of the whole Scene. I reccollect attending a ceremony of the kind in the time of Ferdinand VII, and finding it very imposing though a little tedious. I shall find it less wearisome on the present occasion as I take an interest in every thing in which the young queen is engaged.

My dinner went off much better than I expected. My guests were in high good humor, and lingered after dinner until quite a late hour; which was a pretty good proof that they were pleased. The fact is my cook is good, my wines are good and my servants are good, so that my only solicitude in giving a large dinner is that my guests may be well assorted, so as to chime in with one another; a circumstance which in diplomatic dinners we cannot always secure; as we have to invite part of our guests for official reasons rather than from choice. Hitherto, however, I have always been successful and my dinners have gone off with animation and good humor. Thanks to the activity and excellent management of Lorenzo they are no trouble to me. I have but to name the number of my guests and the style of dinner I wish, and I need take no further thought about the matter.

I have just received a letter from your Uncle E.I.[1] He had come to town on a visit and was surprised to find George Van Wart[2] there, just arrived from England. There was a gathering in Chamber Street to make acquainted with his American Kins folk. He was quite astonished at the number and perplexed to know who was who and which was which. George is in a fair way of becoming quite a favorite among them; he had come over to America they said, "with good feelings, was pleased with every thing, and disposed to be so." How strange it must have been to him to find himself, at twenty five years of age, thus suddenly surrounded by numerous relatives none of whom he had ever seen.

Friday. 21. I returned home yesterday excessively fatigued after being on my legs for several hours attending the Ceremonies at the Palace, when I found your two letters of the 11th & 15th[3] awaiting me; having both come by the same French Courier. I immediately unharnassed myself of my diplomatic uniform and trappings and putting on a robe de chambre took my seat in a deep arm chair and enjoyed your letters in the true style of an epicure. I am concerned, however, to find that you have suf-

fered so much of late from chills and fever, and hope you have succeeded in completely conquering them. I cannot bear to think that you
should lose an iota of that fine health and those fine looks which you had
last Summer. Poor Gabriels condition too gives me deep concern. How
unfortunate that he should have come abroad in such a state of health,
without his good little wife to be with him and take care of him in case
of extremity. Should Dr De Kay go away and leave him behind, his
state will be for some time very lonely and deplorable, until Eliza can
come to him. His constitution, however, has repeatedly rallied in a surprising manner after severe attacks of his malady, and may do so again.
He will have the advantage too of the best of medical treatment in Paris
that his visit to Europe may prove beneficial.

Your two letters give me very few particulars about those two worthy
little women Kate and Susie; I beg you will not be so remiss in future; but
let me know their progress step by step in knowledge and accomplishments. I am glad Kate would not permit herself to be imposed upon by
Dr. De Kay in his attempt to pass himself off upon her for me. I shall begin
to ⟨hope⟩ think she really does retain some reccollection of me; unless
she opposed the Doctors claims out of the mere spirit of contradiction
for you know she was always rather a "contradictory baby."

Your letter of the 11th. gave me some charming particulars about *your
favorite* Mrs Ellis. I was quite amused with the despair of the dress
maker at Mrs Ellis's persistance in wearing the dress of "rich black velvet" about which you are so eloquent. She little thought she was addressing one who had been bitten by the dress and raved about it. I
hope, if ever I am to see Mrs Ellis again, I may have the good fortune
to see her in that dress. Dont think I am bantering your taste my dear
Sarah. I think a dress of the kind is one of the most lady like and becoming that some persons could appear in; and I have no doubt it becomes
Mrs Ellis *à merveille.*[4]

Saturday I had intended to make this a long letter, but I must bring
it to a close abruptly having others to write by this Courier. Give my kind
regards to Mr Storrow Kiss the little women for me & believe me affectionately your uncle

                                                        WI.

ADDRESSED: Madame / Madame Storrow / No 4 Rue de la Victoire / à Paris
MANUSCRIPT: Yale.

1. This letter has not been located.
2. The youngest son of Sarah Irving and Henry Van Wart, George was born in
1818. He lived until 1903.
3. These letters have not been located.
4. Wondrously well.

1835. To Sarah Storrow

Madrid, March 27th. 1845

My dear Sarah,

I received yesterday several letters from home[1] giving me a budget of family news, all of which you have probably heard by the same opportunity, the Steamer of the 1st. Your Mother had had one of those attacks of indisposition to which she is subject in the Spring time, but was nearly restored to her usual state of health. The last date of her letter is the 27 Feb. The piece of news which most surprised me was the engagement of Oscar Irving to be married to Eliza Romeyn.[2] They are to be married some time in the course of April and to go to housekeeping in May. I cannot say that I am displeased with the match. I had supposed Oscar would marry again[3] and felt a little Solicitude as to whom he might marry. This match brings no new and disagreeable member into the family; the parties know each other well, and are calculated to live happily together. Pierre M Irving[4] gives me the news of this engagement, which, he says, he regards on the whole with satisfaction.

Another engagement is that of Alexander Hamilton to the pretty Angelica Livingston.[5] He had a penchant for her before he came to Spain and the liking appears to have been mutual; as she had refused two or three rich offers during his absence. She is well spoken of by those who know her intimately and her preference of my little friend Hamilton to his wealthy rivals, speaks well for her intellect and her disinterestedness. The marriage will not take place immediately. Another engagement is that of Carson Brevoort to a Miss Lefferts,[6] a wealthy heiress of Long Island; a match which gives great satisfaction to his father, as I should suppose a wealthy match would. I shall now look forward to hearing soon of my little friend Hector Ames being pledged to some fair one; and then all the original Legation will be provided for except the *Chef.*

Mr Grinnel has taken Mr Shennards Cottage for two years; so that Julia will still be in the Neighborhood of Sunnyside; though not so near as its inmates could wish.

I have a very pleasant letter from Julia Sanders[7] giving me all the gossip of Washington. Sanders feels some little Solicitude as to his continuance in office under the New administration; but I do not think he will [be][8] displaced. He has acquitted himself well and is much respected in the post office department, and he and his amiable little wife have made themselves many friends in Washington. I sent Sanders some time since a letter reccommending him Strongly to the protection of Mr Dallas the Vice President; who is an old friend of mine. Sanders had received the letter and was about to deliver it.

Friday. Since writing the foregoing I have received Your letter of the 21st and am glad to find no more talk of chills and fever in it. I cannot bear to think that you should lose any thing of the fresh and blooming health that you had last summer. You cannot think what interest I take in every thing you write about Kate and Susie. Your account of Kates sensibility on hearing from her nurse a sorrowful story absolutely brought tears into my eyes, and the next moment I found myself laughing at the rigorous rule she exercises over her dolls, putting them in the dark closet for the least offence. It is this versatility of character ⟨that⟩ ↑which↓ makes the little creature so engaging.—but I would not have her sensibilities played upon too often by doleful stories. Keep her as much as possible a merry happy little girl. There is a notion prevalent in England and the United States that it is important to cultivate the tender and charitable feelings of children by tales of human misery and Suffering; and many books are written with this view: calculated as it is thought, to make very good little boys and girls. I consider all this as apt to produce a mawkish and morbid sensibility, quite opposite to that cheerful healthy robustness of mind most conducive to happiness. Your accounts of dear little Susie make me long to see her. Indeed I have your two lovely children constantly before my mind, and one of the greatest happinesses on earth to me would be to have them in my arms. You ask me if I take Madame Albuquerque and her children out to drive with me as formerly. of late my large carriage is at the Coach makers undergoing some repairs and My Coupè is too small for a family party. I had the two little girls out with me yesterday however. They are lovely children one about Seven and the other six years of age, and made a very pretty appearance with a pink bonnet and a pink face at each window. They received very gracious bows and smiles from some of the Royal family who were driving on the Prado. I thought how I should like to shew off my little Parisian Nieces in this manner.

Mr Livington does not accompany me in my drives; he has horses and a phaeton of his own, and is out either on horseback, or driving his equipage. He is very gentlemanlike, but he has not the ⟨many⟩ companionable qualities of Hamilton; ⟨and we⟩ We live pleasantly together because we do not interfere with one another, having our apartments at each end of a long house, without any necessity of meeting except at dinner time. I think myself fortunate upon the whole in having so correct and gentlemanlike a person for a Secretary of Legation.

I am happy to hear that poor Gabriel has Struggled through the recent access of his malady and is regaining strength. The Season is in his favor; and the arrival of his good little wife will I trust have a most favorable effect upon his health. I beg you to remember me to him most affectionately. I think when he has his family with him he had better establish himself comfortably for a few years in Paris or its vicinity

The Spring has suddenly broke upon us with all its Splendor; that is to say, as far as weather is concerned; for the vicinity of Madrid affords but little opportunity for the Spring to put on its gala dress. The weather, however, is exquisite. Such bright sunshine; such a deep blue sky, and such bland temperature. The prado is gay with equipages and the promenade crowded with all the beauty and fashion of Madrid. I confine my drives at present, to this popular resort, which is somewhat like the Champs Elysees; ⟨so⟩ and amuse myself by observing the passing throngs. In this way, though alone, I am not lonely. Indeed I have been for so much of my life a mere looker on in the game of society that it has become habitual to me; and it is only the company of those I truly like that I would prefer to the quiet indulgence of my own thoughts and reveries. I therefore pass much of my time alone through choice. I breakfast alone, when I read the papers: then pass the morning in my Study, until summoned to my afternoon drive. This I usually take alone, amusing myself, as I before observed, with looking out upon the world. I return home in time to dress for dinner, which I take in company with Mr Livingston, & occasionally a guest or two: and in the evening I take my quiet seat at the Opera, where I need no company to help me enjoy the music. This is the scheme of many of my days; though occasionally diversified by visits to my particular intimates; and evening gatherings at the ↑French↓ Embassy or at Mr O Sheas. My literary occupations have a great effect in recconciling me to a solitary life, and even in making it pleasant; and then I have constantly in view the prospect of being enabled, by present occupation and a little self denial, to return once more to my kindred and early friends, without the necessity of ever more parting from them. Beside I am now at that time of life when the mind has a stock of reccollections on which to employ itself; and though these may sometimes be of a melancholy nature, yet it is a "Sweet Souled Melancholy," mellowed and softened by the operation of time; and has no bitterness in it. My life has been a checquered one, crowded with incidents and personages, and full of shifting scenes and sudden transitions; all these I can summon up and cause to pass before me, and in this way can pass hours together in a kind of reverie. When I was young my imagination was always in the advance, picturing out the future and building castles in the air, now memory comes in the place of imagination, and I look back over the region I have travelled. Thank God the same plastic feeling which used to deck all the future with the hues of fairy land throws a soft coloring on the past, until the very roughest places, through which I struggled with many a heartache, lose all their asperity in the distance.

But what a raphsody I am running into! So now to conclude with a few ⟨necessary facts⟩ brief words. Give my kind regards to Mr King when you see him, and tell him ⟨to⟩ I am glad he is not going to return to the United States to take a place in the Cabinet. There is no ⟨likelihood⟩ doubt that he can remain at Paris as long as he chooses, and I would advise him to get himself well accommodated in comfortable quarters in Paris or its vicinity; where he can make a climate for himself. He will soon get accustomed to Parisian life and will know how to manage it so as to live within his means (official & private) and then he will find there is no city where one can live more pleasantly.

Give my most respectful remembrances to Mrs Ellis (craving her name at the same time as the yankees say.) Tell Mrs Henderson if she does not persuade her husband to buy that farm I'll never be friends with her again. and tell the pretty Miss Fisher I kiss her hand.

With kind remembrances to Mr Storrow and many kisses to the darlings

> Your affectionate uncle
> Washington Irving

MANUSCRIPT: Yale.   PUBLISHED: PMI, III, 373–74 (in part).

1. These and other letters mentioned herein by WI have not been located.
2. The two are first cousins, Oscar (1800–1865) being the son of William Irving, and Eliza (1801–1887), the daughter of Sarah Irving and Richard Dodge.
3. His first wife, Catherine Dayton, had died in March of 1842.
4. In similar fashion Pierre had married his first cousin, Helen Dodge, the sister of Eliza.
5. Angelica Livingston (b. March 16, 1820) was married to Alexander Hamilton on December 10, 1845.
6. Elizabeth Dorothea Lefferts, daughter of Leffert Lefferts of Brooklyn, was married to James Carson Brevoort on October 8, 1845.
7. The wife of Sanders Irving, who is so designated as to distinguish her from Julia Grinnell in the preceding paragraph.
8. WI omitted the bracketed word.

1836. To John C. Calhoun

Legation of the United States / Madrid 2⟨0⟩8th March 1845

No 62 / The Hble / John C. Calhoun / Secretary of State

Sir

The question about the differential duties on American and Spanish flour introduced into the ports of Cuba has continued to be discussed from time to time in the Madrid papers. I have occasionally furnished the writers with such facts, within my reach, which I considered favorable to our interests and had conversations on the subject with the Minister of Finance[1] who appeared to be much perplexed and embarrassed by the representations and intrigues of the flour merchants and speculators of Castile.

I have thought it might be of advantage to call the attention of General Narvaez to this subject, and, at the same time, to make it the occasion of reiterating our general policy with respect to the Island of Cuba. The position of General Narvaez and his active and dominating spirit give him great influence over the affairs of each department and though not technically versed in commercial concerns, he has a quick sagacity, a mother wit, which enables him often to grasp the essential merits of a subject where others are perplexing themselves with details.

I enclose a copy of my note and his reply.[2]

I am Sir / Very respectfully / Your obedient servant.
Washington Irving

DOCKETED: Recd. 8 May. / Mr. Markoe
MANUSCRIPT: NA, RG 59. PUBLISHED: Manning, *Diplomatic Correspondence*, 347.

Only the signature is in WI's handwriting.

1: Alejandro Mon.
2. WI to Narváez, March 10, 1845; Narváez to WI, March 19, 1845.

1837. To Eliza Romeyn

Madrid April 2d. 1845

My dear Eliza

It is some time since I received a letter from you in which you asked me to sit down and write you an answer on the spot. It was pretty much like demanding a mans money on the high way when he has not a farthing in his pocket. I could not have mustered up ideas for a letter at the time had it been to save my life, and ever since my good intentions in the matter have been elbowed aside by a thousand other claims on my pen. I am overtasked at present in literary occupation, striving hard to make up for lost time, ⟨and and to⟩ in regard to my literary undertakings, and having to cope with my official duties; my familiar correspondence is generally made at the expense of the time I should devote to repose and recreation; and thus a sad weariness of flesh and spirit is occasionally produced; while, after all, a mass of correspondence accumulates on my hands which I look at with despair. This I am sure will be a sufficient excuse to you for ↑my↓ not having written as frequently to you as you might wish.

I now take up my pen in consequence of information just received from Pierre M Irving, which has quite taken me by surprise. I allude to your intended change of condition. I hope and trust it will be for the better. You and Oscar know each other well, and from relationship and long intimacy have a thousand sympathies in common. You will only be strengthening old bonds of kindness and esteem by a still dearer tie; and I trust you will both be happier for your union. May god bless you both.

Every budget of domestic news makes me long more and more to be restored to the family circle which is now a little world within itself, and to me worth all the world beside. This is the constant wish of my heart, and the object of all my exertions. I long to be once more back at dear little Sunnyside, while I have yet strength and good spirits to enjoy the simple pleasures of the country and to rally a happy family groupe once more about me. I grudge every year of absence that rolls by. To morrow is my birth day. I shall then be sixty two years old. The evening of life is fast drawing over me; still I hope to get back among my friends while there is yet a little sunshine left.

My letters to your Aunt Paris has[1] kept you all informed of the gay life I am leading, in spite of myself, at Madrid; obliged, willy nilly, to revel in palaces and bask in the sunshine of a court. Still there is more romance about court life in Spain than in any other European country especially in the present era of conspiracies and revolutions. The ⟨marria⟩ question of the queens marriage is again beginning to excite attention; it is the great question on which every thing hinges. The Court will soon depart for Aranjuez, and thence after a time to Barcelona. Whither I shall follow it in its migration I do not know. I have written to Government for instructions on the subject. If left to my own will I would remain in Madrid, to pursue my literary occupations, or perhaps make a brief visit to Barcelona, to pay my respects to the Sovreign.

I am affraid I shall not be able to write to your Aunt Paris by this Steamer; if not, I beg you to give my love to her and tell her she shall hear from me by the next. I am in debt also in letters to Pierre, to Helen, and I believe to half the world. I shall have to call a meeting of my creditors, or to declare myself bankrupt. With affectionate remembrances to "all bodies"

> Your affectionate uncle
> Washington Irving

ADDRESSED: Mrs. Eliza Romeyn / *care of Pierre M Irving* / Bank of Commerce /

New York   POSTMARKED: [*unrecovered*]   DOCKETED: *Legation of the United States Madrid* / Mrs Oscar Irving / from her uncle / Washington Irving
MANUSCRIPT: SHR.

1. WI's error.

1838. To George P. Putnam

Madrid, April 3d. 1845

Dear Sir,

In reply to your letter soliciting my aid in procuring permission from the Authorities of Seville for the disinterment of the remains of the late Mr Bacon, that they may be transferred to his native country, I have to inform you that a like application was made to me some time since, by Mr Burton our Consul at Cadiz. I immediately represented the Case to Genl Shelley,[1] Captain General of Seville, who ⟨was⟩ ↑is↓ attending the Cortes ⟨of⟩ at Madrid, as deputy, and who is my intimate friend. He wrote on the subject to the Ecclesiastical Authorities at Seville; and has received a reply and assures me there will no opposition be made to the disinterment of the body.

Very respectfully / Your friend & Servt
Washington Irving

Geo P Putnam Esqr

MANUSCRIPT: HSA.   PUBLISHED: *Diary 1828–1829*, pp. 105–6.

This letter is written on official stationery with the letterhead "Legacion / de los / Estados Unidos / en / España."

George Palmer Putnam (1814–1872), who became a partner in Wiley and Putnam in 1840, was to become WI's publisher and to bring out the very successful Author's Revised Edition of WI's works in the late 1840's.

1. General Ricardo Shelley (1811–1855) had held a political post in Barcelona earlier. See WI to Edward Everett, October 7, 1842.

1839. To Sarah Storrow

Madrid, April 3d. 1845

My dear Sarah,

I have just received yours of the 29th.[1] and and in replying must begin by one thing which in a manner appertains to business. You say

⟨"⟩Mr King had written by the last courier in reply to my letter. That reply has never come to hand, and the circumstance gives me double concern as involving the loss of a letter from so estimable a correspondent, and as shewing that the diplomatic courier is not to be depended upon. You may remember a letter of mine to you some months since ⟨never⟩ sent by the same conveyance, never reached you: and I have always had doubts whether others written at the same time to other members of the family ever reached their destination. I wish Mr King would have enquiries made on the subject at the Foreign office in Paris and I will do the same at the French Embassy here. I beg you to tell my valued friend Mr King how much I am concerned at the loss of his letter.

I had a letter from Mr Beasley a day or two since, telling me of a person having been nominated in his place as Consul at Havre. His good friend Mr Rives (however) formerly Minister to France, had undertaken to prevent the nomination being acted upon in the Senate. If he has done so this paltry manouvre of Mr Tyler may yet be a *Coup Manqué*[2]

I have just received a letter from Alexander Hamilton written in perfect extacy at the Success of his matrimonial suit. You may reccollect Angelica Livingston who is really a little beauty; and I am told is intelligent and well informed. Her choice of Hamilton in preference to several wealthy suitors speaks well for her heart.

The young lady to whom Carson Brevoort is engaged is a Miss Lefferts, only ⟨daugh⟩ child of Mr Leffert Lefferts; whom Alex. Hamilton denominates "a *wealthy old Gentleman* of Long Island[.]" I can reccollect him a handsome *Young* Gentleman in my youthful days; so as I tell Hamilton, I wish some one else had kept pace with him [in] [*MS blotted*] purse as well as in years.

By the way, talking of old gentlemen, this is my Sixty second birthday. I reccollect the time when I did not wish to live to such an age, thinking it must be attended with infirmity, apathy of feeling; peevishness of temper, and all the other ills which conspire to "render age unlovely;" yet here my Sixty second birthday finds me in fine health; in the full enjoyment of all my faculties; with my sensibilities still fresh, and in such buxom activity, that, on my return home yesterday from the Prado, I caught myself bounding up stairs, three steps at a time, to the astonishment of the porter; and checked myself, reccollecting that it was not the pace befitting a Minister and a man of my years. If I could only retain such health and good spirits I should be content to live on to the age of Methusaleh;[3] ⟨t⟩ my only danger at present is that I am growing ⟨"⟩*too hearty.*⟨"⟩

To day I am to dine at the house of a rich Neighbor, Mr Arcos who has a fine, joyous musical family of young men, so that I anticipate a jovial birthday dinner, and am determined to be as young as any of the party.

You must not keep angling for me for your Swiss tour. I am not to be caught even though you bait your hook with Mrs Ellis and her black velvet dress. I *have* visited Switzerland[4] though I may never have talked about it to you. In my young days I crossed St Gothard, on my return from Italy. The road was not ⟨as⟩ practicable for wheel carriages then as now; so that I crossed on horse back, three days from the Italian valley of the Tesino to the banks of the Lake of the Four Cantons, and a wild picturesque journey it was; from the rich umbragious scenery of Italy to the then terrific pass of the Devils bridge and the dreary valley of Schollenen. I traversed [all][5] of the four Cantons; coasted by some of the Scenes of the exploits of William Tell; visited Lucerne, Zurich, Basle &c and then struck off on my first visit to Paris. I well remember what a home feeling I had in Switzerland. What delight I had again in meeting with log houses among the mountains,—What pretty girls I saw in every village. I am sure I should not see as many now, even though I have the advantage of looking through spectacles. Oh days of my youth! how much younger and greener the world then was than now. And the Women! The world is full of old Women now, they were all young in those times.

And so the gentle, the discreet Mrs Ellis, has really been flirting with General Tom Thumb:[6] and the little hero was ⟨really⟩ annoyed at being caught up in her arms. Upon my word he shewed no more spirit than his name sake of renown,[7] who roared when the young giantess of Brobdignag put him in her mouth. I shall have a very small opinion of the general hereafter, great as may be his fame. I remember his equipage driving through the Streets of Birming[ham?][8] last summer, when he was exhibiting in that City. I had not the curiosity to go to see him having heard that he was not so old by several years as he was represented. I rather suspected him to be a *"hombod;"* but must have been misinformed

Saturday—Apl. 5. My birth day dinner was a very handsome and a very pleasant one. By the way I must give you some account of my host and his family. Mr Arcos ⟨is a very⟩ has made a large fortune by commercial and financial operations in Spain and in Spanish America. He has lived a good deal about the world, and ⟨learnt studied in most a⟩ studied the art of living in his various migrations. He has a great passion for fitting up and furnishing houses; spares no expense in surrounding himself with every comfort and luxury; and when he has rendered his habitation complete so that there is nothing to improve; is very apt to part with it at a sacrafice, and begin another. He has just been rendering an old picturesque but dilapidated house in my neighborhood one of the most convenient, tasteful and enviable in Madrid; and has furnished it in the most exquisite style without regard to cost. His wife who is a native of Chili is a most amiable excellent person. They have four sons all grown up; full of life and spirit, apt at every thing, and admirable musicians. Two of them were the base and tenor of the amateur Italian opera that was got up at the English Embassy just before my arrival in Paris. Their voices are admirable, and their style and method highly approved. In fact they would make fortune on the stage. They (the sons) all speak English well.

The dinner was capital in itself, and admirably got up. The dinner service rich and beautiful It was a large party, ladies and gentlemen, and excepting three, all from America; but from every part of the two continents: ⟨there were⟩ from Mexico, Peru; Chili, Venezuela, Cuba, Brazil, The United States &c quite a singular assemblage. I was seated between mine hostess, who, as I have told you is a most amiable personage, with the remains of great beauty, and a very pretty, sprightly and romantic young lady, native of Madrid with whom I endeavored to pass myself off as rather a gallant young fellow: carefully suppressing the fact that it was my sixty second birth day. The dinner went off gaily and was followed by a very pleasant evening, during which we had a great deal of delightful music, from Antonio and Domingo Arcos, accompanying themselves on a superb piano, and a newly invented kind of organ not bigger than a piano. It was delightful to see the manner in which this family live together, the young men appear more like the brothers than the sons of their Mother; and all ⟨have such a⟩ ↑are so↓ frank & joyous. ⟨manner⟩ This family is intimately linked with our diplomatic corps and generally forms a part of our weekly gatherings

To day I dine with my good friends the O'Sheas; where I am always sure to enjoy myself. Their house is almost like a home to me. Mrs OShea & Madame Albuquerque, who have their apartments under the same roof, are like sisters, so that we see each other almost every day. Tomorrow I am invited to a great dinner at the Weisweilers'; the Madrid connexion of the Rothschilds; so you see I am still in the midst of dissipation; though it ⟨is⟩ now runs upon dinners, instead of balls.

In the course of a few weeks there will be a complete breaking up. The Court will go to Barcelona, ⟨and⟩ many of the Court circle will follow it; others will disperse for the warm weather to the sea side, to watering places, to France &c and Madrid will be almost deserted.

According to your account, Eliza, Gabriels wife will probably arrive in Paris in the course of May. I shall be heartily glad to hear of her arrival. It gives me great concern to receive such bad accounts of the state of Gabriels health, and to think of him seperated from his family, when in such helpless suffering condition[.] I know what it is to be sick and lonely in a strange land; and if I have felt its sadness, who am a bachelor accustomed for a great part of my life to have no one about me who cares for me, what must it be to him who has always lived in the midst of a family, with an affectionate wife to watch by his pillow. Poor fellow—what a pity that he left his comfortable home, to be sick and solitary amidst the gaieties of Paris. However, Elizas arrival will brighten all up, and bring sunshine into his sick chambre. I beg you to remember me to him most affectionately, and tell him how deeply I feel concerned for his situation.

I find by an incidental word in your letter that you are still taking lessons in French of Miss Flanden. I entreat you to continue to do so until you have conquered all the difficulties of the language, so as to converse with perfect ease and freedom. It will be a source of comfort to you for the rest of your life; or rather, a want of such facility in the language will be a cause of perpetual restraint and discomfort to you in all your intercourse with ↑European↓ society as I have experienced and do experience to my cost.

Let me hear all about Kates visit to Tom Thumb.[9] I hope she may not be guilty of the same indiscretion as Mrs Ellis. I rather think she will be inclined to *bang* the general.

With many kisses to her and dear little Susie and kind regards to Mr Storrow

Your affectionate uncle
Washington Irving

ADDRESSED: Madame / Madame Storrow / No 17. Rue du Faubg Poissonniere / a
Paris
MANUSCRIPT: Yale.   PUBLISHED: PMI, III, 374–76 (in part).

1. This and other letters mentioned herein by WI have not been located.
2. A failure.
3. See Genesis 5:27.
4. WI described his travels in Switzerland during May 1805 in great detail in *J&N*, I, 348–405; and in letters to Elias Hicks, May 4–June 19, 1805; to William Irving, May 31, 1805.
5. WI's omission.
6. Charles Sherwood Stratton (1838–1883), an American midget who was managed and exhibited by P. T. Barnum. After a successful run in London in the spring and early summer of 1844, Tom Thumb toured the British provinces. WI probably encountered his carriage in Birmingham when he was visiting the Van Warts. See Raymond Fitzsimmons, *Barnum in London* (New York, 1970), pp. 106–7.
7. WI seems to be fusing the story of Tom Thumb in Henry Fielding's play of 1730 with Gulliver's voyage to Brobdingnag in Swift's *Gulliver's Travels* (1726).
8. WI wrote "Birming."

9. Barnum took Tom Thumb to Paris where he was presented to Louis Philippe
through the good offices of U.S. minister William R. King. The midget performed
in Paris for four months. Scc Fitzsimmons, *Barnum in London*, pp. 115–16.

1840. To Francisco Martínez de la Rosa

Madrid 4th April 1845

His Excy / Don F. M. de la Rosa / etc etc

Sir,

It is with great regret that I find myself called upon to address your
Excy on an occurrence, which, if it has already come to your knowledge,
I am sure, must have caused as much concern to you as it has done to
myself. By a dispatch just received from my Govt I learn that, about
8 o'clock of the evening of the 24th Decemr last, as the Bark Zulette
belonging to Boston in the U. S., having just set sail from Gibraltar
was passing the Spanish fort at Tarifa, under a press of sail, she was
fired into from that fort. The shot passed but a little distance above the
deck, cut some of the rigging and went through one of the lower studding
sails. The following is an extract from the log book of the Bark which
gives a simple statement of the fact, taken down at the time.

Extract from the Log Book of the Bark Zulette of Boston, 1844
"Dec 1844, 24th At 5 P. M. got underweigh from Gibraltar bound to
Boston and proceeded on the voyage. At 8 P. M. passing Tarifa, the
wind east, studding sails set on both sides, going 8 Knots, was *fired at*
from the shore; the shot took off the starboard maintack about three
feet above the sail (the mainsail being clewed up) and went through
the larboard lower studding sail."

Signed—Anthony Killey Junr / Master of Bark Zulette
Signed = David Kelley (Mate)

On the arrival of the Bark in the U. S. the owners and agents made their
complaint to the Govt at Washington. I have, in consequence, received
instructions to lose no time in representing the case to her Majesty's
Govt. and in "demanding an explanation, or the punishment of the officer
who may have been guilty of what appears to be a wanton outrage"

I am sure I need add nothing more to obtain from her Majesty's Govt
all that is just and decorous in the ⟨[*unrecovered*]⟩ case. Their quick
and honorable sensibility to the sanctity of their own flag when violated
on a late occasion, in nearly the same waters, convinces me that they

will be prompt and scrupulous in meting out to others the same reparation which they demanded for themselves.[1]

I have the honor etc
Signed = Washington Irving

MANUSCRIPT: NA, RG 84 (letterbook copy).

1. WI received a prompt reply from Martínez de la Rosa on April 6, 1845, indicating that he had requested details about the incident and would reply as soon as
he had heard (NA, RG 84).

1841. To Francisco Martínez de la Rosa

Madrid ⟨1⟩9th April 1845

His Excy / Don F. M. de la Rosa / etc etc

Sir,
I have just received a letter from the Commodore of the U. S. squadron
stationed at Port Mahon,[1] informing me, that from fortuitous circumstances, that port is at present virtually without an American Consul.

It appears that Mr O. Rich who was U. S. Consul there being obliged
to quit his post on account of ill health, left it in charge of his son
James. M. Rich. The latter has since departed, leaving the Consulate
in charge of Lt J. J. Boyle[2] of the U. S. Navy. The Governor, however,
has officially signified to the American Commodore that he could not
recognize Lt Boyle to act as Consul without the approbation of her
Catholic Majesty.

As Pt Mahon is ↑used as↓ a naval depot by the U. S., it is extremely
important that they should have a Court functionary there; indeed it
is important both to Spanish and American interests, and as Lt Boyle
is a person of high trust and respec⟨s⟩↑ta↓bility, having charge of the
Naval Stores of the depot I would most respectfully urge as a measure
of expediency that his temporary appointment receive the sanction of
her Majesty's Govt until the Govt of the U. S. can have time to receive
information and to act on the premises.

I have the honor to renew etc

Signed = Washington Irving

MANUSCRIPT: NA, RG 84 (letterbook copy).

1. Commodore Joseph Smith (1790–1877), who was in charge of the Mediterranean Squadron until December, 1845.

2. Junius J. Boyle (1802–1870), who had been on Mediterranean duty for about ten years.

1842. To Francisco Martínez de la Rosa

Madrid 10th April 1845

His Excy / Dn F. M. de la Rosa / etc etc

Sir,

It is with extreme regret that I have to call the attention of your Excy to the unjust exactions in some of the Spanish Postoffices on letters arriving from the U. S. in American vessels.

This matter has heretofore been made the subject of repeated complaints by this Legation and to remedy abuses of the kind a Royal order was issued on the 20th July 1832 according to which all letters brought to Spanish ports in *Foreign* vessels and for the carriage of which by sea nothing had been paid by the P. O. department should be distributed and transmitted by the Dept free from all other charges than such as are paid upon letters mailed at the place of landing.

It appears, however, that notwithstanding this order, the abuses still exist and are carried on to a scandalous extent especially as it regards the Port of Malaga. The ships from the U. S. bound to Spain and the Mediterranean generally touch first at Gibraltar or Cadiz where the Captain delivers all letters intended for the Peninsula. Letters thus mailed at Gibraltar or St Roque ought to pay but a very trifling postage at Malaga. Yet our Consul at that port finds single letters coming through that channel from his friends in the U. S. charged with 11 rs. 4 ms. postage as if they had come from England. I enclose the covers of three letters thus overcharged as a specimen.

The greatest abuse, however, occurs in the receipt of letters at Malaga from the U. S., via Cadiz. On one occasion a letter to the Consul, coming through this channel was charged the enormous postage of 28 rs. 20 ms. He remonstrated and informed the post master of the Royal order of 1832. The postmaster pleaded utter ignorance of such an order. A copy of it was subsequently furnished to him whereupon he restored the extra postage. The abuse, however, has since continued and is a source of continual vexation to the American Consul and the commercial houses of Malaga engaged in trade with the U. S. Letters are received at Malaga, via Cadiz, but bearing merely the general and vague stamp *Estados Unidos* without the requisite stamps of the Cadiz and Malaga Post offices with the date of reception. On single letters thus received a postage is levied of 11 rs. 4 ms. It is in vain that the merchants remonstrate; it is in vain that they may shew on the superscription of the letters the name of the very American ship, recently arrived at Cadiz, by which they have been brought. The Postmaster declines making restitution unless the American Consuls will give certificates that the letters have come by American vessels. Thus the American Consul is called upon to satisfy the doubts of the Postmaster, caused by the blunders or bad faith of his own subalterns.

I enclose for the inspection of your Excy the covers of a few of the letters received at Malaga, via Cadiz, and thus vaguely stamped and shamefully overcharged.

I am willing to believe the master himself free from any improper intention, but I cannot help observing that there is something very suspicious in the omission of the stamps of the respective post offices; those "levied marks" by which an error or abuse might be traced to the right door. It looks very much like collusion between the subalterns of the different offices; like a subterfuge to prevent detection and defeat reclamation.

I am sure your Excy will view this matter in its proper light, that you will feel indignant at these petty abuses by which the fair and honorable intentions of her Majesty's Govt are rendered unavailing; that you will be eager to carry into full effect the royal order of 1832 and to relieve the commercial correspondence of the principal ports of Spain from a disgraceful tax imposed upon it by the blunders or peculations of official underlings.

I avail myself etc

Signed = Washington Irving

MANUSCRIPT: NA, RG 84 (letterbook copy).

1843. To Sarah Storrow

Madrid, April 11th. 1845

My dear Sarah,

I have received your letter of the 4th.[1] Giving me an account of the interesting interview between Kate and the little General.[2] I hope she behaved with proper decorum, and did not follow the example of another lady who shall be nameless. I observe a paragraph in a news paper stating that the little General intends to visit Madrid; in which case I shall certainly give him a dinner; and invite Genl Narvaez to meet him.

I am happy to have such good news of poor Gabriel, and that he was likely to be able in the Course of a few days to leave his room. If he can get to the Garden of the Tuileries occasionally, or take a drive to the Bois de Bologne the fine weather and fine Season will act as restoratives. It is a most fortunate circumstance that his spirits do not droop; I had feared they would be completely prostrated. I shall rejoice to hear of the arrival of his excellent little wife.

Your mention of Paris in all the splendor of Spring time and Sunny weather makes me indeed long to be with you to enjoy it. ⟨the ten[?]⟩ I have been there repeatedly in the Spring and know well the enlivening effect of the Season in brightening up every thing with effulgent sunshine and bringing out blossoms and blooming faces and new dresses. And then to see Kate Storrow in her blue silk plaid and her blue bonnet! Heavens and earth! And Susie too; who it seems has cast her *slough* like a little ⟨Sp⟩ Snake in Spring time and come out in short petticoats! You tell me she rejoices in being able to use her feet. Surely she does not pretend to walk already, nor even to stand alone. Though I am ready to believe any thing of her; especially as she has such a wonderful little sister to prompt and instruct her

We are likely to have quite a musical Campaign here. The rival opera houses are strengthening their forces and preparing for vigorous opposition. Ronconi is daily expected, if he has not already arrived; and is to appear next week at the Circo. when we shall have the beautiful opera of the *Straniera*[3]—The other house The *Cruz*, has lately engaged a capital tenor in place of Moriani; who I perceive is performing with great success in London. The same theatre it is said has engaged Fornesari[4] for some part of the year; at the time I presume when the opera houses in Paris and London are closed. This rivalry of the two houses gives ↑us a↓ great ↑⟨w⟩↓ variety of operas and performers; though I could wish one choice company could be culled out of the two. However, I manage to amuse myself very tolerably sometimes at one theatre and sometimes at the other, and the older I grow, and the less disposed and less fitted to mingle with the gay throng of society, the more I bless my stars that such a species of amusement has been invented; where a solitary man with humble means, may take his seat and for a mere pittance, have a mimic world conjured up for his entertainment. A King with all his wealth can command no more. It equals Arabian Enchantment. I am equal to Alladin with his wonderful lamp: without any ⟨sort⟩ risque from a malignant magician—They talk of the stage "holding the mirror up to nature,"[5] why nature was never half so fine. I never saw such nymphs and sylphs in nature as I see in ballets;[6] I never saw people in real life talk, and quarrel and storm in recitative, nor languish and make love in dulcet strains with the accompaniment of an orchestra; and as to Kings and Queens, I have seen numbers of them in real life in my time, but none that could compare with the Kings and Queens of the ⟨stage⟩ theatre.

Saturday.   I am looking anxiously for letters from government, which must determine my movements for the Summer. I have written to know whether it is the wish of Govt. that I should follow the Spanish Court in its ⟨cha⟩ migrations; or whether, if it make a long sojourn in Barcelona, a temporary visit there on my part, merely to shew respect to the Sovreign will not be sufficient. I should delight in passing a long time in that ⟨delightful⟩ ↑beautiful↓ City, but I do not wish to be long absent from Madrid—where I can ⟨follow⟩ pursue my literary occupations more advantageously. I have received a letter from Mr Anguera claiming me as his guest if I come to Barcelona and telling me he has changed his residence and has ample accommodations for me in his new quarters. The Albuquerques will follow the court and pass all the Summer in Barcelona. They have written to have a house taken there for them. The O'Sheas set off in the Course of two or three weeks on their Summer tour; in the Course of which they will visit England and the Rhine; so that if I remain in Madrid my favorite Social resorts will be closed. With my pen, however, to occupy me in the morning and the opera to solace me in the evening; and an occasional drive or ↑a↓ stroll in the Prado and Retiro, I can manage to play hermit through the summer very tolerably.

With kind regards to Mr Storrow and many kisses to the little Miss Ponces,

Your affectionate uncle
Washington Irving

MANUSCRIPT: Yale.

1. This letter has not been located.

2. Tom Thumb, who was mentioned in WI's last letter to Sarah Storrow, April 3, 1845.

3. A two-act opera by Bellini, first performed in Milan on February 14, 1829. See *Grove's Dictionary of Music and Musicians*, I, 608.

4. Luciano Fornasari, an Italian basso who began singing professionally about 1828, with extended engagements in New York, Havana, Lisbon, and London in the next fifteen years. See *Grove's Dictionary of Music and Musicians*, III, 447.

5. See *Hamlet*, III, ii, 24.

6. The Italian opera in the nineteenth century often introduced ballet scenes even though they were not an integral part of the action. This practice was taken from the French, who often used ballet and dancing merely for their spectacular effects. See David Ewen, *The New Encyclopedia of the Opera*, pp. 53–54.

1844.   To Francisco Martínez de la Rosa

Madrid 16th of April 1845

His Excy / The Minister of State

The undersigned Envoy Exy and Minister Pleny of the U. S. has the honor to submit to his Excy Don F. M. de la Rosa, Minister of State the claims of Messrs Fitch Brothers and Co[1] american merchants, resident at Marseilles in France, caused to them in the case of the Dutch Galliot Vrouw Johanna, captured and carried into Palames[2] and Barcelona in the course of last year by a Spanish Guarda costa, under a suspicion of an intention to smuggle arms into Catalonia but liberated after a detention of 54 days.

On board of this vessel were 60 tons of refined sugar owned by the Messrs Fitch Brothers and Co and which they had sold previous to arrival. The purchasers impatient of the long detention of the vessel and fearful of her ultimate condemnation, instituted legal proceedings against the house of Fitch Brothers and Co which were settled by the latter paying 3000 francs as an indemnity.

The undersigned has the honor to enclose a copy of the receipt given to the Messrs Fitch for this sum: the original of which document properly authenticated will be furnished when required. The Messrs Fitch claim of her Majesty's Govt the restitution of this sum as being a loss caused by the wrongful detention of their property by one of her own armed vessels

The justice of this claim appears to the undersigned so evident that he persuades himself it will be immediately admitted by her Majesty's Govt and he only urges that the wrong sustained by the claimants may be rendered as light as possible by the promptness of the redress.

The undersigned etc

Signed = Washington Irving

MANUSCRIPT: NA, RG 84 (letterbook copy).

1. This shipping and merchandising firm composed of Douglas and William Fitch in Marseilles and Asa in New York served as official supplier for the American Navy in the Mediterranean, with a virtual monopoly on American shipping in the area. See Scoville, *Old Merchants of NYC*, I, 58–63. The claim of Fitch Brothers & Co. was set forth in a letter to WI, April 5, 1845 (NA, RG 84).

2. Palamos is a seaport on the northeastern coast of Spain, about eighteen miles east southeast of Gerona.

1845.   To Francisco Martínez de la Rosa

Madrid 16th April 1845

His Excy / Don F. M. de la Rosa / Minister of State

Sir,

I have the honor to acknowledge the receipt of your Excellency's note of the 8th inst. on the subject of certain reclamations made by the Spanish Govt on the Govt of the U. S. for the diminution of the tonnage dues paid by Spanish vessels in the ports of the U. S.

Your Excy observes that a Message from the President of the U. S. brought this matter before Congress in 1840, that a bill was founded thereupon, which received the approbation of the House of representatives and passed to the Senate, but that the matter appears to have been given to oblivion for reasons which have never reached the Spanish Govt.

Your Excy further informs me that orders have, in consequence been given to her Majesty's Minister at Washington to announce to the American Govt after the 1st of August next, the old tariff of tonnage dues will be revived with respect to American vessels arriving in Spanish ports unless the principle of reciprocity is previously observed with regard to Spanish vessels and your Excellency intimates a wish that I would urge my Govt to suitable action in the matter

In reply, I would observe that, in examining the Journals of Congress I find the message of 1840 to which your Excy alludes and the bill consequent thereto which bill appears to embrace all the objects contemplated in the reclamations of the Spanish Govt. . This bill, instead of passing into oblivion, has been brought before Congress in succeeding sessions and appears never to have met with opposition. That it has not passed into a law has not been from any want of good faith and good intentions on the part of the American Govt. nor of favorable dispositions on the part of Congress, but from the extraordinary press of other business and from the thousand fortuitous delays to which the best devised and best intended laws are subject in their passage through legislative bodies and of which your Excy from your parliamentary experience must be fully aware. I shall certainly comply with your Excy's suggestion in urging this matter upon the prompt attention of my Govt.; but I would observe that it is impossible for the Govt to make any alterations in the duties previous to the 1st of August next, Congress not being in session to pass the necessary law. I regret that the resolution taken by her Majesty's Govt had not been announced at an earlier date, prior to the adjournment of that body.

I submit to the consideration of her Majesty's Ministers whether, as the good intentions of the American Govt are apparent in this matter, it would not be advisable to give them a little more time to operate by postponing the measure of countervailing duties to a date subsequent to the next session of Congress especially as the bill which is intended to be passed into a law, provides for the repayment of all tonnage dues levied on Spanish vessels since 1832 contrary to the principle of reciprocity.

I am etc

Signed = Washington Irving.

MANUSCRIPT: NA, RG 84 (letterbook copy); NA, RG 59 (copy).

A copy of this letter was enclosed with WI's despatch no. 63, dated April 17, 1845, to the secretary of state.

1846.   To [James Buchanan]

Legation of the United States / Madrid, April 17th. 1845

No. 63. / The Honble / The Secretary of State / Washington

Sir,

Since my last communication to the Department I have received despatch No 40, enclosing the Commission of Washington Rccd[1] as Consul of the United States for the port of Sagua la Grand, in the island of Cuba. As this port is not one of the four to which the Spanish government limits the admission of foreign consuls. I have forborne to apply for an Exequatur.

In comformity to instructions given in the same despatch I have made a representation to the Spanish government of the Case of the Bark Zulette of Boston, fired upon by the Spanish fort at Tarifa; and have demanded "an explanation, or the punishment of the officer who may have been guilty of what appears to be a wanton outrage."[2]

It happens that the Spanish flag has recently sustained a similar outrage in nearly the same waters, a Spanish guarda costa pursuing a smuggler within the British bounds of Gibraltar, having been fired upon and sunk by the first shot. The circumstance caused great irritation in Spain and a demand for satisfaction of the British government. In my note I have alluded to this circumstance, and while I gave the Spanish government credit for the quick sensibility to the honor of their flag which they had manifested on the occasion I trusted that they would be prompt and scrupulous in meting out to others the same reparation which they demanded for themselves.

In reply the Minister of State has assured me that the matter shall immediately be investigated.

I would observe the rock of Gibraltar is a constant thorn in the side of Spain, and is regarded with great jealousy and heart burning by the Spanish forts in its neighborhood; which are apt to retaliate any real or fancied insult offered to Spanish pride by the British batteries. The Zulette may have been mistaken for a British vessel and treated accordingly. A recent English writer observes of Tarifa, "the insolence of the garrison is unexampled: all vessels which do not hoist colours are at once fired into. This happens frequently with merchantmen and especially those from Gibraltar. They fire even into our men of war. . . . no redress is ever given at Madrid."[3]

I enclose copies of notes which have passed between the Spanish Minister of State and myself[4] on the subject of the delays on the part of our government in complying with the claims of the Spanish government for a diminution of tonnage duties on Spanish vessels in ports of the United States. As the equity of those claims has been admitted by the incipient acts of our government in compliance with them, good policy as well as good faith, require that those acts should be completed and rendered effectual as soon as possible. We cannot complain of delays on the part of Spain in satisfying any of our just demands while a measure of redress, to which she is entitled by acknowledged principles of reciprocity, and national good faith, is allowed to slumber for years in the chambers of Congress: with the apparent risk of proving abortive.

I remain, Sir, / Very respectfully / Your Obt Servt.
Washington Irving

DOCKETED: Recd. 21 May. / Mr. Markoe. [top of page 1] / No 63. W. Irving. Madrid – 17 April 1845
MANUSCRIPT: NA, RG 59.

This entire despatch is in WI's handwriting.

1. Washington Reed of North Carolina was nominated as U.S. consul for Sagua La Grande on February 13, 1845. See Hasse, Index to U.S. Documents, III, 1747.

2. See WI to Martínez de la Rosa, April 4, 1845.

3. See Richard Ford, A Hand-Book for Travellers in Spain, I, 342.

4. See Martínez de la Rosa to WI, April 8, 1845; WI to Martínez de la Rosa, April 16, 1845.

1847. To [James Buchanan]

Madrid 17th April 1845

No 64 / The Hble / The Secretary of State / Washington

Sir

I have the honor to enclose the accounts and vouchers of the Legation for the First Quarter of 1845 showing a balance against the United States of $5.74 which will be carried to their debit on their next account

I am Sir / Very respectfully / Your obedient servant

Washington Irving

MANUSCRIPT: NA, RG 59.

Only the signature is in WI's handwriting.

1848. To Francisco Martínez de la Rosa

Madrid 18th April 1845

His Excy / Dn F. M. de la Rosa. / Minister of State

Sir,

I have the honor to acknowledge the receipt of your Excy's note of the 14th inst. in reply to my request[1] that Mr Junius Boyle be authorized to exercise the functions of U. S. Consul At antim [?] at Mahon.

It is with much concern that I hear of the very irregular conduct of the person who last exercised these functions at that port in arrogating to himself faculties to which he was not entitled and in neglecting those respectful observances towards the local authorities, due to their dignity and to the policy of his own Govt., which is anxious, on all occasions to cultivate the best feelings and relations with Spain.

I would observe, however, that the person who has quitted his post thus unceremoniously was not Mr O. Rich, the Consul, who has filled that office for many years and always, I believe, with great decorum, but his son James Rich, whom he left in charge last year, on being obliged to absent himself on account of ill health and who is a young man apparently little versed in the ways of the world or schooled in official proprieties. I shall not fail strongly to represent to the latter the gross impropriety of his conduct and to the father his great want of consideration in entrusting the office to such incompetent hands.

In the meantime I beg leave to express to your Excy the proper sense I entertain of the very prompt and considerate attention paid to my representation by her Majesty's Govt and of its favorable action in the case, by which much inconvenience to the public service has been prevented.

I take this occasion etc.

Signed = Washington Irving

MANUSCRIPT: NA, RG 84 (letterbook copy).

1. See WI to Martínez de la Rosa, April 9, 1845.

1849. To Messrs. Fitch Brothers & Co.

Madrid 19th April 1845

Messrs Fitch Brothers and Co / Marseilles

Gentlemen

I duly received your letter of the 5th inst. and immediately passed a note to the Spanish Govt.[1] stating the loss you had sustained by the detention of the Dutch Galliot "Vrouw Johanna" by a Spanish Guardacosta and claiming indemnification. I enclosed in my note the copy of the receipt given you for the money you had been obliged to pay to stop legal proceedings and engaged to furnish the original properly authenticated whenever it should be required. I believe the document can be sufficiently authenticated by the Spanish Consul in Marseilles, but I will let you know when I have a reply from the Govt. You may be assured I will do everything in my power to serve your interests in the case and will be happy at any time to render you any other service

I remain gentlemen / Very truly your friend and servt
Signed = Washington Irving

MANUSCRIPT: NA, RG 84 (letterbook copy).

1. See WI to Martínez de la Rosa, April 16, 1845.

1850. To Irving Paris

Madrid April 19th 1845

My dear Irving

I have been unable from the press of other claims upon my pen, to acknowledge earlier the receipt of your kind letter of the 4th. January last.[1] I now write to you on a ⟨mat⟩ subject which I hope may be acceptable to you in the way of business.

The Marquis of Casa Yrujo[2] formerly Spanish Minister to the United States married a daughter[3] of Governor Thomas M'Kean[4] of Pennsylvania. The governor gave his daughter in her marriage portion certain lots of land in Pennsylvania. These the Marchioness at her death bequeathed to her daughter Narcissa who has since married Don Blas St Iago Perrard[5] an officer in the Spanish army. The Perrards have been excessively perplexed about their American property. They have the title deeds all in good order, but they know nothing about the condition or value of their property; and having no knowledge of business have not known how to proceed in the matter. The old Marchioness had a correspondent or two in America who used to look after the property for her; but the press of other concerns have induced them to decline further attention to it. A long illness previous to her death prevented the Marchioness ⟨to⟩ from giving all the explanations necessary to her heirs. The young Marquis of Casa Yrujo,[6] who is the man of business of the family has enough to do to manage his own large fortune, and is at present absent, as Minister in England. Under these circumstances the Perrards have applied to me for advice as I am an old friend of the family; having known them all intimately during my former residence in Spain.[7] It occurred to me that as you were not overwhelmed with business you might be able to attend to this matter, and the suggestion at once seemed to take quite a load of perplexity off of ⟨the⟩ their minds. ⟨of the Perrards.⟩ I enclose the numbers and names of the lotts of land described on the several title deeds. The object will be for you to ascertain their state and condition, their value and, in short, every thing pertaining to them. The persons who used to correspond with the old Marchioness about these lands were a Mr Dunlap[8] of Philadelphia (christian name unknown) and a Mr William Wilkins[9] of Pittsburgh; who lived near them. This latter I presume to be the same who was formerly in the Senate and subsequently Minister to Russia. He is brother in law of Vice President Dallas. You may make enquiries of him by letter; but I should judge it ↑more↓ advisable for you to visit the lands and ascertain by careful inspection and enquiry every thing concerning them. You will of course charge for your expenses and trouble. You will let me know the results of your enquiries and your bill of cost and charges. ⟨If⟩ In any subsequent measures that the Perrards may take with respect to this property I will get you a power of attorney to act in their name. Madame Perrard has inherited large property in Spain and is very wealthy.

⟨The⟩ In any enquiry you may have to make of Mr Wilkins, whether personally or by letter, you may tell him I ⟨[*unrecovered*]⟩ requested you to do so. He is a gentleman with whom I was formerly well acquainted.

This is a mere letter of business so I shall say nothing about family matters excepting my love to your Father & mother and to "all bodies"

Your affectionate uncle
Washington Irving

P. S I think it very probable that the Perrards, if they could get a fair offer for their lands would be glad to ⟨dis⟩ sell them: ascertain what they would be likely to fetch if put at once in the market, and what is their real value. ⟨[*Several words unrecovered*]⟩

MANUSCRIPT: Dr. Noel Cortes.

This letter is written on official stationery imprinted "Legacion / de los / Estados Unidos / en / España."

1. This letter has not been located.

2. Carlos Martínez de Yrujo y Tacon, marques de Casa Yrujo (1763–1824) was Spanish minister to the United States from 1796 to 1806 and later served his government as minister to Brazil and France. See Roberdean Buchanan, *Genealogy of the McKean Family of Pennsylvania* (Lancaster, Pa., 1890), pp. 134–38.

3. Sarah Maria Theresa McKean (1780–1841), a striking beauty and a reigning belle of Philadelphia society, married Casa Yrujo on April 10, 1798. After her husband's death she lived with her children in Madrid. See Buchanan, *McKean Family*, pp. 133–38.

4. Thomas McKean (1734–1817), a signer of the Declaration of Independence, was governor of Pennsylvania from 1799 to 1808.

5. Narcisa Maria Luisa Casa Yrujo (1800–1874) was married on February 14, 1842, to Blas Santiago de Pierrard y Alceda (d. 1872), a lieutenant general in the Spanish army, military governor of the Philippine Islands, and later a member of the Cortes. See Buchanan, *McKean Family*, p. 187.

6. Carlos Fernando Martínez de Yrujo y McKean, duke of Sotomayor (1802–1855), who held various appointments in the Spanish government and was a member of the Cortes after 1838, was Spanish minister to Great Britain from 1844 to 1846. In 1847 and 1848 he was president of the Council of Ministers and first secretary of state (Foreign Affairs), and from 1849 to 1851 he was ambassador to France. See Buchanan, *McKean Family*, pp. 187–89.

7. The marchioness de Casa Yrujo and her daughter Narcisa were part of the circle of friends in Madrid to which WI was admitted on his arrival there in 1826. From February of 1826 through March of 1827 WI records twenty-six meetings with the marchioness and her daughter. See *Journals of WI*, III, 7–59.

8. Possibly James Dunlap (1795–1856), a lawyer and author of *The General Laws of Pennsylvania*.

9. William Wilkins (1779–1865), a judge in the U.S. District Court of Western Pennsylvania (1824–1831), U.S. senator (1831–1834), U.S. minister to Russia (1834–1836), and secretary of war (1844–1845). His second wife Matilda was the sister of George M. Dallas, vice-president with James K. Polk.

1851. To Joseph Smith

Madrid April 19th 1845

Commodore Smith / commanding Medn Squadron.

Sir,

On receiving your letter of the 18th March I immediately made application to the Spanish Govt for the royal sanction of the temporary appointment of Lt Boyle to the Consulate at Mahon.

I have just received a reply from the Minister of State in which he complains of the conduct of Mr Rich in assuming to himself the sole faculty of naming a successor and in departing unceremoniously without observing any of those marks of respect due to the local authorities and consonant with the amicable relations of the two countries It was in consequence of this indecorous and irregular conduct that Gl Sureda[1] felt himself obliged to decline all recognition of the illegal nomination made by Mr Rich until the pleasure of her Majestys Govt should be known and his conduct has been approved by that Govt as strictly correct.

The Minister adds "A pesar de esto y teniendo en consideracion lr[?]mautel[?] ado por vd. en su citada nota me he apresurado a dar las ordenes oportunas al Gobernador de Mahon para que en el caso de no ofrecerse mas inconvenientes en el nombramiento del Sr Boyle que la forma en que se ha verificado, lo autorice desde luego para desempeñar interinamente las funciones consulares, hasta persona que deba desempeñar el Consulado."[2]

I trust, therefore, that by the time this letter reaches you Lt Boyle will have been duly recognized as Consul ad interim

I remain Sir / Very respectfully / Your very obt servant
Signed = Washington Irving

MANUSCRIPT: NA, RG 84 (letterbook copy).

1. The governor of Port Mahon, at which the U.S. Navy supply base was located.

2. Translation: "In spite of that and taking into consideration in your aforementioned note I have hastened to give pertinent orders to the governor of Mahon so that in case no obstacles other than the manner in which it has been carried out present themselves in the nomination of Mr. Boyle he may authorize him immediately to fulfill temporarily the consular functions, until the person who is to fulfill the consulship has been named by the government of the Republic."

1852.   To John Miller

Madrid 22nd April 1845

To John Miller Esqre

Dear Sir

I enclose a draft on Messrs Baring and Co of London payable to your order for 7.4.11 Pounds Sterling being in payment of your account incurred for this Legation for the last Quarter

I am respectfully / your obedient servant
Signed = Washington Irving

MANUSCRIPT: NA, RG 84 (letterbook copy).

1853.   To Catharine Paris

Madrid, April 22d 1845

My dear Sister,

I have just received your letter of March 25. and 27th.[1] and shall endeavor to scribble a hasty reply; though I have other letters to write by the Courier which leaves Madrid in the course of three hours. I am glad to find by your letter that you had nearly recovered your usual state of health and strength after your spring attack. I shall rejoice to hear ⟨fr⟩ of your being once more among the birds and blossoms at the cottage and breathing the sweet country air.

I had heard, as you suppose, before the receipt of your letter, of the intended marriage of Oscar and Eliza,[2] which I suppose has by this time taken place.[3] It has my hearty approbation, and I have no doubt will prove a happy union. Eliza will, as you say, be sadly missed at the Cottage, of which, since your Sarahs departure, she was the life. [He]r [*MS torn*] residence in town, on the other hand, will be a great gain to Helen: and should the two sisters live under the same roof, it might prove a very comfortable family establishment.

I have written a letter on business to your son Irving,[4] ⟨by⟩ which will probably go by the same vessel which brings this. Tell him I have not given the name of the Spanish family correctly. Instead of "Perrard" it should be "de Pierrard."

My health continues to be excellent, though I am continually occupied with my pen. Madrid has been unusually gay this winter, and still continues to be more animated than formerly. I was a few days since at another royal banquet at the Palace; but have given you so many descriptions of these court fêtes that I have nothing new to communicate on the subject. ⟨It w⟩ The dinner was not quite so grand, as to the number of guests, as on a former occasion, but was quite splendid. After dinner we had a concert, at which some of the performers from the Italian opera sang: and Mr Artot,[5] who recently figured in the United States, playd on the violin. We did not leave the palace until half past one oclock. On the 27th. of this month we have a grand Besamanos, it being the day of Queen Maria Christina. On the 1st. of May there is a grand diplomatic dinner in uniform at the French Embassy being the "jour de fête" of Louis Philippe. To day I dine with the British Minister[6]—so you see I still continue in the midst of dissipation.

I have no dispatches from Government to guide me as to my movements in regard to the removal of the court to Barcelona, which takes place ⟨in th⟩ about the middle of next month. Indeed I am quite uncertain as to my continuance in office. I observe that Mr Polk is beset by heavy office seekers; and he will have many important political friends to provide for. Should I be displaced it will bring me back among my relatives and friends sooner than I should come were I left to my own prudential calculations, but perhaps it would turn out all for the best. I await the result of cabinet arrangements without anxiety.

I received letters recently from brother E. I.[7] to which I will reply by a future opportunity. I am glad to find that he has been setting out evergreens. His letters from the Cottage always give me heartfelt satisfaction; for they shew that he enjoys existence there; surrounded as he is by his family, and engaged in healthful and delightful occupations.

You make frequent mention of the amiable attentions you receive from a Miss Tuckerman.[8] I feel them as kindnesses done to myself, and I beg you to tell that very estimable young lady how much I am obliged to her.

I thank you for your suggestion that I should publish my works by subscription—I shall bear it in mind. I ⟨have⟩ am in no hurry about republishing my works, being desirous to get them all in a proper state of revision before I commence.

With love to "all bodies"

Your affect. brother
W.I.

ADDRESSED: Mrs Daniel Paris / Care of E. Irving Esqr / New York   FRANKED: *Legation of United States, Madrid*
MANUSCRIPT: Star P. Myles, Wayland, Massachusetts.

This letter is written on official stationery with the letterhead "Legacion / de los / Estados Unidos / en / España."

1. This letter has not been located.
2. For other details, see WI to Sarah Storrow, March 27, 1845.
3. They were married on April 3, 1845.
4. See WI to Irving Paris, April 19, 1845.
5. Alexander Joseph Montagney (1815–1845), a brilliant Belgian violinist and composer, adopted Artot as his professional name.
6. William Henry Lytton Bulwer.
7. These letters have not been located.
8. This may be Ruth Keating Tuckerman, the sister of Henry T. Tuckerman.

1854. To Sarah Storrow

Madrid ⟨March⟩ April 23d. 1845

My dear Sarah,

I received a day or two since your letter[1] (without date) by post; after having been disappointed last week in receiving none by the French Courier. I sent you no letter last week, having none to answer, and being in no mood for letter writing. I am not in a better mood at present, but I will write, however much against the grain. I presume you have received letters from your Mother by the late arrivals. I have one from her dated towards the end of March; when she had recovered from her usual Spring indisposition and was waiting for settled genial weather to venture abroad. Your accounts of your children delight her, as they do me; so be never sparing of them in your letters to either of us. Your account of poor little Kate sitting by you at the table while you were writing to me, and sighing heavily because obliged to keep silent, amused me extremely. Dear restless little Kate, I wish I had her here to fidget about me. I'd give up pen, paper, books and every thing to devote myself to her.

Your Uncle E. I writes me that Judge White of Whitesborough near Utica, has purchased the Dutcher farm[2] for his son; so that the Hendersons have lost the chance of getting one of the pleasantest situations on the Hudson River, and I have lost the chance of having them for Country neighbors. However, tell Mrs Henderson I dont care two straws about it. tell her I'm rather pleased than otherwise—tell her I am quite pleased and only hope they'll settle in Texas. or the Oregon territory, or any other place at the other end of the world.

We have had more festivities since I wrote to you. A banquet at the Palace, followed by a concert, at which some of the operatic company sang. But I have given you ⟨disper⟩ ↑so many↓ accounts of Court fetes that I have nothing new to say on the subject. Ronconi is here, performing at one of the Theatres[3] and drawing immensely crowded houses.

The Musical rivalry between the two operas goes on with great vigor, much to the entertainment of the public.

The French Ambassador has moved into a very large Hotel; one of the old Spanish family palaces; which he is furnishing in great style. on the first of May (the Day of Louis Philippe) he gives a grand diplomatic dinner, in uniform. On the 27th. of this month, the day of Queen Maria Christina, there will be a besa manos at the Palace, and probably some fete in the evening—These I trust will close our court fêtes for the Season, as the Royal family will probably set off for Barcelona about the Middle of May. I believe I have told you that I have an invitation from Mr Anguera to take up my residence under his roof, should I visit Barcelona this year. All my movements, however, will depend upon my despatches from Government. I should not be surprised at finding myself superceded in office as I observe Mr Polk is making many removals, and several candidates are named for my place. I really think the event by no means ⟨pr⟩ improbable, In that case you will see me sooner than you otherwise would; though of course it would be some ⟨little time⟩ time before my successor would arrive here. I am in hopes of receiving despatches from Government by the French Courier which arrives this day, ⟨which⟩ from which I may be able to judge of the probability of Such an event.

Your uncle E I. informs me that his son Pierres wife has enriched her husband with another daughter.[4] He intimates that Pierre is a little embarrassed by the amount of his riches of this kind. He however, manages to get on tolerably comfortably; having a Salary as Secretary of the Foreign Missionary committee; eked out by an allowance as an assistant to Dr Milner[5] at St Georges Chapel. Pierre is a favorite with the people of St Georges Parish; Dr Milners health is feeble and declining. ⟨so that⟩ ↑and↓ your uncle ↑piously↓ observes "*should Providence see fit to remove him,* it is probable Pierre will succeed him as Rector."— I trust the "heavenly father" will "bring the matter about," in his usual "wonderful way," for the accommodation of your uncles family.

Friday. I was agreeably surprised yesterday by the receipt of a letter from you by the French Courier; for having written to me by post Mail, I did not expect another letter of the same week. I thank you for Julias letter, which I return, and which has given me great pleasure. I have no despatch from Government by the Courier, at which I am a little surprised; as it was high time for me to receive an official letter from the New Secretary of State,[6] apprising me of his appointment. I shall be kept some time longer in doubt as to my continuance in Madrid; but it is not a matter that causes me much anxiety.

From what you say in your letter I shall not be surprised to hear of all "Chamber Street"[7] being suddenly transferred to Paris. It would give me the most heartfelt pleasure to meet them all there. I think it would be an excellent move for your aunt;[8] and can see no objection to it.

I have never received the letter from Mr King which in your letter of *March 29th.* you mention as having been sent by the last Courier. I received a letter from him last week, but it was written long after your letter of March 29th. being dated April 10th. There is nothing in it in reply to my letter to him. This is the Second letter I have received from him since I left Paris. One has certainly miscarried; which I greatly regret. He intimates in his letter a slight doubt of his own continuance in office under the dispensations of Mr Polk; but I am satisfied he may continue in Paris as long as he pleases; and I hope he ⟨will⟩ may find it consistent with his health and happiness to remain there. It would be difficult for us to furnish the French court with a more perfect specimen of the Republican gentleman—and then his niece!

Do not abandon your French Studies under the idea that you can never make yourself fluent in conversation. A little daily practise, if but for *half an hour* at a time, on the difficulties of the language, will vanquish them all. A half an hour, three times a week will do wonders: only let the practise be confined to the difficult points; such as embarrass you in conversation. Practise with your pen on the moods and tenses. The difficulties, after all, are⟨,⟩ but few, a little practise gives you the key to them; and now is the time to practise, while you are new in the language, and have not any confirmed habitudes of speaking incorrectly. A little, a very little present trouble will save you from a world of annoyance for the rest of your life.

Give my affectionate remembrances to Gabriel. I long to hear of the arrival of his family, and that he has his good little wife beside his pillow—

With kind regards to Mr Storrow and many kisses to the dear little women—

Your affectionate Uncle
Washington Irving

ADDRESSED: Madame / Madame Storrow / no 4 Rue de la Victoire / à Paris
MANUSCRIPT: Yale.

1. This and other letters to WI mentioned herein have not been located.
2. This farm was probably owned by the descendants of William Dutcher, a Revolutionary militiaman in Westchester County. See J. T. Scharf, *History of Westchester County*, I, 298.
3. Probably the Circo. See WI to Sarah Storrow, February 27, 1845.
4. Frances Sutherland Irving, born on March 20, 1845, and died on April 24, 1846, was the ninth child and sixth girl of Anna Duer and Pierre P. Irving.

5. James Milnor (b. 1773) was the rector of St. George's Church on Beekman Street from 1816 until his death on April 8, 1844. Apparently WI was unaware of his demise.

6. James Buchanan (1791–1868) had been U.S. senator from Pennsylvania from 1834 until he assumed his duties as secretary of state on March 6, 1845.

7. The residence of the John Treat Irving family (and possibly that of Gabriel Irving) until a few weeks earlier. See WI to Sarah Storrow, March 12, 1845.

8. Mrs. John Treat Irving, Sr.

1855. To Sarah Storrow

Madrid May 2. 1845

My dear Sarah,

I received yesterday your letter of the 25th March,[1] your "Miserable Scrawl" as you call it; but which I read over and over with heartfelt pleasure. I find you begin to talk dubiously about your grand expedition to the Rhine & to Switzerland; about which you used to hold forth so confidently. I could not help picturing ⟨yourse⟩ you to myself like another Christiana Setting forth with all her children on a Pilgrims Progress, and I feared you would be sadly in want of a captain Great Heart[2] to champion you. (I trust you have read the evangelical romance of John Bunyan.) And then how Kate, with her "heady highmindedness," would make out in the civil wars of the Swiss, gave me some doubts and anxieties. I think, upon the whole, you are discreet in bringing your travelling plans within narrower limits; and leaving these distant expeditions until your children have grown larger, and distance has been annihilated by rail roads. As to your Swiss tour you have enjoyed ⟨the⟩ it in anticipation, and that is often the best part of a Scheme of pleasure.

I am still waiting for intelligence from Washington before I make my arrangements for the Summer. Should I conclude to pass it ·here, you need be under no apprehensions of my Suffering from heat. I passed the Summer before last in Madrid in my present quarters; and though out of health at the time, passed it very comfortably. My house is very large; the walls thick and the interior well ventilated. I shut out the glare and the heat of day; remain in my spacious twilight saloons, which are almost as cool as vaults, until the sun has set, and then drive out to enjoy the evenings which are temperate, and the nights which are heavenly. I do not know any thing more bland and delightful than the temperature of the Prado towards midnight in mid summer.

We have just had great festivities at Court in honor of the birth day of Queen Christina.[3] A Besa manos, which was very magnificent but very fatiguing as I had to be on my legs for upwards of three hours in the presence chambre; while all the world passed in review before the throne to pay homage to the Royal family. Two days after there was a grand fête Champêtre at Vista Alegre,[4] a rural possession of Queen Christinas about a Couple of miles from Madrid. The grounds are laid out with groves, shrubberies; walks, canals &c and all kinds of Amusements were prepared; flying horses, swings; ⟨ridin⟩ roundabouts and riding at the ring; shooting with cross bows, gondolas on the Canal &c &c &c nearly a thousand persons, the elite of Madrid were there. ⟨I⟩ We assembled at four Oclock and the pleasure grounds presented a most animated and amusing picture. One old Courtier fell off of a wooden horse and broke his head: a gondola in which was the Countess of Montijo and her party, upset in the Canal (which is nine feet deep) and the ladies, among which was my fair friend Leocadia Zamora, were extricated from the water with some difficulty. In the evening we had fireworks; a concert; and a repast, which last was served up in an immense tent, illuminated, as were several walks of the gardens, with innumerable chinese lamps. The weather was perfect; the trees were all in leaf, the lilacs in flower, and the nightingales in full song. There were bands of music too stationed in different parts of the grounds; playing ⟨the most⟩ popular pieces from fashionable operas. Altogether it was one of the pleasantest and most successful fetes champetre that I have ever witnessed.

Yesterday I was at a splendid dinner given by the French Ambassador in honor of the day of Louis Philippe.[5] The Embassy had recently been removed to the Benevente palace; and the apartments newly and richly furnished and decorated were first thrown open on this occasion. We set down about forty persons to dinner, in full uniform. The table was splendidly set out, and the effect of the whole very brilliant. Now I trust we have got through great fêtes for the season.

A day or two since I had Madame Albuquerques children to pass the day with me; to see a grand religious procession[6] which was to pass the house twice in the Course of the day; in which there were to be children dressed up as Angels &c. Juana undertook to prepare for the entertainment of the young folks; who arrived, with their English nurse between ten and eleven in the morning. The little girls are about six and seven years of age, the boy about the age of Kate. They are beautiful children. I put the house quite at their service and gave them the complete range of it. A lunch was provided for them at twelve oclock, and a dinner at four. Juana took care that every thing was arranged to their liking; and a merry day they passed, sporting about the Saloons and corridors. I enjoyed myself as much as they did, and joined with them in their games; but I often thought, in the course of the day how much my enjoyment would have been heightened had I had Kate and Suzie here to do the honors of my house. These little folks always call me uncle so that I have something of the feeling of home when surrounded by them. I take a peculiar interest in the boy little José, because he is about the age of Kate and an intelligent child, like her, and I think I can guage by him Kates advancement in knowledge and civilization. He is a remarkably fine child. Something of a Spanish face, with large dark eyes, and a rich glowing expression. He is a stout hearted little fellow and full of Spirit; and it is delightful to hear him Speak Spanish; rolling the r's ⟨with⟩ ↑in↓ true Castilian style. He has a great passion for military affairs; his favorite toys are drums, trumpets, swords, and I made him quite happy by giving him a grenadier thoroughly equipped; and now, whenever his sisters play with their dolls he brings forth his "Soldado," and treats him to a tune on the trumpet. After the little folks had had their days revel I sent them out with Juana in the Carriage to take an airing on the Prado and then to return home.

Saturday. I must not omit to notice your account of the "elegant and agreeable" party at the Corbins. I have no doubt that every thing was in the best taste, and that the party went off with *eclat*—How could it ⟨do⟩ be otherwise when Mrs Ellis made her appearance there in "a pink dress with DEEP FLOUNCES"! ! !. By the way you are throwing all my reccollections of that fair lady into confusion. When I left Paris I brought away a distinct image of her in my mind, in her quiet ⟨black dress⟩ suit of mourning with her pale brown hair simply parted on her forehead in classic style; and I thought I would never have her look otherwise. But you have arrayed her in rich black velvet; and you have half hid her features with clusters of ringlets, and now you have so be-pinked and be flounced her, that I almost lose sight of the original idol of my worship in the finery of her decorations.

⟨And the⟩ You are quite poetical too in your *tirade* about spring time at Paris. "The Season of blossoms! !—"the exquisite freshness of the Tuilleries" ↑and Champs Elysees"↓ "—"the air perfumed with Sweets."— "the Park of Monceau with its lilacs in full blow." But what are all these—my dear Sarah—What are the blossoms of the Season—the lilacs of the park—the Sweets of the garden and the flowers of the field—What are all these, my dear Sarah, to Mrs Ellis, "in a pink dress, with DEEP FLOUNCES! ! !"

Give my affectionate remembrances to poor Gabriel. The latter part of your letter represents him as ⟨having⟩ being much better than he had been a day or two previously. I trust to that reaction in his system which has occurred before in his malady; and which has rallied him up in a manner that has surprised his friends. and I trust much to his constittutional cheerfulness and his manly spirit. But I shall nevertheless be rejoiced to hear of the arrival of his excellent little wife.

With kind regards to Mr Storrow and many Kisses to my dear little Kate and Susie.

Your affectionate Uncle
Washington Irving

P.S. I do not mean to Mention Mrs Henderson in this letter. I will never forgive her for not making her husband buy the Dutcher farm— never—dont write me any thing about her—as Kate Irving says, "I hate her."

ADDRESSED: Madame / Madame Storrow / No. 4 Rue de la Victoire / à Paris
MANUSCRIPT: Yale.   PUBLISHED: *Yale Review*, 17 (October, 1927), 116–17 (in part); LFSS, pp. 78–80 (in part).

1. WI probably intended to write "April." This letter has not been located.
2. In part 2 of *Pilgrim's Progress* Christiana, the wife of Christian, sets out on the same journey her husband had undertaken. Captain Greatheart accompanied her.
3. María Christina's birthday was on April 27. See WI to Sarah Storrow, April 23, 1845; and *La Posdata*, April 28, 1845.
4. For other details, see *La Posdata*, April 30, 1845.
5. This banquet was reported in *La Posdata*, May 1, 1845.
6. The feast day of St. Catherine of Sienna (1347–1380) was celebrated on April 30. See H. Pomeroy Brewster, *Saints and Festivals of the Christian Church* (New York, 1904), pp. 218–19; and *La Posdata*, May 2, 1845.

1856. To Francisco Martínez de la Rosa

Madrid 3rd of May 1845

His Excellency / Don Francisco Martinez de la Rosa / Minister of State

Sir,

I have the honor to acknowledge the receipt of your Excellency's note of the 30th April communicating the result of enquiries made into the conduct of the garrison of Tarifa in firing upon the Zulette a merchant vessel of the United States. I feel properly sensible of the promptness with which your Excellency has attended to my representation of this case and of the fair, frank and courteous spirit which characterizes your note; still I must observe that the explanation given by the Commander of the fortress does not convince me that he was justified in firing upon the Zulette. He alleges that several vessels were descried to the Eastward on the 23rd December last, keeping at a great distance during daylight; but that about seven o'clock, one which appeared to be a Frigate, accompanied by several merchant vessels, approached the Fort. That they did not sail with velocity correspondent with the prevailing wind etc.

Now, if your Excellency will advert to the extract from the log book of the Zulette which I had the honor to enclose to you, you will find that she had not been keeping at a distance until nightfall, but had come direct from Gibraltar with an Easterly wind, and of course along the Coast. That, instead of hovering about and lagging in a suspicious manner, she was making the best of her way, directly before the wind, with *studding sails set,* and going at the rate of eight miles an hour. She was thus *sweeping past the Fortress,* in a manner totally incompatible with any hostile or nefarious intention when she was fired into.

Your Excellency observes that the frank and friendly manner in which vessels from the United States are received in the ports of the Peninsula is a guaranty of the good dispositions of her Majesty's Government towards the ⟨Union⟩ States of the Union and has much more significancy that an isolated act resulting resulting[1] from misunderstanding and without any serious consequence. I assure your Excellency that I need no guaranty of the good intentions of her Majesty's Government towards my country; I am satisfied that a reciprocity of amicable feeling exists between the two Governments; but to preserve this enviable state of national amity intact, a rigid eye should be kept upon the conduct of public officers and agents by whose acts those good intentions may be either carried into effect ⟨ed⟩ or defeated. As your Excellency observes, the act of the Commander of Fort Tarifa was attended with no serious result; but that was not owing to any caution on his part. The shot struck the vessel and your Excellency will recollect that a single shot, fired in this same rash, heedless way, on a recent occasion, from one of the batteries of Gibraltar sunk one of the vessels of her Majesty, and caused a loud demand upon the British Government for redress; which demand ↑I believe↓ is still in the course of negotiation.

The fortress of Tarifa is peculiarly situated; on a frontier point of Europe, commanding, under some circumstances, the narrow Strait of Gibraltar, so that ships of all nations, bound to and from the Mediterranean, are often obliged to pass within the range of its batteries. Such a fortress should be confided to none but the most considerate and cautious hands. The following account I find given of it in an English work recently published in London.

"The insolence of the garrison is unexampled; all vessels which do not hoist colours are at once fired into. This frequently happens with merchant vessels, and especially those from Gibraltar. They fire even into our men of war. . . ., no redress is ever given at Madrid."[2]

With this extract, the truth of which appears to be strongly illustrated by the case of the Zulette, I shall leave this subject in the consideration of Her Majesty's government which, I am satisfied, will feel its own honor and interests concerned in a rigid scrutiny into the general conduct of this frontier post. In the meantime I shall forward to my government the note relative to the matter, which I have recently had the honor to receive from your Excellency, and which, as I before observed, breathes a most satisfactory spirit of national good will.

I have the honor to be with high consideration your Excellency's most obedient servant

Signed = Washington Irving.

MANUSCRIPT: NA, RG 84 (letterbook copy); NA, RG 59 (copy).

A copy of this letter was enclosed with WI's despatch no. 65, dated May 4, 1845, to the State Department. Because of its greater attention to detail, it is used as copy-text. It is written on official stationery inscribed "Legacion / de los / Estados Unidos / en / España."

1. WI's secretary inadvertently repeated "resulting."
2. WI quoted the same passage from Richard Ford, *A Hand-Book for Travellers in Spain*, I, 342 in despatch no. 63, dated April 17, 1845, to the State Department.

1857. To [James Buchanan]

Legation of the United States / Madrid, May 4th. 1845.

No 65. / The Hon. / The Secretary of State / Washington.

Sir,

I enclose a copy of a note from the Spanish Minister of State dated 29th. April, by which you will perceive that, in consequence of the representations contained in my note of 8th. April, (a copy of which I had the honor to enclose in Despatch No 63) orders have been sent by the Spanish government to its Minister at Washington, to extend the term, originally fixed for the 1st. of August next, for raising the rates of tonnage duties on American Vessels in Spanish ports to a level with those Still imposed upon Spanish vessels in our ports contrary to the principle of reciprocity; but to extend it no longer than shall appear to him reasonable and requisite for the just fulfilment of the negotiation.

I trust that the government will bear me out in the assurances I have given of its sincere and faithful intentions in this matter; by which I have delayed the contemplated measure of the Spanish government. I trust that the proper action in the case, which has been inexcusably delayed, will take place at an early day of the next session of Congress, and that an act will be passed retrospective in its effects, so as to provide for the repayment of the extra duties imposed upon Spanish vessels since 1832.

I have also the honor to enclose copies of notes which have recently passed between the Minister of State and myself relative to the affair of the Zulette. You will perceive that the commander of Tarifa states, in explanation, that·he fired with ball upon several vessels, on the evening specified; but that it was in consequence of their approaching the fort in a suspicious manner, without displaying lights, or paying any attention to signal guns previously fired.

In my reply, while I consider the explanation somewhat unsatisfactory, I have forborne to follow the matter up with rigor, inasmuch as that the letter, from the owners of the vessel, to the Department of State, leaves me to conclude that—the master of the Zulette had really neglected to observe the forms customary in passing within the bounds of fortified places; and because the extract from the logbook states merely the isolated fact of the vessel being fired into, without giving any of the circumstances which preceded or attended ⟨to⟩ it; and which might take from it all its imputed character of "wanton outrage."

> I have the honor to be / Very respectfully / Your Obt Servt
> Washington Irving

DOCKETED: Recd. 21 June / Mr Markoe [*upper left corner of page 1*] / No. 65. Washington Irving, Madrid, May 4th.
MANUSCRIPT: NA, RG 59.

This entire despatch is in WI's handwriting.

1858. To Brantz Mayer

> Madrid, May 6th. 1845.

Sir,

I have the honor to acknowledge the Receipt of your letter informing me of my being elected an honorary member of the Maryland Historical Society, and enclosing a Diploma.

I beg you will assure the Society of the deep and grateful feeling with which I accept this distinguished mark of their esteem

> I am Sir, / very respectfully / Your obt Servt.
> Washington Irving

Brantz Mayer Esqr

ADDRESSED: Under cover to / Washington / For / Brantz Mayer Esqr. / Corresponding Secretary / of the Maryland Historical Society / Baltimore   POSTMARKED: Washington City D. C. / JUL / 24
MANUSCRIPT: Maryland Historical Society.

The direction for the address is not in WI's handwriting.

Brantz Mayer (1809–1879), a Baltimore lawyer, author, and editor, was one of the founders of the Maryland Historical Society and its president from 1867 to 1871. See Jerry E. Patterson, "Brantz Mayer, Man of Letters," *Maryland Historical Magazine*, 52 (December, 1957), 275–89.

1859. To Reuben Beasley

Madrid May 10th 1845.

Reuben Beasley Esqre / U. S. Consul Havre

Sir,

I enclose a draft on Messrs Greene and Co. Paris payable to your order for 88 res. 90 c being in payment of your expenses incurred for this Legation for the last two Quarters. I remain etc

Signed = Washington Irving

MANUSCRIPT: NA, RG 84 (letterbook copy).

1860. To Sarah Storrow

Madrid May 10th. 1845

My dear Sarah,

I have just received Your letter of May 1 & 3, by *Mail*. I had given up all hope of hearing from you this week as the Courier, which arrived two days since, brought no letter. You mention your disappointment in being one week without receiving a letter; it was because I had received none from you; your letter, which you say should have come ⟨by⟩ through the Foreign office, having been put into the Post office, so as not to reach me in time for a reply by the French Courier. I fancy Antoine[1] is now and then too late at the Foreign office, and sends the letters by mail.

Your intelligence concerning the *King family* is uncommonly full and interesting. You need never fear wearying me however minute you may be in your details about that estimable family. You know my great regard for Mr King and the interest I take in every thing connected with him. I am glad to find that by frequent and close observation you have at last discovered all those excellencies in Mrs E—which struck me at first sight. You will henceforth, I trust, do credit to my quickness of perception where the charms of a lady are concerned. By the way, you describe her admirably, and discriminate those qualities in which she excells, and which give an inexpressible charm to all that she says and does. I am glad at length to know her christian name, and am very well pleased with it. Petruchio, if you will reccollect, rings the changes upon that name, beginning with "Kate the curst"[2] and ending with "the *bonniest Kate in Christ⟨o⟩endom*"—and this last is Mrs Ellis.

And now for our own little Kate. I would fain indulge the belief that she really reccollects "Unty" and all that he said and did—but I fear I am only an ideal being in her mind; kept up by your frequently talking of me. I should like to try her reccollection of me, as uncles do upon the Stage; when they return incog. from a long absence in India or elsewhere. I have a longing desire to see her and little Susie and have them continually in my minds eye. The reccollections of Kates whims and oddities are in fact sources of great amusement to me in my solitary hours, and I often find myself laughing out right as some of them pass through my mind.

I am waiting for letters from Washington to form my plans for the summer. I have received nothing from government since the election of Mr Polk and the formation of the new cabinet, but a ⟨lett⟩ circular from Mr Buchanan dated March 10th. informing me of his appointment. The government in the interim must have received despatches from me which ought to have been replied to; and this silence makes me think that I am being weighed in the balance. Mr Livingston has received letters from his friends, who think I will certainly be recalled. You cannot think it probable—"because it would be so unpopular"—but you my dear Sarah, always over rate me and my importance in the eyes of the public. Beside, political men in the position of Mr Polk are ⟨placed⟩ beset by difficulties and perplexities and have often to do things to which they are disinclined.

Could I consult my own pride, my independence and my inclinations I would long ere this have resigned my post and returned to my friends; but the constant thought of those I have to provide for, cuffs down my pride, and prevents me from sacraficing, to my independence and my inclinations, a post which enables me to keep my little flock at home in decent maintenance. I hope letters by the next Steamer will relieve me from my present incertitude. Whichever way the matter may be determined, my mind will soon be made up to it.

You will have no doubt heard before this that the wedding of Oscar and Eliza took place on the 3d April (my birth day) at the Cottage. They were married by Dr Creighton. Pierre M Irving & Helen, and Julia Grinnel & Ogden Irving[3] were present. The ceremony took place at 12 O Clock, after which they had a neat little collation when the Bride & bridegroom and the visitors set off for the city—and the "young couple" set off the next day on an excursion to New Haven. They were to commence housekeeping on the 1st May—

I received a letter a day or two since from *little John* Schell,[4] as we used to call him; but who must now be a young man of years and discretion. He seems to have thriven in the City of Quincey and to have made a little property, as the family have built a two story brick house on the lots which I furnished them with money to buy. He is now desirous of obtaining a deed from me for the lots which were bought in my name: and to pay me for the same. He says ["]I[5] have endeavored to be industrious and economical and so far have been fortunate, and have acquired some little property most of which has been laid out in the buildings and fixtures. I think I can say without boasting that I sustain a tolerable good character in this place for honesty and industrious habits. I feel very desirous of seeing you once more, and I think, if ever you get back to the united States again, I shall try and make you a visit. My father and our family all send their respects to you."

So much for "little John," who I was sure, if he retained his health, would do well.

To day I dine with Mr Bulwer, who is on the point of departing for England, on leave of absence. Indeed there is about to be a general breaking up of our Society here for the Summer. The Court goes to Barcelona. ⟨Th⟩ My friends the Albuquerques will probably follow it. The O'Sheas set out next week on their Summer tour to be gone until Autumn. The French Ambassador goes for a time to Paris and then joins his family at Barcelona: in a word, if I remain at Madrid I shall be quite alone: but if I am not displaced by govt. I shall be content to remain here and to pursue my literary tasks without interruption.

With kind remembrances to Mr Storrow and many Kisses to my little darlings

Your affectionate uncle
Washington Irving

MANUSCRIPT: Yale.   PUBLISHED: STW, II, 193 (in part).

1. Probably the messenger used by Mrs. Storrow.
2. See Shakespeare, *The Taming of the Shrew*, II, i, 187.

3. Pierre and Henry Ogden Irving (1807–1869) were Oscar's brothers; Julia Grinnell was his sister.

4. John Schell was an eleven-year-old German boy whom WI met on shipboard when he returned to the United States in 1832. Later, after working for WI for three years, he borrowed $100 from him to buy land in Illinois. See PMI, III, 36.

5. WI omitted the bracketed quotation mark.

1861.   To Sarah Storrow

Madrid, May 14th. 1845

My dear Sarah,

I am very desirous that you should know my amiable and excellent friend Mrs O'Shea, whom I have so often mentioned in my letters, and who will pass a few days in Paris in the course of a Summer tour. I have requested her therefore, on her arrival in Paris to send you this note with her address, that you may know where to call upon her.

Your affectionate Uncle
Washington Irving

Mrs. Thomas W Storrow.

ADDRESSED: Madame / Madame Storrow / 4. Rue de la Victoire / à Paris   POST-MARKED: ESPAGNE ST – J. – DE – LUZ / 3 DHC 13 // [*unrecovered*] // [*unrecovered*]   DOCKETED: *May 14th 1845.*
MANUSCRIPT: Va.–Barrett.

1862.   To Sarah Storrow

Madrid, May 16th. 1845

My dear Sarah,

Your letter of the 10th. inst,[1] received yesterday gives me very discouraging accounts about poor Gabriel. I hope your next letter will inform me of the arrival of his good little wife, whose presence will presence[2] will have the most soothing if not salutary effect. I am glad he is lodged at the Neothermes which is a quiet establishment, between court and garden, with freer circulation of air than in most houses in the centre of the city, and where there is attendance suited to invalids.

Yesterday my excellent friends the OShea's departed on their Summer tour, to be absent from Madrid about five months. It is a sad loss to me, for their house was like a home to me. They will pass about a week in Paris; where they will probably arrive in about a fortnight. I have given Mrs O'Shea a letter to you; which she will send with her card, on arriving. I want you to see and know her. She is one of the most amiable excellent women I have ever known; and one for whom I feel the affection of a relative. You need make no "fuss" with her; nor put yourself out of the way to entertain her; but see her and let her see your children, about whom I have often talked with her. Mr O'Shea is full of business and when in Paris has his hands full: and Mrs O'Shea say[s][3] she sometimes feels lonely there; an occasional visit from you therefore I am sure would be agreeable; and you might put her in the way of shopping and making her purchases to advantage.

You tell me Kate was busy with pencil and paper, writing to me. Why did you not send me her scrawl. I would almost value it as much as a letter from yourself. I am quite amused with your picture of her passing off upon poor little Susie the scoldings she sometimes receives from yourself, for making a noise when you are writing.

I am looking daily for letters by the Great Western, which I hope may give me some means of forming an idea whether or not I am to be displaced. The uncertainty in which I am kept is very irksome, as it prevents me from making any plans or arrangements for the rest of the year. I am happy to hear from my worthy friend Beasley that he is not likely to be disturbed; Mr Polk having given General Cass assurance to that effect. Mr King will also no doubt continue in office as long as he pleases, and I hope Mr Wheaton may also retain his post. It could not be more creditably filled.

Mr Oliver of Baltimore was here a day or two since and has gone to Barcelona, on his way back to Paris. He is an intimate friend of Mr King, ↑they↓ having both, when young men, been in the Legation of Mr Pinckney to Russia. He tells me Mr King talks of making a summer visit to ↑one of↓ the watering [places][4] in the Pyrenees, having relinquished the idea of a tour in Switzerland: and that on his return to Paris he means to reduce the expenses of his establishment; in which he will act very wisely. I wish you would ascertain what are his intended movements. I should like, if put in motion by any turn of events this summer, to fall in with him in the Course of my journeyings—though I think the chance a very remote one.

I am finishing this letter on Saturday, after the arrival of the mail; and am disappointed at finding that there is still no news from the United States. The Great Western is unusually long in arriving. With kind remembrances to Mr Storrow, and many thanks to dear little Kate for the letter which you neglected to send me.

Your affectionate uncle
Washington Irving

ADDRESSED: Madame / Madame Storrow / No 4. Rue de la Victoire / à Paris
MANUSCRIPT: Yale.

1. This letter has not been located.
2. WI repeated "presence will."
3. WI omitted the bracketed letter.
4. WI omitted the bracketed word.

1863. To Sabina O'Shea

Madrid May 17th. 1845

My dear Mrs O'Shea,

I am vexed to learn that you were sufficiently at leisure the evening previous to your departure, to receive company; so that I might have passed the evening in your society instead of moping it away in the solitude of my room. I should have seen Mr O'Shea and Willy[1] also, to take my farewell of them. Indeed it did not seem to me as if I had half taken farewell of your self in the morning; remembering after I left you, several things which I wished to have said. But I was stupid and out of order all that day; and the next day was confined to the house by the effects of a slight cold. Yesterday I made a visit to Madame Albuquerque. In ascending the Staircase I felt almost a shock at noticing the door leading to your part of the house, and which always stood so hospitably open, now closed—a mute ↑sign↓ that you had indeed departed.

I sat a long time with Madame Albuquerque and our conversation was almost entirely about you. She feels quite desolate at your departure, and well she may, for never has she had so true and kind a friend and one so worthy of her affection and esteem since her residence in Madrid. In the evening we had a gathering as usual at the French Embassy; where you were missed most sadly. The Countess de Bresson said many kind things of you, as did others of your intimates. In the latter part of the evening the Princess Carini and Madame Weisweiller came in. The latter looked ⟨sweet as usual⟩ rather dull; I presume she wanted your presence to excite her and give her animation. Old Dalbergo took me home in his carriage; he was mourning as usual over his losses; he had lost roundly that evening at Whist: he was losing by the Bourse; he was losing by rail roads; he was losing by mines; in a word he was in a fair way to be ruined. Considering the worthy old man is worth nothing it takes a longer time to ruin him than any man I ever was acquainted with. He puts me in mind of an old lady with a cracked constitution; who began to die when she was thirty years old, and kept on dying to an extreme old age. As D'Albergo last evening seemed a little soured in temper, I have no doubt he will revenge himself on society by another of his big bad dinners. Let us hope stocks may ⟨aris⟩ rise and avert so great a calamity.

I thank you for your kind present of Tea; you cannot think how acceptable it was to me; and how much I relish my breakfast, now that I seem to receive it from your hands.

Lilly Albuquerque² complains bitterly that the faithless Kicky departed without bidding her farewell personally or by message. I have endeavored to console her by alleging the general faithlessness of men; but really I think Kicky begins rather early to play the gay deceiver.

Give my kind remembrances to Mr OShea and the young gentlemen, and believe me, ever, my dear Mrs O'Shea

Very truly yours
Washington Irving

P.S. I am glad to learn that the fan which you accidentally left behind at Mr Bulwers was safely restored to you through the hands of John O'Shea. Though I think Mr Bulwer might have brought it to you himself; but fans and gloves and handkerchiefs are thrown away on some people—they're so dull of apprehension.

MANUSCRIPT: HSA.   PUBLISHED: Penney, *Bulletin NYPL*, 62 (December, 1958), 617–18.

1. A son of the O'Sheas who was to marry Cristina Osorio de Moscosco y Caravajal, duchess of San Lucar la Mayor. See Penney, *Bulletin NYPL*, 62 (December, 1958), 629.

2. A daughter of the Brazilian minister and his wife, who lived in the same building as the O'Sheas.

1864.   To Francisco Martínez de la Rosa

Madrid 19th May 1845

His Excy / Don Francisco Ms de la Rosa / Minister of State

Sir,

I have the honor to acknowledge the receipt of your Excy's note informing me of the intended departure of Her Majesty the Queen and her August Mother and Sister for Barcelona and that you are to follow them in your quality of Minister of State.

Your Excy, in addition, kindly intimates that it is left to my own choice to follow, or not, the Court to that city. I feel properly sensible of this indulgence and assure your Excy that, in whichever way I may avail myself of it, I shall ever be actuated by a profound respect for her Majesty and by a sedulous desire to promote to the best of my abilities the objects of my mission to her Court.

I avail myself etc

Signed . Washington Irving

MANUSCRIPT: NA, RG 84 (letterbook copy).

1865.   *To Messrs. Fitch Brothers & Co.*

Madrid May 22nd 1845

Messrs Fitch Brothers and Co

Gentlemen,

I enclose a copy of a note just received from Mr Martinez de la Rosa Spanish Minister of State by which you will perceive that your claim for damages in the case of the Dutch Galliot Vrouw Johanna is in course of consideration, but that it is necessary for you to authenticate in due form before the Spanish Consul in Marseilles the anticipated sale of the sugar and the amount of indemnity you had to pay to the purchasers in consequence of being prevented from fulfilling the sale in due time by the detention of the Galliot by a Spanish Guarda costa. You will forward to me the documents of the case duly certified by the Consul that I may lay them before the Spanish ⟨Cons⟩ govt.

I am Gentlemen / Very etc
Signed = Washington Irving

MANUSCRIPT: NA, RG 84 (letterbook copy).

1866.   *To Arthur MacCulloch*

Legation of the United States / Madrid May 22d. 1845

Arthur MacCulloch Esq / Consular agent of the U States / Alicant.

Sir,

I have duly received your letters:—public and private of the 16th. inst. vindicating your Self from the charges made against you of having taken an active part against the Spanish government in times of popular commotion. One of the charges struck me at the time as improbable, stating that on one occasion you had actually pointed a cannon against the Queens troops. Still as this was the Second time your conduct in political matters had been gravely called in question, I apprehended you might have been too free in publicly canvassing and condemning the measures of government in regard to seditious movements; an ill timed freedom of speech contrary to the non interference in foreign politics charged by our government upon its foreign agents. I was corroborated in this idea by learning from another source that General Roncali had expressed himself dissatisfied with your excitability in politics. This was told me casually by a person unacquainted with you, and without any intention of injuring you: he being very probably of the same way of thinking with yourself.

I am now convinced that, whatever may be your private opinions, your public conduct has been misrepresented, and that the specific acts charged upon you are false. I am happy to add that Mr Isturiz, the Minister of State, to whom I read your official letter, declared himself perfectly satisfied with it and assured me he should dismiss the matter from his mind.

I am Sir / Respectfully your ob St

W I.

MANUSCRIPT: NA, RG 84 (letterbook copy).

This copy is written in WI's handwriting.

1867. To Francisco Martínez de la Rosa

Madrid 22nd May 1845

His Excy / Don F. Ms. de la Rosa / etc etc

Sir,

I have the honor to acknowledge the receipt of your Excy's note of the 18th inst. informing me of the necessity of the claim of Messrs Fitch, Brothers and Co being substantiated in due form before the Spanish Consul at Marseilles prior to payment being made by her Majesty's Govt.

I was aware that such would be the case and have written for the necessary documents legally authenticated by the Consul; in the meantime the object of my application was merely to have the principle of the claim admitted by her Majesty's Govt, which, from the tenor of your Excy's note, I persuade myself has been done.

As soon as the documents arrive I will have the honor of transmitting them to your Excy.

I avail myself etc

Signed — Washington Irving.

MANUSCRIPT: NA, RG 84 (letterbook copy).

1868.   To Francisco Martínez de la Rosa

Madrid 24th May 1845

His Excy / Don F. M. de la Rosa / Minister of State

Sir,

I regret extremely that it is not in my power to give your Excy an explicit answer as to the future measures of the Govt of the U. S. with respect to the duties on foreign sugars.

There has recently been, as your Excellency must be aware, a change in the Chief Magistrate and the whole Cabinet of the Union. What line of policy the new Administration will pursue in regard to commercial regulations is yet to be developed. Mr Polk, the new President, in his inaugural Speech, has declared himself generally in favor of a moderate tariff, "for the purposes of revenue"; and so discriminated as to impose the lowest duties on articles of the greatest necessity; that is to say, articles essential to the comfort and well being of the largest and poorest classes and the highest duties upon articles of mere luxury consumed only by the wealthy.

How far this discrimination may affect the duties on sugar is uncertain; it may be in favor of common and low priced sugar of which there is a vast consumption even among the laboring classes of the U. S. with whom it is, in fact, almost a necessary of life. The tariff of duties will probably come under the consideration of the next Session of Congress when material alterations may take place under the moderate policy of Mr Polk unless political events and the exigencies of the Govt. should forbid any measure that might tend to diminish the revenue.

I have the honor etc

Signed = Washington Irving.

MANUSCRIPT: NA, RG 84 (letterbook copy); NA, RG 59 (copy).

A copy of this letter was enclosed with WI's despatch no. 66 to James Buchanan, May 25, 1845.

1869. To Sarah Storrow

Madrid, May 24th. 1845

My dear Sarah,

I thank you for the letters of Your Mother & of Marianne Van Wart, inclosed in your last. I have since received a letter from your Mother,[1] of the same date and of pretty much the same tenor with the one to you.

I am indeed surprised by the engagement of Henry Van Wart with our dear little Abby;[2] but we seem doomed to surprises in the matrimonial way in our little circle at home. I trust the match will prove a happy one. Henry will have an amiable intelligent little wife; who will sweeten and enliven his home, which of late must have been peculiarly lonely and desolate.[3] I think the match will be one of the best remedies for the nervous complaint with which he has of late been troubled, and which I have no doubt has chiefly risen from mental causes. I had looked to your letter to bring me tidings of the arrival of Eliza; and was exceedingly disappointed and grieved to find that she was still upon the Ocean; though two Steamers had arrived, which sailed after her departure. By this time she *must* be in Paris; where her presence will be a real blessing to poor Gabriel. Give my best love to her; I have always loved and prized her, but never so much as since the proof she has given of her woman like devotion to her husband, in so promptly setting off alone to cross the Sea and bring comfort and relief to him.

Yesterday we had a grand ceremony; the Queen going in State to close the Cortes; after which the Corps diplomatique repaired to the palace to make a farewell visit to the Queen and her Mother and Sister, who depart this day for Barcelona.[4] We were introduced Severally into the Royal presence; and I have never felt more interested than by this farewell interview, which perhaps may be the last I may ever have with this young virgin queen; as I may be removed from office and may leave Spain before she returns to her Capital and I regret to say, that I still look upon her situation as surrounded by doubt and danger and throne by no means established on sure foundations.

My amiable friend Madame Albuquerque received yesterday intelligence of the death of her father Mr Daniel Oakey. I have not seen her since but shall call on her today. It was quite unexpected, as he was ill but a very few days. The shock ⟨will⟩ must be severe for her, as she has been rather delicate in health and nervous of late. She sets off in the Course of a few days ⟨for⟩ with her family for Barcelona. The absence of her and Mrs O'Shea will leave me quite lonely. Indeed there is a complete breaking up of Society here for the summer. The diplomatic corps disperses in every direction; part will come together again in Barcelona. Even Mr Livingston takes his departure for France in the course of a few days; so you see I shall be perfectly alone. If I can only exercise my pen, however, I shall be ⟨fin⟩ content, and shall turn my liesure and quiet to advantage. Should I be removed from office I shall have enough to do in winding up my concerns and preparing to leave Madrid "for good and all." I do not consider the latter event by any means so improbable as you appear to do, and have made my mind up to it. I see poor Kitt Hughes[5] is at length displaced; and feel extremely sorry for him, for I do not know how he will be able to exist out of diplomacy, which has become a second nature to him. For my part I am heartily tired of all its forms and ceremonies and solemn humbug, and nothing would retain me a moment in ⟨the⟩ office if it were not that I have "a family to provide for,"—a consideration which bends the neck to all kinds of yokes.

So Kate is aspiring to be a "Young lady".—I think you'll have some trouble in keeping her down, now she is getting upon her tiptoes. I long to see her, adorned with all her new airs, and graces which she has acquired since last autumn. You should have persisted in your treatment of Susie for the cure of the propensity to mumble her thumbs. She would soon have cried herself to sleep; and after one or two more crying fits the cure would have been accomplished[.] Matilda Van Warts little girl, as old, if not older that[6] Kate, had ⟨th⟩ still the same trick when I saw her last summer. If not checked it will hang on for years

I am writing very much against the grain—being ⟨ou⟩ quite out of the writing vein and yet having other letters to write by this Same courier.

Give my affectionate regards to Mr Storrow, and to Gabriel & Eliza; and, with kisses for the two little women

Your affectionate uncle
Washington Irving

MANUSCRIPT: Yale.

1. These letters have not been located.

2. Henry Van Wart married his first cousin Abby Irving (1822–1906?), daughter of John Treat Irving, Sr. on September 23, 1845.

3. Probably the reason for Henry's loneliness and desolation was the death of his first wife, Susan Storrow (b. 1807) in September, 1843. She was the sister of Thomas Wentworth Storrow, Jr., Sarah's husband.

4. See La Posdata, May 24, 1845; and La Gaceta, May 24, 1845.

5. Christopher Hughes had served as U.S. chargé d'affaires at The Hague, Netherlands. See Almanach de Gotha pour l'Année 1845 (Gotha, 1844), p. 468.

6. WI probably intended to write "than."

1870. To James Buchanan

Legation of the United States / Madrid May 25th. 1845.

No 66 / The Hon James Buchanan / Secretary of State of the United
States Washington /

Sir,

I have the honor to acknowledge the receipt of your letter of March
10th. informing me of your appointment to the department of State and
of your having entered upon the discharge of its duties.

I enclose a copy of a rejoinder of the Spanish Minister of State to my
note of the 3d. instant relative to the affair of the Zulette. From attentively considering the case I am satisfied that no wanton outrage on our
flag was intended; the darkness of the night preventing the garrison from
knowing to what nation the vessel belonged. Neither does the shot appear
to have been fired wantonly. The suspicions of the garrison had been
awakened by the appearance of a number of vessels, probably smugglers,
hovering at a distance during the day and approaching under convoy
of what seemed to be a frigate at night fall; and this at a time when
rumors were prevalent of conspiracies hatching among Spanish exiles
at Gibraltar, partizans of Espartero; of intended descents upon the Spanish coast, and even of a projected attempt to surprise this very fortress
of Tarifa. In firing upon the vessels, therefore, on their neglecting to
shew lights in reply to his signal guns, the Commander of Tarifa appears
to be justified by the circumstances of the case and by the general usages
of fortified posts. With this view of the affair, which there is nothing in
the meagre log book minutes of the Master of the Zulette to disprove, I
have deemed it inexpedient to press the matter further; lest it should assume a querulous, litigious aspect, quite at variance with the feelings of
our government towards Spain, and with that magnanimous spirit which
should accompany the consciousness of power.

I enclose a note from the Spanish Minister of State inquiring whether
the Government of the United States intends to make reductions in the
"enormous" duties levied on Spanish sugars; as the Minister of Finance,
who has the commercial intercourse of the two nations under consideration, is disposed to regulate his measures accordingly. I am inclined to
think this inquiry has been suggested by the late urgent remonstrances
made against the excessive duties on American flour in the ports of Cuba.
I enclose my reply, which, of course could be any thing but explicit.

The session of the Cortes was closed by the Queen in person on the
23d. instant. I enclose a copy of her speech, and a copy also of the reformed constitution[1] which was promulgated on the same day. The lat-

ter is scoffed at by both absolutists and progresistas; it is an instrument, they say, which gives satisfaction to nobody; for its very devisers consider it a compromise between their consciences and their interests, with which they vainly hope to beguile the people.

I have forborne of late to attempt to trace the tortuous course of Spanish politics where every thing is perplexed with mystery and intrigue; and where even those in power, who have good intentions, find themselves over ruled or under mined by adverse influences. The recent diplomatic transactions with the Court of Rome—for instance, have taken even the cabinet by surprise and nearly produced a convulsion at head quarters.[2] Narvaez suspected that he had been outgeneraled by the Queen mother, and that she had given secret instructions to the Spanish minister at the Papal Court[3] (late her private Secretary) by which the Cabinet has become grieviously compromised. A scene, it is said, ensued between Narvaez and the Queen Mother, and an ↑open↓ rupture was expected; but neither was prepared for such an event, which would have thrown every thing into confusion. A truce took place between them; matters were arranged by compromise; the document sent on from the Papal court in lieu of the anticipated and much trumpeted concordat, was returned as inadmissible, but the supple minister who is suspected of negotiating under double instructions, is continued in the post, from which, in the first moments of wrath, he had been threatened to be hurled with disgrace. It remains to be seen whether, in this diplomatic game, the woman and the priest will not be an over match for the Soldier, bold and wary as he is.

In fact the whole position of this government is forced and false, and has no true foundation in the opinions and affections of the people; it is, therefore, liable to further revolutions.

The Queen, accompanied by her mother and sister, departed yesterday for Barcelona.[4] They will be followed immediately by General Narvaez and others of the Cabinet ministers.

I am sir / Very respectfully / Your obt Servt
Washington Irving

DOCKETED: Recd. 5th. July / Mr Markoe [*upper left corner of page 1*] / No. 66. W. Irving, Madrid. 25 May 1845

MANUSCRIPT: NA, RG 59.   PUBLISHED: Hellman, *WI Esquire*, pp. 314–16; STW, II, 200 (in part).

This despatch is entirely in WI's handwriting.

1. These copies which still remain with the despatch in RG 59, were printed, respectively, in *La Gaceta*, May 24 and 23, 1845, as well as in other Madrid newspapers.

2. The papal document stipulated the return of unsold church lands which had been seized earlier, the incomes of the clergy to be provided by the state but

administered by the church, and independent status for the church in Spain. Both Narváez and Martínez de la Rosa would not agree to these terms. See H. Butler Clarke, *Modern Spain*, pp. 201–2; and *La Gaceta*, May 22, 1845. The issues of church-state relationships brought forth heated comments in the press. *La Posdata* (May 21, 1845) engaged in a polemic with *La Esperanza*, a paper with clerical sympathies, over the confiscations of church lands. On May 20 the same journal, in a front-page editorial, attacked the negotiations with Rome.

3. José de Castillo y Ayensa (1795–1861), a writer, translator of Greek and Roman classics, and a member of the Spanish Academy, was minister plenipotentiary to the courts of Popes Gregory XVI and Pius IX.

4. Plans for the trip to Barcelona had been reported in *La Posdata*, May 17, 1845.

1871.   To Sarah Storrow

Madrid June 5th. 1845

My dear Sarah,

I received this morning by the Courier of the French Embassy, your *two* letters of May 20th. and 30th.[1] I presume the reason I did not get the former one ⟨by⟩ last week was that Antoine delivered it too late at the Foreign office. I was extremely disappointed at getting no letters from you last week and felt some uneasiness; as I had heard from Mr Beasley of poor Elizas having arrived just in time to hear of the death of her husband; and of her having hurried on to Paris to endeavor to get there before the funeral. Dear, excellent Eliza—I feel most deeply for her situation. What a long and anxious voyage she has had; and what dismal news to meet her on her arrival. What a dreary ↑home↓ voyage she has to look forward to, also; but then it will be a short one; and it will be to her home, where she will have a meeting with her children to console and cheer her. I have felt extremely interested by poor Gabriels illness, and affected by the manly patience and even cheerfulness with which he has sustained it. I have felt for you too, my dear Sarah, harrassed as you must have been by ⟨anxiety⟩ sympathy for the poor sufferer and anxiety about the arrival of his precious little wife. Poor dear Eliza—much as we loved and valued her before, how much closer is she drawn to our hearts by her conduct on hearing of the danger of her husband.

You ask my opinion as to an excursion to or rather a sojourn at some bathing place on the sea coast. I have no doubt it would be of great service in restoring your health and bracing your nerves. I doubt whether you would be in time to join your aunt;[2] who has been passing some weeks at Weston, on the sea coast, in the Bristol channel ⟨of⟩ The Isle of Wight, I have only visited transiently for a day or two and do not know how it would be likely to suit you for a lengthened sojourn; though all who have been there for sea bathing speak well of it You would find very good sea bathing at Dieppe or Havre; with the advantage of being so near Paris, that, with the present facilities of conveyance, Mr Storrow ⟨w⟩ might pass much of the time with you, without neglecting business. While you have small children and nurses to take with you you will find it important to circumscribe your travelling as much as possible.

Your information of George Irvings[3] being engaged to be married quite surprises me, as I cannot think of him but as a mere boy. He certainly cannot be of age yet. I presume however, the marriage will not take place immediately.

⟨The⟩ Your letter gave me the first information of the deaths of Mrs Brevoort[4] and Mrs Peter R Schermerhorn.[5]

I hope to hear by your next letter of your having made the acquaintance of my most amiable excellent friend Mrs O'Shea; though you will have little opportunity of knowing her worth from brief interviews amidst the bustle of Paris. She is one to know intimately and quietly. I miss her continually; for she and Madame Albuquerque, who had apartments under the same roof with her, were ⟨my⟩ objects of my daily pilgrimages; and we formed quite a trio. I am sorry to Say the Albuquerques set off for Barcelona in the course of four or five days, and then I shall feel quite desolate. I shall feel this loneliness the more sensibly as I am at present completely idle and listless and have been so for some weeks past; my mind refusing to occupy itself with any literary task; and even revolting from the labor of writing a letter. I hope this will pass away and my mental activity return, otherwise time will hang most heavily on [my][6] hands. I am kept also in a state of irksome suspence as to the intentions of government towards me, and am looking anxiously for letters from Washington which may throw some light upon the subject. ⟨Until⟩ In the mean time I can make no plans nor enter into any arrangements for the rest of the year. I am most heartily sick of this state of dependence upon the will or whim of another; and if I had only myself to think for, would promptly throw up office and live on a crust rather than not be my own master—but I have others to provide for; and am therefore obliged to cling to what, however irksome, furnishes a present competence.

If Eliza is still with you give her my kindest love and tell her how very much I feel for her afflictions. Give my kind regards to your husband and many Kisses to to my dear little Kate and Susie. [end of MS]

ADDRESSED: Madame / Madame Storrow / No 4. Rue de la Victoire / à Paris   POST-
MARKED: JUIN 15. 1845
MANUSCRIPT: Yale.   PUBLISHED: STW, II, 193 (in part).

1. These letters have not been located.

2. Sarah Van Wart.

3. George (January 24, 1824–October 5, 1908), youngest son of John Treat Irving, Sr., married Robertine Blackwell (d. March 3, 1858) on December 9, 1845.

4. Probably Mrs. Henry Brevoort, Sr.

5. Mrs. Peter R. Schermerhorn, the former Sarah Jones (b. 1782), had died on April 28, 1845.

6. WI omitted the bracketed word.

1872. To Francisco Martínez de la Rosa

Madrid June 12th 1845

His Excellency / Don Francisco M. de la Rosa / etc etc

Sir,

In your Excellency's note of the 20th May last relative to the claim of Messrs Fitch, Brothers and Co American Merchants, resident in Marseilles, for indemnification for losses sustained by the capture and detention of the Dutch Galliot, *Vrouw Johanna*, by a Spanish Guarda Costa, you signified that, before her Majesty's Govt could proceed to pay the said claim, it would be necessary that the anticipated sale of the sugar, and the other circumstances giving rise to the claim should be substantiated in due form before the Spanish Consul in Marseilles. This has been done accordingly and I have now the honor to enclose the requisite documents verified by the Consul.

Having thus complied with the requisitions of your Excy, I trust the just and equitable intentions of her Majesty, signified in the note of your Excy will be carried into effect and the redress required by the "Commercial usages of all nations" will be rendered with the promptness essential to render it satisfactory and complete

I avail myself of this occasion to renew to your Excy the assurance of the high consideration with which I have the honor to be

Your obt servant
Signed = Washington Irving.

MANUSCRIPT: NA, RG 84 (letterbook copy).

1873.   To Sarah Storrow

Madrid, June 13th. 1845

My dear Sarah,

I received yesterday your letter of the[1]   inclosing one which you had received from Mrs Ledyard. Her brother (Mr Livingston) was quite amused with her exclamations against the democracy at home; as before her visit to Europe she used to advocate it with great zeal, and to rail at him for being spoiled by residing too long in aristocratic countries. I have no doubt Mrs Ledyard finds a sad contrast in her situation at home with the very agreeable position she enjoyed in Paris. I am glad you have seen my most amiable and estimable friend Mrs O'Shea—to appreciate her properly, however it is necessary to know her intimately, hers is a quiet and endearing worth that grows upon acquaintance and wins the affections. The absence of herself and Madame Albuquerque, has left me quite desolate. The latter departed early yesterday morning with all her family. I have had the children with me repeatedly of late to pass the day; and I shall miss the merry little groupe sporting about my saloons. I should have liked to have had Kate here as a companion to little José who is about the same age, and quite a match for her in intelligence and in winning ways, but as fond of playing the Soldier as she is of playing the fine lady. He is one of the finest little fellows I have ever known. These children all call me uncle and seem to consider me as such; and while they are frolicking about my house I half persuade myself that I am surrounded by my own Kith and kin.

⟨The day before yesterday⟩ ↑A day or two since↓ two young Americans Mr King and Mr Carey, made their appearance here, the latter bringing the long desired print of the Cottage. Mr King dined with me the same day, when I gave a farewell dinner to the Albuquerques. He sets off this Evening on his return to Paris. Mr Carey, who was too ⟨unable⟩ much "travel tired" to dine with me, will remain a little time at Madrid. There have been scarcely any Americans ⟨at yet⟩ at Madrid this year; and it is quite a treat to have a visit from such intelligent gentlemen like young men as these two appear to be.

My letters from home by the Steamer of 16. May, give me reason to think that I shall not be displaced for the present. Such Pierre M Irving, writes me, is the opinion expressed by Mrs Polk, in presence of several persons, one of whom reported it to Treat; and Mrs P. is supposed to be acquainted with affairs of State. I have received despatches from government ↑also,↓ which have cut out work for me, for some little time to come. I have received no instructions to follow the Court to

Barcelona; so I shall not go there; especially as the Queen will not remain there beyond the 10th. or 15th. of July. I have made up my mind, therefore, to remain quietly at Madrid; and have already arranged my house for the Summer; Indeed there are few places where I could be so comfortable during the hot months as in my own mansion; passing my days in the large lofty Saloons, where the heat and glare of day are excluded, and a soft twilight and a bland temperature produced; and driving out in the evening or walking at a late hour in the Prado when the temperature is quite heavenly. Mr Livingston sets off next week, in the Malle poste, for Bayonne, intending to ⟨join⟩ meet his brother and family in the Pyrenees; where he will pass the hot months, I shall, therefore, lead quite a hermit life this summer but if I can only employ myself as I wish, I shall pass it both pleasantly and profitably.

June 14th. I find that George Van Wart returned home by the last Steamer. I regret that he has made so short a sojourn in the United States and cannot concieve why he should hurry home so soon; when spring was just opening, when his brothers marriage was pending, and when he had had no time to look round and inform himself whether there was any chance for him in the way of business. His visit is a match to that of his brother William; one has taken a glance at the United States during the nakedness of Winter the other during the height of Cholera and the dog days. I hope George does not hurry home, like his brother, on account of some love affair; but I am always in a little solicitude about my unmarried nephews; whenever they are at a loss how to get on in the world, they look out for some pennyless helpmate to share their poverty. They almost all ⟨belong to⟩ resemble that species of plants called *creepers*—they never *climb*.

Before this reaches you poor Eliza will be on her way home. She will be much better when travelling than when remaining quiet. The necessity of exerting ⟨this⟩ herself; and the succession of scenes and objects presented to her mind will prevent her dwelling so exclusively on the subject of her affliction—I shall rejoice to hear that she is once more at home in the cheering company of her children.

You did not tell me how Kate acquitted herself when introduced to my friend Mrs O'Shea. I hope she did not contradict by her conduct the high character I had given her. As to Susie, I presume she kicked and rolled for Mrs O'Sheas amusement, those being the two accomplishments on which, according to your accounts, she prides herself.

Has Mr King determined what quarter of Paris he will remove to, after leaving his present establishment?—What becomes of all Mrs Jones' furniture? Has she given up the intention of returning to Paris— Excuse these questions; you know these are matters on which I take a peculiar interest.

I hope your next letters will give me something about Mrs Ellis, and Mrs Henderson (though I forgot I dont mean to say any thing about her, ever—for letting the Dutcher farm slip through her fingers) and Miss Fisher and the rest of your peculiar intimates.

With kind remembrances to Mr Storrow and many Kisses to the two little women

Your affectionate Uncle
Washington Irving

MANUSCRIPT: Yale.

1 WI left blank the space for the date.

1874. To Sabina O'Shea

Madrid June 15th. 1845

My dear Mrs OShea

I have just received your letter of June 7th[1] in reply to mine written a day or two after your departure. I had begun to fear from your long silence that my letter had miscarried or perhaps ↑had↓ fallen into your husbands hands, and been suppressed, according to the old trick of husbands, as laid down in plays and novels. I am loth to suspect Mr O'Shea of such manouvres, but you reccollect the old stage trick he was going to play off on the occasion of the snug little dinner to which you invited me; and which after all he marred by staying and dining at home. Really one cannot be too much on ones guard against these husbands.

I find you have heard that you are to be unhoused in September. The Albuquerques immediately gave up their appartment, and sent all their furniture to my quarters. They left here, with all the children early on Wednesday morning last for Barcelona, and must be by this time in Valencia. Madame Albuquerque told me to tell you that she counted upon your taking a house in which they could have a modest apartment. You would know exactly what would suit her. You cannot be more anxious than she is, to be under the same roof. Her departure in addition to yours, has left me quite desolate. I have not been past your deserted habitation since; and indeed have scarce stirred out except to take an evening drive, being shut out of my old visiting haunt. I believe my very horses would shed tears if obliged to pass by the door without stopping. They will sadly miss their favorite stand in front of the Ayuntamiento where they passed most of the time that they were out of their stable.

I suppose you will have heard, long before this, that Madame de Bresson has presented her husband with a Son. Both mother and child are doing well; and the Ambassador set off the night before last, in the malle post for Bayonne; whence I believe he will repair to Barcelona instead of Paris. The Embassy, therefore, is "closed for the season;" some of its frequenters I fancy have taken to the Casino as a make shift. I saw the worthy old Dalbergo hovering about the latter place at a time when he should have been in bed. The poor old man ⟨has t⟩ according to his own account has been ruined in the late fall of the funds ↑but goes on "burning the candle at both ends;"↓ he is like an Irishman who gets *kilt* in every row and yet survives. Your husband will understand this figure, which sounds somewhat marvellous.

Mr Livingston is much obliged by your kind message to him. He sets off to night in the Malle Poste for Bayonne intending to pass the hot weather in the Pyrenees. Some ten days or a fortnight since I ⟨got⟩ gave a dinner to a number of his young friends of the legations and the fashionable circle, by way of affording him an opportunity of returning their civilities. It was a very gay one, we being all *young fellows* together. After dinner they got up the notion of an amateur bull fight with novillos; several of them, who were foreigners, being persuaded that they could face the bulls as well as the Spaniards. I presumed it to be a young mans bravado which would end in smoke; but to my surprise they carried their project into effect, and that in the course of a very few days. You will have seen an account of the affair most probably, in the Spanish papers. It took place at a Casa del Campo of a Mr. Faguada, a mile or two out of Madrid. Don Francisco and his family presided; and there w⟨ere⟩as quite a brilliant display of ladies of the fashionable circle. I felt really uneasy, fearing that some unfortunate circumstance might take place, or something awkward and absurd, which might expose the young gentlemen to ridicule; and I was the more anxious as Mr Livingston took [a][2] leading part in the affair; was to be one of the Espadas, and insisted on having some of the novillos of a greater age than was deemed prudent. All, however, went off without any serious accident. The aficionados, though most of them had never officiated before, acquitted themselves with great courage and some of them with considerable dexterity: ⟨and as⟩ Mr Livingston escaped unscathed; after having killed one of the most dangerous bulls with great success; and after having siezed a younger one by the horns and thrown him on his back, besides two or three other feats of courage and strength; but I confess I was glad when the dangerous amusement was at an end and my Secretary was safe at home again.[3] I find I am ⟨some ho⟩ in some manner mixed up in the affair; one of the newspapers stating that the *Embaxador de los Estados Unidos,* Mr Livingston, signalized himself on the occasion. This comes you see of my being such a wild swell of a fellow, and keeping such young company. It is well you had left Madrid before this *funcion* took place; I am sure Quique would have been among the *Espadas,*[4] and, as the Irishman said, would have *extinguished* himself.

Give my kind remembrances to the Messrs OSheas, old and young and believe me, with sincerest regard, your friend

Washington Irving

P.S. My last letters from the United States give me reason to think that I shall pass the next winter in Madrid.

ADDRESSED: Madame / Madame O'Shea / aux Soins de Messrs H Ganneron & Co / Banquiers / à Paris   POSTMARKED: [*unrecovered*] / 15 / Juno. / 1845 // PARIS / 27 / Juin / 45   DOCKETED: Washington Irving's *letters* / ⟨October 13th⟩[*at other end of envelope*]

MANUSCRIPT: HSA.   PUBLISHED: Penney, *Bulletin NYPL,* 62 (December, 1958), 618–19.

1. This letter has not been located.
2. WI omitted the bracketed letter.
3. "Another account of this event of June 10 is to be found in the staid official paper *Gaceta de Madrid* (June 12, 1845, pp. 3–4), taken from *El Heraldo.* The patronesses were the countess of Montijo, mother of the empress-to-be Eugènie, the fair Leocadia Zamora, and others, who presented beautiful ornaments for the bulls' heads (*moñas*). Don Francisco, the queen's uncle, and his august family occupied the principal box. The first of the six young bulls (*novillos*), from a breeding farm at Colmenar Viejo, was Mosquito, aged sixteen months. The contestants represented twelve different nations" (Penney, *Bulletin NYPL,* 62 [*December, 1958*], 630–31).
4. The "espada" is the fighter who kills the bull.

1875. To Francisco Martínez de la Rosa

Madrid June 18th 1845

His Excy Dn F. M. de la Rosa / etc

The undersigned Envoy Exty and Minister Pleniy of the U. S. of America has the honor to invite the attention of Dn F. M. de la Rosa her Majesty's First Minister of State and of Foreign Affairs to the following statement.

On the 7th day of October[1] last the Supreme Authorities of Cuba issued a decree authorizing the importation, duty free of lumber and other articles necessary for building and of corn, corn flour, beans, Irish potatoes and rice. This decree, by its terms, was to continue in force six months from its date. Its object was to relieve the distress occasioned by a dreadful hurricane which had visited the city of Havannah and its environs,[2] demolishing houses and destroying the fruits of the earth. The Decree urges in the strongest terms, the "immeasurable calamities" which called for speedy relief; the horrible distress which threatened all classes if assistance were not promptly afforded and at the same time it expresses an assurance that the "magnanimous heart" of the Queen of Spain could not but condole with the people of Cuba when she should hear of their distress and could not but approve of all that had been done to alleviate it.

On the faith of this decree and of the confident conviction expressed in it that her Majesty would give it her approbation, the Merchants of the U. S. with a promptness required by the exigencies of the case, imported into Havanna the materials necessary for rebuilding the houses of the suffering people and the articles of provisions necessary for their subsistence.

While this trade was in full activity the decree which had given impulse to it was annulled, without one ⟨t⟩ moment's previous notice, on the 20th February 1845, by the promulgation of the fact that Her Majesty had refused to give it her sanction; and that the ⟨formalities⟩ ↑former duties↓ must thenceforth be levied. As many shipments had been made in the U. S. of articles embraced by the Decree, under the confident belief that it would continue in force until the 7th day of April, severe losses have been the inevitable consequence.

The undersigned has stated this case briefly, simply and dispassionately, for the facts themselves speak with an eloquence that needs no coloring of language. With the motives and policy of her Majesty in reversing a decree dictated by humanity and apparently by the best colonial interests of Spain, the Govt of the U. S. is conscious that it has nothing to do; but it has a deep concern in everything which affects the Commercial intercourse between the two countries and cannot passively see it disturbed by capricious legislation. Indeed there is such manifest injustice in annulling this Decree without any previous notice; it is so much in contradiction to the Commercial usages prevalent among enlightened nations; that the undersigned is tempted to hope there may have been some oversight and inadvertency in the case, which may since have been remedied by some voluntary act of her Majesty's Govt..

The undersigned will content himself, therefore, for the present, with informing his Excy, Don F. M. de la Rosa, that it is the opinion of the President of the U. S. that those citizens of the Union who imported any of the articles embraced in the Decree into Havanna between the 20th of Feby and the 7th of April 1845, without knowledge at the time of their departure from the U. S. that the decree had been annulled, are ⟨all⟩ entitled to be indemnified by the Spanish Govt for the losses which they may have sustained; and the undersigned is instructed to express the confidence felt by his Govt that prompt and effectual measures will be taken by her Majesty's Ministers to yield such indemnication.

The undersigned avails himself etc

Signed = Washington Irving.

MANUSCRIPT: NA, RG 84 (letterbook copy).

1. According to the instructions WI received from James Buchanan, the date was October 8, 1844. See Buchanan to WI, May 9, 1845, in *The Works of James Buchanan*, ed. John Bassett Moore, 12 vols. (New York, 1960), VI, 155–56.

2. This violent storm began during the evening of October 4 and continued unabated until 10:00 A.M. on October 5. See NYEP, October 26, 1844.

1876. To Sarah Storrow

Madrid, June 20th. 1845

My dear Sarah,

I received yesterday your letter of the 14th.[1] by which I find poor Eliza had set out on her route homeward. I am glad you were able to procure her so faithful and efficient a travelling servant. I long to hear of her being once more at home, with her children. Thank heaven, conveyances are nowadays so rapid that time and space are almost annihilated. In a fortnight from the time I am now writing she will in all probability be restored to her family, ⟨at⟩ ↑and↓ at rest from her lonely and dreary wanderings.

I had a letter Some days since from my amiable friend Mrs O'Shea on which she speaks of having made your acquaintance, she says "⟨f⟩First I must tell you how much I was pleased with Mrs Storrow, her warm, kind manner reminds me so much of you. She immediately came to see me. The following day we all went to see her and her pretty children. Baby is quite a picture, so fair and English looking, in its little short sleeves and bare bosom. Your pet is a very fine child also, full of health. She took more notice of Henrique than of us. I am sorry that our stay is so short and that we are so hurried—having so much to do, which prevents my seeing more of Mrs Storrow, but on our return I hope I may have an opportunity of seeing her oftener."

I am glad you are getting Kates likeness taken for her Grandmama. It will be a delightful surprize to her. I hope the artist has been able to catch the laughing expression of her eyes; as to giving an idea of the eternal fidget which characterizes her; that is beyond the reach of his art. How often I wish I had little Kate here; my saloons would afford fine scope for her perpetual motion, and how she would enliven my existence! I have been in a state of mental torpor for some time past; unable to apply myself to any thing; and as my social resorts are shut up, and my most intimate friends gone I find time occasionally hang[s]² very heavy on hands; which it never does when my mind is in a state of activity. In this mood Kate would be a perfect Godsend to me, and we would play *high jinks* from morning till night. I long too to see Susie; who is growing in grace with me continually. It seems to me as if I have a perfect idea how she must look and act. I hope Kate takes good care of her education. Does she ever put her in the Corner as she used to put her dolls?

Mr Livingston set off in the Malle poste on Sunday night last for Bayonne; and ⟨by⟩ ↑at↓ this time must be in the Pyrenees: I have, therefore, the house entirely to myself; and should not be ill pleased to be alone if I could but occupy myself. I trust, however, the writing vein will return before long and then time will pass rapidly. It is in these listless intervals that I feel my absence from my family and friends— when I am wasting so much of life unprofitably and joy⟨ous⟩↑less↓ly³ that might be passed so happily in their society. But I comfort myself with the thoughts that this is the last year of my exile; for go things as they may, life with me is running too much to a remnant to allow any further waste.

You complain of the heat in Paris; here we have unexampled weather for the season—Cool and showery. I have not as yet put on summer clothes. There is every probability of a short summer.

Saturday. 21. I have just received a letter from Madame Albuquerque by which I find the family were all safely arrived at Valencia, and in a couple of days were to set off in a Steamer for Barcelona. The expedition by sea is nothing, but I had felt a little anxious about the journey by land, in a Spanish ⟨mid Summer⟩ diligence and in Midsummer, with four children. It was even worse than your contemplated tour of the Swiss mountains with your two *pappooses.*

The absence of the Court from the Capital will be much abridged. The Queen is to return to Madrid about the middle of next month;⁴ so that we shall be likely to have Court fêtes and ceremonies in the dog days, which will be rather irksome. The abdication of Don Carlos in favor of his son, and the manifesto of the latter;[5] together with rumors of plots and conspiracies, have convinced the ⟨Cabinet⟩ Ministers that it is unwise for the Sovreign ⟨to be away from⟩ ↑and part of the Cabinet to be↓ travelling about in the provinces, and that it is best to centralize their force in the Capital. If ⟨Mr Livingston⟩ Mr Sumner continues to visit you, however, he can put you up to all the mysteries of Spanish politics, he being a kind of amateur conspirator.

Kiss the darling little women for me and remember me kindly to Mr Storrow

Your affectionate uncle
Washington Irving

P.S. Until further advices write to me by the mail. The Courier of the French Embassy for the present, will proceed to Barcelona—[6]

ADDRESSED: Madame / Madame Storrow / No 4. Ruc de la Victoire / à Paris
MANUSCRIPT: Yale.

1. This letter and the one from Mrs. O'Shea mentioned in the next paragraph have not been located.
2. WI omitted the bracketed letter.
3. WI probably intended to write "joylessly." Someone, perhaps WI before sending the letter, has written "less" over the "ous" of the word.
4. For the queen's travel plans, see *La Posdata*, June 12, 1845.
5. On May 18 the pretender, Don Carlos abdicated in favor of his son, who accepted the rights to the crown from his father and took the title of count de Montemolin. The Carlists hoped that the count (1818–1861) could marry Isabella II and unite the opposing factions; but the queen, after studying his picture, declared, "I will not marry a man with a squint." See John D. Bergamini, *The Spanish Bourbons*, p. 233; and Aronson, *Royal Vendetta*, p. 50. First mention of Don Carlos's abdication appeared in *La Posdata*, June 2, 1845, along with his son's manifesto of May 23. News of these events was sent to *La Esperanza*, but the government forbade publication. The manifesto was finally published in *La Posdata*, June 5, 1845.
6. This postscript is written vertically along the left margin of page 1.

1877. *To Gurdon Bradley*

Legation of the U States / Madrid June 25th. 1845

Gurdon Bradley Esq / Consul of the U. S. / Mayaguez. Porto Rico

Sir,

I am instructed by the Department of State to investigate the circumstances of the case of the American Schooner Siam, and to take such steps as may be necessary to secure redress and indemnity. It appears that this vessel, having sustained serious damage at Sea, was condemned on survey and ordered by you to be sold; but that the public authorities of Mayaguez interfered and forbade the sale, whereupon the captain and yourself formally abandoned the vessel. Under these circumstances the agents in behalf of those interested have sought the interposition of government.

There is nothing, however, in the documents sent to me by the department to shew upon what grounds the public authorities of Mayaguez proceeded in prohibiting the sale of the vessel excepting the following paragraph in a letter of the agents to the Secretary of State:

"Cap. Byard informed us that the plea made by the authorities was that the treaty made by our government with Spain provided for cases of the kind, and they were acting in conformity"

This information is too vague and unsubstantiated to afford any support to a claim for indemnification. As I presume that the reasons given by the authorities for their interference must exist in official writings, I will thank you, Sir, to forward to this Legation authenticated copies of the same; or such legal and documentary evidence as may serve to elucidate this point; the elucidation of which I consider essential to a proper understanding of the case and to an efficient application for redress

> I am Sir / Very respectfully / Your ob St
> W I.

(N B. A copy of the above was sent to the agents Messrs. Mears & Clark. Boston.)

Manuscript: NA, RG 84 (letterbook copy).

1878.   *To James Buchanan*

Legation of the United States / Madrid, June 25th. 1845

No 67. / The Hon. James Buchanan. / Secretary of State. Washington,

Sir,

I have duly received Despatches Nos. 42 and 43. The former relates to the case of the Schooner Siam, which I am required to investigate and "to take such steps as may be necessary to secure redress and indemnity; provided the result of my enquiries should render it clear that complainants are entitled thereto"

To understand this case, and to make an efficient application for redress, it appears to me necessary to be clearly informed of the grounds on which the public authorities of Mayaguez proceeded in interdicting the sale of the Schooner. The plea intimated by Captain Byard as having been set up by them, that they were acting in conformity with treaty provisions appears to me too absurd and groundless to have been officially advanced; and and[1] leaves to me to apprehend other reasons for their conduct which have not been reported to the department. At any rate, it is to be presumed that the interdict of the sale was formally announced in writing, and specified the motives for such an act; or that the Consul took official steps to acquaint himself with those motives before he proceeded to abandon the vessel. It is singular that no documentary evidence on this head appears among the papers furnished to the department.

I have, therefore, written to the Consul at Mayaguez[2] for authenticated documents, or other evidence calculated to elucidate this point, and have sent a copy of my letter to Messrs Mears & Clark, the agents at Boston. Until I receive the required information on this head it appears to me useless to bring the matter before the Spanish government

Despatch No 43 (accompanied by documents) relates to injuries resulting to citizens of the United States from the annulling, by the Spanish government, of the decree of the Supreme authorities of Cuba, authorizing the importation of certain articles into the island for six months, free of duty. I passed a note to the Spanish government some days since, in conformity with your instructions, but as yet have received no reply. The Belgian Chargé d'affaires is making an urgent representation on the same subject, and it is vigorously advocated in the *Cronica*, a paper recently set up here and devoted to colonial interests; especially those connected with the island of Cuba; and to which paper I occasionally furnish facts and intelligence.

It is extremely difficult, however, to get any questions of this kind attended to by this government at present. The disjointed state of the Cabinet, part at Madrid and part at Barcelona, interrupts the regular course of business: while the complicated negotiations with the Court of Rome; the perplexed question of the marriage of the Queen: the agitations and alarms caused by the recent abdication of Don Carlos and the manifesto of his son; the reports of plots conspiracies internal and external; and the disasterous fluctuations of the funds; in which some persons high in place are supposed to be implicated; all these distract the attention and disturb the minds of ministers and render them heedless of all affairs but such as are immediately important to their political existence.

I am, Sir, / Very respectfully / Your Obt Servt
Washington Irving

DOCKETED: Recd. 21 July. / Mr Markoe [*upper left corner of page 1*] / No. 67. W.
    Irving. Madrid 25 June 1845.
MANUSCRIPT: NA, RG 59.

This despatch is entirely in WI's handwriting.

1. WI repeated "and."
2. See WI to Gurdon Bradley, June 25, 1845.

1879. To Catharine Irving

Madrid June 26. 1845

My dear Kate

I have merely time to Scrawl a little letter in reply to your most
welcome one of April 21.[1] Do not imagine that it was from any thing
said by your father in his letters that I took up the idea that the Cottage
might prove a lonely residence to you all during the long winter months.
Your father appears to be always happy there himself, and to suppose
every body happy around him. He has mentioned with pleasure too,
the occasional visits you have all of you made to town and the kindness
you have experienced from your friends. I got the idea from solicitude
casually ⟨?thou?⟩ expressed by others lest you might all feel the difference between the social life of the Cottage during the summer months
and the monotony and dullness of winter. And I have long felt a solicitude of the Kind myself. While I was at home among you I could
occasionally give a little stir and animation to domestic life; though
even then, not so much as I wished: but since my departure I cannot
but think the winters must prove tedious.

I have been relieved, therefore, the last winter, by finding you ⟨wer⟩
had all opportunities for weeks together of participating in the social
life and innocent amusements of the city; and trust you will be able
to do so still more the next winter. Arrangements might even be mad[e][2]
for your all passing the winter months in town among your relatives;
making ↑them↓ pecuniary compensations; and leaving a mere garrison
at the Cottage. ⟨By⟩ In this way you might all vary the scene without
material encrease of expense. I love the cottage; but only because I
considered it a happy family nestling place. When it ceases to be so
it loses its value and I shall be the first to counsel an abandonment of
it. You must not mew yourselves up there under an idea that it is my
wish. My sole wish is that you should all be happy; and I know you
all to be such dear good girls that you may be safely left to consult
your own inclinations. Therefore make all your domestic arrangements
to suit yourselves.

I have been deeply concerned of late by the illness and death of poor Gabriel at Paris: and even still more at the mental sufferings of his excellent little wife; during her long and anxious voyage, and on her arriving too late even for his dying bed! I long to hear of her being once more at home ⟨to⟩ with her children and friends, after her sad, sad wanderings. She is of a most noble nature and is to be loved and prized the more she is known.

I shall be anxious to hear how you all pass the Summer; now your old neighbors have returned after a fashionable car⟨r⟩eer in Paris. I want to know, also, how Julia Grinnell likes the Shennard ⟨?es?⟩ Cottage; and whether you are able to keep up a tolerably frequent intercourse.

Tell your father I have received his letter of April 15.th[3] giving a statement of the fiscal affairs of the Cottage; which is very satisfactory. I am glad to find that the pigs and poultry pay for their boarding and lodging; and especially that the turkeys are so much more productive on being suffered to play the vagabond. I am glad also to hear that you have a good gardener, and that the garden flourishes. In fact the garden and the poultry yard furnish occupation and amusement in a little establishment like Sunnyside—I will write to your father by another opportunity

Give my love and benediction to all the household—

Your affectionate Uncle
Washington Irving

P. S. Tell your father in his annual report he has made no mention of Vaney.

MANUSCRIPT: SHR.

1. This letter has not been located.
2. WI omitted the bracketed letter.
3. This letter has not been located.

1880. *To Sarah Storrow*

Madrid June 29th. 1845

My dear Sarah,

Your letter of the 21st.[1] having gone with the Courier to Barcelona, where the French Ambassador is at present, did not reach me until this morning (Sunday) instead of Thursday last. Send your letters through the post office until I direct otherwise.

Do not lay any more temptations in my way to come to Paris. I need none greater than the longing desire I have to see you and your children. In remaining, alone, at my post, I am making a severe sacrafice of my inclinations, but I do it from a conviction of its importance to the welfare of those dependent upon me. I have told you how important it is to my plans and prospects that I should devote the remaining time I may remain at this place, to the uninterrupted exercise of my pen; do not then seek to shake a resolution conscientiously formed and essential to my own self contentment; nor ⟨to⟩ hold forth pictures of enjoyment which only cost me a greater sacrafice of inclination to forego.

I am glad that the painter has succeeded in entrapping a likeness of fidgety little Kate. I wish I could see it before its transmission to the United States—I shall be desirous to hear of its first exhibition to grandmama. I believe all you say of dear little Susie, and beg you to give me as many anecdotes and descriptions as you can of both her and Kate; You cannot imagine how delightful these little details are to me, and how brief they seem. I am sure I shall love Susie as much as I do Kate. The very contrast in their characters pleases me. I delight in the picture you present of Susie's sweet gentle happy nature; while I love Kate for her very excitability and restlessness, and because she is a little of a "limb." I see by your letter Kate is beginning to enter the "Grande Monde." Not exactly dining out, but dropping in at ⟨evening⟩ Soirees, and making visits at Chateaux. I hope to have an account of her excursion to Chateau Thurmheysen at Enghien.

I am highly edified by your account of the Wilson christening, and of Mr Kings assuming the responsible office of Godfather. Is the child a boy or girl, and does it inherit its mothers beauty?—Though I do not know whether you belonged to the party of true believers, who considered her beautiful. I am glad to see Mr King remains firm in the faith.

When does Mr King set off on his Summer tour? I want to hear of Mrs Ellis' getting away from the ennervating summer heat of Paris and being among the bracing airs of the Swiss mountains. I trust Mr King will do what you say he promises,—write to me when he arrives among the Pyrenees. If circumstances should occur to dislodge me from Madrid, I should like to meet the travellers there: though at present I do not see any likelihood of it.

The Summer here, has so far been quite cool; unusually so. The heats are now beginning; but in my spacious apartment I do not suffer from them. I have been heavy and inert for some time past, however, and incapable of literary occupation; or indeed of any close mental application: a scientific friend suggested to me that I was bilious and reccommended me regimen and a few pills. His prescription has been successful, and I ⟨som⟩ feel as if I had emerged from a cloud. I now take exercise on foot, for an hour or two before breakfast, in the early freshness of the morning; remain in the house (all) during the heat of the day drive out in the evening and again take exercise on foot, in some of the public walks. This with a light diet keeps me in excellent order. In fact I was getting *too hearty.*

We have had a great treat here for some time past in Ronconi; who, being seen in high relief, in various characters, appears to greater advantage than among the rival artists of the Paris opera. He has shewn great talent both in Serious and Comic parts. His quack doctor Dulcamara, in the Elizir d'Amore,[2] is admirable and his Nabuco (Nebuchadnezzar) in the opera of the same name, has brought down thunders of applause.

Remember my kindly to Mr Storrow. Kiss the dear little women for me.

Your affectionate uncle
Washington Irving

MANUSCRIPT: Yale.

1. This letter has not been located.
2. Donizetti's *Elisir d'Amore* was first produced in Milan on May 12, 1832. See *Grove's Dictionary of Music and Musicians*, II, 929.

1881. *To Francisco Martínez de la Rosa*

Legation of the United States / Madrid June 30th. 1845

His Exy. Don F M. de la Rosa / &c &c &c

Sir

I have the honor to transmit to your Excellency, herewith, the commission of Mr Simeon M Johnson,[1] appointed by the President of the United States Consul for the Port of Mantanzas, in the island of Cuba; and to request that a Regium Exequatur be issued.

I beg leave to repeat, in this instance, the suggestion which I had the honor to offer in my note of the 23d. of February last (in the case of Mr Wright, appointed Consul for St Iago de Cuba) and which suggestion met with the approbation of your Excellency, that as a measure of expedition, and to save the time usually lost in collecting information in the Colony respecting the fitness of a consular candidate and transmitting it to Madrid, the Exequatur be forwarded, at once, to the competent authorities in the Island of Cuba, to be delivered to Mr Simeon M Johnson as soon as it shall appear, on due investigation, that it is expedient to grant it to him.

I have also the honor to solicit Her Majestys Exequatur for Mr Nicholas B Boyle,[2] appointed by the President of the United States Consul for the port of Mahon in the island of Minorca; and whose commission is likewise transmitted herewith.

I take this occasion to renew the assurance of the high consideration with which I have the honor to remain

Your Excellencys Obt Serv
W. I.

MANUSCRIPT: NA, RG 84 (letterbook copy).

This copy is in WI's handwriting.

1. Johnson of Michigan was nominated as U.S. consul for Matanzas on December 18, 1845. The request for the exequatur seems to have occurred before the formal nomination was made. See Hasse, *Index to U.S. Documents*, III, 1746.

2. Boyle of Washington was likewise nominated as U.S. consul for Port Mahon on December 18, 1845, after the request for his exequatur. See Hasse, *Index to U.S. Documents*, III, 1747.

1882.   To Messrs. Baring Brothers & Co.

Legation of the United States / Madrid July 1t. 1845

Messrs Baring Brothers & Co. / London

Gentlemen,

Enclosed I send you a draft on yourselves for Four hundred and Sixty four Pounds Seventeen shillings and Six pence, on account of Salary due me ⟨by⟩ ↑from↓ the Government of the United States; ⟨and⟩ ↑also↓ a ⟨like⟩ draft for twenty pounds on account of the contingent expenses of this legation—The aggregate amount ⟨of these bills ↑drafts↓⟩ you will please to hold subject to ⟨my drafts or the drafts⟩ ↑the disposition of myself or↓ of Mr Pierre M Irving of New York.

I remain Gentlemen / Very respectfully / Your obt Sert
Washington Irving

DOCKETED: Drafts on Messrs / Baring Brothers & Co. / £464.17.6. Salary / £20: Contingencies / *July 1. 1845*
MANUSCRIPT: SHR.

Accompanying this letter were the following drafts:

Legation of the United States / Madrid July 1. 1845

Messrs Baring Brothers & Co / London

Please pass to my credit the sum of Four Hundred and Sixty four Pounds, Seventeen shillings and six pence and charge the same to the Government of the United States on account of my diplomatic salary

Your obt Servt.
(Washington Irving)

£464.17.6

Legation of the United States / Madrid July 1t 1845

Messrs. Baring, Brothers & Co

Please pass to my credit the sum of Twenty Pounds, and charge the same to the Government of the United States on account of the contingent expenses of this Legation

Your Obt Servt
(Washington Irving)

£20-:- -:-

Each of these drafts has "Copy" written vertically across them, and WI's signatures have lines drawn through them.

1883. *To James Buchanan*

Legation of the United States / Madrid, July 1st. 1845.

No 68. / The Hon. James Buchanan. / Secretary of State. Washington

Sir,

I enclose the accounts and vouchers of this Legation for the Second Quarter of 1845. Shewing a balance in favor of the United States of $24.18/100, which will be carried to their credit in the next account.

As I am apprehensive there may have been inaccuracies in some of my preceding accounts I will be much obliged to you for a statement of my account from the Auditor of the Treasury.

Very respectfully / Your Obt Servt
Washington Irving

DOCKETED: Recd. 2 Augt. / Mr. Markoe
MANUSCRIPT: NA, RG 59.

This letter is in WI's handwriting.
The lower left margin has the following penciled notes: "Mr. Z. / Please / show this / to Mr. P. / Have a / St made out / Account requested / Sent from the 5th. / Auditor's office, on / the 13th. Aug. 1845, to / Mr. Irving, agreeably / to his wish as expressed above"

1884. To James Buchanan

Legation of the United States Madrid July 10th. 1845.

No. 69. / The Honble / James Buchanan / Secretary of State. / Washington.

Sir,

I have recently received Dispatches Nos. 44, and 45. containing the Consular Commissions of Simeon M. Johnson for Matanzas, and Nicholas B. Boyle for Port Mahon in Minorca, and have made application for the royal Exequaturs.

I have received no reply as yet to my note to the Minister of State claiming restitution of duties wrongfully imposed on American merchandize shipped to Cuba, under the "duty free" decree. Indeed, the absence of part of the Cabinet with the Court at Barcelona interrupts the whole course of business. I have forborne to follow the Court to Barcelona this year having received no instructions from Government on the subject, and there being a probability that the royal sojourn in that city would be very short: Should the absence of the court from the Capital be prolonged, I may find it expedient to pay it a brief visit to prevent being thought wanting in respect.

It is now decided that the Queen will depart from Barcelona toward the latter part of this month, but will visit the Basque Provinces before her return to Madrid,[1] and will repair to the Coast for the benefit of sea bathing. This measure has been strongly opposed by the ministers, and disapproved by the press generally,[2] who have thought it extremely important to have the court, and Cabinet concentrated at Madrid, at the present critical juncture. The Queen mother however had resolved upon the expedition to the Basque Provinces and she has carried her point. It is probable that she is actuated merely by a mother's solicitude for a daughter's health; the physical condition of the Queen, and the critical point of life at which she has arrived, calling for the most careful, and assiduous treatment.

The public, however, consider the Queen Mother a great manouverer, and suspect a covert design in every movement. They consider the projected journey into the Basque Provinces as having some connexion with her matrimonial schemes, for her royal daughters. Maria Cristina has long been desirous that her daughter Isabella II should marry the Count de Trap⟨p⟩ani, and Louis Philippe had at length consented to it, finding that he could not secure the hand of the Queen for one of his own sons. The shrewd Monarch is said to have consented, on condition that his son the Duke of Montpensier should have the hand of the Queen's sister, the

Infanta. In this he has shewn his usual forecast. The constitutional infirmities of Queen Isabella make it not unlikely that she will die early,
and without progeny; in such a case her sister would succeed to the
throne. The royal journey into the Basque provinces therefore is thought
to be projected by the Queen Mother to bring about a meeting between
her daughters, and the French princes, who are about to visit the Pyrenees.

With respect to the marriage of the Queen, there is ⟨a⟩ continual plot,
and counterplot, so that the game is perpetually changing. It is now
said that the Trap⟨p⟩ani match is given up by the Court of Naples; being
found to be so generally unpopular in Spain. A *Coburg* Prince[3] is now
talked of. There have been diplomatic conferences on the subject, it is
said, at Paris, between Mr. Bulwer, the British Minister at this Court,
and Mr. Guisot. It will have the English interest in its support, and Louis
Philippe in his growing spirit of accomodation to the views of England
is said to incline in favor of it; provided always that the Duke of Montpensier have the hand of the Infanta.

In the mean time, another candidate is suddenly brought into the field,
supported by Narvaez, and the Cabinet, and likely to be popular with
the nation. This is the Infante Dn. Enrique, Duke of Seville,[4] and second
son of the Infante Dn. Francisco. He is about twenty years of age, a captain in the Navy, and in command of a Brig of War. Report speaks favorably of him; he has acquitted himself well in the studies, and duties of
his profession, and this implies intelligence, instruction, and manly qualities. Narvaez managed that he should visit Barcelona in his vessel of
war during the sojourn of the young Queen at that port. Here he was
received with great distinction; Narvaez gave him a grand dinner; as
did Martinez dela Rosa; he was fêted by the local authorities, dined at
Court, and the young Queen visited his vessel in some degree of state.
He is now the theme of eulogium in most of the ministerial papers; nor is
it likely he will meet with opposition from the others, as he is a Spaniard
by birth, and of the Bran↑c↓h of the royal family which has been inclined to liberal principles. A newspaper is about to be set up in Madrid,
under the auspices of the Ministers to enforce his pretensions. Dn. Francisco, also, and his family, who have hitherto been half overlooked by
royalty, have suddenly been invited to repair to St. Sebastian, during
the Royal sojourn there;[5] Dn Enrique of course is included in the invitation. This also has probably been managed by Narvaez as a check to the
Queen Mother. The latter now finding the Trap⟨p⟩ani match likely to
be entirely defeated is anxious to postpone the marriage of her daughter, until she shall have arrived at a more mature age; until her health
is established, and her constitution developed and confirmed. In this she
is certainly right. The marriage of the Queen at her present immature

age might be productive of domestic, and public evils, which it is needless to enumerate. All these, however, may be set at defiance by politicians; who are only actuated by present expediency, so that to settle this matrimonial question, which is so fruitful of difficulties and dangers, the poor young Queen may be hurried into an early marriage, which may hurry her into an early grave.

From the foregoing statement it will be perceived that a variance still exists between Narvaez, & the Queen Mother: indeed there has been a contest for supremacy between them almost ever since the return of Maria Cristina to Spain, and in nothing have they been more completely opposite than in respect to the Trapini match.

In bringing forward the Infante Enrique, however, Narvaez has something more in view, that[6] mere dislike to Trapani, and opposition to Queen Christina. He feels the necesity of strengthening his own position, and the position of his cabinet, and hopes, by supporting a member of the liberal branch of the royal family to conciliate the progresista party. He feels that he has completely lost favor with that party since he came into power. He engaged in the insurrection of 1843, as the leader of a section of that party, under the pretext of freeing the ultra liberals from the supposed, or rather the pretended, oppression of Espartero, and with a prospect of carrying out a *"juste milieu"* in Spain as Louis Philippe had in France. Since his elevation to power, however, the impetuosity of his temper, and his disposition to domineer ha⟨d⟩s at times caused him to trample on constitutional forms, and privileges, and to be guilty of acts of the sheerest despotism.—Such for instance was the recent arrest ⟨by his orders⟩ of two writers for a public journal; who were hurried away under military guard to Cadiz to be transported to the Phillipine Islands;[7] a despotic act which has resounded throughout the Peninsula. Now Narvaez is an enemy to Despotism, excepting when practised by himself, and in this instance only gave way to a paroxysm of his ungovernable temper. His friends have attempted to palliate his conduct by insinuating that the persons arrested had been suspected of conspiring against government; but it is well known that the real offence was a wound inflicted upon the general's vanity. They had given a burlesque account of his pomp, and style on a public occasion, with some ludicrous allusions to his person and his *wig*. This was not to be tolerated by a man arrived at a *certain age*, yet still a general gallant, and particularly ambitious of the smiles of the ladies.

Vanity in fact is Narvaez' besetting weakness, It overlays his bolder, and better qualities, and by its indirect operations has contributed greatly to lessen his stand in public opinion. He is prodigal, and ostentatious in his style of living. Has his palaces, and state equipages; gives princely fetes, and entertainments at which royalty is sometimes present, and lives far beyond his ⟨means⟩ income or his ostensible means. It is true his past services were rewarded by the Queen Mother, under the advice of the French Embassador, with the round sum of $100.000—but this was insufficient to cope with his vain glorious prodigality. Among other equivocal modes of replenishing his coffers he has leagued himself with certain of the principal Stock brokers of Madrid, and has engaged in some of those speculations in the funds, which have shaken society to its centre. These gambling operations have become matters of notoriety, and have injured him with the public. They have injured him too, with his main dependance, the Army, who detest everything in a commander which may appear sordid or mercenary. Unfortunately for the general he has too many dangerous enemies in that army, disappointed rivals, who gladly trumpet forth, and exaggerate anything, which may destroy the military prestige of his name.

Thus vanity has contributed indirectly, but greatly, to diminish the general's individual weight with the public, and his moral force in the government. He feels therefore the necessity of some expedient to sustain his political eminence, and to enable him to keep the Queen Mother in check, who has the advantage of him in being permanent in her elevated position.

But indeed, it is not the General alone, the whole Narvaez Cabinet needs propping. It occupies a mere isthmus between the absolutists (including the Carlists) on the one side, and the Progresistas on the other. This isthmus is continually narrowing. It has been shored up by the army, but even the army of late has ceased to be altogether a certain dependance, many of the officers being Carlists, and whole regiments of doubtful loyalty—Under these circumstances the bringing forward, and supporting a progresista candidate for the Royal hand is certainly an expedient of the Narvaez cabinet to prop its tottering fortunes.

The negotiations with the Court of Rome continue envelloped in doubt, and mystery, and are a source of humiliation to the Cabinet, and the Nation. The cross ↑purposes in this quarter↓ are attributed to the secret maneuvres of the Queen Mother, and add to her unpopularity; though she may have been actuated ↑in her intermeddlings↓ by conscientious motives, anxiety for the papal recognition of her daughter, as Queen of Spain, and a desire to expiate her own sins, and weaknesses by zealous promotion of the interests of the Church. The public say she is conscience stricken, and conscience bound, and that the Pope takes advantage of it.

It seems there are two parties in the Sacred college of Cardinals, one called the "Political," which is disposed to keep pace with the age, and to render the yoke of the church easy to her somewhat restive children; the other the "theocratic" party, intent upon reinstating the chair of St.

Peters in all the sway, religious, political, and fiscal, which it exercised in the days of Gregory VII. Unfortunately the cause of liberal principles has sustained a great loss in the recent death of the Cardinal Cappacini,[8] who was head of the Political party, and might have inclined the Pope to a liberal line of policy; his death leaves full scope for the councils of Cardinal Lambuschini,[9] who, beside being Secretary of State, is head of the theocratic party. This party is guided in its policy towards Spain by an intriguing knot of Carlist prelates, priests and laymen, Spanish emigrants, who came to Rome under the banner of the late Bishop of Leon;[10] and who represent their native country, as the most promising theatre for the great theocratic plan of retrocession.

It is unfortunate that at such a juncture, the Spanish government should have sent out Mr. Castillo y Ayense as their envoy to the Papal Court, a man of limited capacity, and completely subservient to Maria Christina. The consequence is that he has played a double part, openly acting in conformity to Cabinet instructions, and secretly, at the behest of the Queen Mother, subscribing to all the requisitions of Cardinal Lambuschini.—The negociation has thus been rendered of very difficult arrangement, nor would it be surprising if Rome, in case of persisting in her imprudent exactions, should lose altogether her supremacy in Spain.

The financial affairs of the Peninsula continue in a most embarassed state. Mon, the Minister of Finance, bears an unimpeachable character for integrity, though many of his opponents pronounce him an empyric; as physicians, however skillful, are apt to be pronounced, who have to deal with desperate cases, and rotten Constitutions. He has undertaken to reduce to order the immense chaos of national debts, and administrative abuses; but has set to work with scanty funds, slender public credit, and the distant hope of a loan; which may be deferred, if not defeated by the vicissitudes of political events, and of the government itself.[11] He has the marriage question, with all its perplexities to contend with, and the still more dangerous task of levying about twenty millions of dollars of new taxes by a new process. He certainly deserves high credit for the attempt; perhaps in other, and more settled times, it might have been attended with success; that it will be so now is more than problematical.

Having alluded to the Madrid Stock exchange, which at present has such an immense influence on the morals and fortunes of society, I would observe that it is not governed by the ordinary rules of such institutions.[12] Political events have comparatively small influence upon its fluctuations. Its supporters are not, as in other countries, holders of stock as a permanent investment to derive their income from the interest. They are solely, and purely gamblers with more or less Capital. They combine among themselves occasionally to play for a rise, or a fall, and are pretty sure to effect their purpose. When no combination of the kind exists, the funds are stagnant, or at a low price. It will take some years of tranquility, & good administration to induce people to invest Capital in Spanish Stock as a source of regular income. Gambling will go on in the mean time creating, and destroying mushroom fortunes. It is the mania of the day.—

A better spirit of enterprize however is awakening in the country. During the late breathing spell of comparative tranquility, a disposition has been evinced to explore, and develope the immense internal resources of the Peninsula, and to introduce those improvements prevalent in other parts of the world. The home capital which for a long time has remained dormant, is becoming active: foreign Capital is pouring into the Country, the ancient Mines are being reopened, others sought for; rail road companies are forming; in a word it needs but a few years of peace, and tolerable government to effect a total change in the Peninsula; to restore external credit, and internal prosperity, and to elevate the nation to a level with the rest of Europe. The country, say certain of the old political augurs, has been long in a state of transition, moral, material, religious, and political. It is now undergoing its vital crisis, and one year more may solve the riddle of its future fortunes—

I must apologize for the long and rambling disquisition into which I have unconsciously been betrayed. I had intended merely to touch briefly upon the main points of Spanish politics, but the whole is a complicated web, into which it is difficult to venture, without getting completely entangled; and in which one is obliged at times to be prolix in order to be explicit.

I am, Sir, / Very respectfully / Yr. obt. St
Washington Irving

DOCKETED: Recd. 2 Augt. / Mr. Markoe
MANUSCRIPT: NA, RG 59.   PUBLISHED: Hellman, *WI Esquire*, pp. 316–23; STW, II, 187 (in part).

Only the signature is in WI's handwriting.

1. This trip was confirmed in *La Posdata*, July 7, 1845.

2. Adverse comments resulted in an issue of *El Espectador* being confiscated and in the arrest and banishment to the Philippines of Fernando Corradi and Juan Perez Calvo, newsmen working for *El Clamor Publico*. See *La Posdata*, May 26, 27, 29, 30, 1845.

3. Prince Leopold, as WI suggests, had the support of Queen Victoria and Prince Albert. See John D. Bergamini, *The Spanish Bourbons*, p. 222.

4. Enrique, duke of Seville (1823–1870) was the younger brother of the effeminate Francisco de Asis, duke of Cadiz, who subsequently married Isabella on October 10, 1846. See Aronson, *Royal Vendetta*, p. 56.

5. See *La Posdata*, June 8, 1845.

6. WI probably intended to write "than."

7. See note 2.

8. Francisco Cappacini (1784–1845), who, after completing his theological work, studied physics and astronomy and became director of the observatory at Naples. He later became a diplomat for the Holy See, with assignments in the Low Countries, Munich, Vienna, Naples, and Portugal.

9. Luigi Lambruschini (1776–1854), who was made a cardinal in 1831, helped to formulate the statement on the dogma of the Immaculate Conception.

10. Joaquin Abarca y Blanque (1780–1844), who was named bishop of Leon by Ferdinand VII in 1824, later broke with the king and supported the Carlist movement. Forced to flee Spain, he went to Italy and retired to a Dominican convent near Turin, where he died. See Vincente Carcel Orti, *Politica eclesial de los gobiernos liberales españoles (1830–1840)* (Pamplona, 1975), pp. 114–24, 470–71.

11. The royal decree on the reorganization of the Ministry of Finance is published in *La Posdata*, June 19–28, 1845. Plans for financial reform are also discussed on the first page of *La Posdata*, July 2, 1845.

12. New regulations for the stock exchange were published in *La Posdata*, July 2–3, 1845.

1885.   To Sarah Storrow

Madrid July 10th. 1845

My dear Sarah,

I thank you over and over again for your long and most acceptable letter of the 28th. June;[1] which was some little time reaching me; the Courier having come by the way of Barcelona. As the French ambassador has left that City the Courier will resume the route direct between Paris and Madrid; so you may continue to write to me through the foreign office.

I am very much obliged to Mr King for the kind interest he evinces in my being suffered to remain undisturbed at my post. I am gratified to find that the feeling I have toward him is reciprocated. I do not think now that it is likely I shall be displaced, at least for the present year. I wish I could feel that I was turning the year to better account, but I begin to fear I shall fall short of all my literary anticipations. The official claims on the exercise of my pen, and the ever recurring tax of letter writing exhaust almost all the time and mood that I should otherwise devote to ⟨literary⟩ the task of composition—and in fact the inclination to that task is continually growing weaker—I feel at times as if I would gladly renounce the pen for ever: and I almost think I would; if I could get on without it.

I have received letters a few days since from home: one from your Mother just after her return to the Cottage; and full of delight at having got back among the birds and honeysuckles. These letters from sweet little Sunnyside make me at times quite homesick and I feel as if, did it regard myself alone, I could live on bread and water so that I could get back among my friends; among those whom I love and who love me.

Still, do not think I am suffering from loneliness and depression. The course of life I have for some time adopted has had the finest effect upon my health and spirits. I continue to sally forth early in the morning, generally between five and six, and, and² take exercise for two and three hours in the open air; rambling in the Retiro, or in other of the public walks, in and about the city. The mornings are generally fresh and delightful. In the evenings I drive out just before sunset, on the hills which enjoy the cool breezes from the Guadarama mountains; and there alight and walk for an hour or so; after which I return to the Prado, and take a promenade there before going to the opera. I have wished for you in some of my evening drives. The prospects from the hills are really grand; though melancholy; over vast lonely regions, variously tinted, but inclining to the autumnal brown; with the Splendid line of Guadarama Mountains, closing the scene; all clad in purple and some of them yet tipped with snow; with the Sun setting behind them;—and then such evening skies—The moment I get out on these hills I feel that I am in another region. the air is so light and elastic, and the breezes so bracing and refreshing. The very loneliness of the vast landscape is inspiring; and when it is animated it is by ⟨scenes of thes⟩ picturesque groupes suited to the scene and characteristic of Spain. Bands of Muleteers with their *Cavalgadas*;³ Travellers on horseback, with guns slung behind their saddles, and looking more fit to rob than to be robbed. or now and then a lumbering Spanish travelling carriage; drawn by half a dozen mules; with jingling bells; and escorted by as many rough looking fellows with blunder busses—I think you would enjoy one of these lovely evening drives with me even more than a drive in the Bois de Bologne: there is so much character in every thing around— And oh! what I would give if I could have you and your dear little ones here, with me—I then could make myself quite happy at Madrid.

I envy Mr King his having a favorite niece to travel with him—I have nearly lost the passion for travelling, but, with such a companion, I could travel to the worlds end. There is no merit in either Mr King or myself being "kind uncles" considering what neices we have.

A letter which I received from London this morning mentions that Mr McLane⁴ is appointed Minister to the Court of St James. Can this be true? I have seen no mention of any thing of the Kind in the American news papers; nor do my letters from home speak of it. I should be delighted if it were the case; but I cannot help doubting it.

I am sorry you are to lose Mrs. Hacquet; though I think she is right to get as far as possible out of the way of being importuned by that paltry animal her husband. I wish she could be completely divorced from him, and he left to shift for himself. I beg you when next you see Mrs Hacquet to remember me to her most Kindly.

How does Kate get on in speaking. Does she speak equally well in French and English, and does she keep the languages distinct? She must now be able to talk quite fluently, without getting in a bother and a pet at not being understood. I should suppose that Susie, also, begins to use her legs to more purpose than mere Kicking. Does she begin to walk, or does she still content herself with rolling?

Kiss the dear little women for me and remember me Kindly to your husband

Your affectionate Uncle
Washington Irving

MANUSCRIPT: Yale.   PUBLISHED: STW, II, 189–90 (in part).
1. This and other letters mentioned in this letter have not been located.
2. WI repeated "and."
3. WI's misspelling of "cabalgatas," cavalcades.
4. Polk had offered Louis McLane the post of U.S. minister to London in early June, 1845, with the hope of using his diplomatic skills to negotiate a settlement of the Oregon question. WI had served as secretary of the legation in London under McLane from 1829 to 1831. See Munroe, *Louis McLane*, pp. 254–55, 291, 514.

1886. *To John Miller*

Legation of the U S. / Madrid, July 12th. 1845

John Miller Esqr

Sir

I enclose a draft on Messrs. Baring Brothers & Co. payable to your order, for eight pounds 7/4 ½p Sterlg. being the amount of your postage account, ↑against this Legation,↓ for the last quarter

very respectfully / Your Obt St
W I.

P. S. The Passport Seal is extremely well ⟨both⟩ designed and executed. The Ink box, cushion &c did not come with it. I have had to provide myself with those articles here.

MANUSCRIPT: NA, RG 84 (letterbook copy).

This copy is in WI's handwriting.

1887.   To Horatio Sprague

Madrid July 12th. 1845.

Horatio Sprague Esqr / Consul of the U States Gibraltar

My dear Sir,

I received yesterday your letter of the 24th. June informing me that you had forwarded the letter for Manilla by the Steamer Oriental for which I am much obliged to you.

With respect to Mr Josiah Raymond, he must have become aware, long since, that no Royal Exequatur can be obtained for him as Consul of the United States for ⟨Matanz⟩ Manzanilla, in Cuba; as I addressed a circular dated 19th February last, to him and other candidates for consulates in Cuba, informing them that the Spanish Government had come to the determination not to admit foreign consuls in any but four ports of the Island, viz, Havanna, Matanzas, St Iago de Cuba and Trinidad

&c &c &c
W I.

MANUSCRIPT: NA, RG 84 (letterbook copy).

This copy is in WI's handwriting.

1888.   To James J. Wright

Legation of the U S. / Madrid. July 17th. 1845

James J Wright Esq / Consul of the U. S. / St Iago de Cuba

Sir,

I herewith forward to you your Exequatur received this day from the Department of Foreign Affairs together with the original commission Signed by the President of the United States.

I had been led to believe that my suggestion to the Minister of State, ↑in your case would be adopted, viz↓ that your Exequatur should be forwarded directly to the authorities of the Island, to be delivered to you as soon as they should be satisfied of the expediency of granting it. This would have saved some months of delay in collecting information and forwarding it to Madrid. It appears, however, the old plan has been adhered to, notwithstanding its inconveniencies

I am Sir / Respectfully / Your obt Servt
W I.

MANUSCRIPT: NA, RG 84 (letterbook copy).

This copy is in WI's handwriting.

1889. To Francisco Martínez de la Rosa

Legation of the U States / Madrid, July 24th. 1845

His Excellency / Don Francisco M de la Rosa / &c &c &c

Sir

I have the honor to transmit herewith the commission of Mr John W. Holding,[1] appointed by the President of the United States Consul for the Port of Sant Iago de Cuba, and to request that a Regium Exequatur be issued.

I have the honor to remain

With high consideration / Your Excellencys Obt Servt
W I.

MANUSCRIPT: NA, RG 84 (letterbook copy).

This copy is in WI's handwriting.

1. John W. Holding of Maryland was nominated as U.S. consul for Santiago de Cuba on December 18, 1845, to replace James Wright, who had died. Again WI has applied for the exequatur before the formal nomination to Congress. See Hasse, *Index to U.S. Documents*, III, 1748.

1890. To George Read

Legation of the U States / Madrid July 27th 1845

George Read Esqr / Consul of the U S. Malaga

Dear Sir,

I have to acknowledge the receipt of your letter of the 21 inst. enclosing copies of your consular returns for the half year ending June 30th. and of the Statement of exports from your port for the same term.

I have also to acknowledge, ↑with many thanks,↓ the receipt of the historical document relative to the Carthusian Convent famous for the wine of the Priorat The document is curious in itself and must have additional relish for those who have the good fortune to be acquainted with the wine which grows under the auspices of the Convent.

I am my dear Sir / very truly yours
Washington Irving

Manuscript: NA, RG 84 (letterbook copy).

This copy is in WI's handwriting.

1891. To Francisco Martínez de la Rosa

Legation of the United States / Madrid, August 2d. 1845.

The Undersigned, Envoy Extraordinary and Minister Plenipotentiary of the United States of America has the honor to acknowledge the receipt of the note of his Excellency M ⟨Fernandez⟩ ↑Francisco↓ Martinez de la Rosa First Minister of State and of Foreign affairs ↑of Her Catholic Majesty↓ stating the case of the American Brig Pavillon des Etats Unis.

According to this statement it would appear that while the said Brig was at anchor in the port of Coamo in the island of Porto Rico ↑taking on wood and water↓ the Captain obtained a "moratoria" of two days, to recover two of his crew who had deserted; that on the very first day of the term ↑thus granted,↓ without waiting for the recovery of the deserters, he suddenly set sail, without paying his port dues; leaving at the same time his ships papers in the hands of the Captain of the port. That the deserters were found on the following day and ↑were↓ delivered, ↑or surrendered themselves↓ into the hands of the ↑United States↓ Consul of Ponce,[1] who requested that the Ships papers might likewise be given up to him, and that the authorities would proceed in accord with him in the business. That the latter part of his request was refused by the authorities on the ground that it would be allowing a foreign agent to mingle himself in their acts of government and permitting him to exceed his attributes which were limited to those of a mere commercial agent: and that the Ships papers would not be given up until the port dues had been paid.

If the Undersigned has rightly understood the Statement he would observe, that there is something inexplicable to him in the sudden departure of the Captain of the Brig without waiting the recovery of the deserters (apparently so much desired) and without receiving his ships papers the want of which might subject him to serious difficulties and losses in the subsequent course of his voyage It does not seem to the undersigned that the mere saving of the port dues would be a sufficient object to induce such a course of conduct; however fraudulently the Captain might be inclined. There is, apparently, some link wanting in the chain of circumstances to give congruity to the whole. The Undersigned therefore waits in the hope of receiving from the Consul at Pons or from other parties concerned in the affair, explanations which may furnish this link, and clear up what now appears to him inexplicable. In the mean time he has transmitted to his government a copy of the note which he had the honor to receive from his Excellency on the subject

The Undersigned avails himself of the occasion to renew to his Excellency the assurance of his distinguished consideration

(Signed) W Irving.

MANUSCRIPT: NA, RG 84 (letterbook copy).

This copy is in WI's handwriting.

1. J. C. Gallaher of Pennsylvania was U.S. consul for Ponce, Puerto Rico at this time. See Hasse, *Index to U.S. Documents*, III, 1747.

1892. *To Sarah Storrow*

Madrid Aug 2d. 1845

My dear Sarah,

I was quite surprised a day or two since to receive a letter from you dated from Southampton. (July 18th.) Your previous letter July 5th.[1] merely Said that you had *almost* determined to leave Paris on the following Saturday for Havre: which place you had chosen in preference to Dieppe because if circumstances favored, it would be more convenient to cross to the Isle of Wight. Perhaps you may have written an intervening letter which has never come to hand.

I wish I could have been with you at Southampton, to have rambled about the place and its vicinity. It is a fine old English town, and somewhat historical. I reccollect being much pleased ↑on my first visit,↓ with the approach to it by land, ⟨on my first visit⟩, through the pleasant valley of the Itchin. It was then skirted by old picturesque mansions of red brick, with court yards, grass plots and flower beds before them, which you saw through large iron gateways. There seemed also to be an abundance of nice, trim, pretty English nursing maids, with their fresh, blooming frolicksome little charges—very important groupes in English landscape. I suppose you know that Southampton is the place where Canute[2] is said to have forbade the Sea to wet him; which replied by giving his Majesty a complete drenching. They used to shew the ⟨old⟩ ancient wall beneath which the Monarch took his seat. I suppose it has been pulled down. The old part of the town at that time was full of ⟨q⟩ quaint houses; with bow windows projecting like noses from them. Close beside the city gate was the effigy of Sir Bevis of Hampton;[3] whose heroic exploits as recorded in old Story books used to delight me in my boyhood.

I presume you visited the beautiful ruins of Netley Abbey,[4] in the neighborhood of Southampton ———[5] but now I reccollect; you have been to Southampton before: on your way from London to Paris, and must have noticed all these things when they had more novelty for you than they can have at present.

I do not wonder you find England quiet and death like ⟨after⟩ in comparison with France, especially on Sunday. It takes time to get accustomed to this stillness; and to the reserved, shut up look of the people and their habitations. I reccollect how much I was struck, after residing several years in England, with the contrast presented on crossing from Southampton to Havre. I landed at Havre on a pier swarming with women in red dresses, ⟨high⟩ flaunting caps and wooden shoes, all gossipping and chattering like a flock of parrots. Instead of the shut up look of Southampton here the houses seemed turned out of doors; the doors and casements open, tags and rags fluttering from the windows; the family in the Street, and no body at home but parrots and monkeys. After a long experience, however, of both sides of the channel I give a decided preference to France as a residence. As you say, I feel more at home there. It is in fact, more the home of the Stranger than England. The mode of living is less restrained and formal; you may live as you please without supervision, or Supercilious remark. Beside, England is growing less and less a pleasant residence for an American. A rancorous prejudice against us has been diligently inculcated of late years by the British press and it is daily producing its fruits of bitterness. I could never again live in England with the home feeling I once enjoyed there. No, No, give me "la belle France" that bright, gay, good humored country, for a residence.

I am quite amused with Kates passion for Cathedral architecture; which tempted her to play the part of Goody two shoes in the ⟨chu⟩ Cathedral of Rouen. I am delighted too to find that both of the little folks are such good travellers; but one main reason is, they are in such pure and excellent health. Half and more than half of the waywardness and fretfulness of children arises from puny frames and disordered stomachs; the result of motherly indulgence. I trust you will always continue to observe the same healthful system as to air, exercise, diet &c with your children. As Kate is now becoming more and more an intellectual little being you must observe a simplicity of diet for her mind as well as her body. Do not accustom her too early to artificial pleasures and excitements. Let her amusements be as simple as possible   do not carry her too much to sights and shows and Spectacles. Paris is a great show box and perpetual fair, where the mind gets too early palled with wonders, and the sensibilities blunted by excitements. Kate is naturally excitable and needs no extra stimulants. be as sparing as possible of those ⟨amuse⟩ exciting amusements and spectacles with which Paris abounds. Mr. Storrow knows the delightfully quiet and simple manner in which his sisters were brought up in the very centre of Paris; and the excellent effect it had upon their characters and manners. I wish your two little girls could be brought up in the same manner; retaining ⟨the⟩ freshness of feeling and simplicity of tastes and habits, though surrounded by all the refinements and falsities of art.

I have received this morning a letter from "Jock"[6] as you call him. I wrote to him some time since to make enquiries about landed property in Pennsylvania, belonging to ↑a lady of my acquaintance,↓ a descendant of ↑the late↓ Gurran M'Kean but now residing in Madrid. I was in hopes, and still am, that it might throw some business into his hands. He complains sadly of the dearth of business. Still he gets some; and I hope he may have faith and fortitude enough to hold on. Law business is always of slow growth; but when once it begins to grow, it is apt to keep on and encrease. It is free also from the risks and harrassing cares of commerce. He tells me that Professor Renwicks family has employed him lately and compensated his labors liberally. When he can get employ from such sources it shews that his character is becoming known and appreciated.

I think it probable this letter will find you fixed at Havre and enjoying the pure breezes of the Cote. I am sorry to find that Mr Beasley is absent for the summer. His presence there would have contributed greatly towards making your residence agreeable.

I am amused with the quiet elopement of Mrs Walsh; and with the philosophic acquiescence of Mr Walsh. By the bye, I have never heard of that promised and prognosticated Soiree going into effect, whereat you were to meet with all the notorieties of Paris. I hope the Consulate has proved more productive than it seemed likely to be: and that the family has been able to keep up the comfortable and pleasant style of living with which they commenced.

I continue to brave the summer heat in excellent Style; or rather to evade it. The copious exercise I have taken, morning and evening for weeks past ⟨[unrecovered]⟩ has put me quite in good training. I do not know when I have been in better health. I only wish I had a companion to ⟨share⟩ accompany me on my walks. I enjoy them however though alone; and pass a couple of hours ↑delightfully↓ before breakfast in the shady walks of the Retiro with the beautiful prospect of the Guadarama mountains in the distance; reminding me, in their aerial tints, of the distant views of the Catskill.

About the Middle of this Month I expect the Albuquerques will return to Madrid; and then I will have a domestic circle to resort to, and little fairy visitors to enliven my home.

Give my kind remembrances to Mr Storrow and kiss the dear little travellers for me.

Your affectionate Uncle
Washington Irving

P. S. As Kate, I presume, does not keep a journal of her travels, I trust to you to give me particulars ⟨concerning⟩ of her adventures and observations; also let me know every step of Susies progress in accomplishments. Her last achievement was smelling to a flower; which certainly was more elegant and ladylike than either Kicking or rolling. Let me know how the little women are dressed for travelling; whether they amuse themselves by noticing objects as they pass. In a word gossip as much as you can about your children and your letters will be sure to interest and delight me.

MANUSCRIPT: Yale.

1. These letters have not been located.
2. This story about Canute, a Dane who was king of England from 1016 to 1035, is told in Holinshed's *Chronicles*.
3. Bevis was the son of the earl of Southampton, whose wife caused him to be murdered and his son to be sold as a slave.
4. Netley Abbey, a Cistercian Abbey founded in the thirteenth century by Henry III, lay about three miles southeast of the city.
5. WI inserted the long dash.
6. Irving Paris, Sarah's brother. His letter has not been located.

1893. To Francisco Martínez de la Rosa

Legation of the U States / Madrid Aug 4th. 1845

His Excellency / Don F M. de la Rosa / &c &c &c

Sir

In conformity with the suggestion in Your Excellencys note of the 20th. May last, I obtained and transmitted to you documents duly authenticated before the Spanish Consul at Marseilles, substantiating the claim of Messrs Fitch. Brothers & Co to be indemnified for losses sustained in consequence of the detention of the Dutch Galeot Vrouw Johanna by a Spanish Guarda Costa.

I was led to expect from the tenor of your Excellencys note that, the illegality of the detention of the Vrouw Johanna being admitted, the production of those documents would be followed by the prompt payment of the claim in question: indeed the merits of the case were so extremely clear and simple that there did not appear to be a reasonable pretext for delay.

Nearly three months have elapsed, however, without my hearing any thing further on the subject from Her Majestys government, I would observe to your Excellency that this delay of redress, where the injury and injustice have been tacitly acknowledged, is in itself a grevious wrong; and is a wrong on the part of the government, whereas the original act was the error of one of its officers

I trust I will not have again to address your Excellency on a subject where a proper consideration for the dignity of Her Majestys government should prompt such immediate action

I avail myself of this occasion to renew to your Exy the assurance of my distingd consideration

Your Exys Ob St
W I.

Manuscript: NA, RG 84 (letterbook copy).

This copy is in WI's handwriting.
A note in pencil after the letter: "The above claim paid in 1846"

1894. To Irving Paris

Madrid Aug 7th. 1845

My dear Irving

I received a few days since your letter of June 23d. on the subject of the Pierrard property.[1] I am affraid I have troubled you in the matter to no purpose It appears that just about the time that the Pierrards applied to me on the subject Madame Pierrards brother, the Duke of Sote Mayor (Spanish Minister at London) suddenly moved in the matter and wrote out to Mr Calderon de la Barca, Minister at Washington, to reccomend him some agent in the United States, who would attend to the business. Mr Calderon reccommended a Mr Dunlap or Dunlop, a lawyer of Philadelphia; and the Duke consequently wrote to the Pierrards to join with him in a power of attorney to be sent out to Mr Dunlap. It is singular that both the Duke and his sister, after having neglected this matter for years should suddenly and simultaneously have moved in it, without consulting each other.

The Pierrards would prefer that the matter should be put into your hands; they have written to the Duke of Sote mayor on the subject and ⟨have⟩ waited for his reply before they forward the power of attorney. I have told them that I had no doubt Mr Dunlap would manage their affairs ⟨with⟩ to their Satisfaction: and that his residence in the State of Pennsylvania would ⟨give him⟩ enable him to do it with more facility that you could. They still however seem disposed to give you the preference; though I think it probable the Duke will decide in favor of Mr Dunlap

I had been induced to throw this matter onto your hands because by a former letter to me you appeared to be in want of employment; and I thought it might be attended with profit. From your last letter I am inclined to think it might be attended with more trouble and vexation than profit; the property lying in a distant part of another state; and occupied perhaps by Squatters, whom it might be difficult to dislodge. I shall not, therefore, regret if the power of attorney is given to Mr Dunlap.

I am glad to find that you get occasionally a little law business, enough to cause a "faint revival of your hopes" and that you have such good clients as the Renwick family. The profession of the Law, like that of medicine, requires great patience and perseverance and a fixed residence. The gains at first are very small, and they are slow in encreasing, but when once they begin they keep on. It is a profession free from the harrassing cares; and risks and the fatal reverses of commerce. It may not make a man wealthy; but at least it does not break his rest and break his heart, as the vicissitudes of commerce are apt to do. I hope therefore, you will still keep on. You have intelligence and capacity for business, and a rectitude of principle that will always inspire confidence. Such qualifications will gradually become known, and when known will have their proper appreciation and effect on such an immense place of business as New York.

I hope your journey into Clinton County may prove satisfactory, and that you may succeed in making the lands there productive. I am glad to see that your father maintains his post through the various changes of the Custom House, and trust he will continue to hold it. I am sure if he loses it, it will not be through lack of staunch German fidelity to his trust.

I shall endeavor to write to your mother by the Steamer which will take this letter; if I do not, it will be because my pen is overtasked by other claims upon it.

Remember me affectionately to your father and believe me my dear Irving, with the strongest interest in your wellfare

Your affectionate uncle
Washington Irving

MANUSCRIPT: Va.–Barrett.

1. WI had written to him about this matter on April 19, 1845.

1895.   To Alejandro Mon

Legation of the U States / Madrid, Aug 9th. 1845

His Exy. Alexr. Mon / Minister of Finance.

Sir,

Your Excellency cannot but be fully aware of the serious losses sustained by citizens of the United States who made heavy shipments to the Island of Cuba in the course of last winter, on the faith of a decree of the Supreme authorities of the island admitting certain articles free of duty for the space of three months; but who found their merchandize on its arrival subjected to the old duties, in consequence of an act of Her Majestys government carried into effect in the interim, and without due notification, annulling the aforesaid decree.

The government of the United States, keenly alive at all times to every thing which may affect the rights of its citizens and disturb the harmonious relations of the two countrys, could not but be deeply aggrieved by an irregular act, which took the confiding American merchant by surprise and was calculated to impair that confidence and security in commercial intercourse which it is the interest of both governments to sustain inviolate

I received instructions from my government therefore, to make urgent remonstrances against this irregular proceeding on the part of Her Majestys government, manifestly unjust in itself and in contradiction to the commercial usages prevalent among enlightened nations. I was instructed, furthermore, to say that the government of the United States felt confident that prompt and efficacious measures would be taken by Her Majestys goverᷠnᷠment to redress the wrongs thus occasioned; and I was instructed to intimate that, in the opinion of the President of the United States, those citizens who had imported any of the articles embraced in the decree into the Havanna between the 20th of February and the 7th. of April 1845, without knowledge at the time of their departure from the United States that the decree had been annulled, were entitled to be indemnified by the Spanish government for the losses they had sustained.

I accordingly on the 15th. June last addressed a note to the foregoing purport to his Excellency Mr Francisco M de la Rosa, Her Majestys first Minister of State; and I trusted that the gravity of the case; the obvious justice of the claim presented, and the importance attached to it by the government of the United States would have procured instant and satisfactory attention to my communication. It is with surprise and regret, therefore, that I find nearly two months suffered to elapse without the least notice being taken of my note, and without even the receipt of it being acknowledged.

To address a second note to the Minister of State appears to me, under present circumstances, useless if he suffered the first to lie unregarded, when he was present in the Capital, it is not likely he would pay more attention to a second, now that he is attending Her Majesty in the distant provinces. Under these circumstances, and knowing the earnestness with which my government looks for a speedy adjustment of this matter, I have deemed it expedient to press it upon the attention of your Excellency.

I will merely observe that it is a case in which nothing is gained by delay; on the contrary, it grows in importance under silence and neglect; so that an act which, if promptly remedied, might be palliated as the unintentional result of hurry or inadvertency, may be tacitly aggravated into a serious cause of offense

I have the honor to be,

> With high consideration, / Your Excellencys Obt St.
> W. I.

MANUSCRIPT: NA, RG 84 (letterbook copy).

This copy is in WI's handwriting. Another copy was enclosed with WI's despatch no. 71, August 23, 1845, to James Buchanan.

1896. To Catharine Paris

Madrid, Aug 9th. 1845

My dear Sister,

I have been a very bad correspondent of late, and have suffered your last letter[1] to lie by me upwards of a month unanswered but you know how much my pen is tasked at present and I am sure will excuse me. I am passing the Summer quite alone at Madrid; almost all my intimates and acquaintances are absent, some with the Court, others on tours or at watering places; every body deserts Madrid during the heats of Summer. Yet this has been a very temperate Season, and I find greater heat prevailing every where else than here. To be sure it is always scorching hot in the Sun; but it is quite a different temperature in the shade. In my saloons, where sun and mid day air are excluded, the thermometer has generally been at 72 degrees and rarely as high as 75 and at night the temperature in the bed rooms is perfect. I have been in the practice for some weeks past, to sally out before Six Oclock in the morning and to pass a couple of hours taking exercise in the Shady walks of the Retiro, or other public promenades. I then remain all day in the house, very lightly clad, until ⟨between⟩ ↑near↓ Seven Oclock in the evening, when I drive out, some distance ⟨in⟩ ↑from↓ the City to where the hills catch any breeze that may be stirring, and there again I take exercise on foot. After which if I do not go to the opera I take a late promenade on the Prado. Thus I manage to get a great deal of air and exercise, without exposing myself to the Summer heat.

My evening drives though lonely are pleasant. You can have no idea of the neighborhood of Madrid from that of other cities. The moment You emerge from the gates you enter upon a desert. Vast wastes as far as the eye can reach, of undulating and in part hilly country; without trees or habitations; green in the early part of the year, and cultivated with grain, but burnt ⟨up⟩ by the summer sun; ⟨and [*one line unrecovered*]⟩ into a variety of browns, some of them rich though sombre. A long picturesque line of mountains closes the landscape to the west and north; on the summits of some of which the snow lingers even in mid summer. The road I generally take, though a main road, is very solitary; now an[d][2] then I meet a group of travellers on horse back, roughly clad, with muskets slung behind their saddles and looking very much like the robbers they are armed against; or a line of Muleteers from the distant provinces, with their mules hung with bells and tricked out with worsted bobs and tassels; or a goatherd, driving ⟨home⟩ his flock of goats home to the city for the night to furnish milk for the inhabitants. Every groupe seems to accord with the wild half savage scenery around; and it is difficult to realize that such scenery and ⟨such⟩ groupes should be in the vicinity of a populous and ancient capital. Some of the sun sets behind the Guadarama mountains, shedding the last golden rays over this vast melancholy landscape, are really magnificent.

I have had much pleasure in walking on the Prado on bright moonlight nights. This is a noble walk within the walls of the city and not far from my dwelling. It has alleys of Stately trees, and is ornamented with fine fountains decorated with Statuary and Sculpture. The Prado is the great promenade of the city. One grand alley is called the Saloon and is particularly crowded. In the Summer evenings there are groupes of ladies and gentlemen seated in chairs and holding their *tertulias* or gossipping parties until a late hour; but what most delights me are the groupes of children, attended by their parents or nurses who gather about the fountains; ⟨and⟩ take hands and dance in rings to their own nursery songs. They are just the little beings for such a fairy moonlight scene. I have watched them night after night, and ⟨performed their⟩ only wished I had some of my own little nieces or grand nieces to take part in the fairy ring. These are all the scenes and incidents that I can furnish you from my present solitary life.

I am looking soon for the return of the Albuquerques to Madrid, which will give me a family circle to resort to. Madame Albuquerque always calls me Uncle and I endeavor to cheat myself into the idea that she is a niece; she certainly has the kindness and amiableness of one; and her children are most entertaining companions for me. She has felt much the death of her father whom she had hoped to see once more on her return to the United States.

Your letter from the Cottage brings with it all the reccollections of the place; its trees and shrubs; its roses and honeysuckles and humming birds. I am glad to find that my old friend the cat bird still builds and sings under the window. You speak of Vaneys barking too; it was like suddenly hearing a well known but long forgotten voice, for it is a long time since any mention has been made of that most meritorious little dog.

You speak of the affection with which the girls have welcomed you back to your old quarters, and of the kind attention with which they treat you. They are dear good girls and I love them all the better for it; though it is nothing but what was to be expected from their affectionate natures. I consider you, however, my representative at the cottage and all kindness shewn to you I feel as shewn to myself. I shall one day have to task their kindness in person, when I too become infirm; and it is soothing to see, from their conduct to you, what I have to expect. I am glad you find the medical Services of Dr Law so efficacious. He is a worthy man and appeared to me to be judicious and careful in his practise; it is very satisfactory to have such a trust worthy physician in a country neighborhood.

Sarah sent me for my perusal a delightful letter which she had received from Julia Grinnell. Julia appeared to be well pleased with her Cottage near Yonkers, and it is fortunate, since she could not have Mr Jones house, that she got within a pleasant drive of Sunny side. These letters about home make me at times quite home sick; I long to be once more among my kith and kin, where I feel interested in all around me, and can persuade myself that they take an interest in me. My heart seems almost starved at Madrid by being kept in such short commons among strangers. However, this is the last year of my exile.

I find, from a delightful letter just received from Helen Pierre, that Oscar and Eliza have entered upon housekeeping and have already had two ⟨gir⟩ of the girls from the Cottage on a visit; and moreover that they have a snug little room fitted up for brother Ebenezer when ⟨call⟩ he visits the city, ⟨we⟩ and called his room. I shall not readily forget this kindness shewn to *my family.* And Oscars son Natt has gone with Uncle Nat[3]—I trust they will suit each other and that Uncle Nat will find in the lad a most reliable *bottle companion.*

Tell brother E. I that I have received ⟨his⟩ two or three letters from him which lie unanswered; but which shall be answered in the fullness of time. Give my affectionate remembrances to your husband, who I hope will survive all the changes of Custom house administration give my love to all the girls from Kate even unto Charlie and believe me ever my dear Sister

Your affectionate brother
Washington Irving

MANUSCRIPT: Yale.   PUBLISHED: PMI, III, 376–78 (in part).

1. This and the letters from Helen and Ebenezer Irving mentioned later have not been located.

2. WI omitted the bracketed letter.

3. Nathaniel Paulding Irving (1826–1869) was Oscar Irving's older son, named after his grandmother Julia's brother, Nathaniel Paulding, who was a wine merchant.

1897. To Sarah Storrow

Madrid, Aug 9th. 1845

My dear Sarah,

I am very much fagged by *pen work*, so must get you to put up with a very brief scraw[l][1] in reply to your long and delightful letter[2] from Frascatis Hotel, treating of your visit to the Isle of Wight and other agreeable Subjects. How much I feel our Separation whenever you give me an account of your travels; I think we are so suited to travel together; or rather I should have my old romance of travel so much revived by having you for a companion. I should delight too in having the little women to attend to; for you know the ways and whims of children are a perpetual amusement to me. Kate above all others, is my caprice, from her thousand little fidgetty peculiarities. I shall almost regret when she grows to be a "reasonable being"

By your letter it would appear that Mr Beasley is returned from Bordeaux and once more at his little Snuggery the *"Juste Milieu"* I am glad to hear it. You will find him a most cordial neighbor. I beg you to give him my most affectionate remembrances. I wish I was nestled with him for a little while just now, that I might make some excursions with you about the neighboring country. What a penance it is to be cooped up thus in a place like Madrid, surrounded by a desert and from whence there are no excursions. However it is the last summer I shall pass here; and the last year I shall be severed from my friends.

I return you Julias letter which I have read with great pleasure. I have likewise had a long letter from Helen Pierre, giving me a budget of family News. How these letters draw me homeward! I long to be once more in the Midst of the family connexions where I can visit from one to the other, and every where meet kind looks and kind hearts; beings that I love and that love me. It seems as if a return to such a circle will almost repay me for the social sterility in which I have so long existed.

I hope while you are at Havre you will profit by your vicinity to the Sea and take saltwater baths. I think you will find them very strengthening. The pure sea breezes, also, which you enjoy on the Côte are quite reviving. I find by my letters from New York they have been suffering greatly from heat there: only think of ninety degrees of Farenheit in the dining room and ninety three in the bed room, at a Hotel on Staten Island, where they go for the sake of *air*—While in the hottest days this summer the thermometer in my saloons has not risen above seventy five; while my bed rooms are at nights of a delightful temperature. However, the Spanish houses are calculated for hot weather; and this summer has been uncommonly temperate.

I am longing for the return of the Albuquerques, that I may have a family circle where I may resort; I trust they will be here in the course of ten or twelve days. My kind friends the O'Sheas will not be back until ⟨the⟩ late in the Autumn

Oscar and Eliza have gone to housekeeping and seem to have commenced on a kind, warm hearted plan. Two of the girls from the Cottage have already been on a visit to them; as has Julia Grinnell; and a snug little room is set apart for your uncle Ebenezer whenever he shall come to town and is called to his room. God bless them! I wish I had a big bag of money to lay at their door—but I shall find some way or other of proving to them how Sensible I am of this kindness to *my family*

Farewell my dear Sarah. Kiss the darling little women for me; dont let Kate forget me and teach little Susie my name as soon as she can talk.

Your affectionate uncle
Washington Irving

ADDRESSED: Madame / Madame Storrow / No 4. Rue de la Victoire / à Paris
MANUSCRIPT: Yale.

1. WI omitted the bracketed letter.
2. This and the letter from Helen Irving mentioned in the third paragraph have not been located. The Grand Hôtel Frascati was located on the beach near the battery at the entrance to the harbor at Le Havre. See Karl Baedeker, *Northern France*, p. 56 and map on opposite page.

1898. To Francisco Martínez de la Rosa

Legation of the U States / Madrid, Aug 12th. 1845

His Exy. / Don Francisco M de la Rosa / &c &c &c

Sir

It is with much regret that I find myself again obliged to urge the action of Her Majestys Government in a case long since, and repeatedly, presented for its consideration[.] I allude to the case of Michael Drawson Harang, a citizen of the United States, claiming the restitution of several thousand dollars wrongfully exacted by the Intendente of the Island of Porto Rico, from the proceeds of the Sale of the estate of Luis Alexander Harang, deceased, under the title of *derechos de extraccion,* and in contravention of treaties existing between the United States and Spain.

The claimant who represents the heirs of the deceased, first attempted, many years since, to get redress from the tribunals of the island, but was put off with the declaration that the case, with all its documents, had been referred to Her Majestys government at Madrid. To Her Majestys government, therefore, he addressed himself, through my predecessor M. Vail, but with no better success, so that, on my taking charge of this legation, I found the claim among the matters especially charged by my government, upon my attention. I accordingly addressed a note on the 24th. of September 1842 to Count Almodovar, then Minister of State and of Foreign affairs, giving a full statement of the case, and complaining of the delay that had already occurred in its adjustment. Count Almodovar in reply observed, that, finding the claim pending before the tribunals of Porto Rico, he had ordered enquiries to be made in the matter, the result of which he would communicate to me.

A year and eight months elapsed without my receiving any further communication from Her Majestys government on the subject. I therefore on the 16 June 1844 addressed a note respecting it to His Excellency the Marques of Viluma, then Minister of State. He retired from office before he had time to reply. I made a verbal representation of the case to General Narvaez who held the office *ad interim*. With his characteristic promptness he wrote me a note dated the 20th July, informing me that, on the same day, the Minister of Finance had been written to, with urgency, for information in the premises, and that, as soon as he should receive such information he would send me an explicit answer. I was also assured, about the same time, at the department of State, that a reply was actually in the course of preparation. General Narvaez, however, ceased to have charge of the department of State and, with his relinquishment of it, apparently ceased all further attention to this case; the promised reply having never been forwarded to this legation, nor any any[1] other communication made on the subject by Her Majestys Government.

Thus for nearly ten years has this claim been in a manner bandied backward and forward between the Colonies and the mother country, and between tribunals and departments; answers have been promised to this legation but have never been sent, and there would seem to be a disposition to evade all definite action in the case and tacitly to consign it to oblivion.

The respect, however, which this legation owes to itself and to the government which it represents, will not permit it passively to acquiesce in such inattention to a matter which has so repeatedly been made the subject of earnest communications and I now most respectfully, but urgently, claim from Her Majestys government that explicit answer in the case which has so long been promised.

I have the honor to be,

        With high consideration, / Your Excellencys Obt Servt

                                       W. I.

MANUSCRIPT: NA, RG 84 (letterbook copy).

This copy is in WI's handwriting.

1. WI repeated "any."

1899. To George P. Putnam

                                   Madrid, August 13, 1845.

Geo. P. Putnam, Esq.

Dear Sir:

I have to acknowledge the receipt of your letter of July 7th as well as one, on the same subject, dated 1st March last,[1] from your House in New York.

I do not know any House in which I would confide more implicitly than in yours for fair and honorable dealing; but it has one disadvantage in respect to a new work; you publish on both sides of the water, and your cheap New York editions would stand very much in the way of a bargain with a London publisher.

The terms you offer are very probably liberal, in the present state of the "literary market" but they show how the want of an international copyright, by inundating the country with foreign works, published at so low a rate as scarcely to yield a profit to the publisher, is calculated to starve native literature.

However, I have nothing now at present that I am prepared to launch before the public; neither am I willing just now that any of my former works should be published separately.

I am preparing a complete edition of my works,[2] with corrections, alterations, additions, and when in a sufficient state of forwardness, it is my idea to make an arrangement for the whole, (and perhaps for any new writings I may have ready for the press) either by disposing of the copyrights, or by turning them out collectively for a term of years, at a yearly consideration.

I think I can then show, when I come to make such an arrangement, how, in the hands of an extensive publishing house, my writings may be made available in a variety of ways. They are voluminous, yet varied; they may be published collectively and separately; they may be thrown into various forms, series of titles, of essays, of sketches; they may form parts of series of similar writings by other authors, etc., all of which arrangements and modifications I would undertake to superintend.

If, hereafter, I can make a satisfactory arrangement of this kind with your House, I assure you there is none with which I would be more happy to deal.

I am, dear Sir, / Very respectfully, / Your friend and servant,
Washington Irving.

PUBLISHED: G. H. Putnam, *A Memoir of George Palmer Putnam* (New York, 1903), pp. 138–40.

1. These letters have not been located.
2. This was to be the Author's Revised Edition, which Putnam's published in fifteen volumes between 1848 and 1850.

1900.   *To Sarah Storrow*

Madrid, Aug 14th. 1845.

My dear Sarah,

I have just received your long delightful letter of 7th. ↑(Four days since I received that of July 31.)↓[1] How kind it is to keep up such a frequent correspondence with one so far away, when you have such darling objects at hand to engross your time and your affections. You complain of the length of time which had elapsed since you had heard from me; I trust you have before this ⟨written⟩ Received a couple of letters which I wrote one on the 2d. and the other on I believe the 9th. of Aug.

I am glad you are so well pleased with Havre, as it is a place to which you can get with such facility from Paris, and where you can be so much at your ease; beside commanding so many advantages as to health and recreation. I have always had a great liking for Havre; partly from old associations, and there is no place where I should more have liked to pass part of the summer with you. I am glad too it proves so beneficial to all your healths; as you will now know where to repair to when you find strength and appetite flagging. I am glad Susies temper only gives way at meal times. It is a sign it is an affair of the Stomach instead of the heart: a keen appetite rather than a cross temper. The delightful sea breezes of the Cote have a most potent effect upon the appetite as I have often had occasion to experience. How much I was struck with the first view from that Cote; and I never have ceased to enjoy it. I wish I had it now within reach to vary my morning rambles.

I know no sea port that has such a beautiful scite close by for rural residences. You are at such a short distance from the City; it lies almost at your feet; you see all the movements of the port, the arrival and departure of vessels; it is a complete animated picture; and at the Same time you are nestled away aloft, among groves and gardens; have all the quiet and retirement of the country and inhale the invigorating breezes of the ocean.

It was fortunate you had the worthy little captain to act as Cicerone to you on your first rambles about the Cote. He is almost a feature of Havre; having frequented it throughout almost the whole of his life. I shall look for an account of the breakfast on board of the Oneida; and only wish I could be there to partake of it.

I am amused with the idea of Kates dreaming; or rather, with her having any notion what dreaming was; or in what it differed from reality. And then the idea of her dreaming of little Tom Pouce—I suppose he is quite her hero of romance.

I want to know if Kate still does penance occasionally in the dark closet; or if she has got quite above all correction of the kind; and whether she ever attempts to shut up Susie in the closet as she used to shut up her dolls; which I believe were two thirds of the time doing penance.

Poor Pampolino Thorne![2] What troubles and cross purposes he has with his rebellious family. As I wish him well, notwithstanding all his folly, I hope the daughter, who is about to be married, has made a good choice; the chances however are against her. Thorne must now ⟨beg⟩ feel more and more what Sacrafices he has made of real happiness and substantial respectability, to empty shew and fashion. The report has got about that he is almost ruined in fortune. I do not believe it; but if his family breaks up into seperate establishments the fortune that has enabled them to live in style must be broken up too; or some of the parties will be almost destitute. The very rumor of ruin, however, has despelled the prestige with which Thorne had managed to surround himself, and people now shrug their shoulders when they talk of him; and unless he can continue to give fetes he will find his saloons deserted. I hope he may carry home property enough to live respectably in his own country; and may have gained experience enough to make a wise use of it. He carries home with him, however, some domestic inmates that will give him trouble; and he leaves behind the pearl of his family, Madame de Varenne, who appeared to me a most amiable and estimable person.

Aug 16. I have just recd. a letter from Charles A Davis[3] (Major Jack Downing) who is in London for the first time, enjoying himself greatly and delighted with every thing around him. It is probable you will see him in Paris as he intends passing some little time there. He had intended when he left home, to visit Spain but I fear he has given up the idea. I should be delighted to see him here. Mrs Jack Downing, is not with him I believe, so that you will not have the pleasure of meeting ⟨which⟩ with her in Paris.

I doubt whether the McLanes will visit Paris. They paid it a brief visit when they were in Europe before; but did not seem much pleased; ⟨Neither⟩ Mr McLane does not ⟨t⟩ Speak French; and I doubt whether Mrs McL. does. All Paris therefore passed before them, as it were, in dumb show. You yourself must be aware how much Paris has gained upon you in its delights since (thanks to your indefatigable study) you have made yourself mistress of the language.

I have been expecting the return of the Albuquerques, but they still linger at Barcelona from the almost impossibility of securing an apartment in Madrid, they having had to give up their former one, prior to leaving the Capital. It is astonishing how Madrid is filling up with inhabitants and how difficult it is to meet with apartments; though new houses are building in every direction. In the present emergency I have written to the Albuquerques urging them to come on at once and take up their quarters with me until they can look round and find an apartment to suit them. I have ample room for the whole of them (⟨;⟩ for Spanish houses are not cramped up like houses in Paris) and I shall be delighted to have them all under my roof. I have been leading such a lonely life of late, in the midst of crowds, that my heart seems half famished for the want of social sympathies. I long to have beings about me for whom I feel a real regard and who I trust have the same for me; with whom in short I can feel that I am a *fellow creature*. Madrid is a place where a stranger is always a stranger. I do not speak this merely from my own experience; for in my own case I should attribute it in a great measure to a shyness which sometimes isolates me among strangers; and requires to be overcome by cordiality; but I find the same remark made by ⟨other⟩ almost all the foreigners I have met here some of whom have lived here for years. Certainly when I leave Madrid there will be no cordial ties painfully broken between me and any of its native inhabitants; though I shall bear them general good will. They have been civil to me[.] I cannot blame them for not caring for me; especially as I have taken no pains to interest them

However, I do not at any time nor in any place, care for a large circle of acquaintance. It is rather a tax upon my time, my spirits and my convenience; but I require social intercourse with a few; and a *very few* are sufficient for me. Their intimacy is heartfelt and confiding. If I could have you and your children with me I could content myself even at Madrid.

I see by your late letters you have Miss Tessier[4] for an occasional visitor. Does she admire the babes as much as ever; I presume so by your appearing to value her visits.

Let me hear how Kate relishes sea bathing. I do not think it worth while to bother poor little Susie with it. The air bath of the Cote appears to be quite Sufficient for her, as she ⟨has⟩ is in such good looks and ⟨likes?⟩ has such an angry appetite. I really long to see the dear little woman; and I keep a list of all her growing accomplishments; rolling on the carpet, kicking, sucking her thumb and smelling to a flower! I beg you to let me hear of every new one.

your affectionate uncle
Washington Irving

P.S. I received a letter about a month since from a Mr Samuel I Hunt of New York, but actually in Paris, and who told me he had a letter of introduction to me from Mr Grinnell. He was desirous of making a tour in Spain, with his wife and daughter in the latter part of August, and wished to know whether it would be safe for females, to come to Madrid and travel in the interior. I have let him know ↑that↓ the roads throughout the greater parts of Spain have been ⟨rendered⟩ freed from robbers of late, by the institution of a "garde civile" or Gendarmerie; but that ladies must make up their minds to put up with many privations and inconveniences.

Do you know any thing of Mr Hunt and his family. If they are agreeable people I should be well pleased to see them here.

Remember me kindly to the Gibbs's[5]

ADDRESSED: Madame / Madame Storrow / no 4. Rue de la Victoire / à Paris
MANUSCRIPT: Yale.

1. These letters and that from Charles A. Davis mentioned later have not been located.

2. WI may be referring to Colonel Herman Thorn, whom he met in Paris in 1842. See WI to Catharine Paris, June 10, 1842.

3. Charles Augustus Davis (1795–1867), a New York merchant and humorist whose letters of J. Downing had created a sensation with their satire against Andrew Jackson when they appeared in the New York *Daily Advertiser* in 1830.

4. A young lady from Philadelphia visiting in Paris, mentioned in WI to Sarah Storrow, February 21 and March 12, 1845.

5. Perhaps the family of Thomas Gibbes, whose daughter Charlotte married John Jacob Astor III on December 19, 1846. For other details see WI to Sarah Storrow, February 15, 1847.

1901. *To James Buchanan*

Legation of the United States / Madrid Aug 23d. 1845

No 71 / Hon James Buchanan / Secretary of State, Washington

Sir,

I have the honor to acknowledge the receipt of Despatch No 47, with its enclosure.

I transmit herewith a copy of a note addressed to Mr Martinez de la Rosa, concerning the long pending case of Michael Drawson Harang. Also a note to Mr Alexander Mon, Minister of Finance, relative to the nullification of the Cuba decree. The reply of Mr Mon, herewith sent, states that the matter is undergoing investigation; a usual reply with the Spanish government when pecuniary indemnity is required.

The royal tour to the Basque provinces has so far been unattended with any adverse political circumstances. The Biscayons both in town and country appear to be gratified by the visit ⌐of their youthful Sovereign,⌐ and flattered by the frank and confiding manner in which she moves among them. Her tour, therefore, may strengthen her cause and render her popular in that hitherto doubtful part of her dominions.[1]

The meeting of the Cabinet ministers at Saragossa,[2] instead of producing a crisis, had the effect of clearing up misunderstandings and welding them more firmly together. Indeed their common safety would seem to forbid discord or disunion; being assailed from all quarters; even by many of their former adherents. The Queen Mother is supposed to have a controlling influence at present over the affairs of the cabinet.

For some days past Madrid has presented a singular Scene; a kind of passive insurrection.[3] The merchants and tradespeople have made common cause against the new law of taxes or contributions. At first they proceeded by the way of memorials to the queen; but, fearing these would be of no avail; they agreed to shut up shop and suspend all business, until their prayer was granted. The authorities had taken timely measures to prevent any scarcity of provisions by providing extra supplies of bread and butchers meat, and they furthermore, on the first day of the movement, rendered it penal for those who dealt in articles of subsistence to keep their shops closed. Troops were stationed in various parts of the city and others patrolled it day and night, to prevent any tumult. The inhabitants however do not appear in general to have contemplated any thing more than a passive resistance to the law. Some idlers and ruffians as usual attempted to get up commotions; and a life or two were lost and a few persons wounded; but all attempts at riot were easily suppressed. Many persons have been arrested, most of whom will probably be liberated when the agitation is past. One unfortunate taylor, who threw a brick at the Gefe Politico (or chief of the Municipal authorities) has been made a severe example of being tried ↑(by a military tribunal)↓ condemned and shot within three days after the offence had been committed: though the Gefe Politico, himself, interceded for a mitigation of the sentence.

These prompt and energetic measures have had their effect. To day most of the shops are open and business is resuming its usual current. The city is quiet, but gloomy and discontented. It has received a mortifying proof how completely it is under the iron hand of military rule. If there were, in fact, any revolutionary schemes connected with this public movement they have been frustrated: and the devisors have been made sensible how difficult it is without a national militia and a progresista municipality to get up a pronunciamento.

> I am Sir / Very respectfully / Your Obt Servt
> Washington Irving

DOCKETED: Recd. Sept. 22 / Mr. Markoe [*upper left corner, page 1*] / No. 71. W. Irving. Madrid. 23 Aug. 1845
MANUSCRIPT: NA, RG 59.

This entire despatch is in WI's handwriting.

1. The queen proceeded from Barcelona to Cervera to Saragossa to Pamplona to San Sebastián, where she arrived in August. See *La Gaceta*, July 2 to August 5, 1845.

2. See *La Posdata*, July 31, 1845.

3. For details, see *La Posdata*, August 18–23, 1845.

1902. *To Sarah Storrow*

Madrid Aug 29th. 1845

My dear Sarah,

I believe I have suffered a week to elapse without writing to you, but in fact I have not had time. The Albuquerque family ⟨f⟩ left Barcelona ten or twelve days since and set out for Madrid, expecting, from the tenor of my letters that I had secured an apartment for them. In the mean time the proprietor of the apartment disappointed me, and to my dismay I found the whole family of the Albuquerques, man woman and child; bag and baggage, on the road without a home to come to. In this emergency I prepared quarters for them in my own house, which is sufficiently ample to quarter a regiment. Here then they have been with me for Several days past. You may easily concieve what a change it has made in my late lonely habitation. It is now full of life and bustle. 1 am once more in the bosom of a family and it seems almost as if it were my own family; for the children all call me Uncle and seem to consider me as such. Madame Albuquerque always does the same; and I almost persuade myself that she is one of my thousand and one nieces. As the Albuquerques are at a loss where to find a habitation in the present crowded state of Madrid; and as I have the prospect of leaving here at all events in the Spring—We are talking of an arrangement which would be mutually accommodating, ↑viz↓ for me to transfer the whole establishment to them, in the same way that Mr Vail transferred it to me. I retaining a géte[?] in the house and the office of the Legation there, as long as I may remain in Madrid. This would relieve me from all the perplexities and sacrafices and delays of breaking up an establishment and disposing of the furniture &c; and leave me at liberty to march at a moments warning. Dont you think it would be an excellent arrangement?

I received the day before yesterday your letter of the 19th.[1] and am delighted with the happy spirit which breathes throughout it. You have a fund of happiness my dear Sarah in your own genial and Susceptible nature: so easily pleased; and with such a relish for simple and innocent pleasures. I am glad you are so well satisfied with Havre. It is a favorite place with me and I think it is one of the very best you could resort to in Summer You have pure bracing and enlivening sea breezes; the freshness and quiet of the country; and ⟨the⟩ no Royal nor Aristocratical neighbors to look you down and to ride over you Every thing around you is in harmony with your own condition. The ⟨excu⟩ occasional visit to Havre is really ⟨an⟩ ↑a pleasurable↓ excursion for Mr Storrow; ⟨which has the character of a party of pleasure rather than⟩ His daily journey to and from Versailles must have cut up his time, and degenerated into something of a fag. I regret I could not be of your party to breakfast on board of the Oneida; and that I could not be with you to explore the country within the reach of a days excursion about Havre. It is full of beauty and historical interest.

I am scribbling this in spite of frequent interruptions; having young folks about me who have as little respect for my literary avocations as ever little Kate had. By the bye they have heard me talk so much about little Kate that they have formed a kind of acquaintance with her, and often ask questions concerning her.

Give my love to her and to dear little Susie whose sweet temper appears to be sharpening in the Sea breeze. I am quite amused with the idea of her striking Kate; it is quite an act of rebellion. I dont dislike her shewing a little Spirit.

With kind remembrances to Mr Storrow

Your affectionate Uncle
Washington Irving

MANUSCRIPT: Yale.

1. This letter has not been located.

1903.   To Charles Callaghan

Madrid Aug 31, 1845

Charles Callaghan Esq / Philadelphia

Sir

In reply to your letter of July 31st[1] I would observe that I know of nothing on the subject to which you refer that is not already known to the Department of State; to which I would refer you for any information you may require in the premises. From that Department alone I can receive instructions as to any Steps which may be deemed expedient in this matter

I am Sir very respectfully / Your Ob St
W I.

MANUSCRIPT: NA, RG 84 (letterbook copy).

This copy is in WI's handwriting.

1. In his letter Callaghan had requested information about the manner in which the Spanish government planned to pay the interest on the indemnity debt falling due on February 14 and August 14, 1845 (NA, RG 84).

1904.   To Sarah Storrow

Madrid Sept 6th. 1845

My dear Sarah,

This is the country of revolutions and one has just taken place in my own domains. I have made a transfer of my establishment (furniture &c) to the Albuquerques with whom I shall live *en famille* for the residue of my residence in Madrid; having the intention to send home my resignation, so as to be Relieved from my post by the opening of Spring; if not before. I retain a small part of the apartment, and maintain the office of the Legation there. This arrangement suits us all admirably. The Albuquerques have a commodious well furnished house ready provided for them, at a time when they were at their wits end to find a habitation; and I ⟨de⟩ am saved all the trouble, delay and sacrafice of breaking up and selling off an establishment by piece meal. In the mean time being now relieved from the responsibilities of house keeping I have resolved upon making a brief visit to Paris and shall set off in the Malle Poste with Lorenzo on the evening of the ninth; so that [you][1] will see me within a very few days after the Receipt of this letter. I wish nothing to be said of ⟨this⟩ my Coming, as I shall have to be for a part of the time *incog*. In fact I have to see Mr Brewster or some other skillful dentist and transact some very troublesome business with him, which may oblige me to keep out of sight for some days. If I can I will arrange to pass the time with my friend Beasley; provided he is reinstated in his house in Havre. This is a very embarrassing matter which I have deferred as long as I dare. You will say nothing about it. When it is all over I will pass a brief time with you and then return to Madrid until regularly relieved from my post by a successor. When we return Lorenzo undertakes the superintendance of Mr Albuquerques household, ⟨as he has⟩ in the same capacity that he has lived with me. The faithful Juana likewise remains as Housekeeper and ladys maid; and my excellent cook retains his office, so that I shall have my old servants about me. At present I am living delightfully in the Albuquerque family; and feel quite as if I were among relatives.

I defer all further discussions until we meet when I shall have the inexpressible pleasure of once more seeing you and your dear little ones. Give my affectionate remembrances to Mr Storrow

Your affectionate Uncle
W.I.

P. S I have just received your long and delightful letter of the 29th[2] giving me a host of amusing particulars about the little people which make me more eager than ever to see them.

⟨There will⟩

You need not trouble yourself ⟨about⟩ to make arrangements for my reception should Marianne[3] be with you ↑while I am in Paris↓ I can readily find quarters in some hotel not far off

ADDRESSED: Madame / Madame Storrow / 4 Rue de la Victoire / a Paris

MANUSCRIPT: Yale.   PUBLISHED: PMI, III, 378–79   (in part).

1. WI omitted the bracketed word.
2. This letter has not been located.
3. Probably Marianne Van Wart, Sarah's English cousin.

1905.   To James Buchanan

Paris. Oct 1t. 1845

The Hon. / James Buchanan / Secretary of State. Washington.

Sir,
    The sudden recurrence of a Herpetic malady which has afflicted me more or less ↑during↓ ⟨for⟩ a great part of my residence in Madrid; induced me to make a hasty journey to Paris for the benefit of medical advice ↑and treatment↓ before the approach of winter. I shall set out on my return as soon as I find myself in travelling condition, which I trust will be in the course of a fortnight; in the mean time the business of the Legation will be faithfully attended to by the Secretary, Mr Jasper H Livingston

I am Sir, / Very respectfully / Your Obt Servt
Washington Irving

DOCKETED: Mr. Markoe
MANUSCRIPT: NA, RG 59.

1906.   To John Miller

Paris 11th October 1845

John Miller Esqre, London

Sir,
    I enclose a draft ⟨payable⟩ on Messrs Baring and Co payable to your order for £6..15..6d being the amount of your postage account against this Legation for the last Quarter

Very respectfully / Your obt servant
Signed—Washington Irving

MANUSCRIPT: NA, RG 84 (letterbook copy).

1907. To Sabina O'Shea

[October 31, 1845]

My dear Mrs O'Shea

I have to go out at an early hour today on business but will be with you between one and two oclock.

Very truly yours
Washington Irving

⟨Saturday⟩ ↑Friday↓ Oct. 31 [1845]

ADDRESSED: Madame / Madame O'Shea / Hotel de Bristol / Place Vendome
    DOCKETED: 31st. October — —
MANUSCRIPT: HSA.   PUBLISHED: Penney, *Bulletin NYPL*, 62 (December, 1958),
    619.

The date was determined by the perpetual calendar.

1908. To Catharine Paris

Paris Nov 1t 1845

My dear Sister,

I have suffered a long time to elapse without writing to you but in fact I have been *Spell bound* in respect to letter writing and have written to scarcely any body. I even now take my pen at the eleventh hour, to scrawl a hasty line merely to break the spell.

A letter to Pierre written early in September[1] informed you all of the sudden transfer of my establishment at Madrid to my good friends the Albuquerques. It was an arrangement satisfactory to all parties excepting to my poor servants, who at first were quite in consternation. Madame Albuquerque agreed to retain Lorenzo, the cook, and Juana; Lorenzo was to accompany me in my visit to Paris and on his return to take charge of the household as before. ⟨He?⟩ Poor Juana was at first quite inconsolable. She could hardly be reassured that I intended to return from Paris and for several days could hardly speak to me without the tears coming into her eyes. She said she had hoped always to remain with me until she was married to her cousin; ⟨[*unrecovered*]⟩ (who is studying medicine and to whom she is to be married on his being admitted to practise.) On my taking leave she hung round me and cried like a child. She is an excellent and most respectable girl and has proved a most faithful servant. Madame Albuquerque has promised to be all kindness to her and I am persuaded she will keep her word. My old coachman Pedro remains in the household until my return—unless the carriage & horses are previously disposed of.

Lorenzo and myself travelled as usual by Malle Poste to Bayonne. There I ⟨booked⟩ hired a carriage and posted to Bordeaux; making a little tour however along the skirts of the Pyrenees to Pau² the birthplace of Henry the fourth,³ ⟨one⟩ and one of the most beautiful places as to prospects and scenery in the South of France; thence I proceeded to the ⟨Riv⟩ banks of the Garonne; ⟨and⟩ to the little town of Tonneins, and thence along the course of that River to Bordeaux. My visit to Tonneins and the banks of the Garonne was induced by reccollections of my youthful days. On my first visit to Europe, when I was but about twenty one years of age, my first journey was up along the banks of this river on my way to Montpelier; and the Scenery of it remained in my memory with all the magic effects of first impressions. ⟨This was a pleasant pa?⟩ I had pleasant travelling companions in the diligence, among them was a young French officer not much older than myself, returning home on leave of absence. When the diligence stopped in the country towns to change horses ⟨we⟩ the passengers used to stroll through the streets; making observations, and chatting ⟨in with Fren⟩ with French sociability with every one they met. As we were strolling in this way through the streets of Tonnein,⁴ we came to a house where a number of girls were quilting. The windows were low ⟨so th⟩ and open so that we had a full view into the room. My companions entered into lively conversation with the girls who were very merry. The latter were particularly amused with my broken French. At length one of them asked who I was; and was informed by one of my companions that I was an English prisoner whom the young officer had in charge—and what would be done with me—"Oh; thrown into prison—perhaps shot!—" In an instant all the gaiety of the kind hearted creatures was at an end. There were ejaculations of pity on all sides—"I was so young!—So far from my family & friends &c &c—" I happened to be thirsty and asked for a glass of water. They flew to serve me; brought wine and fruit, and as the dilligence drove up obliged me to fill my pockets with the latter. Some of them got round the young officer to intercede in my behalf and to charge him to be kind to me. It was a shame to leave them with such painful impressions. I am convinced the poor young English prisoner remained a melancholy theme of gossip among the good people of Tonneins.

The reccollection of this incident induced me to shape my course so as to strike the river just at this little town. A beautiful place it is; situated on a ⟨height⟩ high *cote,* commanding a wide view of the Garonne and the magnificent and fertile region through which it flows[.] I found all ⟨the⟩ ↑my↓ early impressions of the beauty of the scenery fully justified; and almost felt a kindling of the youthful romance with which I once gazed upon it. As my carriage rattled through the quiet streets of Tonnein and the postilion smacked his whip with the French love of racket I looked out for the house where forty years before I had seen the quilting party. I believe I recognized the house; and I saw two or three old women who might once have formed part of the merry groupe of girls; but I doubt whether they recognized in the ↑stout↓ elderly gentleman thus rattling in his carriage through their streets the pale young English prisoner of forty years since

My journey brought on an irritation of my old malady with a return of which I had been troubled before leaving Madrid. I was obliged to lie by two days at Bordeaux. Then proceeded in a steamer by sea to Nantes; then ascended the Loire in steamers through very beautiful and historical scenery; and at Orleans took the rail road to Paris; where I arrived quite the worse for a fortnight of fatiguing travel. For some time I was obliged to keep quiet ⟨and re⟩ having a bilious attack beside a pretty troublesome turn of my old malady. I have now, however, got the better of both, and trust to be able in the course of a few days to return for the last time to Madrid.

I have found Sarah in excellent health and looks; and her children every thing that could be wished. I have had the pleasure too of finding Marianne here, who, however, set off yesterday on her return home.

I have ↑just↓ received a budget of letters from home; from Charlie, from your Irving, from Pierre &c[5]—to which I will reply when more in the vein.

I trust this letter will find you restored by cool and bracing weather; to your usual health and free from that nervousness, which the Summer heats had brought upon you. I have scrawled at greater length than I thought I should be able to do when I sat down to write. The hour is come to send off the letter to Mr Storrows counting house to be forwarded—and I can only conclude with love to all bodies

Your affectionate brother
Washington Irving

Manuscript: SHR.   Published: PMI, I, 71–72 (in part).

1. This letter has not been located.
2. Pau is about sixty-three miles east of Bayonne.
3. Henry IV became king of France in 1589.
4. WI sometimes neglected to include the final *s* on "Tonneins."
5. These letters have not been located.

1909. To Sabina O'Shea

[November 4, 1845]

My dear Mrs O'Shea,

I send you an american work in which you will see the professional character of Mons. Jobert de Lamballe[1] fully set forth. He appears to be a surgeon of high qualifications.

Very truly yours
Washington Irving.

Tuesday, Nov. 4th. [1845]

MANUSCRIPT: HSA.   PUBLISHED: Penney, *Bulletin NYPL*, 62 (December, 1958), 619.

The year has been determined by the perpetual calendar.

1. Antoine Joseph Jobert de Lamballe (1799–1867), a highly respected French physician and professor.

1910. To Catharine Ellis

[Paris, November 6, 1845]

My dear Mrs Ellis,

I send you the engraved portrait of Columbus[1] which I spoke of last evening; and also the pamphlet illustrative of it. The portrait appears to me to possess very fair claims to authenticity.

Very truly yours
Washington Irving

Paris Nov. 6th. [1845]

MANUSCRIPT: Andrew B. Myers.

Catherine Ellis, the niece of William R. King, U.S. minister to France, served as official hostess for her bachelor uncle. As his frequent references to her in his letters suggest, WI was very favorably impressed with her.

1. This was a copy of a recently discovered oil portrait of Columbus, an engraving of which was given to WI by Edmond François Jomard, principal of the Royal Library in Paris. According to Thacher, Jomard had discussed the portrait in *Bulletin de la Société de Géographie*, 3d ser. 3, 369. When WI speaks of the "pamphlet," he may be referring to this article. See John Boyd Thacher, *Christopher Columbus, His Life, His Work, His Remains*, 3 vols. (New York, 1967), III, 47, 62. WI later describes the painting of Columbus in letters to Joseph E. Bloomfield, October 28, 1851, and to William C. Bryant [December 20[?], 1851].

1911.   To Henry O'Shea

Paris, Nov. 11th. 1845

My dear OShea

Mrs O'Shea is getting on as well as could be expected considering that she drives three doctors in hand, and each pulls a different way. One gave her a sad panic the other day. He represented her case as ⟨a⟩ critical; told her that it was an affair for the whole winter; that she must not stir out; must keep perfectly quiet and undergo very painful treatment. I accordingly found her lying on a sopha; frightened out of sleep and appetite and nervous to a degree. So she continued for three days during the absence of her first Physician; who was occupied with the accouchement of the princess de Joinville. When he returned he succeeded in persuading her that the council of the rival physician was all humbug, and assured her she might drive out & enjoy air and sunshine, without fear of harm. She has accordingly resumed her drives; begins to talk cheerfully; and even to laugh again, and is none the worse for it. The name of the Doctor who was for her "lying up" for the winter ⟨was⟩ is *Job*art. I fancy he thought to make a job of it. He ought to be President of the ⟨laying up⟩ "lying up hospital" if there is such an institution. She now talks of reducing her establishment to one Doctor, and I am in hopes will get hearty in spite of him.

I see her every day and shall continue to pay her every attention consistent with propriety—more could not be expected from me.

While I am thus attentive to your wife during your absence I would reccommend my own interests to your kind attention at Madrid. As I have no doubt you have the flesh pots of Egypt at your command I wish you would now and then dip in the ladle for me. I can at any time command a few thousand dollars in case of need, and will really feel greatly obliged to you if you can conveniently use them as seed corn to produce an abundant crop.

Give my regards to Willy and believe me very faithfully yours

Washington Irving

Henry O'Shea Esq / &c &c &c

Docketed: Washington Irving / Novber. 11th. 1845.
Manuscript: HSA.   Published: Penney, *Bulletin NYPL*, 62 (December, 1958), 620.

1912.   To Sabina O'Shea

[November 13, 1845]

My dear Mrs O'Shea,

As I have not heard from you to the contrary I presume the engagement holds good for the theatre this evening. If so, what is your dinner
hour.

I hope you have good news from Mr O'Shea

Very truly yours
Washington Irving

Thursday, Nov. 13th. [1845]

ADDRESSED: Madame / Madame O'Shea / Hotel de Bristol   DOCKETED: 13th.
Novber.
MANUSCRIPT: HSA.   PUBLISHED: Penney, *Bulletin NYPL*, 62 (December, 1958),
620.

1913.   To Pierre M. Irving

[Paris,] Nov. 15, 1845

He[1] is very anxious about the state of our affairs with England. The
Oregon question is becoming more and more difficult of adjustment. * * *
Much will depend upon the temper and language of the forthcoming Mes-
sage of Mr. Polk.

PUBLISHED: PMI, III, 380.

1. Louis McLane, the U.S. minister at London, who had tentatively planned to
visit Paris, where he hoped to confer with WI.

1914.   To Sabina O'Shea

[November 15, 1845]

My dear Mrs O'Shea

The day is so damp and dismal that I doubt whether you will feel
inclined to drive to the Bois de Bologne[.] I will, therefore, crave your
indulgence to excuse me from calling on you at two oclock; and will devote the day to paying off some visits which are weighing on my con-

science and which I dare not postpone longer without risk of giving offence.

I have a letter from Mr Livingston who tells me Mr O'Shea celebrated his return to Madrid by passing an incredible number of times at cards at the Ambassadors.

Yours very truly
Washington Irving

Saturday, Nov. 15. [1845]

ADDRESSED: Madame / Madame O'Shea / Hotel dé Bristol   DOCKETED: 15th.
Novber.
MANUSCRIPT: HSA.   PUBLISHED: Penney, *Bulletin NYPL*, 62 (December, 1958), 620–21.

1915. To Catharine Paris

Paris Nov 30th. 184⟨6⟩5

My dear Sister

I am still lingering in Paris waiting to See Mr M'Lane who talks of coming here in the course of three or four days and who is very desirous of meeting me. I am equally desirous of seeing and conferring with him. He is in a very anxious, responsible ⟨situation⟩ position, and full of doubts and apprehensions about our gathering difficulties with England. After I have seen him and passed a few days with him in Paris I shall set off for Madrid.

As Sarah is writing to you by this Steamer she will give you all the household news. She is looking extremely well, and her children are in fine health. Kate is a very intelligent child, and of a noble affectionate disposition. She exerts a complete sway over me. ⟨The⟩ Little Susie is fair and fat; with beautiful eyes of a most pleasant expression. She has just learnt to run about, and she and Kate form the prettiest groupes imaginable as they play together. You may well console yourself, in your separation from Sarah, with the assurance that her lot is a most prosperous and happy one. Her domestic establishment is a very genteel one; perfectly suited to her circumstances, and goes on most harmoniously; she is domestic in her habits and tastes; and has a choice set of American intimates by whom she is highly prized and respected.

We are looking ⟨forward⟩ anxiously to the letters by the next steamer for accounts of your health. The last letters from home mentioned your having had an attack of influenza; which it was hoped would put an end to your nervous complaint of sleeplessness. I am in hopes the next accounts from you will be more favorable than those contained in your late letters. No doubt the long summer heats have had an unset[tl]ing[?] effect upon your nerves. It was a Summer to prostrate the most iron constitution.

I have received a long and delightful letter from Helen,[1] but am not in the vein to answer it at present. In fact I scrawl this letter at the last moment, merely that the steamer may not go without something from me to the family, but I was never less in the mood for letter writing. You must give my love to "all bodies" and say that when I am in the proper vein I will write to them all.

I am my dear Sister

Your affectionate brother
Washington Irving

MANUSCRIPT: Yale.

1. This letter has not been located.

1916.   To James Buchanan

Paris Decr. 12th. 1845.

The Hon James Buchanan, / Secretary of State. Washington.

Sir,

The time having elapsed which I had allotted to myself to remain abroad when I accepted the mission of Envoy Extraordinary and Minister Plenipotentiary to the court of Spain, I now most respectfully tender to the President of the United States my resignation of that post.

The unexpected manner in which I was called to this high trust from the retirement of private life, without reference to any political considerations; and the cordial manner in which I was welcomed to it by my countrymen of all political creeds, have ever made me regard it as the crowning honor of my life. I have endeavored to discharge its duties to the best of my abilities, though I regret to say my endeavors have occasionally been counteracted by the derangement of my health. In now offering my resignation I am actuated by no party feeling, nor any indisposition to aid in carrying out the foreign policy of the present administration; but solely by an earnest desire to return to my country and my friends.

Communications, which I have had with Mr King and Mr M'Lane, have induced me to protract my sojourn in this city, and may carry me to

London, in the idea that I may be able to render some service in the present crisis of our affairs with England. I will indulge, however, in no idle delay; but, should I find my continuance in these parts of no utility, will return forthwith to Madrid, there to await the arrival of my successor

I remain, Sir,

Very respectfully / Your Obt Servt
Washington Irving

DOCKETED: *Washington Irving's / resignation as Minister / in Spain [written vertically at upper right corner, page 4] / W. Irving. (Paris) 12 Dec. 184⟨6⟩5*
MANUSCRIPT: NA, RG 59. PUBLISHED: Hellman, WI *Esquire*, p. 324; STW, II, 193 (in part).

1917. To Sabina O'Shea

[December 13, 1845]

My dear Mrs O'Shea

I read your note in a great hurry last evening just as I was going out to dinner, and as it was not very distinctly written I understood it that you had the opera box for thursday evening.

I did not discern my mistake until after my return home when I reread your note. It was very provoking; for I might have got away from my party at an early hour and indemnified myself for a tedious dinner by a cosey evening with you and Papa Quique at the opera.

I beg you will write more distinctly another time, for I should be outrageous at another such a blunder.

I am affraid I shall not get to Lady Dorothea Campbells on Friday evening. I am jaded with dissipation and long for a little quiet dull hum drum life, by way of repose.

I called on you yesterday but you had not returned from your drive. I will endeavor to call on you today and hope to be more fortunate.

My duties to Papa Quique

Yours ever very truly
Washington Irving

Thursday. 13 Decr. [1845]

MANUSCRIPT: HSA. PUBLISHED: Penney, *Bulletin NYPL*, 62 (December, 1958), 621.

The year has been determined by the perpetual calendar.

1918. To ——

Paris Decr 16th. 1845

Dear Sir,

Absence from Madrid has prevented your letter of Octr. 30th.[1] from reaching me in due season.

Your account of the first voyage of the Splendid packet Ship,[2] which the owners have thought proper to call after me, is highly gratifying. I hope her succeeding voyages will be as prosperous and profitable as her first has been brilliant.

The good feelings and good wishes expressed by your fellow passengers toward myself, and which you say you are deputed to communicate to me, call for my most heartfelt acknowledgements. To merit such good will has ever been the leading object of my life, being ever more desirous of being liked than admired.

With many thanks for the kind expressions on your own part contained in Your ⟨encl⟩ letter[.] I am, my dear Sir,

Very truly & respectfully / Your obliged
Washington Irving

[*name cut out*] Esq

MANUSCRIPT: SHR.

1. This letter has not been located.
2. The movements of this ship seem not to be advertised in the NYEP in the fall of 1845. On July 29, 1848, George Templeton Strong records in his diary that he went to Whitestone in the *Washington Irving*. See *The Diary of George Templeton Strong*, ed. Allan Nevins. and Milton Halsey Thomas, I, 325.

1919. To Benjamin Perley Poore

Paris, Dec 20h. 1845

Dear Sir.

Indisposition has prevented an earlier reply to your note of the 15th. inst.

I am glad to hear that you are pursuing the vein of historical research so successfully opened by Mr Brodhead The documents you mention relative to the discovery of america must be full of interest.

I have no ⟨facts⟩ material facts relative to Pinzon other than those published in my works: should I be able to obtain any on my return to Madrid I will communicate them to you.

I wish the State of Massachusetts would authorize you to extend your researches to Spain. That country is a perfect mine of historical riches; with respect to Europe as well as America[.] I was anxious for Mr Brodhead[1] to come on these while I was there: and I have regretted continually that my official occupations and my broken health prevented me from making in person the varied researches I had contemplated.

Wishing you every possible success in your interesting and honorable pursuits I remain my dear Sir:

With great respect / Yours very truly
Washington Irving

MANUSCRIPT: Va.–Barrett.

Benjamin Perley Poore (1820–1887) was a journalist and popular biographer. Using the name "Perley," he wrote a column for the Boston *Journal* between 1854 and 1884 reporting on political events in Washington, D.C.

Attached to WI's letter is one from Barclay Dunham to Mrs. Borland, dated December 28, 1895, indicating that the letter was found in his desk and belongs to Mrs. Borland. Dunham observes that Poore "was appointed in 1845 to select and transcribe documents in France bearing upon the history of Mass."

1. John Romeyn Brodhead had searched for documents relating to the early history of New York in the archives of Northern Europe. See WI to William H. Seward, July 11, 1842.

1920. To Pierre M. Irving

[Paris], Dec. 29, 1845

I have deferred my return to Madrid, and am in the midst of preparations for a visit to England, where my friends think I may be of more service, during the present crisis,[1] than in Spain. I shall remain in England three or four weeks, part of which I shall pass at Birmingham, and will then set out for Madrid, there to await the arrival of my successor. I send my resignation by this steamer.

The President's Message,[2] though firm and unflinching on the subject of the Oregon question, has not been of a tone to create any *flare-up* in England. I think he is justifiable in the view he takes of that question, and believe that the present Cabinet of Great Britain would be well disposed to entertain the proposition which was so haughtily rejected by Mr. Packenham.[3] I still hope the matter may be settled by negotiation; but, should England provoke a war upon the question as it stands, I am clearly of opinion that we have the right on our side, and that the world will ultimately think so.

PUBLISHED: PMI, III, 380–81.

1. Since WI was a former associate of McLane's in the London legation from 1829 to 1831 and was acquainted with many political leaders and with the niceties of diplomatic procedure, he was a distinct asset for McLane in his negotiations. As WI indicates in later letters, McLane planned for him to prepare a convincing statement of the U.S. position on Oregon, to be published as a pamphlet.

2. In his message to Congress on December 2, 1845, Polk asserted the U.S. claim to all of Oregon; he recommended termination of the Anglo-American convention for joint occupation of the entire territory; he recommended extension of U.S. jurisdiction over all settlers in Oregon; he recommended military protection of the Oregon Trail and establishment of an Indian agency west of the Rocky Mountains. See Senate, *Congressional Globe*, 29th Cong., 1st sess., pp. 6–7.

3. Richard Packenham (1797–1868), British minister to the United States, without consulting the Foreign Office in London, rejected Polk's offer to accept the 49th parallel as the northern boundary of Oregon, whereupon Polk withdrew the offer and claimed all of the region west of the Rockies from California to Alaska as belonging exclusively to the United States. See Munroe, *Louis McLane*, pp. 517–18.

INDEX